D0241571

CONTENTS

WELCOME TO CAREERS 2011

When you first start choosing your future career it can seem a daunting and complicated process. There are so many different jobs with new ones emerging all the time; how do you begin to search for something that would suit you?

Finding all the information you need to help with your career choices can therefore be difficult – and when you find it, it is not always easy to understand.

We all have different values, interests and ambitions so *Careers 2011* lists all of the most important aspects for young people searching for a future career to help make the process of choosing a career path much easier.

Within *Careers 2011* you will find brief but detailed entries on hundreds of different jobs, each of which includes entry requirements, advantages and disadvantages, working conditions, your future prospects, a description of the type of person suited to the area of work and a money guide. In addition, there are case studies describing how someone got to where they are today and their personal feelings about their job.

Although you can go straight to the pages on the jobs you're already interested in, to get the most from using *Careers 2011* we suggest you first read the opening section, as this will explain more about the content and how to use the publication.

We are confident that *Careers 2011* offers a new approach, is interesting and is easy to use. More importantly, however, it will help you to find the answers to the questions that matter to you.

- Which careers will suit me?
- What qualifications will I need?
- How much can I hope to earn?
- What's the future likely to hold?
- Will the studying be worthwhile?

Take a look at the sample job profile overleaf to see how you can use this book to find out exactly what you need to know.

We hope you enjoy using *Careers 2011* and wish you all the best with your future career choices.

The Trotman team.

An example job profile

All of the job profiles in *Careers 2011* are laid out in the same style with the same sections. This is an example job profile showing you what each section refers to and the information they contain.

Heading/job title

This refers to the title of the job you will find on the page. Some job profiles are very closely linked so they have been merged together so the heading will have each job title that is going to be covered in the profile.

What the work involves

These opening bullet points will give you a quick overview of what the job is like.

The type of person suited to this work

Within this category you will find lots of information to help you match your own strengths, weaknesses, likes and dislikes to the individual job.

Sadly it is very common for someone to start a job not knowing everything they'll be expected to do. They might then be confronted with something they find either too hard or not enjoyable; this might mean leaving a job they studied a long time for. To make sure this doesn't happen to you, think carefully about the information provided here and whether it matches your skills, experience and personality.

Working conditions

This section explains where you can expect to work, whether it's outside or inside, in an office or travelling around the country, for the career that interests you. It also tells you the typical working hours you can expect and whether you will be expected to work at weekends, evenings and on shifts. This will give you a good idea of the day to day life you can expect on the job.

Future prospects

This section shows you where you could progress to within a certain career. This may be in terms of climbing the career ladder, or branching into new territory as a career

sector develops and changes. Of course, no one can predict the future of any career sector completely but important changes to the economy, reductions and increases in labour force as well as technological advances will have an impact upon how a sector develops. This information will give you a balanced view of where your future could take you in any given career.

Advantages/disadvantages

It's important that, when choosing a career, you have a well-rounded and honest view of what the work will be like. This section gives you some of the most common good and bad points about a job so that you can decide if a job matches up to your expectations.

PAYROLL MANAGER

Administration, Business, Office Work and Financial Services

CRCI: IA

What the work involves

- Payroll managers are employed by organisations to arrange and manage employees' salaries.
- You will ensure that each member of staff receives the correct amount on the correct date. When doing this you will take into account laws regarding tax, national insurance, sick pay and maternity/paternity leave.
- Your tasks will include keeping records of hours worked, calculating repayments for salary advances or student loans, calculating pay, pensions and tax deductions.
- As you progress from payroll clerk to payroll supervisor and payroll manager you will gradually take on more responsibilities, such as managing and delegating tasks to a team of payroll clerks, and creating and documenting payroll policies.

Qualifications and courses

You will not be required to have any specific qualifications to become a payroll clerk, supervisor or manager. However employers prefer candidates with GSCEs (A*–C) including English and maths.

The Diploma in Business, Administration and Finance or even NVQs, Levels 2 to 4 in Financial Services or 2 and 3 in Payroll Administration could all be useful for entry into this line of work.

You will train on the job. The Institute of Payroll Professionals (IPP) provides an Advanced Diploma in Payroll and Business Management. Further qualifications also include a BTEC Advanced Certificate in Payroll Techniques or a BTEC Advanced Award in Payroll Procedures.

The type of person suited to this work

As you will be in contact with many employees and work alongside other payroll staff, you must enjoy working with other people and be able to work in a team.

You should be sensitive in your approach to discussing earnings with employees, and treat their information with confidentiality.

As you will be responsible for maintaining records and large amounts of information you must be organised and methodical in your work.

You will need strong numerical and IT skills as you will be working with figures and working on computerised systems.

You should also be able to multi-task and work to tight deadlines.

Working conditions

From Monday to Friday you will work around 37 hours per week. You might have to work overtime, especially at the end of a financial year which can be a busy time.

You might have the option of working part-time or flexible hours and there may even be opportunities for job-sharing.

You will be largely office-based. You will have a desk from which you will answer the phone, send emails and make calculations. You may have to attend meetings at times.

Future prospects

You will enter this profession as a payroll clerk and after you have gained a few years' experience and qualifications you will be able to progress to payroll supervisor and payroll manager.

These roles will involve more responsibility and managerial tasks such as liaising with HM Revenue and Customs, organising training for other members of payroll staff and being involved in business strategy.

Advantages/disadvantages

You will be working with a variety of people as you will potentially be working with each employee within an organisation.

At times the administrative nature of your work may become repetitive and monotonous.

Money guide

As a payroll clerk your starting salary can be around £13,000 to £16,500 per year.

In a supervisory position you can earn from £18,000 to £23,000 a year.

If you progress to a role as a payroll manager you can earn £40,000 or more a year.

Related opportunities

- Accounting Technician/Finance Clerk p19
- Pension Administrator p52

Further information

Association of Accounting Technicians (AAT)
140 Aldersgate Street, London EC1A 4HY
0845 863 0800; www.aat.org.uk; info@aat.org.uk

Institute of Payroll Professionals (IPP)
Shelly House, Farmhouse Way, Monkspath, Solihull B90 4EH
0121 712 1000; www.payrollprofession.org;
info@payrollprofession.org

City&
Guilds

www.cityandguilds.com/myperfectjob

Entry level

This number corresponds to the *Careers 2011* level of qualification you need to start your career in a particular job. For more information about what the entry levels in *Careers 2011* mean, see the next page.

Qualification and courses

This section looks in detail at the most common ways to enter a profession and the qualifications and courses you will need to take. If there are different qualifications available depending on whether you live in England, Scotland, Wales or Northern Ireland, these variations will be listed here to.

As qualifications and courses change often, we would recommend that you use the Further information section addresses to get more advice on which qualifications you will need to give yourself the best chance of entering your chosen careers.

Money guide

For some people one of the most important things they'll consider before undertaking a new course, qualification or a career is 'how much can I expect to earn?'

To help you we have included:

- the most up-to-date information about pay scales
- where possible, what you can expect at entry, intermediate and senior levels
- any regional differences.

Related opportunities

This section lists jobs that are similar in style and the skills that they require to the job profile you are looking at. This is to give you lots of options to choose from if you haven't decided which career interests you the most.

You might not have considered or heard of some of these before, so it will help you to broaden out your ideas further.

Further information

Listed here are the contact details of organisations, helplines, websites and other ways to help you continue your research into your chosen job areas.

CRCI

CRCI (Connexions Resources Centre Index)

These codes show you where you will be able to find additional information about the job title within school, college, university or community-based careers information areas.

Qualifications: what do the entry levels in Careers 2011 mean?

You will see that every job profile in this book has an entry level number assigned to it. This refers to the lowest qualification level that you need to achieve in order to enter the profession. In this book, the levels range from 1 to 8 and each job profile entry level number listed is the lowest one you need in order to gain access to a particular career.

The number shown indicates the level of qualification you are most likely to need:

■ to enter the job and

■ to enter the job and to train while working.

The qualifications grid

Opposite is a grid which shows what the levels in *Careers 2011* refer to in terms of qualifications that you can take in England, Wales, Northern Ireland and Scotland.

The information from three qualifications frameworks has been incorporated into this table; the Qualifications and Credit Framework (QCF), the Scottish Credit and Qualifications Framework (SCQF) and the Framework for Higher Education Qualifications (FHEQ).

Because the frameworks all have their own levels please be aware that this grid cannot accommodate subtle differences between the frameworks and you should refer directly to the websites below for more information.

The Qualifications and Credit Framework (QCF)

The QCF has now replaced the NQF (National Qualifications Framework) and is the basis of the qualifications grid on the following page. The framework contains both academic and vocational qualifications offered in England, Wales and Northern Ireland from Entry level to Level 8.

The Framework for Higher Education Qualifications (FHEQ)

The FHEQ includes higher education qualifications from Certificates of Higher Education through to Doctoral degrees. It applies to qualifications offered in England, Wales and Northern Ireland and includes five levels, each indicated by a letter corresponding with the initial of the main qualification offered at that level.

The Scottish Credit and Qualifications Framework (SCQF)

The SCQF is a 12-level framework including vocational, occupational and academic qualifications offered in Scotland. It covers all levels including further and higher education, from Access through to Doctoral degrees.

Each framework is under continuous review, but information in this book was correct at the time of writing.

For further details and the most up-to-date information, refer to the following websites:

■ QCF: www.qcda.gov.uk;
www.accreditedqualifications.org.uk;
www.wales.gov.uk; www.ccea.org.uk

■ FHEQ: www.qaa.ac.uk/academicinfrastructure/fheq

■ SCQF: www.scqf.org.uk

Key

Qualifications that are available in England, Wales, Northern Ireland and Scotland.

Qualifications that are available in England, Wales and Northern Ireland.

Qualifications that are available in Scotland.

Careers 2010 Level	Rough equivalent framework level	General and academic qualifications	Vocational and occupational qualifications
Entry level	QCF Entry Level Skills for Life at entry level SCQF Access Levels 1–3	**Entry Level Certificate SQA Access 1, 2 Access 3, Foundation Standard Grade National Certificate**	**National Progression Award (start at SCQF Level 2)**
1	QCF Level 1 SCQF Level 4	*GCSE grade D–G 14–19 Foundation Diploma Skills for Life Key Skills level 1* **Intermediate 1 General Standard Grade National Certificate**	NVQ/SVQ Level 1 *BTEC Introductory Certificate/ Diploma Level 1 Certificate OCR Nationals* **National Progression Award**
2	QCF Level 3 SCQF Level 5	*GCSE grade A*–C 14–19 Higher Diploma Skills for Life Key Skills level 2* **Intermediate 2 Credit Standard Grade National Certificate**	NVQ/SVQ Level 2 *Level 2 Certificate/Diploma BTEC First Certificate/Diploma Apprenticeship BTEC Nationals OCR Nationals* **National Progression Award**
3	QCF Level 3 SCQF Level 6	*A level Key Skills level 3 14–19 Advanced Diploma Advanced Extension Award Mathematics Extended Project International Baccalaureate* **Scottish Higher**	NVQ/SVQ Level 3 *A levels in applied subjects Level 3 Certificate/Diploma BTEC National Award/Certificate/ Diploma Advanced Apprenticeship (England) BTEC Nationals OCR Nationals City & Guilds Level 3* **Modern Apprenticeship (Scotland, Wales, Ireland) Professional Development Award**
4	QCF Level 4 FHEQ Level C SCQF Level 7	Certificate of Higher Education *Key Skills level 4* **Scottish Advanced Higher Higher National Certificate**	NVQs*/SVQ Level 3 *Level 4 Certificate/Diploma BTEC Professional Diplomas, Certificates and Awards City & Guilds Licentiateship* **Professional Development Award**
5	QCF Level 5 FHEQ Level I SCQF Levels 8 and 9	Bachelor's degree Diploma of Higher Education *Diploma of Further Education* Foundation Degree Higher National Diploma	NVQ/SVQ Level 4* Higher National Certificate/Diploma (HNC/HND) *BTEC Professional Diplomas/ Certificates/Awards National Diploma in Professional Production Skills Level 5 Certificate/Diploma City & Guilds Full Technological Certificate (FTC)* **Professional Development Award**
6	QCF Level 6 FHEQ Level H SCQF Level 10	Bachelor's degree with Honours Graduate Diploma Graduate Certificate	*NVQs* Level 6 Certificate/Diploma BTEC Advanced Professional Diplomas/Certificates/ Awards City & Guilds Graduateship* **Professional Development Award**
7	QCF Level 7 FHEQ Level M SCQF Level 11	Master's degree Postgraduate Diploma (PgDip) Postgraduate Certificate (PgCert) Integrated Degree *Diploma in Translation*	NVQ/SVQ Level 5* *Level 7 Diploma/Fellowship Level 7 Advanced Professional Certificate BTEC Advanced Professional Diplomas/Certificates/Awards City & Guilds Membership* **Professional Development Award**
8	QCF Level 8 FHEQ Level D SCQF Level 12	Doctorate	Specialist awards and diplomas from professional bodies *City & Guilds Fellowship* **Professional Development Award**

Job families

The jobs in this book have been divided into job families to make it easy for you to go straight to the right section and find the job you are interested in. At the beginning of each job family section is an introduction to the career sector and a list of all the jobs that will appear in the section. You will also find information on other similar job families and where to find them in the book.

There are 20 job families in *Careers 2011* which are:

  Administration, Business, Office Work and Financial Services

 Building and Construction

 Catering and Hospitality

 Computers and IT

 Design, Arts and Crafts

 Education and Training

  Engineering, Manufacturing and Production

 Environment, Animals and Plants

 Healthcare

 Languages, Information and Culture

 Legal and Political Services

 Leisure, Sport and Tourism

   Marketing, Advertising, Media, Print and Publishing

 Performing Arts

 Personal and Other Services including Hair and Beauty

 Retail, Sales and Customer Services

 Science, Mathematics and Statistics

 Security and Armed Forces

 Social Work and Counselling Services

Transport and Logistics

What do the icons mean?

The icons used in this book are the same as those used in the CRCI (Connexions Resources Centre Index) and they will appear at the beginning of each section to make it easy and clear to see exactly which job families are being covered.

Administration, Business, Office Work and Financial Services

To work in this sector you often need to have a great head for numbers and be very good at managing your time effectively. The variety of jobs in this family is huge, so you could work in a large, busy office or you could work for yourself dealing with clients from a host of different professions. Many jobs require you to have an eye for detail as you could be compiling reports and advising organisations on how they could work more effectively or safely or organising other people's time and schedules. In all cases, you should be highly motivated and organised. If you enjoy this responsibility and like the idea of the challenge of keeping a business running like clockwork there are many jobs that would suit you in this sector.

For further information see *Careers Uncovered: E-Commerce* and *Real Life Guide: Business, Administration and Finance*, published by Trotman.

For a full list of jobs in this section turn to page 15.

Building and Construction

The jobs in this sector are very varied; some require a high level of personal fitness, while for others, a creative flair is essential. You may be interested in working on a construction site with a team of people and for this you would need to demonstrate excellent personal safety and be happy to work outside in all weathers. Alternatively, maybe your interest lies in buying and selling property or maybe working in an office is more your sort of thing. All the jobs in the sector require someone with a great eye for detail who is very good at working with others.

If you would like to read further information about this industry and how to go about starting your career please see *Real Life Guide: Construction* and *Real Life Guide: Plumbing* both published by Trotman.

For a full list of jobs in this section turn to page 69.

Catering and Hospitality

Working in this sector, you will meet a wide variety of people and probably need to be a very strong team player. For some of the jobs, you need to be outgoing, confident and sociable and may end up working early mornings or late nights. For many jobs in this sector you need to be very meticulous when it comes to standards of cleanliness and tidiness. Workers in the sector thrive on providing an impeccable service and ensuring customers are completely satisfied and are given a wonderful experience whether that be in a restaurant, hotel or bar.

For further information about training for and starting your career in this industry see *Real Life Guide: Catering* and *Real Life Guide: Hospitality & Events Management*, published by Trotman.

For a full list of jobs in this section turn to page 133.

Computers and IT

This sector is still fairly new and so it is expanding all the time, creating new jobs for a whole range of people. You may have a mathematical brain or a real creative ability – or a bit of both! Essentially, you must be passionate about computers to consider working in this sector. You could be working directly with clients and customers, helping them to rectify problems with their computers or you could be researching and developing the latest console for the games market. In all cases you need to keep right up to date with the latest technologies and IT developments as well as people's tastes, interests and hobbies to enjoy working in this sector.

If you want more information about working in this sector see *Real Life Guide: Information & Communications Technology* and *Careers Uncovered: The Internet* both published by Trotman.

For a full list of jobs in this section turn to page 149.

Design, Arts and Crafts

The idea of turning your arts and crafts hobby into a career may be one you like the thought of. Jobs in this sector can involve working in any medium, from textiles to jewellery to metalwork or children's toys. Some jobs may involve you researching current styles and trends and creating your own designs whereas others will involve working to a set brief set out by your customer to create a bespoke product. You may find yourself working for a company but many people in this industry are self-employed working for a range of clients. This means you need to be very organised and have brilliant communication skills to ensure you can give your clients exactly what they want. People working in this industry are extremely passionate about their careers and have a real sense of perfectionism to produce a beautiful finished article.

If you would like more information about training for and getting started in a career in this field see, *Getting Into Art and Design Courses*, *Careers Uncovered: Design* and *Real Life Guide: Creative Industries*, all published by Trotman.

For a full list of jobs in this section turn to page 167.

Education and Training

To work in this sector you need to be motivated and enthusiastic about other people's learning, whether it's adults or children. There are jobs suitable for people with all levels of qualification, but whatever your entry level you will need to be interested in keeping up to date on the latest developments in education and will enjoy working with other people. If you choose to teach, the range of subjects available is huge so whatever your interest – languages, art, sciences, cooking, sports – you can become a teacher in that field. Jobs in this sector require a multitude of skills including: creativity, imagination, numerical skills, good communication and organisational skills and, in some cases, having a lot of patience!

If you would like more help with starting your career in education and training please see the *Careers Uncovered:*

Teaching and *Real Life Guide: Childcare*, both published by Trotman.

For a full list of jobs in this section turn to page 189.

Engineering, Manufacturing and Production

There are a number of highly-skilled jobs available in this job family and workers need to be creative and methodical, combining brilliant technical skill with spatial awareness. Engineers are very well qualified indeed so you should be willing to study hard for good qualifications. Jobs in this sector can take you into a range of different fields, from scientific research to car production to working out at sea; there's something for anyone who has an inquisitive mind and a high level of technical capability. Another attractive element of this industry is that you can work with an enormous variety of different materials. You may be interested in food production but equally your passion could lie in working with aircraft or marine manufacture. People in these professions share the ability to concentrate for long periods of time and work meticulously on a job to finish it to a high standard. Some will also be highly trained with specialist equipment which may sometimes be hazardous to use so a high level of personal safety awareness is vital.

For further information on working in this area see *Real Life Guide: Electrician*, *Real Life Guide: Engineering Technician*, *Real Life Guide: Manufacturing & Product Design* and *Real Life Guide: The Motor Industry*, all published by Trotman.

For a full list of jobs in this section turn to page 211.

Environment, Animals and Plants

Some people working in this sector spend a lot of their time outdoors. This means the jobs are perfect for those of you who don't want to spend every day behind a desk in an office, although this is not to say that you will not need to spend time writing reports and keeping a log of research findings or clients' information. Workers in this sector are passionate about animals or about caring for and maintaining the environment. You will sometimes work in unpredictable settings, especially if you are working outside or have close contact with animals. You should also have brilliant people skills especially if you find yourself responsible for the welfare of someone else's animal. You should be someone who is very observant and interested in the natural world, not just from a welfare point of view but also from an economic one; many jobs in this sector involve using the environment for financial gain but increasingly industry is interested in doing so responsibly.

If you would like more information about jobs in this sector see *Getting Into Veterinary School*, *Real Life Guide: Working Outdoors* and *Real Life Guide: Working with Animals & Wildlife*, all published by Trotman.

For a full list of jobs in this section turn to page 253.

Healthcare

If you are keen to pursue a career in healthcare you must be compassionate and enjoy either caring for people or deciding what treatment they should receive. There is such a wide variety of jobs available in this sector simply because you can specialise in absolutely any aspect of human healthcare. Maybe you're interested in working with athletes or perhaps working with children interests you more. You could be part of the rehabilitation process after an illness or injury or find yourself working as a mental health therapist. Many jobs require a lot of training and you can expect to work in some highly-pressurised and sometimes distressing situations. Workers in healthcare are extremely dedicated and enthusiastic about their careers, which rarely constitute a 9–5 job. You can expect every day to be different and you should relish the challenges working with people of all ages can bring.

For more information about training for and working in healthcare see *Careers Uncovered: Medicine*, *Careers Uncovered: Nursing and Midwifery*, *Careers Uncovered: Psychology*, *Getting Into Medical School*, *Getting Into Dental School*, *Getting Into Physiotherapy Courses*, *Getting Into Psychology Courses* and *Real Life Guide: Care*, all published by Trotman.

For a full list of jobs in this section turn to page 287.

Languages, Information and Culture

If you are really interested in history or perhaps would like to use another language as part of your career, a job in this sector could be right for you. The jobs in this family are quite varied in terms of whether you would work with other people or by yourself. You could find yourself working in a range of different places, from museums to antiques fairs to conferences as an interpreter. Some of the jobs in this family are more unusual and are perfect for those of you who want a fascinating job that allows you to indulge in your passion for historic artefacts and artwork or languages and foreign countries. To excel in this sector you should have an inquisitive mind, be meticulous in your work and enjoy carrying out research. If you are keen to work with languages you should also be willing to travel in order to improve your language and your knowledge of the culture and history.

For a full list of jobs in this section turn to page 343.

Legal and Political Services

Are you interested in justice and fairness for all? Do you relish the opportunity to speak out for what's right and enjoy the challenge of persuading others that everyone needs an equal voice? Maybe you find the Law a fascinating subject and you feel you would enjoy a challenging career where the rewards are a good salary and a real sense of achievement when your hard work pays off. If so, a job in this sector could be what you are looking for. Workers in this sector are fiercely passionate about their careers and have more often than not, completed a lot of training and worked hard to establish themselves in this competitive field. You need to be driven and thrive on pressure and tight deadlines; this is a sector for someone who is ambitious and very talented at working tactfully with people.

For more information about training for this sector as well as where to begin job hunting, read *Careers Uncovered: Law* and *Getting Into Law*, both published by Trotman.

For a full list of jobs in this section turn to page 361.

Leisure, Sport and Tourism

This sector relies on a motivated, up-beat and out-going workforce for its success. You will need to show that you can work very well with other people, providing them with an excellent service when they want to enjoy themselves on holiday or if they are keen to improve their fitness and sporting ability. If you are keen to work with professional sports players or become one yourself you should be very aware of how to keep the body fit while avoiding injury. It's also important that you can keep a level head as you will often be responsible for other people's welfare. You should be warm and friendly but also able to maintain a high level of professionalism at the same time. You should also demonstrate you have patience and tact and be clued up on health and safety regulations.

If you would like to read more about getting a job in this area see *Careers Uncovered: Sport and Fitness*, *Careers Uncovered: Travel Industry*, *Real Life Guide: Sport and Active Leisure* and *Real Life Guide: Travel & Tourism*, published by Trotman.

For a full list of jobs in this section turn to page 383.

Marketing, Advertising, Media, Print and Publishing

Do you consider yourself to be a great communicator? Are you interested in working in an exciting and often fast-paced environment with passionate, driven and ambitious individuals? If so, a career in this industry could be right for you. People who work in this sector are exceptionally motivated and are willing to put in long hours often on low starting wages because of their love of the job. While you need to be good at preparing your work alone, people who work in this sector tend to be very good at working with others and build up strong professional relationships as part of their job. You should have a great sense of creativity and imagination and be good at putting your ideas on paper, but you will often also need strong business acumen as many of your decisions will be made from an economical point of view as well as a creative one.

If you think this is a career you would like to find out more about why not read: *Careers Uncovered: Journalism*, *Careers Uncovered: The Music Industry*, *Careers Uncovered: Media* and *Real Life Guide: Creative Industries*, published by Trotman.

For a full list of jobs in this section turn to page 401.

Performing Arts

This job family contains a wide range of exciting jobs for those of you who want to work in theatre, music, on screen or behind the scenes. People working in this sector do so because they are passionate and creative and love the arts. Jobs can be scarce, so you will need to demonstrate that you are willing to work very hard but the rewards of being part of a fantastic production can be huge. You won't necessarily be confined to working in one place as your job may take you on tour all over the world. There are also jobs available in this sector for those of you who are more technically minded – sound and lighting engineers also play a vital role in this industry as do people who have trained in fashion and textiles. Make up artists also play a major role in theatre, television and music production.

If you would like to know more about how you can enter the world of performing arts see *Careers Uncovered: The Music Industry*, *Careers Uncovered: Performing Arts* and *Real Life Guide: Creative Industries*, published by Trotman.

For a full list of jobs in this section turn to page 433.

Personal and Other Services including Hair and Beauty

This is a very wide job family and covers everything from hairdressing and beauty to cleaning to wedding consulting. You can enter this career sector with a host of different skills and qualifications. What all of the jobs have in common is that they provide a particular service that a customer has asked for so you need to be good at listening to others and giving customers exactly what they want – people in this sector have a brilliant way with people. You should also demonstrate creativity and strong practical and technical skill as many of the jobs in this family require you to use specialist equipment, and have knowledge of health and safety.

If this is a sector you would like to know more about, see *Real Life Guide: The Beauty Industry* and *Real Life Guide: Hairdressing*, published by Trotman.

For a full list of jobs in this section turn to page 457.

Retail, Sales and Customer Services

Jobs in this sector are suited to those of you who are very good at communicating with others and are interested in making your customers happy. Maybe you're interested in working with food and want to give your customers high quality, fresh produce. Your interest may lie in fashion retail and you could spend your time providing style advice. You should also be commercially minded and think about how your work relates to the success of the company you work for. Jobs in this sector also involve maintaining standards such as safety and quality to ensure guidelines are met, so a practical outlook can be useful.

For more information about a career in this sector read *Real Life Guide: Retail*, published by Trotman.

For a full list of jobs in this section turn to page 477.

Science, Mathematics and Statistics

Do you have a very mathematical brain? Are you logical in how you approach tasks? Maybe you are fascinated by scientific advances and would like to be involved in future discoveries? People who work in this sector can spend long periods of time carrying out meticulous research. You may find yourself working for a variety of employers, from the health service to a cosmetics company or even a charity. You should be willing to work on your own but also be happy to present your findings in reports to others. People in this sector are very highly skilled individuals who have often been through a lot of training, and possess a questioning and inquisitive mind.

For a full list of jobs in this section turn to page 503.

Security and Armed Forces

Working in this sector may give you many incredible experiences and opportunities not open to most people. You need to be an excellent team player and in some instances you may find yourself in a potentially dangerous situation. Working in this sector you can expect to spend your day absolutely anywhere! Some roles involve a lot of office work whereas others can involve spending a lot of your time on the road, or even at sea. If you're looking for a job that will be exhilarating but are able to remain calm and professional under pressure this sector could offer you a lot of opportunities.

If you would like to know more about working in this field, see *Real Life Guide: Armed Forces*, *Real Life Guide: The Police Service* and *Real Life Guide: The Fire Service*, published by Trotman.

For a full list of jobs in this section turn to page 539.

Social Work and Counselling Services

People who work in this sector are dedicated to caring and talking through people's problems and anxieties to improve their general well-being and their future prospects in life. The work requires a lot of patience, an open mind and a friendly and approachable personality. You could be helping people who are distressed and need help and guidance but equally you may be helping people who want to move on to the next stage in their careers or educational choices. Either way, you should be someone who enjoys helping people change their lives for the better. If you are interested in working in this field you need to show that you are compassionate and very good at communicating with people from all walks of life and of all ages. You should also be someone who can maintain a strong sense of professionalism as you could be in a position of trust and you must be very respectful of your clients' privacy.

If this is a career that interests you, you can find more information here: *Real Life Guide: Care*, published by Trotman.

For a full list of jobs in this section turn to page 567.

Transport and Logistics

The jobs in this sector are immensely varied because of the wide range of transport and communication links that exist today to keep our lives running. You could need a high level of technical knowledge in this sector especially for jobs such as a pilot or a train driver. But you could also be great at keeping attention to detail and maintaining schedules if logistics is more where your interest lies. Jobs in transport and logistics require very efficient and practical people to ensure that our infrastructure continues to run smoothly and safely. You may need to cope well under pressurised situations. As you will probably have contact with the general public you should be good with people, and have a calm, professional manner.

If this job family covers jobs that you would like to read about in more detail, see *Real Life Guide: Distribution & Logistics* and *Real Life Guide: Passenger Transport*, published by Trotman.

For a full list of jobs in this section turn to page 591.

Where to go for more help

Below is a brief explanation with some contact details of the main organisations that can help you find out more about the career you are interested in.

England
The Connexions Service
Designed to offer every young person the 'best start in life', the Connexions service is available across England for 13- to 19-year-olds and provides information, advice and guidance on all aspects that affect you. The range of issues covered includes careers, education, training and all life issues such as health, leisure and housing information. The service is managed locally and you should contact your local partnership to see if you can make an appointment to speak to a Connexions Personal Adviser.

For more information:
www.connexions.gov.uk

Connexions Direct
Offering a telephone support service and detailed website, Connexions Direct can help you with information and advice on issues such as your career and learning options, money, health, housing, and relationships with family and friends. It can also let you know about activities you can get involved in.

You can contact Connexions Direct on:
Freephone: 0808 001 3219
Text phone: 08000 968 336
Text Message: 07766 4 13 2 19
www.connexions-direct.com

Please check with your local authority for more information on the career service provider in your area.

Northern Ireland

If you want advice from a careers adviser you can attend one of the 35 JobCentres and Jobs and Benefits Offices throughout Northern Ireland. Here you will get information on all aspects of work, education and employment issues. Careers Advisers visit schools regularly and you should speak to your careers teacher to arrange a careers interview. If you have left school you should contact your local JobCentre to make an appointment to speak to a Careers Adviser. There are also 28 Careers Service Support Units spread throughout the region offering access to Careers Advisers and resources, and the Careers Service NI website is packed with information.

Tel: 028 9044 1781
www.careersserviceni.com

Scotland
Careers Scotland
Careers Scotland is available to both young people and adults looking for information about careers, education or employment options. If you want to meet a trained adviser you can either visit one of the 100 centres that are available across Scotland or visit the Careers Scotland website.

For more information contact:
Freephone 0845 8 502 502
Textphone: 0141 889 8581
Typetalk: 18001 0845 8502 502
www.careers-scotland.org.uk

Wales
Careers Wales
Offering help both to young people and to adults, Careers Wales provides advice on any issues you have related to careers, work, education or training.

Youth Gateway
In addition to the help and advice Careers Wales has available, they have now introduced Youth Gateway. This is designed specifically for you if you are aged 16–19 and looking for advice about training, employment and education. You will get help from Careers Advisers and Personal Advisers who are working together to make sure you get the help you need.

For further information on both Careers Wales and Youth Gateway see:
www.careerswales.com

CLIC
CLIC is an information and advice service for young people in Wales. It offers help and guidance on a range of issues from education and employment to relationships, health and housing.

For more information see:
www.cliconline.co.uk

England, Wales and Northern Ireland
learndirect
If you need advice on any aspect of your careers, training or educational options try contacting learndirect. learndirect has trained advisers who can discuss your options over the phone or you can attend one of the many learndirect centres available throughout England, Wales and Northern Ireland. Their help is available to anyone of any age, although it is mainly aimed at adults.

If you want some more information or advice contact:
0800 101 901
www.learndirect.co.uk and www.learndirect-advice.co.uk

Administration, Business, Office Work and Financial Services

To work in this sector you need to have a great head for numbers and be very good at managing your time effectively. Jobs in business and finance can be fast-paced and exciting and workers in all four of these areas are highly motivated and enjoy working in an office environment.

In this section we look at the following jobs:

For similar jobs to this job family please go to the section: *Legal and Political Services* on page 361.

ACCOUNTANT

What the work involves

- Accountancy involves keeping and analysing financial records for companies or individuals, helping them to increase their profits including advising on financial planning and development, tax returns and future costs and budgets.

- You will keep detailed accounts and internal audits and produce regular statements on whether the company's systems are efficient and cost effective.

- There are three main areas of accounting and within each sector you can either become a certified or a chartered accountant. Chartered accountants work to a globally recognised standard and are often sponsored by their employer to achieve this qualification.

Industrial and commercial

- Employed directly by a company, you will provide them with a range of services.

- You will help to plan the company's development by predicting costs, benefits and risks.

Private practice

- You will work for a specialist accountancy firm that offers services to clients.

- Smaller practices usually work for local businesses. However, accountancy firms can be huge and some companies provide services to multinational corporations.

Public sector

- Working for public bodies such as the NHS, universities and local authorities, you will offer advice on tax, financial problems, raising money, financial ICT systems and management consultancy.

- Your role will be to help provide an efficient, quality service that is within the budgets set by the government.

The type of person suited to this work

As you will be giving presentations and working with people at all levels, you will need excellent written and verbal communication skills. Much of your work will include dealing with confidential reports and financial information, so you will need to be honest and reliable. You will also need to be able to work under pressure and to deadlines, be prepared to study in your own time and to continue to keep up to date with new developments.

A knack for figures and an interest in how businesses work will be essential. You will need research skills and the ability to process and analyse complicated financial information. You will be a problem-solver, producing written reports showing your findings and conclusions.

Working conditions

You could work in an organisation of any size and will generally be office based, spending a lot of time using ICT, sitting at a desk or meeting clients. Smart dress will be required.

Depending on your role, you might have the opportunity to travel both in this country and abroad to meet clients so a driving licence could be useful. You might need to be prepared to spend time away from home.

Although you will normally work office hours from Monday to Friday, you might need to work extra hours at busy times, especially during February to March (the end of the financial year).

Future prospects

The growing importance of information technology is having a major impact on the accountancy sector. Access to faster communication systems means more major companies are becoming global, which in turn will have an impact on the numbers required within the accountancy sector. If

accountancy is your chosen route, it is recommended you think very carefully about the area you would like to focus on at an early stage of your career.

In the long term you could choose to become self-employed, offering consultancy services to clients.

Industrial and commercial

There is a high demand for trainees with opportunities throughout the country, but as you would probably be working for a larger organisation, you will be based in a city. Once you are qualified and experienced you could move into highly paid senior management positions, or you could choose to move to a larger company for promotion.

Private practice

You could work for a small company, offering a personal service to local businesses and individuals or for a huge multinational firm. Job opportunities are good and there is a high demand for qualified accountants.

Public sector

The public sector covers a wide range of services, including education, healthcare and social services. Government changes mean that budgets are increasingly held at local level, for example schools now manage their own finances, opening up opportunities across the country.

If you do well, you can move into high-level management jobs.

Advantages/disadvantages

If you work within the right organisation you can expect to earn extremely high salaries. To achieve this you will need to be very dedicated and able to cope with a lot of responsibility, stress and pressure. Accountancy is a varied career and there are many opportunities both in this country and abroad. You will need to be committed and determined to cope with training, studying and taking exams whilst you work.

Money guide

Successful accountants can earn very high salaries but a lot will depend on your level, experience and location. The highest salaries are within London and the south-east of England, the lowest are in Northern Ireland, Scotland and the north-east of England.

Private practice

As a graduate just beginning your training you can earn between £18,000 and £25,000 per year depending on where you work and your responsibilities.

Recently qualified graduates earn between £29,000 and £50,000.

When fully qualified, with several years' experience, and perhaps a specialist area of work, salaries can increase to £80,000+.

Public sector

A trainee usually starts on £16,000–£25,000 per year. On completion of training you could earn between £28,000 and £50,000.

Fully qualified senior managers can earn £50,000–£150,000 per year, while directors could earn £150,000+.

Your salary will depend on the type of organisation you work for, the qualification you have studied, and your location. ACCA qualified accountants typically earn more than those with CAT. Accountants working in London can expect to earn up to 20% more than in other areas.

Related opportunities

- Accounting Technician/Finance Clerk p18
- Actuary p20
- Auditor p21
- Bank Manager p23
- Financial Adviser p39
- Insurance Broker p42

Further information

Association of Chartered Certified Accountants
29 Lincoln's Inn Fields, London WC2A 3EE
020 7059 5000; www.acca.co.uk; info@accaglobal.com

Qualifications and courses

Most people start with a degree (usually 2.2 classification or higher). If your degree is in accounting or a related subject you may be exempt from certain papers for some of the professional qualifications. Due to an increase in global companies, graduates with language degrees are in high demand.

The minimum entry requirements for a degree are normally 2 A levels/3 H grades and 5 GCSEs/S grades (A*–C/1–3), including maths and English, or equivalent. HNC/HND in accounting or a business-related subject followed by a top-up degree may be another route into the profession.

It is possible for school leavers, with a minimum of 4 GCSEs/S grades, including English and maths, to follow a vocational training route. This is normally offered by the Association of Accounting Technicians (AAT) and The Chartered Institute of Management Accountants (CIMA), who offer the Technician route to qualification. There are varied exam requirements, depending on qualifications offered at entry.

Accountants hold a qualification from a recognised accountancy body: Association of Chartered Certified Accountants (ACCA), Institute of Chartered Accountants in England and Wales (ICAEW), Institute of Chartered Accountants in Scotland (ICAS), Institute of Chartered Accountants in Ireland (ICAI), Association of International Accountants (AIA). The Chartered Institute of Management Accountants (CIMA) and the Institute of Financial Accountants (IFA) provide qualifications for management accountants and financial accountants working in all sectors.

Accountants working in the public sector usually hold the Chartered Institute of Public Finance and Accountancy (CIPFA) qualification.

ENTRY LEVEL 4

Institute of Chartered Accountants in England and Wales
Chartered Accountants Hall, Moorgate Place, London
EC2R 6EA
020 7920 8100; www.icaew.co.uk

Institute of Chartered Accountants of Scotland
CA House, 21 Haymarket Yards, Edinburgh EH12 5BH
0131 347 0100; www.icas.org.uk

Institute of Financial Accountants
Burford House, 44 London Road, Sevenoaks TN13 1AS
01732 458080; www.ifa.org.uk; mail@ifa.org.uk

ACCOUNTING TECHNICIAN/ FINANCE CLERK

What the work involves

- Accounting technicians are responsible for financial issues including company expenditure, tax returns and payroll.

- Your work will include collecting and analysing information, keeping records and writing reports.

- In a large firm, you will probably work as part of a team and support qualified accountants. In a smaller company, you might cover a wider range of tasks and be responsible for most of the finances.

- Once you are qualified you could specialise in a specific financial area, for example insolvency or tax analysis.

The type of person suited to this work

You will need to be confident with numbers, and have the ability to gather, analyse and record information accurately when under pressure from deadlines.

Good verbal and written communication skills are also essential, as you will often have to explain complicated financial issues to clients in a clear manner.

You must be willing and committed to further study in order to pass your technician exams. You will be expected to continue learning throughout your career, as it is important for accounting technicians to keep up-to-date with changes in financial law.

Good ICT skills are also important, as most of the work is computer based.

Working conditions

You will normally work standard office hours from Monday to Friday, however at busy times you might need to put in extra hours over evenings or weekends.

Most work will be office-based, although you may also travel to meetings with clients within your working day so a driving licence could be useful.

Future prospects

Although the finance industry employs a lot of people, the majority do not hold many professional qualifications. This means there is a skills shortage within the sector, so the higher the qualifications you gain the better your career prospects.

Prospects for promotion are good, and working in a smaller company may also give you the opportunity to take on more responsibility and work at a more senior level earlier in your career. Alternatively, you could choose to become self-employed, or train as a chartered accountant.

Advantages/disadvantages

You will usually be working in a team environment, which means that you will build strong relationships.

The work can be slightly monotonous.

Qualifications and courses

There are no formal academic requirements for entry to the role of an accounting technician, but some GCSEs/S grades (A*–C/1–3), including English and maths, are desirable. Other useful qualifications include the Diploma in Business, Administration and Finance, A levels, BTEC Awards and HNC/HNDs in subjects such as accounting, finance and business. City & Guilds also offer Levels 1–3 in Book-keeping and Accounts.

The Association of Accounting Technicians (AAT) and Association of Chartered Certified Accountants (ACCA) award accounting technician qualifications, which are usually studied part time at college or work. These are available at three NVQ/SVQ stages: Level 2 (Foundation), 3 (Intermediate) and 4 (Technician). You might be exempt from some levels with relevant qualifications.

The AAT also offers a diploma for those who are unable to find a work placement whilst they study. This has three stages: Certificate in Accounting (Foundation), Advanced Certificate in Accounting (Intermediate) and Diploma in Accounting (Technician). Technician status is awarded on completion of all three components.

The Certified Accountancy Technician (CAT) qualification, awarded by ACCA, combines a year's practical experience with exams at three levels.

Money guide

As a trainee, working towards gaining foundation level qualifications, you can expect to earn £11,000–£19,000 per year. When fully qualified, earnings range from £14,000 to £29,000. Once you have gained experience and progressed to a management level, or if you are successfully self-employed, you could earn up to £49,000.

Related opportunities

- Accountant p16
- Pensions Administrator p53
- Bank Cashier/Customer Adviser p22

Further information

Association of Accounting Technicians
140 Aldersgate Street, London EC1A 4HY
0845 863 0800; www.aat.org.uk; aat@aat.org.uk

Association of Chartered Certified Accountants
29 Lincoln's Inn Fields, London WC2A 3EE
020 7059 5000; www.acca.co.uk; info@accaglobal.com

City&
Guilds

www.cityandguilds.com/myperfectjob

TRAINEE ACTUARY/ ACTUARIAL SUPPORT

Here's Holly Saxon's story:

After studying Actuarial Science at the University of Canterbury at Kent, Holly worked in a number of roles before making the move to Mercer in London.

When and why Holly chose an actuarial career

"After over two years working for an insurance company and investment house in roles not related to actuarial science or mathematics I realised that a move into an actuarial career was definitely the right career move for me."

What the job entails

"I work in the retirement, risk and finance department in London. Day to day work includes calculating pension values for individuals and group schemes, and carrying out test cases for our clients. Other work involves preparing company valuation reports, designing new spreadsheets for client use, valuing assets and liabilities for client planning and various other projects."

What makes Holly good at her job

"A mathematical background and a good understanding of Excel is an advantage, although training is provided. The ability to work under your own initiative and be able to work to tight deadlines is fundamental. Good planning and organisational skills and the ability to switch between tasks when requested or deadlines demand is also highly important."

What Holly personally gets out of it

"The responsibility of managing my own work and meeting deadlines as part of a team. The sense of equality in the department and high level of communication skills between colleagues. The ability to work in a professional environment and the opportunity to learn something new everyday."

How Holly achieves a work/life balance

"I organise my time well and try to plan my workload in terms of deadlines and priorities and how long a piece of work may take. Planning is crucial. Often work is allocated with very short notice and needs to be done instantly, so I always need to plan well ahead for ongoing projects. Working in London not only gives me the opportunity to progress my career, but also has a fantastic social scene with many bars and restaurants, theatres and lots of other events to help me unwind at the end of a long day."

Holly's future plans

"To qualify as an actuary and continue my work at Mercer. I would like to become a scheme actuary with expertise in pensions and investments."

Holly's advice for others considering an actuarial career

"Be sure that it is definitely what you want to do. A top company will have high expectations and demands of you but it is a great challenge. Also, there are the professional exams to consider which take up a lot of time and hard work as well as the job itself. If you're prepared to work hard in a professional environment and be rewarded for your efforts then you'll be set for great success."

ACTUARY

What the work involves

- Actuaries calculate financial risk. Using statistics and knowledge of investments, law, business and economics, they make financial predictions to help design products such as insurance and pensions.

- As an actuary you would help set insurance prices based on statistics, probability and risk.

- You would also use your knowledge to help companies make long-term financial decisions.

- You might work in insurance, life assurance, pensions, investments or for the government.

The type of person suited to this work

You must be good with numbers and enjoy solving complicated mathematical problems. You should also be analytical, able to think logically, and be skilled at problem solving.

You will need to have excellent communication skills as you must explain complicated financial issues in a clear and understandable way to clients.

Actuaries must pay close attention to detail and work to deadlines. You must keep up to date with new developments, such as the laws governing the industry.

You will be expected to dress formally and have excellent ICT skills.

Working conditions

Most actuaries work within life assurance companies and numbers in general insurance are increasing rapidly. Although the profession is growing, entry is competitive and you will most likely need relevant work experience. Jobs are available throughout the country but most are based in Edinburgh, London and the south-east.

As a trainee you will have to study in your own time but once you are qualified you could work abroad and might be able to work part time.

Future prospects

Most actuaries work within life assurance companies and numbers in general insurance are increasing rapidly. Although the profession is growing, entry is competitive and you will probably need relevant work experience. Jobs are available throughout the country but most are in Edinburgh, London and the south-east.

As a fully qualified actuary you can work within a specialism or in a consultancy, or you could travel as your qualifications will be recognised all over the world. Within larger companies there are opportunities for promotion to very senior positions.

Advantages/disadvantages

Training after university takes up to 6 years and involves studying while working full time. However, actuaries are in demand. There are good promotion prospects and the pay is

Qualifications and courses

Most people enter this career with a degree in maths or a related subject; some entrants have a postgraduate qualification in actuarial science or a professional qualification from the Institute of Actuaries (England and Wales) or the Faculty of Actuaries (Scotland).

Normal entry requirements for a degree course are 2 A levels/3 H grades and 5 GCSEs/S grades (A*–C/1–3), or equivalent. For a degree in maths, this will include an A level/H grade in a maths subject.

You could become a trainee actuary after A levels or Scottish Highers. The minimum entry requirements are 2 A levels including a mathematical subject at grade B, or 3 Scottish Highers including maths at grade A.

To help gain a trainee post you may study by distance learning. Trainee positions usually last 3–6 years. To qualify as an actuary you need to enrol as a student member of the Faculty and Institute of Actuaries while working and studying for professional exams at the same time.

Trainees with a degree or diploma in actuarial science/ studies may be exempt from various training. Other degrees may give exemption from certain exam papers.

good and UK qualifications are recognised everywhere so you have the option to work abroad.

Money guide

As a graduate trainee you can expect a salary between £30,000 and £40,000 per year. Newly or part-qualified staff can expect £50,000–£75,000. Senior staff can earn up to £100,000 and it is possible to earn £170,000+. Salaries vary based on location and specialism, and are expected to be higher in London and the south-east of England.

Related opportunities

- Accountant p16
- Financial Adviser p39
- Stockbroker p66
- Risk Manager p62

Further information

Association for Consulting Actuaries
St Clement's House, 27–28 Clement's Lane,
London EC4N 7AE
020 3207 9380; www.aca.org.uk

Institute and Faculty of Actuaries
Staple Inn Hall, High Holborn, London WC1V 7QJ
020 7632 2100; www.actuaries.org.uk;
careers@actuaries.org.uk

AUDITOR

What the work involves

- You will be a fully qualified accountant specialising in audit work, exploring all aspects of a business, talking to staff and ensuring that the paperwork and accounts give a true picture of the company's finances.

- Internal auditors work for a company preparing their accounts for external auditors to check. They are also responsible for assessing other risks, not just finances.

- All businesses and government departments must be externally audited by law.

- As an external auditor you will create an independent report for a company, stating that the accounts are true and accurate and recommending possible improvements to the business.

The type of person suited to this work

You must be happy working with numbers and interpreting statistics and be a thorough and methodical person.

As you will be using your skills and experience to solve financial problems you need to enjoy researching all aspects of a business.

It is important that you have excellent communication skills so that you can present your findings clearly, both verbally and in writing. You should also be able to work effectively as part of a team and with the company you are auditing. You should be well organised, able to work under pressure, meet deadlines and have excellent ICT skills.

Working conditions

Large companies have internal auditors who prepare their accounts for inspection. External auditors are based temporarily in the firms they are auditing, so they may have to travel and stay away from home. A driving licence can be useful.

You will work normal office hours but might have to work evenings and weekends.

Future prospects

There is an increasing demand for qualified auditors. As an internal auditor you could work for a business or government department, work for yourself or as a consultant.

External auditors are employed by accountancy firms, the National Audit Office (the Accounts Commission in Scotland) auditing central government departments, or the Audit Commission working with public sector organisations such as local authorities or the NHS.

Advantages/disadvantages

Accountancy training takes 3–5 years after university and involves studying in your own time. Usually you will need work experience to support an application.

Qualifications and courses

In order to become an auditor, you will need to obtain a professional accountancy qualification (see p17).

Most entrants to this profession are graduates.

Private accountancy firms audit companies in the private sector and some public sector organisations. A chartered accountancy qualification with CIPFA, ACCA, ICAEW, ICAS, ICAI or CIMA is required.

Public sector auditing is usually carried out by national audit bodies such as the Audit Commission, the National Audit Office, Audit Scotland and the Northern Ireland Audit Office. A chartered accountancy qualification with CIPFA, ACCA, ICAEW, ICAS, ICAI or CIMA is required.

External auditors join a company as a graduate and study for a professional qualification with one of the above accountancy bodies. Degrees in maths, accountancy or economics may be useful.

The National Audit Office has a 2 year programme for school leavers which leads to an Association of Accounting Technicians (AAT) qualification. Internal auditors can come from a variety of academic backgrounds. Prior experience in finance or business is an advantage. The Diploma in Internal Audit Practice is offered by the Institute of Internal Auditors; entry is either with a degree or recommendation by an employer.

Money guide

As a graduate starting training you could earn £15,000–£25,000 per year. This could rise to £30,000–£45,000 a year when you are qualified. A senior manager can earn between £50,000 and £90,000, and even up to £150,000. Salaries can be up to 20% higher in London.

Related opportunities

- Accountant p16
- Actuary p20
- Chartered/Company Secretary p26
- Financial Adviser p39

Further information

Association of Chartered Certified Accountants
29 Lincoln's Inn Fields, London WC2A 3EE
020 7396 5800; www.acca.co.uk; info@accaglobal.com

Chartered Institute of Management Accountants
26 Chapter Street, London SW1P 4NP
020 8849 2251; www.cimaglobal.com;
cima.contact@cimaglobal.com

Institute of Internal Auditors – UK and Ireland Ltd
13 Abbeville Mews, 88 Clapham Park Road, London SW4 7BX
020 7498 0101; www.iia.org.uk; studentsupport@iia.org.uk

BANK CASHIER/ CUSTOMER ADVISER

What the work involves

- Bank cashiers/customer advisers work for banks and building societies, and are the first point of contact for customers with enquiries or complaints.

- You may be working in a branch dealing with customers face to face, or you could be based in a contact centre liaising with them over the phone or by email.

- You will be handling customers' accounts, including the paying in and withdrawing of money using computerised systems.

- You will also be expected to sell the company's products and services, which will involve working to set sales targets.

The type of person suited to this work

You will need excellent customer service skills so that you can process their requests efficiently, and also gain their trust in order to advise them on a range of financial products.

You must be confident working with figures and ICT, and working to targets.

As you will be handling money, you should be trustworthy and able to work accurately, paying close attention to detail.

Since you will be working as part of a team, a helpful and positive attitude coupled with the ability to use your own initiative is valuable.

Working conditions

In a branch you will probably work normal office hours, and Saturdays if the bank is open. Call centres usually offer a 24 hour service, so you should expect to work shifts that include nights and weekends.

Part-time and flexible working hours are commonly available.

You should be well presented, and will usually be required to wear a uniform.

Future prospects

Job opportunities in the financial sector are currently depleted due to the economic downturn, with a trend of bank mergers and the closing of high street branches. Despite this, opportunities are still available, especially given the recent trend for re-opening UK call centres as a drive to attract customers.

You could specialise in an area such as mortgages or pensions, or gain further professional qualifications in order to train as a financial adviser or bank manager.

Advantages/disadvantages

Looking after customers and helping to solve their queries can be interesting and rewarding.

Banks offer well-structured training programmes on entry, and you will have a clear route of career progression.

Qualifications and courses

You need a minimum of 4 GCSEs/S grades (A*–C/1–3) including English and maths, or equivalent qualifications

Other useful qualifications include City & Guilds Awards in Customer Service Levels 1, 2 and 3, City & Guilds Levels 2 and 3 Certificate and Diploma in Business and Administration, the IFS Level 2 Diploma in Introduction to Financial Services, any BTEC national qualification in Business or Personal and Business Finance, and CCN Level 2 and 3 Awards in Introduction to Financial Services.

Most banks also offer a variety of trainee programmes for A level or graduate entrants. You will usually need either 2 A levels or a higher second class degree in any subject. Competition for places is intense, so some relevant work experience could be helpful.

You can also enter this career by doing an Apprenticeship in Financial Services.

Because of the economic downturn, entry into this profession is more competitive than ever before.

Money guide

You could expect to earn between £11,500 and £14,000 in your first couple of years as a trainee. With several years' experience you could be earning up to £24,000. Senior customer advisers, especially those who have specialised in a certain financial area, can earn £30,000+.

You may receive bonuses for meeting sales targets, and most employers also offer packages that include cheaper mortgages, pensions, loans and insurance.

Related opportunities

- Financial Adviser p39
- Bank Manager p23
- Accounting Technician/Finance Clerk p18
- Pensions Adviser p54

Further information

IFS School of Finance
IFS House, 4–9 Burgate Lane, Canterbury, Kent CT1 2XJ
01227 818609; www.ifslearning.ac.uk;
customerservice@ifslearning.ac.uk

Financial Services Skills Council (FSSC)
51 Gresham Street, London EC2V 7HQ
0845 257 3772; www.fssc.org.uk; info@fssc.org.uk

www.cityandguilds.com/myperfectjob

BANK MANAGER

What the work involves

- Bank managers are responsible for running branches of retail, commercial or corporate banks.

- You will be accountable for staff recruitment, motivation and training, as well as meeting budget and sales targets for products and services.

- You will be required to keep up-to-date with a range of financial products, and market your services to individuals and businesses.

- Attending meetings and preparing reports on branch operations for both staff and head office will also be important tasks.

The type of person suited to this work

Bank managers work with people at all levels, so excellent verbal and written communications skills are essential.

You will be expected to deal with customers on a daily basis, as well as leading and motivating your team, both of which require confidence, organisation, negotiation skills, initiative and the ability to think on your feet.

You should be comfortable working with numbers as you will have to meet budget and sales targets, and calculate profits.

Working conditions

You will usually work normal office hours and occasional Saturdays, in keeping with the opening hours of your bank. If you manage a call centre, you will probably be required to work shifts in order to provide a 24 hour service to customers.

As well as working in an office, you will occasionally travel to visit clients at their business premises, so a driving licence could be useful.

Future prospects

Despite recent bank mergers, the number of management positions has stayed quite stable. As a branch manager, you could progress to become a regional manager, or use your skills and experience to work in the company's head office. You could also specialise in areas such as training, human resources or marketing.

London is one of the leading financial centres of the world and offers the best opportunities for pursing a high-level career. There are also numerous roles located overseas.

Advantages/disadvantages

This challenging, fast-moving industry offers many opportunities in various sectors including telephone and internet banking, and also in various organisations including supermarkets which are now offering banking services.

Within investment and merchant banking you can earn extremely high salaries.

You will need to meet challenging targets in an increasingly

Qualifications and courses

ENTRY LEVEL 2

Most entrants hold a degree or equivalent qualification. You will need at least a 2.2 Honours degree to secure a place on a graduate management training scheme. Relevant subjects such as maths, business studies, economics or accountancy are often preferred. Training lasts 18–24 months. For degree entry you will need at least 2 A levels and 5 GCSEs. The Diploma in Business, Administration and Finance may also be useful. It's advisable to study a foreign language if you wish to apply to an international bank.

You can start work in a bank in a service role with GCSEs (A*–C) and then progress your way to management by studying for professional qualifications. The IFS School of Finance Professional Diploma in Financial Services Management, Certificate in Personal Finance or the Certificate/Diploma in Financial Studies may all be useful.

competitive market which is sensitive to changes in the national and global economy.

Money guide

Graduates on bank management training schemes can expect to make £19,500–£25,000.

With qualifications and experience this increases to £26,000–£50,000. Senior staff, such as area managers, can earn salaries of £50,000–£100,000. Merchant and investment bankers can earn higher salaries still.

You may get bonuses for meeting targets. Additional benefits usually include cheaper mortgages, pensions, loans and insurance.

Related opportunities

- Accountant p16
- Financial Adviser p39
- Insurance Broker p42

Further information

IFS School of Finance
IFS House, 4–9 Burgate Lane, Canterbury CT1 2XJ
01227 818609; www.ifslearning.ac.uk;
customerservices@ifslearning.ac.uk

Chartered Institute of Bankers in Scotland
Drumsheugh House, 38b Drumsheugh Gardens,
Edinburgh EH3 7SW
0131 473 7777; www.charteredbanker.com;
info@charteredbanker.com

City&
Guilds

BUSINESS ADVISER

What the work involves

- Business advisers provide independent advice to an array of small and medium-sized businesses or enterprises (SMEs), in order to improve the success of a business.

- You will provide advice on prospective business plans and recommend relevant specialist services and suppliers that could support the venture.

- You may run workshops and seminars that offer basic support and information for new or existing businesses.

- You will need to be informed about more than one area of business, but will often choose to specialise in an area, such as marketing and public relations (PR), accountancy and taxation, and law.

The type of person suited to this work

You will need to have a good understanding of a variety of business environments and sizes, whilst being able to use this knowledge through offering advice on current business issues, geographical trends and financial help available to support new or failing businesses.

You need to be logical and objective, yet approachable and enthusiastic. You will need the ability to manage a variety of projects whilst consistently meeting tight deadlines.

Working conditions

Hours tend to follow the national average of between 37 and 40 hours a week, working 9am–5.30pm, Monday to Friday. Should there be weekend or evening events to attend then these hours will increase.

You will be mostly office based, with occasional visits to client premises, suppliers' or to networking events. There are also self-employment consultancy opportunities available, which would allow you to work from home.

Future prospects

With approximately 12,000 business advisers in the UK, this is a thriving industry, with opportunities nationwide. Vacancies are posted on enterprise and business support organisations' websites, and in publications, such as IBC's journal, *Business Adviser*.

It is important to gain accreditation, such as the IBC's internationally recognised Certified Management Consultant (CMC) Award, which can be applied for after gaining three years' practical experience. Through this, business advisers are eligible to join the national register for business support professionals.

Advantages/disadvantages

Employment as a business adviser allows for a certain amount of autonomy, whilst the using of initiative in an advisory position is often rewarding.

It is important to gain recognised awards, such as the CMC

Qualifications and courses

There are no specific entry qualifications but advisers must have substantial business experience. Many advisers have prior experience running a business or working as a management consultant. Others have expertise in a key area of business, such as senior management, marketing or finance.

You may want to start off with GSCEs and A levels in applied business or business studies before gaining practical experience in the industry. The Diploma in Business, Finance and Administration may also be useful. Business-related degree courses and diplomas that include a year in industry are recommended.

The Institute of Business Consulting (IBC) provides professional qualifications for business advisers including a Certificate in Management Consultancy Essentials and a Diploma in Business Support.

Bodies, such as IBC, Technology Means Business and the Small Firms Enterprise Development Initiative (SFEDI) have begun regulating and accrediting business advisers. You will be required to purchase professional indemnity insurance provided by the IBC before offering your services.

from the IBC, in order to prove to clients that you are a certified adviser with business experience.

Money guide

Business advisers can expect around £20,000 a year.

This will increase to £30,000 through the gaining of experience.

For senior positions, salaries are over £50,000.

Related Opportunities

- Regeneration Manager/Economic Development Officer p60
- Management Consultant p50
- Project Manager p56
- Company Director p30

Further information

Institute of Business Consulting (IBC)
Chartered Management Institute, 4th Floor, 2 Savoy Court, London WC2R 0EZ
020 7497 0580; www.ibconsulting.org.uk

National Federation of Enterprise Agencies (NFEA)
12 Stephenson Court, Fraser Road, Priory Business Park, Bedford MK44 3WJ
01234 831623; www.nfea.com

City&
Guilds

www.cityandguilds.com/myperfectjob

School Profile

LIVERPOOL BUSINESS SCHOOL

ONLY A FIVE minute walk from the centre of Liverpool you'll find Liverpool Business School (LBS), one of the leading parts of Liverpool John Moores University (LJMU). A modern and dynamic educational establishment, the School is set around tranquil gardens and boasts an award-winning, state-of-the-art learning resource centre. With over 30 years' experience to draw on, this large Business School has over 5,000 students enrolled on undergraduate, postgraduate and professional programmes.

LBS offers a range of degree programmes spanning a number of areas, including: Accounting and Financial Management, General Business and Management, Human Resource Management, Information & Library Management, Marketing, and Public Relations.

At undergraduate level, LBS offers:

- BA Business Studies
- BA Accounting and Finance
- BA Marketing
- BA International Business and Languages
- BA Public Relations and Languages
- BA Business and Economics
- BA Business and Public Relations

LBS has a team of extremely experienced academics who use the latest and most modern student-centred methods of teaching on all courses. The School is continually exploring new ways in which it can improve the employability of its graduates and it places considerable emphasis on the practical nature of its programmes. For example, a number of students were this year able to study for the Chartered Management Institute (CMI) Level 5 Certificate in Management and Leadership alongside their sandwich year placement. Through this initiative the students were able to gain new and invaluable skills, making them more attractive to future employers. One of the students said:

"I am so delighted to be doing the CMI Level 5 Certificate in Management and Leadership as part of my course, it is a unique opportunity that has really put me ahead of the game now in the graduate market.

"I have been given a real chance to gain so many new and practical work skills.

"I know that by the time the placement is finished there will be many things that I achieved to take away with me."

LJMU is a truly international university with over 24,000 students from all over the world. The University has embarked on a major campus redevelopment programme to ensure that LJMU truly is a 21st century university. The £24 million Art & Design Academy – the biggest investment in arts education in the UK today – is the first of our major projects to be completed.

If you want to have a great university experience, graduate with a respected qualification and secure the skills and 'know-how' that will help you climb the professional career ladder, then you should choose Liverpool Business School at LJMU.

For more information about Liverpool Business School contact the BLW Admissions Team on 0151 231 3999 or email: BLWadmissions@ljmu.ac.uk. Alternatively, you can visit the website at www.ljmu.ac.uk/lbs

CHARTERED/COMPANY SECRETARY

What the work involves

- This is a vital administrative and managerial role. You will have a high level of responsibility.

- You will be in a very senior position advising executives and directors on finance and company law.

- You will be responsible for the legal reports all companies are required to keep, reporting to Companies House and other institutions such as the Stock Exchange.

- You will be responsible for running board meetings and could be responsible for financial planning, accounts, wages, human resources and all administrative and ICT systems.

The type of person suited to this work

You will need excellent communication skills to be able to work with people at all levels. You should be interested in business and have a thorough knowledge of how your organisation works. You will need to understand complicated legal and financial issues and be able to use your knowledge to solve problems, maximise efficiency and advise ways of improving and developing the company.

You should be highly organised, able to deal with several tasks at once and pay close attention to detail. You will analyse figures and accounts and work to strict legal guidelines. You must be confident giving presentations to high-level staff.

Working conditions

Most of your work will be office-based, attending lots of meetings, including working at other sites and outside organisations, which could involve some travel and possibly going abroad.

You will normally work office hours but will have a heavy workload and a lot of responsibility; you will need commitment and dedication to work overtime and meet deadlines.

To be successful, a high level of personal and professional integrity is important.

Future prospects

The Companies Act 2008 means that private companies are no longer legally required to have a company or chartered secretary. Despite this change, businesses will still have to meet a range of legal requirements so most will continue to employ a company secretary.

An experienced company secretary will have opportunities to work in highly paid jobs in a range of organisations, and you could go on to specialise or could become a self-employed consultant.

Advantages/disadvantages

This is a high-level career which is interesting, varied and challenging. You will use a wide range of skills and

Qualifications and courses

You will need a degree, Foundation degree, HNC/HND or equivalent to enter and train in this career.

At least 1 A level/2 H grades or equivalent are required for entry onto a HNC/HND course, while degree courses require 2 A levels/3 H grades and 5 GCSEs/S grades (A*–C/1–3) or equivalent.

You will need to become a member of the Institute of Chartered Secretaries and Administrators (ICAS), by taking their International Qualifying Scheme. This has four stages: Certificate in Business Practice, Diploma in Business Practice, and the Professional Programme Parts 1 and 2.

To become an associate member (ACIS), you will need at least 3 years' work experience (6 if you have not got a degree).

After at least 5 years (8 if you have not got a degree), and when you are working at a very senior level, you can become a Fellow of the Institute (FCIS).

ICSA offer courses for extra qualifications, which can be done full or part time depending on your job and responsibilities.

knowledge, prospects are good and earnings can be high. But you will have to take on a lot of responsibility and work long hours; you might have to prepare information for directors if the company is doing badly.

Money guide

Graduates starting out can expect to earn anything between £28,000 and £32,000 per year. With some experience you can earn between £45,000 and £70,000. Very experienced secretaries can earn between £80,000 and £130,000.

Related opportunities

- Accountant p16
- Barrister/Advocate p363
- Company Director p30
- Auditor p21

Further information

Institute of Chartered Secretaries and Administrators
16 Park Crescent, London W1B 1AH
020 7580 4741; www.icsa.org.uk; info@icsa.co.uk

Companies House
Companies House, Crown Way, Maindy, Cardiff CF14 3UZ
0303 1234 500; www.companieshouse.gov.uk,
enquiries@companies-house.gov.uk

Council for Administration
6 Graphite Square, Vauxhall Walk, London SE11 5EE
020 7097 9620; www.cfa.uk.com; info@cfa.uk.com

CIVIL SERVICE/LOCAL GOVERNMENT ADMINISTRATOR

What the work involves

- Administrators deal with company paperwork via filing, photocopying and faxing, and also store and update information on computer systems.

- Civil service administrators work for specific national government departments, such as planning or environmental.

- You will be required to deal with members of the public and high-level government staff, as well as carrying out normal administrative duties.

- If you work in local government, you are more likely to work across a range of areas such as leisure, environment and public health.

The type of person suited to this work

You will need excellent organisational skills as you will be responsible for administering numerous important projects at a time. The ability to use your initiative, prioritise your workload, and work on your own are also essential.

A high level of accuracy and attention to detail is required in order to keep good records and produce clear correspondence.

Since you will be liaising with team members, the public and high level government staff daily, excellent verbal and written communication skills are vital.

You will need to be able to understand complex information, much of which can involve specialist terminology.

Working conditions

You will probably work normal office hours, and most offices operate a flexitime policy. There are also opportunities for part-time work.

Future prospects

The civil service has an established training and development programme, and is keen to reward hard work and effort with promotion or pay rises in keeping with their grading system.

Local government administrators can continue working upward to a senior administrative level, or diversify into a different career. For example, if you became interested in housing policy, you could undertake appropriate training to become a housing officer or similar.

Advantages/disadvantages

Public sector work offers good holidays, flexible working hours and excellent perks.

Even without advanced qualifications there are opportunities to progress into higher level jobs.

In the initial stages of employment and training, work can be repetitive.

Qualifications and courses

ENTRY LEVEL 4

The majority of entrants have a degree/HND. Degrees in related subjects such as business and management, legal studies, social administration, social policy or politics may give you an advantage.

A Civil Service Fast Stream scheme is open to all graduates, which allows a more focused and rapid career progression from administrative to management level.

School leavers with Level 2 qualifications can go straight into the Civil Service, although they will usually begin by working as an office junior and train on the job to become an administrator. 5 GCSEs/S grades (A*–C/1–3) are normally required, including English and maths. Equivalent qualifications such as an NVQ/SVQ Level 1 or 2 in administration are accepted.

Some departments will require you to undertake a criminal records bureau check prior to commencing employment. You will need to be a UK national, a Commonwealth citizen or have dual nationality (with one being British).

Money guide

Local government administrators can start on a salary of £12,000–£18,500. For graduates, a higher starting salary of £16,000–£21,000 is typical.

With experience, you could earn from £20,000 to £30,000 as a local government administrator.

Salaries for civil service administrators are slightly higher, starting between £15,000 and £27,000. After 4 or 5 years' experience, your salary could rise to £40,000.

Related opportunities

- Personal Assistant p55
- Project Manager p56
- Secretary p63

Further information

Civil Service
Most recruitment is via individual departments and agencies; CivilServiceJobs@cabinet-office.x.gsi.gov.uk

Local Government Association (LGA)
Local Government House, Smith Square, London SW1P 3HZ
020 7664 3131; www.lga.gov.uk; info@lga.gov.uk

City& Guilds

www.cityandguilds.com/myperfectjob

CIVIL SERVICE OFFICER (EXECUTIVE AND ADMINISTRATION)

What the work involves

Civil servant

- Civil servants provide support to government ministers. They are employed by a variety of departments, such as industry and agriculture, revenue, benefits and pensions, the department that issues driving licences or the central administrative, policy and support services.

Executive officer

- A civil service executive officer is the equivalent of a junior manager, with specific activities including the managing of a small team, helping with staff training, advising members of the public and investigating those that are believed to be breaking the law.

Administrative assistant/officer

- Administrative assistants/officers take care of the administration that is required to ensure that government offices are able to operate efficiently.

- Available positions are usually found in the following areas: working in a minister's private office, working in consumer research and advice, a job involving finance or procurement and working in marketing or public relations.

- There are also some opportunities in departments such as human resources, neighbourhood renewal, social justice and European and international relations.

- Specific tasks undertaken involve the updating of records on computers, answering public enquiries, replying to incoming letters and helping with statistics and accounts.

The type of person suited to this work

You should have a neutral interest in governmental affairs, and enjoy providing a service to members of the public.

You must be able to work both independently and as part of a team, as much of the work requires liaising with different departments and working on individual assignments with the received data. In addition to this, those wishing to become executive officers or administrative officers should have management and leadership skills, alongside excellent communication abilities.

You will need to understand government and local authority legislation, and to be able to explain it clearly to those who have limited understanding.

Much of the information that you will be come into contact with is of a confidential nature and so you must be appreciative of privacy rules and discreet when processing confidential information for members of the public.

You will often be working to deadlines, so must be calm, prepared and capable throughout these pressurised situations.

Working conditions

Civil servants usually work between 35 and 37 hours a week, Monday to Friday. There are flexitime schemes in place for all government employees, allowing members of staff to occasionally vary their working hours in order to gain extra holiday time through working overtime.

Hours may occasionally increase during busier periods, should this be suitable for individual employees. 20% of employees work part time, and job share is also widely available, with working parents able to work only during school terms.

All of these positions are office based, with some being open to visits from the public that require the services of government officials. It would occasionally be necessary for executive officers to visit members of the public or organisations.

The dress code tends to be smart/casual, with a relaxed office environment that aims to ensure all employees feel supported in order to reduce stress. 25 days holiday are usually available, and there are even opportunities for career breaks or secondment, which allow for the gaining of experience in a different department for a set amount of time before returning to your permanent position.

Future prospects

The civil service offers a clearly defined promotion structure, with experienced executive officers being able to apply for senior posts after a period of working in their contracted position and gaining experience in relating departments.

Should employees join the civil service through the Fast Stream entry plan, promotion to more senior posts is often awarded after only 3–5 years, due to the intense training scheme.

If an executive officer has at least 2 years' experience and was employed through means other than the Fast Stream service, they are eligible to be nominated as an applicant to the In-service Fast Stream system once they have demonstrated the appropriate skills and abilities.

Through the gaining of experience, civil service administrative assistants can apply for promotion to the role of administrative officer, and once in this position, to executive officer. Executive officers are in a position of junior management and once in this position there are further opportunities for progression.

In all departments of the civil service there is a clear promotional strategy, with it also being possible to cross over into similar departments should the available route of progression not be of interest.

Advantages/disadvantages

The advantages of joining the civil service are the various promotional opportunities on offer, alongside rewarding salaries and the opportunity to help members of the public in a relaxed, yet challenging working environment.

There are many ways in which employees can improve their working experiences through flexitime or even secondment.

The public sector is often viewed as a low paid vocation, with limited budgets sometimes meaning an increased work load when colleagues go on leave or progress to other positions and funds are not available for the replacement of that person.

Money guide

For executive officers, starting salaries are often in the region of £21,000 a year, with those who have gained more experience earning up to £28,000. Through gaining knowledge and by highlighting personal skills and capabilities, officers can be promoted to a higher salary of around £34,000.

Upon appointment, an administrative assistant can expect to earn £15,000 a year, with this increasing to around £20,000 a year. Once experience has been gained within the sector of employment, experienced administrative officers are able to earn up to £25,000 a year.

It should be noted that those who are based in London are usually paid at a higher rate, although all those employed by the Civil Service benefit from a variety of schemes. Included in this is a pension scheme and even discounts on sports and social facilities or the benefit of a subsidised canteen.

Related opportunities

- Health Records Clerk p307
- Project Manager p56

Further information

Civil Service Fast Stream, Application Helpdesk
Pilgrims Well, 427 London Road, Camberley GU15 3HZ
01276 400333; www.faststream.gov.uk

Government Skills
Cabinet Office, Admiralty Arch, The Mall, London SW1A 2WH
020 7276 1611; www.government-skills.gov.uk

National School of Government
Sunningdale Park, Larch Avenue, Ascot SL5 0QE
01344 634000; www.nationalschool.gov.uk

Qualifications and courses

For a position as an executive officer it is not necessary to have a degree, although entry requirements tend to vary between departments so you are advised to contact the sector you are interested in directly. Applicants are increasingly being considered on the merits of their competencies and skills, alongside the amount of experience a candidate might have for the particular job being applied for. Candidates who hold an Honours degree can apply for the Fast Stream service which will lead to faster promotion to a more senior level.

In order to gain relevant work experience it is recommended that you view the Civil Service Recruitment Gateway, as you will find opportunities in a variety of departments and agencies, and even the possibility of a day visit to see whether the working environment is of interest.

Prospective employees will be invited to attend an interview and may even be required to complete a range of tests designed to highlight ability in numeracy, writing, communication and interpersonal skills, along with decision-making and analytical skills.

In order to gain a position as an administrative assistant, it is usually necessary to have at least 2 GCSEs (A*–C), including English and often maths, or equivalent qualifications. Should you not hold these minimum qualifications, the opportunity to present abilities through a written test is sometimes provided.

For those wishing to apply for a position as an administrative officer it is usually necessary to have at least 5 GCSEs (A*–C), including English and often maths, or equivalent qualifications. Many applicants wishing to become a civil service administrative officer hold 2 or more A levels, or equivalent, or even a degree.

Should prospective applicants not wish to pursue a degree route, the Diploma in Business, Administration and Finance and the Diploma in Public Service would be useful. In addition to this, Apprenticeships and Advanced Apprenticeships allow for practical training in a chosen area of work.

There are also Young Apprenticeships available for 14- to 16-year-olds.

COMPANY DIRECTOR

What the work involves

■ As company director you will have responsibility for every aspect of your business. You will be responsible for setting the company's aims and polices and ensuring that it achieves these as efficiently as possible.

■ You might own the company or head a board of directors. In a large company you will probably lead a team of managers who specialise in specific areas such as sales, finance or product development but you will have overall responsibility.

The type of person suited to this work

The ability to analyse problems, find solutions, make decisions and think through their long-term effects is vital. You will need excellent communication skills to motivate staff and help sell your ideas, products and services to your customers and investors.

You should be highly motivated and prepared to work long hours. You must be able to prioritise, work to deadlines, supervise others, take advice and respond to change.

An excellent knowledge and understanding of your business and its markets will be necessary to make your company successful.

Working conditions

You will probably be office based but will attend a lot of meetings with customers, financial and legal advisers, and staff. You should be prepared to work long hours and to travel in the UK and abroad.

Although you will probably be advised by a team of experienced and knowledgeable managers, you will make the final decision and must be prepared to take risks and accept consequences.

Future prospects

Once you are at manager level, you can take professional courses to develop your skills and become a member of the Institute of Directors. IOD members may become qualified as Chartered Directors. There is the opportunity for progression to Chief Executive and then Chair of an organisation. You could also become a part-time non-executive director for other organisations.

If you are successful, there is no limit to what you can achieve.

Advantages/disadvantages

You can get enormous rewards and satisfaction from seeing the company grow and succeed.

You could start your own business based on a personal interest or skill.

You will have huge responsibility and need to be dedicated, hard working and able to cope with failure as well as success.

Qualifications and courses

There is no set route to becoming a company director, but you will usually need experience at senior management level.

You could enter the company at any level and with qualifications and work experience progress up to management-level jobs and then to director.

You could start on a management trainee scheme after taking Level 3 qualifications, but probably after doing a degree. The degree could be in a specialist subject related to the company's business, such as engineering, or you could do a business-related degree.

The Institute of Directors (IOD) and the Chartered Management Institute (CMI) offer courses for the professional development of managers, or you may be able to take them through a professional institute related to your business.

Once you have got management experience you could take a Master's degree in Business Administration.

You may be able to do NVQs/SVQs in Management at Levels 3 and 4 on a management training scheme. Level 5 NVQs/SVQs are available in specialist areas including Operational Management.

Money guide

Earnings will vary enormously depending on the size and success of the business. A trainee manager starts on about £20,000 a year. With a year or two of experience, this can rise to around £40,000+. Directors of large private companies can earn between £50,000 and £1,500,000 plus huge bonuses, or as the owner of your own successful company you could become extremely rich. Salaries tend to be higher in London.

Related opportunities

■ Accountant p16
■ Chartered/Company Secretary p26
■ Financial Adviser p39
■ Management Consultant p50

Further information

Chartered Management Institute
Management House, Cottingham Road, Corby NN17 1TT
01536 204222; www.managers.org.uk;
enquiries@managers.org.uk

Institute of Directors
116 Pall Mall, London SW1Y 5ED
020 7839 1233; www.iod.com

www.cityandguilds.com/myperfectjob

COMPLIANCE OFFICER

What the work involves

- Compliance officers work for financial services organisations, and are responsible for aiding senior management in ensuring that their firm is complying with the rules set by the Financial Services Authority (FSA).

- Alongside this you will investigate complaints from clients that relate to possible breaches of these rules.

- You will explore the ways in which business efficiency can be improved within the FSA rules through the monitoring of sales processes, checking of paperwork and telephone recordings.

The type of person suited to this work

You will need to have an enquiring, analytical mind, enjoy analysing information and be interested in the legal aspects of selling financial products.

It is important that you are an easily approachable person with good communication skills and excellent report writing skills.

The job may be quite demanding and so you should be able to work well under pressure and be capable of working on a variety of projects at one time, whilst remaining organised and informed.

Working conditions

Compliance officers are generally office based, with attendance at meetings being a regular occurrence. They might have to travel around the country, or even overseas for an international company.

Generally, a compliance officer will work in the region of 37 hours a week, 9am to 5pm, Monday to Friday. However, changes to FSA policy may mean that extra hours need to be worked in order to implement changes.

Future prospects

Competition for FSA training posts is high, however you will be entering one of the fastest growing areas in financial services. There are around 9,000 compliance officers in the UK and many other positions involved with compliance, which highlights that the future is alive with prospects.

As you progress within this role you will have the opportunity to experience greater levels of responsibility and roles within management.

Advantages/disadvantages

There are chances for progression within this vocation and opportunities to work from home as a consultant.

You may feel under pressure at times and will often be asked to explain changes to the financial system in a clear and concise way.

Qualifications and courses

ENTRY LEVEL 4

While there are no set qualifications for this profession, most employers prefer candidates with a relevant degree in accountancy, auditing or law. Professional qualifications in investments, insurance or banking are also useful.

Entry requirements for financial degree programmes vary, but are usually a minimum of 2 A levels/3 H grades and 5 GCSEs/S grades (A*–C/1–3), including maths and English.

Many employers offer in-house training programmes. Trainees will work under the supervision of an experienced colleague, whilst gaining qualifications through part-time study, including distance learning.

Should you wish to train before entering the workplace, there are a number of professional bodies that offer relevant qualifications. Recommended courses are: the Diploma in Investment Compliance, offered by the Securities & Investment Institute; a Certificate, Diploma or Advanced Diploma in Financial Planning, offered by the Chartered Insurance Institute; the CeFA, offered by the IFS School of Finance.

Compliance qualifications are also available through the International Compliance Association (ICA), in association with the Warwick University Business School. These vary from introductory courses to programmes designed for those with 3 years' experience in the industry and/or a relevant degree.

Money guide

Although rates of pay vary depending upon geographical location, compliance officers can expect a starting salary in the region of £25,000–£40,000 a year.

As you gain more experience your salary will increase to around £50,000 a year.

Should you wish to progress further, you can expect to earn over £80,000 a year as a Head of Compliance.

Related opportunities

- Auditor p21
- Financial Adviser p39
- Risk Manager p62

Further information

The Financial Services Authority (FSA)
25 The North Colonnade, London E14 5HS
020 7066 1000; www.fsa.gov.uk

International Compliance Association (ICA)
Wrens Court, 52–54 Victoria Road, Sutton Coldfield,
Birmingham B72 1SX
0121 362 7534; www.int-comp.org

Compliance Institute
107 Barkby Road, Leicester LE4 9LG
0116 246 1316; www.complianceinstitute.co.uk

CREDIT ANALYST

What the work involves

- Credit analysts deal with both personal and business credit. They assess the individual circumstances of the application, using statistical and accounting criteria in order to decide the extent of the risk involved when lending.

- Much of the work involves administration and figure work, due to a need for the analysis of given data and the writing of reports and presentations.

- To thoroughly assess an application, an analyst must have an understanding of legal, compliance and business issues. For instance, a business application would be considered against economic growth and the country's financial stability.

The type of person suited to this work

You should have an interest in the financial sector and have a general and varied knowledge of the business world. Much of the work deals with statistics and so analysts need computer skills and the ability to work with spreadsheets and specialist statistical software packages.

You need to have good organisational and both verbal and written communication skills so that you can explain concepts to non-specialists.

Working conditions

Daily working hours range from 9am to 5pm or 5.30pm, Monday to Friday. There may be times when you will be required to work extra hours. However, there are also opportunities for part-time working.

Generally, credit analysts are based in offices, with much of their work involving computer based activities and the monitoring of the financial markets, with the occasional need to present changes in the market to senior staff.

Future prospects

There are currently more vacancies than applicants, with job opportunities being stable. This vocation holds many avenues for promotion or progression into other areas of banking. Most opportunities are available in London, West Yorkshire, Cardiff and Scottish cities.

Vacancies are published in *The Banker* and *The Economist*. The Institute of Financial Services (IFS) School of Finance, the Chartered Financial Analyst Institute (CFA) and the Institute of Credit Management (ICM) Recruitment Consultancy post vacancies on their websites.

Advantages/disadvantages

There are many opportunities, with routes for promotion and progression being advantageous and salaries being rewarding.

Credit analysts often have to make difficult decisions about awarding or denying credit; this could make it a high pressured job when in a corporate environment.

Qualifications and courses

Credit analysts usually have a degree and enter the profession through a graduate training scheme. Suggested degree courses include economics, business studies, maths and statistics. Also recommended are subjects that include a high level of numerical content, for instance computer science, physics and electronics. Professional qualifications in areas such as accountancy improve career prospects.

In order to be accepted onto one of the above degree courses, prospective students need at least 5 GCSEs/S grades (A*–C/1–3) and 2 A levels/3 H grades. However, most degree courses will ask for qualifications above this minimum suggestion.

The larger commercial and investment banks offer career training programmes for mature candidates. There are also some professional bodies that offer relevant qualifications, such as the IFS School of Finance and the ICM.

Credit analysts are expected to take part in Continuing Professional Development (CPD), which involves reading relevant journals and undertaking skills-related courses.

Much of the work involves being office based, using a computer to track market changes and scrutinise statistics.

Money guide

Credit analysts can expect to earn between £22,000 to £25,000 a year when newly appointed, with this rising to between £35,000 and £60,000 a year with experience. Due to the progression opportunities being good in this profession, a senior analyst for a major corporation can expect to earn more than £90,000 a year when part of a senior management team. Additional benefits could include subsidised mortgages, pensions, private healthcare and share option schemes.

Related opportunities

- Accounting Technician/Finance Clerk p18
- Bank Manager p23
- Economist p34
- Insurance Broker p42
- Insurance Underwriter p45

Further information

Chartered Financial Analyst Institute (CFA)
10th Floor, One Canada Square, London E14 5AB
020 7531 0751; www.cfainstitute.org

Financial Services Skills Council (FSSC)
51 Gresham Street, London EC2V 7HQ
0845 257 3772; www.fssc.org.uk

Institute of Financial Services (IFS) School of Finance
IFS House, 4–9 Burgate Lane, Canterbury CT1 2XJ
01227 762600; www.ifslearning.com

DEBT COLLECTOR

What the work involves

- Debt collectors are employed to recover assets for the organisation that is owed the money.

- The debtor is firstly contacted by letter or telephone, they then receive a personal visit should this not work, and are finally contacted by a solicitor if the matter remains unresolved.

- The five areas of specialism include consumer debt collection, commercial debt collection, international collection, legal collection, and debtor tracing.

- Specific activities include helping debtors by arranging payment through instalments and becoming involved with debt collections that have entered the legal system.

The type of person suited to this work

The job of a debt collector can often be challenging and sometimes confrontational, so a person entering this profession needs to be resilient, determined and skilled in all forms of communication. Empathy with the debtor's situation is required at times and is often just as important as assertiveness and the ability to negotiate a suitable solution for both parties.

Debt collectors require commercial awareness and an understanding of consumer and credit law, should they be involved in legal collections. Knowledge of the financial and credit industries, and numeracy and IT skills will also be of benefit.

Working conditions

Commercial debt collectors work from 9am until 5pm, Monday to Friday. It may sometimes be necessary to work extra hours, in this case in order to meet monthly collection targets.

In comparison, consumer debt collectors may work from 8am to 9pm, Monday to Saturday. However, these hours are usually part of a flexible shift system.

Most debt collectors will be office based and work in teams; in comparison field agents are often based at home and are self-employed, often visiting debtors' homes or places of work.

Future prospects

You will be entering an ever increasing profession that employs around 10,000 people, with employment opportunities existing throughout the UK.

Due to the UK being a capitalist, consumer society, overdue debt is a constant problem, with this allowing for good opportunities in the future of debt collecting.

This is one of few professions that will benefit from the current economic crisis.

Advantages/disadvantages

The job can often be confrontational and challenging, with consumer debt collectors sometimes working unsociable hours.

However, the salary is often rewarding and helping debtors arrange more manageable repayments can often be gratifying.

Qualifications and courses

ENTRY LEVEL 2

This vocation does not require specific qualifications. However, employers may look for GCSEs (A*–C) in English and maths. The Diploma in Business, Administration and Finance may also be useful.

If you want to progress to management roles you will need a degree with an element of credit management. For degree entry you will need at least 2 A levels and 5 GCSEs (A*–C).

There are a variety of vocational courses available, with the Institute of Credit Management (ICM) providing professional qualifications, such as the ICM Diploma in Credit Management. There is also the City & Guilds Diploma in Debt Collection, which is offered by the Credit Services Association (CSA). In addition to this, the CSA offers courses on features of debt collection, and includes information on how to deal with abusive debtors and telephone collection techniques.

Prospective debt collectors could also take part in Credit Management Training courses, with topics including cash collection and DIY legal action. CMT also offer a Level 4 Diploma in Credit Management accredited by NCFE. This awards participants with an MACP (Diploma) as well as membership of the Association of Credit Professionals for the first year.

Money guide

The general starting wage for a debt collector is usually £14,000 a year, with this increasing to £30,000 through the gaining of experience. Through becoming self-employed and establishing a successful business, debt collectors could earn more than £35,000 a year. When working for a company, target related bonuses may be given on top of basic salaries.

Related opportunities

- Bailiff/Enforcement Agent p362
- Debt Counsellor/Money Advice Caseworker p572
- Financial Adviser p39
- Private Investigator p556

Further information

Credit Management Training Ltd (CMT)
The Old Surgery, Church Street, Cropwell Bishop, Nottingham NG12 3BY
0115 989 9997; www.cmtltd.co.uk

Credit Services Association (CSA)
Wingrove House, Ponteland Road,
Newcastle upon Tyne NE5 3AJ
0191 286 5656; www.csa-uk.com

The Institute of Credit Management (ICM)
The Water Mill, Station Road, South Luffenham, LE15 8NB
01780 722900; www.icm.org.uk

ECONOMIST

What the work involves

- Economists play a vital role in a country's financial stability, with the government, financial institutions and major businesses taking heed of their advice.

- Economists research and analyse a variety of mathematical modelling techniques and data, with the information received being used to identify and predict economic changes.

- Many economists work alone, although much of their work will be through consultation with statisticians, civil servants, and marketers.

The type of person suited to this work

The work of an economist takes into account many factors and so it is necessary for them to have an interest in current affairs, politics, social welfare and business, alongside economics. Much of the job centres on the researching and analysing of market trends, so a methodical and accurate, self-reliant nature is essential, as often they are required to advise and report on situations through their own interpretation. Economic information reported in an unambiguous way will be sought; due to this economists must be able to communicate their understanding of a situation in a clear and concise way.

Working conditions

Economists tend to work regular office hours, between 9am and 5.30pm, Monday to Friday. However, some related sectors could require extended hours due to the work topic being unpredictable. For those that work in the Civil Service and similar sectors, flexibility may be allowed in relation to hours worked, with part-time work and job sharing being an option.

Economists are mostly office based, with the occasional need to travel to meet clients or to be present at conferences and seminars, to which they may need to contribute.

Future prospects

This profession holds many exciting opportunities, such as the chance to progress to an economic adviser after only three to four years, based on your ability and drive. Many economists choose to become self-employed or to work abroad with multinational companies after gaining experience and establishing a reputation.

120 new assistant economists are employed by the GES each year through September and February recruitment. The Bank of England also offers opportunities through their 3-year Analyst Career Training programme.

Advantages/disadvantages

This job offers fantastic career prospects, with there being opportunities for progression in a short amount of time once training has been completed.

Qualifications and courses

ENTRY LEVEL 5

You will need a 2.1 degree or higher in economics. A joint degree in economics and another related subject such as law, politics, finance, maths, or even a business studies degree with a high economic content, is often acceptable. Many employers are also increasingly requiring candidates to hold a postgraduate degree.

Entry on to a degree usually requires at least 2 A levels, including maths and preferably economics. Five GCSEs (A*–C), including maths and English are necessary prior to this. For entry on to a postgraduate degree you will need a 2.1 Honours degree.

On top of academic achievement, knowledge of a foreign language may aid employment prospects, as would relevant work experience. With regard to this, the Government Economic Service offers work experience placements, as does the Bank of England. These include internships, sponsorships, sandwich placements, gap year placements and vacation work placements.

The salary is highly competitive, when compared to other professions, and the working hours are relatively average.

Tight deadlines, political pressure and the need to juggle different projects can make the job a demanding one.

Money guide

New assistant economists start on a respectable wage of £25,000 a year, with this increasing to approximately £37,000 through the gaining of experience. Once they have progressed to senior level, economists could earn around £60,000 or more, with top economists in finance and consulting having the earning potential of £250,000.

Related opportunities

- Accountant p16
- Actuary p20
- Mathematician/Research Scientist (Maths) p527
- Statistician p536

Further information

Bank of England
Threadneedle Street, London EC2R 8AH
020 7601 4444; www.bankofenglandjobs.co.uk

Government Economic Service (GES)
HM Treasury, 1 Horse Guards Road, London SW1A 2HQ
020 7270 4571/5073; www.ges.gov.uk

Royal Economic Society
School of Economics & Finance, University of St Andrews, KY16 9AL
01334 462479; www.res.org.uk

ENVIRONMENTAL HEALTH PRACTITIONER/OFFICER

What the work involves

- Some environmental health practitioners are responsible for all aspects of environmental health in their local areas, while others specialise in either food safety, housing conditions, workplace health and safety, or environmental conditions.

- Your tasks might include developing public health policies, carrying out inspections in premises such as restaurants, houses and workplaces to identify any hazards and ensure that relevant laws are being followed, and educating and advising the public and businesses.

- You will also carry out investigations of accidents or outbreaks and contaminations.

The type of person suited to this work

You must be interested in finding ways of improving public health, and will need a scientific and logical approach to collect and assess evidence and use it to identify and solve problems. Excellent written and verbal communication skills are vital for explaining regulations clearly and simply to a wide range of people.

You have to be able to handle challenging situations, for example when confronting noisy neighbours. You must be able to enforce the law when necessary.

You need to be comfortable working both alone and as part of a team.

Working conditions

You will be office-based, but spend a lot of time visiting homes and businesses such as restaurants and factories in your local area. Some of the places you visit will be smelly, dirty or potentially dangerous and you will sometimes have to wear protective clothing.

You will probably work a normal working week from Monday to Friday, but you will occasionally need to work evenings and at weekends.

Future prospects

Job opportunities are good as there is a strong demand for environmental health practitioners. Most jobs are with local authorities, but you could also work for central government agencies such as the Food Standards Agency, or for environmental protection consultancies, the NHS, holiday companies or the food industry.

With experience, you could progress to higher levels such as senior, principal or chief environmental officer. Self-employment and working abroad are also options.

Advantages/disadvantages

It can be challenging dealing with people who are angry, for example when enforcing regulations.

Qualifications and courses

To become an environmental health officer, you will need a BSc or MSc in environmental health accredited by the Chartered Institute of Environmental Health (CIEH) or the Royal Environmental Health Institute of Scotland (REHIS).

Entry to a first degree normally requires 2 A levels/3 H grades including a science subject, plus 5 GCSEs/S grades (A*–C/1–3) including English, maths and science, or equivalent. Entry to the MSc requires a first degree in a relevant science or technology subject accredited by the CIEH or REHIS, or equivalent.

It is also necessary to complete a 9–12 month work placement. This can be incorporated into a first degree through a sandwich year or completed after graduation in England and Wales. Successful completion of all the training requirements leads to the Environmental Health Officers' Registration Board Certificate and graduate membership of the CIEH.

In Scotland, at least 48 weeks of the training period must be with a local authority, supervised by REHIS. Training may be undertaken during university holidays or after graduation. Successful completion of all the training requirements leads to the REHIS Diploma in Environmental Health.

You will have the satisfaction of protecting the health and safety of people and improving their quality of life.

You may have to face some distressing sights.

Money guide

Starting salaries are around £20,000+ per year for local authority environmental health officers. This can increase to around £35,000 with experience.

Senior staff can earn up to £65,000 a year.

Salaries in the private sector vary. Environmental health officers working for private companies may earn more than those in local authorities, but this is not always the case.

Related opportunities

- Food scientist/technologist p518
- Health and Safety Adviser p40
- Health Promotion/Education Specialist p306
- Trading Standards Officer p498

Further information

Chartered Institute of Environmental Health
Chadwick Court, 15 Hatfields, London SE1 8DJ
020 7928 6006; www.cieh.org

Royal Environmental Health Institute of Scotland
19 Torphichen Street, Edinburgh, EH3 8HX
0131 229 2968; www.rehis.org; contact@rehis.com

EQUALITY AND DIVERSITY OFFICER

What the work involves

- Your role is to ensure that businesses and public organisations do not discriminate on disability, race, gender, sexuality, age or religion.

- You will make sure that services such as education and health are accessible to everyone.

- You will promote positive images of all groups and promote diversity in all company literature.

- You will advise on how to attract job applicants from all sections of the local community and ensure the company is following all the relevant legislation.

The type of person suited to this work

You should be committed to working for change, be persuasive and good at negotiating. At the same time you need to be a good listener, be sensitive and diplomatic in the way you deal with people and situations.

You will need excellent communication skills and should be confident in giving presentations, advising management and delivering training.

You will need to be able to understand all the relevant equal opportunities laws and regulations and be able to apply them to all policies and procedures within the company, offering advice on any new developments and how to implement them.

For some jobs you might need specialist skills such as being able to speak another language.

Working conditions

Much of your time will be office based doing normal office hours. However, you will probably do quite a bit of evening and weekend work too, organising special events and working with community groups.

You may visit other businesses and organisations, so a driving licence may be useful.

Future prospects

Opportunities are increasing but competition is strong. Government departments, local authorities, universities, trade unions and other large companies employ specialist equal opportunities advisers. In smaller companies the work is covered by the human resources department.

You could progress into management and will develop specialist knowledge and experience, so you could work for yourself offering a consultancy service to companies who want to ensure they are working within equal opportunities legislation.

Many public services are focusing upon delivering services to asylum seekers and immigrants. This means many organisations are employing officers to work specifically with these minority groups.

Qualifications and courses

It is possible to enter this career with qualifications at Levels 2 or 3, but most people have a degree, HND or equivalent, and you will need relevant experience. Degrees and HNDs in education, business administration and human resource management are all relevant to this career. A BA Honours degree in Education and Diversity is available at Sheffield Hallam University.

Most people enter this role through experience working in law, human resources, social work or teaching. Many equal opportunities advisers are members of the Chartered Institute of Personnel and Development (CIPD).

Relevant postgraduate courses include race relations or disability studies. These qualifications can be beneficial in acquiring a senior level position.

The CIPD offer short courses for further study, including Discrimination and the Law, and The Psychology of Diversity. A number of short courses are also run by colleges and training centres and include Equal Opportunities (Good Practice) and Equal Opportunities (Legislation).

Advantages/disadvantages

You will be working for a cause you feel passionately about and could be making a real difference to people.

The work can be stressful – you will be dealing with sensitive issues and may be working with people who do not share your beliefs or who have no desire to change.

Money guide

Starting salaries are around £18,000 per year. With experience you can expect up to £40,000. Those in senior positions in large companies can earn over £60,000.

Related opportunities

- Human Resources/Personnel Officer p41
- Training Manager p68

Further information

Equality & Human Rights Commission
Arndale House, Arndale Centre, Manchester M4 3AQ
0161 829 8100; www.equalityhumanrights.com;
info@equalityhumanrights.com

Equality Commission for Northern Ireland
Equality House, 7–9 Shaftesbury Square, Belfast BT2 7DP
028 9050 0600; www.equalityni.org;
information@equalityni.org

ERGONOMIST

What the work involves

- An ergonomist creates designs that aid society, for instance, a chair for comfort and ease or a social environment that accounts for the disabled and the elderly.

- Designs are informed by biomechanics, physiology, psychology, engineering, industrial design, and IT.

- Ergonomists consult with other professionals, including design engineers, production engineers, health and safety practitioners, computer specialists and industrial physicians.

The type of person suited to this work

An interest in the human body and mind, and the ways in which designs can aid quality of life, is an important part of this profession. Ergonomists need to be creative, enquiring and observant in order to meet the needs of society, whilst being approachable and communicative when liaising with supporting professionals ensuring observations are relevant in contemporary society. In order to create the best designs possible, ergonomists must be resilient and unremitting in their search for a perfect design, whilst being analytical and methodical in their research and conclusions about the needs of society.

Working conditions

The general working hours of an ergonomist are usually 9am to 5pm, Monday to Friday. However these hours may vary or increase slightly should attendance be required at research projects, or if approaching deadlines require more manpower. It is possible to be self-employed in this line of work, and through this the hours worked may vary further.

Working environments are variable, with offices usually being the primary base, whilst visits to places of work, such as factories, offices or construction sites, or laboratories might be necessary.

Future prospects

By gaining specialist experience with an organisation it is possible to move on to another company by way of progression. Willingness to change geographical location enhances ergonomists' ability to advance within this industry.

Self-employment is a common option for ergonomists, as there is often work with consultancy firms, or they can become a self-employed ergonomic consultant. There are also opportunities in teaching, training, or working abroad.

Advantages/disadvantages

Society's interest in ergonomics is increasing due to a renewed interest in health and safety, and personal welfare through well

Qualifications and courses

Entry to this profession requires either a BSc degree in Ergonomics from Loughborough University or a degree in a related subject such as biology, engineering, design, medicine. If you graduate in one of the above related degrees you will need to follow this up with a postgraduate course in ergonomics.

For a BSc degree in Ergonomics you will need at least 3 A levels. Useful subjects include maths, physics, biology and psychology.

Relevant work experience is recommended as entry onto degree courses as well as into the industry is competitive.

The Ergonomics Society encourages newly qualified ergonomists to take part in their work experience scheme, 'Opening Doors', with many other organisations across the UK offering schemes that are helpful to those entering the profession. It is also advised to join the Ergonomics Society to make useful contacts.

designed products which aid the body, both psychologically and physiologically.

There may not be as many chances for promotion in this profession as with others, unless you are with a large company.

Money guide

Although figures may vary depending upon geographical region and employer, graduates entering the profession can expect to earn between £17,000 and £25,000 a year. This will rise to between £25,000 and £40,000 through the gaining of experience in the professional field. Senior ergonomists who are near the top of their field can expect to earn £40,000–£50,000.

Related opportunities

- Consumer Scientist p513
- Health and Safety Adviser p40
- Product Designer p185

Further information

The Ergonomics Society
Elms Court, Elms Grove, Loughborough LE11 1RG
01509 234904; www.ergonomics.org.uk;
www.ergonomics4schools.com

Loughborough University
Department of Human Sciences, Loughborough, LE11 3TU
01509 223013/223036; www.lboro.ac.uk

Ergonomics and Safety Research Institute (ESRI)
Garendon Building, Holywell Park, Loughborough LE11 3TU
01509 22 6900; www.lboro.ac.uk/research/esri

ESTATES OFFICER

What the work involves

■ Estates Officers manage, refurbish and uphold land and property that belongs to private landlords, local authorities and organisations involved in land and property owning.

■ Specific activities include the management of an organisation's property portfolio, such as ensuring the amount of rent being paid is sufficient, dealing with tenancy agreements/applications, checking that properties are not being maltreated, and organising any necessary building repair or environmental work.

■ Letting, buying and management are areas of specialism.

The type of person suited to this work

This job is suitable for someone that is able to communicate well in order to co-ordinate the work of colleagues, and has good negotiating skills when discussing tenancy agreements and the terms of a contract. Organisation is of importance when overseeing a portfolio of properties for a client, with an appreciation for detail being paramount when examining a property, proposed legal documents or finances. It is often necessary to be analytical when dealing with written and numerical information, and the ability to write clear and concise reports and presentations is an important requirement of the job.

Working conditions

Working hours tend to be from 9am to 5pm, Monday to Friday. As with many jobs, extra hours may need to be worked in order to attend committees or meet deadlines, although there are also opportunities for flexitime, job sharing and part-time work. This job is mostly office based, although site visits to portfolio buildings may involve being outside in all weathers, a lot of walking, and the climbing of ladders.

Future prospects

Self-employment or employment with a commercial business may be the most sustainable career path for estate officers, due to local authorities privately contracting work to outside companies. Health authorities, civil service departments, university estates departments, charities and the Office of Government Commerce also provide work opportunities.

Opportunity for promotion is more likely in larger estates businesses and departments, with progression leading to appointment as the head of a unit, a specialist area, or department.

Advantages/disadvantages

This position holds a fair amount of responsibility, with the use of leadership qualities and organisational skills on a regular basis increasing the chances of promotion.

Qualifications and courses

A degree is not always necessary for this job, although an increasing number of applicants hold a degree or diploma. Entry to a degree is usually with at least 2 A levels and 5 GCSEs (A*–C), including English and maths. The Diploma in Construction and the Built Environment may also be useful.

You may choose to do an Apprenticeship in Surveying and follow the surveying track or the property and maintenance track.

Many estates officers have qualifications as chartered surveyors or surveying technicians, with there being a wide range of entry routes for these professions. A list of relevant qualifications is available on the Asset Skills website at www.assetskills.org.

Although mostly office based, estate officers often have to make visits to buildings within their remit, which may mean having to work outside in all types of weather.

Money guide

When first entering the profession, a junior estates officer can expect to earn between £18,000 and £27,000 a year. Through the gaining of experience and further qualifications, this amount soon rises to around £33,000 a year. Heads of units, specialist areas or departments often have an income of around £43,000 a year.

Related opportunities

■ Civil Service Officer (Executive and Administration) p28
■ Chartered Surveyor p84
■ Facilities Manager p98
■ Health Service Manager p308

Further information

The College of Estate Management
Whiteknights, Reading RG6 6AW
0118 921 4696; www.cem.ac.uk

Institute of Revenues Rating and Valuation (IRRV)
41 Doughty Street, London WC1N 2LF
020 7831 3505; www.irrv.org.uk

Royal Institution of Chartered Surveyors (RICS)
Surveyor Court, Westwood Way, Coventry CV4 8JE
0870 333 1600; www.rics.org

www.cityandguilds.com/myperfectjob

FINANCIAL ADVISER

What the work involves

- Financial advisers offer client consultations on a wide range of financial issues including mortgages, pensions and investments.
- You will also be producing reports and annual summaries for clients to keep them up to date with their financial situation.
- Tied advisers work for a financial institution, like a bank, advising clients on their services.
- Independent advisers sell products and services offered by a range of companies.

The type of person suited to this work

Good communications skills are essential in order to explain complex financial matters simply to your clients.

You will need to enjoy working with numbers, and have the ability to analyse and understand technical financial information.

You should be honest and reliable. This will allow you to gain the trust of your clients and subsequently sell your products.

You must be self-motivated and organised with good ICT skills.

You will also need an understanding of the relevant financial laws, and to keep up with changes in the industry.

Working conditions

You will usually work standard office hours, but you should be prepared to work longer hours at busy times.

Tied advisers usually work some Saturdays, and independent advisers may have to work evenings and weekends to suit their clients.

You will be expected to dress formally, and to visit clients in their homes or offices so a driving licence would be useful.

Jobs are available throughout the UK, but the majority are based within London and the south-east.

Future prospects

The demand for financial advisers is growing as people increasingly take charge of their own pensions and finances.

Financial advisers work in insurance companies, banks and other businesses, and there is also the option of being self-employed.

Promotion prospects are good, and there are opportunities to take additional qualifications and move into management jobs. You could also specialise in a particular area, perhaps training others or marketing products.

Advantages/disadvantages

Pay and prospects are good; you can specialise in specific financial areas, such as savings or pensions, or become self-employed.

Qualifications and courses

There are no specific entry routes, and requirements depend on the employer. 2 A levels/3 H grades and 5 GCSEs/S grades (A*–C/1–3), including English and maths, are the minimum requirements. Communication and personal skills are also essential.

Useful qualifications include the Diploma in Business, Administration and Finance, the BTEC National Award in Personal and Business Finance, the BTEC Diploma in Business and the Edexcel Level 3 Award in Providing Financial Advice.

Apprenticeships in Providing Financial Services with a track in general insurance or retail banking are available.

On-the-job training is provided, with additional study undertaken part time or through distance/online learning. This is regulated by the Financial Services Authority.

The Chartered Insurance Institute, CIOBS and Institute of Financial Services offer more specialised qualifications, for example the Certificate in Mortgage Advice and Practice.

The job comes with a high level of responsibility, and you will be under pressure to sell products and meet targets.

Money guide

Salaries are often based on performance and meeting targets, so the rates vary between companies. Most financial consultants work either on a fee or commission basis. Starting as a trainee you could earn £19,000–£30,000 per year. Salaries of £35,000–£70,000 are possible if you have a few years' experience and are meeting targets. For the most successful advisers, a salary of £80,000–£120,000+ is possible.

Related opportunities

- Bank Manager p23
- Business Adviser p24
- Stockbroker p66

Further information

Financial Services Skills Council
51 Gresham Street, London EC2V 7HQ
0845 257 3772 www.fssc.org.uk; info@fssc.org.uk

IFS School of Finance
IFS House, 4–9 Burgate Lane, Canterbury CT1 2XJ
01227 818 609; www.ifslearning.ac.uk;
customerservice@ifslearning.ac.uk

Chartered Institute of Bankers in Scotland (CIOBS)
Drumsheugh House, 38b Drumsheugh Gardens, Edinburgh EH3 7SW
0131 473 7777; www.ciobs.org.uk; info@ciobs.org.uk

HEALTH AND SAFETY ADVISER

What the work involves

- You will help maintain a safe workplace by developing and implementing health and safety policies and procedures.

- You will inspect premises and ways of working, ensuring all relevant regulations are followed.

- The work involves investigating and reporting on accidents and giving specialist advice and training to staff on health and safety issues such as fire regulations and dealing with dangerous chemicals.

The type of person suited to this work

You must be investigative, diplomatic and able to visualise the big picture of how a company works and how they can improve.

You will need to understand technical and operational processes and be able to explain your findings and recommendations in a clear and straightforward way.

You should be thorough, methodical and able to understand and apply relevant regulations.

You will also need good ICT and administrative skills and need to be reasonably fit for working safely on large outdoor and industrial sites.

Working conditions

You will be office based but depending on where you work, may have to spend a lot of time visiting factories and building sites. This could mean having to wear protective clothing, working outdoors in all weathers and at heights or in hot, noisy conditions.

You will work normal office hours but many need to be on call at other times in case of emergencies.

Future prospects

The government and European Union are producing more regulations and guidelines to help companies ensure a safe working environment for staff. This means that opportunities are increasing as employers need help implementing and monitoring new legislation.

Many health and safety advisers work in engineering, construction and manufacturing; there are also opportunities to specialise or do consultancy work. It might be necessary to switch jobs in order to be promoted.

Advantages/disadvantages

The work can be varied and you will be instrumental in helping to save people's lives. You will be dealing with important issues that affect people's safety and wellbeing, so there is a lot of responsibility.

Money guide

Starting salaries can range from £20,000 to £24,000 per year. With experience salaries can increase to around £33,700.

Qualifications and courses

Entry to this career normally requires an industry-recognised qualification, which can be a degree, diploma, or equivalent professional qualification. It is possible to gain experience first or alongside taking qualifications, for example at an operational level, in a scientific or technical field. Health and safety advisers are normally corporate members of the Institute of Occupational Safety and Health (IOSH).

Many local authorities and councils also offer Advanced Apprenticeships in occupational health and safety providing relevant training with an employer.

The main professional qualifications are the newly revised National Diploma awarded by the National Examining Board in Occupational Safety and Health (NEBOSH), and the NVQ/SVQ Level 4 in Occupational Health and Safety Practice.

Entry to the NEBOSH Diploma requires an approved qualification in health and safety accredited at Level 3 or above. Evidence of relevant work experience may also be needed.

Salary levels vary according to the sector you work in. In areas such as local government you could earn up to about £35,000 a year, but with experience and working in a high-risk industry such as construction or oil and gas, you could earn over £45,000 a year.

Related opportunities

- Environmental Health Practitioner/Officer p35
- Human Resources/Personnel Officer p41
- Road Safety Officer p624
- Trading Standards Officer p498

Further information

Institute of Occupational Safety and Health
Highfield Drive, Wigston LE18 1NN
0116 2 573100; www.iosh.co.uk

Health & Safety Executive
Rose Court, 2 Southwark Bridge, London SE1 9HS
www.hse.gov.uk; hse.infoline@natbrit.com

British Safety Council
70 Chancellors Road, London W6 9RS
020 8741 1231; www.britishsafetycouncil.co.uk;
mail@britsafe.org

City&
Guilds

www.cityandguilds.com/myperfectjob

HUMAN RESOURCES/ PERSONNEL OFFICER

What the work involves

- Human resources officers are responsible for recruiting the right staff for jobs at all levels and helping them get the training and development that they and the company need.

- You will be involved with negotiations between staff and trade unions on issues such as pay and conditions.

- You will also be involved with discipline, complaints and redundancy.

The type of person suited to this work

You will work with people at all levels, including staff who could be angry or upset, so you will need excellent communication skills.

You should be interested in people and be able to solve problems. You will need to help with negotiations between staff and managers over issues such as pay and conditions.

You may be involved with disciplinary procedures and redundancies which can be very stressful. In these situations you will need to be tactful and diplomatic.

You will have to understand and implement employment legislation, manage a budget, write clear and accurate reports, be organised and methodical and be able to work under pressure.

Working conditions

You will work standard officer hours, 9am–5.30pm, Monday to Friday, although you might need to work extra hours during busy periods. You will visit the different locations and sites of your organisation so that people get to know and trust you, which could also involve being outdoors or in noisy, dirty places.

You must be able to work well with others as you will probably be working as part of a human resources team.

Future prospects

All types of businesses employ HR staff but it's a popular and competitive career so work experience is vital. Many HR officers have a degree but you could work your way up from an administrative role.

You may get more responsibility in a small company but have better prospects in a larger one. You will need to take professional qualifications and could work abroad or become a self-employed consultant.

Advantages/disadvantages

This is a rewarding career if you are interested in people and helping them to develop their skills. You can study for professional qualifications and gain promotion. However, you will be involved in solving disputes between staff and the company, which can be stressful and you might have to make staff redundant.

Qualifications and courses

ENTRY LEVEL 3

There are no minimum entry requirements for this career, but most human resources officers have a degree or postgraduate qualification. Relevant subjects include business studies, human resource management, management, social administration and psychology.

Employers are likely to ask for 5 GCSEs/S grades (A*–C/ 1–3), including English and maths, and some A levels/H grades.

Personnel assistants or administrators can take the Chartered Institute of Personnel and Development's Certificate in Personnel and Practice (CPP) or Certificate in Training Practice (CTP), usually part time at college. The CIPD also offers NVQ/SVQ Level 3 in Personnel Support, a work-based equivalent to the CPP. Either route makes you eligible for Associate membership of the CIPD.

With a degree or HND you train on the job, usually taking CIPD professional qualifications. Some degrees and postgraduate qualifications give exemptions from parts of the Professional Development Scheme (PDS). The PDS has four parts: Leadership and Management, People Management and Development, Specialist and Generalist Personnel and Development, and Applied Personnel and Development.

Some companies offer a graduate training scheme. Usually a 2.2 or 2.1 in any subject is required for these schemes, although degrees in human resources and business may be more relevant.

Money guide

Salaries start at around £22,000–£26,000 per year. Once qualified and with experience, you could earn £30,000–£45,000. Senior staff and HR Managers can earn over £60,000 a year.

Related opportunities

- Recruitment/Employment Agency Consultant p59
- School Administrator/Secretary p203
- Training Officer p68
- Work-based Training Instructor p209

Further information

Chartered Institute of Personnel and Development
CIPD House, 151 The Broadway, London SW19 1JQ
020 8612 6200; www.cipd.co.uk

Employment National Training Organisation (ENTO)
Kimberley House, 47 Vaughan Way, Leicester LE1 4SG
0116 251 7979; www.ento.co.uk; info@ento.co.uk

People Management
17–18 Britton Street, London EC1M 5TP
020 7324 2729; www.peoplemanagment.co.uk

INSURANCE BROKER

What the work involves

- Insurance brokers act as an agent between clients and insurance companies. They advise on the best policies to meet the client's needs and negotiate deals.

- Retail insurance involves general claims whereas wholesale insurance involves more complicated claims such as sourcing cover for the royal family's jewels.

- You will use your knowledge and skills to gauge the risks and costs involved to set a price.

- You will also collect premiums and process all of your accounts.

The type of person suited to this work

Brokers need excellent verbal and written communication skills in order to obtain information, negotiate deals, sell policies and explain complicated financial issues to clients in simple terms. It is essential to be detail oriented and good with numbers.

You will also need to be personable, honest and trustworthy in order to gain your client's confidence. It's essential to be persuasive as well as you want to secure the best deal for your client. You should be able to manage your time well as you will work on multiple projects at once. Good ICT skills are also important.

Working conditions

Brokers could work in a high-street location, selling policies to the public, or in an office where customers call for quotes or claims updates. You will spend a lot of time on the phone, visiting customers and sourcing new business.

Although you will work normal office hours you might need to work the occasional Saturday to meet your client's needs.

Smart dress is important as you must be presentable when meeting with clients.

Future prospects

As a broker you could work in a small company, dealing with a wide range of services, or specialise in a specific area such as household or risk management insurance within a larger organisation.

With experience you might choose to move into a management role or become an account executive dealing with more complex claims and visiting clients on their own sites. You also have the option to train further and become a chartered broker.

Advantages/disadvantages

The insurance industry offers good career prospects and chances for promotion.

Insurance qualifications gained in the UK are respected worldwide allowing you to work abroad.

Qualifications and courses

ENTRY 3 LEVEL

Although there are no formal entry requirements, most organisations prefer at least 2 A levels/3 H grades and 2 GCSEs/S (A*–C/1–3), including English and maths for entrance to a junior position.

Many candidates are graduates in related subjects including accounting, maths, finance, business and economics. Larger companies offer specialised training schemes for graduates.

Apprenticeships at Levels 2 and 3 in providing financial services are also available as an entry route with options to pursue financial advice, general insurance or long-term care insurance.

The Chartered Insurance Institute (CII), the Institute of Financial Services (IFS), and British Insurance Brokers' Association (BIBA) run relevant courses for new entrants. Additional qualifications are offered by the IFS, which are particularly relevant for those seeking to work in financial planning.

Recruiters generally look for entrants with no criminal record.

The work can involve a lot of responsibility and stress as you will be dealing with huge sums of money and sometimes major disasters.

Money guide

Trainee insurance brokers with mainly administrative duties start on £15,000–£22,000 per year. This could increase up to £40,000 with 3–5 years' experience. You could earn £70,000+ as a senior insurance broker. Your pay may vary based on where you live with higher salaries normally in London. Your salary may also be based on commission.

Related opportunities

- Loss Adjuster p49
- Financial Adviser p39
- Insurance Underwriter p45

Further information

Chartered Insurance Institute
42–48 High Road, London E18 2JP
020 8989 8464; www.cii.co.uk; customer.serv@cii.co.uk

British Insurance Brokers' Association
John Stow House, 18 Bevis Marks, London EC3A 7JB
0844 770 0266; www.biba.org.uk; enquiries@biba.org.uk

Financial Services Skills Council
51 Gresham Street, London EC2V 7HQ
0845 257 3772; www.fssc.org.uk/directions

Case study

discover
risk
.co.uk

DISCOVERING RISK: INSURANCE

Here's Hannah Woolford's story

Hannah is a Commercial Business Developer at Allianz where she has been able to gain professional qualifications. Hannah is responsible for looking after several brokers and must visit and develop her relationship with these brokers on a regular basis.

How Hannah progressed at Allianz

"I joined Allianz after completing my A levels. Most of my career has been in Claims where I worked my way up to Technical Claims Handler. I then took a secondment, looking at offshoring, which involved a visit to our office in India. When I returned I decided to move to operational roles and took on a role as a Team Leader, then Claims Business Consultant looking after large clients. I then moved to a Commercial function nine months ago to develop my commercial awareness."

What a typical working day involves

"As a Business Developer I have a number of brokers to look after. My main duties involve visiting these brokers regularly, developing relationships with them and building our business. I regularly review performance of their accounts and discuss innovative ways of working with them. I also get involved in visiting agencies who may want to open an account with Allianz. This role involves a lot of co-ordination internally and externally to ensure my brokers get the best service to meet their needs and ours."

How Hannah's role fits into the wider picture

"My role is all about building lasting relationships, listening to brokers' needs and working with them to make sure our offering suits them and their clients. Like any good business, Allianz has growth targets and my role is to identify where I can obtain growth as well as retain existing business. There are many insurers out there all wanting to do business with brokers so I need to make sure we stand out as a major player."

The most challenging part of Hannah's role

"The biggest challenge I face is prioritising visits and work and making sure I always book time out to deliver on my actions from my meetings. It is a challenge to please all people at all times, which is why honesty and managing expectations is key."

What makes Hannah good at her job

"You need to be very organised and a people person who can communicate with different people at all levels. You also need to be flexible and be comfortable challenging ideas."

The professional qualifications Hannah has attained

"I have completed my ACII and BA in Financial Services. Allianz have been very supportive towards my professional qualifications."

The main benefits of working in Risk

"Insurance offers many opportunities. Working for a large company I have been lucky to change roles and drive my career in the direction I have wanted – there are always job opportunities or secondments available. You get to make a difference and it is great to meet people. The market is big but everyone knows everyone else, so it is a great profession to be part of."

If you want to find out more about a career in Risk, simply visit www.discoverrisk.co.uk or email discover@cii.co.uk.

INSURANCE SURVEYOR

What the work involves

- You will provide insurance companies with relevant information about a site that may affect their decision to accept requests for insurance cover.

- You will investigate sites that need to be insured and prepare reports detailing the risks and recommend ways underwriters can reduce these.

- Your reports will enable underwriters to decide whether or not to accept these risks and what terms and conditions should go into their policies

- You may specialise in one of four areas: Engineering; Fire and Perils; Burglary; or Liability.

The type of person suited to this work

You will come into contact with a diverse range of people and must be able to communicate complicated and technical information in a clear way. You should be honest in order to build your clients' trust and you should have excellent negotiation skills.

An investigative nature will help you survey a variety of risks and you will need to be able to pay close attention to detail and work efficiently under pressure when writing up your reports for insurance companies. Workloads can be heavy so you should be self-motivated and organised.

Good ICT skills are essential.

Working conditions

Most of your time will be spent investigating a variety of sites which could include industrial plants, engineering plants, oil rigs and construction zones. These can be potentially dangerous and polluted and may require you to work at heights. You will need to wear business attire when greeting your customers but change into protective gear when surveying the site.

You will most likely work Monday to Friday during normal office hours but might need to work evenings or weekends depending on your customers' availability. Working from home will give you greater flexibility and is increasingly favoured over being office based.

Future prospects

Career prospects may be affected by the financial climate. However, insurance risks are a high priority for many companies and jobs are currently in demand.

You may choose to specialise in one area of risk such as business interruption or travel overseas to work for a global insurer dealing in international risks.

You could be promoted to corporate risk manager or head of department but this will mean a less hands-on role. Many surveyors also move out of insurance and into the public sector.

Qualifications and courses

ENTRY LEVEL 4

Most employers will expect you to have a degree or HND. Subjects such as science and risk management will be useful. If you want to specialise in engineering insurance you will need an engineering degree.

Although requirements vary between universities and colleges, most degree courses require at least 5 GCSEs (A*–C) and 2 A levels.

You may apply for a graduate training scheme at many large insurance companies. These will require a 2.2 degree or equivalent.

If you complete a Higher Diploma in Business, Administration and Finance you may be able to get a job as an assistant and be promoted to insurance surveyor while studying for professional qualifications such as the CII Diploma in Insurance.

All trainees are required to be CII Associates. You must complete the CII Certificate, Diploma or Advanced Diploma in Insurance in order to apply.

Advantages/disadvantages

You will always be developing and growing in knowledge as no two days will be alike. You also have the chance to meet new people and to travel the world.

Sometimes customers may prove difficult to work with. Visiting hazardous sites on a regular basis can be physically and emotionally demanding.

Money guide

Starting out, insurance surveyors earn between £20,000 and £22,000 a year. With a few years' experience you can earn between £28,000 and £40,000 a year.

If you are a specialist, for example in liability insurance, a manager or head of department, you can earn up to £65,000 a year. This could rise to £100,000 if you work in London. Many employers also offer additional benefits such as medical insurance.

Related opportunities

- Building Surveyor p79
- Civil/Construction Engineer/Civil Engineering Technician p85
- Insurance Underwriter p45

Further information

Lloyd's of London
1 Lime Street, London EC3M 7HA
020 7327 1000; www.lloyds.com; enquiries@lloyds.com

The Chartered Insurance Institute (CII)
42–48 High Road, London E18 2JP
020 8989 8464; www.cii.co.uk

INSURANCE UNDERWRITER

What the work involves

■ Underwriters decide whether or not applications for insurance cover (risks) should be accepted, as well as assessing the size of risks to work out premiums.

■ In all negotiations you should make a profit for your company and protect them from losses.

■ In order to do this you will need to research, interview specialists, analyse statistics and write up policy wording, often inserting additional conditions.

■ You should always keep records of the policies you write.

The type of person suited to this work

Underwriting is a specialist job that requires an in-depth knowledge of risk in order to make predictions from applications. You will need excellent attention to detail, along with numeracy skills, in order to solve complex problems and prepare accurate and detailed reports.

You must be able to work well under pressure and make quick, difficult decisions. You should have a good sense of judgement and be trustworthy when handling confidential information.

Negotiation and communication skills are essential when arranging deals with brokers.

Working conditions

Underwriters' work is mainly office based and travel is rare although commercial underwriters will occasionally travel to meet clients. You will work Monday–Friday but might need to stay late at the office to meet deadlines. Most underwriters do have the option to work on flexitime which means you can shape your hours around what works best for you.

You will spend most of your time at a computer researching and writing up reports. You may need to investigate dangerous or distressing situations at times.

Future prospects

As you gain experience you will attract more difficult and complicated cases which will enable you to earn a promotion or switch companies more easily. Many underwriters choose to move into management or training roles or specialise in one type of insurance such as aviation.

You may wish to set up your own broking company, switch to reinsurance or train in sales and sell insurance packages which can prove to be a profitable option.

Advantages/disadvantages

Underwriters are constantly researching risks and are therefore learning new information every day which makes the job exciting. It offers excellent benefits.

Qualifications and courses

Most companies require a minimum of GCSEs/S grades (A*–C/1–3), including English and maths for entrance to a junior position. This could include a Diploma in Business, Administration and Finance.

Many companies offer graduate training schemes that require a 2.1 degree for entry. Degrees in business, statistics, law, accounting, financial services and economics are useful.

A Level 2 Apprenticeship and Level 3 Advanced Apprenticeship in providing financial services are also available as entry routes with options to pursue general insurance.

The Chartered Insurance Institute (CII) offers certificates, diplomas and advanced diplomas in insurance for new entrants. You will need to complete the Lloyd's and London Market Introductory Test (LLMIT) if you wish to work in London.

You may feel under pressure as you must make difficult decisions regarding risks often at short notice. Insurance can be a tough industry to work in during a recession.

Money guide

Starting salaries for underwriters range from £15,000 to £30,000 a year. If you're experienced and have a Diploma in Insurance you can reach a salary of £50,000. With an Advanced Diploma in Insurance and managerial duties you can expect to earn £70,000+. Lloyd's of London underwriters can earn £300,000+.

Benefit packages are also common including discounted personal insurance and subsidised mortgages.

Related opportunities

■ Actuary p20
■ Insurance Broker p42
■ Insurance Surveyor p44

Further information

The International Underwriting Association of London
3 Minster Court, Mincing Lane, London EC3R 7DD
020 7617 4444; www.iua.co.uk; info@iua.co.uk

The Chartered Insurance Institute
42–48 High Road, London E18 2JP
020 8989 8464; www.cii.co.uk

Financial Services Skills Council
51 Gresham Street, London EC2V 7HQ
0845 257 3772; www.fssc.org.uk/directions

INVESTMENT ANALYST

What the work involves

- The main job of an investment analyst is to inform other professionals, such as stockbrokers, traders and fund managers, about the best and worst investments for making a profit.

- Sell-side analysts assess an individual company's financial output and report this to private investors and unit trust fund managers

- Buy-side analysts research investment opportunities for pension funds, investment banks, and insurance and life assurance companies.

- Activities include analysing the economic stability of various countries, predicting the movement of share prices and taking account of economic implications, such as warfare.

The type of person suited to this work

This job is suitable for someone that has an interest in current affairs, and the impact these have on the financial markets. A certain amount of research is required in order to make informed, accurate decisions on possible financial opportunities, with the presentation of these requiring tenacity and self-belief. The pressured environment and the constant need to be reliable requires someone who can be resilient and trustworthy when calculating risks and forecasting trends. In order to present findings in an effective way, employees need to be good communicators who have initiative and are numerically skilled.

Working conditions

This profession requires employees to work long hours, often starting work before 7am in preparation for the opening of the London Stock Exchange and closure of Far Eastern markets, and working until after 6pm. These hours could change, or even increase, for analysts that need to cover markets operating in different time zones.

Future prospects

There are annual recruitment opportunities for graduates in large companies, with application deadlines usually being in November or December of the year before the graduate programme starts.

Opportunities for promotion are related to individual performance, with 7–8 years of service seeing an analyst progressing to the position of company vice-president; or executive director after 10–15 years. Should an individual or team appear to be performing extremely well, there are often competing companies that will poach successful employees.

Advantages/disadvantages

This is an extremely well paid job that allows for progression within a relatively short amount of time.

Qualifications and courses

ENTRY 5 LEVEL

To enter this profession you usually need at least a 2.1 degree. Relevant ubjects are economics, accountancy, maths and statistics, with a second language being recommended. In order to be accepted on to a desired degree course, most applicants will need at least 2 A levels and 5 GCSEs (A*–C).

A relevant postgraduate qualification is also recommended. The internationally recognised Chartered Financial Analyst (CFA) qualification or a Master's in Business Administration (MBA) are recommended. Alongside this, internships in the summer of the second year of a degree can help; as many as 60–95% of interns are offered full-time employment.

Should you choose not to study for a degree, possible entry routes are as a junior researcher or administrator, which allows for progression to a position as an analyst. Applicants should ensure that they have good A levels and relevant commercial experience.

Due to the fast moving stock market and the handling of vast sums of money, this job can often be highly pressured, yet rewarding.

An extremely high level of concentration is needed.

Money guide

A junior analyst can expect to be paid around £25,000–£40,000 a year. With experience, analysts' income could rise to around £80,000 a year, with a senior analyst (usually a vice president or director), earning around £130,000.

In addition to this, analysts often receive performance-related pay, with there being the possibility of substantial bonuses, low-rate mortgages, medical insurance, and life and pension cover.

Related opportunities

- Credit Analyst p32
- Economist p34
- Stockbroker p66

Further information

Association of Certified International Investment Analysts (ACIIA)
Feldstrasse 80, Buelach, Zurich CH-8180 Switzerland
www.aciia.org

Financial Services Authority (FSA)
25 The North Colonnade, London E14 5HS
020 7066 1000; www.fsa.gov.uk

Securities & Investment Institute (SII)
8 Eastcheap, London EC3M 1AE
020 7645 0600; www.sii.org.uk

Organisation profile

THE INSTITUTE OF LEGAL EXECUTIVES

Legal secretary

The Institute of Legal Executives (ILEX) is the largest and oldest professional and education body for legal secretaries and paralegals in England and Wales.

Many Legal Executive lawyers started off as legal secretaries, paralegals or legal support staff and have gone on to develop a full career as a lawyer by qualifying through ILEX. However legal secretaries and paralegal/legal support staff enjoy fulfilling careers in their own right. So whatever your ambitions, why not choose the UK's leading qualifications?

If you wish to train as a qualified legal secretary or legal support staff member then we have the qualification for you. Together ILEX and City & Guilds offer the law sector's leading qualifications for legal secretaries and paralegals which are available for study through over 100 approved City & Guilds centres nationwide. Over 20,000 people have chosen these qualifications to advance their career.

Reflecting the National Occupational Standards in Administration, the programmes are now considered a benchmark for those aspiring to or working in a legal environment as secretaries or personal assistants. They offer a flexible route with no entry requirements (although a Grade C or above in English Language GCSE is desirable) and are assessed by task based assignments.

Specially produced course books are available, and the City & Guilds/ILEX Level 2 Certificate in Vocational Paralegal Studies can be used as part of your entry criteria to study as a Legal Executive lawyer with ILEX.

City & Guilds approved centres are available nationwide. To find your nearest centre, simply contact your regional City & Guilds office (details on www.cityandguilds.com) or email paralegal@ilex.org.uk

Legal secretaries and paralegals are also eligible to apply to become members of ILEX. The grades and fees for 2010/11 are as follows.

Student member – for those wishing to enter the legal profession; those who have no relevant legal qualification; or those with less than three years' work experience of a predominantly legal nature. Annual subscription fees of £50 are payable, plus a one-off initial registration fee of £35.

Affiliate member – for those with at least one ILEX Level 3 unit qualification, or who have completed a relevant legal qualification at Level 2, or gained at least three years' work of a predominantly legal nature. Annual subscription fees of £100 are payable, plus a one-off initial registration fee of £35.

For more information on ILEX qualifications or to receive information on your nearest study centre, please call +44 (0)1234 841000 or email info@ilex.org.uk, or visit www.ilexcareers.org.uk

LEGAL SECRETARY

What the work involves

- Secretaries provide help with administrative tasks such as arranging meetings, making travel arrangements and updating filing systems.

- You will also help lawyers, legal executives and paralegals with specialist tasks such as studying different parts of the law for cases and making notes at court, police stations and appointments with clients.

- You will be responsible for typing legal documents and arranging statements and paperwork for court.

- Secretaries may also manage cases in fields such as debt recovery.

The type of person suited to this work

You will need to be very organised, have fast typing skills and a good grasp of spelling, grammar and punctuation. You must also have a high level of accuracy as you will be dealing with confidential legal documents. A legal secretary will have to be aware of different legal terminology and processes and possess excellent research skills. You should be able to work to tight deadlines and be friendly, polite and helpful at all times.

Working conditions

You will work normal office hours (9am–5pm) and will spend a great deal of time using a computer as well as other office equipment. You may also have to attend court to make notes, deliver legal documents and attend meetings, at which times you will need to be well presented. You could also make visits to police stations. This job may also require you to show clients around the organisation.

Future prospects

After gaining 2 years' experience, it is possible to become an Associate member of the Institute of Legal Secretaries and PAs. You could progress to a role as senior secretary, personal assistant or office manager. In a bigger organisation, there is a higher chance of promotion into a senior role. With further training, you can become a legal executive, paralegal or licensed conveyancer. Some secretaries study for a law degree in order to become a solicitor or barrister.

Advantages/disadvantages

Part-time work is available.

With further qualifications, there is the opportunity to progress into related legal careers.

The job can be repetitive.

Tight deadlines and a heavy workload can be very stressful.

Qualifications and courses

ENTRY 2 LEVEL

There are no set entry qualifications, although many employers look for GCSEs/S grades (A*–C/1–3) in English and maths. A lot of employers also ask for previous administrative experience or a relevant qualification. You could take an NVQ at Levels 1–4 or a City & Guilds qualification at Levels 2 and 3 in business. A City & Guilds Diploma is also available in Keyboarding, Text Production Skills and Office Procedures, as well as an OCR Certificate in Text Processing. An Apprenticeship in Business and Administration could also be useful.

You could also study for The Institute of Legal Secretaries and PAs Legal Secretaries Diploma or a course in Conveyancing, Family Law or Wills, Probate and Administration. The Institute of Legal Executives also provides the Level 2 Certificate and the Level 3 Diploma for Legal Secretaries.

Money guide

Salaries depend on the location and size of the employer. Higher salaries are often available in London and other big cities. A legal secretary in their first job can expect £13,000–£16,000 a year. With experience, this can rise to £25,000 a year. Legal secretaries with extensive experience and qualifications can earn up to £37,000.

Related opportunities

- Personal Assistant p55
- Receptionist p58
- Bilingual Secretary p349

Further information

Institute of Legal Secretaries and PAs
20 Portland Square, Bristol BS2 8SJ
0845 643 4974; www.institutelegalsecretaries.com;
info@institutelegalsecretaries.com

Institute of Legal Executives
Kempston Manor, Kempston, Bedford MK42 7AB
01234 841000; www.ilex.org.uk

The National Association of Licensed Paralegals
Kennington Business Park, 1–3 Brixton Road,
London SW9 6DE
020 3176 0900; www.nationalparalegals.com

City&
Guilds

www.cityandguilds.com/myperfectjob

Become instantly more attractive

WHAT IS WORLDSKILLS?

WorldSkills is the largest international vocational skills competition in the world where every 2 years, around 1,000 young people from 50 countries are chosen to represent their country and compete against each other in what can only be described as a 'skills olympics' setting. The competition runs in over 40 vocational skills ranging from mechatronics and web design to floristry and jewellery, plumbing and bricklaying to hairdressing and confectionery.

Participants battle against the clock, and in front of a live audience, working on briefs set by international skills experts.

UK Skills are the only UK representative in the competition, responsible for selecting and training Team UK.

Who can take part?

UK Skills find the best skilled people in the UK through a series of regional and national skills competitions called WorldSkills UK.

Last year, over 5,000 people registered to enter a regional and national competition, out of these, winners are celebrated at the end of each competition and out of those, outstanding competitors are then considered to potentially go on to represent the UK through a series of shortlisting competitions. Medal ceremonies celebrate the success of competitors as well as the support of their tutors, colleges, training providers and employers.

In the UK, competitions are open to all ages, however, at WorldSkills competitors must be 26 years old or under and either a student, trainee or employee.

Getting involved in WorldSkills whether at a regional / national and international level is a unique and invaluable learning experience for all competitors. Most competitors go on to excel in their chosen careers as a result of the experience.

To find out the criteria for entering a competition – visit www.worldskillsuk.org or follow us on facebook: WorldSkills UK – Official

UK success at WorldSkills

In September 2009, Team UK travelled to Calgary, Canada, to compete in the 40th WorldSkills Competition

Managed by UK Skills, the 26 strong team of highly talented young people came 6th in the world on medal count, bringing home 3 Gold, 6 Bronze and 14 Medallions for Excellence – meaning that the competitors surpassed the international points standard.

To ensure that Team UK continue this winning streak, UK Skills are currently working with partners to ensure that we identify the best in the UK that can potentially go on to represent the UK at the next WorldSkills.

To recap Team UK's best moments at WorldSkills Calgary – visit www.worldskillsteamuk.org

WorldSkills London 2011

Currently, the UK are gearing up to when they host the next WorldSkills which will take place on 5–8 October 2011 at ExCeL London. The event aims to host over 50 countries, 1,000 competitors and reach up to 250,000 people. Visitors to the event will be encouraged to have 'have a go' and try the trades of their choice. Students will also be able to speak to past competitors about studying towards vocational qualifications and their competition experience.

City & Guilds are Premier Sponsors of this unique event and will be on offer to talk to students about vocational qualifications available.

To find out more about this unique event, please visit www.worldskillslondon2011.com

City & Guilds

City & Guilds is the UK's leading body dedicated to vocational learning. We offer over 500 qualifications in 28 industry areas so that learners can gain the skills and knowledge they need to fulfil their career ambitions.

In operation for the last 130 years, 20 million people in the UK have City & Guilds qualifications and we award a further 1.5 million qualifications to learners every year.

City & Guilds qualifications are the ideal grounding, not only for work, but for competition across a vast range of industries, and at the very highest standards.

City & Guilds qualifications are valued by employers because they are developed in conjunction with key industry bodies – so they are relevant and up to date. Many leading businesses and organisations, such as Honda, Tesco and the London Underground, work with us to train and develop their staff.

For more information about the work of City & Guilds, visit our website www.cityandguilds.com.

AQA – City & Guilds Diplomas

Why not gain an insight into an industry before you commit to a career. We have 14 different Diploma qualifications for you to choose from to start you on your journey to success.

The Diplomas are exciting qualifications for 14–19 year olds, which combines class work with hands on experience and can be studied as one of the 3 main educational pathways alongside GCSE's and A Levels. This is your chance to learn in an exciting, creative and enjoyable way.

As well as studying the main subject area of your interest such as Engineering, Hair and Beauty Studies, Creative and Media or Environmental and Land-based Studies you will also develop transferable skills that are needed in everyday life such as:

Functional Skills – the practical skills in English, mathematics and ICT that have been identified as vital to enable young people to succeed

Additional and Specialist Learning – the opportunities for learners to specialise in particular areas and take up complementary studies. This can include options such as languages, music or science which relate to individuals' needs, interests and ambitions

Projects – specific tasks which are designed to support each learners individual talents progression and development

10 days' Work Experience – this is your chance to show what you have learned and put it into practice

The Diplomas will develop your skills which employers and universities say is needed including; planning, research, presentation and communication skills.

Visit www.diplomainfo.org.uk to find out about the Diplomas that we have available for you.

Become instantly more attractive

City&
Guilds

discover
risk
.co.uk
Do you have an
ENQUIRING
mind?
Have you got an enquiring mind?
Do you ask more questions than you can answer?
Want to know more?

Your best route to becoming a lawyer

"There are many benefits to becoming a lawyer through **ILEX**, and the gaps between being a solicitor, barrister or legal executive lawyer are fast diminishing: I can now become an advocate*, a judge or a partner in a law firm."

■ No full-time study required: complete your ILEX qualifications part-time or by distance learning. You can earn and learn at the same time to avoid student debt

■ Places as a trainee Legal Executive may be available when formal training contracts or pupillages aren't

■ Legal Executive lawyers who wish to dual qualify as solicitors are usually exempt from the SRA's 2-year training contract

■ You can represent your clients in court if you study to be a Legal Executive Advocate

■ Legal Executive lawyers are eligible to apply for judicial appointment and to become partners in legal disciplinary firms.

■ Salaries vary according to your location and area of law. Starting salaries are usually £15,000 to £28,000 per year whilst qualifying. When you've finished your ILEX qualifications you can expect to earn up to £38,000. Fully qualified Legal Executive lawyers can expect to earn £35,000 - £55,000, and you can earn much higher.

Law is the most popular subject for all university applications, so each year around 80% are rejected.

Established in1963, the Institute of Legal Executives (ILEX) provides a cost-effective alternative way of obtaining law qualifications without completing a degree (although graduates of law or other subjects can still choose to become a lawyer via the ILEX pathway).

ILEX is recognised by the Ministry of Justice as one of the three main approved ways of becoming a qualified lawyer (alongside Barristers and Solicitors).

Over 80,000 people have chosen the ILEX route. Why not join them?

Join up now

Contact 01234 841000
or email: info@ilex.org.uk

www.ilexcareers.org.uk

LOSS ADJUSTER

What the work involves

- Loss adjusters are independent specialists who work for insurance companies, investigating and advising on large or complicated claims or where there is a dispute.

- During your work you will visit premises, check damage and inspect reports from other professionals such as the fire service or police force to assess whether loss resulting from an incident is covered by the insurance policy.

- On completing your research, you will recommend the size of payments and offer advice to both claimants and insurers.

- You could be investigating numerous claims, including those caused by flood, fire, theft, fraud or accident.

The type of person suited to this work

You will be communicating with distressed claimants on a daily basis, so you will need excellent communication skills in order to be sympathetic whilst maintaining a professional distance.

Part of your job will be resolving disputes between organisations and/or individuals, which will require you to be calm and focused in order to make impartial decisions based on evidence.

You could be dealing with a number of complex cases at once, so good time management and organisational skills are an attribute.

Working conditions

You will usually work normal office hours, although it is not uncommon for adjusters to be called to look at premises in the evening or at weekends in emergency cases.

The majority of work is office-based, but you will have to travel to sites within the local area or overseas to make assessments.

You may be asked to assess the potentially distressing aftermath of situations such as fires, earthquakes, train crashes and robberies, in which case you must be emotionally prepared.

You will be required to wear relevant safety equipment when on site.

Future prospects

Loss adjustment is a highly competitive area of work but opportunities are increasing.

You could work in a large firm, which may allow you to focus on a particular area of interest early on and could create an excellent route of career progression into a management role.

Smaller insurance firms usually hire loss adjusters on a case-by-case basis, so you also have the opportunity of working on a freelance basis. With experience, you could set up your own firm.

Qualifications and courses

All entrants must have GCSEs (A*–C) in English and maths. However, most candidates are increasingly graduates/HND holders. A degree in a subject such as accountancy, insurance studies, law, statistics, surveying, economics or business studies could put you at an advantage.

However, relevant practical experience is equally as important as academic qualifications. You could start out as a claims technician and with experience and professional qualifications gained on the job you can progress to a loss adjuster.

Most qualified loss adjusters become Associate Members of the Chartered Institute of Loss Adjusters (CILA). To take the CILA exams, you need to be an ordinary member of the CILA, have at least 2 years' work experience in the office of a member company, and have a relevant professional qualification.

To become an ordinary member of the CILA, you need to be 21 or over and working for a company or an independent loss adjusting firm.

Advantages/disadvantages

Loss adjusters working for Lloyd's of London, who specialise in major risks, can earn extremely high salaries.

Insurance is a major industry in the UK and overseas, so this career offers plenty of international opportunities.

Money guide

A junior loss adjuster can expect to be paid around £18,000–£24,000 a year. With experience and the relevant professional qualifications this can increase to £25,000–£40,000 a year. At senior levels it is possible to earn £60,000–£100,000.

The work can involve a lot of responsibility and stress, dealing with huge sums of money and sometimes assessing major disasters such as plane crashes.

Related opportunities

- Accountant p16
- Actuary p20
- Insurance Broker p42
- Financial Adviser p39

Further information

Chartered Institute of Loss Adjusters (CILA)
Warwick House, 65/66 Queen Street, London EC4R 1EB
020 7337 9960; www.cila.co.uk; info@cila.co.uk

Financial Services Skills Council
51 Gresham Street, London EC2V 7HQ
0845 257 3772; www.fssc.org.uk; info@fssc.org.uk

MANAGEMENT CONSULTANT

What the work involves

- You will work with organisations and companies helping them to develop and improve their efficiency, services, products or staffing.
- This might involve observing and evaluating working practices, researching information, training staff or developing new ways of operating.
- You will need extensive knowledge of the sector you are working within.
- Consultants can work for a private consultancy organisation, be members of a specialised team or be freelance/self-employed.

The type of person suited to this work

You must be dynamic, confident and self-motivated. You will need to be able to research information, talk to staff and develop a thorough knowledge of an organisation. You must be good at identifying problems and problem solving. You may need to develop training programmes.

You will need excellent communication skills for writing reports, dealing with staff and presenting information.

You may have to review budgets and make savings, which may result in redundancies or spending cuts. Therefore you will need to have good financial skills, be able to justify your decisions and cope with any criticism.

Working conditions

A lot of your time will be spent travelling to different companies, so you will probably have to spend time away from home.

Working to deadlines can be stressful. The work can be pressured as you will have to taking responsibility for high-level decisions which could have far-reaching consequences.

You could be self-employed, work for a private consultancy service or be part of a team of company improvement specialists.

Future prospects

The consultancy market in the UK has grown to become the largest in Europe as many private and government organisations have reduced costs by cutting management staff and employing consultants for specific tasks. Many different types of organisations require management consultants, but competition is intense.

To succeed you will need to deliver an excellent service, build a reputation and be able to secure new contracts and work to deadlines.

Advantages/disadvantages

This is a rewarding, varied and interesting career with lots of opportunities. Salaries can be high and you may be able to

Qualifications and courses

ENTRY LEVEL 5

Entry to this profession generally requires an Honours degree (minimum 2.1). Any subject is usually acceptable, but if you have a degree in business, management, maths, economics or a related area, this can be an advantage. Typical minimum entry requirements for a degree are 2 A levels/3 H grades and 5 GCSEs/S grades (A*–C/1–3).

A postgraduate qualification, such as an MBA (Master's in Business Administration), can be an advantage; entry usually requires a good first degree, and substantial work experience may also be required.

Mature entry may also be possible through relevant work experience in management or a related area. Some entrants have an accountancy qualification with one of the main accountancy bodies.

Training is usually provided on the job, which may include the chance to study for an employer-sponsored MBA. The Institute of Business Consultancy (IBC) offers professional training courses, including the Certified Management Consultant Award (CMC). For the latter, candidates need to be Associate Members of the IBC with appropriate qualifications and at least 3 years' experience as a management consultant.

travel. This job can be stressful and demanding, and hours can be long and unpredictable.

Money guide

If you are freelance or self-employed you will probably be paid per day and your earnings will depend on your success. Entry level consultants may earn up to £27,000, after several years' experience this can rise to around £50,000. Senior consultants can earn over £90,000 and may also receive commission and bonuses.

Related opportunities

- Company Director p30
- Equality and Diversity Officer p36
- Financial Adviser p39
- Human Resources/Personnel Officer p41

Further information

Chartered Management Institute
Management House, Cottingham Road, Corby NN17 1TT
01536 204222; www.managers.org.uk;
enquiries@managers.org.uk

Management Consultancies Association
60 Trafalgar Square, London WC2N 5DS
020 7321 3990; www.mca.org.uk

Institute of Business Consulting
4th Floor, 2 Savoy Court, Strand, London WC2R 0EZ
020 7497 0580; www.ibconsulting.org.uk

MEDICAL RECEPTIONIST

What the work involves

- Medical receptionists book appointments for patients, organise the appointment diaries, answer the telephone and take messages.

- You will be responsible for greeting patients when they arrive, making sure they are in the right place, and answering their queries.

- You will also carry out some general administrative work, such as preparing patients' notes and files, dealing with post and typing letters.

The type of person suited to this work

It is important that you are well presented, friendly and reassuring. You will be the first point of contact for patients, so need to make a good first impression.

Excellent communication skills are required as you will be interacting with patients and other medical staff all day, in person and by telephone.

You will need to be well organised and efficient, as you might be dealing with several queries at once and will need to make sure they are all dealt with as quickly and accurately as possible.

As you will be helping sick, ill or distressed patients it is important to be sympathetic and discreet when dealing with their problems.

Working conditions

You will be working standard office hours, Monday to Friday. However you may work shifts including the weekends and evenings if your place of work offers extended opening hours.

You will spend most of your time in an office, sitting or standing at a desk, and looking at a computer screen.

Future prospects

Medical receptionists are needed all over the UK, so there are good job prospects. Most are employed by the NHS but there are opportunities in the private sector.

Progression in this career is relatively easy. With some training you could become a medical secretary or move into a supervisory or managerial role.

Advantages/disadvantages

Helping people, who are sick or distressed, will bring great job satisfaction.

You will have to deal with patients who could be angry or distressed which could be upsetting.

This job will be great for you if you enjoy meeting new people.

Qualifications and courses

There are no minimum entry requirements, although employers may ask for 5 GCSEs/S grades (A*–C/1–3), including English and maths or NVQs/SVQs at Levels 1 or 2. Work experience in an office or in customer service may be helpful.

The Diploma in Business Administration or Society, Health and Development, City & Guilds Level 2 Certificate in Medical Reception or EDEXCEL Level 2 NVQ in Support Services in Health Care may be useful.

Apprenticeships/Skillseekers in business and administration may be available for candidates aged 16–24.

Medical receptionists are trained on the job, and may be encouraged to undertake further training. The Association of Medical Secretaries, Practice Managers, Administrators and Receptionists offer several training courses including the Certificate in Health Service Administration and the Intermediate Diploma in Medical Reception.

Money guide

You might have a starting salary of around £13,000 a year, and with experience this could increase to about £16,000.

Senior positions or those with extra responsibilities might pay around £20,000.

Related opportunities

- Personal Assistant p55
- Hotel Receptionist p143
- Secretary p63
- Travel Agent p399

Further information

Council for Administration
6 Graphite Square, Vauxhall Walk, London SE11 5EE
020 7091 9620; www.cfa.uk.com; info@cfa.uk.com

Association of Medical Secretaries, Practice Managers, Administrators and Receptionists
Tavistock House North, Tavistock Square, London WC1H 9LN
020 7387 6005; www.amspar.com; info@amspar.com

City&
Guilds

www.cityandguilds.com/myperfectjob

PAYROLL MANAGER

What the work involves

■ Payroll managers are employed by organisations to arrange and manage employees' salaries.

■ You will ensure that each member of staff receives the correct amount on the correct date. When doing this you will take into account laws regarding tax, national insurance, sick pay and maternity/paternity leave.

■ Your tasks will include keeping records of hours worked, calculating repayments for salary advances or student loans, calculating pay, pensions and tax deductions.

■ As you progress from payroll clerk to payroll supervisor and payroll manager you will gradually take on more responsibilities, such as managing and delegating tasks to a team of payroll clerks, and creating and documenting payroll policies.

The type of person suited to this work

As you will be in contact with many employees and work alongside other payroll staff, you must enjoy working with other people and be able to work in a team.

You should be sensitive in your approach to discussing earnings with employees, and treat their information with confidentiality.

As you will be responsible for maintaining records and large amounts of information you must be organised and methodical in your work.

You will need strong numerical and IT skills as you will be working with figures and working on computerised systems.

You should also be able to multi-task and work to tight deadlines.

Working conditions

From Monday to Friday you will work around 37 hours per week. You might have to work overtime, especially at the end of a financial year which can be a busy time.

You might have the option of working part-time or flexible hours and there may even be opportunities for job-sharing.

You will be largely office-based. You will have a desk from which you will answer the phone, send emails and make calculations. You may have to attend meetings at times.

Future prospects

You will enter this profession as a payroll clerk and after you have gained a few years' experience and qualifications you will be able to progress to payroll supervisor and payroll manager.

These roles will involve more responsibility and managerial tasks such as liaising with HM Revenue and Customs, organising training for other members of payroll staff and being involved in business strategy.

Qualifications and courses

You will not be required to have any specific qualifications to become a payroll clerk, supervisor or manager. However employers prefer candidates with GSCEs (A*–C) including English and maths.

The Diploma in Business, Administration and Finance or even NVQs, Levels 2 to 4 in Financial Services or 2 and 3 in Payroll Administration could all be useful for entry into this line of work.

You will train on the job. The Institute of Payroll Professionals (IPP) provides an Advanced Diploma in Payroll and Business Management. Further qualifications also include a BTEC Advanced Certificate in Payroll Techniques or a BTEC Advanced Award in Payroll Procedures.

Advantages/disadvantages

You will be working with a variety of people as you will potentially be working with each employee within an organisation.

At times the administrative nature of your work may become repetitive and monotonous.

Money guide

As a payroll clerk your starting salary can be around £13,000 to £16,500 per year.

In a supervisory position you can earn from £18,000 to £23,000 a year.

If you progress to a role as a payroll manager you can earn £40,000 or more a year.

Related opportunities

■ Accounting Technician/Finance Clerk p18
■ Pension Administrator p53

Further information

Association of Accounting Technicians (AAT)
140 Aldersgate Street, London EC1A 4HY
0845 863 0800; www.aat.org.uk; info@aat.org.uk

Institute of Payroll Professionals (IPP)
Shelly House, Farmhouse Way, Monkspath, Solihull B90 4EH
0121 712 1000; www.payrollprofession.org;
info@payrollprofession.org

City& Guilds

www.cityandguilds.com/myperfectjob

PENSIONS ADMINISTRATOR

What the work involves

- As a pensions administrator you will be responsible for the general management and maintenance of pension schemes and life insurance policies.

- You will answer queries from customers by telephone or email and complete the necessary associated administration. This can include information on policies in general, tax relief entitlement, cash sums on retirement and options for benefit transfer.

- You will undertake a variety of administrative tasks such as calculating pension forecasts, processing pension contributions and keeping up-to-date records.

- When a policy has to be paid out, in case of retirement or a death, you will organise all of the paperwork and arrange the payment of lump sums.

The type of person suited to this work

You should enjoy methodical, detailed work.

You will have strong mathematical and IT skills in order to work out calculations and check databases for information.

As you will be dealing with the public a great deal you should be friendly and polite and be able to explain detailed policies in laymen's terms.

You should have an interest in the financial sector and tax regulations and keep up-to-date with economic developments.

As you will be maintaining records and referring back to them frequently you must have excellent organisation skills.

You must be able to multi-task and prioritise your workload.

Working conditions

You will work Monday to Friday, 35 hours a week. At times you may be required to work overtime at weekends or in the evenings. You are likely to be able to work part-time or flexible hours or organise job sharing.

You will be office-based which will have a certain layout and benefits depending on the organisation you work for.

You will have a mainly sedentary working lifestyle, sitting at a desk using computers and answering the telephone.

Future prospects

A good deal of on-the-job assessment and training is required throughout your career, for example pensions companies must assess staff involved in pension schemes due to the Financial Services Authority (FSA) requirements.

With experience and further qualifications you may be promoted to team leader or a management position. There may also be opportunities to move across to pension advice or consultancy where you will provide information and guidance regarding financial planning and employee benefits.

Advantages/disadvantages

Each day you will have to deal with a variety of different queries from customers.

Qualifications and courses

ENTRY LEVEL 2

The entry requirements can vary widely. The minimum academic requirement are at least 4 GCSEs (A*–C) in English and maths. The Diploma in Business, Administration and Finance might be useful.

Advanced Apprenticeships in Providing Financial Services are available. There are two tracks available: pensions administration or pensions advice and you will work towards the NVQ Level 3 in Retail Financial Services.

You might be required to gain professional qualifications as you work. The Pensions Management Institute (PMI) offers qualifications for administrators involved in occupational pension schemes such as the NVQ in Public Sector Pensions Administration and Diploma in Pensions Calculations (DPC). The PMI also provides Associateship examinations that cover the whole of pension management and administration. For more information visit the PMI website.

If you are an administrator involved with personal pension schemes you might need to gain one of the following qualifications: the Chartered Insurance Institute (CII) Certificate in Financial Administration or the PMI Diploma in Member Directed Pension Scheme Administration.

Some aspects of your work may be repetitive.

Money guide

As junior administrator you can earn from £14,000 to £18,000 per year.

With experience you can earn from £19,000 to £25,000 per year.

In a senior role or as a team leader you can earn up to £40,000 per year.

Related opportunities

- Accounting Technician/Finance Clerk p18
- Bank Cashier/Customer Adviser p22
- Pensions Adviser p54
- Insurance Broker p42

Further information

The Chartered Insurance Institute
42–48 High Road, London E18 2JP
020 8989 8464; customer.ser@cii.co.uk; www.cii.co.uk

The Pensions Management Institute
PMI House, 4/10 Artillery Lane, London E1 7LS
020 7247 1452; www.pensions-pmi.org.uk;
enquiries@pensions-pmi.org.uk

City&
Guilds

www.cityandguilds.com/myperfectjob

PENSIONS ADVISER

What the work involves

- Pension advisers help individuals and organisations to choose, create and manage a pension plan that is most suited to their needs.

- You will work in-house, or as a consultant for businesses and other organisations, to set up and maintain pensions that will suit all employees whilst remaining within budget.

- As you will work with and train a team of pension advisers and administrators you will need to understand and keep up-to-date with the latest changes in financial and tax regulations.

The type of person suited to this work

As you will be working closely with the public you should have excellent communication and interpersonal skills in order to explain complex policies in laymen's terms in a polite, friendly manner.

You should have a genuine interest in answering consumers' financial queries.

You must have strong numerical skills in order to make accurate financial estimates and economic forecasts and IT skills to keep records of current policies and procedures.

You should be able to lead a team as you may manage a group of advisers and administrators. You must have excellent organisational skills and pay attention to detail.

Working conditions

You will work around 40 hours a week, Monday to Friday. You may have to be flexible with your hours to suit clients who need weekend or evening appointments.

You will be mainly office-based but you might occasionally have to travel within the UK to meet with clients and organisations or to liaise with other financial advisers.

Future prospects

As the financial sector is constantly changing and adjusting its regulations, and you must be aware of new developments, you will be subject to training and continuing professional development (CPD).

You may be promoted to senior roles, progress to other advisory roles in financial areas in actuarial firms, with accountants or solicitors for example. You may also be able to become self-employed.

Advantages/disadvantages

Your work will be diverse as you will meet with different customers on a daily basis and tailor your advice to each new client.

Some aspects of your work might be stressful, particularly if you are on performance-related pay.

Qualifications and courses

ENTRY LEVEL 4

You will usually need to have a degree, Foundation degree, diploma or at least a HND. Most managers are graduates. Relevant subjects include business, accountancy and finance. For entry to a degree you will need at least 2 A levels and 5 GCSEs (A*–C) including English and maths.

The Diploma in Business, Administration and Finance or an Apprenticeship in Retail Financial Services or Advising on Financial Services may be useful. Some organisations run graduate training programmes. Most require a 2.1 degree.

Before being able to give advice, all pensions advisers and managers need to be registered with the Pensions Management Institute (PMI), pass professional qualifications and must be 18 years old.

Possible professional qualifications include CII Certification, the Award and Diploma in Financial Planning, Certificate in Life and Pensions, NVQs in financial advice and service and the IFS School of Finance's Certificate for Financial Advisers. PMI also offers a range of qualifications.

It is sometimes possible to start out as an administrator within the industry and then progress to pensions adviser or manager with experience and professional qualifications.

Money guide

In a trainee or graduate role you might have a starting salary of £15,000–£25,000 per year.

With 5 years' experience you can earn £25,000–£30,000 a year.

If you work in a senior role for a large firm you can earn up to £80,000 per year.

You may also be eligible for performance-related pay and some bonuses.

Related opportunities

- Actuary p20
- Accountant p16
- Financial Adviser p39
- Pensions Administrator p53

Further information

Pension Careers
Unit 6, The Quadrangle, 49 Atalanta Street, London SW6 6TU
020 7565 7900; sales@pensioncareers.co.uk;
www.pensioncareers.co.uk

The Pensions Management Institute
PMI House, 4/10 Artillery Lane, London E1 7LS
020 7247 1452; enquiries@pensions-pmi.org.uk;
www.pensions-pmi.org.uk

PERSONAL ASSISTANT

What the work involves

- Personal Assistants ease the workload of senior managers and directors, allowing businesses to run more efficiently.

- You may make decisions on behalf of your manager, represent your manager at events as well as manage projects and confidential information.

- It will be your job to organise efficient administrative systems, both paper and ICT based.

- You will maintain diaries, take minutes, answer phone calls, greet visitors, write letters and arrange meetings and travel.

The type of person suited to this work

Excellent organisational skills are essential. You will constantly be juggling several things at once and need to be adaptable, efficient and able to work to deadlines. You will have to follow instructions but also use your initiative and prioritise your own work. You will need a good knowledge of the company you work for and may have to deal with budgets. You will be representing your manager so you will need good written and verbal communication skills.

You should be discreet and reliable as you may be dealing with confidential information. You will need to be accurate and have excellent ICT skills.

Working conditions

You will work in an office, usually doing normal office hours but may have to work longer at times to meet deadlines. You may have to go to other premises for meetings and will be expected to dress fairly formally.

Personal assistants work in all types and sizes of organisations and companies. You could be working in a very small business or a large company with smart, modern offices, or anything in between.

Future prospects

There are opportunities throughout the UK.

Being a PA can be the first step in some very competitive careers such as the media, but these types of jobs will be popular.

With experience you could work for a more senior manager or move into another area of the company, such as human resources. You could also manage a team of junior administrators.

With language skills you could work abroad, or you could become self-employed providing 'virtual' PA services using the internet.

Advantages/disadvantages

The job can be varied and interesting with a lot of responsibility. If you get along well with your manager, the

Qualifications and courses

There is no set minimum qualification required although some GCSEs/S (A*–C) may be advantageous, including English. Some employers may expect a Bachelor's degree or equivalent. A business-related BTEC HND or degree could help you find a position with greater responsibilities.

You may find it useful to have NVQ Level 2 and/or 3 in Business and Administration, a Diploma in Business, Administration and Finance or a secretarial qualification from City & Guilds. Apprenticeships are also available in Business, Administration and Law.

Previous experience in other administrative or clerical roles is vital.

You should be computer literate and able to use a variety of computer software. Extra skills such as shorthand, audio typing or a foreign language can also be helpful.

work can be rewarding. On the other hand, the work can also be demanding and your contributions may not always be recognised across the organisation.

Money guide

Salaries vary according to the size and type of company you work for and you will probably earn more in London and the south-east of England. A starting salary is around £17,000 per year. With experience you could earn around £24,000–£28,000 per year. A senior personal assistant with a lot of experience and responsibility, probably in a large company, could earn £30,000+ per year.

Related opportunities

- Customer Service Assistant/Manager p483
- Public Relations Officer p422
- Receptionist p58
- Secretary p63

Further information

Council for Administration
6 Graphite Square, Vauxhall Walk, London SE11 5EE
020 7091 9620; www.cfa.uk.com; info@cfa.uk.com

Institute of Professional Administrators
6 Graphite Square, Vauxhall Walk, London SE11 5EE
020 7091 2606; www.inprad.org; info@inprad.org

City & Guilds

www.cityandguilds.com/myperfectjob

PROJECT MANAGER

What the work involves

- Many project managers specialise in a particular area, such as the managing of commercial business improvements.

- In the course of a job, a project manager will liaise with the client, create a timescale, a budget plan that keeps to agreed standards, and choose a capable project team.

- You will need to access specialist software for scheduling, risk analysis, costing and estimating.

The type of person suited to this work

The project manager is relied upon to co-ordinate the operations of his team and solve any problems that may arise. Due to this, it is necessary for people thinking of entering this profession to enjoy team work and have strong people management, communication, and organisational skills. In order to solve any problems which may arise, a project manager must be logical and methodical, especially when under pressure.

In addition to this, the job of a project manager requires good computer skills and an ability to understand complex information and control budgets, whilst working on several other projects.

Working conditions

A certain amount of variation must be allowed for from these hours due to variety in projects. However, generally, hours range from 9am to 5pm, Monday to Friday. Like many jobs, the meeting of deadlines may mean these hours are occasionally increased.

Managers are often office based, with the occasional need to visit sites or clients to check progression. Should a manager be working on a project abroad, it may be necessary to spend prolonged periods of time away from home.

Future prospects

By becoming a project manager you will be joining a growing industry, with the Association for Project Management (APM) having over 15,500 members. Upon entering the profession, most people will make up part of the project support team, progressing to team leader after the gaining of experience, which gradually leads to a position as project manager. There are promotional opportunities to senior management posts from here, although this may mean changing companies, with some managers setting up their own consultancy business.

Advantages/disadvantages

This job allows for variety due to there being many different projects to work on. Although this may cause the employee to feel pressured, the rewards of the completed project may be of greater benefit.

Qualifications and courses

There are no formal academic requirements but all entrants need experience in commerce, business, management, engineering, construction, ICT or science. This experience could range from an Apprenticeship to a postgraduate degree.

A Foundation degree, degree or postgraduate qualification in project management combined with construction or civil engineering would be useful.

Entry to degrees requires at least 2 A levels/3 H grades and 5 GCSEs/S grades (A*–C/1–3), or equivalent.

You could also study while working through online or part-time courses offered by the Association for Project Management, the Information Systems Examination Board or the Project Management Institute.

Salaries are very rewarding and the expansion of the industry indicates that this is fast becoming a thriving industry with long term employment prospects.

Money guide

For people entering this profession, the starting salary ranges from around £20,000 to £27,000 a year. This is usually for people that are part of the support team on a project, with salaries rising to £30,000–£60,000 a year for experienced project managers. For larger and higher profile projects, salaries can rise to more than £75,000 a year, with there often being opportunities for bonuses when a deadline or objective has been met.

Related opportunities

- Civil/Construction Engineer p85
- Business Analyst p150
- Construction Supervisor/Manager p90
- Quality Manager p57
- Risk Manager p62

Further information

Association for Project Management (APM)
Ibis House, Regent Park, Summerleys Road,
Princes Risborough HP27 9LE
0845 458 1944; www.apm.org.uk

Chartered Management Institute
Management House, Cottingham Road, Corby NN17 1TT
01536 204222; www.managers.org.uk

Information Systems Examination Board
First Floor, Block D, North Star House, North Star Avenue,
Swindon SN2 1FA
01793 417417;
www.bcs.org/BCS/Products/Qualifications/ISEB

QUALITY MANAGER

What the work involves

- Quality managers are employed by an organisation to ensure that quality assurance aims are met in relation to products or services; this includes legal compliance levels and customer expectations.

- Practices include monitoring and advising on existing systems in order to consistently improve current standards, and publishing data and reports that inform management.

- Quality managers must ensure that the company they are working for is applying the required level of environmental and health and safety standards.

- Encouraging staff to adhere to new doctrines and legislation is fundamental.

The type of person suited to this work

This job is suited to someone that has an interest in securing and improving standards of quality. In order to do this, it is necessary to have good communication skills in order to influence and persuade others to follow set regulations and uphold required standards. Problems may arise due to complicated legislation and staff lacking interest and so quality managers must be resilient and create ways in which models of quality can be easily understood and adhered to. An organisation's customers must be listened to and so quality managers must be adaptable and approachable.

Working conditions

Normal working hours apply when employed by the government or a bank, although a position in engineering, production or retail could involve shift work. Offices and laboratories are where most are based, although those with experience often become consultants to smaller firms once they have gained enough experience to be self-employed.

It may be necessary to travel to different clients during the working day, or even to stay overnight.

Future prospects

There are around 25,000 quality managers in the UK, with employment opportunities ranging across business, production, commerce and public sector organisations. Opportunities for progression to managerial and board room levels are ever increasing due to the rising importance of health and safety, and customer expectation.

Quality managers can decide whether to specialise in a particular area or whether to progress to a position of management in other sectors; these include production, health and safety, technical sales, and customer relations.

Advantages/disadvantages

This is an important job, with quality managers being in charge of the levels of service provided to customers and clients. With the importance of this job ever increasing, the work carried out can be rewarding and respected.

Qualifications and courses

ENTRY LEVEL 4

Most entrants hold a degree or postgraduate degree. Useful subjects include polymer science/technology, textile technology, business/ management, engineering or physical/mathematical/ applied science. You can also complete an HND in a similar subject as above or in materials science, printing, clothing technology, or food science/technology.

The general entry requirements for a HND are 1 A level and 4 GCSEs (A*–C) or equivalent.

Entry without a degree or HND is often possible when an applicant is moving across from another vocational field involving quality or management. The qualifications provided by The Chartered Quality Institute would provide the necessary skills for a manager qualified in an area such as accountancy, law, engineering or marketing. These qualifications are the Certificate in Quality (Level 3) and the Diploma in Quality (Level 5). The Chartered Management Institute offers the Diploma in Quality Management (Level 4).

Career progression or movement to self-employment is possible. However, quality legislation is constantly updated and so it is important to keep up to date.

Money guide

Quality managers can expect a starting salary in the region of £18,000–£23,000 per annum, with this increasing after 10–15 years to between £25,000 and £43,000 through experience and progression to senior level. Should you make it to a level similar to that of a director, salaries could reach £50,000–£70,000.

Related opportunities

- Operational Researcher p532
- Project Manager p56
- Quality Control Inspector p241
- Statistician p536

Further information

British Quality Foundation
32–34 Great Peter Street, London SW1P 2QX
020 7654 5000; www.quality-foundation.co.uk

Chartered Management Institute
Management House, Cottingham Road, Corby NN17 1TT
01536 204222; www.managers.org.uk

The Chartered Quality Institute (CQI)
12 Grosvenor Crescent, London SW1X 7EE
020 7245 6722; www.thecqi.org

RECEPTIONIST

What the work involves

- You will be greeting visitors, signing them in and out of the building, checking they know where they are going and answering any queries.

- You will be responsible for answering the telephone, transferring calls and taking messages, as well as managing queries via email.

- You may also manage incoming and outgoing post and handle cash transactions.

The type of person suited to this work

You will create the first impression of your organisation, so it is vital that you should be friendly, welcoming, outgoing and well presented.

Excellent communication skills are essential as you will be solving problems and queries for visitors and other members of staff.

You will need to be able to remain calm under pressure and balance a heavy workload, as the reception desk could get very busy at times.

Good organisation skills and efficiency are needed for dealing with visitors' queries swiftly and accurately.

Working conditions

Receptionists are based at a reception desk, with access to a phone and computer. You will normally work standard office hours Monday to Friday, but this does depend on the opening hours of your place of work. You may need to work evenings and weekends.

There are usually opportunities to work part time or temporary contracts.

Future prospects

All types of organisations employ receptionists including law firms, banks, garages, leisure centres and veterinary practices; therefore there are good job prospects across the UK.

Reception work offers progression into other areas such as office or customer service work; you will develop a good range of transferable skills.

You may be able to progress to a managerial role or supervisory position after a few years' experience and further training.

Advantages/disadvantages

This is a great job if you enjoy meeting people and providing good customer service.

Some people you encounter may be rude or angry if they have a problem with the company you work for.

Qualifications and courses

There are no minimum entry requirements, although employers are likely to ask for 5 GCSEs/S grades (A*–C/1–3), including English and maths or NVQs/SVQs at Levels 1 or 2. ICT skills and office experience will also be an advantage.

The Diploma in Business, Administration and Finance may be useful for this career; it also includes practical work experience. City & Guilds offer several training courses such as Level 2 Diploma in Reception Operations and Services, and an NCFE is available at Levels 1 and 2 in Customer Service.

Apprenticeships/Skillseekers in business administration may be available for candidates aged 16–24.

Training will be done on the job by a senior receptionist, and many employers encourage further study. Courses available are the NVQs/SVQs in Customer Service Levels 2–3, or business and administration Levels 1–4.

There are good opportunities to enter other professions such as office or secretarial work.

Money guide

Starting salaries are around £12,000, with experience this can increase to £16,000–£17,000.

Senior receptionists with extra responsibilities may earn £25,000+.

Related opportunities

- Personal Assistant p55
- Medical Receptionist p51
- Secretary p63
- Travel Agent p399

Further information

Council for Administration
6 Graphite Square, Vauxhall Walk, London SE11 5EE
020 7091 9620; www.cfa.uk.com; info@cfa.uk.com

London Chamber of Commerce and Industry
33 Queen Street, London EC4R 1AP
020 7203 1881; www.londonchamber.co.uk;
lc@londonchamber.co.uk

City&
Guilds

www.cityandguilds.com/myperfectjob

RECRUITMENT/EMPLOYMENT AGENCY CONSULTANT

What the work involves

- Working for an agency, you will help companies recruit the right staff for permanent and temporary jobs through advertising, networking, headhunting and referrals.

- Your work will include carrying out a preliminary interview and background check and then helping suitable candidates to find work to suit their skills and experience.

- You will assess people's skills to help them decide on the type of work they want, and may suggest further training, which could be available through your company.

- You will spend time making contacts with new companies to sell your agency's services.

The type of person suited to this work

You will be selling your agency's services so will need to be well presented with excellent sales ability.

You will probably be working on commission so should be able to remain calm when working to tight deadlines.

You will need to be persuasive as it is essential that employers continue to use your agency. You may need to be persistent if they do not respond after a first approach.

Working conditions

Office hours will often be long as you might have to speak to clients outside working hours.

You will be doing a lot of work on the phone and some agencies are internet based. You may need to visit employer premises, so could need a driving licence. You will probably work in a team and be expected to dress smartly.

Future prospects

Opportunities depend on the economy and which sectors are hiring new staff.

You could work for a specialist agency, for example supplying medical staff but may need experience within that sector first. Some people work as 'head hunters', actively searching out people for specific high-level jobs.

With good results you could be promoted to senior consultant and then branch manager.

You may go on to start your own agency or you could move into a related area such as human resources.

Advantages/disadvantages

You will meet people at all levels and will get satisfaction from helping them find the right job or career.

Working on commission can be stressful and clients and businesses can be demanding. This is a very competitive career and your success will depend on your sales ability.

Qualifications and courses

You can enter this career with qualifications at Level 2 but people often have Level 3 or 4 qualifications. Entrants come from various backgrounds such as sales, marketing or customer service. The Diploma in Business, Administration and Finance could be useful.

There are also graduate schemes available. Although most subjects are welcome, a degree in human resources or business can improve your chances.

Trainees receive training on the job, and may take courses accredited by the Recruitment and Employment Confederation (REC). The REC's Certificate in Recruitment Practice is designed for new entrants or those who have no formal training or qualifications. The Diploma in Recruitment Practice is aimed at consultants with a year's experience, or those with A levels, a degree or equivalent. Passing the Diploma gives you full membership of the REC and eligibility for the degree in Recruitment Practice at Middlesex University Business School. However, it is not crucial to have these professional qualifications.

Some consultants take the Chartered Institute of Personnel and Development examinations, for example, the CIPD Certificate in Recruitment and Selection.

Money guide

Consultants often get commission and a small basic salary. They earn their commission when they successfully get new business or place staff. Progression depends upon meeting sales targets. Trainees start on between £14,000 and £20,000 per year. When you are qualified and have experience you can earn up to £26,000. Senior consultants can earn £32,000 and managers can earn £40,000+. You could earn extra bonuses or commission. You will earn more in London and the south-east of England.

Related opportunities

- Human Resources/Personnel Officer p41
- Marketing Manager/Director p414
- Secretary p63

Further information

Recruitment & Employment Confederation
15 Welbeck Street, London W1G 9XT
020 7009 2100; www.rec.uk.com; info@rec.uk.com

Chartered Institute of Personnel and Development
CIPD House, 151 The Broadway, London SW19 1JQ
020 8612 6208; www.cipd.co.uk

Employment National Training Organisation
4th floor, Kimberley House, 47 Vaughan Way,
Leicester LE1 4SG
0116 251 7979; www.ento.co.uk

REGENERATION MANAGER/ ECONOMIC DEVELOPMENT OFFICER

What the work involves

- Regeneration managers aim to improve living environments in areas such as: dilapidated residential areas where local industries have closed down, areas of low income and high unemployment, and areas with poor access to healthcare and education.

- Specialist fields include economic development, planning, surveying, and housing.

- The extent of involvement ranges from the presentation of an idea, to ensuring that the project is completed on time and on budget and the generation of financial support and planning permission.

The type of person suited to this work

It is necessary to have an interest in the ways in which communities and living environments can be improved when deciding upon whether to become a regeneration manager. Due to this profession involving a lot of negotiation with a variety of people, you will need good communication skills and should be able to influence people towards contributing in a positive way. Regeneration managers often need to be strict with budgets and able to solve problems that may arise; both of which need a strong will and an ability to deliver results in a set amount of time.

Working conditions

Generally, working hours are typical of those for an office job, with the amount of hours worked usually being around 37 a week, with the occasional need to attend a residency meeting during the evening or at weekends. Employment with local councils tends to be employee focused, with most offering part-time or job-sharing contracts, alongside flexitime schemes.

Although mostly based in an office, regeneration managers will need to travel to sites that are undergoing the regeneration process in order to meet with residents, clients and agencies.

Future prospects

The government is currently committed to improving community areas through regeneration schemes, making this a very positive vocation to get involved with; especially whilst there is a current shortage of people who have the combination of skills required for this job.

Opportunities are available within the following employers: local authorities and government agencies, regional development agencies and English Partnerships, the government's national regeneration agency. There are also employment possibilities with private consultancies, housing associations and property developers.

Advantages/disadvantages

Both the public and private sector are becoming involved in regeneration projects, with opportunities opening up in senior management roles through the gaining of experience.

Qualifications and courses

You will need a degree and possibly experience within regeneration. Recommended subjects are urban studies, housing, and planning, with related subjects including geography, social studies and economics. Entry for a degree requires at least 2 A levels/ 3 H grades plus 5 GCSEs/S grades (A*–C/1–3), including English and maths. Postgraduate study may be of benefit.

The Diploma in Environmental and Land-based Studies and a Foundation degree in Sustainable Communities are also available.

You should also gain relevant work experience or voluntary environmental work in order to improve career and employment prospects. Areas such as housing, planning, urban design, or surveying would be best. Knowledge of government regeneration policy and the main sources of funding will also strengthen applications.

The Homes and Communities Academy offers a means to study and work at the same time through its 2-year paid graduate development programme.

This job may become extremely challenging when convincing people that regeneration is positive, especially when they have lived in a location for a certain number of years.

Money guide

To begin, regeneration managers can expect a salary in the region of £22,000 a year, with this steadily increasing to £40,000 through the gaining of experience. Through a progression to senior management, regeneration managers have the ability to earn around £60,000 a year, depending on their level of responsibility.

Related opportunities

- Building Conservation Officer p77
- Chartered Surveyor p84
- Project Manager p56
- Town Planner/Town Planning Technician p128

Further information

British Urban Regeneration Association (BURA)
4th Floor, 63–66 Hatton Garden, London EC1N 8LE
020 7539 4030; www.bura.org.uk

English Partnerships, Corporate Headquarters
110 Buckingham Palace Road, London SW1 9SA
0207 881 1600; www.englishpartnerships.co.uk

Improvement and Development Agency for Local Government
Layden House, 76–86 Turnmill Street, London EC1M 5LG
020 7296 6600; www.idea.gov.uk; www.lgtalent.com

REGISTRAR OF BIRTHS, DEATHS, MARRIAGES AND CIVIL PARTNERSHIPS

What the work involves

- Registrars record all births, stillbirths, marriages, civil partnerships and deaths in an area, making sure all details are accurate.

- After a birth, you will interview parents, record the baby's name and date of birth and issue a birth certificate.

- After a death, you will interview relatives before issuing a death certificate and inform the coroner or procurator fiscal if anything seems suspicious.

- You will interview people planning to marry or enter a civil partnership to check they can legally do so, and conduct marriage and civil partnership ceremonies.

The type of person suited to this work

You will need to be a good listener, be discreet and communicate effectively. It is also important to judge how people are feeling and be sympathetic, without becoming emotionally involved.

Attention to detail is vital to ensure that all legal requirements are carried out. You may need patience to explain procedures to people who are unclear about them. Other key skills include information handling, ICT and public speaking.

Confidence is important when conducting marriage and civil partnership ceremonies, and good judgement to decide if people are telling the truth. It's important to be flexible in dealing with different situations and people of various cultures.

Working conditions

You will be based in the registrar's office for your district. You will work a 37-hour week, but this will often include Saturdays. You may also need to be on call to work evenings, Sundays or bank holidays.

You may travel to conduct marriages or civil partnership ceremonies so a driving licence is useful. You might attend ceremonies within a hotel or other public places.

Computers are becoming increasingly important but good handwriting is often a requirement. You will be sitting down for most of the time.

Future prospects

There are about 1750 registrars in England and Wales and about 500 in Scotland. There are very few vacancies for this kind of work. Part-time work may be possible.

You would usually start as an assistant and be promoted to registrar, but promotion opportunities are limited. You will have opportunities for in-house training and could move into other administration-based careers.

Qualifications and courses

In England and Wales, there are no set entry requirements for this career. A good general standard of education is expected, including English and maths. GCSEs are increasingly preferred and if working in Wales, candidates require GCSE Welsh.

Applicants from certain professions are prohibited from becoming registrars, including doctors, midwives, ministers of religion, funeral directors and anyone working in the life assurance industry.

In Scotland, candidates need 3 GCSEs/S grades (A*–C/ 1–3), including English. Assistant registrars must be 18 and registrars must be 21.

Candidates take the examination of the Association of Registrars in Scotland and obtain a Certificate of Proficiency in the Law and Practice of Registration. At least 2 years' experience is required before the certificate can be awarded.

Advantages/disadvantages

The work is varied and no two days are the same; you will meet many different people at their happiest or saddest moments.

You will work some weekends and bank holidays and may be on call at other times.

You will probably be well respected as this is seen as an important community position to hold.

Money guide

You would earn around £17,000–£19,000 per year when starting. £20,000–£30,000 is usual as an experienced superintendent. Up to £45,000 is possible at the most senior levels.

Related opportunities

- Court Administrative Officer p368
- Court Clerk/Sheriff's Clerk p377
- Legal Executive p373

Further information

General Register Office
Identity and Passport Office, Trafalgar Road, Southport PR8 2HH
www.gro.gov.uk

Association of Registrars of Scotland
Secretary, Registration Area Office, Municipal Buildings, College Street, Dumbarton G82 1NR
01389 738351

Local Government Careers
www.lgcareers.com

RISK MANAGER

What the work involves

- Risk managers are responsible for assessing the different risks that could prevent a business, or project within a business, from being viable. They identify, analyse, control and monitor each risk for the safety of the business.

- Risks can be different in each organisation; financial companies are concerned with market risks, safety and environmental risks are important in industry, and even the health service need to identify risks to patients and staff.

- You will be doing a variety of tasks including risk surveys and investigations, designing strategies to prevent risks, and presenting all of your findings to the head of the business.

The type of person suited to this work

You will need to have indepth knowledge of the organisation that you work for, and excellent research skills to be able to identify potential risks.

Good problem-solving skills will be essential for creating strategies to manage any risks, as will knowledge of regulations which are relevant to your company.

It is important to have good communication skills, both written and verbal, as you will need to write up reports of your findings and present these back to your colleagues or clients.

Being persuasive and tactful will help you convince people to support your view of how to deal with a potential risk.

Working conditions

You will be working around 37 hours a week, Monday to Friday; however you might need to work extra hours if you have a heavy workload.

Although the majority of your time will be spent in an office, you might need to visit sites which could be dangerous, or industrial locations such as engineering plants and building sites.

It would be helpful to have a driving licence and your own vehicle for travelling between sites.

Future prospects

There are jobs available across the UK, with risk managers being employed in both the private and public sector; these may include banks, local authorities, engineering firms and the emergency services. There is currently a shortage of financial risk managers, so this area may be a good starting point for your career.

Promotions are possible from risk manager to chief risk officer; you might need to move around different companies though to gain enough experience. You can also go into self-employment as a consultant or trainer. There are promotional possibilities to senior positions through the gaining of experience, with opportunities increasing throughout the UK when specialising in a technical field or industry sector.

Qualifications and courses

The majority of risk managers have a degree. Any subject is relevant but it may be an advantage to have a degree in risk assessment, health and safety, law or auditing. Entry to a degree is with a minimum of 2 A levels/3 H grades and 5 GCSEs/S grades (A*–C). You can study the Institute of Risk Management's (IRM) Certificate in Risk Management or a postgraduate degree if your first degree is not in a relevant subject

General requirements for entry onto a degree course are at least 2 A levels and 5 GCSEs (A*–C), or equivalent qualifications.

Training is done by the employer and further study is required. The IRM offers the International Certificate in Risk Management and the International Diploma in Risk Management which leads to IRM membership. Risk managers working in insurance can study towards the Chartered Insurance Institute Advanced Diploma, and others choose to study towards the National Examination Board for Occupational Safety and Health qualifications. As a risk manager it is important to commit to continuing professional development; the IRM has a programme that can be followed and leads to Fellowship.

Advantages/disadvantages

This is an exciting and varied career as you can work in a range of sectors from financial to the emergency services.

There could be dire consequences if you make a mistake and neglect a risk.

There are opportunities to be self-employed as a consultant and to travel abroad.

Money guide

Starting salaries are between £22,000 and £30,000, with experience this can increase to around £35,000–£70,000. The top risk managers may earn £200,000+ in specific areas such as finance.

Related opportunities

- Actuary p20
- Chartered Surveyor p84
- Insurance Broker p42
- Insurance Surveyor p44

Further information

Association of Insurance and Risk Managers
6 Lloyd's Avenue, London EC3N 3AX
020 7480 7610; www.airmic.com

The Institute of Risk Management
6 Lloyd's Avenue, London EC3N 3AX
020 7709 9808; www.theirm.org

SECRETARY

What the work involves

- Secretaries are responsible for giving clerical assistance to professionals in order to ensure the efficient running of an organisation.

- Your job will include typing letters and reports, setting up and updating filing systems, taking care of diaries and travel arrangements as well as coordinating meetings and appointments.

- You will also have to liaise with staff and customers and deal with incoming mail and telephone calls.

Farm

- You will deal with the financial administration related to running a farm such as putting together budgets, dealing with the staff payroll, looking into government grants, maintaining records of livestock and crops, as well as more typical responsibilities as described above.

- You will also need to be aware of current health, safety and environmental regulations and ensure that these are enforced on the farm.

Medical

- You will be based in a GP's surgery or hospital and undertake general clerical work as well as more specific medical tasks such maintaining patient records and seeing if samples from examinations are correctly labelled and delivered.

The type of person suited to this work

You must be organised, efficient and able to multi-task. You will need a good grasp of spelling, grammar and punctuation as well as a fast typing speed. You should have excellent communication skills and be friendly, helpful and discreet, especially when dealing with confidential information. It is important that you are IT literate, have a good attention to detail and are able to work towards tight deadlines. The ability to work on your own, as well as part of a team, is also essential. Numerical skills are an advantage as your role may include dealing with financial tasks.

A medial secretary must also be considerate and sensitive to patients' feelings when giving them confidential information. A farm secretary should also be aware of how a farm is run.

Working conditions

Your working hours will typically be from 9am–5pm, although longer hours will be needed during busy periods. Part-time and temporary work is widely available. You will probably be located in an open plan office, and you will spend the majority of your day on the phone and working at a computer.

Farm

You may have to work evenings and weekends at certain periods in the year when the workload is high. Offices are based in rural locations, so you will need a driving licence.

Medical

You will be based in a GP surgery, hospital or other medial organisation. You could have to work early mornings, evenings or Saturdays.

Future prospects

You could progress in a bigger company to a job with a more senior manager, or to a role as a personal assistant. You could find a role in human resources, sales or marketing. With experience, many secretaries are working as a virtual assistant from home. If you work for a smaller company, you might have to find a different employer to progress in your career.

Farm

After gaining experience, you could become self-employed. You could also find a job in management within the agricultural industry.

Medical

After gaining further experience and qualifications such as an AMSPAR Diploma (Level 5) in Primary Care Management, you could progress to a role as a practice manager. You could become a senior medical secretary or a junior manager in a bigger healthcare trust. However, there are fewer posts as many hospitals now outsource work formerly completed by secretaries.

Advantages/disadvantages

You can use your experience in a particular company or department to gain a promotion.

Part-time and temporary work is widely available in this line of work.

This job could be a practical way of using your skills and interests.

Tight deadlines and a heavy workload can make this job stressful. It can be repetitive.

Money guide

You can expect a starting salary of £14,000–£18,000 when working outside London, and £19,000–£25,000 in London. Salaries increase to around £30,000–£40,000 after 10–15 years. Roles in banking and finance are more highly paid than those in the media, charities and smaller companies.

The starting salaries for medical secretaries in the NHS are £15,190–£18,157. After gaining experience, this can increase to £17,732–£21,318. The salary for a personal assistant in the NHS can reach up to £26,839.

As a farm secretary, you could start on £14,000. With experience this can reach £28,000.

Secretaries with experience who are self-employed or work on a big estate can earn £28,000+.

Related opportunities

- Personal Assistant p55
- Receptionist p58
- Bilingual Secretary p349

Further information

Institute of Chartered Secretaries and Administrators
16 Park Crescent, London W1B 1AH
020 7580 4741; www.icsa.org.uk; info@icsa.co.uk

Institute of Agricultural Secretaries and Administrators
Stoneleigh Park, Kenilworth, CV8 2LG
024 7669 6592; www.iagsa.co.uk; IAgSA@IAgSA.co.uk

Association of Medical Secretaries, Practice Managers, Administrators and Receptionists
Tavistock House North, Tavistock Square,
London WC1H 9LN
020 7387 6005; www.amspar.co.uk; info@amspar.co.uk

The Council for Administration
6 Graphite Square, Vauxhall Walk, London SE11 5EE
020 7091 9620; www.cfa.uk.com

www.cityandguilds.com/myperfectjob

Qualifications and courses

Employers look for GCSEs/S grades (A*–C/1–3), including English. A GCSE in business studies and the Diploma in Business, Administration and Finance could be helpful. Good ICT skills and a typing speed of 45 wpm are also often required by employers. School leavers often study for a secretarial or business administration qualification, including NVQs in Business and Administration at Levels 1–4, the OCR Higher Diploma in Administrative and Secretarial procedures or the Pitman Diploma and Advanced Diploma in Secretarial Studies. Foundation degrees in Business and Finance, BTEC National Certificates and Diplomas in Business and Apprenticeships are also available. Senior or executive secretaries are often members of the Institute of Chartered Secretaries and Administrators or take a course approved by the Chartered Institute of Personnel and Development. You could also study for a degree or HND in Secretarial Studies, Government/Public Administration, or Business/Management. There are also secretarial courses for graduates at private colleges.

Farm

There are specific farm secretary courses available from agricultural colleges and recognised by the Institute of Agricultural Secretaries and Administrators. The City & Guilds/NPTC Level 3 Certificate in Rural Administration is also on offer. A book-keeping or accounting qualification could be helpful. Courses are run by the Association of Accounting Technicians and The Institute of Certified Bookkeepers.

Medical

Employers often look for an Advanced Diploma of the Association of Medical Secretaries, Practice Managers and Administrators (AMSPAR). You will need 4 GCSEs/S grades (A*–C/1–3) to get onto this course. A British Society of Medical Secretaries and Administrators Certificate in Medical Secretarial Studies is another relevant qualification.

STOCK MARKET TRADER

What the work involves

- Traders use their knowledge of the market to make the highest possible profit on behalf of investors by buying and selling shares, bonds and other assets.

- There are three types: market traders operate on behalf of clients; sales traders highlight new financial ideas, but take direct orders from clients; and proprietary traders make investments for banks.

- You will deal with large sums of money, so your decisions must be quick and well-informed; due to this, you will need to build strong contacts in order to be successful in this business.

The type of person suited to this work

You should have enthusiasm for the financial sector and enjoy a working environment that is highly performance related.

Alongside this, you will need to be extremely confident and full of informed initiative, whilst having the ability to cope with the constant pressure of trading with large sums of money that belong to other people.

As well as demanding accuracy, skilled analysis and responsibility, the job also requires that you are physically forceful and competitive, an excellent verbal communicator and a team player.

Working conditions

Traders often need to begin work at 7am in order to be informed about developments that have happened in foreign markets overnight and to be ready for the 8am opening of the London Stock Exchange, often not finishing their working day until 5pm.

The highly pressurised trading arena involves the monitoring of markets on a screen, and the making of deals on a phone. This communicative tool has made the environment less noisy, although it still remains competitive and ruthless.

Future prospects

Given the current financial climate, opportunities for traders are severely limited.

Once in the industry however, there are many opportunities for progression. The gaining of experience and qualifications allows for promotion to an analyst, being put in charge of a team or gaining the responsibility of a new trading desk. These positions often lead to associate, senior associate and director level.

Many traders change career after a few years due to the highly pressurised working environment.

International offices are common with investment banks, bringing an opportunity to work in foreign arenas.

Advantages/disadvantages

This is an exciting and often hugely rewarding job that would

Qualifications and courses

You will need at least 2.1 degree or higher, in a subject that has a strong numerical focus to it, such as economics, business studies, accountancy, maths, science or engineering. Minimum requirements for degree courses are often at least 2 A levels and 5 GCSEs (A*–C), including English and maths, or equivalent qualifications.

It is also a good idea to try and gain an internship or financial work experience, alongside the submission of a speculative application, which shows you have researched the industry. Major investment banks offer graduate training schemes.

The Diploma in Business, Administration and Finance or the IFS Certificate or Diploma in Financial Studies could be useful.

never become boring due to the constant changes in the financial market.

The highly pressurised environment can often be stressful and means the professional duration of a stock market trader is generally less than those in another profession.

Money guide

The starting salary of a stock market trader is usually between £30,000 and £40,000 per annum, with this quickly rising to over £100,000 a year through the gaining of experience.

Some traders at the height of their profession can earn more than £200,000 a year. However it must be noted that these are figures for markets in London, and other regions will sometimes pay far less than these top figures.

In addition to these impressive salaries are large bonuses, up to 100 per cent of a salary, non-contributory pensions and mortgage subsidies.

Related opportunities

- Investment Analyst p46
- Risk Manager p62
- Stockbroker p66

Further information

Financial Services Authority (FSA)
25 The North Colonnade, London E14 5HS
020 7066 1000; www.fsa.gov.uk

Financial Services Skills Council (FSSC)
51 Gresham Street, London EC2V 7HQ
0845 257 3772; http://careers.fssc.org.uk, www.fssc.org.uk

London Stock Exchange
10 Paternoster Square, London EC4M 7LS
020 7797 1000; www.londonstockexchange.com

STOCKBROKER

What the work involves

- Stockbrokers work for individuals or companies investing their clients' money to make them a profit by buying and selling stocks, bonds and shares.

- You will be managing investments, advising your clients on investing their money and trading on behalf of your clients, often dealing with huge amounts of money.

- You will have to keep up to date with economic trends, interpret market information, and predict how a company's stocks and shares are likely to perform.

The type of person suited to this work

To succeed as a stockbroker you must be confident, determined, competitive and outgoing.

You will have to predict trends in a constantly changing market and take risks with huge sums of money so must be decisive and able to remain calm under pressure. You will need to be personable, trustworthy and honest with a good reputation.

You will need excellent ICT skills and will be expected to work long hours and to dress smartly.

Working conditions

You will be office based, acquiring much of your market information from computers and doing much of your work by telephone. Hours are long: you will probably start early and finish late in order to accommodate international markets in different time zones. You will most likely work over the weekend as well. Much of your day will be spent in a very busy, tense and pressurised environment.

Future prospects

You could be working for a firm which specialises in this work or for other financial institutions such as banks or building societies. Your career will develop by taking on more responsibilities and more important clients.

Competition for jobs is intense so work experience is vital. Economic changes can happen fast so jobs are not always secure.

This is a high pressure job and many stockbrokers finish their careers in their 40s. You could move into other areas within finance such as fund management or become self-employed as a consultant.

Advantages/disadvantages

The hours are long and the work is very pressurised and stressful.

It is a very competitive job and you will need to be tough and determined to succeed.

The work can be exciting and rewarding and is extremely well paid.

Qualifications and courses

ENTRY LEVEL 5

You will normally need at least a 2.1 degree, particularly in such subjects as economics, business studies, maths, physics, accountancy or law. Increasingly, in a very competitive market, possession of a postgraduate qualification such as an MBA (Master of Business Administration) or a Master's in subjects such as business or economics, together with another language, will prove very useful.

Typical entry requirements for a degree course are 2 A levels/3 H grades and 5 GCSEs/S grades (A*–C/1–3) or equivalent; specific subjects may be required.

Individuals with relevant experience may be able to move into stock broking from an analyst, research or investment banking role and graduates are allowed to register for the Chartered Financial Analyst (CFA) Institute's exams before starting in stock broking. Advanced Apprenticeships are also possible.

Graduate trainee positions are available on an annual basis from major investment banks. It's important to apply in late October/early November for these roles starting the following summer or autumn.

Many companies have their own, very detailed selection procedures, including psychometric and aptitude testing. New entrants must be registered by their employer as an 'authorised person' with the Financial Services Authority (FSA).

Money guide

You could earn £24,000–£35,000 a year when you first start work and training after university, with a fairly small number of clients.

With experience you could earn between £45,000 and £80,000. After many years of experience and depending on location, some stockbrokers can earn over £150,000. In addition to their salary, stockbrokers also receive bonuses on the trade they do and can earn substantially more.

Related opportunities

- Accountant p16
- Bank Manager p23
- Economist p34
- Financial Adviser p39

Further information

London Stock Exchange
10 Paternoster Square, London EC4M 7LS
020 7797 1000; www.londonstockexchange.com

Financial Services Authority
25 The North Colonnade, London E14 5HS
020 7066 1000; www.fsa.gov.uk

TELEPHONIST

What the work involves

■ Telephonists work at a switchboard, answering calls, connecting callers to the right person and advising them on which department or person they need to speak to.

■ You will be responsible for a caller's first impression of your company. Your job will include taking messages, testing phone lines and reporting faults.

■ You may need to respond to out-of-office calls left on answering machines.

■ You might do other reception duties such as meeting and dealing with visitors, taking deliveries and other clerical work.

The type of person suited to this work

You will need a professional and friendly telephone manner, a clear and polite voice and good listening skills.

Excellent customer service is essential. You must be assertive with impatient and rude callers while at the same time remaining calm and understanding even when you are busy. You should be someone who enjoys working with people in a team and who can work quickly and accurately.

It's also important to have a good understanding of how your organisation works in order to answer calls effectively.

Working conditions

Most of your work will be in an office or telephone room, probably with other people. You might be based at a reception desk.

Although you will probably work normal office hours, you might need to be at work to take calls before the company opens. Some switchboards provide a 24-hour service which means working shifts including nights and weekends.

You will be wearing a headset and using computer databases and automated switchboards.

Future prospects

Most large or medium-sized companies need people to answer their phones and provide a reception service, so job opportunities are good. You could work in finance, industry, schools, government, NHS, emergency services or transport companies and call centres.

You may lead a team of other telephonists or move into a job in telesales. You could become a senior telephonist receiving training in customer service skills and gaining administrative experience. You could then move into a wide range of jobs working in business administration in offices or with the public.

Qualifications and courses

There are no formal entry requirements for this work, but 5 good GCSEs/S grades (A*–C/1–3), including English language and maths, are a distinct advantage. Basic computing skills or an ICT qualification are also useful.

Many colleges offer courses in customer service and telephone skills at Levels 1–3.

Most training is done on the job. You employer may support studying the NVQ at Levels 1–4 in Customer Service.

Advantages/disadvantages

On a busy switchboard you will be working under pressure and could be working shifts.

Dealing with the public means staying polite and calm no matter what happens.

You will gain valuable customer service and administration skills to help you progress.

Money guide

As a trainee your starting salary is normally around £12,000 per year. With more experience this rises to £16,000+. Earnings could reach £17,000+ for a senior switchboard operator with experience. Earnings could reach £21,000+ for a senior switchboard operator who has experience and more responsibility, perhaps supervising other staff.

Related opportunities

■ Call Centre Operative p482
■ Court Administrative Officer p368
■ Receptionist p58
■ Secretary p63

Further information

Council for Administration
6 Graphite Square, Vauxhall Walk, London SE11 5EE
020 7091 9620; www.cfa.uk.com

Institute of Customer Service
2 Castle Court, St Peter's Street, Colchester CO1 1EW
01206 571716; www.instituteofcustomerservice.com

e-skills UK
1 Castle Lane, London SW1E 6DR
020 7963 8920; www.e-skills.com; info@e-skills.com

www.cityandguilds.com/myperfectjob

TRAINING MANAGER

What the work involves

- You will be responsible for making sure your company's staff have the skills and knowledge they need to make the business as efficient as possible.

- Some of your work will involve looking at how to provide the best training at the lowest cost – from different options such as in-house, distance learning, ICT packages or college courses.

- You will also deliver training yourself or organise other trainers to do this. You will have to write reports and make presentations assessing the value of training.

The type of person suited to this work

You should be interested in people and in helping them to develop and improve their skills. You will need to be able to pass on your knowledge and expertise in a lively, interesting way by designing imaginative and varied training that appeals to everyone.

You will need to be organised and able to plan ahead, meet deadlines and assess the effectiveness of training. To do this you will need excellent ICT skills and an understanding of costs and budgets.

Working conditions

You will usually do normal office hours but may have to work longer at busy times or attend residential, evening or weekend events.

You will be based in an office, probably working as part of a team, but will spend a lot of your time out and about – delivering training, finding training venues, going to meetings and visiting staff in their work places.

Future prospects

Training managers come from a variety of backgrounds as they often become experts in their own field before moving into training people within the industry, but it is possible to start as a graduate trainee.

There are opportunities all over the country as all types of organisations have training managers. Developments in new technology and more on the job training have increased the need for staff training. More companies are using consultants to deliver training to their staff so opportunities to become a self-employed consultant are increasing. It is also possible to gain promotion or move into related areas.

Advantages/disadvantages

The work can be varied and you will have the satisfaction of passing on your expertise to help people learn and develop.

You may need to work hard to motivate staff who are having to do training they are not interested in or do not feel they need.

Qualifications and courses

There are no formal requirements for entry into this profession, but some employers may require relevant vocational qualifications, such as an NVQ/SVQ at Level 3 in Direct Training and Support, or a degree or HND in a subject such as business studies, management, training or personnel.

Training managers are often trained in house but there are some relevant courses of study. The Chartered Institute of Personnel and Development (CIPD) offer a range of relevant courses, including: the Advanced Certificate in Learning and Development Practice, the Advanced Certificate in Managing Organisational Learning, and a Professional Development Scheme. The latter consists of four modules, completion of which allows the candidate to become a graduate member of the CIPD.

Other relevant NVQs/SVQs include: Management and Development of Learning Provision, and Training and Development Strategy at Level 5.

Postgraduate qualifications in training and development are also available. Entry usually requires a degree, a relevant professional qualification, or equivalent work experience.

Money guide

Starting salaries are around £18,000–£21,000 per year. As an experienced and qualified training officer you can earn £28,000–£55,000. This could rise to £60,000 a year in some companies for a training manager with responsibility for other staff. Salaries vary, depending on experience and the size of the company.

Related opportunities

- Human Resources/Personnel Officer p41
- Further/Higher Education Lecturer p196
- Work-based Training Instructor p209

Further information

Chartered Institute of Personnel and Development
CIPD House, 151 The Broadway, London SW19 1JQ
020 8971 6200; www.cipd.co.uk

Lifelong Learning UK
5th Floor, St Andrew's House, 18–20 St Andrew Street, London EC4A 3AY
0300 303 1877; www.lluk.org; enquiries@lluk.org

City&
Guilds

www.cityandguilds.com/myperfectjob

Building and Construction

Are you interested in working on a construction site with a team of people? Maybe your interest lies in buying and selling property and working in an office is more your sort of thing. All the jobs in the sector require someone with a great eye for detail, creative flair and someone who is very good at working with others.

In this section we look at the following jobs:

For similar jobs to the ones in this section why not have a look at *Engineering, Manufacturing and Production* on page 211.

CONSTRUCTION PROFESSIONAL

Make a positive impact on our world with a career as a construction professional

A career in the construction industry can offer much more than just building sites and hard hats. A career in construction offers the chance to shape the future in a big way. And, for those who are concerned about defining issues like climate change and energy efficiency, a career in construction offers one of the few opportunities to make a direct impact.

Michael Brown, Deputy Chief Executive at the CIOB, says: "Sustainability and the environmental agenda are very important in construction, where we are creating solutions through energy efficiency in buildings. Construction is fundamentally about people and how we live, our environment and how we build for people.

"People will always need buildings and that demand won't decline. As our awareness of issues such as climate change increases so does the appetite for a greener and more sustainable built environment. Through a career in construction it is possible to create legacies that form the very essence of tomorrow's society."

Career opportunities as a construction professional

The built environment offers diverse career and work opportunities. These can range from thinking how to utilise the latest technology to create sustainable buildings, how to preserve historic buildings for future generations, to planning and implementing reconstruction projects following natural disasters such as earthquakes.

A wide variety of roles are available within the construction industry

There are a wide variety of roles within the construction industry including architects, engineers, surveyors, site managers, project managers and planners. These roles offer you an international passport – giving you the opportunity to work anywhere in the world.

The Chartered Institute of Building

The Chartered Institute of Building has been established for over 175 years and just as its founder members shaped the skyline of Victorian Britain, so its 42,000 members continue to do so today. CIOB members have played leadership roles in the construction of some of the world's most iconic buildings, including the Palace of Westminster, Sydney Opera House, the Petronas Twin Towers in Kuala Lumpur, Beijing 'Bird's Nest' National Stadium and the Millennium Dome.

Our members have left their mark . . . will you leave yours?

www.ciob.org

ARCHITECT

What the work involves

- Architects design new buildings and the spaces around them. They also design changes to existing buildings.

- Your work will include agreeing design briefs with clients, researching development sites, deciding which materials to use for particular buildings and drawing technical plans.

- You will also be responsible for testing new ideas, obtaining planning permission and inspecting building work while it is in progress

- You could specialise in a particular field such as building heritage and conservation, sustainable and environmental design, or project management.

The type of person suited to this work

You must be able to produce creative, detailed designs that meet the needs and wishes of your clients and other people in the community.

You will need excellent verbal communication skills for working with other professionals, such as surveyors, planners and builders, and for presenting your ideas to them and your clients. You also have to be organised and have good research and problem-solving skills.

As you will use computer-aided design (CAD) in your work, ICT skills are also useful.

Working conditions

Although architects are based in offices, you will go out to visit construction-sites and meet clients. You will need to pay attention to health and safety regulations when on-site. A driving licence may be necessary.

You are likely to work regular office hours, although to meet deadlines you might have to do some work at weekends and during the evenings.

Future prospects

Generally, you would start work in a private architect's practice to gain wide experience of the work, but you may also work for other employers, such as local or central government, later on.

Self-employment is common for qualified and experienced architects.

In the long term, your career will be dependent on your experience, ability and competence. If you decide to remain in private work you could progress to associate level and possibly become a partner. Some of the larger architectural practices win international contracts so you could work on projects abroad.

Advantages/disadvantages

There may be problems to overcome when making design decisions. For example, there might be conflicting needs and views to deal with.

Qualifications and courses

ENTRY LEVEL 5

Professional architects must have chartered membership of the Royal Institute of British Architects (RIBA) and registration with the Architects Registration Board (ARB). The main route to qualification is via a RIBA/ARB-recognised degree. Minimum entry requirements are 2 A levels, which should be drawn from academic fields of study. In addition you must have passed at least 5 GCSEs including English, maths and a science. Equivalent qualifications such as a National Certificate/Diploma may be accepted.

Candidates without the usual entry requirements for a degree may be able to take a foundation year at a school of architecture instead.

Training as an architect takes 7 years. Candidates undertake a 5-year degree programme, divided into three parts. Part 1 takes 3 years and Part 2 takes 2 years. A year is spent working in an architect's office after both Part 1 and Part 2. Candidates then take the Part 3 examination in Professional Practice and Management, leading to chartered membership of RIBA.

If you have passed Part 1, you may be able to join an architectural practice as an architectural technician.

There is personal satisfaction in dealing with these problems and creating designs for buildings that will influence the landscape for many years to come.

Money guide

There are no set pay scales for this work but you can generally earn more if you work in the private sector rather than the public sector. On starting out, with RIBA Part 3 qualifications, you could earn around £25,000–£35,000 per year. Average salaries for experienced architects are from £30,000 to £40,000. Senior architects can earn more than £45,000.

Related opportunities

- Architectural Technician p73
- Architectural Technologist p74
- Construction Supervisor/Manager p90
- Town Planner/Planning Technician p128

Further information

Architects Registration Board
8 Weymouth Street, London W1W 5BU
020 7580 5861; www.arb.org.uk

Royal Incorporation of Architects in Scotland
15 Rutland Square, Edinburgh EH1 2BE
0131 229 7545; www.rias.org.uk

Royal Institute of British Architects
66 Portland Place, London W1B 1AD
020 7580 5533; www.architecture.com

School Profile

FACULTY OF ART, ARCHITECTURE AND DESIGN
University of Lincoln

The Faculty of Art, Architecture and Design houses two Schools:

- The School of Art and Design
- The School of Architecture

The two Schools offer a comprehensive range of visually creative subjects at undergraduate, taught postgraduate and postgraduate research levels.

SCHOOL OF ARCHITECTURE

The **Lincoln School of Architecture**, housed in the award winning Rick Mather designed building on the main Lincoln campus, was originally established in the 1930s in Hull. Today it offers a multidisciplinary 3D design environment, founded on the research and consultancy interests of its staff, having developed an international reputation. The School has benefitted over the years from substantial investment in its facilities which include dedicated design studios, workshops and information technology suites. Modern computer-aided design facilities reinforce the School's progressive and vibrant establishment, preparing students for the creative opportunities of today's world.

Undergraduate courses offered:-

BA (Hons) Architecture RIBA/ARB Part 1 and 2
BA (Hons) Design for Exhibition and Museum
BA (Hons) Interior Design

BA (Hons) Design for Exhibition and Museum shares its first year with BA (Hons) Interior Design, both of which have common links with BA (Hons) Architecture. Design for Exhibition and Museum is a very successful niche course, taking its skill set from disciplines in both Architecture and Design, to allow students to graduate fully equipped to enter into a highly competitive 3D design industry. Interior Design at Lincoln is very much a programme specialising in Interior Architecture or Spatial Architecture, the design of existing space.

For further information on any of these courses, please contact the Faculty of Art, Architecture and Design at aadenquiries@lincoln.ac.uk or telephone 01522 837171.

Web links:-

University website	www.lincoln.ac.uk/aad
School of Architecture website	www.lincoln.ac.uk/lsa
School of Art and Design website	www.lsad.co.uk

UNIVERSITY OF
LINCOLN

ARCHITECTURAL TECHNICIAN

What the work involves

- You will be responsible for liaising between the construction and design teams, making sure everyone is up to date with the latest project developments.

- You will gather and organise all of the technical information which will be required throughout the project.

- You will prepare drawings, plans and specifications using CAD (computer-aided design) software and also by hand.

- This is essentially a support role; you will be providing assistance to the other members of the team including architects, architectural technologists, surveyors and engineers. You will enable them to complete their work as efficiently as possible.

The type of person suited to this work

You need good drawing skills, both hand and computer-aided design (CAD). You will need an ability to visualise in three dimensions.

You must also be able to develop a scientific and technological knowledge of building materials. You will need to understand building regulations and techniques and be able to explain them to others.

You will need to be able to work well alone, as well as having good verbal communication skills for working with other professionals, such as architects, surveyors and engineers.

Your organisational, research and problem-solving skills will need to be excellent.

Working conditions

Architectural technicians are based in offices, but you may visit sites to inspect work in progress. You will need to be aware of health and safety regulations when on-site and will be expected to wear safety clothing. When working on site you will be outdoors in all weathers and may need to climb ladders or scaffolding. You may need a driving licence. You are likely to work normal office hours (9am–5pm, Monday to Friday), although you might have to work late and at weekends on some projects.

Future prospects

An architectural technician may take further CIAT-accredited training to develop their skills and apply to work as an architectural technologist.

You could choose to work in private practice or alternatively within the public sector in an area such as local government, research practices, education or central government. You may need to change employers in order to progress.

There is also the possibility to work freelance or on short contracts.

Advantages/disadvantages

As you will be the main point of contact between contractors

Qualifications and courses

ENTRY 5 LEVEL

The most common route into this career is to complete a HNC/HND or a Foundation degree in a relevant subject such as architecture or building technology. HND/HNC courses usually require applicants to have at least 1 A level (relevant subjects include physics and maths) as well as a GCSE grade A*–C in your A level subject. You should also have another 3 or 4 GCSEs grade A*–C or equivalent including maths, English and a science subject.

You can also complete a degree; however most employers will not expect applicants to be graduates.

To become a qualified architectural technician you will need to apply to become an Associate Member (ACIAT) of the Chartered Institute of Architectural Technologists (CIAT). In order to achieve this you must first complete The CIAT's POP record. In order to achieve this you need to carry out 2 years of supervised work experience and be assessed against CIAT's professional standards.

and clients, when things get heated you will be in the middle of it.

If you work for a larger company you will have the opportunity to work on a range of projects which will keep your job interesting.

Money guide

Technicians can expect a starting salary of £18,000.

After 3 years' experience you could earn between £22,000 and £28,000 a year.

Project managers may earn over £40,000 a year.

Earnings vary widely depending on location and the individual employer.

If you work as a freelance architectural technician you can expect to earn between £15 and £25 an hour.

Related opportunities

- Architect p71
- Architectural Technologist p74
- Cartographer p82
- Surveying Technician p125
- Town Planner/Planning Technician p128

Further information

ConstructionSkills
Bircham Newton, King's Lynn PE31 6RH
01485 577577; www.cskills.org; www.bconstructive.co.uk

Chartered Institute of Architectural Technologists
397 City Road, London EC1V 1NH
020 7278 2206; www.ciat.org.uk

Chartered Institute of Building
Englemere, Kings Ride, Ascot SL5 7TB
01344 630700

ARCHITECTURAL TECHNOLOGIST

What the work involves

- You will be responsible for ensuring that the architect's design is translated into a functioning building.

- You will be involved right from the start, helping to liaise with the client and the architect and advise them on any issues that might affect the build.

- You will make sure that the more practical elements of the build run smoothly, by ensuring that the right materials are used and that all legal requirements and building regulations are met.

- You will have a leading role within the construction team including developing project briefs, coordinating, negotiating contracts and providing guidance.

The type of person suited to this work

You need good drawing skills, both hand and computer-aided design (CAD). You will need an ability to visualise in three dimensions.

You must also be able to develop a scientific and technological knowledge of building materials. You will need to understand planning regulations and construction law, and be able to explain them to others.

You will need good communication skills for working with other professionals. Your organisational, management, research and problem-solving skills will need to be excellent.

Working conditions

Architectural technologists are based in offices, but you may visit sites to inspect work in progress. You will generally be working 9am–5pm but you might need to work extra hours to meet deadlines. You will need to be aware of health and safety regulations when on-site and will wear safety clothing. On-site work can be cold and wet, or hot and dusty as you will be outdoors in all weathers. You may need a driving licence.

Future prospects

Architectural technologists, with CIAT qualifications and experience, may set up their own practice or work in a partnership with other architectural technologists or architects.

It is also possible to progress within private firms to more senior positions or move to other companies which attract larger and possibly international contracts. Promotion is generally easier within larger firms but you may still need to change employers in order to progress.

Advantages/disadvantages

There may be problems to solve at any time during the architectural process, for example issues with the supply of the right materials.

It is rewarding to make your contribution to the design and construction of buildings that will influence the landscape for many years to come.

Qualifications and courses

ENTRY LEVEL 4

The preferred route to becoming an architectural technologist is to complete a degree which has been accredited by the Chartered Institute of Architectural Technologists (CIAT). There are about 29 of these degree programmes and they are listed in CIAT's careers handbook.

You could alternatively complete an NVQ/SVQ Level 4 in architectural technology or a related industry degree such as architecture, architectural engineering, building services engineering, building/construction, built environment studies, civil and structuring engineering, computer-aided engineering and surveying.

Completion of a HNC/HND in Construction or a Foundation degree in Architectural Technology will enable you to become a qualified architectural technician. Once you have had more than 10 years' experience and successful completion of CIAT's professional standards assessment you could become an architectural technologist.

You could choose to complete postgraduate study in architectural technology; however this is not a requirement of the profession.

If you can complete relevant work experience this would be extremely beneficial. You can find relevant placements on the CIAT website and in their publications and in other industry publications and websites.

Money guide

Generally salaries are higher in London and the south.

A junior technologist can expect to earn between £15,000 and £22,000 a year.

After 3 years' experience you should be earning between £24,000 and £28,000 a year.

Once you are in a senior position and have been working for 10 years your salary should be somewhere between £35,000 and £42,000 per year.

Related opportunities

- Architect p71
- Architectural Technician p73
- Cartographer p82
- Town Planner/Planning Technician p128

Further information

ConstructionSkills
Bircham Newton, King's Lynn PE31 6RH
01485 577577; www.cskills.org; www.bconstructive.co.uk

Chartered Institute of Architectural Technologists
397 City Road, London EC1V 1NH
020 7278 2206; www.ciat.org.uk

AUCTION PROPERTY CONSULTANT

What the work involves

- You will be responsible for valuing property and land, from listed buildings to new builds, assessing the current market and organising the property or land to be auctioned off.

- You will be meeting prospective clients, researching their property or land, attending the auction and getting the best price for the client.

- You will need to make detailed reports of the property you value, and report back to your client. You might also have other duties including, advising clients how auctions work and of any other services your company offers.

The type of person suited to this work

You will need excellent communication skills to successfully run an auction, and be firm when settling a bid.

Being lively, outgoing and confident will help when you have to address a large crowd of people; a clear and authoritative voice will be beneficial.

You will need good observational skills for valuing land and property, with a good knowledge of the property market. You will need to keep up to date with current property laws.

Working conditions

You will work around 37 hours a week, Monday to Friday, with the possibility of working evenings and weekends, depending on when the auction is.

You will spend a lot of time in an office, but you will be out and about on a daily basis, meeting clients and valuing properties. You will need to work in all weather conditions, and travel around regularly – a driving licence and vehicle will be very useful.

Future prospects

There are jobs available across the UK, with international auction houses being based in London. There is currently a need for property auctioneers due to the increase in popularity of property auctions, therefore job prospects are good.

You can progress into a senior auction role, or managerial position. It may be possible to move into different areas of auctioning, such as livestock or antiques.

Advantages/disadvantages

Auctions are fast paced and lively events; this job offers an exciting day's work!

It could be frustrating when an auction doesn't go the way you planned, and profit isn't made.

You get great job satisfaction when you auction off a property successfully.

Qualifications and courses

There is no specific entry route for this career, although you will need a degree in a land management or property related subject to join a company as a trainee. You could study for a degree in Property and Valuation accredited by the Royal Institution of Chartered Surveyors (RICS) and join a surveying firm, or you could enter a different area, such as estate management, and train as a chartered surveyor on the job. Entry to a degree is normally with 5 GCSEs/S grades (A*–C) and a minimum of 2 A levels/3 H grades.

The National Association of Valuers and Auctioneers (NAVA) in partnership with the University of Wolverhampton offer a Foundation degree in Auctioneering and Valuation.

Training is done on the job, under the supervision of a senior consultant. NAVA offer property auction workshops to help develop trainees' skills. The National Federation of Property Professionals (NFoPP) has a Level 3 Technical Award in Real Property Auctioneering, which is available through distance learning.

It is important to commit to a continuing professional development programme to keep your skills and knowledge up to date with property law and auctioning methods.

Money guide

The amount that you earn does depend on which type of organisation you work for and where it is located. For example an auction house may pay less than a private chartered surveyor company.

You could start on £15,000 while training, with experience this could increase to £25,000. After several years of experience you could earn £30,000–£40,000 per year.

Those who are particularly successful can earn £60,000+.

Related opportunities

- Auctioneer p348
- Estate Agent p96
- Surveying Technician p125

Further information

Royal Institution of Chartered Surveyors
Parliament Square, London SW1P 3AD
0870 333 1600; www.rics.org

National Federation of Property Professionals
Arbon House, 6 Tournament Court, Edgehill Drive, Warwick CV34 6LG
01926 496800; www.nfopp.co.uk

BRICKLAYER

What the work involves

- Bricklayers build and repair external and internal walls.

- You will use a range of materials including bricks, stones and mortar as well as specialist tools to build walls that often include ornamental and decorative effects.

- Jobs include building houses as well as office buildings, other public venues, shopping centres and stadiums.

- You will spend a lot of your time outside doing manual work.

The type of person suited to this work

As the work requires you to move around a lot and lift materials, you must be physically fit. And you must not mind working at heights.

You need to be able to follow plans and work with accuracy and attention to detail, so that the walls you build are structurally perfect and create the right visual effect.

You also need to work in a team with other bricklayers and those in other construction trades and professions.

Working conditions

You will often be working outdoors and in all weather conditions. This can mean being cold and wet in the winter and hot and dusty in the summer.

To keep yourself and others safe you will need to observe health and safety regulations, which will include wearing protective clothing.

You are likely to work a normal working week, although weekend and evening work is common.

Future prospects

There are currently plenty of opportunities to enter bricklaying as construction is the largest industry in the UK. You can also enter into bricklaying by joining and training with the Army (Royal Engineers).

In the long term, you could progress to technical, supervisory and managerial roles. You can also become an instructor in a training school. The construction industry has one of the highest percentages of self-employment and bricklayers are no exception. Many have set up their own businesses, often working on smaller, local contracts.

Advantages/disadvantages

The work can be physically demanding for some people.

Bricklayers are in demand particularly in the south-east of England.

This is a great career if you like being outdoors, doing practical and creative work.

Money guide

Salaries for trainees range from £7,000 to £13,000 a year, according to the level of training. Once you have achieved

Qualifications and courses

Apprenticeships/Skillseekers are open to those aged 16–24. Some GCSEs/S grades (A*–E/1–5) are normally required in subjects such as English, maths, science and technology. In England and Wales, a Construction Apprenticeship Scheme allows you to study for NVQ Levels 2 and 3. There is no upper age limit for this scheme. Vocational qualifications include: BTEC Introductory Certificate and Diploma in Construction; BTEC First Diploma in Construction; City & Guilds Certificate in Basic Skills (6081). Bricklayers who train on the job can work towards NVQs/SVQs in Trowel Occupations at Levels 1–3 specialising in Bricklaying.

ConstructionSkills' On-Site Assessment and Training (OSAT) programme or the Experienced Worker Practical Assessment (EWPA) offer unqualified bricklayers the opportunity to receive a nationally recognised NVQ. New Deal offers taster courses and placements with an employer for at least 26 weeks. It may be possible to stay on and study for NVQs/SVQs. To qualify you must be aged 18–24 and unemployed for more than 6 months, or 25 or over and unemployed for 18 months.

NVQ/SVQ Level 2 qualifications you can expect to earn around £17,000 per year. Experienced and qualified bricklayers can earn £25,000+. Overtime is often available, and on some projects there are bonuses based on outputs, which can lead to higher earnings. If you are self-employed you have more freedom to negotiate your rate of pay with your clients.

Related opportunities

- Building Technician p80
- Dry Stone Waller p93
- Stonemason p123

Further information

ConstructionSkills
Bircham Newton, King's Lynn PE31 6RH
01485 577577; www.cskills.org; www.bconstructive.co.uk

The Scottish Building Apprenticeship and Training Council (SBATC)
Crichton House, 4 Crichton's Close, Edinburgh EH8 8DT
0131 556 8866; www.sbatc.co.uk

Federation of Master Builders (FMB)
Gordon Fisher House, 14–15 Great James Street, London WC1N 3DP
020 7242 7583; www.fmb.org.uk

www.cityandguilds.com/myperfectjob

BUILDING CONSERVATION OFFICER

What the work involves

- Building conservation officers protect and restore buildings of special historical or architectural interest, such as houses, churches, windmills, factories and lighthouses.

- You will be involved in planning the development of listed buildings and sites, recommending buildings for conservation, writing reports on their condition, making schedules and estimates for work required and giving advice to architects, local authorities or planning committees on building conservation.

- You might have to source suppliers or craftspeople who work with specialised or traditional building materials.

The type of person suited to this work

You will be working to restore historical buildings and sites so it is important that you are interested in history, architecture and construction and have an understanding of historical architecture, building methods and techniques.

You will also have excellent communication skills as you will need to coordinate the many different aspects involved in the development of one site. You must have excellent verbal and written skills as you might need to give presentations to planning authorities or government agencies to persuade them to follow your advice.

Working conditions

Your work is occasionally office-based, but much takes place outdoors on site. This can be dusty and dirty, working at heights and confined spaces in adverse weather conditions. Protective clothing, including hard hats and safety boots, is necessary as you may be visiting buildings in poor repair.

Travel during the day with the occasional overnight stay may be necessary. Working as consultant may involve travel all over the UK or visiting sites in remote areas so a car and driver's licence are useful. Working hours include regular extra hours but not weekends or shifts.

Future prospects

Positions as historic inspector or conservation office can be found in local authorities, district and county councils.

You may be promoted to senior conservation officer or managerial roles. Promotions are limited in small organisations.

There are many opportunities in national government organisations such as English Heritage, the National Trust, the Victorian Society or the Georgian Group.

As a qualified and experienced professional you can be self employed. With substantial experience and industry contracts you can become involved in consultancy work which focuses on advisory and design work.

Qualifications and courses

ENTRY LEVEL 5

Most entrants are graduates and will have studied relevant subjects such as planning, building, construction, civil engineering, surveying, architecture, design or history of art. Courses in architectural heritage and conservation and building conservation and management are offered by some universities. Many graduates will have a postgraduate degree as it is quite a specialist area.

Entry with an HND is possible, or alternatively you can enter as a planning technician and after gaining experience and training become a historic buildings inspector or a conservation officer.

Training is usually provided on the job but employers look for candidates with experience. You could volunteer with the National Trust or a national amenity society.

Advantages/disadvantages

As building conservation officers work to protect and conserve listed buildings, you will gain a great deal of satisfaction from working to ensure the survival of such sites.

Buildings are often in a poor state of repair and building sites may be hazardous.

Money guide

Starting as a trainee or an entry level position you can expect a salary of £18,000–£24,000 depending on your experience. Local authority trainees start on Scale 5 or 6, generally lower than those of historic buildings inspectors employed by central government bodies.

At senior level, with 10–15 years in a role, you can earn £26,000–£40,000.

Related opportunities

- Architect p71
- Building Surveyor p79

Further information

The Institute of Historic Building Conservation
IHBC Business Office, Jubilee House, High Street, Tisbury SP3 6HA
01747 873133; www.ihbc.org.uk

The Society for the Protection of Ancient Buildings
37 Spital Square, London E1 6DY
020 3733 1644; www.spab.org.uk; info@spab.org.uk

City&
Guilds

www.cityandguilds.com/myperfectjob

BUILDING SERVICES ENGINEER

What the work involves

- Building services engineers are responsible for each aspect of energy-using building services such as lifts, lighting, heating, air-conditioning, water supply, ventilation and electrical supply.

- You will design and plan services that are efficient, cost effective and sustainable and in the interest of public safety.

- You will also be responsible for organising and supervising the installation and maintenance of these services and you will work with architects and clients to reduce the environmental impact.

- Although the industry is becoming increasingly multidisciplinary, you will probably specialise in mechanical engineering, electrical engineering or public health.

The type of person suited to this work

You should have a good grasp of maths and physics as you will have to plan each stage of a building service system.

You will need good problem-solving skills, and excellent communication and interpersonal skills so that you can work in a team and with those involved in other aspects of a building's design and construction.

You should have an aptitude for design and technical drawing, model making and show proficiency working with computers and computer-aided design (CAD) software.

Working conditions

Your time will be divided between office-based work, such as planning, designing and estimating costs of projects, and spending time on site, coordinating installation or managing existing systems.

You may work on sites such as airports, hospitals, industrial plants, domestic housing, leisure pools, hotels and cinemas. For this you might need specialist skills.

You will usually be expected to work more than the average office hours but not weekends or shifts. Some roles require on-call availability in case of emergencies.

You may have to travel within a day but overnight stays are uncommon.

Future prospects

Opportunities in this field are numerous, with demand for building services engineers usually exceeding supply.

Promotion to a managerial role such as team leader, project manager or department manager is likely, which will involve pay increases. You can then go on to become a company director or partner.

As a chartered engineer you may establish yourself as an independent consultant.

Qualifications and courses

To enter this profession you will need a relevant degree, subjects include building services engineering, mechanical engineering, maths and physics. Entry to a degree is usually with 2 A levels/3 H grades with a least one in maths or a science, entry is also possible with the Advanced Diploma in Engineering or Construction and the Built Environment.

Accredited HNDs or Foundation degrees in engineering or technology can be used to progress to full degree courses or trainee posts.

As a trainee you will need to complete Initial Professional Development (IPD) to become a professional engineer, you can train for this through your employer.

You can then work towards Incorporated Engineer (IEng) or Chartered Engineer (CEng) status, and commit to a continuing professional development (CPD) programme to keep your skills up to date.

Advantages/disadvantages

The profession has been traditionally separated into electrical and mechanical roles, but it is now becoming increasingly multidisciplinary.

This profession depends heavily on the economic climate of the construction industry, so you need to be aware of this, as it will affect your chances of employment.

Money guide

Your starting salary could range from £17,500 to £24,000.

At senior level your salary can rise to £30,000–£52, 000 and even £70,000.

Related opportunities

- Architect p71
- Civil/Construction Engineer/Civil Engineering Technician p85

Further information

The Chartered Institution of Building Services Engineers
222 Balham High Road, London SW12 9BS
020 8675 5211; www.cibse.org

The Institution of Engineering and Technology (IET)
Michael Faraday House, Stevenage SG1 2AY
01438 313 311; www.theiet.org

City& Guilds

www.cityandguilds.com/myperfectjob

BUILDING SURVEYOR

What the work involves

- Building surveyors work on new building projects, and also suggest ways to improve or enhance existing structures.

- You could work on residential and commercial building projects, and will advise on a number of areas including design, restoration, sustainability and repairs.

- You may also be responsible for ensuring that buildings meet health, safety and access regulations.

The type of person suited to this work

Since the job involves explaining ideas and negotiating with industry professionals and clients, good communication skills are vital. You will produce detailed reports, so a good standard of written English is required.

You will need excellent time management skills and a head for figures to ensure that projects come in on time and within budget.

You will need a logical, analytical and practical approach to work, along with the ability to organise and manage a team.

As much of the work involves computers and electronic equipment, you will need to have good ICT skills.

Working conditions

Working hours are normally 9am–5pm, although longer hours and evening meetings with clients are not uncommon. Most surveyors divide their time equally between office-based work and external client meetings, site visits and surveys. These travel commitments mean it is helpful to have a driving licence and transport.

When on-site you will need to stick to health and safety regulations and be prepared to get muddy, wet and cold.

You may occasionally be called to give evidence in court proceedings concerning a breach of building regulations, which can be stressful.

Future prospects

At the moment prospects are not as good as they once were as the sector has been affected by the financial crisis.

You could work for a variety of employers including surveying practices, construction companies, government departments, and mortgage and property companies, both throughout the UK and internationally. Freelance and consultancy work are also a possibility.

With experience, you could become a partner in a company or establish your own firm. You could also specialise in an area that interests you, such as advising on the restoration and improvement of historical or architecturally valuable buildings.

Advantages/disadvantages

Surveying provides a varied career as each day is different and there are a range of areas to work in.

Qualifications and courses

ENTRY LEVEL 5

All building surveyors hold a relevant degree on entrance to the profession. You may study full time at university for a Royal Institution of Chartered Surveyors (RICS) accredited degree in a relevant subject. The Chartered Institute of Building (CIOB), the Association of Building Engineers (ABE), and the British Institute of Facilities Management also offer professional qualifications.

Candidates with a non-accredited degree, or a degree in a non-vocational subject can take a postgraduate conversion course that has been accredited by the RICS.

The Chartered Surveyors Training Trust offers work-based training for young people aged 16–24 in London and the south-east of England. Applicants must have a minimum of 4 GCSEs (A*–C) or equivalent.

Graduates who have completed a year in industry as part of their degree have an advantage in the job market.

Many surveyors are self-employed and enjoy the flexibility of working freelance.

Sometimes you will need to work extra hours to meet deadlines, or if you are working towards promotion.

Money guide

Graduate surveyors can expect a salary of £18,000–£20,000, which can rise to £24,000 in London-based roles.

With experience you could earn up to £30,000, and if you became a partner in a firm this could rise to £70,000+.

Some companies offer additional benefits such as a company car, mobile phone and pension scheme.

Related opportunities

- Quantity Surveyor p115
- Rural Property Practice Surveyor p118
- Civil/Construction Engineer/Civil Engineering Technician p85

Further information

Royal Institution of Chartered Surveyors (RICS)
Parliament Square, London SW1P 3AD
0870 333 1600; www.rics.org/careers; contactrics@rics.org

Chartered Institute of Building (CIOB)
Englemere, Kings Ride, Ascot SL5 7TB
01344 630700; www.ciob.org.uk; reception@ciob.org.uk

www.cityandguilds.com/myperfectjob

Building and Construction

CRCI: BB

BUILDING TECHNICIAN

What the work involves

- Building technicians support the work of construction professionals including surveyors and construction managers.

- Your work will vary depending on your employer, but might include planning work schedules, drawing up plans and estimating project costs.

- A building technician is also responsible for buying materials, checking that plans meet building regulations, measuring and preparing construction sites, and supervising work on site.

The type of person suited to this work

Organisational skills are essential as you ensure each construction job is completed accurately and efficiently. Mathematical and ICT skills are important for calculating costs, taking measurements and using computer-aided design.

You must have an understanding of the technical aspects of construction. You must be dependable and will need strong communication skills for working with suppliers, site teams and other professionals.

Working conditions

You may work on construction sites or in an office. Building technicians often divide their time between the two. When on site you will need to wear a safety helmet, overalls and boots at all times.

You are likely to work regular hours, but you may also have to start early, finish late or work at weekends on occasion as well as spend time away from home for various projects.

Future prospects

There are about 20,000 building technicians in the UK and currently a shortage of qualified applicants for the steady supply of vacancies.

Building technicians work for employers such as contractors, construction companies, property developers, surveyors' practices as well as the public sector.

With experience and further qualifications, you may be promoted to a higher position such as building/construction manager. You may also choose to specialise in an area of expertise such as buying or drafting.

You may also have the opportunity to work abroad.

Advantages/disadvantages

It can be stressful having to work to deadlines.

Your work will be varied and interesting and you will be an integral part of the team producing all sorts of different buildings.

Qualifications and courses

ENTRY LEVEL **3**

Building technicians normally need to train to NVQ/SVQ Levels 3 or 4. It is possible to train as a building technician with an employer as a construction apprentice. Most apprentices start between the ages of 16 and 18, although entry is possible after this. They usually need a minimum of 4 GCSEs/S grades (A*–C/1–3), including maths and science or technology, or equivalent.

HNDs in Building Studies or similar subjects can be studied over 2 years full time. Applicants should ideally have a science A level/H grade. Introductory courses to a career at technician level include BTEC National Certificate/Diploma or Scottish Group Award in Construction.

You can apply for a ConstructionSkills Inspire Scholarship if you plan to pursue a construction-related degree. This includes a 10 week placement as well as a grant to support university study.

Many companies run training schemes, day-release study (for HNC and Chartered Institute of Building exams), time spent on building sites, in-house training courses, and the Construction Industry Training Board (CITB) Technician Training Scheme.

Money guide

Starting out you can expect to earn around £14,500 per year. This can rise to £25,000 for building technicians with an increased level of experience. Up to £30,000 is possible for experienced senior building technicians.

Related opportunities

- Architectural Technician p73
- Architectural Technologist p74
- Construction Supervisor/Manager p90
- Surveying Technician p125

Further information

ConstructionSkills
Bircham Newton, King's Lynn PE31 6RH
01485 577577; www.cskills.net, www.bconstructive.co.uk

Chartered Institute of Building
Englemere, Kings Ride, Ascot SL5 7TB
01344 630700; www.ciob.org.uk

The Association of Building Engineers
Lutyens House, Billing Brook Road, Northampton NN3 8NW
0845 126 1058; www.abe.org.uk

City&
Guilds

www.cityandguilds.com/myperfectjob

CARPENTER/JOINER

What the work involves

- Carpenters/Joiners make, put in place or repair the wooden parts of buildings.

- You may make and install floorboards, skirting boards, cupboards, partitions, windows and doors.

- You will work with different types of wood and use specialist hand tools such as hammers, chisels and planes, as well as power tools like jigsaws and sanders.

- You will either work in a workshop or on site with other building professionals.

The type of person suited to this work

You must have good practical skills and enjoy working with your hands and different tools.

You will be expected to follow plans and work carefully with attention to detail so that the structures you make fit into place correctly. As you will need to take measurements and calculate angles and dimensions, you will have to be good at maths and be accurate.

You should be physically fit in order to move around and lift materials.

You must be able to work in a team with other carpenters and those from the other construction trades.

Working conditions

You may work in a workshop or on construction sites, or divide your time between the two.

This can be heavy, dangerous and dusty work. You will need to keep to health and safety regulations, which may include wearing protective gear such as safety goggles and a mask. You are likely to work a normal working week, usually with an early start, although weekend work may also be required.

Future prospects

Across the UK there are around 240,000 carpenters/joiners, but employers are finding it difficult to recruit well-qualified and experienced carpenters. Many qualified carpenters are self-employed or work as sub-contractors.

With experience, you could move into a related occupation like shopfitting, kitchen fitting or furniture making, or you may progress to training, technical, supervisory and managerial levels.

Advantages/disadvantages

Work can be seasonal; working fewer hours in the winter or jobs being cancelled are common.

You will develop a lot of new skills, and can specialise in certain areas such as listed buildings.

You get a sense of achievement when you see your woodwork in place in a building.

Qualifications and courses

You will normally need 3–5 GCSEs/S grades (A*–E/1–5), preferably including English, maths, science and technology. Once employed, you can work towards NVQs/SVQs and City & Guilds qualifications, both on the job and at college.

Three year Apprenticeships are available for school leavers. Diplomas and NVQs can be studied without an apprenticeship, or alongside practical working by attending a training centre or college.

NVQs/Diplomas at Levels 2 and 3 can be studied in Site Carpentry and Wood Machining and NVQs at Levels 2 and 3 in Shopfitting Site Work

City & Guilds certificates are available in Basic Carpentry and Joinery Skills (6111); Carpentry and Joinery (5859); Fine Woodwork (5770) and Machine Woodworking (5860).

The Construction Awards Alliance runs a Foundation Certificate in Building Craft Operations. Young Apprenticeships may be available through the Construction Industry Training Board for 14–16 year olds.

Money guide

Trainees can earn between £12,500 and £16,000 per year. Qualified carpenters can earn between £25,000 and £30,000. Very experienced joiners could have an income of £35,000+. Overtime is often available, and on some projects there are bonuses based on outputs, which can lead to higher earnings.

Related opportunities

- Building Technician p80
- Construction Operative p88
- Window Installer p132

Further information

Institute of Carpenters
3rd Floor D, Carpenters Hall, 1 Throgmorton Avenue, London ECZN 2BY
020 7256 2700; www.instituteofcarpenters.com

British Woodworking Federation
55 Tufton Street, London SW1P 3QL
0870 458 6939; www.bwf.org.uk

www.cityandguilds.com/myperfectjob

CARTOGRAPHER

What the work involves

- Cartography involves collecting, evaluating and displaying information gained from a variety of sources, including satellite technology, to create or update maps and navigation charts.

- This is achieved by using artistic, scientific, ICT and technological methods.

- Part of your job will involve travelling around and carrying out surveys.

- You will often use sophisticated information technology for a range of tasks – from collecting to displaying the information.

The type of person suited to this work

You will need to be artistic, have good ICT, scientific and mathematical skills, and an interest in geography.

It can take months to produce one sheet of a map, so you need to be patient, dedicated and able to concentrate on one piece of work. A high level of accuracy and attention to detail is needed in this job so that the map provides the best possible information for the user.

You need to be willing to keep up with new techniques and experiment with new ways of producing maps throughout your career.

Working conditions

You are likely to work normal office hours at a workstation where you will have access to a computer.

You will use graphics software and the different information collected by surveyors or other specialists to produce your maps. You may have some surveying duties which will mean travelling around the country.

Future prospects

Most work is available in government departments, such as Ordnance Survey, the Hydrographic Office and the Meteorological Office. You may also work for local authorities, universities, councils, commercial map publishers, oil companies and motoring organisations.

After gaining experience, you could become a freelance cartographer, provide consultancy services or work within higher education as a tutor.

If you are interested in working abroad, there are opportunities to work in cartography all over the world.

Advantages/disadvantages

You can get great satisfaction from producing a map that looks good and is user friendly. Potentially, a large number of people could use your maps.

When deadlines are near you might have to work late.

The work is varied and combines a variety of subject areas, from design to geography to maths.

Qualifications and courses

The usual entry requirement for a cartographer is a relevant degree. Useful degree subjects include geography, geographical information systems, urban/land studies, surveying and mapping sciences. GCSE/S grade maths is generally needed for entry to these degrees, and an A level/H grade in science, maths or geography might be required.

It is useful to hold a postgraduate qualification in a relevant subject, for example cartography, geographical information systems or remote sensing.

Entrants receive on-the-job training in relevant software and techniques. Government departments that employ cartographers have their own training schemes. It is also possible to work towards an NVQ/SVQ at Levels 3 and 4 in Spatial Data Management.

The minimum entry requirements for a cartographic technician are GCSEs/S grades (A*–C/1–3), including maths, English and a science. In practice, most entrants have A levels/H grades, and some enter with a National Certificate/Diploma or HNC/D in a relevant area.

It may be possible for people entering as school leavers to study for a Certificate/Diploma or HNC/D by day release, while training on the job; this is through the Royal Air Force or Ordnance Survey

Money guide

When starting out you can earn around £18,000–£20,000 per year. With 3–5 years' experience you can get £20,000–£29,000. It is possible for experienced or senior cartographers to earn up to £45,000. Earnings vary depending on the region, type of employer, your qualifications and experience.

Related opportunities

- Architect p71
- Geographer p520
- Land/Geomatic Surveyor p107
- Town Planner/Planning Technician p128

Further information

British Cartographic Society
The Royal Geographical Society, 1 Kensington Gore, London SW7 2AR
020 7591 3000; www.cartography.org.uk

The Survey Association
Northgate Business Centre, 38 Northgate, Newark-on-Trent NG24 1EZ
01636 642840; www.tsa-uk.org.uk; office@tsa-uk.org.uk

Association for Geographic Information
5 St Helen's Place, Bishopsgate, London EC3A 6AU
020 7036 0430; www.agi.org.uk

CEILING FIXER

What the work involves

- As a ceiling fixer you will fit suspended ceilings into new and existing large commercial or public buildings.

- Your work will include fitting a ceiling grid in place and inserting tiles, by using tools such as metal cutters and screwdrivers.

- The ceiling is fitted to the concrete floor of the room above and may hide wiring and systems such as air conditioning.

- Because your job requires you to work at heights, you will need to be up to date on safety training.

The type of person suited to this work

As most of your work will be done on ladders you will need to be comfortable working at heights. You will also need to be physically fit to do the necessary climbing, carrying and bending.

You need to be thorough and accurate. An understanding of technical plans is essential and you will need to be able to follow instructions. Numeracy skills are also important to measure materials and calculate weights. As you will work alongside other ceiling fixers, electricians, heating and ventilating fitters, painters and decorators you need to be a good team player. However you will also need to prioritise your own time effectively.

Working conditions

You will need to drive to various construction sites so a driving licence will be useful. The sites you work on will be mainly indoors and you will most likely work from a ladder in confined spaces.

You will need to take safety precautions for yourself and your colleagues and you will be expected to wear protective clothing such as a hard hat, boots and overalls. You are likely to work Monday to Friday, normal office hours, although overtime work at the weekends might be available.

This could be dusty work, which might be difficult if you suffer from some allergies.

Future prospects

There is currently a shortage of qualified ceiling fixers in the construction industry.

You will most likely start out as a tradesperson. With experience, you may progress to a supervisory or managerial position, or perhaps run your own company. You could become a subcontractor.

Advantages/disadvantages

Working at heights may be demanding for some people.

It is satisfying to see the transformation that takes place when you have worked on fitting a ceiling and hidden away unsightly features such as air conditioning.

Qualifications and courses

No specific qualifications are required, although GCSEs/S grades or a BTEC Introductory Certificate/Diploma in Construction may be useful. Maths, design and technology, science and English are useful subjects.

You will be trained on the job while working towards qualifications. This may also involve going to a college or training centre on day or block release.

NVQs/SVQs in Interior Systems (Ceiling Fixing) at Levels 1, 2 and 3 and Foundation, Higher and Advanced Diplomas in Construction and the Built Environment are available. Apprenticeships might be available to those aged 16–24.

You can also train by doing a Construction Industry Training Board (CITB) Construction Apprenticeship Scheme in Ceiling Fixing or a Construction Craft Apprenticeship which is run by ConstructionSkills. Alternatively, you could complete the appropriate Construction Skills Certification Scheme (CSCS).

Money guide

Trainees generally earn between £8,600 and £14,500 a year. When starting out as a newly qualified ceiling fixer you can expect to earn around £18,000 per year. With a Level 3 NVQ, this can reach up to £21,000. For those with lots of experience, a salary of £27,000 is possible. Overtime is often available, and on some projects there are bonuses based on outputs, which can lead to higher earnings.

Related opportunities

- Construction Operative p88
- Painter and Decorator p110
- Plasterer p112
- Roofer p117

Further information

ConstructionSkills
Bircham Newton, King's Lynn PE31 6RH
01485 577577; www.constructionskills.net;
www.bconstructive.co.uk

Association of Interior Specialists
Olton Bridge, 245 Warwick Road, Solihull B92 7AH
0121 707 0077; www.ais-interiors.org.uk;
info@ais-interiors.org.uk

City&
Guilds

www.cityandguilds.com/myperfectjob

CHARTERED SURVEYOR

What the work involves

- As a chartered surveyor you will specialise in a particular field of surveying. This can be in building, construction, planning, the environment or quantity surveying.

- You will have a variety of tasks to do such as examining plans, designs and project briefs, taking measurements, recording and analysing data and interpreting it through charts, maps or diagrams.

- You may oversee entire construction projects, where you will ensure that specifications are met, calculate supplies needed, and advise clients on the purchase, sale or development of property or land.

- You will spend time negotiating, advising and explaining designs and construction issues with clients.

The type of person suited to this work

You should have an interest in construction, architecture, landscape and the environment.

As you may be a go-between between construction workers and clients you will need to act as a negotiator, have a hands-on approach to problem-solving and be able to delegate tasks.

As you may be involved with several large, complex projects at the same time you must be highly organised and methodical in your work and have a keen eye for detail.

Working conditions

You will probably work 9am–5pm, Monday to Friday. You may have to work longer hours to meet deadlines. You can work part-time.

You will be based in an office but also spend a good deal of time on site.

Depending on the specialised field in which you work, you might have to work in all weathers and wear protective clothing when on site.

You may have to travel for your work purposes, abroad and within the UK. For this a driving licence is strongly recommended.

Future prospects

You may follow a formal promotion structure to gain senior management roles.

You may choose to become self-employed or to join a private practice.

As a qualified chartered surveyor and member of the RICS you will have to take part in Continuing Professional Development (CPD). For this you must accumulate 60 hours of CPD every 3 years.

Qualifications and courses

ENTRY LEVEL 5

You must become a member of the Royal Institution of Chartered Surveyors (RICS). For this you must complete a RICS-accredited degree course or a postgraduate conversion course. Degree entry requires 5 GCSEs (A*–C), 3 A levels or the relevant BTEC/SQA national awards or the equivalent qualification. The Diploma in Construction and the Built Environment will be useful. After completing an RICS-accredited course you must gain practical experience before you will be fully qualified.

If you do not have the appropriate A levels or GCSEs you can take HNC/HND courses or Foundation degrees which can then be supplemented by an RICS-accredited degree course.

You can also train on the job as part of the Chartered Surveyors Training Trust scheme. This is available to those aged 16–24 who have 4 GCSEs (A*–C) or equivalent.

You will be required to undertake continuing professional development (CPD) to keep up to date with surveying trends and skills.

Advantages/disadvantages

Employers may provide benefits such as a company car and bonuses.

There is significant competition for graduates wishing to gain entry to some areas of chartered surveying.

Money guide

As a graduate your starting salary may be from £15,000 to £22,000 a year.

Average salaries can be £40,000 a year and the high earners can expect £100,000 or more a year.

Related opportunities

- Architect p71
- Land/Geomatic Surveyor p107
- Surveying Technician p125
- Town Planner/Planning Technician p128

Further information

The Association of Building Engineers (ABE)
Lutyens House, Billing Brook Road, Weston Favell, Northampton NN3 8NW
0845 126 1058; www.abe.org.uk; building.engineers@abe.org.uk

Chartered Surveyors Training Trust
16th Floor, The Tower Building, 11 York Road, London SE1 7NX
020 7871 0454; www.cstt.org.uk; cstt@cstt.org.uk

Royal Institution of Chartered Surveyors (RICS)
Parliament Square, London SW1P 3AD
0870 333 1600; www.rics.org

CIVIL/CONSTRUCTION ENGINEER/ CIVIL ENGINEERING TECHNICIAN

What the work involves

Civil engineer (consulting)

- You will be designing and developing plans for construction projects such as roads, tunnels, bridges, railways, reservoirs, pipelines and major buildings.

- Your work could span many areas including waste management, coastal development and geotechnical engineering.

Civil engineer (contracting)

- You will take the consulting civil engineer's designs and make them into a reality at ground level, overseeing and managing the construction project.

- This will include recruiting a team, sourcing materials, managing budgets and ensuring that the project is completed on time.

Civil engineering technician

- You will be responsible for providing technical support to the civil engineer, which may include producing costing estimates for a project and helping with recruitment.

- The role will also include aspects of land and quantity surveying, as well as the production of design drawings.

The type of person suited to this work

Regardless of the area you decide to work in you will need to enjoy finding creative, but workable, solutions to problems.

You will need to be happy and confident when using computers to produce designs, work out budgets and undertake research.

You should also be good at maths and science so that you can make accurate calculations and understand the different building materials available to you.

You will also have to be able to think three dimensionally, so that you can visualise and design different buildings and structures.

Written and verbal communication skills are important as you will have to write reports, explain your designs to clients and other professionals, and supervise construction staff.

Your will work as part of a team, so you must be able to communicate with people at all levels including other professionals and clients.

An understanding of environmental building issues, such as the use of energy efficient materials and land protection, is of increasing importance.

Working conditions

Working hours are typically longer than the average working week and can include early morning and evening work onsite. Weekend or shift work is rare for civil engineers, although civil

engineering technicians can be required to remain on 24 hour call for some projects.

Your work will involve both being indoors and out onsite. When working onsite you will need to stick to health and safety regulations and be aware of your own and colleagues' safety. You will have to wear safety clothing including a helmet.

You could work in dangerous places including working up ladders or on scaffolding, or in difficult environments.

When you are in your office, you will be based at a workstation where you will use a computer with specialised software and

possibly a drawing board. You will attend meetings and speak to clients on the phone or in person.

It is also likely that you will have to work away from home from time to time, including projects abroad, but the extent of this will depend on the size of the company you work for and the type of contracts they attract.

Future prospects

Around 100,000 professional civil engineers work in the UK for a range of employers including health trusts, local authorities, central government, energy suppliers including water, gas, nuclear and electricity companies, contractors, consultancies and transport networks.

Work is available on a variety of projects including the building of new schools, hospitals and the upgrading of public transport networks.

Many UK civil engineering companies also operate globally, increasing the opportunities to work overseas. The range and size of opportunities open to you will depend on the size of the company you work for, and the types of contracts won.

Civil engineering technicians can undertake job-related training and study for more qualifications to become full civil engineers.

There is scope to undertake further study and specialise in areas such as environmental engineering, coastal and marine engineering, geotechnics or tunnelling.

With experience, you can progress into management or possibly associate/partnership positions within UK or international companies, management and chief engineer jobs in public services work, provide training or consultancy services, or choose self-employment.

Advantages/disadvantages

You will play an important part in the design and construction of buildings and structures throughout the world.

Seeing your ideas being built is satisfying.

Having an engineering background and qualifications are keys to entering other non-engineering careers at senior levels.

There is the opportunity to become self-employed, or work overseas.

Work is varied, each day is different and you will be meeting and dealing with a wide range of people.

Sometimes the hours can be long and you might have to juggle a number of projects.

Money guide

Starting salaries for civil engineers, either contracting or consulting, are between £16,000 and £21,000. This will increase to around £24,000 when fully qualified.

With a few years' experience, civil engineers can earn between £35,000 and £45,000.

Qualifying as a member or fellow of the Institution of Civil Engineers (ICE) can see salaries for civil engineers rise to £60,000+.

Civil engineering technicians start on about £14,000, and this will rise to £25,000 with a few years' experience. Senior technicians can earn £30,000+, and if you train as a civil engineer your earning potential will increase as above.

Earnings vary among regions and employers. Salaries are generally higher in London and other large cities.

Related opportunities

- Building Surveyor p79
- Insurance Surveyor p44
- Town Planner/Planning Technician p128
- Architect p71

Further information

The Engineering Careers Information Service (ECIS)
14 Upton Road, Watford WD18 0JT
01923 238 441; www.enginuity.org.uk,www.semta.org.uk

Engineering Council UK (ECUK)
246 High Holborn, London WC1V 7EX
020 3206 0500; www.engc.org.uk

Institution of Civil Engineers (ICE)
1 Great George Street, London SW1P 3AA
020 7222 7722; www.ice.org.uk; careers@ice.org.uk

Women into Science, Engineering and Construction (WISE)
2nd Floor Weston House, 246 High Holborn,
London WC1V 7EX
020 3206 0408; www.wisecampaign.org.uk;
info@wisecampaign.org.uk

www.cityandguilds.com/myperfectjob

Qualifications and courses

Entrants to Civil Engineering are usually graduates, although there are opportunities to progress from craft or technical level.

The main route to becoming an engineer is a degree in the relevant branch of engineering, or a closely related subject. The normal minimum entry requirements for an engineering degree are 3 A levels or 5 H grades including maths and a science, usually physics or chemistry. Equivalent qualifications such as BTEC/SQA National qualifications may be accepted.

Candidates who do not have the relevant A levels or equivalent may gain entry to an engineering degree by taking a 1 year foundation course. Foundation courses are offered by universities and are sometimes taught at local partner colleges.

It is possible to enter engineering after taking GCSEs and progress to technician or professional level by studying part time for an HNC/D or NVQ/SVQ Levels 4 or 5. It is also possible to gain a position as a trainee technician within a company straight after GCSEs, although you will need at least grades A*–C in English, maths and science. There are also BTEC and SQA national certificates or diplomas which will give you the relevant qualifications and which can be studied at any age.

Apprenticeships may be available for candidates aged between 16–24 years.

Professional engineers can be chartered or incorporated members of one of the engineering professional bodies, for example the Institution of Civil Engineers (ICE) or the Chartered Institution of Building Services Engineers (CIBSE). These professional bodies also accredit BEng and MEng degrees.

The usual requirement for chartered status is an accredited MEng degree, or equivalent. For incorporated status, a 3 year accredited BEng or BSc degree or an HND or equivalent, plus an additional period of learning (matching section) is required.

CONCRETER

What the work involves

- Your job will aid in the construction of drives and pathways, floor slabs, foundations, columns and beams.

- You will initially level and compact the ground to prepare it for concreting.

- You will take early-morning deliveries of concrete, place it on the prepared ground, vibrate it to remove air trappings, and wrap it in polythene sheeting in order to cure it.

- At times you might need to mix cement, stone and water to make concrete.

The type of person suited to this work

You should have a careful, methodical approach to your work and have good hand skills.

Maths skills are important as you will be calculating quantities for materials.

You should enjoy working outdoors, as part of a team or on your own.

Being fit and active is essential as you will be required to work long and at times hard hours.

You need to be aware of health and safety requirements when working on site.

Working conditions

Your work will be site based, largely undertaking manual labour in dirty or dusty surroundings.

You will work 37 hours a week, including some early mornings and late nights.

You could work on a building site, motorway, private driveway or the interiors of large buildings.

You will use traditional hand tools such as shovels as well as machinery such as cement mixers and drillers.

Protective clothing is needed.

Future prospects

You can move into specialised areas of work such as concrete spraying or concrete repair. It is also possible to progress to a managerial or supervisory role.

After gaining experience, many concreters choose to become self-employed. You could start your own company or work on a labour-only basis for a contractor.

You can work for building and engineering contractors, local authorities and public organisations.

Job opportunities are available abroad, as well as throughout the UK.

Advantages/disadvantages

You have the opportunity to earn good money if you work hard.

Qualifications and courses

You can work as a trainee concreter and learn on the job as soon as you leave school. Apprenticeships are available. It would be helpful to have GCSEs (A*–E) including maths, design, technology and English.

You can work towards Level 1 and 2 NVQs in Trowel Occupations, Erection of Precast Concrete, Specialist Concrete Occupations, Concrete Repair or Sprayed Concrete.

Foundation Construction Awards are available if obtaining experience in the workplace for NVQs is a challenge.

Colleges offer these awards along with an Apprenticeship.

There is an increased risk of injury on construction sites. The cement in concrete can cause burning or inflammation and you should avoid contact with the skin.

Money guide

As a trainee you can expect to earn around £12,500. With experience this can rise to £20,000–£25,000. Concrete sprayers with a lot of experience can earn up to £30,000. Salaries can be boosted by bonuses and overtime. You may earn more if you set up your own contracting firm.

Related opportunities

- Bricklayer p76
- Construction Operative p88
- Plasterer p112

Further information

The Chartered Institute of Building
Englemore, Kings Ride, Ascot SL5 7TB
01344 630700; www.ciob.org.uk/home

The Concrete Centre
Riverside House, 4 Meadows Business Park, Station Approach, Blackwater, Camberley GU17 9AB
01276 606 800; www.concretecentre.com;
enquiries@concretecentre.com

Women and Manual Trades
52–54 Featherstone Street, London EC1Y 8RT
020 7251 9192; www.wamt.org; info@wamt.org

www.cityandguilds.com/myperfectjob

CONSTRUCTION OPERATIVE

What the work involves

- Construction operatives support the work of other construction workers by doing various practical tasks.

- Your work might include digging trenches, moving building materials and tools, putting up signs and safety barriers, helping to lay drains, and paving roads.

- You will also mix and lay cement as well as operate construction equipment and vehicles.

The type of person suited to this work

As the work requires you to lift heavy materials and be on the move a lot you must be physically fit. You must also not mind working at great heights or depths.

You need to be able to follow and carry out instructions and work well in a team with other labourers and professionals. It is essential to be hands on, flexible and trustworthy.

Working conditions

You will be working both indoors and outdoors in all weather conditions. The work is often dusty and dirty and may be difficult for people suffering from allergies.

You will need to pay attention to both your own and your colleagues' health and safety. You will be expected to follow procedures for each type of work you do, including the wearing of protective clothing.

You may work a normal week, although evening and weekend work may also be available, and you might need to start early or finish late for some projects as well as work away from home at times.

Future prospects

Building projects, new builds and renovations can't happen without construction operatives so they are in strong demand when business is doing well.

You could work for the public sector, contractors or local authorities.

You may progress to a specialist craft career such as carpentry or bricklaying or advance to a supervisory role. You have the option of becoming self-employed or working abroad.

Advantages/disadvantages

The work can be physically demanding at times.

You have the opportunity to learn a wide range of skills and work on a different project every day. You are important on site as you pave the way for tradespeople to complete their tasks.

Money guide

As a trainee starting out you can expect to earn around £9,000–£15,500 per year. As a skilled construction operative

Qualifications and courses

Your training will be given mainly on the job by experienced labourers/construction operatives and tradespeople.

There may be opportunities to work towards NVQs/SVQs at Levels 1 and 2 in Construction and Civil Engineering Services and in Specialised Plant and Machinery Services while you are working.

City & Guilds offers a certificate in Basic Construction Skills (6051), BTEC certificates and diplomas are available in construction as well as a ConstructionSkills Foundation Certificate in Building and Craft Occupations.

You can also train by doing a 2 year Construction Apprenticeship Scheme. You can choose to do an extra year for a Level 3 Construction Diploma. If you are a full-time student doing a construction-related course you can qualify for a programme-led apprenticeship (PLA) and can gain experience up to NVQ Level 2.

you could earn £16,000–£18,000. Overtime is often available, and on some projects there are bonuses based on outputs, which can lead to higher earnings. Skilled operatives may be able to earn more than £20,000 on some projects.

Related opportunities

- Bricklayer p76
- Building Technician p80
- Mastic Asphalter p108
- Plasterer p112

Further information

ConstructionSkills
Bircham Newton, King's Lynn PE31 6RH
01485 577577; www.cskills.net; www.bconstructive.co.uk

Federation of Master Builders
Gordon Fisher House, 14–15 Great James Street, London WC1N 3DP
020 7242 7583; www.fmb.org.uk

Women and Manual Trades
52–54 Featherstone Street, London EC1Y 8RT
020 7251 9192; www.wamt.org; info@wamt.org

www.cityandguilds.com/myperfectjob

CONSTRUCTION PLANT OPERATOR

What the work involves

- Construction plant operators operate and maintain different forms of plant (machinery) used for tasks such as moving soil and building materials, flattening the earth and preparing concrete.

- You may operate bulldozers, excavators, diggers, cranes and fork-lift trucks.

- In larger organisations you may specialise in operating one type of plant. For example, crane operators control the machine to load and unload materials, working in conjunction with a signaller on the ground.

The type of person suited to this work

As you will often handle large and complex machines, you need to be good with your hands and have keen safety awareness. You will also need good mechanical knowledge.

You need to stay focused and communicate with your workmates so that you can operate safely.

If you are working on cranes, you need to be comfortable working at heights, be alert and be a skilled driver.

Working conditions

You will work outdoors and on a variety of sites. Expect to get hot, dusty and dirty in the summer and cold, muddy and wet in the winter.

You will have to stick to health and safety regulations and wear a protective helmet and boots.

You are likely to work a normal working week from Monday to Friday, but you may also work extra hours at weekends. Some construction firms operate longer hours during the summer months and shorter during the winter. You might have to travel away from home on some contracts.

A driving licence (often a large goods vehicle category C licence) is essential for crane operators.

Future prospects

Work is available across the UK with crane-hire companies, manufacturers, local authorities and construction companies. For operators specialising in engineering work there is a high concentration of jobs available in the Midlands and in the North of England.

With experience, you may progress to using a wider range of plant, and you may supervise or train plant operators or work as a safety inspector. You may also choose to specialise in operating one type of plant.

With experience and financial backing, it may be possible to start your own construction plant operation or hire business.

Advantages/disadvantages

Working on construction sites can be noisy, dusty and dirty although you will have safety gear such as ear protectors. Working at heights may be demanding for some people.

Qualifications and courses

ENTRY 1 LEVEL

There are no set academic entry requirements, although GCSEs/S grades or equivalent in English, maths and science or technology are useful, along with equivalent vocational qualifications. It is also possible to take NVQs/SVQs at Levels 1 and 2 in Specialised Plant and Machinery Operations and Construction Plant and Equipment Supervision at Level 3.

The minimum age to operate plant is 18, but 17-year-olds may work under supervision while they are training.

Crane operators usually enter this career through an apprenticeship with 12 weeks at the National Construction College East and 2 years on site with an employer, leading to an NVQ Level 2 in Plant Operations.

The Construction Plant Competence Scheme (CPCS) card is required to operate most categories of plant, including cranes. New applicants must pass a health and safety test and technical test for a 'red' CPCS card which allows trainees to work on site. After working 300 hours and completing an NVQ/SVQ you can obtain a 'blue' card.

It is a skilled and varied career where you are responsible for some awesome machinery. It can be satisfying to be able to control the machinery efficiently and safely.

Money guide

As a trainee you can expect to earn around £15,000 per year. This can rise to £28,000 with qualifications and experience. Operators of special types of crane may earn up to £40,000. Overtime is often available, and on some projects there are bonuses based on outputs.

Related opportunities

- Demolition Operative p92
- Construction Operative p88
- Highways Maintenance/Road Worker p104

Further information

ConstructionSkills
Bircham Newton, King's Lynn PE31 6RH
01485 577577; www.cskills.net; www.bconstructive.co.uk

The Association of Building Engineers
Lutyens House, Billing Brook Road, Weston Favell, Northampton NN3 8NW
0845 126 1058; www.abe.org.uk; building.engineers@abe.org.uk

**City&
Guilds**

www.cityandguilds.com/myperfectjob

CONSTRUCTION SUPERVISOR/ MANAGER

What the work involves

■ Construction supervisors/managers run both new build and maintenance construction sites.

■ Your duties will include planning the build, preparing the site, arranging deliveries, and checking quality and cost of building materials and equipment.

■ You will also have the responsibility for overseeing the construction project, hiring and managing staff, making sure everyone is safe on site, and solving problems when they arise.

■ You will need to report directly to whoever is paying for the work to be done and keep them updated on progress.

The type of person suited to this work

You have to be able to plan ahead and have good management and problem-solving skills so that projects run smoothly. Numeracy skills are important in order to budget your projects.

You will use computer software packages to plan workflow, so ICT skills are also useful.

You need to be a good communicator, energetic, hard working and diplomatic in order to motivate and manage your staff effectively. You must be able to develop an in-depth knowledge and understanding of all aspects of the construction business.

Organisational skills are essential and you should be prepared to take responsibility for anything that happens on your site.

Working conditions

You will be based on construction sites and are likely to work from a portable office. You will work outdoors in all weathers.

You may work a normal working week, but you may also have to start early, finish late or work at weekends on some projects. As some companies win contracts all over the UK, you might have to work away from home.

Future prospects

There is a shortage of qualified construction managers and supervisors across the UK. There are opportunities on a wide range of projects including multi-million pound builds.

You may work for contractors, construction companies, project management companies, surveyors' practices, public services, utility companies or retailers.

With experience, you may be promoted to work as a contract manager on bigger and more prestigious projects. You could teach or work as a health and safety inspector.

You may also be able to work abroad.

Advantages/disadvantages

It will be great to know that you can begin with an empty

Qualifications and courses

The normal entry qualification to be a construction manager is a degree, HND or Foundation degree. Relevant subjects include construction project management, building services and construction management. For entry to a degree, 5 GCSEs/S grades (A*–C/1–3), including maths and science and 2 A levels/3 H grades are normally required.

It may be possible to work your way up from technician level. The NVQ/SVQ Level 3 Construction Site Supervision and Level 4 Construction Site Management are open to anyone with experience in building site supervision and management. Technicians can also study part time towards an HNC or degree.

Recently qualified graduates are likely to continue training on programmes designed for professional and managerial staff. The Chartered Institute of Building (CIOB) runs a Professional Development Programme (PDP) leading to corporate membership of the Institute.

piece of land and leave a finished construction behind, a relatively short time later.

When there is a tight deadline to meet and a problem arises, the work can be stressful – particularly as many projects are on large but tightly planned budgets.

Money guide

Salaries for graduate trainees start from £20,000 per year. This can quickly rise to £26,000–£37,000 for managers with experience. For managers running the largest projects £40,000+ is possible. Earnings vary depending on geographical location and your particular employer.

Related opportunities

■ Architectural Technician p73
■ Building Surveyor p79
■ Building Technician p80
■ Civil/Construction Engineer/Civil Engineering Technician p85

Further information

ConstructionSkills
Bircham Newton, King's Lynn PE31 6RH
0844 844 0046; www.cskills.net; www.bconstructive.co.uk

Chartered Institute of Building
Englemere, Kings Ride, Ascot SL5 7TB
01344 630700; www.ciob.org.uk

City&
Guilds

www.cityandguilds.com/myperfectjob

DAMP PROOFER

What the work involves

- You will provide guidance and solutions to people in residential or commercial properties who experience damp problems.

- You also may need to install damp-proof courses to buildings. This is a horizontal layer of water-repellent/ proof material that prevents moisture rising from the ground up the walls.

- You will need to be able to install damp-proof courses to old and new buildings. In new buildings this is laid as walls are constructed by the bricklayers.

The type of person suited to this work

As you will be working on buildings or engineering projects, you should have an interest in construction and architecture.

You should have good problem-solving skills and relish new challenges. You should be able to work in a team and cooperate with colleagues and customers.

You need to have a keen eye for detail and have good practical skills to operate drills and specialist machinery such as moisture meters to check damp levels.

You should also have good health and have an understanding of health and safety protocol.

You should be willing to travel.

You will need good written and communication skills to give and follow instructions and guidelines.

Working conditions

You will usually work 38 hours a week, Monday to Friday. You may have to work overtime and this could include evenings and weekends. These hours will vary depending on where you are working, who you are working for and even the weather.

You will have to do a lot of travelling to each new site. A driving licence and car would be useful.

Your work will be largely outdoors, so can be affected by the weather.

Future prospects

You can find job opportunities with the 1,500 damp proofing contractors across the UK. You can also find employment in related fields such as timber treatment, waterproofing and pest control.

With experience you will be eligible for promotion to remedial treatment surveyor or supervisory posts. The BWPDA runs its own training courses for surveyors and technicians and with an NVQ/SVQ Level 2 in insulation and remedial maintenance you can apply for occupational assessment under the Construction Skills Certification Scheme (CSCS Card).

You may become self-employed.

Qualifications and courses

There are no set academic requirements. However GCSE English and maths (A*–E/1–5) are an advantage as you will need to calculate quantities, make estimates and keep written records. The Diploma in Construction and the Built Environment might be useful.

No colleges provide apprenticeships specific for damp proofing. Some private companies, involved in Investors in People, may consider apprenticeships.

Young Apprenticeships, Apprenticeships and Advanced Apprenticeships are available in England. They are organised differently in Scotland, Wales and Northern Ireland. Pay rates vary according to area and industry. On-the-job training is provided by experienced damp proofers. Damp-proof installer companies may provide courses on safety awareness.

Technicians can take short courses at the British Wood Preserving and Damp Proofing Association. You can study for the Level 2 NVQ in Insulation and Building Treatments. You must have a Construction Skills Certification Scheme card to work on a building site.

Advantages/disadvantages

As a damp proofer you will have plenty of opportunities to travel around the UK and abroad.

You may have to work in uncomfortable weather conditions and antisocial working hours.

Money guide

Your starting salary may be around £12,000 a year but the average salary of a damp proofer is about £25,000. With specialised skills and training you can earn up to £35,000 or more.

Related opportunities

- Building Technician p80
- Concreter p87
- Thermal Insulation Engineer p127

Further information

The Wood Protection Association
5C Flemming Court, Castleford WF10 5HW
www.wood-protection.org; info@wood-protection.org

The Institute of Specialist Surveyors and Engineers
Essex House, High Street, Chipping Ongar CM5 9EB
0800 915 6363; www.isse.org.uk

www.cityandguilds.com/myperfectjob

DEMOLITION OPERATIVE

What the work involves

- Demolition operatives demolish or dismantle buildings and structures. You will assess structures and plan for the safest and most efficient way to demolish them.

- You will prepare sites, put up fencing and scaffolding, strip out fittings, and remove, sort and grade reusable materials.

- You will use a variety of tools such as chisels, crowbars and axes for hand demolition of brick and stone and you may also use specialised machinery including pneumatic drills, steel girders, chain saws and even explosives for bigger jobs.

The type of person suited to this work

As you will be involved in the construction industry you should have an interest in building, construction and the environment.

You should have a high level of fitness as your work can be quite physical at times, lifting and carrying, and you should be able to work at heights.

You will also need good manual skills to operate equipment and tools and an aptitude for more delicate tasks such as hand demolition.

You should be willing to work as part of a team and be conscious of your safety and that of those around you.

Working conditions

You will normally work 39 hours per week. This will frequently include weekends and overtime.

As you will be working on construction sites you should be willing to work outdoors in dirty, dusty, noisy conditions in all weathers. This will also involve lifting, bending and working at heights.

You will need to wear protective equipment including helmets, boots, gloves and goggles which will be provided by the employer. You may also be required to wear breathing equipment for some jobs.

Future prospects

There are opportunities for demolition operatives on many building and development projects throughout the UK. You can find employment in specialist companies which may be based nationally but many companies are based in urban and traditionally industrial areas of the UK.

Advantages/disadvantages

Although it is unusual to be self-employed in this profession, with experience you can set up your own contracting business.

At times your work can be strenuous and potentially hazardous if you do not follow safety procedures.

Qualifications and courses

ENTRY 1 LEVEL

No formal qualifications are required to be a demolition operative. However GCSEs/S grades (A*–E/1–5) in maths, science subjects and English may be useful. The Diploma in Construction and the Built Environment may be relevant for this job.

You can enter via the ConstructionSkills Demolition Plant Operative Apprenticeship, if you are under 16. There is also a specialist Apprenticeship, for people who work in demolition but do not handle machinery.

Most training is done on the job, with special attention given to health and safety. You can study for the NVQ at Level 2 in Demolition and Demolition Plant. Other NVQs are available for specialist work such as the Level 2 in Removal of Hazardous and Non-Hazardous Waste.

You will need a Certificate of Competence of Demolition Operatives (CCDO) card, to prove you are qualified to carry out the job.

Money guide

Starting salaries range from around £12,000 a year.

With experience you should earn £18,000.

As a senior operative you can earn around £20,000.

You may earn significantly more with overtime or for operating plant machinery.

Demolition operatives have nationally recommended minimum rates of pay.

Related opportunities

- Construction Operative p88
- Quarry Worker p243
- Roofer p117
- Scaffolder p119

Further information

ConstructionSkills
Bircham Newton, King's Lynn PE31 6XG
0300 456 7701; www.cskills.org

National Federation of Demolition Contractors
NFDC Resurgam House, Paradise, Hemel Hempstead HP2 4TF
01442 217144; www.demolition-nfdc.com

City & Guilds

www.cityandguilds.com/myperfectjob

DRY STONE WALLER

What the work involves

- Dry stone walls are built as boundaries in rural landscapes, and sometimes in gardens and parks. Unlike other walls, they are built without the use of mortar or cement.

- You will build new walls and maintain and rebuild existing walls, using the existing stone or newly quarried stone.

- You will prepare foundations, set up a frame and lay stones, as well as strip out any existing wall or stones.

- You will need to be able to use tools such as hammers, sledgehammers, pick axes and tape measures.

The type of person suited to this work

You need to be thorough, methodical and good with your hands. Being physically fit is essential as you will be lifting and carrying heavy stones. You will also need endurance and self-motivation as you will most likely be self-employed.

An eye for design is useful for creating decorative effects. You may also need to work in a team with other dry stone wallers.

You will need to respect the plants, animals and insects that live within, on or around the walls and other parts of your working area so having an interest in conservation and the environment is useful.

You should also be aware of health and safety regulations.

Working conditions

Your work will be physically demanding and take place outdoors in most weather conditions. The work may also be dusty and dirty.

You will need to wear protective gear such as boots, strong gloves and safety goggles.

Your working hours are likely to vary according to daylight hours and when the work is available. You may need to work weekends.

Future prospects

Dry stone walling is prospering due to the increased interest in conserving walls and the growth in artistic landscape projects. With a demand for walls on farms, parks and gardens, work is available in all rural areas of the UK for skilled dry stone wallers.

Employment is possible with organisations such as National Parks and The National Trust – although most experienced dry stone wallers are self-employed.

You can begin by working for an experienced dry stone waller and gain the necessary skills before working for yourself.

Many experienced wallers travel around the UK to complete projects. A few wallers combine this work with traditional bricklaying work.

Qualifications and courses

No specific qualifications are required. You can train with an experienced dry stone waller or do a land-based training course that includes dry stone walling. Lantra Certificates at Levels 1 and 2 are available in Dry Stone Walling.

The Dry Stone Walling Association of Great Britain (DSWA) runs a National Certification scheme at 3 levels (Initial, Intermediate and Advanced) which is open to anyone, including complete beginners.

Lantra offer an Apprenticeship in Dry Stone Walling (England and Wales). Apprentices work towards NVQ Levels 1 and 2 in Environmental Conservation and the Lantra Level 2 Certificate in Dry Stone Walling. There are no formal entry requirements to an Apprenticeship; commitment to a career in dry stone walling is more important. The Apprenticeship normally takes 12 months.

Advantages/disadvantages

The work can be physically demanding. It is rewarding to use craft skills to build dry stone walls that are not only functional, but also enhance the landscape and become part of our heritage.

You also have the chance to be creative when producing decorative effects.

Money guide

The normal starting point for new entrants is around £8,000 per year. For dry stone wallers with some experience £10,500–£14,500 is possible. For very skilled dry stone wallers up to £21,000 is likely. Earnings vary widely across the UK.

Related opportunities

- Bricklayer p76
- Construction Operative p88
- Stonemason p123
- Thatcher p126

Further information

Dry Stone Walling Association of Great Britain
Westmorland County Showground, Lane Farm, Crooklands, Milnthorpe LA7 7NH
01539 567953; www.dswa.org.uk

Lantra
Lantra House, Stoneleigh Park, Coventry CV8 2LG
0845 707 8007; www.lantra.co.uk

www.cityandguilds.com/myperfectjob

ELECTRICIAN

What the work involves

■ Electricians install and inspect the wiring systems in all kinds of buildings (residential and commercial) and mechanical equipment.

■ You will follow detailed diagrams and plans when checking and installing new systems. Once installed you will test them to make sure they are safe.

■ You may work on quite complex wiring systems, ranging from security circuits and computer networks to traffic lights and other street lighting.

The type of person suited to this work

Normal colour vision is essential. You must also have the practical skills to be able to use tools such as pliers, screwdrivers and drills.

You will need to be physically fit as the work involves bending, stretching, kneeling and generally being active. It can also involve working at heights, so you must be comfortable with this.

You should have the ability to follow wiring diagrams and work within strict safety regulations.

An aptitude in maths and physics is a significant aid.

You may work alone or in a team, but either way you will be talking to customers and explaining electrical problems, so good communication skills are an asset.

Working conditions

You may work a normal working week from Monday to Friday, but most electricians work 37–40 hours including evenings and weekends to accommodate the needs of their customers.

Electricians work in a variety of locations from people's homes to offices or building sites. You will almost certainly need a driving licence.

The work can be dusty and dirty.

You will need to keep to health and safety regulations, as otherwise working with electricity can be exceedingly dangerous.

Future prospects

Employment prospects for new trainees are still good, although a halt in construction projects following the financial crash has affected the job market slightly.

Work is available in housing associations, general building companies and public services such as local authorities and health trusts.

With further qualifications and experience, you can progress to approved grade and then technician grade, which will increase your earning potential.

You may hold a supervisory or management position, and owning your own company is also an option.

There are also opportunities to work abroad.

Qualifications and courses

An appropriate Level 3 NVQ and a technical certificate are needed. The most common route is through an Electrotechnical Advanced Apprenticeship. This offers training to NVQs in Electrotechnical Services, Panel Building and Electrical Machine Rewind and Repair.

Entry requirements are 3 GCSEs/S grades (A*–C/1–3) including English, maths and science or the Higher Diploma in Construction and the Built Environment or Engineering. You must pass a selection and a colour vision test; entry is quite competitive.

Those experienced in areas like electronics may qualify for entrance onto a training course. Colleges and private organisations offer their own courses, but candidates must show practical work ability. Other qualifications include the City & Guilds Engineering Systems Maintenance Course, the BTEC National Certificate in Engineering or the NVQ/SVQ in Engineering Maintenance Level 3.

Advantages/disadvantages

You are providing a vital service and it is particularly rewarding to solve problems for people.

Seeing a job through from start to finish is satisfying.

Many electricians are self-employed so you could have increased control over your life/work balance.

Money guide

The Joint Industry Board (JIB) for the Electrical Contracting Industry sets salary rates and travel allowances for apprentices and qualified electricians.

As an apprentice you could start from £10,000. Once qualified, this will rise to between £20,000 and £25,000. Experienced electricians can earn £30,000+. Rates in London are generally higher.

Related opportunities

■ Carpenter/Joiner p81
■ Plumber p113

Further information

SummitSkills
Vega House, Opal Drive, Fox Milne, Milton Keynes MK15 0DF
01908 303960; www.summitskills.org.uk

Scottish Electrical Charitable Training Trust (SECTT)
The Walled Garden, Bush Estate, Midlothian EH26 0SE
0131 445 5659; www.sectt.org.uk; admin@sectt.org.uk

City&
Guilds

www.cityandguilds.com/myperfectjob

ELECTRICIAN

Here's Steven Bastien's story

After training as an electrician Steven studied for City & Guilds qualifications and then went on to become an NICEIC Approved Contractor. He has now set up his own company and is responsible for a variety of projects from emergency callouts to major building projects such as Tower Bridge and the NEC in Birmingham.

How Steven realised he wanted to be an electrician

"When I was younger, during the weekends I would accompany my electrician uncle on his jobs in London, to earn extra pocket money. I was about 14 and I found it interesting working in different types of buildings and areas. The excitement and adventure of going to different places and meeting different people made it enjoyable.

Until the age of 16 I continued working with my uncle at weekends. I learnt how to install new electrical installations and rewire properties. At first, the jobs I did were mainly manual, moving furniture, lifting up carpets and floorboards etc. Sometimes I would get the opportunity to chase out walls to bury cables. I also had to pack away the tools at the end of the day, and make sure none were missing!

As time went on, I realised I really enjoyed electrical work. It made me feel important and made me feel valued. I felt good about myself. I felt I was doing something which was a skilled trade . . . so becoming an electrician was a straightforward choice. I was advised by my careers adviser and teachers what subjects would be best to study; these subjects were science, maths, English, history and geography."

How Steven qualified as an electrician and progressed in his career

"After leaving school, I studied at college for two years, taking relevant City & Guilds qualifications. I studied very hard to make sure I would pass – which I did with a distinction and passes. I then applied to electrical companies for an electrical apprenticeship. I was successful and was offered a 5-year JIB Apprenticeship. It was here I gained a vast amount of experience in the electrical field, working in offices, schools, factories and shops. I carried on at college where I continued my studies to gain more qualifications in Electrical Installations.

Three years later I became a Qualified Electrician. I then decided to become even more adventurous by becoming self-employed. This gave me the opportunity to work on major building projects throughout the UK. I worked in a variety of places such as Fleet Street, working for different newspapers. I even worked on a building which had a helicopter pad on top of it. That was quite exciting! I also worked on the first tower block of Canary Wharf. I worked on Tower Bridge, the NEC in Birmingham, the first Toyota Car Factory in the UK, and many more.

I then started working for local authorities, carrying out maintenance work as well as emergency callouts. Callouts give you a good feeling as you have helped someone.

Recently, I have formed my own company – Facelift Electrical Services Ltd – and successfully became an NICEIC Domestic Installer. I then became an NICEIC Approved Contractor which involved me taking more qualifications."

Steven's advice for others considering a career as an electrican

"I can now say to any young person who would like to become an electrician, that it's a very enjoyable and satisfying career. It's great when you see the beginning of the project and see it through to the end. It's great to know you were part of that project being completed."

For further information visit www.niceic.com or call 0870 013 0382.

ESTATE AGENT

What the work involves

- An estate agent's job is to sell property for their clients, earning a fee for their work

- This may involve finding suitable properties for people to view and showing them around properties.

- When a buyer is found, you will help the buyer and seller to agree a price for the property.

The type of person suited to this work

You will need excellent listening and speaking skills so that you can recommend suitable properties to potential buyers. You also have to be good at negotiating so that you can help buyers and sellers to agree prices for properties.

You must be confident dealing with people and prepared to work hard to achieve sales.

As you will be dealing with figures when valuing properties or negotiating prices, you will need numeracy skills and an interest in keeping up to date with what is happening in the housing and property markets.

Working conditions

Some of your time will be spent in the branch office, and the rest of the time you will be visiting properties, so a driving licence is needed.

Estate agency branches are often modern and open-plan with up-to-date equipment. You will spend a lot of your time working at a computer and speaking to your customers on the phone.

This can be very stressful work as you will have sales targets to reach and your earnings will depend on your selling ability.

You are likely to need to work at weekends and evenings (with some time off during the week instead).

Future prospects

Estate agents are located throughout the UK but there tend to be fewer opportunities in a poor housing market.

If you do well and gain experience and qualifications, there are opportunities for promotion – especially in larger estate agencies. For example, you may move from trainee to negotiator, then to senior negotiator and on to branch manager.

Advantages/disadvantages

The work can be stressful if you are finding it hard to meet sales targets, especially if you are working on a commission-only basis in a slowing housing market. However, the financial rewards can be high if the property market is booming.

Money guide

Earnings vary widely depending on region and may be affected by the number of sales you make. Bonuses and commission

Qualifications and courses

No formal qualifications are required to become an estate agent. However, it is useful for entrants to have GCSEs grades (A*–C) or equivalent. Most entrants start as a trainee negotiator and undertake an NVQ qualification in the Sale of Residential Property. However, a degree, Foundation degree or HND in subjects like property management and real estate management can increase your chances of employment.

Training can be done on the job. It may involve studying for qualifications such as Technical Awards in Sale of Residential Property, Residential Letting and Property Management and the Technical Award in Commercial Property Agency, through the National Federation of Property Professionals (NFOPP).

Diploma programmes from the NFOPP in Residential Estate Agency, Residential Letting and Property Management, and Commercial Property Agency are intended for those with around 3 years' experience. Both the Technical Awards and the Diplomas may be studied by distance learning, or part time at a college.

An Apprenticeship in Property Services and a Diploma in Construction and the Built Environment are also available.

Qualifications are also offered by the Royal Institution of Chartered Surveyors (RICS).

payments are often added to salaries. Some estate agents work for commission only. Starting salaries for new entrants are between £10,000 and £20,000 a year. This can rise to £20,000–£55,000+ for experienced advisers, negotiators and managers.

Related opportunities

- Auction Property Consultant p75
- Property Valuer p114
- Planning and Development Surveyor p111

Further information

Asset Skills (Sector Skills Council in property services, housing, cleaning services and facilities management)
2 The Courtyard, 48 New North Road, Exeter EX4 4EP
0845 678 2888; www.assetskills.org

National Association of Estate Agents
Arbon House, 6 Tournament Court, Edgehill Drive, Warwick CV34 6LG
01926 496800; www.naea.co.uk

City & Guilds

www.cityandguilds.com/myperfectjob

FABRICATOR

What the work involves

- Fabricators manufacture, assemble and install structural frames of buildings.

- You will extend and adapt existing buildings or work on manufacturing the entire frame work for new ones. This may include houses, public buildings, swimming pools, airport terminal buildings and caravans.

- Your work will be influenced by architectural demands and advances. The need for thermal performance, speed and versatility in architecture means that traditional forms of construction such as concrete, steel and glass are being replaced with new, more efficient materials.

- You will probably work with a diverse range of materials such as aluminium, PVC foam, timber, natural stone and fibreglass.

The type of person suited to this work

As a fabricator you should have an interest in machinery and the construction industry.

You will be working on site or in a manufacturing plant and as this may include physical labour you should be fit and have good manual skills.

You should also enjoy working as a team and have excellent knowledge and awareness of health and safety practices.

You should be organised and know how to plan ahead.

Working conditions

You will typically work 39 hours per week Monday to Friday. This may vary depending on the project you are working on. You may also be required to do shifts and overtime and work evenings and weekends.

You may work in a variety of locations; outdoors, indoors and at heights. Weather conditions may make this work uncomfortable or delay work.

As a fabricator you might have to operate machinery such as mobile cranes.

Future prospects

As you gain experience you will have the opportunity to specialise in a certain area of fabrication. This could be as an aluminium fabricator (curtain walls, windows, and frames), a conservatory fabricator (working with timber, aluminium or PVC to erect conservatories) or a window fabricator (working with frame makers and door makers building offsite manufactured rooms that can be assembled onsite).

As you accumulate experience you can progress to higher level positions such as supervisors or you may also choose to become self-employed.

Qualifications and courses

ENTRY LEVEL 1

There are no specific entry qualifications. However GCSEs or S grades (A*–E/1–5) in English and maths are useful. Science and design and technology are useful as you must have an understanding of calculations, measurements and theory. The Diploma in Construction and the Built Environment will be relevant.

ConstructionSkills may provide apprenticeships. You will be assessed on literacy and your ability to work at heights. You will take an aptitude exercise on maths and problem solving.

Construction apprentices learn practical skills under the supervision of skilled fabricators, as well as taking courses at a college or training centre. These include NVQs/SVQs such as Level 1 in Construction and Civil Engineering Services, Level 2 and 3 in Fabrication and Welding Engineering, Level 2 and 3 in Carpentry and Joinery and Level 4 in Construction Site Management.

A Construction Skills Certification Scheme card is needed to work on a building site.

Advantages/disadvantages

New and exciting developments and improvements in materials and technology mean that your work is likely to include scope for diversity and creativity.

Your work at times may be physically very demanding.

Money guide

Your starting salary may start around £15,000 a year.

Related opportunities

- Building Technician p80
- Carpenter/Joiner p81
- Ceiling Fixer p83
- Structural Engineer p124

Further information

ConstructionSkills
Bircham Newton, King's Lynn PE 31 6RH
www.constructionskills.net

National Association of Shopfitters
NAS House, 411 Limpsfield Road, Warlingham CR6 9HA
01883 624961; www.shopfitters.org

City&
Guilds

www.cityandguilds.com/myperfectjob

FACILITIES MANAGER

What the work involves

- Facilities managers are responsible for the management and administration of premises, including offices, schools and commercial properties.

- You will provide a safe and efficient work environment for staff by implementing procedures to improve facilities, reduce costs and increase productivity.

- Your day to day work will depend on the type of organisation you work for, but will include a broad spectrum of tasks such as coordinating and managing central services, organising mail receipt and despatch, arranging contractors for security, or supervising cleaning and catering.

- You must be able to respond to all problems that arise unexpectedly, and react to them appropriately and efficiently.

The type of person suited to this work

As you will be coordinating many different aspects of an organisation, or many organisations in one location, you need to be highly organised. You should be able to meet deadlines and have strong problem-solving skills.

You will lead a team so you should have excellent negotiation skills and strong written and verbal communication ability.

You should also be aware of environmental issues affecting premises and how budgets are planned and controlled.

As you will be working with a variety of different people you should have good customer service skills.

Working conditions

Your hours will vary depending on the organisation you work for but on average you will work from 9am–5pm. You will mainly be office-based, but you will move around a lot to inspect and supervise various projects throughout the location you work in.

You may have a permanent contract or work on a fixed-term contract. At times you may be required to be available at any time in the event of emergencies.

Future prospects

You may begin as an assistant in a particular support field such as IT, HR, finance or purchasing or health and safety and then progress to functional manager, senior manager and director positions.

You can work as a facilities manager in-house or join a facilities management provider or consultancy. This will provide a variety of projects and responsibilities but will not have the same level of stability.

It is recommended that you seek opportunities in different organisations to secure promotion.

Advantages/disadvantages

Prospects for career development can be excellent. If you are hardworking, flexible, and efficient, have commercial acumen and the ability to juggle tight budgets you can progress to higher level management jobs.

Qualifications and courses

ENTRY LEVEL 4

Many entrants to this profession are graduates who have studied property and land-based subjects such as estate management or surveying.

Others gain experience in relevant fields such as construction, building services, engineering or hospitality to acquire skills for facilities management.

You can take vocational courses in facilities management. These include appropriate NVQs/SVQs or professional qualifications from the British Institute of Facilities Management (BIFM). You can also study for a Foundation degree (developed by Asset Skills) or an HND in facilities management.

Work experience is recommended and employers will seek candidates with good experience. For graduates year long placements are invaluable.

Entrants to facilities management also come from other areas of employment using relevant skills and experience. Many of these entrants have backgrounds in office management and administration, building services and engineering, customer services and the armed forces.

You may find it difficult to move from an in-house role to a position with a service provider as there is a perceived difference in outlook and experience.

Money guide

Starting salaries may range from around £14,000 to £20,000 per year.

An experienced facilities manager can earn between £25,000 and £35,000 a year.

Senior facilities managers can earn in excess of £40,000.

Related opportunities

- Building Services Engineer p78
- Health and Safety Adviser p40
- Quality Manager p57

Further information

British Institute of Facilities Management (BIFM)
Number One Building, The Causeway, Bishop's Stortford CM23 2ER
0845 058 1356; www.bifm.org.uk; info@bifm.org.uk

Chartered Management Institute
Management House, Cottingham Road, Corby NN17 1TT
01536 204222; www.managers.org.uk;
enquiries@managers.org.uk

City& Guilds

www.cityandguilds.com/myperfectjob

Case study

THE FLOORING TRADE

Here's Matthew Blackbourn's story

On the job training has formed a key part of 22-year-old Matthew's journey into the flooring trade, fitting carpets and other floor coverings in domestic homes. He firmly believes that ensuring you begin your working life with a reputable, established company is vital. Matthew has supplemented the experience he has gained on site with training courses through FITA, after which he applied to become a "Masterfitter" in Carpet via the NICF. Although he has a passion for installation and gets a true buzz from a job well done, Matthew hopes to grow more in to the management side. However, his positive experience of training has also led him to have ambitions to become an instructor and put something back.

For Matthew the future in flooring is bright and full of opportunity.

What the job entails

"Working for a small business in the domestic market means that the range of tasks involved are enormous. I generally find myself fitting floors during the day and enjoy the diversity of products and skills I have to employ. I also like working with the public and when we are busy I tend to help out with measures in the evenings. More recently, I have started to get involved with pricing and ordering stock etc.

The commercial sector is of course slightly different with work typically taking place in offices, hospitals and schools. Generally, on a bigger scale, some of the contracts involve materials worth many thousands of pounds. Main contractors are often working to tight timescales and obviously floor layers have to enjoy working in a team in what is often essentially a construction environment. As well as a craft and a skill, floor laying is becoming increasingly technical and finding the solution to meet the needs of a client (many working on fast track projects) are some of the demands and challenges of the 'on site' role."

What you need to suceed

"Flexibility, good communication, as well as an obvious natural tendency towards good practical skills, are all qualities required to succeed in the flooring industry. The ability to use your own initiative, as well as work in a team, is often an advantage.

Practical on site experience will always be required, but formal qualifications such as an NVQ level 2 in floor laying are recognised qualifications that can currently be gained through a number of routes including a modern apprenticeship. This can be supplemented with short training courses through organisations such as FITA as both an introduction, as well as a career building strategy."

For further information or advice contact:

The Contract Flooring Association (CFA)
Telephone: 0115 941 1126

The Flooring Industry Training Association (FITA)
Telephone: 0115 950 6836

The National Institute of Carpet & FloorLayers (NICF)
Telephone: 0115 958 3077

FLOOR LAYER/FINISHER

What the work involves

■ Floor layers fit various rooms and buildings with many different types of flooring, such as vinyl, wood, carpet, tiles, rubber or plastic.

■ You will decide on the best material to use for the particular type of floor.

■ You will use various tools to prepare the surface, cut the flooring material to size and lay the floor.

■ You will work from technical plans and diagrams in order to lay and fit each floor correctly.

The type of person suited to this work

To do this work you will need accurate numerical skills in order to calculate the exact amount of flooring material you will need for each job.

You should be physically fit as you will spend a lot of time lifting and carrying materials, or working on your hands and knees.

You may work alone for some smaller jobs, but you must also be able to work in a team with other construction professionals for larger jobs.

Good planning skills are helpful when organising your workload, and you should be happy meeting and talking to lots of different people.

Working conditions

You will usually work normal Monday to Friday office hours, but you may also need to work through the night or over weekends on some contracts, so that you can lay floors without disrupting the work of shops and businesses.

Most of your work will be spent indoors in a variety of locations including people's homes, hospitals, offices and construction sites, some of which will be dirty and dusty.

This is mobile work, so a driving licence is useful.

Some contracts may involve absence from home overnight or for longer periods of time.

Future prospects

There are good prospects for finding work as a trainee floor layer because there is a shortage of floor layers nationwide.

Once you have qualified, work will be available within small or large flooring companies or contractors across the UK.

You may choose to specialise in using one type of flooring material such as tiles or laminates.

With experience, you can progress to technical, supervisory or managerial posts. Or you could set up on your own as a self-employed floor layer.

Qualifications and courses

No specific qualifications are required, although GCSEs/S grades (A*–E/1–5) in maths, design and technology, science and English are useful. The Diploma in Construction and the Built Environment may be relevant.

You will be trained on the job while working towards qualifications. You may go to a college or training centre on day or block release.

The Construction Industry Training Board (CITB) offers an Apprenticeship Scheme in Foor Laying for entrants aged 16–24 and a Construction Award in Floor Covering.

Fast-track short courses from independent providers like the Flooring Industry Training Association and NVQs/SVQs in Floor Covering at Levels 1–3 are also available. You might need a Construction Skills Certification Scheme card.

Advantages/disadvantages

An attractive and well-laid floor can transform a room. The ability to use your skills and a range of materials to create this effect can give you great job satisfaction.

You will spend a lot of time travelling to and from jobs, and may need to spend time away from home on big flooring projects.

Money guide

Starting rate for trainees is around £12,500 per year. With an NVQ earnings can rise to £14,500+, and as a fully qualified floor layer you could earn about £20,000. Highly skilled, experienced floor layers can earn salaries of up to £30,000.

Earnings vary among employers and in different parts of the country. Salaries in London are higher. Many floor layers are self-employed and earnings will depend on the ability to win contracts.

Related opportunities

■ Carpenter/Joiner p81
■ Glazier p101
■ Plasterer p112
■ Roofer p117

Further information

ConstructionSkills
Bircham Newton, King's Lynn PE31 6RH
01485 577577; www.cskills.org

The Flooring Industry Training Association (FITA)
4c St Mary's Place, The Lace Market, Nottingham NG1 1PH
0115 950 6836; www.fita.co.uk; info@fita.co.uk

City&
Guilds

www.cityandguilds.com/myperfectjob

GLAZIER

What the work involves

- Glaziers use specialist cutting and fixing tools to cut glass to the correct size and fit it into place.

- You might fit glass into houses, shop fronts, office blocks or roofs.

- You might be working on new buildings or replacing existing or broken glass.

- You will use your knowledge to choose a suitable type of glass for each job.

The type of person suited to this work

You will be measuring and cutting glass accurately so that it fits perfectly into the frame. As you will be using different hand tools a practical ability will be necessary.

You will also need to be physically fit so that you can carry glass and be comfortable working at heights (sometimes extreme heights).

You may work alone for some jobs, such as in people's homes, but you must also be able to work and communicate with other glaziers, especially when working on large jobs with big, heavy panes of glass.

Working conditions

You will work indoors and outdoors in many different locations. A driving licence may be useful.

You will need to work safely and be aware of your own, the public's and your colleagues' safety when carrying, cutting and fixing glass.

You may work normal working hours during the week, but you may also need to work at weekends and during evenings, possibly offering emergency cover for households and businesses when replacing broken glass.

Future prospects

Work is available with glazing and construction companies throughout the UK and the demand for trained glaziers is high. The range of jobs in glazing work is also increasing to include specialist areas, for example automotive glass repair and replacement

After gaining sufficient experience, you may progress to technical or supervisory levels, or you could decide to start your own glazing business. The majority of glaziers are self-employed.

Advantages/disadvantages

Working at extreme heights may be demanding for some. You will get to work in a variety of locations on a wide range of projects. Cutting tools and glass can be dangerous, so you will have to be aware of health and safety regulations. You could be called out at all hours for emergency jobs.

Qualifications and courses

To work as a glazier you need to have a ConstructionSkills Certification Scheme (CSCS) card or be registered with an affiliated scheme. This scheme requires an NVQ Level 2 and the completion of a health and safety test.

GCSEs or equivalent, vocational qualifications such as a Diploma in Construction and the Built Environment and Manufacturing and Product Design can improve your chances of getting work. Maths, English and technology subjects are useful for the parts of the job that involve measurements and calculations, and for theoretical training. 2 to 3 year Apprenticeships or traineeships are also available.

You can train and gain vocational qualifications while you work. You will be taught practical skills and may spend time off-site at a college or training centre.

You are likely to work towards NVQs in glass-related subjects. These include Glazing, Automotive Glazing, and Fenestration Installation and Surveying at both Levels 2 and 3.

Money guide

Newly qualified glaziers earn round £14,000. With experience, glaziers can expect to earn £28,000. Those highly skilled, with experience and extra responsibilities, such as emergency call-outs, might achieve up to £35,000.

Related opportunities

- Building Technician p80
- Carpenter/Joiner p81
- Ceiling Fixer p83
- Window Installer p132

Further information

Proskills UK
Centurion Court, 85b Milton Park, Abingdon OX14 4RY
01235 833844; www.proskills.co.uk

Glass Qualifications Authority
Provincial House, Solly Street, Sheffield S1 4BA
0114 272 0033; www.glassqualificationsauthority.com

Glass and Glazing Federation
44–48 Borough High Street, London SE1 1XB
0870 042 4255; www.ggf.co.uk

City&
Guilds

www.cityandguilds.com/myperfectjob

HEATING AND VENTILATING ENGINEER/ GAS SERVICE TECHNICIAN

What the work involves

Heating and ventilating engineer

- Heating and ventilating engineers install equipment such as pipework and boilers for systems including central heating, hot and cold water services, and gas supplies in industrial and commercial buildings.

- Your work will include cutting, bending and joining pipes that will need to withstand high pressures, so welding is an important part of the work.

- When you have installed a system, you will test it to make sure that everything is working properly.

Gas service technician

- Your job will be to install, maintain, repair and test gas appliances such as fires, cookers, heating systems and industrial equipment.

- Once installed you will test the appliances and give advice.

- You could work in private homes or on business premises.

The type of person suited to this work

Heating and ventilating engineer

You must be a practical person so that you can use the equipment for the job. Understanding and following diagrams is an essential part of the work, so you need a logical, mechanically minded approach to your work. You will also need to be good at maths for making calculations.

It can be physically demanding work, as you will be bending, kneeling and working in tight spaces. You also need a head for heights and a safety-conscious attitude, because you will often be working from ladders and scaffolding.

Teamwork and communication skills are also important when you are installing large systems.

Gas service technician

You will need excellent practical skills, enjoy using tools and making things work. Some work will involve finding faults – this area needs people who like investigating and working out why things go wrong.

Gas appliances are potentially dangerous, so you should be very thorough and reliable. As you will be working in homes you should be personable and presentable when dealing with clients.

Working conditions

A lot of your time will be spent indoors, but you will also need to work on various construction sites. You will need to wear safety gear such as a hard hat, goggles and gloves.

You may work a normal working week, but there may be times when you will work weekends and evenings to avoid disruption to clients or if you provide emergency cover. You may also be expected to work away from home on various contracts.

Future prospects

Heating and ventilating engineer

There is currently an acute shortage of skilled heating and ventilating engineers with around 56,000 currently working in the UK.

Once you undertake training and are qualified, work will be available with specialist heating and ventilation companies, or organisations such as the NHS or local authorities. Many qualified fitters also become self-employed, joining up with other engineers to offer sub-contracting services.

There are good prospects for advancement to supervisory roles and it is possible for you to become a heating and ventilating technician. If you take additional qualifications and higher education, progression to professional engineering level is also possible. There are also opportunities to work overseas.

Gas service technician

There is a shortage of gas service technicians. You can work for national or private companies or become self-employed. In larger companies you can progress up to supervisory posts or apply for training posts at local colleges or within private organisations.

Advantages/disadvantages

Working in cramped and awkward spaces can be uncomfortable.

Transforming a building from an empty shell into a warm, comfortable environment can be rewarding.

Career progression opportunities are excellent.

There is demand across the country for work in this area.

Money guide

Heating and ventilating engineer

The Heating and Ventilating Contractors' Association (HVCA) publishes recommended salary rates. Overtime is often available, which can lead to higher earnings.

As a new fitter you could start at around £11,500 per year. As a qualified building services graduate you could earn £21,000–£25,000.

With experience and additional responsibilities, you could earn £35,000–£45,000.

Gas service technician

New apprentices earn around £12,000 per year which, after training, can rise to between £17,000 and £25,000. The most experienced can earn up to £33,000+. It is also possible to earn extra for overtime and shift work.

Related opportunities

- Mechanical Engineer p234
- Gas Network Engineer p226
- Plumber p113
- Thermal Insulation Engineer p127

Further information

SummitSkills
Vega House, Opal Drive, Fox Milne, Milton Keynes
MK15 0DF
0800 068 8336; www.summitskills.org.uk

Building Engineering Services Training Ltd
The Priory, Stomp Road, Burnham SL1 7LW
0800 917 8419; www.best-ltd.co.uk

Heating and Ventilating Contractors' Association
Esca House, 34 Palace Court, London W2 4JG
020 7313 4900; www.hvca.org.uk

Building Engineering Services Training Ltd (Scotland)
Unit 4, Bush House, Penicuik EH26 0BB
0131 445 5900; www.best-ltd.co.uk

Gas Safe Register
PO Box 6804, Basingstoke RG24 4NB
0800 408 5500; www.gassaferegister.co.uk

www.cityandguilds.com/myperfectjob

Qualifications and courses
Heating and ventilating engineer

Most employers train young entrants through Apprenticeships/Skillseekers. 4 GCSEs/S grades (A*–C/ 1–3), including maths, English and science subject may be required for entry to these. You will also need to pass a colour vision test and selection test.

Training for Apprentices/Skillseekers includes attending college on day or block release. You will work towards NVQ/SVQ Level 2 in Mechanical Engineering Services: Heating and Ventilation Installation, progressing to NVQ/ SVQ Level 3. NVQs/SVQs cover industrial, commercial and domestic installation, and maintenance of components.

The same NVQ qualifications are available to adults, but for entry to these you may be required to be in related work or have relevant experience.

Other training includes: City & Guilds Certificate in Energy Efficiency for Domestic Heating (6084), for domestic fitters; and the Oil Firing Technical Association for the Petroleum Industry's (OFTEC) training scheme for those working with oil-fired equipment.

It's also possible to achieve higher level qualifications including NVQ Level 4 and foundation and Master's degrees which can lead to professional membership of the Chartered Institution of Building Services Engineers (CIBSE).

Gas service technician

At least 4 GCSEs/S grades (A*–C/1–3) including English, maths and sometimes science or technology subjects are normally required for entry to this career. Practical subjects such as metalwork and woodwork are useful.

Apprenticeships/Skillseekers are available for people aged 16–24. Apprentices work towards NVQ/SVQ in Domestic Natural Gas Installation and Maintenance, awarded by City & Guilds. Gas service companies also run their own apprenticeship schemes.

Trainees must gain registration with the Gas Safe Register. To become registered, trainees need to work towards the NVQ/SVQ in Domestic Natural Gas Installation and Maintenance at Level 2 or 3, or complete equivalent in-house training with a company. Technicians with qualifications or training other than the NVQ/SVQ must complete ACS (Accredited Certification Scheme) assessments.

Gas service technicians have to demonstrate their gas safety competence on a 5-year cycle by successfully completing nationally agreed Accredited Certification Scheme (ACS) assessments.

HIGHWAYS MAINTENANCE/ ROAD WORKER

What the work involves

- Road workers' tasks include building new roads, re-routing or widening existing roads, and repairing potholes and cracks in roads.

- You will also have other duties such as putting up warning signs and barriers, controlling the movement of traffic near the work site, laying kerbstones and pavements, and gritting roads in the winter.

- You will work with numerous building materials including concrete, tarmac and paving slabs.

- You will use a range of tools and equipment in your work, including specialised, heavy machinery such as diggers and rollers.

The type of person suited to this work

You must have a good standard of fitness, as the work involves a lot of hard, physical work and requires you to lift and carry heavy materials.

Practical ability with tools such as picks and shovels is useful, as is experience of operating equipment such as cement mixers, diggers and rolling machines.

As much of your work will be undertaken as part of a team of road workers and supervisors, it is important that you can get along with colleagues at all levels.

Working conditions

You are likely to work a normal 37 hour working week, although you may also work weekends and evenings to avoid disrupting traffic.

You will need to be aware of the danger of traffic and health and safety for yourself and your colleagues. Onsite, you will wear protective clothing such as a safety helmet, fluorescent jacket and boots.

Future prospects

Road workers may work for local authorities or, as work is increasingly contracted out, for specialist road-building or civil engineering companies.

Work is available across the UK. Some work is short-term or seasonal. You could become self-employed and work on contract basis.

As you develop and gain experience and qualifications, you may go on to lead a small team or become a supervisor.

Advantages/disadvantages

You will be helping to maintain and improve the safety of the roads in your local area, which can be personally rewarding.

You will be outdoors doing physically demanding work in all weathers, so can expect to get hot in the summer and cold in the winter.

Qualifications and courses

There are no formal entry requirements for this work, but GCSEs/S grades in maths, English and design and technology may be helpful. Personal skills and physical fitness are usually more important than qualifications.

Your training will be given mainly on the job by experienced road workers.

You may be able to work towards NVQs/SVQs in Construction and Civil Engineering Services, Highway Maintenance at Levels 1 and 2, Road Building at Level 2 and Winter Maintenance Operations at Level 2 whilst you are in employment.

To become a qualified site operative, you need one of the following: a City & Guilds award in Street Works, Excavation and Reinstatement; an SQA National Award in Excavation and Reinstatement; or a CABWI award in Street Works Excavation and Reinstatement.

If working with plant machinery, you will need to be 18 or over. A driving licence will also be required, and an LGV licence may be needed for some jobs.

Money guide

Trainee road workers start at around £12,000 per year. With experience you could get £15,000–£17,000.

The highest-earning road workers with a lot of experience and relevant qualifications can expect around £19,000+.

You can increase your earnings with overtime and shift work.

Related opportunities

- Concreter p87
- Demolition Operative p92
- Bricklayer p76
- Construction Operative p88

Further information

ConstructionSkills
Bircham Newton, King's Lynn PE31 6XG
01485 577577; www.bconstructive.co.uk, www.cskills.net

The Street Works Qualification Register (SWQR)
The Optima Building, 58 Robertson Street, Glasgow G2 8DQ
0845 270 2720; www.swqr.org.uk

www.cityandguilds.com/myperfectjob

HOUSING OFFICER

What the work involves

- You will manage and maintain rented housing, usually for a housing association or local authority.

- Tasks include assessing housing needs in an area and making policies to provide for them, allocating housing to applicants, planning property maintenance and repair.

- You will also need to set rents, and deal with tenants who are behind with their rent as well as resolving neighbourhood disputes and answering tenants' enquiries.

- You will find yourself working with a range of different people which could include vulnerable people or those in particularly bad situations economically.

The type of person suited to this work

As most of your work will involve talking and listening to people, you will need excellent communication skills. You should also be able to work with and relate to a variety of people, including other professionals and tenants.

Maths and numeracy skills are useful for dealing with rental payments, maintenance and repair costs, and budgets.

It is important to keep up with developments in a range of housing and tenant welfare issues, be flexible and be able to solve problems as and when they arise.

You will also need to be able to work as part of a team as well as on your own.

Working conditions

Many housing officers are based in an office, but regularly travel to make property inspections, visit tenants or attend meetings. You should be prepared to deal with rude and aggressive tenants.

As some of your work will involve travelling, a driving licence and your own vehicle is required for many posts. Although you will normally work standard office hours, you might have to do some unsocial hours and weekend work.

Future prospects

The employment situation is stable at the moment as social housing is a growth area with organisations taking on a number of new trainees as well as experienced staff. Work is available in towns and cities throughout the UK.

Employers look favourably on work experience or voluntary work in housing.

Most housing officers work for local authorities and housing associations, but you may also work for other employers such as voluntary organisations, property companies, private landlords and housing trusts. You may also be able to specialise in a particular area such as neighbourhood management or welfare benefits.

Qualifications and courses

It is possible to enter at an administrative level with GCSEs/S grades (A*–C/1–3) and study part time while working. Many people enter with an HNC, Foundation degree, degree or postgraduate qualification in housing studies and social policy.

The National Certificate in Housing Studies is often taken before the HNC in Housing. For entry to a Foundation degree in Housing Studies, at least 2 A levels/3 H grades are required.

Housing Officers whose degrees do not include a work placement will be expected to gain appropriate industrial experience before they become a member of the Chartered Institute of Housing. The CIH also offers courses which can be studied part time and through distance learning, these include Level 3 Certificate in Housing and the Professional Diploma in Housing.

After gaining experience, you could progress into a more senior role such as principal housing officer or housing manager.

Advantages/disadvantages

It will be your responsibility to resolve complicated issues like misuse of property or disputes between residents.

Helping people find a home can be personally rewarding.

Money guide

Starting salaries are about £18,000 per year. This can rise to £25,500–£30,000 for experienced housing officers. Up to £38,000 is usual for housing managers. £50,000+ can be achieved in the most senior posts.

Related opportunities

- Welfare Benefits Adviser/Welfare Rights Caseworker p588
- Residential Warden p582
- Social Care Worker/Social Worker p583

Further information

Chartered Institute of Housing
Octavia House, Westwood Way, Coventry CV4 8JP
024 768 51700; www.cih.org

Scottish Federation of Housing Associations
Pegasus House, 375 West George Street, Glasgow, G2 4LW
0141 332 8113; www.sfha.co.uk

City&
Guilds

www.cityandguilds.com/myperfectjob

LAMINATOR

What the work involves

- Laminators work with polymer composite materials to make a variety of products such as hockey sticks, snowboards, canoes, car bodies, yachts and aircraft cabin interiors.

- You will follow a brief for the design of a product, taking into consideration any requirements regarding strength, colour and finish. You will then choose the appropriate material to be pressed, sprayed or poured into a mould, prior to it being shaped into the final product.

- You will work with traditional materials such as wood laminates, fibre glass and resin, and new products such as Kelvar.

The type of person suited to this work

You should have a keen interest in design and technology, engineering and materials science.

You should like practical work and have practical skills to handle tools and use specialist machinery.

You should have initiative, follow a brief and work to a deadline. You should also be interested in, and keep up to date with, technological advancements in laminate materials.

You should like to work in a team.

You need to be reasonably fit and have good vision for monitoring quality and noticing detail.

Working conditions

Your working hours will depend heavily on the project you are working on. Typically it can range from 37 to 40 hours but will vary according to the rate of your work and deadlines.

You will usually work in an environmentally controlled building. This means that the temperature is controlled and maintained to help resin harden quickly. Air is changed frequently to remove dust and the strong smell of resin.

You will be required to wear full protective clothing.

Future prospects

You may be employed by an engineering consultancy that undertakes installation projects for companies.

With experience and training there are opportunities to be promoted to roles such as technician and senior technician, or to move into design, research or development work for specialist composite laminate manufacturers.

Advantages/disadvantages

You may have the opportunity to work on products that are on the cutting edge of design such as speed boats, Formula 1 racing cars and craft for the air force and the military.

Qualifications and courses

No formal qualifications are required. However, some GCSEs/S grades might be required and can be useful, as you must have an understanding of design and technology, and calculations. The Diploma in Engineering, Manufacturing and Product Design might be relevant.

Some employers will take on apprentices. Apprenticeships require 4 GCSE/S grades (A*–C/1–3) in maths, science or technology. CITB-ConstructionSkills provides guidance on apprenticeships.

On-the-job training is provided. You can also undertake further training at college through courses that focus on the theoretical parts of your job, first aid, and health and safety. Available courses are NVQs at Level 2 in Polymer Processing Operations and Performing Engineering Operations.

BTEC National Certificates/Diplomas in Polymer Processing and Materials Technology are available.

With 4 years' experience, relevant NVQs/SVQs or a BTEC certificate/diploma, you could apply for membership of the Institute of Materials, Minerals and Mining.

There is a shortage of laminators, so many employers seek adults with previous relevant experience and will provide further training to technician level following an NVQ/SVQ Level 3 training route.

Your work will frequently be dusty and involve the use of strong industrial chemicals which may be hazardous if handled incorrectly.

Money guide

A salary for an apprentice laminator starts at around £7,000 a year.

As you gain experience and qualifications this may increase to £18,000.

A senior laminator can earn up to £25,000 per year.

Related opportunities

- Marine Craftsperson p231
- Polymer Technologist p240

Further information

British Plastics Federation
5–6 Bath Place, Rivington Street, London EC2A 3JE
020 7457 5000; www.bpf.co.uk

Institute of Materials, Minerals and Mining
1 Carlton House Terrace, London SW1Y 5DB
020 7451 7300; www.iom3.org

LAND/GEOMATIC SURVEYOR

What the work involves

- Land/geomatic surveyors collect and analyse information to map the land and/or sea, which is then used when planning construction and civil engineering projects.

- You will use satellite images, GPS, digital mapping and other equipment to produce surveys that record features such as contours, materials below the Earth's surface and man-made objects.

- You will use technical software such as CAD to record and present the data you have gathered. You will also have to interpret data from maps and plans and explain it to clients.

The type of person suited to this work

You will be working with both clients and other professionals on a daily basis, so excellent verbal and written communication skills will be needed to present and explain complex information.

As much of the work involves using technical equipment and producing maps, plans and reports using specialist computer software, you will need to have very strong analytical and ICT skills with specific knowledge of geographical information systems (GIS) and AutoCAD.

Working conditions

Working hours are usually 9am–5pm, but you might need to work unsocial hours to ensure projects are finished within set deadlines. Weekend or shift work can also be required for certain projects.

You will frequently work away from home. You will be paid more for overseas work, and most contracts are on a short-term basis although multinational companies offer good long-term opportunities.

Self-employment is an option, but finding work is not always easy so most surveyors choose to work in salaried employment.

Future prospects

Prospects are good as there is a national shortage of land/geomatic surveyors. Most graduates start as a junior surveyor, from which there is a natural progression to surveyor and then on to a team management position. You could alternatively undertake further study and gain a qualification as a chartered surveyor.

You can specialise in a number of areas including offshore engineering and exploration, or cartography.

Advantages/disadvantages

You will have the opportunity to travel throughout the UK and overseas.

You could be playing a key role in land and environmental development.

A considerable amount of time is spent outdoors so be prepared to get cold, wet and muddy.

Qualifications and courses

ENTRY 5 LEVEL

Most entrants have completed a Royal Institution of Chartered Surveyors accredited degree in subjects like surveying and mapping science, geomatics or geographic information systems as well as a period of supervised instruction. An HND or Foundation degree in Applied Science, Land/estate Surveying or Civil Engineering is also accepted, although you would start in a slightly lower position in a company.

If you wish to specialise in a particular area, such as offshore engineering, a postgraduate qualification may be helpful in acquiring a job.

Once qualified, many surveyors work towards achieving chartered status and undertake further courses and assessment through bodies such as the Institution of Civil Engineering Surveyors (ICES) and the Royal Institution of Chartered Surveyors (RICS). This usually takes between 4 and 5 years.

Modern Apprenticeships in Land/Geomatics Surveying are also available. You will work towards gaining an NVQ.

A Construction Skills Certification Scheme (CSCS) white card may be needed. You will need to take a health and safety test.

Money guide

Starting salaries for non-graduates are £13,000–£15,000. For newly graduated land surveyors salaries fall between £16,000 and £20,000. If you also hold a qualification in chartered surveying, your starting salary would rise to £27,000–£34,000.

With several years' experience you could earn £40,000–£50,000. At a senior level, either as a manager or a partner, salaries can reach £44,000–£72,000.

Salaries are highest in London, or if you work overseas.

Related opportunities

- Rural Property/Practice Surveyor p118
- Planning and Development Surveyor p111
- Insurance Surveyor p44
- Town Planner/Planning Technician p128

Further information

The Chartered Institution of Water and Environmental Management
15 John Street, London WC1N 2EB
020 7831 3110; www.ciwem.org

Institution of Civil Engineering Surveyors
Dominion House, Sibson Road, Sale M33 7PP
0161 972 3100; www.ices.org.uk; education@cices.org

MASTIC ASPHALTER

What the work involves

- You will work with material called mastic asphalt, a mixture of limestone and bitumen which turns to liquid when heated.

- You will inspect a site, clean it, lay out membranes and guides and then spread hot liquid asphalt onto the area. It will cool into a protective waterproof surface.

- You will work on surfaces such as dams, landfills, riverbank protection, car parks, bus stations, pathways and the roofs of buildings.

- You will use various specialised tools such as boilers, mixers and cylinders in order to prepare surfaces and apply the asphalt.

The type of person suited to this work

You need to have good practical skills to be able to spread and form the mastic asphalt. Maths skills will be useful too, for calculating quantities of materials.

It is important to be able to understand plans, follow instructions and work well in a team.

As it is an active job you must be physically fit, and you must be happy climbing and working at heights. Agility is essential and you should be able to work quickly but accurately.

Working conditions

You will mainly work outdoors, although some of the work may be under cover. You will travel regularly between sites.

You will need to wear protective gear such as a safety helmet, gloves and boots.

If you suffer from claustrophobia, vertigo or breathing problems, this work might be difficult for you.

You are likely to work a normal working week, although you might need to work evenings and weekends as well.

Future prospects

Most opportunities are with specialist mastic asphalt contractors. Self-employment is also common if you are skilled.

You can work your way up to become a supervisor, manager or trainer in large companies, or set up your own contracting business. You may need to move between employers for promotion.

Advantages/disadvantages

Working at heights on roofs, or in cramped conditions when working in tanks or underground spaces, can be demanding for some people. There is the possibility of fumes and accidental burns in this line of work.

You will develop a range of skills and work on a variety of surfaces.

Qualifications and courses

To train in this field, it is useful to have some GCSEs/S grades (A*–E) in English, maths, design and technology, or vocational qualifications such as the Diploma in Construction and the Built Environment, the BTEC Introductory, First Diploma or Certificate in Construction or Foundation, Intermediate and Advanced levels in Construction Awards.

Most entrants complete the Construction Industry Training Board (CITB) Construction Apprenticeship Scheme in Mastic Asphalting. This scheme takes 2–3 years and apprentices complete either an NVQ Level 2 or 3 in Mastic Asphalt and the CSkills Awards Level 2 Diploma in Mastic Asphalting.

If you decide to specialise in roofing, it would be helpful to undergo examinations from the Institute of Roofing.

Mastic asphalters employed on construction sites require a Construction Skills Certification Scheme (CSCS) card. This demonstrates that the holder has health and safety training, as well as aiming for competence in a particular occupation (usually requiring an appropriate NVQ or equivalent).

Money guide

£10,000 per year is average for a trainee starting in this work. With experience you could earn around £25,000. £30,000+ is possible for supervisory workers. Overtime is often available, and on some projects there are bonuses based on outputs, which can lead to higher earnings. Travelling expenses will be reimbursed.

Related opportunities

- Building Technician p80
- Floor Layer/Finisher p100
- Roofer p117
- Thatcher p126

Further information

ConstructionSkills
Bircham Newton, King's Lynn PE31 6RH
01485 577577; www.constructionskills.net;
www.bconstructive.co.uk

Mastic Asphalt Council
PO Box 77, Hastings TN35 4WL
01424 814400; www.masticasphaltcouncil.co.uk

www.cityandguilds.com/myperfectjob

NAVAL ARCHITECT

What the work involves

■ As a naval architect you will be responsible for the design, construction and repair of marine vessels and offshore structures, including merchant ships, submarines and offshore drilling platforms.

■ You will coordinate a team of engineers working on a project.

■ You will ensure that the structure you are working on is safe and seaworthy, within budget and to the specifications laid out in the design brief.

■ Your work will depend on the specialism you choose, but you could prepare architectural designs, work with computer or 3D models, source materials or evaluate the safety of the design.

The type of person suited to this work

As you will be working with others and as part of a team you will need to have good written and verbal communication skills.

As you will be coordinating various aspects of a project such as budget, location and facilities you must be organised and efficient in you work.

You must also be able to lead a team and work to a deadline.

You should also have strong ICT and numeracy skills and a keen eye for detail.

Working conditions

You will work average office hours, 5 days a week. However you might have to work extra hours to meet deadlines.

You may be office based while working on design work or visiting construction sites, docks and shipyards within the UK or overseas. Shipyards, docks and marinas can be noisy and dirty. If you are working onboard a craft you may encounter fumes, heat and noise and have to work in all weather conditions. You may be required to wear protective clothing.

Future prospects

As a naval architect you can become self-employed, work for a company or organisation, or work as a design consultant. Organisations such as the Royal Institution of Naval Architects (RINA) provide continuing professional development (CPD) courses which are essential for progression in this job.

You can move up from technical roles to general management roles and then senior roles or directorships. Your career development will depend on the qualifications you have and the specialism you choose to go into.

Advantages/disadvantages

There is a lot of opportunity to work abroad for a ship surveying company, on contract, or you may work on a large scale project abroad.

Competition for jobs as a naval architect is high.

Qualifications and courses

You must have a degree in engineering, marine technology, naval architecture or another similar subject; many degrees are accredited by the Royal Institution of Naval Architects (RINA). 2 A levels/H grades including physics and maths, and 5 GCSEs/S grades (A*–C) are needed, the Diploma in Engineering may also be useful.

If you have a BTEC HND/NHC you can transfer to an engineering degree. A Master's degree in engineering can improve your chances of finding a job. The Ministry of Defence has a Defence Engineering and Science Group Graduate Scheme, although it is competitive. You may be able to join a marine engineering Apprenticeship straight from school, through the Royal Navy or local ship builders.

On-the-job training is provided, with extra courses available to reach fully qualified naval architect. These are run by the RINA and the Institute of Marine Engineering, Science and Technology. After significant work experience, membership of RINA and registration as a Chartered or Incorporated Engineer with the Engineering Council UK is possible.

Money guide

Your starting salary as a naval architect can be from £20,000 to £24,000 per year. With some experience this can increase to £35,000, and with extensive experience you can earn up to £75,000.

Related opportunities

■ Aerospace Engineer p212
■ Electrical Engineer p221
■ Marine Engineer p232
■ Merchant Navy Engineering Officer p613

Further information

Defence Engineering Science Group (DESG)
Ministry of Defence
01225 449368; www.desg.mod.uk; sit-desgmktman@mod.uk

The Royal Institution of Naval Architects (RINA)
10 Upper Belgrave Street, London SW1X 8BQ
020 7235 4622; www.rina.org.uk; hq@rina.org.uk

UK Resource Centre for Women in Science, Engineering and Construction
2nd Floor, Weston House, 246 High Holborn, London WC1V 7EX
020 3206 0404; www.wisecampaign.org.uk

PAINTER AND DECORATOR

What the work involves

- Painters and decorators improve the interior and exterior of people's homes and other new or old buildings.

- They also paint large structures such as bridges.

- Your work will include preparing surfaces by making sure they are clean and smooth, applying primers, undercoats and topcoats of paint, and putting up wall coverings such as wallpaper.

- You will use a range of tools including brushes, rollers and spraying equipment.

The type of person suited to this work

You need to be good with your hands, and particularly skilful when using fine decoration techniques. You will also need an eye for colour and design and an interest in décor and current trends.

You need to be friendly, personable and able to work well in a team.

You will need to be fit and active as you will have to climb ladders and carry tools and equipment. You should not mind working at heights.

You must be able to measure accurately so that you can work out how much paint and other material you will need.

Working conditions

Most of the work is indoors, but some is outdoors. You will regularly work on ladders or on scaffolding. It is important that you follow health and safety regulations, which might include wearing a mask to prevent you from breathing in paint fumes.

You are likely to work a normal working week, although weekend work and overtime are common. You may need a driving licence.

Future prospects

There are good employment opportunities for painters and decorators in the UK at the moment.

You can work for painting and decorating companies or building contractors. Painting and decorating companies may offer a range of work or may specialise in work such as domestic, commercial, new build or industrial.

After gaining experience, it is possible to progress to a supervisory role or become self-employed.

Advantages/disadvantages

Working at extreme heights may be difficult for some people.

It can be rewarding to see the improved look of a newly painted building or structure and you have the opportunity to be creative.

Qualifications and courses

It is useful to have some GCSEs/S grades (A*–E/1–5) in subjects such as maths, design and technology and English. You could also enter with a vocational qualification, such as a BTEC Introductory Certificate/Diploma in Construction.

Construction Apprenticeships offer a training programme leading to NVQ/SVQ Level 3. Apprenticeships are validated by the Construction Industry Training Board (CITB).

Most training is done on the job whilst attending college to obtain qualifications such as NVQs/SVQs in Painting and Decorating (Levels 2/3), CITB Intermediate/Advanced Construction Award in Decorative Occupations, or City & Guilds (6217–03) Level 1 Certificate in Basic Construction Skills (Painting and Decorating). The CITB Construction Award in Painting and Decorating allows those who have difficulties in gaining work experience to train for an NVQ.

A Construction Skills Certificate Scheme (CSCS) card is mandatory for painters and decorators working on constructions sites. All applicants need to have a relevant NVQ/SVQ qualification and to pass a health and safety test. Trainees who are working towards an NVQ Level 2 or a construction award can apply for a Trainee Card (Craft and Operative).

Money guide

Apprentices under the age of 19 can earn up to £14,439 a year. New entrants/trainees can expect to earn between £12,000 and £15,000 per year.

NVQ Level 2 or 3 qualified painters and decorators can earn between £18,000 and £21,000.

Decorators with specialist skills and supervisory duties can earn £25,000 or more.

Overtime is often available, and on some projects there are bonuses based on outputs.

Related opportunities

- Construction Operative p88
- Plasterer p112
- Signwriter/Signmaker p186
- Wall/Floor Tiler p129

Further information

Painting & Decorating Association
32 Coton Road, Nuneaton CV11 5TW
024 7635 377; www.paintingdecoratingassociation.co.uk

www.cityandguilds.com/myperfectjob

PLANNING AND DEVELOPMENT SURVEYOR

What the work involves

- Planning and development surveyors develop and manage new building or refurbishment projects.

- You will create proposals and oversee projects from conception through to completion.

- You will be responsible for recruiting team members for each project, as well as liaising with external industry professionals throughout.

- You will also give valuations on properties and developments, advise clients on financing options for their building plans, and prepare their applications for planning permission.

The type of person suited to this work

As you will be managing team members, briefing other professionals and dealing with clients on a daily basis, well-developed communication and negotiation skills are required.

Good numeracy skills, coupled with scientific aptitude, are essential to successfully write proposals and manage financial details within a project. An understanding of legal matters within the building and construction industries is helpful, as is an interest in the environment, architecture, history or preserving the natural landscape.

Working conditions

You may have to work longer than the standard 35 hour week, but weekend and shift work is unusual.

Although there is some day to day travelling involved, overnight stays are also uncommon.

Most jobs are found in cities where there is a high level of commercial activity. You could work for public sector or private companies, which range in size from very small practices up to large multinational firms. Work in the public sector is becoming increasingly flexible, with part time work and career breaks available.

Future prospects

Your career progression should be very straightforward; from graduate trainee, to surveyor, to senior surveyor, and up to associate or partner with several years' experience. If you progress to become an equity partner you will earn a high salary and also get a cut of the company's profits.

If you work in the public sector, you could enhance your career prospects with a Royal Town Planning Institute (RTPI) qualification, or develop a more specialised career in an area of surveying in which you are particularly interested.

Advantages/disadvantages

Work is varied and you have the opportunity to travel within the UK and overseas.

Qualifications and courses

This profession is open to all graduates, although further academic and vocational qualifications from the Royal Institution of Chartered Surveyors (RICS) must be gained before you can qualify as a chartered planning and development surveyor.

Some degree and HND subjects offer exemption from the academic stages of the RICS assessment, and these include surveying, planning, and land/estate/property management. Entry requirements for most degree/HND courses are a minimum of 5 GSCEs (A*–C), 3 A levels or the relevant BTEC/SQA national awards (or equivalent).

If your first degree/HND is in a subject completely unrelated to surveying, you will need to take an RICS approved conversion course prior to starting training. Occasionally, larger organisations will employ graduates with unrelated degrees and allow them to undertake a conversion course during their employment.

Although you might need to work extra hours, weekend work is rare.

You will have a lot of responsibility, which can be stressful at times.

Money guide

New graduates can start on salaries of between £18,000 and £23,000, the higher end of which is generally confined to London-based positions.

Fully qualified surveyors can earn upwards of £35,000, with £50,000 being average after a few years' experience.

If you went on to become a partner in a firm, you could be earning £80,000+, with an additional share of profits on top.

Chief executives in the largest, London companies can earn between £350,000 and £800,000.

Related opportunities

- Land/Geomatic Surveyor p107
- Rural Property/Practice Surveyor p118
- Civil/Construction Engineer/Engineering Technician p85
- Town Planner/Planning Technician p128

Further information

Royal Institution of Chartered Surveyors (RICS)
Parliament Square, London SW1p 3AD
0870 333 1600; www.rics.org/careers; contactrics@rics.org

Institution of Civil Engineering Surveyors
Dominion House, Sibson Road, Sale M33 7PP
0161 972 3100; www.cices.org.uk

PLASTERER

What the work involves

- There are three types of plastering that you could do: solid, fibrous or dry lining.

- Solid plastering involves the application of plaster or cement to internal and external walls, ceilings and floors.

- Fibrous plastering involves making ornamental plaster work, such as the kind you see on decorative ceilings.

- Dry lining involves the use of plasterboard to construct walls or partitions and then skimming over the joins with plaster making them ready for decoration.

The type of person suited to this work

To be able to use your tools skilfully, you need to be good with your hands. An ability to use basic maths for calculating the amounts of materials you will need for a job is also helpful.

You will need to be able to work in a team with other plasterers, and with those in other construction trades.

You should be physically fit, as the work is very active and can be tiring. It can also be dusty when working with the plaster powder; this may be difficult if you suffer from certain allergies. You will be climbing ladders and possibly scaffolding, so you must not mind working at heights.

Working conditions
Solid/dry lining

Most of the work for solid plasterers and those doing dry lining work is indoors, although you might have to work outdoors if working on exteriors. You will work from ladders and scaffolding.

Fibrous

Most fibrous plasterers work in workshops, although you may also install your work on-site.

All plastering requires an understanding and appreciation of health and safety regulations, which includes wearing protective gear. You may work a normal working week, although you might need to start early or finish late, and weekend work may also be available.

Future prospects

Because the building industry is cyclical there may be less of a demand for plasterers during a recession. Shortages of qualified plasterers do exist however in the south and south-east of England. Besides being employed by specialist plastering firms and building contractors, you can also work in the cultural heritage or public sectors.

After you have gained sufficient experience, you could progress to technical, supervisory or managerial roles or become self-employed.

Advantages/disadvantages

Working at heights may be difficult for some people.

Qualifications and courses

To be eligible for an apprenticeship you will need some GCSEs/S grades in subjects such as English, maths, design and technology. Construction Apprenticeships offer a structured training programme leading to NVQ/SVQ Level 3. Apprenticeships are validated by the Construction Industry Training Board (CITB) and last 3 years in England and Wales, and 4 years in Scotland.

Most training is done on the job whilst attending college to obtain qualifications such as NVQs/SVQs in Plastering (Levels 1, 2 and 3), or City & Guilds certificates in Basic Construction Skills – Plastering (6217–04). NVQ Level 3 entitles you to craftsperson status. A Diploma in Construction and the Built Environment is also relevant for plasterers.

Construction Skills Certification Scheme (CSCS) cards are required by plasterers employed on construction sites to demonstrate that they have health and safety training and are competent in their field.

You will be able to work in a variety of locations, especially as a solid plasterer. There are opportunities to be creative when producing fibrous plaster work.

Money guide

As a trainee you could earn around £14,000 per year. With a Level 2 qualification this can rise to £18,500 and with Level 3 the minimum is £21,111. Experienced plasterers can earn up to £35,000 or more. Overtime is often available, and on some projects there are bonuses based on outputs.

Related opportunities

- Building Technician p80
- Mastic Asphalter p108
- Wall/Floor Tiler p129

Further information

ConstructionSkills
Bircham Newton, King's Lynn PE31 6RH
01485 577577; www.cskills.net; www.bconstructive.co.uk

Federation of Plastering and Drywall Contractors
1st Floor, 8/9 Ludgate Square, London EC4M 7AS
020 7634 9480; www.fpdc.org

Scottish Building and Training Council (SBATC)
Crichton House, 4 Crichton's Close, Edinburgh EH8 8DT
0131 556 8866; www.sbatc.co.uk

www.cityandguilds.com/myperfectjob

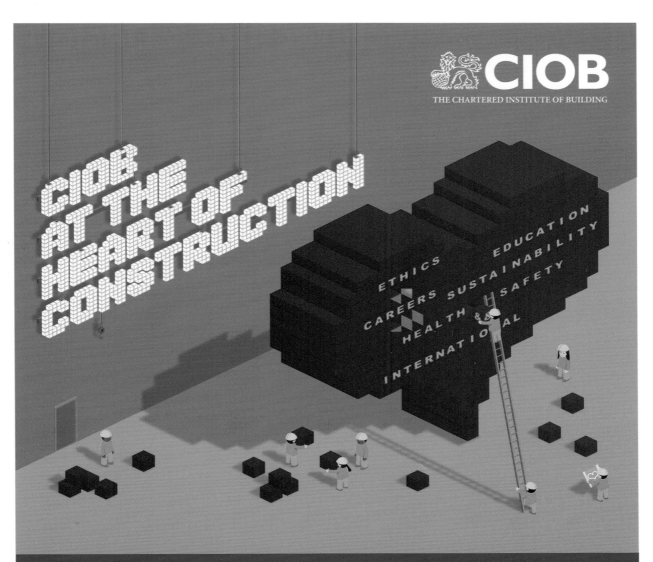

Fancy building a brighter future?
Why not think about a career in construction?

If you thought a career in construction was all about hard hats and bricks and mortar, then think again. It is first and foremost about people and the promotion of the built environment as central to quality of life for everyone everywhere.

A career in construction is an international passport that can give you the opportunity to work anywhere in the world. It also offers career progression and the chance to influence and really make a impact on social and environmental agendas.

So if you think you'd like a career that's diverse, innovative, inspiring and where you can really make a difference to the way in which people live, then why not think about a career in construction.

Construction careers can offer diverse and exciting work opportunities such as:

■ Thinking about how to utilise the latest technology to create sustainable buildings

■ How to preserve historic buildings for future generations

■ Planning and implementing reconstruction projects after natural disasters like earthquakes

■ Planning new roads to help people get from A to B more efficiently

If you would like to find out more go to
www.ciob.org

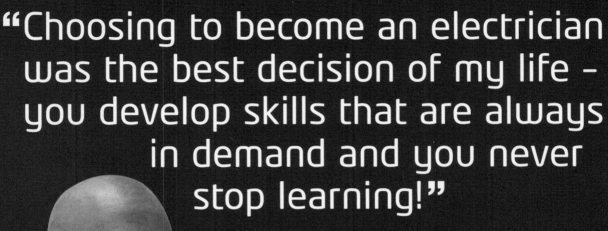

Considering a career in flooring?

A job within the flooring industry is a trade to be proud of and often very lucrative. Whether it be fitting floors in residential or commercial environments, the opportunities for individuals with good practical skills and an eye for detail are endless.

Whilst school leavers should, wherever possible, gain their skills from formal programmes like apprenticeships, they can also choose to supplement this through organisations such as FITA, the Flooring Industry Training Association, www.fita.co.uk, who offer practical training courses to suit all levels of experience, from real beginners just getting started in the industry to upskilling courses aimed towards the more seasoned professional.

The Contract Flooring Association (CFA) and the National Institute of Carpet and Floorlayers (NICF) offer guidance on all aspects of floor fitting to companies and individuals. For more information on the world of flooring from the leading trade associations representing the commercial and domestic markets visit their websites at www.cfa.org.uk and www.nicfltd.org.uk.

Whatever path you choose, from laying that perfect floor to estimating, planning and even self employment, with experience and skills the future is bright in flooring!

For further information or advice contact:

The Contract Flooring Association (CFA)
Telephone 0115 941 1126

The Flooring Industry Training Association (FITA)
Telephone: 0115 950 6836

The National Institute of Carpet & Floorlayers (NICF)
Telephone: 0115 958 3077

CONTRACT FLOORING ASSOCIATION
cfa

fita
THE FLOORING INDUSTRY
TRAINING ASSOCIATION

N I C F
National Institute of Carpet & Floorlayers

Tomorrow

Today

See where a Rolls-Royce apprenticeship could take you.

As a Rolls-Royce apprentice you'll carry out mission-critical work, earning while you learn from the engineers and scientists behind the world's most important power systems. Like our revolutionary LiftFan technology and a swivelling jet pipe, which together allow the F-35B fighter to land vertically. Join the team that sets the standard.

Trusted to deliver excellence

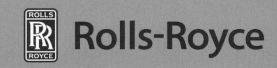

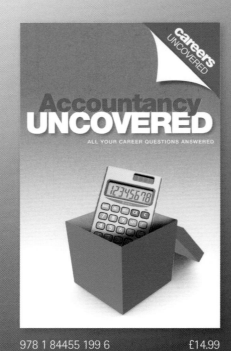
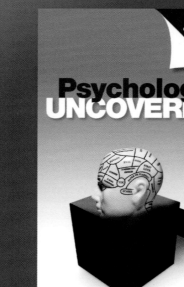

LEARN IN THE SOMERSET COUNTRYSIDE!

BRIDGWATER COLLEGE

The Cannington Centre was known for many years as Cannington College, which was established in 1921 and had a long-standing reputation as a one of the key providers in the land-based education sector. In September 2004, Cannington College merged with the local tertiary education provider, Bridgwater College, a move which secured a substantial investment package to significantly improve the facilities.

The countryside location of the Cannington Centre makes it an ideal choice for students wanting to pursue a land-based education. The rural environment creates a calm and relaxed atmosphere, which students find very satisfying and conducive to learning. The teaching facilities comprise a range of purpose-built accommodation within beautifully maintained grounds. Class sizes and tutor groups are usually small, which allows every student to have individual attention from their lecturers.

The provision is comprehensive and so the student profile is varied, in terms of age, gender and nationality. Combined with the factor that many students opt to live on-site, tutor groups tend to form strong units and many lasting friendships are established.

ANIMAL MANAGEMENT CENTRE

This facility provides superb theory and practical rooms, as well as a dog-grooming salon, kennel and cattery block. It is home to a large animal collection, along with an external aviary, alpaca enclosure, wild fowl pond and animal paddocks.

EQUESTRIAN CENTRE

The Equestrian Centre is an approved BHS riding school and all instructors are BHS qualified. The facilities include an indoor and outdoor arena, stable blocks and a range of College horses. Group riding and jumping lessons are available as well as specialist instruction in dressage and show jumping. For more information visit www.canningtonequestriancentre.co.uk

ACTIVITY CENTRE

This is a fun packed outdoor facility full of high and low rope challenges and climbing activities. For more information visit www.canningtonactivitycentre.co.uk

RODWAY FARM

The 200 hectare mixed farm is our largest real work experience facility. We have a dairy herd of 250 high-yielding Holsteins, a flock of 200 ewes and a brand new state-of-the-art milking parlour and a refurbishment to the value of over £1 million. The farm also offers many opportunities for countryside skills, such as hedge laying and dry stone walling.

WALLED GARDENS

The Walled Gardens are a training facility and are also open to the public; they were officially opened by HRH Prince Edward in April 2009. With a botanical glasshouse, plant shop, tea rooms and extensive gardens, they are an outstanding facility for Horticulture students, as well as a great visitor attraction, having recently achieved the Visitor Attraction Quality status. For more information visit www.canningtonwalledgardens.co.uk

GOLF COURSE

Our golf facilities are used for teaching Sports Turf Management and training our Golf Academy students. They are also available for use by staff and students at reduced rates. They include a nine hole, 18 tee course, a ten bay fully automated driving range and a club house with a pro's shop. For details visit www.canningtongolfcentre.co.uk

LEARNING RESOURCES CENTRE & IT

All students have access to a wide range of support resources, including the Library, which houses 20,000 books, journals, newspapers, DVDs and CDs, and a careers library. There is also access to networked computers, scanners, photocopiers and the internet. All students are welcome to use their own laptops with wireless connection to the College network.

STUDENT COMMON ROOM AND ENTERTAINMENT

The Student Liaison team makes sure there are plenty of entertainment and events for day and residential students. Typical activities might include paintball and laser quest trips, DVD nights, hockey, football, rugby, rounders, pool competitions, karting, cinema trips, bowling, skittles, Wii competitions, swimming and College parties. The Common Room has pool and table tennis tables, jukebox, refreshments bar, games machines and much more. Cannington Centre students can also participate in all events organised at the Bridgwater Centre.

RESIDENTIAL ACCOMMODATION

Many students choose on-site residential accommodation if they live too far away to travel daily or if they are studying a course which involves out of hours duties. The accommodation consists of 120 mainly modern study bedrooms, most with en-suite facilities and all with internet access points. All accommodation has security controlled access, CCTV and 24 hour security support. For more information contact Student Support on (01278) 441233.

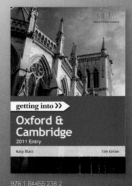

PLUMBER

What the work involves

- Plumbers install, maintain and repair plumbing, heating and water systems in various locations including people's homes and public buildings.

- You will use a range of hand and power tools, such as wrenches, cutters and welding equipment.

- You will also be responsible for routine check ups on appliances such as boilers.

- When you have completed a job, you will need to test the system to make sure that everything is working properly.

The type of person suited to this work

Good practical skills are essential. You must be careful and accurate and follow instructions to ensure that systems work properly and safely. Analytical and problem-solving skills are also important.

You might be bending, kneeling and squeezing into tight spaces so it would help if you were physically fit. You need to be comfortable working at heights.

You need to be a team player but also willing to work alone. You should keep a good appearance and have excellent communication skills when dealing directly with customers.

Working conditions

You will work both indoors and outdoors, possibly within confined spaces and at heights. Travelling will be required for jobs so it would be useful to have a driving licence and your own vehicle.

You may work a normal working week but, if your organisation offers a 24/7 call-out service, you need to be available all times of the day, any day of the week.

Future prospects

Work is available across the UK, so job prospects are good.

With additional training and Gas Safe registration, you could move into gas central heating installation and repair. You could also move into a related career such as heating and ventilation, refrigeration or air conditioning.

You can progress to supervisory, training or managerial positions after a few years' experience. Also, many plumbers choose to set up their own business.

Advantages/disadvantages

You could be called out at all times of night and day, to deal with plumbing emergencies, which can be difficult for those with family commitments.

Being able to solve a difficult problem and make a customer happy can be very rewarding.

Money guide

The Joint Industry Board for Plumbing Mechanical Engineering Services (JIBPMES) agrees wage rates.

Qualifications and courses

To train as a plumber, either on the job or via an Apprenticeship you will normally need 3 or 4 GCSEs/S grades (A*–C/1–3) preferably including English, maths, and science and technology. Equivalent qualifications, such as an Intermediate 2 in Construction and the Built Environment, SGA Intermediate in Construction or BTEC First in Construction may also be accepted. The Diploma in Construction and the Built Environment or in Engineering may be relevant. Entrants for Apprenticeships or training schemes will need to pass a selection test and have their colour vision tested.

Trainees can work towards a City & Guilds NVQ Levels 2 and 3 in Mechanical Engineering Services: Plumbing (Domestic), City & Guilds Technical Certificates Levels 2 and 3 Plumbing Studies. Most training is done on the job whilst attending college.

Gas Safe registration and possession of a Gas Safe ID card is a legal requirement for anyone installing or repairing gas fittings or appliances.

Overtime is often available, which can lead to higher earnings.

You can start at around £10,000 per year as a first-year apprentice.

This can rise to £15,000–£17,000 in the final year of training. When qualified you could get £19,500–£21,000.

With experience you could expect anything between £20,000 and £30,000.

Earnings for self-employed plumbers can be much higher. Top earners can get £35,000–£40,000 or more. Salaries are highest in London and the south-east of England.

Related opportunities

- Construction Operative p88
- Gas Network Engineer p226
- Heating and Ventilating Engineer/Gas Service Technician p102
- Refrigeration Engineer/Technician p116

Further information

SummitSkills
Vega House, Opal Drive, Fox Milne, Milton Keynes MK15 0DF
01908 303960; www.summitskills.org.uk

Chartered Institute of Plumbing and Heating Engineering
64 Station Lane, Hornchurch RM12 6NB
01708 472791; www.ciphe.org.uk

www.cityandguilds.com/myperfectjob

PROPERTY VALUER

What the work involves

- As a property valuer you will assess the value of property (buildings, land or personal items) for a client and give them advice on how the property may be sold, loaned, taxed, acquired by a company or made part of a compensation claim.

- You will assess new commercial and industrial property and reassess existing property that has been altered and improved.

- You will provide reports on your valuations which may be important if property becomes part of legal negotiations or insurance claims.

- You may have to run live auctions where you will sell items that you have valued, or you may pass them to a specialist.

The type of person suited to this work

You should have a keen interest in property valuation law and taxes.

You must have strong numerical skills to make accurate calculations, such as working out taxes or analysing accounts.

As you may be hired by a company on a freelance basis, you must be organised and able to work on your own initiative.

You need to have excellent written and verbal communication skills in order to communicate with clients, employers and government bodies and contact those in the locality as you assess a particular property.

Working conditions

You will work about 35–40 hours per week, Monday to Friday. You may have to work weekends depending on the project or your employer.

You will be mainly office-based but will frequently have to visit and inspect properties or meet clients.

As you might need to travel locally to visit clients or inspect properties you might need a driving licence.

Future prospects

There are many opportunities in the UK. You may work for an estate agent in order to value property that is being sold, rented or mortgaged. You may find opportunities in the Valuation Agency assessing property for local authorities and government departments.

Valuers are also needed by HM Revenue and Customs (HMRC) where you will value property and land that must be taxed when it is sold or bought.

Qualifications and courses

There are no formal qualifications required to become a property valuer but entrants are usually graduates or hold at least HND or HNC qualifications. Entry requirements vary depending on the employer.

If you become a property valuer you should become a member of a professional body such as the Royal Institution of Chartered Surveyors (RICS) or the Institute of Revenues, Rating and Valuation (IRRV). You will find a full list of accredited degree and diploma courses on the RICS website.

You can take an accredited postgraduate degree or diploma course in an auctioneering/valuation subject. Please see the Royal Institution of Chartered Surveyors for a full list. You may have to combine these courses with work experience and further professional qualifications.

Advantages/disadvantages

Usually you will combine your role as a valuer with other roles such as estate management, surveying and even auctioning.

Property and land valuations may become part of compensation claims which could take a long time to sort out.

Money guide

Your starting salary can be from £18,000 to £21,000 a year.

With experience this can increase to £27,000–£36,000.

You can find salaries of £42,000 each year.

Related opportunities

- Auction Property Consultant p75
- Estate Agent p96
- Loss Adjuster p49
- Insurance Surveyor p44

Further information

The Institute of Revenues Rating and Valuation (IRRV)
41 Doughty Street, London WC1N 2LF
0207 831 3505; www.irrv.net

National Association of Valuers and Auctioneers
Arbon House, 6 Tournament Court, Edgehill Drive, Warwick CV34 6LG
01926 417 774; www.nava.org.uk; member@nava.org.uk

Royal Institution of Chartered Surveyors (RICS)
Parliament Square, London SW1P 3AD
www.rics.org; contactrics@rics.org

QUANTITY SURVEYOR

What the work involves

- Quantity surveyors are responsible for calculating costs, issuing contracts, keeping projects to time and within budget, managing subcontractors and arranging payments for work.

- You will need a good understanding of building regulations to ensure that projects meet the required standards of quality and safety.

- You could work on a wide variety of projects from residential developments to hospitals or sports stadiums.

The type of person suited to this work

You must have a high level of numeracy and the ability to manage financial projects as you will be responsible for all the financial details of projects. Good negotiation skills are also important, as you must agree contracts and prices with workers and contractors.

Excellent verbal and written communication skills are vital for leading and motivating the onsite team, liaising with clients and subcontractors, and producing accurate and detailed progress reports.

Finally, a good understanding of business and legal matters in relation to the building and construction industry is needed, since you will be responsible for ensuring that all projects meet current regulations and standards.

Working conditions

Working hours are slightly longer than average and will include early starts, late evenings and weekend work.

You will usually be office-based, although it is not uncommon for the office to be in the form of a temporary hut onsite. Travel to client meetings and other projects is also expected.

Self-employment is possible, and many companies use freelance quantity surveyors on projects. There is also the opportunity to travel overseas.

Future prospects

Your opportunities are likely to lie within local authority or government departments, private practices, building contractors, property companies or commercial organisations both in the UK and abroad.

With experience, you can undertake a more comprehensive project management role and have the satisfaction of taking a job through from conception to completion. There is also a natural progression from quantity surveying to commercial management.

Advantages/disadvantages

Working on numerous projects and with a range of people makes the job varied.

Qualifications and courses

ENTRY LEVEL 4

Most employers look for candidates who have a degree, particularly in quantity surveying or a related subject such as maths or physics. If your degree subject is completely unrelated, you will need to take a postgraduate conversion course that is recognised by the Royal Institution of Chartered Surveyors (RICS).

An HND in a related subject such as building/construction, civil engineering or urban and land studies is also valued by employers and may gain you employment as a surveying technician from which you can study for more qualifications to become a full quantity surveyor. A range of RICS recognised part time and distance learning courses are available.

Entry without a degree or HND is sometimes possible, although unusual. You would have to work your way up through the industry, undertaking relevant courses and gaining qualifications as you go.

Once you are in employment, you will need to become a member of the RICS and this is achieved through attaining both an approved degree in quantity surveying, and also completing the Assessment of Professional Competence (APC) which requires at least 2 years' practical, work-based experience.

There are good opportunities for career progression and specialisation.

Hours are longer than average, with occasional weekend work.

Money guide

Starting salaries for quantity surveyors can range from £17,000 to £25,000, whether in private practice or working for local government. If you have gained chartered status, you can expect a considerably higher starting salary.

At a senior level salaries reach £45,000, but can be considerably more for those in partner positions in private firms.

If you undertake shift work or are required to travel extensively, allowances are often paid on top of your basic salary.

Related opportunities

- Building Surveyor p79
- Insurance Surveyor p44
- Civil/Construction Engineer/Civil Engineering Technician p85
- Town Planner/Planning Technician p128

Further information

ConstructionSkills
Bircham Newton, King's Lynn PE31 6XG
01485 577577; www.cskills.net; www.bconstructive.co.uk

Royal Institution of Chartered Surveyors (RICS)
Parliament Square, London SW1P 3AD
0870 333 1600; www.rics.org; contact@rics.org

REFRIGERATION ENGINEER/ TECHNICIAN

What the work involves

- Your work as a refrigeration engineer will involve the design, installation and repair of refrigeration equipment and air conditioning systems.

- Refrigeration engineers aim to create and maintain comfortable working/living environments in offices and homes that are both energy-efficient and safe.

- Your work in commercial buildings and factories will be to provide refrigeration systems that keep food at the correct, safe temperature.

- You will be called out to undertake repairs and maintenance, estimate costs of construction and installation projects, carry out inspections on existing equipment, and give advice on adjustments and improvements.

The type of person suited to this work

It is important that you like hands-on work and have a practical approach to problem-solving.

You should be interested in the building services industry and keep up to date with relevant developments in legislation and technology.

Written and spoken communication skills are important as you will be in contact with clients and planning projects.

You should have an aptitude for maths and physics and have strong technical skills.

Working conditions

You will normally work around 37 hours a week and how this is spread over a week may vary. However you might have to work longer hours during the summer which is peak time for refrigeration engineers.

You will be office-based to plan visits to sites and organise jobs, but you will also visit various locations such as offices, shopping centres or factories to complete practical jobs such as maintenance, repair and installation.

You may also work in refrigeration transport, on specially adapted vehicles such as trucks, aircraft and fishing vessels or in vehicle workshops.

On certain visits you might have to wear protective clothing or equipment.

Future prospects

As you gain experience in the field you will find opportunities for progression to supervisor and managerial roles.

To improve your skills you may take further qualifications such as NVQs in Building Services Engineering at Levels 3 and 4 in refrigeration and air conditioning specific topics. Such courses also act as a stepping stone to the Chartered Institution of Building Services Engineers (CIBSE).

Qualifications and courses

Entry is usually through apprenticeship. To qualify you are likely to need 4 GCSEs (A*–C) in English, maths, physics and design and technology. The Diploma in Engineering is also helpful. You will learn on the job for 3–4 years.

Apprentices can gain NVQs, Levels 2 and 3, in Mechanical Engineering Services and Refrigeration and Air Conditioning, and in health and safety procedures. Arrangements for apprenticeships are different in Scotland, Wales and Northern Ireland.

Further qualifications such HNCs/HNDs in Refrigeration and Air Conditioning, the BTEC National certificate/ diploma, and Foundation degrees in Building Services Engineering are available. You could also apply to be a member of the Institute of Refrigeration.

You can add further experience with further qualifications and work towards becoming an incorporated or chartered engineer.

Advantages/disadvantages

There are opportunities to work abroad as UK qualifications are internationally respected.

You may also be required to do overtime work and to be on call overnight and on weekends.

Money guide

Starting salaries are around £14,000–£18,000 a year.

This can increase to around £20,000–£30,000 with experience and qualifications.

Salaries can be as high as £50,000 per year.

Related opportunities

- Electrical Engineer p221
- Electrician p94
- Civil/Construction Engineer/Civil Engineering Technician p85

Further information

Institute of Refrigeration (IOR)
Kelvin House, 76 Mill Lane, Carshalton SM5 2JR
020 8647 7033; www.ior.org.uk

www.cityandguilds.com/myperfectjob

ROOFER

What the work involves

- Roofers remove old roofs and replace them, cover new roofs and repair existing ones.

- You will have a choice of roofing materials to work with, such as tile, slate, felt, thatch and sheet. You could specialise in flat or pitched (sloping) roofs or work on both.

- When working on flat roofs you will need to spread a waterproof bitumen layer. On all types of roofs your work will involve measuring and cutting materials, layering them on the roof and using mortar or cement to seal it.

- You could also conduct lead work or liquid applied roofing.

The type of person suited to this work

You need to have good practical skills and be physically fit, so that you can climb ladders and scaffolding and carry roofing materials. You must be comfortable working at heights.

It is important to be able to understand plans and follow instructions. You should be a team player with good communication skills when dealing with customers.

It will also be useful to be interested in building construction and to enjoy being outdoors.

Working conditions

You will work outdoors on roofs in various locations from people's homes to historic cathedrals and construction sites. The work can be dusty and dirty.

As you will be working up ladders, on scaffolding or on the roof itself, you will need to pay close attention to all health and safety procedures, which includes wearing protective gear such as a safety helmet and boots.

You are likely to work a normal working week, although extra work may be available at weekends.

Future prospects

There is a good demand for qualified roofers across the UK at the moment. Work is available within roofing companies, contractors, local authorities, roofing material suppliers and other public organisations. Self-employment is common.

You can decide to specialise in using one type of roofing material (such as slate) or you can train to become skilled in using several types.

You may work your way up to technical, supervisory and managerial levels. After you have gained enough experience, you could start your own roofing company.

Advantages/disadvantages

Working at heights may be difficult for some people.

It is satisfying to produce a lasting structure that is functional and looks good.

Qualifications and courses

To train as a roofer it is useful to have some GCSEs/S grades (A*–E/1–5) or a vocational qualification. Maths, English, craft, design and technology are all relevant subjects.

The Construction Apprenticeship Scheme (CAS) offers a structured training programme leading to NVQ/SVQ Level 3. Apprenticeships are validated by the Construction Industry Training Board (CITB) and last 3 years in England and Wales, and 4 years in Scotland.

Most training is done on the job whilst attending college to obtain qualifications such as NVQs/SVQs in Roofing Occupations and City & Guilds Certificates.

Many employers on construction sites require workers to have a Construction Skills Certification Scheme (CSCS) card. This demonstrates that the holder has health and safety training.

You could get to work on some impressive projects such as fitting the roof on a new football stadium.

You will gain an understanding of other construction work, such as joinery.

Money guide

The Building and Allied Trades Joint Industrial Council (BATJIC) agrees minimum wage rates annually. Trainee salaries are about £13,500 per year. After NVQ/SVQ qualifications this rises to around £16,000. As a trained roofer with qualifications you can earn £16,500–£25,000. £26,000+ is possible for very experienced roofers who are self-employed.

Overtime is often available, and on some projects there are bonuses based on outputs, which can lead to higher earnings.

Related opportunities

- Building Technician p80
- Construction Operative p88
- Scaffolder p119
- Thatcher p126

Further information

ConstructionSkills
Bircham Newton, King's Lynn PE31 6RH
01485 577577; www.cskills.net; www.bconstructive.co.uk

The Institute of Roofing
Roofing House, 31 Worship Street, London EC2A 2DX
020 7448 3858; www.instituteofroofing.co.uk

www.cityandguilds.com/myperfectjob

RURAL PROPERTY/PRACTICE SURVEYOR

What the work involves

- Rural property/practice surveyors manage properties in the countryside such as farms and estates.

- You will supervise staff, oversee finances, value rural land and property, and organise auctions.

- You will give advice to rural landowners on how to develop the land and farms to gain more profit, without disturbing the local environment. You will also advise on the buying and selling of properties, on farming grants and subsidies and how national and EU law affects their business.

The type of person suited to this work

Excellent communication skills are needed as you will need to negotiate and liaise with people of all ages and backgrounds.

You must have an analytical mind and a clear writing style in order to explain complex statistical information.

A good understanding of rural issues, including knowledge of crops, is essential in order to assess a client's economic viability with accuracy.

Problem-solving and forward-planning skills are also essential to keep on top of a heavy workload.

Working conditions

Early morning and weekend work is common as you need to adapt around rural events such as harvests.

You will mostly work outdoors. If you are office based, it will be in rural market towns or villages. You should be prepared to drive and travel regularly.

Future prospects

Your career path is narrow but progression can occur very quickly. In larger companies, there may be the opportunity to specialise in areas such as agriculture or renewable energy use in the countryside. By contrast, a smaller company could give you a greater range of projects which will build broader experience. With 10–15 years of experience, you could become a partner in a firm.

Advantages/disadvantages

You will be based in peaceful rural locations.

You will be instrumental in developing the future of the countryside and rural industries.

Hours can be long and you should expect to regularly work early mornings and weekends.

Money guide

Average earnings for new graduates are between £15,000

Qualifications and courses

ENTRY LEVEL 5

This sector is open to all graduates, although a degree in a related subject such as agriculture, forestry, estate management or land management is particularly useful. Most degree courses require 5 GSCEs (A*–C), 2 A levels or relevant BTEC/SQA national awards (or equivalent). Relevant A levels include geography, economics, business studies and maths. Degree courses accredited by the Royal Institution of Chartered Surveyors (RICS) will reduce the length of time you will have to spend in professional training by a year.

If your first degree was in an unrelated subject, the College of Estate Management offers a postgraduate conversion course that can be studied by distance learning.

If you have a relevant HND or Foundation degree, then you can qualify for Associate status. However, a degree is necessary to qualify for Chartered status.

Once qualified, you will need to complete the Assessment of Professional Competence during your first 2 years of employment, in order to gain Chartered status.

and £23,000. With experience, this rises to £28,000 a year. A senior chartered surveyor can receive a salary of £45,000+.

Compared with other surveying roles, rural property salaries are fairly low and the opportunity to earn £50,000+ is rare.

Additional benefits such as a company car or health insurance are sometimes offered by employers, and subsidised accommodation may be available for surveyors managing a farm or estate.

Related opportunities

- Auction Property Consultant p75
- Building Surveyor p79
- Land/Geomatic Surveyor p107
- Civil/Construction Engineer/Civil Engineering Technician p85

Further information

Agricultural Development and Advisory Service
Woodthorne, Wergs Road, Wolverhampton WV6 8TQ
0845 766 0085; www.adas.co.uk

Department for Environment, Food and Rural Affairs
Eastbury House, 30–34 Albert Embankment, London SE1 7TL
0845 933 5577; www.defra.gov.uk

Royal Agricultural College
Stroud Road, Cirencester GL7 6JS
01285 889912; www.rac.ac.uk; admissions@rac.ac.uk

SCAFFOLDER

What the work involves

- Scaffolders put up scaffolding so that new constructions, or the maintenance of existing buildings and structures such as bridges, can take place.

- You will put together metal tubes, fittings and wooden or metal platforms to create the scaffolding.

- You will use tools such as swivel spanners and spirit levels in your work.

- You may also put up spectator stands, stages and rigging for outdoor concerts and events.

The type of person suited to this work

Safety is the main priority in scaffolding. You need to ensure that it is safe for the people who will be working on it, passers-by, workmates and yourself. For this reason, you have to be able to keep your concentration, have good practical skills, be well organised and be able to follow instructions and take measurements accurately.

You must be physically fit so that you can lift and carry equipment up and down ladders and, of course, you must be happy working at heights.

You also need to be able to work as part of a team of scaffolders.

Working conditions

You will be working mainly outdoors in most weather conditions, often at great heights.

You will need to wear protective equipment such as a hard hat, boots and a safety harness.

You may work a normal working week from Monday to Friday, although you might need to start work early or finish late. Extra hours at weekends may also be available.

Future prospects

There is a good demand for scaffolders across the UK and opportunities with specialist scaffolding firms and building contractors as well as oil and power companies.

You may progress from basic to advanced scaffolder, and then on to supervisory and managerial positions. Some experienced scaffolders set up their own businesses. If you possess computer-aided design skills, progression to project design and management is possible.

You may also work in other countries.

Advantages/disadvantages

This can be physically challenging work and working at heights can be demanding for some people.

You will get to work in a variety of locations and you might have the chance to put up scaffolding for major sports and music events, or for film sets.

Qualifications and courses

There are no set entry requirements, but it may be useful to have some GCSEs (A*–E) or a vocational qualification, such as the BTEC Introductory Certificate or Diploma in Construction.

Training is normally provided on the job with part-time attendance at college or training centres to get qualifications.

Scaffolders can work towards NVQs at Levels 1–3 in Accessing Operations and Rigging, the QCF Level 2 Diploma in Scaffolding or The Construction Industry Scaffolders Record Scheme (CISRS) Basic and Advanced Cards.

The CISRS card system ensures that operatives are properly trained and sufficiently experienced to work safely and correctly. An 18 month Apprenticeship will provide you with the CISRS Basic card and a QCF Level 2 Diploma in Scaffolding. With 6 months' scaffolding experience, the Scaffolding Basic Part 1 and 2 courses, and the NVQ at Level 2 in Accessing Operations and Rigging Scaffolding, will also qualify you for the CISRS Basic card.

For the Advanced CISRS Card, scaffolders must have a Basic Card, 12 months' subsequent experience and complete the 10 day Advanced Scaffolding course and the NVQ in Accessing Operations and Rigging Scaffolding at Level 3.

Money guide

Starting as an Apprentice or trainee you can expect to earn £12,500–£13,000 per year.

With qualifications you could get £16,000–£23,000. Very experienced scaffolders can earn £25,000 or more. Overtime is often available, and on some projects there are bonuses based on outputs, which can lead to higher earnings.

Related opportunities

- Building Technician p80
- Construction Operative p88
- Roofer p117

Further information

ConstructionSkills
Bircham Newton, King's Lynn PE31 6RH
01485 577577; www.constructionskills.net

National Access and Scaffolding Confederation
4th Floor, 12 Bridewell Place, London EC4V 6AP
020 7397 8120; www.nasc.org.uk

SHOPFITTER

What the work involves

■ As a shopfitter you will create and install the interiors and exteriors of commercial buildings such as shops, banks, offices, restaurants and hotels.

■ You may be working from designs made by an architect or designer, or you might have to research and prepare your own design drawings.

■ You will prepare, assemble and finish joinery and metalwork according to the design, before bringing each part together and assembling them on site.

■ You will probably specialise in a particular area. These include a metal fabricator, cutting and shaping metal components; a wood machinist, using specialist machinery to cut precise parts for joiners.

The type of person suited to this work

As you will be working in a workshop or on site you should have a keen interest in practical work and have good hand skills.

You should also be interested in design and construction.

You should have an eye for detail and a high level of concentration.

You should have a certain level of fitness as you will be required to work long and at times, hard hours.

As you will be taking measurements and making calculations frequently you should have good spatial awareness and an aptitude for maths.

Working conditions

You will normally work around 40 hours per week. Your work may be in an office, a workshop, a machine shop or a paint shop. You may have to travel to work onsite and this may involve working away from home at times. You can often do overtime work.

You may have to work irregular hours, overnight or at weekends to accommodate clients – work may need to be done during the night when premises are closed.

Onsite work may be dusty, dirty and noisy and usually involves physical work such as lifting and bending.

Future prospects

When you have been trained and qualified and have gained experience you may choose to set up your own business.

Advantages/disadvantages

This is a diverse profession because as a shopfitter your work will change according to the project that you are working on. This could include working with a variety of materials such as

Qualifications and courses

You can begin as a trainee in a specific area such as shopfitting joiner, wood machinist or metal fabricator.

No formal academic qualifications are required but some employers might require GCSEs (A*–E) in English, maths and a science. GSCEs in art, design and technology might also be useful. The Diploma in Construction and the Built Environment, City & Guilds qualifications in woodworking and BTEC certificates in construction are also relevant.

You could begin as an apprentice with a shopfitting company. This leads to NVQs/SVQs in Shopfitting Levels 2–4 which will include training onsite work, bench work and site management. Apprenticeships in Shopfitting and Construction are available.

With experience you can apply for membership of the National Association of Shopfitters for further training. A Construction Skills Certification Scheme card is needed to prove you are qualified.

wood, glass, aluminium and plastic and you may also be working with many other professionals involved in construction such as engineers, architects, electricians and plumbers.

Your work can be hard and hours long.

Money guide

Your starting salary may be around £9,000 a year.

As a qualified shopfitter you may earn £18,000 a year and as an experienced shopfitter around £23,000 or more.

Related opportunities

■ Builder's Merchant/Assistant p480
■ Carpenter/Joiner p81
■ Furniture Manufacturer p225

Further information

ConstructionSkills
Bircham Newton, King's Lynn PE31 6XG
01485 577577; www.ckills.org

National Association of Shopfitters
NAS House, 411 Limpsfield Road, Warlingham CR6 6HA
01883 624961; www.shopfitters.org

www.cityandguilds.com/myperfectjob

SITE MANAGER/ CLERK OF WORKS

What the work involves

■ As a site manager/clerk of works you will be responsible for supervising all the onsite aspects of a construction contract.

■ You must ensure that good standards are maintained and that work is carried out efficiently and on time.

■ You will inspect and monitor materials, procedures and work so that the client is guaranteed quality and value for money.

■ You will also act as a superintendent, advising contractors about aspects of work and solving problems as they arise.

The type of person suited to this work

You should have an interest in construction.

You need to be responsible, organised and honest as you may be in control of projects involving large teams of workers and a variety of materials.

You should enjoy working outdoors and in all weather conditions.

You need to be physically fit and have a head for heights.

You should have excellent communication skills, be able to lead a team and to establish appropriate working relationships with contractor's staff.

You will need a keen eye for detail and to be thorough and vigilant in maintaining quality standards of work and material.

Working conditions

You will usually work around 40 hours a week, Monday to Friday. However you will frequently have to work at the weekend and during the evening depending on deadlines.

You will be based in a site office which will usually be a temporary structure. You will have to spend much of your time outdoors in all weather conditions.

When you are inspecting a site you might have to wear protective clothing such as a hard hat and work boots.

You may have to climb ladders and scaffolding or in tunnel construction, work underground.

Future prospects

As an experienced clerk of works you must take Continuing Professional Development. This is so that you can keep up-to-date with advances in areas such as new materials, practices, law and regulations, and health and safety issues.

Clerks of works can move up to roles in site management or other management roles in the construction industry.

You may have the opportunity to become self-employed and to work abroad.

Qualifications and courses

There are no set qualifications to become a clerk of works/site manager. However experience in a relevant industry is necessary such as construction or civil engineering. It is not normally something you can begin as soon as you leave school.

As well as experience you might need certain construction and civil engineering qualifications. This might include City & Guilds qualifications, NVQs Level 2 or 3, BTEC/SQA national award, a BTEC higher national award or a foundation or honours degree.

When you are working you can gain NVQs in Site Inspection at Levels 3 and 4. As you accumulate qualifications you can achieve levels of membership of the Institute of Clerks of Works: Student, Licentiate and Member; although this is not essential it is increasingly sought by employers. To enter each level of membership you will need to have a relevant qualification, a report of your professional history and a materials identification test.

Graduates may be taken on by companies as apprentices where they will learn on the job.

Advantages/disadvantages

You can choose to specialise in particular areas such as building, civil engineering or mechanical and electrical installations.

On-site inspection may be dusty, dirty and noisy.

Money guide

Your starting salary may be at around £20,000 a year.

With experience as a clerk of works you can earn over £25,000 a year and senior clerks may earn more than £35,000.

Related opportunities

■ Building Surveyor p79
■ Civil/Construction Engineer/Civil Engineering Technician p85
■ Construction Supervisor/Manager p90

Further information

Chartered Institute of Building
Englemere, Kings Ride, Ascot, Berkshire SL5 7TB
01344 630 700; reception@ciob.org.uk; www.ciob.org.uk

The Institute of Clerks of Works (ICW)
28 Commerce Road, Lynch Wood, Peterborough PE2 6LR
01733 564033; www.icwgb.org

City&
Guilds

www.cityandguilds.com/myperfectjob

Building and Construction

CRCI: BB

STEEPLEJACK

What the work involves

- Steeplejacks work on high structures including power station chimneys, cooling towers, oil refineries, factories and church spires.

- Your work on these structures will include climbing to high places with your tools to complete routine maintenance and repairing jobs or renovation projects.

- You will plan each job carefully. To ensure a safe and accessible working environment you will put in ladders, specialist scaffolding or industrial rope access (abseiling), work platforms (cradles) and bosun's seat (harness) and fall arrest devices.

- You will be working on both historic buildings and modern constructions, in urban and rural areas.

The type of person suited to this work

You should be organised as you will have to plan each project so that you know which safety equipment to use and which tools are required when you reach your elevated working area.

You absolutely must have a good head for heights to do this job and it is equally important that you can work in small or confined spaces (chimneys).

You will enjoy working outdoors in all weather conditions.

You will have good hand skills for installing rigging and using tools.

You will be very conscious of, and committed to, health and safety procedures.

Working conditions

Your working hours and shifts can vary and you might have to work during the evenings and weekends.

Your work will be physically demanding as it will involve rigging, climbing, carrying ladders and tools and working with your hands.

You will need to wear protective clothing and headgear.

You may have to work on industrial chimneys which can be extremely dusty, requiring respiratory equipment.

Future prospects

As a steeplejack you will probably work for construction firms that specialise in steeplejacking. These tend to be based in London, Middlesbrough, Manchester, Nottingham, Bristol, Cardiff, Edinburgh and Glasgow, and are likely to seek local employees.

With experience you will be eligible for promotion to a role as a supervisor or manager within a firm. With significant experience you can become self-employed, although this is not common.

You may be able to travel and increasingly you can find work abroad.

Qualifications and courses

There are no formal entry qualifications for this job but you will find it useful to have GCSEs/S grades (A*–E/1–5) in maths, English, science and technology for calculations, measurements and theory work. The Diploma in Construction and the Built Environment could also be useful.

Young entrants can train on the job with an employer or as an apprentice with an approved apprenticeship scheme. ConstructionSkills provide such opportunities. You will take aptitude tests in maths and problem solving and will be assessed for literacy and ability to work at heights. You will be sponsored by an employer and spend 6 months (over 2/3 years) at the residential National Construction College where you can gain NVQs in Accessing and Rigging, Levels 2 and 3, Key Skills Level 1 and various other CITB courses such as Health and Safety, Working at Heights certification and First Aid Certification.

If you are training with an employer you can also gain NVQs in Construction in Accessing and Rigging and Steeplejacking, Levels 2 and 3, at approved colleges and training centres.

Advantages/disadvantages

Currently in the UK there are there are between 800 and 1,000 steeplejacks. As a qualified steeplejack you may find work easily and there are plenty of opportunities in this area.

Your work may be hampered by weather conditions for example high winds may prevent access to structures and delay completion of projects.

Money guide

Your starting salary can be from around £15,000 a year. As an experienced steeplejack you may earn around £22,000 a year. If you become a senior engineer you can earn over £28,000 a year.

Related opportunities

- Bricklayer p76
- Scaffolder p119
- Stonemason p123

Further information

The Association of Technical Lighting and Access Specialists
4c St Mary's Place, The Lace Market, Nottingham NG1 1PH
0115 955 8818; info@atlas-org.uk; www.atlas.org.uk

City&
Guilds

www.cityandguilds.com/myperfectjob

STONEMASON

What the work involves

- Stonemasons cut and shape stone and fix it to buildings. Some work on new buildings, but many work on restoring and repairing old ones.

- There are three types of stonemason. Banker masons cut, shape and carve the stone, fixer masons assemble and fix stones into place and monumental masons make things such as plaques and headstones.

- While the work is manual and strenuous it is also highly creative.

The type of person suited to this work

Banker mason

As a banker mason, you have to be good with your hands to cut, shape and carve stone accurately. You also need artistic skills for producing decorative finishes.

Fixer mason

You must be physically fit so that you can lift the stones, although you will use special equipment to lift the heaviest ones. You must not mind working at heights.

Monumental mason

In this sector, you will be working closely with the funeral industry, so you need to be sensitive to people's requirements and have a good eye for design. It is also useful to be interested in architecture and history, as much of the work involves restoring old buildings.

Working conditions

Banker masons mainly work in a workshop, while fixer masons work on-site in all weather conditions and restoration masons work on monuments and listed buildings, often at heights.

All masonry work can be dusty and noisy and unsuitable for people who have allergies. You will need to follow health and safety procedures, including wearing protective clothing such as a mask, a hard hat and boots.

You are likely to work a normal working week, although extra work at weekends may also be available.

Future prospects

There is good demand for stonemasons in the UK.

You can choose to work for stonemasonry companies and larger building contractors. If you work for a small stonemasonry company you are likely to have to do both banking and fixing work.

After training you can decide to specialise in new building or restoration work. You can also specialise as a memorial mason, making and carving gravestones or take on supervisory and managerial roles.

Qualifications and courses

Training is provided on the job with part-time attendance at college or training centres to gain relevant NVQs/SVQs. Apprenticeships/Skillseekers may be available for those aged 16–24.

NVQs/SVQs at Levels 2 and 3 are available in relevant subjects (e.g. Architectural Stonemasonry, Carving, Heritage Skills), as well as City & Guilds Certificates. There is also a City & Guilds Diploma in Advanced Stonemasonry and the new NVQ/SVQ Level 3 in Heritage Skills. The Construction Industry Training Board (CITB) Construction Award in Stonemasonry allows those who have difficulties in gaining work experience to train for an NVQ.

Many employers on construction sites require workers to have a Construction Skills Certification Scheme (CSCS) card.

Advantages/disadvantages

The physical nature of the job, including working at heights, may be strenuous for some people.

You may have the opportunity to work on impressive restoration projects such as those on cathedrals.

It can make you proud to produce work on a building that will be admired for many years.

Money guide

As a new entrant you could earn between £8,000 and £14,400 per year. When trained and with some experience you could earn between £18,000 and £21,500. Senior and experienced stonemasons can achieve up to £30,000. Overtime is often available, and on some projects there are bonuses based on outputs.

Related opportunities

- Bricklayer p76
- Building Technician p80
- Dry Stone Waller p93

Further information

National Heritage Training Group
Carthusian Court, 12 Carthusian Street, London EC1M 6EZ
0300 456 5517; www.nhtg.org.uk

Stone Federation Great Britain
Channel Business Centre, Ingles Manor, Castle Hill Avenue, Folkestone C20 2RD
01303 856123; www.stone-federationgb.org.uk

www.cityandguilds.com/myperfectjob

STRUCTURAL ENGINEER

What the work involves

- Structural engineers design structures that are strong, durable and able to withstand the high pressure they are placed under.

- You will work with architects on the design and construction of a variety of structures including bridges, tunnels, domestic houses, office blocks or sports stadia.

- Among other tasks you will calculate the loads and stresses of a structure, analyse potential problems and test digital models to examine how they will endure influences such as wind, gravity and earth tremors.

- You will investigate soil conditions, visit construction sites, and undertake projects that involve demolition or repair of a structure.

The type of person suited to this work

You should be interested in the construction industry.

You should have an aptitude for problem-solving and analytical thinking.

You should also have strong skills in maths, physics and ICT.

You must have a keen eye for detail and accomplish your work efficiently and with the utmost accuracy.

You will need to be good at technical drawing and have 3D concept skills.

You must be able to work in a team as well as being able to work with other professionals from across the construction industry.

Working conditions

You will work a total of approximately 40 hours a week, Monday to Friday. At times you might have to work on the weekend.

You will work both in an office and out on site. This can be in all weather conditions and you will have to wear protective clothing such as a hard hat.

You will frequently have to travel from site to site and a driving licence may be useful for this.

Future prospects

Many employers provide training schemes for new structural engineers which allow you to work towards the specific core objectives necessary for you to achieve professional status, during your work placement.

You may follow a formal progression structure within an engineering organisation.

You can become self-employed although chartered status is necessary if you want to start up your own business.

Advantages/disadvantages

Despite the recent decline in the construction industry, many

Qualifications and courses

Structural engineers normally have a degree in engineering or a highly numerate science degree. This could be a 3-year BEng degree in structural engineering, civil engineering or general engineering and when you have completed this course you can directly become an incorporated engineer. To gain status as a chartered engineer you will need further academic qualifications.

To become a chartered engineer you will need a 4 year MEng degree in structural engineering, civil engineering or general engineering, accredited by the Engineering Council UK (ECUK). When you have qualified you will work alongside engineers as you train.

A Higher National Diploma in construction, civil engineering or other engineering subject must be combined with further studies before you acquire chartered or incorporated engineer status.

If you take a course that is not accredited you can go on to take an accredited postgraduate degree. A specialist Master's programme in structural engineering will allow you to increase your depth of knowledge in the discipline.

Apprenticeships may be available at technician level which will allow you to train on the job and take courses to gain qualifications and achieve incorporated and chartered status.

construction projects are planned in London and the South East.

Money guide

A typical starting salary is around £22,000.

With several years' experience this can rise to £36,000 and in a senior role of structural engineering you can earn in the region of £50,000.

Related opportunities

- Architect p71
- Civil Engineer p85
- Quantity Surveyor p115
- Surveying Technician p125

Further information

Association for Consultancy and Engineering (ACE)
Alliance House, 12 Caxton Street, London SW1H 0QL
020 7222 6557; consult@acenet.co.uk; www.acenet.co.uk

ConstructionSkills
Bircham Newton, King's Lynn, Norfolk PE31 6XG
01485 577577; www.cskills.org

The Institution of Structural Engineers (IStructE)
11 Upper Belgrave Street, London SW1X 8BH.
020 7235 4535; www.istructe.org.uk

SURVEYING TECHNICIAN

What the work involves

- Surveying technicians work alongside chartered surveyors, providing hands-on support across the full range of surveying specialisms including building, land, rural and commercial.

- You will be expected to carry out a range of administrative tasks associated with each project, such as putting together contracts and writing reports.

- You will also be using complex computer programs and technical equipment both onsite and in the office in order to create reports and survey drawings, and to assess various aspects of each project.

The type of person suited to this work

You will be working closely with other professionals and clients at all levels, so the ability to communicate both verbally and in written documents is vital.

Because you will be dealing with very specific technical issues in each project, you will need to have an accurate and methodical approach to work, good numerical skills and the ability to multi-task and think on your feet.

You will need a good level of ICT skills, and confidence in using the wide range of sophisticated equipment required for the job.

Knowledge of business, law and health and safety-related regulations are also desirable.

Working conditions

Working hours usually follow those of a normal office job, but you will occasionally be called to work early mornings, evenings and at weekends during busy times or for certain site visits.

Most of the work is office based, but you will also spend time working onsite. This means you must be prepared to get cold, wet, muddy and dusty, and wear appropriate safety equipment at all times.

You will be carrying out a lot of complex technical tasks which require excellent concentration and can be quite tiring.

Future prospects

You could work with central or local government, large construction firms, smaller surveying companies or even financial businesses, and art and antiques auction houses.

You could progress to become a consultant, a partner in a firm or even move into related sectors such as town planning or chartered surveying with the right qualifications. Self-employment is also an option.

Advantages/disadvantages

You will be providing invaluable support on a number of important projects, so should have job satisfaction.

Qualifications and courses

ENTRY 5 LEVEL

Entry to this profession is usually with a degree or diploma, preferably one that is accredited by the Royal Institution of Chartered Surveyors (RICS). For a degree course, the usual qualifications needed are a minimum of 1 A level or a relevant BTEC/SQA National award. You can also obtain a job by studying towards NVQ Level 4 in quantity surveying practice, valuation, spatial data management or town planning whilst doing work experience.

To become a chartered member of RICS you need to complete a 2 year Assessment of Professional Competence (APC).

The Chartered Surveyors Training Trust offers work-based training for young people aged 16–24 in London and the south-east of England. Applicants must have a minimum of 4 GCSEs (A*–C) or equivalent.

Once you have qualified as a surveying technician, further training is possible in the form of NVQs through which you could specialise in an area such as construction or the built environment.

There is the opportunity to become self-employed, or work overseas.

Earning potential is not as high as some other roles in surveying.

Hours can be long and unpredictable at busy times.

Money guide

Starting salaries range from £17,000 to £21,000 per year. With experience, this will rise to £24,000–£30,000. Becoming a partner in a firm can see earnings increase to £40,000+. Salaries are generally higher in London.

Related opportunities

- Quantity Surveyor p115
- Chartered Surveyor p84
- Construction Supervisor/Manager p90
- Civil/Construction Engineer/Civil Engineering Technician p85

Further information

Chartered Surveyors Training Trust
16th floor, The Tower Building, 11 York Road,
London SE1 7NX
020 7871 0454; www.cstt.org.uk; cstt@cstt.org.uk

Royal Institution of Chartered Surveyors
12 Great George Street, Parliament Square, London
SW1P 3AD
0870 333 1600; www.rics.org/careers; contactrics@rics.org

Association of Building Engineers
Lutyens House, Billing Brook Road, Weston Favell NN3 8NW
0845 126 1058; www.abe.org.uk;
building.engineers@abe.org.uk

THATCHER

What the work involves

- Thatching is the covering of roofs with plant stems such as water reed, combed wheat reed and long straw.

- Your tasks will include removing old thatched roofs and replacing them, thatching new roofs and repairing or re-thatching existing thatched roofs.

- Your work will involve using many different tools, including mallets, hooks, needles, knives and shears.

- As thatchers work outside all year round, your hours will differ depending on the season.

The type of person suited to this work

You need to have good practical skills to be able to use the specialised tools and equipment, and to develop an expertise in the craft. You must also be physically fit so that you can climb ladders and scaffolding whilst carrying thatching materials. You will need to be comfortable working at heights.

It is important to be able to measure roofs accurately so you can work out the required amount of thatching material. Communication skills are necessary for talking to customers and planning officers. You will also need to be interested in learning a traditional rural craft.

Working conditions

You will work outdoors on roofs in rural locations in most weather conditions. The work can be dusty, which can be difficult if you suffer from certain allergies.

It is important that you follow health and safety procedures closely when working on roofs.

Your working hours are likely to vary according to when the work is available. This can be seasonal work, meaning you will be busiest during the spring and summer months when the weather is best.

Future prospects

There are about 500 thatcher businesses in the UK and, as about a half of all thatched buildings are protected and need to be re-roofed every 15–20 years, there is a steady demand for thatching work. However, there is fierce competition for training vacancies and some thatchers have another job to supplement their income. Not all areas of the UK have thatched buildings so you might have to relocate to find work.

It can take a number of years to become highly skilled. Many thatchers become self-employed once they are fully trained.

Advantages/disadvantages

Working at heights may be demanding for some people and potentially dangerous.

It is rewarding to work in an ancient craft and create thatched roofs that are both functional and decorative.

If you have allergies, this work could be difficult for you.

You may need a second job to supplement your earnings.

Qualifications and courses

There are no set entry requirements. It may help to have GCSEs/S grades (A*–E/1–5) in English, maths and ICT, which are useful for running small businesses. The Diploma in Construction and the Built Environment could be useful for this type of work.

Herefordshire College of Technology has a New Entrants Training Scheme aimed at candidates aged 16–25 working in rural areas. Candidates must have recently started working in the industry and be based in a rural area. The scheme takes 2 years and leads to NVQ/SVQ Level 2 in Thatching. An optional third year leading to NVQ/SVQ Level 3 is available, which places greater emphasis on the skills of thatching, covering the detailing and decorative effects.

The Construction Industry Training Board offers a Construction Award in Thatching which takes 2 years. Once completed you can progress to the NVQ at Level 2.

Money guide

Earnings vary according to the county and employer. A trainee earns around £14,000 a year. An experienced thatcher can earn £17,000–£23,000. £35,000+ is possible for very experienced thatchers able to negotiate their own contracts. Self-employed thatchers have more freedom when it comes to what they can charge.

Related opportunities

- Dry Stone Waller p93
- Mastic Asphalter p108
- Roofer p117
- Stonemason p123

Further information

Lantra
Lantra House, Stoneleigh Park, Coventry, CV8 2LG
024 7669 6996; www.lantra.co.uk

National Heritage Training Group
Carthusian Court, 12 Carthusian Street, London
EC1M 6EZ
0300 456 5517; www.nhtg.org.uk

Thatching Advisory Services
The Old Stables, Redenham Park Farm, Redenham, Andover SP11 9AQ
01264 773820; www.thatchingadviseryservices.co.uk

THERMAL INSULATION ENGINEER

What the work involves

- You will use various types of insulation to either prevent heat loss or keep heat out within different types of products and equipment, such as boilers, pipework, refrigeration or air conditioning.

- The types of insulation you will use will be dependent on the actual project but could involve silicate or foam.

- You will measure, cut and shape insulating materials to fit around pipes, boilers and duct work. Once the item is insulated, you will cover it using sheet metal or another cladding material.

- You will assess clients' needs and advise them on the best plan to solve their insulation problem.

The type of person suited to this work

You may be exposed to some potentially dangerous materials, so you must follow health and safety regulations carefully.

Much of the work involves strenuous lifting, balancing and climbing up scaffolding, so you will have to be physically fit.

The ability to work in a team and get on with other people will be important as you will often work alongside other professionals from the construction and engineering industries.

You should be able to understand instructions, have a practical approach to your work and enjoy using manual skills.

Working conditions

You could be working indoors or outside at heights, in places that are cramped or difficult to access.

You may be exposed to harmful substances and be working in dusty and dirty environments, so you will wear protective clothing, like goggles and sometimes a face mask.

You will normally work a standard 38-hour week, but overtime and evening or weekend work might be required.

Travelling around the country to visit different sites and projects may be necessary.

Future prospects

The energy conservation industry is expanding and there is growth in the demand for qualified thermal insulation engineers to work on a wide range of engineering and construction projects.

After gaining training and experience, you could find a job within building, building service engineering or specialised energy conservation companies.

Within the larger companies it might be possible to progress into supervisory posts and work abroad can be available.

Qualifications and courses

Although no formal qualifications are required, employers usually require GCSEs/S grades in English, maths, science and an engineering or construction subject.

It is possible to enter this career from an Apprenticeship opportunity if you are aged 16–24.

You will have to pass an entry test after which you will undertake on-the-job and off-the-job training at college. Your employer could use a training programme provided by the Insulation and Environmental Training Agency.

It is also helpful if you can evidence some practical work experience when applying.

NVQs/SVQs in Thermal Insulation Engineering are available at Levels 2–3, Level 2 certificate in Thermal Insulation and Key Skills in Communication, Application of Number and IT are also available to aid a job application.

Advantages/disadvantages

You will be working alongside people from different industries.

You will need many different skills to complete one job.

You may need to stay away from home – this could be difficult if you have family commitments.

Opportunities are good and overseas work may be possible.

Money guide

Whilst training, your earnings will range from £9,000 to £16,000 a year. With qualifications this rises to between £19,000 and £22,000. Senior thermal insulation engineers can earn up to £30,000. Expenses may be paid when you need to stay away from home during a project.

Related opportunities

- Damp Proofer p91
- Gas Network Engineer p226
- Heating and Ventilating Engineer/Gas Service Technician p102
- Plumber p113

Further information

ConstructionSkills
Bircham Newton, King's Lynn PE31 6RH
0300 456 7577, www.cskills.org, www.bconstructive.co.uk

www.cityandguilds.com/myperfectjob

TOWN PLANNER/ PLANNING TECHNICIAN

What the work involves

Town planner

- You will manage and develop urban or rural areas to best serve the population. When deciding how to use the land, you will take into account commercial, social, environmental and heritage needs.

Town planning technician

- You will support the work of town planners.

- You will carry out surveys, map areas, record information, analyse and present reports, and provide advice on planning permission.

The type of person suited to this work

You will need excellent communication skills as you will need to explain your ideas clearly and produce comprehensive written reports.

You must be organised with good research, problem-solving and analytical skills to investigate the potential effects of different proposals for land use.

Specialist skills required include competency in graphic design, desktop publishing and familiarity with computer-aided design (CAD), geographical information systems (GIS) and cartography.

Working conditions

Regular office hours are likely, although you may sometimes need to attend meetings in the evening.

Most town planners are based in offices but often go out on site visits. A driving licence might be necessary.

Future prospects

There is a huge demand for more qualified planners in the UK and overseas.

Most employers are local authorities and planning consultancies, but opportunities also exist within central government, construction companies and environmental organisations. With experience, you may be promoted to senior or chief town planner, or move into related careers such as recreation management, market research or property development.

Advantages/disadvantages

It is satisfying to deal with public problems and to improve the environment in which people live and work.

It can be frustrating to compromise on planning initiatives. Dealing with angry or upset members of the public can be difficult.

Money guide

The starting salary for a trainee technician can range from £15,000 to £17,000, and can reach about £25,000

Qualifications and courses

Town planning technician

There are no set qualifications, but at least 4 GCSEs (A*–C) including English and maths, are usually required. Many entrants also have A levels, Foundation degrees or other qualifications. The Diploma in Construction and the Built Environment or in Environmental and Land-based Studies may also be useful. Planning technicians are trained on the job and may also undertake part-time study. Technical Membership of the Royal Town Planning Institute (RTPI) requires a recognised qualification at NVQ Level 3 or higher and 2 years' work experience.

Town planner

It is necessary to have a RTPI accredited qualification such as a first degree or a postgraduate qualification. For degree entry you will need 2 A levels and at least 5 GCSEs (A*–C), including English and maths. Some institutions also offer a 12 month fast track course. The Diploma in Construction and the Built Environment or in Environmental and Land-based Studies may also be useful. For entry to a postgraduate course, a related degree in subjects such as geography, architecture or statistics is required. Full membership of the RTPI is given after completion of an accredited qualification, and 2 years' relevant work experience.

when qualified. Experienced technicians can earn up to £32,000.

Newly graduated town planners could earn 16,000–£28,000. Senior planners can earn £20,000–34,000. Principal planners or heads of a team can earn £29,000–£41,000. Chief planning officers, heads of department and company directors can earn £50,000–£80,000.

Local authorities, especially in London and the south east, pay the higher amounts in these salary ranges if there is a shortage of planners.

Related opportunities

- Land/Geomatic Surveyor p107
- Planning and Development Surveyor p111

Further information

Royal Town Planning Institute
41 Botolph Lane, London EC3R 8DL
020 7929 9494; www.rtpi.org.uk

Royal Town Planning Institute in Scotland
57 Melville Street, Edinburgh EH3 7HL
0131 226 1959; www.rtpi.org.uk/rtpi in Scotland

WALL/FLOOR TILER

What the work involves

- You will fit tiles in various locations, from bathrooms and kitchens to hospitals and swimming pools.

- You may work with many kinds of tile including ceramic, stone, glass, terracotta, granite, marble and mosaic.

- First you will set out (mark) an area by calculating the amount of tile and adhesive needed. You will then use bench-mounted or hand tools to cut the tiles to the correct size and shape.

- You will level the surface with plaster, cement or sand, fix the tiles in the correct position and then fill in the gaps with grout.

The type of person suited to this work

Maths skills are essential as you will need to measure and calculate how much material you will need. You must work carefully and accurately. It is important to match colours and patterns, so a flair for design is useful.

You need to be physically fit for carrying the materials, and for working on your hands and knees.

You need to be able to work on your own initiative as well as in a team. You should be presentable and pleasant when dealing with customers.

Working conditions

You will work mainly indoors in a variety of locations, including people's homes, offices, factories and construction-sites. A driving licence might be useful.

You may work a normal working week, but you may also need to work evenings or weekends so that you can tile walls and floors without disrupting businesses.

As you will use special cutting tools and adhesives, you will need to be aware of health and safety procedures.

Future prospects

Work is available with specialist tiling companies and building contractors, or you may choose to become self-employed, providing services to individuals or sub-contracting to organisations. Demand for tilers depends on the economy.

It is possible to specialise in using one type of tiling, for example flooring tiles, mosaic work or bathrooms.

With experience, you may progress to technical, supervisory or managerial positions.

Advantages/disadvantages

You will be on your hands and knees, sometimes working in dusty, dirty or cramped conditions.

The work is varied and you can achieve spectacular results using coloured and textured tiles to decorate walls and floors.

Qualifications and courses

ENTRY 1 LEVEL

No specific qualifications are required, although GCSEs/S grades (A*–E) may be useful in subjects like maths, technology or English. Similar subjects may be needed to be eligible for an Apprenticeship or equivalent vocational qualifications like the Edexcel Introductory Certificate or the Diploma in Construction and the Built Environment.

Certain schools also offer 14–16-year olds the Foundation Certificate in building craft operations by the Construction Awards Alliance (CAA).

You will be trained on the job while working towards qualifications. This may also involve going to a college or training centre on day or block release.

NVQs in Wall and Floor Tiling at Levels 2 and 3 are available.

Apprenticeships may be available to those aged 16–24. In Scotland, applicants for a construction Apprenticeship need to take a selection test.

It is becoming increasingly necessary to have a Construction Skills Certification Scheme (CSCS) card to work in construction. Eligibility for this card depends on your qualifications and experience. Check the CSCS website for more details on this scheme.

Money guide

Salaries are around £18,000 per year and this can rise to £26,000 with experience. £40,000 is possible for the highest earners. Overtime is often available, and on some projects there are bonuses based on outputs, which can lead to higher earnings.

Related opportunities

- Building Technician p80
- Carpet Fitter p462
- Floor Layer p100
- Construction Operative p88

Further information

ConstructionSkills
Bircham Newton, King's Lynn PE31 6RH
01485 577577; www.bconstructive.co.uk;
www.constructionskills.net

The Tile Association
Forum Court, 83 Copers Cope Road, Beckenham BR3 1NR
020 8663 0946; www.tiles.org.uk

City&Guilds

www.cityandguilds.com/myperfectjob

WASTEWATER TREATMENT PLANT OPERATOR

What the work involves

- Water treatment plant operators monitor wastewater as it goes through various treatment processes which remove harmful substances. They ensure that treated water is returned to the water cycle and that wastewater is removed and destroyed as appropriate.

- You will be responsible for the operation and maintenance of the plant, ensuring that septic tanks, filters and screens are disinfected, checking water samples, and adding treatment micro-organisms and chemicals to the water when necessary.

- You will conduct tests on samples, take readings from monitors and adjust treatment equipment as necessary.

- You will work with a team composed of a supervisor, senior technicians, engineers and a manager.

The type of person suited to this work

You need to have a passion for the environment, science and technology.

You need to be able to communicate effectively and work well in a team.

You should be able to follow health and safety regulations.

You must be organised and methodical as you will be testing samples to ensure that harmful substances are removed from the water cycle.

You also need to be happy to work with new technology which you will use on a daily basis.

It is important that you are fit and active as you may be doing practical strenuous work at times, such as cleaning and maintenance.

Working conditions

You will work approximately 37 hours a week. Overtime may be possible but part-time work is rare. You will probably have to work shifts as water treatment plants operate 24 hours a day. You may have to join a call-out rota to cover nights and weekends.

You will be based indoors in control rooms but some of your work will involve being outside in all weather conditions. You may also have to carry out work at heights or in confined spaces.

Protective clothing is provided. This may include a breathing apparatus, and should be worn to prevent contact with harmful substances.

Future prospects

After gaining experience, you could progress to a role as a supervisor and from there to roles as an inspector, a superintendent or a plant manager. You may also choose to move into a related area such as treatment plant design.

Qualifications and courses

There are no formal academic qualifications required to become a wastewater treatment plant operator. However some companies seek employees with a minimum of 4 GCSEs/S grade (A*–E/ 1–5) in maths, English and a science or technology subject.

You can train by doing a Water Industry Apprenticeship. The minimum age is generally 18. You may also pursue a Diploma in Environmental and Land-based Studies.

You can also take a course with City & Guilds to improve your skills, including the Level 2 Certificate for Water Sector Competent Operators.

An important qualification for a wastewater treatment plant operator is the NVQ in Operating a Process Plant (Water), Level 2. You can also gain an NVQ in Utilities Control Centre Operations, Level 2. You may choose to pursue an HND/C or degree which will qualify you for more senior roles.

You can also take a Higher National Certificate, Diploma or degree which will allow you to move to higher positions.

Advantages/disadvantages

You may find opportunities to increase wages by taking extra shifts, going on stand-by and doing overtime.

Your working environment in the plant may be smelly and wet.

Money guide

Your salary as a trainee can start at around £11,000 a year.

With experience you can earn from £16,000 to £22,000.

As a supervisor you may earn more than £25,000.

Related opportunities

- Brewery Worker p220
- Oil/gas Drilling Engineer p238
- Water/Sewerage Network Operative p131

Further information

Energy and Utility Skills Limited
Friars Gate, 1011 Stratford Road, Shirley, Solihull
B90 4BN
0845 077 9922; enquiries@euskills.co.uk;
www.euskills.co.uk

City & Guilds
1 Giltspur Street, London EC1A 9DD
enquiry@cityandguilds.com; www.cityandguilds.com

Water UK
1 Queen Anne's Gate, London SW1H 9BT
020 7344 1844 www.water.org.uk

WATER/SEWERAGE NETWORK OPERATIVE

What the work involves

- Water/sewerage network operatives lay, maintain and repair the pipework that carries drinking water, waste water and sewage.

- Your tasks might include digging trenches in roads and relaying them afterwards, putting up barriers and warning signs, laying pipes, repairing leaks, clearing blockages and installing water meters.

- You will use a range of tools such as welding equipment to join pipes together and machinery such as mechanical diggers.

The type of person suited to this work

You must have good practical skills and be mechanically minded so that you can use tools, equipment and machinery effectively. You must be able to follow health and safety regulations as working on-site can be dangerous. You will have to follow plans and instructions accurately, so that systems are installed correctly and safely.

You must be fit and active for bending, kneeling and carrying materials and equipment.

You will have to deal with complaints from the public, who might be upset that their water services are disrupted. You must also be able to work in a team with other water/sewerage network operatives. You may need a driving licence.

Working conditions

You will work outdoors in all weather conditions. The work can be dusty, dirty and wet, as well as smelly.

You will need to follow strict health, safety and hygiene regulations, which may include wearing a breathing apparatus, a safety helmet, boots and gloves.

You may work normal working hours or shifts, but the particular hours you work will vary according to the needs of the job and the hours of daylight available. You may be on-call 24/7 in case of emergency repairs.

Future prospects

There is strong demand for water/sewerage network operatives because the privatised water companies, who manage water supply and sewerage disposal, are investing money in developing their systems.

You can find work with water companies and construction firms across the UK.

After gaining experience, you could progress to a role as team leader or supervisor.

You could move into related areas such as water distribution inspection work.

Qualifications and courses

There are no formal entry requirements, but you might need 4 GCSEs/S grades (A*–C/1–3) including maths, English, science or technology.

Relevant experience, for example in site maintenance work, is useful. Registration in an appropriate safety passport scheme could be required by many employers to be able to work on-site.

Entrants are trained on the job, and may work towards vocational qualifications. An NVQ/SVQ Level 2 is available in Water Distribution. CABWI offers a range of relevant NVQs, including Distribution Control Level 2, Operating Process Plant (Water) Level 2, Leakage Control Level 3 and Maintaining Water Supply Level 3.

Apprenticeships/Skillseekers may be available for people aged 16–24. The scheme starts with basic preliminary training, with apprentices usually working towards NVQs/SVQs at Level 2 in subjects such as customer care, water distribution, construction and technical drawing.

Advantages/disadvantages

The work can be physically demanding for some people, and it can get smelly if you are working on sewerage systems.

Helping to provide people with an essential service can be rewarding.

Money guide

Trainees earn around £10,000–£11,000 a year. This can rise to £17,000 for fully trained operatives with 1 year's experience. With additional experience earnings can increase to £25,000 or more. Earnings vary depending on your employer and in which part of the country you work.

Related opportunities

- Construction Operative p88
- Gas Network Engineer p226
- Plumber p113

Further information

Energy and Utility Skills
Friars Gate Two, 1011 Stratford Road, Solihull B90 4BN
0845 077 9922; www.euskills.co.uk

Water UK
1 Queen Anne's Gate, London SW1H 9BT
020 7344 1844; www.water.org.uk

www.cityandguilds.com/myperfectjob

WINDOW INSTALLER

What the work involves

- Window fitters install windows into new and existing buildings.

- You will use hand and power tools to take out any old windows and fit new ones. You will work with materials such as glass, plastic and wood.

- Once you have fixed a new window into the allocated space, you will need to give it a weatherproof seal.

- Your job may also involve fitting doors and conservatories, and weatherboarding.

The type of person suited to this work

You will need good practical hand skills for using tools and you will need to be physically fit as you will be lifting and carrying windows. Maths skills are essential in order to make accurate calculations and fit frames properly.

You should be safety conscious and comfortable working on ladders.

You may work on your own for some jobs, but you will often work with one other window fitter or in a small team, so you must be able to work with others. You should also be able to get on with customers, because you will spend a lot of time on their premises.

Working conditions

You will work indoors and outdoors in a variety of locations, and you will be working in most weather conditions. A driving licence may be useful.

You will need to pay attention to health and safety, especially when working with glass, and be happy clearing up after your work has finished.

You are likely to work normal working hours during the week, but overtime may be available at weekends.

Future prospects

Work is available throughout the UK. There is an increasing demand for double-glazed windows and for conservatories so job prospects are high.

After gaining sufficient experience, you may progress to team leader or supervisory positions. You could also run your own window-fitting business. You may choose to specialise in fire-proof glazing or film application (applying film to glass for privacy). There are also openings within the sales and marketing sides of the industry.

Advantages/disadvantages

Lifting and carrying windows and working at heights may be difficult for some people.

You will get to travel to many different locations in your job.

It is satisfying to make customers happy by improving the

Qualifications and courses

There are no formal entry requirements, but you might need some GCSEs/S grades; English, maths and technology are useful or equivalent qualifications such as the Diploma in Construction and the Built Environment.

Apprenticeship/Skillseekers may be available for people aged 16–24. Applicants normally need GCSEs/S grades (A*–E/1–5), or an equivalent qualification such as Intermediate GNVQ or First Diploma. Proskills, the Sector Skills Council, is currently promoting Apprenticeships in the glass industry.

Initial training is provided by employers and covers removing and fitting window frames, health and safety, customer relations and relevant paperwork.

You can gain vocational qualifications while you work. You will be taught practical skills and may work towards NVQs/SVQs in Fenestration Installation at Level 2, Fenestration Installation and Surveying at Level 3, and Glazing Installation and Maintenance at Levels 2–3.

Glass Training Limited (GTL) provides a list of relevant glass related NVQs on their website.

appearance, value and function of their buildings by installing and repairing windows.

Money guide

You can expect an average salary of around £14,000–£18,000, once you have qualified. £22,000–£26,000 is likely to be earned by a competent installer, and £30,000 could be earned by supervisors or managers. Earnings will depend on where you work and the size of the organisation.

Related opportunities

- Carpenter/Joiner p81
- Carpet Fitter p462
- Ceiling Fixer p83
- Glazier p101

Further information

Proskills UK
Centurion Court, 85b Milton Park, Abingdon OX14 4RY
01235 833844; www.proskills.co.uk

Glass and Glazing Federation
44–48 Borough High Street, London SE1 1XB
0870 042 4255; www.ggf.co.uk

City&
Guilds

www.cityandguilds.com/myperfectjob

Catering and Hospitality

Working in this sector, you will meet a wide variety of people and probably need to be a very strong team player. Workers in the sector thrive on providing an impeccable service and ensuring customers are completely satisfied and are given a wonderful experience whether that is in a restaurant, hotel or bar.

In this section we look at the following jobs:

For similar jobs to the ones in this section why not have a look at *Leisure, Sport and Tourism* starting on page 383 and *Retail Sales and Customer Services* from page 477.

BAR MANAGER/LICENSEE/ PUBLICAN

What the work involves

- Your duties will include the recruitment, training and management of staff. You will also deal with the accounts, stock replenishment, and maintaining links with suppliers and business development.

- You will need to keep up to date with any changes to licensing laws and other legal requirements such as health and safety or fire safety regulations, and ensure that your customers and staff adhere to them.

- In addition, you will demonstrate a high level of customer service to ensure client satisfaction.

The type of person suited to this work

It is essential to have excellent communication skills and to enjoy meeting and speaking to people of all ages. A confident, professional attitude is needed to deal with customer or supplier problems.

Being physically fit and able to stay on your feet all day is helpful. You should be practical, flexible and good at multi-tasking.

Good numeracy skills are expected as you will be managing cash on a daily basis. Finally, you should keep up to date with legal requirements, and enforce those that affect you.

Working conditions

Although pubs, clubs and bars can remain open for 24 hours a day, most only extend their hours at weekends or for special events.

You will work long hours in an environment which can be busy, noisy and hot. You will be required to stand for lengthy periods and lift and carry heavy items such as barrels.

You may have to deal with demanding or difficult customers who are intoxicated. Changes to smoking legislation have resulted in the need to provide outside facilities, where problems might occur.

Future prospects

A publican can own, lease or become a tenant of their premises. You can be a manager on behalf of a brewery of different premises like high street chains, family establishments, café bars or themed pubs and restaurants across the country.

With experience, you could progress to managing a nightclub or even manage a bar overseas.

Advantages/disadvantages

The hours will be long and irregular, which might affect your personal life.

You will have to deal with drunk customers, who may be difficult or aggressive, on a fairly regular basis.

Qualifications and courses

You can start as a bar person from the age of 18, and progress to a supervisory or management position. NVQs/SVQs are available in Bar Service (Level 2), in Food and Drink Service (Level 2), Hospitality Supervision (Level 3) and On-Licensed Premises Management (Level 4). The BTEC First and National Certificate/Diploma in Hospitality or the Diploma in Hospitality are also relevant. You could study for an HNC/HND, Foundation degree or degree in a related subject such as hospitality management with licensed retail or take an apprenticeship in Drinks Service.

In England and Wales new entrants to on-licensed premises are required by law to take the Level 2 National Certificate for Personal Licence Holders. This is available from the British Institute of Inn-keeping Awarding Body (BIIAB). In Scotland, you must take the Scottish Certificate for Personal Licence Holders from the BIIAB.

Money guide

Earnings vary according to the location, type and size of the premises you work in.

The average starting salary for a trainee manager is £14,000–£15,000, but with experience this can increase to between £22,000 and £30,000.

If you work within a very successful and large establishment, it is possible to earn up to £50,000.

Related opportunities

- Brewer Worker p217
- Catering/Restaurant Manager/Maître d'hôtel p135
- Hotel Manager p141
- Waiting Staff p146

Further information

British Institute of Innkeeping
Wessex House, 80 Park House, Camberley GU15 3PT
01276 684449; www.biiab.org

British Beer and Pub Association
Market Towers, 1 Nine Elms Lane, London SW8 5NQ
020 7627 9191; www.beerandpub.com

Wine & Spirit Education Trust
International Wine & Spirit Centre, 39–45 Bermondsey Street, London SE1 3XF
020 7089 3800; www.wset.co.uk

City& Guilds

www.cityandguilds.com/myperfectjob

CATERING/RESTAURANT MANAGER/ MAÎTRE D'HÔTEL

What the work involves

■ You will manage, train and employ staff in a kitchen or restaurant. A maître d'hôtel is specifically responsible for running a hotel restaurant.

■ Part of your work will involve planning menus, checking stocks of food and drink and ordering fresh supplies when needed. You will be expected to handle paperwork, manage budgets and organise staff rotas.

■ You will be responsible for the health and safety of both your staff and customers.

The type of person suited to this work

You will be dealing with kitchen staff, suppliers and other business professionals, so you should be confident and have excellent communication skills. It is essential to provide good customer service at all times.

As you will be involved with preparing food for the public you will be required to follow and keep up-to-date with health and safety laws. You will also need an interest in service delivery and food.

Good management skills, including an understanding of the different roles undertaken by your staff, are essential. Exceptional organisational abilities are also necessary.

You will also need good numeracy skills as you will be managing a budget and working out stock quantities.

Working conditions

Much of your time will be spent in your kitchen or restaurant, which can get very hot and busy. Expect to be on your feet for long periods of time.

You might wear a uniform or protective clothing and regularly work unsocial hours. It is important to follow high standards of food safety and hygiene.

It is possible to work as a catering manager in the Armed Forces, in which case you might find yourself working in challenging environments, anywhere in the world, in a variety of climates.

Future prospects

Currently there is a shortage of restaurant managers across the UK so prospects are good. The sector offers a wide range of career opportunities and quick progression. However, it will help your career if you work in increasingly bigger and well-known premises.

Some restaurant/catering managers move on to running their own businesses, either a restaurant or private contract catering company.

Advantages/disadvantages

You will be working in a fun and lively atmosphere.

Qualifications and courses

You can start in a job as a kitchen assistant, waiter/waitress, chef or cook and work your way up. People working in the industry can take NVQs/ SVQs, for example Hospitality Supervision at Level 3.

Many hotels and hotel chains offer training schemes. It may be possible to join a scheme with A levels/H grades or equivalent, but the usual requirement is a degree or HND/C in a relevant subject (for example hospitality management, hospitality and catering, hotel management, international hospitality management). Minimum requirements for degree entry are usually 5 GCSEs/S grades (A*–C/1–3) and 2 A levels or 3 H grades. Postgraduate courses are also available.

You might have the chance to organise the catering for special events such as weddings or parties.

This can be a very busy job where you will be doing several tasks at the same time.

Hours are long and will include weekend or evening work.

Money guide

Salary rates vary depending on the type and size of restaurant, location and level of responsibility. Salaries tend to be higher in London and large cities.

Starting salaries for assistant managers are £15,000–£25,000. With experience, and in a large restaurant, this can rise to £35,000–£50,000.

A senior manager in the most successful premises can earn £50,000–£70,000.

Related opportunities

■ Food Safety Officer p139
■ Events and Exhibition Organiser p411
■ Kitchen/Assistant Supervisor p145

Further information

People 1st
2nd Floor, Armstrong House, 38 Market Square, Uxbridge UB8 1LH
01895 817000; www.people1st.co.uk

Institute of Hospitality
Trinity Court, 34 West Street, Sutton SM1 1SH
020 8661 4900; www.instituteofhospitality.org

www.cityandguilds.com/myperfectjob

Catering and Hospitality

CRCI: C

CELLAR TECHNICIAN

What the work involves

- You will set up and maintain the systems that keep alcoholic and soft drinks at a consistent quality in pubs, hotels and other sites.

- Visiting a range of locations, you will install equipment such as high-pressure gas systems, and check that they are compatible with existing water, electricity supply or drainage systems.

- You will undertake regular maintenance checks to make sure that everything works properly, train the staff on how to operate it and deal with any problems.

The type of person suited to this work

You will need good practical skills and the confidence to work and operate different systems quickly and efficiently. As you will be handling heavy equipment, a good level of physical fitness is helpful. Good communication skills are useful, as is a confidence in your ability to do the job well.

As you will be providing a service on behalf of your company for lots of different licensed premises you will need to have excellent customer care skills.

Working conditions

You will spend lots of time driving from site to site. Some of your work will be attending emergency call-outs which could include evenings and weekends. The extended pub opening hours might mean this includes 24-hour call-out duties.

You will work in dark, cramped conditions using specialist tools and equipment such as electrical testing devices.

Future prospects

There is a steady demand for experienced cellar technicians. The main employers are breweries, drink-dispensing equipment manufacturers and soft drinks manufacturers. Many applicants come from the licensed trade who have watched the job and become interested. It is therefore useful to have pub experience or relevant qualifications before applying.

With experience you can apply for senior/managerial posts or move into other areas of the licensed or food and drink sector such as sales.

Advantages/disadvantages

This job combines meeting and training people and lots of practical work.

You might have to travel long distances to reach customers.

You might work in uncomfortable conditions, for example when fitting a new dispensing system in a cellar.

Qualifications and courses

It is necessary to have a British Institute of Innkeeping Awarding Body (BIIAB) Level 2 National Certificate for Cellar Service Installation and Maintenance. The Certificate is awarded after the completion of a 5 day course and modular examinations.

Once you have acquired a certificate, you can take NVQs in Cellar Service at Level 2 and Drinks Dispense Systems (installation and maintenance) at Level 3. Some employers prefer candidates with GCSEs in maths, science or technology subjects.

The following qualifications are also useful: NVQ Levels 2 or 3, City & Guilds or BTEC First or National awards. Some employers in particular may prefer electrical or electronic engineering.

Employers provide training that covers areas such as health and safety, customer care, refrigeration, checking systems and working with equipment. Cask Marque offers a 1-day course in cellar management.

Money guide

The starting salary is normally around £18,000 per year. With experience this can increase to £25,000–£30,000. The highest salary for a cellar technician is about £35,000. You might also be paid overtime for emergency call-out duties or for working in the evenings or at weekends.

Related opportunities

- Bar Manager/Licensee/Publican p134
- Brewery Worker p220
- Plumber p113

Further information

British Soft Drinks Association
20–22 Stukeley Street, London WC2B 5LR
020 7430 0356; www.britishsoftdrinks.com

People 1st
2nd Floor, 38 Market Square, Uxbridge UB8 1LH
01895 817000; www.people1st.co.uk

City & Guilds

www.cityandguilds.com/myperfectjob

CHEF/SOUS CHEF

What the work involves

- Chefs and sous chefs cook for restaurants, cafés, bars, cruise ships and catering firms. Some also work for specialist food companies, helping to create new products.

- You will coordinate kitchen activities and supervise the preparation of food by your team of kitchen staff.

- Commis chefs are trainee chefs. Sous chefs are second in command of the kitchen. They will be required to recruit and train kitchen staff.

- Planning new menus and dishes, checking stocks of food and drink and dealing with suppliers are also included in the sous chef role.

The type of person suited to this work

Kitchens can be hot and hectic environments, therefore you need to be able to remain calm under pressure.

Good team working, communication and multi-tasking skills are important to ensure the smooth running of the operation. As you are responsible for the health and safety of your team, you must also be vigilant at all times.

You should have excellent cooking skills, be very creative and have a passion for food. It is also helpful if you want to try out new things and set trends. Good numeracy skills are also required to measure ingredients, and in order to manage budgets and stock levels.

Working conditions

Most of your work will be within a kitchen, which will be hot, busy and noisy. You will be required to use equipment and cutting tools that can be dangerous if not used correctly.

As you will be preparing food you will need to wear protective clothing and pay attention to health and hygiene.

Hours are unsociable and include evenings and weekends. Part-time work can be found. However you will normally work about 40 hours a week in a shift pattern, which might affect your personal life.

Future prospects

In many areas of the UK there is a shortage of chefs, due to an increasing number of establishments opening and a lack of chefs with the required skills and qualifications.

Starting as a commis chef you will help in different sections of the kitchen. With experience you can progress to sous chef, where you act as deputy to the chef and manage a section of your own, or head chef.

Gaining significant experience may allow you to open your own business or even become a lecturer.

Advantages/disadvantages

Preparing high-quality food is very rewarding and will be a memorable event for your customers.

Qualifications and courses

No academic qualifications are required to enter this profession. Most training is on the job and you will be taught by an experienced chef whilst you work in the kitchen. It is possible to work your way up with enough kitchen experience.

You could take a GCSE in Catering, Apprenticeship in Hospitality, Level 2 or 3 City & Guilds Diploma in Professional Cookery, Level 2 or 3 NVQ in Professional Cookery or a Diploma in Hospitality.

You can study for NVQs/SVQs (Levels 2/2–3) in Food Preparation and Cooking, and it can be helpful to gain a food hygiene certificate whilst working towards becoming a chef.

Further qualifications are also available, including degrees or Foundation degrees in Professional Culinary Arts and Culinary Arts Management.

You will have the opportunity to combine creativity with practical skills.

This type of work requires you to work long hours including weekends and evenings.

You will be on your feet for much of the time in a hot and busy environment.

Money guide

Salaries vary according to the type of employer, geographic area and your experience and reputation. Where there are chef shortages, salaries are higher.

Salaries start at £12,000–£16,000 per year for a commis chef, rising to £25,000 as a chef de partie and £30,000 as a sous chef.

Executive chefs can earn £60,000+.

Related opportunities

- Catering/Restaurant Manager/Maître D'hôtel p135
- Food Safety Officer p139
- Kitchen Assistant/Supervisor p145

Further information

Institute of Hospitality
Trinity Court, 34 West Street, Sutton SM1 1SH
020 8661 4900; www.instituteofhospitality.org

People 1st
2nd Floor, 38 Market Square, Uxbridge UB8 1LH
01895 817000; www.people1st.co.uk

www.cityandguilds.com/myperfectjob

CONCIERGE

What the work involves

- Concierges work as part of the front of house team in a hotel, apartment block or corporate organisation.

- You will be responsible for greeting guests, assisting with their baggage, answering questions, giving advice or directions, and generally making them feel as comfortable as possible.

- If you work in a hotel you must keep up-to-date on events and functions in the hotel, and may be asked to book tickets and organise travel for guests.

- You may manage a team of other concierges, reception or door staff. Some organisations may require you to undertake extra services such as shopping and pet walking/sitting.

The type of person suited to this work

As you will be the first port of call for guests and visitors to the establishment you work for, you should enjoy meeting new people and working in a busy environment.

You must be polite, friendly, helpful and informative at all times.

You should have an interest in the catering and hospitality industry.

You need to have a practical approach to problem solving and be able to remain calm.

As you will be entrusted with important errands and messages you must be responsible and reliable.

You should also have a certain level of strength and fitness to carry bags and work long shifts.

Working conditions

You will work 40 hours a week on average. This will mainly be shifts of 12 hours and will include working at night, early mornings and weekends.

You may have a desk or an office, where you will use the telephone or computer, but you will spend the majority of your time on your feet in the reception area meeting and helping guests, or running errands within the establishment or around the local area on behalf of guests.

You may be required to lift heavy bags.

Usually your employer will provide you with a uniform.

Future prospects

Establishments may have formal progression routes and this may consist of moving up from a position as a porter to deputy head concierge, head concierge and then up again to front office management positions.

You may also transfer to another discipline within hospitality and even set up your own business.

You may travel abroad as there are international opportunities within certain establishments, such as hotels.

Qualifications and courses

ENTRY 1 LEVEL

There are no formal academic requirements. A foreign language will be useful. Useful qualifications include the Diploma in Hospitality or Travel and Tourism as well as the Level 2 Award in Principles of Customer Service in Hospitality, Leisure, Travel and Tourism.

You will usually start in a front of house role such as porter or receptionist and with experience progress to the role of concierge. You could train in-house or through an Apprenticeship in Hospitality.

You will learn and train as you work. This may include gaining knowledge of the establishment's policies and techniques in waiting and room service. You can also work towards NVQs at Level 1 in Hospitality and at Level 2 in Multi-skilled Hospitality Services.

Previous work experience in catering or hospitality is recommended.

Advantages/disadvantages

You will meet new people each day and will be responsible for a wide variety of guests or visitors and their requirements.

You may have to work long and unsociable hours.

Money guide

Your starting salary as a concierge can be from £12,000 a year.

As you gain experience over the years you can earn around £20,000 a year.

If you reach the position of head concierge of a four–five star establishment you could earn up to £25,000 or more.

Related opportunities

- Customer Service Assistant Manager p483
- Personal Assistant p55
- Receptionist p58

Further information

Institute of Hospitality
Trinity Court, 34 West Street, Sutton, Surrey SM1 1SH
020 8661 4900; www.instituteofhospitality.org

People 1st
2nd Floor, Armstrong House, 38 Market Square, Uxbridge UB8 1LH
01895 817000; www.people1st.co.uk

City& Guilds

www.cityandguilds.com/myperfectjob

FOOD SAFETY OFFICER

What the work involves

- You will advise those working in catering/food premises by providing information on the safe presentation, preparation and storage of food for public consumption.

- Your role will be to investigate outbreaks of food-related illnesses and implement hazard warnings in places such as butchers, retailers and restaurants.

- You will enforce accurate food labelling.

- You will also advise schools and businesses on food regulations as well as nutritional awareness.

The type of person suited to this work

You need excellent communication skills as you will be advising and educating people of all backgrounds on food safety and nutrition. You should be able to explain technical information in a simple and clear way. You must also be tactful when investigating food poisoning and other hazardous issues.

It's important to be analytical and methodical in your work. Good attention to detail is essential. You need to be able to juggle many different jobs at once and be a confident decision maker.

Working conditions

Although you will be office based, most of your time will involve travelling to businesses, restaurants, schools and homes, following up complaints and giving advice. A driving licence is essential.

The places you investigate may be smelly and unpleasant at times. You will need to wear protective clothing such as masks, hair protection and boots. You will work normal office hours, but some evenings and weekends may be required.

Future prospects

Due to the rise in mass manufacturing of food and fast food outlets, the need for food safety officers has remained steady. You may be employed by a local authority or by a food company.

Outside of Scotland, most food safety officers begin as environmental health officers and specialise later. In Scotland, inspection and food hygiene is undertaken by registered food safety officers.

With experience you can progress to senior positions within food safety or return to other areas of environmental health. You could also set up your own consultancy.

Advantages/disadvantages

This job offers flexibility and variety. You have a chance to make a difference to public health.

Investigations can be difficult at times as you might need to close down a business.

Qualifications and courses

To become a food safety officer outside Scotland, you will first need to train as an environmental health officer.

Candidates need a BSc or MSc in Environmental Science accredited by the Chartered Institute of Environmental Health (CIEH) or the Royal Environmental Health Institute of Scotland (REHIS). Entry to a first degree normally requires 2 A levels/3 H grades including a science subject, plus 5 GCSEs/S grades (A*–C/1–3) including English, maths and science. Entry to the MSc requires a first degree in a relevant science or technology subject. Before qualifying as an environmental health officer, graduates must undertake a minimum of 48 weeks' practical training. During this time you will complete a required Experiential Learning Portfolio (ELP).

The Diploma in Society, Health and Development or the Diploma in Environmental and Land-Based studies may also be useful before starting a degree.

Food safety officers working in Scotland must meet the requirements of the Scottish Food Safety Officers' Registration Board. Candidates for the Higher Certificates in Food Premises Inspection and Food Standards Inspection must have a minimum of an HND in Food Science or Food Technology.

Money guide

Starting out within a local authority you may earn around £24,000 a year and earn up to £31,000 with experience. Depending on the organisation you work for you could earn up to £38,000 a year as an experienced food safety officer.

Senior consultants earn £45,000+. If you are self-employed, daily rates range from £250 to £460 per day.

Related opportunities

- Environmental Health Practitioner/Officer p35
- Health and Safety Adviser p40
- Meat Hygiene Inspector p489

Further information

Chartered Institute of Environmental Health
Chadwick Court, 15 Hatfields, London SE1 8DJ
020 7928 6006; www.cieh.org

Royal Environmental Health Institute of Scotland
19 Torphichen Street, Edinburgh EH3 8HX
0131 229 2968, www.rehis.org

www.cityandguilds.com/myperfectjob

HOTEL/ACCOMMODATION ROOM ATTENDANT

What the work involves

- You will clean, tidy and prepare guest rooms to a high standard. This could include cleaning bathroom and toilet areas and other parts of the hotel.

- Work involves stocking up levels of supplies as they are used and keeping records of any items of lost property left in rooms.

- Using a trolley or cart, you will move supplies of linen, towels and other items around the hotel.

- You will also check for maintenance problems or damage to hotel property.

The type of person suited to this work

As much of the work involves cleaning areas of the site and moving supplies around, you will need a good level of physical fitness. You will also need to be well organised, enthusiastic and able to work quickly to get all your tasks completed on time.

You must have a polite and friendly manner when liaising with guests. In order to keep up standards of cleanliness, you must have a good eye for detail. As you will be cleaning areas around guests' personal belongings, you should be very honest and trustworthy.

Working conditions

This is physical work so expect to be on your feet for much of the time, using cleaning equipment and pushing a cart from room to room.

You will be working with cleaning fluids and other cleaning equipment on a daily basis, which could affect those with skin problems.

You will probably work shifts and may need to work early mornings, late at night and at weekends.

Future prospects

There are around 46,000 hotels in the UK employing 280,000 people. However, these figures do not include the other options in this area such as bed and breakfasts or leisure facilities. Larger employers provide staff with good training and development support. The number of top level hotels is increasing, and is expected to grow further as we get nearer to the London Olympics in 2012.

You could also work abroad, for an international hotel or in a resort. With experience, you could go on to work as an accommodation manager or housekeeper.

Advantages/disadvantages

Some employers allow you to live on site and will provide your meals.

There are opportunities to gain seasonal and holiday work. This type of job is also available on a part-time basis.

Qualifications and courses

There are no minimum entry requirements for this job. Some companies prefer to employ people aged over 18.

Employers provide on-the-job training when you first start work, usually under the supervision of a more experienced member of staff. This could include aspects such as safe lifting methods and furniture and carpet cleaning.

It may be useful to gain an NVQ/SVQ Level 2 in Housekeeping or Levels 1 and 2 in Cleaning Support Services. City & Guilds also offers VRQ Levels 1–3 in Accommodation Operations and Services.

You could undertake Apprenticeships/Skillseekers to enter this area of work.

To progress to the role of accommodation manager or staff supervisor work, you could study for an NVQ/SVQ Level 3 in Hospitality Supervision.

On the days when many guests are arriving and leaving this can be very busy work.

Money guide

Earnings vary according to employer and location and may be based on hourly rates working out to a minimum of £7,100 a year at age 16. If over 21 you will earn a minimum of £11,500 a year. With experience you may earn £15,000 a year. Guests often leave tips for room attendants, which you may share with other staff or be allowed to keep yourself.

Related opportunities

- Cleaner p464
- Hotel Manager p141
- Hotel Porter p142
- Housekeeper/Accommodation Manager p144

Further information

Institute of Hospitality
Trinity Court, 34 West Street, Sutton SM1 1SH
020 8661 4900; www.instituteofhospitality.org

People 1st
2nd Floor, Armstrong House, 38 Market Square,
Uxbridge UB8 1LH
01895 817000; www.people1st.co.uk

www.cityandguilds.com/myperfectjob

HOTEL MANAGER

What the work involves

- You will manage the services and staff of your hotel, ensuring that it is a successful business and gains new customers to make a profit.

- You will be responsible for checking that the buildings and grounds of your hotel meet health and safety and other standards.

- Your work could involve promoting and developing the hotel to increase numbers of customers.

- You could work in all types of hotel, from a small private one up to large national or international chains.

The type of person suited to this work

As you will manage budgets and cash flow, you will need a good level of numeracy and the confidence to handle large quantities of money. Communication skills are very important as you will be organising staff and dealing with guests. You will be working in a sociable and busy environment, so you will need to enjoy meeting lots of different people.

You should be well organised and able to meet targets. Strong customer service and good business skills are essential, as is flexibility, as you will be working long and unsocial hours.

A knowledge of tourism is useful.

Working conditions

This work involves working long hours that include evenings and weekends. You might spend some of your evenings living-in so you can be on-site in case of emergencies. You are also likely to work shifts.

Some members of the public can be rude and aggressive so you will need to maintain a calm professional manner at all times.

You will need to have a smart appearance and you might have to wear a uniform.

Future prospects

Hospitality is a developing sector and there are about 46,000 hotels of all kinds throughout the UK employing over 280,000 people. After a difficult period the hotel sector is showing signs of growth with around a fifth of hotel staff reaching managerial roles.

With experience, you could work overseas, open your own hotel or progress from hotel management into other areas of a company such as human resources, finance and IT.

Advantages/disadvantages

Live-in accommodation is offered with some jobs.

There are opportunities to travel and work overseas.

You can progress to be a manager of a large hotel relatively quickly.

Qualifications and courses

No specific academic qualifications are required, as it is possible to enter the industry at a lower level and work your way up. You can study part time towards NVQ/SVQ Level 1 and 2 in Catering and Hospitality and Level 3 Supervisory Management.

Apprentices undertake on-the-job training and work towards NVQ/SVQ Level 1 and 2 in Catering and Hospitality and Level 3 Supervisory Management.

It is possible to join with previous hotel experience and through attending fast-track training schemes. Knowledge of a second language can be useful.

The Institute of Hospitality (formerly the Hotel and Catering International Management Association) offers a selection of courses for staff in specific roles.

Many entrants to this profession have a degree, HNC/D or postgraduate qualification, and enter as management trainees. Relevant degree subjects include Hospitality Management and Hotel and Catering Management.

Money guide

Salaries will depend on the size, reputation and location of the hotel in which you work. London and the south-east of England pay the highest.

Assistant/trainee managers earn between £12,000 and £19,000 per year. As a deputy manager you could earn £21,000–£30,000.

An experienced manager could earn anything from £25,000 to £50,000 with salaries of £100,000+ possible for the largest London hotels.

Related opportunities

- Bar Manager/Licensee/Publican p134
- Catering/Restaurant Manager/Maître d'hôtel p135
- Holiday Representative p389
- Housekeeper/Accommodation Manager p144

Further information

Institute of Hospitality
Trinity Court, 34 West Street, Sutton SM1 1SH
020 8661 4900; www.instituteofhospitality.org

Springboard UK
3 Denmark Street, London WC2H 8LP
0845 293 2515; www.springboarduk.net

City&
Guilds

www.cityandguilds.com/myperfectjob

HOTEL PORTER

What the work involves

- As a porter, you will greet hotel guests, answer the phone, take reservations and deal with general enquiries.

- You will also be responsible for moving guests' luggage to and from rooms.

- If you work as a night porter, you will look after the security and safety of the hotel site.

- As a head porter in a large hotel, you will be responsible for a team of porters that will include night, conference and kitchen porters.

The type of person suited to this work

As you will be working with hotel guests, you will need good customer service skills and a smart appearance. Good communication skills and an ability to work as part of a busy team are also important.

You may be asked to undertake duties at short notice, so you will need a flexible and enthusiastic attitude.

Being responsible for the security of the hotel site and guests' belongings means that you must be aware of security issues and be honest and reliable. You must be fit and active as you will be doing a lot of lifting and carrying.

Working conditions

This work can be physically demanding as you will spend a lot of time on your feet. It is very important that you keep up a smart appearance. You might have to wear a uniform.

You could work shifts, split shifts or standard hours. You may live in and possibly be on call. If you work as a night porter your working hours may affect your personal life.

Future prospects

You can work in hotels all over the country. Part-time and seasonal work is also available. There is also the possibility of working abroad.

Smaller hotels tend to employ one porter so you would need to move to larger hotels if you want to progress, so being flexible can be helpful. In larger companies, you could work towards a job as a head porter or a reception-based role.

Advantages/disadvantages

In some hotels, you would be able to live in on-site.

This job can fit educational commitments by offering seasonal opportunities.

You will have the opportunity to meet many different people.

Some hotels prefer to employ mature individuals.

Qualifications and courses

There are no minimum entry requirements for this job although some employers prefer individuals with a good general education. Good communication skills, ICT skills and some customer service experience could be useful.

A driving licence can be helpful. Some employers prefer individuals to be over 18 years of age as you may be required to serve alcohol.

Many hotels will provide training to new staff, whether or not they have previous experience. This is usually gained over a few weeks or longer, under the supervision of a more experienced member of staff.

It is possible to gain qualifications whilst working, including the NVQs Level 1 and 2 in Front Office and the Level 2 Award in Principles of Customer Service. You could undertake an Apprenticeship/Skillseekers to enter this area of work.

Money guide

Salary levels vary according to the type of hotel you work for and geographic location. Starting salaries are about £11,500 per year.

This can rise to £12,000–£15,500 with experience. Head Porters in large hotels could earn up to £22,000. You can also earn more through tips from guests.

Related opportunities

- Concierge p138
- Hotel/Accommodation Room Attendant p140
- Housekeeper/Accommodation Manager p144
- Receptionist p58

Further information

Institute of Hospitality
Trinity Court, 34 West Street, Sutton SM1 1SH
020 8661 4900; www.instituteofhospitality.org

People 1st
2nd Floor, 38 Market Square, Uxbridge UB8 1LH
01895 817000, www.people1st.co.uk

City&
Guilds

www.cityandguilds.com/myperfectjob

HOTEL RECEPTIONIST

What the work involves

- You will be responsible for welcoming guests to the hotel, checking them in and out, managing any requests and allocating them a room.

- You will also prepare your guests' bills, taking payments and handling foreign exchange. You will answer the telephone, take messages and bookings and inform guests about the local area.

- Hotel receptionists work closely with other members of staff to ensure the smooth running of the hotel. In a large hotel you may be working within a team of receptionists whereas in a small hotel you may be working alone and have extra duties including housekeeping and waitressing.

The type of person suited to this work

You should be a friendly, welcoming and well-presented person as you will be the first point of contact for hotel guests.

Good communication skills are essential as you will be interacting with all types of people and a polite telephone manner will be necessary when making calls and taking messages.

You will be very busy at times but will have to stay calm and polite even under pressure, making sure that each guest gets the service they expect.

It would be helpful to be knowledgeable about the local area and the hotel. Being able to speak a foreign language would also be desirable, as you might have foreign guests staying at the hotel or you may want to work overseas.

Working conditions

Hotels are open 24/7, this means you most probably will do shift work to make sure the reception desk is manned at all times. There are opportunities to work part time or seasonally.

You will work behind the reception desk the majority of the time, where you will have access to a computer and a telephone. You might be provided with a uniform.

Future prospects

The tourism industry is growing, with hotels being built all over the UK; this means more job opportunities are available.

As a hotel receptionist you could progress to being a supervisor or manager of a team of receptionists, or choose to work in a different aspect of the hotel such as event organisation.

There might be opportunities to work overseas, especially if you speak another language.

Qualifications and courses

There are no minimum entry requirements, although employers are likely to ask for 5 GCSEs/S grades (A*–C/1–3), including English and maths, the Diploma in Hospitality may also be useful. Having some office work experience and computer skills would be helpful for this career.

Further training is usually provided by the employer, and new entrants often work under the supervision of more experienced reception staff. Courses available include NVQs/SVQs in front office Levels 1–2 and in multi-skilled hospitality services Levels 2–4.

Advantages/disadvantages

You could get to work in hotels overseas, and travel the world.

Some people you meet may get angry if their plans are disrupted. This could be frustrating, especially if it is not your fault.

This is a varied and active role, which will be great for people who like to keep busy.

Money guide

Your salary may depend on the location and size of the hotel you work for. Starting salaries are from £11,000 to £15,000 a year. This can increase to £18,000 after gaining experience. Senior receptionists or those in supervisory roles can earn up to £25,000. Normally, meals and accommodation are extra benefits included in the salary.

Related opportunities

- Personal Assistant p55
- Sales/Retail Assistant p494
- Secretary p63
- Travel Agent p399

Further information

Institute of Hospitality
Trinity Court, 34 West Street, Sutton SM1 1SH
020 8661 4900; www.instituteofhospitality.org

People 1st
2nd Floor, Armstrong House, 38 Market Square,
Uxbridge UB8 1LH
01895 817000, www.uksp.co.uk; www.people1st.co.uk

www.cityandguilds.com/myperfectjob

HOUSEKEEPER/ ACCOMODATION MANAGER

What the work involves

■ You will be in charge of a team of cleaners and will ensure that all rooms on your premises are clean, tidy and hospitable. You may work in hotels, conference centres, private households, hospitals, care homes and university halls of residence.

■ You will manage a housekeeping budget, recruit and train staff as well as organise work rotas and duties.

■ You will inspect rooms, take care of repairs, and ensure linens, soaps, towels and other necessities are always in stock.

■ You will sort out lost property and file maintenance reports.

The type of person suited to this work

Excellent management skills are essential. You will be responsible for training staff and making sure they work to a high standard, so good verbal communication skills are also important.

Good business sense and an ability to manage budgets are useful.

Working conditions

Although you will have an office, you will be on your feet for much of the time. You might be expected to live on-site and work unsocial hours. You will use a range of cleaning chemicals and equipment that could cause problems if you have skin allergies.

Future prospects

There is scope for developing a career in management in this area, but you have to work your way from junior or deputy housekeeper to senior housekeeper. In larger hotels, you could go on to a role in head office, in areas such as human resources or training. There are also opportunities in facilities management.

International companies could provide the opportunity to work overseas. With enough experience, you could go on to own and run a hotel.

Advantages/disadvantages

You will have to work some unsocial hours, which could affect your personal life.

Some employers will allow you to live on-site and larger hotel and leisure companies provide leisure and restaurant discounts to staff.

Money guide

A salary of £12,500 per year is typical for those working in a small budget-class hotel. A graduate trainee

Qualifications and courses

It is possible to enter this career without academic qualifications, but employers will want to see evidence that you are organised and have good customer service skills. Many entrants start out as room attendants and work their way up. Most employers will require you to be at least 18 years old to start work.

Apprenticeships in Hospitality and the Diploma in Hospitality might be helpful.

HNCs/HNDs, Foundation degrees or degrees in subjects such as hospitality or hotel management can be useful. You will need a degree if you want to be accepted onto a management training scheme at a large hotel chain.

Training usually takes place on the job. You can study for qualifications through the Institute of Hospitality, including the Business Skills Certificate for Hospitality, Leisure and Tourism (Level 2), the Certificate in Management for Hospitality, Leisure and Tourism (Level 3) and the Diploma in Management for Hospitality, Leisure and Tourism (Level 4).

accommodation manager can earn £17,000–£21,000 per year. £18,000 is the average salary for this job. Salaries of up to £40,000 are possible for head housekeepers working in the largest London-based hotels. Salaries may not be as high if accommodation is provided.

Related opportunities

■ Cleaner p464
■ Hotel/Accommodation Room Attendant p140
■ Hotel Manager p141
■ Hotel Porter p142

Further information

Institute of Hospitality
Trinity Court, 34 West Street, Sutton SM1 1SH
020 8661 4900; www.instituteofhospitality.org

People 1st
2nd Floor, 38 Market Square, Uxbridge UB8 1LH
01895 817000; www.people1st.co.uk

Springboard UK
3 Denmark Street, London WC2H 8LP
020 7497 8654; www.springboarduk.org.uk

www.cityandguilds.com/myperfectjob

KITCHEN ASSISTANT/ SUPERVISOR

What the work involves

Kitchen assistant

- You will keep the kitchen clean, wash-up equipment, peel and chop fruits, vegetables and meat and check on stock levels. You will also prepare quick, simple dishes.

Kitchen supervisor

- Kitchen supervisors are experienced, trained chefs who oversee the running of a kitchen and hire, train and manage all kitchen staff.

- You will plan menus, order ingredients, oversee food preparation, presentation and quality control and contact suppliers to place orders and negotiate prices.

The type of person suited to this work

Kitchens are hectic and it is essential to have good team-working, communication and multi-tasking skills to ensure the smooth running of the operation.

Supervisors need to be assertive, patient and composed as they have to delegate tasks, resolve disputes, negotiate prices, keep records and stay in control of a team.

Kitchen assistants need to be on time for work, able to follow directions and to work efficiently at a fast pace.

You must adhere to and impose strict health and safety procedures and standards of hygiene.

Working conditions

Most kitchen assistants work part time on a shift system including split shifts and overtime. Supervisors generally work a 40-hour week. All kitchen staff should be prepared to work holidays and weekends.

Kitchens can often be noisy, clammy and cramped places to work. You will need to wear an apron, hairnet and protective gloves to ensure food is not contaminated.

While both kitchen assistants and supervisors will spend most of their time standing and lifting heavy items, supervisors will also have a small office in which they organise their paperwork.

Future prospects

Kitchen workers are constantly in demand. You may work in a wide range of settings from restaurants, bars and hotels to hospitals, schools or the armed forces.

Kitchen assistant

You may progress to an assistant chef or move into food service or bar work.

Kitchen supervisor

You may be promoted to general manager or head office manager. You may also choose to set up your own independent restaurant or catering company.

Qualifications and courses

Kitchen assistant

ENTRY LEVEL 1

There are no minimum qualifications. Previous catering experience is helpful. Qualifications such as the GCSE in Food Technology, Diploma in Hospitality and Level 1 Certificate in Hospitality Industry are also useful.

Most employers provide on-the-job training in basic cookery techniques and food hygiene. You can also take a City & Guilds certificate in Food Preparation whilst you work. In Scotland the SQA National Qualification in Health and Food Technology is available.

Kitchen supervisor

To become a supervisor you will need experience as a fully trained chef. There are no formal requirements but you will need to have trained as a commis chef or a kitchen assistant first.

Many employers seek candidates with previous experience or NVQs Level 1 or 2 in Catering. HNCs/ HNDs, degrees or postgraduate qualifications in hospitality will increase your chances of being hired.

Advantages/disadvantages

Working with a team in a fast-paced kitchen can be both fun and exciting. Some employers provide free meals and you have the option to work on a flexible basis.

You may need to work long shifts at unsocial times. The work can be stressful and physically demanding.

Money guide

Kitchen assistant

If you work a 40 hour week your salary can range from £10,046 for those aged 18–21, to £12,064 per year for those 22 and older. With experience you may earn up to £16,700.

Kitchen supervisor

If you start out as a chef you can earn between £14,000 and £23,000 a year. As a supervisor you may earn up to £25,000 and with experience this can rise to £45,000.

Related opportunities

- Chef/Sous Chef p137
- Waiting Staff p146

Further information

Institute of Hospitality
Trinity Court, 34 West Street, Sutton SM1 1SH
020 8661 4900; www.instituteofhospitality.org

www.cityandguilds.com/myperfectjob

WAITING STAFF

What the work involves

Waiter/waitress

- You will take food orders from customers and provide meals, through table or counter service.

- You will provide accurate bills for meals and take payment from customers. Before and during your shift you will probably have to keep the eating area clean and prepare tables for customers.

Butler

- You will work in a private household where you will be responsible for arranging travel and security, providing and serving food and welcoming visitors.

- You will usually work within a wealthy household, including those of famous celebrities or royalty.

Sommelier

- You will be responsible for the provision of wines or other alcoholic beverages such as spirits.

- You will be expected to attend tastings and to design a wine list or cocktail menu.

- It is important to understand how beverages complement food in order to aid customer selection. You will need to serve beverages correctly at the expected temperature.

The type of person suited to this work

Waiter/waitress

As you will be working with the public, you should possess a polite attitude, a neat appearance and good customer service skills.

You may have to explain parts of the menu to customers, so an interest in food and drink is useful.

You will need a good memory and communication skills to take food orders correctly from customers and pass them on to kitchen staff. You should be happy to work as part of a team.

The ability to work with numbers and deal with cash is important. You must work to a high standard of health and hygiene at all times.

Butler

In addition to the above skills, you should be very well presented, honest and reliable. Your employers will expect you to be dedicated, loyal and completely trustworthy as you will be responsible for their day-to-day security and their home when the family is away.

Sommelier

It is essential to be enthusiastic about wines and have an interest in food. You should understand tasting notes and demonstrate a thorough knowledge of wines and beverages from all over the world.

Working conditions

Waiter/waitress

This role includes shift work and you will have to work unsociable hours, including evenings and weekends.

It is essential to have lots of energy for this role as you will be on your feet for most of the time, carrying heavy plates and dishes.

Most waiting staff service a number of tables at once and have to remember different customer requests. It is important to have the ability to remain calm in the face of customer complaints.

You will be required to wear a uniform and may be exposed to a hot, noisy kitchen environment. You will be expected to work to a high standard of cleanliness at all times

Butler

You will probably work within luxurious surroundings in the UK or abroad and will normally live in and have your own quarters.

You may be required to stay in and care for the home whilst your employer is away, and you may also escort them overseas and travel extensively.

Sommelier

You will probably wear a uniform and work shifts, including weekends and evenings, until the early hours of the morning.

You will spend most of your time front of house and should be energetic and have high hygiene standards.

You may have the opportunity to travel domestically and internationally to attend tastings.

Future prospects

Waiter/waitress

The hospitality industry is growing in the UK, with further expansion predicted. As a result there is a strong demand for waiting staff with good customer service skills and experience in the UK and overseas.

With experience, you could become junior or head waiter. Larger employers such as hotel chains increasingly provide formal training and support for staff, and may allow inter-departmental movements.

Butler

Opportunities to become a butler are increasing. You are more likely to get a job if you are willing to be flexible and take on other responsibilities, such as those of a personal assistant, or provide some childcare services. Many catering firms provide butler services and there is demand from contract caterers, hotels and financial institutions.

Many of the jobs are overseas and the most successful butlers are willing to travel.

Sommelier

There are a growing number of opportunities to work in a variety of outlets in the UK and abroad. An increasing number of women are entering the profession.

With experience it is possible to progress to a higher managerial position in the hospitality industry or start your own business in the wine sector.

Advantages/disadvantages

Waiter/waitress

Catering staff are often provided with uniforms, free meals and on-site accommodation.

The role can be physically draining.

Butler

Your job could include lots of travelling and the opportunity to live in the luxurious homes of the rich and famous.

This job can affect your personal life as it is difficult to be off duty.

Sommelier

You may have the opportunity to travel within the UK and abroad.

Working long and unsociable hours can affect your personal life.

Money guide

Waiter/waitress

Salaries will depend on the location, size and reputation of your employer. Starting out you can expect around £10,000 per year. With experience this rises to £14,000.

If you become a section head, or sommelier, this will increase to £19,000–£25,000+.

In most jobs you would receive tips from customers in addition to your salary.

Butler

Your salary will depend on your experience and your employer. Starting salaries are around £15,000 per year and this can increase to between £20,000 and £45,000 with experience. The most successful can achieve £75,000.

In addition, you will be provided with free accommodation and meals.

Sommelier

Salaries will depend on the location, size and reputation of the organisation you work for. Starting out you can expect around £13,000 per year, with experience this rises to £30,000.

A head sommelier could earn £40,000+

Earnings can be increased with tips and bonuses. Live-in accommodation and free meals may also be provided.

Related opportunities

- Steward/Cruise Ship Purser p626
- Housekeeper/Accommodation Manager p144
- Kitchen Assistant/Supervisor p145

Qualifications and courses

Waiter/waitress

No minimum qualifications are required. However communication and numeracy skills are important. The Diploma in Hospitality or an Apprenticeship in Food and Drink Service could be useful.

It is possible to gain NVQs/SVQs Levels 1–2 in Catering and Hospitality. You could also work towards NVQs/SVQs in Food and Drink Service Levels 1–3 or Hospitality Supervision at Level 3.

High profile employers may require staff with experience in fine dining and silver service. The Academy of Food and Wine Service provides short courses.

Butler

No formal qualifications are required, however hospitality experience is essential. Qualifications in general hospitality and catering are well regarded. The Diploma in Hospitality could be useful.

It is possible to attain a City & Guilds Level 2 Diploma for Butlers as well as NVQs in Food and Drink Service at Level 2 and Hospitality Supervision at Level 3.

Some large institutions such as hotel chains provide formal training. You will probably need a driving licence and a second language may be useful.

Sommelier

There are no minimum qualifications but you must be 18 years or over to serve alcohol. Relevant experience and fluency in a foreign language, especially French, is also useful.

Certain employers require qualifications from Level 1 Foundation Certificate in Wines to a Level 5 Honours Diploma from the Wine & Spirit Education Trust (WSET).

NVQs/SVQs are also available in Food and Drink Service. Diplomas are available in Hospitality, Professional Food and Beverage Service (Level 2) and Wines and Spirits (Level 4). You could also take an Advanced Certificate in Wines and Spirits (Level 3).

Further information

Institute of Hospitality
Trinity Court, 34 West Street, Sutton SM1 1SH
020 8661 4900; www.instituteofhospitality.org

Springboard UK
3 Denmark Street, London WC2H 8LP
020 7497 8654; www.springboarduk.org.uk

Wine & Spirit Education Trust (WSET)
International Wine & Spirit Centre, 39–45 Bermondsey Street, London SE1 3XF
020 7089 3800; www.wset.co.uk

CRCI: C   Catering and Hospitality

Computers and IT

This sector is still fairly new and so it is expanding all the time, creating new jobs for a whole range of people. You may have a mathematical brain or a real creative ability – or a bit of both! Essentially, you must be passionate about computers to consider working in this sector. You need to keep right up to date with the latest technologies and IT developments as well as people's tastes, interests and hobbies to enjoy working in this industry.

In this section we look at the following jobs:

BUSINESS ANALYST

What the work involves

- You will be responsible for inspecting businesses, to see if there are any improvements to be made or current problems that can be solved using information technology. Your aim is to generate higher efficiency and profits for the company.

- You will work with managers in order to learn more about the organisation structure and the technology it uses. You will map out a new business plan and train staff on how to implement it.

- You will ensure that project deadlines and budgets are met on time.

The type of person suited to this work

Your understanding of how businesses work is the key to being a successful business analyst – you will be aware of the need to balance costs with solutions.

You will also need to be a good negotiator, able to influence managers who may not understand how the new solutions or products you are suggesting can benefit their businesses.

Excellent communication skills are crucial because you will need to put across your ideas in meetings and in written reports.

You will also need a strong knowledge of what is available in the technology market and how it works in order to develop project briefs.

Working conditions

You will work standard office hours, although work at evenings and weekends will be necessary when projects are near to completion. You will spend a lot of time meeting and working with other members of the project team. It is likely that your job will also involve travelling to meet clients at all stages of the project and you may be away from home for several days at a time.

Future prospects

There are vacancies in all areas of business including finance and retail. Employers also include specialist management consultancies, software houses and computer companies.

There is a growing market for business analysts with the right combination of skills and talents. Analysts with e-commerce technology skills and experience are in particular demand, due to the continued growth of internet use in business.

Progression is possible into senior analyst jobs and on to project management or consultancy work.

Advantages/disadvantages

You can get a real sense of satisfaction from producing successful solutions that transform a business.

Qualifications and courses

The majority of entrants have a degree, Foundation degree or HNC/D in a relevant subject, for example e-business/commerce, accountancy, business studies or computer science.

A sponsored degree from e-skills UK is available. This is focused on learning through project work in teams with external mentors from sponsoring organisations such as BT, CA, Ford, Fujitsu, Hewlett Packard, IBM, Morgan Stanley and Aviva.

The normal minimum entry requirements for degrees are 2 A levels and 5 GCSEs (A*–C), and for Foundation degrees or HNC/Ds, 1 A level and 3 GCSEs (A*–C). Maths might be a required subject.

Another funded route that may be available is the Higher Apprenticeship in ICT. This leads to a full Honours degree in addition to vocational, technical and Key Skills qualifications and work experience. A Diploma in Business, Administration and Finance or Information Technology or a BTEC National Diploma in an ICT or business subject could be helpful.

There often has to be a trade-off between the solution you would like to recommend and the limitations put down by your client who has a tight budget.

Money guide

£17,000–£25,000 per year is usual for starting salaries. This can rise to £30,000–£45,000 with experience. Senior business analysts can earn £60,000 or more. Additional benefits may include profit sharing, performance-related pay and a car.

Related opportunities

- Internet/Web Professional p158
- Software Developer/Programmer p161
- Systems Analyst p163
- Technical Sales Specialist p164

Further information

British Computer Society
North Star House, North Star Avenue, Swindon SN2 1FA
01793 417424; www.bcs.org

Institute for the Management of Information Systems
5 Kingfisher House, New Mill Road, Orpington BR5 3QG
0700 002 3456; www.imis.org.uk

e-skills UK
1 Castle Lane, London SW1E 6DR
020 7963 8920; www.e-skills.com

COMPUTER GAMES DESIGNER

What the work involves

- Using storyboards and flowcharts, you will present your ideas for a new computer game to a panel for acceptance or rejection.

- If it is accepted you will manage all aspects of the playing experience, from scripts to programming and from animation to sound effects and music.

- You will work with a team of specialists, such as programmers and graphic artists, to produce a prototype.

- Once a computer games play-tester has picked out any flaws and if the panel think it is a winner, it will go into full development by your team.

The type of person suited to this work

To be a top-class computer games designer you will need creativity and an ability to see how ideas fit together. You will also have a passion for and knowledge of the computer games market.

Your ideas need to be technically viable and cost effective, so you will need a broad understanding of computers and games consoles, multimedia and the internet.

You will need to be a team player to work with specialists such as graphic designers to make sure that their part of the project fits in with the final version of the game.

Working conditions

You will be mainly based in an office or studio working with other members of the games project team.

Although you will work Monday to Friday, you might need to work overtime on evenings and weekends to meet deadlines.

Future prospects

Employers are specialised companies producing games for PCs or games consoles such as the Xbox or PS2. This market is expected to grow as the computer games industry is a profitable global business.

It is a popular career choice so entry is competitive. You will need talent and project/people management skills in order to be promoted from junior to designer and then to lead designer.

There may be opportunities to work abroad. Progression is possible into management or consultancy work.

Advantages/disadvantages

Games designers say it is enjoyable creating entertainment for a living. It is a young business and the rewards can be high. It can be tough when a game does not sell or receives poor reviews. It is stressful producing a game for a timed release such as the Christmas market.

Qualifications and courses

Many employers will ask for a degree, Foundation degree or HND plus a portfolio of game projects or design. Relevant industry experience is a must and many people work initially as a tester of quality assurance in a games studio.

Useful degree subjects include computer games technology, computer arts, or computer animation. At least 2 A levels/3 H grades or equivalent might be required or preferred for entry to related degrees.

A funded route that may be on offer in your area is the Higher Apprenticeship in IT. This leads to a full Honours degree in addition to vocational, technical and Key Skills qualifications and work experience. An Apprenticeship in Quality Assurance and Games Production is also available.

Training programmes are on offer for graduate entrants from any discipline.

The new 14–19 Diploma in IT is available at Levels 1–3 and focuses on competencies relevant to IT professional work. Level 3 is equivalent to 3.5 A levels.

Money guide

£19,000 per year is usual for starting/training salaries in this area of work for designers with prior industry experience. This can then rise to £25,000–£35,000 with more experience. £35,000–£55,000 is possible for senior games designers to earn. Additional benefits usually include profit sharing and performance-related pay or a bonus.

Related opportunities

- Interactive Media Designer p157
- Internet/Web Professional p158
- Software Developer/Programmer p161
- Website Designer/Developer p166

Further information

British Computer Society
North Star House, North Star Avenue,
Swindon SN2 1FA
01793 417424; www.bcs.org

Institute of IT Training
Westwood House, Westwood Business Park,
Coventry CV4 8HS
0845 006 8858; www.iitt.org.uk

www.cityandguilds.com/myperfectjob

Computers and IT

CRCI: D

COMPUTER HARDWARE ENGINEER

What the work involves

- You will be responsible for developing, installing and repairing computer hardware – the computer itself rather than the applications or software.

- You will be designing computer components, including microchips and circuit boards, and testing these systems.

- When repairing a fault or upgrading a machine you will open up the computer and use tools to install upgrades or replace faulty parts.

- You may specialise in installing new computer systems and training the people who use them.

The type of person suited to this work

You will need both technical skills and practical ability. Building your own computer system and repairing friends' machines is something you will probably already be doing in your spare time.

You should be a good problem solver. You will need to be able to identify what is wrong and put it right within a strict deadline as your customer may be losing money while you do the repair.

It's important to be inquisitive and adaptable as you will need to absorb new information quickly in order to solve many repairs. You should pay close attention to detail and be thorough and accurate in your work.

Often working on your own, you will need to be reliable and able to work unsupervised.

Working conditions

You might be based in a workshop, or in an office, but many engineers travel to customers' premises or homes.

You will work a 37- to 40-hour week, but as businesses need major work to be done in the evenings and at weekends you will have to work shifts or be on a call-out rota.

Future prospects

Computer hardware engineers are employed by computer manufacturers, computer service firms and by a range of large organisations such as banks, hospitals and universities.

This is a stable area of work because computers need regular repairs or upgrades to improve performance or capacity.

Promotion could be to team leader or supervisor and then on to senior engineer. Self-employment as a freelance/consultant engineer is possible.

Advantages/disadvantages

Your job will be varied as few technical problems are ever the same. It is rewarding to get a computer up and running again. Your customer may have a service agreement requiring you to put the problem right in a fixed period of time, which can be stressful.

Qualifications and courses

ENTRY LEVEL 3

A degree, Foundation degree or HND/C is usually required to work as a computer hardware engineer, but it is possible to start at basic technical support level and work your way up. Useful degree subjects include computer systems engineering or electronic engineering.

The normal minimum entry requirements for degrees are 2 A levels/3 H grades and 5 GCSEs/S grades (A*–C/1–3). For technical degrees, maths, technology or a science subject may be required.

You may choose to enter this career through an Apprenticeship in IT and Telecoms Professionals.

Training programmes are on offer for graduate entrants from any discipline. Engineers must ensure their technical knowledge is always up to date by completing the Continuing Professional Development course.

Money guide

When you begin work as a computer hardware technician you can expect your starting/trainee salary to be around £18,000 per year. This could then increase once you have experience to around £19,000–£25,000. Salaries can rise to between £35,000 and £40,000 at senior level.

Related opportunities

- Computer Technical Support Person p155
- Software Developer/Programmer p161
- Software Engineer p162
- Telecommunications Technician p165

Further information

e-skills UK
1 Castle Lane, London SW1E 6DR
020 7963 8920; www.e-skills.com

Engineering Careers Information Service
SEMTA House, 14 Upton Road, Watford WD18 0JT
0800 282167; www.enginuity.org.uk

City& Guilds

www.cityandguilds.com/myperfectjob

COMPUTER HELPDESK ADVISER

What the work involves

- You will answer telephone calls or emails from computer users who are having technical problems.

- You will ask the customer to take certain actions to try to correct the fault.

- You will log the query and give the customer a job number.

- If the problem is too complex to sort out by phone or email you may arrange for a technician to repair faulty hardware or arrange delivery of replacement software.

The type of person suited to this work

You should have a lot of tact and patience when dealing with frustrated customers over the phone.

You need good verbal and listening skills to be able to guide a customer to take the action they need to put a problem right.

You should enjoy challenges, and be able to think quickly and logically. To solve a problem you might have to move from idea to idea and approach it from different directions.

You will need to be keen to learn and keep up to date with your employer's new products.

Working conditions

You will be sitting in front of a screen wearing a headset to talk to customers. You may be based in a call centre with lots of activity and background noise.

Employers will usually give you frequent breaks from the screen to make your job less stressful.

You will work 37–40 hours a week usually in shifts often including weekend and evening work.

Future prospects

You will most likely be employed by computer hardware and software manufacturers or internet service providers who offer support to their customers.

Support work has grown rapidly in recent years, but helpdesks are sometimes sourced outside the UK by employers looking for lower costs.

This is a job with a high turnover as it is often used as a stepping stone to move into the software industry.

Promotion to supervisory and management work is possible. You could also move into sales or become self-employed.

Advantages/disadvantages

You will get useful training in computers and software, and it is rewarding to resolve a problem.

The job can be stressful because customers can be angry and frustrated by the time they ring you.

Qualifications and courses

It may be possible to enter as a trainee or apprentice with GCSEs/S grades, including English, maths, science and ICT. It is also possible to enter with an Applied A level or BTEC National qualification in ICT or Computing.

Many people enter this career with no formal qualifications but with relevant computer knowledge and good customer service experience. However, some employers prefer you to have a qualification such as a degree, HNC/HND in computing or BTEC National Diploma. A degree would be an advantage in entering a training scheme as a specialist.

You could also study for a Higher Apprenticeship in IT. This leads to a full Honours degree in addition to vocational, technical and Key Skills qualifications and work experience.

The Help Desk Institute offers recognised qualifications for people working in the sector; these include the Customer Support Representative, the Support Centre Analyst, and the Support Centre Desktop Support Technician Certificates.

Money guide

When you start in this profession you can expect to be on £15,000–£16,000 as a starting/trainee salary. This can rise to £18,000–£23,000 once you have gained more experience in the industry. £30,000+ is possible at supervisory level.

Related opportunities

- Computer Technical Support Person p155
- Database Administrator p156
- Computer Operator p154
- Technical Sales Specialist p164

Further information

British Computer Society
1st Floor, Block D, North Star House, North Star Avenue, Swindon SN2 1FA
01793 417424; www.bcs.org

Institute of IT Training
Westwood House, Westwood Business Park, Coventry CV4 8HS
0845 006 8858; www.iitt.org.uk

City&
Guilds

www.cityandguilds.com/myperfectjob

CRCI: D **Computers and IT**

COMPUTER OPERATOR

What the work involves

- ICT or computer operators work for organisations that operate a multi-user computer system to store, manage and present their data.

- Your main responsibility will be starting up, running, closing down, cleaning and backing up data on your employer's multi-user computer system.

- You will be updating and running database programs and tasks prepared by programmers or database managers.

- Routine recording and reporting of any errors you spot to your manager or ICT specialist will also be your responsibility.

The type of person suited to this work

You must have a good typing speed and a good attention to detail to enter accurate and reliable data. Good observational skills are needed to ensure that errors and therefore costly problems and delays are avoided.

It is important that you are organised and practical, as this job will involve backing up data and cleaning the equipment.

You will also need to be good with figures as most databases have lots of data in number format.

You should have a good understanding of hardware and software as you will be working with complex systems.

Working conditions

You will be based in an office, maybe alongside a noisy computer server. This job will involve sitting in front of a computer for most of the day so you should be aware of health concerns such as eye strain and your sitting position.

You will probably work office hours, Monday to Friday. Shift work is also common in this job.

Future prospects

Vacancies are often in big organisations, such as banks, retailers, universities, hospitals and government departments, which have large multi-user databases.

Job opportunities are decreasing. ICT systems are now usually networked and data put in by authorised computer users with support from a specialist database or network manager.

If you have experience and additional training, it is possible to progress to a role as senior operator, shift leader and then database or network manager. You could also work as a self-employed contractor.

Advantages/disadvantages

This job is starting to disappear as content management programs become more user friendly and more employees at all levels input data as one of their work tasks.

Qualifications and courses

You do not need specific entry qualifications for this job, but GCSEs/S grades (A*–C/1–3) in subjects such as maths, English and IT are an advantage. Employers may prefer customer service skills.

Useful qualifications include BTEC National Awards in computer- and business-related subjects.

The Help Desk Institute (HDI) offers recognised qualifications for people with or without experience working in the sector.

If you are aged 16–24 you could enter IT work through an Apprenticeship route. You would then work towards NVQs/SVQs Levels 2 or 3 in information technology.

Trainee computer operators can start as an Apprentice and develop skills as they work. The British Computer Society (BCS) offer professional qualifications for those who wish to improve their existing skills

Training is usually provided by employers on the job.

The Diploma in IT is available at Levels 1–3 and focuses on competencies relevant to IT professional work. Level 3 is equivalent to 3.5 A levels.

Money guide

Starting salaries are around £14,000–£18,000 per year as a Computer Operator. Once trained as an operator and with experience, you could earn around £25,000+. At managerial level an operator can earn between £30,000 and £50,000.

Related opportunities

- Computer Technical Support Person p155
- Database Administrator p156
- Network Manager p160
- Secretary p63

Further information

British Computer Society
North Star House, North Star Avenue, Swindon SN2 1FA
01793 417424; www.bcs.org

e-skills UK
1 Castle Lane, London SW1E 6DR
020 7963 8920; www.e-skills.com

Institute for the Management of Information Systems
5 Kingfisher House, New Mill Road, Orpington BR5 3QG
0700 002 3456; www.imis.org.uk

City&
Guilds

www.cityandguilds.com/myperfectjob

COMPUTER TECHNICAL SUPPORT PERSON

What the work involves

- You will work for an organisation, offering specialist technical support to its computer users.

- You might install new systems and upgrades and train staff in their use.

- Initially, you might try to resolve the problem by telephone or email, only going out to the user's workstation if necessary.

- You will try to fix the problem but if the hardware is under guarantee you will call out the manufacturer's service engineer.

The type of person suited to this work

You will need to be both technical and practical to resolve hardware or software problems.

You will also need to be a good communicator – able to explain technical language to inexperienced users.

You need to cope well with stress and deadlines. You will be under pressure to get the problem sorted quickly so that staff can get back to work. A keenness to stay up to date is vital – you will be expected to be the expert.

Working conditions

You will probably be based in an office with a technical workshop attached.

Your employer may have several sites you need to travel between, sometimes in different parts of the UK.

You may have to work shifts to cover your employer's hours of operation, which may be 24/7, or to install or repair equipment outside office hours.

Future prospects

The main employers are large organisations such as banks, retail chains, and hospitals who require their large computer networks to be functional during working hours.

With experience, promotion could be to team leader, network manager/administrator or on to network development. You could also become self-employed and offer contract services to big companies.

However, there has been a reduction in the number of technical support positions due to the shift in ICT companies offering remotely managed services and the recession.

Advantages/disadvantages

If you take advantage of the training on offer, this broad-based job can lead to jobs at a higher level in the ICT industry.

You will be under pressure to sort out colleagues' problems quickly.

Qualifications and courses

The majority of technical support staff have a relevant qualification and work experience. The Computer Technology Industry Association (CompTIA) A+ Certification and courses by the Service Desk Institute are available. Those with little ICT experience or more than 1 year's work experience, can obtain qualifications from The Help Desk Institute (HDI).

It would be helpful to have at least 4 GCSEs/S grades (A*–C/1–3), including maths and English. It is also possible for school leavers to enter this work via an apprenticeship.

Acceptable entry qualifications include the BTEC National Certificate or Diploma in IT, Levels 2–3 NVQs for IT Practitioners/Professionals and IT certificates or diplomas offered by OCR, City & Guilds and the British Computer Society. Some candidates enter with a Foundation degree or degree or HNC/D in computing, computer science or a related subject.

Microsoft, Linux, Unix, Oracle and Cisco offer certification courses in their own products such as the Microsoft Certified Software Engineer (MCSE) qualification or the Microsoft Certified Systems Administrator (MCSA) qualification. These qualifications are the most broadly accepted technical certifications.

Money guide

£16,000–£20,000 per year is usual for starting/trainee salaries. This can rise to £25,000 with experience. £35,000+ is possible at supervisory level. Additional benefits may include a car.

Related opportunities

- Computer Hardware Engineer p152
- Computer Helpdesk Adviser p153
- Network Manager p160
- Technical Sales Specialist p164

Further information

British Computer Society
North Star House, North Star Avenue, Swindon SN2 1FA
01793 417424; www.bcs.org

e-skills UK
1 Castle Lane, London SW1E 6DR
020 7963 8920; www.e-skills.com

City&
Guilds

www.cityandguilds.com/myperfectjob

DATABASE ADMINISTRATOR

What the work involves

- Your job is to ensure that databases are accurate, accessible and secure. If a huge amount of information needs to be stored with the capacity to search and access specific parts of the data, a database will be used. For example, a hospital uses a database to manage information about its patients.

- To keep the data secure you will back up the content regularly, train users and issue them with passwords.

- You may also be responsible for setting up and testing a new database.

The type of person suited to this work

Databases function to provide people with the information they require to do their jobs, so you will need effective communication skills.

You should be a good negotiator. To train users to input or access a new or modified database you will need to be able to convince them that these changes will benefit them.

To set up or develop a database you will need to be very technical with a high level of programming knowledge. You will also need to be a good listener, able to find out what the database users want including the new design they wish to achieve.

Working conditions

You will be based mainly in your own office although in some cases the work can be carried out at home or in a place of your choice using laptops and broadband wireless technology.

Your employer may have several sites you need to travel between, sometimes in different parts of the UK.

You may have to be on-call to deal with problems outside your normal working hours.

Future prospects

The main employers of database administrators are large organisations, such as banks and retailers. You could also work for a specialist ICT firm providing a complete database service to customers.

This is a growth area because increasing numbers of businesses are developing databases for their websites to allow customers to look at information about their goods online and then go on to buy them.

With experience, you could specialise in network development or move into consultancy work.

Advantages/disadvantages

If you are methodical and analytical, you will enjoy the complex job of writing a new database. It can be frustrating though when database users cause problems by not keeping their information up to date or by leaving vital parts out.

Qualifications and courses

ENTRY LEVEL 4

The usual entry qualification for this work is a degree, Foundation degree or HNC/D in a relevant subject, for example computer science, software development, operational research, e-commerce technology or maths. Other qualifications may be acceptable, such as BTEC National Diplomas and NVQs/SVQs.

The normal minimum entry requirements for degrees are 2 A levels/3 H grades and 5 GCSEs/S grades (A*–C/1–3), and for Foundation degrees or HNC/Ds, 1 A level/2 H grades and 3 GCSEs/S grades (A*–C/1–3). For technical degrees, maths/science may be required.

A funded route that may be on offer in your area is the Higher Apprenticeship in IT. This leads to a full Honours degree in addition to vocational, technical and Key Skills qualifications and work experience.

Entry without a degree may be possible if you have significant programming experience and knowledge. Training programmes are on offer for graduate entrants from any discipline including the Graduate Professional Development Award (GPDA). Database managers may also take manufacturers' courses in particular operating systems/packages.

Money guide

£18,000 per year is usual for starting salaries as a database administrator. This can rise to £30,000–£40,000 once you have gained experience. £50,000 and above is possible at a supervisory level.

Related opportunities

- Computer Operator p154
- IT Trainer p159
- Network Manager p160
- Software Developer/Programmer p161

Further information

British Computer Society
North Star House, North Star Avenue,
Swindon SN2 1FA
01793 417424; www.bcs.org

e-skills UK
1 Castle Lane, London SW1E 6DR
020 7963 8920; www.e-skills.com

City&
Guilds

www.cityandguilds.com/myperfectjob

INTERACTIVE MEDIA DESIGNER

What the work involves

- Interactive media designers use a mix of visuals, sounds, animation, text and effects to produce multimedia and communication tools such as interactive websites and virtual reality DVDs.

- You will work with a team to develop a brief, finding out what your client wants and determining how to find the best solution, and creating simulations along the way to show the client your ideas.

- Your role will also involve planning, coordinating and overseeing the whole project as well as testing, integrating and, if needed, installing at the customer's site.

The type of person suited to this work

Your creative skills need to be outstanding for this job. Every project will be different and you will need the vision to be able to think about what a client wants to achieve with a multimedia project and then develop ideas to produce a solution.

You need to be good at working in a team and motivating others to achieve tight deadlines. You must be organised, have a keen eye for detail and possess good drawing skills.

You should have excellent presentation and communication skills, as you might need to bid against other designers to win contracts for new projects.

Working conditions

You will spend time working in an office or studio at your workstation, but you will also be working with your project team and meeting customers. You may also have the opportunity to work from home.

You may have to travel regularly to clients, to meet and present your solutions to them.

Although you will work normal hours from Monday to Friday, when you are preparing a bid or a deadline is approaching you will need to work overtime.

Future prospects

Employers include specialist multimedia consultancies, internet service providers, e-learning specialists, software houses and hardware manufacturers.

Interactive media is a growing industry and designers who have an understanding of both technical and creative aspects are currently in demand.

Once experienced you could become self-employed, or work on a contract or consultancy basis. You could also move into management or training.

Advantages/disadvantages

This job uses cutting-edge technology and is a young, vibrant industry. The pace of development means you will

Qualifications and courses

Entry is often by means of a degree, Foundation degree or HNC/D in a relevant subject such as graphic or multimedia design.

The normal minimum entry requirements for degrees are 2 A levels/3 H grades and 5 GCSEs/S grades (A*–C/1–3), and for Foundation degrees or HNC/Ds, 1 A level/2 H grades and 3 GCSEs/S grades (A*–C/1–3). For technical degrees, mathematics/science may be required.

Entry without a degree, Foundation degree or HNC/D usually requires practical experience in the field and a portfolio of relevant samples.

You may choose to do a Higher Apprenticeship in IT which will lead to a full Honours degree in addition to work experience.

Training programmes are on offer for graduate entrants from any discipline including the Graduate Professional Development Award (GPDA). The British Computer Society and The Institute for Management of Information Systems also offer qualifications.

never be able to stand still. You will have to keep up to date and keep learning to stay on top of the game.

Money guide

£15,500–£22,000 per year is usual for starting salaries. The average salary for an experienced interactive media designer is £31,800+, more in London. Highly experienced, you could earn £45,000+. The more skills and experience you have to offer, the more you can earn.

Related opportunities

- Internet/Web Professional p158
- Software Developer/Programmer p161
- Software Engineer p162
- Website Designer/Developer p166

Further information

e-skills UK
1 Castle Lane, London SW1E 6DR
020 7963 8920; www.e-skills.com

British Interactive Multimedia Association
Briarlea House, Southend Road, Billericay CM11 2PR
01233 658107; www.bima.co.uk

www.cityandguilds.com/myperfectjob

INTERNET/WEB PROFESSIONAL

What the work involves

- You might work in or supervise a team of staff who design, program and maintain the various pages that make up an internet site.

- In a small company, you might be the programmer, designer and master/manager of the site.

- You might write content or develop a content management program for authorised staff to contribute material.

The type of person suited to this work

You must have a good attention to detail and be able to carefully check your work. You will need to set up secure data entry checking systems and regularly test them for faults. You must be able to respond quickly and calmly when faults occur, such as the wrong prices being matched to the wrong products on a shopping site, and be able to work efficiently to fix them.

It will be your responsibility to create your own website or maintain one from the group of sites you work with. Creativity is important, as is accuracy; you need to make sure the site is easy to use.

Excellent management and communication skills are vital as you may be required to lead a project team at senior level.

Working conditions

You will be mainly office based, using a computer to manage the site. You may have to move around your company's site to train, meet with managers and discuss site improvements.

You will work a 37–40 hour week, normally Monday to Friday, but if you are working to maintain and support a 24/7 site you will work shifts as part of a team to cover all hours.

Future prospects

Websites are big business, with growing numbers of organisations using them to share information, market themselves, sell goods or services and advertise jobs.

You could work for web-based retailers, travel companies, the multimedia industry, local and central government and financial companies.

After gaining experience, you could progress to project management level. A talented web professional could move into freelance or website development consultancy work.

Advantages/disadvantages

This is an expanding market with high rewards on offer if you are creative and have technical skills.

The work can be pressured as you will have responsibility for the internet site of your company.

Qualifications and courses

The usual entry qualification for this work is a degree, Foundation degree or HNC/D in a relevant subject, such as e-business/commerce, e-systems design/technology, 3D design, graphic design, computer science or related areas.

The normal minimum entry requirements for degrees are 2 A levels/3 H grades and 5 GCSEs/S grades (A*–C/1–3), and for Foundation degrees or HNC/Ds 1 A level/2 H grades and 3 GCSEs/S grades (A*–C/1–3).

Another funded route that may be on offer in your area is the Higher Apprenticeship in IT. This leads to a full Honours degree in addition to vocational, technical and Key Skills qualifications and work experience.

Training programmes are on offer for graduate entrants from any discipline, including the Graduate Professional Development Award (GPDA). This offers training and accreditation to IT professionals working in the industry. It includes e-skills, internet services delivery and industrial management and practice.

Money guide

£18,000–£22,000 per year is usual for starting salaries as an internet or web professional. This can rise to around £35,000 with experience. £40,000+ is possible for senior web managers with additional responsibilities. £50,000+ is achievable for project managers.

Related opportunities

- Database Administrator p156
- Interactive Media Designer p157
- Network Manager p160
- Software Developer/Programmer p161

Further information

e-skills UK
1 Castle Lane, London SW1E 6DR
020 7963 8920; www.e-skills.com

British Interactive Media Association
The Lightwell, 12–16 Laystall Street, London EC1R 4PF
020 784 36797; www.bima.co.uk

www.cityandguilds.com/myperfectjob

IT TRAINER

What the work involves

- IT trainers give people user skills, for example, in applications such as Word, Excel or desktop-publishing packages. You may also train people in advanced computer skills such as programming languages.

- Planning courses, preparing learning materials and setting up the computers ready for a session will be part of your typical day.

- You will give presentations and network some materials. You will demonstrate the software being taught and assist students with any problems.

- Evaluating what has been learned and changing future learning materials as required will also be part of your job.

The type of person suited to this work

The constant release of new IT products guarantees a future for trainers but only if you are keen to stay up to date. You will need lots of self-discipline to do research and prepare learning materials.

As e-learning and virtual classroom technology expands, more students are being taught over the internet. Therefore, you will need to be up to date with e-learning tools, technologies and processes.

This job is about helping others to learn. Whether you train face to face or by virtual technology, you will need strong interpersonal and communication skills. Students can be sensitive to criticism and need to be motivated and encouraged.

Working conditions

You may be based in a training centre or you may travel to clients' premises to train their staff on-site.

Although your hours will be usually Monday to Friday, you will need to spend time preparing learning materials and working some evenings and weekends to fit in with students' timetables.

Future prospects

Employers such as hardware and software manufacturers, IT consultancies, training organisations and colleges employ IT trainers. There is a strong demand for trainers, especially in the South-East.

This is rarely a first job. Most trainers have gained experience in other areas of computing first.

Experienced IT trainers can move into self-employment as consultants. Promotion into supervisory or management roles may be possible.

Advantages/disadvantages

It can be personally rewarding when you succeed in making a student understand a difficult subject. This job can be

Qualifications and courses

To work as an IT trainer you need to first gain the relevant skills and experience in IT yourself.

Although no set qualifications are required, it might be an advantage to have a degree, Foundation degree or HNC/D in a relevant subject, for example computer science, e-business/commerce or software engineering.

The normal minimum entry requirements for degrees are 2 A levels/3 H grades and 5 GCSEs/S grades (A*–C/1–3), and for Foundation degrees or HNC/Ds, 1 A level/2 H grades and 3 GCSEs/S grades (A*–C/1–3).

You could enter this job without a degree if you have got significant experience and training in IT.

The Institute of IT Training is the certification awarding body for a range of courses in e-learning training skills offered by the Training Foundation.

Through the Institute of IT Training you can qualify as Certified Training Practitioner.

The new 14–19 Diploma in IT is available at Foundation, Higher and Advanced level which focuses on competencies relevant to IT professional work

badly affected when the economy is depressed as training is often the first thing businesses cut back on in difficult times.

Money guide

Starting salaries are usually £18,000–£23,000 per year. With experience, you could earn £24,000–£30,000. At senior levels, with management responsibilities, it is possible to earn £40,000+. Self-employed trainers work for set fees either per day or per training course and can earn over £30,000.

Related opportunities

- Business Analyst p150
- Network Manager p160
- Secondary School Teacher p205
- Work-based Training Instructor p209

Further information

Institute of IT Training
Westwood House, Westwood Business Park,
Coventry CV4 8HS
0845 006 8858; www.iitt.org.uk

The Chartered Institute of IT
1st Floor, Block D, North Star House, North Star Avenue,
Swindon SN2 1FA
01793 417424; www.bcs.org

www.cityandguilds.com/myperfectjob

Computers and IT

CRCI: D

Computers and IT

CRCI: D

NETWORK MANAGER

What the work involves

■ You will design, set up and maintain a network of computers and any linked equipment such as printers. This could be in just one building or extend across different sites.

■ Managing access to and the security of your network, you will put in place and monitor firewalls, password systems and antivirus software.

■ It will be your responsibility to solve the network users' problems.

■ In large organisations you could manage a team of ICT technicians and carry out duties such as training staff, organising work rotas and allocating staff duties.

The type of person suited to this work

You need to have excellent communication skills in order to explain technical issues clearly and simply to computer users who need to get back onto the network.

Technical ability and determination are needed for this job. You might develop and write software programs for your network and need to be logical to work out how to sort out any problems.

Network solutions are developing very quickly so you will need to be prepared to carry on learning to keep up your expert status.

Working conditions

You will work standard office hours, though longer hours can be required when installing systems or on-call.

You will use a computer to manage the system. You may need to work in the same room as a noisy mainframe server.

You may have to move around your company's site to attend meetings, train staff and resolve problems.

Future prospects

Most organisations use networks to enable their staff to work together, communicate and share resources from their own workstations. Employers include industry, retailers, schools and universities, hospitals, local and central government and financial companies. You could work within an organisation as a network manager, or as part of an external IT agency and work in many different companies.

Promotion could be into the job of senior network manager and then project manager. A talented network manager could also move into freelance or network design consultancy work. Other possibilities include lecturing or training.

Advantages/disadvantages

You will feel valued because communication and the sharing of information are central to the effective running of any organisation.

This job can be stressful as problems will need to be solved quickly so that users can go back to work.

Qualifications and courses

ENTRY 5 LEVEL

Entry is usually by means of a degree, Foundation degree or HNC/D in a relevant subject, for example control and network computing, software engineering, artificial intelligence or computer science. The normal minimum entry requirements for degrees are 2 A levels /3 H grades and 5 GCSEs/S grades (A*–C/1–3), and for Foundation degrees or HNC/Ds, 1 A level/2 H grades and 4 GCSEs/S grades (A*–C/1–3). For technical degrees, maths/science may be required.

A Higher Apprenticeship in IT may be available in your area. This leads to a full Honours degree in addition to vocational, technical and Key Skills qualifications and work experience.

Training programmes on offer to graduates from any discipline include the Graduate Professional Development Award. This offers training and accreditation to ICT professionals in work.

The Diploma in IT is available at Levels 1–3 and focuses on competencies relevant to ICT professional work. Level 3 is equivalent to 3.5 A levels. Other useful qualifications include the City & Guilds Level 4 Higher Professional Diploma in Information Management using ICT, the Institute for the Management of Information Systems Foundation Diploma or accredited qualifications from CISCO and Microsoft.

Money guide

Starting salaries are usually from about £24,000 per year. With experience you could earn from £30,000 to £50,000. Senior network managers can earn £60,000+. Additional benefits may include profit sharing or performance-related pay.

Related opportunities

■ Computer Hardware Engineer p152
■ Computer Technical Support Person p155
■ Database Administrator p156

Further information

British Computer Society
North Star House, North Star Avenue, Swindon SN2 1FA
01793 417424; www.bcs.org

e-skills UK
1 Castle Lane, London SW1E 6DR
020 7963 8920; www.e-skills.com

City& Guilds

www.cityandguilds.com/myperfectjob

SOFTWARE DEVELOPER/ PROGRAMMER

What the work involves

- You will be designing, developing and testing computer software for your clients to improve their business' productivity and efficiency. You may also improve existing software by analysing and fixing any problems. Your clients could be companies from the finance, insurance, retail or building industries.

- You will work closely with a team of other programmers and designers to develop a detailed specification for the software and present this back to your client.

- You will write the programming code for the new software from scratch or adapt an existing code.

- You will then be responsible for testing and maintaining the software, and making sure your client is happy with the new system.

The type of person suited to this work

You will need to have excellent ICT skills, with an in-depth knowledge of up to date packages and software coding techniques.

You must be a good communicator, as you will be working with other ICT professionals and members of staff.

Being logical and having a knack for problem solving will be vital in this work, as you will need to come up with new programming codes and restore existing ones.

Working conditions

Most software developers/programmers work normal office hours. If there is a deadline to meet you might work overtime or at the weekend.

You will be based in an office, with access to a software development system, i.e. a computer. You might need to travel around the country when meeting clients.

Future prospects

Software developers/programmers are employed by a variety of industries; these include retail, finance, engineering and government bodies.

You can progress into senior or management roles, or work as a contracted IT consultant. Some software developers/programmers become self employed or become trainers.

Advantages/disadvantages

You will need to keep up to date with new and developing ICT techniques; this could prove difficult if you wanted a career break.

There are great opportunities for promotion, leading to senior management roles and consultancy.

Qualifications and courses

Entry is usually by means of a degree, Foundation degree or HNC/D in a relevant subject, for example programming, software engineering or computer science, or a degree with modules in computer graphics or html and Java programming.

The normal minimum entry requirements for degrees are 2 A levels/3 H grades and 5 GCSEs/S grades (A*–C/1–3), and for Foundation degrees or HNC/Ds, 1 A level/2 H grades and 3 GCSEs/S grades (A*–C/1–3). For technical degrees, maths or science may be required.

Entry with a degree in an unrelated subject area is possible; many employers recruit graduates from all disciplines. However as the industry is competitive it may be beneficial to take a conversion course or postgraduate course in a computing subject.

Entry without a degree, Foundation degree or HNC/D is unusual unless you have substantial experience in programming work and experience of designing or programming websites using new media. A strong portfolio will be required.

Further study is available, from in-house training to professional qualifications. These include the Information Systems Examination Board (ISEB) qualifications at foundation, practitioner and higher level which cover business analysis.

Money guide

£26,000 a year is the average starting salary; this can increase to £35,000–£47,000 once you have gained several years' experience. Senior and management roles can pay up to £70,000.

Related opportunities

- Internet/Web Professional p158
- Interactive Media Designer p157
- Website Designer/Developer p166

Further information

British Interactive Media Association
The Lightwell, 12–16 Laystall Street, London EC1R 4PF
020 7843 6797; www.bima.co.uk

www.cityandguilds.com/myperfectjob

Computers and IT

CRCI: D

ENTRY LEVEL 4

CRCI: D   Computers and IT

SOFTWARE ENGINEER

What the work involves

- Software engineers test and evaluate software that helps computers to run effectively. You may also develop new software such as computer games, operating systems and business applications.

- As well as providing technical support to businesses and organisations, you may also build new computer systems for them from scratch.

- You will debug software when it is faulty and constantly research new technologies to find the best solutions.

- You will work with computer codes and will usually specialise in either systems or applications.

The type of person suited to this work

You will need technical, practical and creative ability. It will be useful if you write your own programs or have built your own computer system.

You should be an excellent problem solver. You will need to be able to anticipate problems and work out ways to prevent them.

You must be patient and methodical to be able to produce accurate work when your deadline is close and your tests are not going well.

Your teamwork and communication skills should be strong as you will be working with a project team. At higher levels you will be giving presentations or lectures.

Working conditions

You may be based in a laboratory, a research and development unit, or a workshop.

At project management level you may travel nationally and internationally to meetings and conferences. You will work a 37- to 40-hour week but you will need to be flexible and put in extra hours at key times.

Future prospects

There is a strong demand for software engineers in many sectors, including academia, government research, computer manufacturing, software development and electronics and telecommunications.

You will have more opportunities if you are both creative and technical.

You will start work as a junior member of a project team. With experience you could move into lecturing or project management. You might also choose to become an IT consultant or work as a contractor.

Advantages/disadvantages

Your team's work could make the headlines. New products and cutting-edge research, such as the building of world-

Qualifications and courses

ENTRY LEVEL 5

The usual entry qualification is a degree or a Master's in a relevant subject, for example computer science, artificial intelligence or electronic engineering. Some employers will expect a doctorate.

The normal minimum entry requirements for degrees are 2 A levels/3 H grades and 5 GCSEs/S grades (A*–C/1–3). Required subjects usually include maths and physics.

Should you have no formal qualifications, there may be the opportunity of an Apprenticeship in IT within your area. Otherwise Access courses are generally available if you wish to progress to a degree.

Training programmes are on offer for graduate entrants from any discipline. Engineers must ensure their technical knowledge is always up to date by completing continuing professional development courses.

The new 14–19 Diploma in IT is available at Levels 1–3 and focuses on competencies relevant to IT professional work. Level 3 is equivalent to 3.5 A levels.

class supercomputers, are of international interest. Solutions to problems do not happen quickly. It can be really frustrating to retest hundreds of times and still not get the result you are looking for.

Money guide

Starting salaries are usually from £18,000 to £25,000 per year. With experience you can expect to get between £25,000 and £35,000. At senior levels you can earn between £40,000 and £60,000+.

Related opportunities

- Computer Hardware Engineer p152
- Software Developer/Programmer p161

Further information

e-skills UK
1 Castle Lane, London SW1E 6DR
020 7963 8920; www.e-skills.com

City& Guilds

www.cityandguilds.com/myperfectjob

SYSTEMS ANALYST

What the work involves

- You will prepare a brief of what your client wants a computer system to do and then translate this brief into recommendations for IT solutions.

- To determine the system needed you will use performance monitoring or sizing tools. You will then design, cost and recommend suitable hardware/ software solutions.

- If purpose-built software is needed, you may write it or brief a programmer on your team.

- You will go on to install and test the configuration you have developed.

The type of person suited to this work

An excellent all-round knowledge of ICT, including hardware and software, is vital. You will also have to keep up to date with new ICT products as you will be expected to be the technical expert.

Your teamwork and communication skills will need to be good as you will be working with business clients and colleagues such as business analysts and programmers to produce the best value system as a team.

To make systems that work well and enhance profitability and efficiency for your customer, you will also need to be a problem solver who understands how businesses work.

Working conditions

You will be mainly based in an office, working with other members of the project team. You will have to travel to clients at all stages of the project and may be away for several days when installing and testing the new system.

Although your hours will be usually Monday to Friday, you will need to work some evenings and weekends to meet deadlines.

Future prospects

Employers include software and systems houses, ICT consultants as well as organisations in sectors such as commerce, finance and banking, retail and health.

You could move from this broad-based job to specialise either in offering ICT solutions for business, or a technical area such as software or website development.

Progression is possible into a senior analyst role, project management or consultancy work. The speed of advancement depends upon the size and type of organisation you work for.

You could become an independent consultant.

Advantages/disadvantages

It is rewarding to put together hardware and software to create a unique solution designed for your customer. Clients tend to set very stressful, demanding briefs to deliver the right solution both at the lowest cost and in the shortest time possible.

Qualifications and courses

A degree, Foundation degree or HND/C is usually required. Useful degree subjects include computing or e-systems design and technology. 5 GCSEs (A*–C), including English and maths, and 2 A levels, including maths are usually required for these degrees. Entry is still open to those with arts and humanities degrees providing they pass an IT aptitude test. Postgraduate courses in IT may be helpful to these applicants.

A new sponsored degree from e-skills, Information Technology Management for Business, is available. This is focused on learning through project work in compact teams with external mentors from sponsoring organisations.

The Higher Apprenticeship in IT may be available in your area. This leads to a full Honours degree in addition to vocational, technical and Key Skills qualifications and work experience. Apprenticeships are also available in this field.

Late entry is often possible for those who have developed computer skills working in other fields, though starting salaries will probably be lower.

It would be helpful to have either a Diploma in Information Technology, NVQ Levels 2, 3 and 4 in Information Technology, a BTEC National Diploma in Computer Studies or ICT, a City & Guilds course in Information Technology or a BTEC Higher National Diploma in Computing.

Money guide

Starting/training salaries are usually from £25,000. With experience, you could earn from £35,000 to £45,000. In a senior position, salaries of £50,000+ are possible.

Related opportunities

- Business Analyst p150
- Database Administrator p156
- Network Manager p160
- Software Developer/Programmer p161

Further information

e-skills UK
1 Castle Lane, London SW1E 6DR
020 7963 8920; www.e-skills.com

Institute for the Management of Information Systems
5 Kingfisher House, New Mill Road, Orpington BR5 3QG
0700 002 3456; www.imis.org.uk

Institute of IT Training
Westwood House, Westwood Business Park,
Coventry CV4 8HS
0845 006 8858; www.iitt.org.uk

TECHNICAL SALES SPECIALIST

What the work involves

■ You will talk to customers interested in your product, finding out what they are looking for, answering technical questions and explaining how the product works.

■ You will then present what the client requires to an in-house technical team and work on adapting the product to suit the client.

■ Presentation of the finished product to your client is an important part of making the sale.

The type of person suited to this work

It is essential to be personable and persuasive. You will also need good verbal and written communication skills as you will be dealing with customers as well as writing up reports and proposals.

You must be able to clearly explain technical jargon to customers who may have no technical knowledge. Equally, you will need to understand all the technical specifications of your products as some of your customers will be experts.

It is a competitive market so you will need to be good at selling, negotiating and building customer loyalty. You will also need to be up to date with all the products out there so that you know the competition.

Working conditions

You might be based in an office, dealing with customers by phone or email, or in a retail outlet, selling direct.

If you specialise in selling to retail chains or organisations, you will spend a lot of time driving and in meetings. A driving licence will be useful.

Your hours will depend on your customers. Your employer may operate a shift system to deal with queries and sales from early until late, 7 days a week.

Future prospects

Employers include large ICT companies producing and retailing products such as mobile phones, computer hardware and software. Large specialist ICT retailers also employ technical sales staff.

The demand for new ICT products continues to grow but new competitors are always entering the market. Strong areas of demand include secure wireless broadband and mobile working.

You might be able to gain promotion to a supervisory or sales management role, or work as an IT consultant, a lecturer or contractor.

Advantages/disadvantages

If you close a deal at a good price or sell extras such as a service contract, you could be paid a bonus. Selling can be

Qualifications and courses

You will usually need a degree, Foundation degree or HNC/D in a computer-related subject to enter this job.

The normal minimum entry requirements for degrees are 2 A levels/3 H grades and 5 GCSEs/S grades (A*–C/1–3), and for Foundation degrees or HNC/Ds, 1 A level/2 H grades and 3 GCSEs/S grades (A*–C/1–3). Maths may be a required subject.

A funded route that may be on offer in your area is the IT and Telecoms Professionals Apprenticeship.

Experience in sales is extremely useful. If you have a sales background and want training in IT you can pursue a City & Guilds Level 4 Higher Professional Diploma in Information Management using ICT or a BTEC National Certificate/Diploma for IT Practitioners.

Initial training is usually intense as you will need to gain a thorough technical knowledge of your employer's products and their preferred communication style.

The Diploma in IT is available at Levels 1–3 and focuses on competencies relevant to IT professional work. Level 3 is equivalent to 3.5 A levels.

very stressful, with high sales targets to achieve. It is frustrating if you have to spend a lot of time with a customer without it resulting in a purchase.

Money guide

£22,000–£25,000 per year is usual for starting salaries. This could rise to £40,000 with experience. Sales managers can earn more than £70,000. Additional benefits may include profit sharing, performance-related pay, mobile phone, laptop and a car.

Related opportunities

■ Business Analyst p150
■ Computer Helpdesk Adviser p153
■ IT Trainer p159
■ Sales/Retail Assistant p494

Further information

British Computer Society
North Star House, North Star Avenue, Swindon SN2 1FA
01793 417424; www.bcs.org

e-skills UK
1 Castle Lane, London SW1E 6DR
020 7963 8920; www.e-skills.com

Institute of Sales & Marketing Management
Harrier Court, Lower Woodside LU1 4DQ
01582 840001; www.ismm.co.uk

TELECOMMUNICATIONS TECHNICIAN

What the work involves

- Telecommunications technicians install, test and repair networking and communications technology and systems across a range of applications, including mobile phones, telephones, satellite and radio networks, and aerials.

- Your day to day tasks will vary but you may be assembling, installing and testing telecommunications equipment; laying copper and fibre optic wire in the street or other sites; setting up or repairing networks.

- You may also be involved in designing or consulting on plans for telecommunications systems.

The type of person suited to this work

You should be interested in maths, IT, electronics and communications.

As you will be working in a team and explaining technical terms to customers you should have good communication and customer service skills. You should also have good writing skills to write up reports and produce statistics.

As you may be installing systems and laying wires which may involve heavy lifting and carrying, digging or using ladders you should be fit and have a good head for heights.

Working conditions

You will work 9am–5pm, Monday to Friday. You may be required to work shifts which may include evenings, weekends or to be available on-call. Overtime may be necessary to complete projects or meet deadlines.

You may be based in a factory workshop or in a control centre from where you will travel to complete projects which may be in homes, offices or outdoors.

Future prospects

To progress as a telecommunications technician you can apply to become a professionally recognised engineering technician (EngTech) or ICT technician (ICTTech).

With experience and qualifications you may be promoted to senior technician or supervisor. With further experience, qualifications and skills you can apply for incorporated and chartered engineer status.

You can become self-employed, or work on a contract basis.

There are numerous opportunities to work abroad.

Advantages/disadvantages

You may be in a diverse working environment as new and exciting developments in technology are occurring rapidly.

You may have to work outdoors in uncomfortable weather conditions.

Qualifications and courses

You can enter this profession as an apprentice, where you will be supervised by a qualified telecommunications technician. Apprenticeships usually last for 2 years. You can work towards NVQs Level 2–3.

The IT and Telecoms Professionals Apprenticeship requires that candidates have 4 GCSES (A*–C) which must include English, maths, science, technology, or a BTEC First diploma in a relevant subject.

You can also take a vocational course such as a BTEC National Certificate or Diploma, HND or a Foundation degree in a relevant subject such as telecommunications, technology, electronics or computing. City & Guilds also offer a Level 2 Certificate in Communications Cabling and a Level 3 Diploma in ICT Communications System.

You might also find the Diploma in Information Technology useful for this field.

Depending on the company you work for, continuing in-service training may be available. This can be combined with specific manufacturers' courses and vendor qualifications such as the networking qualifications offered by CISCO and Microsoft.

Money guide

Your starting salary will begin around £12,000 a year. With experience and qualifications you can earn up to £32,000 a year. The most experienced technicians can earn in the region around £40,000+ a year.

Related opportunities

- Computer Hardware Engineer p152
- Electrical Engineer p221
- Network Manager p160

Further information

The Institute of Telecoms Professionals
Sunbury TE, Green Street, Sunbury-on-Thames TW16 6QJ
01932 788861; enquiries@theitp.org; www.theitp.org

The Institution of Engineering and Technology
Michael Faraday House, Six Hills Way, Stevenage SG1 2AY
01438 313311; postmaster@theiet.org; www.theiet.org

City & Guilds

www.cityandguilds.com/myperfectjob

WEBSITE DESIGNER/ DEVELOPER

What the work involves

- You will be responsible for designing and coding a website, in charge of both the graphic and technical developments.

- You will use your computer expertise and creativity to make sure the website works properly and is attractive to users.

- You will work closely with your clients to make sure you understand what they want the website to look like, what features it needs and what purpose it has.

The type of person suited to this work

You will need to have very good IT skills, and be trained in graphic and website coding software packages.

Creativity is also a must, as you will be designing and coding websites that will need to be attractive, modern, easy, and fun to use.

Good communication skills are important, as you will need to explain clearly to your clients your designs and plans.

Most web designers/developers work as part of a team; you will need to work well with others as well as independently.

Working conditions

Your typical working week will be 9am–5.30pm, Monday to Friday, however you might need to work extra hours to complete projects and reach deadlines.

You are most likely to be working in an office, with other colleagues, or from home if you are self-employed. There will be some travelling involved when meeting clients so it would be useful to have a driving licence.

Future prospects

Website development is expanding. There are growing numbers of small businesses using the web to share information, market themselves, sell goods or services or advertise jobs.

There are jobs available across the UK, but with a greater concentration in London and the South-East. Some web designers/ developers have the opportunity to work abroad.

There are promotion opportunities to senior levels in a company, such as head of a design team, some web designers/ developers choose to move into training, or become self-employed.

Advantages/disadvantages

You can take great pride in your work; it is satisfying to see your finished website, knowing you are the person who created it.

You need to make sure you are up to date with new design trends and software, which could be challenging.

Qualifications and courses

There is no set entry route into web design/ developing. A degree or HND in an IT or design course will make you more attractive to employers, but some will be more interested in your experience and portfolio of work.

Degrees in design and web content management are offered by most universities; BTEC HNC/HNDs in computing subjects are available from colleges, which can be studied full or part time. Some courses offer one year of work experience with an IT company, which allows students to build a strong portfolio of work.

Postgraduate courses, such as the MSc in Multimedia, are available if your first degree is not IT related. Further study is available for IT professionals, with courses being offered by the British Computer Society and City & Guilds.

Your clients could be relying on you to create a website that will generate them more business; this means there is greater pressure on you to do an excellent job.

Money guide

You may start on around £20,000, with this rising to £30,000 after several years of experience. Senior web designers/ developers could earn up to £50,000. Web designers/ developers working for large companies as consultants may earn £60,000+.

Related opportunities

- Business Analyst p150
- Internet/Web Professional p158
- Interactive Media Designer p157
- Software Developer/Programmer p161

Further information

The Chartered Institute for IT
1st Floor, Block D, North Star House, North Star Avenue, Swindon SN2 1FA
01793 417417; www.bcs.org

The UK Web Design Association
www.ukwda.org

e-skills UK
1 Castle Lane, London SW1E 6DR
020 7963 8920; www.e-skills.com

www.cityandguilds.com/myperfectjob

Design, Arts and Crafts

The idea of turning your arts and crafts hobby into a career may be one you like the thought of. Jobs in this sector can involve working in any medium, from textiles to jewellery to metalwork or children's toys. You may find yourself working for a company but many people in this industry are self-employed working for a range of clients. This means you need to be very organised and have brilliant communication skills to ensure you can give your clients exactly what they want.

In this section we look at the following jobs:

For similar jobs to these have a look at these sections: *Marketing, Advertising, Media, Print and Publishing* on page 401 and *Performing Arts* starting on page 433.

ANIMATOR

What the work involves

- Animators produce images that appear to come to life on the screen, both creatively and commercially, for use by TV companies, games developers, in advertising, on websites, and in films.

- There are 4 specialisms: traditional (2D drawn), 2D computer generated, 3D computer generated and stop frame or stop motion. In all of these styles you will work to create a continuous story.

The type of person suited to this work

You will need strong creative flair and imagination to develop new ideas for animated stories and characters.

You must have excellent computer skills; a knowledge of software such as Flash, Maya and After Effects is essential. However modelling and life drawing are still important.

You must be patient, have a keen eye for detail and be able to work in a team as well as under pressure. Problem-solving skills are also necessary in a job where you might need to adapt to technical challenges.

Working conditions

Your working environment will depend on the type of animation you do. In some jobs, you will work with tools to hand-create images or forms in different materials. You could be on your feet (using your hands) all day: bending, lifting and shaping models.

Many new animation jobs involve work with specialist CAD packages at a PC console – sometimes with colleagues. Most of your work will be done during normal office hours except when projects have tight deadlines!

Future prospects

This is a highly competitive field. Although there are some opportunities for traditional drawing-based animators, the main area of growth is in computer generation. Most recruiting now comes from games developers.

Once within the industry, contracts are usually short term, but it is possible to move from working as a key animator, to an animation director role. At senior levels, you would have more creative input and be less directly involved with the technical side. With experience, you could set up as a freelance animator or start your own company.

Advantages/disadvantages

This type of work can be highly satisfying, providing opportunities to develop your own creative ideas and style. Animation is rising in popularity amongst the public. Many animated films are highly successful at the box office.

Qualifications and courses

Entry usually requires an HND, Foundation degree or degree in animation, art and design, or a related area; a relevant postgraduate qualification can be an asset. Entry requirements vary so it is best to check with individual institutions.

A portfolio of relevant work, demonstrated by a show reel, is essential. Unpaid work experience as a general or animation assistant for a company is a good way to build up relevant skills.

Entry to the profession without a degree/HND may be possible, by starting off as a runner fulfilling basic tasks for an employer, however most are graduates.

With experience, you could work towards an NVQ/SVQ Level 3 in Animation Assistance; Skillset vocational courses for the industry are also available in Design for the Moving Image at Levels 2, 3 and 4.

In more commercial jobs, you would need to produce work under pressure to meet a client's requirements.

Money guide

BECTU, the union for broadcasting, film, theatre, entertainment, leisure, interactive media and allied sectors, sets minimum wage guidelines for the industry, but animators negotiate their own rates and may receive more depending on the project. A new animator can expect to earn £20,000 a year. An experienced animator could earn £30,000 a year. Senior animators can expect to earn £40,000+ a year. Contact BECTU for details of current freelance salaries.

Related opportunities

- Cartoonist p169
- Fine Artist/Sculptor p173
- Graphic Designer p176
- Photographer/Photographic Stylist p418

Further information

Skillset
Focus Point, 21 Caledonian Road, London N1 9GB
0808 030 0900; www.skillset.org/animation

Guild of British Animation
26 Noel Street, London W1T 9PV
020 7434 2651

Broadcasting Entertainment Cinematograph and Theatre Union
373–377 Clapham Road, London SW9 9BT
020 7346 0900; www.bectu.org.uk

CARTOONIST

What the work involves

- You will plan and draw original cartoons and captions. These can be single images, whole cartoon strips or entire books.

- You will promote and market your work, for example by sending out samples to newspapers and advertising through the internet.

- Cartoonists create images for greetings cards, adverts, book illustrations, magazines, newspapers and websites.

- A small number of cartoonists are employed to run regular cartoon features in newspapers or other media but others maintain a 'web comic' of their work.

The type of person suited to this work

Creativity and an excellent sense of humour are essential. You should have a wild imagination and be up to date with current trends. Cartoon ideas often draw on situational humour or arise in quick response to headline news.

Even if you use a software art package, good drawing skills are very important. You may have to work to deadlines so need to be well organised, with good business management skills. Self-motivation is important.

As you will be sending out examples of your work to potential employers, you will need to be able to deal with rejection.

Working conditions

Most professional cartoonists work on a freelance basis, either in a studio or from home. This can be isolating as many work alone. Much of your time will be spent at a drawing board or a computer where you will either sit or stand using the materials required.

If you are self-employed you will have the freedom to set your own working hours. You might need to attend meetings with clients or potential employers, which could involve travelling long distances and working longer hours.

Future prospects

Most cartoonists work on a freelance basis for a number of employers at the same time. Some work as animators for companies that develop games and other ICT resources.

You could also be employed by publishers, advertising agencies, television studios, newspapers, magazines or theme parks. With experience you could run workshops in schools, libraries and museums. You could also specialise in one form of cartoon such as political or comic strips.

You could also move into other areas such as illustration or graphic design.

Qualifications and courses

ENTRY LEVEL 3

A strong portfolio and relevant experience are usually more important than formal qualifications. Most entrants have an HNC/D or degree in an art and design subject, such as graphic design, illustration or fine art.

There are a small number of cartooning qualifications available through distance learning courses, including a Cartoon Diploma course. These can help you develop your cartooning skills and provide feedback on your work.

In England, Wales and Northern Ireland, many students take a 1-year Art Foundation course as preparation for entry to an art and design degree course. 5 GCSEs (A*–C) and a relevant A level are usually required. In Scotland the first year of an Art and Design degree course equates to the Foundation year.

Advantages/disadvantages

Because cartoonists are usually paid for individual pieces of work, they have little job security especially at the start of their careers.

You would have the satisfaction of creating original work and seeing it in print.

Money guide

Salaries vary widely. It is possible to earn higher levels of pay by doing commercial work for greetings cards and adverts. Cartoonists starting out in full-time employment can expect to earn around £15,000–£20,000 per year. If you become established, well known, and are in demand for your work, you could earn up to £50,000. Cartoonists are usually paid on a freelance, one-off basis. Cartoonists creating work to illustrate books can earn royalties from sales.

Related opportunities

- Animator p168
- Fine Artist/Sculptor p173
- Graphic Designer p176
- Signwriter/Signmaker p186

Further information

Arts Council of England
2 Pear Tree Court, London EC1R 0DS
0845 300 6200; www.artscouncil.org.uk

The Cartoon Art Trust
The Cartoon Museum, 35 Little Russell Street, London WC1A 2HH
020 7580 8155; www.cartoonmuseum.org

Creative and Cultural Skills
The Leathermarket, Weston St, London SE1 3HN
020 7015 1800; www.creative-choices.co.uk/visualarts

Design, Arts and Crafts

CRCI: E

Design, Arts and Crafts

CRCI: E

COSTUME DESIGNER

What the work involves

- You will design, buy or hire the clothes and accessories worn by casts in films, plays and TV dramas.

- You will read scripts, research the period and setting of a production and come up with original sketches to best represent the director's vision. You will then decide which fabrics and materials to use. You could also be involved with making or overseeing costume production.

- You will be responsible for organising fittings and ensuring that costumes are delivered on time, are comfortable and within budget. Depending on the size of the production, you may also manage a team of costume professionals.

The type of person suited to this work

Creativity and originality are essential. Having the skills to draw designs by hand and to use specialist CAD software when required are also very important.

You should also have a meticulous eye for detail, and demonstrate a passion for costume history, fashion and the arts. It's important to be a good communicator and to work well in a team.

You must be organised to ensure that projects are carried out on time, within budget and as requested. As deadlines can be tight, you should also have the ability to work well under pressure.

Working conditions

Hours are long and irregular, including evenings and weekends.

It is possible to work for production companies, however most costume designers are freelancers. Therefore you will be required to travel around the UK and even overseas.

You will normally work within a studio using drawing tables, computers, cutting tables and sewing machines. This can be dusty and the cutting required can be dangerous.

It is likely that you will be standing for long periods of time, and may carry out some heavy lifting.

Future prospects

Costume designer vacancies are rarely advertised and most work is centred in major cities such as London and Manchester. It is essential for costume designers to have a strong portfolio and to build up good contacts.

If you work for a large organisation such as the BBC you could progress to head of department or to head of wardrobe for a theatre company.

Advantages/disadvantages

It's rewarding to see your original work in the public domain and you can work flexible hours.

Meeting tight deadlines can result in high stress levels.

Qualifications and courses

Most people have a Foundation degree, degree, or postgraduate diploma in a related subject such as art, fashion or performing arts. Most entrants begin their careers as costume makers and wardrobe trainees to gain practical experience.

A City & Guilds qualification is also available in Design and Craft – Theatre Costume at Levels 2 and 3. There are some formal training schemes, such as the BBC Design Trainee Scheme in costume design and you can study wardrobe assistance at FT2 – Film and Television Freelance Training.

It is useful to take courses in Computer Aided Design (CAD) and Photoshop to gain more desirable skills.

ENTRY LEVEL **4**

Money guide

Industry salaries vary depending on type of employer and geographical location.

New entrants to the profession can expect to earn about £18,000 per year, rising to £25,000–£40,000 per annum with experience.

The most experienced costume designers can earn £40,000+ per year.

Freelancers can expect to earn about £700 per week.

Related opportunities

- Fashion Designer/Milliner p172
- Display Designer/Window Dresser p171
- Tailor/Dressmaker p246

Further information

Costume Society of Great Britain
28 Eburne Road, London N7 6AU
www.costumesociety.org.uk

Department for Culture, Media and Sport
2–4 Cockspur Street, London SW1Y 5DH
020 7211 6200; www.culture.gov.uk;
enquiries@culture.gov.uk

Design Council
34 Bow Street, London WC2E 7DL
020 7420 5200; www.designcouncil.org.uk

City& Guilds

www.cityandguilds.com/myperfectjob

DISPLAY DESIGNER/ WINDOW DRESSER

What the work involves

- Using your technical design skills, you will plan and design eye-catching window or shop front displays for shops, businesses and other organisations.

- You will work closely with clients to make sure that your designs meet their requirements.

- Once you have identified materials and props for a window display, you will design an arrangement to create a striking theme or effect.

- You might also provide advice to other shop branches or organisations on successful display design.

The type of person suited to this work

It is important to have strong creative ability, as well as excellent technical drawing and CAD skills. You need to have excellent communication skills to be able to balance your vision with that of your client and work with a wide range of people.

Certain roles will require you to keep up with new trends and products in fashion and culture. You must also be numerate, as one of your responsibilities will be to manage project budgets. A good level of fitness is also needed as assembling displays can be tiring.

Working conditions

Normally, you will be working indoors with different hand tools, materials, fabrics and the products to be displayed in the window or display. The work can often be pressured due to strict deadlines. You might have to work late especially in the build up to holiday seasons such as Christmas.

The job can involve a great deal of manual work. You will do lots of lifting and be on your feet for long periods, which can be very tiring. A driving licence would be useful as you will have to travel to meet suppliers and visit exhibitions and different company stores.

Future prospects

There are a range of opportunities, for example working for specialist display consultancy firms, large retailers, museums and other visitor attractions.

You will probably start as a junior and progress to a more senior position as supervisor, head designer, merchandiser and possibly department manager.

If you work for a multinational company, the opportunity may arise to work abroad. You could also go on to teach or lecture in design-related subjects.

With experience, some display designers set up their own businesses or provide consultancy support to other organisations.

Qualifications and courses

There are no minimum qualifications for this type of work. However, many entrants will have done an accredited course.

Many different courses are available. Degree courses in Visual Merchandising usually require 2 A levels/H grades and 5 GCSEs/S grades (A*–C/1–3) or equivalent. Foundation degrees typically require 1 A level/H grade and 5 GCSEs/S grades (A*–C/1–3) or equivalent. Other courses include City & Guilds Level 2 award and the Fashion Retail Academy Level 4 Diploma in Visual Merchandising. Qualifications are also available from the British Display Society. It is also possible to take an ABC Level 3 qualification as well as an OCR Level 3 Certificate or Diploma in Visual Merchandising. The Diploma in Creative and Media may also be useful.

A portfolio of art and design work is usually required. Experience in display and the retail or exhibition sector can also be helpful.

Advantages/disadvantages

This type of work can be pressured due to tight deadlines. You will have the satisfaction of seeing very visible results from your work. Many people will enjoy your displays and give you positive feedback. You could get the chance to work with special effects like animatronics.

Money guide

Starting salaries are around £15,000 per year. Earnings can rise to £25,000 with experience. £50,000+ is possible for top designers at the most senior levels.

Related opportunities

- Retail Buyer p492
- Interior Designer p179
- Model Maker p182
- Retail Manager p493

Further information

British Display Society
14–18 Heralds Way, Town Centre, South Woodham Ferrers CM3 5TQ
020 8856 2030; www.britishdisplaysociety.co.uk

Design Council
34 Bow Street, London WC2E 7DL
020 7420 5200; www.designcouncil.org.uk

www.cityandguilds.com/myperfectjob

FASHION DESIGNER/ MILLINER

What the work involves

- Using your design sense and knowledge of textiles and other materials you will develop clothing, shoes and accessories. This could include articles such as babywear or sports clothes. A milliner specialises in creating headwear.

- You will specialise in haute couture, ready-to-wear or high street fashion.

- You will be responsible for analysing trends in fabrics, colours and shapes.

- As well as creating initial designs by hand and with computer aided design (CAD), you may also oversee the manufacture of these items.

The type of person suited to this work

It is essential to have the creativity and the imagination to develop original designs.

Having the skills to draw designs by hand and to use specialist CAD software is also very important. You should also have technical skills, such as pattern cutting and a good eye for design, colour and detail.

These abilities should be balanced with good business sense and the competency to see a project through.

You should have excellent communication, negotiation and organisational skills to ensure that projects are carried out on time, within budget and as requested.

Working conditions

This can be very stressful work, especially during the lead up to shows. Expect to work very long hours and to change ideas up until the last minute.

You will work alone, or in a small team, within a studio. The environment can be dusty and the cutting required can be dangerous.

You will also spend some of your time visiting textile producers and clients at their premises, which could be overseas.

Future prospects

Most designers work in and around the fashion hub of London.

Career progression depends upon the individual's talent and reputation. You will most likely start as a design assistant and progress to a role as a designer. With experience, it is possible to become a senior or head designer or work in an area such as style consultancy or fashion journalism. There are fewer opportunities for promotion for a milliner, due to the smaller size of this industry.

The UK industry has an excellent international reputation, offering progression to work overseas if desired.

Qualifications and courses

Entry to this profession is rare without a degree, Foundation degree or HNC/HND, in a relevant subject such as fashion, textiles or millinery. A postgraduate degree will help those who wish to specialise in a particular area, such as menswear and enable students from other academic backgrounds to show their commitment to working in the industry.

It could also be helpful to take a City & Guilds Level 1, 2 or 3 award in Millinery.

Most entrants are young, and have a diverse portfolio that encompasses the breadth of their design capabilities.

It is essential to acquire experience in the industry, even if unpaid, to gain contacts and demonstrate your commitment. Some graduates gain experience with European or American designers before aiming to break into the UK market.

Advantages/disadvantages

Seeing your original ideas in the public eye is satisfying.

You will have the opportunity to travel and meet interesting people of different nationalities.

Meeting tight deadlines in the lead up to shows can result in stress.

Money guide

Earnings vary according to type of employer and location. Your salary will be determined by your success and the most famous designers earn huge amounts. However, those starting out can expect to earn around £14,000–£22,000 per year, rising to an average of £25,000–£45,000 with 5 years' experience. At senior level you could earn £45,000–£80,000.

Related opportunities

- Display Designer/Window Dresser p171
- Illustrator/Technical Illustrator p178
- Interior Designer p179
- Model Maker p182

Further information

Design Council
34 Bow Street. London WC2E 7DL
020 7420 5200; www.designcouncil.org.uk

www.cityandguilds.com/myperfectjob

FINE ARTIST/SCULPTOR

What the work involves

- Fine artists work with various media such as oil paints and charcoal to create two-dimensional pieces of various sizes. Sculptors create three-dimensional pieces and use materials like clay, stone and metal.

- You will be responsible for promoting your work to sponsors, galleries and other organisations, by networking or issuing publicity material.

- You might organise solo or joint exhibitions in a variety of venues to showcase your work. Some residencies are available in institutes such as schools and prisons.

The type of person suited to this work

As you will be creating original works of art, you will need strong artistic and technical skills, well-developed powers of observation and a vivid imagination.

Self-belief and motivation are important, as it takes perseverance to turn an original idea into a finished piece. Sculptors will also require a high level of manual dexterity.

Many artists are self-employed, necessitating good business sense and organisational skills.

Good communication skills will help you to convince galleries to show and sell your work. An ability to network and make contacts in the art world is also useful.

Working conditions

You will work in a studio, research your work on location, or teach workshops at a residency. The majority of your time will be spent alone and you will most likely set your own hours.

Many artistic materials are dusty, oily or may stain and, even wearing overalls, you can expect to get dirty.

You might have to work with solvents and other chemicals, which can adversely affect those with sensitive skin or allergies.

Sculptors will work with dangerous tools such as knives, chisels and welding equipment.

Future prospects

This job demands confidence and persistence as few artists and sculptors earn their full living from art alone. You could earn additional income by working in related areas including arts education, community development and in art galleries.

A developing artist should join networks to make contacts. It is possible to sell your work through a number of galleries, shops, workshop co-operatives, studios and increasingly the internet. You could progress from showcasing your work in a group exhibition to securing a solo exhibition. You could eventually own your own studio, secure an

Qualifications and courses

Most artists have formal qualifications such as a degree in fine art, or an HNC/HND or degree in art and design. Postgraduate qualifications in fine art are also available. Sculptors usually have a fine art degree with a specialisation in sculpture. Entry requirements vary. Some institutions require A levels/H grades in relevant subjects, while others accept students on the strength of their portfolio.

It is possible to gain NVQ/SVQs in the following subjects: Arts Development and Teaching (Levels 3 and 4) and Visual and Applied Arts Practice Level 4.

For sculptors, training usually occurs on the job under the supervision of an experienced professional.

agent and have your work displayed in national and international art fairs.

Advantages/disadvantages

Your work is fulfilling and you will have the pleasure of seeing customers enjoy and appreciate your art.

It can be an isolated way of life and may not always lead to recognition and it may be difficult earning a living.

Money guide

It is possible to earn a regular income from your work, but this is more likely with experience.

Many artists have another job to provide a more stable source of income. Some teach part time, while others might work on a commission basis on community projects.

New artists can expect to earn about £22,900 a year, rising to £37,000 with 10 years' experience.

Sculptors can earn £26,000 per year for a residency.

Related opportunities

- Animator p168
- Cartoonist p169
- Graphic Designer p176
- Illustrator/Technical Illustrator p178

Further information

Arts Council of England
14 Great Peter Street, London SW1P 3NQ
0845 300 6200; www.artscouncil.org.uk

Scottish Arts Council
12 Manor Place, Edinburgh EH3 7DD
0131 226 6051; www.scottisharts.org.uk

Department for Culture, Media and Sport
2–4 Cockspur Street, London SW1Y 5DH
020 7211 6200; www.culture.gov.uk

GEMMOLOGIST

What the work involves

- Gemmologists work with diamonds, gems, precious stones and other ornamental materials.

- You will identify such materials and examine their quality. This may involve assessing or grading the cut of the stone, or identifying flaws or imitations (stones that are made of synthetic or artificial materials).

- You are likely to work for a jewellery house where you will be involved in making evaluations for customers and clients, and buying and selling stones.

- You may also be employed by an insurance company where you will make appraisals for those who wish to insure their jewellery.

The type of person suited to this work

It is important that you have an interest in rocks, gems and crystals, design, the earth sciences and geology.

You should also have a keen eye for detail as you will have to look for the slightest qualities to make valuations and identify stones.

As your work will mainly be hands-on you should be good with your hands and have good eyesight and memory.

You should be trustworthy and happy to work in high-security environments.

Working conditions

Your working hours will depend on the type of organisation that you work for. Retail jewellers work around 40 hours a week, including weekends.

You could work in an office, laboratory, workshop or studio. If you become involved in mining or travelling to gem markets you might have to work in remote and uncomfortable conditions.

You will use specialist equipment such as lenses, refractometers, spectroscopes and microscopes to examine gemstones.

Due to the nature of your work, you will have to adhere to strict security protocol, including locked doors, barred windows, armed guards, CCTV surveillance and alarm systems.

Future prospects

After you have finished your training and gained qualifications and experience, you may move up to senior management positions.

You may find opportunities in wholesale organisations, retail operations such as jewellery houses, and insurance companies.

There may be opportunities to work abroad.

With significant experience and good contacts you may become self-employed, work as a consultant or set up your own business as a jewellery maker or designer.

Qualifications and courses

There are no set entry requirements, however many entrants are graduates of relevant subjects such as art, craft, earth sciences, geology, sciences, physics in particular, and technology. The Diploma in Creative and Media could also be helpful.

If you have a qualification in a geological subject, and experience in a relevant field such as diamond mining, you could train as a gemmologist. Other useful qualifications include a degree in a geoscience subject such as geology, geophysics or geochemistry or a degree in gemmology and applied mineralogy from Kingston University. A BTEC National Diploma in Gemmology is available from Birmingham City University.

You are likely to train on the job and study for qualifications on a part time basis. This may take 1–4 years. The Gemmological Association (GEM-A) offers qualifications (in conjunction with Kingston University) which combine theoretical and practical work.

Jewellery courses and qualifications are available in many institutions throughout the UK.

Advantages/disadvantages

As a self-employed gemmologist your work may involve travel to mines, markets and international gem-selling centres such as Africa, Russia, Australia, Thailand, Brazil or Madagascar.

As you may be working with valuable materials you might have to work in restricted, high security environments.

Money guide

Starting salaries for gemmologists are around £12,000 a year.

As an experienced gemmologist you can earn between £25,000 and £35,000 a year.

You can earn more than £50,000 a year in a senior position.

Related opportunities

- Gold/Silversmith/Engraver p175
- Jeweller p487
- Materials Scientist p526

Further information

British Jewellers Association
Federation House, 10 Vyse Street, Hockley,
Birmingham B18 6LT
info@bja.org.uk; www.bja.org.uk

The Gemmological Association (GEM-A)
27 Greville Street, London EC1N 8TN
020 7407 3334; info@gem-a.com; www.gem-a.info

Jewellery and Allied Industries Training Council (JAITC)
Federation House, 10 Vyse Street, Hockley,
Birmingham B18 6LT
www.jaitc.org.uk

GOLD/SILVERSMITH/ ENGRAVER

What the work involves

- Gold/silversmiths create large and small items such as boxes, figures, picture frames and clocks in gold and silver.

- Engravers will create and insert or engrave images, words or patterns onto stone, glass, metal or wood.

- You will be required to work with your hands and use specialist equipment.

- You may create objects commissioned by jewellers or individual clients, or develop your own craft pieces to sell through galleries and craft shops.

The type of person suited to this work

This job demands dexterity and conscientiousness. A technical and creative approach is useful to help you to plan a piece and decide on the amount of material needed.

An artistic flair is essential in this type of work, as is the ability to see a project through from start to finish. You will need considerable patience to undertake delicate and sometimes repetitive work with specialist materials and equipment.

If you run your own business you will need a confident and determined approach so that you can promote yourself and your products. Financial and business skills are also needed.

Working conditions

You will probably work in a workshop or studio – either with other craftspeople or on your own. You may work in a shop and have meetings with customers to discuss pieces of work.

You will use specialist tools for heating, cutting, bending and shaping the metals, which can be dangerous if used incorrectly. You will therefore need to wear eye, face, hand and possibly ear protection for some jobs.

Future prospects

This is a competitive area due to the high cost of silver and gold, and the limited demand for glass and metal engraving.

However, stone engravers are sought by stone masonry firms which are doing less hand-carving than before.

You could work for a specialist company or a shop. With experience and funding, you could set up your own studio/ shop to sell individual pieces.

Advantages/disadvantages

This type of work provides the intense satisfaction of creating attractive and lasting objects.

Because you will be working with expensive materials, there is very little room for mistakes.

Working with materials such as glass and metal can be challenging and time-consuming.

Qualifications and courses

No formal educational qualifications are required, but GCSEs in art and design or design and technology are useful.

Many different formal qualifications in design crafts as well as art and design are available such as City & Guilds certificates, BTEC qualifications, UAL Foundation Diplomas and HNDS. Foundation degrees in 3D Design and Applied Arts and the Diploma in Creative and Media might be useful.

For the creative side of engraving, there are degrees and Master's degrees in metalwork, jewellery making and silversmithing. Entry for a degree usually requires a portfolio of work, an art and design Foundation course and/or a relevant BTEC National Diploma.

The National Association of Goldsmiths has created many courses, designed to complement a traineeship. Many can be undertaken by distance learning.

Training is done on the job, working with an experienced goldsmith, silversmith or engraver. There is no age limit for entry to training.

Money guide

Many goldsmiths/silversmiths work on a part-time basis either for themselves or for jewellers.

You could start out as a full-time employed designer earning £12,000+ per year, rising to £20,000–£25,000.

Engravers should expect to earn £10,000–£14,000 to begin with. This can rise to £16,000–£20,000 with experience. Top earners can expect to earn £30,000.

Related opportunities

- Jewellery Designer p180
- Model maker p182

Further information

British Jewellers' Association
Federation House, 10 Vyse Street, Birmingham B18 6LT
0121 237 1110; www.bja.org.uk

Crafts Council
44a Pentonville Road, London N1 9BY
0207 806 2500; www.craftscouncil.org.uk

Institute of Professional Goldsmiths
PO Box 668, Rickmansworth WD3 0EQ
www.ipgold.org.uk

www.cityandguilds.com/myperfectjob

GRAPHIC DESIGNER

What the work involves

- Graphic designers produce original images and designs for use in published or other materials, such as leaflets, brochures, websites, logos and stationery. Most work is now done on computer, although manual techniques are also occasionally used.

- You will need a thorough understanding of clients' needs in order to develop appropriate designs for specific projects.

- You will be responsible for producing time and budget schedules, and ensuring that they are adhered to.

The type of person suited to this work

It is essential to have a strong creative flair, the imagination to develop original designs and a good eye for layout. Having the skills to draw designs by hand and to use industry-specific graphics or multimedia software packages is also important.

You should also have good communication skills, including the confidence to present ideas to colleagues and clients.

It is likely you will work in a fast-paced environment with tight deadlines and will need to be a good multi-tasker, who works well under pressure.

Organisational skills are essential to ensure that projects are carried out on time, within budget and as requested.

Working conditions

Most of your work will take place at a computer and drawing board within a studio. However, you may undertake external research in order to gain inspiration for a project and you will also be required to attend client meetings to present your ideas.

The majority of graphic designers work 37 hours a week, from Monday to Friday. You will be expected to work supplementary hours in order to meet deadlines. Part-time work is available and many designers become freelancers having gained significant experience.

Future prospects

In the UK there are about 40,000 businesses in this growing sector, with over half being in London and the South East. The diversity of graphic design qualifications available has resulted in increased competition for positions.

There is the possibility to work for a range of clients in an agency or in-house for a large organisation such as a bank. Junior designers can progress to senior and eventually a director role. With experience there are many freelance opportunities.

Qualifications and courses

(Entry Level 4)

Most entrants have a degree or diploma in a subject like graphic design, or art. For a degree you need 5 GCSEs (A*–C) and a BTEC National Diploma or a Foundation Diploma in Art and Design, and possibly 2 A levels, including an art related subject. The Diploma in Creative and Media, Foundation degrees, design apprenticeships and NVQs in Design are also available.

A diverse portfolio is also needed. In the absence of formal qualifications, a keen interest and an exceptional portfolio may secure a trainee post.

Advantages/disadvantages

You will have the opportunity to be creative and hone your business skills simultaneously.

The creation of original work and seeing your ideas being used in the public eye is satisfying.

Competition is becoming increasingly fierce as the number of available qualifications in this field rises.

Meeting tight deadlines can result in high stress levels.

Money guide

Earnings vary according to the type of employer and geographical location. Large organisations tend to offer higher salaries.

A junior designer can expect to earn £11,000–£18,000 a year. This may rise to £25,000 with experience.

A creative director can earn £65,000+.

It is possible for a highly regarded freelancer to amass up to £40 per hour.

Related opportunities

- Advertising Art Director p403
- Animator p168
- Cartoonist p169
- Illustrator/Technical Illustrator p178

Further information

Department for Culture, Media and Sport
2–4 Cockspur Street, London SW1Y 5DH
020 7211 6000; www.culture.gov.uk

Design and Art Direction
9 Graphite Square, Vauxhall Walk, London SE11 5EE
020 7840 1111; www.dandad.org

Design Council
34 Bow Street, London WC2E 7DL
020 7420 5200; www.designcouncil.org.uk

School Profile

SCHOOL OF ART AND DESIGN
University of Lincoln

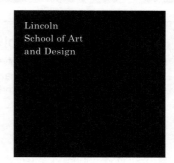

The **Lincoln School of Art and Design**, at the University of Lincoln, founded in the 1860s, provides a range of exciting, popular and well-regarded courses in Art and Design disciplines, taught by experienced and committed staff in various sites across the historic part of the city. Many of the courses are vocational in nature, with strong industry links, and with regular field trips, both nationally and internationally, students are often able to exhibit their work outside of Lincoln, such as in London, Milan and Shanghai. Our students are also regular winners of international awards such as D&AD, MPA Roses Student Creativity, New Designers and Brahm SH.

Undergraduate courses offered:-

BA (Hons) Animation

BA (Hons) Conservation and Restoration

BA (Hons) Contemporary Lens Media (Photography and Moving Image)

BA (Hons) Creative Advertising

BA (Hons) Fashion Studies

BA (Hons) Fine Art

BA (Hons) Graphic Design

BA (Hons) Illustration

BA (Hons) Interactive Design (Web design, moving graphics, sound)

BA (Hons) Jewellery and Object (new for 2010)

BA (Hons) Product Design (3D design)

For further information on any of these courses, please contact the Faculty of Art, Architecture and Design at aadenquiries@lincoln.ac.uk or telephone 01522 837171, or visit the School Blog at www.lsad.co.uk

Web links:-

University website	**www.lincoln.ac.uk/aad**
School of Art and Design website	**www.lsad.co.uk**
School of Architecture website	**www.lincoln.ac.uk/lsa**

UNIVERSITY OF
LINCOLN

ILLUSTRATOR/ TECHNICAL ILLUSTRATOR

What the work involves

- You will create original illustrations for published material such as books, magazines and greetings cards. You may also create images for TV and the internet.

- You will work with specialist design software, pen and ink and other media to develop strong designs.

- Your work will include attending client meetings, agreeing payments and contracts, and working to fulfil specific clients' requirements.

- Technical illustrators design accurate graphics or illustrations to accompany and clarify often complex technical information in product and systems manuals, training information, presentations and technical websites.

The type of person suited to this work

You will need strong design skills, a creative flair and imagination for illustration work.

Technical illustration necessitates high attention to detail and strong technical drawing skills to plan and create accurate images.

You should also be able to work well with computer design software.

Sharing ideas and working around another person's vision or 'brief' demands good communication skills.

As many illustrators/technical illustrators work on a self-employed basis, you will need the confidence to promote your services as well as good business and financial sense.

You will require a good knowledge of legal issues in order to protect your copyright and licence rights.

Working conditions

You are likely to work in a shared studio or at your own premises. Technical illustrators occasionally work in offices, and some illustrators are employed in publishing or design houses, but freelancing is increasing.

You will probably use paints and adhesives which may cause respiratory problems or skin allergies for susceptible people.

Future prospects

The internet and email have made it easier for illustrators to promote themselves and find work, and it is now possible to gain work from clients based overseas.

Some people choose to specialise in competitive areas such as medical, botanical or technical illustration.

To subsidise their income, some illustrators also teach, lecture or work in other related areas. A small number write and illustrate their own books. Others supplement their salary by selling illustrations and paintings through galleries.

Qualifications and courses

ENTRY LEVEL 3

Most professional illustrators have an HNC/HND, Foundation degree or degree in art and design related subjects such as graphic design, fine art and fashion. The Diploma in Creative and Media could be helpful. A strong portfolio is essential, and an excellent portfolio can be a substitute for academic qualifications.

Technical illustrators are required to demonstrate a good knowledge of science and/or technology depending on your desired specialisation.

Training is provided on the job, and can lead to specialisation in such areas as technical illustration or medical illustration.

The Association of Illustrators (AOI) offer practical advice to illustrators and run training seminars on business and computer related subjects.

Advantages/disadvantages

This type of work provides the satisfaction of seeing your work in print and often in the public domain.

Working on a freelance, job-by-job basis can be an insecure way to make a living. Generally, illustrators have a second job to support them during quiet periods.

Money guide

Salaries vary according to employers and individual projects. Projects can range from one image to a series of illustrations. Illustrators may be paid per project, by the hour or by the day. Hourly pay is around £35.

Income for employed new entrants is around £14,000–£18,000 per year. Experienced illustrators could earn £20,000–£30,000. With 10 years' experience, the best known can earn in excess of £40,000 per year.

Related opportunities

- Fine Artist/Sculptor p173
- Cartoonist p169
- Graphic Designer p176
- Medical Illustrator p181

Further information

Association of Illustrators
2nd Floor, Back Building, 150 Curtain Road, London EC2A 3AT
020 7613 4328; www.theaoi.com

Institute of Scientific and Technical Communicators
(ISTC) Airport House, Purley Way, Croydon CR0 0XZ
020 8253 4506; www.istc.org.uk

INTERIOR DESIGNER

What the work involves

- Interior designers create specific, co-ordinated styles for homes, commercial spaces and other buildings.

- You will be required to assess spaces, produce detailed designs, increasingly using computer-aided design (CAD) software, and choose suitable materials for the project, which may include upholstery, wallpaper, furniture and decorative objects

- You will need to get a good understanding the client's needs, and also negotiate fees with them.

- You will provide supervision to ensure that the project is completed accurately and is in accordance with the budget and schedule.

The type of person suited to this work

It is essential to have a strong creative flair and the imagination to develop original designs. Having the skills to draw designs by hand and to use specialist CAD software when required are also very important.

You will be required to keep up-to-date with changes in design and architecture, and to understand building regulations.

These abilities should be balanced with good business sense and the competency to see a project through.

You should also have good communication, negotiation and organisational skills to ensure that projects are carried out on time, within budget and as requested.

Working conditions

The main employers in this sector are design and architectural firms. However many designers are self-employed and part-time work is possible.

Many client meetings occur in the evenings and at weekends. You could be working on several contracts at the same time and tight deadlines can result in stress and may necessitate extra working hours.

Your work will be divided between meeting clients in their own premises and working in your studio, or other work space.

Smart dress is expected and protective clothing may be required on-site.

Future prospects

The contribution of design towards the UK economy is very important and the significance of this intensely competitive sector continues to grow.

Although many interior designers work for design and architectural companies, some are freelance and many choose self-employment, either immediately after graduation or after gaining work experience.

Gaining significant experience can result in progression to a partner role in a consultancy.

The UK industry has an excellent international reputation offering progression to work overseas if desired.

Qualifications and courses

ENTRY LEVEL 3

Entry is rare without an HNC/HND, Foundation degree or degree in art or design; 5 GCSEs (A*–C) and 2 relevant A levels are usually required. Many applicants also complete a Foundation Diploma in art and design.

In the absence of formal qualifications, an exceptional portfolio may secure a trainee post within a design or architectural firm.

City & Guilds qualifications are also available in Interior Design and CAD skills.

Advantages/disadvantages

The creation of original work and seeing your ideas being used in a practical or decorative way is satisfying.

Working as a freelance designer can result in greater flexibility.

You will have to adapt your ideas to fit the client's requirements.

Money guide

Junior interior designers can expect to earn between £22,000 and £26,000 per year.

Senior designers can earn £30,000+ per year, while directors can earn up to £75,000 per year.

In contrast, earnings for self-employed designers can be very low, particularly at the beginning. Freelancers typically earn from £18 per hour upwards.

Related opportunities

- Display Designer/Window Dresser p171
- Illustrator/Technical Illustrator p178
- Model Maker p182

Further information

British Interior Design Association
Units 109–111 The Chambers, Chelsea Harbour, London SW10 0XF
020 7349 0800; www.bida.org

Design Council
34 Bow Street, London WC2E 7DL
020 7420 5200; www.designcouncil.org.uk

Chartered Society of Designers
1 Cedar Court, Royal Oak Yard, Bermondsey Street, London SE1 3GA
020 7357 8088; www.csd.org.uk

City& Guilds

www.cityandguilds.com/myperfectjob

JEWELLERY DESIGNER

What the work involves

- Jewellery designers are involved in each aspect of the production of decorative pieces of jewellery, made of gold, silver, precious metals and stones.

- You will research the design and the function of a piece; its symbolism, the materials used, the cost, the potential buyer and even current trends.

- You will prepare detailed drawings which you or a craftworker will construct using traditional crafting methods or using high-tech machinery. A design may be for a one-off piece or part of a range of pieces.

- You will undertake tasks such as stone cutting and setting, model-making, mounting, engraving, enamelling, welding, chain-making, cleaning and polishing.

The type of person suited to this work

You should have a strong interest in art, design and craftwork. As your sales may be influenced by the current design marketplace you should keep up-to-date with jewellery fashion and design trends.

You must have a keen eye for detail and patience as you will be working with small scales and intricate and delicate designs.

You will need to be organised and self-motivated as you will probably be working on a variety of projects at the same time.

You should also be able to visualise two-dimensional designs as three-dimensional objects.

Working conditions

If you are employed by a company you will usually work 39 hours a week, Monday to Friday, including late nights or weekend work when deadlines are approaching.

You can also work on a freelance basis or become self-employed. If you are self-employed you are likely to work on commission and produce designs specifically tailored to the client's requirements.

You may work in a studio which can be bright and airy or in a large workshop, which may be noisy and dusty. You must wear protective clothing.

Future prospects

As you gain experience and build up a good reputation you may be able to become self-employed. To stay ahead in the industry you should attend trade fairs and exhibitions.

As an employed goldsmith or silversmith you may be able to progress to management positions or retail positions such as international buyer.

Advantages/disadvantages

You may be able to work from your own designs and see your creations become popular pieces.

Qualifications and courses

There are no academic requirements in order to become a jewellery designer. However many courses and programmes are available which may help you to develop your skills.

You can take GCSEs in art and design or design technology which will help you to gain entry to this profession or to higher level courses. These include HNDs, Foundation degrees or degrees in art and design or craft making such as goldsmithing, silversmithing, and jewellery design. It may be possible to move across from another relevant subject such as fashion design, textile design, fine art, or applied arts if you build up a suitable portfolio.

If you are interested in gold and silver craftwork specifically you may benefit from a BTEC National Certificate or Diploma course in Design Crafts which are available at some colleges.

However, qualifications are not as important as craft skills. Work placements can help you to accumulate experience of the jewellery industry and build up a network of contacts which will help you to develop skills and find buyers and sellers for your work.

As a self-employed jewellery designer you may find that without the right support system in areas such as promotion, marketing and sales it can be difficult to become established.

Money guide

As a graduate your salary can start at around £15,000 but this can increase to £25,000 or more with experience.

Your salary will depend greatly on factors such as whether or not you are self-employed, experienced and have enough success to gain a reputation within the industry.

Related opportunities

- Gold/Silversmith/Engraver p175
- Fashion Designer/Milliner p172
- Product Designer p185

Further information

The British Jewellers Association
Federation House, 10 Vyse Street, Birmingham B18 6LT
info@bja.org.uk; www.bja.org.uk

Crafts Council
44a Pentonville Road, London N1 9BY
0207 806 2500; education@craftscouncil.org.uk;
www.craftscouncil.org.uk

City&
Guilds

www.cityandguilds.com/myperfectjob

MEDICAL ILLUSTRATOR

What the work involves

- Medical illustrators create annotated or labelled images to provide visual information to professionals and trainees working in medical care, research and education.

- You may also work as a medical photographer or video producer (digital technician), or combine all these functions in one role.

- You will have to record images of patients and develop graphics for health/medical publications such as information leaflets and websites. You could work in wards, operating theatres, pathology labs, mortuaries and clinical exam centres.

Qualifications and courses

ENTRY LEVEL 4

A national register for medical illustrators was formed in 2010. Qualified clinical illustrators are now required to register with the Health Professions Council (HPC) and will need to have a degree or postgraduate degree in clinical photography.

The Medical Artists' Educational Trust postgraduate Diploma in Medical Art is available in Manchester and London. Entrants require a degree and a relevant portfolio. Completion results in membership of the trust.

Medical illustrators usually enter the profession as trainees and learn on the job while working towards a medical illustration qualification.

The type of person suited to this work

Good visual sense and attention to detail is very important.

You should have excellent technical skills to work with equipment such as videos and cameras, and will have to work creatively yet accurately with computer design packages.

As you will have to record images of patients, a sensitive, tactful and ethical approach is necessary. You should also have a knowledge of physiology and anatomy.

Also required is the ability to communicate with all sorts of people, some of whom could be very ill. You must be able to cope with upsetting situations and sights, for example, if visiting someone who is terminally ill.

Working conditions

You may be based within a group of hospitals and other centres and have to travel regularly between these. During the day you will visit theatres, wards, training centres and mortuaries – all of which could involve distressing sights and intense odours. You may have to be on call at night to photograph emergency operations.

Using a computer and software design packages, you will work within an office or studio to prepare and produce images and visual information. You may also have to record laboratory results.

Future prospects

Whilst this is a relatively small and quite competitive area of work, there is a steady need for accurate medical visual information.

Gaining a range of technical skills and experience rather than specialising in one area could open more opportunities.

After training, it is possible to progress within one organisation to head of department or you could go on to provide freelance services for medical establishments or medical and scientific publications.

Advantages/disadvantages

This job gives the satisfaction of providing valuable visual information to help medical professionals and their patients.

You may have the opportunity to freelance, which offers flexibility.

You will work with sick and sometimes distressed patients and may have to deal with upsetting sights.

You may have to be on call at night in order to photograph emergency operations.

Money guide

£16,500 per year is usual for trainee illustrators.

With experience, senior medical illustrators can earn around £30,000+.

Up to £50,000 is possible for a head of department in a university teaching hospital.

Medical illustrators in large universities could be employed on a number of pay scales covering technicians, medical laboratory officers, or sterile services technicians. Check with the universities for more details.

Related opportunities

- Fine Artist/Sculptor p173
- Graphic Designer p176
- Illustrator/Technical Illustrator p178
- Photographer/Photographic Stylist p418

Further information

Association of Illustrators
2nd Floor, Back Building, 150 Curtain Road,
London EC2A 3AT
020 7613 4328; www.theaoi.com

Health Professions Council (HPC)
Park House, 184 Kennington Park Road,
London SE11 4BU
020 7582 0866; www.hpc-uk.org

Institute of Medical Illustrators
29 Arboretum Street, Nottingham NG1 4JA
0121 338 8492; www.imi.org.uk

MODEL MAKER

What the work involves

- Working with materials such as fibreglass, resin, wood and rubber you will create three-dimensional images or models.

- You will construct detailed and accurate models of buildings, prototypes of items, engineering products and figures for museums, TV or film companies.

- You will work with clients to develop their ideas into a convincing and practical model, deciding which materials to use.

- You will plan the model using technical drawings or computer software

The type of person suited to this work

You will need a strong creative flair to visualise and develop models. Producing detailed models out of fragile materials demands tremendous patience and good technical skills. You should have a logical approach, in order to plan and create accurate work.

The tasks will demand great attention to detail and good eyesight. A feel for and interest in design will enable you to create well-planned models.

You will also need a basic knowledge of maths and the ability to understand technical drawings. The capacity to work effectively with computer design packages is increasingly important in this area of work.

Working conditions

Most model makers work standard office hours, but evening and weekend work may be required to meet deadlines.

Your work will be carried out in a studio, where you will wear protective clothing to suit the materials and tools you are using. This could include eye, ear and skin protection. Sometimes you may be based in an office, planning models with specialist design software.

You may need to travel around the UK or overseas to meet clients and assemble or install models for them.

Future prospects

Most model makers work within London and the South-East. Whilst this is quite a small area of work, demand is stable.

You could focus on architectural model making and work for a large architectural practice, or work for museums to create historical models for display purposes. However, most model makers work on a freelance basis and are paid on a contract-by-contract basis.

Some model makers choose to set up their own business after developing a strong portfolio and good reputation.

Qualifications and courses

There are no formal entry requirements. However, most entrants complete a model-making course and a portfolio of work is usually required.

The ability to work with your hands, using specialist tools, is required.

There are a wide variety of courses available including a City & Guilds Level 2 Progression Award in Applying Engineering Principles, ABC Level 3 Award in Model Making and Presentation, and degrees in three-dimensional design. Entry requirements vary but are very competitive and most institutions will expect some GCSEs/S grades in subjects such as maths, design and technology, and physics. At least 2 A levels (or equivalent) in a relevant subject are required for degree courses. Foundation courses are available in Art and Design which can aid applicants to build up a portfolio of work. Entry via an Apprenticeship/Skillseekers programme may be possible.

Advantages/disadvantages

This job can provide the satisfaction of developing original work.

You will need to create highly detailed work to fairly limited deadlines, which can be stressful.

Money guide

Starting salaries are around £18,000–£20,000 per year. With experience this rises to around £22,500–£30,000. At senior level, with many years of experience, you could earn up to £45,000.

Related opportunities

- Fine Artist/Sculptor p173
- Graphic Designer p176
- Signwriter/Signmaker p186
- Toymaker/Designer p188

Further information

Design Council
34 Bow Street, London WC2E 7DL
020 7420 5200; www.designcouncil.org.uk

Creative and Cultural Skills
Lafone House, The Leathermarket, Weston St, London SE1 3HN
020 7015 1800; www.creative-choices.co.uk/design

www.cityandguilds.com/myperfectjob

MUSICAL INSTRUMENT MAKER/ REPAIRER/PIANO TUNER

Design, Arts and Crafts

CRCI: NJ

What the work involves

- You will make, repair and service musical instruments such as pianos, flutes and violins. This can involve replacing worn-down or broken parts or checking for the cause of specific faults.

- You will work with customers and deal with repair requests or commissions for new instruments.

- Piano tuners check the condition and pitch range of different types of pianos by undertaking assessments using specialist equipment. This could range from fine tuning to obtain 'concert pitch', to significant maintenance work.

The type of person suited to this work

A passion for music and a practical understanding of how musical instruments function is essential. They are complex objects so you will need a good eye for detail and a patient approach. In addition, piano tuners should have excellent hearing.

Strong technical skills will enable you to design, create or repair instruments.

You will need to be dexterous and confident in working with your hands and in using materials such as wood and glue.

You need to have excellent communication and interpersonal skills in order to deal with customers.

Working conditions

You will work with a range of specialised tools in the workshop of a specialist company or from home if self-employed.

With larger instruments, such as pianos, organs or timpani, you will need to visit private homes and other locations (such as concert halls, theatres or music studios) to do repairs on-site. It would be useful to have your own driving licence and transport.

You need to have strong manual handling skill. This job may be difficult for people with skin or respiratory conditions due to some of the specialist materials used.

Future prospects

This is a specialised area of work, but you could work for educational music departments, major orchestras, opera houses and theatres, rehearsal studios, retailers, and individual musicians.

Some musical instrument makers/repairers specialise in a specific area such as classical guitars or make more unusual instruments to customer requests.

A lot of people are self-employed and some music shops will publicise local repairers, instrument makers and tuners, rather than employing their own.

Qualifications and courses

Musical instrument maker/ repairer

You need to have GCSEs/S grades in relevant subjects, such as design and technology, plus a professional qualification. These range from City & Guilds certificates to degrees.

Specific vocational qualifications are available in music technology, musical instrument making, and musical instrument technology and repair. Some courses allow specialisation in certain types of instruments such as strings or woodwind.

Piano tuner

Piano-tuning courses are available. The School of Violin, Woodwind and Piano Technology at Newark College offers a piano tuning and repair programme. Students learn about the tuning and repair of pianos as well as the practicalities of running a small business.

Advantages/disadvantages

Many musical instrument repairers/makers/piano tuners are freelance and work on a project-by-project basis, which can create some job insecurity.

This career has excellent fringe benefits as you could work for some of the best musical talents in the UK.

Money guide

In some parts of the country there is not sufficient work for full-time employment so earnings will depend on your location, the local music scene and your specialism.

You could earn £16,000–£20,000 per year once trained. The most experienced people can earn up to £30,000+.

Related opportunities

- Musician p446
- Music Teacher p199
- Art Therapist p292
- Model Maker p182

Further information

Crafts Council
44a Pentonville Road, London N1 9BY
020 7806 2500; www.craftscouncil.org.uk

Institute of Musical Instrument Technology
Northfield House, 11 Kendal Avenue South, Croydon CR2 0QR; www.imit.org.uk

Pianoforte Tuners' Association
PO Box 1312, Lightwater, Woking GU18 5UB
0845 602 8796; www.pianotuner.org.uk

PICTURE FRAMER

What the work involves

- You will plan and create attractive and protective surrounds or frames for prints, paintings, photographs and three-dimensional objects.

- Working with specialist equipment and materials you will create strong, high-quality frames.

- Helping customers choose the most suitable style and size of frame will be part of your job, as will advising them on the most practical and appropriate method of framing and glazing the artwork.

- If you work on a self-employed basis you will need to promote your services to potential customers.

The type of person suited to this work

Creativity is essential in order to design the frame. You will also need good customer service skills. Technical skills and the ability to work safely with potentially dangerous equipment are highly important.

Paying attention to detail and taking a pride in your work will ensure that you produce high-quality frames. You will need to be able to work under pressure as short deadlines can be a part of this job. You should also be commercially aware. If self-employed, you will require business, financial and marketing skills to be successful.

Working conditions

You could work in a shop or workshop. When working in the shop you will have to deal with customers who can sometimes be rude or confrontational, if dissatisfied. Workshops can be noisy and busy.

Picture framers generally work 40 hours a week, with weekend work often needed and overtime during busy periods. Many picture framers work on a part-time basis.

Picture framers work with potentially dangerous equipment such as specialist cutting machinery so you will need to be aware of health and safety requirements.

Future prospects

Success depends upon the skills and reputation of the individual.

Many picture framers set up their own studios or shops where they also sell works of art and artists' materials. Others work solely in framing and are employed in larger workshops – mass-producing framed prints and mirrors. There is the possibility of promotion to supervisor or manager in bigger companies. Some picture framers take additional training so that they can teach part time.

Advantages/disadvantages

This job provides the satisfaction of creating enduring and high-quality items.

This is precise, careful work that demands a lot of patience.

Qualifications and courses

There are no formal educational requirements. However, most people have a relevant qualification or related experience as a picture framer requires specific skills and techniques. Courses are available from local colleges and education services which are often part time and run from 8 weeks to a year.

An interest and experience in woodwork or metalwork would be useful. GCSE grades (A*–E), certificates, diplomas, NVQs, Foundation degrees or degrees can also be an advantage; relevant subjects include art and design and craft, design and technology. A Diploma in Creative and Media is also available.

Training is usually done on the job.

Picture framers are able to work towards the Fine Art Trade Guild Commended Framer (GCF) qualification, which involves both practical and written assessments. In order to work with high-value items, framers need to be trained to conservation standards.

Money guide

Your salary will depend on where you work and your employment situation. The starting salary is usually about £12,000 per year. This rises to £15,000–£20,000 with experience. If you work in a specialist shop or work as a manager you could earn £25,000+. Earnings for self-employed framers vary depending on location and expertise.

Related opportunities

- Antiques Dealer p478
- Conservator/Restorer p350
- Gold/Silversmith/Engraver p175
- Model Maker p182

Further information

Fine Art Trade Guild
16–18 Empress Place, London SW6 1TT
020 7381 6616; www.fineart.co.uk

Institute of Conservation
1st floor, Downstream Building, 1 London Bridge, London SE1 9BG
020 7785 3807; www.icon.org.uk

City&
Guilds

www.cityandguilds.com/myperfectjob

PRODUCT DESIGNER

What the work involves

- Product designers create products and improve the design, functionality or cost efficiency of existing products. These could be day-to-day products like tables, or specialist ones like medical equipment.

- You will decide upon a design brief with your client and carry out research on similar products and consumer behaviour. You will use both traditional drawing techniques, as well as specialist computer software in order to develop appropriate designs.

- You will select materials, produce models and ensure that the project is completed on time and to budget.

The type of person suited to this work

This job requires both creativity and technical expertise.

You should have a good eye for design as well as technical drawing and ICT skills. It is important to understand how different materials and production methods function.

You should also have good communication skills and an understanding of clients' needs and consumer behaviour.

Problem-solving and organisational skills are essential to ensure projects are completed on time and within budget.

Working conditions

The majority of product designers work 37 hours a week, Monday–Friday. You will be expected to work extra hours in order to meet deadlines. Part-time work is available.

Most of your work will take place in a bright, clean studio or office. However, you will undertake some experiments and material testing in lab conditions, using some dangerous cutting and construction tools. In addition you might have to visit production factories, which may be dusty and noisy.

Future prospects

Product designers work in manufacturing firms and design companies, which produce material for a variety of sectors. Employment is available all over the UK, but most design consultancies are based in London and the South-East.

There is strong competition for entry level jobs; however there is a shortage of experienced product designers with a high level of technical expertise. Experienced designers may have the opportunity to work abroad or freelance. You could progress to a role as senior designer or manager.

Advantages/disadvantages

You will have the opportunity to use your imagination and your technical skills. The creation of original work that is used by the public is satisfying.

Competition for entry level jobs is fierce. Meeting tight deadlines can be stressful.

Qualifications and courses

Entry to this profession is rare without an HNC/HND, Foundation degree or degree in product design, industrial design or a related subject. Degree courses last 3 or 4 years and some include a year-long industrial placement. Design courses can be centred on the art or engineering sides of product design. A general art Foundation course for 1 year is sometimes taken by those choosing the art-based route.

Entry requirements for a degree are usually 2 A levels and 5 GCSEs (A*–C). For an HND, you should have an A level in an art and design related subject and 3 GCSEs (A*–C). A BTEC qualification in Art and Design or 3D Design or a Diploma in Manufacturing and Product Design, Creative and Media or Engineering could also be useful.

A postgraduate qualification may be particularly useful in specific sectors and with certain European clients.

Previous experience through industrial placements, freelance work or design competitions is very useful.

Money guide

Earnings vary according to the type of employer and geographical location. Large organisations tend to offer higher salaries.

Starting salaries are around £14,000–£20,000 per year. This may rise to £20,000–£40,000 with experience. Senior product designers can earn £45,000+ and the most skilled and experienced account directors can achieve up to £60,000.

Related opportunities

- Manufacturing/Production Engineer p230
- Toolmaker p249
- Toymaker/Designer p188

Further information

Chartered Society of Designers
1 Cedar Court, Royal Oak Yard, Bermondsey Street, London SE1 3GA
020 7357 8088; www.csd.org.uk

www.cityandguilds.com/myperfectjob

Design, Arts and Crafts

CRCI: E

SIGNWRITER/SIGNMAKER

What the work involves

- You will design, plan and produce signs with graphic images, lettering and logos to publicise companies, attract customers and draw attention to specific locations.

- You will work closely with customers to develop appropriate, appealing designs that match their requirements.

- You could work with any number of different materials and methods; from plastics to glass to sketching as well as computer aided design (CAD).

- You will produce signs for shop fronts, roadsides, hospitals, vehicles and even boats!

The type of person suited to this work

As you will be creating signs to interest or warn people, you will need strong graphic design skills. A creative flair and drawing skills are also important. You will need an understanding of the materials you work with and good manual skills.

You must be methodical and have strong attention to detail so that your signs are accurate. Technical skills will allow you to work with a range of equipment. ICT skills are increasingly important. Good written and verbal communication skills will help you to meet clients' requirements accurately and avoid expensive errors.

Working conditions

You could work within a studio or manufacturing site, which can get messy and noisy. You might attend meetings with customers and make site visits. Much of your time will be spent drafting signs at a computer using special software.

You may work with large or small-scale specialist equipment, with printing inks and chemical finishes, which can affect people with skin or respiratory conditions. You will need to wear protective clothing and face masks.

Future prospects

This is a fairly competitive area; however, the demand for high-quality signs from a range of organisations means that there are many opportunities. You could work in the more commercial side of signwriting, within a specialist company on the design or manufacturing side, or you could work within the more creative, hand-crafted side of the industry.

Some signwriters go into set design for theatre. With experience, you could start your own business – perhaps specialising in pub or restaurant signs.

Advantages/disadvantages

This kind of work can provide opportunities to be creative and to use your imagination to help customers, for example

Qualifications and courses

There are no formal educational requirements, but relevant vocational qualifications can be useful. NVQs/SVQs at Levels 2 and 3 are available in Signmaking.

Training is usually done on the job.

Many employers offer Apprenticeships/Skillseekers for people aged 16–24. Applicants normally require 4 GCSEs/S grades (A*–D/1–4), including maths, English language, a science and an art and design subject, or other evidence of aptitude.

It is also possible to take a full- or part-time course in signwriting and signmaking. Or you can specialise in this area after taking a general Art and Design course such as a Foundation Degree or a HND/C.

when designing a company logo. You might need to travel frequently to visit a range of locations, to take measurements or photographs. You have the option of working abroad.

Money guide

Trainees and apprentices are most likely to start at around £12,000. With experience, signwriters can earn £17,000–£24,000 per year. With management responsibilities you could earn up to £30,000. Self-employed signwriters will earn more.

Related opportunities

- Cartoonist p169
- Fine Artist/Sculptor p173
- Gold/Silversmith/Engraver p175
- Graphic Designer p176

Further information

British Sign and Graphics Association
5 Orton Enterprise Centre, Bakewell Road,
Peterborough PE2 6XU
01733 230033; www.bsga.co.uk

ccskills
4th Floor, Lafone House, The Leathermarket, Weston St,
London SE1 3HN
020 7015 1800; www.ccskills.org.uk

The Faversham House Group Ltd
Faversham House, 232a Addington Road,
South Croydon CR2 8LE
020 8651 7100; www.fhgmedia.com

City&
Guilds

www.cityandguilds.com/myperfectjob

STAGE/SET DESIGNER

What the work involves

- Stage/set designers are responsible for the visual elements of a theatre (stage designer), TV or film production (set designer) including sets, locations and possibly props and costumes.

- From background research, you will be required to create original ideas which accurately reflect the relevant style and historical period of the piece.

- Working closely with the production team, you will oversee the development and installation of the sets and ensure that everything is delivered on time and within budget.

The type of person suited to this work

It is essential to have a strong creative flair and a good eye for design. Having the skills to use specialist CAD software, to draw designs by hand and to create scale models when required is also very important.

You should be detail driven and demonstrate a passion for history, culture and the performing arts.

These abilities should be balanced with good communication skills to aid leadership and self-promotion.

Organisational skills are important to ensure that projects are carried out on time, within budget and as requested. As deadlines can be tight, you should also have the ability to work well under pressure.

Working conditions

Designers either work directly for the production company or freelance. Working hours are long and unsociable and travel may be involved. You will be expected to work supplementary hours in order to meet deadlines.

Your work will be divided between being in a studio designing and building models of the sets, and consequent supervision or involvement in their creation. Normally this happens behind the scenes in theatres, television studios or purpose-built warehouses.

You will work on large pieces, which necessitate the use of ladders and scaffolding.

Future prospects

Stage designers work for theatres and opera houses and may have the opportunity to oversee a travelling production. There is fierce competition for entry level positions.

Set designers can work for the BBC or one of the 1,500 production firms in the country.

Part-time work is difficult to find and although there are many freelancers in the industry, work can be sporadic.

Advantages/disadvantages

The creation of original work and seeing your ideas being used in the public eye and in high profile productions is satisfying.

Qualifications and courses

It is possible to enter the industry as a craft assistant in a design studio and work your way up. However, most people have an HND, a degree, or postgraduate diploma or degree in theatre design or a related art and design subject.

For a degree you should have 2 A levels, a BTEC national diploma/certificate in a relevant subject, 5 GCSEs (A*–C) and a good portfolio. For an HNC/D you are normally required to have 1 A level. The Diploma in Creative and Media might also be useful.

It is helpful to obtain experience before entering this highly competitive profession as it highlights commitment to the industry. This can be achieved by means of an unpaid placement, freelance work, involvement in student productions or design competitions.

Working as a freelancer can result in greater flexibility.

Competition for entry level jobs is fierce and a strong portfolio and good networking skills are important.

Meeting tight deadlines can result in high stress levels.

Money guide

Newly qualified assistant designers in a theatre can expect to earn about £15,500 per year. This may rise to £20,000 for a resident head designer position and those with the most experience can earn about £40,000.

Many designers are freelancers. Their earnings will be dependent on individual ability and contract sizes. According to the Broadcasting Entertainment Cinematographic and Theatre Union (BECTU) the current minimum rate for a freelance art assistant is £280 per week.

Related opportunities

- Costume Designer p170
- Interior Designer p179
- Model Maker p182
- Production Assistant/Runner (TV, Film and Radio) p421

Further information

Design Council
34 Bow Street, London WC2E 7DL
020 7420 5200; www.designcouncil.org.uk

The Society of British Theatre Designers
Theatre Design Department, Rose Bruford College, Burnt Oak Lane, Sidcup DA15 9DF
020 8308 2664; www.theatredesign.org.uk

City&
Guilds

ENTRY
4
LEVEL

Design, Arts and Crafts

CRCI: E

TOYMAKER/DESIGNER

What the work involves

- You will design, plan, test and create toys for babies, children and even adults!

- As a traditional toymaker, you could use early designs to make toys by hand, such as doll houses and rocking horses. If working for a large manufacturer you will help develop new products based on original ideas and sketches.

- You will spend time promoting your work and design services to clients and customers. Your work could be sold in shops or at craft fairs and toy fairs.

The type of person suited to this work

As you will be developing original ideas, you will need creative flair. Practical design skills and an active imagination will help you create long-lasting and functional toys. A genuine interest in how individuals respond to toys will help you design appealing items that sell well.

If creating objects by hand, as many toymakers do, you will need good manual handling skills and an understanding of the materials you work with. Knowledge of and skills in 3D design are fast becoming essential.

If self-employed, you will also need good business and financial skills and the confidence to promote your work.

Working conditions

Most toymakers/designers spend a lot of time in a workshop, planning and developing their products. Some of the materials used can be dangerous so you might need to wear protective clothing and masks.

If employed as a toy designer by a manufacturer, you may work purely with computer design software and create, rather than construct, your designs.

Future prospects

Public interest in traditional toys and games is growing. You could work on a self-employed basis, making and designing toys. Some toymakers/designers own shops where they sell their own handmade toys. A growing number sell their products at craft fairs, on the internet or by mail order.

A small number of toymakers also restore antique toys. There is steady demand for innovative toys in high street shops and you will always have an emerging potential market for new products! There may be opportunities in buying, marketing and business development amongst large toy manufacturers.

Advantages/disadvantages

This work provides the enjoyment of creating fun, attractive objects.

It can take time to build up a business, if working on a self-employed basis. Competition is high and vacancies for toy designers are limited at manufacturing companies.

Qualifications and courses

ENTRY 3 LEVEL

There are no formal entry requirements, but many entrants have a background in art and design, and HND or degree qualifications can be an advantage. Relevant subjects include art and design, graphic or three-dimensional design, creative arts and craft and model making.

In England, Wales and Northern Ireland many students take a 1-year Foundation course as preparation for entry to an art and design degree; 5 GCSEs (A*–C) and a relevant A level are also usually required. In Scotland the first year of a degree equates to the Foundation year.

There are various courses available, such as Foundation degrees in three-dimensional design and creative arts, and degrees in craft studies. Institutions sometimes have links with toy manufacturers, which can provide a useful first step into the industry. Degree entry requirements are usually 2 A levels/3 H grades or equivalent.

Money guide

Starting salaries for toy designers working for toy manufacturers range from £10,000 to £15,000 per year. With experience and working in a large company this can increase to £23,000–£35,000. As a top designer you could get up to £45,000. Traditional toymakers are usually self-employed and salaries will depend on the success of the business.

Related opportunities

- Animator p168
- Carpenter/Joiner p81
- Model Maker p182
- Picture Framer p184

Further information

British Toymakers Guild
PO Box 240, Uckfield TN22 9AS
01225 442440; www.toymakersguild.co.uk

Design Council
34 Bow Street, London WC2E 7DL
020 7420 5200; www.designcouncil.org.uk

Crafts Council
44a Pentonville Road, London N1 9BY
020 7806 2500; www.craftscouncil.org.uk

City& Guilds

www.cityandguilds.com/myperfectjob

Education and Training

To work in this sector you need to be motivated and enthusiastic about other people's learning, whether it's adults or children. If you chose to teach, the range of subjects available is huge so whatever your interest – languages, art, sciences, cooking, sports – you can become a teacher in that field. Jobs in this sector require a multitude of skills including: creativity, imagination, numerical skills, good communication and organisational skills and, in some cases, having a lot of patience!

The following jobs are covered in this section:

For similar jobs to the ones in this sector turn to *Social Work and Counselling Services* on page 567.

COMMUNITY EDUCATION OFFICER

What the work involves

- Community education officers provide all members of the community with information on, and access to, educational and developmental programmes.

- You will identify the needs and interests of the community, and sensitively and creatively organise a variety of suitable activities and courses to improve learning, career and personal development opportunities.

- You will plan projects and outreach programmes, liaise with community and local authority groups, and recruit and train staff. At a senior level your job will involve policy development and negotiating funding.

- You may work in areas of social deprivation or high unemployment, or with certain disadvantaged groups such as ethnic minorities or the homeless.

The type of person suited to this work

You should have a genuine interest in helping people and charitable work.

As you will be liaising with communities as well as official government and voluntary bodies you must be able to communicate with a variety of different people and situations, both casual and formal, whilst maintaining a professional approach.

You should be a good listener and have a practical, optimistic approach to problem solving.

You will need to show initiative in your approach to your work but you will also require patience as many projects are long-term developments rather than quick-fix solutions.

Working conditions

You will probably work flexible hours as many posts are short-term contracts because their existence is heavily dependent on funding. This can be difficult as many projects require long-term support. There is plenty of opportunity for part time work and flexible hours but these may involve working during the evening and at weekends.

You will have an office based in a community centre, a local authority or a college, from which you will travel to the surrounding region.

Future prospects

You will receive formal training once you have secured a post consisting of short courses that will develop skills or examine new issues such as health development or training.

You may find that postgraduate MA programmes in community studies and education are beneficial to your progress. NVQs and diploma qualifications in relevant subjects such as youth and community work will boost your opportunities for progression.

Qualifications and courses

ENTRY 5 LEVEL

You can gain entry to this profession as a graduate, a Diplomate or with a HND/Foundation degree. A qualification in a relevant subject such as community education, sociology, social sciences or educational studies may give you an advantage.

Normally employers seek candidates who have combined their qualification with voluntary community experience.

If you accumulate significant experience but have no qualifications it may be possible for you to achieve a post in the voluntary sector involving recreational activities for example. However, it is likely that you will be required to have academic qualifications to secure a senior level role. Some undergraduate and postgraduate courses provide part time or distance learning and many employers will support you while you are studying.

You can gain experience when you are a student to learn about the sector and decide if it is an area you would like to work in. Information and advice about voluntary work is available from local volunteer bureaux, student volunteer centres and the YouthNetUK online volunteer service.

Advantages/disadvantages

You will provide communities and their members the educational opportunities they require for personal or career growth which can be highly rewarding.

Your work may be frustrating at times as certain aspects such as the establishment of courses and programmes will depend on the availability of funding.

Money guide

If you work for the public sector you will earn around £20,000–£25,000 on average. This may be lower if you work in the voluntary sector. With experience and qualifications you can progress to a senior post where you may earn in the region of £30,000–£35,000.

Related opportunities

- Social Care Worker/Social Worker p583
- Volunteer Manager p587
- Youth and Community Worker p589

Further information

Workers' Educational Association
Corporate Services, 3rd Floor, 70 Clifton Street, London, EC2A 4HB
020 7426 3450; national@wea.org.uk; www.wea.org.uk

City& Guilds

www.cityandguilds.com/myperfectjob

DANCE TEACHER

What the work involves

- Planning dance lessons for pupils which adhere to a syllabus or curriculum set out by a school, or lead to a dance qualification.

- Helping your pupils to develop their fitness and agility and ensuring that they do so safely without causing injury to themselves or others.

- Entering pupils into examinations.

- Choreographing dance routines, as well as choosing music and costumes.

The type of person suited to this work

You need to have a high level of fitness and stamina and be able to demonstrate complicated dance moves and positions to your pupils. You should also be very enthusiastic about music and the performing arts in general and possess good rhythm and balance. As a teacher of any subject it is imperative that your communication skills are impeccable but for dance teachers this is especially important because you need to ensure that everyone in your class is dancing safely and not likely to injure themselves or others. Creativity and self-discipline are very important traits to possess as well.

Working conditions

If you are employed in the state school sector you will be working during the school day, however it is likely that you will run classes after school in the early evening as well. This is certainly true of the private sector.

If you are a freelance teacher you can expect to need to travel as you will work at a variety of different venues; from schools and colleges to theatres and community centres.

Future prospects

As a dance teacher you can progress to becoming self-employed and even to running your own dance school. There are also other performing arts sectors you could branch into such as choreography. For experienced dance teachers there is the possibility to branch into community work as a dance therapist working with people from all walks of life.

Advantages/disadvantages

You will always be active as part of your job so you will stay fit and healthy and will not be stuck behind a desk all day.

Your work will often be fun as it is a very creative and expressive art form.

You may injure yourself from constantly dancing and this could jeopardise how much you could work.

Qualifications and courses

To become a dance teacher you would typically have a degree in a dance related subject or a HND or Foundation degree.

There are also many vocational qualifications in dance available at specific dance and performing arts institutions.

If you want to go on to teach in a state school you will need to obtain Qualified Teacher Status (QTS). This can be achieved by doing a PGCE after your degree or some degrees in dance subjects which hold QTS status themselves. Working as a dance teacher in the private sector requires being accredited by the Council of Dance Education and Training.

It might become stressful preparing for a big performance especially if you are working with children who can be unpredictable.

Money guide

Starting salaries as a dance teacher can vary widely and this will also be influenced by whether you work in a state or private school. Typically, starting salaries in the state sector are £19,000. This can progress to around £30,000–£34,000 with experience and lots of responsibility.

If you run your own private dance school you could earn £50,000 and more.

Related opportunities

- Choreographer p437
- Dancer p440
- Music teacher p199
- Primary School Teacher p202
- Secondary School Teacher p205

Further information

Council for Dance Education Training
Old Brewer's Yard, 17–19 Neal Street,
London WC2H 9UY
020 7240 5703; www.cdet.org.uk

Imperial Society for Teachers of Dancing
22/26 Paul Street, London EC2A 4QE
020 7377 1577; www.istd.org

National Dance Teachers Association
NDTA, PO Box 4099, Lichfield WS13 6WX
01543 308618; www.ndta.org.uk

CRCI: F   **Education and Training**

Education and Training

CRCI: F

EARLY YEARS SPECIALIST/ NURSERY WORKER

What the work involves

- Within a nursery or private home, early years specialists/nursery workers look after young children, from newborn babies up to the age of 8, ensuring they are safe and comfortable.

- Much of your work will involve feeding, changing, dressing and bathing babies, and helping older children to develop in areas such as language, art, practical skills and music.

- You will plan the day to include play, exercise, meals and rest, to keep children healthy and mentally stimulated.

The type of person suited to this work

It is essential to enjoy caring for young people and to be outgoing, with a friendly manner towards children and adults alike. You also need to be patient and tolerant to deal with different types of behaviour.

Planning activities needs imagination and creativity, and it is helpful to be good at art, practical tasks and singing.

You will need to be flexible, enjoy team working and be comfortable working with many different types of people from all cultures and backgrounds.

Working conditions

The majority of nursery workers work 40 hours a week, however hours can vary depending on parents' requirements. Most of your work will be indoors in a nursery, school, hospital or private home. You may 'live in' if you are a nanny in a private home.

The work involves bending, lifting and playing with children so you need to be physically fit.

Future prospects

Nursery workers work in nurseries, schools and hospitals, and as nannies in private homes.

With the large rise in working mothers, there is high demand for qualified childcare staff throughout the UK. Sometimes, there are opportunities to travel, particularly in private work.

You can start to train straight from school or after gaining experience in other types of work.

Promotion prospects are limited. You could take further training to enter paediatric nursing or primary school teaching.

Advantages/disadvantages

The work is varied and rewarding.

As well as children, you will have the opportunity to work with adults.

The hours can be long, particularly in nanny work, and you might have to work shifts and weekends.

Qualifications and courses

Academic qualifications are not necessary, although GCSEs (A*–C), especially in English and maths are helpful. The Diploma in Society, Health and Development could also be useful.

There is a framework of nationally accredited nursery worker qualifications in England and Wales. Typical qualifications include CACHE Level 3 Diploma in Child Care and Education; BTEC National Diploma in Children's Care, Learning and Development and NVQ/SVQ Level 3 in Children's Care, Learning and Development. Apprenticeships in Children's Care, Learning and Development may also be available.

In Scotland, registration of nursery workers has been introduced. Early years practitioners with qualifications such as SVQ Level 3 or an HNC can register with the Scottish Social Services Council (SSSC). Support workers, qualified to SVQ Level 2 or equivalent, can register from October 2008.

All applicants must pass a Criminal Records Bureau check.

Money guide

Expect to start on around £9,000–£11,500 per year. You can earn £14,000–£17,000 with experience.

Salaries can rise to rise to £35,000+ for a senior post. £25,000+ a year, with accommodation and food, is possible for a nanny working in a private home.

Related opportunities

- Childminder p569
- Children's Nurse p294
- Healthcare Assistant p576
- Teaching Assistant/Learning Support Assistant p208

Further information

CACHE
Apex House, 81 Camp Road, St Albans AL1 5GB
0845 347 2123; www.cache.org.uk

Care Commission
Compass House, 11 Riverside Drive, Dundee, DD1 4DY
0845 6030890, www.carecommission.com

www.cityandguilds.com/myperfectjob

EDUCATION AND CHILDCARE INSPECTOR

What the work involves

- You will use your extensive experience gained from working in schools, colleges, nurseries or youth service settings, to undertake inspections.

- You might inspect early years learning, or focus on secondary education and preparation for work organisations. Inspections cover special schools and out-of-school learning units.

- Inspectors look at the quality of teaching, curriculum, standard of leadership and pupils' achievement levels.

- During the visit, you will contribute to the inspection report, which is then made available for everyone to read on the internet.

The type of person suited to this work

You must be knowledgeable about the types of organisations you will be inspecting. You should be observant and possess a high level of integrity. Strong analytical skills are essential. You will be gathering evidence and interviewing a variety of people so you need to be an effective communicator and be able to make appropriate and fair judgements.

It's important to work to a high standard but also to work quickly and to deadlines.

Good ICT and report writing skills are also important.

Working conditions

You will visit organisations across the country and will need to spend long periods of time away from home.

Most of the work takes place in classrooms or offices where you will speak to head teachers, pupils, parents, governors and the other professionals linked to the organisation.

Most inspectors are freelance.

Future prospects

You could be working for Ofsted, Tribal Inspections, Serco Education and Children's Services or the Centre for British Teachers Education Trust. These organisations have offices in London, Bristol and Manchester although most inspectors work from home.

Inspectors working for Ofsted are called HMIs (Her Majesty's Inspectors). AIs (Additional Inspectors) work for other organisations under contract to Ofsted. Early years inspectors specialise in education for under fives. AIs can apply to be HMIs, and early years inspectors can be promoted to adult and senior children's services. There is also the chance to be promoted to managerial level in all groups.

Advantages/disadvantages

This job offers you the chance to use your experience to make sure that the right quality of provision is in place in an institution.

Qualifications and courses

Registered inspectors in England and Wales, and inspectors in Scotland, must be qualified as teachers, or have 5 years' experience in advising or inspecting.

Qualified Teacher Status (QTS) is gained through Initial Teacher Training (ITT). The two main routes are a first degree followed by a Postgraduate Certificate in Education (PGCE) or a first degree (BEd/BA/BSc) leading to QTS.

Registered inspectors also need to have 3 years' experience in a leadership or a managerial role, and a relevant qualification. Many inspectors are ex-head teachers or childcare managers.

Training for inspectors is provided by the Office for Standards in Education (Ofsted) in England, Estyn in Wales, HM Inspectorate of Education in Scotland, and the Department of Education for Northern Ireland.

You have the chance to travel around the country.

It's challenging when you need to give an 'inadequate' judgement to an institution.

Money guide

Inspectors generally earn the same as advisers employed by local authorities. Pay varies, depending on the level of work. Early years inspectors are usually employed by private organisations, salaries vary but as a guide starting salaries are around £28,000. HMIs can earn £48,500–£62,000 per year for full-time employment, with pro rata for part time. AIs can earn £300–£500 per day and have expenses paid.

Related opportunities

- Education Officer p194
- Further/Higher Education Lecturer p196
- Primary School Teacher p202
- Secondary School Teacher p205
- Work-based Training Instructor p209

Further information

Ofsted
Royal Exchange Buildings, St Ann's Square, Manchester M2 7LA
0845 640 4040; www.ofsted.gov.uk

HM Inspectorate of Education in Scotland
Denholm House, Almondvale Business Park, Almondvale Way, Livingston EH54 6GA
01506 600 200; www.hmie.gov.uk

www.cityandguilds.com/myperfectjob

Education and Training

CRCI: F

EDUCATION OFFICER

What the work involves

- Education officers prepare educational materials and resources for visits of school students to galleries, museums or other organisations.

- A museum education officer is responsible for designing and delivering the museum's educational programme to primary and secondary schools.

- An environmental education officer is responsible for raising awareness of environmental issues, promoting sustainability and conservation and teaching a wide range of age groups about the natural world.

- It will be your responsibility to increase public awareness about new exhibitions and events, and to update the educational sections of your website by producing lesson materials and careers information.

The type of person suited to this work

As an education officer, you will need self-confidence and an ability to talk to young people in a way that will interest and excite them. You must be bright, interesting, humorous, have lots of patience and a willingness to listen.

You will always be busy, so you will need good organisational skills, as well as excellent written and verbal communication skills. An understanding of ICT and confidence in handling budgets will also be useful.

Working conditions

Your time will be spent in an office or lecture room, on the exhibition floor of a museum or gallery, or visiting local schools where you will represent your organisation. You might wear a uniform or protective clothing.

Depending on your organisation, you might spend some of your time outdoors in all weathers, for example at a zoo or community farm. You might do some evening work, especially if you work with community groups.

Future prospects

Entry to this profession is very competitive, but there is a steady increase in the number of educational jobs available in organisations.

Alongside traditional exhibits, learning through demonstrations, videos, talks and other presentations is being introduced by education officers as interactive experiences increase in popularity.

Advantages/disadvantages

This offers an opportunity to be involved in teaching without being in the classroom.

You will contribute to making a visit to your organisation a more memorable one for everyone.

You will be juggling lots of different tasks at once.

Qualifications and courses

To work as an education officer in a museum or gallery, a degree or HND is required. Useful degree subjects include history, archaeology, anthropology, museum studies, cultural studies, history of art and education. Museums favour certain degree subjects that are particular to their collection e.g. history of art for the Burrell Collection in Glasgow.

An environmental education officer will require a degree in a biological or environmental science eg ecology or zoology. It is also possible to enter this position with an HND in a related area such as countryside management.

Qualifications and/or experience in teaching or community education are useful, and may be required. Relevant work experience is essential in order to secure a paid position.

Postgraduate qualifications are available in relevant subjects such as museum studies and heritage management. Entry to these courses requires a degree in any subject, and, normally, some related work experience. A Postgraduate Certificate in Education (PGCE) is useful for museum education officers working with school children, as it demonstrates a good understanding of the requirements of the national curriculum.

Money guide

Museum education officers working in large prestigious museums or educational adventure establishments in full-time positions can earn £15,000–£20,000 per year. With substantial experience this rises to £25,000–£35,000. Environmental education officers can expect to earn £15,000–£19,000 to begin with. This rises to £22,000–£30,000 at senior level. Education assistants who work alongside education officers can earn £13,000–£18,000.

Related opportunities

- Arts Administrator/Manager p347
- Learning Mentor p198
- Museum/Art Gallery Curator p356

Further information

GEM – Group for Education in Museums
Primrose House, 93 Gillingham Road, Gillingham ME7 4EP
01634 853424;www.gem.org.uk

City& Guilds

www.cityandguilds.com/myperfectjob

EDUCATION WELFARE OFFICER

What the work involves

- You will work with young people who are not attending school, and their families, to support them back into education.

- It will be your responsibility to issue education supervision orders, school attendance orders and truancy schemes. You may have to prosecute parents of children who continue to truant despite your efforts to help the children to return to school.

- You will help families get all the benefits they are entitled to, such as free school meals, clothing or transport.

- As a link between families and schools, you will try to improve existing relationships – writing reports, attending meetings and case conferences.

The type of person suited to this work

As there can be many reasons for poor attendance at school, such as fear of bullying, caring responsibilities at home or difficulty in coping with school work, it is important to be open-minded and to listen impartially to school staff and parents. You will also need to be strong enough to prosecute a family if it becomes necessary.

You must enjoy working with young people and see the value in education, because you might have to convince parents who do not share your views.

You will also have to keep up to date with legislation and you must be able to work on your own and as part of a team.

Working conditions

You will have an office base, but most of your time will be spent visiting young people and their families at home or looking for young people in the local area, so a driving licence is useful.

You may go to other agencies' offices to attend meetings and case conferences.

Families may view your interventions as interfering rather than assisting; you must always consider your safety.

Future prospects

There are about 4,500 education welfare officers in England, Wales and Northern Ireland. In Scotland, they are called attendance officers.

There is a promotion structure within local authorities and you can become a senior education welfare officer, team leader or manager. There is also the opportunity to become a specialist, for example dealing only with primary school pupils. With further training, you can do similar work in care and social services.

Advantages/disadvantages

You will have the satisfaction of helping people – sometimes quite profoundly.

Qualifications and courses

There are a number of routes into this profession. Candidates generally have relevant work experience, for example in special education, counselling or youth work.

A degree in social work or a qualification in education welfare, social work, youth and community work or teaching is now insisted upon by certain local authorities.

Degree courses usually require a minimum of 2 A levels/ 3 H grades and 5 GCSEs/S grades (A*–C/1–3) or equivalent, including English and maths.

Apprenticeships and the Diploma in Society, Health and Development may also be useful. An NVQ in Learning, Development and Support Services for Children, Young People and Those Who Care for Them (Level 3 or 4) is also available.

A number of additional skills and aptitudes are valuable for entry to this work, for example skills in advising/ counselling work or caring for people, high-level skills in communication, decision-making, ICT and information handling, as well as working with others.

You may have to work in the evenings to find parents at home.

Some people may be abusive and you may find yourself in stressful situations.

Money guide

You will earn around £18,000–£21,000 per year on entry. With experience you could earn up to £32,000. This rises to £36,000 and £55,000 for a senior education welfare officer.

Related opportunities

- Careers Adviser p568
- Social Care Worker/Social Worker p583
- Youth and Community Worker p589

Further information

General Social Care Council
Goldings House, 2 Hays Lane, London SE1 2HB
020 7397 5100; www.gscc.org.uk

Northern Ireland Social Care Council
7th Floor, Millennium House, 19–25 Great Victoria Street, Belfast BT2 7AQ
028 9041 7600; www.niscc.info

www.cityandguilds.com/myperfectjob

CRCI: V **Education and Training**

FURTHER/HIGHER EDUCATION LECTURER

What the work involves

Lecturer in further education (FE)

- You will teach students aged 16+, on vocational (work based) or academic (general) courses at a further education college the information and skills they need to achieve their qualifications.

- As well as teaching your main subject you will also be a tutor helping students with their personal development and career planning.

- You will also arrange work placements with local companies, visit students to monitor and assess their progress, act as a student mentor and meet your colleagues to develop courses.

Lecturer in higher education (HE)

- As a higher education lecturer you will teach undergraduate or postgraduate students at a university or franchised college.

- As well as delivering lectures you will take tutorials, act as a consultant for individual research projects and run seminars on topics related to the department's research interests.

- To maintain your professional knowledge you will carry out research in your specialist area, and submit papers for publication in academic journals and periodicals.

The type of person suited to this work

Lecturers need to be patient and interested in helping people of all ages to learn and increase their knowledge by developing their ability, skills and interests. It is also important to be comfortable talking to large groups of students.

If you choose to lecture in HE, you are likely to have already done research work and completed a thesis. You must be very interested in your subject and how facts support hypotheses and theories. To be able to help your students learn you will also need to enjoy debating and arguing different ideas and concepts.

FE lecturers often have extensive practical experience of their specialist area before entering the profession.

Working conditions

Most of your time will be teaching in either lecture theatres, classrooms, labs or workshops. For some practical subjects you might spend some of your time outdoors.

When not teaching you will be office based, using a computer for research, writing papers, reports and analyses, and marking students' work.

Although you are likely to work mostly during the day, you might have to work at night and occasionally, weekends.

Depending on your institution, you will mostly work term time, although FE conditions are changing to all year round.

Future prospects

There are a number of progression routes open to both type of lecturer.

For FE lecturers there are opportunities to enter other areas of teaching, financial work, quality improvement and human resources. In addition, you could also look to take more senior positions within your current or another college such as a senior lecturer or head of department. However, tight college budgets have led to a cut in management positions.

As an HE lecturer, some of your options will depend on the size and financial status of your institution. There is evidence to show that taking a career break can be a disadvantage as this can reduce your ability to do the research work which is so important if you are to build your reputation. Sabbaticals, however, are considered to be positive as they will enable you to spend time doing research. HE lecturers can apply for promotion within their own or other institutions, undertake consultancy, enter the media or do public speaking. You could also find part-time work providing advisory or training services or start your own business. There is strong competition for permanent jobs, especially in certain arts subjects. 40% of lecturers have short, fixed-term contracts. There is a demand for lecturers in engineering, construction and ICT. Progression follows the structure of senior lecturer, reader, research fellow, professor, chair and dean.

Advantages/disadvantages

This is a rewarding profession in which you can witness a student's progression.

You are a professional teacher, but in a less-structured, formal environment than a school.

In HE, it can be hard to follow up your own research interests when you have to set up and help run demonstrations or tutorials for undergraduates, while marking essays and assignments.

In FE, you could teach students of all ages with many different reasons for studying.

Money guide

Most full-time FE lecturers start their career within the range of £18,000–£23,000 per year. With several years' experience or promotion to senior level this rises to £35,000+. Those employed on part-time or sessional basis earn £15–£30 per hour.

HE lecturers are paid more, with starting salaries after a PhD ranging between £25,000 and £30,000. After gaining experience, this can rise to £33,000–£45,000. Senior lecturers can earn up to £56,000. Salaries for both jobs are dependent on the research of your department, links with local businesses and the size and status of your university/college. Salaries are typically £3,000–£4,000 per year higher in London.

Related opportunities

- Primary School Teacher p202
- Secondary School Teacher p205
- Work-based Training Instructor p209

Further information

Lifelong Learning UK
5th floor, St Andrew's House, 18–20 St Andrew Street, London EC4A 3AY
0870 757 7890; www.lifelonglearninguk.org

University and College Union
Carlow Street, London NW1 7LH
020 7756 2500; www.ucu.org.uk

www.cityandguilds.com/myperfectjob

Qualifications and courses
Lecturer in further education

ENTRY 5 LEVEL

New entrants must have a relevant degree, Foundation degree or HND. Entry is also open to professionals with significant work experience and a qualification at Level 3 in the subject they wish to teach. You will need to register with the Institute for Learning.

In England and Wales, within 5 years of commencing teaching you must also acquire a Certificate or Diploma in Teaching in the Lifelong Learning Sector, a Certificate in Education or a Postgraduate Certificate in Education. If you do not have any of these qualifications when you start lecturing, you must take the Preparing to Teach in the Lifelong Sector award in your first year.

You will generally need a QCF Level 4–6 qualification for entry to a Diploma or CertEd programme, and a degree for entry to a PGCE. You will normally also need at least a Level 3 qualification in the subject you wish to teach.

Lecturer in higher education

HE lecturers need a 1st or 2.1 Honours degree, Master's degree and must have or be working towards a PhD.

For posts in academic subjects, a record of research and publication is required. Teaching experience whilst working towards a PhD is also valuable. Lecturers in vocational subjects should have several years of relevant work experience.

Opportunities to study for a postgraduate qualification followed by a fellowship or lecturing post can arise for research assistants.

Lecturers normally receive further training from their employer's institution. The Higher Education Academy accredits in-service programmes for lecturers.

Education and Training

CRCI: F

LEARNING MENTOR

What the work involves

- You will support people whilst they are learning to overcome obstacles and meet their targets.

- Working on a one-to-one basis, you will listen to their difficulties and offer various solutions.

- You will help everybody you work with to succeed in and enjoy their learning experience.

- You will also work with the teachers and parents of the student you are focusing on.

The type of person suited to this work

To be a good learning mentor, you will need to have experience of the subject you mentor, along with an understanding of different styles of studying. You should enjoy helping and listening to people and have good communication skills. You should be patient and willing to listen.

The best mentors are those who can be a critical friend, know the benefits of learning and can explain them to the people they work with.

It will also help if you have had first-hand experience of the issues yourself and an appreciation of the difficulties people face. You should be able to handle emotional-stress, be adaptable, non-judgemental and encouraging.

Working conditions

You can work on a part- or full-time basis with people at school, home or sometimes at a college, university or training centre. You might be employed on a term-time only basis or all year round. Some of your work might involve weekends and evenings – this will depend on the organisation you work for.

You will meet in a quiet, confidential area where you will examine workbooks and essays, talk over any issues and offer help.

Future prospects

There are opportunities to progress to management roles or even to head of year at some schools. You may choose to study further and become a teacher, youth worker or social worker. You could also specialise in various areas including working with refugee families or children with behavioural disorders.

Advantages/disadvantages

This job involves a variety of roles – friend, confidence builder and motivator.

Results have shown how important this job can be in helping learners to succeed.

You will be working with students without being a teacher.

Qualifications and courses

ENTRY LEVEL 4

There are no formal entry requirements for this career. However, most entrants have a degree, HND or equivalent vocational qualification. The NVQ Level 3 in Learning, Development and Support Services for Children and Young People is a minimum requirement for many local authorities.

Relevant degree subjects include social sciences, psychology and National Curriculum subjects, particularly English and maths.

Experience of working with young people is required, and experience in a related area such as social work, counselling or teaching is useful.

Newly-appointed learning mentors take part in a 5-day national initial training programme provided by The Children's Workforce Development Council.

It may be possible to work towards a Foundation degree or NVQ/SVQ Level 3 or 4 in Learning, Development and Support Services. The Level 4 NVQ/SVQ is normally required to become a learning mentor coordinator.

All candidates are required to undergo a Criminal Records Bureau check.

Money guide

Within schools, salaries for newly appointed mentors range between £14,000 and £17,000 per year. With experience, you can expect this to increase up to £25,000, and as a senior mentor up to £40,000.

Related opportunities

- Careers Adviser p568
- Special Educational Needs Teacher p206
- Youth and Community Worker p589

Further information

Mentoring and Befriending Foundation
1st floor, Charles House, Albert Street, Eccles, Manchester M30 0PW
0161 787 8600; www.mandbf.org.uk

Learning Mentors
CWDC, 2nd floor, City Exchange, 11 Albion Street, Leeds LS1 5ES
0113 244 6311; www.standards.dfes.gov.uk/learningmentors

City& Guilds

www.cityandguilds.com/myperfectjob

MUSIC TEACHER

What the work involves

- Music teachers are either classroom teachers in primary or secondary schools where they help pupils to develop vocal, instrumental skills and performance technique; or private or visiting teachers, giving instrumental, theory or voice tuition.

- You will be teaching an appreciation of musical theory and composition, musical development and different composers' works.

- You will be expected to plan lessons, organise groups such as orchestras, and you might have to prepare students for external exams.

The type of person suited to this work

You should be patient, have a caring attitude towards others and an interest in drawing out and developing individuals' potential in learning about music.

Excellent communication skills are important, as are firmness and commitment, imagination and creativity.

You have to be well organised, flexible and able to change plans and the sequence of lessons to accommodate unexpected events.

It is important to be comfortable in maintaining discipline and be confident when speaking to large groups of young people and other professionals.

Working conditions

Music teachers work indoors in all kinds of settings within public and private sector schools and learning centres, and in their own or pupils' homes as tutors.

Classroom teachers will usually work 8.45am to 3.45pm, with some evening and weekend work required for tuition, rehearsals and concerts.

It is likely that you will work evenings and weekends, and part time work is common. Private music teachers should expect to carry out some travelling and you may be expected to lift and carry heavy musical instruments.

Future prospects

After gaining experience, you could become head of the music department, an advisory teacher or a local authority inspector.

Many private teachers combine this work with composing, performing or directing choirs/orchestras, and career breaks are common. If you can play the piano and have excellent sight reading, you could accompany students at examinations and recitals.

Advantages/disadvantages

Teaching is a rewarding profession in which you can witness a student's progression.

You will be kept very busy with preparation, classes, marking and assessing, analysing coursework, communicating with examining bodies, meetings and ordering materials.

Qualifications and courses

ENTRY LEVEL 4

Music teachers working in state schools must have Qualified Teacher Status (QTS). There are two main routes to QTS: a first degree, such as a music degree, followed by a Postgraduate Certificate in Education (Professional Graduate Diploma of Education in Scotland) qualifies candidates to teach; a BEd degree such as music with primary teacher training combines a degree and QTS training.

In addition, music teachers must be able to demonstrate a good standard of musicianship, usually grade 7/8 from an Associated Board on a first instrument and grade 6 on a second.

Graduate diploma courses offered by conservatoires are equivalent to degrees but would need to be followed by a 1 year PGCE.

If you are not teaching in state schools then entry routes can vary.

There are no set qualifications for private music teachers; however it is essential that you have excellent music competence and knowledge of your instrument. The Incorporated Society of Musicians (ISM) offers a diploma, which can be related to the instrument you wish. Rockschool offers a music educator course, which will help to demonstrate your commitment to the teaching and learning process.

Money guide

Starting salaries for classroom teachers are £20,000–£24,000. With experience this can rise to £29,000–£33,000. With Advanced Skills Status teachers can earn £34,000–£59,000. For private teachers the Musicians' Union recommends a rate of £25.40 an hour. Generally, wages are between £20 and £30 per hour depending on reputation, experience and location.

Related opportunities

- Education and Childcare Inspector p193
- Further/Higher Education Lecturer p196
- Teaching Assistant/Learning Support Assistant p208

Further information

Incorporated Society of Musicians (ISM)
10 Stratford Place, London W1C 1AA
020 7629 4413; www.ism.org

Musicians' Union
33 Palfrey Place, London SW8 1PE
020 7840 5504; www.musiciansunion.org.uk

Rockschool Ltd
Evergreen House, 2–4 King Street, Twickenham, Middlesex, TW1 3RZ
0845 460 4747; www.rockschool.co.uk

CRCI: F   Education and Training

NVQ/SVQ ASSESSOR

Education and Training

CRCI: F

What the work involves

- NVQ/SVQ assessors work alongside trainees to ascertain their current knowledge, and from this formulate a plan for their development.

- You will offer feedback on their progress as they gain experience and take their NVQ/SVQ qualifications.

- You will observe how trainees do different tasks and measure their achievements against the standards for the qualification.

- You will also read through each trainee's portfolio of evidence, checking that tasks are undertaken.

The type of person suited to this work

It is essential to demonstrate an interest in other people and a commitment to helping them to progress.

You will need to motivate and encourage all kinds of individuals – some of whom will not have enjoyed school and find training difficult.

Excellent communication skills are important for the amount of speaking, questioning, listening and reporting that is involved.

In addition you should be organised and able to interpret the different standards in ways that are helpful to those who are learning. You should also have an interest in the area you are assessing.

Working conditions

You will have access to an office where you will use a computer to update learner records and check portfolios. You will also spend lots of time travelling to meet employers and trainees at their places of work.

Depending on your specialist area you could have very early starts (for example assessing bakers at work) or late finishes (assessing car finishers working nights).

It is necessary to keep up-to-date with the changes and developments in your occupational area.

Future prospects

The government is currently encouraging learning through work-based qualifications and school/college leavers now have more opportunities to pursue Apprenticeships, National Traineeships or Skillseekers.

There is currently a national shortage of skilled professionals in this area, and there will be increasing need for NVQ/SVQ assessors in the future. This may result in more firms and organisations having a team of specialists who train other employees in their particular area of expertise e.g. health and safety.

Advantages/disadvantages

This work involves being at the centre of improving the skills levels of the workforce.

You will spend lots of your time meeting, speaking to and getting to know other people.

Qualifications and courses

It is necessary to have between 2 and 4 years' occupational experience, and often a vocational qualification, in the subject or work area to be assessed. For this reason it is not possible for school or college leavers to enter this area straight away. Many training practitioners choose to work towards NVQ/SVQ assessor qualifications.

It is necessary to have an assessor qualification, either A1 (Assesses Candidates Using a Range of Methods) or A2 (Assesses Candidates' Performance Through Observation), which are carried out whilst you are working and take 6 to 12 months to complete. To obtain the qualification, you need to build up a portfolio of evidence from your work with NVQ/SVQ candidates.

Some courses only accept candidates who have been nominated by their employer and have extensive experience in the specialist area and a Level 2 qualification (or higher) in the area.

Qualified assessors can carry out further training to work as NVQ/SVQ verifiers. Verifier qualifications are V1 (conduct internal quality assurance of assessment process) or V2 (conduct external quality assurance of assessment process).

Depending on your specialist area, you might have to work unsociable hours in order to assess candidates in their workplace.

It can be challenging to motivate and encourage candidates who do not enjoy learning to achieve an academic qualification.

Money guide

Average starting salaries are between £16,000 and £20,000.

More experienced assessors can expect to earn up to £25,000 per year which can increase beyond £35,000 for the most senior positions.

It is also possible to do this work on a freelance basis. Rates start at £225 or more per day.

Related opportunities

- Driving Instructor p603
- Human Resources/Personnel Officer p41
- Further/Higher Education Lecturer p196
- Training Manager p68

Further information

Qualifications and Curriculum Authority
53–55 Butts Road, Earlsdon Park, Coventry CV1 3BH
0300 303 3010; www.qca.org.uk; info@qca.org.uk

City& Guilds

www.cityandguilds.com/myperfectjob

PLAY WORKER/ HOSPITAL PLAY SPECIALIST

What the work involves

■ Play workers and hospital play specialists are responsible for ensuring that children between the ages of 5 and 15 play in a safe environment.

■ Your will encourage children and young people to learn through play by giving them the freedom to explore and get to know themselves.

■ Hospital play specialists use play to entertain children and help them to deal with their experiences in hospital. This includes using play to prepare them for treatments and diverting their attention from unpleasant procedures. You may work with severely disabled children.

The type of person suited to this work

Imagination and creativity are needed to do this job well. It is essential that you like being with children of all ages, understand what they like to do and recognise how they change as they develop.

You should be positive and patient with lots of energy and stamina. As the safety of the children will be your responsibility, you will need high levels of concentration and to stay alert at all times.

A hospital play specialist needs to be sympathetic to the needs and issues of each child, have some understanding of medical conditions, and must be able to cope with distressing situations.

Working conditions

As many opportunities operate after school or during holidays you will normally work in the early evening, at weekends and in school holidays. Many jobs are seasonal and most are part time.

Play specialists work in children's hospitals, children's wards and outpatients' clinics. You may take children on trips or visit them in their homes, so you might need a driving licence.

Future prospects

This area of work is rising in importance and is part of the National Childcare Strategy, which recognises the significance of giving young people opportunities to improve their lives through education, sport and leisure.

With the increased number of working parents, the need for out-of-school carers has grown.

There is currently an increase in the number of hospital play specialist posts available nationally. Most opportunities are with NHS hospitals but you could also work in hospices or community paediatric teams.

Qualifications and courses

Most people enter this career as a play assistant for which you will need an NVQ Level 3 qualification in Childcare.

Relevant courses include the CACHE Certificate in playwork and NCFE Certificate in playwork, both at Level 2, and the CACHE Certificate and Diploma in Childcare and Education. NVQs/SVQs are available.

To become a qualified hospital play specialist, you must be aged 20 or over and will need the Edexcel BTEC Professional Development Diploma in specialised play for sick children and young people, approved by the Hospital Play Staff Education Trust (HPSET). Applicants must have an appropriate qualification in a subject such as childcare, nursery nursing, drama or music therapy, occupational therapy, teaching or social work, and at least 3 years' recent experience of working with children in a group setting.

There are also Apprenticeships available in health and social care and children's care which would be useful starting points when entering this career.

Advantages/disadvantages

Helping children who are ill to enjoy themselves can be extremely rewarding.

Hospital play specialists may have to deal with sad and distressing situations.

Money guide

Starting salaries for hospital play specialists are £17,316 to £20,818 per year. With experience or promotion, salaries can increase up to £26,123. As a senior manager, it is possible to achieve salaries up to £35,000.

Related opportunities

■ Childminder p569
■ Youth and Community Worker p589

Further information

CACHE
Beaufort House, Grosvenor Road, St Albans AL1 3AW
01727 818616; www.cache.org.uk

www.cityandguilds.com/myperfectjob

Education and Training

CRCI: F/JG

Education and Training

CRCI: F

PRIMARY SCHOOL TEACHER

What the work involves

- You will teach young children the key subjects of English, maths and science as well as ICT, history, religious education, geography, art, languages and physical education.

- In a state school, you will teach young children reading, writing and numeracy following the frameworks outlined in the National Curriculum. Private schools can set their own teaching guidelines.

- You will prepare resources for structured play and social development work.

- Primary schools admit pupils aged five to eleven and have children of a wide range of abilities in the same class.

The type of person suited to this work

You must be calm and caring in order to deal with different types of behaviour. You should also be assertive and able to uphold discipline as you will be responsible controlling the behaviour of a large group of children.

Planning activities requires creativity. You need to have excellent organisation and communication skills, as well as a high level of fitness. It is also important to be able to encourage and motivate your students – no matter how small their achievements are.

Working conditions

The majority of primary school teachers work 50+ hours a week. Teachers have 12–13 weeks holiday per year, when the school closes. However, preparation for lessons and marking is often completed during this time, as well as at evenings and weekends during term-time. Extra responsibilities include parents' evenings, after-school activities and school inspections. You will be based in a classroom and will have a great deal of freedom over your teaching timetable for the day. It is also possible to gain part-time supply work.

Future prospects

You could become a coordinator of your specialist subject, or work with teachers in nearby schools as an advanced skills teacher in England and Wales or a chartered teacher in Scotland. The National College for Leadership of Schools and Children's Services provides programmes which offer greater salaries and responsibilities to gifted teachers. Progression to deputy head/head can be reached in 10 years. Other options include jobs in local or national government such as Ofsted inspector. Some teachers offer private tutoring or prepare educational texts.

Advantages/disadvantages

Being responsible for your students' educational development can be very rewarding.

You will have long holidays.

Qualifications and courses

You can enter this career with a Bachelor of Education degree or a BA/BSc degree with Qualified Teacher Status.

Alternatively, after obtaining an Honours degree, you could complete a Professional Graduate Certificate in Education or, at Master's level, a Postgraduate Certificate in Education. In Scotland you can complete a Professional Graduate Diploma in Education.

You can also study for qualifications whilst working in a school. In England and Wales, if you have a degree it is possible to apply for the Graduate Teacher Programme. This takes between 3 months and a year to complete. If you have a HND, Foundation degree or an equivalent qualification you can apply for the 2-year Registered Teaching Programme which leads to a degree.

It is also necessary to gain classroom experience to be accepted onto these programmes.

Once you have qualified, you need to undertake an induction period and then register with the General Teaching Council.

This job is demanding as you will have to carry out many duties including marking, preparing lessons and teaching.

Work will often have to be completed in the evening and at weekends.

Money guide

Starting salaries in England, Wales and Northern Ireland are £20,627 per year and increase to £30,148 with experience. You can expect a higher salary in London. The starting salary in Scotland is £20,427, rising to £32,583. After gaining a promotion, salaries in all areas can increase to £35,121.

Advanced skills teachers earn from £35,794 to £54,417. Chartered teachers can expect up to £39,942.

Related opportunities

- Education and Childcare Inspector p193
- Further/Higher Education Lecturer p196
- Teaching Assistant/Learning Support Assistant p208
- Work-based Training Instructor p209

Further information

Training and Development Agency for Schools
Portland House, Stag Place, London SW1E 5TT
0845 600 0991; www.tda.gov.uk

www.cityandguilds.com/myperfectjob

SCHOOL ADMINISTRATOR/ SECRETARY

What the work involves

- School administrators/secretaries are responsible for greeting visitors and answering telephone calls.

- You will develop administrative systems (both paper and ICT based) to keep information organised and easily accessible.

- In some schools you might also collect money for lunch and school trips, and could be in charge of the sick room.

The type of person suited to this work

You will be highly organised and efficient with excellent written and verbal communication skills. You should be confident dealing with people at all levels, including teachers, students and their guardians, and you might need to work with people who are ill, angry or upset.

You should have an excellent telephone manner and possess keyboard skills, knowledge of ICT packages and information systems.

You must be responsible, able to prioritise your workload, be flexible and use your initiative. You should also be able to work calmly under pressure, meet deadlines and handle confidential information.

Working conditions

You will usually be office based, doing normal school hours (8.30am–4pm). You will use a range of office equipment, including computers, photocopiers, telephones and fax machines.

School offices are open to visitors and pupils and can be very busy. On a reception desk, you will be responsible for greeting visitors and showing them to their meeting room or contacting colleagues. Business dress is often required.

Many school secretaries work part time and do not work at all during the school holidays.

Future prospects

In the UK, there are about 55,000 administrators employed in nursery, primary and secondary schools. There are job opportunities in all areas of the country, although jobs can be competitive as the working hours and holidays are appealing.

Much of the work is part time and there are not usually many opportunities for promotion, but you could go on to become a teaching assistant or move on to secretarial work outside the education sector.

Advantages/disadvantages

If you have family commitments there are part-time opportunities. The hours and holiday allowances are attractive.

The work can be routine and repetitive.

Qualifications and courses

ENTRY LEVEL 2

There are no formal entry requirements but you will likely need 5 GCSEs (A*–C) or equivalent and a good standard of maths and English. Adult entry is common and many entrants have several years of office experience. A new Diploma in Business, Administration and Finance is also available in various colleges.

You will need keyboard and word-processing skills. Other ICT skills and shorthand are also useful. Training is mostly on the job and some schools will require you to carry out external training.

It is possible to study for the National Certificate in Educational Administration at the School of Educational Administration (SEA). This course has been accredited by the Qualifications & Curriculum Authority and can be undertaken in 2 years by distance learning.

In addition an NVQ in Business and Administration at Levels 1–4 is available, and City & Guilds offer an award or certificate at Level 2 or Diploma at Level 3 in Support Work in Schools.

Money guide

On average you could earn £15,000 if you are new and working full time in a state school. This could rise to around £23,000+ if you are working in a large secondary school and have additional responsibility or staff to manage. The most experienced people in this profession can expect to earn up to £40,000. Salaries in private schools vary.

Related opportunities

- Arts Administrator/Manager p347
- Personal Assistant p55
- Receptionist p58

Further information

School of Educational Administration
Earlstrees Court, Earlstrees Road,
Corby NN17 4HH
01536 399007; www.admin.org.uk

www.cityandguilds.com/myperfectjob

SCHOOL BUSINESS MANAGER/ BURSAR

What the work involves

- You will be responsible for the financial and strategic planning, human resources and environmental issues of a school or college.

- The term 'bursar' is common in independent schools; in the state sector you might also be called a school business manager or finance manager.

- Your role will include the staff pay, recruitment, and managing contracts with cleaning and maintenance companies. You will also have to keep all the school premises' insurance documents up to date.

- In independent schools, you will also set fees and distribute bursaries, scholarships and awards.

The type of person suited to this work

You need a polite yet firm approach and excellent communication skills as you will deal with the head teacher and senior staff, other professionals (auditors, company managers, etc) as well as parents and students.

You should have a head for figures and be happy using computers and financial software. You need to be very organised in order to oversee all of your responsibilities.

Working conditions

Normally, you will work in an office sitting at a desk. Here, you will have access to a computer and spend lots of time talking to people – both in or outside of your organisation.

You will attend lots of meetings with the head teacher and other professional staff – sometimes staying late to give reports to your school's governing body.

You may also need to work during the evenings and in school holidays.

Future prospects

Most bursars progress to the job after working in either a private financial organisation, after being an accountant or occasionally after working their way up from within a school/college.

With experience, bursars can move to larger organisations or return to the private sector. You could also work in British schools overseas.

Posts are advertised in local and national level publications such as the *Times Educational Supplement*. Jobs are also posted on the National Bursars Association (NBA) website.

Advantages/disadvantages

The work is varied and you will be able to use your own initiative.

You will have the opportunity to work with people of all ages and backgrounds.

Qualifications and courses

Most entrants have experience in related fields, and many hold a degree or professional qualification. Management experience in education, accountancy or personnel is of value.

Qualifications such as NVQ Level 3 or 4 in Administration or Management, or SVQ Level 3 or 4 Business Administration or Management, may be an advantage.

For people already in posts, the National College for School Leadership offers a Bursar Development Scheme. The Certificate of School Business Management is aimed at newly-appointed bursars or those in school administration posts, and the Diploma of School Business Management is intended for experienced bursars/business managers.

The Independent Schools' Bursars Association offers training for those working in independent schools.

The National Bursars Association (NBA) offers the MSc in Educational Leadership, which is a three year course which can be studied through Distance Learning. Postgraduate courses in subjects such as education business management are available.

Money guide

The salary range for bursars differs greatly depending on where you work and the size and type of institution you work in. The average starting salary in a state school or college is £22,000–£20,000 per year, rising to £50,000+ with experience.

In the independent sector, salaries are higher and it is possible to earn between £70,000 and £100,000.

Related opportunities

- Accountant p16
- Accounting Technician/Finance Clerk p18
- Financial Adviser p39

Further information

National Bursars Association
First Floor Offices, 140 Wood Street, Rugby, Warwickshire CV21 2SP
01788 573300; www.nasbm.co.uk

Independent Schools' Bursars Association
Units 11–12 Manor Farm, Cliddesden RG25 2BJ
01256 330369; www.theisba.org.uk

www.cityandguilds.com/myperfectjob

SECONDARY SCHOOL TEACHER

What the work involves

- You will be a specialist in one or two subjects and teach students from ages eleven to nineteen.

- You will also take on the role of form tutor and be responsible for encouraging personal development and good behaviour.

- In state schools, you will follow the National Curriculum.

- Private and independent schools are not required to follow the National Curriculum and are free to set their own educational standards.

The type of person suited to this work

You must be patient, caring and have excellent communication skills in order to relate to and teach your pupils. You must be imaginative and creative to design lessons which capture your students' attention. You should also be assertive and able to maintain discipline with large groups of young people. It is important that you are highly organised as this jobs involves a lot of marking and lesson planning.

Working conditions

You will be based in a classroom and will teach classes from about 9am until 3 or 4pm. However, you will have to come in early, stay late and work from home in order to carry out preparation for lessons and finish marking pupils' work. Schools are usually open for 39 weeks of the year, but teachers often carry out preparatory work during the holidays. In addition, teachers often go on school strips or visit students on work placements. Modern foreign language and PE teachers should be prepared to go on school trips overseas.

Future prospects

There are shortages of maths, science, ICT, design technology and religious education teachers. You could progress to a role as a Key Stage coordinator, the head of a department or year group, or work with teachers as an advanced skills teacher (chartered teacher in Scotland). You could also go into teacher training, advisory work or become a schools inspector. The National College for Leadership of Schools and Children's Services provides greater salaries and responsibilities to gifted teachers.

Advantages/disadvantages

Helping your students to learn and progress can be very rewarding.

You will have long holidays.

Pupils can sometimes be difficult and disruptive.

You will have to work from home in order to finish marking and preparing for lessons.

Qualifications and courses

You can take a Bachelor of Education degree or a BA/ BSc degree with Qualified Teacher Status (QTS).

Alternatively, you can do any degree and then a Postgraduate Certificate in Secondary Education or a Professional Graduate Diploma in Education in Scotland.

Many employment-bases routes to QTS are also available for people who want to work in school and also qualify. The 2-year Registered Teacher Programme is for people with an HND, Foundation degree or equivalent. The School-centred Initial Teacher Training lasts for one year and the Graduate Teacher Programme takes between 3 months and 1 year. Both schemes are aimed at graduates.

In the Teach First Scheme, after 2 years of teaching, graduates can move on to the public or business sector or remain in teaching.

All teachers in state schools must register with the General Teaching Council.

Money guide

In England, Wales and Northern Ireland, the salary band for newly qualified teachers is from £20,627 (£25,000 in central London) and rises to £30,148 (£34,768 in central London). In Scotland, the salary band is from £19,878 to £31,707. Starting salaries will depend on your qualifications, previous experience and the specific role. A Distant Learning Allowance of £1,536 and a Remote Schools Allowance of £971 or £1,791 are also available.

Related opportunities

- Education and Childcare Inspector p193
- Further/Higher Education Lecturer p196
- Teaching Assistant/Learning Support Assistant p208
- Work-based Training Instructor p209

Further information

General Teaching Council Scotland (GTCS)
Clerwood House, 96 Clermiston Road,
Edinburgh EH12 6UT
0131 314 6000; www.gtcs.org.uk

Training and Development Agency for Schools
City Tower, Piccadilly Plaza, Manchester M1 4TD
0845 6000 991; www.tda.gov.uk

www.cityandguilds.com/myperfectjob

Education and Training

CRCI: F

SPECIAL EDUCATIONAL NEEDS TEACHER

What the work involves

- Teachers for special educational needs help children with disabilities, learning difficulties or emotional or behavioural problems to achieve their best.

- You might also work with exceptionally gifted children.

- Working with educational psychologists, social workers, other teachers and learning support workers, you will assess each child's individual needs and draw up an Individual Education Plan (IEP).

- In each of these teaching jobs, you will accompany students on visits and trips, help them understand the world around them, and teach life skills to give them greater independence.

The type of person suited to this work

You must be patient and determined in order to deal with challenging behaviour and solve communication problems with pupils. You should be observant and must be able to recognise and praise efforts and achievements, however small.

You need to be kind and have excellent communication skills as well as a commitment to drawing out and developing individuals' potential in learning. You have to be well organised, flexible and able to change plans and the sequence of lessons to accommodate unexpected events.

Working conditions

There are opportunities all over the UK. You may be based in one school or work in teams covering a number of institutions. Part-time work is possible if you are registered with your local authority. Freelance or self-employment is less common.

You will work 39 weeks a year in school. Hours are usually 9am–4pm Monday to Friday. Additional hours will be required to create lesson plans and attend meetings.

Future prospects

There are over 150,000 SEN teachers in the UK. Most work in mainstream schools, whilst others work in special schools like hospital schools, pupil referral units, youth custody centres and community homes. There is a shortage of skilled candidates.

SEN teachers working in a mainstream school may have the opportunity to be promoted to special education needs co-ordinator. You could also progress to a role as a special needs assessor in a local education authority.

Advantages/disadvantages

Helping children with disabilities, learning difficulties or emotional or behavioural problems and knowing that you helped them to progress is extremely rewarding.

You will be kept very busy with duties including preparation, classes, marking and assessing, analysing coursework,

Qualifications and courses

ENTRY LEVEL 5

It is generally necessary to have 2 years' teaching experience in a mainstream school before training to become a teacher for pupils with special educational needs. In England and Wales it is necessary to have qualified teaching status (QTS) or a teaching qualification in Scotland. In order to obtain these you should have a Postgraduate Certificate in Education, a Bachelor of Education (BEd), or a BA or BSc with QTS.

You must have relevant qualifications if you are teaching children with visual, hearing or multi-sensory impairments The Training and Development Agency for Schools provides courses that cover specific subjects such as maths and science, and ways of teaching these to children with special educational needs. It also offers courses which raise awareness of SEN teaching methods and practices.

Postgraduate qualifications are available in subjects such as special educational needs, specific learning difficulties (dyslexia), and visual impairment. You can study part time or by distance learning.

Qualified teachers of hearing impaired pupils require CACDP Stage 1 in sign language, or equivalent. Qualified teachers of visually impaired pupils must be proficient in Braille.

communicating with examining bodies, meetings and ordering materials, which can be stressful.

Money guide

Starting salaries depend on the employer, location, level of qualifications and responsibilities.

Salaries can start at £20,500–£30,500. With experience you can earn between £31,000 and £33,000. With added responsibility and additional points, you can achieve up to £37,000.

Related opportunities

- Education and Childcare Inspector p193
- Further/Higher Education Lecturer p196
- Work-based Training Instructor p209

Further information

National Association for Special Educational Needs
4/5 Amber Business Village, Amber Close, Amington, Tamworth B77 4RP
01827 311500; www.nasen.org.uk

City& Guilds

www.cityandguilds.com/myperfectjob

TEACHER OF ENGLISH TO SPEAKERS OF OTHER LANGUAGES

What the work involves

- You may be based in the UK or overseas and will teach English to students who are not native speakers. The term Teachers of English to Speakers of Other Languages (TESOL), is only used when the students are in the UK. Teaching English as a Foreign Language (TEFL) is used if you are teaching students abroad.

- You will teach students of every age who want to learn to speak English, for educational, cultural or business reasons.

- It is your responsibility to demonstrate your passion for the English language as well as inspiring and encouraging your students.

The type of person suited to this work

It is absolutely essential to have an excellent grasp of the English language. You should be patient and have an interest in developing individuals' learning potential. Good communication skills are important, as is commitment and imagination.

You have to be well organised, and flexible. You must be able to recognise and praise efforts and achievements. You should be comfortable in maintaining discipline and be confident when speaking to large groups.

Working conditions

If you teach English as a foreign language, you may work in this country or abroad, teaching in community and learning centres, commercial and industrial settings. Hours vary according to the employer, however evening and weekend work is common.

Future prospects

There is always a need for EFL teachers to cope with the high demand of people who wish to learn English. However, competition is fierce for full-time positions. Most EFL teachers are employed overseas on temporary contracts during the academic year. They may return to the UK to teach during the summer.

It is possible to progress to become a course director or course co-ordinator. With experience, you could get involved in teacher training or set up your own private language school.

Advantages/disadvantages

This is a very busy and demanding job. You will have to deal with preparation, teaching, marking, and different examining bodies.

Teaching is a rewarding profession in which you can witness a student's progression and know that you

Qualifications and courses

It is becoming increasingly necessary to have a degree to enter this occupation, especially in England. Useful subjects are English, linguistics, modern foreign languages and education.

In addition, you will need a CELTA (Cambridge Certificate in English Language Teaching to Adults) or a Cert TESOL (Trinity College London Certificate in Teaching English to Speakers of Other Languages).The Cert TEFL (Certificate in Teaching English as a Foreign Language) from International House is designed for those who do not have English as a first language.

Higher-level courses are also available for people with a Certificate qualification and at least 2 years' TEFL/TESOL experience: DELTA (Cambridge Diploma in English Language Teaching to Adults) and the Trinity Licentiate Diploma. Experienced teachers with a degree and/or TESOL qualification can also study for a Master's in TESOL.

If candidates wish to teach in a state school, a teaching qualification must be held (degree or PGCE).

played a major role in helping them to master the English language.

Money guide

If you work within the UK you can earn £13,000–£18,000 per year, but short-term contracts are usual and opportunities are often seasonal. Senior positions attract salaries of between £18,000 and £30,000. Top earners can expect a maximum of £36,000, which is likely to entail management duties. If you work outside the UK, your salary is likely to be much lower. Some contracts include flights, accommodation and extra bonuses.

Related opportunities

- Education and Childcare Inspector p193
- Further/Higher Education Lecturer p196
- Teaching Assistant/Learning Support Assistant p208

Further information

Cambridge ESOL
1 Hills Road, Cambridge CB1 2EU
01223 553355; www.cambridgeesol.org

www.cityandguilds.com/myperfectjob

CRCI: F

Education and Training

TEACHING ASSISTANT/ LEARNING SUPPORT ASSISTANT

What the work involves

- Teaching/classroom assistants help pupils to learn by supporting the teacher and, sometimes, by describing the work in a more visual way or reading questions aloud.

- You may be required to plan and deliver parts of a lesson for the main teacher, working together to make the best use of time and resources.

- Some teaching/classroom assistants will offer one-to-one support to students with learning difficulties or disabilities.

The type of person suited to this work

In this work, you need to like children to help them make the most of their time in school.

You will need lots of patience and possess the ability to stay calm, as all pupils have their off-days when they are noisy or upset. Sometimes, you will work with students who need extra help so you should have an interest in young people who have special needs.

Working conditions

Many learning support assistants work in mainstream schools, but some are employed in independent schools, in residential institutions for students with special needs or specialist colleges.

You will normally work between 8.30am and 4.30pm, although you might have to attend meetings after this and sometimes at weekends.

Future prospects

Recent changes to teachers' workload have involved freeing them from some administrative tasks so they have more classroom time. This has increased the need for teaching assistants working across the UK.

Often, teaching assistants train to become teachers themselves, and there are Initial Teacher Training courses especially for teaching assistants. Special needs learning assistants may specialise in helping young people with a particular disability.

Advantages/disadvantages

This can be a very rewarding job, as you will witness students' educational development and growth. You might help students take steps towards independent living.

You will be very busy, so you might have to snatch meetings with colleagues to share information.

Qualifications and courses

Previous relevant experience, for example in nursing, is an advantage. Candidates need to be at least 18 years old.

Level 2 pre-entry certificates for teaching assistants are offered by CACHE, NCFE, Edexcel (BTEC) and ABC. CACHE, NCFE and Edexcel (BTEC) also offer a Level 3 Certificate, aimed at experienced teaching assistants. Apprenticeships in Supporting Teaching and Learning in Schools are available which lead to NVQs at Levels 2 or 3.

You will be trained on the job. Local authorities in England and Wales may provide additional training.

Upon entry you can work towards NVQ Level 2–3 in Teaching Assistants or SVQ Level 2–3 in Classroom Assistants. There are also NVQs/SVQs in Early Years Care and Education. Teaching assistants in England can work towards Higher Level Teaching Assistant (HLTA) status.

A number of colleges and universities offer Foundation degrees. Anyone who will be working with children must undergo a CRB police check.

Money guide

Pay levels are set by local authorities or sometimes by school governors, so the rate can vary across regions. The rate for a HLTA is set by the local authority. The starting salary for this profession is normally between £12,000 and £16,000 per year. With experience, if you become a unit manager or work with young people with severe difficulties, you could earn up to £21,000.

Related opportunities

- Childminder p569
- Play Worker/Hospital Play Specialist p201
- Primary School Teacher p202
- Secondary School Teacher p205

Further information

Training and Development Agency for Schools
151 Buckingham Palace Road, London SW1W 9SZ
0845 6000 991; www.tda.gov.uk

CACHE
Head Office, Apex House, 81 Camp Road, St Albans AL1 5GB
0845 347 212; www.cache.org.uk

www.cityandguilds.com/myperfectjob

WORK-BASED TRAINING INSTRUCTOR

What the work involves

- You will work alongside employees, in their workplace or in a training centre, and teach them new skills or develop their existing skills.

- You will liaise closely with the employer's training or human resources manager in order to ascertain the type of training needed and organisational aspects.

- It is likely that you will specialise in an area such as IT, management, personal development, customer service or craft.

The type of person suited to this work

It is essential to demonstrate a real interest in helping people to learn and progress.

You must be patient, organised and up to date with the latest developments in your occupational area. Good ICT skills will also be helpful.

Excellent communication skills are important for the large amount of speaking, questioning, listening and reporting that are involved.

Working conditions

You will work in an office where you will use a computer to prepare lessons and update learner records. However, you will also spend lots of time travelling to meet employers and learners at their workplaces.

You will work normal office hours, Monday to Friday.

Future prospects

New media and different ways of working mean that there is a continual need to help businesses and industry develop the right people to carry out new work tasks.

All companies today are expected to develop their workforces and the government is currently encouraging learning through work-based qualifications, and school/college leavers now have a wider range of opportunities to pursue such as Apprenticeships.

Promotion to a training manager or consultant is possible with experience and further qualifications such as NVQs at Levels 4 and 5.

Advantages/disadvantages

This work involves being at the centre of improving the skills levels of the workforce.

You constantly have the opportunity to learn new things.

It can be challenging to motivate trainees who don't have an interest in achieving an academic qualification.

Qualifications and courses

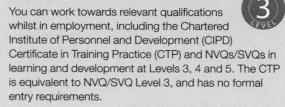

You can work towards relevant qualifications whilst in employment, including the Chartered Institute of Personnel and Development (CIPD) Certificate in Training Practice (CTP) and NVQs/SVQs in learning and development at Levels 3, 4 and 5. The CTP is equivalent to NVQ/SVQ Level 3, and has no formal entry requirements.

The higher level NVQs/SVQs and the CIPD Professional Development Scheme are appropriate for people in training manager posts.

Postgraduate qualifications are available in subjects such as education and training management, training and development, mentoring and coaching. These can usually be studied part time or by distance learning, and entry requirements are a degree or equivalent professional qualification.

Training practitioners can also work towards gaining NVQ assessor qualifications. Entry requirements are at least 2 years' occupational experience in the subject or work area to be assessed.

Associate teachers at further education colleges or organisations funded by the government need a Certificate in Teaching in the Lifelong Learning Sector. Full teachers need to take a 1-year course to obtain the Diploma in Teaching in the Lifelong Learning Sector.

Money guide

Salaries vary depending on the type and size of employer and location. Larger salaries are possible if the specialised skill you teach is in high demand. Starting salaries are about £16,000 a year. With experience this can rise to £18,000–£25,000. Top earners can expect £26,000 a year.

Related opportunities

- Human Resources/Personnel Officer p41
- Further/Higher Education Lecturer p196
- Training Manager p68

Further information

Chartered Institute of Personnel and Development
CIPD House, 151 The Broadway, London SW19 1JQ

www.cityandguilds.com/myperfectjob

Engineering, Manufacturing and Production

There are a number of highly skilled jobs available in this job family and workers need to be creative and methodical and combine brilliant technical skill with spatial awareness. You may be interested in food production but equally your passion could lie in working with aircraft or marine manufacture. People in these professions share the ability to concentrate for long periods of time and work meticulously on a job to finish it to a high standard. Some will also be highly trained with specialist equipment which may sometimes be hazardous to use so a high level of personal safety awareness is vital.

This section looks at the following jobs:

AEROSPACE ENGINEER

What the work involves

- Aerospace engineers research, design and manufacture space vehicles, satellites, missiles and aircraft.

- You can specialise in mechanical, electrical or electronics engineering, and within these areas you can focus on airframes, hydraulics, materials and structures, or engines.

- Your work might involve research, design and manufacture, or experimenting with new materials.

- You may also undertake flight test programmes, and maintain and improve fleets of aircraft all over the world.

The type of person suited to this work

You should have a logical mind and be good at problem solving. You should also be good at maths, and be able to produce good drawings and diagrams, as well as being able to interpret them well.

Your verbal and written communication skills should also be good, as you'll need to communicate ideas effectively. Teamworking skills are essential, but you must also be able to take on responsibility and work independently.

You'll be expected to keep up to date with new technology and developments in the industry, and for some roles you need to have normal colour vision.

Working conditions

It's usual to work 37–40 hours a week, but this depends a lot on project deadlines and what's currently taking place: hours can be longer.

Work usually takes place in clean quiet laboratories, but visits to production areas are essential and these areas are usually dirty and noisy.

Visits to airfields also take place, where you might be required to inspect and test the functions of the aircraft.

Future prospects

There are good opportunities for promotion in aerospace engineering. The skills you will require will make you suitable for higher positions even in other branches of engineering, and many aerospace engineers move into management positions or research roles as their career progresses.

Some aerospace engineers work independently as consultants, and others find work abroad for foreign governments or aircraft construction companies.

Advantages/disadvantages

You may have to work long hours, evenings and weekends. Stress levels can also be high if you're trying to meet deadlines.

The starting salary is relatively high, and you can work your way up to a good wage with time and experience.

Qualifications and courses

ENTRY LEVEL **4**

Most entrants are graduates, and many have studied Aeronautical Engineering as a degree. BEng degrees last 3 years and MEng last 4. You will need at least 5 GCSEs (A*–C) and 3 A levels, including maths and physics for entry to a degree.

A postgraduate degree will give you an advantage as will prior work experience. For example, doing a voluntary work placement at an industrial company would be helpful.

It is possible to enter at a lower level by beginning to train for a craft or technician job straight from school. Apprenticeship schemes usually require good GCSE grades in English, maths, and physics.

Many companies offer graduate training schemes and the chance to work towards an engineering licence through the Civil Aviation Authority.

Once you have a degree and some experience you can apply to the Engineering Council to receive chartered status.

Money guide

Starting salaries for graduates tend to range from £20,000 to £25,000 per year.

Depending on your professional status, you can work your way up to £40,000 per year as an experienced engineer.

Senior engineers might earn over £50,000.

Related opportunities

- Mechanical Engineer p234
- Electrical Engineer p221

Further information

The Engineering and Technology Board
2nd Floor, Weston House, 246 High Holborn,
London WC1V 7EX
020 3206 0400; www.etechb.co.uk

The Institution of Engineering and Technology
Michael Faraday House, Six Hills Way,
Stevenage SG1 2AY
01438 313311; www.theiet.org

Royal Aeronautical Society
4 Hamilton Place, London W1J 7BQ
020 7670 4325/6; www.aerosociety.com

City&
Guilds

www.cityandguilds.com/myperfectjob

Organisation profile

ROLLS-ROYCE APPRENTICESHIPS

"The best part of the Rolls-Royce apprenticeship is you're learning from the best to be the best."

Gurjit Johal – Plant Design Engineer

Join the team that sets the standard

Why Rolls-Royce?

Because we set the standard, that's why.

Others may talk about achieving the impossible; we go out there and do it.

We've broken the sound barrier, produced engines that fly passengers around the world in record time and transported rescuers to previously unreachable places. We've even designed turbines that generate enough energy to power a city the size of New York.

It takes 39,000 people, including some of the world's most respected engineers, to make all this possible. Each one of us shares a fascination with how things work, and a passion for wanting to make them work better. Want to join us?

Go further with the Rolls-Royce of apprenticeships

The Rolls-Royce Apprenticeship Scheme, which was recently described as "outstanding" by Ofsted inspectors, is designed to help you reach your full potential.

As one of our apprentices, you'll carry out mission-critical work, earning while you learn from the engineers and scientists behind the world's most important power systems.

Studying theory one day, the next putting it into practice, you'll have real responsibility from day one – and a steep learning curve. At the same time, you'll have the support you need to help you succeed. Plus the privilege of working with some of the world's best technology and practices.

Start your journey to becoming a world-renowned engineer

You can join us at just 14 as a Young Apprentice, combining your apprenticeship with school work, or wait until you're 16 and over and become a full-time apprentice. You can also opt for a Practical Apprenticeship, where you'll be hands-on, or a Technical Apprenticeship where you'll be mostly on the computer, problem solving.

Either way, you'll earn while you learn and there's a high possibility that we'll sponsor you for your degree.

What's more, when your apprenticeship finishes, you'll be off to a fantastic start – with all the skills, experience and confidence you need for a full-time role. Plus, with the retention rate for Rolls-Royce apprenticeships currently 98% (the national average is 65%), you can look forward to an exciting career with us.

See where a Rolls-Royce apprenticeship could take you, visit www.rolls-royce.com/apprenticeships

Case study

ROLLS-ROYCE APPRENTICESHIP

"I'm furthering my education while gaining invaluable work experience and being paid."

Rachel Freestone
Advanced/Modern Apprenticeship in Mechanical Engineering

Rolls-Royce's apprenticeships are a genuine alternative to university. Combining classroom study with on-the-job training, they offer two routes to becoming a world-renowned engineer – practical and technical.

Here's Rachel Freestone's story

Rachel Freestone chose the practical route. She explains why. "The Technical Apprenticeship is more theoretical. You're in the office, on the computer, which isn't me. I'm more hands-on and like being on the shop floor."

Now in the second year of her 3.5-year apprenticeship, it's easy to see Rachel loves what she does. She comes alive when she talks about engines and it's surprising to think that, when younger, she wanted to be a hairdresser.

"This is much better than being a hairdresser", Rachel confides. "It's great to work with an engine from the start – from stripping it – to the end where it's tested. You learn about the engine in depth, especially since you're taught by amazing engineers who really know their stuff. You study one day; the next you put what you've learnt into practice. It's brilliant."

So what's the biggest highlight of her apprenticeship so far? Rachel smiles, "It's got to be when I first helped assemble the EJ200, a gas turbine engine which powers the Eurofighter Typhoon. It was the first engine I worked on in my career – amazing!"

Rachel concludes, "I never really saw myself going to university. But, with Rolls-Royce, I'm currently studying for my HNC – and they may even sponsor my degree. The way I see it: what's the point of getting into debt at uni when you can earn while you learn with a good job at the end?"

See where a Rolls-Royce apprenticeship could take you, visit www.rolls-royce.com/apprenticeships

ASSEMBLER

What the work involves

- You will work on an assembly line within a factory or workshop, or at a bench. You could work on products within sectors as diverse as: engineering, furniture production, soft-furnishings, domestic electrical equipment, vehicles or electrical circuit boards.

Assembly line

- You will produce products or components as they arrive at your work area. Sometimes they may not stop, but keep moving along a belt or route in the factory.

- As the line needs to keep going at a set speed, you will be required to work at the same pace as everyone else.

Bench

- Using hand tools, and in some cases simple machinery, you will carry out specific assembly tasks or create a finished product.

The type of person suited to this work

You will need to have practical skills and enjoy making or repairing items.

In order to construct your product or components you will have to follow diagrams and instructions and be able to work quickly and precisely.

You need good interpersonal skills and a solid work ethic.

As it can be repetitive work you must be able to focus on the same task many times a day.

Working conditions

Assembly line

You can expect to be in a large factory – in some sectors this could be noisy, dirty and busy and in others, such as the electronics industry, it would be clean and dust-free.

Some assembly lines require 24/7 production; if so, you will normally work a shift pattern.

Bench

You will be sitting or standing using the tools and machinery positioned around you. If you need to use a soldering iron for assembly it can be hot work and may cause fumes.

You can also work part time.

Future prospects

The largest employers of assemblers are the electrical, electronic and information technology industries.

As machines are increasingly replacing some of the assembly work that used to be done by people, jobs are reducing. However there is still demand for assemblers to work on assembling products that are too intricate to be done by machine, or for assembling very small batches of goods.

Qualifications and courses

There are no formal entry requirements for this work. Key Skills, GCSEs/S grades in English, maths and practical subjects or vocational qualifications in engineering/manufacturing can be useful.

The Diploma in Engineering, Manufacturing and Product Design would be relevant for work in this area

Apprenticeships/Skillseekers may be available to enter this area of work.

ENTRY LEVEL 1

With experience, you may be able to progress into a supervisory role or other areas of manufacturing such as quality control. You could also go on to train as an engineering craft worker.

Advantages/disadvantages

Whilst carrying out repetitive tasks, you must be able to concentrate and maintain a fast pace of work for long periods of time.

Your surroundings may be dirty and noisy.

Due to advances in technology, the need for workers will continue to drop.

Part-time work is also available, which is attractive to people with families wanting to supplement their income.

Money guide

Starting salaries for assemblers are on average £10,000–£12,000 per year. For experienced assemblers salaries can range from £12,000 to £17,000. Very skilled and experienced assemblers in certain parts of the industry, such as automotive assembly, can earn £20,000+. Productivity bonuses are commonly used as an incentive and will increase salaries.

Related opportunities

- Food Processing Operative p224
- Mechanical Engineer p234
- Welder p251

Further information

Semta
14 Upton Road, Watford WD18 0JT
01923 238441; www.semta.org.uk

Proskills UK
Centurion Court, 85B Milton Park, Abingdon OX14 4RY
01235 833844; www.proskills.co.uk

City & Guilds

Engineering, Manufacturing and Production

CRCI: NJ

BLACKSMITH

What the work involves

Artist blacksmith

- You will produce decorative pieces such as gates and furniture.
- You may create specially commissioned pieces such as a stairway for a building project.

Industrial blacksmith

- You will produce functional objects for use by companies such as fire escapes and security screens.
- You may specialise in an area such as agricultural engineering or security.

The type of person suited to this work

All blacksmiths mostly work alone so you should be able to use your initiative.

Much of your time will be spent on your feet using different hand tools, often near to the forge which will be very hot. You will need to be very responsible, as the tools and materials that you will be working with can be dangerous.

Artist blacksmith

Having a creative flair will help you to use your materials imaginatively.

Industrial blacksmith

You will need an understanding of the way products function and how different metal properties will affect the end product.

Working conditions

All blacksmiths will work with various metals and will use different hand and bench tools and a forge. This will result in conditions that can be noisy, dirty and sometimes cramped.

You will spend much of the time on your feet. You will wear protective clothing such as gloves, ear protectors and goggles.

Artist blacksmith

You will mainly work in rural areas.

Industrial blacksmith

You will be working in mines, docks and with engineering companies.

Future prospects

Artist blacksmith

With experience you may move on to work for a museum or heritage centre.

Industrial blacksmith

As you are more likely to work within a company you might progress to supervisory or managerial posts.

Qualifications and course

ENTRY LEVEL 1

Training can be by an apprenticeship or college course. Some courses may require specific GCSEs/S grades and forge-work experience. HNDs and degrees in creative aspects of blacksmithing are available. Two A levels/3 H grades and 5 GCSEs/S grades (A*–C/1–3) are required for entry.

The National Crafts Training Programme combines on-the-job training with periods of block-release study at the college, and lasts from 2 to 3 years. Herefordshire College of Technology also operates a New Entrants Training Scheme in forge work.

Most blacksmiths however are self-employed. Future success will rely on your ability to gain orders and build a reputation.

Advantages/disadvantages

Much of the work is done alone and can be isolating.

The work is tiring, but when you have created what a customer requires it can be satisfying too.

If you are involved in a creative project such as a commissioned sculpture, it can be very rewarding.

Money guide

There are currently no agreed minimum rates for apprentice blacksmiths so salaries can vary widely. Starting salaries generally range from £11,000 to £16,000 a year. Once training has been completed you could earn £25,000+ a year depending on regional differences. Highly experienced blacksmiths earn over £50,000 a year.

Related opportunities

- Farrier p266
- Sheet Metal Worker p245

Further information

British Artist Blacksmiths Association
Anwick Forge, 62 Main Road, Anwick, Lincoln NG34 9SU
01526 830303; www.baba.org.uk

National Association of Farriers, Blacksmiths and Agricultural Engineers
The Forge, Avenue B, 10th Street, Stoneleigh Park, Coventry CV8 2LG
024 7669 6595; www.nafbae.org

Worshipful Company of Blacksmiths
48 Upwood Road, London SE12 8AN
020 8318 9684; www.blacksmithscompany.org.uk

City&
Guilds

www.cityandguilds.com/myperfectjob

BREWERY WORKER

What the work involves

- You will make and package beer, stout and lager for a variety of outlets, including shops and pubs.

- You will be involved in the whole brewing process, from measuring out ingredients to labelling and loading the finished product.

- You will work as part of a team supervised by a technical brewer.

The type of person suited to this work

You will need to enjoy working in a team, and be aware of the health and safety regulations to keep yourself and others safe at work.

The work is quite physically demanding, you will be lifting and operating heavy machinery so will need to be fit and healthy.

Good numeracy skills will be helpful when measuring out ingredients and checking the amount of products produced.

Working conditions

Most large breweries have a shift system in place for their workers. You will usually work around 40 hours a week, and can work overtime if necessary.

You will be working with machinery and fermenting ingredients, therefore overalls, gloves and goggles may be worn to limit contamination and to keep you safe.

Future prospects

After a few years of experience you can move into a supervisory or management role, in charge of a team of brewery workers.

Often brewery workers study further to become craft technical brewers.

Advantages/disadvantages

Due to the decline in breweries across the UK, it can be difficult to find work; many smaller breweries are family run so employ very few staff.

Working in a brewery can be smelly, hot and physically demanding; this may be stressful or tiring at times.

Working in a team of other brewery workers creates a lively and fun atmosphere.

Making beer, stout and lager is a satisfying job role as you know you are creating beverages that people enjoy drinking.

Qualifications and courses

ENTRY 1 LEVEL

There are no set entry requirements for this career. Having GCSEs/S grades in English, maths and science may be helpful. Sometimes it is possible to start with a role in packaging operations and progress to brewery worker.

There may be an Apprenticeship/Skillseekers available in food manufacture which leads to this career.

Brewery workers can train on the job and study for NVQs at Levels 1, 2 and 3 in food manufacture. Brewing Research International (BRI) offers specialist courses in brewing techniques and the Institute of Brewing and Distilling also offers short courses in drink manufacture.

Money guide

The amount you earn does depend on the location and size of the brewery you work for. Average starting salaries are around £15,000, with this rising to £22,000 with a few years' experience.

Senior brewery workers or those in supervisory roles may earn £29,000+.

Related opportunities

- Biotechnologist p508
- Cellar Technician p136
- Craft Technical Brewer p220

Further information

Institute of Brewing and Distilling
33 Clarges Street, London W1J 7EE
020 7499 8144; www.ibd.org.uk

www.cityandguilds.com/myperfectjob

CRCI: NC

Engineering, Manufacturing and Production

CAD DRAUGHTSPERSON

What the work involves

- You will produce the drawings and instructions that will enable others to create structures, equipment or components.

- Using a computer-aided design (CAD) workstation you will draw up technical drawings for components or sections of a structure, or for different products.

- Depending on the specialism of the company you work for, you may design part of a structure as large as a factory or bridge, or a component as small as an electronic circuit.

The type of person suited to this work

You should be patient and accurate, and have a good understanding of different production processes.

You need to be organised and methodical in your work and be able to work to tight deadlines.

Good ICT, technical drawing and numerical skills are essential. You will need to be able to solve design problems in a creative way and should be comfortable and confident communicating your work to others.

Working conditions

Most of your work will be done sitting in front of your computer or drawing board, in an office or design area.

You will work office hours but you might need to work overtime when deadlines are close.

Sometimes you will visit the shop floor or factory area where the product you are designing is being made – which could be noisy, hot and dirty. However your own workspace will be quiet as a lot of concentration is required.

Future prospects

A wide range of employers recruit CAD draughtspeople; including aeronautical, civil, electrical, mechanical and marine engineering companies, central and local government and the public utilities such as water and electricity supply.

All construction and manufacturing companies across the UK need trained draughtspeople which means they're in constant demand

You can progress on to senior, supervisory and team-leader work with experience and training. With further training you could become an architect or a chartered engineer.

There are opportunities to work abroad.

Advantages/disadvantages

As much of your work involves using your drawing board or computer, your eyes could get tired and strained.

Qualifications and courses

You can enter this job as a trainee technician with an employer, through an Advanced Apprenticeship/Skillseekers scheme. Most entrants are aged 16–19, but entry is possible up to the age of 24. Applicants require 4 GCSEs/S grades (A*–C/1–3) or equivalent including maths and science or technology.

Alternatively, you can take relevant pre-entry qualifications such as a BTEC First Certificate in Engineering or First Diploma in Manufacturing Engineering, National Certificate/Diploma in Manufacturing Engineering, or a City & Guilds Level 2 award in CAD, and gain entry at technician level.

Qualifications that can be obtained through on-the-job training include NVQs/SVQs at Level 3, BTEC National Certificates or Diplomas, or a City & Guilds Certificate.

If you want to progress, you can move to supervisor level within your own company or elsewhere. With experience, it may be possible to do this work on a freelance basis, being contracted by smaller companies who do not employ their own draughtsperson.

Money guide

Earnings will be affected by the type of industry you work in and your location.

General starting salaries are around £18,000 per year.

With experience, and working in one of the higher paying industries, you can earn up to £30,000.

At senior level you can earn more than £40,000.

Related opportunities

- Architectural Technician p73
- Architectural Technologist p74
- Graphic Designer p176

Further information

Engineering Careers Information Service
SEMTA House, 14 Upton Road, Watford WD18 0JT
0800 282167; www.enginuity.org.uk

Chartered Institute of Architectural Technologists
397 City Road, London EC1V 1NH
020 7278 2206; www.ciat.org.uk

City&
Guilds

www.cityandguilds.com/myperfectjob

CHEMICAL ENGINEER

What the work involves

- You will devise low-cost, safe and environmentally friendly methods that will transform raw materials into products such as fuel, pharmaceuticals, plastics and toiletries.

- You might research ways to improve the future of our planet which could include discovering renewable energy sources or producing replacement human organs.

- You might work in manufacturing and help design and construct plants for mass production of products. You will then oversee the running of the plant and the quality of its products.

The type of person suited to this work

You will need to have good oral and written communication skills in order to brief colleagues and compile useful and extensive reports from research you have undertaken. This includes good project management skills.

In keeping with this, an analytical mind and ability to problem solve are helpful when designing and testing products or equipment in the plant itself.

You will also need to be creative, in order to come up with cost-effective products and solutions to problems.

An aptitude and interest in chemistry is also recommended, as is a good understanding of engineering and mathematics.

Working conditions

Working hours are normally fairly standard from Monday to Friday although you might have to work extra hours on occasion, particularly if you are developing a new product, and this can include evenings and weekends.

You will usually work in a plant, laboratory or research establishment so conditions can vary from peaceful, sterile labs to noisier factory floors.

You might need to wear appropriate safety equipment for certain aspects of the job.

Future prospects

Jobs are available across the UK in a range of industries, from pharmaceuticals to oil and gas.

Opportunities for progression and promotion are great; you could obtain a position in senior management or a project leader role.

Chemical engineers are encouraged to achieve chartered or incorporated status.

Advantages/disadvantages

You will gain further qualifications and skills as you develop in your career, and have the opportunity to work in a range of industries as well as abroad.

Working in a sterile lab environment, or a noisy factory, can be off-putting.

Qualifications and courses

This career is open to all graduates with a degree in physical or applied sciences, and engineering. Specific subjects such as chemistry, chemical engineering, applied chemistry and polymer science may improve your chances further. HNDs in similar subjects are also considered although you might have to start as a technician and work up to the position of chemical engineer as you gain further qualifications. You will need a minimum of 5 GCSEs/Highers (A*–C/1–3) including English, maths and science, and 2 A levels/Highers in order to gain a place on an engineering or related degree/HND course.

Your degree or HND must be IChemE accredited by the Engineering Council UK (ECUK) if you want to qualify as a chartered (CEng) chemical engineer. Qualifying will add considerable scope to your career potential.

Entry without a degree or HND is uncommon, although an Advanced Apprenticeship in engineering could lead to a role as an engineering technician or enable you to take a relevant degree. The Diploma in Engineering could also be useful.

Chemical engineers, once working, need to commit to a programme of continuing professional development (CPD) to make sure their skills are kept up to date.

ENTRY LEVEL 4

Money guide

Typical starting salaries range from £20,000 to £26,000. With experience and gaining a more senior role in the company, you can expect to earn £45,000–£47,000. If you achieve chartered status, you could earn £60,000+.

Related opportunities

- Environmental Engineer p223
- Mechanical Engineer p234
- Manufacturing/Production Engineer p230

Further information

The Career Engineer
Beaumont House, Kensington Village, Avonmore Road, London W14 8TS
0845 241 4022; www.thecareerengineer.com

SEMTA
14 Upton Road, Watford WD18 0JT
01923 238 441; www.semta.org.uk

British Chemical Engineering Contractors Association
1 Regent Street, London SW1Y 4NR
020 7839 6514; www.bceca.org.uk

City & Guilds

www.cityandguilds.com/myperfectjob

CRAFT TECHNICAL BREWER

What the work involves

- You will be overseeing the whole brewing process, managing the brewery workers and monitoring the condition of the brewing equipment.

- Technical brewers are responsible for checking the quality of raw materials and testing the product regularly for texture, taste and appearance. In a large brewery you may specialise in a certain area of brewing.

- You will be responsible for developing new brewing methods, and designing and developing new beers, stouts and lagers.

The type of person suited to this work

You will need to be scientific, with an enquiring mind and a particular interest in biochemistry. Both a practical ability and an interest in engineering are also useful.

Leadership and interpersonal skills are needed as you will be managing a team of brewers. Good written communication skills are also needed as you will be responsible for writing reports, keeping records and presenting new brewery methods to your colleagues.

Working conditions

As brewing is a continuous process, you will work shifts including nights and weekends. Usually you will work no more that 40 hours a week.

Some technical brewers will need to be on their feet all day, checking the brewing process, in hot and noisy conditions. Some time will be spent in an office though, organising paperwork and making reports on production, stock qualities and budgets.

Future prospects

You can progress to managerial roles and senior brewer positions in a large brewery. Some brewers can choose to set up their own microbrewery.

There are opportunities to work abroad.

Advantages/disadvantages

Due to the decline in breweries in the UK, competition for positions is high. The highest concentration of jobs is in the east of England and London; this may mean relocating.

This is an interesting, and diverse role, which can lead to good promotions and self-employment.

Working night shifts in a hot and smelly environment may be tiring and stressful.

Qualifications and courses

Trainee technical brewers usually have a degree or postgraduate qualification. Degrees in brewing and distilling, food studies, biochemistry and biology are all relevant. Entry requirements for a degree are 5 GCSEs/S grades and at least 2 A levels/ H grades.

Starting out as a brewery worker or production assistant and progressing to technical brewer may also be possible. Usually only GCSEs/S grades are needed to start in these roles. The Diploma in Manufacturing and Design may be useful as well.

Work experience in a brewery will help an application as a technical brewer.

Technical brewers usually have further training when they begin work. The Institute of Brewing and Distilling offers a range of courses for general brewing and specialist subjects, these include general certificate in brewing, distilling and packaging, diploma in brewing modules and master brewing modules.

Money guide

Starting salaries are around £19,000 per year; this can increase to £25,000–£30,000 with some experience. Senior brewers working in a large brewery may earn up to £40,000.

Related opportunities

- Biotechnologist p508
- Cellar Technician p136
- Brewery worker p217

Further information

Institute of Brewing and Distilling
33 Clarges Street, London W1J 7EE
020 7499 8144; www.ibd.org.uk

Brewing Research International
Lytell Hall, Nutfield RH1 4HY
01737 822272; www.brewingresearch.co.uk

www.cityandguilds.com/myperfectjob

ELECTRICAL ENGINEER

Engineering, Manufacturing and Production

CRCI: GE

What the work involves

- Electrical engineers research, design and develop a range of electrical equipment.

- You will be making, testing and servicing all types of electrical equipment and machinery, and as such will be involved in projects from conception to completion.

- You will usually work on projects with a team of professionals, such as contractors and engineers from other industries.

- You will also be liaising with clients and contractors about the development of each project, which will include preparing reports and giving presentations.

The type of person suited to this work

You should have excellent mathematical ability and a very analytical mind in order to successfully design and develop complicated new electrical systems. A logical approach to problem solving is also beneficial.

You will need good communication skills, both verbal and written, for working alongside team members and clients. This will include explaining and talking through projects, as well as compiling written reports and leading presentations.

You must have normal colour vision and natural manual dexterity.

Working conditions

Although electrical engineers usually work within the normal working week, you may find that you will need to work additional or unsociable hours in order to solve problems and meet project deadlines.

Your time will be divided between office-based and on-site work, and you can expect to travel on a daily basis so a driving licence is useful.

Conditions on-site can often be dirty, cramped and potentially hazardous, so you should be prepared to get your hands dirty and wear safety equipment.

Future prospects

There are no set pathways of career progression for electrical engineers, and many decide to stay in a purely engineering role for the duration of their working life.

Alternatively, there are possibilities of going into project management, becoming a consultant, or taking on a more managerial role within a company.

Advantages/disadvantages

Your work will be undertaken at a mixture of indoor and outdoor locations, so you won't be stuck in the office on a daily basis.

You will play an instrumental role in developing new and increasingly safe electrical equipment for a variety of important functions.

Qualifications and courses

You will need a degree in a subject such as physics, maths, computer science or electrical engineering. You will need at least 2 A levels and 5 GCSEs (A*–C), including maths and science for degree entry.

Graduate apprenticeships are available which allow you to study for a degree and work at the same time. You could also work on a gap year.

You could train to become a technician straight from school through an apprenticeship. You will need good GCSEs (A*–C) in English, maths, science or technology. The Diploma in Engineering or in Construction and the Built Environment may also be helpful. In order to become an engineer though you will need to study for a degree.

Scholarships, sponsorships and placements are available. See the Institution of Engineering and Technology website for more information.

To become a professional engineer, you will need to take a Master's degree to gain incorporated (IEng) or chartered (CEng) status.

Hours can be long and unpredictable, especially when nearing completion of a project.

Money guide

The starting salary for an electrical engineer can range from £17,000 to £25,000. With 10–15 years' experience, your salary could rise to £40,000+.

Within engineering, salaries vary greatly according to location (London usually yields the highest wages) and the size of the company that you work for. Some companies also offer excellent benefit packages and bonus schemes in addition to a basic wage.

Related opportunities

- Telecommunications Engineer p247
- Mechanical Engineer p234
- Civil/Construction Engineer/Civil Engineering Technician p85
- Electrician p94

Further information

The Institution of Engineering and Technology
Michael Faraday House, Stevenage SG1 2AY
01438 313 311; www.theiet.org; postmaster@theiet.org

City&
Guilds

www.cityandguilds.com/myperfectjob

ELECTRICITY DISTRIBUTION WORKER

What the work involves

- Electrical distribution workers are responsible for installing, checking and maintaining all machinery and equipment that supplies electricity to commercial and residential properties.

- You will be working on the overhead lines, masts, and underground cables that run from power stations and connect all the electricity networks together.

- You could work as a cable jointer who mainly works on the underground cables, an overhead line worker, or an electrical fitter who installs, tests and repairs equipment in the regional electricity substations.

- You will be working on a variety of projects from small scale domestic problems to regional electrical concerns.

The type of person suited to this work

You will need to be practical and good with your hands as you will be using a variety of tools and undertaking fiddly tasks.

You should be reasonably fit with a head for heights, as some jobs may require lifting and carrying heavy equipment or working high above the ground.

You must have normal colour vision and pay meticulous attention to detail.

Since you will be working with live electricity, you must be aware of your own safety and that of others around you. You may need to wear protective equipment at times.

Working conditions

Although you will usually work an average of 37 hours a week, these may well be over shift patterns including evening and weekends. You should also expect to work overtime on occasion in order to complete projects on time.

The work can be physically demanding as you will be bending and carrying large cables and equipment.

You may work outdoors in damp and muddy trenches, and can expect to be carrying out tasks in cramped conditions from time to time.

Future prospects

As an electricity distribution worker, you will have various options open to you as you progress in your career. You may go on to become a supervisor or manager and be responsible for a team of workers. Alternatively, you could move into another related craft job within the industry.

Your career prospects could be improved further by studying for additional qualifications as you work, such as an NVQ Level 4 or BTEC National Certificate in electrical engineering, or even starting on a related degree course.

Qualifications and courses

ENTRY LEVEL 2

Most people start in this career as an apprentice. Although there are no set qualifications, most employers look for at least 4 GCSEs/S grades (A*–C/1–3) including English, maths and a related subject such as science, design and technology or engineering. Apprenticeships are open to those aged 16–24 and could last up to 4 years. You will undertake a mixture of on-the-job practical training and college based study.

The Diploma in Engineering or an HND in a relevant subject may also prove beneficial.

On completion of your training, you could work towards becoming a registered engineering technician which will increase your earning potential. You could work towards an NVQ Level 2 or 3 in Electricity System Technology Engineering, or a Technical Certificate from BTEC or City & Guilds.

Advantages/disadvantages

You will be on site for the majority of your time so won't be cooped up in an office.

Possibilities for career progression or diversification are good.

Although you might have to work irregular hours, nights away from home are uncommon.

Conditions can be unpleasant, due to weather or space constraints.

Money guide

Starting salaries for an apprentice are around £8,000, and will rise to around £18,000 near the completion of training. With experience, your salary could increase to between £19,000 and £25,000. As a senior electricity distribution worker, especially if you become a team supervisor or manager, you could earn £30,000+.

Related opportunities

- Gas Network Engineer p226
- Electrician p94
- Electrical Engineer p221

Further information

Engineering Council UK
246 High Holborn, London WC1V 7EX
020 3206 0500; www.engc.org.uk

The Institution of Engineering and Technology
Michael Faraday House, Stevenage SG1 2AY
01438 313 311; www.theiet.org; postmaster@theiet.org

City & Guilds

www.cityandguilds.com/myperfectjob

ENVIRONMENTAL ENGINEER

What the work involves

- Environmental engineers work on projects concerning waste management, land reclamation and pollution control, and liaise with a variety of clients from local authorities to private property developers.

- You will visit and assess numerous sites in relation to their environmental impact, and will have to explain your findings to clients via presentations and reports.

- You may also have to communicate the environmental issues of a project or site to the general public, green groups and regulatory authorities.

The type of person suited to this work

You should have excellent mathematical ability and a very analytical mind in order to successfully carry out complicated procedures and calculations to assess sites and projects.

A swift and logical approach to problem solving is also beneficial when dealing with often unforeseen environmental complications.

You will need good communication skills, both verbal and written, for working alongside team members and clients.

Good negotiation skills are also helpful as you might need to reach compromises over projects with local government officials, residents or clients.

Working conditions

You will usually work about 39 hours from Monday to Friday, although it is not uncommon to work additional or unsociable hours should problems occur or if deadlines need to be met on a project.

Your time will be divided between office-based and on-site work, so you can expect to travel on a daily basis. Because of this, a driving licence is essential.

You will work in all weather conditions on-site, so should be prepared to get cold and muddy. You will also have to adhere to site safety regulations and wear relevant protective clothing.

Future prospects

As environmental concerns become an increasingly important aspect of construction projects across the globe, there are good prospects and opportunities within this field for career progression.

With experience, you could move into consultancy and set up your own firm. Alternatively, you could specialise in an area such as treatment of industrial waste, or provision of drinking water in developing countries.

You could work in a small company, or in much larger multinational firms. There are also numerous opportunities to work on projects abroad.

Advantages/disadvantages

You will be responsible for minimising the environmental impact of building projects and protecting the wellbeing of the natural surroundings, which will be rewarding.

Qualifications and courses

ENTRY LEVEL 4

Most employers require a degree in a relevant subject such as civil or environmental engineering. You may be considered if you have studied another engineering subject, or something related such as physics, applied physics or maths. You will need at least 2 A levels and 5 GCSEs (A*–C), including maths and physics for degree entry.

You can also enter with an HND in a relevant subject such as general engineering, civil engineering, environmental engineering, applied physics or computing and IT. Some employers do prefer graduates, however, so supplementing your HND with work experience is highly recommended.

Apprenticeships are occasionally available to candidates following completion of A levels by which companies sponsor candidates through their degree programme.

To become a professional engineer, you will need to take a Master's degree to gain incorporated (IEng) or chartered (CEng) status.

Working on potentially controversial developments could lead to confrontation with local residents or clients.

There are excellent opportunities to work overseas, or set up your own company.

Money guide

The starting salary for an environmental engineer can range from £18,000 to £24,000. With a few years' experience, your salary could rise to £30,000–£40,000. Senior environmental engineers can earn £60,000+.

Related opportunities

- Environmental Health Practitioner/Officer p35
- Marine Engineer p232
- Mechanical Engineer p234

Further information

Environmental Careers
The Chartered Institution of Water and Environmental Management (CIWEM), 15 John Street, London SC1N 2EB
020 7831 3110; www.ciwem.org

Engineering Council UK
246 High Holborn, London WC1V 7EX
020 3206 0500; www.engc.org.uk

The Career Engineer
Trinity Mirror Digital Recruitment, One Canada Square, London E14 5AP
0845 241 4022; www.thecareerengineer.com

City&
Guilds

www.cityandguilds.com/myperfectjob

FOOD PROCESSING OPERATIVE

What the work involves

- Food processing operatives can be involved in one of many areas of food processing. These include freezing, canning, baking, drying, cooking, chilling, pasteurising, or a combination of several of these processes.

- Since much of the work above is carried out by machines, you may be involved in operating the machinery, and you might also be expected to carry out basic maintenance on it.

- You might be involved in the production of the food, for example placing different components of foodstuffs in containers.

- Packaging and labeling are other tasks that you might be required to carry out.

The type of person suited to this work

It's helpful if you have an interest in food and food processing.

You should be good at working in a team, and be able to respond quickly to problems that may arise. You need to be able to stay alert and perceptive at all times, even if tasks are mundane or boring. Good ability to concentrate and observe what's going on around you will really help with this.

Good literacy and numeracy skills are also essential, and you'll need to be able to follow instructions easily, both written and spoken. A thorough understanding of health and safety requirements is also an advantage.

Working conditions

You will be working in a factory environment most of the time. This will involve standing in a production line, as well as bending and lifting.

Temperature in the factory varies according to the processes taking place, and could be very warm or quite chilly.

You'll almost certainly be required to wear special clothing, such as overalls and hats, and a high level of personal hygiene is essential.

You can expect to work 37 to 40 hours a week, usually on a shift system which may include weekends. Overtime is often available.

Future prospects

Progression within the food and drink industry is relatively common, and if committed you stand a good chance of moving up in your company or moving to others.

You can progress to supervisory and management positions quite quickly. Most managers in this sector started out as a food processing operative or something similar.

Advantages/disadvantages

The working environment may not always be pleasant: it can be very hot or very cold. Work may be mundane at times, and the salary isn't very high.

Qualifications and Courses

There are no set qualifications. Some employers will ask for basic levels of literacy and numeracy.

If you want to progress into a supervisory role, you might need GCSEs (A*–E) in English, maths, science or food technology.

An Apprenticeship in Food Manufacture or the Diploma in Manufacturing and Product Design may also be useful.

Some companies will require you to be 18 or over to start work.

Most training will take place on the job. Practical skills will be taught, as well as general health and safety, and food safety.

You can improve your skills by taking an NVQ/SVQ (Level 1–4) in Food and Drink Manufacturing Operations.

With time, you can work towards progressing to a management role or supervisory position. At an operative level, you can choose to move to different areas of food production, such as baking, freezing or brewing.

There are usually plenty of jobs available in this sector, and prospects for promotion are good. If you work your way up jobs become more interesting and better paid.

Money guide

Salaries start at about £11,500 per year, but some apprentices might earn less.

This can rise to £15,000 per year as you gain experience.

Supervisors and managers can earn £18,000 upwards.

Related opportunities

- Brewery Worker p220
- Meat Process Worker p233

Further information

Food and Drink Federation
6 Catherine Street, London WC2B 5JJ
020 7836 2460; www.fdf.org.uk

Improve Ltd
Ground Floor, Providence House, 2 Innovation Close, Heslington, York YO10 5ZF
0845 644 0448; www.improveltd.co.uk

Scottish Food and Drink Federation
4A Torpichen Street, Edinburgh EH3 8JQ
0131 229 9415; www.sfdf.org.uk

www.cityandguilds.com/myperfectjob

FURNITURE MANUFACTURER

What the work involves

■ Furniture manufacturers construct pieces of furniture, either using machinery or by hand.

■ This involves cutting and shaping individual parts of each piece, then assembling them to make a finished item.

■ You may then have to smooth and finish items, getting them ready for sale.

■ Once you've done the above, you'll usually be asked to add handles and hinges, and sometimes to upholster the furniture too.

The type of person suited to this work

You must be practical and good with your hands. You should also have excellent eyesight and full colour vision. Hand-to-eye coordination is a must.

Your physical strength should be reasonably good, as you'll need to lift and carry things.

You must be able to take orders, and to work under supervision, as well as being good at team work.

Some jobs will require artistic ability, and all will require you to be accurate, careful, and above all patient.

Tasks may become repetitive, but you need to be able to stay focused all the time.

Working conditions

You'll be working in a factory, so the environment may be noisy. Most jobs require you to stand in a production line all day, and the air may be dusty and smell strongly of the products used to treat finished furniture. Protective clothing is usually worn, including ear protectors and face masks for many jobs. Many jobs involve standing for long periods, lifting heavy weights, and bending.

It's normal to work a 39 hour week, but overtime is sometimes necessary if the factory has a delivery deadline, or during seasonal peaks.

Future prospects

Promotion is a possibility, and many manufacturers move into more senior roles within companies, managing projects and gaining responsibility.

Others choose to specialise in specific areas of furniture manufacture, for example furniture restoration, craft cabinet making, or even furniture design.

Some furniture manufacturers choose to teach their craft, or set up their own business.

Advantages/disadvantages

If you're interested in your craft and willing to put a little time in, a career in furniture manufacture can really grow, and so can your salary.

Qualifications and courses

Most employers don't require any specific qualifications, but some ask for GCSEs (A*–E). You may need to pass an eye sight and colour vision test.

Apprenticeships in Wood Making and in Making and Installing Furniture are available. The Diploma in Manufacturing and Product Design may also be helpful.

Training usually occurs on the job. As a trainee you could follow a part-time course in college and gain a relevant qualification. This could be a City & Guilds Certificate in Manufacturing Furniture, or one of many NVQ qualifications including Production of Furniture and Furnishings, Making and Installing Furniture, Making and Repairing Hand-Crafted Furniture and Furnishings, and Making and Installing Production Furniture. There is also a City & Guilds qualification available in Furniture Crafts.

This job can be satisfying if you enjoy building and making things and are good at DIY.

Working on constructing the same item over and over again can get repetitive.

Money guide

Most operatives start on a salary of around £12,000 per year.

Once you've gained some experience, this might increase to about £15,000 per year.

If you become highly skilled, you can expect to earn £20,000 upwards.

Related opportunities

■ Carpenter/Joiner p81
■ Shopfitter p120

Further information

Association of Master Upholsterers and Soft Furnishers
Francis Vaughan House, Q1 Capital Point Business Centre, Parkway, Cardiff CF3 2PU
029 2079 3508; www.upholsterers.co.uk

British Furniture Manufacturers Association
Wycombe House, 9 Ambersham Hill, High Wycombe HP13 6NR
01494 523021; www.bfm.org.uk

FFINTO
67 Wollaton Road, Beeston, Nottingham NG9 2NG
0115 9221200; www.ffinto.org

www.cityandguilds.com/myperfectjob

Engineering, Manufacturing and Production

CRCI: NL

GAS NETWORK ENGINEER

What the work involves

- Gas is transported from its supply points (called beaches) to domestic and industrial customers by a network of pipes and meters that will be your responsibility to fit and maintain.

- To gain access to pipework you will probably need to dig a hole in a road, garden or pavement.

- You will be responsible for the safety of yourself and others when carrying out work. This will include putting up warning signs, barriers and traffic control if needed.

- You may have to deal with emergency gas leaks.

The type of person suited to this work

You will normally work in a small team, so you should enjoy working with and be able to get on with people. You will be meeting new customers each day, so being polite and courteous are also important skills.

This can be a physically demanding job. You will be using digging and excavating tools and pipe-laying equipment. You will also have to understand and follow technical instructions and drawings.

When the job is complete, you will have to ensure the finished surface is safe and as good as it was when you started, so you should be tidy and efficient.

Working conditions

You will be working in a team outdoors in all weathers. You will normally work a 37–40 hour week, overtime and weekend work will be expected on a rota basis.

You will be using equipment which can be physically demanding and you will get dirty. As this can be dangerous work you will wear protective clothing such as high-visibility and fireproof clothing, steel toe-capped boots and head gear.

Future prospects

The National Grid coordinates and monitors the gas distribution network in the UK. There are four gas distribution companies; National Grid Distribution, Wales and West Utilities, Northern Gas Networks and Scotia Gas Networks (operating in the south of England as Southern Gas and in Scotland as Scotland Gas Networks). There is currently a demand for gas network engineers due to an extensive 30-year pipeline replacement programme.

With experience and training, you could progress to a technician, supervisory or management position where you would be responsible for a number of teams.

Advantages/disadvantages

You will be working outside in all weathers.

You may have to deal with complaints from angry customers about holes in their road.

Qualifications and courses

You will normally start as a trainee or an apprentice. There are no formal qualifications required. However, entry to gas network engineering Apprenticeships requires a minimum of 4 GCSEs/S grades (A*– C/1–3), in maths, science, English and a practical technical subject.

The Diploma in Engineering could be helpful.

It is necessary to have a safety passport from Safety Health and Environment Awareness.

It's also useful to have some experience in engineering or building work. A lot of adults are recruited through this route.

Once employed you can work towards NVQs at Levels 1, 2 and 3 in Gas Network Operations. After completing an NVQ Level 3 it is possible to apply for HND/degree or higher level NVQs. Graduate engineering and management training schemes are also available.

It is also possible to undertake a 3 year National Grid Advanced Apprenticeship.

Having a clean driving licence is increasingly important.

Giving the public a gas supply for their homes and businesses can be rewarding.

Money guide

Whilst training, workers can earn £10,000–£11,000 per year.

Upon qualification and with experience this rises to £17,000.

As a team leader or with more responsibility you can expect your salary to increase to £25,000.

Salaries may be boosted significantly with payment for overtime and shift work.

Related opportunities

- Construction Operative p88
- Construction Plant Operator p89
- Plumber p113
- Water/Sewerage Network Operative p131

Further information

Northern Gas Networks
1100 Century Way, Colton, Leeds LS15 8TU
0845 6340508; www.northerngasnetworks.co.uk

Scotland Gas Networks
Inveralmond House, 200 Dunkeld Road, Perth PH1 3AQ
0845 070 1432; www.scotiagasnetworks.co.uk

www.cityandguilds.com/myperfectjob

LAND-BASED ENGINEER

What the work involves

- Land-based engineers design, develop, test and modify agricultural and horticultural equipment in order to ensure that these industries stay up-to-date.

- You will need to carry out extensive research into the needs of those using the equipment you are producing, as well as assessing and limiting the environmental impact of your projects.

- You will also be called upon to compile reports and undertake presentations on your work, as well as offering expert advice to clients and other professionals.

The type of person suited to this work

You will need to have great ingenuity in order to find solutions to problems, or design new equipment to aid agricultural and horticultural processes.

Alongside this, you will need excellent communication skills in order to understand the needs of your clients and translate them into designs and instructions for your team.

Good ICT skills, problem-solving abilities and a flexible approach to work are also essential in order to cope with the various demands that differing projects will make of you.

Working conditions

You will usually work a normal working week, although occasional overtime may be necessary to complete projects to deadline.

Although you will be office-based for the majority of the time, there will be some onsite and field work so that you can assess projects and carry out tests on equipment.

Because of the onsite work, you may find that you have to work outdoors in unpredictable weather in conditions that are cold, wet and muddy.

You will also need to wear relevant safety equipment whilst onsite.

Future prospects

There are opportunities for land-based engineers to work all over the world, undertaking a variety of projects from food production in the UK to creating effective water supplies in areas of the developing world.

You could work in a large multinational organisation, or a smaller company. Larger firms offer greater scope for career progression, and you could soon be managing your own projects and moving up the career ladder. Smaller firms offer less opportunity for progression, so you might have to move to another company in order to develop in your field.

Advantages/disadvantages

You will be working towards developing and preserving the landscape and rural life for future generations.

Qualifications and courses

ENTRY LEVEL 5

This career is open to all graduates with a degree in engineering. Subjects such as agricultural engineering, environmental engineering, ergonomics or mechanical engineering may improve your chances. HNDs in similar subjects are also considered for entry level positions, and employers may be willing to support further study to take you to degree level. You will need a minimum of 5 GCSEs (A*–C) including English, maths and science, and 2 A levels for degree entry.

Your degree or HND must be accredited by the Institution of Agricultural Engineers (IAgrE), or a similar licensed body of the Engineering Council UK (ECUK) if you would like to progress to qualifying as a chartered (CEng) or incorporated (IEng) engineer. Qualifying in either will add considerable scope to your career potential.

You could also start out as a technician by doing an apprenticeship and studying while you work. The Diploma in Environmental and Land-Based Studies may also be useful.

Each day will present new problems and challenges, so the work will always be interesting and stimulating.

You will be working with a variety of people from many professional sectors and areas of the community.

On average, you will earn less than engineers in other industries.

Money guide

Salaries for graduates typically range from £18,000 to £24,000. Once you have gained experience and qualified as a chartered or incorporated engineer, your salary could rise to between £35,000 and £55,000. Additional allowances and benefits are usually given for overseas work.

Related opportunities

- Agricultural Scientist p254
- Environmental Engineer p223
- Land Geomatic Surveyor p107
- Product Designer p185

Further information

British Agricultural and Garden Machinery Association
Middleton House, 2 Main Road, Middleton Cheney OX17 2TB
01295 713344; www.bagma.com; info@bagma.com

Engineering Council UK
246 High Holborn, London WC1V 7EX
020 3206 0500; www.engc.org.uk

City&
Guilds

www.cityandguilds.com/myperfectjob

Engineering, Manufacturing and Production

CRCI: GB

LOCKSMITH

What the work involves

- You will sell, install and fix the locks of houses, cars and businesses for your customers.

- You will use specialist machinery to cut replacement keys for locks.

- Advising on, repairing and installing security and closed-circuit television systems may be part of your job.

The type of person suited to this work

If you have ever been locked out of your home or a car you will know how distressing it can be. As a locksmith you will have to be calm and patient – reassuring your customers whilst providing a prompt and reliable service. Good communication skills are important in this job.

Your customers and employer will also expect you to be totally trustworthy and honest.

To do this job you will have to enjoy using your hands, different tools and equipment. You should enjoy practical tasks and be able to offer solutions to security problems. Carpentry or general engineering skills are also helpful.

Working conditions

If you work in a shop you will probably have a 40-hour Monday–Saturday week. Self-employment is possible.

If you, or your employer, offer a 24 hour call-out service, you could be working at all times of day or night. Where you work will depend on your customers and could include working outdoors in all weathers.

You may work mainly from a van that holds your tools, and do lots of driving.

Future prospects

Employers include independent small locksmiths, larger national companies offering a 24-hour call-out emergency service, specialist security companies, DIY hardware stores and shoe repairers which offer a key-cutting service.

Progression for locksmiths is mainly achieved by becoming self-employed and building up a profitable business. It is also possible to progress into more specialist areas of work such as safe engineering.

Advantages/disadvantages

This can be a varied job. You will never know what your next job will be, or where you will have to go.

Meeting the public can be interesting and knowing you've helped people can be rewarding.

Working all hours of the day and night can be difficult and call-outs to replace locks after burglaries can be distressing.

Qualifications and courses

ENTRY LEVEL 2

There are no formal educational requirements, but most applicants will be required to hold GCSEs/S grades (A*–C/1–3) in English, mathematics and preferably a practical subject like craft or technology.

Some locksmiths take on trainees – contact local locksmiths to see if they require new staff.

The Master Locksmiths Association (MLA) offers a General Locksmithing course at their training centres.

To apply you will have to be a member of the British Locksmithing Institute (BLI). Individuals can apply for student membership of the BLI without any prior experience, and then study for 1 year to be become an Advanced Student.

The British Locksmiths & Keycutters Association also runs a range of courses and membership grades.

NVQs at Levels 2 and 3 are available in Providing Security or Emergency and Alarm Systems. Courses on Security and Emergency Alarm Systems are also provided by City & Guilds and BTEC.

Money guide

As a trainee you can expect to earn around £12,000–£14,000 per year. With experience this can increase to £25,000. Many locksmiths choose to become self-employed. Earnings will then depend on individual charges and company success. Earnings will be affected by regional differences; more can be expected in the larger cities as 24-hour call-outs will be more common.

Related opportunities

- Carpenter/Joiner p81
- Glazier p101

Further information

Master Locksmiths Association
5D Great Central Way, Woodford Halse, Daventry NN11 3PZ
01327 262255; www.locksmiths.co.uk

British Locksmiths and Key Cutters Association
3 Murrow Lane, Parson Drove, Wisbech PE13 4JH
0845 644 5397; www.blka.co.uk

Skills for Security, Security House
Barbourne Road, Worcester WR1 1RS
0845 075 0111; www.skillsforsecurity.org.uk

City & Guilds

www.cityandguilds.com/myperfectjob

MACHINIST

What the work involves

- Engineering machinists make engineered parts from various materials, such as metals or heavy and lightweight plastics.

- You could be making parts for a variety of products, from domestic appliances and machines to wind turbines and aeroplane engines.

- You will be using a range of machinery, including grinding and cutting machines, drills and presses. Increasingly, computer numerically controlled (CNC) machinery is being used which combines some of the manufacturing processes.

- You will need to interpret complicated engineering drawings in order to assess which materials, tools and machines to use to produce each part.

The type of person suited to this work

You will need to have good eyesight, excellent co-ordination and sound practical ability in order to operate machinery safely and accurately.

Good mathematical skills and the ability to read complicated engineering drawings and interpret them into a 3D part are essential.

You should have good communication skills as you will mainly be working in a team environment.

A good level of physical fitness is also beneficial as the job involves lifting heavy materials and standing or bending over machinery for the majority of the day.

Working conditions

Working hours are usually around 38 per week, Monday to Friday, although you will usually start early in the morning and finish early in the afternoon.

Some larger companies operate 24 hour production, and in this case you would be required to work shifts which could include evenings and weekends. Conditions in factories and workshops are usually fairly pleasant, although can be noisy at times.

Because you are operating machinery you will also need to wear appropriate safety equipment at all times.

Future prospects

There are jobs available for machinists all over the country, although the majority are found in larger cities and within general mechanical engineering companies.

With experience, you could be promoted to become team leader or supervisor, and if you gain further qualifications you could go on to specialise in areas such as design.

As there is currently a shortage of machinists in the engineering sector, job prospects are good.

Qualifications and courses

Entry into this career is usually between the ages of 16–18 via an Advanced Apprenticeship in Engineering. Most employers require candidates for apprenticeships to have at least 4 GCSEs/S grades (A*–C/1–3) including English, maths, a science subject, and either technology/engineering or a related subject.

As an apprentice, you will undertake several months of learning skills and studying away from the workplace in order to build up your skill level. You will then spend 2–3 years working for a company whilst also attending college and studying towards an NVQ Level 3 or higher in Engineering Production.

Entry for older candidates is possible, although they must be able to demonstrate some relevant experience and skills. Some employers will also be willing to support you in working towards gaining an NVQ Level 3 qualification.

Advantages/disadvantages

Jobs are available throughout the UK and there is little travelling involved, so you will rarely be absent from home for any period of time.

It is a physically demanding job, with large amounts of time spent standing or bending over machinery and lifting heavy materials and equipment.

You may have to work unsociable hours due to early starts or unpredictable shift patterns.

Money guide

The starting salary for an apprentice machinist will be between £6,000 and £8,000. Once you have qualified, your salary should rise to around £16,000–£18,000. With several years' experience, and as you move into a more senior position within a company, your salary could increase to £25,000+.

Related opportunities

- Civil/Construction Engineer/Civil Engineering Technician p85
- Motor Vehicle Technician p235
- Sheet Metal Worker p245
- Toolmaker p249

Further information

SEMTA
14 Upton Road, Watford WD18 0JT
01923 238441; www.semta.org.uk

www.cityandguilds.com/myperfectjob

Engineering, Manufacturing and Production

CRCI: GF

MANUFACTURING/PRODUCTION ENGINEER

What the work involves

- Manufacturing engineers design, implement and maintain manufacturing processes.

- You will be consulting with other professionals, such as design engineers, in order to produce high quality products efficiently and with minimum cost.

- You could work in a variety of industries, including food and drink, fashion, and pharmaceuticals.

- You could work across a project from design and research to after-sales care, and as such you will be using a variety of manufacturing equipment and computer systems on a daily basis.

The type of person suited to this work

You should be able to work as part of a team with a variety of people, as you will be liaising with other professionals on a daily basis to discuss product ideas and manufacturing solutions.

You should be good at analysing and solving problems in order to understand and stay ahead of potential manufacturing issues. The ability to prioritise your workload is also beneficial.

Strong numerical skills are essential.

Working conditions

You will usually work 37 hours per week, but this often includes evening and weekend work. Extra or unsociable hours can be expected when a new production process is being tested, or if the company you are working for operates a shift system.

You will divide your time between office-based work, meetings and time spent on the shop floor/in the factory. When on the shop floor, you might have to wear relevant safety equipment or protective clothing.

Future prospects

You could work in a variety of manufacturing sectors, building diverse experience that will help you move across industries and sectors within manufacturing, taking up managerial or marketing roles.

Alternatively, you could specialise in a certain area (such as pharmaceuticals or clothing) and move into production management or consultancy, drawing upon your unique knowledge and experience to motivate and advise others.

There are also numerous short-term contracts available for manufacturing engineers, which would allow you to become self-employed.

Advantages/disadvantages

Manufacturing engineers enjoy one of the most creative roles in the engineering sector, with great input into product design and final function.

If you work in a large company, there may well be opportunities to travel in the course of your employment.

Qualifications and courses

The most common entry route is with a relevant degree in an engineering subject. For degree entry, you will need 3 A levels/Highers (including maths and physics) and 5 GCSEs/S grades (A*–C/1–3). You can also enter this career via an Apprenticeship, full details are below.

HNDs in similar subjects are also considered by employers, but you will have to start in a lower position and undertake further study towards degree level qualifications whilst working.

You could start as an apprentice and train to be a technician. To apply you will need at least 3 GCSEs (A*–C), including English, maths and science. GCSEs in engineering or design and technology may also be useful. The Diploma in Manufacturing and Product Design could also be helpful.

Scholarships and sponsorships may be available for entrants wishing to pursue a degree. You can find out more information from the Institution of Mechanical Engineering.

You may work evenings and weekends on a regular basis, although absence from home overnight is rare.

Money guide

The average graduate starting salaries on completion of initial training range from £20,000 to £24,000. With 5–10 years' experience, you could earn up to £37,000. Senior manufacturing engineers can expect to earn £45,000+.

Related opportunities

- Chemical Engineer p219
- Electrical Engineer p221
- Mechanical Engineer p234
- Textile Operative p248

Further information

Institution of Mechanical Engineers
1 Birdcage Walk, London SW1H 9JJ
020 7222 7899; www.imeche.org.uk

SEMTA
14 Upton Road, Watford WD18 0JT
01923 238 441; www.semta.org.uk

The Institution of Engineering and Technology
Michael Faraday House, Stevenage SG1 2AY
01438 313 311; www.theiet.org; postmaster@theiet.org

www.cityandguilds.com/myperfectjob

MARINE CRAFTSPERSON

What the work involves

- A marine craftsperson takes part in the building and repair of many different kinds of ships and boats.

- Repairers and shipbuilders work with big vessels such as ferries, dredgers, tugs, submarines, tankers and warships.

- Boat builders work with smaller boats, like wooden dinghies, sailing boats, narrow boats and powerboats.

- Both crafts require you to work from a design to create the ship or boat. This has usually been created on a computer, and you work at marking and cutting out shapes, welding, and cutting and bending steel and other materials.

The type of person suited to this work

You should be a good team worker, and a good communicator.

A practical, logical and problem-solving mindset is essential, as you'll not only be required to interpret drawings and plans but will also need to solve problems on the job quickly and intelligently.

You should also be good with numbers, and have good eyesight and good physical fitness.

Working conditions

Marine craftspeople tend to work a normal 37 hour week, but overtime is usually available. Some urgent repair jobs may take place overnight and during weekends, but this is relatively rare.

Working conditions

Working at heights is normal, and you will probably spend the majority of your time indoors.

Future prospects

As you gain experience, it may be possible to progress to a position such as supervisor or inspector. You could also work towards becoming workshop manager.

Another option is to use your experience to become self-employed in areas such as boat building and repair.

Some people choose to gain further qualifications and become a marine engineering technician.

Advantages/disadvantages

If you have an interest in practical work and building things, and in ships and maritime matters, then this job can be really enjoyable. It can be really satisfying to create something you're passionate about.

The grubby working conditions might not sit well with everybody, so if you want to work in a clean and tidy environment your skills may be better suited elsewhere.

Qualifications and courses

ENTRY LEVEL 2

Many employers ask for GCSEs (A*–G) in English, Maths and a science or related subject. Sometimes employers will ask for further qualifications, or even set an aptitude test. The Diploma in Engineering would provide you with all the training required.

Many enter this profession by doing an apprenticeship in the ship-building industry.

You can take an engineering-related vocational course at college, such as an NVQ or BTEC, which will enable you to apply for an Advanced Apprenticeship.

You can undertake a mixture of on-the-job and classroom-based training, which most employers will be willing to fund. Training usually starts with health and safety regulations and an induction course, followed by basic skills including selecting materials, interpreting drawings, how to use relevant tools and developing skills.

Possible boat-building qualifications you can take include NVQs in Boat Production and Support Services, Boat Building and Maintenance, and a City and Guilds Certificate in Boat Building, Maintenance and Support.

You could also take a specialist degree in Leisure Boat Design and Construction.

Money guide

As an apprentice at the age of 18, you'll probably earn about £8,000 a year. Once you're qualified, the average salary is about £20,000 a year. Experienced marine craftspeople who have worked their way up may earn about £30,000 a year.

Related opportunities

- Civil/Construction Engineer/Civil Engineering Technician p85
- Marine Engineer p232
- Merchant Navy Engineering Officer p613

Further information

British Marine Federation
Marine House, Thorpe Lea Road, Egham TW20 8BF
01784 473377; www.britishmarine.co.uk

The Institute of Marine Engineering, Science and Technology
80 Coleman Street, London EC2R 5BJ
020 7382 2600; www.imarest.org

SEMTA
14 Upton Road, Watford W18 0JT
0800 282 167; www.semta.org.uk

www.cityandguilds.com/myperfectjob

MARINE ENGINEER

What the work involves

- Marine engineers design, construct and maintain ships' seafaring equipment, as well as developing and preserving offshore systems.

- You could work in a shipbuilding company, on board ships and submarines, in marine surveying, in an oil company, or in the leisure industry.

- You will work across a range of engineering disciplines, including electrical, construction and mechanical.

- You will work closely with naval officers, architects, other professionals and team members.

The type of person suited to this work

You will need excellent communication skills, both verbal and written, in order to manage and lead your team as well as liaise with other professionals and clients.

Excellent maths and ICT skills are essential, as is an ability to solve problems under pressure. Prioritising your workload through careful planning and project management is also very important.

You should be good at working within a team, especially as you might have to live and work with colleagues in confined areas when undertaking projects on boats or submarines.

Working conditions

You could work anywhere from an office to a boatyard, or even on a submarine, and many jobs involve a combination of office-based and onsite work.

If you are working on projects on a ship or offshore installations, living accommodation can be tight and you will probably need to spend time away from home.

The job involves climbing and lifting equipment so you will need to be physically fit.

Future prospects

Prospects are good for marine engineers. You could work for a variety of companies, from small shipping businesses, to leisure cruise liners, through to joining the Royal Navy.

When you have gained skills and experience, you could go on to specialise in project management or marine research, or even work as a consultant.

There are plenty of opportunities to work abroad.

Advantages/disadvantages

There are a huge variety of employment options available to you, from conservation projects to defence systems.

You will work in numerous diverse areas, and with many different people, so the work will always be interesting and fresh.

You may be working in cramped, uncomfortable conditions for long periods of time. This includes living and working with colleagues 24 hours a day on certain projects.

Qualifications and courses

Entry to this career is with a relevant degree in marine engineering, marine technology, offshore engineering or naval engineering. Entry to a degree course usually requires at least 5 GCSEs/S grades (A*–C/1–3) and 3 A levels/4 H grades, including maths and a science subject.

You can also enter the industry with an HND in a relevant subject such as general or marine engineering, or marine technology. Entry requirements for an HND course are usually 1 A level or a BTEC National Certificate in a relevant subject.

You could undertake an Apprenticeship as a marine engineering technician and work towards becoming a marine engineer, undertaking additional training and qualifications on the job.

The Merchant Navy Training Board offers a number of training and sponsorship schemes for entrants at GCSE, A level, undergraduate or graduate stages of their education. Graduate applicants must have degrees in a scientific subject.

The Royal Navy accepts applications for engineering officers from candidates in their final year of university.

Money guide

As a graduate marine engineer, you could expect to earn around £23,000. With a few years' experience, this can rise to £36,000. Experienced and highly skilled marine engineers can expect to earn £50,000+. Some companies also offer excellent benefit packages and bonus schemes in addition to a basic salary.

Related opportunities

- Electrical Engineer p221
- Environmental Engineer p223
- Marine Craftsperson p231
- Mechanical Engineer p234

Further information

Institute of Marine Engineering Science & Technology
80 Coleman Street, London EC2R 5BJ
020 7382 2600; www.imarest.org

Merchant Navy Training Board
Carthusian Court, 12 Carthusian Street, London EC1M 6EZ
www.mntb.org.uk; enquiry@mntb.org.uk

Engineering Council UK
246 High Holborn, London WC1V 7EX
020 3206 0500; www.engc.org.uk

www.cityandguilds.com/myperfectjob

MEAT PROCESS WORKER

Engineering, Manufacturing and Production

CRCI: NC

What the work involves

- Meat process workers do everything from herding animals, to slaughtering, to cutting up carcasses, to packaging and grading meat and ensuring it is free from contamination and ready to sell to the public. You could specialise in either of the following roles:

Abattoir operative

- You will slaughter animals for food.
- After the animals have been humanely killed, you will separate the edible meat from the waste.

Meat manufacturing operative

- You will manufacture meat products.
- You may also weigh, wrap and label the meat.

The type of person suited to this work

This can be distressing and smelly work, so you should be prepared to cope with blood and mess.

As you will have to do lots of lifting and operating machinery, you will need to be physically fit and able to be on your feet for long periods at a time.

You should have a responsible attitude as you may use dangerous knives and machinery. You also need to be aware of your personal cleanliness as you are part of a food production process.

Working conditions

Refrigerated areas are cold and all areas need frequent cleaning and so may be wet. You will be expected to wear protective clothing, including footwear and hairnets.

You will normally do a 40-hour week, although shift and part-time work are possible.

Future prospects

Abattoir operative

With experience you could apply for senior positions or look to move to related areas such as butchery, retail, or food marketing. Other options are jobs in quality control, health and safety consultancy or self-employment.

Meat manufacturing operative

With experience you could apply for supervisory, quality control and management jobs or move into related areas of work such as retail butchery.

With the right experience, qualifications and training you may be able to progress into work on the meat inspection teams employed by the Meat Hygiene Service (MHS) – part of the Food Standards Agency.

Qualifications and courses

ENTRY LEVEL 1

There are no formal entry qualifications for these jobs. However, GCSEs/S grades in English and maths are useful, particularly if you want to move up to supervisory, inspection or technical level. You could work towards NVQs/SVQs at Levels 1–3 in Meat and Poultry Processing or Meat and Poultry Plant Operations and then onto an NVQ/SVQ at Level 4 in Meat Processing Management. The Meat Training Council offers other courses.

If you would like to work as a meat manufacturing operative the new Diploma in Manufacturing and Product Design will be helpful.

To work at an abattoir you must be aged 18 or over, and be licensed by the Meat Hygiene Service (MHS), a division of the Food Standards Agency.

Advantages/disadvantages

This can be cold, smelly and dirty work. The job can be repetitive and monotonous.

You will be part of a team and often there is a good working atmosphere.

Money guide

Abattoir operative

The minimum salary for trained adults is around £12,000 per year, rising to £15,000 with experience. Experienced abattoir workers with supervisory duties may earn up to £22,000.

Meat manufacturing operative

The starting salary is usually about £11,000 per year. Experienced meat manufacturing operatives earn up to £18,000 per year.

Related opportunities

- Butcher p481
- Kitchen Assistant/Supervisor p145
- Meat Hygiene Inspector p489

Further information

Meat Training Council
PO Box 141, Winterhill House, Snowdon Drive, Milton Keynes MK6 1YY
01908 231062; www.meattraining.org.uk

City& Guilds

www.cityandguilds.com/myperfectjob

MECHANICAL ENGINEER

What the work involves

- Mechanical engineers design, develop and maintain the moveable parts of all equipment, ranging from those in small household appliances up to large machinery or vehicles.

- You will probably work on a project from conception to completion, so will be involved with all aspects from design and development through to final manufacture.

- You could work in a number of industries, including manufacturing, sport, medicine or transport.

- You will also have to manage budgets, resources and people on each project.

The type of person suited to this work

You will need an exceptionally high level of scientific knowledge and technical ability in order to design mechanisms and solve practical problems as they occur in the development process.

Good communication skills, both verbal and written, are essential for dealing with colleagues, other professionals and clients on a daily basis. You will also be required to produce detailed reports and occasional presentations.

Excellent organisational skills and the ability to work under pressure are a must, as are good ICT skills including knowledge of computer-aided design (CAD).

Working conditions

You will usually be required to work longer hours than those of the average working week, but evening or weekend work is rare.

You will be based mainly in an office although you will also spend a good amount of time on site, whether in a factory, workshop, hospital or other building. Despite this travel, overnight absence from home is uncommon.

You will need to wear a smart suit or similar whilst in the office, but appropriate safety equipment when on site.

Future prospects

Job opportunities for mechanical engineers are found throughout the UK, particularly in larger towns and cities. With experience, you could become self-employed and undertake freelance work which will give you greater flexibility over your work/life balance.

Alternatively, you could go on to increasingly senior engineering posts, or even set up your own consultancy.

Some engineers choose to move into a more business-orientated role within their company such as sales or HR.

There are also excellent opportunities for working abroad.

Advantages/disadvantages

It is exciting to be at the forefront of creating new products and finding solutions to mechanical problems across numerous industries.

Qualifications and courses

Most employers require a first degree in a relevant subject such as mechanical, nuclear, aeronautical, civil or computer-aided engineering. However, it is also possible to start as a technician for which you can enter via an Apprenticeship (see below). For entry at engineer level you will need 2 A levels and 5 GCSEs (A*–C), including maths and physics for entry.

You could start out as a technician with GCSEs (A*–C) in English, maths and science by training as an apprentice or by taking a college course. You will work towards an NVQ Levels 1–3 in Performing Engineering Operations, Mechanical Manufacturing Engineering or Technical Services.

You will be working on a variety of projects and meeting a range of people, so the work is rarely boring.

There are excellent opportunities for career development, including the option of working overseas.

You may have to work long hours to meet project deadlines.

Money guide

Starting salaries for mechanical engineers can range from £19,000 to £28,000, although the average is around £22,000.

With 10 years' experience, your salary could increase to £40,000–£55,000+.

Within engineering, salaries vary greatly according to location (London usually yields the highest wages) and the size of the company that you work for. Some companies also offer excellent benefit packages and bonus schemes in addition to a basic salary.

Related opportunities

- Clinical/Biomedical Engineer p296
- Electrical Engineer p221
- Marine Engineer p232

Further information

Engineering Council UK
246 High Holborn, London WC1V 7EX
020 3206 0500; www.engc.org.uk

Institution of Mechanical Engineers
1 Birdcage Walk, London SW1H 9JJ
020 7222 7899; www.imeche.org; enquiries@imeche.org

www.cityandguilds.com/myperfectjob

MOTOR VEHICLE TECHNICIAN

What the work involves

- Motor vehicle technicians are responsible for the maintenance and repair of all vehicles, including cars, motorbikes, lorries and coaches.

- You will need to carry out routine jobs such as servicing, as well as identifying technical problems, and advising customers as to which repairs are necessary and the costs involved.

- You will work on a variety of different mechanical and electrical systems and use a range of tools and equipment.

The type of person suited to this work

You will need an excellent technical and mechanical knowledge of most motor vehicles, on which you can build when in employment.

You will be working in a team and with the general public, so will need excellent communication skills in order to get along with colleagues and advise customers.

Full colour vision, a good level of fitness, and the ability to think quickly and work methodically are all essential.

You will also need good ICT skills in order to understand and fix the computerised equipment in vehicles.

Working conditions

You will usually work 40 hours per week, just above the national average. Regular working hours are usual, but shift work, weekend work and overtime are not uncommon.

If you specialise in repairing broken down vehicles, you might have to travel to their location at any time of day or night.

You will usually work in a garage, which can be noisy at times and very cold in winter.

You will need to wear overalls and other safety equipment to protect you and your clothes whilst you work.

Future prospects

Being a motor vehicle technician provides good career opportunities as demand is relatively high all over the UK. This means you could work in a large city or a small village, for a large company or a tiny independent garage.

Within a larger organisation, you could progress to a senior or supervisory level as a technician, or alternatively move into a management or training role.

There is also the option of setting up your own repair business, although the initial costs of hiring and equipping premises can be expensive.

Advantages/disadvantages

There is demand for technicians throughout the UK, so you should be able to find a job in the location of your choice.

Qualifications and courses

ENTRY LEVEL **2**

Although you do not need any formal qualifications to begin training as a motor vehicle technician, most employers (especially the larger companies) prefer you to have at least 4 GCSEs/S grades (A*–C/1–3) including English, maths and a science.

There are several ways to enter the industry at a trainee level. You could undertake an Apprenticeship and learn on-the-job whilst gaining qualifications at college. Alternatively, some larger employers have dedicated training facilities for their employees at which you can learn the skills you need.

You could also undertake a course at college. Many colleges will also have links to local employers which could be a route into work experience or employment. Relevant courses include NVQ Levels 2 and 3 in Vehicle Maintenance and Repair, Motorcycle Maintenance and Repair, Vehicle Fitting and Auto Electrical. City & Guilds also offer useful courses in vehicle maintenance and automotive vehicle servicing and repair. BTEC National Certificates and Diplomas are also available in Vehicle Technology.

Hours are generally fairly regular, and you won't need to be away from home overnight.

You may have to work in cold, damp or cramped conditions which can be unpleasant.

Money guide

As a trainee motor vehicle technician, you could expect to start on around £11,000. As you gain experience and qualifications, this will rise to £16,000–£18,000. With 5–10 years' experience and even some specialised skills, you could earn £23,000+. Garage owners and self-employed technicians can earn considerably more.

Related opportunities

- Electrician p94
- Highways Maintenance/Road Worker p104
- Sheet Metal Worker p245
- Welder p251

Further information

GoSkills
Concorde House, Trinity Park, Solihull B37 7UQ
0121 635 5520; www.goskills.org; info@goskills.org

The Institute of the Motor Industry
Fanshaws, Brickendon, Hertford, SG13 8PQ
01992 511 521; www.motor.org.uk; imi@motor.org.uk

City& Guilds

www.cityandguilds.com/myperfectjob

Engineering, Manufacturing and Production

CRCI: GJ

NUCLEAR ENGINEER

Engineering, Manufacturing and Production

CRCI: GE

What the work involves

- Nuclear engineers work mainly in the large-scale production of nuclear energy, although they can be involved in smaller industrial or medicinal projects.

- You could alternatively work in developing effective nuclear waste management systems.

- You could also lecture and train other people on the subject of nuclear power.

The type of person suited to this work

You will need excellent communication skills, both verbal and written, in order to manage and lead your team as well as liaising with other professionals and clients. You should also enjoy working as part of a team.

You should possess an analytical mind and a logical approach to problem solving. Excellent maths and ICT skills are also essential.

Because you will be working with nuclear hazards, you must be able to take responsibility for your own safety and that of your colleagues.

Working conditions

You will usually work a normal 37 hour week, although you may be required to put in additional hours as project deadlines approach. If you work in a nuclear power station, your hours will usually adhere to a 7-day shift system.

The majority of the work will be indoors, either in a power plant, laboratory, office or factory.

You may have to work in hot, cramped conditions and will have to wear protective clothing in certain situations. As you will be working with radioactive substances, you will also need regular medical check-ups.

Future prospects

Prospects are good for nuclear engineers, especially given the government's new drive to increase nuclear power production in the forthcoming years.

The majority of nuclear engineers work in large power plants and companies, although you could work in medical research or in the field of nuclear waste disposal. With continued study and increasing experience, you can move into more senior positions within any company and discipline.

Advantages/disadvantages

Nuclear power is a growing industry, so employment opportunities will increase accordingly.

You have the opportunity to work freelance after building significant experience, so you can achieve a suitable work/life balance for yourself.

You will be working in an environmentally controversial industry, which has the potential to upset friends and family.

Qualifications and courses

ENTRY LEVEL 5

The most common entry qualifications are BEng and MEng degrees in mechanical, electrical or control system engineering. You could enter with a related degree such as maths, physics or science. You will need at least 5 GCSEs (A*–C/1–3) and 3 A levels, including maths and a science.

You can also enter the industry with an HND in a relevant subject such as general engineering, civil engineering, maths or physics. Entry requirements are usually 1 A level or a BTEC National Certificate in a relevant subject.

Graduate apprenticeships may also be available, which bring together study at a degree or postgraduate level with work-based learning.

Most nuclear engineers will work towards chartered status. You will need a MEng degree and must be registered with the Engineering Council.

If you are over 35 and do not have relevant qualifications you can do a course through the Nuclear Institute (NI) or the Institution of Engineering and Technology (IET).

Money guide

As a newly qualified graduate nuclear engineer, you could expect to earn around £24,000.

With 5–10 years' experience, coupled with professional association membership, you should earn between £35,000 and £45,000. As a senior chartered engineer, you could earn £55,000+.

Some companies also offer excellent benefit packages and bonus schemes.

Related opportunities

- Aerospace Engineer p212
- Chemical Engineer p219
- Electrical Engineer p221
- Mechanical Engineer p234

Further information

The Nuclear Industry Association
Carlton House, 22a St James's Square, London SW1Y 4JH
020 7766 6640; www.niauk.org; info@niauk.org

SEMTA
14 Upton Road, Watford WD18 0JT
0845 643 9001; www.semta.org.uk

City& Guilds

www.cityandguilds.com/myperfectjob

OFFSHORE DIVER

What the work involves

- Offshore divers work in deep water on structures for the oil and gas industry.

- You will be responsible for creating, inspecting and carrying out repairs on constructions such as offshore platforms and pipelines.

- Divers often have knowledge of specialist engineering or scientific methods such as welding.

- You might have to help with the construction of offshore wind farms.

The type of person suited to this work

You must be fit, active and a very strong swimmer as diving is very physically demanding. You must be able to follow health and safety regulations. You will need to be able to work well in a team and on your own.

You need to be able to concentrate and cope with diving conditions which can be dangerous and exhausting. You must have quick reactions in order to cope with any potential emergencies or dangers.

Working conditions

Working conditions are cold, dark and may be cramped. It is necessary to wear protective clothing and breathing apparatus. Jobs may be located abroad.

Offshore divers will be based on ships or rigs, where you may stay overnight. Offshore divers who undertake saturation diving could live in diving bells for up to 28 days.

Diving is a dangerous job due to the potential hazards of decompression and accidents when underwater.

Working hours for divers are irregular and depend on the job. A lot of divers work just 120–180 days per year.

Future prospects

Opportunities are available with construction or civil engineering companies.

The growth of offshore wind farms and the oil and gas sector has led to a huge rise in the demand for experienced offshore divers around the world. However, finding work as an offshore diver may be hard at first as employers favour divers with experience.

You could progress to a supervisor or a shore-based operations manager. Another possibility is to set up your own diving school or shop.

Advantages/disadvantages

There is a strong demand for experienced, offshore divers.

Salaries can be high for experienced, saturation divers.

Qualifications and courses

There are no set requirements to start diver training, although you must pass a medical test. A qualification in recreational diving and GCSEs/S grades in English and maths would be useful. You must have a qualification certified by the Health and Safety Executive in offshore diving or offshore bell/saturation diving.

To become an offshore diver you must have a science or engineering degree and undergo offshore safety training. NVQs in welding or non-destructive testing would be helpful.

You will also need to pass a basic offshore safety induction and emergency training (BOSIET) course. It is essential that you also have a first aid certificate.

If you study a degree in offshore or coastal engineering or marine science, then you will also be taught how to dive.

The high levels of fitness and health needed for diving can make this a short career.

There is a risk of accidents when underwater.

Money guide

The majority of divers are paid daily or by the job. Divers who work in civil engineering can earn £70–£175 per day. After gaining experience, divers working for the oil industry can earn £300 a day, while deep-sea divers can earn £1,000 a day.

Offshore divers earn about £30,000 a year. With a lot of experience this can rise to £46,000+.

£150,000 a year is possible for senior saturation divers who work the North Sea.

Related opportunities

- Civil/Construction Engineer p85
- Marine Engineer p232
- Police Officer p552
- Royal Navy Officer p561

Further information

Health and Safety Executive – Diving Operations
Caerphilly Business Park, Caerphilly CF83 3GG
0845 345 0055; www.hse.gov.uk

Underwater Centre
An Aird, Fort William PH33 6AN
01397 703786; www.theunderwatercentre.co.uk

International Marine Contractors Association
52 Grosvenor Gardens, London SW1W 0AU
020 7824 5520; www.imca-int.com/careers

ENTRY LEVEL 5

Engineering, Manufacturing and Production

CRCI: U

Engineering, Manufacturing and Production

CRCI: GI

OIL/GAS DRILLING ENGINEER

What the work involves

- Drilling engineers plan, schedule and supervise the drilling process behind creating oil and gas wells.

- You will be involved in the drilling project from the initial planning and design of the well, through to its completion and eventual closure.

- You could be working on land, or on sites out at sea, depending on where the reserves are situated.

- You could also have to undertake certain administrative tasks, such as drawing up contracts and planning and managing the budget of each project.

The type of person suited to this work

Excellent communication and interpersonal skills are needed for teamwork and to build strong relationships with other professionals and clients.

You should have a high level of numeracy and good IT skills, as well as scientific understanding of related fields such as geology and chemistry.

You will need to have excellent planning, organisational and problem solving skills to successfully run a project.

Working conditions

The work is both mentally and physically demanding, especially in the early years when you could be working 12 hour shifts on off-shore oil rigs. Conditions are noisy, wet, cold and inhospitable at times.

Living standards on the rigs are good, with excellent sports and social facilities.

Opportunities for office-based work increase once you have gained a few years' experience in the field.

Future prospects

Careers can move quickly over a short period of time, and within a few years you could find yourself in control of projects worth up to £10 million.

Typically, after 2–4 years working on projects all over the world you can settle into an office-based design role.

You could progress to a management position within an oil company, or undertake independent consultancy work.

Advantages/disadvantages

Travelling around the world and working closely with colleagues on the rigs can prove to be exciting, rewarding and challenging.

The harder you work the faster your career will progress and the better your opportunities will become.

Oil drilling in particular operates in some of the most dangerous and hostile areas of the world, so your safety could be threatened on a daily basis.

Qualifications and courses

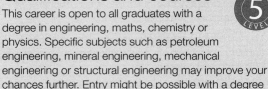

This career is open to all graduates with a degree in engineering, maths, chemistry or physics. Specific subjects such as petroleum engineering, mineral engineering, mechanical engineering or structural engineering may improve your chances further. Entry might be possible with a degree in geology or natural science.

Most entrants to graduate training programmes for the larger oil companies will have gained a high 2.1 in their subject, and MEng degrees are preferred. A postgraduate MSc in Offshore or Petroleum Engineering may increase your chances of employment.

Entry requirements for engineering or related degrees are a minimum of 5 GCSEs/Highers (A*–C/1–3) including English, maths and science, and 3 A levels/Highers. Alternative entry qualifications may include relevant BTEC National Diplomas, Access courses and the Diploma in Engineering.

As much of the work takes place overseas, a basic knowledge of another language is desirable.

Money guide

Salaries for graduates typically range from £25,000 to £35,000, with the larger salaries coming from the big oil companies. After 5 years, you could be earning £45,000–£55,000+. Engineers in managerial roles could earn up to £70,000.

Salaries are performance based, and the location of your projects will influence the amount you are paid. Most companies give additional benefits or allowances for overseas work.

Related opportunities

- Civil/Construction Engineer/Civil Engineering Technician p85
- Environmental Engineer p223
- Mechanical Engineer p234

Further information

Oil Careers
Westhill Business Centre, Arnhall Business Park, Westhill AB32 6UF
01224 330500; www.oilcareers.com; uk@oilcareers.com

www.cityandguilds.com/myperfectjob

PAPER MANUFACTURER/ TECHNOLOGIST

What the work involves

- Paper manufacturers work with the equipment and systems that turn wood pulp and other materials into many different kinds of paper.

- Your role can vary greatly depending on which sector you decide to work for within the paper mill.

- You might be operating the machine that breaks down the raw materials, managing what's going on inside, adding chemicals, checking consistency, or adjusting the controls.

- You could also be managing the steam system that dries the paper, controlling it in reels, or overseeing the packaging process.

The type of person suited to this work

If you'd like to be a paper manufacturer or technologist, you need to be good with your hands, and good at team working and communication with others.

Being able to act on your own initiative is important, and you should have an accurate and methodical mindset.

Following plans and diagrams is a big part of the job, so you should be confident in this, and the ability to work with chemicals is also important.

Working conditions

This kind of work usually takes place in shifts. You could be working daytimes, evenings, nights or weekends depending on your company, and it may well be a combination of them all.

It's normal for your working hours to add up to 38–40 per week, and overtime is usually available and often encouraged.

You'll be working on the factory floor most of the time, in the control room. This is so that you can monitor the processes being carried out by the machines you're looking after.

Future prospects

There are opportunities for progression within the industry. With experience you can apply for positions at technician and supervisor level, which can turn into engineering roles.

If you choose to you can also move around in the industry, changing to a career in management or sales, for example.

Roles and jobs such as these might require additional qualifications which you may be able to pursue.

Qualifications and courses

ENTRY LEVEL 2

There are no formal entry qualifications, but having GCSEs (A*–E) in English, maths and science will help. You can start straight from school, working your way up and training on the job as an apprentice. You could enter at a higher level, if you hold a HNC or HND in a subject such as engineering. You will need 1 A level in science or maths or a BTEC National Certificate/Diploma to start. The Diploma in Manufacturing and Product Design may also be useful.

You could study towards an NVQ in a subject such as Engineering or Combined Working Practices. There are also courses in paper technology.

Advantages/disadvantages

Opportunities to progress are good in this job, and even if you come straight from school and work on the factory floor, you could move up to sales or management relatively quickly: keep this in mind.

The work may be a little mundane to start with.

Money guide

Trainees earn around £12,000 a year, but this can be boosted with overtime.

This can increase to £22,000.

Related opportunities

- Chemical Engineer p219
- Manufacturing/Production Engineer p230
- Textile Operative p248

Further information

Confederation of Paper Industries
1 Rivenhall Road, Swindon SN5 7BD
01793 889600; www.paper.org.uk

The Paper Industry Technical Association (PITA)
5 Frecheville Court, Bury, Lancashire BL9 0UF
0161 764 5858; www.pita.co.uk

Proskills UK
Centurion Court, 85b Milton Park, Abingdon OX14 4RY
01235 432032; www.proskills.co.uk

City& Guilds

www.cityandguilds.com/myperfectjob

Engineering, Manufacturing and Production

CRCI: NH

POLYMER TECHNOLOGIST

What the work involves

■ Polymer technologists use polymer materials, such as plastics, rubber, adhesives, resins and fibres, to manufacture products.

■ You will use these materials to make a wide range of products, including toys, casings for mobile phones, medical devices, tyres, wetsuits and hoses.

■ You might also use composite polymer materials in place of traditional materials such as metal in e.g. the manufacture of car bodies or aircraft wings.

■ You will be responsible for developing the moulds used to form materials during manufacture. This is a job that requires specialist skills as a minor flaw could ruin an entire product.

The type of person suited to this work

You should have a strong interest in materials science, chemicals and engineering and a good understanding of manufacturing processes and construction methods.

You should also be interested in design and technology and be familiar with computer aided design.

You will need to be able to analyse projects or problems that arise and have strong numeracy skills.

As you will be part of a team, or leading a team you will need strong communication skills.

You should also be able to take initiative and find a solution when you are confronted with a problem.

Working conditions

You will work between 35 and 40 hours per week, Monday to Friday. It may be necessary for you to work overtime to meet deadlines. Overtime and weekends will increase your pay accordingly.

Your time may be divided between the office, the laboratory and the factory. This may involve travel.

You will wear protective clothing at times.

Future prospects

Polymer science is a growing industry; there are many opportunities for promotion.

You could work for a variety of companies, including manufacturers of medical equipment, toy companies, or aerospace engineering firms.

You could choose to specialise in a specific area such as vehicle manufacturing, aviation or medical equipment.

Advantages/disadvantages

You won't be stuck in an office all day, and may have the opportunity to travel locally and abroad as part of your work.

Hours can be long and unsociable at times.

Qualifications and courses

ENTRY LEVEL 5

Most entrants to this profession have a first degree in a related subject. This could be polymer science, materials engineering, or materials science. However the minimum entry is a BTEC Higher National Diploma/Certificate in polymer processing, manufacturing engineering and materials technology. For entry into a degree course you will need at least 5 GCSEs (A*–C) and 2–3 A levels including chemistry, maths or physics.

Vocational qualifications may be helpful as would the Diploma in Manufacturing and Product Design.

Postgraduate courses in materials engineering or polymer technology may be available after you have taken a first degree in engineering or science. Graduates may also apply for programmes in companies where they will be trained as a full-time employee. Work placements may also be available for those on sandwich courses.

For those without the required scientific or engineering background some universities provide one year foundation courses in preparation for degree courses.

Those with relevant experience are welcomed into the industry and part time study towards a HND is possible.

Money guide

A starting salary for a polymer technologist is around £14,000.

The average salary is between £22,000 and £26,500 but this can rise to £39,000.

Related opportunities

■ Aerospace Engineer p212
■ Chemical Engineer p219
■ Manufacturing/Production Engineer p230
■ Materials Scientist p526

Further information

British Plastics Federation
5–6 Bath Place, Rivington Street, London EC2A 3JE
020 7457 5000; www.bpf.co.uk ; reception@bpf.co.uk

The Institute of Materials, Minerals and Mining
1 Carlton House Terrace, London SW1Y 5DB
020 7451 7300; www.iom3.org

The Polymer Innovation Network
1 Carlton House Terrace, London SW1Y 5DB
020 7451 7404; www.polymerinnovate.com

QUALITY CONTROL INSPECTOR

What the work involves

- Quality control inspectors work in a variety of industries such as engineering, food, pharmaceuticals and clothing, where manufacturing procedures must be monitored to ensure that products meet specified standards.

- You will test products as they go through each stage of production by observing, measuring, and weighing samples, and comparing results against specified requirements.

- You will also work to ensure that quality and safety standards are maintained by checking and testing materials sourced from external suppliers.

- You will write reports on the testing that you carry out and help to come up with solutions to any problems or inconsistencies that arise.

The type of person suited to this work

As you will be regularly inspecting products and manufacturing processes you must be highly organised, methodical and have a keen eye for detail.

You will be responsible, thorough and be able to solve problems efficiently.

You will have an aptitude for communicating with others and for advising and compelling people to improve standards. You will have good written skills for writing up reports on testing methods and results.

You should also have an interest in the science and technology of the industry that you are monitoring.

You should have a strong interest in health and safety issues and procedures.

Working conditions

You will work 35 to 40 hours per week, this will often include shift work, weekends and nights.

You could work in a laboratory or an office. You will also frequently visit factory floors or warehouses to monitor production processes or meet with staff.

These factories may be clean and bright or noisy and dirty.

Protective clothing is required in laboratories and may be required on factory or warehouse visits.

Future prospects

When you have some experience you may progress to roles as a team leader, supervisory roles, quality management roles or move across to technical sales or production management.

Qualifications and courses

Most entrants to this profession have prior experience in a relevant industry; you might have started your career in a production role, for example.

Employers usually seek applicants with 4 GCSEs/S grades (A*–C/1–3) which should include maths, English and a science subject.

As a Quality Control Inspector you will specialise in a particular sector such as aerospace or pharmaceuticals. For this you may require A levels/H grades, a BTEC/SQA national qualification, an HNC/HND or a degree in science or technology.

Apprenticeships may be available in areas such as engineering, food and drink processing. You will be able to learn on the job and possibly take courses at a college or training centre to further your skills.

With experience as a Quality Control Inspector you can take courses to increase your skills, including the City & Guilds Certificate in Quality Assurance and the Chartered Quality Institute's (CQI) Certificate in Quality. The latter allows you to apply for associate membership of the CQI.

Advantages/disadvantages

There may be opportunities for travel and work abroad as a Quality Control Inspector.

You may become self-employed.

Due to developments in technology companies are increasingly using advanced equipment to monitor standards.

Money guide

Salaries for this job can start at £20,000 per year. When you have gained some experience this can rise to £24,000. As you gain responsibility you can earn from £30,000 to £35,000 depending on the industry in which you are working. If you work as a freelance high-technology quality control inspector specialist, you can earn between £40,000 and £60,000.

Related opportunities

- Laboratory Technician p524
- Quality Manager p57
- Trading Standards Officer p498

Further information

Chartered Quality Institute
12 Grosvenor Crescent, London SW1X 7EE
020 7245 6722; www.thecqi.org; info@thecqi.org

SEMTA
14 Upton Road, Watford WD18 0JT
0845 643 9001; www.semta.org.uk

ENTRY LEVEL 2

Engineering, Manufacturing and Production

CRCI: NJ

QUARRY MANAGER

What the work involves

- Quarrying involves opencast mining to extract minerals and other materials to manufacture goods such as chemicals.
- Your job will involve managing all the staff in the office and the quarries.
- On-site, you will inspect the quality of the minerals and other products mined, ensure production is on schedule and check equipment.
- In the office you will manage the sales department, look after the budget, produce performance reports and plan changes to the production system when different materials are needed.

The type of person suited to this work

You will need to have good communication skills as you will be liaising with a wide range of people. You must also have a good technical knowledge of the production system in quarries. You should be business-minded with excellent management skills.

You will need to be aware of health and safety legislation as well as government regulations and ensure that these are followed on-site. It is important to have a good understanding of technical drawings and plans.

Working conditions

You will be on call in case of emergency. You will typically spend 2 days on-site and 3 days based in an office. You must wear protective clothing such as helmets and ear protectors when on site and be prepared to work in all weathers.

Future prospects

After gaining experience, it might be possible to progress into a managerial role in area operations. There is also the possibility of working abroad. It would be helpful to become a member of the Institute of Quarrying. It has a professional development system which ranges from student to fellowship levels. Career prospects can be improved by further qualifications in management and quarry legislation. It will be necessary to take jobs at different quarries to improve career progression, unless you work for a big company.

Advantages/disadvantages

You will have a high level of responsibility.

You will spend time working outdoors.

Long hours, including work on weekends are common in this industry.

Working conditions on sites are dirty, dangerous and noisy and sites are often based in rural areas.

Qualifications and courses

ENTRY 5 LEVEL

You will need a degree or HND. Subjects such as minerals engineering, environmental sciences, geology or mining engineering are very useful. You will typically need at least 2 A levels in sciences and 5 GCSEs (A*–C). Master's degrees are also available in Quarry Management. You could also take a year long industrial placement with a big organisation as part of your degree.

Graduate management schemes with large organisations typically look for a degree in quarry engineering, IT or business. Work experience on a quarry site would be very useful.

The Mineral Products Qualifications Council (MPQC) offers many useful qualifications in risk assessment, supervising safety in quarries, quarry safety inspections and understanding quarries regulations. Entrants will typically acquire professional accreditation with the Institute of Quarrying or the Institute of Materials, Minerals and Mining.

Money guide

Salaries will depend upon the location of the site and the employer. Bonuses can boost salaries.

A new assistant quarry manager can earn £23,000 or more.

£35,000 is a typical starting salary for a quarry manager and a unit manager who is in charge of a number of quarries or a big quarry can earn £50,000 or more.

Related opportunities

- Construction Operative p88
- Demolition Operative p92
- Quarry Worker p243

Further information

Institute of Quarrying
7 Regent Street, Nottingham NG1 5BS
0115 945 3880; www.quarrying.org

Institute of Materials, Minerals and Mining
1 Carlton House Terrace, London SW1Y 5DB
020 7451 7300; www.iom3.org

Proskills UK
Centurion Court, 85b Milton Park, Abingdon OX14 4RY
01235 833844; www.proskills.co.uk

QUARRY WORKER

What the work involves

■ There are many types of quarry worker. A machine operator controls heavy equipment whilst a plant and process operator is focused on the screening plant.

■ Shotfirers are responsible for explosives and drillers are responsible for creating holes for explosives and investigation.

■ Truck drivers, maintenance workers and laboratory technicians are also needed to undertake quality control and investigate samples from the site.

The type of person suited to this work

You need to be strong, fit and active to do this job. You must also follow safety regulations at all times due to the dangers that could arise when using heavy machinery.

You need to be able to work well with others as teamwork is a big part of this job. An interest in mechanical work is also crucial. Quarry workers should enjoy working outdoors and be prepared to do so in all weathers.

Working conditions

You will often work in shifts, which will include early mornings and late nights. Floodlights will be switched on during these periods. You should be prepared to travel for long periods of time to reach sites, as they are predominantly located in rural areas.

Working conditions are often dirty, noisy, muddy and dangerous. Protective clothing such as helmets and ear protectors must be worn at all times. Work will often include a lot of carrying and climbing.

Future prospects

Roughly 1,000 quarries exist in the UK. Although each local authority will have a quarry, the majority of them are located in the East Midlands and south-west of England.

After gaining experience, you may be able to progress into a role as supervisor or manager. With further study, you can apply for jobs as laboratory or quality control technicians. Drivers, mechanics and fitters can undergo training to become drillers or shotfirers.

Advantages/disadvantages

You could use powerful machines such as drills and excavators or explosives.

You will work outdoors.

Working conditions are muddy, noisy and dangerous.

Travel times to work can be fairly long as sites are often located in remote, rural areas.

Qualifications and courses

ENTRY LEVEL 1

This job does not have any formal educational requirements. However, employers generally look for at least 5 GCSEs/S grades (A*–C/1–3). Relevant subjects include English, maths, science and technology. The Diploma in Engineering or Construction and the Built Environment could be useful. Apprenticeships in Extractive and Mineral Processing Operations may be on offer in your area. You can also take a Level 3 Certificate or Diploma in the Extractives and Mineral Processing Industries.

Once on the job, you could also work towards NVQs at Levels 1–3 in Mineral Processing Industries, Level 2 in Plant and Operations (Extractives), Levels 1–2 in Specialized Plant and Machinery and Level 2 in Drilling Operations. An NVQ at Level 3 in Blasting Operations or equivalent is needed to work with explosives. Courses are also available from the Mineral Products Qualifications Council (MPQC). A LGV licence would be helpful.

Money guide

Salaries will depend upon the location of the site and the employer. They can also be boosted by extra payments from overtime, bonuses and shift work. The starting salary for an operator is about £13,000. After gaining experience and training this can rise to £25,000. If you are a specialist with significant experience, or progress to a role as a manager, you can earn £40,000+.

Related opportunities

■ Construction Operative p88
■ Demolition Operative p92
■ Quarry Manager p242

Further information

Institute of Quarrying
7 Regent Street, Nottingham NG1 5BS
0115 945 3880; www.quarrying.org

Institute of Materials, Minerals and Mining
1 Carlton House Terrace, London SW1Y 5DB
020 7451 7300; www.iom3.org

Proskills UK
Centurion Court, 85b Milton Park, Abingdon OX14 4RY
01235 833844; www.proskills.co.uk

City& Guilds

www.cityandguilds.com/myperfectjob

Engineering, Manufacturing and Production

CRCI: GI

RAILWAY FITTER/ ELECTRICIAN

What the work involves

- A mechanical fitter will maintain and service the traction and rolling stock, plant, machinery and passenger coaches. You could also repair station equipment such as customer lifts and hoisting equipment.

- An electrical fitter will work alongside mechanical fitters and other engineers, specialising in the electrical side of the maintenance and servicing work. You will work on the traction and rolling stock, plant machinery and passenger coaches.

- A multi-skilled fitter will have a combination of both of the sets of skills held by mechanical and electrical specialists; you will be able to work in either aspect.

The type of person suited to this work

You should enjoy working with your hands, diagnosing faults and working out solutions. You will be comfortable using different hand tools and equipment and enjoy working in a team alongside other fitters.

Physically fitness is important as you will be on your feet, working at your bench or directly within the various railway stock.

You should be happy to follow verbal and written instructions, be able to read and understand technical drawings and diagrams and have a responsible attitude to health and safety.

Working conditions

Much of your work will take place within heated workshops or depots. Depending on your work you might have to visit jobs which are outdoors, for example near to railway sidings or within a station. On these occasions it might be cold and dark.

As many of the work places are in remote areas, having your own transport is often essential.

You will have to wear protective clothing and be happy working in cramped places, using lots of bending and lifting.

You will have a 37-hour working week, with shifts that cover early, late, evening and weekend working. Also, you might need to be 'on call' for emergencies outside of your working hours.

Future prospects

Many specialist maintenance companies carry out work for operating companies and engineering companies, making new traction units and carriages.

Well-developed promotional and in-service training programmes exist which help fitters to progress to supervisor, technician, team leader and management levels.

Qualifications and courses

It is sometimes possible to start as a trainee straight from school, but a better route of entry is through an Apprenticeship/Skillseekers scheme. Entry requirements are usually 3–5 GCSEs/ S grades (A*–C/1–3) including English, maths, science and technology. You will also need to pass a medical exam and an aptitude test may be set.

NVQs/SVQs in Rail Transport Operations, and Railway Engineering: (Traction and Rolling Stock) at Levels 2 and 3 are available.

An ability to drive, with access to personal transport, is often required

Advantages/disadvantages

The rail industry is beginning to expand – so demand will increase for new recruits.

Training and career routes are well developed.

Due to the range of jobs within the railway industry it is possible to move sideways into other related job areas.

Money guide

During an Apprenticeship you will receive around £12,000 per year. With experience and qualifications you can get £14,000–£22,000. Very skilled and experienced railway fitters can earn £30,000+ per year.

Overtime and free or reduced rail travel are also common.

Related opportunities

- Mechanical Engineer p234
- Rail Track Maintenance Operative p621
- Rail Signalling Technician p620
- Train Driver p629

Further information

Network Rail
Kings Place, 90 York Way, London N1 9AG
0845 711 4141; www.networkrail.co.uk

Engineering Council UK
246 High Holborn, London WC1V 7EX
020 3206 0500; www.engc.org.uk

GoSkills
Concorde House, Trinity Park, Solihull B37 7UQ
0121 635 5520; www.careersinpassengertransport.org

City & Guilds

www.cityandguilds.com/myperfectjob

SHEET METAL WORKER

What the work involves

- Sheet metal workers produce parts for a number of important items ranging from vehicles and aeroplanes, through to electrical equipment and common domestic appliances.

- You will be using complex engineering drawings as a guide to marking out and cutting each piece.

- You will also be operating a variety of machines including hand-powered tools, cutting and pressing devices, and increasingly also computer numerically controlled (CNC) devices.

The type of person suited to this work

You should have good communication skills as you will be working as part of a team so building good relationships with colleagues is important.

Good numerical skills and the ability to interpret complicated technical drawings are essential for making accurate calculations and creating precise parts.

You should have a good level of fitness as you will be expected to lift large items and operate heavy machinery. Good eyesight and excellent practical skills are also required in order to use tools and equipment safely.

Finally, you should have good ICT skills as computer-operated machinery is increasingly used in this role.

Working conditions

You will usually work standard hours during the week, although shift work and overtime is also common. If you are producing bespoke items for a customer to a tight deadline, you may be required to work overnight on occasion.

Work is usually undertaken in a factory or workshop. You will spend the majority of your time at a bench so will be bending over for most of your day. The work also involves lifting, and spending hours on your feet. You will be required to wear appropriate safety equipment at all times.

Future prospects

Prospects are good for sheet metal workers. Once your initial training is completed, you could go on to work towards qualifying as an engineering technician. Alternatively, you could become supervisor/manager of an engineering workshop which provides increased responsibility and salary. Because of demand, opportunities are available on small and large projects both in the UK and overseas.

Advantages/disadvantages

You will be working with a variety of materials and tools, which will enable you to build specialist understanding and knowledge quickly.

Working hours usually fall within the week, so you will rarely be called in to work over weekends.

Qualifications and courses

You will need to have at least 5 GCSEs/S grades (A*–C/1–3), including maths, English and a science subject. The Diplomas in Engineering; Construction and the Built Environment; or Manufacturing and Product Design may all be useful.

Apprenticeship and Young Apprenticeship opportunities may be available.

The Engineering Construction Industry Training Board (ECITB) offers a fast-track Advanced Apprenticeship under the National Apprenticeship Scheme for Engineering Construction (NASEC).

You can study at college for qualifications such as City & Guilds awards or a BTEC in subjects such as manufacturing engineering and fabrication and welding.

If you are looking to enter this profession as an adult, then training is available through the National Skills Development Scheme (NSDS). No qualifications or previous experience is required for this programme, but you should already be working in a job that is related to that of a sheet metal worker.

Money guide

As a trainee sheet metal worker, you could earn between £8,000 and £11,000. Once fully qualified, this will rise to around £14,000. With between 3–5 years of experience, you could expect to earn between £20,000 and £23,000. Highly skilled sheet metal workers who are fully competent with using computer-controlled equipment can earn up to £27,000.

Related opportunities

- Assembler p215
- Blacksmith p216
- Welder p251

Further information

Engineering Construction Industry Training Board
Blue Court, Church Lane, Kings Langley WD4 8JP
01923 260000; www.ecitb.org.uk; ECITB@ecitb.org.uk

SEMTA
14 Upton Road, Watford WD18 0JT
01923 238441; www.semta.org.uk

www.cityandguilds.com/myperfectjob

Engineering, Manufacturing and Production

CRCI: NE

TAILOR/DRESSMAKER

What the work involves

- Tailors and dressmakers can design and make made-to-measure, bespoke items of clothing.

- Tailors usually make structured items such as suits, jackets and coats. Dressmakers can make a range of clothing, from day dresses and casual trousers to ball gowns and wedding dresses.

- You will be working with numerous materials, including silk, linen, cotton and polyester, and will also use equipment such as sewing machines, scissors, tape-measures and pins.

The type of person suited to this work

Since you will be dealing with a range of people, including clients and suppliers, you will need to have excellent interpersonal and verbal communication skills.

Understanding how different cuts, styles and colours flatter various shapes and figures is important for customer satisfaction, as is maintaining a smart/fashionable appearance.

Working conditions

You can expect to work 37–40 hours a week. Saturday and weekend work is common as that is when most of your clients will be available for meetings and fittings.

You could be situated in a workshop, small factory or work from home if you are self-employed.

A reasonable level of physical fitness and flexibility is required, as you will be bending and kneeling when measuring customers and fitting clothes. You may also need to lift and carry heavy rolls of fabric.

A lot of the work is very detailed, so you will need a high level of accuracy and good eyesight.

Future prospects

You could work for a small or large company, and create high fashion or more classic pieces. You can also opt to be self-employed.

In larger companies, you may be promoted to a supervisory position, and there may also be the opportunity to diversify into pattern cutting or design.

There are opportunities to travel and work overseas, especially if you are involved in fashion and haute couture tailoring or dressmaking.

Advantages/disadvantages

You will be undertaking very creative work with lots of scope to use both your talent and imagination on a daily basis.

Fashion is a fast-paced, interesting and potentially lucrative industry to be working in.

Qualifications and courses

(Entry Level 2)

The main route into tailoring or dressmaking is straight from school. No experience is necessary as all training is provided on the job by more experienced colleagues.

A demonstrable aptitude for design, sewing and art is usually sought be employers, as are GCSEs (A*–E) in English, maths, textiles or art.

If you are specifically looking to train as a prestigious Savile Row tailor, you could join the Bespoke Tailoring Apprenticeship programme run by Newham College. It lasts four years and teaches you all you need to know to become a top tailor, including pattern cutting, garment construction and sewing by both machine and hand.

A number of courses are available on a full or part time basis, or via distance learning, including: BTEC Awards, Certificates and Diplomas in Textiles, Fashion, Art and Design, and ABC Level 3 Diplomas in Production or Handcraft Tailoring.

Money guide

The average starting salary for both tailors and dressmakers ranges from £10,000 to £13,000.

With 3–5 years' experience, your salary could rise to £14,000–£18,000.

Senior tailors or dressmakers, especially those located on Savile Row or who work in high fashion, could earn £40,000+.

Related opportunities

- Fashion Designer/Milliner p172
- Textile Operative p248

Further information

Newham College of Further Education
East Ham Campus, High Street South, London E6 6ER
020 8257 4000; www.newham.ac.uk;
ExternalEnquiries@newham.ac.uk

ABC Awards
Robins Wood House, 1 Robins Wood Road, Aspley,
Nottingham NG8 3NH
0115 854 1616; www.abcawards.co.uk;
enquiries@abcawards.co.uk

City&
Guilds

www.cityandguilds.com/myperfectjob

TELECOMMUNICATIONS ENGINEER

What the work involves

- Telecommunications engineers are responsible for designing, testing and overseeing the installation of all telecommunications equipment and facilities.

- You could work across a variety of engineering fields, including electronics and construction, providing technical guidance and offering solutions to other professionals and clients.

- You will be responsible for the management of telecommunications projects, which includes planning budgets, recruiting a team and implementing onsite safety.

- You will also produce written reports and verbal presentations in order to keep both your team and your clients up-to-date on how each project is progressing.

The type of person suited to this work

Good communication skills are essential for managing and briefing your team, as well as negotiating with clients and explaining complex technical information to them in a clear and simple manner.

You should have an analytical mind and be excellent at problem-solving. The ability to work efficiently under pressure and organise your workload effectively is also essential.

Working conditions

You will usually work a normal week of about 37 hours from Monday to Friday. Occasionally additional hours may be required, particularly as you progress to more senior positions.

Your working hours may be fairly flexible and you will not always be office-based, as the industry is seeking to promote working from home and part-time opportunities.

You will need to spend time onsite, checking and overseeing the installation of telecommunications equipment. In these instances, you may find yourself working outdoors or in cramped conditions. You will usually be required to wear appropriate safety equipment as well.

Future prospects

As the telecommunications industry is continually expanding and improving, job prospects for engineers in this sector are good.

Working in this fast-paced industry will require you to undertake further training throughout the course of your career in order to stay up-to-date with new products, techniques and developments.

As you progress, you could study to achieve professional status as a chartered engineer (CEng) which will improve your earning potential. If you work within a company, you could move into increasingly senior positions as your experience grows.

Qualifications and courses

Most employers require a relevant degree in a related subject such as telecommunications, electronic engineering, computer science, physics or maths.

It is possible to enter with an HND in a relevant engineering subject, but you will only be able to take a role at technician level. From there, you can supplement your on-the-job experience with further qualifications in order to achieve a relevant degree.

Many employers also look for candidates who have a postgraduate qualification such as a MEng or suitable MSc. A PhD could also help you enter the industry at a more senior level than that of a graduate trainee.

Advantages/disadvantages

Hours are generally regular, and there are increasing opportunities to work from home or undertake part-time hours.

In such a rapidly changing industry, you will be learning continually as you progress so the job will not become monotonous.

You will have to spend time on site which may involve working in cold, muddy conditions, at heights, or in cramped and uncomfortable surroundings.

Money guide

Starting salaries for graduate trainee telecommunications engineers are between £18,000 and £25,000 per year. After 5–7 years, this can rise to £30,000–£40,000. If you reach a senior level and gained chartered status, you can expect to earn £50,000+.

Some companies also offer excellent benefit packages and bonus schemes in addition to a basic salary.

Related opportunities

- Electrical Engineer p221
- Civil/Construction Engineer/Civil Engineering Technician p85
- Electrician p94

Further information

The Institution of Engineering and Technology
Michael Faraday House, Stevenage SG1 2AY
01438 313 311; www.theiet.org; postmaster@theiet.org

www.cityandguilds.com/myperfectjob

Engineering, Manufacturing and Production

CRCI: GE

TEXTILE OPERATIVE

What the work involves

- Textile operatives manufacture carpets, prepare the yarns of fibres to be woven or knitted (which may involve carding and combing or chemical processing), spin yarn on a machine, or even make fabric on a loom.

- You will carry out basic maintenance on your machinery, make sure you have a supply of raw materials and keep your work area clean and tidy in accordance with health and safety regulations.

- You may also work on finishing processes such as dyeing or waterproofing fabrics.

The type of person suited to this work

You will need to be practical in order to operate the machinery skilfully and responsibly. In keeping with this, you should have good concentration as you will be doing repetitive tasks for long periods of time.

Manual dexterity and good spatial awareness, coupled with excellent eyesight and in the majority of cases full colour vision, are also requirements for carrying out tasks such as spinning or weaving textiles.

A reasonable level of personal fitness, an understanding of and adherence to work place health and safety rules, and enjoyment of working in a team are also attributes.

Working conditions

Although you will work an average 37–40 hours per week, you will usually be doing shift work which is likely to involve early mornings or later evenings. Overtime and part-time work is also available.

You will usually work in a textile factory, which should be light and well-ventilated, although the machines can be noisy and you will have to wear relevant safety equipment at all times.

It can be physically tiring, as you will spend the majority of your time standing over your machine or walking between the various pieces of equipment you are using.

Future prospects

The opportunities for textile operatives are good, as there has been increasing demand for textile production in recent years so a larger number of people are gaining employment at entry level and progressing more quickly to supervisory or managerial positions.

If you gain experience in using a variety of machines and performing a range of tasks, you will find your prospects improve accordingly.

You could also choose to move into quality control or sales once you have gained a full knowledge of the textile industry.

Advantages/disadvantages

You will be putting your practical skills to good use creating a range of textiles for various purposes.

Qualifications and courses

Although there are no specific entry requirements for this position, there are several courses available that would build valuable understanding of the industry and what the role would involve. Courses include GCSE art and design (including a textiles module), Edexcel BTEC Introductory Certificate/Diploma in Art, Design and Media, Edexcel Level 1 BTEC First Certificate in Art and Design. The Textile Centre of Excellence also offer a Technical Certificate in Textiles that provides a flexible, distance learning programme.

Once qualified, the Textile Institute (TI) offers a range of qualifications for professional development from Licentiate to Fellow level. Alternatively, ABC offers a variety of courses in sewing, manufacturing and textiles, as do City & Guilds at Levels 1–3.

Apprenticeships with textile manufacturers may also be available.

The work can become monotonous.

Hours can involve unsociable shift work in the early morning or evening.

Money guide

Starting salaries for new entrants range from £10,000 to £12,500. With a couple of years' experience and increasingly diverse skills, you could earn between £13,000 and £17,000.

Once you have become a multi-skilled senior operative you could earn up to £20,000.

If you work shifts, or undertake overtime, earnings could be higher. Piecework payments (awarded for high production volume) can also boost earnings.

Related opportunities

- Tailor/Dressmaker p246

Further information

The Textile Institute
1st Floor, St James's Buildings, Oxford Street, Manchester M1 6FQ
0161 237 1188; www.textileinstitute.org;
tiihq@textileinst.org.uk

Society of Dyers and Colourists
Perkin House, 82 Grattan Road, Bradford BD1 2JB
01274 725138; www.sdc.org.uk

City & Guilds

www.cityandguilds.com/myperfectjob

TOOLMAKER

What the work involves

- Toolmakers make specialist tools and devices that are used to cut, shape, mould and form various materials for use in the production of all items from domestic appliances to aeroplanes.

- You will work with a range of materials, including metals and plastics.

- You will also be using complex engineering drawings as a guide to marking out and cutting each piece.

- You will be operating a variety of machinery including drills, grinding and milling machines, cutting and pressing devices, and increasingly also computer numerically controlled (CNC) equipment.

The type of person suited to this work

Good hand-to-eye co-ordination and a keen eye for detail will be beneficial when operating machinery, and to check the quality of the tools produced. Because you will be making extremely precise devices, it is essential to be able to spot any faults or errors before the tools are despatched to customers.

Good numerical skills and the ability to interpret complicated technical drawings are essential for making accurate calculations and creating precise parts.

Finally, you should have good ICT skills as computer-operated machinery is increasingly used in this role.

Working conditions

You will usually work 39 hours per week from Monday to Friday, although some larger companies operate shift patterns so evening and weekend work may be necessary.

Work is usually undertaken in a tool room within a factory or workshop. This means that you will be working in a fairly quiet environment, away from the main factory machinery.

You will normally stand for the duration of your working day, which can be tiring.

You will be required to wear appropriate safety equipment at all times.

Future prospects

Prospects for toolmakers are good, and there are employment opportunities in most parts of the UK.

After gaining 5–10 years' experience as a toolmaker, you could move into a supervisory role within a company, overseeing production within a tool room or workshop. This could then lead into a management position.

You could also undertake further qualifications in order to work towards employment as an engineering technician, which could in turn lead to undertaking a degree course in order to become an engineer of some kind.

Qualifications and courses

You will need to have at least 5 GCSEs/S grades (A*–C/1–3) or equivalent, including maths, English, science and technology.

Most people start on the Advanced Apprenticeship in Engineering scheme on completion of school or college. You will spend several months at a training centre and then spend 2 or 3 years working within your company whilst also attending college.

If you have difficulty finding an apprenticeship, there is also the option of taking an NVQ that is related to engineering.

Entry opportunities for adults are limited unless you have significant previous experience, as companies generally just train up existing employees when necessary.

Advantages/disadvantages

You will be making tools which are vital for the construction of important equipment ranging from aeroplanes to washing machines.

You will be using both your practical skills and your mental abilities daily.

The work can be physically exhausting, as you will spend the majority of your day on your feet.

Money guide

Starting salaries for toolmakers range from £15,500 to £17,000 a year. With a few years' experience, you could expect to earn around £25,000. Highly skilled toolmakers, who are fully competent with using computer-controlled equipment, can earn up to £35,000.

Related opportunities

- Motor Vehicle Technician p235
- Sheet Metal Worker p245
- Welder p251

Further information

SEMTA
14 Upton Road, Watford WD18 0JT
01923 238441; www.semta.org.uk

Engineering Council UK (ECUK)
246 High Holborn, London WC1V 7EX
020 3206 0500; www.engc.org.uk

www.cityandguilds.com/myperfectjob

Engineering, Manufacturing and Production

CROI: GF

VEHICLE MAINTENANCE PATROLLER

What the work involves

- Vehicle maintenance patrollers travel to motorists who have broken down in order to diagnose the problem with the vehicle and fix it if possible. If repair isn't possible, you will need to tow the vehicle to the nearest garage.

- You will be responding to urgent calls from a central control centre, and may need to reassure worried or shaken motorists.

- You will be driving a van or truck, and operating a range of electronic equipment alongside general tools and car parts.

The type of person suited to this work

You will need excellent communication skills in order to explain to motorists what is wrong with their vehicle and what can be done to fix it. You may be required to reassure people who are distressed or upset following an accident.

The ability to think quickly when assessing vehicles at the roadside is necessary.

You should be good with your hands as you will be operating various tools and machines and undertaking fiddly jobs from time to time.

Working conditions

An average working week comprises 39 hours, usually worked on a shift system including evening and weekend work. You may also be required to remain on standby on occasion.

Since the majority of work is undertaken on the road, a driving licence is essential. Depending on the vehicle you drive, you may also need an additional HGV or LGV licence. You will be working on the roadside in all conditions, including hazardous weather such as snow and fog, so must wear relevant safety equipment at all times.

Future prospects

Vehicle maintenance patrollers enjoy a variety of employment options. You could work for a large, well known national organisation such as the Royal Automobile Club (RAC) or the Automobile Association (AA), or for a smaller garage providing a localised breakdown service.

With experience you may progress to a supervisory role in a larger organisation, in which you will oversee and develop the performance of a number of breakdown engineers across a region.

In larger organisations, you could also move into a managerial or senior administrative position.

Advantages/disadvantages

You will be providing a valuable and well appreciated service to people every day.

Qualifications and courses

Vehicle maintenance patrollers are qualified vehicle technicians, and as such must hold NVQ Levels 1 and 2 in motor vehicle maintenance and repair along with having a minimum of 3 years' relevant experience in motor vehicle repair.

You will need a clean driving licence, and pass a driving assessment, aptitude test and medical exam. Most employers will expect you to have at least 4 GCSEs (A*–E), including English, maths and science.

NVQs are available in roadside assistance and recovery, which encompass all aspects of the job including assessing the vehicle and carrying out minor repairs at the roadside.

Some of the larger organisations offer induction programmes that allow new entrants to train on the job and learn skills such as customer service techniques, alongside building their technical knowledge. They may also support study for relevant NVQs.

There is great job satisfaction in being able to repair a vehicle at the roadside and send a happy customer on their way.

You will spend long periods of time on your own, which can get boring and lonely.

Money guide

The starting salary for a qualified vehicle breakdown engineer is around £25,000. With 3–5 years' experience, you could expect this to rise to £30,000–£33,000. Senior engineers, including those working in supervisory positions within larger companies, can earn up to £40,000.

Related opportunities

- Assembler p215
- Motor Vehicle Technician p235

Further information

The Automobile Association
Member Administration, Contact Centre, Lambert House, Stockport Road, Cheadle SK8 2DY
0870 600 0371; www.theaa.com

Royal Automobile Club
8 Surrey Street, Norwich NR1 3NG
01922 727 313; www.rac.co.uk/careers/

Institute of Vehicle Recovery
Top Floor, Bignell House, Horton Road, West Drayton UB7 8EJ
01895 436 426; www.theivr.com; mail@theIVR.com

City& Guilds

www.cityandguilds.com/myperfectjob

WELDER

What the work involves

■ Welders work with metals and heavy duty plastics, which they join together using heat to form plates, pipes and other items.

■ You could use a number of welding techniques that are either classed as manual, semi-automatic or fully mechanised. You will most likely specialise in one of these areas as opposed to working across all three.

■ You may have to work from technical drawings, using them as a guide by which to weld components together.

The type of person suited to this work

You will need good hand-to-eye co-ordination, coupled with manual dexterity, to successfully operate your tools and machinery.

You should be willing to work responsibly within strict health and safety guidelines, and to look out for the safety of others in your team. This will prove especially important when you are called upon to work unsupervised.

Working conditions

Hours are usually 37 per week, and often operate on a shift pattern. Opportunities for overtime work are common.

You could find yourself working in almost any location, from standard factory or workshop roles to onsite jobs which could be outdoors or even under the sea. This means you might have to work in confined spaces which can be uncomfortable.

You will also need to wear safety equipment, including protective goggles to shield your eyes from UV light and sparks, and also fire resistant aprons and gloves.

Future prospects

There are excellent employment opportunities for welders throughout the UK, although the majority are found in fairly industrial areas.

Employers are mostly small and medium-sized firms, although some larger companies do also employ welders. There is also the option to be self-employed.

As you gain experience within a company, you could move into a supervisory role. Alternatively, you could undertake further qualifications in order to specialise in a particular area of welding, or work towards a career as an engineer.

Advantages/disadvantages

Practical work, where you can see the result of your efforts, is extremely rewarding.

Career prospects are good, with opportunities throughout the UK.

You will be operating machinery that is potentially dangerous.

Qualifications and courses

Most employers expect you to have least 5 GCSEs/S grades (A*–C/1–3) or equivalent, including maths, English and a science subject.

The most common route into this career is undertaking an Apprenticeship or Advanced Apprenticeship after school. Most apprentices spend several months learning their initial skills off site at a training centre.

Alternatively, you can take related NVQs or BTEC Certificates and Diplomas at college in order to gain knowledge prior to entering the industry. Relevant qualifications include NVQ Level 2 in Fabrication and Welding Engineering, NVQ Level 3 in Welding (pipework) and Welding (plate), the Welder Approval Certificate which is the industry-recognised qualification, a BTEC in Manufacturing Engineering, or completing Vocationally Related Qualifications (VRQs) in Welding at Levels 1, 2 and 3.

Money guide

Trainee or apprentice welders can start at about £8,000, rising to £13,000 as they gain qualifications. Once qualified, you could earn around £22,000.

With experience and increased levels of skill you could earn £40,000 and above, especially if you work on specialised projects or overseas.

Salaries and additional benefits vary according to the region you are working in, and the company you are employed by.

Related opportunities

■ Blacksmith p216
■ Civil/Construction Engineer/Civil Engineering Technician p85
■ Sheet Metal Worker p245
■ Toolmaker p249

Further information

Engineering Construction Industry Training Board
Blue Court, Church Lane, Kings Langley WD4 8JP
01923 260 000; www.ecitb.org.uk; ecitb@ecitb.org.uk

The Welding Institute
Granta Park, Great Abington, Cambridge CB21 6AL
01223 899 000; www.twi.co.uk; twi@twi.co.uk

www.cityandguilds.com/myperfectjob

Engineering, Manufacturing and Production

CRCI: GF

Environment, Animals and Plants

Jobs in this sector are perfect for those of you who don't want to spend every day behind a desk in an office, although this is not to say that you will not need to spend time writing reports and keeping a log of research findings or clients' information. Workers in this sector are passionate about animals or about caring for and maintaining the environment. You should also have brilliant people skills especially if you find yourself responsible for the welfare of someone else's animal. You should be someone who is very observant and interested in the natural world, not just from a welfare point of view but also from an economic one; many jobs in this sector involve using the environment for financial gain but increasingly industry is interested in doing so responsibly.

We look at the following jobs in this section:

For similar jobs to the ones in this section turn to *Leisure, Sport and Tourism* starting on page 383.

AGRICULTURAL SCIENTIST

What the work involves

- Agricultural scientists carry out research to improve current farming techniques in crop production and the breeding and managing of livestock.

- Using biology, biochemistry or chemistry, you will become a specialist in one area such as the study of soil, viruses, fungi, pests or genetics.

- You will conduct tests, analyse the information and then write up reports.

- You could also teach farmers and companies that sell seeds or chemicals about your findings.

The type of person suited to this work

You must have an aptitude and a passion for science and the environment, especially biology and chemistry. You will need strong communication skills as you will initially liaise with farmers and other growers to find out about their agricultural problems. You should be innovative and have strong research skills as you will spend the majority of your time in a laboratory or in the field, developing new solutions. It is important to be patient, methodical and organised as progress in some research projects can take a very long time.

Working conditions

You will work 35–39 hours a week. It may be necessary to work early mornings, late evenings and weekends. You will be based either in an office or a laboratory. Shift work could be needed when conducting experiments in the laboratory. When working in laboratories or on farms you must wear protective clothing. If you have hay fever, pollen or dust allergies or allergies related to animals, this work could be tough for you. A driving licence would be helpful as you might have to travel to farms or greenhouses.

Future prospects

Opportunities for general research are declining, although they are rising in some fields like genetic engineering. There is strong competition for jobs. Vacancies are available with local and national government, manufacturers of animal feed, fertilisers and chemicals and research organisations. After gaining experience, you could become a lecturer in a university, school or college. You may be able to use your communication skills and shift into sales-related work for production companies

Advantages/disadvantages

This job is perfect for those with a passion for plants and wildlife.

You will be able to conduct scientific research and practical work.

Qualifications and courses

ENTRY 5 LEVEL

You will need a degree in an area such as agriculture, biological science, horticulture, soil science or animal nutrition. Training is also provided on the job. Entry requirements for a degree are typically a minimum of 2 A levels/H grades, including maths and chemistry or another science, or equivalent as well as GCSEs including English, maths and science. It can be useful to have a postgraduate qualification such as a Master's degree in animal production, soil science or seed and crop technology.

It will also be necessary to have some work experience on a farm or in horticulture. It could be useful to take a Diploma or Certificate in Agriculture.

Job opportunities are falling in some areas.

It can take a long time to see any progress in some research projects.

Money guide

Salaries will depend on your location and employer. Certain private companies and the majority of public organisations have a structured pay scale.

The starting salary for an agricultural scientist is £17,000–£22,000. With experience, this can increase to £30,000–£40,000.

If you progress to a senior role such as a department head, it is possible to earn up to £55,000.

Related opportunities

- Botanist p509
- Chemist p510
- Ecologist p515
- Laboratory Technician p524

Further information

Lantra
Lantra House, Stoneleigh Park, Coventry CV8 2LG
024 7669 6996; www.lantra.co.uk

Institute of Biology
9 Red Lion Court, London EC4A 3EF
020 7936 5900; www.iob.org

Department for Environment, Food and Rural Affairs
Customer Contact Unit; Eastbury House;
30–34 Albert Embankment; London SE1 7TL
0845 933 5577; www.defra.gov.uk

AGRONOMIST

What the work involves

- Agronomists are specialists who work towards producing crops of the highest quality and productivity.

- You will become an expert in areas such as irrigation, drainage, plant breeding, soil classification, soil fertility and wood control.

- You will study any factors which could affect the crop such as the weather and water supply.

- You will carry out experiments, examine the results and then complete reports.

The type of person suited to this work

You must have a high level of expertise in science, especially biology and an interest in the environment. You need to be good at problem solving and have excellent research skills. You should be comfortable working on your own and as part of a team. You must have strong analytical and communication skills in order to turn your research into practical solutions and explain them to farmers or businesses. It is important that you are methodical, practical and patient as it may take a long time to conduct successful experiments.

Working conditions

You will spend a lot of time working outdoors. You will also carry out experiments and tests in laboratories and write up reports in an office. Hours are generally 9am–5pm, Monday to Friday, although you might have to work extra hours to complete some experiments.

Travel to different locations such as farms can be necessary for some agronomists. Protective clothing is needed as you will probably work with hazardous equipment. This job may not be suitable for those with pollen or dust allergies. Good colour vision may be needed for certain jobs.

Future prospects

Job prospects are better for agronomists in certain fields such as genetic engineering. A lot of agronomists work for the government, research organisations and agricultural development organisations as well as businesses that produce seeds, chemicals or food products.

After gaining experience, it is possible to become self-employed and work as a consultant. Lecturing in universities is another option. You could also progress to a role such as a manager in a research agency or a project supervisor.

Qualifications and courses

ENTRY LEVEL 5

You will need a degree in a relevant subject such as agronomy, crop science or agriculture. Typical entry requirements are a minimum of 2 A levels/ H grades, including a science and GCSEs/S grades including science. It can be useful to have a postgraduate qualification such as a Master's degree in soil science or seed and crop technology.

On the job training is provided. Work experience on a farm is very useful. The Diploma or Certificate in Agriculture may be helpful. A driving licence is often needed.

Advantages/disadvantages

You will have the opportunity to work outdoors.

Scientific research and practical work are combined in this role.

Conducting successful experiments can take a long time and requires patience.

You will often have to wear protective clothing.

Money guide

Salaries vary according to the location and type of employer.

The starting salary for an agronomist is around £16,000–£20,000. After gaining experience, this can reach £25,000–£35,000. If you progress to a senior role, you can expect a salary of up to £45,000.

Related opportunities

- Botanist p509
- Chemist p510
- Ecologist p515
- Laboratory Technician p524

Further information

Lantra
Lantra House, Stoneleigh Park, Coventry CV8 2LG
024 7669 6996; www.lantra.co.uk

Institute of Biology
9 Red Lion Court, London EC4A 3EF
020 7936 5900; www.iob.org

Department for Environment, Food and Rural Affairs
Customer Contact Unit, Eastbury House;
30–34 Albert Embankment; London SE1 7TL
0845 933 5577; www.defra.gov.uk

Environment, Animals and Plants

CRCI: HA

ANIMAL BEHAVIOURIST

What the work involves

- Animal behaviourists advise owners whose pets have developed inappropriate and dangerous behaviour.

- Although working with all domestic animals, you would probably focus on dogs, cats and horses. Typical problems include aggressive behaviour, soiling or destructiveness. You will also aid owners in achieving general control over their pets.

- You could be connected to a veterinary practice, work in kennels, catteries and welfare societies or be freelance.

The type of person suited to this work

You will need a strong interest in animals, their care and welfare. As this job also involves working with the owner, you will have to be able to communicate with people too! Whilst dealing with the owner you should be able to maintain a certain level of tact. Working with animals can be messy and smelly work, so you must be prepared to get dirty.

You will also need to have lots of patience and the ability to remain calm. You should be good at science, especially biology and have a certain degree of business acumen along with the ability to keep records and accounts.

Working conditions

This work takes place in clinics and clients' homes and so a driving licence would be extremely helpful. You could be indoors or outside in all weathers.

Some jobs will involve evening and weekend work, especially if you visit your clients and animals in their own homes. Most animal behaviourists are self-employed and set their own hours.

The work can be dusty, dirty and physically demanding, so you will need to be fit and active. This profession can be difficult for those who suffer from allergies.

Future prospects

Although demand across the canine and equine areas has increased due to television programmes and press coverage there are still very limited career opportunities for this job. Some of the larger animal welfare charities are starting to employ staff with these skills, however most are self-employed and running their own practices. Other options include lecturing and writing papers on animal behaviour.

Advantages/disadvantages

You will be working with animals, perhaps helping them to have a better quality of life.

Pet owners can be more difficult than their pets!

This job offers the opportunity for self-employment.

It can be difficult to build up a client list, which will affect your income.

Qualifications and courses

Membership of the Certificated Clinical Animal Behaviourists (CCAB) which is administered by the Association for the Study of Animal Behaviour (ASAB) requires a degree or postgraduate qualification in a biological or behavioural science.

The Association of Pet Behaviour Counsellors (APBC) also requires the acquisition of a degree for membership.

Typical entry requirements consist of 2 A levels/3 H grades (which should include biology and/or another science subject) and 5 GCSEs/S grades (A*–C/1–3) including English and maths.

In order to gain entry to a postgraduate course, applicants will normally require a first degree in a relevant subject, such as animal science, biology, psychology veterinary science or zoology.

Money guide

Many working in this area are self-employed, average fees are around £20–£50 for each consultation.

Once qualified, you can expect a salary of around £15,000 per year.

Depending on experience you could expect to earn between £25,000–£35,000 a year. The highest paid animal behaviourists may exceed this amount.

It is unusual for an animal behaviourist to make a full time living from this industry. Many supplement their income by lecturing or writing articles.

Related opportunities

- Animal Physiotherapist p257
- Dog Trainer/Handler p261
- Kennel Worker p274
- Veterinary Surgeon p283
- Zookeeper p285

Further information

Association of Pet Behaviour Counsellors
PO Box 46, Worcester WR8 9YS
01386 751151; www.apbc.org.uk; info@apbc.org.uk

ASAB Membership Secretary
School of Psychology, University of St Andrews,
St Mary's College, South Street, St Andrews KY16 9JP
www.asab.nottingham.ac.uk; susan.healy@st-andrews.ac.uk

City&
Guilds

www.cityandguilds.com/myperfectjob

ANIMAL PHYSIOTHERAPIST

What the work involves

- Animals suffer from joint and muscular pain in the same way that humans do. As a result animal physiotherapy has become a regular part of animal care.

- You would be used by many domestic pet owners and even more so by horse owners.

- Techniques you will use may include soft tissue mobilisation, ultrasound (including long-wave), neuromuscular stimulation, joint mobilisation, magnetic field therapy, hydrotherapy and massage.

The type of person suited to this work

This job involves working with the owner so you will have to be able to communicate with people too!

Working with animals can be messy and smelly, so you must be prepared to get dirty. You should expect the work to be occasionally distressing, especially if the animal is injured or dies.

You will need to have good dexterity and be physically fit. You should have experience of working with animals and the ability to match treatments with problems.

Working conditions

You will be working in clinics, clients' homes, farmyards and/or stables. You could be indoors or outside in all weathers.

A driving licence is essential for some posts and you will normally wear protective clothing. This job will probably involve some heavy lifting and you will need to be physically fit.

Some assignments will involve evening and weekend work, especially if you visit your clients and animals in their own homes. As most animal physiotherapists are self-employed, working hours must be flexible to suit the client.

Future prospects

This profession is extremely competitive and employs very small numbers. Work experience will improve your chances of employment.

Some of the larger animal welfare charities and veterinary surgeries employ animal physiotherapists; however most are self-employed running their own practices. To be successful you will need to build up a client list and have good business skills. There is not a structured career path in place.

With experience you could work as a lecturer or consultant.

Advantages/disadvantages

You will be working with animals, perhaps helping them to have a better quality of life.

There is the opportunity for self-employment.

Some heavy lifting will be required.

Some aspects of the job may be messy and smelly.

Qualifications and courses

ENTRY LEVEL 4

To qualify as a chartered animal physiotherapist, you can complete a degree in human physiotherapy. You will need the highest level A levels/H grades in maths and science for entry. Upon completion of the degree you then can choose to either spend a further 2 years (at least) gaining work experience with a practising chartered animal physiotherapist, or study part time for the PG Dip or MSc in Veterinary Physiotherapy with the Royal Veterinary College.

Alternatively, you can choose to complete an animal physiotherapy course, such as a certificate in animal physiotherapy offered by the National Association of Veterinary Physiotherapists (NAVP). Entry requires a suitable first degree such as equine sciences; veterinary nurses with 4 years' experience are also considered. This programme lasts 2 years.

The College of Animal Physiotherapy also offers a diploma in animal physiotherapy. This course lasts 1–2 years part time. If you successfully complete this course you will be accepted to the International Association of Animal Therapists.

Money guide

Many working in this area are self-employed, average fees are around £35–£70 for each consultation of 1 hour.

The average starting salary is about £18,500 per year, this can increase to around £20,000–£25,000 with experience. As a senior animal physiotherapist or consultant you could earn up to £65,000 a year.

Related opportunities

- Animal Behaviourist p256
- Masseur p315
- Physiotherapist p330
- Veterinary Surgeon p283

Further information

Association of Chartered Physiotherapists in Animal Therapy
Morland House, Salters Lane, Winchester SO22 5LP
01962 844390; www.acpat.org

National Association of Veterinary Physiotherapists
43 Heath Avenue, Rode Heath, Stoke-on-Trent ST7 3RY
01270 876115; www.navp.org.uk

The College of Animal Physiotherapy
Tyringham Hall, Cuddington, Aylesbury HP18 0AP
01844 290545; www.tcap.co.uk

City&
Guilds

www.cityandguilds.com/myperfectjob

ANIMAL WELFARE OFFICER

What the work involves

- You will work for an animal protection organisation or local authority offering a 24/7 service. You will undertake rescue work, but you will also visit and advise pet and animal owners. You may need to investigate cases of abuse.

- You will be on call to collect stray and injured animals or animals at risk, possibly from dangerous situations.

- You will promote animal welfare in your area, and may be responsible for caring for any animals taken in by the organisation you work for.

The type of person suited to this work

You will find yourself in situations that could be potentially dangerous, so you will have to be aware of your own, the public's and the animals' health and safety. Some work will be distressing, especially if the animal is in pain or has been mistreated.

Although you will often work on your own, you may well work within a team, especially in rescue situations. You will need excellent communication skills with the ability to remain calm in a crisis.

Working conditions

Each day will be different; you could be in a factory, private house, animal establishment or outdoors up to your waist in water.

You will spend a lot of your time travelling around your area driving a van. You will probably have to work shifts including evenings and weekends.

Animals can bite and kick, especially when they are frightened, so you will have to use your skills to make sure they remain safe and that you do not put yourself at risk. You will not be able to do this work if you suffer from animal or dust-based allergies.

Future prospects

You could work for a number of animal charities such as the RSPCA or the Blue Cross, or for a local authority. Within the RSPCA you can be promoted from animal welfare officer to inspector, with more responsibility over animal cruelty cases.

There may be possibilities of working overseas, providing support to local people in disastrous events such as earthquakes or informing local people about animal welfare.

You can also move into other related jobs such as local authority dog and animal warden, kennel and cattery work.

Qualifications and courses

There are no formal entry requirements for this position but it would be an advantage to have experience working with animals, through voluntary work. GCSEs/S grades (A*–C/1–3) in English and maths will be helpful and a clean full driving licence would also be beneficial.

To be recruited by the RSPCA you will need a full driving licence and 5 GCSEs/S grades (A*–C/1–3) including English and a science subject. Physical fitness is as important as academic qualifications; you have to be able to swim 50m fully clothed. The RSPCA has its own 12-month training course including animal welfare legislation, basic veterinary training, rescue situation techniques, interview and communication techniques, animal handling and public speaking. The Diploma in Work-Based Animal Care is also available to be studied whilst you work.

Advantages/disadvantages

You will have the satisfaction of rescuing animals that are being abused and mistreated.

Some people will be abusive and you may come across dangerous situations.

It is rewarding to know you have made a difference to the quality of animals' lives and given them a chance to be re-homed.

Money guide

Starting salaries as a trainee animal welfare officer are around £15,000 per year.

This can increase to around £18,000–£25,000 per year with experience.

Related opportunities

- Dog Trainer/Handler p261
- Kennel Worker p274
- Trading Standards Officer p498
- Veterinary Nurse p282

Further information

Royal Society for the Prevention of Cruelty to Animals
Wilberforce Way, Southwater, Horsham RH13 9RS
0300 1234 555; www.rspca.org.uk/home

Scottish Society for the Prevention of Cruelty to Animals
Kingseat Road, Halbeath, Dunfermline KY11 8RY
0300 0999 999; www.scottishspca.org

ARBORICULTURAL WORKER/ TREE SURGEON

What the work involves

- You will carry out all kinds of work on the trees, shrubs and hedgerows in private and public gardens, parks, roadsides and on paths.

- You will be responsible for planting new trees and shrubs, taking direction from a landscaper or garden designer.

- Using chainsaws, hand tools, ladders and other specialised climbing equipment, you will use your knowledge of trees to make them safe, help them grow or increase the light available for other species.

The type of person suited to this work

You must have practical skills and be happy using potentially dangerous machinery and tools. You will also have to be interested in trees and the problems that can occur with them.

This job is physically demanding and will include lifting, cutting and climbing so you will need to be strong and agile. You would need to observe health and safety rules and be happy working in a team or on your own. You will need excellent communication skills to deal with customers and explain what work needs to be done.

Working conditions

You will be outdoors in all weathers, hanging from ropes and using dangerous tools like a chainsaw.

If you suffer from pollen and dust allergies or vertigo, this work will be difficult for you. You will have to wear protective clothing and be very safety conscious.

Future prospects

Demand for experienced workers has risen due to greater public interest and concern for the environment. Opportunities are available with the National Trust, contractors, landowners or private employers.

With further qualifications you could enter senior or managerial positions, but this might involve moving to larger organisations.

With experience you could set up your own business.

Advantages/disadvantages

The work can be hazardous so you must obey safety regulations.

You will be outside working in all weathers.

You could do very long hours in the summer and shorter hours in the winter, which may affect your earnings.

Money guide

Salaries will depend on whether you are working for a contractor or are self-employed. You will probably earn more

Qualifications and courses

Entry is through a combination of on-the-job work experience and qualifications. There are NVQs/SVQs available in Forestry and Arboriculture at Levels 1 and 2, which include workplace assessment. The Diploma in Environmental and Land-based Studies could be useful.

ENTRY LEVEL 2

BTEC National qualifications in Forestry and Arboriculture and the Royal Forestry Society Level 2 Certificate in Arboriculture are available. The NPTC Level 2 Certificate of Competence to Climb Trees and Perform Aerial Rescue, the NVQ Level 2 in Arboriculture and Apprenticeships may be helpful. You could also take a Competence-Based Craft-Level Award in Chainsaw Assessments & Pesticide Application.

Some employers require GCSEs and might ask for a degree. Degrees are available in arboriculture but a degree in a related horticultural subject could also be accepted.

Short part-time and full-time courses are available at land-based colleges for further education in chainsaw use, maintenance of equipment, health and safety and climbing techniques. A Competency Certificate from the National Proficiency Training Council or Scottish Skills Testing Service is needed to work on your own or with machinery.

The Royal Horticultural Society also offers short courses leading to Arboricultural Association certificates and Lantra-accredited apprenticeships.

The National Trust can help in organising work experience placements. The Woodland Trust and the British Trust for Conservation Volunteers provide volunteer opportunities.

in the south-east of England. Starting salaries are around £12,000 per year. This rises to around £14,000–£24,000 with experience. Those who are self-employed can earn £30,000+.

Related opportunities

- Countryside Ranger p260
- Forest Worker/Officer p268
- Gardener/Garden Designer p270
- Horticultural/Garden Centre Worker/Manager p273

Further information

Lantra
Lantra House, Stoneleigh Park, Coventry CV8 2LG
024 7669 6996; www.lantra.co.uk

www.cityandguilds.com/myperfectjob

COUNTRYSIDE RANGER

What the work involves

- By patrolling the countryside throughout the year you will monitor the success and progress of the plants, animals, fencing and buildings in your care.

- You will be responsible for the safety and enjoyment of any visitors, answer their queries and help them get the most from their visit.

- You will keep a record of any work that is carried out, along with inspections, accidents and incidents.

The type of person suited to this work

You will need to enjoy being outdoors and have a strong interest in wildlife and the countryside.

To ensure the future of your area you will need to provide information to the public which could include talking to potential funding organisations or local politicians. You will therefore have to be confident speaking in public and have excellent written and spoken communication skills. You might have to write reports and sometimes undertake research.

To find work you might have to start with some voluntary or community-based work, so it's important that you are keen and willing.

Working conditions

Most of your work will be outdoors, driving or walking around your area. You will be working in all weathers and despite protective clothing you will be, at times, cold and wet or hot and dusty. This is physically demanding work and is likely to involve walking over difficult terrain.

You are likely to work longer hours during the spring and summer, especially if there are animals or plants that require protection.

This work can be difficult if you suffer from pollen or dust allergies.

Future prospects

Once employed within the industry it is likely that you will need to move from employer to employer in order to progress.

Many jobs are offered on temporary contracts or on a seasonal basis.

After gaining experience, it is possible to enter lecturing, consultancy or research work. You could also progress to the role of officer or a more managerial position, which would be more office based. You might choose to move to leisure management, agriculture or horticulture work.

Advantages/disadvantages

You will spend a lot of time in the open air combining your interest in the countryside with work!

You could be working in remote areas.

It is a very competitive area to enter so unpaid experience can be vital.

Qualifications and courses

There are no set entry qualifications, but GCSEs or higher-level qualifications in science and geography may be required. The Diploma in Environmental and Land-Based Studies could be useful.

Relevant courses include NVQs/SVQs at Levels 2 and 3 in Environmental Conservation and BTEC/SQA National Certificates and Diplomas in Countryside and Forestry, Conservation, Countryside Skills or Countryside Management. You will require 1 A level and relevant work experience to gain entry to these.

Most training is done on the job. Courses for professional development are provided by Lantra National Training Organisation.

A driving licence is essential. Employers prefer applicants aged 21 or over.

Money guide

These figures are only approximate and may vary depending on location and employer.

Initial salaries are between £9,000 and £13,000 per year. With experience this can rise to around £20,000 a year. The most senior countryside rangers can earn over £25,000 per year. You may also be given additional payments if you are required to work unusual hours.

Related opportunities

- Environmental Conservation Manager/Officer p262
- Farm Manager p263
- Forest Worker/Officer p268
- Gamekeeper p269

Further information

Lantra
Lantra House, Stoneleigh Park,
Coventry CV8 2LG
0845 707 8007; www.lantra.co.uk

British Trust for Conservation Volunteers
Sedum House, Mallard Way, Potteric Carr,
Doncaster DN4 8DB
01302 388888; www.btcv.org.uk

Natural England
1 East Parade, Sheffield S1 2ET
0845 600 3078; www.naturalengland.org.uk

City&
Guilds

www.cityandguilds.com/myperfectjob

DOG TRAINER/HANDLER

What the work involves

Dog trainer

- You could support security staff, the police force or animal charities such as the Guide Dogs for the Blind. Your work will be divided between training the dogs and their human carers.

- You might run one-to-one and group classes on obedience training for dogs.

Dog handler

- Working as a team, you will search buildings, vehicles and open spaces for such things as people, illegal drugs, firearms or evidence. You may protect property including private property or military establishments.

- You might attend large-scale disturbances to control crowds or search for casualties at disaster scenes.

The type of person suited to this work

You may need to house and care for your dog from puppyhood right to the time it retires 7–10 years later. You will require a stable home environment.

Most police dog work involves attending incidents, so you will need to be able to stay calm in an emergency. You will need to be patient, self-confident, alert and observant.

Dog trainer

You will need to be patient and a good teacher. You will need to have a good imagination to make classes fun and also be physically fit.

Working conditions

If you work with domestic owners you will probably be self-employed and work from a community setting like a village hall.

Dogs are used in dangerous situations and so you will be at risk of injury.

Future prospects

The main employers are the police, armed forces and customs and excise. Some other organisations employ a few dog handlers, for example the fire service, security companies and search and rescue services.

This job is fiercely competitive as many handlers stay in the job for life.

There is also the option of self-employment or lecturing on dog training courses.

Advantages/disadvantages

There is the possibility of self-employment.

You may at some point be bitten or scratched.

Qualifications and courses

Dog handler

ENTRY LEVEL 2

Dog handling is usually a second career. Employers such as HM Customs and Excise, the police, the army and the fire service expect you to start in mainstream work first before applying.

You could start as an apprentice and work towards a Diploma in Work-Based Animal Care. There is also an ASET Level 2 National Award in Security Dog Handling. You are required by law to have a Security Industry Authority (SIA) licence.

Dog trainer

After working as a handler you can then apply to become a trainer. Some organisations, such as the police, require 3 GCSEs (A*–C), including English and maths. Voluntary work is recommended.

Foundation degrees and degrees are available in animal behaviour and training and animal studies.

You will form a strong bond with your dog.

It is really rewarding when the dog you have trained catches a criminal, or finds dangerous drugs or explosives.

Money guide

Domestic dog trainers earn around £15,000 a year. Police dog trainers make about £21,000 which can rise to £30,000 with experience. If you are self-employed your earnings will depend on your success.

On average dog handlers earn between £15,000 and £25,000 a year depending on experience. Extra allowances are paid when the dog lives with and is cared for by you.

Related opportunities

- Animal Behaviourist p256
- Animal Welfare Officer p258
- Racehorse Trainer p278
- Police Officer p552

Further information

Police recruitment information
0845 608 3000; www.policecouldyou.co.uk

Armed Forces Careers RAF
22 Unthank Road, Norwich NR2 1AH
01603 614616; www.rafcareers.com

Association of Pet Dog Trainers
PO Box 17, Kempsford GL7 4WZ
01285 810811; www.apdt.co.uk

City & Guilds

www.cityandguilds.com/myperfectjob

Environment, Animals and Plants

CRCI: HC

ENVIRONMENTAL CONSERVATION MANAGER/OFFICER

What the work involves

- Environmental conservation officers/managers preserve and protect important wildlife areas, including nature reserves and sites of special scientific interest.

- You will achieve this through methods such as raising awareness of the issues that affect the natural environment, monitoring species to see which require protection, and gathering evidence of pollution.

- You will advise authorities and communities on the effect developments will have on the natural environment.

- Managers are responsible for the hiring, training and supervising of staff. You will also be in charge of the way budgets are spent.

The type of person suited to this work

In order to pursue this career you must have an interest in and a passion for environmental conservation.

You should have strong observational skills. You will also need to be physically fit. You should be capable of conducting research, have strong communication and negotiation skills, both in person and on paper and the ability to speak in public.

You might have to be involved in enforcing environmental laws and so you will have to be able to remain calm and logical.

Working conditions

You will spend some of your time in an office environment and the rest working outdoors.

Working hours will vary depending on the season, but the average is about 40 hours a week. This is not a 9am–5pm job and working weekends, evenings and bank holidays is common.

You might be required to travel between sites and so a driving licence may be useful. As an officer you may be provided with protective clothing.

Future prospects

Officers may progress into a managerial position, for example countryside manager or senior officer. In order to gain this kind of promotion you will need to gather qualifications and experience. However, promotion opportunities can be hard to come by.

You may also be able to specialise in an area of conservation which could increase your employment potential.

Advantages/disadvantages

You will have to work outside in all weathers.

This job has many elements to it and so every day will be different.

You will have to enforce environmental legislation which might place you in heated situations.

Qualifications and courses

Most entrants have completed a degree; however it is possible to enter this profession with a HND, Foundation degree, A levels or equivalent. A postgraduate qualification would be beneficial as this field is highly competitive.

Subjects such as environmental science, biological sciences (e.g. zoology), environmental conservation, countryside management and earth sciences (e.g. geography) would all be relevant.

Generally degree programmes require applicants to have achieved at least 2 A levels and 5 GCSEs grades A*–C or equivalent. Entry requirements do vary so it is important to check with the individual institution.

You will also have to demonstrate your commitment to this career, which you can do by completing work experience placements within conservation groups or wildlife trusts.

An alternative route into this industry is to start as a ranger or warden, gather experience and then apply for an environmental conservation officer post. There are Apprenticeships available for this particular career.

Money guide

These figures will vary depending on location, employer and sector. Your salary will increase as you gain responsibility. The average starting salary for an environmental conservation officer is between £19,500 and £21,500 per year. With experience this can increase to between £24,000 and £32,000. Those who excel in the field can earn up to £36,000 a year.

Related opportunities

- Countryside Ranger p260
- Landscaper/Landscape Manager p276
- Landscape Architect/Designer p275

Further information

BTCV, Head Office
Sedum House, Mallard Way, Potteric Carr,
Doncaster DN4 8DB
01302 388 883; information@btcv.org.uk; www.btcv.org.uk

City& Guilds

www.cityandguilds.com/myperfectjob

FARM MANAGER

What the work involves

- You will be responsible for the overall running of a farm. This includes making the decisions about which crops to grow or livestock to raise.

- You will supervise the work of your staff, keep up to date with farming developments and oversee the economic side of the business.

- You will have to communicate with government officials, farming suppliers and feed merchants and your customers who could be major supermarkets or small local shops.

- You will keep farm records up to date such as the budget and where crops and livestock are sold to and bought from.

The type of person suited to this work

You should have a passion for science, the environment and business, combined with a strong understanding of farming and a desire to learn.

You will also need an appreciation of health and safety and the ability to recruit, develop and retain your staff, as well as run the business of the farm.

You should be capable of motivating staff, be computer literate and work well when under pressure.

Working conditions

Farm managers tend to work long hours, with particular times of year being exceptionally busy, for example harvest or lambing season. This job involves early mornings.

Managers will spend a lot of their time doing accounts and making sure the farm is operating profitably, but will also need to muck in with general farm work during busy periods. On smaller farms this may be a regular occurrence. The outdoors work will involve heavy lifting and will be dirty, smelly and/or dusty.

Future prospects

Competition for jobs is intense and career progression is likely to involve moving from one part of the country to another. With substantial experience and qualifications it is possible to progress into other related areas of agriculture, such as plant breeding, crop protection, plant trials or genetics. These opportunities are available within private companies or academic/research organisations. Training or research opportunities are also possible. There could be the chance to work abroad.

Advantages/disadvantages

You will spend a lot of time in the open air caring for living and growing things.

At some times of the year your social life may be restricted.

Qualifications and courses

There are no formal entry requirements but most that enter this area do so with an HND, degree or other higher level qualification. Courses are available in agriculture, agricultural science, land and property management, and agricultural engineering. A levels/H grades or their equivalent, often including a science subject will be required. Postgraduate courses are also available which will require a relevant degree or HNC/D and experience.

It is possible to enter with an NVQ/SVQ in Agriculture Crop Production or Livestock Production Level 3, Agriculture (Livestock Management) Level 4 or Agricultural and Commercial Horticulture (Crop Management) Level 4. Candidates should also have previous experience of farm work, and most degree-level courses include sandwich placements for this purpose. A driving licence is essential.

You will get to combine business acumen and an understanding of nature.

Your future can depend on things outside of your control such as bird flu or foot and mouth disease.

Money guide

Average salaries are around £16,500. With experience this can increase to between £24,000 and £30,000. Managing a large farm, once enough experience has been gathered, may increase this to over £50,000. Some jobs include rent-free accommodation and a vehicle. There is a set minimum wage, decided upon by the Agricultural Wages Boards for England and Wales, Scotland and Northern Ireland.

Related opportunities

- Parks Officer p277
- Fish Farmer p267
- Forest Worker/Officer p268
- Horticultural/Garden Centre Worker/Manager p273
- Farm Worker p264

Further information

Lantra
Lantra House, Stoneleigh Park, Coventry CV8 2LG
0845 707 8007; www.lantra.co.uk

National Federation of Young Farmers' Clubs (NFYFC)
YFC Centre, 10th Street, Stoneleigh Park, Coventry CV8 2LG
024 7685 7200; www.nfyfc.org.uk

www.cityandguilds.com/myperfectjob

Environment, Animals and Plants

CRCI: HA

FARM WORKER

What the work involves

Livestock

- You will work on farms or estates caring for livestock such as cows, sheep, poultry and pigs. You could specialise in one type of animal depending on the nature of the farm.

- You will need to feed and handle the animals, clean their living spaces and food and water troughs, as well as unload and load the livestock for transport.

- You will tend to ill livestock, give them proper medication and help out with birthing procedures.

- Depending on where you work you could also milk cows and shear sheep.

Crops

- You will work on arable farms, ploughing, planting, sowing, fertilising, spraying and harvesting a variety of crops.

- Sometimes you will hand pick crops and other times you will use machinery such as balers and combine harvesters.

- You could work with crops such as wheat, barley and oats, vegetables, non-food crops like linseed and flax, or energy crops used for heat and power generation.

- You will also be responsible for looking after ditches, hedges and machinery.

The type of person suited to this work

You should be practical and good with your hands. A love of the outdoors and an interest in the environment is essential. Working on a farm can often involve 24-hour care so you need to be willing to put in long hours when needed. You should be strong, active and adaptable.

A good knowledge of plant and/or animal care is important. You may need to work out weights and other calculations so good numeracy skills are also useful. Much of the materials and machinery you will work with could be dangerous so you need to be able to follow instructions and to work with care and caution.

Working conditions

Farm work is seasonal so you will be busier at certain times of the year such as during lambing and harvesting. At these times you can expect to work 16 hour days. You will normally work 40 hours a week year round including evenings, early mornings and weekends. You will work in all weathers and will often be expected to live on or near the farm.

Livestock

The work on all livestock farms can be smelly, dusty and dirty. You will often need to wear protective footwear and clothing. If you work on a poultry farm you will work in buildings with controlled temperatures and humidity.

Crops

You will need to wear ear protection when operating agricultural machinery. You will also need to wear protection when working with chemicals.

If you drive a tractor you will be sitting down for long periods at a time. Your job can be physically demanding and will involve a lot of standing, bending, lifting and carrying.

Future prospects

All farm workers may be promoted to supervisory roles or train further and become farm managers. Most farms are small however, employing only up to 10 people, so you might need to move from farm to farm in order to be promoted. There are also opportunities to work overseas.

Livestock

Livestock farms are mostly centred in western parts of the UK. A rise in farmers' markets means that demand for meats is high and your opportunities are plentiful. You could work as a dairy, beef, sheep, pig or poultry worker. You could also specialise even further. For instance, a poultry worker may move on to breed exotic birds such as guinea fowl.

Crops

Crop farms are mostly centred in eastern parts of the UK. Opportunities are dependent on arable land, climate and local markets. You could work with vegetables, cereals or root crops. You could also specialise in non-food crops such as pharmaceuticals, oils or materials such as hemp.

Advantages/disadvantages

You will work in all weathers outdoors which means you could be working in dry and sunny or cold and wet conditions.

Working on a farm, especially during busy seasons, can be physically exhausting.

It's an amazing experience to tend to and watch an animal give birth. It's also rewarding to reap an abundant harvest.

Mucking out livestock pens or digging ditches for crops can be dirty and unpleasant.

Money guide

The Agricultural Wages Board sets minimum wages for farm workers based on qualifications, age, experience and responsibility. If you start out as a trainee at 16 years old you may earn between £7,158 and £12,000 a year. If you are 19 or older you may earn between £9,673 and £14,986 a year. With experience and leadership responsibilities this could rise to £19,000 a year.

Many farm workers are paid per hour on a flexible or part-time basis. You can earn anywhere from £5.81 to £8.64 per hour. Apprentices will earn between £95 and £170 per week.

Many employers will provide you with free or low-rent accommodation. Overtime pay is also common which will increase your salary.

Related opportunities

- Farm Manager p263
- Gamekeeper p269
- Fish Farmer p267

Further information

Department for Environment, Food and Rural Affairs
Nobel House, 17 Smith Square, London SW1P 3JR
0845 933 5577; www.defra.gov.uk

Lantra
Lantra House, Stoneleigh Park, Coventry CV8 2LG
0845 707 8007; www.lantra.co.uk; www.afuturein.co.uk

National Federation of Young Farmers' Clubs
YFC Centre, 10th Street, Stoneleigh Park, Coventry CV8 2LG
024 7685 7200; www.nfyfc.org.uk

Edexcel Ltd
190 High Holborn, London WC1V 7BH
0870 240 9800; www.edexcel.org.uk

Qualifications and courses

There are no set entry requirements for this job but many employers will expect you to have work experience such as a weekend or summer job on a farm. GCSEs/S grades in English, maths and science may be useful for gaining promotion and higher pay.

The Diploma in Environmental and Land-Based Studies or an Apprenticeship in Agricultural Crops and Livestock may be helpful. You could also do a BTEC Certificate or Diploma in Agriculture.

Livestock

Lantra offers a variety of livestock courses including Cattle Hoof Trimming, Lamb Hypothermia and Animals in Transit. You can train while on the job and work towards NVQs Levels 1–3 in Livestock Production or a Diploma in Animal Care.

You may choose to do an HNC in Poultry Production at the Scottish Agricultural College. Poultry husbandry courses are also available at many land-based colleges

Crops

The Royal Agricultural College offers degrees in Organic Farming, Crop Production and Agricultural Science. You could also take a National Proficiency Tests Council accredited course in Tractor Driving or Pesticide Use.

Many employers will allow you to train on the job and you can work towards NVQs Levels 1–3 in Agriculture, Mixed Farming and Crop Production.

ENTRY LEVEL 1

CRCI: HA   Environment, Animals and Plants

FARRIER

What the work involves

- Farriers shoe, trim and care for the feet of horses.

- As well as the skills of removing and fitting new shoes, you will have to keep up to date with new practices and know about horse anatomy and illnesses that can affect horses' feet.

- You would often work in partnership with vets to treat leg and joint problems.

The type of person suited to this work

You should enjoy being around horses and have the right temperament to handle them. You will need to get on with your customers and deliver high-quality care to them and their horses.

You will have to enjoy being outdoors working in all weathers, often in a muddy environment. This work is both practical and physical, so you will need to be strong to do manual work using lots of hand tools and have good metalworking skills.

Working conditions

Weekend work is common and emergency cover can be needed at any time.

Your days will involve driving to each customer, working with the horses and returning to your forge to prepare shoes and collect materials. In the summer months your hours will be long, especially when more people are riding their horses. This can be hot, tiring work, especially if fitting shoes to a difficult horse.

You could work from a blacksmith's forge or travel to farms and stables and work out of a mobile workshop.

Future prospects

Riding is a very popular activity and there are stables all around the country. There are about 2,500 farriers who are mostly self-employed. There is high competition for each apprenticeship. Larger riding schools, stables and horse breeders can offer permanent jobs. You could progress to become a senior farrier or into a managerial role.

Some farriers supplement their earnings by undertaking blacksmithing whilst they build up their farriery client list.

Advantages/disadvantages

This is a great job if you want to work with horses without riding.

It's a satisfying skill to have; using your hands.

The work is physically demanding and can result in back injuries.

Qualifications and courses

Younger trainee farriers are required to take an Advanced Apprenticeship with an FRC Approved Training Farrier (ATF). They must be at least 16 years old and hold a Forging Certificate. There are no entry requirements for the Access to Farriery course. It is also necessary to undertake a medical examination and look for an Approved Training Farrier to recommend you to the Farrier Training Agency and complete the apprenticeship with. This takes 4 years and 2 months.

The course combines on-the-job training with periods at a FTA-approved college. At the end you will also be awarded a NVQ Level 3 in Farriery, the Diploma of the Worshipful Company of Farriers and be eligible for registration with the Farriers Registration Council.

A Foundation degree in Farriery for those who are already qualified and working is also available.

A driving licence is required.

Money guide

When starting out you can expect a salary of around £8,500 per year.

Once qualified, you can earn between £10,000 and £20,000, depending on your success and the number of customers you have. Some experienced and popular farriers can earn over £35,000.

Related opportunities

- Animal Behaviourist p256
- Blacksmith p216
- Farm Manager p263
- Racehorse Trainer p278

Further information

Farriery Training Agency
Sefton House, Adam Court, Newark Road,
Peterborough PE1 5PP
01733 319911; www.farrier-reg.gov.uk

Worshipful Company of Farriers
19 Queen Street, Chipperfield,
Kings Langley WD4 9BT
01923 260747; www.wcf.org.uk

City&
Guilds

www.cityandguilds.com/myperfectjob

FISH FARMER

What the work involves

- As a fish farmer you will raise fish from small (juvenile) fry until they reach saleable size. The most common fish to raise are salmon and trout.

- You will feed, check for disease and protect them from predators. You will finally net the catch and pack them for market.

- Some farms specialise in producing the breeding stock: the fingerlings (the tiny fish that other farmers bring to saleable size).

- Some shellfish farms in coastal locations also produce oysters, scallops and mussels.

The type of person suited to this work

You will need to be a practical type with the ability to learn a lot about fish and be happy to get wet and dirty. Much of this work is scientific in approach, so you should have good observational skills to be able to identify anything that might affect the quality and success of the fish in your care.

You will need to be patient, hard working and persevere if things are tough. This work is difficult and long-term security is not guaranteed.

If you become a manager, in addition to your practical ability, you will also have to have good business and administrative skills.

Working conditions

Working with fish is the same as any animal-based work, which means they need care and attention 24/7. You are likely to work on a rota basis with 2 days off every week and work very long hours including early mornings, late evenings and weekends.

You will be outdoors in damp, cold conditions having to cope with all types of weather. Some of the work will be unpleasant and will involve the sight of blood.

Future prospects

With the problems related with sea fish stocks, fish farming is becoming quite important.

Like other farming enterprises, fish farms are vulnerable to price fluctuations, so predicting the future is risky. Around 7,500 people are employed in the industry, most of whom are based in Scotland. There are 300 trout farms located in Scotland, southern and central England and north Yorkshire.

With experience you may move into a research related role involving scientific and technical work. You could also start up your own farm or work abroad.

Advantages/disadvantages

You will spend a lot of time in the open air. You will have the satisfaction of producing an in-demand product.

There are only limited areas where the work is available and you may often work unsocial hours.

Qualifications and courses

Applicants do not necessarily need formal educational qualifications, but most employers require GCSEs (A*–C).

A BTEC First Diploma in Fish Husbandry is available to those with 4 GCSE/S grades (A*–C/1–3); students can then progress to the National Diploma in Fish Management or the Scottish group Award in Fishery Studies.

BTEC and SQA Higher National qualifications can be taken in Fish Farm Management, Aquaculture or Fishery Studies.

Training can be done on the job with attendance at short courses. Entrants may work towards NVQs/SVQs at Levels 2 and 3 in Fish Husbandry, or may study by distance learning for the Institute of Fisheries Management Diploma.

Degrees in aquaculture/fisheries studies, biology, marine and freshwater biology are available.

In Scotland, entry is available through Skillseekers.

Money guide

Fish farm worker

Starting out you can expect to earn around £13,000–£14,000 per year. Average earnings for those with experience are between £13,000 and £20,000.

Manager

Experienced managers can expect up to £45,000.

Related opportunities

- Countryside Ranger p260
- Farm Manager p263
- Skipper/Fisherman/woman p279

Further information

Institute of Fisheries Management
22 Rushworth Avenue, West Bridgford,
Nottingham NG2 7LF
0115 982 2317; www.ifm.org.uk

British Trout Association
The Rural Centre, West Mains, Ingliston EH28 8NZ
0131 472 4080; www.britishtrout.co.uk

www.cityandguilds.com/myperfectjob

Environment, Animals and Plants

CRCI: HA

FOREST WORKER/OFFICER

What the work involves

Forest worker

- Work includes planting trees, felling trees, managing weeds, maintaining fencing and carrying out tree surgery.

- In addition, you will use tools, drive vehicles and repair any broken fences.

Forest officer

- You will plan and manage the annual programme of your forest. This includes organising the clearing of areas, planting and felling trees, and overseeing general maintenance.

The type of person suited to this work

This can be dangerous work as you will be using heavy machinery. It is important that you can follow instructions and enjoy being outdoors.

Forest officer

You will have to be organised as you will be planning jobs months in advance. You will need both technical skills and theoretical knowledge of forests and wildlife.

Working conditions

Forest worker

You will probably work a standard Monday–Friday week with overtime and weekend work during the busier summer months. You will have to be aware of health and safety legislation as this can be dangerous work, using potentially hazardous tools.

Forest officer

Much of your time will be spent outdoors but you will also work indoors planning jobs for your staff to follow. You are likely to do a lot of travelling, whilst you check the different areas under your responsibility and a driving licence would be helpful as many of these places are isolated.

Future prospects

The range of employers open to you includes the Forestry Commission, private landowners and estates, local authorities and large companies. Career progression is likely to involve moving, as promotion is rare within all but the largest employers. Many contracts are short term so you need to have a flexible approach to employment opportunities. With significant experience, self-employment as a consultant or trainer is possible.

Advantages/disadvantages

It's a perfect job if you love the outdoors.

As in all jobs with plants, you are often at the mercy of the weather.

Qualifications and courses

ENTRY 2 LEVEL

Forest worker

There are no formal entry requirements but at least 2 GCSE/S grades (A*–C/1–3) or a forestry qualification would be an advantage. These include: NVQs/SVQs in Forestry (Establishment and Harvesting) Level 2 and Treework (Forestry Establishment or Forestry Harvesting) Level 3; BTEC/SQA in Forestry and Arboriculture and Countryside Management (Woodland Management).

The National Proficiency Tests Council (NPTC), the Scottish Skills Testing Service (SSTS) and Lantra award competence certificates in skills such as operating chainsaws and carrying out chemical spraying.

Forest officer

Entry is with a Foundation degree, HND, degree or postgraduate qualification in forestry. For entry to a degree, 2 A levels/3 H grades, normally including maths or a science, and 3 GCSEs/S grades (A*–C/1–3) are required. At least 1 A level/H grade or equivalent is required for entry to an HND or Foundation degree.

Money guide

Forest worker

You are likely to earn around £12,200 per year when starting out. This rises to around £18,000 with experience. If you are a supervisor you could earn up to £26,500. Some employers also provide subsidised accommodation.

Forest officer

Forestry Commission salaries for officers start between £18,500 and £23,000 per year, with experience it can rise to £35,000 or more.

Related opportunities

- Countryside Ranger p260
- Gardener/Garden Designer p270
- Rural Property/Practice Surveyor p118

Further information

Forestry Commission
Silvan House, 231 Corstorphine Road, Edinburgh EH12 7AT
0845 367 3787; www.forestry.gov.uk

Institute of Chartered Foresters
59 George Street, Edinburgh EH2 2JG
0131 240 1425; www.charteredforesters.org

City&
Guilds

www.cityandguilds.com/myperfectjob

GAMEKEEPER

What the work involves

- As a gamekeeper you would work on a large country estate, where shooting for sport is part of the estate business. You will also play an important role in managing the land.

- You will be responsible for providing birds and other animals such as deer or hares for the clients to shoot, or possibly fish to catch.

- This is achieved by raising game birds and releasing them into the wild once they are mature enough, and protecting game from its natural predators such as magpies and rats.

- You may also plant and protect crops, clear the land, and keep rivers clean.

The type of person suited to this work

You must have an unsentimental approach to wildlife as this job involves the killing of animals for sport. To enable the clients to get the most from their day, you will need to be a good communicator and be able to offer advice about gun usage and how to hit targets successfully.

Physical fitness and stamina are essential. You must be alert and possess excellent practical skills. You must be happy to work on your own for long periods of time.

Working conditions

You will be outdoors in all weathers and seasons. Your hours will be flexible and will involve weekend working and late/early starts. You will spend long periods of time on your own, doing lots of walking to check the estate and the progress of the game.

You will be handling and using guns, traps and poisons so will have to be confident using them and very aware of your own safety and that of others.

This work will be difficult for those who suffer from allergies to animals, pollen or dust.

Future prospects

Most of this work is within remote parts of the country or on large country estates. There is strong competition for jobs, so it is best to take a few training courses before applying.

With further skills in shoot-management or land management you can be promoted to head of estate, with experience and dedication you can advance from trainee keeper to head keeper quickly.

Advantages/disadvantages

This job combines outdoor physical work with lots of practical skills.

You will spend a lot of time alone.

You might be provided with a house.

Qualifications and courses

No formal qualifications are needed for this role. However, 3 GCSEs/S grades (A*–C/1–3) may be an advantage. Voluntary or relevant work experience is very useful.

Training is generally on the job, but there are some courses available to applicants who wish to progress.

City & Guilds offer the National and Advanced National Certificate in Environmental Conservation (Countryside Management); National Certificate in Gamekeeping Level 2 and the Certificate in Land-based Studies Level 1.

NVQs/SVQs are available in Gamekeeping and Wildlife Management at Levels 2 and 3. A BTEC National Award is available in Gamekeeping. The Diploma in Environmental and Land-Based Studies and BTEC National Diploma in Countryside Management are also available.

An HNC is available in Gamekeeping and Wildlife Management. Candidates would need practical experience and/or the National Award in Gamekeeping.

Foundation degrees are available in Countryside and Environment (Gamekeeping) at several colleges. These generally require a National Diploma or 2 or more A levels for entry. Apprenticeships/Skillseekers could be available for those aged 16–24.

Money guide

Starting salaries for new entrants are around £12,700 per year. With experience you may earn between £13,000 and £18,500. Head gamekeepers can expect up to £21,500.

Related opportunities

- Countryside Ranger p260
- Farm Manager p263
- Farrier p266
- Forest Worker/Officer p268

Further information

British Association for Shooting and Conservation
Marford Mill, Rossett, Wrexham LL12 0HL
01244 573 000; www.basc.org.uk

Game and Wildlife Conservation Trust
Burgate Manor, Fordingbridge SP6 1EF
01425 652381; www.gct.org.uk

City&
Guilds

www.cityandguilds.com/myperfectjob

Environment, Animals and Plants

CRCI: HC

GARDENER/ GARDEN DESIGNER

What the work involves

Gardener

- Gardeners work in a wide range of settings, from large gardens such as those in stately homes and National Trust properties, to small urban parks and private gardens.

Garden designer

- You will advise clients on how to improve the look and planting of their garden. You will present your ideas as a series of plans, and supervise a landscape contractor to turn your design into reality.

The type of person suited to this work

Gardeners need to be physically fit and confident in using hand tools.

You must be creative and able to picture how a piece of bare or neglected ground can be transformed into something beautiful.

As a garden designer, drawing and ICT skills will be useful, as will an extensive knowledge of plants and the environments they need.

Working conditions

Gardeners mostly work outdoors. There will be a lot of physical work, lifting large pots and bags of peat, and digging and clearing beds.

Garden designers will spend most of their time in a studio designing and researching garden plans. You will spend some time outdoors overseeing practical tasks.

Future prospects

Gardener

Many gardeners are self-employed offering services to both the public and private sectors. If you work for a local authority, with experience, you could move on to supervisor or manager jobs, especially if you gain further qualifications. Gardeners can also train to be garden designers.

Garden designer

Half of all designers work in private practice. Some specialise in certain types of design such as planting, landscaping, etc. Some designers choose to be self-employed offering services to private home owners.

Advantages/disadvantages

Designers can mix creative, practical and outdoor work.

Your work will depend on the weather.

You may work in beautiful places (or create them if you are a designer).

Qualifications and courses

Gardener

There are no set requirements for entry to this career. GCSEs (A*–C) would be useful. Courses are available to those who wish to progress and include a Diploma in Land-based Studies and NVQs/SVQs in Environmental Studies. The Royal Horticultural Society (RHS) have a general examination, which allows entry onto the Advanced National Certificate in Horticulture.

Garden designer

Although there are no formal requirements for this job, a design-orientated qualification is an advantage. Many garden design courses are offered at land-based colleges and some art colleges too. Courses include NVQs/SVQs. Degrees in garden design and related subjects are also available. The Institute of Gardening offers a Diploma in Horticulture which can be studied at home.

Money guide

Gardener

Gardeners working for a local authority start at around £10,000–£12,000 per year. With experience this can rise to £20,000+, especially if you have management duties. If self-employed you will agree an hourly rate with your customer.

Garden designer

As a guide, trainee rates start at between £10,000 and £15,000 per year. Designers' pay will depend entirely on how well they can market themselves and generate work; many are self-employed and charge around £30–£60 per hour.

Related opportunities

- Groundsperson/Greenkeeper p272
- Horticultural/Garden Centre Worker/Manager p273
- Landscape Architect/Design p275

Further information

Royal Horticultural Society
80 Vincent Square, London SW1P 2PE
0845 260 5000; www.rhs.org.uk

City&
Guilds

www.cityandguilds.com/myperfectjob

GROOM/STABLE HAND/ STUD HAND

What the work involves

Groom/stable hand

- You would be responsible for the health and welfare of the horses in your care. You would groom, feed, muck out and tack up.

- You could be based within a riding school, competition or livery yard, racing stable or veterinary hospital. You may have the opportunity to ride and even compete.

Stud hand

- This is a specialised area of work, you will be working with stallions, brood mares and young stock.

- You will use your understanding and knowledge of breeding lines to help owners breed a foal that meets their requirements.

The type of person suited to this work

As well as having lots of patience and the right temperament to be with the horses, you will need communication and team-working skills to work with your colleagues, owners and stable visitors.

Most of your work will be outdoors undertaking hard physical, dirty work. You will have to be happy to get your hands dirty by mucking out, grooming and cleaning tack. The hours are long and the pay can be low!

Working conditions

You will spend most of your time outdoors lifting heavy bags of feed, hay and bedding. You will carry tack, clean up the yard or ride. In the summer the work can be hot, dusty and smelly. In the winter it is cold, wet and muddy.

You will wear protective clothing and, as this work can be dangerous you must be aware of your own and others' safety. Horses can kick and bite.

You can expect to work 24/7 especially if you live-in including some holidays and weekends.

Future prospects

Groom/stable hand

With experience it is possible to specialise. Competition grooms (show-jumping, dressage and eventing) are in demand. Gaining your HGV driving licence can increase opportunities. Most grooms progress to more successful yards that compete internationally or keep more expensive and quality horses.

Stud hand

Interest in breeding quality British horses and ponies has increased due to European competition. Stud work is therefore rising in importance and those with skills are in demand.

Qualifications and courses

Groom/stable hand

Full-time courses include BTEC National Diploma in Horse Care or Equine Studies and NVQ in Equine Studies; NVQ/SVQ Levels 1–3 in Horse Care and Horse Care Management, the British Horse Society (BHS) stage 1–4 exams; and the Association of British Riding Schools (ABRS) certificates and diplomas. A driving licence is useful.

Stud hand

There are no formal entry requirements. Some knowledge of stable work and horse care is expected. Candidates under the age of 19 may enter as a trainee stud hand and work towards an NVQ Level 2. Training is free and starts with a residential course at a Centre, then continues in the workplace. Some people choose to enter as a working pupil; this option is especially popular within competition yards.

ENTRY LEVEL 1

Advantages/disadvantages

You really need to be a horse lover. If you are you will put up with the disadvantages!

Pay can be low and stables can be in remote locations.

Injury risks are high in all horse activities and this could affect your long-term career security.

Looking after horses is not a 9am–5pm job.

Money guide

The horse industry has a reputation for low salaries and long hours. As a starting salary you can expect to be on the minimum wage up to around £10,500 per year. This can rise to between £15,000 and £16,000 for the most experienced. As head groom you can expect £20,000 or more. If you live-in, free or supplemented board and lodging is common.

Related opportunities

- Farrier p266
- Race Horse Trainer p278

Further information

British Horse Society
Stoneleigh Deer Park, Kenilworth CV8 2XZ
0844 848 1666; www.bhs.org.uk

City& Guilds

www.cityandguilds.com/myperfectjob

GROUNDSPERSON/ GREENKEEPER

What the work involves

- Your main role will be to prepare and maintain the grounds used for different sports. Although you might work on synthetic surfaces for games like hockey, most of the time you will be working with grass.

- You will cut, treat, weed and prepare the surface before each game, match or event.

- You will be responsible for outlining the playing areas with tape or marking compound, ensuring that they adhere to the regulations by the appropriate sport governing body.

- You will put up posts, nets and other equipment where needed.

The type of person suited to this work

You need specialist horticultural knowledge, combined with an understanding of the different sports and what the competitors of each sport need.

You will also need lots of stamina to do a range of other jobs from putting up nets, to applying fertilisers.

Working conditions

You will have to work flexible hours including evenings and weekends. You will need to be active with a strong eye for detail. If you suffer from pollen allergies this work might be difficult.

You will spend a lot of your time outdoors, working in all weathers, although when repairing and maintaining the equipment you will probably be in a workshop. You will need to wear protective clothing.

Future prospects

The range of potential places for you to work is increasing and demand for staff is growing. You could work in a professional sports club, local authority education or sports and leisure department, hotel, university or college.

With additional qualifications and experience you could apply for promotion to supervisor or team leader, head groundsperson and then an area manager. Bigger companies offer greater promotion opportunities.

It is possible to progress into a position in leisure management or estate management.

Advantages/disadvantages

This job offers the opportunity for your work to be seen by thousands of people!

It offers non-sportspeople a chance to get involved with sport.

Money guide

A trainee groundsperson will start at around £10,000 per year. Once qualified, this rises to £14,000. With

Qualifications and courses

There are no set qualifications required for this role and training generally takes place on the job. However, relevant courses include the Diploma in Environmental and Land-based Studies, the Level 2 National Certificate in Sports and Amenity Horticulture, the Level 3 Advanced National Certificate in Sports and Amenity Turf Management, or BTEC National Awards, Certificates and Diplomas in Horticulture. An Apprenticeship in Amenity Horticulture is also available. You could also undertake Level 2 and 3 work-based Diplomas in Amenity Horticulture or a Level 4 NVQ in Sports Turf Management.

Foundation degrees in sports turf and golf course management are available. Entry requirements for degrees in sports turf science and management are 2 A levels/3 H grades and 5 GCSEs/S grades, including English and maths (A*–C).

The Institute of Groundsmanship offers three levels of courses covering practical greenkeeping, scientific principles of groundsmanship, and grounds management.

The British and International Golf Greenkeepers Association offers various training courses, including a Master Greenkeeper Certificate Scheme which acknowledges qualifications and expertise in golf course management.

experience this can increase to £18,336–£22,400. Senior staff can expect £32,000+. Staff responsible for major sporting venues can receive higher salaries. Employers could also offer accommodation on-site or bonuses for overtime.

Related opportunities

- Gardener/Garden Designer p270
- Horticultural/Garden Centre Worker/Manager p273
- Lifeguard p390
- Forest Worker/Officer p268

Further information

Institute of Groundsmanship
28 Stratford Office Village, Walker Avenue,
Wolverton Mill East, Milton Keynes MK12 5TW
01908 312511; www.iog.org

British International Golf Greenkeepers Association
BIGGA House, Alne, York YO61 1UF
01347 833800; www.bigga.org.uk

City&
Guilds

www.cityandguilds.com/myperfectjob

HORTICULTURAL/ GARDEN CENTRE WORKER/MANAGER

What the work involves

Horticultural worker

- You will look after the plants, check for disease, feed, water, prune and spray them.

- To produce new stock, you will plant out cuttings and seedlings. You will also pot-up and pack plants.

Horticultural manager

- As manager you will supervise, train and recruit staff and look after the day-to-day running of the organisation.

- You will decide which plants to grow, manage the budgets and ensure deliveries are despatched on time.

Garden centre worker/manager

- You will maintain display areas and give customers advice.

- You will look after the stock, water and feed the plants, ensure public spaces are safe, unload deliveries and spend time on the tills.

The type of person suited to this work

Much of your day will involve carrying, bending and working with the plants, so you will need to be physically fit.

You will be outdoors for much of the time working in all weathers, doing dirty work. These jobs could be difficult if you suffer from pollen or dust allergies.

Working conditions

You will often have to work weekends and late evenings.

Horticultural worker/manager

You will generally do a 40-hour Monday–Friday week, with additional hours at busy times.

Garden centre worker/manager

You will spend time outdoors, in all weathers. You could spend some time indoors in the sales area.

Future prospects

There is a constant demand for workers, especially for those with experience. Horticultural jobs are available within major plant producers, national parks, public gardens and local and national garden shops/nurseries. After gaining experience and qualifications you could progress to a role as supervisor, manager or buyer for garden centres, work as a freelancer or start up your own shop.

Advantages/disadvantages

There is a good mix of practical and managerial work.

These jobs combine lots of skills and can be very rewarding.

This is an expanding market with lots of opportunities.

Qualifications and courses

Horticultural worker

There are no formal entry requirements for horticultural work, but certain employers look for GCSEs/S grades (A*–C/1–3) including science, or a BTEC First Diploma in Horticulture. There are a number of vocational qualifications that could be useful, including qualifications in horticulture from the Royal Horticultural Society at Levels 1–3. There are also Foundation degrees and degrees in Horticulture. A Kew Diploma from the Royal Botanical Gardens can be obtained after 3 years. They also offer a 3-year Kew Apprenticeship.

Horticultural manager

In addition to those courses above you could gain: NVQs/SVQs in Management or Supervisory Management and an HND/BSc in Horticulture with Business Management. The Royal Botanical Gardens at Kew offer International Diploma courses in Botanic Garden Management.

Garden centre worker/manager

To work within a garden centre, qualifications in both horticulture and customer service are an advantage. NVQs/SVQs in Customer Service Levels 1–3 can be taken. It can be useful to have a Lantra Award Level 3 Diploma in Retail Knowledge (Garden Retail).

Money guide

Starting salaries are around £12,000–£15,000 per year. With experience this rises to around £18,000–£20,000.

Horticultural/garden centre manager

Starting salaries are around £16,000 per year rising to £21,000 for graduates. Qualified and experienced managers can earn between £22,000 and £40,000.

Related opportunities

- Arboricultural Worker/Tree Surgeon p259
- Gardener/Garden Designer p270

Further information

Institute of Horticulture
Capel Manor College, Bullsmoor Lane, Enfield EN1 4RQ
01992 707025; www.horticulture.org.uk

www.cityandguilds.com/myperfectjob

KENNEL WORKER

What the work involves

- There are lots of types of kennels including: boarding, pet sanctuary, breeding and quarantine kennels for animals brought from overseas.

- As well as cleaning the kennels, you will feed, exercise and check on the dogs' (and sometimes cats') health.

- You might need to complete some administration work including answering the phones, taking payments and keeping records when medicine is administered or if any behavioural problems are displayed.

- In a pet sanctuary you might be required to show prospective owners around and answer any questions they have on animal care.

The type of person suited to this work

You will need to enjoy spending time outdoors and not mind getting dirty. Some of the animals you will be working with might have behavioural problems or nervous dispositions and so you will need to be calm and patient.

You will require a good level of fitness as you will spend a large part of the day being active.

You should have strong communication skills and the ability to work well alone or as part of a team.

A good knowledge of small pet care is vital.

Working conditions

This is physically demanding work involving walking dogs and cleaning the kennels. You may work shifts and your hours will probably include evenings, weekends and public holidays.

Many animals will be frightened and confused so they could be aggressive, you will therefore have to be aware of your own and others' safety.

You will spend a lot of time outdoors in all weathers and the work can be smelly, dirty and noisy.

Future prospects

There are approximately 3,500 kennels, but with recent changes in quarantine laws numbers employed within this job have reduced. However, you could work for national charitable organisations such as the RSPCA, Guide Dogs for the Blind Association or a private breeder. The Army and Police recruit service and civilian kennel staff.

In a larger kennel there may be the opportunity to progress to the position of supervisor or manager.

Advantages/disadvantages

This is not a 9am–5pm job and the unusual hours may affect your social or family life.

There is the possibility of being attacked by an animal.

There is an opportunity to become self-employed by opening your own kennel.

Qualifications and courses

There are no formal educational requirements although some employers will favour candidates with GCSEs/S grades A*–C in English and/or maths. NVQ/SVQ Levels 1–3, BTEC National Qualifications in Animal Care and the City & Guilds Advanced National Certificate in Animal Care may be useful.

The Animal Care College also offers training programmes which may prove helpful. The Guide Dogs for the Blind Association can provide work experience for applicants aged over 18. They also require a full UK driving licence for all Puppy Walkers. Hearing Dogs for the Deaf also recruit volunteer puppy socialisers from people who have experience of looking after young dogs and have an approved home.

Apprenticeship/Skillseekers available for those aged 16–24.

Lantra have developed several Apprenticeship/Skillseekers schemes for those aged 16–24. Training takes place on the job and is given by the manager or an experienced staff member.

Money guide

Pay will depend on the nature of your employer, however most start at levels around £8,000. If you are working for a private kennels £12,000–£15,000 is likely. For animal charities and larger organisations you may get more. The RSPCA offers a minimum of £10,500 to its kennel workers (animal care assistants). You may be provided with accommodation and extra pay could be offered for overtime.

Related opportunities

- Animal Welfare Officer p258
- Dog Trainer/Handler p261
- Veterinary Nurse p282
- Zookeeper p285

Further information

Guide Dogs for the Blind Association
Burghfield Common, Reading RG7 3YG
0118 983 5555; www.guidedogs.org.uk

The Animal Care College
Ascot House, High Street, Ascot SL5 7HG
01344 636436; www.animalcarecollege.co.uk

www.cityandguilds.com/myperfectjob

LANDSCAPE ARCHITECT/ DESIGNER

What the work involves

- You will design or develop a new or existing outside space. You will then make a plan, saying what plantings should be included, and calculate the cost.

- You would then see the project through to completion by supervising the work on-site.

- Although you will understand garden design you will also have an understanding of civil engineering, horticulture and planning law.

- You could work on projects aimed to regenerate towns and cities and developments to help combat climate change.

The type of person suited to this work

You will have to enjoy being outdoors and want to make a difference to the environment. You will be interested in making, building and constructing hard landscaping but will appreciate and understand the impact that different plants can have. You should be physically strong and able to use machinery and hand tools. You must be creative, artistic and have strong computer skills. You will need to be happy in the open in both the summer and the winter and be prepared to spend time away from home on some jobs. You should have solid communication and negotiation skills.

Working conditions

Landscape architects spend a lot of time in the design studio sitting at a computer and drawing board or attending meetings on-site at clients' premises. You could spend about a quarter of your time at the project site, supervising operations. Some of your time will also be spent on the phone dealing with contractors and suppliers. Site work will involve being outdoors in all weather. Average hours are about 37 per week Monday to Friday. You may spend some time away from home.

Future prospects

Due to the impact of home improvement programmes, designing and developing gardens is now a popular and growing business. However, it can be a competitive area so many choose self-employment.

Organisations who recruit landscape staff include local authorities, botanical gardens, large private estates, the National Trust, English Heritage, building contractors and landscape design houses.

If you choose to become self-employed your success will depend upon finding customers, the quality of your work and how quickly you can build your reputation.

Advantages/disadvantages

There is a good mix of practical hands-on work with planning, design and meeting people.

You will get satisfaction from knowing your work will have an impact on future generations.

Qualifications and courses

ENTRY LEVEL 5

You will need a degree in landscape architecture or a degree in any subject with a relevant postgraduate qualification. In order to gain entry to a degree course you will usually need at least 2 A levels/ 3 H grades and 5 GCSEs/S grades (A*–C), or a diploma in an environmental and land-based subject. In order to gain access to a postgraduate course you will usually need to complete an honours degree in a relevant subject.

Entrants who have completed a course accredited by the Landscape Institute (LI) can work towards chartered membership of the LI through the Professional Practice Examination.

Courses are also available at land-based colleges of further education, who offer a range of BTEC National qualifications in relevant subjects.

You could get wet, cold, hot and dusty.

You will not be able to do this work if you suffer from pollen or dust allergies.

Money guide

Salaries vary depending on location and employer.

Starting salaries for assistants in local government are around £20,000 per year.

Salaries for the more experienced could range from £24,000 to £45,000 a year.

When working as a principal landscape architect in local government this figure could increase to about £38,500 per year.

If you work in private practice these figures could increase substantially.

Related opportunities

- Town Planner/Planning Technician p128
- Architect p71
- Ecologist p515
- Landscaper/Landscape Manager p276

Further information

Landscape Institute (LI)
PO Box 651, Redhill RH1 9AJ
020 7299 4500; www.landscapeinstitute.org

Landscape Design Trust (LDT)
Bank Chambers, 1 London Road, Redhill RH1 1LY
01737 779257; www.landscape.co.uk

City& Guilds

www.cityandguilds.com/myperfectjob

LANDSCAPER/ LANDSCAPE MANAGER

What the work involves

Landscaper

- You will do the practical work of turning a landscape architect's plan into the finished thing.

- You will operate machinery, carry out planting schemes, put up fences, create ponds, lay paths, construct decking and make terraces.

Landscape manager

- You will use your specialist knowledge to advise others on the development and maintenance of a wide range of landscapes such as historic gardens, motorway verges and public parks.

- Duties include deciding where to place features like footpaths and play areas, overseeing the people contracted to carry out work and completing reports and budget management.

The type of person suited to this work

You will have to enjoy being outdoors and want to make a difference to the environment. You will be interested in making, building and constructing hard landscaping but will appreciate and understand the impact that different plants can have. You will need to be physically strong and able to use machinery and hand tools.

An understanding of the laws surrounding the environment and the countryside is essential.

Working conditions

Landscaper

You will be outdoors in all weathers creating the design and working on landscape maintenance. There is a lot of physical labour involved such as heavy lifting, operating machinery and digging. You will need to wear protective clothing.

Landscape manager

You will work in an office for a lot of your time, but you will also go out for meetings to check and supervise work on-site. On average you will work 37 hours a week, though overtime may be required. You may need to spend time away from home.

Future prospects

The types of organisations who recruit landscape staff are local authorities, botanical gardens, large private estates, the National Trust, English Heritage, building contractors and landscape design houses.

Landscape Managers in government can follow a structured career path, in other organisations you may find yourself moving companies in order to progress. Self-employment is also an option.

Qualifications and courses

Landscaper

There are no required qualifications but relevant GCSEs, National Proficiency Tests Council (NPTC) Certificates, BTEC and RHS Certificates/Diplomas in Horticulture are useful. Apprenticeships and the Diploma in Environmental and Land Based Studies may be helpful.

A driving licence is often required.

Landscape manager

Although there are no set qualifications this is still an extremely competitive industry. A HNC/HND, degree or postgraduate qualification in a relevant subject such as garden design would prove valuable. The Landscape Institute has accredited some degree courses.

Advantages/disadvantages

You will get satisfaction from knowing your work will have an impact on future generations.

You could get wet, cold, hot and dusty.

You will not be able to do this work if you suffer from pollen or dust allergies.

Money guide

Landscaper

Starting rates are generally between £12,000 and £16,000 per year and range from £19,000 to £20,500 for those with experience. Senior landscapers with additional responsibilities can get up to £45,000.

Landscape manager

The starting salary would be around £20,000 and this can rise to between £24,000 and £38,500 with experience. Rates for those who are self-employed will depend on their personal success. Work may be seasonal.

Related opportunities

- Forest Worker/Officer p268
- Groundsperson/Greenkeeper p272
- Landscape Architect/Designer p275

Further information

Landscape Institute
33 Great Portland Street, London W1W 8QG
020 7299 4500; www.landscapeinstitute.org

www.cityandguilds.com/myperfectjob

PARKS OFFICER

What the work involves

- You will supervise the gardeners and horticulturists who maintain and look after local parks, sports and recreation centres, gardens and public places.

- As well as planning new planting schemes you will organise staffing rotas and plan annual work programmes.

- You will be responsible for the recruitment and monitoring of your team, as well as budget control.

- You will have to liaise with your employer, normally local government, and other department colleagues.

The type of person suited to this work

To do this work you must be organised, be able to plan ahead and manage people. You will need technical and practical horticultural skills, have an understanding of budgets and be an effective negotiator. You should have a good understanding of plants and how to present outside spaces so they look good all year round.

To do this job you will need to be physically fit and passionate about your work.

Working conditions

You will normally work for a local authority Monday–Friday, but at busier times, particularly in the spring and summer, you may do extra hours.

You will be provided with protective clothing and will have to ensure health and safety rules are followed by your teams. If you suffer from asthma, pollen allergies or some skin conditions this work might be difficult for you.

A small part of your job will be indoors at a computer in an office where you will spend time ordering plants and materials.

Future prospects

Most parks officers are employed by a local or county council. A small number are employed by companies who win park management contracts.

It is likely that you will start your career as a gardener or horticulturist and then progress to parks officer once you have gained sufficient experience. You may also move into department or divisional management within local/county authorities.

Advantages/disadvantages

This is a mixture of indoor and outdoor work, using a variety of skills.

You will use your experience and knowledge to make a difference in your community.

You might have to wait for opportunities to become available or be willing to move to progress.

Qualifications and courses

No formal qualifications are required for this work although 5 GCSEs/S grades (A*–E/1–5) will be helpful. The Diploma in Environmental and Land-based Studies could also be useful.

Many park officers begin as gardeners/horticulturists. NVQs/SVQs in Amenity Horticulture at Levels 1–2 are available and are useful qualifications to take at the early stages of your career.

Land-based colleges offer a range of horticulture qualifications which will be useful, including the Royal Horticultural Society (RHS) General Examination, City & Guilds Advanced National Certificate in Horticulture (ANCH), BTEC and SQA National qualifications.

Once you are employed as a parks officer, NVQs/SVQs in Amenity Horticulture and training skills are available at Levels 3–4.

Money guide

As a parks officer your earnings will depend on the size of your employing authority and the number of sites you are responsible for.

If you work for a local authority you will normally receive around £17,000–£18,000 per year. With experience you could earn up to £27,000. At senior level you could earn £40,000+.

Related opportunities

- Arboricultural Worker/Tree Surgeon p259
- Countryside Ranger p260
- Groundsperson/Greenkeeper p272
- Horticultural/Garden Centre Worker/Manager p273

Further information

Local Government Careers
www.lgcareers.com

Institute for Sport, Parks and Leisure
Abbey Business Centre, 1650 Arlington Business Park, Reading RG7 4SA
0844 418 0077; www.ispal.org.uk

Convention of Scottish Local Authorities
Roseberry House, 9 Haymarket Terrace, Edinburgh EH12 5XZ
0131 474 9200; www.cosla.gov.uk

City & Guilds

www.cityandguilds.com/myperfectjob

RACEHORSE TRAINER

What the work involves

■ Trainers usually own or lease their stables and train horses for owners as well as owning horses themselves. Most trainers start as jockeys or assistant trainers and progress to running their own yard.

■ You will have to ready the horses for races by increasing their stamina, technique and fitness. In order to do this you will have to create training regimes.

■ To be successful you will work closely with all of those in your team including other professionals such as vets and farriers.

The type of person suited to this work

You should have a strong interest in horse racing, a flair for business and an inherent talent for training horses. You will need the ability to communicate well and be a strong leader and manager of people.

You will have to love being around and caring for horses and have lots of patience and the right temperament to work with them.

You will need to enjoy working outside, in all weathers as this is where most of your duties will take place. You should be the kind of person who doesn't mind getting their hands dirty. You will require a certain level of fitness.

Working conditions

Much of your work will take place outdoors. In the summer months it may be hot, smelly and dusty, whereas in winter it could be cold, wet and muddy. You will also spend some time in an office environment. When riding you will wear a hard hat and a body protector. Horses can be unpredictable and so there is a certain level of risk involved. The hours are long and may include weekends. There will also be some travel involved if you are required to attend race meetings.

Future prospects

There are around 500 licensed trainers in the UK. Before you are granted a licence the Jockey Club expects several years' experience as an assistant trainer. Your success will then depend on attracting and retaining the owners of good quality horses, and lots of luck! You will need to build up a strong client base in order to progress. Owning your own successful yard may allow you to take on staff to complete some of the more mundane tasks.

Advantages/disadvantages

This can be an extremely lucrative profession.

Injury risks are high in all horse activities. This could affect your long-term career security.

Looking after horses is not a 9am–5pm job and the hours may affect your social or family life.

Qualifications and courses

Racehorse trainers need to be licensed with the Jockey Club. There are three types of licence: a Combined Jump and Flat Licence, a Jump Only Licence and a Flat Only Licence. All candidates for a trainer's licence must hold an NVQ Level 3 in Racehorse Care and Management and should attend three 1-week modules: Racehorse Management; Business Skills for Racehorse Trainers; and Staff Management.

Trainers must have spent at least 2 years in an assistant trainer position; previous experience in a racing yard or as a jockey is desirable. Some people choose to enter as a working pupil; this option is especially popular within competition yards.

Money guide

As you are likely to be self-employed your earnings will depend on the size and success of your yard.

As a guide, a trainer can earn anything from £15,000 per year to over £50,000 if they are very experienced and have a good record of winning.

You will decide on your own fees and these will be dependent on a variety of factors including costs and the market rates.

Related opportunities

■ Groom/Stable Hand/Stud Hand p271
■ Farm Manager p263
■ Farrier p266

Further information

Association of British Riding Schools
Queen's Chambers, 38–40 Queen Street, Penzance TR18 4BH
01736 369440; www.abrs-info.org

British Horse Society
Stoneleigh Deer Park, Kenilworth CV8 2XZ
0844 848 1666; www.bhs.org.uk

British Racing School
Snailwell Road, Newmarket CB8 7NU
01638 665103; www.brs.org.uk

City& Guilds

www.cityandguilds.com/myperfectjob

SKIPPER/ FISHERMAN/WOMAN

What the work involves

- You will spend anything from a few days to several weeks at sea.

- You will drop the nets, wind them in, sort the catch and then box it up. If your vessel has the facility you might help to process fish on board by gutting and filleting.

- You might keep watch, steer the ship and use winching gear. Duties may also include vessel maintenance and cooking.

- As a skipper you will be in charge of the vessel, including health and safety, navigation, paperwork, crew management and management of business arrangements.

The type of person suited to this work

This work is very practical, physically demanding and can involve being away from home for periods of time.

As you will be at sea in dangerous and treacherous conditions, experiencing all types of weather, you should be able to cope with whatever you come up against but remain positive and focused.

Working conditions

This is a very tough outdoor job. You will be out in the wind and the rain, summer and winter getting wet and cold.

Fishing is the most dangerous industry in the UK, with big machinery and rough seas producing a combination of risks which must be treated with great caution. You will have to work long hours at sea, often for substantial periods away from home and conditions below deck may be basic and cramped. There could also be some heavy lifting and carrying.

Future prospects

There are two job progression routes. The first is from deckhand to ship's mate and then skipper. The other is to begin as an engineer watch-keeper and progress to second engineer, then chief engineer.

Jobs are located around the coasts of Scotland, the south-west and eastern England. Many are part of family-owned businesses which have been in existence for generations, making it difficult to find work. Some are seasonal meaning long-term security can be difficult.

Advantages/disadvantages

You will spend a lot of time onboard your boat at sea working as part of a small team.

Due to periods at sea, your social and family life may be difficult. Jobs are limited to certain locations in the UK.

Qualifications and courses

ENTRY LEVEL 2

New entrants must take the Marine Coastguard Agency approved basic Safety Training course. This programme consists of four 1-day courses in sea survival, first aid, fire fighting and basic health and safety.

Most people enter through one of 15 Catching Sector Group Training Associations (GTAs) in the UK. The Seafish Industry Training Division also provides new entrant training programmes. Apprenticeships/Skillseekers opportunities might be available for those aged 16–24.

Skippers have to take the Marine Coastguard Agency certificates which cover different levels of competence, before they can take charge of a fishing vessel.

Open Learning Modules are available allowing fishermen, from deckhands to skippers, to develop their skills and knowledge on board rather than in the classroom.

Money guide

Earnings from fishing can be very variable, as pay often includes a share of the profit, which often depends on weather conditions. New entrants can expect to receive around £10,000 per year as a starting salary. With experience this can rise to up to £25,000.

Skippers are generally self-employed so their earnings will depend on the success of their team and good weather. Some very experienced skippers can earn between £40,000 and £100,000 a year.

Related opportunities

- Coastguard p542
- Fish Farmer p267
- Merchant Navy Deck Officer/Rating p610

Further information

Maritime and Coastguard Agency
Seafarer Training and Certification Branch, Spring Place, 105 Commercial Road, Southampton SO15 1EG
023 8032 9231; www.mcga.gov.uk

Scottish Fishermen's Federation
24 Rubislaw Terrace, Aberdeen AB10 1XE
01224 646944; www.sff.co.uk

City& Guilds

www.cityandguilds.com/myperfectjob

CRCI: HA   Environment, Animals and Plants

STOCKMAN/STOCKWOMAN

What the work involves

- You will undertake the practical duties on a farm, caring for livestock, such as pigs, poultry, cattle and/or sheep, and possibly crops as well.

- You will be required to keep track of animals' breeding cycle in order to know when mating or artificial insemination should take place. You will also be responsible for caring for the animals through pregnancy and the birthing process.

- You may also complete general tasks such as farm maintenance.

The type of person suited to this work

You must enjoy being outdoors in the countryside, working in all weathers. As you will be caring for animals you should have an interest in the environment. If you are allergic to pollen or animals this work will be very difficult for you.

You will have to be fit and active, able to be on your feet all day and prepared to work very long hours, especially during the summer months. If your animals become ill, you will have to be prepared to be with them and administer drugs when needed.

Working conditions

This job involves a lot of time outdoors; you will be out in the wind and the rain, summer and winter. Farming is not a 9am–5pm job and is very physical work; you may be expected to work weekends, evenings and public holidays as animals need constant care. You can expect to work around 39 hours a week and at particular times of the year this may increase. A lot of the work you will be doing is smelly and dirty. Animals can be unpredictable and at times dangerous.

Future prospects

The main concentration of livestock farming is in the west of the UK. Experienced stockmen/stockwomen with training can become supervisors or unit managers without having to buy their own farms. However opportunities are scarce and promotion unlikely unless you work on a very large farm. In order to progress you can complete diplomas or degree courses. There is the opportunity to set up your own business as a farmer or farm contractor.

There are opportunities for stockmen/stockwomen to work abroad.

Advantages/disadvantages

You will spend a lot of time in the open air caring for living things.

At some times of the year your social life may be restricted.

You will usually be given free accommodation or subsidised rent.

Your future can depend on things outside of your control such as bird flu or foot and mouth disease.

Qualifications and courses

ENTRY 1 LEVEL

Formal qualifications are not normally needed but relevant work experience is useful. It might be a good idea to do some casual work at weekends and evenings while still at school. Apprenticeships/Skillseekers may be available for those aged 16–24. The pay for these apprenticeships will vary depending on location and employer.

Qualifications in agriculture could be useful. Qualifications for livestock farming include a BTEC National Certificate or Diploma in Agriculture (Livestock) and Animal Management (Care), BTEC National Awards in Agricultural Production, NVQs at Level 1 in Agriculture, Levels 2 and 3 in Livestock Production and Levels 1 to 3 in Animal Care, SQA National Course in Livestock Production and the National Proficiency Test Council (NPTC) National and Advanced National Certificate in Agriculture.

Money guide

These figures will vary depending on location and employer.

A stockman/stockwoman in their first year should earn at least £6,976 increasing to £13,730 with qualifications and experience. Once fully qualified and with extra supervisory responsibilities this may increase to over £20,000.

Some jobs include accommodation with subsidised rent and the possibility of overtime. The accommodation is generally an estate house or farm cottage.

Related opportunities

- Farmhand p264
- Gamekeeper p269
- Zookeeper p285

Further information

Lantra
Lantra House, Stoneleigh Park, Coventry CV8 2LG
0845 707 8007; www.lantra.co.uk

Department for Environment, Food and Rural Affairs
Nobel House, 17 Smith Square, London SW1P 3JR
08459 335577; www.defra.gov.uk

National Federation of Young Farmers' Clubs
YFC Centre, 10th Street, Stoneleigh Park,
Coventry CV8 2LG
024 7685 7200; www.nfyfc.org.uk

City& Guilds

TAXIDERMIST

What the work involves

- As a taxidermist you would make lifelike representations of animals, birds and fishes using the skin of a dead creature.

- You could spend time observing the animal in its natural environment taking photographs or drawing them.

- You would remove the skin of the animal to preserve it, while keeping as much of the original colour and texture as possible.

- The body of the animal is then modelled by using a range of rather sculptural techniques, sewing and gluing pieces into place and then stretching the finished skin over the model.

The type of person suited to this work

This is very time-consuming work, which requires an understanding and appreciation of wildlife. You will have to be good with your hands, be patient and have an eye for colour and detail.

You will have good observation skills, but you will not be able to be squeamish as it can involve working on animals that have been in accidents. This can be lonely work, so you will need to like your own company.

Working conditions

You could work in your own home, within the conservation department of a museum or at a workshop. Working from home means that you can set your own hours; however, if you choose to work for an employer you will probably do 37 hours, Monday–Friday.

You will use different hand tools and materials, from real animal products such as teeth and claws, to man-made products.

Future prospects

There are very few opportunities for professional taxidermists as this is a very small profession. Many people do this as a hobby rather than for employment.

You could work for a national or local museum or a national taxidermy company. If you work within a museum you might also do other conservation work with biological specimens. It is likely that you would have to move into managerial jobs to get promotion.

In recent years there has been a slight growth as opportunities abroad – particularly in the USA and Africa – have become available.

Advantages/disadvantages

This combines using your artistic and practical ability with your understanding of animal anatomy.

Qualifications and courses

ENTRY LEVEL 2

There are no set qualifications for this work, but at least 3 GCSEs/S grades A*–C/1–3 including English, maths, art, biology and/or a technical subject or equivalent are normally needed for entry to a junior museum post in taxidermy.

Lengthy on-the-job training, by watching an experienced taxidermist, is required. Some commercial taxidermy firms may offer apprenticeships which are generally over 3–5 years.

Courses in subjects such as animal anatomy, biology, natural sciences or specimen conservation would prove useful for this work, as would good knowledge of wildlife.

If you want to be a professional taxidermist you need to register with the Department for the Environment, Food and Rural Affairs (DEFRA) and follow their strict guidelines for the collection of specimens.

The Guild of Taxidermists runs seminars and demonstrations suitable for those with some taxidermy experience. Independent taxidermists also occasionally offer short and residential courses for varying fees.

The general public can learn a lot about species by looking at your work, which is satisfying.

If you suffer from allergies or are squeamish, it could be difficult working with animal skins.

Money guide

Those who are self-employed can expect a low income that may need to be supplemented with additional part-time work. As a trainee you could expect to get around £12,000 per year. If you are employed by a museum, earnings are generally between £16,000 and £28,000. Higher salaries around £50,000 are available for senior managers.

Related opportunities

- Archaeologist p345
- Embalmer p467

Further information

Guild of Taxidermists
c/o Lancashire County Museum, Stanley Street,
Preston PR1 4YP
www.taxidermy.org.uk

Department for Environment, Food and Rural Affairs
Eastbury House, 30–34 Albert Embankment,
London SE1 7TL
0845 933 5577; www.defra.gov.uk

Environment, Animals and Plants

CRCI: HE

VETERINARY NURSE

What the work involves

- Veterinary nurses assist vets in their work by helping to treat animals suffering from disease and injury.

- As well as carrying out simple treatments such as dressings and nail trimming, you will examine blood and urine samples, give injections, prepare and help in the theatre and sterilise the instruments after use.

- You might also work in reception giving an initial assessment of animals, ordering drugs and arranging future appointments.

- Most nurses also undertake the day-to-day care of animals recovering from treatment within veterinary hospitals.

The type of person suited to this work

You will have to be passionate about animals and want to help them. To do this, you will need to learn about different diseases and treatment. Although lots of animals get better, some of this work will be distressing. This means you will have to work in a practical and unsentimental way.

As much of your work will also involve working with the animals' owners, you will need to be sympathetic and have excellent communication skills to explain what is happening.

If you do not like the sight of blood, or suffer from an animal-based allergy, this job will be difficult for you.

Working conditions

Although there are still lots of general practices that deal with small animals (dogs, cats, rabbits, etc), many more are becoming specialist centres as animal hospitals or large animal practices (cows, horses, sheep), and some are working with just horses or zoo animals. Your working conditions will depend on the type of practice you work in.

Future prospects

You could be employed by zoos, wildlife centres, animal welfare centres, veterinary hospitals and charities such as the People's Dispensary for Sick Animals (PDSA).

With experience you could progress to become a supervisor, practice manager or head nurse, or move into related areas such as research. You could also lecture, specialise in an area such as animal behaviour or become a veterinary drugs company representative.

Advantages/disadvantages

You will get to help sick animals which will rely on you for their care.

It is an interesting job with lots of variety.

It can be stressful and distressing.

You may have to work irregular hours which will affect your social life.

Qualifications and courses

ENTRY LEVEL 2

You can follow a Veterinary Nursing training scheme recognised by the Royal College of Veterinary Surgeons (RCVS). This is available as an Apprenticeship if you are aged 16–24.

The scheme lasts 2 years, and consists of practical training and attendance at college. It leads to NVQs at Levels 2 and 3 and, following 2 years' approved employment, the RCVS Certificate of Veterinary Nursing.

Entry requirements are 5 GCSEs (A*–C) including English language, maths and a science. Trainees must be at least 16 years old. There is strong competition for a place on this scheme. For those without these qualifications, an alternative route may be through the BTEC National Diploma in Animal Management and Basic Skills at Level 2 in Application of Number or the ABC Certificate for Animal Nursing Assistants and Key Skills in Application of Number and Communication at Level 2.

You can do a 3- or 4-year degree course in Veterinary Nursing, which includes the full RCVS training. A level biology is normally required. Equivalent qualifications such as the National Diploma in Science may also be accepted.

Work experience with a veterinary practice or an animal charity would be helpful.

Money guide

New entrants can expect to earn about £12,000 per year.

With experience this rises to around £14,000–£20,000.

Head nurses or supervisors generally earn £25,000 or more, depending on the size and type of their practice.

Related opportunities

- Animal Welfare Officer p258
- Dog Trainer/Handler p261
- Veterinary Surgeon p283
- Zookeeper p285

Further information

British Veterinary Nursing Association
Suite 11, Shenval House, South Road, Harlow CM20 2BD
01279 408644; www.bvna.org.uk

www.cityandguilds.com/myperfectjob

VETERINARY SURGEON

What the work involves

- A vet treats animals that are suffering because of disease or injury. They administer vaccinations, prescribe drugs and deliver newborn animals. They also advise owners on caring for their animals.

- You might carry out surgical operations and be involved in the inspection of livestock and meat.

- Some vets work in local practices and others become specialists carrying out complex surgery on a certain part of the anatomy or become an expert for a particular animal.

The type of person suited to this work

You will need to be able to learn large amounts of complex scientific information and apply it to treating animals.

Some of your work will be sad or distressing, so you will have to work in a practical and unsentimental way. You must have good communication skills to talk to the owners.

Working with large animals is physically demanding work, so you will need to be fit. If you dislike the sight of blood or suffer from animal allergies, this job will not suit you.

Working conditions

Your working conditions will depend on the type of practice that employs you. In small-animal practice you will spend a lot of time in the surgery. Working with farm livestock and horses, you will be out on the road visiting your patients. Some of this work will be unpleasant or smelly and involve travelling long distances to get to the animals. Some of your work may be dangerous as animals can be unpredictable. You will work long hours and be on call to cover emergencies.

Future prospects

There are around 20,000 registered vets in the UK. The majority of these work in private practice.

Once you are qualified, finding a first job is not too difficult. You will normally join an established practice and would hope eventually to become a partner (effectively part-owner) of a practice. This would probably involve buying your way in.

Some vets work for the government or for firms researching and producing animal pharmaceuticals.

Advantages/disadvantages

The training is long and very competitive to enter.

It can be a very stressful but rewarding job, with lots of responsibility.

In this career you will never stop learning – more experience will make you a better vet.

You will have to deal with the death of some of the animals you treat, including times when you put them down.

Qualifications and courses

Vets must obtain a degree in veterinary science/veterinary medicine approved by the Royal College of Veterinary Surgeons (RCVS). Normal minimum entry requirements are 3 A levels/4 H grades including chemistry and 1 or 2 from biology, physics and maths. A good range of GCSE/S grades (A*–C/1–3) are required.

Degree courses usually last 5 years but courses may include an optional additional year in which students gain an Honours degree in a related science subject. All courses include the 38 weeks of practical experience required by RCVS.

Before being able to work as a veterinary surgeon, you must register with the Royal College of Veterinary Surgeons (RCVS).

Money guide

Salaries are dependent on the type of practice you work in and its location. The figures below are a rough guide.

Newly qualified vets earn around £31,000 per year. This might also include a car and free accommodation.

With 5–10 years' experience, this rises to £40,800+ (including rewards).

A senior partner can expect to earn up to £100,000.

Related opportunities

- Animal Behaviourist p256
- Hospital Doctor p311
- Farm Manager p263
- Veterinary Nurse p282

Further information

Royal College of Veterinary Surgeons
Belgravia House, 62–64 Horseferry Road,
London SW1P 2AF
020 7222 2001; www.rcvs.org.uk

British Veterinary Association
7 Mansfield Street, London W1G 9NQ
020 7636 6541; www.bva.co.uk

www.cityandguilds.com/myperfectjob

Environment, Animals and Plants

CRCI: HC

WATER BAILIFF/KEEPER

What the work involves

- Water bailiffs work outdoors, maintaining lakes or rivers and everything that lives in them, for the purpose of legitimate recreational use.

- You'll confront two main problems in your work; breaches of the law and ecological problems.

- You will basically be a gamekeeper for water. Water bailiffs have the same powers of search and arrest as police officers. You would mostly be looking out for poachers and lawbreakers, and you'll be granted a warrant by the Environment Agency.

The type of person suited to this work

Ideally, you should be a friendly yet firm person, able to deal with members of the public effectively and politely, sometimes in difficult disciplinary situations.

An interest in the environment and working outdoors is really useful, as is knowledge of waterways. You need to be aware of the main environmental threats, and understand the basics of how ecosystems maintain themselves, and know about fish diseases and biology.

You also need to know about fishery law, not only in the UK (although this is most useful), but also at EU level. Be aware that it may even be different at local level, for example if you live in Scotland.

Working conditions

You will spend the majority of your time outside, patrolling areas either in a car, by boat or on foot.

You will usually work 37–39 hours per week, which will involve night shifts and weekends. Part time or seasonal work is also available.

The work is physical and tiring. You may have to pursue offenders across rough terrain on foot, and could find yourself wading through cold rivers and ponds. For this reason, you will probably spend your days in waterproofs, wellies, and even lifejackets.

Future prospects

Once you're working for the Environment Agency, many possibilities arise. You will have the opportunity to become a team leader within the agency, and this may lead to promotion and managerial opportunities.

Another option would be to move into related areas of work, such as fish farming or gamekeeping. Once you have a little experience in the area it will be possible to choose what interests you most, and in which direction you want your career to progress.

Advantages/disadvantages

This can be a really satisfying and exciting job, and if you're the kind of person who loves being outside and finds the idea of

Qualifications and courses

In England and Wales, there are no set requirements for those wishing to become water bailiffs. In Scotland, there is a training module that you need to pass, set by the Institute of Fisheries Management. In Northern Ireland, you need at least 5 GCSEs at C grade or above, and these have to include English and Maths.

Medical examinations usually need to be passed, and many people work their way into the industry by working unpaid for angling clubs to begin with.

This is a popular second career, and if you want to get into the field then any experience you can gain in gamekeeping, security work, police work, or farm work will be advantageous.

The Scottish IFM offers a course in Fisheries Management. You can choose between a 1-year certificate or a 2-year diploma, covering all aspects of working with fish and pondlife. You can also follow an NVQ in Fisheries Management if you choose to do so.

a desk job a nightmare, you'll probably thoroughly enjoy it. It's good if you like your own company, and that of the great outdoors.

It can be lonely, and conditions can be hard if you're not naturally a country person. You need to be prepared for all weather conditions, and work can be cold, wet, and tiring.

Money guide

Salaries vary, and can range from around £14,500 to £25,000 upwards per year.

Related opportunities

- Countryside Ranger p260
- Forest Worker/Officer p268
- Fish Farmer p267
- Gamekeeper p269

Further information

Environment Agency
Rio House, Waterside Drive, Aztec West, Almondsbury, Bristol BS32 4UD
08708 506506; www.environment-agency.gov.uk

Institute of Fisheries Management
22 Rushworth Avenue, West Bridgford, Nottingham NG2 7LF
0115 982 2317; www.ifm.org.uk

City&
Guilds

www.cityandguilds.com/myperfectjob

ZOOKEEPER

What the work involves

- You could work in a zoo, safari, wildlife or birdlife park or aquarium where you will care for animals ranging from mammals, birds, reptiles, amphibians and fish to invertebrates.

- You will provide food, water and fresh bedding for the animals in your care. You will clean out their enclosures and check for signs of injury or disease.

- Many zoos stress the importance of conservation and education and some of your work may involve leading tours and giving presentations to visitors.

- You will keep records of animals' feeding, health and behaviour and keep an eye out for their safety.

The type of person suited to this work

You need to be patient, observant and like handling and being around animals. Some of this work is physically demanding so you will have to be active. Some animals you will work with could be dangerous, so you will have to respect them and be aware of your own and others' safety.

Working conditions

Animals require 24/7 care, you will work 5–6 days a week, normally on a shift system including early mornings, late evenings, weekends and bank holidays, especially during busy periods.

Your work will be physically demanding and often dirty. A uniform will be provided. If you suffer from allergies, this work will be difficult for you.

Some centres close for parts of the year which means your work could be seasonal.

Future prospects

There are 350 zoos and animal parks throughout the UK employing around 3000 people full time. Expect to move for work or promotion. You may choose to specialise and work with one species. You could also be promoted to senior keeper or head keeper.

You may also choose to move into related work such as becoming an RSPCA inspector.

Advantages/disadvantages

This can be difficult work to enter and progress in.

The financial rewards can be small.

You will be working with the most unusual or exotic animals.

The role of zoos as centres of breeding and supporting conservation has increased recently, so you could undertake important work.

Money guide

Pay will depend on your location and type of animal park.

Qualifications and courses

No specific qualifications are required although GCSEs/S grades (A*–C/1–3), especially in English and science subjects, will be useful.

However, it is becoming increasingly necessary to gain qualifications as this is a very competitive area.

General animal care and management courses available include the City & Guilds Level 2 National Certificate in Animal Care, Advanced National Certificate in the Management of Zoo Animals and Advanced National Diploma in Animal Management at Level 3.

Alternatively you could take BTEC Awards, Certificates and Diplomas at Level 3 in Animal Management or ABC Awards and Diplomas in Work-based Animal Care at Levels 1 to 3.

Foundation degrees or BSc Honours degrees in subjects like zoology are also available. Sparsholt College in Hampshire offers a Foundation degree in Zoo Resource Management for people in relevant employment.

Apprenticeships may be available if you are aged 16–24. Previous experience of zoo work is highly recommended, through a volunteer programme or holiday job.

Many jobs include free or subsidised accommodation. Trainees can start at about £10,000–£13,000 per year. With experience, this can rise to £17,000. Senior keepers earn around £17,000–£30,000 a year.

Related opportunities

- Animal Welfare Officer p258
- Dog Trainer/Handler p261
- Veterinary Nurse p282
- Veterinary Surgeon p283

Further information

Association of British Wild Animal Keepers
Chessington Zoo, Leatherhead Road,
Chessington KT9 2NE
01372 731555; www.abwak.co.uk

British and Irish Association of Zoos and Aquariums
Regents Park, London NW1 4RY
020 7449 6351; www.biaza.org.uk

City&
Guilds

www.cityandguilds.com/myperfectjob

ENTRY LEVEL 2

CRCI: HC   Environment, Animals and Plants

Healthcare

If you are keen to pursue a career in healthcare you must be compassionate and enjoy either caring for people or deciding what treatment they should receive. There is such a wide variety of jobs available in this sector simply because you can specialise in absolutely any aspect of human healthcare. Many jobs require a lot of training and you can expect to work in some highly pressurised and sometimes distressing situations. Workers in healthcare are extremely dedicated and enthusiastic about their careers, which rarely constitute a 9am–5pm job.

We look at the following jobs in this section:

For similar jobs to the ones in this section turn to *Science, Mathematics and Statistics* on page 503 and *Social Care and Counselling Services* on page 567.

ACUPUNCTURIST

What the work involves

- Acupuncturists work from ancient Chinese holistic guidelines. They treat medical illnesses and imbalances of energy by inserting very fine needles into identified pressure points on the human body.

- You will need to talk to patients about their problems, taking plenty of notes, in order to explore their lifestyle and emotional state, and then assess all of these factors to determine a suitable treatment.

- In addition you may carry out procedures such as burning herbs on needles, and passing small electric currents through them.

The type of person suited to this work

You must be very personable, with excellent communication skills in order to elicit trust and personal information from your patients, as well as being able to explain the techniques you are using to them.

Being comfortable with close and physical contact is also important when examining and treating your patients.

You will need an analytical mind in order to understand each patient's problem and formulate a beneficial course of treatment.

As you will probably be running your own business, you will need excellent business acumen in order to successfully take on aspects such as marketing, accounting, and administrative tasks.

Working conditions

Hours vary and tend to fit around the needs of clients. This usually involves evening and weekend work.

You could work from your own rented treatment room, from home, in your patients' homes, or in hospices, health clinics and addiction treatment centres. As you may work across a number of locations, a driving licence is really useful.

You'll usually be working on your feet, standing and bending a lot.

Conditions have to be clean and sterile, and there are strict health and safety guidelines to adhere to.

Future prospects

If you are self-employed, the success of your career depends on your reputation and marketing skills. If you build up a strong client base there are plenty of opportunities for expansion and even setting up your own health clinic.

Many practising acupuncturists choose to teach their subject, or carry out research and write articles for books and magazines.

You could work abroad, although qualifications for practice vary from country to country.

Qualifications and courses

Careers in acupuncture usually begin with an accredited training course, and this can vary from a 3 year part-time course to full-time degree that can last up to 4 years. You will need at least 5 GCSEs and 2 or 3 A levels. Science subjects are useful. Successful completion of a course leads to professional membership of the British Acupuncture Council.

Courses vary, but generally cover topics such as anatomy and physiology, techniques and acupuncture points, ethical issues, clinical experience, and advice on setting up a practice. Some courses are even available at postgraduate and doctorate levels.

Advantages/disadvantages

This can be a really rewarding career, especially if you like being with people and enjoy helping them.

You may hear distressing stories and have insight into some upsetting personal lives, so need to be able to leave work at work.

Money guide

Earnings in acupuncture depend a lot on your situation, marketing ability, and experience.

As a newly-qualified acupuncturist starting up your own practice, you'll probably earn around £12,500 per year.

Once you've started to build up clients and gain experience, you can expect something like £18,000–£30,000 a year.

If you grow your business into a large established practice, your earnings may rise to about £40,000 a year.

Related opportunities

- Chiropractor p295
- Counsellor p571
- Homeopath p310

Further information

The Acupuncture Society
27 Cavendish Drive, Edgware HA8 7NR
0773 4668 402; www.acupuncturesociety.org.uk

The British Acupuncture Accreditation Board
63 Jeddo Road, London W12 9HQ
020 8735 0466; www.baab.co.uk

British Acupuncture Council
63 Jeddo Road, London W12 9HQ
020 8735 0400; www.acupuncture.org.uk

ADULT NURSE

What the work involves

- Adult nurses assess the needs of each patient in order to plan a care programme for them.

- You will observe how they progress on this treatment plan, and modify it as necessary as they improve or otherwise.

- You will also give patients practical care such as administering medicines and injections, changing dressings, and checking blood pressure.

- You could work in a variety of positions, including a community or occupational nurse, or as a healthcare assistant.

The type of person suited to this work

You will be working with patients from all sectors of the community who will have a wide range of problems, so it is essential to remain non-judgemental and sympathetic.

You will need excellent communication skills in order to interact with patients, explaining care plans and illnesses, and also calming those who are angry or distressed.

You will also need to be very practical, with good manual dexterity for undertaking precision jobs such as taking blood, and also helping patients with everyday things like washing and cooking.

Working conditions

You will usually work 37.5 hours per week, although overtime hours are available. If you are working in a hospital, these hours will encompass night and weekend shifts.

You could work in a number of locations, including hospitals, GP surgeries, prisons, hospices and in patients' homes. If you are required to travel around in the local community on a daily basis, a driving licence may be useful. Adult nurses in hospitals work in specific wards, such as intensive care or accident and emergency.

Future prospects

There is currently a shortage of trained adult nurses, so employment prospects are very good.

The majority of job opportunities lie within the NHS, although other employers include private hospitals, the armed forces, hospices and nursing homes, and the prison service.

With experience and additional qualifications, you could specialise in a subject of interest to you such as neurology or cardiology, and go on to become a nurse consultant.

UK nursing qualifications are recognised across the globe, so there are also opportunities to work abroad.

Advantages/disadvantages

Working with a wide range of people, helping them to get better or become more independent, is both rewarding and enjoyable.

Qualifications and courses

All nurses must hold a degree or diploma in nursing that has been recognised by the Nursing and Midwifery Council. Degree courses usually require at least 3 A levels or equivalent, alongside 5 GCSEs/S grades (A*–C/1–3) including English, maths and a science subject. Entry for a diploma is slightly lower at just 5 good GCSEs or equivalent. If you do not have any formal qualifications, Access courses are available in health and social care, and these will give you the experience and qualifications necessary to apply for a degree or diploma course.

Graduates with a relevant degree in biology or another health-related subject may apply for an accelerated programme, which on average lasts about 2 years.

It is also possible to join a nurse cadet Apprenticeship if you are aged between 16 and 19. These usually last 2 years and will provide you with an NVQ Level 3 or Access course pass. Continuing Professional Development (CPD) is vital for nurses to keep their skills and knowledge up to date.

There are opportunities to work flexible hours or part time. Career breaks are common and the NHS runs specialist courses to get nurses who have had a break back up to speed quickly.

You may have to deal with distressed, angry or violent patients.

Money guide

As a newly qualified nurse, you can expect to earn around £17,700. With experience and additional responsibility, such as becoming a sister or charge nurse, your salary can increase to between £24,800 and £29,000.

If you specialise in a particular area and undertake the training to become a nurse consultant, you could earn up to £65,000.

Related opportunities

- Learning Disabilities Nurse p314
- Mental Health Nurse p317
- Health Visitor p309
- Hospital Doctor p311

Further information

The Nursing and Midwifery Council
23 Portland Place, London W1B 1PZ
020 7333 9333; www.nmc-uk.org

Royal College of Nursing
20 Cavendish Square, London W1G 0RN
020 7409 3333; www.rcn.org.uk

NHS Careers
PO Box 2311, Bristol BS2 2ZX
0345 606 0655; www.nhscareers.nhs.uk

CRCI: JI | Healthcare

ANAESTHETIST

What the work involves

- Anaesthetists are doctors who have undergone further training in anaesthesia.

- You will prepare and administer drugs to make patients unconscious and pain free during surgery. You will monitor patients during the procedure and bring them back to consciousness afterwards. You will also give local anaesthesia to specific areas of the body.

- In addition you will give pain relief after surgery, to seriously ill patients or during procedures such as childbirth.

- Anaesthetists also work in intensive care, resuscitation and pain management.

The type of person suited to this work

Anaesthetists need excellent communication skills to care for patients; you need to be both reassuring and a good listener in order to explain to patients the procedures you will perform. You should also be able to work well in a team with other medical staff and be able to both give and follow instructions.

You should be able to stay calm in an emergency and make decisions under pressure. You will need to be able to use complicated equipment and administer powerful drugs safely and accurately.

Finally, you must be prepared to undergo a long programme of education and training in order to gain the in-depth knowledge and skills necessary to become an anaesthetist.

Working conditions

Anaesthetists work in operating theatres, wards, clinics and accident and emergency departments within hospitals.

You will work directly with patients and as part of a medical team and will handle potentially dangerous drugs and equipment.

You will work shifts and be on an on-call rota, which includes working at nights, at weekends and on bank holidays.

Future prospects

There are opportunities throughout the UK, mainly within the NHS but also in private hospitals and clinics. Promotion to consultant posts is very competitive. Anaesthetists may work in sub-specialities such as paediatrics, obstetrics, cardiac surgery, resuscitation or intensive care.

Once fully qualified you will probably be expected to teach and examine students and trainees and to carry out research.

Advantages/disadvantages

Being responsible for the safety of patients in your care and dealing with emergency situations means that this is a very demanding job.

It is rewarding to be able to help patients through surgery and other medical procedures by providing pain relief.

Qualifications and courses

The initial training is the same as that required to become a hospital doctor (see p311); candidates must complete a medical degree recognised by the General Medical Council (GMC). This requires very high A level/H grade results, including chemistry and other science subjects. Competition for a medical school place is very high.

After completing a medical degree, candidates must undergo specialist postgraduate training for 7 years in anaesthesia, intensive care medicine and pain management while working under supervision. After completing the training programme, trainees receive a Certificate of Completion of Training (CCT) and become eligible to have their names added to the General Medical Council's register.

Money guide

Salary levels in the NHS may vary in different locations; the figures below are a guide.

As a trainee you can earn between £29,411 and £46,246. Junior hospital doctors usually earn a supplement on top of their basic salary.

Consultant anaesthetists can earn from £74,000 upwards.

Some senior consultants can earn up to £176,000.

Earnings are often more through private practice work.

Related opportunities

- General Practitioner p305
- Hospital Doctor p311
- Pathologist p325
- Psychiatrist p335

Further information

NHS Careers
0645 606 0655; www.nhscareers.nhs.uk

British Medical Association
BMA House, Tavistock Square, London WC1H 9JP
020 7387 4499; www.bma.org.uk

Association of Anaesthetists of Great Britain and Ireland
21 Portland Place, London W1B 1PY
020 7631 1650; www.aagbi.org; info@aagbi.org

The Royal College of Anaesthetists
Churchill House, 35 Red Lion Square, London WC1R 4SG
020 7092 1500; info@rcoa.ac.uk

AROMATHERAPIST

What the work involves

- Aromatherapists use essential oils to improve the health and wellbeing of clients.
- You'll be required to look into the medical history of all your clients, discussing their lifestyle, diet, exercise, allergies and stress levels.
- Using information gathered, you'll decide on blends and mixes of oils appropriate for the needs of the client.
- You will administer oils to the skin by massage, provide instructions for aftercare, and maintain records of each of your clients.

The type of person suited to this work

You must be very personable, with excellent communication skills in order to elicit trust and personal information from your patients, as well as being able to explain the techniques you are using to them.

Being comfortable with close and physical contact is also important when examining and treating your patients.

You will need an analytical mind in order to understand each patient's problem and formulate a beneficial course of treatment.

As you will probably be running your own business, you will need excellent business acumen in order to successfully take on aspects such as marketing, accounting, and administrative tasks.

Working conditions

Aromatherapists tend to be self-employed, and so working conditions vary. You could rent a treatment room in a health clinic, gym or leisure centre, work from home, or travel to patients' homes to provide treatment.

Hours depend on individual schedules and the needs and demands of clients. You should expect to work evenings and weekends. Part-time hours are a possibility.

Rooms and workspaces must be clean and quiet, and most aromatherapists tend to wear white clothes.

You will be bending, stretching, and spending most of the day on your feet.

Future prospects

Success in aromatherapy depends on effective business skills. If you build a strong client base and market your business well, your practice will grow into a successful business.

You could train in another relevant practice such as homeopathy, reflexology, or counselling, which could attract more clients.

If you like the idea of working abroad, you can even take your skills overseas. Just make sure the country you choose recognises your qualifications.

Qualifications and courses

Professional training courses are the standard method of entry and you usually have to be 18 or over to enrol on one. Courses are available from certificates to degrees; 5 GCSEs/S grades (A*–C/1–3) and 2 A levels/3 H grades are usually required for entry. Prior experience in a related profession like massage will help your application.

The General Regulatory Council for Complementary Therapies have devised national occupational standards for aromatherapy (NOS). Some courses will not qualify you for practice, so be sure that the course you choose is certified by the Aromatherapy Council.

Most courses include modules on anatomy, physiology, pathology, therapeutic relationships, along with both the theory and practice of aromatherapy. You'll also cover the practicalities of being a practising aromatherapist, from legal and ethical issues to business studies and understanding practice.

Advantages/disadvantages

This can be a really rewarding career, especially if you like being with people and enjoy helping them.

There is a lot to remember in aromatherapy, so it requires a calm and intelligent person to remember all the oils and administer them carefully.

Money guide

Whilst the process of building up the practice is taking place, salary can be quite low – between £5,000 and £10,000 a year. This should increase to about £18,000–£20,000 a year once you've gained some experience. Once you have a well-established practice, your annual income can range between £25,000 and £30,000.

Related opportunities

- Acupuncturist p288
- Beauty Therapist p459
- Homeopath p310

Further information

Institute for Complementary and Natural Medicine
Can-Mezzanine, 32–36 Loman Street, London SE1 0EH
020 7922 7980; www.i-c-m.org.uk

The General Regulatory Council for Complementary Therapists
Office 6, Slington House, Rankine Road, Basingstoke, RG24 8PH
0870 314 4031; www.grcct.org

Healthcare
CRCI: JA

ART THERAPIST

CRCI: JB

Healthcare

What the work involves

- Therapists use all kinds of art to help clients who may have difficulty in expressing themselves through the medium of words.

- You may work closely with people suffering from mental health problems, emotional problems, or those with drug and alcohol addiction, helping them to recover. People with speech and language difficulties also benefit from art therapy.

- You will create a safe environment where patients feel free to express themselves and their feelings and move on positively.

The type of person suited to this work

If you want to work with people with emotional and psychological difficulties, you need to be a calm, caring, understanding and trustworthy person.

You will need a lot of patience, excellent communication skills, and a very sensitive nature.

These skills need to be combined with strong artistic ability: you have to be a creative thinker prepared to take on the responsibility of helping clients who may be in a great deal of emotional pain. An interest in all forms of art is also essential.

If you plan on starting your own business, you'll need good marketing and accounting skills.

Working conditions

These depend on who you choose to work for. If being employed by the NHS appeals to you, hours are likely to be 37.5 per week, with weekends free.

If you work in private practice, your hours will vary and will probably include evenings and weekends.

If you're an art therapist, you'll probably have to travel around to give therapy, so a driving licence is really useful. You could work in hospitals, prisons, clinics and community centres.

Surroundings for therapy must always be warm, light and comfortable, so you can expect this to be your working environment.

Future prospects

If you work for yourself, you can grow and expand your business by building up a solid client base and making good contacts.

If you choose to work for the NHS, you could be promoted to management positions, becoming a specialist, head of profession, or consultant.

You might decide you'd like to specialise within a particular area, such as mental health of palliative care. Alternatively, you could combine art therapy with another complementary treatment such as psychotherapy.

Qualifications and courses

Most people who choose to go into art therapy have a first degree in art and design or a related subject, but all have taken a Master's degree in the subject. Make sure you enrol on one that has been approved by the Health Professions Council. You must be at least 23 years old at time of entry. To apply for a Master's, you will need a strong portfolio, and at least a year's experience in working in health, education or social care. Institutions sometimes consider graduates from other disciplines, notably psychology and teaching.

A Master's degree course lasts 2 years full-time, or 4 years part-time. Many areas are covered, including psychodynamics, psychopathology of art, contemporary art therapy and practice skills.

You will have to have art therapy yourself as part of training, and will also be expected to spend 120 days on clinical placement during the course.

Advantages/disadvantages

If you have both a love of art and a desire to help people this will prove a very rewarding career. Opportunities for progression are good, and experiences can be enriching and very fulfilling; there will never be a boring day at work.

You will have to deal with people who are in pain or mentally unstable, which can be extremely upsetting.

Money guide

In the beginning, you will earn about £25,000 a year working for the NHS, probably less through setting up your own practice. As you gain experience this figure will rise to about £40,000 a year. If you get into a management or supervisory role, you can earn around £45,000 a year.

Related opportunities

- Clinical/Health Psychologist p570
- Counsellor p571
- Learning Disabilities Nurse p314

Further information

The British Association of Art Therapists
24–27 White Lion Street, London N1 9PD
020 7686 4216; www.baat.org

Health Professions Council
Park House, 184 Kennington Park Road, London SE11 4BU
020 7582 0866; www.hpc-uk.org

NHS Careers
PO Box 2311, Bristol BS2 2ZX
0345 606 0655; www.nhscareers.nhs.uk

AUDIOLOGIST

What the work involves

- Audiologists examine patients to identify and assess hearing and balance disorders.

- As an audiologist, you will use specialist equipment to test patients and assess their problems and needs.

- You will also fit hearing aids and give treatment and advice to patients on how to improve and manage their conditions.

- Audiologists usually work in one of four main areas: paediatrics, adult assessment and rehabilitation, special needs groups, and research and development.

The type of person suited to this work

As an audiologist you will need to speak clearly and be easily understood by people who are lip reading.

You will need to be a caring person with excellent communication skills to deal sensitively with patients of all ages and backgrounds, listening to them and explaining the tests and procedures you are doing.

You should also be flexible and able to work as part of a team.

You will need to be practical to operate specialist equipment and take a logical, scientific approach to your work and be able to assess patients' needs and conditions correctly, keep accurate records and provide solutions and practical help.

Working conditions

Most audiologists work as part of a hospital team but you could also be based in a clinic or visit patients in their homes or in care homes or schools. You could also be involved in teaching and research work in a university.

You will probably work Monday to Friday but could have to be on call and cover shifts including nights, weekends and bank holidays.

Future prospects

Audiology is a rapidly developing area of healthcare, there is a shortage of qualified staff so job prospects are good.

There are opportunities within the NHS throughout the UK. There are also jobs available in research and in private hospitals.

You could specialise in one area such as paediatrics or adult rehabilitation.

Within the NHS you could progress to higher grades, where you will have more responsibility including managing and training others.

Qualifications and courses

ENTRY LEVEL **5**

The professional qualification for audiologists is a 4-year BSc degree in Audiology. The entry requirements for an audiology degree are 3 A levels/5 H grades or equivalent including at least 1 science subject, maths or psychology.

You will spend the first 2 years of the course at university. During year 3, you will work in a placement in an audiology setting. The final year will be spent back at university learning about more advanced aspects of audiology.

It is also possible to enter this profession with a degree in another appropriate subject and a Master's in audiology.

Advantages/disadvantages

You may need to deal with people suffering from an illness or disorder, such as those with dementia, and this can be emotionally draining at times.

It is fulfilling to know that you are using your skills to improve people's hearing and balance, providing them with a better quality of life.

Money guide

The NHS sets rates for audiologists. There are extra payments available, for example if you work in London.

Trainees start on NHS band 5: £20,225–£26,123 per year. Once qualified this rises to band 7: £29,091–£38,352.

Senior posts have a salary range at bands 8–9 of £37,106–£93,098.

Related opportunities

- Occupational Therapist p319
- Physiotherapist p330
- Rehabilitation Worker p580
- Speech and Language Therapist p338

Further information

NHS Careers
0345 606 0655; www.nhscareers.nhs.uk

British Academy of Audiology
PO Box 346, Resources for Associations, Association House, South Park Road, Macclesfield SK11 6SH
01625 504066; www.baaudiology.org; admin@baaudiology.org

British Society of Audiology
80 Brighton Road, Reading RG6 1PS
01189 660622; www.thebsa.org.uk; bsa@thebsa.org.uk

CRCI: JF | Healthcare

CHILDREN'S NURSE

What the work involves

- Children's nurses work specifically with babies and young people up to the age of 18.

- You will also be working closely with the parents and family of your patients, providing support, education and advice on treatment and care plans.

- You will take medical histories from children and their families, devise a care plan for them with the help of other medical professionals, and record their treatment procedures and outcomes in detailed records.

- You will also have to carry out procedures such as checking blood pressure, taking temperatures, dressing wounds and taking blood samples.

The type of person suited to this work

You will need to be a very warm, approachable person in order to gain the trust of young patients and their families, who will be understandably concerned about their child. At the same time, you must be highly professional and authoritative at times in order to handle difficult children.

You should be a patient teacher, as you will need to demonstrate treatment techniques to both your patients and their parents or carers. You will also need to motivate them to continue treatment at home.

Working conditions

On average, you will work 37.5 hours per week and this will usually include early morning, evening, night and weekend work as part of a shift-based rota. Part time and flexible hours are commonly available.

You could work in children's wards within NHS hospitals, in specialist hospitals, hospices and GP surgeries. You may also work in various locations throughout the community such as visiting patients at home, or in care homes and schools.

You will usually be required to wear a uniform and suitable sterile clothing for certain procedures, such as gloves and an apron.

Future prospects

As you gain experience, you can undertake further training and specialise in a certain area such as neurological or cardiovascular conditions in children. You could eventually become a nurse consultant.

Alternatively, you could apply for team leadership roles such as sister, or move into general NHS management.

Advantages/disadvantages

Working with children, helping them to get better, managing their treatment and easing their suffering, is extremely rewarding.

Qualifications and courses

ENTRY LEVEL 5

All nurses must hold a degree or diploma in nursing that has been recognised by the Nursing and Midwifery Council. Degree courses usually require qualifications of at least 3 A levels or equivalent, alongside 5 GCSEs/S grades (A*–C/1–3) including English, maths and a science subject. Entry for a diploma is slightly lower at just 5 good GCSEs or equivalent, as above.

If you do not have any formal qualifications, Access courses are available in health and social care, and these will give you the experience and qualifications necessary to apply for a degree or diploma course.

Graduates with a relevant degree in biology or another health-related subject may apply for an accelerated programme, which on average lasts about 2 years.

It is also possible to join a nurse cadet Apprenticeship if you are aged 16–18. These usually last 2 years and will provide you with an NVQ Level 3 or Access course pass, from which you can apply for a place on an accredited degree programme.

There are plenty of opportunities to work part-time in order to fit your job around your own family commitments.

It can be upsetting to deal with distressed children.

Money guide

Starting salaries for newly qualified children's nurses are around £20,000. As you gain experience, this will increase to between £24,000 and £32,000. With increasing seniority, you could earn around £40,000. Nurse consultants can earn as much as £65,000.

Related opportunities

- Adult Nurse p289
- Learning Disabilities Nurse p314
- Speech and Language Therapist p338
- Occupational Therapist p319

Further information

The Nursing and Midwifery Council
23 Portland Place, London W1B 1PZ
020 7333 9333; www.nmc-uk.org

Royal College of Nursing
20 Cavendish Square, London W1G 0RN
020 7409 3333; www.rcn.org.uk

NHS Careers
PO Box 2311, Bristol BS2 2ZX
0345 606 0655; www.nhscareers.nhs.uk

CHIROPRACTOR

What the work involves

- Chiropractors work with joints, bones and muscles, using hands and other physical tools, as opposed to drugs, in order to treat patients.

- You could treat a variety of ailments, including back and neck problems, joint stiffness, postural and muscular complaints, headaches and sports injuries.

- Techniques include massage, movement, and applying ice or heat to troublesome areas.

- You will also need to carry out full patient examinations, listen to their concerns and complaints, and record detailed notes of each consultation.

The type of person suited to this work

You should have exceptional communication skills, as you will need to listen to patients carefully in order to understand their complaint, and explain the techniques you are using to them simply.

You will need to be professional and approachable in order to inspire confidence and trust in your patients.

Good organisation and commercial awareness are essential if you are to run your own successful business.

Working conditions

Working hours are usually the standard 9am–5pm from Monday to Friday, although some flexibility may be required to suit the needs of clients. Many clinics and practitioners are increasingly offering early morning, evening, and weekend appointments.

Most chiropractors work either in a specialist clinic, a doctor's surgery, at home or at the houses of their clients. This means you could be working alongside other chiropractors or healthcare professionals, or alone.

It is a physically demanding job, so you will have to ensure your own fitness levels remain high in order to avoid work-related injuries.

Future prospects

The chiropractic profession is gaining medical credibility and growing rapidly, so there are increasing opportunities within the sector but also an increasing number of graduates competing for clients.

Most chiropractors are self-employed or work in private practice. A few are employed by the NHS.

Numerous options are open to you as you gain experience. You could choose to specialise in a specific area, such as children or sports injuries, you could set up your own practice, or you could teach.

Qualifications and courses

In order to practise as a chiropractor, you must complete a degree course that has been recognised by the General Chiropractic Council (GCC). You must be 18 years old to start training, and entry requirements are at least 3 A levels/Highers or equivalent, including biology or another related subject. For candidates who do not meet these requirements, year-long preliminary courses are available as an entry route to the full degree.

More mature applicants, looking to move into chiropractic as a second career, are considered for degree courses without the usual entry qualifications providing they have relevant experience or knowledge of science.

You must undergo an Advanced Criminal Records Bureau check prior to acceptance on a course, as you will be working with children and vulnerable adults.

Advantages/disadvantages

Each day you will be meeting new people and relieving their physical aches and ailments, which gives great job satisfaction. Being self-employed can be extremely stressful. Your earnings are dependent on the number of clients you attract, which can vary greatly from month to month. You will also have to do your own administration, including filling out complicated tax forms.

Money guide

Newly-qualified chiropractors may earn up to £22,000, although if you are self-employed this figure could vary depending on your initial success in attracting clients.

With experience and once you have built a good reputation, your salary could rise to £40,000.

Once you are in a senior position, either as a partner or running your own practice, you could earn £70,000+.

Related opportunities

- Osteopath p323
- Physiotherapist p330
- Masseur p315

Further information

General Chiropractic Council
44 Wicklow Street, London WC1X 9HL
020 7713 5155; www.gcc-uk.org

British Chiropractic Association
59 Castle Street, Reading RG1 7SN
0118 950 5950; www.chiropractic-uk.co.uk;
enquiries@chiropractic-uk.co.uk

CRCI: JB   Healthcare

ENTRY LEVEL 5

CLINICAL/BIOMEDICAL ENGINEER

What the work involves

- Clinical engineers design and maintain medical equipment such as scanners, x-ray machines, pacemakers, heart rate and blood pressure monitors, equipment for surgery, and instruments used in medical research.

- You would work on testing equipment, and collaborate with hospital staff installing and teaching them how to use the equipment.

- All kinds of engineers, from physicists to computer scientists, work on many different parts of the process.

The type of person suited to this work

If you're looking to go into this field, you need to have a natural interest in both electronic and mechanical engineering, and in health and medical issues.

Along with this interest, you'll need to be skilled in engineering and have in-depth knowledge of your subject.

You should be good at problem solving, and be used to keeping up to date with developments in the science and medical research world.

Working conditions

You could work in a hospital or laboratory, depending on the nature of the work. Those working in hospitals might have to work on-call, and are often on standby duty; laboratory hours tend to be more fixed.

The usual working hours for clinical engineers are Monday to Friday, and you would normally be working 37.5 hours a week.

Future prospects

There are good opportunities for progression and promotion for clinical and biomedical engineers.

With the right experience, you can move into management and senior management jobs, and if you're working for the NHS you could be promoted to consultant level. If you don't want to stay with the NHS, you can look for jobs with medical equipment manufacturers.

Advantages/disadvantages

This career requires real skill and education, and it can be a really rewarding experience building up this knowledge, studying for your degree, and putting it into practice.

You're helping people by building and maintaining medical equipment, and doing a job that's really worthwhile.

It can be stressful at times, and working in a hospital environment won't suit everybody.

Qualifications and courses

ENTRY LEVEL 5

You will need either a 1st or 2.1 degree in a subject such as mechanical, electronic or electrical engineering. A degree in medicine or physical or engineering science may be acceptable. For entry you will need at least 3 A levels or equivalent, including maths and physics.

Mature students without relevant qualifications may be considered if they have significant work experience in this area or complete an Access course.

Once employed, you will probably start training in a large teaching hospital. Graduate recruitment schemes which are accredited by the Institute of Physics and Engineering in Medicine (IPEM) are available, most of which last 4 years with the final 2 spent specialising in a particular area. Upon finishing the first 2 years of the course, you're awarded a Postgraduate Diploma, then after at least 4 years in a training post you can apply to be a member of the Health Professions Council.

You will need to commit to a programme of Continuing Professional Development (CPD).

Money guide

Starting salaries are usually around £23,000 a year for an NHS trainee.

If you become a state registered clinical scientist with the NHS, this will probably increase to something between £28,000 and £36,000.

If you work your way up to a senior position, you'll be on the same wage as consultants, and might be earning anything between £40,000 and £90,000.

Related opportunities

- Biotechnologist p508
- Clinical Scientist p512
- Medical Physicist p316

Further information

Association of Clinical Scientists
c/o The Association for Clinical Biochemistry,
130–132 Tooley Street, London SE1 2TU
020 7940 8960; www.assclinsci.org

Clinical Scientist Recruitment Centre
239 Thorpe Park, Peterborough PE3 6JU
0871 433 3070; www.nhsclinicalscientists.info

CRITICAL CARE SCIENTIST

What the work involves

- Critical care scientists support other medical staff caring for critically ill patients by maintaining and operating life-support equipment in intensive care units.

- You will work with equipment such as ventilators, brain monitors, blood filtration machines, electrocardiograms (ECGs) and infusion devices. Your job will involve setting up this equipment, taking readings, checking the equipment is working correctly, repairing it and ordering more supplies if not.

- You will use diagnostic techniques to help the medical team assess a patient's needs and condition.

- You will also need to keep detailed reports of all your work for patients' records.

The type of person suited to this work

You will need compassion and excellent communication skills to work with patients and their relatives at a time of intense stress, and be able to explain things simply and clearly.

You will need to be practical with good technical skills to operate complex equipment and will need to be able to concentrate for long periods of time, as patients' lives will depend on you.

Working conditions

Critical care scientists work as part of a team in the intensive care unit of a hospital using specialist equipment and machinery.

You will need to work to strict health and safety regulations ensuring that infections and diseases are safely contained.

You will normally work shifts, which include nights, weekends and bank holidays.

Future prospects

This is a small but growing profession with opportunities within the NHS throughout the country. Job prospects are good as there is a shortage of applicants for job vacancies.

Many critical care scientists are involved in research and teaching, as well as in practice.

Advantages/disadvantages

It will be emotionally and physically demanding working under pressure in emergency situations.

It is extremely rewarding to help patients recover.

You will have a varied working day; using your technical skills and having contact with patients.

Qualifications and courses

There are no formal entry requirements, but most hospitals expect a good general education and may prefer 4 GCSEs/S grades (A*–C/ 1–3). Critical care technology is moving towards becoming a degree-entry career.

Many candidates enter with higher qualifications, for example A levels, Advanced Highers or a BTEC National qualification in science subjects or electronics. The Diploma in Society, Health and Development may be useful for this career.

Degrees in life sciences, science, maths or electronics are a good grounding for this type of work. A degree in physiological measurement is available.

Trainee scientists train on the job, with other colleagues and senior members of staff to teach them. Part-time study is encouraged; there are vocational and postgraduate degrees available in clinical physiology.

Money guide

The NHS sets pay rates for critical care scientists (on the sterile services technician pay scale).

Critical care scientist trainees earn up to £17,257 per year. Once qualified and with experience this rises to £25,829–£35,000.

Specialists and heads of department can earn up to £65,657.

If you work in London your salary may be higher.

Related opportunities

- Audiologist p293
- Medical Physicist p316
- Sterile Services Technician p340
- Operating Department Practitioner p320

Further information

Skills for Health
2nd floor, Goldsmiths House, Broad Plain, Bristol BS2 0JP
0117 922 1155; www.skillsforhealth.org.uk; office@skillsforhealth.org.uk

NHS Careers
0345 606 0655; www.nhscareers.nhs.uk

Society of Critical Care Technologists
6 South Bar, Banbury OX16 9AA
01295 273559; www.criticalcaretech.org.uk

ENTRY LEVEL 2

Healthcare

CRCI: JF

DENTAL HYGIENIST

What the work involves

- Dental hygienists are predominantly concerned with oral hygiene and help prevent tooth decay and gum disease in their patients.

- Your work will include scaling and polishing teeth, putting in temporary fillings, taking impressions and X-rays, and applying protective coatings to teeth to prevent decay.

- You will be using a range of instruments, including scraping devices and drills.

- You will instruct patients on the appropriate way to floss and brush as well as advise them on their diet.

The type of person suited to this work

You will need to have excellent communication skills and be warm and reassuring as you treat patients of all ages, advising them on oral care.

You will need to combine good scientific knowledge with a personable approach to your work in order to motivate patients and convince them to stick to dental routines. A genuine desire to help people is essential.

You will need good eyesight and precise manual skills so that you can carry out detailed dental work with delicate instruments. An ability to stay focussed for long periods of time is also important.

Working conditions

You will usually work a 37-hour week from Monday to Friday, although occasional evening and Saturday morning work may be required according to practice opening hours. Part-time work is also available.

If you work for a community dental service you may travel to see patients in various locations such as schools and residential homes. You may also work out of a mobile clinic.

Surgeries are clean and well-lit. You will need to wear a white coat, surgical gloves, a face mask and eye protection for various procedures.

Future prospects

Although the majority of hygienists work in dental surgeries, you could also work for a community dental service, in a hospital, or for the Defence Dental Agency (DDA), providing dental treatment for the British Armed Forces around the world.

You may be promoted to practice manager or go on to become an orthodontic therapist. You could also become self-employed and work across several practices, undertaking part-time hours in each, or teach a dental hygiene training course.

Advantages/disadvantages

You will meet all kinds of people which can create a diverse and interesting working day.

Qualifications and courses

You will need to register with the General Dental Council (GDC) prior to working as a hygienist. To do this, you will need either a 2-year full-time Diploma in Dental Hygiene and Therapy or a 3-year full-time BSc degree in Oral Health Science approved by the GDC. There are 13 dental schools in England which offer these.

Minimum entry requirements for these courses are 5 GCSEs (A*–C), including English, maths and a science related subject, plus 2 A levels. Some schools may accept a GDC recognised qualification in dental nursing in place of A levels.

You may do a Foundation degree in an oral health science to prepare for entry to a degree course.

As you will work with children and vulnerable adults you will need a Criminal Records Bureau check prior to training.

It's satisfying to see a patient's condition improve based on your advice.

You may come across anxious patients who may be difficult to calm down.

Money guide

Recent graduates working in an NHS practice may earn £24,000 in their first few years as a dental hygienist. Once you have gained several years' experience, you could earn between £26,000 and £29,000 per year.

If you work in private practice, have considerable experience and a good reputation, you could earn up to £48,000.

Related opportunities

- Dentist p302
- Dental Therapist p301
- Orthodontist p322

Further information

British Society of Dental Hygiene & Therapy
3 Kestrel Court, Waterwells Business Park, Waterwells Drive, Quedgeley GL2 2AT
0870 243 0752; www.bsdht.org.uk; enquiries@bsdht.org.uk

British Dental Association
64 Wimpole Street, London W1G 8YS
020 7935 0875; www.bda.org; enquiries@bda.org

NHS Careers
PO Box 2311, Bristol BS2 2ZX
0345 606 0655; www.nhscareers.nhs.uk

DENTAL NURSE

What the work involves

■ Dental nurses assist dentists in all aspects of clinical life and patient treatment.

■ You will be expected to prepare the surgery each day and for each patient, ensuring that all instruments are to hand and sterilised ready for use.

■ You will also assist in dental procedures by holding suction devices in the patient's mouth, ensuring that they are comfortable throughout their treatment, and giving patients pre- and post-operative advice.

■ You may also take responsibility for the day to day running of the surgery, including maintaining stock and ordering equipment, and undertaking some administrative duties.

The type of person suited to this work

You should have excellent interpersonal skills as you will be dealing with patients on a daily basis, many of whom may be anxious about forthcoming treatment and in need of kindness and reassurance.

Good eye-sight and manual dexterity are helpful when aiding in procedures, as is a calm approach to jobs and the ability to react quickly and calmly to unforeseen situations.

As you will be working closely with a dentist and other colleagues, you will need to enjoy being part of a team environment.

Good time management and organisational skills are necessary in order to fulfil the range of duties you will be expected to undertake.

Working conditions

You will usually work from 8am to 5.30pm Monday to Friday, and some evening or weekend work may be required. Part-time work is often available.

If you work in a hospital, you may be asked to remain on-call over weekends and provide emergency cover at any time of day or night.

Dental nurses are also employed by the salaried primary care dental service (SPCDS) to work in local communities, assisting with patient care in various locations such as mobile clinics, schools and residential homes.

You will have to wear a uniform, and relevant safety equipment such as surgical gloves and a face mask.

Future prospects

Once qualified, you could continue your studies in order to gain further qualifications that will allow you to take on additional responsibilities such as sedation of patients and radiography.

Another option is to train to become a specialist orthodontic dental nurse, or a dental hygienist.

Some dental nurses also move into teaching roles and train student nurses.

Qualifications and courses

ENTRY LEVEL 3

The General Dental Council (GDC) stipulates that entrants need to study for recognised qualifications in dental nursing. Many of these courses require GCSEs/S grades (A*–C/1–3) in English, maths and a science subject for entry. The Diploma in Society, Health and Development may also be relevant.

Qualifications recognised by the GDC are the Certificate of Higher Education in Dental Nursing, the City & Guilds Level 3 Award in Dental Nursing, the SQA Level 3 in Dental Nursing, the National Examining Board for Dental Nurses (NEBDN) National Certificate examination, or a Certificate of Proficiency in Dental Nursing from a recognised dental hospital.

The Armed Forces also offer several routes into dental nursing.

Advantages/disadvantages

You will be working in pleasant, clean environments helping to treat patients and maintain a high standard of dental care across the UK.

Hours are usually standard and regular, with the opportunity to work part-time for a better work/life balance.

Money guide

These salaries are based on those found in the NHS, and they may vary according to your employer and the location in which you work.

Student dental nurses can start on a salary of between £15,000 and £17,750.

Once qualified, you could expect to earn between £17,000 and £21,000.

If you reach a more senior position, such as team leader or nurse specialist, your earnings could rise to £26,000–£33,000.

Related opportunities

■ Dentist p302
■ Dental Hygienist p298
■ Adult Nurse p289
■ Healthcare Assistant p576

Further information

British Association of Dental Nurses
PO Box 4, Room 200, Hillhouse International Business Centre, Thornton-Cleveleys FY5 4QD
01253 338 360; www.badn.org.uk; admin@badn.org.uk

General Dental Council
37 Wimpole Street, London W1G 8DQ
020 7887 3800; www.gdc-uk.org ; CAIT@gdc-uk.org

City&
Guilds

www.cityandguilds.com/myperfectjob

Healthcare

CRCI: JC

DENTAL TECHNICIAN

Healthcare

CRCI: JC

What the work involves

- Dental technicians make and repair dental accessories such as braces, crowns and false teeth. You could work across all three areas, or specialise in just one.

- You will follow detailed prescriptions, written by a doctor or dentist, in order to create individual, patient-specific appliances.

- You will use a variety of materials for crafting each device, including gold, steel, porcelain and plastic.

- You will also use numerous technical instruments in order to accurately carve, mould or wire each accessory.

The type of person suited to this work

You will be producing extremely delicate, precise devices so you will need excellent manual dexterity, good eye-sight and full colour vision.

It helps to have some artistic ability so that you can make items such as false teeth and crowns look as natural and aesthetically pleasing as possible.

You will need to be able to concentrate on a task for lengthy periods of time, and maintain a high level of accuracy throughout.

You should also be comfortable understanding and interpreting complex technical instructions in order to create them as 3D devices.

Working conditions

You should expect to work between 37–40 hours per week. Hours usually fall on weekdays but if you work in a hospital dental unit you might have to work evenings and weekends to cover emergency clinics.

You will be working in a laboratory, either within a hospital, dental practice, or independent commercial facility.

You will be expected to wear protective clothing and safety equipment when undertaking certain tasks.

Future prospects

Dental technicians usually work for commercial laboratories that produce equipment for a number of different practitioners in an area. These range in size from smaller businesses to large companies.

Other employers include hospital dental units, the Royal Army Dental Corps (RADC), the RAF, and the Royal Navy. There is also the option to be self-employed, although this is relatively uncommon.

Within larger companies, prospects for promotion are good.

Advantages/disadvantages

You will have job satisfaction in knowing you are producing high quality dental devices to improve a patient's dental health or appearance.

Qualifications and courses

ENTRY LEVEL 4

You will need to register with the General Dental Council (GDC) prior to working as a dental technician, and to do this you need to pass a qualification that is recognised by them. These include the BTEC National Diploma, a Foundation degree, or a BSc(Hons) degree in dental technology.

Entry requirements for the BTEC National Diploma are at least 4 GCSEs/S grades (A*–C/1–3) or equivalent, including English, maths and a science related subject. For a Foundation degree in dental technology, you will need 4 GCSEs/S grades (A*–C/1–3) or equivalent, and an A level. Entry requirements for a BSc(Hons) course are 5 GCSEs/S grades (A*–C/1–3) or equivalent, and 2 A levels/3 H grades including a science related subject.

You can work as a trainee in a laboratory or hospital whilst you study to obtain a relevant qualification that will enable you to register as a practising dental technician.

The Armed Forces recruit dental technicians, but you will need to be fully qualified at the time of applying, and be under 29 years of age.

It is important to commit to a programme of continuing professional development (CPD) to keep your skills up to date.

It is not the most sociable job in the world. Although you will be working in a laboratory with other professionals, you will be responsible for you own projects and have no patient contact.

Money guide

As a newly-qualified dental technician, you could expect to earn in the region of £20,000–£26,000.

With experience you could earn up to £30,000, and if you specialise in a particular area this could increase further to between £33,000 and £35,000.

As a senior technician, you could earn around £40,000.

Related opportunities

- Dentist p302
- Dental Hygienist p298
- Dental Nurse p299
- Dental Therapist p301
- Orthodontist p322

Further information

The British Institute of Dental and Surgical Technologists
4 Thompson Green, Shipley BD17 7PR
0845 644 3726; www.bidst.org

City&
Guilds

www.cityandguilds.com/myperfectjob

DENTAL THERAPIST

What the work involves

- Dental therapists, or oral health practitioners, perform both clinical and educational dental tasks.

- You will not only perform a hygienist's role such as scaling and polishing teeth, but you will also remove plaque from the root surface of the mouth and carry out fillings and nerve treatments on both adult and deciduous (milk) teeth.

- You will educate patients on proper diet and ways to brush and floss their teeth.

- You could also need to administer a supervised local anaesthetic.

The type of person suited to this work

As you will treat everyone from children to the elderly you will need to be adaptable, good-natured and encouraging. Your patients must feel comfortable with you and trust you.

You need to be a clear and motivational communicator in order to educate patients on proper dental care.

It's essential to have both a solid understanding of biology as well as a sincere interest in the wellbeing of your patients. You will need endurance, the ability to focus for long periods of time and a precise hand for carrying out detailed procedures.

Working conditions

You will work in a clean and bright environment. Your hours will be standard, Monday to Friday but you might need to work the occasional Saturday morning or evening surgeries. It might be possible to work freelance or on a part-time basis.

You might need to travel to schools or residential homes to visit patients if you are employed by a community dental service. This may include working from a mobile clinic.

For most procedures you will need to wear protective gloves, a facemask and uniform.

Future prospects

Good job opportunities exist for dental therapists throughout the UK. You may be employed by a general practice (private or NHS), a dental school, a cosmetic surgery, a salaried primary care dental service or with a Primary Care Trust.

You could be promoted to a dental practice manager or become a researcher or lecturer. With further training you could also specialise in health promotion. You might choose to set up your own dental practice.

Advantages/Disadvantages

It's rewarding to see a patient satisfied at the end of their treatment.

Qualifications and courses

ENTRY LEVEL **5**

You will need to register with the General Dental Council (GDC) prior to working as a dental therapist. To do this, you will need either a diploma in dental therapy (often combined with a diploma in dental hygiene) or a degree in oral health sciences approved by the GDC.

Minimum entry requirements for these courses are 5 GCSEs (A*–C), including English, maths and biology, plus 2 A levels. Some schools may accept a GDC recognised qualification in dental nursing in place of A levels. You must be aged 18 to apply.

As you will work with children and vulnerable adults you will need a Criminal Records Bureau check prior to training.

In addition to all of the training applied to a dental hygienist you will also need clinical skills training in how to do fillings and extract deciduous teeth.

You work will be varied as each patient's case will be unique.

The job can be demanding as you must deal with the public all day.

You might find it difficult to win a patient's trust.

Money guide

Starting out as a therapist in the NHS you can earn between £20,710 and £26,839 a year. As a specialist you may earn up to £33,436 a year.

Advanced therapists may earn up to £39,273 a year.

Your salary may increase based on your employer and where you live. If you are self-employed you will be able to negotiate your salary.

Related opportunities

- Dental Hygienist p298
- Dental Technician p300
- Dentist p302

Further information

British Association of Dental Therapists
8 Salmon Fields Business Village, Royton, Oldham OL2 6HT
0845 257 3487; www.badt.org.uk

General Dental Council
37 Wimpole Street, London W1G 8DQ
020 7887 3800; www.gdc-uk.org

NHS Careers
PO Box 2311 Bristol BS2 2ZX
0345 606 0655; www.nhscareers.nhs.uk

CRCI: JC Healthcare

DENTIST

What the work involves

- Dentists are trained to recognise, diagnose and treat all problems that affect the teeth, gums and mouth.

- You will examine teeth and carry out appropriate treatments, such as fitting or replacing fillings, scraping away plaque, polishing and removing teeth, as well as educating patients about good oral habits in order to prevent disease or decay.

- You will also need to keep detailed dental records for each patient, alongside managing your staff and, if you are a practice manager, looking after the practice budget.

The type of person suited to this work

You will need to have excellent communication skills in order to inspire your team and build good relationships with your patients, who will represent all ages and backgrounds.

You should also be compassionate and sympathetic, as you will encounter patients who are nervous or anxious about their treatment and you will need to be able to soothe and reassure them.

You will need good eye-sight, concentration and manual dexterity to successfully carry out complicated and delicate procedures.

If you intend to run your own practice, you will also need good business acumen.

Working conditions

If you work in a dental surgery, you should have regular Monday to Friday hours, and may even enjoy some flexibility within this framework.

Dentists who work in hospitals will usually work longer hours, including weekends, and will have to adhere to an on-call rota.

You could work across the community, travelling to provide treatment in locations such as schools and retirement homes.

You will need to wear protective, hygienic clothing such as a white coat and surgical gloves when dealing with patients.

Future prospects

Most dentists are self-employed, working in general practice across the UK. Some work for the NHS, and some take on a mixture of private and NHS patients. A recent surge in dental graduates has increased competition in this sector. There is still demand for graduates across the UK, but this is mostly within the NHS which is viewed by some as a less lucrative career move than private practice.

You could undertake further training to specialise in a field such as orthodontics or maxillofacial surgery.

Advantages/disadvantages

The majority of dentists are self-employed and work in the private sector, so you have a good amount of control over the hours you work and the patients you see.

Qualifications and courses

ENTRY LEVEL 5

Fourteen dental schools offer degrees approved by the British Dental Association with the standard programme lasting 5 years. You will need at least 3 good A levels or equivalent, including chemistry and biology and 5 GCSEs (A*–C).

If you have good A level results, but not in the required subjects, you can apply for a 6 year programme that includes an initial 30 week course that will get you up to speed in chemistry, physics and biology.

If you already have a degree in another subject it is possible to take an accelerated degree lasting only 4 years. To qualify you will need a 2.1 first degree, and have relevant qualifications in biology and chemistry.

Once you have completed your degree you will have 1 year of vocational training and will also need to commit to a programme of continuing professional development (CPD) to remain registered with the General Dental Council.

There are excellent opportunities for rapid career progression or further training if you want to specialise in a specific area.

You will mainly be undertaking routine check-ups and very standard procedures, so work can feel monotonous at times.

Money guide

Salaries for recently graduated, trainee dentists in general practice start at around £28,000. If you start your career in the NHS, your salary will be slightly lower at about £26,000.

Experienced dentists in general practice can earn £100,000+, especially if they run their own surgery.

If you reach consultant level in a hospital, your salary could exceed £150,000.

Related opportunities

- Orthodontist p322
- Dental Hygienist p298
- Dental Nurse p299
- Dental Technician p300
- Dental Therapist p301

Further information

British Dental Association
64 Wimpole Street, London W1G 8YS
020 7935 0875; www.bda.org; enquiries@bda.org

The General Dental Council
37 Wimpole Street, London W1G 8DQ
0845 222 4141; www.gdc-uk.org

NHS Careers
PO Box 2311, Bristol BS2 2ZX
0345 606 0655; www.nhscareers.nhs.uk

DIETITIAN

What the work involves

- Dietitians use their scientific knowledge of food to provide advice and information about diet and nutrition.

- You will give advice to a broad range of people, such as hospital patients, caterers, sports professionals and the general public.

- You will help people improve their health and prevent disease by making changes in their diet.

- Dietitians might work in industry developing food products and or even in the media.

The type of person suited to this work

You will need expert knowledge of the science of food and nutrition, and how this relates to the body. You must have excellent communication skills to be able to give practical information and advice to a range of people, from school children to food manufacturers.

You will need to be caring, supportive and non-judgemental, and able to understand the needs and issues of individuals, especially if you are working with sick people. You should have good motivational skills so that people can follow your advice and make the changes that you recommend.

Working conditions

You could work in a range of locations such as hospitals, laboratories, offices and sports centres.

You are likely to work a standard working week from Monday to Friday, although in hospitals you may be called in to work at weekends and on bank holidays.

In most jobs you will be working directly with people who can be ill, distressed or reluctant to take your advice.

Future prospects

The British Dietetic Association has over 5,000 members, and the profession is growing. There are opportunities across the UK and abroad, but competition for jobs is fierce.

Most dietitians work in the NHS, but there are also many opportunities in areas such as sports nutrition, the food and pharmaceutical industries, scientific research, education and journalism. You could become self-employed working as a consultant or see private clients.

In the NHS, you could go on to specialise in areas such as cancer care, or with particular groups such as children or the elderly. You could also move into management.

Advantages/disadvantages

People might be unable or unwilling to take on your advice, which can be frustrating.

Qualifications and courses

ENTRY LEVEL 5

To become a dietitian, an approved degree or postgraduate qualification (PgDip/MSc) in dietetics or human nutrition and dietetics is required. You must then register with the Health Professions Council in order to practise. You will need 2–3 A levels/3 H grades including chemistry and another science and GCSEs/S grades (A*–C/1–3) including English and maths, or equivalent, for entry to a degree in dietetics.

Entry requirements for a postgraduate diploma are typically an Honours degree in a science subject with an acceptable level of biochemistry and human physiology, along with a good command of spoken and written English.

Mature applicants can complete an Access course in science to be accepted into a degree programme.

Some institutions expect applicants to have visited a dietetic department before applying for a place.

It is rewarding to see improvements in people when they put into practice the information and advice you have given them.

Money guide

Starting salary for an NHS dietitian is around £20,500, rising to £26,100 per year.

Salaries for senior grade dietitians can be £29,000–£40,000.

There are higher grades for chief members of staff, or for work outside the NHS. You may earn more if you work in London.

Related opportunities

- Health Visitor p309
- Health Promotion/Education Specialist p306
- Sport and Exercise Scientist p339
- Food Scientist/Technologist p518

Further information

Skills for Health
2nd floor, Goldsmiths House, Broad Plain, Bristol BS2 0JP
0117 922 1155; www.skillsforhealth.org.uk;
office@skillsforhealth.org.uk

NHS Careers
0345 606 0655; www.nhscareers.nhs.uk

British Dietetic Association
5th Floor, Charles House, 148–149 Great Charles Street
Queensway, Birmingham B3 3HT
0121 200 8080; www.bda.uk.com

Healthcare

CRCI: JG

DISPENSING OPTICIAN

What the work involves

- Dispensing opticians use prescriptions from optometrists to supply and fit glasses.

- The work includes measuring the patient's face to ensure the glasses will fit and advising on lenses and frame styles to suit them and their prescription.

- The optician checks the finished glasses meet the original specifications and supplies them to the patient and will also do repairs.

- Some dispensing opticians take further training to supply and fit contact lenses.

The type of person suited to this work

Interpreting prescriptions requires specific scientific expertise.

You will be advising and listening to customers of many different ages and backgrounds, and working as part of a team with other professionals, so you will need excellent communication skills. It will be your responsibility to take measurements and repair glasses so manual skills are necessary.

You will need to be business minded if you choose to set up your own practice.

Working conditions

Most dispensing opticians work in high-street opticians. Financial and management challenges may arise if you are self-employed.

You may work 35–40 hours a week from Monday to Saturday (with some time off during the week instead). You may have to work on Sundays and bank holidays or in shifts, including weekends, in big chains.

Future prospects

Most dispensing opticians work for high-street companies. Some work is available in hospitals. Registration with the GOC will allow you to work in other countries.

With experience, you may specialise, for example in supplying and fitting contact lenses or low vision aids. You could also train new entrants.

You may also be promoted into a management position within a high-street optical chain. With experience, some opticians choose to run their own practices. However, increasing numbers of dispensing opticians are choosing to work for franchises rather than run an independent practice due to the growing threat from big high street chains.

Advantages/disadvantages

It can be stressful having to meet sales targets in some opticians.

If you enjoy combining scientific knowledge with working with the public, this job could be good for you.

Qualifications and courses

You must be registered with the General Optical Council (GOC). To qualify, you must complete an appropriate training course, pass the Professional Qualifying Examinations of the Association of British Dispensing Opticians (ABDO), and undergo a pre-registration year working under the supervision of a qualified optician.

You could take a 3 year degree course in optical management, ophthalmic dispensing, or a related area. Alternatively, 2 year diploma courses or Foundation degrees in ophthalmic dispensing are available. Typical entry requirements for a degree or Foundation degree are 2 A levels/3 H grades, normally including relevant science subjects, and 5 GCSEs/S grades (A*–C/1–3) including English, maths and science. For a diploma, you will need at least 5 GCSEs (A*–C) including English, maths and a science, or equivalent.

You could start as a trainee with a qualified optometrist and work towards part-time qualifications. ABDO offers a 3 year distance learning course and certain colleges offer a 3 year day-release programme for those in suitable employment.

Money guide

Salary levels vary enormously and are usually higher for opticians with management responsibility.

Starting salaries are around £12,000–£17,000 per year. With experience this can rise to around £28,000 per year.

Practice managers or those who are qualified to fit contact lenses can earn £30,000+.

Related opportunities

- Optometrist p321
- Pharmacist p326

Further information

NHS Careers
0345 606 0655; www.nhscareers.nhs.uk

Association of British Dispensing Opticians
199 Gloucester Terrace, London W2 6LD
020 7298 5100; www.abdo.org.uk;
general@abdolondon.org.uk

General Optical Council
41 Harley Street, London W1G 8DJ
020 7580 3898; www.optical.org; goc@optical.org

**City&
Guilds**

www.cityandguilds.com/myperfectjob

GENERAL PRACTITIONER

What the work involves

- General practitioners (GPs) diagnose various health problems, physical or emotional, within their local community.

- You will be talking to and examining patients in order to find out what is wrong with them, and then deciding on how to treat them. This could include giving them advice, prescribing medicine or referring patients to a specialist doctor.

- You may occasionally have to perform minor surgery such as removing moles or warts.

- You are responsible for educating your patients about how to live a healthy lifestyle and prevent illness.

The type of person suited to this work

You will need to have excellent communication skills in order to gain the trust of your patients and build good relationships with them. You should be able to put them at their ease quickly whilst maintaining a professional attitude.

You must have excellent scientific and medical knowledge in order to assess problems quickly and reach a suitable diagnosis, all within the time limit of a 15 minute appointment.

You should have an enquiring mind as you will need to continually update your knowledge and learn about new techniques and medicines in order to keep up-to-date in this fast moving discipline.

Working conditions

You will usually work normal hours from Monday to Friday, although increasingly surgeries are offering evening and weekend appointments which you might have to cover on a rota basis.

GPs are practice-based in small or large surgeries within cities, towns and rural areas.

You may also have to spend some time on call, visiting patients at home at any hour of the day or night.

GPs have to adhere to time and budget constraints, which can make the work stressful and demanding.

Future prospects

As a general practitioner you will be able work anywhere in the UK, in a larger practice with healthcare professionals from a number of disciplines, or a smaller surgery.

You could undertake work for the NHS, enjoy the freedom of self-employment, or opt for a combination of the two.

Advantages/disadvantages

The training period prior to qualifying as a GP is, on average, 10 years.

Dealing with a number of patients with varying complaints each day can be stressful, but helping them to recover is rewarding.

Qualifications and courses

ENTRY LEVEL 6

To become a GP you must first take an undergraduate degree in medicine with the standard programme lasting 5 years. You will need at least 3 good A levels/Highers or equivalent, including chemistry and biology. Most medical schools also require applicants to sit the UK Clinical Aptitude Test (UKCAT).

If you do not have science A levels, some universities offer a 6 year programme that includes an initial 'pre-medical' 30 week course that will get you up to speed. If you already have a 2.1 degree in another subject, some medical schools offer an accelerated degree in medicine lasting only 4 years.

On completion of your degree, you will then undertake 2 years on a Foundation programme of work-based training, which includes placements in a number of specialist areas such as surgery, paediatrics and general medicine. You must then complete a further 3 years' training in hospital and practice environments before qualifying for a place on the GP register.

Money guide

During your Foundation years in a hospital, you could expect to earn about £21,000, plus additional extras for working longer hours or nights. Once you are in training as a GP, this should rise to between £29,000 and £45,000 depending on your experience level.

Qualified, salaried GPs can earn between £50,000 and £80,000. If you are self-employed this could rise to £80,000–£120,000.

Related opportunities

- Hospital Doctor p311
- Surgeon p341
- Pharmacist p326

Further information

Royal College of General Practitioners
14 Princes Gate, London SW7 1PU
0845 456 4041; www.rcgp.org.uk; careers@rcgp.org.uk

British Medical Association
BMA House, Tavistock Square, London WC1H 9JP
020 7387 4499; www.bma.org.uk

General Medical Council (GMC)
Regent's Place, 350 Euston Road, London NW1 3JN
0845 357 3456; www.gmc-uk.org;

City& Guilds

www.cityandguilds.com/myperfectjob

CRCI: JH | Healthcare

HEALTH PROMOTION/ EDUCATION SPECIALIST

What the work involves

- Health promotion/education specialists aim to promote and improve public health in line with national recommendations.

- You could work with organisations such as schools or directly with individuals, groups or communities or you could be developing community policies.

- Your work might include advising individuals on how to make lifestyle changes such as taking more exercise or giving up smoking, encouraging organisations like workplaces, schools and hospitals to improve diets and promote health, and developing partnerships with communities to improve public health.

- Your role might involve liaising with the press and compiling features to encourage healthy living.

The type of person suited to this work

You must be able to encourage individuals and communities to change their lifestyle. It is important to have excellent communication and negotiation skills as a large part of your job will involve dealing with people from school children to community members and policy makers.

You must be creative in order to find different ways to persuade people and organisations to make changes. It is also necessary to have good research and writing skills in order to put together clear reports. You will need to be supportive and non-judgemental and able to relate to the needs of a wide range of people, communities and cultures. You must have good organisational skills to run and manage projects.

Working conditions

You could work in many different places such as health centres, local authority buildings, hospitals, workplaces and fitness centres.

You are likely to have a normal working week, Monday–Friday. Some employers offer flexible working schemes.

Travel within a working day is common as you will need to attend meetings, for example at local schools or community groups.

Future prospects

This is a very competitive industry and you will probably need to do work experience.

Most health promotion/education specialists work for the NHS, health promotion agencies, local authorities, or in social and community settings. You can progress to management roles or go into research and lecturing in health promotion.

Advantages/disadvantages

Changing people's habits can be difficult and take a long time.

Working to tight deadlines and targets can be very stressful.

Qualifications and courses

Entrants need a degree. Courses in health promotion, health studies, public health, social science, environmental health or related subjects provide an advantage. Entry requirements for degrees are usually a minimum of 2 A levels/3 H grades and 5 GCSEs/S grades (A*–C/1–3) or qualifications such as the Diploma in Society, Health and Development or BTEC qualifications in health and social care. More senior posts generally require a postgraduate diploma or MSc in Health Promotion. If you have a Nursing Diploma or a related Foundation degree, there is the option to take a BSc top-up course in Health Promotion.

It may be possible to train on the job for recognised qualifications. The Open University offers certificates in Health Promotion and Promoting Public Health: Skills, Perspectives and Practice. Some colleges run a Health Studies Access Course, for candidates without the necessary entry requirements.

It is possible to enter the profession through related fields. It is advisable to undertake relevant voluntary work.

The Society of Health Education and Health Promotion Specialists maintains a voluntary register for specialists in this field, and recommends degree and postgraduate courses to its members.

Seeing improvements in public health when people put into practice the information and advice you have provided is very rewarding.

You will have the opportunity to work with many different people.

Money guide

In the NHS starting salaries when qualified are between £19,683 and £31,779 per year.

More experienced and senior staff can earn £32,000–£43,000 and managers £60,000+.

With some employers, there may be extra payments available, for example if you work in London.

Related opportunities

- Dietitian p303
- Environmental Health Practitioner/Officer p35
- Health and Safety Adviser p40
- Youth and Community Worker p589

Further information

Faculty of Public Health
4 St Andrews Place, London NW1 4LB
020 7935 0243; www.fphm.org.uk; enquiries@fph.org.uk

NHS Careers
0345 606 0655; www.nhscareers.nhs.uk

HEALTH RECORDS CLERK

What the work involves

- Health administrators and records clerks are responsible for preparing and maintaining records of patients' medical notes, including details about the medicines they take and any other care needs.

- You will be collating, organising and archiving relevant notes and documents in each patient's file, and also ensuring that they are easily accessible for other healthcare professionals.

- You will be working with both paper documents and electronic records, which will include using equipment such as computers, photocopiers and scanners.

- You will also undertake other administrative duties, such as making and rearranging patients' appointments, sorting incoming correspondence and covering reception from time to time.

The type of person suited to this work

You will be working within a team of healthcare professionals as well as dealing with patient enquiries, so you should be personable and have excellent communication skills.

You will need a good level of numeracy and ICT skills as much of the work involves handling numerical information and working with various computer programs. As you will be dealing with a variety of tasks each day, you will need to have good organisational skills and be able to prioritise your workload.

You will be working with confidential information so must be discreet at all times.

Working conditions

You will usually work a 37 hour week from Monday to Friday, although occasionally some jobs require employees to work shifts. Part-time opportunities are common.

As you will be moving and transporting large, heavy piles of paper files around the hospital or practice, you will need to be reasonably strong and fit.

The majority of the work is office-based, although you might need to courier documents to various departments within your building. You will be expected to look fairly smart, although a business suit is unnecessary.

Future prospects

Although the NHS is the biggest employer of administrative staff, there are also opportunities in smaller GP surgeries, private hospitals and voluntary organisations.

Increasingly, the NHS is providing a more structured career path for administrators. This means you could progress to a supervisory or managerial role within your department, move sideways to work in another branch or hospital, or move into supporting a specialist area such as neurology or gastroenterology.

Qualifications and courses

Most employers require candidates to have at least 5 GCSEs/S grades (A*–C/1–3) or equivalent, including English and maths.

The Society, Health and Development Diploma could be useful. Apprenticeships might also be available for candidates aged 16–24. Previous administrative experience will give you an advantage.

As you will be working with children and vulnerable adults, you will need to pass a Criminal Records Bureau (CRB) check. Training is done on the job; you may also be offered the chance to study for extra qualifications such as the NVQs at Level 2 in Healthcare and Level 3 in Business Administration. The Institute of Health Record and Information Management offers several courses in healthcare administration including the Certificate of Technical Competence.

Advantages/disadvantages

You will be providing an essential service to both patients and other healthcare professionals by ensuring the smooth running of behind the scenes operations.

You can expect to have a heavy workload at times.

Hours are regular and there is plenty of opportunity for part-time work which fits in around family commitments.

Money guide

The starting salary for a health authority administrator or health records clerk usually starts at £12,000–£16,000. As you gain experience over a few years, this should rise to between £15,000 and £18,000. If you move into a more senior supervisory or management position, you can expect to earn up to £30,000.

Salaries do vary according to your employer and where you work in the UK. Some employers offer additional benefits such as a pension scheme.

Related opportunities

- Adult Nurse p289
- Pharmacy Technician p328
- Health Visitor p309

Further information

Institute of Health Record and Information Management
744A Manchester Road, Castleton, Rochdale OL11 3AQ
01706 868 481; www.ihrim.co.uk; ihrim@zen.co.uk

www.cityandguilds.com/myperfectjob

CRCI: JE   Healthcare

HEALTH SERVICE MANAGER

What the work involves

- You will help run GP surgeries, hospitals and other health centres, either within the NHS or private sector.

- Your job will be varied, you might be controlling finances, managing staff, producing reports on performance, overseeing buildings, and buying equipment.

- There are specific areas that managers can work in, these are clinical, financial, human resources, ICT, and facilities, and you can also be a practice manager who runs GP surgeries.

The type of person suited to this work

Strong leadership skills and a likable personality will be essential for managing people. Good communication skills are important as you will be interacting with a variety of people – professionals and patients.

You should be comfortable making important decisions, be logical in your approach to problems and have good negotiation skills.

You must have excellent writing skills to produce detailed reports and be comfortable working with figures, as you may be responsible for budgets and resources.

Working conditions

You will work standard office hours, Monday to Friday, but you could be on call for emergencies or work weekends if your place of work is open.

Most of the time will be spent in an office, in hospitals, GP surgeries or in health centres. It is useful to have a driving licence as you might be travelling between sites or to attend meetings.

Future prospects

There is a structured career path if working in the NHS, promotion is gained by moving into different departments and areas of management.

The NHS Gateway to Leadership is available for managers with substantial experience. This fast-track programme enables you to become a chief executive within 5 years.

In private health care there are stages of promotion which can also be followed.

With experience you may choose to take your managerial skills into another industry or become a consultant.

Advantages/disadvantages

You will be in a very responsible position, which could be daunting and stressful.

You will gain valuable skills which are transferable.

You will meet and help lots of different people, which brings job satisfaction.

Qualifications and courses

You can become a manager by starting out at administrative level and progressing to management. For entry level positions 5 GCSEs/S grades (A*–C/1–3) or more commonly 2–3 A levels or equivalent are needed. The Diploma in Society, Health and Development may be useful.

The Association of Medical Secretaries, Practice Managers, Administrators and Receptionist (AMSPAR) offer a Certificate and Diploma in Primary Care Management at Levels 2–5 through City & Guilds.

Entry to the NHS graduate management training scheme is with a 2.2 degree in any subject, or higher education professional qualifications in health or management that you can apply to if you have a degree such as the NVQ at Level 5 in Management or Diploma in Nursing.

There are tests, an interview and a National Leadership Challenge that need to be passed before being accepted. The scheme covers general, finance, human resources and ICT.

The private sector also has graduate management schemes. With BUPA and BMI healthcare you need a 2.1 in any degree or equivalent to enter.

Money guide

If you go through the NHS graduate training programme your starting salary will be £22,000 a year.

Managers in catering or projects can earn between £24,831 and £33,436.

Senior managers can earn up to £79,031, with chief executives earning £150,000+.

Private salaries tend to be around the same amounts.

Related opportunities

- Accountant p16
- General Practitioner p305
- Human Resources/Personnel Officer p41
- Archivist/Records Manager p346

Further information

NHS Careers
0345 606 0655; www.nhscareers.nhs.uk

Institute of Healthcare Management
18–21 Morley Street, London SE1 7QZ
020 7620 1030; www.ihm.org.uk; enquiries@ihm.org.uk

NHS Graduate Management Training Scheme
0845 300 1426, www.nhsleadtheway.co.uk

City&
Guilds

www.cityandguilds.com/myperfectjob

HEALTH VISITOR

What the work involves

- Health visitors work with people of all ages, backgrounds and cultures in various settings such as residential homes, schools, GP surgeries and village halls.

- You will provide advice on issues ranging from problems in children's sleep or feeding patterns, to postnatal depression, bereavement, or relationship problems and your primary patients will be parents with babies and young children.

- You will also be involved in organising community events designed to promote health and wellbeing.

The type of person suited to this work

You will be working closely with patients so you will need excellent communication skills.

You must be trustworthy, understanding, reassuring and professional in order to inspire confidence in your patients, mainly parents, and allow them to share their problems and concerns with you openly. You should also be able to motivate them to make important lifestyle changes on occasion.

You must be able to prioritise a heavy workload, and maintain discretion when dealing with confidential information.

Working conditions

You will usually work a 37 hour week from Monday to Friday, and flexible hours or part-time work are often available. You will work in a variety of locations, including schools, GP surgeries, health centres and residential homes. Because this will require a good deal of travelling within the local area, a driving licence is usually required.

You will encounter patients who are extremely difficult or distressed at times, which can be upsetting.

Future prospects

All health visitors work for the NHS, and they can be based in larger areas such as cities and towns, or work across villages and rural communities.

Career progression could take the form of managing a team of health visitors, moving into a role as a consultant nurse, specialising in a particular area of nursing, education or research, or even taking up a position in general management within the NHS.

Advantages/disadvantages

You will be offering healthcare advice and treatment across the community, including to those who may otherwise not be able to reach a doctor or hospital very easily such as the elderly.

There are opportunities to work part-time or on a job share basis, which would allow you to work around other commitments.

You may have to deal with difficult, potentially threatening patients, which can be frightening and upsetting.

Qualifications and courses

All health visitors must be registered nurses or midwives. To become a nurse or midwife, you must complete either a degree or diploma in nursing or midwifery that is recognised by the Nursing and Midwifery Council. Generally, you will need 5 GCSEs/S grades (A*–C/1–3) or equivalent, and 2 A levels or equivalent. The degree course lasts 3 or 4 years. Entry requirements for a diploma course are slightly lower at 5 GCSEs/S grades (A*–C/1–3) or equivalent. Full time diploma courses last 3 years.

It may also be possible to undertake an apprenticeship or similar training scheme. Those available are Young Apprenticeships (for candidates aged 14–16), Apprenticeships and Advanced Apprenticeships (for entrants aged 16–24). Most apprenticeships last 2 years, during which you will gain an NVQ Level 3 in nursing. This would give you the qualifications necessary to study for a full diploma course. Access courses are also available to those without the necessary entry requirements.

Once you have completed your training as a nurse, you will need to undertake a further degree-level course in public health nursing. These last 1 year full time, or are available as a 2 year part-time option.

Money guide

The starting salary for a newly qualified health visitor is usually around £24,831.

Once you have gained a few years' experience, this will rise to £25,000–£30,000.

Senior health visitors, who have supervisory or managerial duties across a team, can earn around £39,273.

Related opportunities

- Occupational Therapist p319
- Adult Nurse p289
- Paramedic p324
- Midwife p318

Further information

Nursing and Midwifery Council
23 Portland Place, London W1B 1PZ
020 7637 7181; www.nmc-uk.org; advice@nmc-uk.org

Royal College of Nursing
20 Cavendish Square, London W1G 0RN
020 7409 3333; www.rcn.org.uk

www.cityandguilds.com/myperfectjob

CRCI: JI   Healthcare

HOMEOPATH

What the work involves

- Homeopaths use highly dilute doses of natural remedies to treat patients for a variety of ailments ranging from simple headaches to complicated emotional issues, addiction and disease.

- You will need to take into account not only patients' physical symptoms, but also their psychological and emotional state, as well as their lifestyle.

- You will be working with a variety of patients of all ages, backgrounds and cultures.

- You could undertake general cases, or specialise in areas such as fertility and drug addiction.

The type of person suited to this work

You will need excellent communication and listening skills in order to quickly build a rapport with patients and encourage them to discuss their problems and concerns honestly.

As you will need to build your own practice and find clients from scratch, you must have good business acumen, confidence and motivation.

You should also be well-organised and methodical, as you will need to undertake your own administration and keep detailed, informative patient notes.

Working conditions

You will be self-employed and reliant on your clients, so will find that you mainly work at evenings and weekends (especially when newly qualified) in order to fit around their lifestyles.

You could work in a clinic with other healthcare professionals, in an alternative therapy centre, in your own home, or you could travel to see patients in their houses.

Patient appointments can take anywhere between 45 minutes and an hour and a half, so the work is mentally and emotionally draining. Because of this, most homeopaths only work part-time.

Future prospects

Alternative therapy has increased in popularity in recent years. This means that there are more people willing to explore it as a means of treatment, but also that there are an increasing number of practising homeopaths. Competition for clients, especially in the early years, can be great.

The majority of homeopaths are self-employed, although there are opportunities in independent surgeries, private hospitals, and in one of the five homeopathic NHS hospitals in the UK. With experience you could use your knowledge to teach in a university or college, or write related books and articles.

Advantages/disadvantages

Spending time talking to patients about their concerns and alleviating their ailments is extremely rewarding.

Qualifications and courses

ENTRY LEVEL 3

Although it is not compulsory to hold a qualification, it is unlikely that you will attract many patients if you are not registered with one of the UK regulatory bodies, the best known of which is the Society of Homeopaths.

In order to register, you will need to complete an accredited degree or diploma which leads to the qualification of Licentiate in Homeopathy. Entry requirements are usually 5 GCSEs/S grades (A*–C/1–3) or equivalent, and a degree will need the above and at least 2 A levels/3 H grades. The Diploma in Society, Health and Development may also be relevant for this career. Degree courses can be taken full time over 3 years, or part time over 4.

Qualified healthcare professionals can undertake shorter accredited courses in homeopathy at various universities, each of which is regulated by the Faculty of Homeopathy.

If you are self-employed, overheads such as renting clinic space and buying remedies and other equipment will eat into your earnings.

You must be commercially aware in order to successfully market your business, and be prepared to do your own complicated tax forms.

Money guide

Most homeopaths charge their patients directly by appointment. They usually ask between £35 and £70 per hour. A newly qualified homeopath who is just starting to build a reputation and attract clients could earn between £6,000 and £10,000 a year.

With a few years' experience, this could rise to £30,000.

Related opportunities

- Acupuncturist p288
- Chiropractor p295
- Osteopath p323
- Aromatherapist p291

Further information

The Society of Homeopaths
11 Brookfield, Duncan Close, Moulton Park, Northampton NN3 6WL

British Homeopathic Association
Hahnemann House, 29 Park Street West, Luton LU1 3BE
01582 408675; www.trusthomeopathy.org; info@britishhomeopathic.org

Alliance of Registered Homeopaths (ARH)
Millbrook, Millbrook Hill, Nutley TN22 3PJ
01825 714 506; www.a-r-h.org; info@a-r-h.org

HOSPITAL DOCTOR

What the work involves

- Hospital doctors work in either NHS or private establishments, diagnosing illnesses, treating patients and monitoring their care.

- You may treat patients yourself or, having assessed them, refer them to their GP or another healthcare professional.

- You will work in one of over 60 specialisms, which include cardiology, general medicine, paediatrics, orthopaedics and psychiatry.

- You will also be required to carry out surgical operations within your specialism, for example fitting a pacemaker if you are in cardiology. You may also be responsible for teaching medical students.

The type of person suited to this work

You must have excellent communication skills as you will be dealing with both patients and other healthcare professionals on a daily basis.

When handling patients, you should be empathetic, non-judgemental, professional and down to earth.

You should be good at working under pressure, making sensible decisions and solving problems whilst thinking on your feet.

You will need a good academic understanding of science and medicine so that you can apply this knowledge to patients to accurately and effectively solve their complaints.

Working conditions

Generally you can expect to work longer hours than in most other professions, although new guidelines prohibit doctors from working more than a 48 hour week. You will usually work on a shift pattern of days and nights, and will need to be on call on occasion.

You will be working in a consulting room, on the wards and in operating theatres. Conditions are usually quiet and clean, although things can get very fast paced during times of emergency.

You will also be required to attend numerous meetings and conferences across the UK, Europe, and perhaps the world.

Future prospects

Once you have completed your 2 year foundation period as a junior doctor, you can choose to follow a specialist subject such as gastroenterology or geriatric medicine. You will then follow a training programme in your specialism in order to pass the necessary exams to become a consultant.

Increasingly, senior level hospital doctors undertake managerial responsibilities, alongside teaching and mentoring work with students or junior doctors.

Qualifications and courses

ENTRY LEVEL 5

All entrants to become a hospital doctor need to hold a degree in medicine, earning the qualification of a Bachelor of Medicine and Surgery. Courses normally last 5 years and you will need at least 3 A levels/3-grades 1 including chemistry and biology, along with good GCSEs/S grades (A*–C/1–3) or equivalent, including English, maths and science to gain entry.

If you don't have the relevant A levels, some universities offer a 6 year medical degree, the first year of which consists of a 30 week course designed to get you up to speed. Graduates from another discipline could also apply for a 4 year, fast-track medical degree programme.

Once you have gained your first degree, you will need to complete a 2 year foundation programme within a hospital, where you will gain on-the-job experience of a number of specialist fields. On completion of this, you can begin training as a hospital doctor in your chosen area.

Advantages/disadvantages

You will be responsible for finding out what is wrong with people, helping them get better, and making them comfortable throughout their illness, which is very rewarding.

Hours can be long and unpredictable, so it can be difficult to get a satisfactory work–life balance.

Continuous developments in medicine and medical technology mean that you will be continually learning and developing throughout your career.

Money guide

Starting salaries for junior doctors in their foundation years range from £20,700 to £25,800. Once you are in speciality training, you will earn between £44,000 and £69,000, depending on which stage you have reached.

Once you reach consultant level, you could earn between £70,000 and £170,000.

Related opportunities

- Surgeon p341
- General Practitioner p305
- Adult Nurse p289
- Children's Nurse p294
- Pharmacist p326

Further information

British Medical Association
BMA House, Tavistock Square, London WC1H 9JP
020 7387 4499; www.bma.org.uk

NHS Careers
PO Box 2311, Bristol BS2 2ZX
0345 606 0655; www.nhscareers.nhs.uk

Healthcare

CRCI: JH

Healthcare

CRCI: JI

HOSPITAL PORTER

What the work involves

■ Hospital porters transport patients, equipment and other items to where they need to go within the hospital.

■ One of your main tasks will be to move frail and ill patients between departments and wards, while keeping them safe and comfortable.

■ You will transport patients using wheelchairs and trolleys.

■ You may also have a variety of other tasks such as delivering mail and moving medical equipment and supplies.

The type of person suited to this work

Hospital porters need to be responsible and reliable with a positive attitude to make sure that people and equipment are transported to the correct part of the hospital on time. You should be able to follow instructions and work well as part of a team.

Patients may be distressed or in pain so you must be caring and sympathetic and be able to reassure them and keep them comfortable.

Physical fitness is important, because you will walk long distances during your shift and you will have to lift and move patients and equipment.

Working conditions

You will work with patients and other staff, mainly indoors, although you might need to travel to other hospital sites to make deliveries.

You will need to pay attention to health and safety when lifting and handling people and equipment.

Porters usually wear a uniform and often need to work shifts, which includes working nights, weekends and bank holidays.

Future prospects

Most jobs are within NHS hospitals, although there are also posts within private hospitals. There are opportunities throughout the country but they can be competitive in some areas.

With experience you could become a supervisor and then take management qualifications for promotion to head porter or porter manager. You could also do further training to move into related careers, such as healthcare assistant or ambulance work.

Qualifications and courses

There are no formal entry requirements for this job, but applicants must be literate and have good all-round communication skills.

There is no set minimum age, but most applicants are at least 18 years old, and there are good opportunities for mature entrants.

Candidates usually have to pass a medical examination, and may be required to take a physical fitness test.

Experience of volunteer hospital portering work, or of paid or voluntary work in another area of healthcare or another job that involves contact with the public, can be useful.

A driving licence may be required.

Advantages/disadvantages

The work can be physically demanding and stressful at times.

You will meet a variety of people and the job is active and busy.

It is satisfying to play a vital role within a hospital; without porters a hospital would not be able to function.

Money guide

The NHS sets national pay rates for hospital porters.

Earnings start at around £12,517–£13,253 per year.

With experience this can rise to around £15,950. Team leaders can get up to £17,732.

Extra payments are available for working extra hours.

Related opportunities

■ Hotel/Accommodation Room Attendant p140
■ Hotel Porter p142
■ Paramedic p324
■ Sterile Services Technician p340

Further information

Skills for Health
2nd floor, Goldsmiths House, Broad Plain, Bristol BS2 0JP
0117 922 1155; www.skillsforhealth.org.uk;
office@skillsforhealth.org.uk

NHS Careers
0345 606 0655; www.nhscareers.nhs.uk

www.cityandguilds.com/myperfectjob

IMMUNOLOGIST

What the work involves

- Immunologists work with the body's immune system. They study functions and use the knowledge gained to treat and control illness and disease.

- You might work on developing vaccines against diseases such as HIV or meningitis.

- You could also find yourself studying the causes of allergies and looking at ways to stop the human body rejecting transplanted organs.

The type of person suited to this work

If you're thinking of becoming an immunologist, you naturally need to be interested in medicine and healthcare, and the way the body works.

You should have a logical, scientific mind and be good at solving problems, as well as being good at biology and science subjects in general.

You may spend years researching one area or topic, and so will need to be patient and enjoy in-depth research work.

You'll often have to work in teams, so should enjoy this but equally be able to use your initiative and work independently. If you choose to lecture, your communication skills need to be excellent.

Working conditions

Working hours will vary depending on your employer, but will generally fall into the average 9am–5pm Monday to Friday pattern. During busy periods you may be required to work overtime.

Work tends to take place in a laboratory environment, often in sterile conditions. You'll probably be required to wear appropriate clothing, and this often includes a white coat, face mask and rubber gloves. If you choose to lecture, the environment will be very different, and you'll spend most of your time in classrooms and lecture theatres.

Future prospects

Once you're a researcher, you can work your way towards a promotion to lecturer, then senior lecturer and so forth, up to professor and head of department.

If you follow the NHS pathway, the career progression structure is very clear. You basically work your way up the grades, from A to B to C.

Other options to consider include scientific writing and publishing, or working on drugs trials and quality assurance. You could also progress to sales, finance and management positions within the biotechnology industry.

Qualifications and courses

ENTRY LEVEL 5

All immunologists hold a relevant degree in immunology or a related science subject such as medical microbiology, biomedical science, or genetics. Most institutions require at least 5 good GCSEs and 2 A levels (including biology) for entrance. The Diploma in Science may also be relevant for this career.

You'll need at least a 2.1 degree and a postgraduate qualification is required for many NHS positions. You can also enter the profession through working in a pathology laboratory straight from school (i.e. after A levels), but this route is less common.

You can enter this profession as a mature student, and there are Access courses available which can help those who are out of practice at education prepare for a degree.

Once you're in the industry, there is plenty of training on offer. Many employers train you in house, and with the NHS you can apply for a post as a Grade A Clinical Scientist Trainee. Some programmes lead to a Master's degree, and contribute to the requirements for membership of professional bodies.

Advantages/disadvantages

This is a skilled profession, and training and progression can be really rewarding, especially in such an interesting job. There's also the added advantage that you'll be helping people. The job can be stressful and demanding, and the work is by no means easy.

Money guide

As a new graduate in an NHS training post, you'll probably earn around £24,000. Once you gain experience, this can increase to about £38,000 a year. If you work your way up to a senior position, you may earn up to £90,000 a year.

Related opportunities

- Clinical Scientist p512
- Biomedical Scientist/Medical Laboratory Assistant p507
- Hospital Doctor p311

Further information

British Society for Immunology
Vintage House, 37 Albert Embankment, London SE1 7TL
020 3031 9800; www.immunology.org

Grade A Clinical Scientists Recruitment Centre
239 Thorpe Park, Peterborough PE3 6JY
0871 4333070; www.nhsclinicalscientists.info

CRCI: TD   Healthcare

LEARNING DISABILITIES NURSE

What the work involves

- Learning disabilities nurses work with people with learning disabilities in order to teach them new skills and support them in becoming as independent as possible.

- You will be assessing patients and devising suitable care plans for them, as well as supporting their families or carers by helping them implement development strategies, and arranging for them to take a break from their responsibilities when necessary.

- You will work in a range of locations, including people's houses, care homes and schools.

The type of person suited to this work

You will need excellent communication skills in order to develop a good relationship with patients and colleagues alike. You will also need to be a good, and patient, teacher in order to successfully help your patients learn new skills.

You should be compassionate and empathetic so that you can understand your patients' feelings and frustrations, whilst maintaining a professional attitude so that you can distance yourself from your work at the end of the day.

You will need both physical and mental stamina in order to support your patients fully.

Working conditions

You will usually work 37 hours a week, and these will commonly include evening, night and weekend work. Part-time work and flexible hours are frequently available.

As you will be working in the community, you will spend time travelling to and from patients' homes, schools, clinics and residential homes. Because of this, a driving licence may be required. You may also accompany and support clients as they undertake everyday tasks such as going to the shops or the gym, booking a holiday, travelling on public transport or even going to work.

Future prospects

Most learning disabilities nurses are employed by the NHS, although there are also opportunities in the private sector and with local authority healthcare teams.

You may undertake further training that could allow you to specialise in an area that particularly interests you, such as education or cognitive disability.

You could go on to become a team leader, supervisor, or even a nurse consultant. Alternatively, you could move into research or teaching.

Advantages/disadvantages

You will be providing a life enhancing service for a number of people in your local community.

Qualifications and courses

All learning disabilities nurses must undertake a degree or diploma recognised by the Nursing and Midwifery Council. Degree courses last 3 or 4 years and you will need 5 GCSEs/S grades (A*–C/1–3) or equivalent, and 2 A levels/3 H grades to gain entry. Entry requirements for a diploma course are slightly lower at 5 GCSEs/S grades (A*–C/1–3) or equivalent. Full time diploma courses last 3 years. Graduates with a relevant degree in biology or another health-related subject may apply for an accelerated programme, which on average lasts about 2 years.

It may also be possible to undertake an apprenticeship or similar training scheme. Most apprenticeships last 2 years, during which you will gain an NVQ Level 3 in Nursing.

Access courses are available to those without the necessary entry requirements, as is the Nurse Cadet scheme which is a 2 year training programme that is sufficient qualification for entry onto a degree or diploma course.

There are good opportunities for career development or diversification, as well as the option of flexible working hours to suit your lifestyle and personal commitments.

You may encounter difficult or abusive patients, which can be distressing and unpleasant.

Money guide

The starting salary for a newly qualified learning disabilities nurse is around £21,000. With a few years' experience, this could rise to £25,000–£35,000. If you specialise or become a nurse consultant, you could earn up to £60,000.

Salaries do vary according on your employer and where you work in the UK. Some employers offer additional benefits such as a pension scheme.

Related opportunities

- Adult Nurse p289
- Children's Nurse p294
- Health Visitor p309
- Occupational Therapist p319

Further information

NHS Careers
PO Box 2311, Bristol BS2 2ZX
0345 606 0655; www.nhscareers.nhs.uk

Nursing and Midwifery Council
23 Portland Place, London W1B 1PZ
020 7333 93334; www.nmc-uk.org; advice@nmc-uk.org

MASSEUR

What the work involves

- A masseur uses massage as a therapy to relieve clients of pain or stress.

- As a masseur, you're trained in techniques and movements that have proven therapeutic effects and aid the healing process.

- Some practitioners specialise in specific areas of the body, whilst others work on the entire body.

- Many practitioners are self-employed and either work from home or run their own salons.

The type of person suited to this work

You will need to be good with people, and have a reassuring friendly manner.

You will need to be able to explain what you're doing clearly, and have to be able to respond to your client effectively and calmly. You should be very comfortable with close physical contact, and have good manual dexterity.

You should have excellent concentration skills, as the work demands great physical and mental energy.

You will need good organisational skills, as you may well end up running your own business. This will also require confidence and good business acumen.

Working conditions

If you work in a beauty clinic, you will usually do a 40 hour week, whilst self-employed masseurs can opt for fewer hours. Either way, you will have to work around your clients' lifestyles, which means working evenings and weekends.

You could work in hospitals, beauty salons, health spas, care homes, leisure centres, and clients' homes. You could also work from home, or even set up your own clinic.

Treatment rooms should be (and usually are) clean, warm and peaceful. You may often play calming music or use aromatherapy oils to add to the experience.

Future prospects

Once you've gained some experience, you can think about setting up your own practice, provided you have the business sense to do so.

You might also decide you'd like to learn about a similar profession such as reflexology or aromatherapy so that you can offer your clients a wider range of services. You could even teach massage, if you're prepared to study for a teaching qualification.

Advantages/disadvantages

If you like working with and helping people you should really enjoy this work. It's a good opportunity to use your skills, and you can really see the results.

The work can be tiring, and you need to be physically fit to do a good job and enjoy it properly.

Qualifications and courses

There are no set requirements to enter this profession, but many authorities recommend you should have at least 5 good GCSEs to enrol on a course.

The course you choose will need to be recognised by the General Council for Massage Therapy, and include beauty therapy, Swedish massage, holistic massage, and anatomy and physiology. Awarding bodies include ITEC and VTCT.

Once you start training, you'll not only cover massage itself, but also first aid, health and safety, employment law, and assessing clients.

You could begin on the path to massage by following an apprenticeship in beauty therapy. If you already have experience of work in health and beauty, you can enter this field as a second career: many people choose to do this.

Once you're fully qualified you can choose to become a member of a professional body and register with the General Council for Massage Therapy. This will keep you up to date with developments in the field, and you may receive additional training. You can also expand your repertoire by studying related areas of massage such as sports therapy.

Money guide

When you start out, you'll be earning about £11,000 a year.

This can rise to £15,000 with experience.

If you work your way up to specialist and work in a private practice, you could earn over £40,000 a year.

Related opportunities

- Acupuncturist p288
- Aromatherapist p291
- Physiotherapist p330

Further information

Complementary and Natural Healthcare Council
83 Victoria street, London SW1H 0HW
020 3178 2199; www.cnhc.org.uk

General Council for Massage Therapy
27 Old Gloucester Street, London WC1N 3XX
0870 850 4452; www.gcmt.org.uk

ITEC
2nd Floor, Chiswick Gate, 598–608 Chiswick High Road, London W4 5RT
020 8994 4141; www.itecworld.co.uk

www.cityandguilds.com/myperfectjob

Healthcare

CRCI: JA

MEDICAL PHYSICIST

What the work involves

- Medical physicists use their expert knowledge of physics to diagnose, prevent and treat disease.

- You will be using specialist equipment and techniques to investigate patients' illnesses, this includes X-rays, radiography, ultrasounds, MRI machines, radiotherapy, and laser therapy.

- You may be designing, developing and maintaining equipment, and advising medical staff on its use or planning the correct treatment for a patient using specific equipment.

- Your role may also involve patient contact, explaining procedures and results.

The type of person suited to this work

Medical physicists need to have expert skills in physical sciences and the ability to use their skills to solve problems and improve the diagnosis and treatment of disease.

You should have excellent research skills, be able to work accurately and be willing to take responsibility for decisions which will have a direct effect on patients. You will need good communication skills to explain complex procedures clearly to patients, and to work as part of a team. You must also be prepared to keep up with the latest developments and continue to learn new skills.

Working conditions

Most medical physicists work in hospitals and laboratories and some have contact with patients on wards or in clinics.

You will need to work safely with the equipment and chemicals in the laboratory, some of which can be hazardous.

You are likely to work a normal working week from Monday to Friday, but might have to work outside normal hours and have to travel to conferences.

Future prospects

The number of medical physicists is increasing, although trainee posts are competitive and you might have to relocate for some specialist roles. Most jobs are in the larger NHS hospitals throughout the UK. There are also some opportunities in the medical equipment industry, private hospitals and medical research institutes.

Within the NHS there is a recognised career path and you could even reach consultant level. Employment in the private sector is less structured.

Advantages/disadvantages

Some parts of the work could be routine at times.

You will be playing an important role in the overall healthcare of the patients, as you will be contributing to the diagnosis and treatment of their diseases.

Qualifications and courses

Candidates will need a 1st or 2.1 degree in a physical science, acceptance with a degree in subjects, such as physics, medical physics or electrical engineering may be possible. Entry to a relevant degree course requires at least 3 A levels/ H grades, plus 5 GCSEs/S grades (A*–C/1–3), including English and maths. It is almost essential for medical physicists to have physics and maths at A level/H grade, or equivalent qualifications.

An MSc, PhD or industrial experience may also be useful.

Candidates go into the profession as trainees. The training programme lasts 2 years, and includes study for an MSc in medical physics. Successful completion of Part I training allows candidates to then apply for an advanced trainee post.

Advanced trainee medical physicists undertake 2 years of training in a specialist field. On completion, they are eligible for registration with the Health Professional Council to work in the NHS and apply for Corporate Membership of the IPEM.

Money guide

As a trainee you could expect a salary between £24,000 and £30,000 per year.

With several years' experience and with training, you could earn around £38,000 per year.

Senior posts can have a salary of around £50,000–£80,000+.

Rates in the private sector and in London may be higher.

Related opportunities

- Hospital Doctor p311
- Radiographer p336
- Radiologist p337
- Physicist p533

Further information

Skills for Health
2nd floor, Goldsmiths House, Broad Plain, Bristol BS2 0JP
0117 922 1155; www.skillsforhealth.org.uk; office@skillsforhealth.org.uk

NHS Careers
0345 60 60655; www.nhscareers.nhs.uk

Institute of Physics and Engineering in Medicine
Fairmount House, 230 Tadcaster Road, York YO24 1ES
01904 60821; www.ipem.ac.uk; office@ipem.ac.uk

MENTAL HEALTH NURSE

What the work involves

■ Mental health nurses care for people with mental health problems both in hospitals and within the wider community, helping patients come to terms with their problems by listening to them as they talk through their illness and anxieties, and helping them overcome these limitations.

■ You will also work with a patient's friends and family where possible to create a stable and proactive network around the individual, and also to provide support to those closest to him/her.

■ You could encounter patients with problems including stress-related conditions, eating disorders, drug and alcohol dependency, and personality disorders.

The type of person suited to this work

You will need excellent communication skills in order to develop a good relationship with patients and their families, and other healthcare professionals. You must be extremely observant and attentive in order to spot any minor changes in a patient's condition and manage them before they trigger undesirable results.

You should be non-judgemental and empathetic in order to understand your patients' feelings and frustrations, but maintain a professional attitude.

Working conditions

You will usually work 37 hours a week, and these will commonly include evening, night and weekend work. Part-time work and flexible hours are frequently available. You could work in a hospital, in the community, or undertake a mixture of both.

If you work across the community, you will travel to a variety of places including patients' houses, hostels, day centres and drug dependency units. Because of this necessity to move between locations, a driving licence may be required.

Future prospects

Most mental health nurses are employed by the NHS, although there are also opportunities in the private sector and in local social services teams.

You may undertake further training that could allow you to specialise in an area that particularly interests you, such as drug abuse.

You could go on to become a team leader, supervisor, nurse consultant, or even into a general NHS management position. Alternatively, you could move into research or teaching.

Advantages/disadvantages

You will be providing a life enhancing service for a number of people in your local community.

Qualifications and courses

All mental health nurses must undertake a degree or diploma recognised by the Nursing and Midwifery Council. The degree course lasts 3 or 4 years and you will need 5 GCSEs/S grades (A*–C/1–3) or equivalent, and 2 A levels/3 H grades to gain entry. You do not need A levels for a diploma course. Graduates with a relevant degree in biology or another health-related subject may apply for an accelerated programme, which on average lasts about 2 years.

It might also be possible to undertake an apprenticeship or similar training scheme. Most apprenticeships last 2 years, during which you will gain an NVQ Level 3 in Nursing.

Access courses are available to those without the necessary entry requirements, as is the Nurse Cadet scheme which is a 2 year training programme that is sufficient qualification for entry onto a degree or diploma course.

After gaining a few years' experience, you should have the option of flexible working hours that will suit your lifestyle and personal commitments.

You may encounter difficult or abusive patients, which can be distressing and unpleasant.

Money guide

The starting salary for a newly qualified mental health nurse is between £20,000 and £25,000.

With a few years' experience, this could rise to £27,000–£38,000.

If you specialise or become a nurse consultant, you could earn up to £65,000.

Salaries do vary according on your employer and where you work in the UK. Some employers offer additional benefits such as a pension scheme.

Related opportunities

■ Learning Disabilities Nurse p314
■ Adult Nurse p289
■ Health Visitor p309
■ Occupational Therapist p319

Further information

NHS Careers
PO Box 2311, Bristol BS2 2ZX
0345 606 0655; www.nhscareers.nhs.uk

Royal College of Nursing
20 Cavendish Square, London W1G 0RN
020 7409 3333; www.rcn.org.uk

CRCI: JI Healthcare

MIDWIFE

What the work involves

- Midwives help and support women and their partners from early pregnancy, through the antenatal period, during the labour and birth, and also for up to a month after the baby has been born.

- You will be responsible for monitoring your patient throughout her pregnancy, providing advice and support on issues ranging from nutrition, through to methods of childbirth, and breastfeeding.

- You will deliver babies, or assist in the birthing process.

- You will also be responsible for identifying high risk pregnancies and arranging specialist care and provisions where necessary.

The type of person suited to this work

You must be an excellent communicator as it is essential to form a good relationship with patients, their partners, and other healthcare professionals. You need to be friendly and caring in order to gain the trust and confidence from the women under your guidance.

As childbirth is strenuous, messy and unpredictable, you should be able to stay calm in pressurised situations, think on your feet, and have good mental and physical stamina.

You should have a high attention to detail when carrying out your work and completing extensive up-to-date patient notes.

Working conditions

You will usually work 37 hours a week, and these will commonly include evening, night and weekend work. You may also be on-call at times. Part-time work and flexible hours are frequently available.

You could be based in the maternity unit of a hospital or in a birth centre. Midwives are also increasingly affiliated with GP surgeries and other health centres.

You will probably spend a good amount of time travelling from your place of work to your patients' homes, so a driving licence could be helpful.

Future prospects

You can undertake further training that could allow you to specialise in an area that particularly interests you, or to move into a related profession such as neonatal nursing.

Other opportunities include undertaking research, or training and teaching student midwives.

Advantages/disadvantages

Supporting women and families through pregnancy and childbirth is both rewarding and fulfilling.

This job can be distressing as you will have to deal with complications in pregnancy and labour.

Qualifications and courses

You must study for a qualification that is recognised by the Nursing and Midwifery Council.

You could take a full-time, 3-year degree course in midwifery. This is available at universities throughout the UK and entry requirements vary. Generally, you will need 5 GCSEs/S grades (A*–C/1–3) or equivalent, and 2 A levels, one in a science subject. The degree course can also be studied part time.

It may also be possible to undertake an Apprenticeship or similar training scheme. Those available are Young Apprenticeships (for candidates aged 14–16), Apprenticeships and Advanced Apprenticeships (for entrants aged 16–24). Most apprenticeships last 2 years, during which you will gain an NVQ Level 3 in nursing. This will give you the qualifications necessary to study for a full degree course.

Foundation degrees lasting 2 years are available for those who do not have the relevant qualifications to move straight into a midwifery degree. Once this has been completed they can move onto the full degree course. An Access course can also be taken by those with no formal qualifications to prepare for the degree.

For qualified nurses who are looking to move into midwifery, an 18-month fast track course is available.

Money guide

The starting salary for a newly qualified midwife is between £19,000 and £21,000. With a few years' experience, this could rise to £24,000–£34,000. If you specialise or become a consultant midwife, you could earn up to £65,000.

Salaries are higher in London; you will also receive allowances for on-call duties.

Related opportunities

- Adult Nurse p289
- Children's Nurse p294
- Health Visitor p309
- Occupational Therapist p319

Further information

The Royal College of Midwives
15 Mansfield Street, London W1G 9NH
020 7312 3535; www.rcm.org.uk

Nursing and Midwifery Council
23 Portland Place, London W1B 1PZ
020 7333 9333; www.nmc-uk.org; advice@nmc-uk.org

OCCUPATIONAL THERAPIST

What the work involves

- Occupational therapists help people overcome physical, psychological or social problems arising from illness or disability.

- You could see patients with problems stemming from conditions such as multiple sclerosis or Parkinson's, those with physical and mental disabilities or issues, and those who are affected by drug and alcohol use.

- You will help patients with everyday tasks such as washing, cooking and even going to work. Your care will focus on what patients can achieve, rather than on their disabilities.

- Your job will include writing treatment plans, giving advice on practical issues such as disability equipment, teaching coping strategies and using activities to stimulate your patients.

The type of person suited to this work

You must have excellent interpersonal skills as you will need to inspire trust and confidence in patients with a range of problems, including some who are difficult, anxious or unpredictable. You will need to be patient, caring, and sensitive to your patients' needs, concerns and expectations.

You should have both mental and physical stamina as you will need to provide hands-on support to patients as well as coping with their emotional issues.

You should be a natural problem-solver with a flexible and creative approach to your work. The ability to motivate your patients and other professionals is also essential.

Working conditions

Most occupational therapists work a normal working week from Monday to Friday, although you might have to work evenings and weekends to provide a 24 hour community service.

You may work in a variety of locations, such as hospitals, people's own homes, residential homes, prisons and workplaces. A driving licence may be useful since you will need to travel between these locations during the day.

Working with clients can be emotionally demanding and physically tiring.

Future prospects

Demand for occupational therapists is high, but you may still find that there is competition for jobs in certain areas.

You could be employed by the NHS, private hospitals, local authorities, charities or voluntary agencies. There are also opportunities to work abroad.

With experience, you could move into a more clinical position or take up a research post. Alternatively you could progress to a managerial role within the NHS, or opt to teach within your field.

Qualifications and courses

ENTRY 5 LEVEL

To become an occupational therapist, you need a degree or postgraduate diploma in occupational therapy approved by the Health Professions Council (HPC). You must also be registered with the HPC in order to practise in the NHS.

For degree entry, you will normally need at least 2 A levels/3 H grades including a science, preferably biology, human biology or psychology and 5 GCSEs/S grades (A*–C/1–3), or equivalent. The Advanced Diploma in Society, Health and Development may also be relevant.

A degree in occupational therapy normally takes 3 years. An accelerated 2-year diploma programme is available for graduates in other subjects who have experience in health or social care.

In-service courses are available for those employed as occupational therapy support workers or technical instructors. Courses are studied part time and lead to professional qualification as an occupational therapist.

Before you can register with the HPC, you must undergo a Criminal Records Bureau (CRB) background check.

Advantages/disadvantages

It is very rewarding to be able to help people to overcome difficulties and achieve their goals.

You could specialise in a variety of areas such as rehabilitation, learning disability or paediatrics.

The work can be emotionally and mentally demanding.

Money guide

Starting salaries for newly qualified occupational therapists are usually around £20,000. With 3–5 years' experience, this can rise to about £33,000. If you move into a more senior role, perhaps encompassing supervisory or managerial responsibilities, your earnings could increase to between £37,000 and £50,000.

Related opportunities

- Health Visitor p309
- Learning Disabilities Nurse p314
- Mental Health Nurse p317

Further information

British Association/College of Occupational Therapists
106–114 Borough High Street, London SE1 1LB
020 7357 6480; www.cot.org.uk; careers@cot.co.uk

NHS Careers
PO Box 2311, Bristol BS2 2ZX
0345 606 0655; www.nhscareers.nhs.uk

CRCI: JG   Healthcare

OPERATING DEPARTMENT PRACTITIONER

What the work involves

- Operating department practitioners work alongside surgeons, anaesthetists and other staff before, during and after operations.

- Before surgery you will help calm a patient's anxiety, plan treatment, sterilise equipment and bring the patient to the operating theatre. During surgery you will monitor effects of the anaesthetic, pass tools to surgeons, take care of surgical wounds and dispose of soiled dressings.

- After surgery you will bring patients to the recovery unit, monitor their wellbeing, provide pain relief and evaluate care.

- It will be your responsibility to anticipate the needs of your colleagues and respond effectively.

The type of person suited to this work

You will need the scientific knowledge and practical skills to prepare specialist equipment and drugs. You will be helping with operations so you cannot be squeamish.

You must pay close attention when monitoring patients because their lives depend on it. You need to be able to react quickly and accurately if the patient experiences any complications.

Excellent communication skills are essential and you will need to be caring and sensitive.

Working conditions

You will mainly work in operating theatres, anaesthetic areas and recovery rooms in hospitals.

You will need to follow hygiene procedures closely and wear a sterile gown and gloves during operations and be able to stand for long periods.

You will usually work shifts which may include working at nights, at weekends and on bank holidays. You might also have stand-by or on-call duties.

Future prospects

There is a shortage of trained operating department practitioners, so job prospects are excellent. Most employment is available with the NHS throughout the UK. There are also opportunities in private hospitals.

You could progress into higher grade posts which involve more responsibility for managing and training others. There are also opportunities to enter research or teaching.

Advantages/disadvantages

The work can be stressful at times and you will see some unpleasant things.

Qualifications and courses

Entry into this work requires a Diploma of Higher Education (DipHE) in Operating Department Practice approved by the Health Professions Council (HPC). Courses are available throughout the UK and generally last 2 or 3 years. The normal minimum entry requirements are 5 GCSEs/S grades (A*–C/1–3) preferably in English, maths and/or a science based subject or equivalent, but some institutions might require AS levels or A levels/H grades.

It is also necessary to undergo a medical test, an occupational health screening and a criminal records check.

The minimum age for entry is 18, and adult entry is common. Access courses may be taken prior to diploma programmes.

Entrants often have experience of other types of hospital work, for example as a healthcare assistant, and apply to become operating department practitioners later.

It is rewarding to be part of a team improving people's health and saving lives.

You could work in a range of areas, such as resuscitation, intensive care or day surgery.

Money guide

Starting salaries for qualified staff in the NHS are around £20,710–£26,839 per year.

With experience you can earn up to £33,436 per year. It is possible for a higher-level theatre practitioner to earn up to £39,273.

Related opportunities

- Paramedic p324
- Critical Care Scientist p297
- Sterile Services Technician p340

Further information

Skills for Health
2nd floor, Goldsmiths House, Broad Plain, Bristol BS2 0JP
0117 922 1155; www.skillsforhealth.org.uk;
office@skillsforhealth.org.uk

NHS Careers
0345 606 0655; www.nhscareers.nhs.uk

College of Operating Department Practitioners
1 Mabledon Place, London WC1H 9AJ
0870 746 0984; www.aodp.org; office@codp.org.uk

OPTOMETRIST

What the work involves

- Optometrists examine patients' eyes for disease or abnormalities, and carry out vision tests.

- Your work will include shining a light on the retina, and using reading charts and other instruments to diagnose a patient's needs.

- You will determine prescriptions and may also supply and fit glasses or contact lenses.

- You will look out for signs of diabetes and other eye diseases and refer patients to surgeons when needed.

The type of person suited to this work

Examining eyes and diagnosing problems requires a high level of scientific knowledge and a high attention to detail.

Fitting contact lenses and handling instruments requires good technical skills.

You need to have excellent communication and listening skills to deal with patients of all ages and backgrounds. You will need to put patients at ease and explain procedures simply and clearly to them.

You should have good interpersonal skill as you will have to work as part of a team with other professionals.

Working conditions

Optometrists work in high-street opticians and hospitals, in examination rooms which usually have no natural light and often have to be quite dark. You will undertake 10 to 20 half an hour eye examinations per day.

You will probably have a normal working week from Monday to Friday, but may need to work on Saturdays as well.

Future prospects

Job prospects are good but vary throughout the UK. You may work for a chain of opticians, an independent practice, or a hospital. You could also do related work with lens manufacturers.

With experience, you may specialise, for example in children's vision, low vision or contact lenses. You could choose to run your own practice. There are also opportunities to move into research and university teaching.

Advantages/disadvantages

The work can be routine and repetitive at times.

If you enjoy combining scientific knowledge with working with the public, this job could be good for you.

Working closely with patients can be demanding.

Money guide

Optometrists in private practice start on around £16,500 per year and can earn up to around £40,000 with experience, but salaries can be a lot higher.

Qualifications and courses

The only route into optometry is through professional qualifications.

The Professional Qualification Examination of the General Optical Council (GOC) is in two parts. Part One of the Professional Qualifying Examination involves gaining a degree.

Accredited degrees are offered at several universities. Entry requirements may vary according to the institution. Candidates are normally expected to have 5 GCSEs (A*–C), including English, maths and physics or double award science, and 3 A levels including at least 2 from biology, maths, physics and chemistry, or equivalent.

After graduation, new entrants must follow a pre-registration year of supervised clinical experience. Part Two of the Professional Qualifying Examination is taken during the training year. After qualification, trainees are eligible to register with the GOC and as Members of the College of Optometrists.

There are many advanced courses that allow qualified optometrists to specialise in other areas. Courses can include paediatric vision, vision therapy and sports vision.

Qualified and experienced optometrists can earn up to £50,000 in NHS hospitals.

Consultants can earn up to £75,000 in NHS hospitals and more in the private sector.

Related opportunities

- Dentist p302
- Dispensing Optician p304
- Hospital Doctor p311
- Physiotherapist p330

Further information

General Optical Council
41 Harley Street, London W1G 8DJ
020 7580 3898; www.optical.org; goc@optical.org

College of Optometrists
42 Craven Street, London WC2N 5NG
020 7839 6000; www.college-optometrists.org; optometry@college-optometrists.org

www.cityandguilds.com/myperfectjob

Healthcare

CRCI: JJ

ORTHODONTIST

What the work involves

- Orthodontists are concerned with the growth of teeth and jaws, specifically correcting irregularities or abnormalities in either area.

- You will be responsible for rectifying cosmetic and physical problems in your patients, resulting in a considerable improvement in their quality of life.

- The most common procedures that you will carry out involve fitting and maintaining fixed or removable braces, and extraction of teeth. You may occasionally have to carry out jaw surgery.

- You will also need to examine the mouths and teeth or your patients, take x-rays and impressions, and keep detailed medical records of their treatment.

The type of person suited to this work

You will need to have excellent communication skills in order to gain the trust of your patients and build good relationships with them.

You will be working with and possibly managing other professionals, so you should also enjoy working in a team environment and motivating those around you.

Good eyesight and manual dexterity are essential for undertaking fiddly tasks such as fitting and tightening braces or performing jaw surgery. The ability to maintain your concentration during occasionally lengthy procedures is also important.

Working conditions

If you work in private practice you can generally expect to do normal office hours, although some orthodontists choose to work evenings and weekends to suit their patients' lifestyles. Those working in hospitals must be more flexible, occasionally undertaking emergency shifts and being on-call.

You will have to wear a white coat or tunic, along with surgical gloves and a mask when working on patients in order to maintain high levels of hygiene and safety.

Future prospects

There is a constant demand for orthodontists in both the private and public sector, so career prospects are good.

Jobs can be found across the UK in both large cities and smaller towns. You could work in the NHS or as a self-employed professional.

There are opportunities in order to specialise in certain areas of orthodontics, such as adult cosmetic dentistry or children's corrective orthodontics.

Advantages/disadvantages

The majority of orthodontists are self-employed and work in the private sector, which gives you greater control over your working hours and salary.

Qualifications and courses

ENTRY LEVEL 7

All orthodontists must first qualify as a dentist. The standard degree programme lasts 5 years and you will need at least 3 good A levels/Highers or equivalent qualifications, including chemistry and biology. GCSE/S grade results may also be taken into account, and at least 8 passes (A*–C/1–3) are required for consideration.

If you have good A level results, but not in the required subjects for entrance onto the degree course, you can apply for a 6 year programme that includes an initial 30 week course that will get you up to speed.

Once you have qualified as a dentist, you will need to gain 2 years of clinical experience before applying for a place on an orthodontic course. Orthodontic training combines academic study with hands-on training in a hospital, and lasts 3 years full time. You will then sit the Membership in Orthodontics (MOrth) exam to qualify as an orthodontist.

If you are looking to progress to become a hospital consultant, you will need to undertake a further 2 years' training and pass the Intercollegiate Specialty Fellowship Examination.

You will be correcting physically obvious imperfections in your patient's teeth and jawline, and seeing the subsequent improvements in their health and happiness will be rewarding.

A lot of your patients are likely to be children, who may well be anxious and frightened of many procedures which can be upsetting.

Money guide

Generally, salaries start at around £28,000–£30,000. Working in a specialist private practice, you could earn £40,000+. If you run your own practice, you could earn in excess of £150,000.

Related opportunities

- Dentist p302
- Dental Hygienist p298
- Dental Technician p300
- Surgeon p341

Further information

British Orthodontics Society
12 Bridlewell Place, London EC4V 6AP
020 7353 8680; www.bos.org.uk

British Dental Association
64 Wimpole Street, London W1G 8YS
020 7935 0875; www.bda.org; enquiries@bda.org

NHS Careers
PO Box 2311, Bristol BS2 2ZX
0345 606 0655; www.nhscareers.nhs.uk

OSTEOPATH

What the work involves

- Osteopaths work on the musculo-skeletal system of their patients, rectifying problems with all areas of the body including the circulatory, gastro-intestinal and nervous systems.

- You will focus on understanding each patient's problem through talking to them, observing their movements and carrying out physical examinations.

- You will then rectify the problem using a serious of manipulative techniques on the muscles and bones of your patient, such as stretching the muscles, mobilising the joints and realigning bones.

The type of person suited to this work

You will need a highly developed sense of touch and strong observational skills in order to identify points of slight weakness or pain in your patients. Logic and problem-solving abilities will also help you diagnose correctly and treat the problem creatively where necessary.

You will need excellent communication skills so you can develop a good relationship with patients in order to inspire their trust and confidence.

The work can be very physical, so you should also have a good level of fitness.

Working conditions

You could practise in a variety of locations including leisure centres, therapy centres, private clinics, hospitals and even your own home.

If self-employed you will have complete control over the hours you work. Most professionals offer evening and weekend appointments as well as those during the day, as these tend to be more convenient for patients.

Future prospects

As awareness of osteopathy grows, there is increasing demand for qualified and registered professionals, so career opportunities are correspondingly positive. Most osteopaths are self-employed, and usually start out by working as an associate in a practice to establish a reputation and solid client base. After a few years, many then go on to set up their own practice.

You could also choose to specialise in an area of particular interest to you, such as treating sports injuries or problems resulting from childbirth.

Advantages/disadvantages

You will be providing a highly effective, natural alternative to drugs and surgery for your patients.

You will work with a variety of people and encounter a wide range of new complaints and challenges on a daily basis.

Qualifications and courses

ENTRY LEVEL 5

All osteopaths must be registered with the General Osteopathic Council (GOsC) before they are legally allowed to practise. In order to register, you must hold a recognised qualification in osteopathy. Most recognised courses are at degree level. Each takes 4 years when studied full time, and 5 on a part-time basis. For entry onto these courses, most of the universities require at least 5 GCSEs/S grades (A*–C/1–3) or equivalent and a minimum of 2 A levels, with chemistry or biology preferred.

Many people train in osteopathy as a second career. If you have relevant experience in healthcare or hold medical-related qualifications prior to commencing your degree, you may be exempt from parts of the course. Short courses are available for fully qualified healthcare professionals.

You may need to work long hours which can be tiring. If you are self-employed this can be stressful as your income is not predictable and you have to handle all your own marketing, accounts and expenses.

Money guide

As the majority of osteopaths are self-employed and work varying hours, it is difficult to predict an exact level of earnings at any stage. Generally, most charge between £25 and £50 for a 30–45 minute session.

Newly qualified osteopaths in a practice can expect to earn £10,000–£20,000 in their first couple of years. With experience, you could see this increase to around £30,000.

If you run your own practice or work in a well-established one, your salary could rise to £35,000–£65,000 per year.

Related opportunities

- Chiropractor p295
- Physiotherapist p330
- Acupuncturist p288
- Homeopath p310

Further information

General Osteopathic Council
176 Tower Bridge Road, London SE1 3LU
020 7357 6655; www.osteopathy.org.uk;
contactus@osteopathy.org.uk

British Osteopathic Association
3 Park Terrace, Manor Road, Luton LU1 3HN
01582 488455; www.osteopathy.org; boa@osteopathy.org

The British School of Osteopathy
275 Borough High Street, London SE1 1JE
020 7089 5316; www.bso.ac.uk

CRCI: JB | Healthcare

PARAMEDIC

What the work involves

- Paramedics provide a rapid response to 999 calls reporting medical emergencies.

- You will be the first healthcare professional to reach a patient and as such must assess their condition and administer immediate treatment.

- You will need to resuscitate and stabilise patients using a variety of methods and equipment, including life support techniques, oxygen, drugs and occasionally performing minor operations such as tracheotomies.

- You will also have to make notes of all the treatments administered so you can brief hospital staff.

The type of person suited to this work

You must have good communication skills and a caring disposition to successfully soothe and comfort patients.

You should be mature, responsible and non-judgemental so that you can relate to people from a wide range of ages, backgrounds and cultures.

You must be able to keep your head in a crisis, as you will be making life and death decisions on a fairly regular basis.

A good level of physical fitness is required for lifting and carrying both patients and equipment. Mental stamina is also essential for coping with occasionally horrific and frightening circumstances.

Working conditions

You will work 37.5 hours a week on rotational shifts. This means you will work nights, weekends and on public holidays regularly. Part-time work is commonly available.

You will either work for a local ambulance service or be based at a hospital, but you will travel to a range of locations in response to emergency calls. You should be prepared to undertake treatment of patients in unfamiliar and potentially dangerous situaitons.

Because you will be responsible for full or shared driving responsibilities of your vehicle, you need a full, clean driving licence.

Future prospects

Career prospects for paramedics are good. Once you have completed your training and gained 3–5 years' experience you could be promoted to a team leader.

Further promotion can take you into management posts within the ambulance service, although you will need to supplement your work experience with further relevant qualifications to achieve this level.

You could also move into related careers such as nursing or occupational therapy.

Advantages/disadvantages

Providing rapid response in emergency situations means that you really will be responsible for saving lives on a weekly basis.

Qualifications and courses

All paramedics must be registered with the Health Professions Council (HPC). There are two approved routes you can follow. You could apply to an ambulance service trust for a role as a student paramedic, and they will put you through an approved course. Training takes between 2 and 5 years to complete. You will need at least 5 GCSEs/S grades (A*–C/1–3) or equivalent including English and maths. The Higher Diploma in Society, Health and Development could also be relevant.

Alternatively you could apply for an approved degree or diploma in paramedic science which can take from 2 to 4 years. Entry requirements are usually at least 1 A level or equivalent. For a full degree, you need 2/3 A levels, including a science.

A full clean driving licence will be required. You will need to pass a Criminal Records Bureau check, fitness test, and medical assessment.

You could find yourself confronted with very difficult patients; those who are frightened, angry, or under the influence of drugs and alcohol may be violent and hostile to treatment.

You will have to work unsociable hours fairly regularly.

Money guide

Salaries for student paramedics range from £17,000 to £20,000. Once qualified, this should rise to around £25,000. With a few years' experience, you could earn £26,000–£30,000.

If you have undertaken the relevant training to take on responsibilities at a senior level, you could earn £33,000–£39,000.

Related opportunities

- Hospital Doctor p311
- Adult Nurse p289
- Midwife p318
- Occupational Therapist p319

Further information

British Paramedic Association
The Exchange, Express Park, Bristol Road, Bridgwater TA6 4RR
01278 420014; www.britishparamedic.org

The Ambulance Service Network
c/o The NHS Confederation, 29 Bressenden Place, London SW1E 5DD
020 7074 3200; www.nhsconfed.org/networks/ambulanceservice

NHS Careers
PO Box 2311, Bristol BS2 2ZX
0345 606 0655; www.nhscareers.nhs.uk

PATHOLOGIST

What the work involves

- Pathologists are doctors who have undergone further training to specialise in pathology.

- As a pathologist you will detect and diagnose diseases and help to identify sources of disease and reduce the risk of it spreading further.

- You could work in one of many branches including haematology (studying diseases of the blood), histopathology (studying tissue samples removed for diagnosis, and determining cause of death by performing post-mortems and autopsies) and immunology (studying diseases and conditions of the immune system).

- You will spend a lot of time in a laboratory, but will also work directly with patients.

The type of person suited to this work

To be a pathologist you should be able to use your medical knowledge and training to diagnose patients' conditions. You must have problem-solving skills and pay close attention to detail when carrying out laboratory assessments.

You should be kind and caring in order to gain your patient's trust, with excellent communication skills to be able to listen to them carefully and explain their conditions and treatments in a clear, simple way.

You will need to complete a long period of education and training in order to gain the in-depth knowledge and skills necessary for this job.

Working conditions

You will normally work within a hospital as part of a medical team working both in a laboratory and with patients. You will need to work safely in the laboratory and wear protective clothing such as a lab coat and gloves.

There will be long hours and you are likely to work in shifts and be on an on-call rota, which includes working at nights, at weekends and on bank holidays.

Future prospects

Most pathologists work within the NHS throughout the UK. There are also opportunities in industry, working for private companies.

You could decide to specialise further in particular areas of the work such as forensic pathology or transfusion medicine. You could also move into academic work, carrying out research or teaching students.

There are also similar careers in pathology for clinical and biomedical scientists, but they do not treat patients.

Qualifications and courses

As for hospital doctors (see p311), candidates complete a medical degree recognised by the General Medical Council (GMC).

Following a medical degree and the 2-year Foundation programme, pathologists begin specialist training, which can last from 5–6 years.

On completion of the training, pathologists are awarded the Certificate of Completion of Specialist Training (CCST), which enables them to work as consultants.

Advantages/disadvantages

The work can be emotionally demanding because it includes dealing with patients who have life-threatening conditions.

Your work can be vital in finding an accurate and early diagnosis for patients, which can help to save lives.

Money guide

Salary levels in the NHS have a national rate, but this can also vary in some areas.

Pathologists in speciality training can earn from £29,411 to £46,246 a year.

Consultant pathologists can earn up to £74,000 with experience.

If you are a senior consultant you can earn anything up to £170,000. You could also earn additional benefits based on merit.

Related opportunities

- Anaesthetist p290
- Psychiatrist p335
- Radiologist p337

Further information

Skills for Health
2nd floor, Goldsmiths House, Broad Plain, Bristol BS2 0JP
0117 922 1155; www.skillsforhealth.org.uk;
office@skillsforhealth.org.uk

NHS Careers
0345 606 0655; www.nhscareers.nhs.uk

Royal College of Pathologists
2 Carlton House Terrace, London SW1Y 5AF
020 7451 6700; www.rcpath.org; info@rcpath.org

CRCI: JH   Healthcare

PHARMACIST

What the work involves

- Pharmacists work in one of three areas: hospital, community or industry.

- Hospital pharmacists are responsible for buying, manufacturing, dispensing and supplying medicines to in and out-patients. You will ensure that patients receive the most appropriate treatment in the correct dosage.

- Community pharmacists work in high-street pharmacies both in large cities and small rural villages. You will supply medicines over the counter, make up doctors' prescriptions, and advise people on general health-related queries.

- Industrial pharmacists work for pharmaceutical companies. You will be discovering, developing, manufacturing, testing and marketing new drugs.

The type of person suited to this work

You should be a strong communicator, as you will be advising patients on choosing medications and clearly explaining how to administer them. You will also need to be comfortable working in a team with other pharmacy staff or healthcare professionals.

You will need in depth medical knowledge as well as problem solving skills in order to prepare medications for patients and advise them on what to take for minor ailments.

Accuracy and attention to detail are essential when selecting, preparing, measuring and labelling medicines.

Working conditions

Hours will depend on where you work. Community and industrial pharmacists will usually work 39 hours per week from Monday to Friday, although Saturday work is increasing in order to meet patients' requirements. Hospital pharmacists may need to work shifts in order to provide a 24 hour service. There are opportunities to work part time.

You could be working in a shop, hospital or laboratory, and may occasionally be required to travel in order to provide a service to nursing homes and community health centres/clinics.

Future prospects

Opportunities for pharmacists are good as there is currently a shortage, particularly in hospitals.

You will be able to choose from a range of working environments including community shops and large hospitals.

As you gain experience, you could choose to combine your work with other responsibilities such as teaching. You could also go on to write about pharmaceutical matters.

Advantages/disadvantages

You will be working with a range of patients and colleagues, so your work will be varied and rewarding.

You can choose to work in a more relaxed retail environment, in the bustle of a hospital, or in a professional industrial setting.

Qualifications and courses

All candidates who wish to become pharmacists need to hold a degree in pharmacy in order to gain the necessary M.Pharm qualification. Throughout the UK, there are 25 schools of pharmacy at which you can study for a degree that has been approved by the Royal Pharmaceutical Society of Great Britain (RPSGB).

The degree course lasts 4 years, and most universities require at least 3 A levels or equivalent, including chemistry and biology, along with at least 5 GCSEs/S grades (A*–C/1–3) including English, maths and science.

It is not possible to start work as a pharmacist with just an HND qualification. You could, however, gain employment as a pharmacy technician to gain experience whilst you study for a degree level qualification.

Prior to registration as a pharmacist, entrants have to complete a year in industry, where they will work either as a community, hospital or industrial pharmacist and gain experience. You will then have to pass the RPSGB's registration examination prior to becoming a fully qualified, registered pharmacist.

You may have to work evenings and weekends in order to provide a good level of service to patients and healthcare professionals.

Money guide

Starting salaries for pharmacists range from £25,000 to £28,000. With 5–10 years' experience, you could expect to earn up to £38,000 if you are working in industry, and £35,000 for community and hospital based roles.

If you reach a very senior level, you could expect to earn over £55,000 in a community position, and £70,000+ if you are working in industry or within a hospital.

Related opportunities

- Pharmacologist p327
- Biochemist p506
- Pharmacy Technician p328
- Hospital Doctor p311

Further information

Royal Pharmaceutical Society of Great Britain
1 Lambeth High Street, London SE1 7JN
020 7735 9141; www.rpsgb.org.uk; enquiries@rpsgb.org.uk

The Association of the British Pharmaceutical Industry
12 Whitehall, London SW1A 2DY
0870 890 4333; www.abpi.org.uk

NHS Careers
PO Box 2311, Bristol BS2 2ZX
0345 606 0655; www.nhscareers.nhs.uk

PHARMACOLOGIST

What the work involves

- Pharmacologists study the effect of drugs on the body. Their work includes discovering, researching, developing and testing new drugs and medicines.

- You will study the actions of drugs via computer simulations, or in biological tests in cells and tissues, or in animals and human volunteers.

- You could specialise in a number of areas, including neuropharmacology or clinical pharmacology.

The type of person suited to this work

You should be a strong communicator with the ability to both work within a team, and also lead and motivate your colleagues in order to drive projects.

You will need excellent analytical skills as you will be gathering and interpreting complex information, and since the majority of equipment used to undertake experiments is computer-based it is essential to have good ICT skills.

You should be adaptable and creative in order to develop and modify experiments by which to successfully understand the effectiveness of a wide variety of drugs.

Working conditions

You will usual work from 9am to 5pm during the week, but occasionally may have to work evenings and weekends in order to monitor the more complex experiments.

You will be working in a laboratory environment, usually within a university, government or commercial research centre, or a pharmaceutical company. This means that the environment is generally clean and quiet, and you may be required to wear protective clothing when undertaking certain experiments.

Future prospects

Although the industry is competitive, once you have gained a position as a pharmacologist the opportunities for career progression are good. You could work within a university, undertaking research and gaining a PhD, and then perhaps moving into a position as a lecturer. Within commercial laboratories, experience will lead to increased responsibility and subsequently managerial opportunities.

Advantages/disadvantages

It is a competitive industry so gaining an entry level position is difficult. Once you are in though, prospects are excellent and career progression rapid.

You will be working towards developing new drugs that will enhance thousands of people's quality of life across the globe.

You will have to experiment on animals, which may be upsetting.

Qualifications and courses

ENTRY 5 LEVEL

Because the work is incredibly scientific, most entrants to pharmacology have a relevant degree in a subject such as pharmacology, biomedical sciences, biochemistry, molecular and cell biology, chemistry or biology.

Most universities require 3 A levels or equivalent, including chemistry and biology, for entrance onto a degree course. At least 5 GCSEs/S grades (A*–C/1–3) or equivalent, are also required.

It is possible to enter this career with a relevant HND, but this is uncommon and you would have to start in a lower position and gain qualifications as you work. Entry requirements for an HND are usually 5 GCSEs/S grades (A*–C/1–3) or equivalent, including English, maths and science.

Because competition is so fierce in this industry, many new entrants hold a postgraduate qualification as well as an undergraduate degree. These include research courses in related subjects such as pharmacology. Undertaking a PhD also gives candidates essential lab experience, which is viewed favourably by employers.

Pre-entry work experience within a pharmaceutical company is also desirable as it demonstrates your enthusiasm and commitment.

Money guide

Starting salaries range from £21,000 for pre-doctoral roles, to £28,000 for those with a PhD. After approximately 10–15 years' experience, you can expect to earn anything from £30,000 to £100,000 depending upon your employer and where you work in the world.

Commercial salaries tend to be higher than those offered by academic institutions, and holding a PhD will generally increase your earning potential by 25%.

Related opportunities

- Pharmacist p326
- Biochemist p506
- Toxicologist p537

Further information

British Pharmacology Society
16 Angel Gate, City Road, London EC1V 2PT
020 7239 0171; www.bps.ac.uk

Association of the British Pharmaceutical Industry
12 Whitehall, London SW1A 2DY
0870 890 4333; www.abpi.org.uk

CRCI: JK   Healthcare

PHARMACY TECHNICIAN

What the work involves

- Pharmacy technicians work under the supervision of a qualified pharmacist, helping to prepare, supply and dispense medications, whilst also advising on how to take them.

- You will also be responsible for monitoring stocks of medicines, checking expiry dates and reordering supplies as necessary.

- You could work in a retail environment as a community pharmacy technician, within a hospital, or in a commercial pharmaceutical lab.

- You will be working with a variety of healthcare professionals, including pharmacists, doctors and nurses, and could also have a good amount of contact with patients.

The type of person suited to this work

You will need to be a strong communicator, as you will be advising patients on choosing medications and explaining how to administer them clearly. You will also need to be comfortable working in a team with other pharmacy staff or healthcare professionals.

You should be good with figures and calculations, and also be extremely accurate in order to ensure that you are making and labelling medications correctly, and also keeping detailed records of each patient's medication needs.

You must be able to be mature and tactful when dealing with patients who will present a variety of unusual complaints, and always remain non-judgmental.

Working conditions

Hours will depend on where you work. Community pharmacy technicians usually work 39 hours a week from Monday to Saturday. Industry and hospital technicians work a 37 hour week, but may be required to cover evening and weekend shifts on occasion.

You could be working in a shop, hospital or laboratory, and may occasionally be required to travel in order to provide a service to nursing homes or community health centres and clinics.

When working in a hospital or industrial laboratory, you may be required to wear sterile clothing such as gloves and a gown.

Future prospects

You could work in a community context, within a small local pharmacy or a larger well-known chain. Alternatively, you could be in a NHS or private hospital, or based in a prison or working for the Armed Forces.

If you work in a hospital, you could move into a specialised, supervisory role after gaining a few years' experience. Additionally, many clinical pharmacy technicians in hospitals are now more involved with patients, undertaking ward rounds and other such duties.

Qualifications and courses

ENTRY LEVEL 2

Most employers ask for 5 GCSEs/S grades (A*–C/1–3) or equivalent, including English, maths and at least 1 science subject. BTEC awards in health and social care and the Diploma in Society, Health and Development might be useful as well.

You will start in a trainee post within either a community pharmacy or a hospital, working under the supervision of a qualified pharmacist whilst also studying for an NVQ Level 3 in Pharmacy Services.

Once you have gained your qualifications and experience as a pharmacy technician, you can register with the Royal Pharmaceutical Society of Great Britain.

Advantages/disadvantages

You will be working with a range of patients and colleagues, so your work will be varied and rewarding.

You can choose to work in a more relaxed retail environment, in the bustle of a hospital, or in a professional industrial setting.

You may have to work evenings and weekends in order to provide a good level of service to patients and healthcare professionals.

Money guide

Starting salaries for trainee pharmacy technicians are usually around £17,000.

With 5–10 years' experience, and having gained a more senior position, you could earn between £20,500 and £28,000.

If you become a team manager within the NHS, your salary could reach £39,000.

Related opportunities

- Pharmacist p326
- Sterile Services Technician p340
- Health Records Clerk p307

Further information

Royal Pharmaceutical Society of Great Britain
1 Lambeth High Street, London SE1 7JN
020 7735 9141; www.rpsgb.org.uk; enquiries@rpsgb.org

The Association of Pharmacy Technicians UK
4th Floor 1, Mabledon Place, London WC1H 9AJ
020 7551 1551; www.aptuk.org; website@aptuk.org

City&
Guilds

www.cityandguilds.com/myperfectjob

PHLEBOTOMIST

What the work involves

- Phlebotomists are specialist medical laboratory assistants who collect blood samples for analysis to help diagnose diseases.

- You will take blood samples from patients as painlessly as possible, label samples and make sure they are taken promptly and safely to a laboratory for examination.

- You will need to keep accurate records and enter data in a computer system.

- It's your responsibility to ensure samples are not mixed up or contaminated.

The type of person suited to this work

Phlebotomists need to be practical and good with their hands to take blood without harming the patient or disturbing nursing care. You need to pay close attention to detail and work carefully as any errors could affect results.

It is important that you are able to communicate well with a range of people from children to the elderly. Some people are scared of having their blood taken, so you need to be able to reassure them.

Working conditions

You will carry out your work in hospital wards, out-patient departments and in the community. You will also spend time working in laboratories.

You will need to pay close attention to health and safety to prevent infection, and will wear a uniform and protective clothing such as gloves.

You are likely to work a normal working day during the week, but you may also need to work at weekends.

Future prospects

Most employment is available in NHS hospitals throughout the UK. There is also similar work available in blood transfusion services, government research departments and university laboratories. Currently there is a shortage of phlebotomists in certain areas including London.

Phlebotomists can progress into managerial and senior roles.

Although there is no route for phlebotomists to progress to a career as a biomedical scientist, you may be encouraged to gain the qualifications that you need to train as one. You can also train to enter other areas of healthcare, such as nursing.

Advantages/disadvantages

Some of your patients will be scared of blood and needles which can make your job difficult.

It can be rewarding to work with patients and play a vital role in helping to diagnose illnesses.

Qualifications and courses

There are no formal entry requirements for this job, but 4 or more GCSEs/S grades (A*–C/1–3), English, maths and science, or equivalent, may be an advantage, and are essential for more advanced work. The Diploma in Society, Health and Development may be relevant to this career.

Training is usually done entirely on the job. After training, you may be awarded a Certificate of Competence, which will allow you to work without close supervision throughout the hospital. You will be trained to National Occupational Standards.

Phlebotomists may be able to work towards related qualifications, such as NVQ/SVQ Medical Assistance Level 2 or City & Guilds Level 2 in Medical Assistance. The National Association of Phlebotomists offers short training courses and workshops.

Money guide

The NHS sets national pay rates for phlebotomists each year; those listed below are a guide only.

Salaries start at £13,233 per year and generally go up to £16,000.

Seniors can earn £17,700–£21,400. Managers can get up to £33,500.

If you work in the private sector or in London you may be paid more.

Related opportunities

- Biomedical Scientist/Medical Laboratory Assistant p507
- Immunologist p313
- Laboratory Technician p524

Further information

Skills for Health
2nd floor, Goldsmiths House, Broad Plain,
Bristol BS2 0JP
0117 922 1155; www.skillsforhealth.org.uk;
office@skillsforhealth.org.uk

NHS Careers
0345 606 0655; www.nhscareers.nhs.uk

The National Association of Phlebotomists
12 Coldbath Square, London EC1R 5HL
020 7833 8784; www.phlebotomy.org;
phlebotomy@btinternet.com

Healthcare

CRCI: JF

PHYSIOTHERAPIST

What the work involves

- Physiotherapists treat patients with problems affecting their muscles, bones, heart, circulation and lungs that have been caused by accident, illness or aging.

- You will assess patients, then decide on an appropriate course of treatment for them. This could include exercise, movement, hydrotherapy, massage or manipulation.

- Sports physiotherapists use the same techniques as those above, but focus solely on treating sports-related injuries.

The type of person suited to this work

You must have excellent communication skills as you will be dealing with both patients and other healthcare professionals on a daily basis. When treating patients, you will need to be able to listen to their concerns, explain the best course of treatment, and motivate them to persevere with their programme.

You will need to have a practical, logical mind in order to think around problems and solve unusual complaints in a creative way.

You must be physically fit, as much of the work can be strenuous and involve a good deal of hands-on contact and muscle manipulation.

Working conditions

You will generally work a 37 hour week, although you should expect to work evenings and weekends to fit in with your clients' lifestyles.

You could be employed by the NHS, private practices and health centres, residential homes, or sports centres and specialist clinics. A good number of physiotherapists opt for self-employment and work in a mixture of locations.

You will need to wear practical clothes, and certain employers may require you to wear a uniform.

Future prospects

60% of physiotherapists are employed by the NHS, although this number is significantly lower for those who have specialised in sports physiotherapy. There are opportunities with numerous other employers such as health clinics and sports centres, and you can be self-employed.

You could go on to specialise in an area such as orthopaedics or geriatric care, or pursue more senior positions. The NHS now offers consultant-level posts for experienced physiotherapists.

Advantages/disadvantages

You will have a great deal of contact with patients and other healthcare professionals so the job is varied and rewarding.

Qualifications and courses

ENTRY LEVEL 5

All physiotherapists must hold a degree that has been recognised by the Health Professions Council (HPC). Full time, and part time courses are also available.

Entry requirements vary according to the university, but you will usually need 3 A levels (A*–C) or equivalent, including biology or similar. You will also need at least 5 GCSEs/S grades (A*–C/1–3) or equivalent, including English, maths and science. The Diploma in Science might also be a useful starting point.

You may also be considered for a university place if you hold a BTEC National Diploma/Certificate in science, applied science, or health sciences or an NVQ Level 3 in a related subject.

Graduates with a related science degree could opt for a 2 year fast-track degree programme, and Access courses are available for entry onto a degree programme for candidates without the relevant science qualifications.

It is recommended to get work experience prior to applying for your degree, as universities look favourably on this.

If you opt for self-employment, you have control over your working hours and the patients you decide to take on.

It is physically demanding work, and working with injured or ill people can also prove emotionally draining.

Money guide

Starting salaries for newly qualified physiotherapists depend on your employer, or whether you are self-employed, but are generally around £20,000. With a few years' experience, you could earn up to £33,000, and at a senior level you could look to earn around £39,000.

Consultant physiotherapists in the NHS earn £50,000+, and those who have specialised in sports physiotherapy can earn up to £55,000.

Related opportunities

- Chiropractor p295
- Osteopath p323
- Acupuncturist p288
- Hospital Doctor p311

Further information

The Chartered Society of Physiotherapy
14 Bedford Row, London, WC1R 4ED
020 7306 6666; www.csp.org.uk

NHS Careers
PO Box 2311, Bristol BS2 2ZX
0345 606 0655; www.nhscareers.nhs.uk

Case study

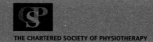

THE CHARTERED SOCIETY OF PHYSIOTHERAPY

PHYSIOTHERAPIST

Here's Nick Southorn's story

Nick decided to study physiotherapy after he realised it would give him the attractive prospect of new challenges each day and would suit the independent nature of his personality. Now qualified, Nick reflects that **"words fail to describe the feeling of first seeing a patient make improvements because of my time with them"** .

Why Nick chose physiotherapy

"While I was thinking about what to study I researched plenty of health careers, like medicine, optometry, pharmacy and nursing. I wanted to join a profession that reflected the active and independent sides of my personality, and physiotherapy fitted that perfectly.

I was attracted by the prospect of new challenges and never having two days the same, and by the chance to form cooperative relationships with patients. The massive range of career prospects amazed me, and the opportunities to progress to a hospital specialist or consultant appealed too."

What Nick's course was like

"The majority of my course was based around a problem solving model and was taught by really experienced and down-to-earth people. The most important lesson I learnt was how to find factual answers based on research and evidence. A lot of it was self-directed and that gave me a sense of control over my study. Some subjects like anatomy, physiology, and biomechanics were taught theoretically in a lecture theatre, and we also had practical lessons that were fantastic for getting to grips with the hands-on stuff."

Qualification for this hugely rewarding career is through a 3-year degree course.

Find out more about entry requirements and university locations at www.csp.org.uk/careers.
Or if you'd prefer a chat, call us on 020 7306 6666.

PODIATRIST

What the work involves

- Podiatrists (also commonly known as chiropodists) are healthcare practitioners responsible for assessing, diagnosing and treating problems relating to the feet and lower limbs.

- The work involves using medical braces to correct deformities, administering local anaesthetics to enable pain free specialist foot treatment, wound care, neurological assessment, skin, nail and bone surgery, care planning and health promotion.

- You will treat a variety of people including those with disabilities and long-term illnesses, children and people with sports related injuries.

The type of person suited to this work

Podiatrists need to be caring and understanding. You should be able to reassure patients of all ages who could be in pain and explain their treatment clearly and simply.

You will also need good communication skills to be an effective part of a healthcare team. You should be able to apply your skills and knowledge to diagnose and solve problems.

You should be good with your hands as you will be using a range of equipment and techniques.

Working conditions

You will most likely work in a clinic but may visit patients in their own homes or in residential care homes at times. You might also need to attend sporting events to treat injured players.

If employed by the NHS you will work 37 hours per week, Monday to Friday; self-employed podiatrists can work flexible hours, including evenings and weekends.

Future prospects

Podiatry offers excellent employment flexibility with the opportunity to work in the NHS, private practice, commerce, leisure, education and occupational health sectors to name but a few.

With experience you might choose to specialise in one area of podiatry such as biomechanics (musculoskeletal disorders), forensic podiatry, working with children or surgery. You could also go on to teach and research in a university or move into management. Many podiatrists even set up their own small private practices.

Advantages/disadvantages

The idea of working with other people's feet may not appeal instantly, but podiatrists generally get great satisfaction from their work.

You will have to deal with people who may be badly injured, very ill and in pain, which could be distressing.

Qualifications and courses

ENTRY 5 LEVEL

To work as a podiatrist, you need to have passed a BSc (Hons) degree in Podiatry (lasting 3 or 4 years) approved by the Health Professions Council (HPC). You must be registered with the HPC in order to practise.

For entry you are generally required to have a minimum of 5 GCSEs (A*–C) or equivalent and 3 A levels/4 Highers, one of which should be a science, preferably biology. Other qualifications may be accepted such as the Diploma in Society, Health and Development or a relevant Access course. Entrants must pass a police background check and a medical screening.

Money guide

Salary levels in the NHS may be subject to change and additional allowances may also be available for those living in or near London.

A new graduate in podiatry would have a starting salary of around £20,000 in the NHS but the earning potential could be in excess of £100,000 depending on which specialism you choose.

NHS podiatrists can earn up to £39,000 at advanced level and £65,657 as a consultant.

Private podiatrists can charge hourly, but their income is dependent on the amount of patients they have and the location of their practice; some can earn up to £105,000+.

Related opportunities

- General Practitioner p305
- Occupational Therapist p319
- Physiotherapist p330
- Prosthetist/Orthotist p334

Further information

Society of Chiropodists and Podiatrists
1 Fellmonger's Path, Tower Bridge Road,
London SE1 3LY
020 7234 8620; www.feetforlife.org

Skills for Health
2nd floor, Goldsmiths House, Broad Plain,
Bristol BS2 0JP
0117 922 1155; www.skillsforhealth.org.uk;
office@skillsforhealth.org.uk

NHS Careers
PO Box 2311, Bristol BS2 2ZX
0345 606 0655; www.nhscareers.nhs.uk

Case study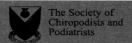

The Society of
Chiropodists and
Podiatrists

PODIATRIST

Here's Joe Parker's story

After graduating from his BSC in Podiatric Medicine, Joe started out as a community podiatrist working in a local health centre dealing with the foot disorders and complaints of the local community. He did this for three years before being moved on to a promoted post where he specialises in children, working in different health centres and hospitals.

What the job entails

"Working with children is a specialist area which covers a variety of foot and gait (walking) complaints. I get referrals from Health Visitors, GPs, Physiotherapists and other Podiatrists. My referrals include children with in-grown toe nails, verrucae and curly toes, but mostly I get children who have flat feet, in-toeing gait or other unusual walking/development problems. I also go out to schools and give Health Promotion talks to pupils on foot health."

A bad day in the office for Joe

"When a child comes into the clinic with a really sore toe and it's so sore that they don't want you to even touch it. Most children don't like getting an injection so won't let you give them a local anaesthetic and it can take you a long time to try and persuade them that you will be able to make them feel better. The parents can put pressure on you also as they know how sore it has been and know that it has become infected."

What makes Joe good at his job

"You need to be very patient and sympathetic towards the children to make them feel relaxed with you to allow you to assess and treat them. Good communication skills are vital to be able to decipher what is wrong. Problem solving skills help you to be able to come up with a management plan that suits you, the patient and the parents."

What Joe personally gets out of it

"It is really rewarding working with children, when that crying child with the sore toe comes back to you smiling as the pain has gone and their foot is better it makes it all worthwhile. Also working as part of a team with the Health Visitors, GPs, Physiotherapist etc is interesting as you are all working together to help your patient.

No two days are the same in this job, there is always something different to do, i.e. one day you could be treating in-growing toenails, the next you are giving exercises to help correct a child with an in-toeing gait. You could also be in the lab making specialist insoles to fit into someone's shoes then going off to give a talk to children in a primary school – there is never a dull moment!"

www.feetforlife.org

The Society of Chiropodists and Podiatrists
1 Fellmongers Path, Tower Bridge Road, London SE1 3LY

PROSTHETIST/ORTHOTIST

What the work involves

Prosthetist

■ Prosthetists design and fit artificial limbs for patients who have lost a limb, have a deformity or who were born without a limb.

■ Work will include taking a cast of the area where the artificial replacement limb will fit and modelling it so that it will be safe and comfortable for the patient. You will also fit and adjust the replacement limb and teach the patient how to use it.

Orthotist

■ Orthotists provide surgical appliances such as arm and leg braces, collars, splints and special footwear for patients.

■ Work will include assessing the patient's problem, designing, fitting and adjusting the orthosis, and helping the patient to use it.

The type of person suited to this work

You must have a good technical knowledge and aptitude of biomechanics and movement. You need to have excellent manual skills in order to take measurements, design devices and do fittings and make adjustments. You should be practical and have a high attention to detail as each device is made to perfectly fit each patient.

It is important to have excellent communications skills and be caring and tactful as you will have to reassure, encourage and explain procedures to your patients.

Working conditions

Opportunities are available in hospitals, clinics and centres for people with disabilities. Some time will be spent in workshops where the prostheses and orthoses are made.

You will generally work normal hours from Monday to Friday, although extra hours are required at busy times. A driving licence is useful if you are working in many different locations

Future prospects

With a shortage of prosthetists and orthotists, job prospects are generally excellent across the UK. Most prosthetists and orthotists work within the NHS but there are also opportunities in private practice, in charities such as the Red Cross and with commercial companies that make devices for NHS hospitals.

With experience, you may specialise in an area such as upper or lower limb prosthetics or spinal orthotics; you could also move into management or carry out research and teaching.

There are also many opportunities to work all over the world – especially in the US. Prosthetic and orthotic work is especially important in development programmes which work with communities affected by war.

Qualifications and courses

Training to become a prosthetist and orthotist takes 4 years, leading to a BSc (Honours) degree recognised by the British Association of Prosthetists and Orthotists and the Health Professions Council. Entry requirements are usually 240 tariff points with 3 A levels, including maths or physics as well as either biology or chemistry, plus 5 GCSEs/S Grades (A*–C/ 1–3). Entry could be granted with qualifications such as AS levels, BTEC Nationals and Higher Nationals or the International Baccalaureate. You could also take a postgraduate qualification in rehabilitation studies

Graduates can either specialise in one area or practise both specialities but must register with the HPC.

Advantages/disadvantages

Working with patients who are upset and in pain can be emotionally demanding.

It is satisfying to be able to see the positive effects that the artificial limbs and surgical appliances have on people's lives.

Money guide

There is no set salary scale for NHS prosthetists and orthotists, but salaries tend to be similar to those in commercial companies.

The starting salary for prosthetists and orthotists is around £20,710–£26,839 per year.

Experienced prosthetists and orthotists can earn £24,831–£33,436.

If you work in the NHS and have management duties, your salary can reach £39,273.

Some seniors in the NHS or those who work for manufacturers can get up to £60,000.

Earnings are generally higher in London.

Related opportunities

■ Medical Physicist p316
■ Occupational Therapist p319
■ Physiotherapist p330

Further information

Skills for Health
2nd floor, Goldsmiths House, Broad Plain, Bristol BS2 0JP
0117 922 1155; www.skillsforhealth.org.uk;
office@skillsforhealth.org.uk

British Association of Prosthetists and Orthotists
Sir James Clark Building, Paisley PA1 1TJ
0845 166 8490; www.bapo.com

PSYCHIATRIST

What the work involves

- Psychiatrists are doctors who have undergone further training in psychiatry.

- As a psychiatrist, you will diagnose mental health problems by talking to patients and carrying out tests. You will then decide on a course of treatment which could include prescribing drugs and talking to patients to help them deal with their problems.

- You will treat people with a range of mental health problems. These include depression, schizophrenia, eating disorders, anxieties, phobias, drug and alcohol abuse, and post-traumatic stress disorder.

- You will probably specialise in one area such as child and adolescent psychiatry, forensic psychiatry or learning disabilities.

The type of person suited to this work

As a psychiatrist you need to be patient and caring. You will need excellent communication skills to listen carefully to people who might be confused or withdrawn. You will help them talk through and come to terms with their problems or illness and should be able to explain their conditions and treatment in a clear, simple way. You will work with relatives and carers, and as part of a team with other medical staff such as psychiatric nurses and occupational therapists.

You will need to be prepared to undergo a long programme of education and training in order to gain the in-depth knowledge and skills necessary to become a psychiatrist.

Working conditions

You could work in a range of locations, including hospitals, people's own homes, schools, residential homes and prisons.

Some psychiatrists have standard office hours. Others work shifts and are on an on-call rota, which includes working at nights, at weekends and on bank holidays.

You will work as part of a team of healthcare professionals.

Future prospects

Most psychiatrists work within the NHS throughout the UK. There is also a small amount of work available in private hospitals, care homes and rehabilitation centres. The armed forces also employ psychiatrists.

There are six specialist areas of psychiatry that you may work in: adult psychiatry; child and adolescent psychiatry; forensic psychiatry; psychiatry of learning disability; old age psychiatry; and psychotherapy.

Entry to psychotherapy is competitive.

You could move into academic work, either carrying out research or teaching medical students.

Advantages/disadvantages

Your patients could be confused or aggressive with a range of difficult problems so the work can be demanding.

Qualifications and courses

To become a psychiatrist you need to qualify as a doctor first. You will therefore need to complete a 5 year medical degree recognised by the General Medical Council (GMC). For a medical degree, you will need good grades in 3 A levels/4 H grades, including chemistry and possibly biology, and GCSEs/S grades (A*–C/1–3). You will also need to pass the UK Clinical Aptitude Test.

After graduating, candidates undertake a 2 year foundation programme before applying for specialist training in psychiatry.

Training as a specialist registrar takes up to a further 6 years, spent training in general adult and old age psychiatry and gaining experience of other specialisms. This leads to the Certificate of Completion of Specialist Training (CCST) and eligibility for entry on the GMC's Specialist Register. It then becomes possible to apply for work as a consultant.

It is rewarding to be able to make a difference to people's lives by helping them to regain their self-respect and happiness.

Money guide

Salary levels in the NHS have a national rate, but this can also vary in some areas.

During training, most junior doctors and senior house officers earn from £22,190 to £27,523.

Consultants earn from around £74,504 and with additional payments and merits it is possible for senior consultants to earn anything up to £176,000.

Different salary bandings, which depend upon the amount of hours worked and the extent of your workload, can boost these figures.

Extra earnings may be available through private practice work.

Related opportunities

- Hospital Doctor p311
- Psychologist p570
- General Practitioner p305

Further information

NHS Careers
0345 606 0655; www.nhscareers.nhs.uk

British Medical Association
BMA House, Tavistock Square, London WC1H 9JP
020 7387 4499; www.bma.org.uk

Royal College of Psychiatrists
17 Belgrave Square, London SW1X 8PG
020 7235 2351; rcpsych@rcpsych.ac.uk

CRCI: JH   Healthcare

RADIOGRAPHER

What the work involves

Diagnostic radiographer

- You will help doctors and surgeons to diagnose diseases and injuries as an essential step towards treating a patient.

- You may use a variety of methods such as X-ray, computed tomography (CT) scanning and ultrasound to create images of body parts and organs.

Therapeutic radiographer

- Working with an oncology team you will use doses of radiation to destroy tumours in cancer patients.

- You will be involved in every aspect of the treatment, including pre-treatment preparation, planning, the delivery of the radiation and follow-up care of patients.

The type of person suited to this work

You should be warm, understanding and adaptable. You must be able to work with both children and adults who are extremely ill. A good communicator, you will need to listen to your patients.

You need to be a quick thinker and be detail-oriented in order to produce accurate images for your patients. Confidence to operate sophisticated computerised equipment is essential.

Working conditions

All radiographers must wear a uniform, and protective clothing for various procedures.

Diagnostic radiographer

You will be based in accident and emergency, operating theatres, wards or imaging units.

These departments need to be staffed 24 hours a day so you will work a shift system including nights and weekends. You should work a total of 37.5 hours a week.

Therapeutic radiographer

You will be based in radiotherapy or oncology centres, outpatient units or at charities such as Macmillan Cancer Support.

Future prospects

You could work for the NHS in a clinic, hospital or oncology centre or work for the Armed Forces or a private practice.

You could be promoted to management roles or become an instructor or researcher. UK radiography qualifications are recognised internationally so you could choose to work overseas.

Diagnostic radiographer

You could specialise in areas such as MRI, ultrasound or nuclear medicine.

Qualifications and courses

ENTRY LEVEL 6

You will need a recognised first degree or postgraduate qualification. Most universities require you to have previous experience in a radiography department. Foundation degrees in health subjects and the BTEC Higher National Diploma in Health could be useful.

Diagnostic radiographer

You must hold a degree in diagnostic radiography. Most courses are 3 years and include a placement. You will need at least 1 A level in a science related subject, preferably biology or physics, for entry onto a course.

Therapeutic radiographer

You will need a degree in radiotherapy or therapeutic radiography. Entry requirements are the same as above. MSc and PhD courses allow graduates to specialise.

Therapeutic radiographer

You could specialise in anything from quality management to treatment planning or palliative care (supporting those with life-threatening illnesses).

Advantages/disadvantages

Each of your patients will be unique, keeping your work interesting.

It is satisfying when you capture the best image possible and contribute to your patients' wellbeing.

Rota work can be difficult as you may be required to work bank holidays and nights.

Money guide

An NHS radiographer can earn between £20,710 and £26,123 a year. Diagnostic radiographers tend to be paid slightly more than therapeutic radiographers.

With experience you could earn up to £32,653. Managers and consultants earn £60,000+.

Your salary might increase if you work for a private practice.

Related opportunities

- Medical Physicist p316
- Critical Care Scientist p297
- Radiologist p337

Further information

The Society and College of Radiographers
207 Providence Square, Mill Street, London SE1 2EW
020 7740 7200; www.sor.org; ifno@sor.org

Radiography Careers
www.radiographycareers.co.uk

RADIOLOGIST

What the work involves

- Radiologists are doctors who have undergone further training in radiology.

- As a radiologist, you will diagnose patients' diseases by using information gained from images such as X-rays, and computed tomography (CT) or magnetic resonance imaging (MRI) scans.

- Radiologists increasingly perform interventional procedures such as biopsies, using image guidance.

- You will also play an important role in identifying sources of disease and reducing the possible risks of it spreading further.

The type of person suited to this work

As a radiologist, you need to care about patients, and you must be able to explain things to them simply and clearly so that they understand their health conditions and any treatments they may need. You will also need good communication skills to work well as part of a team with other medical staff.

Scientific and technical knowledge and an ability to diagnose patients' conditions accurately are also necessary. You will need good eyesight and excellent attention to detail for interpreting images and practical skills for caring for patients and operating equipment.

Working conditions

You will spend a good deal of time studying and training. You will work within a hospital, mainly in the radiology department.

Scientific and technical knowledge and an ability to diagnose patients' conditions accurately are also necessary. You will need good eyesight and excellent attention to detail for interpreting images and practical skills for caring for patients and operating equipment.

Radiologists undergo a long programme of education and training in order to gain the in-depth knowledge and skills necessary.

Future prospects

Career prospects are excellent due to an international shortage of radiologists. Most radiologists work within the NHS throughout the UK. There is also some work available in private hospitals.

You may decide to specialise further in particular areas of the work, or you could move into management. You may also move into academic work, either carrying out research or teaching medical students.

Advantages/disadvantages

The work can be emotionally demanding because you will be dealing with patients who may have life-threatening conditions.

Your work can be vital in finding an accurate and early diagnosis for patients, which can help to save lives.

Qualifications and courses

ENTRY LEVEL 6

Entry to radiology is initially the same as for hospital doctors (see p 311). To enter, candidates complete a medical degree recognised by the General Medical Council (GMC).

Candidates require at least 2 years' post-qualifying experience to enter training as a radiologist, but in practice, competition for training positions is very intense, and many new entrants have more than 3 years' clinical experience and a postgraduate qualification. New entrants must enrol as Members of the Royal College of Radiologists.

Specialist training as a radiologist takes at least 5 years, and leads to the Certificate of Completion of Specialist Training (CCST). At least 4 years of the training are spent in clinical posts, and 6 months' research in any aspect of diagnostic imaging is also included. Trainees must pass all three parts of the Fellowship of the Royal College of Radiologists (FRCR) examination.

The Royal College of Radiologists operates a Continuing Professional Development scheme for qualified radiologists to update their knowledge and skills.

Money guide

You will start off earninig £29,411. The salary for senior house officers with 5 years' experience could be up to £70,000 per year.

Specialists and consultants can earn from £75,000 to £176,000+.

Salary levels in the NHS have a national rate, but this can vary in some areas. Extra earnings may be available through private practice work.

Related opportunities

- Anaesthetist p290
- Hospital Doctor p311
- Psychiatrist p335
- Radiographer p336

Further information

NHS Careers
0345 606 0655; www.nhscareers.nhs.uk

British Medical Association
BMA House, Tavistock Square, London WC1H 9JP
020 7387 4499; www.bma.org.uk

Royal College of Radiologists
38 Portland Place, London W1B 1JQ
020 7636 4432; www.rcr.ac.uk; enquiries@rcr.ac.uk

CRCI: JH

Healthcare

SPEECH AND LANGUAGE THERAPIST

What the work involves

- Speech and language therapists work with patients who have problems speaking, chewing or swallowing.

- You will be responsible for assessing patients, and prescribing a suitable course of treatment.

- You will work with a range of patients including children who need help in developing their speech, people with a speech defect such as a stammer, and those who have trouble eating because of an accident or illness.

- You will also work with each patient's family, partner or carer in order to show them how to support your patient at home.

The type of person suited to this work

You will need excellent communication skills in order to develop a good relationship with patients and colleagues alike. You will also need to be a patient teacher in order to successfully help your patients learn new skills to overcome their problems.

You should be mature and non-judgmental in your approach to patients as you will be dealing with people of varying ages, backgrounds and cultures.

You will work both on your own and within a wider team of healthcare professionals, so you must have plenty of initiative coupled with a good approach to working within a team.

Working conditions

Speech and language therapists usually work 37.5 hours per week from Monday to Friday. Evening, weekend or shift work is rare. There are plenty of opportunities to work part time.

You could work in one or several of a variety of locations, including hospitals, schools, residential homes, health centres, young offenders' institutions and in patients' houses. Since local travel in the community is required, it is useful to have a driving licence.

Future prospects

There is a current shortage of registered speech and language therapists, so job opportunities outweigh the number of candidates.

Most therapists are employed by the NHS and work throughout their local community. Others work for social services, local education authorities, charities and schools. There is a growing trend amongst therapists to be self-employed and treat patients privately. You could progress to more senior supervisory positions, specialise in an area that particularly interests you, or move into research.

Advantages/disadvantages

Speech and language therapists are in great demand, so you will have a greater choice of job opportunities open to you than in some other health-related professions.

Qualifications and courses

All speech and language therapists are registered with the Health Professions Council (HPC). In order to qualify for registration, you must complete an HPC approved training programme.

These take the form of either a degree or a postgraduate qualification in speech and language therapy, human communication or a similar subject. For entrance onto a degree course you will need 3 A levels or equivalent, and 5 GCSEs/S grades (A*–C/1–3) including English, science and maths. The Diploma in Society, Health and Development could also be relevant.

There are also Foundation courses available for those who do not have the relevant qualifications to go straight onto a degree programme, and accelerated 2 year degree courses for students who already have a health-related degree. All courses comprise a balance between academic study and on-the-job training.

Because you will be working with children and vulnerable adults, you will need to undergo a Criminal Records Bureau check and medical screening.

Working closely with patients and seeing them improve under your care and guidance is rewarding.

You may have to work with difficult patients in unfavourable conditions on occasion, such as young offenders' institutions or prisons.

Money guide

As a newly qualified speech and language therapist, you could expect to earn around £20,000. This usually rises quite quickly to £24,000, and, as you gain experience, up to £33,000. Senior therapists can earn up to £43,000, and if you take on significant supervisory and management responsibilities as well you could expect £50,000+.

Related opportunities

- Occupational Therapist p319
- Learning Disabilities Nurse p314
- Health Visitor p309

Further information

Royal College of Speech and Language Therapists (RCSLT)
2 White Hart Yard, London SE1 1NX
020 7378 1200; www.rcslt.org

NHS Careers
PO Box 2311, Bristol BS2 2ZX
0345 606 0655; www.nhscareers.nhs.uk

SPORTS AND EXERCISE SCIENTIST

What the work involves

- Sports scientists work either with athletes to help build their performance or with people who need or wish to improve their health. Clients may also be recovering from illness or injury.

- As a sport or exercise scientist, you require a lot of scientific knowledge, including an understanding of biology, biomechanics, and physiology.

- You also need to have an understanding of psychology, as you might have to assess the mental state of some athletes, and you'll also spend time on performance analysis (usually done with video footage).

- You'll spend some time outside, and also conduct research.

The type of person suited to this work

If you want to be a sports and exercise scientist, above all you need to be a good communicator. Your work will centre on building relationships with people, and you have to be good at listening and aware of your clients' needs.

Aside from this, you need to have a clear writing style to communicate findings, and be good at research and problem solving. You should be good with numbers and statistics, well organised, accurate, and good with computers.

Working conditions

You'll usually work in leisure and sports centres and gyms, usually for 38 hours a week. If you're a sports scientist, some clients may require you outside regular working hours, and part-time work is also available.

You'll also spend a lot of time outdoors, and probably travel too. For this reason, a driving licence is an advantage.

Future prospects

Although there's no specific career path for this job, progression is possible. Building a list of contacts is important, and with the right experience you may be able to work your way up to helping people who play sport at an international level.

You could also teach, or, if you're an exercise scientist you might be able to move into a specific area such as cardiology.

Advantages/disadvantages

This job is really rewarding for those who are interested in exercise and science, and like to be out and about being active rather than sitting still. You have to use your brain and your body, and the job is unlikely to become boring as you'll be working with so many different people.

It can be tiring, and you need quite specialist knowledge that has to be constantly maintained.

Qualifications and courses

Most entrants to this profession have a degree in sports science, but it's also fine if you take a degree in psychology or any kind of physical education. You don't actually need to be very good at sport yourself, although it does help.

To follow a degree in sports science, you usually need good GCSEs and 3 A levels or equivalent. Some of these should be in sciences, especially biology. There's also the option of following an access course before taking a degree, or doing a postgraduate degree in sports science after an initial science degree.

Once you have a relevant degree, you can seek accreditation through the British Association of Sport and Exercise Sciences (BASES), which can help improve job prospects. There is even an option for student membership.

Continuing Professional Development (CPD) and keeping your skills up to date is really important, and there are plenty of opportunities to do this with BASES.

Money guide

Newly qualified, you'll probably earn around £18,000 a year.

As you gain experience, this may rise to about £38,000.

If you work with top athletes, you might earn about £60,000 a year.

Related opportunities

- Leisure/Fitness Centre Assistant/Manager p389
- Sports Coach p393
- Sports Development Officer p394

Further information

British Association of Sport and Exercise Sciences (BASES)
Leeds Metropolitan University, Carnegie Faculty of Sport and Education, Fairfax Hall, Headingley Campus, Beckett Park, Leeds LS6 3QS
0113 283 6162; www.bases.org.uk

English Institute of Sport (EIS)
4th Floor, Byrom House, 21 Quay Street, Manchester M3 3JD
0870 759 0400; www.eis2win.co.uk

SkillsActive
Castlewood House, 77–91 New Oxford Street, London WC1A 1PX
020 7632 2000; www.skillsactive.com/careers

Healthcare

CRCI: JG

STERILE SERVICES TECHNICIAN

What the work involves

- Sterile services technicians work as part of a team responsible for helping to prevent the spread of infections, by making sure that hospital equipment is sterile.

- Your work will involve collecting and cleaning a range of instruments such as syringes.

- You will have to dismantle and examine certain instruments through a microscope before sterilising and then reassembling and testing them afterwards.

- You will work to national standards, operating highly technical machines, and must keep accurate records of your work.

The type of person suited to this work

You will need to be good with your hands, work accurately, pay attention to detail and follow instructions and set procedures carefully.

Sterile services technicians should be very vigilant about hygiene and interested in keeping hospitals and equipment clean and safe for patients and staff. You will work in a team so will need good communication skills. You should also be well organised and able to keep clear, detailed records.

You will be collecting and dismantling machinery so will need to be fit.

Working conditions

You will work in a hospital as part of a team and will have contact with doctors, nurses and other staff. Based in the sterile services department, you will collect equipment from all parts of the hospital and this will involve lifting and pushing trolleys.

You will have to wear protective clothing and may have to work shifts.

Future prospects

Most jobs are in NHS hospitals throughout the UK, but you could also work in a private hospital. Opportunities are good, as there is a shortage of applicants for vacancies.

With experience, you could be promoted to senior technician or supervisor. You could then take professional qualifications and become a sterile services manager. As a manager you could move in to management in other areas of the NHS.

Qualifications and courses

There are no set minimum qualifications to begin work in this position. However, employers will expect you to have a good general standard of education, to have strong reading skills and neat handwriting (for labelling materials and equipment clearly and correctly).

Some employers may prefer you to have 5 GCSEs/S grades (A*–C/1–3). Qualifications such as a BTEC National Certificate or Diploma in Applied Science could also be an advantage. The Diploma in Science will also be useful.

Whilst on the job, you may be encouraged to train for an ASET Level 2 Certificate in Control of Infection and Contamination, or an NCFE Level 2 Certificate in Infection Control.

Advantages/disadvantages

The work can be routine and physically demanding.

You will be making a vital contribution to controlling the spread of potentially deadly infections.

Money guide

Starting salaries are from £13,250 to £16,000 per year, increasing with experience.

As an assistant manager or supervisor you can expect to earn £15,200–£18,160.

Related opportunities

- Hospital Porter p312
- Biomedical Scientist/Medical Laboratory Assistant p507
- Operating Department Practitioner p320

Further information

Skills for Health
2nd floor, Goldsmiths House, Broad Plain, Bristol BS2 0JP
0117 922 1155; www.skillsforhealth.org.uk,
office@skillsforhealth.org.uk

NHS Careers
0345 606 0655; www.nhscareers.nhs.uk

Institute of Decontamination Sciences
Drumcross Hall, Bathgate EH48 4JT
01506 811077; www.idsc-uk.co.uk;
idsc.admin@googlemail.com

SURGEON

What the work involves

- Surgeons work in hospitals, operating on patients in order to remove, isolate or prevent the spread of disease, treat injury, and fix other complaints.

- You will also be responsible for diagnosing problems, taking case histories, talking patients through surgical procedures and advising them on post-operative care.

- You will specialise in operating on specific conditions or diseases relating to a particular system of the body, such as neurological, gastrointestinal or cardiovascular.

- You will see patients on ward rounds and in outpatient clinics, as well as undertaking administrative work, such as updating patient records.

The type of person suited to this work

You will need excellent communication skills in order to develop a good relationship with patients and colleagues alike. You will be required to direct your team through complex surgical procedures in the operating theatre, as well as explaining them to patients in simple terms.

You should have excellent manual and technical skills in order to operate with precision and confidence. As you will be working under immense pressure whilst in theatre, you should also be able to think quickly and clearly when solving problems.

You must be prepared to break news to patients and relatives on occasion, which requires sensitivity and diplomacy.

Working conditions

Most surgeons work extremely long hours which often include nights and weekends. Most of your work will take place in hospitals, working with other health professionals, including other surgeons, nurses, anaesthetists and GPs. You could work in the NHS or in private hospitals, although the majority of surgeons divide their time between the two.

The work is mentally and physically exhausting, as you will need to concentrate for hours at a time and spend a lot of time on your feet.

Future prospects

There are many opportunities to work abroad, particularly in conjunction with specialist charities operating in developing countries.

You will continue to train and learn new skills throughout your career as technology and techniques develop, change and improve. Once you have qualified as a surgeon, you can become a consultant and work within the NHS or in private practice, both of which are lucrative options.

Advantages/disadvantages

You will be personally responsible for transforming and saving a number of lives throughout your career. Jobs don't really get much more rewarding than that.

Qualifications and courses

ENTRY 8 LEVEL

Before commencing training as a surgeon you will need to study for a degree in medicine. Most medical degrees take 5 years; entrants require at least 3 A levels in subjects including chemistry and biology or equivalent, and 5 GCSEs/S grades (A*–C/1–3) or equivalent.

If you do not have science related A levels, you could undertake a 6 year degree programme that includes a preliminary 30 week course to get you up to speed. A 4 year fast-track degree course is available to those who already hold a degree.

On completion of a medical degree, you will need to undertake a 2 year, hospital based foundation programme of general training. At the end of this, you can choose to specialise in surgery. You will then undertake a further 6 years of training in order to pass your surgical exams and qualify for entry onto the General Medical Council specialist register as a surgeon.

The training period is extremely long, often in excess of 12 years, so you have to be extremely dedicated.

You will work long hours and unpredictable hours, which can have an adverse effect on your personal life.

Money guide

Once you have completed your medical degree, you can expect to earn around £23,000 during your foundation years. Once you are in specialist training, you will earn between £44,000 and £69,000, depending on which stage you have reached.

On qualifying to become a consultant, you can earn £70,000+. Senior consultants' salaries reach in excess of £170,000.

Related opportunities

- Hospital Doctor p311
- General Practitioner p305
- Dentist p302

Further information

The Royal College of Surgeons of England
35–43 Lincoln's Inn Fields, London WC2A 3PE
020 7405 3474; www.rcseng.ac.uk

British Medical Association
BMA House, Tavistock Square, London WC1H 9JP
020 7387 4499; www.bma.org.uk

NHS Careers
PO Box 2311, Bristol BS2 2ZX
0345 606 0655; www.nhscareers.nhs.uk

CRCI: JH   Healthcare

TRICHOLOGIST

What the work involves

- Trichologists diagnose and treat diseases and disorders of the scalp and hair, such as hair loss, and dandruff.

- You will talk to patients about their medical history, health and diet and closely examine their hair and scalp.

- You will give advice and recommend treatment, such as using special creams or shampoos.

- You might also refer patients on to other healthcare professionals if appropriate.

The type of person suited to this work

Trichologists need excellent communication skills to speak to patients about their problem and explain the treatment they have recommended. You should be sympathetic and tactful, and able to reassure patients, put them at their ease and listen carefully to their problems.

You will need to have a methodical approach to your work and pay close attention to detail so that you can assess patients' conditions accurately, and plan appropriate treatment.

Working conditions

Most trichologists work in clinics treating patients, or in universities and colleges, and pharmaceutical and cosmetics companies if they are involved in research or teaching.

You will have normal working hours from Monday to Friday, but if you work in private practice you might need to work in the evenings, or occasionally at weekends, to treat people at times that suit them.

The work involves close contact and hands-on treatment of patients.

Future prospects

Many trichologists are self-employed and run their own clinics, either on their own or with another professional. Dermatologists are doctors who have trained in trichology and are usually employed in hospitals.

Trichologists may also go on to work as lecturers in colleges or universities, often in hair and beauty departments.

There are also a number of opportunities to work in research in pharmaceutical and cosmetics companies.

Advantages/disadvantages

Working with patients can be challenging and stressful.

It is rewarding to be able to use your knowledge to treat patients successfully.

Qualifications and courses

The main route into trichology and entry to the register of qualified members of the Institute of Trichologists is by successful completion of the Institute's 2 year training course in trichology (there are limited exceptions to this, for example for doctors (dermatologists) and graduates of HND trichology courses at selected colleges).

Entrants are often mature, though there is no set minimum age. There are no set minimum entry requirements, but the course is academic and scientific in nature and the progress of students is closely monitored.

Successful completion of the Institute's course makes you eligible for admission as an Associate Member of the Institute (AIT). Progression to full membership (MIT) is available upon further study and a minimum of 2 years' professional practice as a trichologist.

To become a doctor (dermatologist), candidates complete a medical degree recognised by the General Medical Council (GMC) as outlined in the doctor entry (see p311).

Money guide

Most trichologists are self-employed and charge clients by the session. Earnings vary widely, depending on how much you charge and how many clients you see. It can also depend on which area of the country you are working in.

Earnings for newly self-employed practitioners may start from about £30 per consultation. Experienced practitioners may earn up to £90 per consultation.

For NHS doctors/dermatologists, you must complete a medical degree; the salary for these posts is outlined in the hospital doctor information page.

Related opportunities

- Hospital Doctor p311
- Hairdresser/Barber p469
- Dietitian p303

Further information

The Trichological Society
1 Kings Mews, London WC1N 2JA
01708 728980; www.hairscientists.org

Institute of Trichologists
24 Langroyd Road, London SW17 7PL
0870 607 0602, www.trichologists.org.uk,
admin@trichologists.org.uk

Languages, Information and Culture

The jobs in this family are quite varied in terms of whether you would work with other people or by yourself. You could find yourself working in a range of different places, from museums to antiques fairs to conferences as an interpreter. Some of the jobs in this family are more unusual and are perfect for those of you who want a fascinating job that allows you to indulge in your passion for historic artefacts and artwork or languages and foreign countries. To excel in this sector you should have an inquisitive mind, be meticulous in your work and enjoy carrying out research.

The following jobs are covered in this section:

For similar jobs to the ones in this section please see *Design, Arts and Crafts* on page 167 and *Marketing, Advertising, Media, Print and Publishing* on page 401.

ANTHROPOLOGIST

What the work involves

- You will study and research the origin and cultural, physical and social developments of humans.

- You will investigate human culture across the world, in terms of its beliefs, values, traditions, social structure and language.

- You will apply specialist knowledge and research skills to find out about the differences between human cultures.

- Anthropologists undertake their research in a wide range of areas such as archaeology, the arts, the environment, biology and religion.

The type of person suited to this work

Whatever job you do as an anthropologist, you will need a strong interest in people and a respectful, flexible attitude to other people's beliefs and customs. You should also enjoy meeting new people and entering different social situations.

Good communication skills are also very important. Strong research skills and an organised approach are useful. ICT skills and a good level of numeracy are also helpful.

You will need an observant approach with an interest in a wide range of subjects.

Working conditions

For research-based work, you might need to visit and stay in different areas. Spending time in other places means that anthropology is not generally a 9am–5pm office-based job.

The work can involve travel in the UK and overseas. Some physical or biological anthropologists work in laboratories analysing and researching samples.

Future prospects

You could gain employment as a researcher on specific projects. Many anthropologists progress within academia by undertaking research and teaching around their specialist interests.

You could also work for government bodies and charities. There are some opportunities to work overseas.

Anthropologists also apply their research skills and training to their work in other areas such as social care, teaching and the health service.

Advantages/disadvantages

This job can provide opportunities to develop and research theories about people and cultures. Anthropology can also provide the chance to meet a variety of people and visit different places.

Field research can be physically demanding and spending time away can be difficult if you have family commitments.

Qualifications and courses

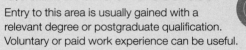

Entry to this area is usually gained with a relevant degree or postgraduate qualification. Voluntary or paid work experience can be useful.

There are limited opportunities to gain qualifications in this area before degree level. A level Sociology and GCSEs cover some aspects of anthropology. For biological anthropology, an A level in Biology may be useful.

Access and degree courses in this area cover subjects such as social anthropology and physical/biological anthropology. Anthropology can also be studied as part of a combined Honours degree with subjects such as archaeology or psychology.

It is also possible to study for a Master's or another postgraduate degree in anthropology following a first degree in any subject.

The Association of Social Anthropologists runs seminars and conferences, and has information on bursaries and awards for anthropology students. Some universities such as Wolverhampton and Brighton have centres for learning and teaching which run courses on sociology, anthropology and politics, although these are aimed at applicants with some knowledge of the subject.

Professionals using their anthropology training in another area such as archaeology are likely to have gained a qualification or degree in their specialist subject.

Researchers in this area are often required to have a relevant postgraduate qualification or the equivalent practical experience.

Money guide

Anthropologists work in a range of sectors, so salaries vary. Starting salaries for graduates are around £21,000+ per year, rising to £26,000 for research assistants/researchers. £25,000–£30,000 per year is usual for lecturers. £28,000–£55,000 is the range for senior lecturers.

Related opportunities

- Archaeologist p345
- Historian p352
- Archivist/Records Manager p346

Further information

Royal Anthropological Institute of Great Britain and Ireland
50 Fitzroy Street, London W1T 5BT
www.theasa.org

Association of Social Anthropologists
PO Box 5233, Brighton BN50 9YW
0121 414 7919; www.c-sap.bham.ac.uk

ARCHAEOLOGIST

What the work involves

- Using your specialist knowledge and skills you will investigate and record physical evidence of the past.

- You will provide practical support on archaeological excavations or 'digs', which might include undertaking basic digging work, project-managing a team or researching evidence found on sites.

- You will develop public understanding of history through presentations, the publication of your findings or teaching in universities or schools.

- You could provide information and advice on how to protect and maintain historical sites.

The type of person suited to this work

You will need a strong interest in history and past cultures. For practical work you will need a patient and careful approach. You should also be observant with an eye for detail. A good level of physical fitness and manual dexterity will be needed when working on digs and handling objects.

The ability to work as part of a team is useful. In more senior jobs, you will need to explain your work to others so communication skills are important. Writing skills will help you to be able to write up reports and keep detailed records. ICT skills are also useful.

Working conditions

Archaeologists often work on sites or digs that are outdoors. Varying weather conditions and the nature of the work make this job physically demanding.

Some archaeologists are based in offices within government bodies, heritage organisations and museums.

Much of your work will be on temporary contracts.

Future prospects

Whatever route you follow, this is a very competitive area in which to develop a career. You will need to gain practical experience on a voluntary or paid basis. With further experience you could project-manage site excavations or work as a researcher analysing excavation findings.

Some archaeologists work for heritage organisations to help preserve historic monuments and buildings. Others go into teaching or follow an academic career.

Advantages/disadvantages

It is likely that you will need to move around different geographical areas to gain practical experience.

There are opportunities to work overseas.

It's rewarding to discover artefacts that can shed ground-breaking light on the past.

Qualifications and courses

Most professional archaeologists have a degree or postgraduate qualification.

Degree entry usually requires 2 A levels, although there are no specific subject requirements. Archaeology can be studied as a single Honours degree or in combination with another degree subject. A small number of Foundation degrees are available in Archaeology. Entry to postgraduate courses requires a good first degree.

It is possible to enter this profession without a degree, although this is becoming increasingly uncommon. The Diploma in Environmental and Land-based Studies could be useful. NVQs at Levels 3 and 4 in Archaeological Practice are also available.

Qualifications in computing, which cover computer-aided design and geographical information systems, can be very helpful due to the increasing use of technology in archaeology.

Voluntary experience on digs is very useful. The key professional bodies can provide details of holiday work experience opportunities. The Archaeology Training Forum (ATF) develops and offers short courses in Continuing Professional Development.

Money guide

£13,700–£15,500 per year is usual for starting salaries.

The average salary for an archaeologist is £23,000.

Senior archaeologists can expect a salary of around £47,000.

Related opportunities

- Archivist/Records Manager p346
- Conservator/Restorer p350
- Further/Higher Education Lecturer p196
- Librarian/Library Assistant p355

Further information

Creative and Cultural Skills
4th Floor, Lafone House, London SE1 3HN
020 7015 1847; www.ccskills.org.uk

Institute of Field Archaeologists
PO Box 227, University of Reading, Reading RG6 6AB
01183 786446; www.archaeologists.net

Council for British Archaeology
St Mary's House, 66 Bootham, York YO30 7BZ
01904 671417; www.britarch.ac.uk

ARCHIVIST/ RECORDS MANAGER

What the work involves

Archivist

■ You will manage and organise stored sets of archives, including records such as documents, maps, films and other items. Many archivists deal with information enquiries and advise on the availability of records. You will ensure that archives are maintained in an appropriate way. You may also conserve documents and prepare them for storage.

Records manager

■ You will be responsible for organising records and information and advising your organisation as to which should be classified, stored or destroyed. You could be dealing with paper based or electronic records.

The type of person suited to this work

Both records managers and archivists manage information so a well-organised and methodical approach is essential. They need strong analytical and IT skills.

Archivists will need an interest in preserving historical records. You may provide information and advice to members of the public so strong communication skills are useful.

Working conditions

Record/archive centres can be modern and spacious, but if based in older buildings, space may be limited.

Accessing records from cramped storage rooms or high shelves can be physically demanding. This job may not suit people with dust allergies.

In archivist roles dealing with enquiries from visitors, the working environment can be very busy.

Future prospects

Archivist

Public records offices, private companies and other organisations need skilled information professionals. With experience, you could progress from an assistant archivist role into senior management.

Records manager

Records managers may need to change employers in order to progress. Consultancy work is an option.

Advantages/disadvantages

Archivist

This job allows you to preserve and protect historical documents.

Employers often offer short-term contracts which can create job instability.

Qualifications and courses

Archivist

Entrants to this profession need a 2.1 Honours degree followed by a postgraduate qualification in Archives and Records Management or Archival Studies. Useful subjects include history, classics, languages and information science. You will need at least 2 A levels and 5 GCSEs (A*–C) for degree entry. Your postgraduate degree must be recognised by the Society of Archivists.

Work experience is an advantage. See the Society of Archivists for opportunities.

Records manager

You will normally require both an Honours degree and a postgraduate qualification in Records Management or in Archives and Records Management. You will need at least 2 A levels and 5 GCSEs (A*–C) for degree entry. Relevant experience is also important. Visit the Society of Archivists' website for opportunities.

Both archivists and records managers may start out as assistants without a degree but will need to study for a degree and postgraduate qualification in order to become professionals.

Records manager

You may have to change employers in order to progress.

You will constantly be learning as computer software and legislation are always changing.

Money guide

£17,000–£24,000 is typical for starting salaries (before gaining a professional qualification). When qualified and with some experience you could earn around £27,000. As a senior archivist it is possible to earn £60,000. Records managers receive a starting salary of about £23,000, with experience this can increase to £26,680–£40,000. With enough experience and within a large enough team you could earn over £70,000.

Related opportunities

■ Archaeologist p345
■ Librarian/Library Assistant p355

Further information

Society of Archivists
Prioryfield House, 20 Canon Street, Taunton TA1 1SW
01823 327030; www.archives.org.uk

City&
Guilds

www.cityandguilds.com/myperfectjob

ARTS ADMINISTRATOR/ MANAGER

What the work involves

■ You will support the development and operation of activities and events in areas such as visual arts, drama and music.

■ You will undertake a range of administrative tasks including coordinating facilities and office management. You may be responsible for booking artists, refreshments, security and ticket sales.

■ Your job could also involve managing funding applications and budgets or writing press releases.

■ Arts administrators are employed in many different organisations such as arts centres, museums, community arts groups, local authorities and theatre companies. If you work for a bigger organisation, you will probably specialise in one administrative field such as public relations or sponsorship.

The type of person suited to this work

Enthusiasm for the arts is essential for this role. You will need a committed approach and be able to take initiative. A good range of administrative, office and ICT skills are also essential. You should be able to communicate well in person and in writing. As you will probably have to manage project budgets, numeracy skills are also useful.

Good organisational and multi-tasking skills are essential. You should enjoy working with a range of people, including artists and members of the public. You should be able to work independently and as part of a team.

Working conditions

Working hours can vary but it is likely that you will need to work some evenings and weekends to attend events.

Working environments vary according to employer. You might be based in a spacious office or have to work in more cramped conditions.

You might be required to travel to meet with artists and to attend performances.

Future prospects

This is a competitive area to get into. Developing expertise in a specific area such as community arts or theatre can be helpful. With experience, you could progress from an assistant administrator role into a more senior job such as general manager or director.

With higher levels of experience, you could provide freelance support or specialise in a particular area such as arts marketing.

Advantages/disadvantages

This job provides the satisfaction of working in the arts.

Many roles are available on a part-time or project basis which can create job insecurity.

You may have to move geographic areas to gain work.

Qualifications and courses

There are no specific entry requirements, but most arts administrators have a degree or HND in an arts subject or business studies.

At degree level, arts management can be studied on its own, or in combination with a related subject such as events management and heritage management. The minimum entry requirements are 2 A levels.

The Diploma in Creative and Media could also be useful.

Postgraduate courses in arts administration/arts management are available. A degree and/or relevant work experience is required for entry to these programmes.

NVQs are available in Cultural Venue Operations and Support at Level 2 and Cultural Venue Administration or Cultural Heritage Operations at Level 3, Cultural Heritage at Level 4 and Cultural Heritage Management at Level 5. Another possible entry route is a creative apprenticeship as it covers community arts management.

Experience in the arts, in administration or business, and ICT skills will be an advantage. It is crucial to gain experience in the arts sector by undertaking work experience, voluntary work, internships or temporary work.

Money guide

Salary levels vary according to the type of organisation you work for.

£12,000 per year is a normal starting salary for an assistant or trainee. When qualified this rises to £15,500. This can rise to £18,500–£30,000 with experience. Senior managers could earn between £25,000 and £50,000. Salaries are higher in London and in other large cities.

Related opportunities

■ Museum/Art Gallery Visitor Services Assistant p358
■ Personal Assistant p55
■ Museum/Art Gallery Curator p356

Further information

Arts Council of England
14 Great Peter Street, London SW1P 3NQ
0845 300 6200, www.artscouncil.org.uk

Scottish Arts Council
12 Manor Place, Edinburgh EH3 7DD
0131 226 6051; www.scottisharts.org.uk

www.cityandguilds.com/myperfectjob

Languages, Information and Culture

CRCI: K

AUCTIONEER

What the work involves

- Auctioneers sell items at auctions, getting the best market price possible for the items they're selling.

- It's your responsibility to make sure the item sells for the best price, both by selling well on the day and by organising and publicising sales in advance.

- You'll be inspecting and valuing items and coming to price agreements with the sellers, making sure that reserves are appropriate.

- On auction days, you'll run through the items on sale, observe customers, and take bids. You may specialise in a particular area, and could be working on anything from antiques and property to livestock and motors.

The type of person suited to this work

You will need to be good with people and communicate well, so that you can interact with customers and successfully sell goods. In addition, you should be outgoing and confident, with excellent knowledge of what you're selling.

You should have excellent observational skills and a good attention to detail, as valuing objects is also a big part of the job. For this reason you also need to be able to think on your feet, and work well under pressure.

You must have shrewd business sense and a good head for figures, as much of your day will revolve around numbers.

Working conditions

You'll usually be working in an auction house, or an office or auction room within. Normal working hours are 9am–5.30pm Monday to Saturday, but be prepared to carry out viewings and valuations during evenings and weekends.

A driving licence is useful as travel may be necessary, for example if you're selling the contents of a large house clearing.

You may also sell livestock and motors outdoors.

Future prospects

Career development relies on building up a list of contacts, and working towards moving to larger more prestigious auction houses.

You may want to become self-employed, or work towards a management position or partnership.

You may also have the chance to travel, as some auction houses have offices abroad.

Advantages/disadvantages

This work is stimulating and challenging, and especially rewarding if you choose to work with items or goods you have a genuine interest in.

Every day will be different, and you will constantly be interacting and communicating with people.

Qualifications and courses

There are no set entry requirements, but most employers prefer candidates with good communication skills and sound GCSEs (A*–C). You can enter the profession by working as a salesroom assistant and progressing to the position of auctioneer. If you want to go into property auctioning, you could start out by gaining experience in valuation work. Some employers will be willing to take you on as a trainee.

The Royal Institution of Chartered Surveyors accredits some degree courses in property and valuation. You can also follow a Foundation degree in Auctioneering and Valuation, or a degree in the Arts Market (offered at Wolverhampton and Kingston universities), or Property and Rural Auctioneering as offered by Cumbria University. Sotheby's Institute of Art also offer an MA in Arts Business.

If you want to work for an international auction house you will need a degree in a subject related to fine arts, for example history of art. For entry onto these courses, you will need GCSEs (A*–C) and at least 2 A levels.

Training is done on the job and you will shadow an experienced auctioneer.

It can be tiring work, and much of the day will be spent on your feet. As the person leading an auction, you have to be 100% alert all the time.

Money guide

Starting salaries for trainees are about £15,000 a year.

As you gain experience, this may rise to about £30,000–£40,000 a year.

If you become a business partner, you might earn over £60,000.

Related opportunities

- Antiques Dealer p478
- Chartered Surveyor p84
- Estate Agent p96
- Rural Property/Practice Surveyor p118

Further information

Livestock Auctioneers' Association Limited
Cobblethwaite, Wreay, Carlisle, Cumbria CA4 0RZ
01697 475433; www.laa.co.uk

National Association of Valuers and Auctioneers
Arbon House, 6 Tournament Court, Edgehill Drive, Warwick CV34 6LG
01926 417774; www.nava.org.uk

National Federation of Property Professionals
Arbon House, 6 Tournament Court, Edgehill Drive, Warwick CV34 6LG
01926 496800; www.nfopp.co.uk

BILINGUAL SECRETARY

What the work involves

- Bilingual secretaries use their language skills to provide administrative support to professionals.

- You will deal with incoming and outgoing telephone calls, emails and faxes in a foreign language, translate reports and take on the role of an informal interpreter.

- It will also be your responsibility to coordinate travel arrangements for visits overseas and make arrangements for foreign visitors.

The type of person suited to this work

You must have the ability to write and speak fluently in English and one foreign language, as well as a good grasp of spelling and grammar.

You should be extremely organised, able to multitask and have a good attention to detail. You must be friendly, helpful and polite and be able to work well as part of a team or by yourself.

It is necessary to have excellent IT and keyboard skills as well as the ability to work under pressure.

Working conditions

You will work standard office hours, though longer hours may be needed at busy periods. You could find part-time or temporary work. Job sharing is also available.

Bilingual secretaries share an office and spend a lot of time on the phone, working on a computer as well as reading and translating documents. It could be your responsibility to deal with members of the public. At senior levels, you might get the opportunity to travel abroad.

Future prospects

Spanish, French and German are most sought after, although there is growing demand for Chinese, Arabic, and Japanese. You could work for an international organisation or any companies which conduct business abroad, though most vacancies are in London and big cities. You can progress to working for a more senior member of staff or to a supervisory role in a bigger company. This job can be a stepping stone into a career in marketing or human resources. You could also work overseas. After gaining more qualifications, you could become a translator or interpreter.

Advantages/disadvantages

You will get the opportunity to use your language skills.

It is possible to use the experience you have gained in a specific company or department to gain a promotion.

This job can be repetitive.

Tight deadlines and a heavy workload can be stressful.

Qualifications and courses

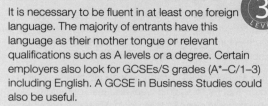

It is necessary to be fluent in at least one foreign language. The majority of entrants have this language as their mother tongue or relevant qualifications such as A levels or a degree. Certain employers also look for GCSEs/S grades (A*–C/1–3) including English. A GCSE in Business Studies could also be useful.

Qualifications specially devised for bilingual secretaries are also available from OCR, LCCI, EdExcel, City & Guilds and SQA.

You could also take a LCCIEB qualification in Business in French, German and Spanish at Levels 1, 2 and 3. The European Computer Driving Licence is also available from the British Computer Society

It would also be helpful to have a specific secretarial qualification such as NVQ Levels 1 to 4 in Business and Administration. Apprenticeships are also available. The Diploma in Business, Administration and Finance could be helpful.

Money guide

A junior secretary can expect around £19,000 a year, with the highest wages offered in London. With considerable experience, this can rise to £42,000. However, this often depends on the sector which you work for.

Jobs in banks or other financial organisations can be much more highly paid than those in the media or charities

Related opportunities

- Secretary p63
- Legal Secretary p48
- Personal Assistant p55
- Receptionist p58

Further information

Institute of Chartered Secretaries and Administrators
16 Park Crescent, London W1B 1AH
020 7580 4741; www.icsa.org.uk; info@icsa.co.uk

The Council for Administration
6 Graphite Square, Vauxhall Walk, London SE11 5EE
020 7091 9620; www.cfa.uk.com

Institute of Professional Administrators
6 Graphite Square, Vauxhall Walk, London SE11 5EE
020 7091 2606; www.inprad.org

Languages, Information and Culture

CRCI: AD

CONSERVATOR/RESTORER

What the work involves

- You will manage the preservation of historical objects and artwork, as well as the care of historic houses and stately homes, applying your specialist knowledge of subjects such as textiles and furniture.

- You will undertake conservation work, treating objects to protect them against wear and tear, or restore objects to as close to their original state as possible.

- Your job might involve managing freelance restorers/conservators.

The type of person suited to this work

The role of preserving valuable collections or buildings requires a good knowledge of culture and history. You will need excellent practical skills, and attention to detail and colour.

Sometimes you will manage other professionals to conserve and restore or speak at public events, so communication skills are essential. Writing skills and ICT skills are important. The ability to work as part of a team is also essential.

Working conditions

Your work is likely to involve handling and treating fragile objects, so good practical skills are important.

You might have to work with specialist materials and equipment, which can affect people with skin conditions.

In most jobs, you will spend much of your time assessing and researching collections on-site both indoors and outdoors. You will work regular office hours Monday to Friday.

Future prospects

Restoration/conservation officers work in museums, galleries and historic houses, often with alternative job titles such as Collections Manager or Curator. Many will have worked as craft conservators/restorers or have gained extensive experience in caring for collections.

You have the opportunity to work anywhere in the world. If you're happy to move around you will find more job prospects. With experience, you could progress into managing a historic house or managing a team in a museum or gallery.

Advantages/disadvantages

This type of work offers the chance to care for valuable historical collections.

Most galleries/museums employ only one person in this role, so you might have to move around to develop your career.

Qualifications and courses

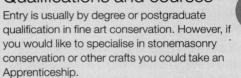

Entry is usually by degree or postgraduate qualification in fine art conservation. However, if you would like to specialise in stonemasonry conservation or other crafts you could take an Apprenticeship.

Degrees and Foundation degrees are available in areas like furniture and buildings. For Foundation degrees, work experience or a range of GCSEs (A*–C) are expected. For degree entry, a Foundation degree or HND or 2 A levels/3 H grades (including chemistry) are normally required. You could also choose to do a Diploma in Creative and Media.

For postgraduate courses you will need a relevant degree, such as science, fine art or art history.

Voluntary experience is useful, and can be gained through the National Association of Decorative and Fine Arts Societies.

Restorers/Conservation Officers can work towards NVQs/SVQs in Cultural Heritage Operations (Level 3), Cultural Heritage (Level 4) and Cultural Heritage Management (Level 5).

Money guide

Salaries vary according to your employer.

As an intern you could earn £15,000 and in your first job you could earn up to £21,000 per year.

This can rise to £36,000 with experience.

Your salary will depend on the high quality of your work. It may be easier to get work in London and other large cities.

Related opportunities

- Archaeologist p345
- Architect p71
- Archivist/Records Manager p346
- Museum/Art Gallery Curator p356

Further information

Creative and Cultural Skills
4th Floor, Lafone House, London SE1 3HN
020 7015 1847; www.ccskills.org.uk

National Association of Decorative and Fine Arts Societies
NADFAS House, 8 Guilford Street, London WC1N 1DA
020 7430 0730; www.nadfas.org.uk

Institute of Conservation
1st floor, Downstream Building, 1 London Bridge, London SE1 9BG
020 7785 3807, www.icon.org.uk

GENEALOGIST

What the work involves

- You will organise and plan research into the history or ancestry of individual families (genealogy) and write reports from your findings.

- You will work with a range of historical information such as newspapers and directories to trace specific facts about family histories.

- Your work could also involve liaising with or supervising the work of researchers.

- Meeting with clients and keeping them updated with your research would also be part of your job.

The type of person suited to this work

As you will be investigating family history, a strong enthusiasm for historical research is essential. You will also need excellent research skills and the ability to understand detailed information. ICT skills will help you work with information management software. You will also need writing skills to produce reports.

You should enjoy meeting a range of people. You will need a good knowledge of historical resources and subject areas. An organised, thorough approach to your work is important. Working with unique historical documents demands good handling skills.

Working conditions

Most genealogists are self-employed and work from home or in offices. However, they spend a lot of their time in public records buildings, undertaking research. The job can involve travel, for example to archive collections.

You will spend a lot of time reading and assessing detailed information.

Future prospects

Genealogy is usually followed as a hobby rather than as a profession. The number of opportunities for work is small so there is a lot of competition.

Most genealogists work on a self-employed basis whilst a small number work for specialist research companies. You can develop knowledge on a specific subject or geographical area and then undertake additional work such as teaching.

Advantages/disadvantages

There are very few job opportunities.

Because the work is often project-based, it can create some job insecurity.

This work gives the satisfaction of providing people with information about their family history and it can be both fascinating and rewarding to tell people details such as they are entitled to an estate.

Qualifications and courses

Most entrants hold a degree and knowledge of social and local history sources are necessary. Knowledge of palaeography (the study of ancient writing and scripts) and Latin are also essential.

Direct entry to this profession is not usual. Entrants normally have qualifications and experience in a related field such as archive administration, librarianship or historical research.

A history degree provides a useful first step and the University Campus Suffolk has a degree in Family and Community History. Blackpool and the Fylde College runs a Foundation degree in History and Heritage Management Studies, which covers genealogy.

The Society of Genealogists provides short courses in genealogy and palaeography both for beginners and for those already working in the field. The Institute of Heraldic and Genealogical Studies provides qualifications including a Certificate, Higher Certificate and Diploma in Genealogy. People who complete these qualifications and with 5 years of experience may be able to progress to Licenciateship of the Institute.

Money guide

Freelance genealogists are usually paid at an hourly rate which can range from £16 to £35.

For more complex projects you may charge a total fee ranging from £35 to £100. Genealogists with a postgraduate qualification can expect to earn £26,500–£35,000 per year.

If you lecture as well you may earn £50,000+.

Related opportunities

- Archivist/Records Manager p346
- Librarian/Library Assistant p355
- Registrar of Births, Deaths, Marriages and Civil Partnerships p61
- Private Investigator p556

Further information

Creative and Cultural Skills
4th Floor, Lafone House, London SE1 3HN
020 7015 1847; www.ccskills.org.uk

Society of Genealogists
14 Charterhouse Buildings, Goswell Road, London EC1M 7BA
020 7251 8799; www.sog.org.uk

Institute of Heraldic and Genealogical Studies
79–82 Northgate, Canterbury CT1 1BA
01227 768664; www.ihgs.ac.uk

Languages, Information and Culture

CRCI: K

HISTORIAN

What the work involves

- You will undertake historical research using ICT, paper-based information and other resources to broaden public and academic understanding of the past.

- You can choose to teach and lecture on specific historical subjects. You could also write articles for professional journals and other publications.

- Heritage organisations sometimes employ historians for research purposes.

- Professional historians can specialise in a specific area of history such as women's history, ancient history or modern history.

The type of person suited to this work

You will need a strong enthusiasm and love for history. You should also have a good knowledge of your specialist subjects. ICT and research skills are essential. You should pay close attention to detail and be accurate in your work.

Excellent verbal communication skills are important for explaining facts to people. Good writing skills are needed for writing up research and articles. Historians need to consider a wide range of theories, so an open-minded approach is important. You should also be well organised to manage and plan your research.

Working conditions

You will spend time in libraries and archive centres. This will involve reading and assessing information. Some historical researchers are based in public records offices.

Historians in an academic role are based in universities.

Undertaking historical research on a self-employed basis can create some job insecurity.

Future prospects

As a professional historian you could go into historical research or follow an academic career path. Many historians combine both roles; they write, teach and carry out research on their specialist area of interest. Others combine historical research with other related areas such as genealogy.

A small number of historians are employed by heritage organisations to provide expert advice and support.

Advantages/disadvantages

This type of work provides the satisfaction of undertaking original research and finding out about the past.

It takes time and dedication to get established as a specialist on a specific historical period or subject.

Qualifications and courses

An MA in History or Historical Archaeology is usually required for work as an archival or historical researcher.

Entry requirements for postgraduate degrees are a first degree in History or related subject such as ancient world studies. Entry requirements for first degrees are generally 3 A levels/5 H grades including history (A*–C).

For a position in a university faculty, a PhD is usually required.

Training courses in historical research are available through the Institute of Historical Research, the Society of Genealogists and the Institute of Heraldic and Genealogical Studies.

Money guide

Earnings vary according to your job.

Historical researchers usually charge by the hour; rates vary from £16 to £50.

Starting salaries for academic posts range from £21,000 to £25,000 per year.

With experience this rises to around £35,000.

At senior academic levels, this could increase to £35,000–£50,000.

Related opportunities

- Archaeologist p345
- Archivist/Records Manager p346
- Genealogist p351
- Museum/Art Gallery Curator p356

Further information

Institute of Historical Research
University of London, Senate House, Malet Street,
London WC1E 7HU
020 7862 8740; www.history.ac.uk

Royal Historical Society
University College London, Gower Street,
London WC1E 6BT
020 7387 7532; www.royalhistoricalsociety.org

Creative and Cultural Skills
Lafone House, The Leather Market, Weston Street,
London SE1 3HN
020 7015 1800; www.ccskills.org.uk

INFORMATION SCIENTIST

What the work involves

■ You will develop, manage and coordinate both electronic and paper-based information systems for a range of organisations and companies.

■ Your job will involve cataloguing, indexing and archiving information. You will also respond to research enquiries, manage intranets and ensure all of your information is up to date.

■ You could work in a range of sectors, including law, education and business and be employed in a variety of roles. For example you could be an analyst or a librarian.

■ You will produce reports, graphs and briefings based on your findings.

The type of person suited to this work

You should be able to work with different forms of information such as databases, the internet and paper resources. You may provide information for members of the public or staff within an organisation so strong communication skills are important. An interest in customer service is useful.

Writing skills and ICT skills are increasingly important. Managing information demands an organised, methodical approach. A good level of numeracy can be useful. You will need to be resourceful and pay close attention to detail.

Working conditions

Information scientists work in offices, resource centres, libraries and other sites. You will be working standard hours, Monday to Friday, and can also be hired on short-term contracts for specific projects.

You could work face to face with members of the public or staff within your organisation. You could also deal with information enquiries over the phone and through email.

Future prospects

Information science is a very broad area. You could begin in an assistant or junior information job and with experience you could progress to working in a management role.

With experience you could specialise and work on a consultancy basis. At the moment there is a demand for specialists in science and computer science. There are also opportunities to work abroad.

Advantages/disadvantages

Depending on the sector you work in, this job can be very fast paced.

Information science skills are transferable to a wide range of job areas.

Money guide

£19,000–£27,000 per year is usual for starting salaries.

With experience this rises to £40,000.

Qualifications and courses

Most professional information scientists are graduates.

The fastest route to professional qualification is via a first degree in subjects such as information management, information studies and information and library studies, which are accredited by the Chartered Institute of Library and Information Professionals (CILIP).

An alternative route to professional qualification is via a degree in any subject, followed by a CILIP-approved postgraduate qualification. Experience of information-related work is advantageous, and may be a requirement for some postgraduate courses. Graduate training opportunities are available for people who wish to pursue a career in this area, and need to gain relevant experience before studying for a postgraduate qualification. Details are available through CILIP.

It is also possible to become a qualified information scientist from a library/information assistant post. CILIP offers a Certification scheme for people with 5 years' experience of information work, or 2 years' experience plus relevant work-based training.

Entrants through both the educational and certification routes may have the opportunity to work towards Chartered membership of CILIP. Candidates for Chartership must have completed an approved period of professional experience.

£72,000+ is possible at senior levels in large commercial organisations.

Information consultants can earn around £400–£500 a day.

Related opportunities

■ Archivist/Records Manager p346
■ Librarian/Library Assistant p355
■ Museum/Art Gallery Curator p356
■ Researcher (Media) p425

Further information

Chartered Institute of Library and Information Professionals
7 Ridgemount Street, London WC1E 7AE
020 7255 0500; www.cilip.org.uk

Association for Information Management
207 Davina House, 137–149 Goswell Road,
London EC1V 7ET
020 7253 3349; www.aslib.com

Arts and Humanities Research Council
AHRC, Whitefriars, Lewins Mead, Bristol BS1 2AE
0117 987 6500; enquiries@ahrc.ac.uk; www.ahrc.ac.uk

Languages, Information and Culture

CRCI: K

INTERPRETER

What the work involves

- Interpreters convert words spoken in one language into conversation or speech in another language.

- Using your knowledge of foreign languages, you will enable speakers of different languages to communicate with each other.

- You could interpret while a person speaks, or make notes and then interpret their statements.

- Interpreters provide services for international political conferences, court hearings, business meetings and public services.

The type of person suited to this work

You must be fluent in at least one, preferably two foreign languages. It is also important to be aware of the culture of these languages. You must have excellent listening skills and the ability to speak clearly.

Interpreting at courts and conferences requires a confident manner. You should keep up to date with current affairs as you will interpret on subjects including business and law. You will need to be discreet as dealing with confidential information may be a part of your job.

Working conditions

Interpreters have to concentrate continuously for long periods, which can be physically demanding.

You will need to travel to different locations at fairly short notice, either abroad or within the UK.

Interpreters work in a range of environments, including high-profile conferences and formal meetings.

Future prospects

This area of work is very competitive with a limited number of full-time opportunities. A small number of interpreters work for international or European agencies. Others are employed by local governments and interpret in courts, hospitals and police stations.

You can choose to work within community organisations, helping people gain access to public services. Many interpreters work on a freelance basis.

There is a greater demand for Chinese, Urdu, Punjabi and east European languages.

Advantages/disadvantages

This type of work provides the opportunity to travel and live abroad.

Due to tight schedules and high levels of travel, this can be a pressured job.

Freelance interpreters often need to take on additional work to support themselves.

Qualifications and courses

Most interpreters have a degree in languages or in translation and interpreting, or a combined degree in languages with a subject such as business. A postgraduate diploma or Master's in interpreting techniques is normally required. Degrees in science, engineering, the environment, business, or politics can be useful for more specialised jobs. For modern language degrees, entry requirements are usually 5 GCSEs (A*–C) and 2 A levels or equivalent, including a modern language.

Fluency in two languages including English is usually required to work as an interpreter.

The Chartered Institute of Linguists (IoL) offers vocational qualifications in a wide range of languages, including the Certificate in Bilingual Skills, the Diploma in Public Service Interpreting at QCF Level 6, and the Diploma in Translation at Level 7. Examinations are open entry, but candidates are expected to have achieved the required level of competence.

CILT, the National Centre for Languages, has developed National Occupational Standards for professional linguists.

Qualified interpreters can work towards membership of the IoL or Institute of Translation and Interpreting. These professional bodies provide further training and development opportunities.

Money guide

Newly qualified interpreters can expect a salary of around £19,000–£25,000 per year.

This can rise to £26,000–£35,000 with experience and £60,000 at senior levels in international or European agencies.

Working freelance, you could charge between £110 and £475 per day.

Related opportunities

- Importer/Exporter p606
- Secretary p63
- Teacher of English to Speakers of Other Languages p207
- Translator p359

Further information

The National Centre for Languages
3rd Floor, 111 Westminster Bridge Road, London SE1 7HR
0845 612 5885; www.cilt.org.uk

Chartered Institute of Linguists
Saxon House, 48 Southwark Street, London SE1 1UN
020 7940 3100; www.iol.org.uk

Institute of Translation and Interpreting
Fortuna House, South Fifth Street, Milton Keynes MK9 2EU
01908 325250; www.iti.org.uk

LIBRARIAN/ LIBRARY ASSISTANT

What the work involves

Librarian

- You will manage collections of books, newspapers and documents and ICT resources in libraries and information services to make them available to visitors.

- You may choose new resources to suit the library or information service you work in. You will also help visitors look for information and use ICT and other resources.

Library assistant

- You will organise and reshelve books and other resources. You may also work on the library counter to help visitors with enquiries and check books in and out of the library. You might deal with petty cash, catalogue new library resources and maintain databases.

The type of person suited to this work

You should enjoy helping people with enquiries and customer care skills are essential. You will also need good research skills and the ability to use resources to locate information. The ability to work with ICT software, the internet and databases as well as explaining these to others is important.

Librarians will need management skills, as well as the ability to work as part of a team. Financial skills will help you manage budgets. You will need an organised approach to your work.

Working conditions

You are likely to work face to face with members of the public or staff within an organisation. Working on a counter, dealing with information enquiries, and lifting and carrying books can all be physically demanding. Library work can be pressured, as you will need to locate and provide information to meet specific requests.

Future prospects

Librarians could progress to a senior level, meaning they would manage a branch library or department. Some librarians move into information management roles within public services or private companies.

Library assistants are employed in library and information services in businesses, community library services and government. Larger organisations provide opportunities to progress into senior roles and take on additional responsibilities.

Advantages/disadvantages

You will be able to exercise your creativity by thinking up ways to promote the library and its resources.

You may need to move geographic locations to develop your career.

This type of work provides the satisfaction of helping people access information and other services.

Qualifications and courses

The fastest route to becoming a qualified librarian is via a degree accredited by the Chartered Institute of Library and Information Professionals (CILIP). The usual entry requirements are 2 A levels/3 H grades (any subjects), but people with experience as library assistants are often admitted to the degree courses with vocational qualifications.

An alternative route is via a degree in another subject followed by a CILIP-accredited postgraduate qualification. Prior experience of library or information work is advantageous, and is a requirement for some postgraduate courses.

Library assistants are often expected to have at least 5 GCSEs/S grades A*–C/1–3 or the equivalent, usually including English. Commercial or industrial libraries may require A levels/H grades.

It is also possible for people working as library assistants to qualify as librarians through a scheme like the one CILIP offers. Senior library assistants can study for a librarianship qualification (degree or postgraduate qualification) accredited by CILIP.

ENTRY LEVEL 2

Money guide

Salaries vary according to the sector in which you are employed, but CILIP recommends the following minimum salaries. Starting salaries range from £19,000 to £23,000. At chartered librarian level, you could earn up to £28,000. A senior academic librarian can earn up to £40,000, and a head of service £47,000+. Most library assistants start on £15,000; with experience this can increase to £18,000. Senior assistants earn over £20,000.

Related opportunities

- Arts Administrator/Manager p347
- Information Scientist p353
- Archivist/Records Manager p346

Further information

Chartered Institute of Library and Information Professionals (CILIP)
7 Ridgemount Street, London WC1E 7AE
020 7255 0500; www.cilip.org.uk

City& Guilds

www.cityandguilds.com/myperfectjob

MUSEUM/ART GALLERY CURATOR

What the work involves

- You will manage and maintain collections of artworks, historical objects or documents. Curators usually have specialist knowledge of a specific historical or cultural field such as women's history, textiles or archaeology.

- You will write and research on the collections in your care.

- You might organise ways in which you can gain funding for your museum/gallery. You will also organise exhibit loans with other museums/galleries.

- You will work with other museum/gallery staff to plan exhibitions using items and information from your collection. You may also give talks to members of the public at special events.

The type of person suited to this work

You will need a good knowledge of history and of your specialist area. You will also need to be able to communicate this information to other staff and to members of the public. You may speak at educational events, so enthusiasm for your subject is essential. You will need good written communication skills for writing reports. ICT skills are increasingly important in this area, for example when managing collection information through specialist databases.

Working conditions

Curators generally work 37 hours a week, however these hours may be extended for special exhibitions and private showings. This job will probably involve weekend or evening work. You may have to be on call to respond to emergencies at the gallery/museum. Working environments also vary depending on the size and how busy a gallery/museum is. There may be some heavy lifting and carrying involved when exhibits need to be moved.

Future prospects

Museum/gallery work is a competitive area in which to develop a career and offers a variety of interesting roles. You could work your way up in some larger organisations, but often you will need to move employers in order to move up the career ladder.

From working as an assistant curator, you could progress into a curator's role. From here you could move on to work as a senior curator or go into managing museums/galleries or historic buildings.

Advantages/disadvantages

This job provides the satisfaction of working closely with works of art and historical objects, some of which can be very valuable.

You will help create exhibitions and then watch the public enjoy them.

Gaining necessary funding may be difficult.

Qualifications and courses

ENTRY LEVEL 5

Entrants should normally have a relevant degree and many candidates increasingly hold a postgraduate qualification in museum, gallery or heritage studies. Useful subjects include archaeology, history of art, art and cultural management or heritage management.

The Diploma in Creative and Media may be a useful pre-entry qualification.

Most degree programmes expect candidates to have achieved 2 A levels and 5 GCSEs (A*–C). For a postgraduate degree you will need at least a 2.1 first degree.

All employers will also require you to have relevant paid or unpaid work experience. See the Museums Association website for ideas and options.

NVQs/SVQs offer an alternative route for people with relevant work experience. NVQs/SVQs are available at Levels 3, 4 and 5 in Cultural Heritage Operations, Cultural Heritage and Cultural Heritage Management.

Many curators continue their studies while working and do a PhD or Master's degree in their specialism.

Money guide

These figures are only approximate and may vary depending on location, sector and employer. The Museums Association publishes salary guidelines each year.

Starting salaries are generally between £15,500 and £23,000 a year. This can increase to between £23,000 and £30,000 a year with experience.

If you reach the level of senior curator you could earn over £30,000.

Related opportunities

- Archaeologist p345
- Events and Exhibition Organiser p411
- Arts Administrator/Manager p347
- Museum/Art Gallery Technician p357
- Museum/Art Gallery Visitor Services Assistant p358

Further information

Museums Association
24 Calvin Street, London E1 6NW
020 7426 6970; www.museumsassociation.org

MUSEUM/ART GALLERY TECHNICIAN

What the work involves

- You will help prepare gallery and museum spaces for temporary exhibitions and collection displays.

- Your work will involve installing audio-visual equipment, such as lighting to suit specific exhibitions. You will also transport objects and artworks to and from exhibition spaces.

- You will provide general technical support to the museums/gallery team as required.

- You might be responsible for maintaining files, mending and cleaning exhibitions and labelling and storing specimens.

The type of person suited to this work

You will need a good range of technical skills to meet the varied practical demands of a museum/gallery environment. As well as providing support for setting up new exhibitions, you will have to deal with practical problems as they arise. The ability to handle fragile or valuable objects and artworks carefully is also useful. You will need a good knowledge of building security and maintenance. You may also be responsible for the fire safety of the gallery/museum. You will be a good team player and have a strong interest in helping people get the most out of their visits to galleries and museums.

Working conditions

Although you may spend some of the time within an office environment a great deal of it will be spent around the museum/gallery. Generally technicians work about 36 hours a week; however you might have to be on call to respond to emergencies at the gallery/museum. You might also have to work longer hours when setting up or dismantling exhibitions. You may have to work some weekends, evenings and bank holidays. You could be required to wear a uniform and/or name badge.

Future prospects

Whilst museum/gallery work is a competitive area in which to develop a career, it offers a variety of interesting roles. You could work your way up in some larger organisations, but often you will need to move employers in order to move up the career ladder.

It is possible to progress to working as a senior or head technician. In larger organisations, you could manage a team of technicians.

Advantages/disadvantages

This job provides the satisfaction of working closely with works of art and historical objects, some of which can be very valuable.

This is a competitive area of work, so you might have to change jobs to receive promotion.

You may have to work some unsociable hours which could disrupt your social or family life.

Qualifications and courses

Experience of working with the public and enthusiasm for museums/ galleries are often valued more by employers than academic requirements. However many large galleries/museums will require at least 4 GCSEs (A*–C). Others prefer candidates with a Foundation degree or degree in museum and gallery studies. Other useful subjects are heritage management, history of art and arts and cultural management. You will need at least 2 A levels and 5 GCSEs (A*–C) for entry to a degree.

You could do the Diploma in Creative and Media or an Apprenticeship in Cultural and Heritage Venue Operations. You could then start as an assistant and work your way up to technician.

Voluntary work experience is recommended and may help you secure a permanent position. See the Museums Association website for ideas and options.

You might be able to gain NVQs/SVQs in Heritage Care and Visitor Services at Level 2 and Cultural Heritage Operations at Level 3 whilst working.

If you will be working with children you will need to pass a Criminal Records Bureau check.

Money guide

These figures are only approximate and may vary depending on location and employer. Larger galleries and museums may pay their technicians a higher rate.

Starting salaries for technicians are generally around £13,000 a year.

You can expect to earn between £15,000 and £17,000 per year once you have gained some experience.

Senior technicians, with added responsibilities, can make over £20,000 per year.

Related opportunities

- Archaeologist p345
- Events and Exhibition Organiser p411
- Museum/Art Gallery Curator p356
- Museum/Art Gallery Visitor Services Assistant p358

Further information

Creative and Cultural Skills
4th Floor, Lafone House, London SE1 3HN
020 7015 1847; www.ccskills.org.uk

Museums Association
24 Calvin Street, London E1 6NW
020 7426 6910; www.museumsassociation.org

Association of Independent Museums (AIM)
4 Clayhall Road, Gosport, Hampshire PO12 2BY
02392 587751; www.museums.co.uk

Languages, Information and Culture

CRCI: K

MUSEUM/ART GALLERY VISITOR SERVICES ASSISTANT

What the work involves

- You will work face to face with visitors to galleries and museums, deal with enquiries and provide information. You will therefore need to keep up to date with information on the material showcased in the museum/gallery.

- Your role will also involve attending and watching over the security of exhibitions and displays.

- You will help set up and dismantle exhibitions. You may also be responsible for museum/gallery security and fire safety.

- You may conduct tours and/or work in the museum/gallery shop.

The type of person suited to this work

You should enjoy meeting and helping people, because you will deal with members of the public on a regular basis. You will need a patient and friendly approach when responding to enquiries and protecting fragile exhibition pieces from over-enthusiastic visitors! You will need a good understanding of fire and security issues. Manual handling skills are useful for setting up and taking down exhibitions. As you may deal with money in a museum or gallery shop, cash-handling skills are useful. You should also be able to work well as part of a team.

Working conditions

You will work around 36 hours a week; this will probably include some weekends, evenings and bank holidays. Generally this job takes place indoors; however there are some open-air museums. You will have to spend a lot of your time on your feet when undertaking security at exhibitions, which can be physically demanding. You might be required to wear a uniform and/or name badge.

Future prospects

Whilst museum/gallery work is a competitive area in which to develop a career, it offers a variety of interesting roles. You could work your way up in some larger organisations, but often you will need to move employers in order to move up the career ladder.

With experience, you could go on to work as a senior attendant/assistant, managing a team of attendants/assistants.

Advantages/disadvantages

This job provides the satisfaction of working closely with works of art and historical objects, some of which can be very valuable.

Because of the public nature of assistant roles, this can be a sociable job.

Qualifications and courses

ENTRY 2 LEVEL

Experience of working with the public and an interest in museums/galleries are more important than formal qualifications for this role. A good general education is usually required and some museums/galleries require at least 4 GCSEs (A*–C) including English and history.

A qualification in tourism and the Diploma in Creative and Media may also be helpful.

You can also enter this career by doing an Apprenticeship in Cultural and Heritage Venue Operations. You may then become a front-of-house administrative assistant and move your way up.

Relevant voluntary or paid work experience is highly recommended. See the Museums Association website for ideas and options.

You might be able to gain NVQs/SVQs in Heritage Care and Visitor Services at Level 2 and Cultural Heritage Operations at Level 3 whilst working.

Money guide

Starting salaries are generally between £11,000 and £13,000 per year. With experience or progression to a senior assistant/attendant role you could earn somewhere between £15,000 and £16,000 a year. It is possible to achieve a salary of over £19,000 per year.

These figures are only a guide, as actual rates of pay may vary, depending on the employer and where people live.

Related opportunities

- Events and Exhibition Organiser p411
- Museum/Art Gallery Curator p356
- Museum/Art Gallery Technician p357

Further information

Museums Association
24 Calvin Street, London E1 6NW
020 7426 6910; www.museumsassociation.org

Association of Independent Museums (AIM)
4 Clayhall Road, Gosport, Hampshire PO12 2BY
02392 587751; www.museums.co.uk

City&
Guilds

www.cityandguilds.com/myperfectjob

TRANSLATOR

What the work involves

- You will convert written text such as letters, reports, leaflets and brochures from one language to another. You will ensure that your translation matches the tone and style of the original text and has a high standard of grammar.

- Your work will also involve meetings with employers to agree projects.

- Translators provide services to specialist translation agencies, private companies, local government bodies and international organisations.

The type of person suited to this work

Translators must work to a high standard of accuracy, so attention to detail is important. The ability to write in your chosen languages in a range of styles is essential. You should also be able to understand and translate complex documents. ICT skills are very useful.

Discretion is important as you may translate confidential information. Being well organised will help you to meet project deadlines. You will need a confident approach to work on a freelance basis and promote your services. Numeracy skills are also useful.

Working conditions

Translators are usually self-employed and based in offices at home, but there are opportunities for translators in companies.

You might attend meetings with employers and colleagues.

This type of work involves close working at a computer and the use of resources such as dictionaries and technical reference books.

Future prospects

As a translator you could work for a variety of employers, translating medical, technical, legal and other documents. Many translators work on a freelance basis.

There are opportunities to work for private companies and international organisations on a permanent basis, in the UK or abroad. Demand for translators is growing, especially due to the upcoming London 2012 Olympic Games.

Advantages/disadvantages

This area of work can provide opportunities to travel and work abroad.

Working on a self-employed project-by-project basis can create some job instability.

Translation can be very demanding due to short deadlines and the constant demand for accuracy.

Qualifications and courses

Most translators have a relevant degree. These include degrees in one or more foreign languages (preferably applied), a foreign language combined with a specialist subject such as business, law, engineering, computer studies, Asian or European studies, or translation or interpreting.

For modern language degrees, 5 GCSEs (A*–C) and a minimum of 2 A levels, with one in a language, or equivalent qualifications are normally required.

Postgraduate courses in translation are available, and usually require a degree in a modern language. The Chartered Institute of Linguists (IoL) offers vocational qualifications in a wide range of languages, including the Certificate in Bilingual Skills (equivalent to A level/H grade) the Diploma in Public Service Interpreting at QCF Level 6, and the Diploma in Translation at Level 7. Examinations are open entry, but candidates are expected to have achieved the required level of competence before sitting an exam.

Fluency in 2 or more languages is required to work as a translator.

Qualified translators can work towards membership of the IoL or Institute of Translation and Interpreting. These professional bodies provide further training and development opportunities.

Money guide

Translators may be paid between £75 and £80 per 1000 words, depending on the language they are translating.

Most positions pay between £18,000 and £21,000 per year. With experience, generalist translators earn around £30,000 and senior translators can earn up to £60,000.

Related opportunities

- Interpreter p354
- Secretary p63
- Importer/Exporter p606
- Teacher of English to Speakers of Other Languages p207

Further information

The National Centre for Languages
3rd Floor, 111 Westminster Bridge Road, London SE1 7HR
0845 612 5885; www.cilt.org.uk

Chartered Institute of Linguists
Saxon House, 48 Southwark Street, London SE1 1UN
020 7940 3100; www.iol.org.uk

Institute of Translation and Interpreting
Fortuna House, South Fifth Street, Milton Keynes MK9 2EU
01908 325250, www.iti.org.uk

Languages, Information and Culture

CRCI: K

Legal and Political Services

If you find the law a fascinating subject and you feel you would enjoy a challenging career where the rewards are a good salary and a real sense of achievement when your hard work pays off, a job in this sector could be what you are looking for. Workers in this sector are fiercely passionate about their careers and have more often than not, completed a lot of training and worked hard to establish themselves in this competitive field. You need to be driven and thrive on pressure and tight deadlines; this is a sector for someone who is ambitious and very talented at working tactfully with people.

In this section we cover the following jobs:

For similar jobs to the ones in this section turn to *Administration, Business, Office Work and Financial Services* on page 15.

BAILIFF/ENFORCEMENT AGENT

What the work involves

- Court bailiffs deliver legal documents such as court summonses to people who owe money and might also take steps to ensure payment.

- Certificated/private bailiffs visit people in debt to recover the money they owe, arranging for removal of their property where necessary.

- In Scotland, officers of court deliver legal documents to people who owe money and take all the legal steps required to get the money paid.

- You might also give advice on how to pay debts.

The type of person suited to this work

As there are strict legal procedures connected with recovering debt, you will need to be sure you are completely up to date with legislation to conduct your work correctly and within legal guidelines.

The work will bring you into contact with many different people, so it's important that you are able to deal with all members of the public.

You will need to be assertive to deal with people's resistance and be persistent to get the job done. Being tactful and able to cope with people under stress is also essential.

Working conditions

You will spend a lot of time travelling and so will need a clean driving licence. Although you will be based in an office, you might have to visit people's homes in the evenings and early mornings to make sure that someone is there.

If you have to remove furniture in payment of debt, you could have to do a lot of heavy lifting, so you will need to be physically fit.

Future prospects

In England and Wales, court bailiffs generally work for the county courts and private bailiffs with magistrates' court orders.

In Scotland, officers of court are called sheriff officers in the sheriff court and messengers-at-arms in the Court of Session.

If you work for the county court you can progress into management or switch to a private firm in which you would also have opportunities to progress into management roles.

Advantages/disadvantages

The work is varied and in different locations; no two days will be the same.

You will meet many different people, some of whom may be difficult to deal with and threatening.

The hours can be long and unsocial.

Qualifications and courses

Employers prefer candidates to have 5 GCSEs/S grades (A*–C/1–3), including English and maths. Applicants must be aged between 21 and 62 but mature candidates, without a criminal record or debt, are often preferred because their life experience may help them deal with difficult situations. A Diploma in Public Services could be helpful.

To become a certificated bailiff, candidates need to obtain a Bailiff's General Certificate. This is issued by a circuit judge. The necessary legal knowledge can be gained by taking the examinations of the Certificated Bailiffs' Association.

To be commissioned as a sheriff officer, candidates need to pass the examinations of the Society of Messengers-at-Arms and Sheriff Officers. The minimum age to be commissioned is 20, but training, which normally takes 3 years, can begin earlier.

You will need a security bond up to the value of £10,000, plus two references for insurance purposes.

Money guide

Starting salaries are around £14,000 per year if you are uncertified. Some firms offer only part-time opportunities.

This rises to £20,000–£25,000 if you are newly certified.

A top rate of £50,000 per year is possible for the very capable and highly experienced.

Private firms may pay you a basic salary plus some form of commission or commission only.

In Scotland you could start at around £17,000; with experience you could earn £26,000–£28,000.

Related opportunities

- Police Officer p552
- Police Support Worker p553
- Security Officer/Manager/Door Supervisor p563

Further information

Enforcement Services Association
Park House, 10 Park Street, Bristol BS1 5HX
0117 907 4771; www.ensas.org.uk

Society of Messengers-at-Arms and Sheriff Officers
11 Alva Street, Edinburgh EH2 4PH
0131 225 9110; www.smaso.org

Association of Civil Enforcement Agencies
513 Bradford Road, Batley WF17 8LL
01924 350 090; www.acea.org.uk; info@acea.org.uk

BARRISTER/ADVOCATE

What the work involves

- Barristers/Advocates give legal advice to solicitors and other professionals and act for clients in certain cases in the high courts.
- You will research information and past cases before giving advice to solicitors on whether a case should go to court.
- In court, you will examine witnesses and present the case for the prosecution or the defence.
- You will also act for clients at tribunals or enquiries if asked to act by a solicitor.

The type of person suited to this work

You will need to research large amounts of information before giving legal advice. You will need to be able to think logically to work out what's important in the case and apply the law to it.

You will need to be confident to speak in court and convince a jury with your arguments, and think quickly when questioning witnesses or defendants. Good writing and speaking skills are needed to prepare your case. Keeping an open mind is important and you must be able to gain people's confidence.

Working conditions

Barristers usually work in offices called 'chambers', and advocates in groups known as 'stables' in the Advocates' Library in Edinburgh.

If you specialise in criminal law, you will spend more time in court than civil law specialists would. As you will travel widely, a driving licence is useful.

Future prospects

Most barristers/advocates are self-employed and it can take around 5 years to establish a practice and become known. After 10–15 years' experience you can apply to 'take silk' to become a Queen's Counsel. This is essential if you want to become a judge in the higher courts. Some people work in central or local government where there is a clear promotion structure.

Advantages/disadvantages

The work is varied and you will get satisfaction when you win a case.

Some cases may put you under pressure, particularly if they attract media attention.

You will sometimes work long hours to meet deadlines.

Money guide

During training or 'pupillage', £11,000–£18,500 per year.

Earnings between £25,000 and £56,000 are normal in the Crown Prosecution Service in England and Wales.

Qualifications and courses

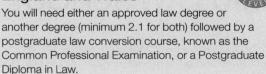

England and Wales

You will need either an approved law degree or another degree (minimum 2.1 for both) followed by a postgraduate law conversion course, known as the Common Professional Examination, or a Postgraduate Diploma in Law.

For vocational entry, you must become a member of one of the 4 Inns of Court and undertake the Bar Vocational Course. You must also complete two 6-month pupillages (a mix of work and training) in Chambers.

Training for the 'bar' continues for 3 years, working in one of the Inns of Court.

Scotland

You will need either an Honours degree in Scottish Law from a Scottish university (minimum 2.1); an Ordinary degree in Scottish Law from a Scottish university with an Honours degree from a UK university (minimum 2.1); or a Scottish Ordinary degree with distinction. You must also undertake a 1-year full-time postgraduate Diploma in Legal Practice at a Scottish university.

For vocational entry, you will need to work for 12–21 months in a solicitor's office and 'devilling' (training with) a member of the bar for 9.5 months, before taking the entry examinations of the Faculty of Advocates.

Advocates will normally practise as a solicitor for 10 years, prior to acting as an advocate.

As an advocate in Scotland you may start at around £11,000; moving up to £24,000–£56,000 in the Procurator Fiscal Service.

The majority of barristers in England and Scotland are self-employed. Earnings can be up to £300,000, sometimes more, depending on experience, location and reputation.

Related opportunities

- Barrister's/Advocate's Clerk p365
- Crown Prosecutor/Procurator Fiscal p371
- Paralegal p378
- Solicitor/Notary Public p382

Further information

The Bar Council
289–293 High Holborn, London WC1V 7HZ
020 7242 0082; www.barcouncil.org.uk

The Faculty of Advocates
Parliament House, Edinburgh EH1 1RF
0131 226 5071; www.advocates.org.uk

Skills for Justice
Centre Court, Atlas Way, Sheffield S4 7QQ
0114 261 1499; www.skillsforjustice.com

CRCI: L **Legal and Political Services**

School Profile

LJMU LAW SCHOOL

The School of Law at Liverpool John Moores University (LJMU) offers a broad portfolio of undergraduate, postgraduate and professional programmes in law, legal practice and criminal justice.

The following degree programmes are available within the School of Law:

LLB (Hons) Law
LLB (Hons) Law and Criminal Justice
BA Single Honours Criminal Justice
BSc Single Honours Forensic Psychology and Criminal Justice
Graduate Diploma in Law (GDL)
LLM International Business & Commercial Law
Legal Practice Course (LPC)
LLM in Legal Practice
MA Criminal Justice
MRes Business and Law

Graduate skills development and work-related learning are embedded in all of our programmes, helping you gain the essential skills and experience demanded by today's employers. The School of Law has invested significantly in staff development, with an emphasis on enhancing the status and quality of teaching and learning. School staff are also engaged in a wide range of law and criminal justice research, and the School hosts the Centre for Criminal Justice.

Lectures are delivered at the John Foster Building and Modular Building within the Mount Pleasant Campus. These buildings boast a range of modern facilities, including 'Hi-Tech' lecture and seminar rooms, a moot room, reading rooms, and a fully equipped IT Suite. The John Foster Building is an 19th Century Listed building and, along with the award-winning Aldham Robarts Learning Resource Centre, is built around an enclosed garden with lawns and benches offering a peaceful retreat in between study.

Student Lawyers at LJMU have done very well over the years in National Mooting Competitions, Client Interviewing, Mediation and National Negotiation Competitions. The teams won the 2007 English Speaking Union – Essex Court Chambers National Mooting Competition and 2008 National Negotiation Championship, reaching the final of the 2009 Client Interviewing and Mediation Competitions.

Additionally, the Student Law Society is a vibrant organisation of law students supporting law students. The Society organises a wide variety of events, such as meet and greets with local legal professionals, public speaking courses and mooting competitions, alongside their social events.

Liverpool John Moores University (LJMU) is a truly international university with over 24,000 students from all over the world. The University has embarked on a major campus redevelopment programme to ensure that LJMU truly is a 21st century university. The £24 million Art & Design Academy - the biggest investment in arts education in the UK today – is the first of our major projects to be completed.

If you want to have a great university experience, graduate with a respected qualification and secure the skills and 'know-how' that will help you climb the professional career ladder, then you should choose the School of Law at LJMU.

For more information about the LJMU School of Law contact the BLW Admissions Team on 0151 231 3999 or email: BLWadmissions@ljmu.ac.uk. Alternatively, you can visit the website at www.ljmu.ac.uk/lbs

BARRISTER'S/ADVOCATE'S CLERK

What the work involves

- Clerks manage the day-to-day work for a group of barristers (England and Wales) or advocates (Scotland).

- An important task will be liaising with solicitors to encourage them to give work to your business.

- You will estimate how much work is involved in a case to see how much time it will take, allocate cases to barristers/advocates and negotiate fees.

- When you first enter this career, you will mainly be preparing accounts, filing and photocopying, and answering the phone.

The type of person suited to this work

As your work will involve meeting lots of people, you will need excellent speaking skills.

Good writing skills are needed for writing letters and preparing notes and reports.

Being good with figures is essential when negotiating fees and preparing accounts.

You will need to be businesslike and have good negotiating skills to bring in work, and confidence to deal with solicitors, court officials and clients.

Your work will involve handling confidential information, which means discretion and tact are necessary. It is also important to be a good team worker and flexible in your approach to work.

Working conditions

You will work mainly indoors in an office, using computers and spending a lot of time on the telephone. However, you might travel in connection with your work so a driving licence is useful.

As you will also be meeting other professionals, you will have to be smartly dressed at all times.

You will typically work standard office hours, Monday to Friday. However, you might have to work evenings and weekends during busy periods.

Future prospects

Competition is fierce for entry to this profession.

Barristers are based in offices known as 'chambers' with one clerk serving more than one barrister; most offices are in London or other large cities. Advocates work in groups known as 'stables' in the Advocates' Library in Edinburgh.

You would start as a junior clerk and progress to clerk with experience. Training will be ongoing throughout your career. With experience you could train for another legal profession or move into general administrative work.

Qualifications and courses

ENTRY LEVEL 2

In England and Wales, barristers' clerks usually require a minimum of 4 GCSEs/S grades (A*–C/1–3), including maths and English. A levels are an advantage. In Scotland (for the Advocate's clerk post) applicants will be at a distinct advantage if they have H grades.

Candidates may join the Institute of Barristers' Clerks (IBC). After completing an appropriate BTEC course and 5 years' service in Chambers, a student can apply for qualified membership of the IBC.

In Scotland, advocates' clerks require a minimum of an H grade in English, and evidence of computer literacy and numeracy. More advocates' clerks are now entering with a HNC/HND or degree. Most training is on the job but candidates are encouraged to take courses organised by Faculty Services Ltd.

Advantages/disadvantages

Your work will be interesting and varied and you will have a lot of responsibility.

Work in the evenings and long hours are necessary when deadlines are approaching.

After further training, you can move into other legal careers.

Money guide

Salaries start at around £12,500, increasing to £16,800 per year. With experience, clerks can earn between £25,000 and £55,000. Senior clerks with a high level of responsibility, in busy chambers, can earn up to £100,000.

In Scotland you can earn between £22,000 and £28,000. As a senior, you can earn up to £45,000.

Related opportunities

- Barrister/Advocate p363
- Court Administrative Officer p368
- Paralegal p378

Further information

Institute of Barristers' Clerks
289–293 High Holborn, London WC1 7HZ
020 7831 7144; www.barristersclerks.com

Skills for Justice
Centre Court, Atlas Way, Sheffield S4 7QQ
0114 261 1499; www.skillsforjustice.com

The Faculty of Advocates
Parliament House, Edinburgh EH1 1RF
0131 226 5071; www.advocates.org.uk

Legal and Political Services

CRCI: L

CRCI: L

Legal and Political Services

CONSTITUENCY AGENT/ POLITICAL RESEARCHER

What the work involves

Constituency agent

- Your job will be to organise the running of the constituency for your political party, including election campaigns. You will arrange meetings, coordinate PR and marketing, and deal with enquiries. As secretary to the local office, your duties will include managing local membership, fundraising and organising volunteers.

Political researcher

- You will research information on political subjects and provide your employer with a coherent briefing of your conclusions. Your duties may include helping to create political speeches, finding sources of expertise on a specific issue and monitoring parliamentary reports.

The type of person suited to this work

You will need a solid understanding of the political system, along with a genuine interest and love of politics. It is important to have strong political opinions whilst understanding that sometimes you must look at the bigger picture.

Key skills for constituency agents are communication, information handling, IT, managing money, management and supervisory skills and working with others.

Key skills for political researchers include tact, IT, resourcefulness, debating abilities, research skills, resilience, communication, articulation and analytical abilities.

Working conditions

Constituency agent

Most of your work will be based in the party office which will be open to the public. However, you will be expected to do lots of travelling both locally and nationally, so a driving licence and car will be useful. You could work evenings, weekends or during the day. Hours could increase during national or local events like elections.

Political researcher

You will be working in an office, normally 9am–5pm although some longer hours might be required to meet specific deadlines. You may need to travel.

Future prospects

Constituency agent

Your prospects could depend on the size of the party you support. Later, you could become a local councillor or Member of Parliament.

Political researcher

This is an excellent starting point for a career in politics. Progression may include becoming an MP. You could take on extra responsibilities and move between public affairs firms in order to achieve promotion.

Qualifications and courses

There are no set entry requirements, although many employers expect candidates to have a 2:1 degree or above. Subjects such as politics, industrial relations, social policy, economics, marketing, public relations or journalism may prove valuable. You will need at least 2 A levels and 5 GCSEs (A*–C) for degree entry.

A postgraduate qualification such as an MSc in Public Affairs and Lobbying, an MPhil in Politics, or an MA in Political Communications would also be helpful.

Experience of working for the party or organisation on a voluntary basis is very important. Experience in other areas is also useful; for example, involvement with a trade union, holding office in a students' union, campaign work for a charity group. In general, candidates must be at least 20 years of age.

Advantages/disadvantages

You will get a good deal of job satisfaction as your work will be making a difference.

You may find this career stressful, particularly when you have to meet project deadlines or when there are elections.

Money guide

Constituency agent

You could expect to earn around £16,000 per year as a starting salary. This can rise to between £28,000 and £35,000 a year, depending on experience and level of responsibility.

Political researcher

Starting salaries begin at about £16,000 a year. This can increase to £20,000 after a year. After 2 or 3 years, in a senior position you could earn up to £24,000 per year.

Related opportunities

- Researcher (Media) p425
- Politician p381
- Welfare Benefits Adviser/Welfare Rights Caseworker p588

Further information

Association of Professional Political Consultants, c/o Precise Public Affairs
The Registry, Royal Mint Court, London EC3N 4QN
www.appc.org.uk

The Chartered Institute of Public Relations (CIPR) Government Affairs Group
52–53 Russell Square, London WC1B 4HP
020 7631 6900; www.cipr.co.uk

CORONER

What the work involves

- You will investigate sudden and suspicious deaths in England and Wales, and decide whether or not an inquest and/or post-mortem are required.

- Coroners preside at inquests and make decisions on whether or not further action is required.

- You will need to work with police and medical services in order to decide whether a person died of natural causes or not and keep detailed records of all proceedings.

- Once you have completed your investigations you must provide families or the relevant authorities with your report.

The type of person suited to this work

Preparing cases involves looking at statements and reports so you need to be able to read and analyse a lot of information. You might need to check points of law and ask for more information, so you must pay attention to detail.

Much of your work will be talking to people, and writing reports, so you need to have excellent speaking, listening and writing skills. Being confident to speak in court and argue logically are important.

You must be organised, able to meet deadlines and handle distressing situations calmly.

Working conditions

You will be based in an office but will spend time in court, at crime scenes and in hospitals. You will usually work normal office hours, however you will need to be available at all times when you are on call.

Although most of your work will be indoors, you will spend time outdoors at scenes of crime and accidents.

Most coroners work part time and spend the rest of their time in private legal practice.

Future prospects

Coroners are appointed and paid for by local councils, but hold office under the crown.

Although at the moment there is no promotion route, the Coroners and Justice Bill has proposed that there be posts such as Senior Coroner and Chief Coroner in the future.

Advantages/disadvantages

The work is varied, carries responsibility and can be satisfying.

You will have contact with many different types of people, some of whom may be difficult to deal with.

There will be a lot of administration and paperwork.

You will be on an on-call rota for evenings, weekends and bank holidays.

Qualifications and courses

Candidates usually start as deputy or assistant deputy coroners and must be qualified lawyers or legally qualified medical practitioners with at least five years' experience.

In order to qualify as a doctor you must complete an undergraduate course which leads to a degree in medicine. To do this you will need 3 A levels (with high grades) and good GCSEs (A*–C). A levels in chemistry and biology are usually required. Entry requirements will differ between universities and so it is best to check with the individual institution.

To train as a lawyer you must complete a qualifying law degree, an undergraduate degree followed by a law conversion course, a senior status law degree or complete exams to become part of the Fellowship of the Institute of Legal Executives. To be accepted onto a law degree you will usually require 2 or 3 A levels and 5 GCSEs grade A*–C (or equivalent).

Aldermen and councillors of local authorities are not eligible for appointment as coroners in their counties or districts until 6 months after the end of their service.

Money guide

Coroners receive an agreed fee, and as a guide, if you work full time as a deputy coroner, you can earn around £25,000 per year.

As a full-time coroner you can expect between £68,000 and £96,500 a year depending on how large the population is that you cover.

Part-time coroners are paid in proportion to the amount of cases they complete; salaries generally vary between £9,600 and £49,000 per year.

Related opportunities

- Barrister/Advocate p363
- Hospital Doctor p311
- Judge/Sheriff p372
- Solicitor/Notary Public p382

Further information

The Coroners' Society of England and Wales
HM Coroner's Court, The Cotton Exchange, Old Hall Street, Liverpool L3 9UF
0151 233 4708; www.coronersociety.org.uk

Ministry of Justice
102 Petty France, London SW1H 9AJ, United Kingdom
www.justice.gov.uk; 020 3334 3555

Department for Constitutional Affairs
Selborne House, 54 Victoria Street, London SW1E 6QW, United Kingdom
020 7210 8500; www.dca.gov.uk

Legal and Political Services

CRCI: L

COURT ADMINISTRATIVE OFFICER

What the work involves

- You will organise all the papers and information for a court hearing so that everything is ready for the judge or magistrate when the hearing starts.

- Booking dates, times and courtrooms for court hearings will be part of your job and you will prepare the timetable for each day.

- You will make sure everyone arriving at court knows where to go and receives the relevant paperwork.

- After the hearings, you will carry out court orders, for example endorsing driving licences, writing adoption orders or collecting fines.

The type of person suited to this work

As you will be responsible for making sure that court hearings run smoothly and everything is ready on time, it is important to be methodical and pay close attention to detail.

As many different people come to court, you need to be polite and helpful so that you can put them at ease and explain things clearly.

If you are working in a finance section, you need to be able to work with figures to deal with fines and costs. You should also have good ICT skills.

Working conditions

Most of your time will be spent indoors in courtrooms and offices in the court. You will be working around 37 hours a week, however overtime may be necessary if there is a hearing in the evening or at the weekend.

You will sit at a desk in an office for the majority of your day. Part-time work is often possible. You may have to travel to different courts, so a driving licence is useful.

Future prospects

Court administrative officers in England and Wales are employed by Her Majesty's Courts Service (HMCS) and move through promotion grades. In Scotland they are often known as court officers and are employed by the Scottish Court Service. Most training is on the job. You may have to move courts to widen your experience. You could move into similar work in the legal field such as legal executive roles or into general administrative work. Promotion to senior administration roles is possible.

Advantages/disadvantages

The work is varied and no two days will be the same.

You will meet and work with many different people.

Some people could be aggressive and threatening, which you could find frightening.

You may have to start early or work late at busy times.

Qualifications and courses

Qualification requirements vary within different regions, but a good general education is required, with 2–3 GCSEs/S grades, including maths and English, depending on the type of court and location. Some areas require administrative, typing, office or computing experience with others also requiring a minimum of one year of relevant office-based experience.

Applicants without formal qualifications may be able to sit an aptitude test or could be considered based solely on relevant administrative experience. New recruits tend to hold A levels/H grades or equivalent qualifications such as the Level 2 or 3 Diploma in Administration and the Diploma in Business, Administration and Finance.

On-the-job qualifications are offered through locally based short courses. NVQ/SVQ Level 2 in Court Administration may be available for those already working as an administration assistant, so they can progress to the role of officer.

Money guide

These figures are only approximate as salaries could vary depending on your employer and location.

Salaries for court administrative officers could start at around £14,000 per year.

With experience, you could earn somewhere between £14,000 and £17,000 a year.

If you progress to become a senior clerk or team leader you could earn over £20,000 per year.

Related opportunities

- Civil Service/Local Government Administrator p27
- Barrister's/Advocate's Clerk p365
- Court Usher/Officer/Macer p370
- Receptionist p58

Further information

Her Majesty's Courts Service (HMCS)
Customer Service Unit, Post point 1.40, 1st Floor,
102 Petty France, London SW1H 9AJ
0845 456 8770; www.hmcourts-service.gov.uk

Scottish Court Service (SCS)
Saughton House, Broomhouse Drive, Edinburgh EH11 3XD
0131 444 3300; www.scotcourts.gov.uk,
enquires@scotcourts.gov.uk

COURT REPORTER/ VERBATIM REPORTER

What the work involves

- Your job could involve attending court hearings, listening and reporting on what is said.

- Using a stenotype machine, or sometimes other recording equipment, you will write down everything a witness says, but you may edit other speakers to correct the grammar.

- Mostly you will work on your own, but in complex cases where lawyers may want a daily transcript of proceedings, you will work in a team of three on a rota basis.

- You could also record proceedings within other legal meetings such as industrial tribunals.

The type of person suited to this work

You need to have excellent listening skills and the ability to concentrate for long periods of time. A fast typing speed, strong attention to detail and a good grasp of punctuation and grammar are needed to ensure that your record is accurate. You must speak clearly when reading back what you have written.

If you do not catch what is said or get behind, you must have the confidence to stop proceedings or ask for something to be repeated.

You need to be able to work on your own when taking a record and in a team as you could work on a rota.

Working conditions

You will operate a steno machine with computer aided transcription systems, a machine with a keyboard layout which enables whole words and phrases to be typed at one stroke.

You might have to travel to different courts, so a driving licence is useful. There is a growing trend in Scotland for court cases to be taped and transcribed afterwards.

Future prospects

You could attend criminal cases in the crown courts, or civil cases in the high courts. You will also be present at other events, including industrial tribunals, public enquiries and in Parliament to record proceedings for Hansard. Some reporters also provide the media industry with subtitles.

Most court reporters are self-employed and there is no defined promotion ladder. Others work for companies contracted to service courts. In England and Wales there is a shortage of trained staff. In Scotland vacancies may decrease due to the shift to taping cases. You could work on television programmes which offer subtitles for viewers with hearing impairments.

Qualifications and courses

Candidates are usually required to have 3–5 GCSEs grades (A*–C), including English. Many entrants also have A levels. Thorough knowledge of English language, grammar and punctuation is also required. Work experience is an advantage.

Applicants need to have qualifications in using shorthand machines. For real-time court reporting you will be expected to have shorthand at 160–200 words per minute. Courses are available through the British Institute of Verbatim Reporters (BIVR). In Scotland all training is done on the job with a mentor.

It is possible after training and 3 years' experience to become a member of the BIVR by taking an examination. Members of the BIVR with deaf awareness training can become accredited Speech to Text (STT) Reporters.

Training for real-time reporting takes about 2 years.

Advantages/disadvantages

You will have contact with a wide range of people.

You will have to concentrate for long periods so the work is demanding.

Work in the evenings is possible to complete reports for the next day.

Money guide

Starting salaries are around £10,000–£15,000 per year. You could earn £24,000 as an experienced real-time reporter, i.e. working in a team of three. In Scotland you could earn up to £19,500. You can expect a daily rate of around £175–£195 if you work freelance. Real-time reporters working freelance can earn £300+ a day.

Related opportunities

- Court Administrative Officer p368
- Paralegal p378

Further information

British Institute of Verbatim Reporters
73 Alicia Gardens, Kenton, Harrow HA3 8JD
www.bivr.org.uk; sec@bivr.org.uk

Sorene Court Reporting & Training Services
73 Alicia Gardens, Kenton, Harrow HA3 8JD
020 8907 8249; www.sorene.co.uk

City&
Guilds

www.cityandguilds.com/myperfectjob

Legal and Political Services

CRCI: L

COURT USHER/OFFICER/ MACER

What the work involves

- Court ushers make sure that everything in the courtroom is ready for proceedings to begin, for example that all papers are ready, glasses and water are on tables and fire exits are clear.

- When people arrive at court, you will meet them and direct them to the right courtroom.

- In court, you will tell people to stand when the judge comes in, call witnesses and administer the right oath to witnesses.

- In Scotland, you will be known as a court officer in the sheriff court and a macer in the supreme courts.

The type of person suited to this work

As courtrooms must be prepared at the beginning of the day, court ushers need to be thorough in their work and pay attention to detail. You must be logical and organised.

You need to be able to work with people of all ages and backgrounds. Some may be nervous, and so it is important to have good speaking skills to explain what is happening and put them at ease. You will also need to be confident and sound in control in court.

It is important to stay calm at all times and be impartial in order to deal with people from both sides of a case.

Working conditions

You will spend most of your time in a courtroom but you might also have an office in the courthouse. In certain jury cases, you might have to stay away from home overnight and you will have to be smartly dressed at all times.

Future prospects

There are not many jobs for court ushers and getting in can be competitive. Most people have experience of other work first, for example within the police or armed services.

You can be promoted to senior and supervisory grades. You could also progress into other administrative jobs within the legal profession or outside.

Advantages/disadvantages

The job will be varied and no two days will be the same.

You might have to stay late or start early if proceedings overrun.

You will meet many different people some of whom may be difficult to deal with.

Qualifications and courses

Whilst no formal qualifications are required, a minimum of at least 2 GCSEs/S grades (A*–C/1–3), or the equivalent, including English, is strongly recommended. Training is conducted on the job, as well as through short courses.

The Diploma in Society, Health and Development could be useful for this role.

The stated minimum age is 21 (16 in Scotland), but most courts prefer to recruit mature people under the age of 63 (60 in Scotland).

A background in the police or armed forces can be an advantage. You will need a Criminal Records Bureau (CRB) check before becoming a court usher.

Money guide

As a starting salary in England and Wales, you can expect to earn around £12,700 per year.

This rises to around £15,400 with experience.

Around £12,000–£13,750 is usual as a macer in Scotland.

Overtime payments for late nights or early starts are often paid.

Related opportunities

- Civil Service/Local Government Administrator p27
- Court Administrative Officer p368
- Receptionist p58

Further information

Her Majesty's Courts Service
5th Floor, Clive House, Petty France,
London SW1H 9HD
020 7210 8500; www.hmcourts-service.gov.uk

Scottish Court Service
Hayweight House, 23 Lauriston Street,
Edinburgh EH3 9DQ
0131 229 9200; www.scotcourts.gov.uk

Skills for Justice
Centre Court, Atlas Way, Sheffield S4 7QQ
0114 261 1499; www.skillsforjustice.com

CROWN PROSECUTOR/ PROCURATOR FISCAL

What the work involves

Crown prosecutor

- You will look at reports from the police and other agencies and decide whether or not crimes in England and Wales should be prosecuted. You will take statements from witnesses before a trial and examine witnesses in court, guiding them through their evidence. You will then sum up the case for the prosecution.

Procurator fiscal

- You will carry out similar duties to crown prosecutors in England and Wales, based on the Scottish legal system. In Scotland, sudden and suspicious deaths are investigated by the Procurator Fiscal Service.

The type of person suited to this work

Preparing cases involves looking at statements so you need to be able to read and analyse a lot of information. You must be able to pay attention to detail.

You must have excellent listening and writing skills. Confidence is needed to make clear and logical arguments in court.

Working conditions

You will be based in an office but will spend time in court. You might also spend time outdoors at scenes of crime and accidents.

Future prospects

Crown prosecutor

There is a clear promotion structure within the service but very few top senior posts. Competition in the CPS is very keen.

Procurator fiscal

Candidates apply to join the Procurator Fiscal Service through the Crown Office. Applicants start as deputes, working under guidance of senior colleagues and gradually taking more responsibility. After a few years, they can apply to become procurator fiscals but promotion is not automatic.

Crown prosecutors and procurators fiscal can transfer into other areas of law such as private practice.

Advantages/disadvantages

The job is interesting, carries responsibilities and can be rewarding.

You will have contact with many different types of people, some of whom may be difficult to deal with.

You will be on an on-call rota for evenings, weekends and bank holidays.

Qualifications and courses

Crown prosecutor

If you are either a solicitor admitted in England and Wales with a full current practising certificate, or a barrister called to the English Bar who has completed pupillage (training) you can apply directly to the Crown Prosecution Service (CPS).

If you are still studying to become a solicitor or barrister you can apply for a trainee scheme run by the CPS, as long as you will have completed your studies by the time the traineeship starts.

Administrative Officers or caseworkers with at least 12 months' qualifying service with the CPS can apply for the Law Scholarship Scheme and Legal Trainee Scheme.

Procurator fiscal

Candidates are solicitors qualified in the Scottish legal system. An LLB degree in Scottish law (or 3 years of pre-diploma training and a pass in the Law Society of Scotland's exams) is required, followed by a Diploma in Legal Practice and 2 years working as a trainee solicitor. Candidates are solicitors qualified in the Scottish legal system. An LLB degree in Scottish law (or 3 years of pre-diploma training and a pass in the Law Society of Scotland's exams) is required, followed by a Diploma in Legal Practice and 2 years working as a trainee solicitor.

The Procurator Fiscal Service offers a few 2-year traineeships, the final stage in qualifying as a solicitor.

Money guide

Crown prosecutor

Crown prosecutors start at £29,000 per year. As a Senior Crown Prosecutor you could earn around £48,000–58,000.

Procurator fiscal

As a procurator fiscal you can earn around £28,000 a year after 2 years as a trainee. You could expect to earn around £40,000–£47,000 with more experience, rising to around £58,000 at the top level.

Related opportunities

- Barrister/Advocate p363
- Solicitor/Notary Public p382
- Paralegal p378

Further information

Crown Prosecution Service
50 Ludgate Hill, London EC4M 7EX
020 7796 8000; www.cps.gov.uk

Crown Office Scotland
25 Chambers Street, Edinburgh EH1 1LA
0131 226 2626; www.crownoffice.gov.uk

ENTRY LEVEL 4

Legal and Political Services

CRCI: L

JUDGE/SHERIFF

What the work involves

- Judges (sheriffs in Scotland) preside over courts and make judgements on what should happen based on the evidence from two opposing parties.

- You will listen to all the evidence and decide on procedures, including whether a piece of evidence can be used, and keep order in court.

- In jury cases, you will instruct and advise the jury on the strength of the evidence before the jury leaves court to consider the verdict.

- You will decide on penalties in criminal courts and on settlements in civil cases.

The type of person suited to this work

As judges make the final decisions in any court case, it is important to be able to grasp facts quickly and analyse the evidence to help make your decision. Judges must think logically and not become emotionally involved.

You should have excellent communication and public-speaking skills. You also need to be a good listener and pay careful attention to the evidence. It is important to have the confidence to make difficult decisions and stick by them. Discretion is needed to deal with classified information.

Working conditions

You will spend much of your time in court but will also have an office with support staff to help you. You will travel between courts and may have to spend time away from home.

You will dress smartly at all times and wear robes in court. Courts are also very formal and have traditions which you must observe.

Future prospects

There are very few openings for judges and sheriffs, which means entry is competitive. Successful candidates have normally followed a long career in law as a barrister/advocate or solicitor.

Most judges work in one type of court, such as a Crown Court or Court of Appeal. Senior positions, such as Lord Chief Justice and Master of the Rolls, are made on the recommendation of the Prime Minister.

In Scotland, most sheriffs work in sheriff courts. A few with experience become supreme court judges in the High Court of Justiciary or the Court of Session.

Advantages/disadvantages

The work is varied and no two days will be the same.

This is a very responsible job, and requires a high amount of intellect and dedication.

Qualifications and courses

ENTRY 7 LEVEL

Candidates are almost always qualified barristers or advocates who have 7–10 years' experience and have progressed to working as a deputy district judge or a recorder. District or circuit judges are usually appointed after 10–15 years' court experience. Judges are appointed by the Judicial Appointments Commission.

After 10–15 years' experience, barristers/advocates may apply to become a Queen's Counsel and may eventually become a High Court judge or a Court of Session judge in Scotland.

Judicial office holders must retire on their 70th birthday.

Sheriffs are required to be qualified advocates (members of the Scottish Bar) with 10 years' experience.

You will meet many different people and hear some cases which will have a high media interest or involve upsetting or distressing evidence.

Some courts work into the evenings.

Money guide

Salaries can vary according to region, but start at around £99,500–£168,000 per year as a senior district judge.

You could earn £138,000 as a circuit judge.

Sheriffs earn around £140,800 per year.

Around £170,000 + is possible as a High Court judge.

Around £239,845 a year is the salary as Lord Chief Justice, the highest legal position in the land.

Related opportunities

- Barrister/Advocate p363
- Crown Prosecutor/Procurator Fiscal p371
- Legal Executive p373
- Solicitor/Notary Public p382

Further information

Judicial Communications Office
11th Floor, Thomas More Building, Royal Courts of Justice, Strand, London WC2A 2LL
www.judiciary.gov.uk

Judicial Appointments Commission
Steel House, 11 Tothill Street, London SW1H 9LH
020 3334 0453; www.judicialappointments.gov.uk

Skills for Justice
Centre Court, Atlas Way, Sheffield S4 7QQ
0114 261 1499; www.skillsforjustice.com

LEGAL EXECUTIVE

What the work involves

- Legal executives work with solicitors, preparing complex cases for them and dealing with straightforward cases themselves.

- You will interview clients, asking questions to help you give them legal advice and explain legal points to them clearly. You will write letters on their behalf, draft contracts and wills and prepare other documents.

- In certain cases, you may represent clients in court or at tribunals.

The type of person suited to this work

Excellent written and verbal communication skills are essential.

Clients will give you confidential information so it is important to be discreet and tactful. You will also need patience as legal points can be difficult to grasp.

When preparing cases, you will be handling large amounts of information, which means it is useful to be a thorough and well-organised worker.

Working conditions

Most legal executives work 37 hours a week, Monday to Friday. You will be based in an office but you may attend court. You will be expected to dress smartly.

You might have to travel to visit clients or legal libraries, so a driving licence is useful.

Future prospects

You could work for solicitors in private practice or in local and central government and industry. Legal executives usually specialise in one area, for example property or business law.

You can train to qualify as a legal executive advocate or as a solicitor, which allows you to follow a case right through to court.

This is a very competitive career, and the majority of entrants are now graduates.

Advantages/disadvantages

You will have the chance to work in a legal environment while studying part time and earning a good salary.

You might have to work under pressure to meet deadlines and possibly work evenings and weekends.

Money guide

Starting salaries for trainee legal executives are around £15,000, rising to nearly £24,000 with experience. Once you have passed ILEX exams you can earn £25,000–£30,500,

Qualifications and courses

You need to undertake academic and practical training to be a legal executive. These examinations are set by the Institute of Legal Executives; practical work experience is gained by working in a legal role. The normal minimum requirements for training are 4 GCSEs/S grades (A*–C/1–3), including English. City & Guilds/ILEX Level 2 Certificate in Legal Studies is a suitable alternative. Many entrants to this career have higher qualifications such as HND/HNCs or a degree.

Students train under the supervision of a solicitor or senior legal executive and studying is carried out on day release or at evening classes. The first part of the course is the Professional Diploma in Law and Practice Level 3, which takes 1–2 years to complete.

Trainees then progress to the Professional Higher Diploma in Law and Practice Level 6. Full training at Level 6 takes 2 years (while working full time) and leads to ILEX Membership. ILEX qualifications can also be taken as part of a Modern legal Apprenticeship scheme.

Some qualifications such as a Law degree may provide exemption from some academic parts of the ILEX qualifications. People with relevant experience can also apply to have their experience approved by ILEX.

In Scotland, there is no direct equivalent to legal executive; staff are known as paralegals or solicitors' assistants. Generally 4 GCSEs/S grades (A*–C/1–3) including English and maths, followed by office experience, are required.

depending on where you work. Legal executives with more experience can earn around £45,000. Senior ILEX Fellows can earn over £60,000.

Related opportunities

- Civil Service/Local Government Administrator p27
- Barrister's/Advocate's Clerk p365
- Solicitor/Notary Public p382

Further information

Institute of Legal Executives
Kempston Manor, Kempston, Bedford MK42 7AB
01234 841000; www.ilex.org.uk

Law Society of Northern Ireland
96 Victoria Street, Belfast BT1 3GN
028 9023 1614; www.lawsoc-ni.org

Law Society of England and Wales
The Law Society's Hall, 113 Chancery Lane, London WC2A 1PL
020 7242 1222; www.lawsociety.org.uk

ENTRY LEVEL 4

CRCI: L | Legal and Political Services

Organisation profile

THE INSTITUTE OF LEGAL EXECUTIVES

Legal Executive Lawyers

The term lawyer is not technically limited to just solicitors and barristers. It means someone qualified and experienced in the law. Legal executives are qualified lawyers in England and Wales who do similar work to solicitors, but specialise in one area of law.

The Institute of Legal Executives (ILEX) offers an exceptionally cost-effective and accessible route to becoming a lawyer. ILEX study fees cost around £6,200 (depending on where the qualifications are studied), which compares exceptionally well to the rising costs of University: Students are now leaving Uni with average debts of up to £30,000 (NUS figures). To become a solicitor or barrister there are post-Uni costs, for example the Bar Professional Training Course (BPTC) (formerly known as the Bar Vocational Course (BVC)) costs from £8,000 to £11,000. Becoming a solicitor costs £5,000 to £10,000 with a law degree, plus another £3,000 to £7,000 for those without a law degree.

Training Contracts and Pupillages are very hard to secure and are currently mandatory. These are not required for the Legal Executive route to becoming a lawyer. As such, becoming a Legal Executive lawyer is viewed as an increasingly appealing alternative to becoming a solicitor or barrister, and exemptions are available from ILEX for those with legal qualifications.

There have been a number of recent changes that put Legal Executive lawyers on a more level footing with barristers and solicitors.

- Under the Legal Services Act 2007, Legal Executive lawyers are 'authorised persons' undertaking 'reserved legal activities', alongside solicitors and barristers.
- Legal Executive lawyers are now able to become partners or managers in Legal Disciplinary Practices (firms of different lawyers with 25% non-lawyer managers).
- Looking ahead, when the relevant sections of the 2007 Act come into force, Legal Executive lawyers will be able to become partners or managers in Alternative Business Structures (firms with external ownership and investment) and set up their own practices.
- Legal Executive lawyers are now eligible to apply for prescribed Judicial posts and become Chairs of Tribunals.
- After taking an additional course, Legal Executive lawyers can undertake Advocacy and represent their clients in court.
- Legal Executive lawyers are Commissioners of Oaths; give advice on compromise agreements; and are able to instruct barristers directly without going through a solicitor.
- Legal Executive lawyers must adhere to a code of conduct and, like solicitors, are required to continue training throughout their careers in order to keep themselves abreast of the latest developments in the law.

Routes to ILEX Qualification

ILEX students usually 'earn whilst they learn' and so take home a salary (usually from £14,000 to £20,000 per year when still qualifying), by working in a law firm whilst studying. Study takes one or two nights a week for the typical four years it takes to do all the ILEX qualifications required, either via a local college or distance learning. On average ILEX students earn around £65,000 during this time.

The ILEX qualifications are set at Level 3 (equivalent to 'A' level) and Level 6 (honours degree level). There is also five years' of work experience required in a legal environment before you can become a fully qualified Legal Executive lawyer. Once qualified, you and your family can attend the ILEX graduation day, complete with mortarboard cap and gown.

Organisation profile

The ILEX route to becoming a lawyer is open to all, though it is recommended that at least 4 GCSEs are held. It is also ideal for those with degrees in law and non-law subject, and those with a BVC or LPC.

For those already holding a qualifying law degree awarded within the last seven years, ILEX offers a Graduate 'Fast-Track' Diploma. This just requires completing two ILEX Level 6 practice units (one of which must relate to the subject areas studied within the law degree), and the ILEX Level 6 Client Care Skills unit to complete academic studies. After five years' relevant work experience (at least two of which must be after completion of the ILEX fast-track qualification) you will be eligible to apply to become a qualified Legal Executive lawyer. This route costs approximately £1,500 to complete.

Non-qualifying law degrees or degrees that have sufficient legal content will be assessed on a subject by subject basis. A full syllabus transcript must be provided with the application to ILEX so that the contents of the qualification can be mapped against the appropriate ILEX unit. If no exemptions are granted, then applicants need to study the two stages of ILEX academic courses (the ILEX Level 3 Professional Diploma in Law and Practice and the ILEX Level 6 Professional Higher Diploma in Law and Practice qualifications) and this usually takes four years of part-time study. However, because the studies are usually through evening classes or by distance learning, this route has the advantage that trainee Legal Executive lawyers can earn a salary whilst qualifying. They must still undertake five years' relevant work experience (again, at least two of which must be after completion of the ILEX academic qualifications) to become a qualified Legal Executive lawyer.

Salaries

Salaries will vary according to location and chosen specialist area of law, but starting salaries are approximately £14,000 a year. Fully qualified Legal Executives can then expect to earn around £35,000 on average across England and Wales, with more being offered for Legal Executives in major cities such as London, where salaries can reach as high as £95,000.

The Institute of Legal Executives
Tel: 01234 841000
Email: info@ilex.org.uk

www.ilexcareers.org.uk

Institute of Legal Executives (ILEX), Kempston Manor, Kempston, Bedford, MK42 7AB.

LICENSED CONVEYANCER

What the work involves

- Licensed conveyancers deal with the legal side of buying, selling, renting and mortgaging of houses, flats, business premises and other property.

- You will draw up the legal documents, known as contracts, that buyers and sellers exchange to make a sale legal.

- Other work includes liaising with lawyers and estate agents involved in the sale and researching details in the contract.

The type of person suited to this work

You will need excellent communication skills to explain complicated legal matters to clients. Being a good team worker is useful to liaise with others involved in a contract.

As legal contracts must be completely accurate, you must be thorough and able to process large amounts of information. You will need good organisational skills to deal with several properties simultaneously.

Working conditions

You will work standard office hours, but may be required to work some late evenings or weekends to meet clients. Your job may be salaried or commission only. Many licensed conveyancers are self-employed.

Future prospects

There are only around 1,000 licensed conveyancers in England and Wales, and very few qualified conveyancers in Scotland. Job opportunities are mainly with legal practices, although since the recession there are fewer places for trainees.

Training is ongoing to cover developments in property law. You could progress into other legal professions, a managerial role or run your own business. Changes in the law now allow conveyancers to take an additional qualification, to add to their licence, and deal with probate. Probate is the legal procedure of administering the money, property and possessions of a person after they die.

Advantages/disadvantages

The work is varied. You will meet different people, though some may be difficult.

You will get satisfaction when clients get their dream home.

You might find it stressful when trying to meet deadlines or clients feel things are moving too slowly.

Money guide

A trainee could earn around £15,000 per year.

With further experience, this rises to £25,000–£40,000. At the more senior levels you might earn £35,000–£55,000. £60,000+ is possible for a partner or an owner of a conveyancing firm.

Qualifications and courses

ENTRY LEVEL 4

England and Wales

Candidates must pass the Council for Licensed Conveyancers (CLC) training and exams. To begin training applicants must be 21 years old and have 4 GCSEs (A*–C), including English. An A level in law is useful. Many applicants will hold a law degree or might have undertaken the Institute of Legal Executives course or the Legal Practice Course for trainee solicitors.

They must have at least 2 years' practical training with a 'qualified employer' and pass the CLC examination. Many students take this as a correspondence course. It is also offered on a part-time basis.

Candidates can then apply for a limited licence. After a further 3 consecutive years you can apply for a full licence.

An Apprenticeship in Business, Administration and Law may also be available.

Scotland

Entrants require a degree in law from a Scottish university or a Diploma/Certificate in legal studies which lasts at least 2 years.

They then undertake a 1 year training contract with an independent qualified conveyancer. After 6 months of training, a Professional Competence Course, which comprises 36 hours of core requirements and 18 hours of electives, must be completed.

For law degrees you need 5 GCSEs/S grades (A*–C/1–3) and 3 A levels/H grades. Some universities require applicants to take the National Admissions Test for Law.

Northern Ireland

The job of a licensed conveyancer is carried out by a solicitor. Solicitors must complete an Apprenticeship programme of 2–4 years, combined with a vocational course. You can complete either a Certificate in Professional Legal Studies or a Postgraduate Diploma in Professional Legal Practice.

Related opportunities

- Barrister/Advocate p363
- Estate Agent p96
- Surveying Technician p125

Further information

Council for Licensed Conveyancers
16 Glebe Road, Chelmsford CM1 1QG
01245 349599; www.conveyancer.org.uk

Law Society of Scotland
26 Drumsheugh Gardens, Edinburgh EH3 7YR
0131 226 7411; www.lawscot.org.uk

MAGISTRATES' COURT LEGAL ADVISER/SHERIFF'S CLERK

What the work involves

Magistrates' Court Legal Adviser (England and Wales)

- You will be a qualified solicitor or barrister with responsibility for advising magistrates in court.

- You will advise on points of law, procedures, penalties and other issues.

Sheriff's clerk (Scotland)

- You might advise on points of law and procedures in any court (civil or criminal).

- You could have a more general administrative role such as handling court complaints and providing statistics for court staff.

The type of person suited to this work

You must have a strong interest in the law and excellent communication skills as you will be expected to advise on a wide range of issues. You must be organised, reliable and able to work quickly and accurately under pressure.

It's important to be impartial and remain detached from emotionally demanding cases. You will need to be discreet to deal with confidential information.

Working conditions

You will normally be located in one court building and will generally work a 37-hour week, from Monday to Friday. However, your working hours may, at times, be irregular due to complex cases. Some courts also open as early as 8.00am and you might need to work weekends. You might travel to different courts so a driving licence is useful.

Future prospects

Her Majesty's Court Service has a set career structure. You could progress to a role as a justices' clerk or a justices' chief executive. You could go on to a role where you train magistrates or manage a team of legal advisers.

In Scotland, sheriff's clerks are employed by the Scottish Court Service. Small rural courts may have only one clerk, while a court in a big city will have several. There is a clear promotion structure within the Scottish Court Service.

Advantages/disadvantages

The work is varied and no two days will be the same.

You might have to work unsocial hours at times.

You might find it hard not to be the decision maker.

Money guide

You can expect around £18,775–£27,137 per year on entry as a Magistrates' Court Legal Adviser.

Qualifications and courses

Magistrates' Court Legal Adviser (England and Wales)

Candidates must be either barristers or solicitors. You will start as a trainee legal adviser.

Barristers need an approved law degree, or a non-law degree followed by the Common Professional Examination (CPE) or a Postgraduate Diploma (PgDL) in Law. They then complete a Bar Vocational Course followed by two 6-month 'pupillages' with an experienced barrister.

Solicitors need an approved law degree or a non-law degree followed by the CPE or a PgD. They can also qualify through ILEX.

Sheriff's clerk (Scotland)

There are no minimum entry requirements but it would be helpful to have S grades (1–3) in maths and English. You could start as an administrative officer and then progress to a role as sheriff's clerk. Fast-track entry to a position as sheriff's clerk deputy is sometimes available to those with a law degree, the Diploma in Legal Practice and 2 years' training with a solicitor.

If you are on Tier One you can receive a salary of up to £45,827 a year and if you reach Tier Two this reaches up to £50,192 a year.

Starting salaries for sheriffs' clerks are about £12,211. This can rise to between £28,000 and £35,000.

Related opportunities

- Barrister/Advocate p363
- Barrister's/Advocate's Clerk p365
- Legal Executive p373
- Solicitor/Notary Public p382

Further information

Her Majesty's Courts Service
Customer Service Unit, Post point 1.40, 1st Floor,
102 Petty France, London SW1H 9AJ
0845 456 8770; www.hmcourts-service.gov.uk

Scottish Court Service
Hayweight House, 23 Lauriston Street, Edinburgh EH3 9DQ
0131 229 9200; www.scotcourts.gov.uk

www.cityandguilds.com/myperfectjob

PARALEGAL

What the work involves

- A paralegal is somebody who is not a qualified lawyer, but whose job involves dealing with a lot of legal issues.

- You may have legal training or experience, and will work in a law firm or similar organisation.

- Your duties will be varied, but will probably involve legal research and drafting documents, as well as other administrative tasks.

- You'll also interview witnesses and clients, and appear in court, often acting on behalf of lawyers. You might specialise in a specific area of law.

The type of person suited to this work

You should have a natural interest in law and current affairs, and be discreet in your work, as you may frequently be dealing with confidential information.

Attention to detail is essential, as is a good command of English, and the ability to communicate well with everybody, from the lawyers you'll be working with to all of their clients.

You should also be patient, understanding, tactful and sympathetic, and be able to work well under pressure.

Organisational skills are essential, as is computer literacy, excellent concentration and a good memory. You also need to be able to understand and absorb a lot of information.

Working conditions

You'll probably be working in an office for about 37 hours a week. However, some of these will be spent visiting clients, which means that a driving licence is useful.

You may spend time in police stations and court, occasionally out of office hours. You may be required to work weekends and bank holidays, if necessary.

Future prospects

Future prospects for a paralegal are good. You can use the knowledge you gain on the job to develop your legal career. If you have the necessary qualifications, you can become a solicitor or barrister, and even work your way up to partner.

With experience, you can take on additional responsibilities and move up within the firm. You may choose to move on to freelance work.

Advantages/disadvantages

Working as a paralegal is stimulating and rewarding, especially if you have an interest in or study law.

It can really give your law career a nudge in the right direction, and is a great option if, for example, you're training to be a solicitor and want to take a gap year or year out.

Occasionally tasks may be a little mundane, and meeting with clients can be stressful.

Qualifications and courses

ENTRY LEVEL 2

You don't need any specific qualifications to become a paralegal, and can start work straight from school. However, most employers prefer you to have some relevant qualifications, for example GCSEs (A*–C), a BTEC in Legal Studies, an NVQ in Business Administration or a Foundation degree in law.

Some employers ask for a HND or degree in law, and others even request the LPC (Legal Practice Course) postgraduate qualification.

Becoming a paralegal is a popular option with those who graduated in law but don't have a training contract to become a solicitor.

Training usually takes place on the job, and you'll be supervised by experienced lawyers. Employers may well encourage you to follow courses in legal training; these are widely available. These might include a HND, BTEC or City & Guilds qualification in law or legal studies.

Money guide

As a paralegal who is starting out, you may earn £14,000–£25,000 a year.

This can grow with experience to £25,000–£40,000 a year.

As a senior paralegal you might be earning over £70,000 a year.

Related opportunities

- Court Administrative Officer p368
- Legal Executive p373

Further information

Institute of Paralegals
2nd Floor, Berkeley Square House, Berkeley Square, Mayfair, London W1J 6BD
020 7887 1420; www.instituteofparalegals.org

Institute of Legal Executives
Kempston Manor, Kempston MK42 7AB
01234 845718; www.ilex.org.uk

The National Association of Licensed Paralegals
308 Canterbury Court, Kennington Business Park, 1–3 Brixton Road, London SW9 6DE
020 3176 0900; www.nationalparalegals.com

City & Guilds

www.cityandguilds.com/myperfectjob

Organisation profile

THE INSTITUTE OF LEGAL EXECUTIVES

Paralegal

The Institute of Legal Executives (ILEX) is the largest and oldest professional and education body for paralegals in England and Wales. The Institute offers an extensive range of qualifications and membership grades aimed at enhancing the career prospects of paralegals working at all levels, whether you are just starting out on your career or hold a law degree.

ILEX now offers a Fast-Track Diploma to graduates with a qualifying law degree, which will cost around £1,900 to complete. Just three units of the ILEX Level 6 qualification are required: If you already hold a qualifying law degree awarded within the last seven years, you just need to study two ILEX Level 6 Practice qualification units (one of which must relate to the subjects you studied within your law degree), and the ILEX Level 6 Client Care Skills unit to complete your academic studies. It is an ideal alternative for those who haven't secured a training contract or pupilage. After five years' relevant legal experience (two of which much have been gained after you complete your ILEX qualification) you will be eligible to become a lawyer. The qualification is usually studied part-time over a 9-month period.

In conjunction with City and Guilds, ILEX also offers a specific range of qualifications aimed at those seeking a career as a paralegal and those working in other legal support roles where knowledge of the law is needed. If you don't already hold a law qualification, these qualifications can also provide you with the opportunity to transfer to the Legal Executive route to become a qualified lawyer.

Together ILEX and City & Guilds offer the law sector's leading qualifications for legal secretaries and paralegals. Over 20,000 people have chosen these qualifications to advance their careers. They are available for study through over 100 approved City & Guilds centres nationwide.

Reflecting the National Occupational Standards in Administration, the programmes are now considered a benchmark for those aspiring to or working in a legal environment as secretaries or personal assistants. The programmes are designed to establish a national standard for those working in a legal environment. They offer a flexible route with no entry requirements (although a Grade C or above in English Language GCSE is desirable) and are assessed by task based assignments.

Specially produced course books are available, and the City & Guilds/ILEX Level 2 Certificate in Vocational Paralegal Studies can be used as part of your entry criteria to study as a Legal Executive with ILEX.

Paralegals are also eligible to apply to become members of ILEX. The grades and fees for 2010/11 are as follows:

Student member – for those wishing to enter the legal profession; those who have no relevant legal qualification; or those with less than three years' work experience of a predominantly legal nature. Annual subscription fees of £50 are payable, plus a one-off initial registration fee of £35.

Affiliate member – for those with at least one ILEX Level 3 unit qualification, or who have completed a relevant legal qualification at Level 2, or gained at least three years' work of a predominantly legal nature. Annual subscription fees of £100 are payable, plus a one-off initial registration fee of £35.

For more information on ILEX qualifications or to receive information on your nearest study centre, please call +44 (0)1234 841000 or email info@ilex.org.uk, or visit www.ilexcareers.org.uk

To find your nearest centre, simply contact your regional City & Guilds office (details on www.cityandguilds.com) or email paralegal@ilex.org.uk

PATENT AGENT/EXAMINER

What the work involves

Patent agent

■ You will advise clients on the law of intellectual property.

■ It will be your responsibility to ensure that inventions put forward do not already exist. The work involves checking that an invention is a new one and not one which already exists.

■ You will prepare specifications for the Patent Office, carrying out any negotiations required and representing the client before the patent examiner.

Examiner

■ You will examine patent applications submitted by patent agents for new inventions, trademarks or a design.

■ You must ensure that patents are granted for new inventions.

■ You will conduct a study on each application to check that it is clear and that it meets legal requirements.

The type of person suited to this work

You will need a thorough knowledge of applying intellectual property to inventions and the laws regarding this sector. You should have strong research skills and a high attention to detail. You must have excellent communication skills in order to explain complex legal issues to your clients. You must be highly organised, decisive and able to multi-task.

Working conditions

You will be based in an office, although patent agents do some travelling in the UK and abroad; a driving licence would be useful.

The majority of your time will be spent researching and writing reports on the computer.

Future prospects

Roughly 750 agents are registered in the UK. Around 80% work in private practices, mostly in the larger towns and cities. Around 20% work with industrial companies or local government agencies.

Patent examiners are civil servants, mostly based in the Patent Office in Newport with a few working in London. The civil service has a formal promotion structure leading to senior patent examiner.

Advantages/disadvantages

This job has a high level of responsibility and is intellectually demanding.

You will get satisfaction from helping new inventions become recognised and being involved at an early stage of the job.

Qualifications and courses

ENTRY LEVEL 5

Patent agent

All patent agents need a degree related to science, engineering or maths. Entry is with at least 5 GCSEs (A*–C) including English and maths, and at least 2 A levels or equivalent. Entry is competitive and most employers look for a minimum of a 2.1.

Patent agents receive specialist training in intellectual property law. Qualified solicitors with experience of working in an intellectual property department or those training to become patent agents may apply to join the Chartered Institute of Patent Agents (CIPA).

A high level of skill in the English language is required, and fluency in foreign languages, especially French and/or German, is a bonus. This is a requirement in order to become a European patent attorney.

A training period and the successful completion of examinations is required for admission to the Register of Patent Agents and the Register of Trade Mark Agents. It usually takes 4 to 5 years to qualify.

The Certificate in IP Law, offered by several universities (typically a 1 to 3 month course) gives exemption from all the Foundation Papers of the CIPA examinations.

Examiner

You must have a good Honours degree in science, maths, engineering or technology. An equivalent professional qualification or corporate membership of a relevant major professional institution may be accepted. It is also essential that you meet the civil service's nationality and residency requirements.

Money guide

The starting salary for a trainee is around £21,500, rising to £27,500 per year with experience. Technical assistants can earn £28,000 and progress to £48,000. Once qualified you could get £52,000–£72,000. With 5 years' experience this rises to £68,000, reaching £95,000+ for senior partners in private practices.

Related opportunities

■ Barrister's/Advocate's Clerk p365
■ Legal Executive p373
■ Solicitor/Notary Public p382

Further information

Chartered Institute of Patent Agents
95 Chancery Lane, London WC2A 1DT
020 7405 9450; www.cipa.org.uk

Intellectual Property Office
Concept House, Cardiff Road, Newport NP10 8QQ
0845 950 0505; www.ipo.gov.uk

POLITICIAN

What the work involves

- MPs represent the people in their local constituencies in Parliament, usually as a member of a political party.

- You will hold 'surgeries' in your local constituency and deal with issues raised by local people at local and national level. MEPs (members of the European parliament) deal with European legislation.

- In Parliament, you will join committees, attend meetings and take part in debates. You will also vote on new policies or laws.

- You may specialise in a particular area, and may hold office in the government or for the Opposition.

The type of person suited to this work

You should be passionate about politics and have strong social beliefs, along with a desire to represent the people of your constituency.

Key skills include: communication, decision making, information handling, supervisory and management skills.

A pleasant manner and the ability to gain people's confidence are also important.

You will be expected to keep up to date with party policies and legislation, which requires being able to deal with large amounts of information quickly and thoroughly.

Working conditions

Your time will be split between your local constituency and Parliament/Scottish Parliament/Welsh Assembly.

MEPs spend one week a month in Strasbourg and much of their remaining time in Brussels.

Politicians tend to work very long hours when parliament is sitting. From the end of July to the beginning of October parliament breaks, so that politicians can spend time in their constituencies. This is an extremely demanding job, with a great deal of responsibility.

There is a lot of travel involved both at home and overseas.

Future prospects

Your job in any parliament will depend on being re-elected, which means it is important to have another career option to fall back on.

Although most MPs represent the local people in their constituencies, they are also involved in the government of their country. You could be offered a post in a ministry, which may lead to appointment as a minister in a particular area. In exceptional circumstances, you could become the leader of your party and maybe even the Prime Minister.

Advantages/disadvantages

The work is varied and challenging, and no two days will be the same.

Qualifications and courses

Any British citizen may stand for election as long as they are over 18 years old. There are no formal minimum educational requirements but many MPs are graduates or hold other professional qualifications. Qualifications in business, law or economics are particularly useful.

It is essential to be actively involved in a political party and experience in areas such as trade union work is helpful.

In Scotland and Wales there are regional members as well as constituency members.

There is a series of selection interviews before candidates can be 'adopted' by their party and their local constituency to stand for election. Candidates must then carry out a successful electoral campaign and be elected by the votes of the local people.

Those disqualified from election are undischarged bankrupts, prisoners of more than 1 year, members of the House of Lords and people holding offices listed in the House of Commons Disqualification Act 1975.

You will get satisfaction, particularly if your party is in power, but also frustration when votes do not go your way.

You will need plenty of stamina to handle the long hours and the job can be pressurised.

Money guide

Basic salary for an MP in the House of Commons is £64,766. Additional allowances are also available for things like travel and communications. Salaries depend on the types of responsibilities. You could earn £144,520 as a cabinet minister. You could earn around £197,689 a year as Prime Minister.

MEPs are paid the same salaries as national MPs in their own countries.

Related opportunities

- Constituency Agent/Political Researcher p366
- Public Relations Officer p422
- Trade Union Official p586
- Welfare Benefits Adviser/Welfare Rights Caseworker p588

Further information

House of Commons Information Office
House of Commons, Westminster, London SW1A 0AA
020 7219 4272; www.parliament.uk

Scottish Parliament
Public Information Services, Edinburgh EH99 1SP
0845 278 1999; www.scottish.parliament.uk

National Assembly for Wales
Cardiff Bay, Cardiff CF99 1NA
0845 010 5500; www.wales.gov.uk

ENTRY 1 LEVEL

Legal and Political Services

CRCI: L

SOLICITOR/NOTARY PUBLIC

What the work involves

Solicitor

■ A major part of your job will be advising clients on legal matters, making a will or setting up a business.

■ In certain circumstances you may represent clients in court, or you might have to instruct a barrister or advocate to act for your client.

Notary public

■ Your main job will be to certify deeds and other documents so that they will be accepted by judicial and public authorities as authentic and legally binding. Notaries public are generally solicitors who combine this function with other legal work.

The type of person suited to this work

You must be able to examine and analyse vast amounts of information and pay close attention to detail.

You need to be discreet to deal with confidential information. It's important to remain impartial.

Working conditions

Most of your work will be in an office. You might spend time in court or have to visit clients, and will need to dress smartly.

You will often be under a lot of stress to meet deadlines.

Future prospects

There is keen competition for traineeships, but there are good prospects for qualified solicitors in private practice, government and industry. You will usually specialise in one area of law and may eventually become a partner in a firm or even become a judge. As a notary public you may decide to start your own company.

Advantages/disadvantages

The work is varied and no two days will be the same.

You might have to work long hours.

Some people may be difficult and unpleasant to work with.

Money guide

As a trainee, you can earn £16,650 per year in England and Wales; in Scotland you start at £19,500 for the first year rising to £22,500 in the second. In Northern Ireland, your salary may start at £14,450.

With experience you may earn between £30,000 and £60,000. Salaries will be higher in London and large cities. Up to £150,000+ is possible as an experienced senior partner of a legal practice. Notaries public are paid set fees for work on individual cases, reflecting the responsibilities of their professional role.

Qualifications and courses

England and Wales

You will need either an approved law degree, or a non-law degree followed by the Common Professional Examination (CPE), the Postgraduate Diploma in Law (PgDL) or the Senior Status Law degree.

Candidates without a degree can take examinations to become Members or Fellows of the Institute of Legal Executives. A Legal Practice Course (LPC) must be completed followed by 2 years of training with a solicitor.

Scotland

You will need either an approved Scottish Law degree, or a good non-law degree followed by a 2-year graduate law degree. Entry is usually with 5 H grades (A–B) including English. Candidates can take 3 years' pre-diploma training and pass the Law Society of Scotland exams.

Entrants must complete a 26-week Diploma in Legal Practice followed by a 2-year training contract with a practising solicitor in Scotland.

Northern Ireland

Solicitors must complete an apprenticeship programme of 2–4 years, combined with a vocational course. You can choose to do either a Certificate in Professional Legal Studies or a Postgraduate Diploma in Professional Legal Practice.

Notary public

In England and Wales qualified solicitors can take a Postgraduate Diploma in Notarial Practice and be approved by the Master of the Faculties to act within a specific area. In Scotland and Northern Ireland solicitors can apply to be enrolled as notaries on qualifying as solicitors.

Related opportunities

■ Barrister/Advocate p363
■ Crown Prosecutor/Procurator Fiscal p371
■ Legal Executive p373

Further information

Law Society of Northern Ireland
Law Society House, 98 Victoria Street, Belfast BT1 3JZ
028 9023 1614; www.lawsoc-ni.org

Law Society of Scotland
26 Drumsheugh Gardens, Edinburgh EH3 7YR
0131 226 7411; www.lawscot.org.uk

Law Society of England and Wales
The Law Society's Hall, Chancery Lane, London WC2A 1PL
0870 606 2555; www.lawsociety.org.uk

Leisure, Sport and Tourism

This sector relies on a motivated, up-beat and out-going workforce for its success. You will need to show that you can work very well with other people, providing them with an excellent service when they want to enjoy themselves on holiday or if they are keen to improve their fitness and sporting ability. If you are keen to work with professional sports players or become one yourself you should be very aware of how to keep the body fit while avoiding injury. You should be warm and friendly but also able to maintain a high level of professionalism at the same time. You should also demonstrate you have patience and tact with people of all ages as well and be clued up on health and safety regulations.

In this section we look at the following jobs:

BETTING SHOP CASHIER/MANAGER

What the work involves

- You will take bets from customers on the outcomes of sporting events and contests, and pay out winnings. You will work out betting odds, the chance of winning or losing, for your customers.

- Cashiers will update display boards with betting opportunities, oversee betting terminals, balance the books at the end of each shift and look out for fraud.

- Managers ensure the shop meets Gambling Commission regulations; deal with disputes and complaints and control profits and costs.

The type of person suited to this work

You need to be alert to gather vital information about race entrants' recent performance ratings and handicaps and have a good understanding of sports.

Customers will keep coming back to place bets in your shop if you are friendly and service-oriented. You need to be good with numbers and money.

Confidence and good verbal and negotiating skills are vital in order to handle difficult customers. Being able to work well under pressure is essential.

Working conditions

You will most likely work up to 40 hours a week although part-time work may be available. Betting shops are open 7 days a week year-round and are usually open until 10pm. Your busiest day will be Saturday and you will need to be prepared to work nights, weekends and holidays.

You will need to wear a uniform or dress smartly.

As an independent bookmaker you will travel long distances to attend all major sporting events and much of your work will be outdoors.

Future prospects

You have the opportunity to work for a chain, an independent shop, a bookmaker business at a racecourse or a national regulatory body such as the Gambling Commission. You can be promoted from cashier to manager with experience.

You could also become a multi-site manager of 15 shops within a city or even an area manager looking after 50 or more shops.

Successful bookmakers often prefer to move into self-employment and may work well beyond normal retirement age.

Advantages/disadvantages

Being involved with people taking risks can create a high-pressure atmosphere.

Some people find the long hours (past 6.30pm in winter and up to 9.30pm in summer) difficult.

Qualifications and courses

There are no formal entry requirements although many betting shop chains may ask for 1 GCSE (A*–C) in maths. You may have to take a basic maths test at interview, focusing on the calculation of percentages, odds and payments.

Some entrants – particularly to trainee management positions – have a degree, HND or Foundation degree. The University of Salford offers degrees in gambling and leisure management.

Experience of customer service is an advantage. Betting shop employees may have opportunities to work towards NVQs/SVQs at Levels 2 and 3 in Customer Service or in Licensed Bookmaking.

Training is provided on the job, and covers areas such as calculating betting odds and payouts, administration, customer service, business skills, managing staff, betting laws and company policies.

By law, you have to be 18 to work in a betting office and you have to be at least 20 to start as a manager.

You may have to handle difficult gamblers who have lost their stake.

You have the opportunity to build a good rapport with customers which can make for an enjoyable workplace.

Money guide

As a cashier you could start out earning between £9,500 and £14,000 full time.

Bookmakers managing small betting shops earn between £15,000 and £30,000. If you manage a range of 100 shops you could earn as much as £45,000 plus bonuses.

If you are a self-employed bookmaker your salary will depend on racing conditions, the number of entrants and gamblers, and the number of events in the calendar.

Related opportunities

- Accounting Technician/Finance Clerk p18
- Entertainment Manager p386
- Croupier p385

Further information

Gambling Commission
Victoria Square House, Victoria Square, Birmingham B2 4BP
0121 230 6666; www.gamblingcommission.gov.uk

Association of British Bookmakers Ltd
Norris House, 4 Norris Street, London SW1Y 4RJ
020 7434 2111; www.abb.uk.com

National Association of Bookmakers
19 Culm Valley Way, Uffculme, Devon EX15 3XZ
01884 841859, www.nab-bookmakers.co.uk

CROUPIER

What the work involves

- Croupiers are responsible for setting up gaming tables, preparing packs of cards and selling gaming tokens to casino-goers.

- You will be greeting customers, inviting them to join games of roulette, black jack or baccarat and explaining the rules if necessary.

- Spinning the roulette or money wheel, shuffling and dealing cards, shaking mini dice cages and encouraging players to place their bets will be part of your role.

- You will also be responsible for announcing and paying out wins, and collecting in lost bets.

The type of person suited to this work

You should have an engaging personality, good interpersonal skills and possess the ability to make customers feel happy and relaxed. Appearance is highly important. You must be smartly dressed, clean and manicured, with immaculately groomed hair.

There might be difficult moments, when people are distressed, even angered by losing, so you must be confident and assertive.

Fluency in another language is an asset.

Working conditions

Casinos open 7 days a week and on holidays from noon to 6am and many are now open 24 hours a day. This means staff work shifts, including the weekends and bank holidays.

On cruise liners, croupiers spend up to 12 months on board, with about 6 weeks vacation. Casinos close when in port, so you do get time ashore in exotic locations!

Future prospects

The number of casinos across Britain is increasing, so prospects are good. Gambling has become better regulated in recent years, and employers really value good staff.

Significant numbers of croupiers are needed to fill jobs on cruise liners, and this can be a favourite choice for experienced croupiers seeking management-level experience. You can progress from croupier to inspector, to pit boss and, finally, manager at any casino.

Advantages/disadvantages

If you are quick and ambitious, you can make rapid progress from croupier to casino manager.

Standing for hours and concentrating on running the games without error, while talking to customers, can be tiring.

Casino-goers drink alcohol, which exacerbates the emotional tension during gaming. Arguments often break out which you must be able to handle according to the rules and regulations governing gaming.

Qualifications and courses

ENTRY LEVEL 1

You will be vetted for a clean criminal record by the Gambling Commission. Unless you hold their Red Licence, you will be barred from the work.

You have to be 18 years old, but there are no specific entry requirements. Prospective employers may set tests at interview.

Most major casino operators run training schemes for entrants, both in-house and externally. To gain NVQ at Level 2 in Casino Operations, entrants may attend a 12-week course available at Blackpool and the Fylde College, London Gaming College and North Warwickshire and Hinckley College. The National Gaming Academy also offers a Foundation degree in Casino Operations Management.

As a croupier with 2 years of experience, you can progress to supervise a number of gaming tables after further training. Floor managers have additional security responsibilities in counting, checking and locking away all the money taken by close of business.

Croupiers with at least 2 years' experience or who enter the work with a BA(Hons) in Gambling and Leisure Management may fast-track to management responsibilities.

Money guide

Starting salaries are £12,500 per year for trainee croupiers. After 2 years, experienced croupiers can earn £18,500–£22,500, but salaries are higher abroad.

Casino inspectors earn between £24,000 and £29,000, casino managers earn slightly more.

Pay scales on cruise liners are similar, but meals and accommodation are free and salaries are often boosted by tips. Salaries in London are higher.

Related opportunities

- Entertainment Manager p386

Further information

British Casino Association
38 Grosvenor Gardens, London SW1W 0EB
020 7730 1055;
www.britishcasinoassociation.org.uk/careers

City&
Guilds

www.cityandguilds.com/myperfectjob

Leisure, Sport and Tourism

CRCI: MA

ENTERTAINMENT MANAGER

What the work involves

- Entertainment managers take responsibility for the schedule of visiting entertainers to a venue, achieving a balance of activities that engage the age, gender, and cultural interests of the audience.

- You will plan, organise, advertise and oversee the running of a full calendar of social events.

- You will contact acts and agents, and negotiate the best possible prices with them. When the events listing is finalised, you will be promoting the programme on a weekly and daily basis.

- You will also be responsible for costing out the entertainment.

The type of person suited to this work

Entertainment managers are people who enjoy life, can think on their feet and can make audiences cry with laughter, if need be. You will need excellent interpersonal and communication skills.

Your organisation depends on you to find reliable acts – often, to a new formula. You have to make quick appraisals to drive home a deal. You need persuasive powers, imagination and considerable personal initiative.

Working conditions

You could be permanently based in a grand hotel or located in a popular resort, on a cruise liner, or with a large company that frequently entertains important clients.

Entertainment managers work invisibly in an office during daylight hours, emerging only after 6pm to manage the flow of evening entertainment and introducing the artists.

There is seasonal work for entertainment managers in all the major holiday centres.

Future prospects

Corporate hospitality is used to create a good relationship between client and service provider. You will have a high-pressured job with considerable responsibility.

As the travel and tourism industry is still growing at a fast rate, there will be increasing need for entertainment to fill evenings for holidaymakers. Memorable evenings – being entertained by stand-up comics or flamenco dancers – encourage them to rebook with the same cruise line, hotel or tour company.

Advantages/disadvantages

You will meet some interesting and entertaining artists.

You will have to work evenings, weekends and bank holidays.

Pressure can build if an act does not show up, so you might occasionally need to fill a gap and prevent the audience from getting irritable.

Qualifications and courses

There are no formal entry requirements for this career, and relevant experience can be more important than qualifications.

Useful courses at further and higher education level include hospitality management, leisure management, events management, management and travel and tourism.

The minimum entry requirements for a degree are 2 A levels/3 H grades and 5 GCSEs/S grades (A*–C/1–3) or equivalent, and for an HND or Foundation degree, 1 A level/2 H grades and 4 GCSEs/S grades (A*–C/1–3).

People working in the industry can work towards NVQs/SVQs in Cultural Venue Operations at Level 2, and Cultural Venue Administration at Level 3. The Educational Development International Level 2 and 3 National Award in live events and promotion is also available.

NCFE offers Certificates at Level 2 in Music Business and in Event Management at Level 3.

Money guide

Generally, travel and recreation work is not well paid.

Entertainment trainee managers can expect to earn £15,000, but between £18,000 and £20,000 per year with experience.

If you hold this post with a large international company, pay and prospects could be much higher, so your earnings might be nearer to £25,000–£35,000.

Related opportunities

- Croupier p385
- Holiday Representative p388
- Theme Park Assistant/Manager p396

Further information

People 1st
2nd floor, Armstrong House, 38 Market Square, Uxbridge UB8 1LH
01895 817000; www.people1st.co.uk

NCFE national awarding body
Citygate, St James' Boulevard, Newcastle upon Tyne NE1 4JE
0191 239 8000; www.ncfe.org.uk

www.cityandguilds.com/myperfectjob

FITNESS INSTRUCTOR/ PERSONAL TRAINER

What the work involves

- Fitness instructors/personal trainers teach people how to exercise in a safe and effective manner, whilst also helping them work towards personal fitness targets.

- You could provide a one-on-one service to your clients, direct and choreograph group fitness activities and classes, or undertake a mixture of the two.

- You could work in a health club, community gym, leisure centre, or a private gym.

- Other duties may include writing individual training programmes for clients, showing them exercise techniques and how to use equipment, and offering advice and guidance on nutrition and other lifestyle related issues.

The type of person suited to this work

You will need excellent interpersonal skills so that you can attract new business opportunities, chat to clients and advise them on fitness and dietary requirements, and build good relationships with other team members.

You must be very enthusiastic about training and fitness in order to motivate your clients and persuade them to persevere with exercise.

You should look smart and fit yourself, so as to promote a good image to existing and potential clients.

You must be innovative in your approach to keeping fit, thinking up new routines for classes, or creating diversity in one-on-one clients' training programmes so people remain enthused and interested in their activities.

Working conditions

Fitness instructors work longer hours than most other professionals, between 38 and 40 hours per week, and these often include early mornings, evenings and weekends to suit the needs of their clients.

Most instructors work on a part time basis, and are affiliated to one or a number of gyms in their local area.

Most instructors wear a uniform of sorts, consisting of matching polo shirt and jogging bottoms.

Future prospects

As society has become increasingly aware of health and fitness issues, the demand for fitness instructors has grown. This trend is set to continue for the foreseeable future, so employment prospects are good.

In certain areas, and in popular high street gyms, competition for jobs can be tough.

With experience, you could move into roles such as fitness manager or sports facility manager. Alternatively, you could build your own fitness consultancy.

Qualifications and courses

No formal academic qualifications are required to work as a fitness instructor or personal trainer, but you do need an industry recognised qualification in order to be placed on the Register of Exercise Professionals (REPs). You will also need to hold public liability insurance.

Qualifications that are approved by REPs include NVQ Level 2 or above in a subject such as instructing exercise and fitness. For entrance onto an NVQ course, you will usually need 4 GCSEs/S grades (A*–C/1–3) or equivalent, including English, maths and a science subject.

Other approved qualifications include degrees in sports science/studies or movement studies, and an HNC/HND in Fitness, Health and Exercise. For entrance onto a degree course, you will need at least 2 A levels or equivalent (including biology), and 5 GCSEs (A*–C) or equivalent. HNC/HND courses require 1 A level and 5 GCSEs (A*–C) or equivalent.

You could choose to do a Young Apprenticeship in Sports Management, Leadership and Coaching.

Advantages/disadvantages

You will play an active role in enhancing many people's lives by introducing them to exercise and ensuring they continue with it. You will see tangible results of your efforts and guidance as people become fitter and slimmer during the course of your work with them.

You will have to work unsociable hours.

Money guide

On average, fitness instructors and personal trainers who are new to the industry earn about £12,000. As you build a reputation and client base over a few years, this should increase to anywhere between £14,000 and £25,000. Highly successful personal trainers, fitness managers and exercise specialists can earn £30,000+.

Related opportunities

- Sports Coach p393
- Outdoor Pursuits Instructor p391

Further information

Register of Exercise Professionals (REPs)
3rd Floor 8–10 Crown Hill, Croydon CR0 1RZ
020 8686 6464; www.exerciseregister.org

City & Guilds

www.cityandguilds.com/myperfectjob

ENTRY LEVEL 2

CRCI: MB   Leisure, Sport and Tourism

HOLIDAY REPRESENTATIVE

What the work involves

■ Holiday representatives meet holidaymakers at airports and other terminals, helping them to locate their luggage and directing them towards the transport that will take them to their accommodation.

■ You will be responsible for checking all the details of each passenger's transport and accommodation to ensure everything is in place for their stay.

■ You will inform customers of important information, including local bus routes, recommended restaurants and sites of interest. You will also sell excursion tickets.

■ You may also be expected to accompany tourists on expeditions, and provide them with holiday entertainment.

The type of person suited to this work

You will need to look smart and have a pleasant, approachable attitude so that customers are comfortable speaking to you.

You will need to be sociable and also very patient, as you will be dealing with customers 24 hours a day for the duration of the holiday season.

You should also have a methodical approach to your work and excellent organisational skills as you will be co-ordinating lots of details for numerous people at one time.

Fluency in the language of the country in which you are working is also an asset.

Working conditions

Working hours vary from day to day, but are usually long and unpredictable. Most reps only have one day off a week, and even then they will be on call in case of a customer emergency.

The work is seasonal, although there are opportunities all year round including beach holidays over the summer months and ski work during winter.

You could work indoors or outdoors.

You will usually have to wear a uniform.

Future prospects

Although there are many vacancies for holiday representatives each year, competition is tough as it is a very popular job.

You could work for a large international travel company or a smaller, more specialist firm. Most opportunities are overseas, although there are a few jobs available in the UK.

With experience, you could move into a supervisory or managerial position. Some representatives also branch out into another area of travel and tourism, such as hotel management or working on a tourist board.

Advantages/disadvantages

You will have plenty of opportunities to work abroad in a number of diverse and exciting areas.

Qualifications and courses

Academic qualifications are not essential, as most employers place higher value on experience in customer service. However GCSEs (A*–C) or equivalent, in subjects such as English, maths, geography and a foreign language can be useful as competition is high. Spanish, French, Italian, Portuguese, Greek and Turkish would be especially helpful.

The Diploma in Hospitality and the Diploma in Travel and Tourism could also be relevant.

Professional courses are available that offer related qualifications. These include: Levels 2–3 Certificates in Travel and Tourism (resort representatives), Travel and Tourism Communication Skills, and Resort Representation; BTEC Intermediate Diploma Level 2 in Overseas Resort Operations.

In some roles you might need specialist knowledge in an area such as archaeology, scuba diving or history, in which case a relevant qualification would be essential.

To work with children, you will need at least 6 months practical experience, a childcare qualification and pass a Criminal Records Bureau check.

You will be dealing with a range of people from all ages and backgrounds on a daily basis, making the work diverse and challenging.

You will have to work long hours which can make the job both physically and mentally exhausting.

Money guide

Starting salaries for holiday representatives are usually around £6,000 per year (£500 per month), with accommodation provided. With experience, representatives can obtain salaries of between £10,000 and £14,000.

If you move into a supervisory or managerial role, your earnings could increase to £18,000+.

Related opportunities

■ Hotel Manager p141
■ Travel Agent p399
■ Tour Guide/Manager p397
■ Air Cabin Crew p594

Further information

Career in Travel
Fusion 2, Parkway, Solent Business Park, Whitley, Fareham PO15 7AB
www.careerintravel.co.uk; RepHelp@careerintravel.co.uk

City&
Guilds

www.cityandguilds.com/myperfectjob

LEISURE/FITNESS CENTRE ASSISTANT/MANAGER

What the work involves

Assistant

- You will help run sports activities, set up equipment and demonstrate its safe use to leisure centre users.

- You will also work on the reception desk issuing tickets, taking bookings, answering enquiries and other tasks specified by your manager.

Manager

- You will oversee the day-to-day work and recruitment of all leisure centre staff, and deal with queries.

- You will meet with company or council reps to discuss budgets, funding sources, marketing issues, and new developments.

The type of person suited to this work

You will need to be friendly and helpful with excellent interpersonal skills. A role as manager will require proven leadership skills. As you will be working within or leading a team you must be able to communicate well. Assistants should be fit and active.

Working conditions

Most of your time will be spent indoors – at the poolside, in a sports hall, at reception or in the office.

You should expect to work unsocial hours – early starts and late finishes.

Future prospects

Due to a growing trend in healthy living, interest in leisure centres is high. You could progress from a role as an assistant to supervisor and then become a manager. After gaining more experience, you could go on to become an area or regional manager. There are greater opportunities for promotion in large organisations.

Advantages/disadvantages

Most leisure centres have a relaxed working atmosphere.

Earnings can be low, unless you start on the trainee management route.

Money guide

Starting salaries are around £10,000 per year rising to £14,500 with qualifications and experience. This can be boosted by overtime and bonuses related to membership as well as weekend and shift work.

The starting salary for an assistant manager is around £12,000–£17,000. A new manager can expect £19,000–£26,000. Managers at senior levels can earn £35,000+. Salaries vary according to the size of the organisation.

Qualifications and courses

ENTRY LEVEL 1

Assistant

Although there are no formal entry requirements, many employers prefer applicants with GCSEs (A*–C) in maths, English and a science and A levels or a BTEC National qualification in Sport or Leisure.

Training is often given on the job, although many courses are offered by the Institute for Sport, Parks and Leisure (ISPAL) and the Institute of Sport and Recreation Management (ISRM). Normally, assistants try for an instructor or coach award in their preferred activity and could be expected to gain a Lifeguard's Certificate. You can also study towards NVQs in Instructing Exercise and Fitness or take an Apprenticeship in Active Leisure and Learning. A First Aid Certificate would be useful.

Manager

A minimum of 5 years' work experience and a related qualification is normally needed. A trainee manager will usually have at least 5 GCSEs (A*–C) and A levels, an NVQ Level 2 in Sport, Recreation and Allied Occupations or a Diploma in Sport and Active Leisure. Many employers also require an NVQ Level 3 in Leisure Management or a BTEC National Certificate/Diploma in Sport. You can also work and study for the ISRM Supervisory Management Certificate and the ISPAL Professional Qualification Scheme.

Foundation degrees, degrees and HNDs are also available in Sport and Leisure Management and Sports Science. Graduate training programmes are often available at large organisations.

Related opportunities

- Fitness Instructor/Personal Trainer p387
- Lifeguard p390
- Outdoor Pursuits Instructor p391
- Sports Development Officer p394

Further information

Institute of Sport and Recreation Management
Sir John Beckwith Centre for Sport,
Loughborough University, Loughborough LE11 3TU
01509 226474; www.isrm.co.uk

City&Guilds

www.cityandguilds.com/myperfectjob

CRCI: MA   Leisure, Sport and Tourism

LIFEGUARD

What the work involves

- Lifeguards are responsible for patrolling and monitoring the water and weather conditions where people are swimming, surfing or boating.

- You will keep watch on public swimming pools or stretches of shoreline to reduce the risk of tragic accidents occurring and taking rapid action to alert the public to danger.

- Your role could involve rescuing people at risk from drowning, assisting them ashore and administering first aid including mouth-to-mouth or CPR (cardiopulmonary resuscitation).

- You will also be involved in informing the public about water safety.

The type of person suited to this work

You must be fit and active, with an interest in canoeing, sailing, swimming, or surfing. You should also have a full understanding of the level of danger in all water activities.

You should be a strong swimmer (able to cover 400 metres of a pool in less than 8 minutes) and have good vision and hearing. The ability to work within a team is also essential. It's important to be observant and be able to respond quickly.

You must be assertive in order to take command and manage dangerous incidents and be able to stay calm in emergencies.

Working conditions

You will either work on the beach or poolside. Either way, you will need to cover early morning and later shifts as part of your hours in order to provide a full emergency service to water users.

You must keep alert and vigilant at all times as when emergency strikes, you have to be ready to act in seconds – not minutes.

Overseas work is possible with holiday companies.

Future prospects

Interest in water sports has grown dramatically and so lifeguards are in great demand.

You could progress into a managerial role such as a pool supervisor, duty manager or general pool manager. You could also qualify as a swimming teacher.

Advantages/disadvantages

Pools and beaches have a relaxed, upbeat atmosphere.

There can be periods of boredom that you have to work through, maintaining vigilance. Accidents can happen at any time.

If working outdoors you could be in danger of overexposure to sunlight.

Qualifications and courses

Lifeguard training is for those aged 16 or over and in possession of a National Pool Lifeguard Qualification (NPLQ) from the Royal Life Saving Society or the Swimming Teachers' Association (STA) Level 2 Certificate for the National Rescue Standard – Pool Lifeguard.

The NPLQ, training covers two assessed units: The Principles of Lifesaving and Swimming Pool Supervision, and The Application of Supervision and Rescue in a Swimming Pool. This training can only take place in a centre approved by the Institute of Qualified Lifeguards.

Training is over 40 hours for the STA. All lifeguards need to hold a valid First Aid Worker Certificate.

Lifeguard qualifications must be renewed every 2 years.

Ocean/beach lifeguards must be aged 18 or over and in possession of the National Beach Lifeguard Qualification or Assistant Beach Lifesaver Award from the RLSS or the National Rescue Standard Beach Lifeguard Awards run through clubs by the Surf Life Saving Association of Great Britain. These courses cover practical ocean rescue skills involving the use of boards and tubes.

Training is also provided by the Royal National Lifeboat Institution. Apprenticeships are also available to entrants aged 16–24.

Money guide

Pay levels vary, depending on employer and patrol times involved.

Starting salaries are around £11,500–£14,000 per year. With experience, pay can rise to £15,000+. Some lifeguards work for local authorities on a part-time basis when rates of pay can vary from £6 to £9 per hour.

Related opportunities

- Leisure/Fitness Centre Assistant/Manager p389
- Outdoor Pursuits Instructor p391
- Sports Coach p393
- Fitness Instructor/Personal Trainer p387

Further information

Royal Life Saving Society UK
River House, Broom, Warwickshire B50 4HN
01789 773994; www.lifesavers.org.uk

Saltwater Training
23 Grenville Road, Padstow PL28 8EX
01841 533076; www.saltwatertraining.com

OUTDOOR PURSUITS INSTRUCTOR

What the work involves

- Outdoor pursuits instructors lead groups of people through a range of challenging activities, designed to help them bond, have fun, learn more about themselves and develop new skills.

- You will work with people of all ages and backgrounds, including those with disabilities, children with special needs, adult recreation groups, and business professionals.

- You will be responsible for guiding these groups though a range of activities.

- You will also be responsible for checking safety equipment, ensuring that group members are comfortable with each activity, and giving practical demonstrations.

The type of person suited to this work

You should have strong leadership skills as you will be required to persuade a group of people who have never met you before to undertake activities that are frightening and push them out of their comfort zone.

You must have an excellent level of physical fitness, alongside good eyesight and hearing.

You must be responsible and maintain continual awareness of the safety of both yourself and those around you.

You should have good communication skills and a personable manner to explain activities clearly.

Working conditions

Hours are generally long and irregular, usually falling over evenings and weekends, including bank holidays. Much of the work is seasonal. Part time hours are commonly available.

Many outdoor pursuits centres are located in the countryside, so a driving licence may be useful in order to travel to and from work with ease. Holding a licence for a passenger carrying vehicle (PCV) may also be helpful.

You should expect to be working outdoors in all weather conditions. Long treks may also involve spending evenings away from the centre, camping in a tent.

Future prospects

Although the outdoor leisure industry is growing, there is still a lot of competition for jobs.

Most opportunities are in independently run activity centres, or those owned by local authorities and charities. There are also jobs available with expedition companies who organise overseas excursions.

Many instructors specialise in a particular discipline, such as canoeing or abseiling, and work freelance across several activity centres.

Qualifications and courses

No formal academic qualifications are required to work as an outdoor pursuits instructor, but employers usually expect applicants to hold 2 or more relevant proficiency or coaching awards in their chosen sporting field. These qualifications should be recognised by the national governing body for the sport, and include courses such as Sports Leaders UK Basic Expedition Leadership Award (BEL), British Canoe Union Level 1 Coach, and the Mountain Leaders Training UK Single Pitch Award. Full-time college courses and degrees are also available that provide relevant qualifications.

As well as holding suitable qualifications, candidates are also expected to be able to demonstrate a history of leading and taking responsibility for others.

You will need to be 18 years old before you can work as an instructor. You will also need to undergo a Criminal Records Bureau check as you will be working with children and vulnerable adults from time to time.

Advantages/disadvantages

You will be helping people to break down boundaries and overcome fear, which will increase their self-reliance and self-confidence.

You will be working with a wide range of people, from all backgrounds and ages, which will give great diversity to your working day.

You will have to work unsociable hours.

Money guide

As an outdoor pursuits instructor, you could expect to earn between £8,000 and £11,000 as a starting salary. As your experience grows, this should increase to around £12,000–£18,000. Once you have reached the level of a more senior instructor, perhaps also developing specialist skills, you could earn £25,000+.

Related opportunities

- Sports Coach p393
- Sports Development Officer p394

Further information

Institute for Outdoor Learning
Warwick Mill Business Centre, Warwick Bridge,
Carlisle CA4 8RR
01228 564580; www.outdoor-learning.org

British Activity Holiday Association
The Hollies, Oak Bank Lane, Hoole Village, Chester CH2 4ER
01244 301342; www.baha.org.uk; info@baha.org.uk

Leisure, Sport and Tourism

CRCI: MB

PROJECTIONIST

What the work involves

- Projectionists work in cinemas and are responsible for operating film screening equipment, ensuring that everything runs smoothly throughout the feature.

- You will also be required to monitor other technical equipment in the cinema, including lighting, heating and ventilation systems, electrical and gas supplies, and ensuring that all fire alarms and extinguishers are in good working order.

- You may work with traditional 20-minute reels of film, or modern digital versions that are stored on a hard drive.

- You will be expected to check that the sound on each film is operating properly, and that it is the right volume.

The type of person suited to this work

You should enjoy working on your own, and watching films, as the majority of your time will be spent alone, operating machinery in the projection room.

You will need good ICT skills in order to use increasingly complicated film screening technology and equipment.

You must be alert and observant so you can pick up on problems quickly, and also have the practical skills and knowledge to solve these issues effectively and under pressure.

You should be able to observe the strict timings given on schedules to ensure each film runs according to plan.

Working conditions

You will work 5 days a week, but hours are generally long and irregular as most cinemas screen films from the afternoon up until late in the evening. Shift work and overtime are common.

You will spend most of your time in a projection room. Most of these do not have windows, but in modern cinemas they are usually air-conditioned. You will be working alone in the projection room for the majority of your shift.

Future prospects

The rise of new multiplex cinemas across the UK has created an excess of jobs for projectionists. Demand currently outstrips supply, so prospects are good.

Opportunities can be found in large cinema chains, or in smaller and often more specialist independent theatres.

In larger organisations, you could be promoted to senior projectionist or an administrative role. Small independent cinemas offer scope for experienced staff to become more involved with the running of the business.

Advantages/disadvantages

If you love cinema, you will enjoy being able to watch films for free.

Qualifications and courses

There are no academic qualifications for this job. You need to be at least 18 years of age in order to show an 18 certificate film.

Many employers also look for candidates who have some knowledge or experience of working with electronic or sound equipment. This could be gained by working as an assistant projectionist for a few months.

There are also short and part-time courses available which could give you the experience needed to go straight into employment as a projectionist. Providers include The National Film and Television School, and The Moving Image Society (BKSTS). The Diploma in Creative and Media may also be helpful.

All employers look for candidates who can demonstrate a real enthusiasm for the moving image. Joining a film club or taking a part-time job in a cinema can give you essential career-related knowledge in this respect.

Apprenticeships may be available to entrants aged 16–24.

You will have the opportunity to work for a number of employers, ranging from large multiplexes screening major blockbusters, to small independent cinemas who may specialise in art-house or international films.

You will be working alone for the majority of the time and your hours will be unsociable, including evenings and weekends.

Money guide

Starting salaries for cinema projectionists tend to be around £12,000.

With a few years' experience, this could rise to about £15,000.

In larger cinemas, if you reach the position of a senior projectionist, you could earn up to £25,000.

Related opportunities

- Lighting Technician p444

Further information

The Moving Image Society
Pinewood Studios, Iver Heath SL0 0NH
01753 656 656; www.bksts.com; info@bksts.com

The National Film and Television School
The Registry, Beaconsfield Studios, Station Road, Beaconsfield HP9 1LG
01494 671 234; www.nftsfilm-tv.ac.uk; info@nfts.co.uk

The British Film Institute
21 Stephen Street, London W1T 1LN
020 7255 1444; www.bfi.org.uk

SPORTS COACH

What the work involves

- Sports coaches provide specialist support, motivation and knowledge to athletes in order to help them attain their best performances and achieve personal goals.

- As a competitive coach, you could work with a variety of levels of athlete, ranging from children's football or netball teams, through to professional and even world class sports professionals.

- At a non-competitive level, you will focus on providing fun and accessible exercise sessions for participants with a range of abilities and fitness levels.

- You will usually coach one specific sport.

The type of person suited to this work

You will need excellent communications skills. You will also need to have good motivational abilities in order to inspire and encourage sports players to push themselves.

You will need an in depth knowledge of your chosen sport, and an understanding of nutrition and physiology is also useful.

It is also essential that you understand a variety of training methods and principles so that you can provide an informed and beneficial service to your clients. Patience and determination are also vital qualities.

Working conditions

You will usually work early mornings, evenings and weekends, as that is when the majority of your athletes will be available.

If you are working in a seasonal sport such as cricket or football, you might have to supplement your income with another job during the quiet months.

You will spend hours on your feet, and might also have to undertake activity in order to demonstrate methods and principles to athletes.

Future prospects

The vast majority of sports coaches working in the UK work on a voluntary or part time basis. Competition for full time positions is fierce, although opportunities may increase in the run up to the 2012 Olympics.

Career prospects will depend on the level of success you achieve in your work. If you gain credibility, you could move into a related development or management position.

You could be self-employed, work for a local authority, or in a school, gym or professional sports club.

Advantages/disadvantages

You will be teaching the sport you love to a range of people, and developing their interest in it.

You may have the opportunity to work with talented athletes.

You will have to spend long periods of time standing outside in all weather conditions.

Qualifications and courses

ENTRY LEVEL 4

All sports coaches must hold a qualification that has been accredited by the National Governing Body (NGB) of their chosen discipline. You can start working towards recognised qualifications at the age of 16, but must be 18 or over to work as an independent coach.

Accredited courses are available directly from the NGB, or you can undertake a college or university course. NGB qualifications are equivalent to studying for NVQs Level 1–4, and no academic qualifications are required. They are usually studied on a part time basis.

Relevant courses at college/university include: BTEC National Certificate/Diploma in Sports Coaching or Leisure Studies; entry requirements are 4 GCSEs (A*–E) or equivalent; BTEC HNC/HND in Leisure Studies, requires 1 A level and 4 GCSEs (A*–C) or equivalent; Foundation degree in Sports coaching, entry requirements vary; degrees in sports science/studies, coaching, and physical education, usually require 2 A levels and 5 GCSEs (A*–C) or equivalent, including English and maths.

Some employers may require a first aid certificate, and if you intend to work with children you must first obtain Criminal Records Bureau clearance.

Money guide

As a newly qualified coach working for an employer, you could earn between £15,000 and £25,000. Experienced coaches who work for a NGB or professional association can earn between £30,000 and £35,000.

If you work at the highest level of your sport, such as coaching Premiership football players, you could earn £100,000+.

Related opportunities

- Fitness Instructor/Personal Trainer p387
- Outdoor Pursuits Instructor p391
- Sports Professional p395

Further information

Sports Coach UK
114 Cardigan Road, Headingley, Leeds LS6 3BJ
0113 274 4802; www.sportscoachuk.org

SkillsActive
Castlewood House, 77–91 New Oxford Street,
London WC1A 1PX
020 7632 2000; www.skillsactive.com

www.cityandguilds.com/myperfectjob

Leisure, Sport and Tourism

CRCI: MB

SPORTS DEVELOPMENT OFFICER

What the work involves

- Sports development officers are responsible for ensuring that sports and related activities are available to people of all ages and abilities.

- You will be promoting the benefits of exercise and encouraging people to live a healthy lifestyle by devising simple but effective strategies that increase participation in sport.

- You will work within the local community, liaising with schools, gyms and social clubs, and also have involvement with larger agencies such as sports national governing bodies (NGBs).

- You may work closely with groups who are usually excluded from sports-related activity, such as disadvantaged youths, prisoners, and disabled people.

The type of person suited to this work

You will need a positive attitude, coupled with a commitment to sport, that will help you to persuade local community members and service providers to back your initiatives.

You will need excellent verbal and written communication skills in order to illustrate your objectives to other professionals. This includes strong persuasive and negotiating skills.

Good ICT and administrative ability will be essential for creating reports, producing material to support your ideas, and keeping accurate records.

Working conditions

You will usually work a 36 hour week within normal office hours. Flexible hours and overtime are often available.

It is not unusual to have to work additional hours during evenings and weekends, attending meetings or networking events.

You will work in an office environment, and also spend time at local schools, clubs and community venues. Since a good deal of travelling is required each day, a driving licence can be helpful.

Future prospects

The pending 2012 Olympics are set to increase demand for sports development officers across the UK as increasing numbers of people are looking for ways to become involved with sport.

You will most likely be working for a local authority, county sports partnership, or NGB. A few opportunities are available in specialist sports colleges.

Career progression for sport-specific development officers is fairly limited; you could be promoted to the role of sports development manager, or become more involved with other community initiatives.

Qualifications and courses

ENTRY LEVEL 5

Although there are currently no specific academic requirements, new entrants to the profession are usually graduates. If you hold coaching qualifications you may be able to start out as an assistant and move your way up.

Relevant first degree subjects include sports science/ studies, physical education, recreation/leisure management, and health and exercise sciences. Most universities require candidates to have 2 A levels, one in a related subject such as biology, and 5 GCSEs (A*–C), including English, maths and a science. Some employers will also accept entrants with relevant BTEC or HNC/HND qualifications in sport, sports science, sports development or another related subject.

Most employers will also require you to have two years' experience in sports development, for example at a leisure centre, a holiday camp or summer school.

Advantages/disadvantages

You will play an active role in enhancing many people's quality of life by providing them with access to sport in their local area. You will be liaising with a variety of people on a daily basis, which should make the work dynamic and interesting.

You will need a resilient approach to your work, as suggestions and plans will often be knocked back or fall through.

Money guide

The starting salary for a newly qualified sports development officer is usually between £15,000 and £17,000. With a few years' experience, your wages could rise to about £24,000. If you reach a management position, you could earn £35,000–£40,000.

Related opportunities

- Sports Coach p393
- Fitness Instructor/Personal Trainer p387
- Outdoor Pursuits Instructor p391

Further information

The Institute of Sport and Recreation Management
Sir John Beckwith Centre for Sport, Loughborough University, Loughborough LE11 3TU
01509 226 474; www.isrm.co.uk; info@isrm.co.uk

Sports Leaders UK
23–25 Linford Forum, Rockingham Drive, Linford Wood, Milton Keynes MK14 6LY
01908 689 180; www.sportsleaders.org

City& Guilds

www.cityandguilds.com/myperfectjob

SPORTS PROFESSIONAL

What the work involves

■ Sportsplayers are paid professionals who compete across the globe in their chosen sport, often in front of an audience.

■ You could compete individually in sports such as boxing, swimming, golf and athletics, or alternatively with a team in sports like football, hockey, cricket and rugby.

■ You will need to spend a great deal of time training in order to maintain a high standard of general fitness, alongside honing your skills in your chosen sport.

■ You may also be required to attend social events, give interviews, and promote the companies that provide you with sponsorship.

The type of person suited to this work

First and foremost, you will need to have an outstanding natural ability for your chosen sport.

From this, you must have the necessary commitment and self-discipline to maintain a continuous training schedule and strict eating regime.

You will need to have a highly competitive nature, but also a polite and pleasant manner in order to get on with team members, fellow players, and coaches.

As well as being physically fit, you must be mentally stable so that you can cope with both the pressure of competition, defeat and disappointment at times.

Working conditions

Competitions and matches usually fall on weekends, although qualifying rounds may take place during the week.

You will usually need to travel to reach competitions, which may involve overnight absence from home.

If you are competing at an international level, you could be away for weeks at a time.

You will need to train most days, and if you are supplementing your professional sports income with a regular job, this will mean working out either early in the morning or in the evening.

Future prospects

Most professional sportsplayers are spotted at an early age by a talent scout or coach. From this point, they build up skills and a reputation through competitions.

Unfortunately, the majority of professionals cannot earn a living playing their chosen sport alone, so you might have to supplement your income with full or part time work.

Sports professionals rarely continue to compete once they have reached their mid-30s, but there are plenty of opportunities to work as a coach or manager, commentator, or even earn money as a TV personality.

Qualifications and courses

You do not need any academic qualifications for most sports. The only exception to this rule is golf, in which the Professional Golfers' Association requires players to have 4 GCSEs/S grades (A*–C/1–3) or equivalent.

You may pursue the Diploma in Sport and Active Leisure or do an Advanced Apprenticeship in Sporting Excellence. This will lead to an NVQ Level 3 and qualifies you to study a sports-related degree.

Across the UK, there are opportunities for gaining additional help and support if you are a promising young athlete. In England, the Talented Athlete Scholarship Scheme (TASS) awards funding of up to £3,500 for sports training. Scotland and Wales also provide similar assistance to young sports stars; their bodies are the Athlete Support Scheme and Elite Cymru.

Advantages/disadvantages

Pursuing your dream as a professional sportsplayer will not feel like work.

The hard work and dedication you put in should be repaid in the form of sporting achievements and acclaim.

One bad injury could ruin your career at a very early stage.

Money guide

If you start your professional career as an apprentice, you will earn about £6,000. You may also receive accommodation and food allowances.

Once you are established as a professional, competing in and winning competitions regularly, you should earn £20,000+.

Highly successful sports professionals working in well-supported sports, such as tennis and football, can earn anything from £100,000 to £5,000,000 and beyond.

Related opportunities

■ Sports Coach p393
■ Fitness Instructor/Personal Trainer p387
■ Outdoor Pursuits Instructor p391

Further information

Talented Athlete Scholarship Scheme
City Sports Centre, off Northumberland Road,
Northumbria University, Newcastle-upon-Tyne NE1 8ST
0191 243 7356; www.tass.gov.uk; info@tass.gov.uk

SkillsActive
Castlewood House, 77–91 New Oxford Street,
London WC1A 1PX
020 7632 2000; www.skillsactive.com

CRCI: MB   Leisure, Sport and Tourism

THEME PARK ASSISTANT/MANAGER

What the work involves

- You will greet customers, check ticket holders' ages and heights, and operate and supervise rides. You may also sell merchandise.

- You must always observe safety rules, and ensure there are no hazards.

- If you are a manager you will need to oversee all the different operations within a theme park, ensure the smooth running of all amusements, the catering operations, the maintenance and surveillance of the park.

- You will also be responsible for recruiting and training staff, managing the budget of the park, and handling any problems that arise.

The type of person suited to this work

Theme park workers should be happy relating to the public, wanting them to have an exciting and memorable experience, but also being aware of and concerned for their safety.

Except for the managers and a few experienced assistants, this is seasonal work, carried out by people who move around the country between casual work opportunities. You must be trustworthy and dependable, with good practical and mechanical skills, and able to follow instructions carefully and safely.

Working conditions

Theme parks are open 7 days a week, and on bank holidays, so you work shifts and get a full day off each week. Assistants are also required to carry out repairs and maintenance on machines each morning and evening.

The manager must inspect the whole site before opening time, taking responsibility for seeing all the necessary safety checks have been done, and that the rides and other facilities are fully staffed.

Future prospects

There is always a high turnover of staff in theme parks, but a core of workers stay on, benefiting from training and increased responsibility which allows them to gain certificates as evidence of their skills.

There is more work in Europe for trained, experienced theme park workers. It helps if you speak another language.

Advantages/disadvantages

This is a specialised line of entertainment and leisure work and might not prove to be a stepping stone to other areas.

You have the opportunity to work anywhere in the world such as at Legoland Denmark or Disneyland USA.

Qualifications and courses

You have to be 18 to start work in a theme park. No formal qualifications are needed, but if your aim is to become a supervisor or manager then it is best to have some GCSEs/S grades in maths, English, ICT and, possibly, DT and sports education. There are work-based qualifications available: NVQs/SVQs in Mechanical Ride Operations at Level 2, and you receive health and safety training from day one. NVQs/SVQs in customer care, catering and sales could also be relevant.

With experience and qualifications, you can progress to team leader and then gain promotion to managerial jobs, taking the ISPAL (Institute of Sport, Parks and Leisure) Certificates and Diploma.

Large parks, such as Alton Towers, need several specialist managers to plan and oversee all the catering, site cleaning and waste management, the ride operations, financial arrangements and marketing.

Money guide

If between 18 and 21 years old you might expect to earn around £9,000 per year when starting out. With experience, this could rise to over £12,000. There might be a few benefits for employees, such as paid overtime, free health insurance and a cash bonus at the season's close.

Managers can earn £22,000–£24,500 per year.

Related opportunities

- Entertainment Manager p386
- Leisure/Fitness Centre Assistant/Manager p389

Further information

British Association of Leisure Parks, Piers and Attractions
Suite 12, 37 Tanner Street, London SE1 3LF
020 7403 4455; www.balppa.org

EQ
Suite E229, Dean Clough, Halifax HX3 5AX
01422 381618; www.thinkeq.org.uk

www.cityandguilds.com/myperfectjob

TOUR GUIDE/MANAGER

What the work involves

- Tour guides are responsible for meeting and greeting parties of people who are taking a holiday, trip, cultural visit or tour together.

- You will accompany the sightseers on their journey and inform them of the historical/environmental/cultural interests of the area they are visiting. You will also assist them if they encounter problems or difficulties.

- Tour managers are responsible for putting together proposals for day trips and excursions in order to attract holidaymakers to the company.

- You will visit destinations to assess their potential as a tour venue, and may also assist tour guides with the delivery of the trip itself.

The type of person suited to this work

Tour guides and managers both need excellent communication skills in order to convey enthusiasm and interest for venues to both customers and potential clients.

You will need good stamina in order to keep up a high level of energy and interest throughout tours.

You will also need to have excellent customer relation skills in order to soothe any disgruntled holiday-makers and reach amicable solutions to problems.

Tour managers should also be methodical in order to put together logistically plausible, suitably detailed plans for excursions.

Working conditions

You may work long hours, and when out on a tour you will be on call for customers 24 hours a day should they need anything.

You could work for a large international company, or a small independent tour provider, but either way your focus will be on promoting the company image and following their tour policies carefully.

You will be expected to wear a uniform when on duty, which usually includes a shirt and tie.

Future prospects

The travel and tourism industry is in a period of expansion, so job prospects for tour guides are good.

You could work in a large international company that runs tours throughout the UK and overseas, or a smaller provider that focuses on specific tourist areas in the UK such as Bath or London.

Competition for work as a tour manager is tough, but if you have built up good skills and knowledge as a tour guide first, you will be in a good position for promotion.

Qualifications and courses

ENTRY 2 LEVEL

Most tour guides and managers are aged 18 or over. Although no formal academic qualifications are required, some GCSEs (A*–C) or equivalent might be useful, particularly in subjects such as English, maths and languages. The Diploma in Travel and Tourism might be useful.

Fluency in another language is important if you intend to work abroad, or work with foreign tourists in the UK.

You can do an Apprenticeship or Advanced Apprenticeship in Travel and Tourism Services. Tour guides can also study towards a number of professional qualifications, which include NVQ Level 2 and Level 3 in Travel and Tourism.

Professional courses for tour managers include full-time HND and degree courses in Travel and Tourism Management, City & Guilds HLQ Level 4 in Travel and Tourism, and a range of related NCFE certificates.

Advantages/disadvantages

You will be dealing with a variety of people of all ages and backgrounds on a daily basis, educating them about areas in which you have an interest.

It can get monotonous as you will be repeating the same spiel over and over again for weeks, months, and even years.

Money guide

Tour guides can expect to start on around £10,000, and with experience this could rise to up to £25,000.

Tour managers generally start on about £16,000, and with experience this rises to around £20,000.

Particularly experienced or specialised tour managers can earn up to £28,000.

Related opportunities

- Holiday Representative p388
- Tourist Information Centre Assistant p398
- Travel Agent p399

Further information

Institute of Travel and Tourism
PO Box 217, Ware SG12 8WY
0844 4995 653; www.itt.co.uk; enquiries@itt.co.uk

International Association of Tour Managers Limited
397 Walworth Road, London SE17 2AW
020 7703 9154; www.iatm.co.uk; iatm@iatm.co.uk

City& Guilds

www.cityandguilds.com/myperfectjob

Leisure, Sport and Tourism

CRCI: MC

Leisure, Sport and Tourism

CRCI: MC

TOURIST INFORMATION CENTRE ASSISTANT

What the work involves

- You will be answering questions in person, over the phone or via the internet, for UK and foreign tourists, business people, local young people and researchers.

- You will provide information, make bookings and reservations, locate accommodation, restaurants and sites of interest, and inform people about forthcoming shows and events in the local area.

- You will hand out leaflets and sell maps, postcards and items of interest from the local area and region. You could also operate a bureau de change.

The type of person suited to this work

You need to have an interest in local matters and in promoting your local area. Good, up-to-date knowledge about places of interest is useful. You should be friendly with good interpersonal skills.

A methodical approach to researching difficult questions is an asset.

Relevant skills include customer-service experience, the ability to research information using the internet, and good verbal communication skills.

It is important to be a good team player and assist your colleagues, even if you are busy.

Working conditions

You will usually work shifts which include the weekends and bank holidays. Tourist information centres are modern, bright spaces that make pleasant work surroundings.

There is quite a lot of standing at the counter and moving to and from storage areas with piles of information leaflets and stock items. You may spend some hours sitting at a computer, researching routes, or B&B facilities in distant locations.

Future prospects

The number of tourist centres has decreased in the recession, but they are located across the whole of the UK, so you should have one local to you.

You could move from a part-time contract into a full-time one and with experience progress to manager or supervisor. You could also choose to become a travel agent or tour guide.

Advantages/disadvantages

There are both busy and quiet times at the counter in tourist information centres.

You could spend a long time on the phone which could get dull.

You will play an important role in promoting both the local region and helping its economy.

Qualifications and courses

No formal educational qualifications are required for this career. Personal qualities are usually more important.

Acute listening and clear speaking skills are essential, and it is very helpful if assistants can use ICT to research information and respond to enquirers via the internet.

Applicants who have GCSEs/S grades (A*–C/1–3) might be at an advantage. A number of TICs are close to international airports or in popular destinations for overseas visitors. In these centres it is valuable if one or more TIC assistants have modern language skills to help newly-arrived tourists, business travellers and foreign visitors. British Sign Language will also be an advantage.

Working as an assistant, you can be assessed for NVQs/SVQs in Tourist Information and Customer Service. Many employees within Tourist Information Centres work towards these awards.

There are also the part-time HLQ Level 4 or BTEC or SQA HNC qualifications in Leisure and Tourism which might be useful for career progression to become a TIC manager. However, it is possible to move into supervisory and managerial positions simply with experience in the work.

Money guide

Starting salaries for full-time staff are around £11,500 per year.

With experience, this can rise to £17,000.

You can earn up to £20,000 as full-time manager of a tourist information centre.

Your salary will most likely be higher in and around London.

Related opportunities

- Holiday Representative p388
- Travel Agent p399

Further information

VisitBritain
1 Palace Street, London SW1E 5HE
020 7578 1000; www.visitbritain.org

VisitScotland
Level 3, Ocean Point 1, 94 Ocean Drive, Edinburgh EH6 6JH
0131 472 2222; www.visitscotland.com

City& Guilds

www.cityandguilds.com/myperfectjob

TRAVEL AGENT

What the work involves

- You will be selling holiday packages to the public and trying to meet your company's sales targets.

- You will be putting together individual holidays for an independent customer or for an organisation that seeks travel, accommodation and entertainment arrangements that are distinct from the travel company's normal holiday packages.

- You will need to contact airline, ferry and rail sales operatives to arrange transport, and make reservations for accommodation, meals, hire cars and entertainment, whether in this country or abroad.

The type of person suited to this work

You will need excellent administrative and research skills to quickly track down, assemble and book all the parts needed for each customer's ideal journey or holiday.

You must have excellent listening and questioning skills in order to find the right holiday package for each individual customer.

If you are friendly, communicative and methodical, with excellent ICT skills, you will suit both your customers' and your employers' needs. It helps if you have a real interest in exploring new places yourself.

Working conditions

You will work indoors, mainly at a desk or behind a counter.

There are numerous details to check over the phone, and tickets, booking confirmations and insurance notes to post out to customers. Almost all the work is done at a computer screen, except for scanning through brochures for holiday deals and consulting transport timetables.

The agency can be very busy at lunchtimes, near to closing time and on Saturdays, before holiday periods. Many sales consultants work part time and there might be only two or three workers in the agency.

Future prospects

With growing interest in travel and holidays abroad, the travel industry now enjoys the highest turnover and numbers of employees of all major business sectors.

There are around 40,000 travel agencies in the UK, so there are plenty of opportunities to advance to a managerial position, or even to start your own independent holiday company offering special-interest holidays.

You can move into other areas of tourism work, such as holiday repping or working as a tour guide, which may enable you to travel the world.

Advantages/disadvantages

A real perk in this work is that you do get some free or discounted holidays.

Qualifications and courses

ENTRY LEVEL 1

Although no formal educational qualifications are needed, it's helpful to have a good standard of education with GCSEs/S grades (A*–C/1–3) in English and maths as a minimum. Skills in geography and ICT are also helpful.

Young people aged 16–24 can train in travel agency work through an Apprenticeship/Skillseekers. You can enter with very few GCSEs/S grades, taking work-based NVQs/SVQs at Levels 2 and 3 in Travel Services. Some of the study is part time at a further education college.

Full-time A level and National Diploma/SQA courses in Travel and Tourism also make an excellent starting point for this work.

There are some full-time management courses offered by TTC Training for those who want to progress to travel agency manager.

The travel industry offers its own examinations – the Association of British Travel Agents Limited (ABTA) Travel Agents Certificate.

There can be long periods sitting at the computer, answering emails, checking flight and booking details, and waiting 'on hold' to confirm bookings, which can be boring.

Money guide

Starting pay for a travel agent is around £12,000 per year.

With experience and some NVQs/SVQs you can earn up to £15,000.

Senior agents receive salaries of around £20,000+.

Although this is a low paying area of work, employees at every level benefit from discounts and can receive commission.

Related opportunities

- Tour Guide/Manager p397
- Holiday Representative p388
- Tourist Information Centre Assistant p398
- Events and Exhibitions Organiser p411

Further information

Association of British Travel Agents Limited
30 Park Street, London SE1 9EQ
www.abta.com

Institute of Travel and Tourism
PO Box 217, Ware SG12 8WY
0844 4995 653; www.itt.co.uk; enquiries@itt.co.uk

City & Guilds

www.cityandguilds.com/myperfectjob

Leisure, Sport and Tourism

CRCI: MC

Marketing, Advertising, Media, Print and Publishing

Do you consider yourself to be a great communicator? Are you interested in working in an exciting and often fast-paced environment with passionate, driven and ambitious individuals? If so, a career in this industry could be right for you. People who work in this sector are exceptionally motivated and are willing to put in long hours often on low starting wages because of their love of the job. You should have a great sense of creativity and imagination and be good at putting your ideas on paper, but you will often also need strong business acumen as many of your decisions will be made from an economic point of view as well as a creative one.

In this section we look at the following jobs:

For similar jobs to the ones in this section turn to *Design, Arts and Crafts* on page 167 and *Performing Arts* on page 433.

ADVERTISING ACCOUNT EXECUTIVE

What the work involves

- You will plan and develop strategies for campaigns to suit different clients' requirements, working for advertising, PR or media agencies.

- You will use a variety of different tactics from TV, newspapers, posters, radio and direct mail to viral and online marketing. It will be your responsibility to ensure that all the campaigns run smoothly, to budget and on schedule.

- Your work will involve liaising between clients and the agency staff, such as designers and budget planners.

- Identifying, approaching and engaging potential clients will also be important.

The type of person suited to this work

As much of your work involves discussions with clients and agency staff, you will need to be flexible, with good communication skills. Having a well-organised approach is essential because you could be running a number of campaigns at the same time.

You will need a strong creative flair and a resourceful attitude. A key ability will be to manage clients' campaigns within budget.

Being a confident team player with an enthusiastic attitude and strong negotiating skills is essential.

Working conditions

You will be based in an office, spending a lot of time at your computer. However, your job will also involve travelling to visit clients and attend meetings. It is almost certain that at times you will have to work under pressure to complete projects within limited time-scales.

You will work standard office hours, but during busy times you will have to work late if required.

Future prospects

Due to the popularity of this sector, competition for jobs is tough. You will need to have particular skills or work experience that make you stand out. It can be difficult to progress due to a lack of higher-level opportunities. The majority of agencies have fewer than 100 employees.

The speed and extent of your career progression will depend on the outcome of your different advertising strategies. With experience, it is possible to progress into a role as account manager and then as account director, where you would have control of the account management department. Another option would be to work as a freelancer or open your own agency.

However, your training will be relevant to the related industries of marketing, market research, business or retail and commerce.

Qualifications and courses

There are no minimum educational requirements, but entry into advertising is very competitive and most entrants are graduates. A degree or HND is often required by large agencies, while smaller agencies also look for relevant work experience.

A range of related courses are available at universities and colleges at HND, Foundation degree, Honours degree and postgraduate levels. Subjects include advertising, marketing, English, communications or advertising/marketing combined with another subject; a sandwich course can be particularly useful.

Training tends to be done on the job. Staff may enrol on an Institute of Practitioners in Advertising (IPA) course if their employer is a member. Some staff may be required to study towards Communication, Advertising and Marketing Education Foundation (CAM) qualifications or Certificates and Diplomas from The Chartered Institute of Marketing.

Advantages/disadvantages

The job is fast-paced, with hectic periods of work which you will need to log. There are opportunities to meet and work with a wide range of people.

It can be rewarding when your clients' campaigns are successful.

Money guide

Salaries vary according to employer and geographical location, although London agencies tend to pay the highest. Starting as a graduate you can expect to earn £17,000–£25,000 a year. £30,000–£37,000 can be expected at senior levels. As an account director, it would be possible to earn £50,000–£80,000.

Related opportunities

- Advertising Art Director p403
- Advertising Media Planner p405
- Marketing Manager/Director p414
- Market Research Executive p413

Further information

Advertising Association
7th Floor North, Artillery House, 11–19 Artillery Row, London SW1P 1RT
020 7340 1100; www.adassoc.org.uk

Communication, Advertising and Marketing Education Foundation
Moor Hall, Cookham, Maidenhead SL6 9QH
01628 427120; www.camfoundation.com

Institute of Practitioners in Advertising
44 Belgrave Square, London SW1X 8QS
020 7235 7020; www.ipa.co.uk

ADVERTISING ART DIRECTOR

What the work involves

- You will design and create effective brand styles and images, with immediate impact, for advertising campaigns to suit clients' requirements.

- Working with specialist software, you will develop new designs, often at short notice, to convey the required mood or tone of a particular campaign.

- Working closely with colleagues, especially copywriters and reprographic specialists, you will make sure your ideas come together.

- You might also be involved in selecting photographers and other professionals to create additional visuals for use in a campaign.

The type of person suited to this work

You will need visual design skills and creative strengths, but also the skills to develop commercial ideas. The capacity to adapt to a client's requirements is also important.

As you will be using software to create new designs, you will need to have up-to-date computer skills.

Much of your time will be spent working in a team, so you will need excellent communication and people skills. Your ideas could be rejected or changed, so a flexible yet confident attitude is essential.

It is important to be able to work to exacting standards, paying close attention to detail.

Working conditions

Most of your tasks will be office-based, sometimes in a studio. You will be seated for long periods at a workstation using a number of computers, and may often be on the phone. Your job will also involve travelling to visit clients and attend shoots.

The majority of your work will be done in normal office hours. However, there will be pressure to complete jobs in the lead-up to contract deadlines and at these times you will be expected to work late.

Future prospects

This is a highly competitive area of work to enter. Although newer agencies exist in some of the larger cities (Manchester, Bristol and Newcastle), the numbers of creative art directors employed are still low. Job opportunities are increasing at the fastest rate in digital/viral marketing.

Normally, agencies hire a team consisting of a copywriter and an art director, so finding a good partner is essential. You will start as a junior creative team member and then could progress to becoming a middleweight art director.

With experience you could move up to work as a senior art director. Some established art directors go on to work on a freelance basis.

Qualifications and courses

While there are no specific entry requirements, most art directors are usually graphic designers trained to HND, degree or postgraduate level. Courses combining elements of graphic design and advertising are particularly useful.

Students generally require at least 2 A levels/3 H grades, 5 GCSEs/S grades (A*–C/1–3) as well as a portfolio of work to get a place on a degree course. Foundation courses are also available. The Diploma in Creative and Media may also be helpful.

Agencies also look for a strong portfolio of work. Work experience or internships may improve chances of entry.

Staff may enroll on an Institute of Practitioners in Advertising course if their employer is a member. The Design & Art Directors Association runs workshops in which participants develop skills and build up a portfolio.

Advantages/disadvantages

This job is rewarding as it offers individuals the chance to influence the images of major companies and brands.

The constant need to develop new ideas can be stressful at times.

Money guide

Salaries vary according to employer and location. The highest earnings are normally in London. Starting salaries at junior art director level are around £18,000–£25,000 per year. With experience and success this can rise to £25,000–£45,000. At senior and very senior levels you could earn £45,000–£150,000. Very few progress to Creative Arts Director and have salaries of over £100,000.

Related opportunities

- Advertising Account Executive p402
- Advertising Media Planner p405
- Copywriter p410
- Graphic Designer p176

Further information

Communication, Advertising and Marketing Education Foundation
Moor Hall, Cookham, Maidenhead SL6 9QH
01628 427120; www.camfoundation.com

Design and Art Directors Association
9 Graphite Square, London SE11 5EE
020 7840 1111; www.dandad.org

Institute of Practitioners in Advertising
44 Belgrave Square, London SW1X 8QS
020 7235 7020; www.ipa.co.uk

ENTRY LEVEL 4

CRCI: O

Marketing, Advertising, Media, Print and Publishing

ADVERTISING MEDIA BUYER

What the work involves

- Advertising media buyers research, identify and negotiate the purchase of media space (e.g. advertising time on television or radio).

- Working for an advertising agency, you will work from a brief laid out by your clients, taking into consideration target audiences, media events and activities, schedules and budgetary constraints.

- You will present proposals, advise creative teams, estimate costs and profits, and monitor and keep records of the progress of your media campaigns.

- You will make media contacts and liaise with other media companies in order to get the best deal and most exposure on behalf of your client.

The type of person suited to this work

You should have a keen interest in media, marketing and advertising and be constantly thinking of new creative ways to approach your work.

As you will need to have a good understanding of your target audiences and markets you should also be interested in the reasons why people purchase certain products or use certain media channels.

You must have good communication skills as you will have to make presentations, draw up proposals and correspond with contacts on a regular basis.

You should have strong organisational skills and be able to work under pressure and within tight deadlines.

You will need to have initiative, drive and be able to work in a team.

Working conditions

You will work around 40 hours a week, Monday to Friday. You may have to work longer hours to meet deadlines. Part-time work or flexible hours may be possible.

You will be mainly office-based although as you gain more experience you will spend more time meeting with clients, making presentations and discussing proposals.

You may have to travel away from home; this could include overnight stays.

The majority of your correspondence with media owners and companies is conducted on the phone, by email or by socialising.

Future prospects

You will usually progress to a permanent position after 1 year in a junior role. Your promotions will depend largely on personal performance and successful campaigns.

You may have to move between agencies in order to progress.

You can take postgraduate qualifications to increase your knowledge about specific aspects of your job such as business or marketing.

Qualifications and courses

Most entrants are graduates of degree or diploma programmes. Relevant subjects include marketing, media studies, statistics and business management. HNDs require 1 A level and 4 GCSEs (A*–C) for entry; degrees require 2 A levels and 5 GCSEs (A*–C). The Diploma in Creative and Media may be useful.

Language skills are helpful, especially for jobs with international companies.

Building up a portfolio of work experience through work placements or volunteering will increase your chances of getting your first job, develop your skills and give you experience in media buying, negotiation, and sales.

After 3–5 years you may gradually take on more account management and responsibilities or you may take a position in data management or account planning.

Advantages/disadvantages

Advances and changes in the media industry mean that you will find new and exciting opportunities to work with multimedia technologies.

This is a highly competitive industry and your work may involve long and stressful hours.

Money guide

As a junior advertising media buyer your starting salary may be from around £15,000 to £20,000 a year.

After you have gained 3 or 4 years' experience you can expect to earn around £25,000–£45,000 a year.

At a senior level you may reach £60,000 a year, but this can vary greatly.

Related opportunities

- Advertising Account Executive p402
- Marketing Manager/Director p414
- Market Research Executive p413
- Public Relations Officer p422

Further information

The Account Planning Group
16 Creighton Avenue, London N10 1NU
020 8444 3692; mail@apg.org.uk; www.apg.org.uk

The Advertising Association
7th Floor North, 11–19 Artillery House, London SW1P 1RT
020 7340 1100; aa@adassoc.org.uk; www.adassoc.org.uk

The Institute of Practitioners in Advertising
44 Belgrave Square, London SW1 X8QS
020 7235 7020; www.ipa.co.uk

ADVERTISING MEDIA PLANNER

What the work involves

- You will research public opinion and interest in a client's product or service to develop new advertising and media campaigns.

- Market research, positive and negative, will form a starting point from which you will plan and develop new advertising strategies for your clients.

- You will need to be very clear when interpreting your clients' intentions.

- The work will require close cooperation with your clients and your creative team in order to create strong and successful advertising.

The type of person suited to this work

As you will be developing fresh advertising ideas, you will need a high level of creativity.

To understand and make use of a range of facts and figures in support of your work, you will need an ability to interpret and analyse trends in data.

As you will have to make presentations to your clients and colleagues at progress meetings, excellent verbal and written communication skills will be essential. Being self-motivated and confident is also important.

Good business skills are helpful and you will need to use clear verbal reasoning when stating your point of view.

Working conditions

Most of your work will be undertaken in an office or at clients' premises. You will be expected to dress formally and be well presented at all times. Although you will work mainly normal office hours, you can expect to work overtime and at weekends during busy periods.

You will have to travel to attend meetings on a regular basis, perhaps staying overnight.

Future prospects

The majority of job opportunities in advertising are based in London although the number of companies in other large cities is growing. Despite this, there are still only around 21,000 people working within the sector of advertising and media, making entry highly competitive. Realistically, account planning makes up only a very small part of the overall advertising/media sector.

If employed by one of the few larger companies – with over 300 employees – it is occasionally possible to work abroad in areas such as Europe. With experience, you could work on a freelance basis or move into market research, design or management.

Advantages/disadvantages

This type of work can provide the opportunity to work for high-profile companies with a Europe-wide or global reach.

Qualifications and courses

Although there are no minimum educational requirements to becoming an advertising media planner, competition is high and most entrants will have a degree. It is rare to get into the profession with less than an HND. Relevant subjects include media studies, business management or marketing. Smaller agencies also tend to require relevant work experience, and a sandwich course can be a particular advantage.

You could choose to do a Diploma in Creative and Media.

Training tends to be done on the job. New account planners may train with the Account Planning Group and Market Research Society, or work towards NVQ/SVQ Levels 3 or 4 in Advertising and Public Relations. You may enrol on a course run by the Institute of Practitioners in Advertising (IPA) if your employer is a member, or take qualifications with the Communication, Advertising and Marketing Education Foundation (CAM).

You will have to develop new ideas, often at relatively short notice. This is a very competitive career and only the most determined will succeed.

Money guide

Starting salaries range from £18,000 to £23,000 per year. Experienced advertising media planners can earn between £25,000 and £45,000. At the most senior level £60,000+ is possible. Some employers provide bonuses if you develop successful campaigns or gain new business. The highest salaries are in London.

Related opportunities

- Advertising Account Executive p402
- Market Research Executive p413
- Marketing Manager/Director p414
- Researcher (Media) p425

Further information

Communication, Advertising and Marketing Education Foundation
Moor Hall, Cookham, Maidenhead SL6 9QH
01628 427120; www.camfoundation.com

Account Planning Group
16 Creighton Avenue, London N10 1NU
020 8444 3692; www.apg.org.uk

Institute of Practitioners in Advertising
44 Belgrave Square, London SW1X 8QS
020 7235 7020; www.ipa.co.uk

CRCI: O | Marketing, Advertising, Media, Print and Publishing

AGENT/LITERARY AGENT

What the work involves

- Agents represent and promote artists and creatives in the film, television, radio, theatre, music and publishing sectors. They can also play a similar role for sporting professionals.

- You will be expected to work proactively to enhance your client's career by securing work and negotiating to ensure that the client attains the best work at the highest fee.

- Literary agents are responsible for assessing the quality and commercial potential of manuscripts submitted by authors.

- You will also have to develop publication and rights agreements with publishers and TV, radio and film producers on their behalf.

The type of person suited to this work

As you will be acting as the link between your client and the world they work in, you will need excellent communication skills. The ability to develop good contacts and a name for reliability is essential. It is also important to develop good working relationships with clients.

You should have a good head for business and an assertive approach will be helpful when it comes to agreeing contracts on behalf of clients.

You should have a good knowledge of the law and how it applies to your client's sector, as they will rely on you for professional advice in this area.

Working conditions

Agents are office-based and can be self-employed or work for agencies.

Although, theoretically, they could work anywhere, most agents are based near London. Literary agents can also be found in Edinburgh, which is an important centre for the UK publishing industry.

Travel is common and you should expect to work 30–40 hours a week, including evening and weekends, as some of your work will involve attending performances and social events to network and raise the profile of your clients.

Future prospects

This is a diverse and extremely competitive area. Agencies are constantly being set up but few stand the test of time. However publishers increasingly prefer to respond to new publication ideas through agents.

Your success will be determined partly by the standard of the clients you represent but, also, by the quality of the advice you can provide to them.

With sufficient experience you might have the opportunity to work abroad in entertainment and publishing hubs such as New York.

Qualifications and courses

Enthusiasm, good industry knowledge and the ability to make good contacts take precedence over academic qualifications.

Many people start out as assistants or administrators and then work their way up to an agent or manager.

However many agencies require experience and qualifications from a related area such as sales, business, music, performing arts or publishing. Many entrants have a degree in a related subject, including business, music or literature. For entry you will need 2 A levels and 5 GCSEs (A*–C).

Contract law knowledge and a second language may be useful in the negotiation of rights deals.

Most literary agents have substantial work experience and/or qualifications in publishing. A degree or postgraduate qualification would be an advantage.

Advantages/disadvantages

You will have the satisfaction of supporting new artists and helping them to succeed.

As you will earn your income from commissions, you will be under pressure to identify and promote new artists.

Unsociable hours and extensive travelling can affect your personal life.

Money guide

Salaries vary widely according to the nature of the agent, the number of artists they work with and the success they have in their field.

Literary agents are paid commission which is usually between 10% and 25% of authors' earnings. New entrants can expect to earn £15,000 in a large agency, progressing to £30,000 with experience. Top agents with prestigious clients can earn £100,000+.

Related opportunities

- Marketing Manager/Director p414
- Public Relations Officer p422
- Publisher/Commissioning Editor p423

Further information

Association of Authors' Agents
Watson, Little Ltd, 48–56 Bayham Place, London NW1 0EU
020 7388 7529; www.agentsassoc.co.uk

The Agents' Association (Great Britain)
54 Keyes House, Dolphin Square, London SW1V 3NA
020 7834 0515; www.agents-uk.com

AUTHOR/SCRIPTWRITER

What the work involves

- Authors write the text for books, magazines, ICT resources and more. This can involve developing initial ideas to create a complete piece, or simply rewriting sections.

- Scriptwriters create text for TV, film, radio and theatre productions.

- As part of the work, you will undertake research using resources such as the internet and libraries.

- Authors often specialise in a particular subject area such as technical writing, science, medicine, cookery, travel or education. A small number of authors write and publish creative works of fiction, poetry or drama.

The type of person suited to this work

It is essential to have an excellent command of the English language and the ability to write with your audience in mind. Having a good imagination and a creative approach is important.

As you will be explaining project ideas to publishers and producers/directors, you will need strong communication skills. However you should also be able to cope with working alone for much of the time.

Many authors work on a self-employed basis, so business awareness and numeracy skills are very helpful.

You will also need to be able to handle rejections from publishers.

Working conditions

The majority of authors and scriptwriters are self-employed and work from home. Most of your time will be spent researching and writing, whilst sitting at a computer for long periods.

It may be necessary to juggle deadlines with other part-time employment taken on to supplement income. Most authors/scriptwriters are employed on a project-by-project basis, so the work provides very little job security.

Most of your work will be undertaken alone, which can be isolating.

Future prospects

Making a living as a professional author can be challenging, and it takes time to develop your writing expertise and specialist areas.

Having an established network of contacts helps.

A variety of support groups, writers' groups and courses exist to help people develop their writing skills. There are opportunities to write and share your work in amateur dramatic groups and writers' circles, some of which publish work on the internet.

At present, short dramas for radio broadcast are actively sought.

Qualifications and courses

ENTRY 3 LEVEL

Authors/scriptwriters are not required to have any specific qualifications, although many are graduates. It may be useful to have a degree in English, journalism, media studies or performing arts.

There are a variety of English and creative writing courses available. These range from degree and postgraduate courses to evening classes designed to improve a writer's technique. Above all it is essential to have a good command of the English language, imagination and originality.

This is a fiercely competitive profession and few authors progress to attain mass-market appeal and a high level of commercial success. For this reason it is often necessary to obtain a second job in order to supplement income.

It is important to be proactive and establish a good network of contacts to aid self-promotion.

Arts Council grants may be available to new authors for work in literature and drama. It is necessary to request such a grant in the form of a written proposal.

Advantages/disadvantages

This type of work can provide the satisfaction of being creative and seeing your work in print and in the public domain.

Not all authors succeed in publishing their work and you might need to take on other types of work to make a living.

Money guide

Earnings vary widely depending on the nature of the writing project, your experience, and your popularity as a writer. Publishers may give a one-off payment for a piece of work or will pay you royalties (a percentage of the sales income of the book). Salaries can be £15,000–£30,000 for authors employed in a commercial environment. You may have a higher income if you are well known and your work is popular.

Related opportunities

- Copywriter p410
- Journalist p412
- Publisher/Commissioning Editor p423
- Technical Author/Medical Writer p426

Further information

BBC Writersroom
Grafton House, 379–381 Euston Road, London NW1 3AU
www.bbc.co.uk/writersroom

Society of Authors
84 Drayton Gardens, London SW10 9SB
020 7373 6642; www.societyofauthors.org

Marketing, Advertising, Media, Print and Publishing

CRCI: PB

CAMERA PERSON (TV/FILM CAMERA OPERATOR)

What the work involves

- Camera operators use digital, electronic and film cameras to capture images for use in films, television programmes or other broadcasts.

- You will work closely with a director or director of photography and will be helped by a 'grip' (a camera assistant) and other crew members such as pullers, clappers, sound engineers and lighting technicians.

- You will understand the technical and creative aspects of filming, including how to work with a script or list of shots, planning shots and shooting images.

- You will have an in-depth knowledge of the equipment you work with, how best to use it, maintain and repair it.

The type of person suited to this work

You must be interested in photography and camera technology. You should also be interested in video, film and TV production.

You will be required to have a certain amount of physical fitness as your work may involve carrying heavy equipment for long periods of time.

As you will be working in a creative environment you will need to have a good imagination and at times an abstract approach to problem solving.

Working conditions

Your working hours will vary greatly. You may be required to work early mornings, late nights and on the weekend. Shooting may be long and run over planned schedules.

You work may be affected by weather, for example some shoots may be cut short, or extended, if they depend on natural light.

You may have to work with cameras on cranes, scaffolding, in moving vehicles or in venues such as concert halls, theatres and sports grounds.

Future prospects

Skillset and regional screen agencies run schemes for those who have some experience and wish to work on a freelance basis within the industry.

Camera operators usually learn most of their skills on the job. However, constantly changing technology means that continuing professional development (CPD) is also essential. Regular training in health and safety is also essential.

Advantages/disadvantages

You may work on a variety of exciting projects, including big-budget films or breaking-news programmes.

Working on location may be dangerous at times, especially if it involves shooting footage for news broadcasts.

Qualifications and courses

To be a TV/film camera operator you do not need any specific academic qualifications. GCSEs (A*–C) in English, maths, science or other relevant subjects might be useful. However the majority of camera operators have higher-level qualifications. Such courses include HNDs, foundation degrees and degrees in film and TV production and photography. The Diploma in Creative and Media might be a useful starting point

You will start as a trainee, runner or camera operator's assistant. You will learn mainly on the job. In practice you will find that technical knowledge, practical skills, experience and contacts are equally as important as your qualifications.

Large companies, such as the BBC, offer work experience placements that will provide you with the opportunity to work with camera equipment or in a set-up studio for example. Camera equipment hire companies or television production companies might also take on work experience candidates.

Film and Television Freelance Training (FT2) offers a technical training scheme which you can use to train as a camera assistant.

City & Guilds offer a Diploma in Media Techniques or Certificate for Audiovisual Industries Induction. The BTEC National Diploma/Certificate in Media Production might help you improve your skills.

Money guide

A starting salary for a trained camera operator is around £13,800. With experience this can increase to £22,000 and £32,000.

As a camera person you are likely to work on a freelance basis or on fixed term contracts and your rate of pay will vary according to each production you work on; for example you could earn £309 for a 10 hour day on a TV drama and £254 for a 10 hour day on TV news.

Related opportunities

- Lighting Technician p444
- TV, Film and Radio Director p428

Further information

BBC Training and Development
201 Wood Lane, London W12 7TS
0370 010 0264; training@bbc.co.uk; www.bbctraining.com

FT2 – Film and Television Freelance Training
3rd Floor, 18–20 Southwark Street, London SE1 1TJ
020 7407 0344; www.ft2.org.uk

COPY EDITOR/SUB-EDITOR/ PROOFREADER

What the work involves

■ Copy editors prepare manuscripts for publication by checking for grammatical errors, spelling mistakes and inconsistencies in style.

■ You might also be responsible for checking the legality of the text.

■ Sub-editors are copy editors who work in newspapers and magazines. They may also create headlines and introductory paragraphs and manipulate text to fit a word count.

■ Proofreaders carry out the final quality checks on texts before publication. They utilise a recognised set of symbols and normally mark changes on a hard copy, but sometimes make alterations on screen using specialist software.

The type of person suited to this work

As you will be responsible for preparing texts for publication, you will pay great attention to detail and take pride in your work. An excellent knowledge of the English language and strong writing skills are expected.

Patience and a methodical approach to your work are also helpful.

If you are working in-house for a publishing or other company, you will need good team-working skills. In addition you will need to be able to deal tactfully with people, for example when explaining changes to authors' manuscripts.

The ability to manage budgets is useful, as is the ability to work to tight deadlines and cope with pressure.

Working conditions

Most copy editors work within offices or are self-employed and work from home. You will spend your time attending meetings with authors, designers, printers, illustrators and colleagues, which may involve some travelling and overnight stays.

At the busiest times you might have to work late to meet copy or production deadlines, but mostly you will work normal working hours.

Future prospects

This is a very competitive area and many copy editors start off in an administrative or related role and work their way up. Sub-editors may become as general reporters.

It may be necessary for in-house copy editors to change their job frequently to aid career progression. With experience you could become a project manager or commission new publications.

Increasingly, copy editors work on a freelance basis for a number of employers.

Qualifications and courses

Although there are no set formal entry qualifications, most copy editors are graduates. Relevant degree subjects include English, publishing, media and journalism. For financial journalism a business studies degree would be useful and to work in technical publishing a science-related degree is recommended. You will need at least 2 A levels and 5 GCSEs (A*–C) for degree entry.

Candidates could be taken on as editorial assistants or trainees to gain experience. Building a portfolio of work and experience is important.

It is also possible to study for a postgraduate qualification in publishing (PgDip or MA).

The Society for Editors and Proofreaders and the Publishing Training Centre offer introductory and advanced training courses on topics such as copy editing and grammar skills. The National Council for the Training of Journalists also offers an introductory sub-editing qualification.

Advantages/disadvantages

The work provides the satisfaction of shaping and improving the style and tone of manuscripts.

You will meet and work with many different types of people.

As you will be making sure a publication is produced on time, this can be a high-pressured job.

Money guide

Earnings vary according to employer and geographic location. Starting salaries are between £16,000 and £22,000 per year. Salaries for experienced editors employed in-house vary between £23,000 and £30,000. The most senior can earn up to £60,000.

Freelance rates vary between £12 and £25 an hour, with higher rates for more complex project management editorial work.

Related opportunities

■ Copywriter p410
■ Publisher/Commissioning Editor p423
■ Journalist p412

Further information

Society for Editors and Proofreaders
Erico House, 93–99 Upper Richmond Road, Putney, London SW15 2TG
020 8785 5617; www.sfep.org.uk

National Union of Journalists
Headland House, 308–312 Gray's Inn Road, London WC1X 8DP
020 7278 7916; www.nuj.org.uk

Marketing, Advertising, Media, Print and Publishing

CRCI: PD

COPYWRITER

What the work involves

- Copywriters create informative, well-constructed text (or 'copy') on a wide range of subjects, from a range of perspectives and for a variety of audiences.

- Advertising copywriters produce text for TV, film, radio, press and internet advertisements.

- You will create copy for websites, company magazines/publications, direct mail, brochures and product information guides.

- Design companies, sales promotion organisations and other companies employ copywriters to write text that promotes their services or products and helps to increase sales.

The type of person suited to this work

As you will be writing copy for a range of uses, you will require excellent writing skills, a strong creative flair and a good imagination. The ability to describe a subject concisely can also be important.

In discussing innovative ideas with your colleagues and clients, you will make valuable use of your strengths in verbal and written communication skills.

You will have to be flexible and willing to alter what you think are good ideas to meet clients' requirements.

It is essential to have good organisational skills, to be able to work well under pressure and to meet tight deadlines.

Working conditions

Many copywriters work on a freelance basis for a number of employers. In-house copywriters will work 9am–5pm from Monday to Friday, within an office or studio environment.

You will spend long periods of time sitting typing, which can be tiring. You will also be expected to attend client meetings, which may involve overnight travel. You will have to work long hours to meet project deadlines, which can be stressful.

Advertising copywriters normally work with an art director, who creates the visual aspect of the campaign.

Future prospects

There are interesting opportunities available, particularly in the website domain, as an increasing number of organisations require innovative copy for service and product promotion.

Competition is fierce but with good contacts, a strong writing style and knowledge of your market, it is possible to make a living in this area.

With experience, some copywriters become freelancers or set up agencies in partnership with other 'creatives'. Other copywriters go on to work in related areas such as public relations and publishing.

Advantages/disadvantages

This job provides the satisfaction of seeing your work in print and in the public domain.

Qualifications and courses

There are no formal entry requirements to be a copywriter, but most entrants have a degree or HND. Relevant subjects include advertising design, English, journalism, communications or media. A postgraduate qualification in copywriting or creative advertising, such as the West Hertfordshire College PG Diploma in Copywriting, can be useful for graduates without a relevant background.

Students generally require at least 2 A–levels/3 H grades and 5 GCSEs/S Grades (A*–C/1–3) to get a place on a degree course. Foundation courses are also available. The Diploma in Creative and Media may be a useful starting point

You will require determination to enter the profession and you will probably need to complete several unpaid work experience placements as a copywriter before being taken on. The most common entry route involves producing a high-quality portfolio and showing this to agencies.

Entry-level jobs are seldom advertised and there are currently no graduate training schemes into the creative side of advertising.

You will be working alongside imaginative colleagues, which can be stimulating.

Copywriting can be stressful because of the need to produce new ideas to tight deadlines.

There may be some job instability if working on a self-employed basis.

Money guide

Earnings vary according to employer and project. Self-employed copywriters may charge hourly rates, by the day, or for individual projects. Starting salaries for full-time roles outside London are around £14,000 per year. London-based, you could start on £18,000. With 3–5 years' experience, you could earn between £32,000 and £40,000. Senior level salaries can range between £45,000 and £200,000+.

Related opportunities

- Author/Scriptwriter p407
- Journalist p412
- Technical Author/Medical Writer p426

Further information

Institute of Copywriting
Overbrook Business Centre, Poolbridge Road, Blackford, Wedmore, BS28 4PA
0800 781 1715; www.inst.org/copy

Institute of Practitioners in Advertising
44 Belgrave Square, London SW1X 8QS
020 7235 7020; www.ipa.co.uk

EVENTS AND EXHIBITION ORGANISER

What the work involves

- As an events and exhibition organiser, you'll be planning and organising events of varying sizes and ensuring that they run to plan on the day.

- You could find yourself organising anything from conferences, seminars and meetings to parties, ceremonies, weddings or even the 2012 Olympics!

- Your role will depend on the event itself, but you might be researching, planning, marketing the event, setting the budget, and sorting out all of the little details that go into planning an event.

- Hours can be late and involve working at weekends – but you may get to attend a free party or two!

The type of person suited to this work

You need to be incredibly well organised.

Work can be tough and stressful, so you need energy and stamina: you should relish taking on a heavy workload, not crumple beneath it.

You should be a team player who is really good at communicating with others.

You need to be creative and have a good imagination, but also have a business mind. Your project management and problem solving skills should be top notch, and you must be able to market, sell and negotiate.

Working conditions

You will be extremely busy and rushing to and from various locations.

You'll usually work office hours, although additional hours are common when events require extra last minute work

Your time will be divided between the office, events venues, and client meetings. You may well have to travel away from home, sometimes abroad.

You'll be working both indoors and outdoors, and may find yourself in hotels, museums, castles, showgrounds. . . the list is endless.

Future prospects

By starting off in roles such as assistant events organiser, you're paving the way and can aim towards positions such as event organiser or manager. From this level you can progress to event director, or even start up your own company.

It is often necessary to move company more than once to progress in this industry.

Advantages/disadvantages

This is an exciting job, and the sense of achievement when an event you've planned is a success is a great feeling.

Planning an event can be stressful, and you might have to work flat out to meet deadlines and make your event a success, sacrificing your evenings and weekends in the process.

Qualifications and courses

There are no set entry requirements for this profession, but many entrants have degrees and postgraduate qualifications. There are relevant courses offered by over 50 higher education institutions in areas such as events management, conference and exhibition management, and hospitality management. Other relevant courses include marketing, tourism, and business. A Diploma in Hospitality is also available.

For entry to one of these courses, you will need 5 good GCSEs (A*–C), including English and Maths and 2 A levels. A foreign language A level is also recommended.

The NCFE Certificate in Events Management is also relevant, and is good if you want to work at a supervisory level or if you're already in the industry and want to move forwards.

The best advantage you can have when you're looking to enter the industry is to gain as much event orgainsing experience as you can of organising events. Try to help with organising charity events, local festivals or anything similar. It'll also give you an idea of whether the job suits you.

Once you're in the industry, there are many training courses available including planning techniques, marketing and crowd safety.

Money guide

As you start out, you might earn between £15,000 and £18,000 a year.

With experience this can grow to £20,000–£40,000 a year.

As an event manager you might earn around £60,000, or even more at the most senior levels.

Related opportunities

- Catering/Restaurant Manager/Maître d'hôtel p135
- Entertainment Manager p386

Further information

Association for Conferences and Events
Riverside House, High Street,
Huntingdon PE18 6SG
01480 457595; www.aceinternational.org

Association of British Professional Conference Organisers
Wellington Park, Belfast BT9 6DJ
028 9038 7475; www.abpco.org

CRCI: O | Marketing, Advertising, Media, Print and Publishing

JOURNALIST

What the work involves

- Journalists research and write stories on subjects such as current affairs, business, health and culture. Broadcast journalists also digitally present these features on radio, television or the internet.

- These stories can immediately become live news articles or features for local and national newspapers, magazines, TV, radio and online broadcasts.

- You will be planning, writing and editing articles in keeping with a house style, usually to very short deadlines.

The type of person suited to this work

As you will be producing articles on a regular basis you will need to thrive on working under pressure.

Strong ICT, written and verbal communication skills are essential for this job and broadcast journalists should have a clear and professional voice.

You should be a highly organised multi-tasker with a good instinct for a potential story and the ability to undertake research through interviews and contacts. You will be expected to research difficult stories and meet hostile people, which can be stressful.

Working conditions

Your work will be dictated by the story you are following. You could visit a range of locations in the working day, often at short notice as news stories unfold.

Overnight travel is often part of this job when chasing a story or undertaking research. You will have to work long, sometimes irregular hours in order to meet publication deadlines. Whilst you may be part of a wider team, you could work alone for much of the time, or in the company of a photographer.

Future prospects

This is a highly competitive area to enter and approximately a third of all journalists work freelance. Many full-time journalists started work as freelancers to establish their reputations.

It is possible to cross over from newspaper/magazine journalism into broadcast journalism as a reporter or presenter. There may be opportunities to work abroad.

Advantages/disadvantages

You will create features that could be read, heard or seen by thousands of people – often beyond the UK.

This profession offers exciting, varied work.

Due to short deadlines, you will have to regularly produce work under pressure.

You might have to get information or photographs to support sad and distressing stories, which could make you unpopular.

Qualifications and courses

The most common route is with pre-entry qualifications. The National Council for the Training of Journalists (NCTJ) accredits HND, Foundation degree and degrees. You could complete an unrelated degree, followed by a 1-year postgraduate course accredited by the NCTJ. The Diploma in Creative and Media might be useful.

A fast-track postgraduate course lasting 18–20 weeks is available at some colleges. New entrants who have completed a pre-entry course will then complete an 18-month training period with their employer.

Direct entry candidates need at least 5 GCSEs/S grades (A*–C/1–3) including English.

Candidates entering into journalism without a relevant qualification are often asked by newspapers to study toward the National Certificate of the National Council for the Training of Journalists. Magazines have their own training courses accredited by the Periodicals Training Council. NVQs/SVQs are also available.

Broadcast journalism is fiercely competitive and entrants should have a strong showreel and work experience in student or community media.

Money guide

Salaries start at £10,000–£15,000 per year at trainee level on a local newspaper. Broadcast journalists can expect to earn £15,000 to begin with and around £17,000 is usual if starting at a magazine. Experienced journalists can earn £22,000–£45,000. The most successful and well-known journalists can earn in excess of £100,000.

Related opportunities

- Author/Scriptwriter p407
- Copywriter p410
- Newspaper/Magazine Editor p417
- Researcher (Media) p425

Further information

National Council for the Training of Journalists
The New Granary, Station Road, Newport,
Saffron Walden CB11 3PL
01799 544014; www.nctj.com

Broadcast Journalism Training Council
18 Millers Close, Rippingale PE10 0TH
01778 440025; www.bjtc.org.uk

National Union of Journalists
308–312 Gray's Inn Road, London WC1X 8DP
020 7278 7916; www.nuj.org.uk

MARKET RESEARCH EXECUTIVE

What the work involves

- You will undertake research to obtain people's opinions on specific products, services or issues and then analyse the results.

- Developing surveys to analyse public opinion on a wide range of subjects or issues will be part of your job.

- You may also interview small groups of people, known as focus groups or panels, to assess in more detail their views on a specific topic.

- You will compile the results of your research in the form of detailed reports or summary analyses to be used by your clients, businesses and other organisations.

The type of person suited to this work

This job is all about people and their opinions, so verbal communication skills are essential. You will also need strong writing skills to create surveys, plan interviews and write reports.

You will need to understand exactly what your client wants to know and think up ways to get this information. A logical and deductive approach to your work is important.

Also, as you will be working with facts and figures and a lot of paperwork you will need to be well organised. Confidence in working with numbers will be useful in helping you to perform statistical analyses. Being aware of the marketplace and what sells is also important.

Working conditions

Market researchers work from offices and attend meetings, presentations and interviews. You could work in a specialist market research agency or department within a larger organisation. Some market researchers work freelance.

The job can involve frequent daily and overnight travel.

This can be a pressured role as you will be required to produce detailed information at short notice. It can be difficult working with the public if they do not want to help you.

Future prospects

The market research industry is worth over £1 billion a year. As well as businesses, many other organisations increasingly depend on market researchers to provide up-to-the-minute facts and figures concerning public opinion on everything from train services to trainers!

After gaining experience as a market research interviewer you can move up to research executive, and then progress to senior research executive. With sufficient experience you could enter a senior management role or set up your own agency.

Advantages/disadvantages

You will work on a variety of projects and meet many different types of people, which can be very interesting. You will have to

Qualifications and courses

ENTRY LEVEL **4**

There are no set qualifications for this role but you will most likely be expected to have an HND or degree. Employers do however tend to look for an outgoing personality and enthusiasm for the job over academic qualifications.

Useful subjects are English, maths, psychology and political sciences. Various universities also offer an Advanced Certificate in Market and Social Research Practice.

The Market Research Society (MRS) also offers a Market Research Society Diploma and, if this is successfully completed, the candidate will be eligible for full membership of the Market Research Society.

NVQs/SVQs are available in Customer Service at Levels 2 and 3 and Marketing Research (Interviewing) at Level 1. These may be useful and some companies may support further study.

MA courses are available in social and market research or in marketing management specialising in market research. Candidates would need to hold a first degree.

work antisocial hours (at weekends or evenings) on a regular basis. The public may not want to speak to you and getting the information needed may be difficult.

Money guide

Starting salaries for interviewers range from £17,000 to £22,000 per year. With 3–5 years' experience this can rise to £26,000-£35,000. Agencies pay £10–£15 per hour. A very experienced market researcher could earn between £40,000 and £80,000.

Related opportunities

- Advertising Media Planner p405
- Marketing Manager/Director p414
- Researcher (Media) p425
- Statistician p536

Further information

Market Research Society
15 Northburgh Street, London EC1V 0JR
020 7490 4911; www.mrs.org.uk

ESOMAR
(World Association for Opinion and Marketing Research Professionals), Eurocenter 2, 11th floor, Barbara Strozzilaan 384, 1083 HN Amsterdam, The Netherlands
+31 20 664 2141; www.esomar.org

International Marketing Research Information
IMRI Ltd, PO Box 7742, Loughborough LE12 8WG
01509 891216; www.imriresearch.com

CRCI: O

Marketing, Advertising, Media, Print and Publishing

MARKETING ASSISTANT/ EXECUTIVE

What the work involves

- Marketing assistants/executives (under the direction of a marketing manager or director) need to promote and raise the profile of ideas, products and services for their clients or organisation.

- You will use a variety of techniques to do this including writing press releases, brochures, advertising, developing promotional material for the web or for TV and radio, poster campaigns or running events.

- You will need to conduct market research which could involve implementing customer surveys and focus groups.

- You will network (sourcing new clients and gaining contacts) regularly and update customer databases with new client details.

The type of person suited to this work

You must be commercially aware and in-tune with consumer behaviour. It's important to understand what motivates people. Imagination and initiative are essential when developing innovative marketing techniques.

Excellent communication and persuasion skills are essential. You need to be confident, adaptable and ambitious in order to succeed.

You need to be organised as many projects will require you to multi-task, working quickly and to a high standard.

Working conditions

You will spend most of your time in an office working normal hours from Monday to Friday. However, you might need to work nights and weekends when running events and campaigns. Most companies will provide you with time off in lieu for working overtime.

You will travel to meet clients and attend exhibitions or launches. You will probably be expected to dress formally.

Future prospects

The majority of marketing vacancies are centred in cities such as London, Manchester and Birmingham. You will work either in-house or for a specialist agency.

With 3–10 years of experience you may be promoted to marketing manager. You could also choose to focus on a particular area such as public relations or advertising. It may be necessary to transfer to a new company in order to increase your chances of promotion.

Advantages/disadvantages

You will be inspired working alongside lively and creative people.

It's rewarding when your campaigns are successful and impact the public or profit your company.

Qualifications and courses

Marketing is highly competitive. While you may become an assistant/executive with relevant work experience or a dynamic personality, you will have an advantage if you are a graduate.

Degrees, HNDs and Foundation degrees in marketing, creative or business studies are particularly useful. You should visit individual college or university websites for entry requirements as these will vary.

A BTEC Higher National Certificate/Diploma is also available in Marketing as is a Diploma in Retail Business.

The Chartered Institute of Marketing (CIM) offers an Introductory Certificate in Marketing for school-leavers and graduates of different disciplines. No qualifications or previous experience is needed.

Internships and work placements are advisable.

A deadline-driven environment can be stressful and demanding.

You could have many campaigns running at once which can be difficult to balance.

Money guide

As a marketing assistant you will earn around £22,000 per year. This may be higher if you work for a professional service. The public sector tends to pay less.

Marketing executives with a few years' experience may earn around £27,000 a year.

Salaries are usually higher in large cities. Bonuses can also increase your salary.

Related opportunities

- Advertising Account Executive p402
- Copywriter p410
- Marketing Manager/Director p415
- Public Relations Officer p422

Further information

Chartered Institute of Marketing
Moor Hall, Cookham, Maidenhead SL6 9QH
01628 427120; www.cim.co.uk

Communication, Advertising and Marketing Education Foundation
Moor Hall, Cookham, Maidenhead SL6 9QH
01628 427120; www.camfoundation.com

City&
Guilds

www.cityandguilds.com/myperfectjob

MARKETING MANAGER/ DIRECTOR

What the work involves

- You will analyse markets and evaluate the competition in order to develop marketing strategies that will promote and increase sales of products, services or ideas. You will also oversee branding.

- You will be responsible for post-campaign evaluations and assessing past strategies. This information will help you to come up with innovative campaigns in the future.

- You will also be responsible for product development and budgeting.

- You will oversee a team of assistants and executives.

The type of person suited to this work

In order to work at a strategic level you must have vision and be a confident and creative decision-maker. You should be diplomatic and persuasive in order to manage your team effectively.

Good business sense and consumer knowledge are essential. You need to have excellent communication and presentation skills. Enthusiasm and imagination will help you to stay ahead of your competitors.

You will be responsible for a project's success and ensuring it is within budget so analytical and numerical skills are also important.

You must be able to cope under pressure.

Working conditions

You will usually work a 37-hour week Monday to Friday but may often stay overtime in order to meet deadlines. As the manager of a campaign you will be in regular contact with the press, printers and designers and will need to travel often. International travel may also be required and you may spend long periods of time away from home.

Otherwise you will be office based, developing strategies and supervising staff.

This can be a stressful and demanding role, as you will be juggling a variety of tasks.

Future prospects

With 10–15 years of experience you may be promoted from marketing manager to marketing director. Postgraduate qualifications will increase your chance of promotion as may a move to another company.

Directors may choose to become self-employed or work as freelance marketing consultants. Alternatively if you work for a global organisation you may choose to take up a leadership role in an office overseas.

Advantages/disadvantages

It's rewarding to see your strategies and campaigns increase profits and raise awareness for your clients.

Qualifications and courses

For management positions employers want to see a good track record and previous experience in marketing. Most managers begin as marketing assistants or executives.

Most employers prefer candidates to have completed the 1-year Chartered Institute of Marketing (CIM) Professional Diploma in Marketing aimed at those wishing to pursue marketing management. To qualify you will need a degree in marketing or the CIM Professional Certificate in Marketing.

If you want to work at a strategic, directorate level you will need a postgraduate qualification. CIM offers a Chartered Postgraduate Diploma in Marketing. To qualify you will need to have completed the Professional Certificate in Marketing or a degree in marketing, and have significant experience as a manager.

NVQs/SVQs up to Level 3 in Marketing Communications and Marketing Products and Brands are also available.

You have the freedom to be creative and innovative in your role.

Clients might dislike your ideas and can be challenging to please.

Working overtime to meet deadlines is stressful and demanding.

Money guide

Marketing managers earn around £30,000 a year. With additional experience you can earn up to £40,000.

Directors working at a strategic level can earn £50,000+. In some sectors this may rise to as much as £100,000.

Your salary may increase with bonuses and you will earn more working for a professional service as opposed to a not-for-profit organisation. Many companies also offer benefits such as gym membership and medical insurance.

Related opportunities

- Advertising Account Executive p402
- Copywriter p410
- Public Relations Officer p422
- Marketing Assistant/Executive p414

Further information

Chartered Institute of Marketing
Moor Hall, Cookham, Maidenhead SL6 9QH
01628 427120; www.cim.co.uk

Communication, Advertising and Marketing Education Foundation
Moor Hall, Cookham, Maidenhead SL6 9QH
01628 427120; www.camfoundation.com

Marketing, Advertising, Media, Print and Publishing

CRCI: O

MODEL

What the work involves

- You could be involved in different types of modelling, such as fashion, photographic or demonstration work.

- You could work in a studio, on location outdoors, at fashion shows or at events such as car shows or conventions.

- It is necessary to build a good portfolio of your work and establish a good reputation within the industry.

- Your job will be to show off new clothing or products to their best advantage in order to help potential customers visualise them being worn or in use.

The type of person suited to this work

This is a very competitive area to find work. You will have to be determined and prepared to deal with disappointment if contracts do not come your way.

Most fashion model agencies have set physical requirements that you will have to meet before you are accepted onto their books.

There is also scope for models with one particularly good feature, such as hands, feet, eyes or hair, to model specific items.

During your work you will meet different types of people, so you will have to be confident and have good communication skills.

Working conditions

The places you will work will depend on the type of modelling that you do and the nature of the contracts you are offered. You might work indoors within a studio, or you could be on location doing catalogue work. This can involve many hours of work to get the correct shot.

You will be on your feet for long periods at a time and will always have to look your best, even if you have been travelling.

The work can be physically demanding, hours spent walking back and forth and posing in awkward positions for long periods can take their toll.

Future prospects

Only the most successful models are always in work. Most are self-employed and have to take up temporary or part-time work when necessary.

To build your reputation, you will have to create a portfolio of work using photos from previous contracts. Your portfolio will need to have a distinct edge to help you win contracts and work.

While top models are very famous and can be rich, there are hundreds more who work for smaller companies and businesses who may earn a lot less.

Most models finish their career in their early 30s.

Qualifications and courses

There are no formal entry qualifications, but a portfolio of photographs is normally required for modelling agencies.

Female models should be at least 5 feet 8 inches (1.72m) tall and should measure around 34–24–34 inches (86–61–86cm). Male models should be at least 6 feet (1.83m) tall. However, some photographic models are required to be smaller or larger than the usual sizes, depending on employer requirements.

There are modelling courses which focus on diet, health and figure correction, deportment, fashion coordination, grooming, catwalk turns and movements, photographic modelling techniques and how to work with agents. There are also fashion-related courses which include business aspects.

Advantages/disadvantages

Only a few models get the top contracts.

You could get to travel around the world.

You will be posing for long periods which could be tiring.

Modelling can be a very glamorous and confidence boosting career.

Money guide

You will probably be self-employed so your earnings will depend on your success in finding regular, well-paid work. Most agencies keep 20% of earnings as commission.

You can expect to start on around £100–£200 per day, rising to £500+ per day for models with experience. Well known and top models can earn very high wages.

Related opportunities

- Beauty Consultant p458
- Beauty Therapist p459
- Fashion Designer/Milliner p172
- Wardrobe Assistant p455

Further information

Alba Model Information
PO Box 588, Southport PR8 9BR
www.albamodel.info

Association of Model Agents
11–20 Fashion Street, London, E1 6PX
020 7422 0699, www.associationofmodelagents.org

London College of Fashion
20 John Princes Street, London W1G 0BJ
020 7514 7400; www.fashion.arts.ac.uk

NEWSPAPER/MAGAZINE EDITOR

What the work involves

- Newspaper/magazine editors are responsible for the coordination of each aspect of a publication.

- You will understand the readership of the publication and include informative, newsworthy articles, entertaining features and high quality images.

- You will work with the editorial, design and advertising departments, as well as journalists, printers and publishers.

- Tasks include editing and proofreading articles and features, assigning journalists to cover stories, commissioning freelance writers for features, meeting with photographers, and conducting interviews.

The type of person suited to this work

You should be able to demonstrate excellent writing skills and a creative flair.

You must have a strong interest in current affairs.

You will have a practical approach to problem solving and remain calm in a crisis situation. You need to show initiative, persistence and decisiveness.

You must pay attention to detail, be meticulous in your organisation and time management and be able to work to a deadline.

You must also have excellent communication skills to be able to delegate tasks and persuade others to meet deadlines.

Working conditions

You will probably work around 40 hours a week, which may include early morning starts, working into the night and even working at the weekend to cover a breaking story. Some large newspapers may offer shift work.

You will be almost entirely office-based which may be noisy and busy at times but you may at times be required to meet with other editors, journalists or photographers outside of the office.

Future prospects

Journalism is a very competitive industry to break into. Work experience, published articles and evidence of commitment to journalism are as important as qualifications.

The typical route to becoming a newspaper/magazine editor is to begin in a junior role as a journalist and work your way up through the editorial department until you are in charge of the content of the magazine or newspaper.

You may also move across and work in PR, press offices or on a freelance basis.

Qualifications and courses

Most entrants are graduates. Relevant subjects include journalism, English, history and politics. However specialist publications might require you to have taken a specific degree, such as science or art. You will need at least 2 A levels and 5 GCSEs (A*–C) for degree entry. The Diploma in Creative and Media might be helpful.

Postgraduate qualifications in journalism can help you to gain entry. The National Council for the Training of Journalists (NCTJ) provides many accredited postgraduate courses. For entry you will need a good first degree, 2.1 or higher.

Building up a strong portfolio by writing for student publications or local newspapers will help you gain a journalism position. From there you can build up experience and contacts and could progress to an editorial role.

Advantages/disadvantages

Your work will be diverse and stimulating as it will involve ever-changing content and working with various people involved with the production of the publication.

You may work in a highly stressful environment, working long, tiring and unsociable hours.

Money guide

Your starting salary as a newspaper editor can be around £14,000 per year if you work for a small local paper. Large regional or national papers will start around £18,000.

This can increase to around £22,000–£40,000 per year with experience.

Senior editors with 10 years' experience can earn around £50,000 or more per year depending on the publication.

Related opportunities

- Copy editor/Sub-editor/Proofreader p409
- Journalist p412
- Publisher/Commissioning Editor p423

Further information

National Council for the Training of Journalists
The New Granary, Station Road, Newport CB11 3PI
01799 544014; info@nctj.com; www.nctj.com

Newspaper Society
8th Floor, St Andrew's House, 18–20 St Andrew Street,
London EC4A 3AY
020 7632 7400; www.newspapersoc.org.uk

CRCI: PD

Marketing, Advertising, Media, Print and Publishing

PHOTOGRAPHER/ PHOTOGRAPHIC STYLIST

What the work involves

- Photographers create photographic images using technical lighting and equipment. Using your eye for design and knowledge of photographic techniques you will create images for a specific brief.

- Photographic stylists help the photographer to design the look of the photograph.

- Many photographers work with digital enhancing techniques to modify and improve, or add interest and illusions to the images they produce.

The type of person suited to this work

You will need a strong visual sense and an eye for what makes a good picture. You will need the technical knowledge and skills to get the most from lighting, studio set-ups and, of course, camera equipment. The use of editing software means that ICT skills are increasingly important.

Strong communication skills and a flexible attitude come in useful when discussing projects with clients, or putting nervous subjects at ease.

To work on a freelance basis, business skills and self-confidence are essential.

Working conditions

You will either be studio or location-based. In a studio you could work with still-life and portraiture. Lighting equipment can be heavy and the work can be physically tiring as you will be on your feet for long periods.

If you work outdoors you could record images for advertising and photo-journalism. This may require patience if the weather or light conditions are not correct for your shot.

Commercial photography is completed to tight deadlines, which can be stressful.

Future prospects

In order to gain the essential skills and an understanding of your specialist type of photography, you could work as a photographer's assistant. Nowadays, positions are even more limited as digital photography has reduced the work of professionals.

With experience you could progress into freelance work or specialise in a particular area such as press, medical or food photography.

Advantages/disadvantages

You will have the satisfaction of using your creativity and technical skills to create original images, which may end up in the public eye.

Qualifications and courses

There are no set academic requirements to become a photographer but the following courses may be useful: A levels in photography; City & Guilds Levels 1–3 in Photo Imaging and Photography; the Diploma in Creative and Media; and an HNC/HND in Art and Design. Applicants will also need a strong portfolio of work comprising between 10 and 15 shots.

Candidates wishing to pursue careers as police, medical or press photographers will need 5 GCSEs/S grades (A*–C/1–3) including English and maths. It is necessary for medical photographers to have a degree or postgraduate certificate in clinical photography and forensic photographers to have 1 A level in science.

The British Institute of Photography's professional qualifying exam requires an HND or a degree. Apprenticeships in Photo Imaging are available through Skillset.

It takes time in this competitive industry to develop contacts, so if you work on a freelance basis you might need a second job to support yourself.

Money guide

As a trainee assistant photographer you can expect to earn about £12,000 per year. This rises to £16,000–£20,000 with experience. £60,000+ is possible at senior levels.

Earnings will vary if you are self-employed or freelance. You are likely to earn between £150 and £600 per day. You may have periods of inactivity and many people have a second job in an area such as teaching to supplement their income.

Related opportunities

- Camera Person p408
- Graphic Designer p176
- Illustrator/Technical Illustrator p178

Further information

Association of Photographers
81 Leonard Street, London EC2A 4QS
020 7739 6669; www.the-aop.org

www.cityandguilds.com/myperfectjob

PRINTER

What the work involves

Machine printer

- Machine printers oversee the production of printed items on machines of various sizes for products such as newspapers, posters, books, etc. You will set up the printing press correctly for the specific job. This includes ensuring that the appropriate plates, paper and inks have been selected.

- You will trial the print run, check for errors and ensure that the quality is up to standard.

Screen printer

- Screen printers create visual images by organising and operating hand- or power-driven screen printing machines which print graphics onto fabrics and paper by forcing ink through a delicate mesh overlay of the stencil design.

- You will be required to prepare the stencils, inks and print processes.

Bookbinder

- Bookbinders are responsible for transforming the printed material into the finished product. Nowadays the majority of bookbinding is a machine orientated process, which involves stitching, stapling, collating, cutting, binding and coating.

Print production planner

- Print production planners are responsible for workflow in the printing firm and ensuring that the efficiency is maximised by checking orders, creating schedules, allocating work, supervising and quality control.

The type of person suited to this work

Printing requires good teamwork and communication skills.

It is usual that your work will involve computers and other types of machinery and equipment so you will need good practical skills and an understanding of ICT.

It is important to have normal colour vision, good hand-to-eye co-ordination and a high level of physical fitness.

You should have a meticulous eye for detail, and you will need to demonstrate art and design skills to convince customers that you can make aesthetically pleasing finished products, from CD covers to pages of pure text or full-colour brochures.

As print runs do not always go smoothly you will need to be adept at problem-solving, have a long concentration span and the ability to work under pressure. Furthermore you should be flexible as some print companies run 24 hour operations and you might have to work shifts at night and at the weekends.

Print production managers should also have good multi-tasking skills, a good head for numbers and the ability to influence people.

Working conditions

In smaller print companies you will normally work office hours, that is 9am to 5pm, but during busy periods you could do additional hours in order to ensure that projects are completed on time. Larger companies tend to run 24 hour operations and you will be expected to work shifts and weekends. Overtime is widely available. Bookbinders may also have the opportunity to work part-time.

Your working environment will depend on your role and the size of the firm. Printshops can be dirty and noisy when machines are functioning. Hazardous chemicals are used in finishes and to wash inks from the press but there is good ventilation to cope with the resulting fumes.

You will be required to adhere to health and safety regulations at all times and use protective gear such as overalls, boots, gloves and ear protectors.

It is necessary to have a good level of physical fitness as you will be standing for long periods of time. Upper body strength is also important as you may be required to carry out some heavy lifting.

Print production planners will work in an office but will also carry out work on the production floor and may have to travel to attend meetings with clients.

Future prospects

The printing, packaging and design industry is the UK's sixth largest manufacturing sector. 316,000 people are employed in over 15,000 companies mostly around London, south-east England, Bristol, Leeds and Glasgow.

At present in the UK there are about 12,000 print companies, which employ about 160,000 people. There are about 30,000 machine printers and bookbinders and 15,000 print production planners.

The majority of the industry comprises small, family-owned enterprises. The industry is sensitive to wider economic issues, such as cheaper rates from foreign print companies, increasing use of electronic resources and seasonal order variations.

Opportunities will depend on your skills and the size and type of your company. Although printers cover all the stages of production, the job of folding machine operator (at the finishing end of the process) is becoming a skills shortage area.

With experience and additional design skills, you could work for a specialist press production company, a design or reprographic house or general printers. To run a printing business takes a high level of business skills, including accounting and sales.

Marketing, Advertising, Media, Print and Publishing

CRCI: PD

Advantages/disadvantages

This job combines creative and artistic skills with technical and computer aided design.

There are good entry opportunities for some printing jobs such as specialist print finishers, which have become skills shortage areas.

Due to the nature of the industry, you might have to move to other parts of the country for promotion.

Many companies now produce high quality publications in-house, so printers need to work with large volumes or specialist niche markets to make a profit.

Money guide

Machine printer

New entrants can expect to earn £15,000. More experienced machine printers can amass £45,000 including shift allowances and bonuses and the highest salaries in this profession are £60,000.

Screen printer

Screen printers can expect to start on £16,000, rising to £24,000 with experience. Top earners can amass £36,000.

Bookbinder

Bookbinders can expect to earn a starting salary of £16,000, rising to £28,000, including shift bonuses, with experience. Those with extensive experience and who lead a team can earn up to £30,000.

Print production planner

New entrants can expect to earn £16,000. With experience, print production planners can amass £30,000 and senior planners can earn £35,000.

Related opportunities

- CAD Draughtsperson p218
- Publisher/Commissioning Editor p423
- Quality Control Inspector p241
- Signwriter/Signmaker p186

Further information

British Printing Industries Federation
Farringdon Point, 29/35 Farringdon Road, London EC1M 3JF
0870 240 4085; www.britishprint.com

Institute of Paper, Printing and Publishing
Runnymede Malthouse off Hummer Road, Egham TW20 9BD
0870 330 8625; www.ip3.org.uk

Scottish Print Employers Federation
48 Palmerston Place, Edinburgh, Scotland EH12 5DE
0131 220 4353; www.spef.org.uk

www.cityandguilds.com/myperfectjob

Qualifications and courses

Although there are no set entry requirements for this career, GCSEs/S grades (A*–C/1–3) in English, maths, science and technologies subjects are an advantage.

Many people enter these professions by means of an apprenticeship. The Diploma in Manufacturing and Product Design might be useful. In addition you can study a relevant college course prior to entry.

Machine printer

As an introduction to the sector you can take a 10-day course run by the Institute of Paper, Printing and Publishing.

You can also work towards NVQs Levels 1–3 in subjects such as machine printing, mechanised print finishing and binding, digital print production, envelope manufacture and carton manufacture.

Screen printer

You can choose to do a college course in printing and graphic communications, printmaking skills, screen printing, graphic printmaking or print media. It is also possible to attain City & Guilds Certificates in Printing and Graphic Communications at Levels 2 and 3, an NVQ in Screenprinting at Levels 2 and 3, an ABC Level 3 Award in Printmaking Skills, Screen Printing, and Screen Printing Skills. Much training takes place on the job with experienced colleagues and many companies provide in-house training schemes.

The Digital and Screenprinting Association, and specialist schools such as London College of Communication also run courses in this area.

Bookbinder

Craft bookbinding is often a second career path. Courses, degrees and diplomas are available in fine bookbinding and repair. NVQs are available in mechanised print finishing and binding at Levels 2 and 3 and hand binding at Level 3.

Print production planner

This job requires maturity and practical industry experience. It is possible to commence as a machine printer and work your way up to this position.

Many print production planners have a degree or diploma in a related subject such as print management, graphic communications, business studies or publishing. For a degree, entry requirements are usually 2 A levels and 5 GCSEs (A*–C). For an HND, you should have 1 A level or a BTEC national diploma in a related subject. You can study for an NVQ in Print Administration at Level 3, which includes modules on health and safety.

The British Printing Industries Federation (BPIF) offers a 12 month distance learning Certificate in Print Management, which is aimed at first-time managers.

PRODUCTION ASSISTANT/RUNNER (TV, FILM AND RADIO)

What the work involves
Production assistant

- Production assistants provide support to the producer and director to help ensure that productions run smoothly and to schedule.

- You will manage a range of key administrative activities, such as organising scripts and filming updates, booking hotels and hiring equipment. You may also be responsible for managing budgets for productions.

Runner

- You will provide a wide range of practical help and support to all members of the production team.

- As well as some administrative work, you will pass messages on and carry equipment and scripts between offices and sets – often, with no prior notice.

The type of person suited to this work
It is essential to be enthusiastic, possess a willingness to learn and a passion for your chosen medium. You should have an interest in learning about all areas of the field and be well versed in recent trends in the industry. You should also enjoy problem-solving and have the ability to work well under pressure and to adhere to strict deadlines.

Working conditions
There are no standard hours in this profession as they vary depending on production size and type. This role requires a great deal of flexibility as during production hours can be long and unpredictable and include evenings and weekends. Many employees are freelancers, shift work is common and you may be required to be on call at all times.

Future prospects
Most opportunities are in London and south-east England, where over half of the TV and film industries are based.

This profession is fast-paced and there is fierce competition for entry level positions. Any relevant work experience will help to secure a position. There are many freelancers in this sector. This usually involves working on several projects simultaneously, and balancing bursts of assignments with quiet periods of inactivity.

Advantages/disadvantages
This is a fast-moving and varied industry with exciting opportunities. These entry level positions are demanding and unglamorous.

Money guide
Earnings in this sector vary greatly according to role, media area, employer and project. Many people are employed on a freelance or contract basis.

Qualifications and courses
Production assistant

No formal qualifications are required but entry is highly competitive, and many entrants are graduates. Understanding of the production process is very important and relevant previous experience is advantageous. Many production assistants begin as runners and work their way up. Useful qualifications include the BTEC Extended Diploma in Creative and Media Production and the Diploma in Creative and Media.

Unadvertised vacancies are common in this field. It is important to be proactive and network to aid self-promotion.

In a bid to create a formal entry path and provide industry-specific education, the UK Film Council and Skillset have joined forces to open specialist training academies and offer advice on professional development.

Runner
There are no formal entry requirements and it is often a key starting point into the TV and film industry.

However it may be advantageous to have a degree in a TV/film production or media related subject and an understanding of the production process. Enthusiasm is essential and it would be beneficial to have gained work experience, even if unpaid.

Production assistant
Starting salaries range between £15,000 and £22,000 per year; with experience you could earn £30,000 per year. Working freelance you could expect around £520 per week.

Runner
New entrants can expect to earn £10,000–£14,000 per year. This can rise to £20,000 with experience.

Related opportunities
- Camera Person (TV/Film Camera Operator) p408
- TV Floor Manager/Film Assistant Director p432

Further information
Broadcasting Entertainment Cinematograph and Theatre Union
373–377 Clapham Road, London SW9 9BT
020 7346 0900; www.bectu.org.uk

Skillset
Focus Point, 21 Caledonian Road, London N1 9GB
020 7713 9800; www.skillset.org

Marketing, Advertising, Media, Print and Publishing

CRCI: PA

PUBLIC RELATIONS OFFICER

What the work involves

- You will manage the image and reputation of organisations by writing publicity materials, studying and advising clients and responding to enquiries or complaints.

- It will be important that you develop and maintain positive working relationships with the local, national and relevant trade press and TV news reporters.

- Public relations (PR) officers work in public relations or communications departments in large organisations and PR companies. Some work on a freelance basis.

The type of person suited to this work

PR is all about maintaining a positive image, so you must be confident and have a smart appearance. You need to have strong communication skills and enjoy liaising with a wide range of people. Written communication and research skills are essential, as are good ICT skills.

You must be able to work effectively under tight deadlines. You should also have a flexible approach in a job where you will manage several projects at once. Financial management skills are also useful.

Working conditions

Most of your work will be within an office where you will have a workstation with computer, access to office equipment and your phone. You will have meetings with clients, colleagues or other professionals. Although you will work normal office hours, longer hours are common in this job, particularly in busy periods.

On a regular basis, you will need to travel to attend meetings, special events and presentations. Working for global companies or high-profile charities may mean some overseas travel.

Future prospects

PR is a growing industry. However, there is strong competition, with often hundreds of well-qualified applicants for one post. You will start as a PR assistant and then progress to a role as an account executive, followed by a move into a senior role.

It is possible to work abroad either within an existing organisation or by moving to one based overseas or with offices abroad. With experience, some PR professionals set up their own companies or work freelance for other organisations.

Advantages/disadvantages

You can be a part of high-profile campaigns. This job can be pressured due to the speed of information releases and the range of activities you will have to juggle. If working for a high-profile organisation, you might have to be on call to respond to unexpected situations or emergencies.

Qualifications and courses

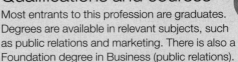

Most entrants to this profession are graduates. Degrees are available in relevant subjects, such as public relations and marketing. There is also a Foundation degree in Business (public relations).

Entry is highly competitive and a postgraduate qualification and previous work experience are an advantage.

Employers provide training, and some have graduate training schemes.

The Chartered Institute of Public Relations (CIPR) offers professional qualifications. Entry requirements for the CIPR Advanced Certificate are a first degree or 2 years' experience and 5 GCSEs/S grades (A*–C/1–3), including English language.

The Public Relations Consultants Association offers a Diploma in Public Relations Consultancy Management. A degree or 2 years' experience in a senior role is required.

The Communication, Advertising and Marketing Foundation (CAM) offers qualifications. The Advanced Certificate requires a degree or relevant experience and 5 GCSEs/S grades (A*–C/1–3), including English and maths or equivalent. For the Higher Diploma, experience and a good educational background are required.

Money guide

Starting salaries are usually around £16,000–£22,000 per year. This rises to £25,000–£35,000 with experience. £40,000–£100,000 is possible as a senior manager/director in a large company. The type of organisation you work for will affect your earnings. The voluntary and charity sector tend to pay less than public or government organisations.

Related opportunities

- Advertising Account Executive p402
- Advertising Media Planner p405
- Journalist p412

Further information

Chartered Institute of Public Relations
52–53 Russell Square, London WC1B 4HP
020 7631 6900; www.ipr.org.uk

Communication, Advertising and Marketing Education (CAM) Foundation
Moor Hall, Cookham, Maidenhead, Berkshire SL6 9QH
01628 427120; www.camfoundation.com

International Public Relations Association
1 Dunley Hill Court, Ranmore Common, Dorking, Surrey RH5 6SX
01483 280130; www.ipra.org

PUBLISHER/ COMMISSIONING EDITOR

What the work involves

- Publishers/commissioning editors plan and manage ranges or lists of books, magazines or ICT resources produced by their department or company. This could include researching consumers' needs and identifying gaps in the company's list of publications.

- You will develop ideas for new publications and respond to proposals from authors. You will also oversee the entire process of developing new publications from an original idea to completed manuscript.

- You may also be responsible for developing marketing strategies to increase publication sales.

The type of person suited to this work

You will need a strong interest in producing books and publications that have extensive commercial appeal.

As you will liaise closely with authors and colleagues, you should enjoy meeting and working with a variety of people. You will also need strong written and verbal communication skills and the ability to encourage people to complete tasks to deadlines. You must be well organised and able to plan ahead.

Working conditions

Most of your work will involve attending meetings or working at a computer within the office of a company or organisation.

You will be expected to liaise with authors, colleagues, designers, ICT specialists and printers either face to face, by email or on the phone.

Although your working week will comprise normal office hours, you can expect to work late at times in order to meet strict publication deadlines or to attend evening events. Business trips, including overnight stays, are a possibility and you could travel abroad.

Future prospects

This is a competitive profession to enter. The main employers are publishing houses, specialist business, professional and educational companies.

Sales and marketing experience can facilitate entrance to this sector. It is possible to set up your own publishing company, although the market is well covered and profit margins narrow.

Currently, the area of greatest expansion is that offered by the internet and digital publishing.

Advantages/disadvantages

You will meet and work with an interesting cross-section of people.

You will be responsible for creating strategies to increase sales of publications, which can be stressful.

Developing new publications can be a lengthy process and requires patience.

Qualifications and courses

The majority of new entrants have gained a degree. You will need at least 2 A levels and 5 GCSEs (A*–C) for degree entry. The Diploma in Creative and Media might be helpful.

A relevant postgraduate qualification, such as an MA or MSc in Publishing is not essential but is advantageous given the competition for places. A 2.1 or higher degree is needed for entry

As this is a senior role, it is unlikely that a new graduate would start as a publisher/commissioning editor. Most entrants begin as an editorial assistant before being promoted to an editor position and then going on to secure a publisher/commissioning editor role.

Specialist training centres such as the Publishing Training Centre provide short courses on different areas of publishing and organisations such as Women in Publishing can provide support to women entering the field.

Entry into the industry is highly competitive and it is important to learn as much as possible about publishing from trade magazines or people in the industry before applying. Experience of writing or editing at a non-professional level can be useful.

Entry into the industry is highly competitive and it is important to learn as much as possible about publishing from trade magazines or people in the industry before applying. Experience of writing or editing at a non-professional level can be useful.

Money guide

Salaries can vary depending on the size and type of employer. Commission and productivity bonuses can be paid, so the more books that are sold, the higher potential earnings can be. Starting salaries in editorial roles can be around £18,000–£28,000 per year (depending on the role). With experience you could earn up to £35,000.

Senior managers and directors of a large publishing company can earn between £48,000 and £80,000.

Related opportunities

- Copy Editor/Sub-editor/Proofreader p409
- Copywriter p410
- Literary Agent p406
- Newspaper/Magazine Editor p417

Further information

Publishers Association
29b Montague Street, London WC1B 5BW
020 7691 9191; www.publishers.org.uk

Publishing Training Centre at Book House
45 East Hill, London SW18 2QZ
020 8874 2718; www.train4publishing.co.uk

Marketing, Advertising, Media, Print and Publishing

CRCI: PD

RECORDING INDUSTRY PRODUCER

What the work involves

■ Recording industry producers are employed by the Artists and Repertoire (A&R) department of a recording company to work with artists to produce successful music tracks or demos.

■ You will discuss ideas with artists and their management, plan new projects, listen to existing tracks and identify areas for improvement.

■ You will be involved in the organisation of each stage of the recording process, including rehearsal time, recruitment of sound engineers, booking studio time, directing the artists, and suggesting alterations that will produce the desired sound.

The type of person suited to this work

You must have excellent communication skills to give instructions to others, persuade people to try your ideas and to build up a good network of contacts.

As you will have to spend long hours in the studio you should have a good ear for music, high stamina, self discipline and patience.

You should also have good planning skills to work out budgets, organise time scales for recording studios and estimate production and post-production costs.

Working conditions

You will work long, irregular hours. This may include working late into the night and at the weekends. Your work may not always be constant and you might have to find other methods of earning money.

You may have to travel within the UK and abroad.

Future prospects

You will probably progress to a production position after several years of working in assistant sound engineer and engineer roles.

At first, you will approach A&R departments with your services until you establish your reputation, usually by producing music that is commercially successful.

Advantages/disadvantages

You may have the opportunity to work with a diverse range of artists and to be a part of the creative process of making music.

Prolonged exposure to loud music may damage your hearing.

Money guide

You can expect a starting salary of around £15,000 per year. With experience and constant work you can earn from £30,000 a year. The top recording industry producers can earn over £100,000 and considerably more.

Qualifications and courses

There are no specific qualifications, although formal music training of some kind is recommended. Work experience and voluntary work for a studio and record companies are vital.

Courses that may help you develop skills and experience include Foundation degrees and degrees in music production, music technology, music practice and music industry management, the BTEC National Diploma in Music Technology, Level 3, or the HNC/HND in Music Production, Level 5 or the Diploma in Creative and Media.

You will need at least 2 A levels and 5 GCSEs (A*–C) for degree entry.

Short music courses are available for young professionals beginning in the music industry such as the BPI seminar, 'Music, It's the Business'.

The Music Producers' Guild (MPG) have created a Knowledge Band and Members' Directory to encourage debate and facilitate future recording industry producers' networking within the industry. The MPG, in association with the Association of Professional Recording Services (APRS), has set up the Joint Audio Media Education Services (JAMES) to allow new entrants to learn from experienced professionals.

You may be paid 'on spec' if you work with an unsigned band. This means that you will be paid if and when the artist is successful.

Usually you will be paid a flat fee, but this will also include an agreed percentage of the sales income. This can be minimal or thousands of pounds.

Related opportunities

■ DJ p442
■ Sound Engineer p450

Further information

BPI British Recorded Music Industry
Riverside Building, County Hall, Westminster Bridge Road, London SE1 7JA
020 7803 1300; www.bpi.co.uk

Music Producers Guild UK Ltd
PO Box 38134, London W10 6XL
020 3239 7606; www.mpg.org.uk

RESEARCHER (MEDIA)

What the work involves

- Researchers develop TV and radio programmes and documentary films by gathering and checking information on specific subjects, people or places.

- You will use the internet and phone, conduct face-to-face interviews and visit different locations to do your research.

- It will be your job to research guests and programme contributors as well as to find relevant images, film clips and music. You could also write and edit programme scripts.

- You will brief the production team on the specific subjects covered by your research in preparation for filming.

The type of person suited to this work

The ability to find accurate, relevant information quickly is central to this role. You will need to be creative and resourceful in order to find the best story angles possible. A flexible approach will help you balance varied tasks and unsociable hours.

You should be persistent, confident and an excellent communicator. You will work to strict deadlines and must be able to stay calm under pressure. Organisational skills are also important. As you will be responsible for gaining permission to access and make use of information, you will need a clear understanding of the law.

The ability to network and build good relationships with contacts is essential.

Working conditions

You will be based in offices or studios to undertake desk research. You will also spend time on research trips to locations in the UK or overseas.

The work usually needs to be completed to strict deadlines which can create a pressured, but fast-moving and interesting working environment.

It is likely that you would have to work at weekends and in the evenings on a regular basis.

Future prospects

Whilst this is a competitive area to get into, researchers are employed in many areas of the media including radio, production companies, TV and film companies. Although the number of roles in terrestrial TV companies has dropped, jobs in the smaller cable and satellite sector are on the rise.

Qualifications and courses

Those with degrees and HNDs are preferred, and subjects such as legal studies, history, journalism and media studies are useful. Relevant work experience and evidence of research skills can be accepted in some cases. The Diploma in Creative and Media could also be helpful.

Work experience is very important. ICT skills and a driving licence are essential.

Many researchers have experience in other areas of the industry or in journalism. A good knowledge of current affairs and media practice can be an advantage.

With experience, you could progress into a role as an assistant producer and then on to working as a producer/programme director.

Many researchers work freelance, getting paid on a contract-by-contract basis.

Some specialise in areas such as documentaries on wildlife, architecture, social history and travel, whilst others concentrate on picture research.

Advantages/disadvantages

You will have to work long and often unsocial hours, which can affect your personal life.

This is a varied job in a fast-moving industry. You could get the opportunity to travel to a range of places.

Money guide

Starting salaries are around £19,000 per year. This may rise to £23,000 with experience. Freelance researchers earn around £650 a week, depending on experience and the employer.

Related opportunities

- Historian p352
- Journalist p412
- Market Research Executive p413
- Archivist/Records Manager p346

Further information

Skillset
Focus Point, 21 Caledonian Road, London N1 9GB
020 7713 9800;www.skillset.org

TRC media
227 West George Street, Glasgow G2 2ND
0141 568 7113; www.trcmedia.org/trcmedia

Marketing, Advertising, Media, Print and Publishing

CRCI: PA

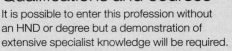

TECHNICAL AUTHOR/ MEDICAL WRITER

What the work involves

- Technical authors/medical writers interpret technical information and communicate it in written language which the intended audience can understand.

- You will create content, commission images, organise and design the layout of the document.

- Technical authors work in various sectors from medicine and defence to business and finance.

- You should be an expert in your specialist sector, but your audience may be novices as well as specialists. For example you may write mass market instructions for a mobile phone, or a medical writer may create a report on clinical trial results for the medical community.

The type of person suited to this work

It is essential to have an excellent command of English and the ability to write concisely and convincingly, with your audience in mind. You should also be detail driven and have a good eye for design.

Having a passion for your specialist sector and an inquiring mind is a necessity. The ability to solve problems, multi-task and to work to deadlines is also important.

Good communication and team working skills are required as you will have to work closely with technical colleagues, such as doctors, as well as liaising with suppliers including printers and translators.

Working conditions

The majority of work will take place at a computer within normal office hours. However supplementary hours may be required in order to meet tight deadlines, and you might have to travel to meet clients.

Having gained experience, many people decide to start up their own business or go freelance, especially as the pay is more attractive.

Future prospects

At present there are 5,000–10,000 technical authors working in the UK in a variety of sectors. There are jobs all over the nation, but more in England than elsewhere. In addition more positions are available in technological clusters e.g. defence in the South West.

It is helpful to establish a network of useful contacts, and mature entry is common as being an expert in your chosen sector is a necessity.

Advantages/disadvantages

This type of work can provide the satisfaction of seeing your completed work in print and sometimes in the public domain.

This profession is likely to be particularly sensitive to the effects of the recession as many technical authors may lose their positions to developers.

Qualifications and courses

It is possible to enter this profession without an HND or degree but a demonstration of extensive specialist knowledge will be required.

Many entrants have a degree or qualification in English, journalism or media studies. Others have qualifications in the area that they wish to specialise in, for example engineering or computer science. Minimum degree entry requirements are usually 2 A levels and 5 GCSEs (A*–C)

Coventry University offers a BA Honours degree in Communication, Culture and Media with an incorporated work placement. In addition the University of Portsmouth offers an MA in Technical Communications which is useful for graduates in science and technology who wish to improve their writing skills. The Institute of Scientific and Technical Communications (ISTC) provides a further list of approved specialist courses.

It is common for mature adults to enter this profession as it necessitates expert knowledge. There is the possibility to study for an open-learning course in Communication of Technical Information at the ISTC, which may be beneficial for mature entrants.

Money guide

Earnings vary widely depending on the technical writer's specialist sector and the size of the employer. However software and telecommunications currently offer particularly attractive salaries.

New entrants can expect to earn about £18,000 per year; with experience this can rise to £30,000.

Top earners in senior roles with extensive experience can amass £50,000+ per year.

Related opportunities

- Copy Editor/Sub-editor/Proofreader p409
- Copywriter p410
- Journalist p412
- Publisher/Commissioning Editor p423

Further information

British Association of Communicators in Business
Suite GA2, Oak House, Woodlands Business Park, Linford Wood, Milton Keynes MK14 6EY
01908 313755; www.cib.uk.com

Institute of Scientific and Technical Communicators (ISTC)
Airport House, Purley Way, Croydon CR0 0X2
020 8253 4506; www.istc.org.uk

E-Skills UK
1 Castle Lane, London SW1E 6DR
020 7963 8920; www.e-skills.com/careers

Industry profile

**LONDON SCHOOL OF
FILM, MEDIA & PERFORMANCE**

CREATIVE AND ENTERTAINMENT INDUSTRIES

New Talent in Constant Demand

Sector growth

Even before the Government's publication of its 2008 document 'Creative Britain: New Talents for a New Economy', the popularity, influence and employment opportunities of the global creative media industries could not be denied. In the UK this sector employs over two million people and contributes 7.3% to Gross Domestic Product.

Leaps forward in digital video, on-demand TV, streaming video and the internet have seen the creative and entertainment industries expanding twice as fast as the rest of the UK economy; recent predictions indicate that it will soon contribute 10% to the national economy.

Globally the picture is equally strong: according to the World Bank, the global creative industries account for more than 7% of the world's economy and are growing by 10% per year.

Contrary to current employment trends, this sector continues to develop and recruit. Its rapid and continuing growth represents huge opportunities for well educated, creative and market-responsive graduates who are in tune with consumer demands.

Indeed, as technological developments continue to integrate entertainment and the media ever more seamlessly into our lives, the demand for high quality content has never been greater. New talent is in constant demand to create high quality, engaging content for viewers to experience across both traditional and newly developing platforms.

British contribution to film and television

Throughout the history of the screen as a cultural and commercial artistic pursuit, British film and television have been recognised worldwide for their record of continued excellence. In quality and cultural influence the UK has always been and continues to be widely respected as exhibiting the highest standards of creativity, discernment, commercial wisdom and, perhaps most tellingly of all, originality.

The topical relevance of these qualities and the growing successes at international awards ceremonies are further testament to these claims. Indeed, the UK is now the world's second-biggest exporter of television programmes. In film also it stands second, with 16% of US sales and 20% of European. UK cinema box office sales for 2008 were the highest since records began.

London — a Creative Hub

London is not only recognised as a creative and cultural hub but is at the heart of the world's fastest-developing general media and specific screen disciplines. Ideas, projects and products that have gone around the world have had their beginnings in this city, often in quite insignificant and unpromising circumstances.

In visual and performance art London has a worldwide reputation which is second to none, and students have access to opportunities which they could never have elsewhere with the same quality of provision and experience.

How to get Ahead

A weakness of many graduates with degrees in media and the creative industries is a lack of understanding of the business of the media, and how their own creative work will be commissioned, developed and marketed. It's important to consider this when choosing a course; a programme that includes professional skills and industry placements will give you the head start you need.

By David Hanson,
Head of London School of Film Media & Performance

TV, FILM AND RADIO DIRECTOR

What the work involves

- Directors manage the process of creating films, radio and TV programmes. This involves both commissioning each project and overseeing the work and schedules of the entire production team.

- You will define the presentation and style of films and productions by making decisions about content, scripting, camera work, editing and acting.

- You will also be required to handle any problems with presenters, actors or production staff, as well as editing the final 'cut' of the show you have directed.

The type of person suited to this work

Working in these competitive sectors can be very demanding and stressful. You should be confident and able to react quickly and calmly to any crises that may arise.

Good verbal communication, interpersonal and team working skills are important, especially as on some jobs you could be away from home on location for weeks at a time. In addition you should have good organisational skills to ensure that projects are carried out on time and within budget.

Working conditions

A good level of physical stamina and fitness is required as this job involves lengthy days spent standing up and carrying, lifting and assembling heavy equipment.

In TV and film you will work on set and on location and will have to cope with changeable outdoor conditions. You will also be expected to be flexible and work at night and at weekends, both during and post-production.

Future prospects

In the UK there are around 110,000 people working in TV and radio, many of whom are freelancers.

Recent financial unrest has resulted in a slow-down in the TV industry with fewer new productions scheduled. The British film industry is coping well, but obtaining finance backing to develop larger productions will get harder.

Entry to the industry is very competitive and excellent technical skills are expected from all applicants.

Advantages/disadvantages

This type of work provides the satisfaction of seeing the results of your work in the public sphere. This is a fast-moving and varied industry with exciting opportunities.

Increasingly, directors are employed on a freelance or short-term contract basis which can lead to job instability.

Contrary to popular belief, this is not glamorous work!

Qualifications and courses

There are no specific entry requirements, but most entrants have a drama, media-related degree or postgraduate qualification.

You could take media, film and television studies at GCSE, BTEC National Diploma, A level, HND, degree and postgraduate level. On the Skillset website you can find their network of Screen Academies and Media Academies providing details of institutions offering the highest quality of film and television studies.

Entry requirements are usually 2 A levels and 5 GCSEs (A*–C) for degree level. For an HND, you should have an A level in an art and design related subject.

Practical work experience is essential and most budding directors create a 'showreel' of self-funded projects to promote their work.

Some organisations, like BBC Talent, offer work experience upon submission of new ideas, which can often lead to full-time employment.

Specialist postgraduate courses in directing are offered at the National Film and Television School. You will need a 'showreel' of work for entry.

Funding and training courses are available from organisations like the UK Film Council.

Money guide

Earnings in this sector vary greatly according to media, location, employer and project. New entrants can expect to earn about £20,000 per year. This may rise to £40,000 with experience. The most successful directors can earn anything up to £200,000.

Many directors are employed on a freelance or contract basis. Rates vary between roles and media area, but are usually paid on a daily basis.

Related opportunities

- Artistic Director p436
- Production Assistant/Runner (TV, Film and Radio) p421
- TV, Film and Radio Producer p430

Further information

BBC Recruitment HR Direct
PO Box 1133, Belfast BT1 9GP
www.bbc.co.uk/jobs

Skillset
Focus Point, 21 Caledonian Road, London N1 9GB
020 7713 9800; www.skillset.org

TV, FILM AND RADIO EDITOR

What the work involves

- Editors play a key role in the post-production process by assembling the final product from captured footage and additional sound and graphics. They are also responsible for storing the footage.

- You will fulfil a brief and liaise closely with the director.

- You will create the flow and pace of a production by using specialist ICT editing equipment to put shots together in a smooth sequence.

- You will ensure the continuity and order of these productions, which may include TV and radio programmes, films, music and corporate videos, and advertisements.

The type of person suited to this work

It is essential to be creative and to have a passion for your chosen medium. You should have a high attention to detail, an inordinate amount of patience and the ability to identify good storytelling techniques.

You will be expected to be well-versed in the latest technological advances in the field, as well as possessing advanced IT skills and the willingness to try new techniques.

Working conditions

In this profession hours vary depending on workload but are typically 9am–5pm, from Monday to Friday. However it should be noted that your personal life may be affected by long and unpredictable hours, which are common in order to meet tight deadlines.

The majority of the work takes place at a computer in an editing suite, and may be carried out alone or with a director. Larger projects may require the assistance of a sound effects editor, music editor as well as assistant editors.

Future prospects

At present there are about 11,000 people working in post-production roles in the UK. This profession is fast-paced and there is fierce competition for entry level positions.

The majority of roles are based in London in post-production companies, independent production firms, broadcasters, and companies in the film and computer software sectors.

Having gained experience, many editors choose to go freelance. This involves working on several projects simultaneously and balancing bursts of assignments with quiet periods of inactivity.

Advantages/disadvantages

This type of work provides the satisfaction of seeing the results of your work in the public domain.

Qualifications and courses

There are no specific entry requirements, but as competition is fierce, many entrants are graduates or hold postgraduate qualifications. Relevant subjects include film, IT, media studies and visual art. You will need 2 A levels and 5 GCSEs (A*–C) for degree entry. The Diploma in Creative and Media might be useful.

It is common to start out as a runner or editing assistant. Practical work experience is essential and you will need a 'showreel' to promote your work.

When choosing a course you should make sure it uses the most advanced equipment, offers work placements and will help you to gain contacts. Skillset, and The British Film Institute list relevant courses and opportunities on their websites.

Entry-level training courses are offered by the BBC as well as independent organisations like FT2, Cyfle, Production Guild, Scottish Screen and Screen Yorkshire.

It is possible to take an NVQ in Electronic and Film Post-Production Editing at Level 2 and Editing at Levels 3 and 4.

This is a fast-moving and varied industry with exciting opportunities.

Increasingly, editors are employed on a freelance or short-term contract basis which can lead to job instability.

Money guide

Earnings in this sector vary greatly according to employer and project. New entrants can expect to earn £15,000–£25,000, rising to £30,000 with experience. The most experienced editors can earn up to £70,000.

The majority of editors are employed on a freelance or contract basis. The Broadcasting Entertainment Cinematographic and Theatrical Union (BECTU) provide a benchmark for current rates.

Related opportunities

- Camera Person (TV/Film Camera Opetrator) p408
- Researcher (Media) p425
- Special Effects Technician p451

Further information

Broadcasting Entertainment Cinematograph and Theatre Union
373–377 Clapham Road, London SW9 9BT
020 7346 0900; www.bectu.org.uk

Skillset
Focus Point, 21 Caledonian Road, London N1 9GB
020 7713 9800; www.skillset.org

Marketing, Advertising, Media, Print and Publishing

CRCI: PA

TV, FILM AND RADIO PRODUCER

What the work involves

- A producer originates ideas, employs pivotal team members, has creative input, gets involved in casting decisions and script editing, and generally oversees the complete production.

- You will be the lead person in TV, film and radio production. They all have a detailed knowledge of the industry, coupled with sound business skills.

- Many producers also play a financial role, approaching initial backers, securing rights and managing the budget throughout production.

- You may also be expected to oversee the final editing process, as well as marketing and distribution plans.

The type of person suited to this work

It is essential to have a strong creative flair and a passion for your chosen medium. A well-rounded knowledge of your sector, spanning technical, creative and commercial aspects is also required.

Excellent communication skills are important and you should have the ability to provide inspiration and motivation for team members. An enjoyment of problem-solving and the ability to work well under pressure will be helpful.

You should also have a good head for figures, and solid negotiation, multi-tasking and organisational skills to ensure that projects are carried out on time, within budget and as requested.

Working conditions

Producers work in a variety of environments including offices, studios and external filming locations.

This role requires a great deal of flexibility, as during production hours can be long and erratic, and travel is often required to assess venues and attend meetings.

Future prospects

At present there are 18,000 TV and film producers in the UK and vacancies tend to be centred in major cities such as London, Manchester and Glasgow.

The main employers are well-known broadcasters such as the BBC, TV and film production firms and production and facilities houses.

Entry to the industry is very competitive and establishing good contacts is essential as many jobs are never advertised and awarded based on the reputation of the producer.

Advantages/disadvantages

This type of work provides the satisfaction of seeing the results of your work in the public domain.

Qualifications and courses

There are no specific entry requirements, but producers need extensive industry experience. Most will have worked their way up the ladder starting out as runners, broadcast assistants or journalists, providing contacts, a well-rounded view of the industry and invaluable knowledge.

Many entrants hold a foundation degree, honours degree or an HND. Useful subjects include film production, communications, broadcasting and drama. You will need at least 1 A level and 4 GCSEs (A*–C) for entry to a Foundation degree or HND and 2 A levels and 5 GCSEs (A*–C) for a degree.

The Diploma in Creative and Media may also be helpful. Skillset and the British Film Institute list courses in producing for film and television.

If you are a radio producer working on news and current affairs shows you will need to have journalistic training. The Broadcast Journalism Training Council can provide more information.

This is a fast-moving and varied industry which can provide exciting opportunities.

Increasingly, producers are employed on a freelance or short-term contract basis which can lead to job instability.

Although you will work with many celebrities, this is not glamorous work.

Money guide

Earnings in this sector vary greatly according to media, role, employer and project.

New entrants can expect to earn between £15,000 and £25,000 per year, rising to £30,000 with experience. The most experienced producers can earn up to £70,000.

Almost half of producers in the industry are freelancers and can earn from £900 to £1300 a week for a 16-week slot.

Related opportunities

- Camera Person (TV/Film Camera Operator) p408
- Production Assistant/Runner (TV, Film and Radio) p421
- TV Floor Manager/Film Assistant Director p432
- Researcher (Media) p425

Further information

BBC Recruitment HR Direct
PO Box 1133, Belfast BT1 9GP
www.bbc.co.uk/jobs

UK Film Council
10 Little Portland Street, London W1W 7JG
020 7861 7861; www.ukfilmcouncil.org.uk

LONDON SCHOOL OF FILM, MEDIA & PERFORMANCE

The London School of Film, Media & Performance is part of Regent's College London, the largest College of private Higher Education in the UK.

LSFMP is ideally situated to provide invaluable practical, hands-on work placements at TV, film and theatre production companies in the heart of London's media-land. With the support of academic staff – media industry practitioners and recognised specialists in creative production – you will develop your skills, make valuable industry connections and enhance your employability.

Our programmes will undoubtedly foster your creative development, but will also ensure that you gain the necessary business skills to succeed in these fast-paced industries. With your unique combination of creativity and business acumen, you will be well placed to produce and market your creative product, liaising and negotiating with a diverse range of individuals across the creative and media sectors.

London is vibrant and dynamic; it is one of the world's great entertainment and creative industry hubs. It's an inspiring place to live and to study. LSFMP is only minutes away from Soho, the West End and live music hotspot Camden, allowing you to get involved in all that London has to offer.

We offer the following courses in the Creative and Media Industries:

■ BA (Hons) Creative Industries (3 years)
■ BA (Hons) Screenwriting & Producing (3 years)
■ BA (Hons) Film, TV & Digital Media Production (3 years – NEW for September 2011 – contact us for details)

BA (Hons) Creative Industries

Our 3-year BA (Hons) Creative Industries degree will develop transferable producing skills which can be applied across the creative media sector. It will also educate you in the mechanics and practices of the creative industries – allowing you to work in both creative and decision-making management roles.

You will learn the basic functions and structures of businesses and the global environment, as well as the effects of politics, economics, the law, social and environmental factors on the media industry arena. You will learn about managing artists in the industry, and will study the media and the law.

BA (Hons) Screenwriting & Producing

The script is the cornerstone of television and film production – from the point of conception through to the realisation of the final work, the script forms the spine, structure and design of the final creative project, and all production ideas, decisions and executions emanate from it.

The 3-year BA (Hons) Screenwriting & Producing degree will help you to become part of the next generation of writers and producers for the screen. You will develop key skills which are essential for the career success of a writer or producer, learning not only how to write effectively but also gaining insight into the commercial and production side of the screen industry.

Both degrees offer industry placements and the option to study abroad.

For more information on creative and media courses at the London School of Film, Media & Performance, scholarships and how to apply, please contact:

LSFMP@regents.ac.uk
REGENTS.AC.UK/LSFMP
Tel: +44 (0)207 487 7505

TV FLOOR MANAGER/ FILM ASSISTANT DIRECTOR

What the work involves

- TV floor managers/film assistant directors are responsible for the coordination of many aspects of the filming process.

- You will ensure that all sets, props and technical equipment are working, in place and set up correctly.

- In situations where the director is away from the set (in the gallery or a broadcast vehicle) you will wear headphones to relay instructions from the director to the crew, actors or audience members.

- You will make sure that everyone involved in the production process knows what to do so that everything runs according to schedule.

The type of person suited to this work

You must be passionate about the media industry, TV and film production in particular.

You should be very organised and able to work under pressure and to a tight schedule.

As you will be working with a variety of people from directors to the most junior crew members, you will need to have good communication skills to create an efficient working environment.

You must have an understanding of the technical and creative aspects of production to ensure that you can deal with problems encountered during the filming or recording stage.

Working conditions

Hours are likely to be long and irregular, including early starts, late nights and weekend work. If you work on feature films, 6 day weeks are common.

You will probably work on a freelance basis, which may involve periods of unemployment between jobs.

You will spend most of your time at work on your feet.

You may have to work outdoors in all weather conditions.

You may have to travel within the UK or abroad, at short notice for varying periods of time.

Future prospects

You may find opportunities to move up to positions as first director and eventually producer or director.

You may also find that you move across into other aspects of the industry such as production or broadcasting.

As you will be working on a freelance basis most of the time you will depend on having a good portfolio of work behind you, having an excellent reputation and making good contacts within the industry to guarantee work.

Qualifications and courses

There are no set academic qualifications. It might be useful to have GCSEs (A*–C) and A levels in subjects such as maths, English, languages or theatre and drama studies. The Diploma in Creative and Media might be helpful.

Degrees or HNDs in relevant subjects such as media studies, drama, photography, film and television will give you an advantage as competition is fierce. You will need 2 A levels and 5 GCSEs (A*–C) for degree entry.

Other qualifications that may help include the BTEC First Diploma or National Certificates in Media and Media Production, City & Guilds Level 3 Diploma in Media Techniques.

Screen Academies and Media Academies, run by Skillset, offer film and television training which will include working towards vocational qualifications. BBC and Channel 4 run similar schemes. See websites for further information.

The most essential requirement is to gain practical work experience. You will probably start as a runner, production assistant, or in a technical role. Employers will seek candidates with a proven commitment to the job and the industry.

Advantages/disadvantages

Your work may involve a diverse range of projects including creative, practical and technical tasks.

You working hours may be long, stressful and unsociable.

Money guide

Your starting salary, in a junior role such as third assistant director, may be around £16,000 a year. As you are promoted to positions as second assistant director you can earn around £25,000 and with experience this can rise to £29,000 a year. First assistant directors can earn in the region of £35,000.

Related opportunities

- Camera Person (TV/Film Camera Operator) p408
- Production Assistant/Runner (TV, Film and Radio) p421
- TV, Film and Radio Director p428

Further information

National Film and Television School
Beaconsfield Studios, Station Road,
Beaconsfield HP9 1LG
01494 671234; info@nfts.co.uk; www.nftsfilm-tv.ac.uk/

Skillset
Focus Point, 21 Caledonian Road, London N1 9GB
0808 300 900; info@skillset.org; www.skillset.org

Interested in a career as a
physiotherapist?

If you...

- like a challenge
- enjoy working with people
- get a buzz from seeing results
- want to promote good health
- have an interest in the sciences
- would like a professional qualification
- and fancy an exciting and varied career for a lifetime

...physiotherapy could be for you

Find out more at www.csp.org.uk/careers
or call 020 7306 6666 for a careers leaflet

THE CHARTERED SOCIETY OF PHYSIOTHERAPY
14 Bedford Row, London WC1R 4ED
www.csp.org.uk

INVESTOR IN PEOPLE

POSITIVE ABOUT DISABLED PEOPLE

Step up, Step forward

For a career in podiatry

If you are looking for a flexible and rewarding career with great earnings potential, step this way.

- 87% graduate employment rate
- Earnings up to £100k plus
- Tuition fees paid for UK & EU students
- NHS bursaries available
- HPC approved courses

www.feetforlife.org

The Society of Chiropodists and Podiatrists
1 Fellmongers Path, Tower Bridge Road, London SE1 3LY

The Society of
Chiropodists and
Podiatrists

LONDON SCHOOL OF
FILM, MEDIA & PERFORMANCE

EXPLORE YOUR CREATIVITY

WITH THE LONDON SCHOOL OF FILM, MEDIA & PERFORMANCE

BA (HONS) CREATIVE INDUSTRIES 3 YEARS

Gain the broad training needed to work at any level in the creative industries, across both creative and decision-making management roles. Includes Industry Skills module, and Industry Placement.

BA (HONS) SCREENWRITING & PRODUCING 3 YEARS

Become part of the next generation of writers and producers for the screen; this degree opens doors to both sides of the film and television industry. Includes Development of a Major Script Project and Industry Placement.

SEPTEMBER ENTRY

SCHOLARSHIPS AVAILABLE / APPLY TODAY
REGENTS.AC.UK/LSFMP

LONDON SCHOOL OF FILM, MEDIA & PERFORMANCE

REGENT'S COLLEGE
Inner Circle, Regent's Park, London, NW1 4NS, UK

T +44 (0) 20 7487 7505
F +44 (0) 20 7487 7425
E lsfmp@regents.ac.uk
W www.regents.ac.uk/lsfmp

LONDON SCHOOL OF FILM, MEDIA & PERFORMANCE

ACT ON AMBITION

WITH THE LONDON SCHOOL OF FILM, MEDIA & PERFORMANCE

ACTING FOUNDATION COURSE 1 YEAR

Gain the skills to audition for drama school or undertake university-level study; this intensive course includes voice & movement and improvisation classes. Includes Mock Audition Workshop with a professional director.

JANUARY AND SEPTEMBER ENTRY

BA (HONS) ACTING & GLOBAL THEATRE 3 YEARS

Develop your acting skills and undertake a challenging study of world theatre cultures. Includes exciting study period abroad.

SEPTEMBER ENTRY

SCHOLARSHIPS AVAILABLE / APPLY TODAY
REGENTS.AC.UK/LSFMP

LONDON SCHOOL OF FILM, MEDIA & PERFORMANCE

REGENT'S COLLEGE

Inner Circle, Regent's Park, London, NW1 4NS, UK

T   +44 (0) 20 7487 7505
F   +44 (0) 20 7487 7425
E   lsfmp@regents.ac.uk
W www.regents.ac.uk/lsfmp

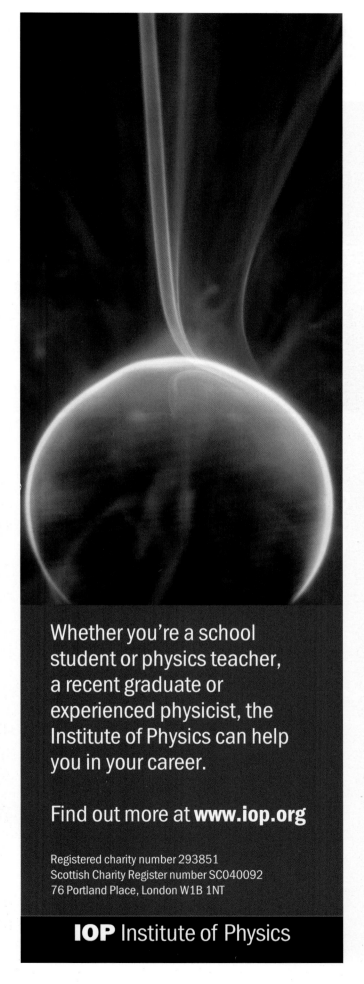

CareersInPassengerTransport.org

Get careers moving with
CareersInPassengerTransport.org

Find out about
- the types of jobs available in passenger transport
- the people who work in the sector
- potential career development and progression

Developed by *GoSkills*, the sector skills council for passenger transport, *www.CareersInPassengerTransport.org* provides the latest information on working in the sector, including an in-depth suite of job profiles and access to a range of case studies. The site will enable you to see the wide variety of roles and opportunities offered by this interesting and diverse sector.

GoSkills

Moving skills forward

Tableware for a restaurant chain

Beer pumps for pubs

X-ray equipment for hospitals

Knickers for a high street store

PR for a global brand

Cans for a fizzy drinks company

Shirts for supporters of a Premier League team

Steering wheels for sports cars

Whatever an organisation spends money on, there's always someone who has to ensure that it's getting best value – that could be you.

THE CHARTERED INSTITUTE OF PURCHASING & SUPPLY®

A CAREER IN PURCHASING & SUPPLY MANAGEMENT IT MAKES YOU THINK.

www.cips.org

Providing a **rewarding** and **adventurous** lifestyle in the **Merchant Navy**

SSTG are looking for aspiring candidates to train as Deck or Engineering Officers working onboard hi-tech modern ships. We are recruiting for more than 30 shipping companies, operating in excess of 300 vessels, so there is plenty of choice.

Various Entry Routes Available:
HNC/HND: requires 4 GCSEs/Standard Grades
Foundation Degree/Hons: requires A Levels/Highers

Sponsorship Package Includes:
* **Course Tuition Fees**
* **Generous Training Allowance**
* **Accommodation Allowance**
* **Travel Costs**

Leave College Debt Free!

Once Qualified Take Advantage of:
* **Unbeatable Travel Opportunities**
* **Generous Leave**
* **Responsibility at Early Age**
* **Great Salary and Career Prospects**

To find out more, contact us

Email: **recruitment@sstg.org**
Tel: **01634 820820**
Fax: **01634 820821**

Ship Safe Training Group Ltd
The Precinct Office, The Precinct, Rochester, Kent, ME1 1SR

Ship Safe Training Group Ltd.
taking you further!
www.sstg.org

Apply online at **www.sstg.org**

Performing Arts

This job family contains a wide range of exciting jobs for those of you who want to work in theatre, music, on screen or behind the scenes. People working in this sector do so because they are passionate and creative and love the Arts. Jobs can be scarce, so you will need to demonstrate that you are willing to work very hard but the rewards of being part of a fantastic production can be huge. There are also jobs available in this sector for those of you who are more technically minded – sound and lighting engineers also play a vital role in this industry as do people who have trained in fashion and textiles.

In this section we look at the following jobs:

ACTOR/ACTRESS

What the work involves

- Actors/actresses perform in front of audiences and this can sometimes include dancing and singing as part of the role.
- There are opportunities for parts in dramatic plays, comedies and musicals on stage as well as on TV and in films.
- You will research your characters, rehearse lines and attend auditions.
- You will also attend costume fittings and make-up sessions.

The type of person suited to this work

Acting is a very competitive area so you should be truly dedicated to this career path. A good memory and level of fitness is important as you will have to learn lines and deal with long hours.

There will be many times when you will be rejected at auditions mainly because you are just not the right face for the part, and so you will need to be able to cope with this and keep trying. Adaptability, self-confidence and creativity are essential.

Working conditions

You will work mainly indoors, in theatres, halls and sometimes studios.

Your hours will be long and irregular, including evenings and weekends.

You could have to travel to different venues for your performances where you might spend time waiting for your part in the performance.

Future prospects

Prospects for success as an actor depend on talent, hard work and a bit of luck.

Some actors go on to work as writers or directors, while others train to teach drama in schools and colleges.

Advantages/disadvantages

The long travelling hours to get to performance venues and then waiting to perform could be boring.

It is a tough, demanding career to enter and to stay in, but once you get regular work it can be very satisfying.

Money guide

Basic rates of pay depend on experience and reputation. Only 6% of actors receive more than £30,000. A lot of actors have second jobs to raise their income.

An actor working in a London West End theatre could expect at least £500 a week while actors in other theatres earn a minimum of £350 a week. Continuous employment is unusual.

Qualifications and courses

Although there are no specific requirements to enter this profession, it is very competitive and almost all actors have some formal training.

The National Council for Drama Training (NCDT) and the Conference of Drama Schools accredits full-time 3 year vocational drama school courses and degrees. Graduates of NCDT-accredited courses who are legally entitled to work in the UK are eligible for Equity membership. Part-time courses and more academic degrees in, for example, drama or theatre studies, are not accredited. Entry is by audition, and A levels or a BTEC National Diploma in Performing Arts are often required.

You can do a degree in acting (or a related subject like drama or performing arts). Acting degrees are offered by drama schools and by universities. Further study, such as an MA or Postgraduate Diploma in acting, is also available. Another option is the Diploma in Creative and Media.

However, experience in the industry is more beneficial than qualifications. It can be helpful to join a local amateur dramatics group and undertake relevant work experience.

As you become recognised as an actor, your income could be much more than this, but it may take many years.

It is important to join Equity, the union for the world of entertainment – as this can help you negotiate fair rates of pay, terms and conditions. Union-negotiated pay scales are on the Equity website.

Related opportunities

- Dancer p440
- Artistic Director p436
- Entertainer p443
- Stage Manager p452

Further information

National Council for Drama Training
249 Tooley Street, London SE1 2JX
020 7407 3686; www.ncdt.co.uk

Creative & Cultural Skills
Lafone House, The Leathermarket, Weston St, London SE1 3HN
020 7015 1800; www.ccskills.org.uk

Equity
Guild House, Upper St Martin's Lane, London WC2H 9EG
020 7379 6000; www.equity.org.uk

Royal Academy of Dramatic Art
62–64 Gower Street, London WC1E 6ED
020 7636 7076; enquiries@rada.ac.uk

LONDON SCHOOL OF FILM, MEDIA & PERFORMANCE

The London School of Film, Media & Performance is part of Regent's College London, the largest College of private Higher Education in the UK. We are a new, vibrant School led by media industry practitioners, academics and recognised specialists in creative production.

Our stunning location in Regent's Park, central London is to be envied, and is fully integrated into our programmes.

Immerse yourself in London's vibrant theatre culture – you will have the opportunity to undertake theatre visits, walks and backstage tours, and will explore London on both a professional and personal basis.

Small classes will nurture your creative development, and will allow for close attention and guidance. Tutors on our Performing Arts courses are experienced professionals from the London theatre community.

We offer the following courses in Performing Arts:

- Acting Foundation Course (1 year)
- BA (Hons) Acting & Global Theatre (3 years)

Acting Foundation Course

This 1 year, intensive Acting Foundation course has been designed to build key acting skills in a relatively short period, as a solid preparation for further study – either at drama school, or university-level study (for example, our 3 year BA (Hons) Acting & Global Theatre).

The course will develop your confidence, will give you industry knowledge, and will prepare you for future auditions as you progress in your career.

The course is structured over two academic semesters. You will be in class for 20 hours per week from Monday to Friday, between 10:00 and 16:00; additional study time will be needed for out-of-class rehearsals, independent study and theatre visits/field trips.

BA (Hons) Acting & Global Theatre

This 3 year degree allows you to develop both your practical acting skills, and your knowledge of the theatre industry through an exciting study of theatre cultures of the world.

This course draws upon the wide range of theatrical expertise of practitioners from both Western and non-Western traditions. You will enjoy Masterclasses, theatre visits and fieldwork. Workshops, practical exercises, scene work, and tutorials develop your performance skills.

You will work under the guidance of a director to explore how a play is structured, issues of potential audience and intended communication, rehearsal strategies, and, above all, creative collaboration between actors, designers and director.

In your second year you will broaden your international understanding of theatre and performance during a Study Abroad Semester at one of the partner universities affiliated with Regent's College; options include Australia, the Czech Republic and the USA.

In addition to subject-specific training, students develop strong transferable skills in team-working, communication, project management, problem-solving, presentation and interpersonal relations.

For more information on Performing Arts courses at the London School of Film, Media & Performance, scholarships and how to apply, please contact:

LSFMP@regents.ac.uk
REGENTS.AC.UK/LSFMP
Tel: +44 (0)207 487 7505

ARTISTIC DIRECTOR

What the work involves

- Artistic directors have control over the artistic interpretation of plays, ballets, operas and other performances.

- You will be responsible for coordinating all the creative elements of each production, including set and costume design, stylistic presentation, the interpretive work of artists, and any musical or choreographic sequences.

- You will liaise with a number of other professionals on a daily basis, including producers, musical directors, technicians, theatre managers, financial backers, performing artists and writers.

- You will select each production, oversee casting, and appear at performances and press events to help generate publicity around each show.

The type of person suited to this work

You will need fantastic artistic and creative vision, that you are able to express both verbally and in written documents. You will also need to have the courage and tenacity to make your vision a reality and present it to an audience.

You must be an excellent leader with the ability to inspire and motivate others. Being able to negotiate with writers, actors and other professionals is an asset.

You should have an in depth knowledge of the theatre, including productions past and present, theatrical trends, and the history of the industry.

Working conditions

Hours can be irregular and you will be employed on a freelance basis through which contracts can be short. Longer fixed-term contracts are available, but they usually only last 3–5 years.

You will be mainly working in theatres and other performance venues. Although the final production may take place on a large stage, you could spend a great deal of time directing scenes from small, offsite rehearsal rooms.

You will mainly work indoors, although certain venues will require you to work outdoors in occasionally inhospitable conditions.

Future prospects

Competition in the theatrical industry is fierce, so you will need talent, dedication, good qualifications and experience.

Since the majority of theatrical work takes place in London you can expect to work there at some period in your career. The city is a base for most freelance directors, although there are opportunities in regional theatres.

As an experienced and admired artistic director, you could set up your own theatre company through which you can stage your performances. Other directors move from theatre into film or television work.

Qualifications and courses

Most artistic directors hold a relevant degree in English, creative/performing arts, drama or theatre studies on entry to the industry. HNDs and Foundation degrees in creative/performing arts or drama/theatre studies are available and may also be useful qualifications to hold prior to entering the theatre. If you are looking to move into the industry after completing your first degree, Birkbeck College, RADA and Mountview offer postgraduate courses in theatre direction.

Of equal importance to professional qualifications are practical skills, acquired through work experience and involvement in school, college or university productions. Since few theatre companies offer in-house training, gaining this practical experience prior to applying for positions is vital.

The Arts Council England runs assistant director schemes for new entrants to the profession, and a few theatres and regional arts councils also offer training bursaries for candidates with exceptional potential.

Advantages/disadvantages

Your creative ability will be the driving force behind the production of visually and technically beautiful or unusual performances.

The industry is extremely competitive so you might have to spend long periods of time working for free or at a minimal wage in order to build enough experience to work as an artistic director.

Money guide

Theatre directors who are working regularly can earn around £19,000. Reaching the level of artistic director should increase your salary to about £23,000. Well-established artistic directors who have built up a good reputation and are in demand across the industry can earn £40,000+.

Related opportunities

- Production Assistant/Theatre Producer p454
- Stage Manager p452
- Actor/Actress p434

Further information

The Directors Guild Trust and the Directors Guild of Great Britain
4 Windmill Street, London W1T 2HZ
020 7580 9131; www.dggb.org

Arts Council England
14 Great Peter Street, London SW1P 3NQ
0845 300 6200; www.artscouncil.org.uk

CHOREOGRAPHER

What the work involves

- As a choreographer, you will create and develop new dance movements for productions such as ballets, opera and musicals.

- Creating a dance means planning the way dancers move to perform beautiful and exciting routines which interpret the music.

- Choreographers work closely with performance artists, musical directors, ballet dance teachers and trainers.

The type of person suited to this work

You will need to have a keen, lively interest in music and movement, and a very well-developed sense of rhythm and timing.

To develop new ballets, dances and shorter dance routines requires an excellent knowledge of past and present pieces, complete understanding of how the body works and of possible movements within dance and the creative imagination to interpret the significance of events and mood changes through physical expression.

Choreographers have responsibility for developing and teaching complicated movements and routines. You will need a good memory, clear communication skills, patience and an ability to get on well with others.

Working conditions

You will mainly work indoors in dance studios, theatres, TV or film studios.

Your initial contacts are likely to be producers, directors and musical conductors. Some choreographers work directly with modern composers, interpreting their music.

As production plans progress, you will start working directly with the performers. You will travel frequently.

Future prospects

Jobs and opportunities can be limited as this is a highly competitive area of work, where experience counts.

It is possible to find opportunities outside mainstream ballet, for example in modern dance companies and developing international venues.

Opera and musicals are becoming reinvigorated through audience demand and both performance areas require choreographers to interpret dance music and contextual pieces as dance routines. You may choose to set up your own dance company.

Advantages/disadvantages

Many hours are spent traveling to different venues – even overseas.

Seeing your finished routine beautifully performed will boost your morale.

Qualifications and courses

There are no formal entry qualifications for this career. GCSEs/S grades and AS/A levels/H grades are available in dance, and some institutions offer a BTEC National Diploma in Performing Arts.

Most choreographers have experience as dance performers prior to becoming choreographers.

Choreography can be studied as an option on some full-time vocational dance courses accredited by the Council for Dance Education and Training, as part of a degree course in dance or as a postgraduate course.

Work experience alongside an experienced practitioner offers a good introduction to choreography and will certainly be taken into account if applying for a dance or choreography-related course.

Enthusiastic reviews will help your career progression.

It will be hard going, and you will need patience and enthusiasm to get the best from dancers.

Money guide

Equity, the performing arts union, recommends a minimum daily sum of up to £130.

You could earn round £12,500 per year if you have just finished at a dance college, or completed a degree or other college courses.

Your salary will reach £20,000 if you have moved into choreography as an experienced dancer.

Experienced, well-known choreographers can earn £50,000, but good salaries will depend on your skills and experience.

Related opportunities

- Dancer p440
- Artistic Director p436
- Make-up Artist p445
- Special Effects Technician p451

Further information

Council for Dance Education and Training
Old Brewer's Yard, 17–19 Neal Street, Covent Garden, London WC2H 9UY
020 7240 5703; www.cdet.org.uk

Dance UK (includes British Association of Choreographers)
The Old Finsbury Town Hall, Rosebury Avenue, London EC1R 4QT
020 4713 0730; www.danceuk.org

Creative and Cultural Skills
Lafone House, The Leathermarket, Weston Street, London SE1 3HN
020 7015 1800; www.ccskills.org.uk

Performing Arts

CRCI: Q

COMPOSER/SONGWRITER

What the work involves

- Composers and songwriters create original music for a variety of uses.

- You could use a variety of tools and instruments when composing or writing, from a pen and paper to advanced computer software programs.

- You may also perform your compositions and songs, although this is most common for composers who are just starting out and those writing for individuals or small groups.

The type of person suited to this work

You will need to have outstanding musical or lyrical talents. You will need dedication, determination and self-discipline as the music industry is extremely tough and knock-backs will be frequent.

You should have a flexible attitude to your work and be willing to take on a range of commissions and assignments in order to build up your experience and reputation.

Working conditions

Composers and songwriters (the former in particular) can expect to work long and unsociable hours writing, rehearsing and performing their work.

Since most musical events take place over evenings and weekends (when most of the working population is free to attend) you can expect to regularly work during these times.

Most composers and songwriters have other jobs in order to fund themselves whilst they establish a name in the music industry.

Future prospects

The music industry is highly competitive, so it can take a long time to gain any recognition for your work. This makes composing a challenging profession to choose and you will need to be extremely resilient.

Most composers or songwriters are self-employed, although opportunities are available with theatrical companies, music publishers and universities.

You could gain great critical acclaim and commercial success, although the majority of composers' and songwriters' work stems from smaller commissions within the media, including writing for television, film and radio.

Advantages/disadvantages

You will be working in a job that you are passionate about, which will be immensely satisfying. If you gain recognition the personal and financial rewards can be excellent.

The industry is highly competitive and chances of success are relatively slim.

Qualifications and courses

Useful qualifications include GCSE and A levels in music, BTEC National Diplomas in music practice or popular music, and relevant degree courses. For entry onto a BTEC National Diploma you will need 4 GCSEs (A*–C) or equivalent. Degree courses usually require 5 GCSEs (A*–C) and at least 2 A levels, preferably with one in music or a related subject, and most usually prefer candidates to have reached grade 8 in an instrument as classified by the Associated Board of Royal Schools of Music.

A wide variety of postgraduate courses are also available. If you are looking to break into the world of classical composition, you are strongly advised to attain a postgraduate qualification.

It is possible, but extremely rare, to achieve success without having undertaken some of the relevant qualifications for this industry.

Money guide

It is very hard to gauge salaries in this industry as so many composers and songwriters are freelance.

If you are commissioned by a large company or orchestra, as a composer you can expect to earn around £500–£1000 for each minute of music you create.

Songwriters could earn around £300 per minute. For title music, jingles and commercials, both composers and songwriters can earn about £350 per minute.

You could also be entitled to royalties from your work.

Related opportunities

- Musician p446
- Singer p449
- Conductor p439

Further information

Arts Council England
14 Great Peter Street, London SW1P 3NQ
0845 300 6200; www.artscouncil.co.uk

The British Academy of Songwriters, Composers and Authors
26 Berners Street, London W1T 3LR
020 7636 2929; www.basca.org.uk

British Music Information Centre
3rd Floor, South Wing, Somerset House, Strand, London WC2R 1LA
020 7759 1800; www.soundandmusic.org

CONDUCTOR

What the work involves

- Music conductors work with musicians and singers to help shape their performance and make sure each musical piece is performed the way it should be.

- You'll be responsible for preparing musical scores for the performance, and taking decisions about how each musical piece should sound.

- You need to understand the role of each performer, and make sure every musician knows which part to play and does so correctly.

- You may work with a wide variety of musicians, both amateur and professional, and these may include choirs and choruses, music students, youth groups and professional artists.

The type of person suited to this work

An interest in music is essential. You should also have good knowledge of music, and be able to play an instrument, preferably the piano.

Good communication skills are vital, as is the ability to work flexibly and with lots of different creative people.

You should also have the command of an additional European language.

Working conditions

Working hours for conductors are varied, and you must be prepared to work whenever and wherever the opportunity arises. Hours include evenings and weekends for both rehearsals and performances.

You will divide your time between working in rehearsal rooms, concert halls, churches, theatres, opera houses and other venues.

A driving licence is useful, as travel is often involved.

It's common to spend a lot of time away from home in venues of a varying standard.

Future prospects

Succeeding in conducting is all about building up your reputation. Once you've proved yourself you can make a name for yourself and start to conduct bigger and better orchestras.

Advantages/disadvantages

If you're musical and want a balance between working independently and working with people, this job may really suit you.

Work can be difficult to come by and there isn't much job security initially.

Qualifications and courses

Most conductors have a degree in music. Most universities require at least 5 GCSEs and 2 A levels, as well as the ability to play an instrument to Grade 7 or 8.

Following completion of a degree, it is usual to undertake a postgraduate course in conducting at music college. Whilst you're doing this, it's a good idea to try and get some work experience as a deputy or assistant conductor.

Most conductors speak at least two European languages. The most useful are English, German, French and Italian.

It's a good idea to attend the seminars run by the Association of British Orchestras; they run many intended specifically for those interested in conducting.

Working as a repetiteur in opera is also a good idea, as you can watch and learn from excellent and experienced conductors.

If you achieve good marks in your conducting studies, keep your eye out for the scholarships offered by organisations such as the Royal Opera House.

Even once you're a qualified conductor, there's always more to learn. Almost all conductors spend their own time studying music theory and constantly keeping up to date with what's going on.

Money guide

Conductors tend to be paid per concert. In the beginning this may be about £380 per concert, and it is likely to increase to about £1000 once you gain experience.

The best conductors can earn about £5000 per concert.

Related opportunities

- Musician p446
- Composer p438
- Music Teacher p199

Further information

Association of British Orchestras
20 Rupert Street, London W1D 6DF
020 7287 0333; www.abo.org.uk

Incorporated Society of Musicians (ISM)
10 Stratford Place, London W1C 1AA
020 7629 4413; www.ism.org

The International Artist Managers' Association (IAMA)
23 Garrick Street, Covent Garden, London WC2E 9BN
020 7379 7336; www.iamaworld.com

Performing Arts

CRCI: Q

DANCER

What the work involves

■ Dancers use the movement and language of their bodies as a way of expressing ideas and emotions to an audience, often accompanied by music.

■ You will focus on any number of styles including street, cultural, modern, contemporary, classical ballet, jazz or tap dance.

■ You might find work in theatres, cabaret clubs, cruise ships or video/TV studios. In addition to performing, you may use dance as a form of education or therapy.

The type of person suited to this work

Anyone entering this area of work must enjoy performing and be very talented to succeed. You must be dedicated to improving technique through daily practice – sometimes, for as long as 10 hours each day.

To be a successful dancer, you need a good sense of rhythm and timing. Being creative and imaginative with routines and choreography is desirable.

It is important that you can cope with setbacks and remain positive and focused.

Working conditions

Most of your rehearsals and performances will take place indoors in studios, schools, theatres or other venues.

While training, most dancers work closely with others in small or larger groups for long hours each day, so it is important that you get on well with all kinds of people.

The job is physically demanding and requires working long hours, often in the evenings and at weekends and will require frequent travel.

Future prospects

Your future prospects as a dancer will largely depend on talent, hard work and luck; competition is always strong. Only a few individuals become top performance artists in solo roles.

If you are employed by a dance company you can progress from chorus to solo parts, but this will be dependent on your skills and dedication. Although dancing is a career for younger people, dance teachers can continue long after they are no longer professional performers, and many leave dancing to set up private dance schools.

Advantages/disadvantages

Dance can be a fantastically rewarding career.

A career as a top soloist can be finished by the age of 30.

Getting paid work can sometimes be difficult.

You will need to stay fit and healthy: injuries can necessitate a complete career change.

Qualifications and courses

You can do a vocational dance performance course at a specialist school such as the Royal Academy of Dance. These courses (Diploma, National Diploma or degree) are usually 3 years in duration. Entry is by audition, interview and a medical, and 5 GCSEs/S grades (A*–C/1–3) are usually required.

For ballet, there are also physical requirements, including height requirements and body proportions.

The Council for Dance Education and Training accredits full-time courses at vocational dance schools.

You can do a degree in dance at a university or college of higher education. A levels/H grades or the equivalent are usually required, and candidates attend an audition.

Some courses offer a teacher-training element. The Royal Academy of Dance and Imperial Society of Teachers of Dancing offer specialist teacher training programmes.

The British Ballet Organisation and the British Theatre Dance Association also offer dance and teacher training qualifications.

Money guide

Salaries for dancers depend on length, type and location of the job. Most dancers are members of the British Actors Equity Association which negotiates performers' salaries and sets a minimum of £336 per week, rising to £360 for experienced dancers. Some dancers are self-employed and set their own rates per contract. Starting full-time employment with a recognised dance company, you should earn up to £18,000 per year. As a soloist, this can rise to £22,000, while principal dancers can earn £36,000+.

Dance teachers are mainly self-employed and receive salaries dependent on the type and size of dance school they work in.

Related opportunities

■ Choreographer p437
■ Theatre Production Assistant/Producer p454
■ Actor/Actress p434

Further information

Council for Dance Education and Training
Old Brewer's Yard, 17–19 Neal Street, London WC2H 9UY
020 7240 5703; www.cdet.org.uk

Royal Academy of Dance
36 Battersea Square, London SW11 3RA
020 7223 0091; www.rad.org.uk

Royal Ballet School
White Lodge, Richmond Park, London TW10 5HR
020 8876 5547; www.royal-ballet-school.org.uk

Industry profile

LONDON SCHOOL OF
FILM, MEDIA & PERFORMANCE

THINKING ABOUT A CAREER IN THE PERFORMING ARTS?

Do you love singing, dancing and acting? Are you on top of the world when you're on stage and in the limelight? Have you been in a drama club, or perhaps been in your very own High School Musical?

Then you might be thinking about a career in the Performing Arts.

Despite the seemingly overnight success of those on Britain's Got Talent and The X-Factor, a career in the Performing Arts requires long-term commitment, determination, self-awareness and a talent for making the most of opportunities. To lay the foundations, many people undertake specialised training.

Getting started

- Not sure if this is the right choice for you? Then consider a 1-year Foundation course. This gives you a taste of the kinds of performance styles in your chosen area. Choose from acting, drama, dance, popular music and creative industries.
- A 2-year BTEC will give you more in-depth experience of the Performing Arts.
- A 3-year BA degree course at a university or college of Higher Education combines performing with academic study, and will equip you for a variety of careers in the creative industries.
- Vocational training takes place in a drama school or a music conservatory. There are fewer than 1000 places for the 22 drama schools in the Council of Drama Schools (CDS). These courses prepare students exclusively for careers in theatre, television, orchestras, opera, film, radio and allied fields.

What job might I do after graduation?

Actor: your performance work may be on stage, screen, TV, radio and in voice-over work. Work is largely freelance and can be very irregular, with long periods of 'resting' between jobs.

Arts Marketing: you develop the publicity material to promote your arts event; you can work freelance or for a company.

Choreographer: the choreographer creates and structures dance pieces for solo performers or group, either as a freelance artist or member of a company.

Dancer: trained in dance styles such as ballet, jazz, contemporary, street dance or modern, a dancer works as a member of a company, as a solo performer and for special events.

Drama Animateur: you work for a theatre company or arts organisation, developing workshops and other drama-related events.

Lighting and Sound Design: graduates with a degree in technical theatre and theatre design, they create the complex lighting and sound effects for theatre, film, and music events.

Musician: whether classical, jazz, rock or pop, musicians work as solo artists as well as in groups and orchestras; you may also find work composing or performing for events, films, or theatre.

Production Assistant: you work alongside a director, designer, or film-maker. Your work is enormously varied as you undertake the different tasks to keep the production running smoothly.

Stage Manager: the Stage Manager works with the theatre director, recording the staging and serving as the liaison between the rehearsal room and the other members of the production team.

Theatre Designer: graduates with a degree in fine art or theatre design, they create the sets, costumes, and props for theatre productions.

By Dr Valerie Kaneko-Lucas
Programme Director, Theatre & Performance Studies
London School of Film, Media & Performance

DJ

What the work involves

■ You will play and mix music for audiences at live venues or on the radio. You could use vinyl, CD, MP3s, turntables, mixers, microphones and amplifiers.

■ Club DJs keep people dancing in bars and clubs. You will create your own sounds and mixes and use lighting and visual effects in time to the beats.

■ As a radio DJ, you will work in a studio playing records and chatting to listeners.

■ VJing is a new form of artistic expression, using a good PC and software to mix/inter-splice sounds with images from video clips and loops, in real time.

■ Mobile DJs play at weddings and other social parties.

The type of person suited to this work

You must have a passion for music, excellent coordination, good communication and listening skills, and a lively outgoing personality.

DJs use the latest in turntables, amplifiers and multimedia, and practise techniques such as mixing, scratching and cross fading to make their live performance interesting.

Sheer hard work and persistence are keys to success. As most DJs are self-employed, basic business skills are an advantage.

Working conditions

As a DJ, you could work in clubs, on radio, in hotels, in holiday camps or at festivals and gigs – even on boats.

You will work long, irregular hours.

High noise levels are an occupational hazard for DJs; you need to take steps to protect your hearing.

Future prospects

Some DJs stay in the job only a short time before moving on. Many work part time alongside a daytime job.

You have to be a self-starter, looking for opportunities, as jobs are rarely advertised. Experienced DJs can get seasonal work in holiday camps. Some move into careers in music production or retail.

Increasingly, DJs are finding opportunities working with VJs who create pop videos.

Advantages/disadvantages

It's rewarding to know you've provided entertainment to make people happy.

There can be heavy equipment to move around, often in the early hours. You may travel considerable distances between venues.

Set-up equipment costs over £1,000.

Qualifications and courses

There is no specific entry route to this job, and no formal qualifications are required.

A BTEC National award in DJ Technology is offered at some colleges of further education, often combined with music technology. The normal entry requirements are 4 GCSEs/S grades (A*–C/1–3). There are also BTEC and Diploma qualifications in Popular Music, Music Technology and Performing Arts that can be useful.

NCFE and City & Guilds also award qualifications in music technology and radio production, offered as short, full-time courses by a few colleges and specialist training centres.

Training in radio skills is offered by CSV Media which runs Media Clubhouses around the UK.

Work experience is highly advisable. A technical career in radio is a good start to becoming a radio DJ and there are many college and hospital radio networks where you can practise.

Some top DJs offer masterclasses; some club DJs allow work-shadowing to gain technical skills.

Money guide

Income varies with the event and venue; your reputation will determine your fee. Your charges/pay should reflect local DJ rates; when starting out, expect a little less!

Depending on the club size, DJs can charge between £50 and £300+ per session.

With your own record releases, fees rise to well over £1,000 in superclubs, while a few top and well established DJs earn £100,000 per year.

Many DJs have another job to boost their income.

Related opportunities

■ Sound Engineer p450
■ Musician p446

Further information

SAE Institute
SAE Institute, 297 Kingsland Road, London E8 4DD
020 792 39159; www.sae.edu

Access to Music
Lionel House, 35 Millstone Lane, Leicester LE1 5JN
0116 242 6888; www.accesstomusic.co.uk

City & Guilds

ENTERTAINER

What the work involves

- Entertainers perform amusing or amazing acts in front of audiences. They include comedians, circus performers, street artists, cabaret performers, dancers, musicians, and magicians.

- You could specialise in one area or skill such as magic, dance or comedy, or you might have several skills that you can combine into one act.

- You will have to source your own props and costumes, attend regular auditions, book venues, rehearse your routine, and also carry out your own promotional work.

The type of person suited to this work

You will need natural confidence and a very outgoing nature in order to present a lively and entertaining act to your audience.

You will need to be extremely talented in your chosen field, be it comedy, music, dance or magic.

You should be good with a wide range of people, as your audience could include members of all ages and backgrounds.

You should have good business awareness and a creative approach to marketing yourself in order to attract interest in your act and increase your bookings.

You must be extremely punctual and reliable so as not to disappoint or annoy a venue or your audience.

Working conditions

Working hours vary. Most performances take place during evenings and weekends, and you may also work morning matinees. You can choose to work full time if you have a number of bookings, or part time in order to supplement your income with that from another job.

You could have regular weekly, fortnightly or monthly jobs, but a great deal of work is on a one-off basis.

You may work across numerous venues throughout the UK (and abroad), so a driving licence would be useful.

Future prospects

The majority of entertainers are self-employed, although there are employment opportunities with circuses, theme park operators and cruise ship companies.

Some may also work with one or more agents, who help with promotion and finding bookings in return for a small fee or commission from earnings.

Overseas work is possible, especially if you work for a cruise ship company or if you have an act that is appreciated across a variety of cultures.

Advantages/disadvantages

You will travel across the UK, and even the world, showcasing your talent to a variety of people to entertain and amaze them.

Qualifications and courses

Entertainers do not need to hold any academic qualifications, although they may be beneficial in honing your skills and proving your ability and commitment to potential employers.

Entry routes are numerous and varied, ranging from entering talent competitions, to working in holiday centres, to performing in local clubs and bars, through to undertaking professional training courses.

Courses that will lead to useful qualifications include: BTEC National Certificates in live entertainment; HND in performance, entertainment and media, Foundation degrees and degrees in entertainment or similar. BTEC entry requirements are usually 4 GCSEs (A*–C) or equivalent. All degree courses require at least 2 A levels or equivalent, 1 in a related subject.

If you are intending to work with children and/or vulnerable adults, you will also be required to undergo a Criminal Records Bureau check prior to starting.

Apprenticeships and Creative Apprenticeships are also available to entrants aged 16–24.

If you are self-employed, you have the opportunity to choose your hours and bookings to fit in around other commitments.

The industry is competitive, and few entertainers are able to pursue their career on a full time basis.

Money guide

Salaries for entertainers vary depending on your genre and level of success. New entrants who have regular work can expect around £10,000.

With experience, you should be paid more per booking and could earn between £12,000 and £20,000.

Well established entertainers, such as those with regular bookings at reputable venues, or regular TV appearances, can earn £30,000+.

Related opportunities

- Singer p449
- Musician p446
- Actor/Actress p434
- Dancer p440

Further information

Spotlight
7 Leicester Place, London WC2H 7RJ
020 7437 7631; www.spotlight.com

The Circus Space
Coronet Street, London N1 6HD
020 7729 9522; www.thecircusspace.co.uk

CRCI: Q   Performing Arts

LIGHTING TECHNICIAN

What the work involves

- Lighting technicians are responsible for creating stage lighting effects, working closely with the set designer and producer.

- You will do lighting for advertising sets, in video production, theatre and broadcasting work.

- You will be responsible for rigging and setting up the lighting, and plotting and programming the lighting requirements.

- It is important to visit venues before productions start and watch rehearsals to get the lighting effects right for live performances.

The type of person suited to this work

Anyone entering this career must have an interest in electrical work and electronics, combined with a strong interest in theatre and performance, or live concerts. You will also need to be physically fit and work well in a team.

Lighting technicians need to have a creative flair as the main aim of this job is to create the atmosphere required by the producer.

In some situations, for example changing or operating spotlights, the tasks could involve working at heights, and would not suit a person who suffers from vertigo.

Working conditions

You will work indoors and outdoors, usually working afternoons, evenings and weekends. You will work with lots of heavy equipment and you may sometimes need to wear protective steel toe-capped boots.

You may have to work in cramped spaces with computerised control systems.

You will often be away from home for weeks and months if you are travelling with a roadshow.

Future prospects

Theatre lighting is usually covered by specialist companies who employ technicians on a short-term contract basis. However, once you are experienced and known in the trade, your opportunity to join the backstage crew of a particular theatre group increases.

Progression as a lighting technician relies on skills and dedication. When in demand, you can become a senior or chief lighting technician and, in some cases, technical manager.

Advantages/disadvantages

You will have irregular working hours, including evening and weekend work – usually, away from home.

Qualifications and courses

All lighting technicians must be fully qualified electricians. Relevant qualifications include the City & Guilds Certificate in Electrotechnology or SVQs Levels 2 and 3 in Lighting (Live Performance). Full-time or part-time college courses are available or you may find a traineeship with a specialist lighting company.

Colleges and universities offer courses in subjects such as lighting technology, lighting design and technical theatre, theatre design and theatre production, which include the study of lighting.

Specialist degrees in lighting design are offered by Rose Bruford College and Central School of Speech and Drama. Drama schools offer degrees and vocational training courses in technical theatre or stage management which include lighting. Many of these are accredited by the National Council for Drama Training.

The BBC offers a central work experience scheme, but places are limited. The Association of British Theatre Technicians offers professional qualifications in Technical Theatre. Apprenticeships/Skillseekers may be available to those aged 16–24.

Seeing your skills and experience light up a set or production will be a great confidence booster.

Money guide

Trainee technicians start at around £9,500 per year. With experience, this rises to around £16,000 for full-time technicians in established theatres. A qualified lighting technician working in television could earn up to £30,000. A number of experienced theatre lighting technicians work freelance earning £300+ per week.

Related opportunities

- Special Effects Technician p451
- Stage Manager p452

Further information

The Association of British Theatre Technicians
55 Farringdon Road, London EC1M 3JB
020 7242 9200; www.abtt.org.uk

National Electrotechnical Training
34 Palace Court, London W2 4HY
www.net-works.org.uk, enquiries@net-works.org.uk

www.cityandguilds.com/myperfectjob

MAKE-UP ARTIST

What the work involves

- Your work will involve applying make-up and arranging hair to produce the right look for male and female artists and performers in films, TV and stage productions.

- You will need to listen to the director in order to create the desired finished look for the individual characters or troupe.

- Most of your work will be done off stage in a make-up or dressing room.

- You could be employed in TV, by a video production company or by a theatre or film company, or be self-employed, perhaps as part of a backstage team.

The type of person suited to this work

Anyone who considers doing make-up work needs to be creative, with the imagination to visualise the finished effect. You will have to pay great attention to detail. The job requires excellent communication skills, as advising colleagues or clients on their image will need a sense of tact.

At times, there will be many people needing to be made up for a particular scene, and you could be working under intense pressure. Self-confidence and an outgoing personality are positive factors in building relationships and succeeding at work.

Working conditions

Most of your work will be indoors in theatres, in studios and, at first, possibly in retail outlets. Long hours and weekend work are common. Doing make-up involves many busy hours spent standing over customers and you will need to be physically fit.

If you are self-employed, you will probably need to provide your own cosmetics.

Future prospects

Although this is not a huge area for employment there will always be a demand for make-up artists. The larger towns and cities present the best opportunities. Although limited, some work could be available in the larger hotels or on cruise ships.

Securing full-time work in TV or video, on a cruise ship, in a hotel, a retail store or with a theatre company are all possible, once you have gained experience. Competition is strong and progression depends upon the reputation, contacts and talent of the individual.

It could be possible to set up your own beauty salon.

Advantages/disadvantages

Working hours may be irregular and unsociable, especially if you do make-up both before and during performances.

Make-up is a highly satisfying job when you see your work on stage or set.

Qualifications and courses

Make-up artists in theatre/TV/film are usually trained in beauty therapy or both hairdressing and makeup, and may have a relevant NVQ or Diploma.

There are a range of specialist further education courses in theatrical and/or media make-up. The Vocational Training Charitable Trust and ITEC offer a Diploma course, and BTEC National Diplomas and Certificates are also available.

The Hairdressing and Beauty Industry Authority and the National Association of Screen Make-Up Artists offer short courses in make-up for TV, film, fashion and theatre.

A number of universities and colleges run HND courses in theatrical and/or media make-up or make-up artistry. A Diploma in Image Styling for Performance, a Foundation degree in Specialist Make-up Design and in Film and TV Make-Up, and a BA (Hons) degree in Make-Up and Prosthetics for Performance are offered at the London College of Fashion. Degrees and diplomas in subjects like fine art/visual art or fashion design or graphic design can be useful. Diplomas are also available in make up artistry and hairdressing.

Money guide

New entrants can expect to earn around £15,000 per year. With experience this can rise to £25,000. The highest paid earn up to £45,000. Employed by a company, you can start on £15,000–£16,000, earning more with specialist skills. Rates for freelances vary from £180 to £250 a day.

Related opportunities

- Beauty Therapist p459
- Beauty Consultant p458
- Hairdresser/Barber p469

Further information

British Association of Beauty Therapy and Cosmetology
Ambrose House, Meteor Court, Barnett Way, Barnwood, Gloucester GL4 3GG
0845 065 9000; www.babtac.com

Make Up Artist magazine
4018, NE 112th Ave, Suite D-8, Vancouver, WA 98682 USA
www.makeupmag.com

Greasepaint
Greasepaint Studio, 143 Northfield Avenue, London W13 9QT
www.greasepaint.co.uk

www.cityandguilds.com/myperfectjob

Performing Arts

CRCI: Q

MUSICIAN

What the work involves

- Whether you work as a classical, popular or armed forces musician, your main responsibility will be to perform to and entertain an audience.

- You will spend the majority of your time practising in order to develop and strengthen your ability on the instrument/s you play.

- You could compose your own material, or play that of other people from a variety of genres.

The type of person suited to this work

You will need to be extremely musical, particularly if you are looking to work as a classical musician.

Throughout the music industry, there is intense competition for jobs. You will need determination, tenacity and resilience in order to cope with knock-backs and persevere.

You will need to be very confident in yourself and your abilities, as well as having considerable stage presence to hold the attention of an audience.

Working conditions

You must be prepared to work long, unsociable hours in a variety of environments, including clubs and bars.

Classical musicians tend to work in locations such as concert halls, theatres, parks and recording studios. Musicians employed by the Armed Forces usually perform for military parades, regimental dinners, state occasions, sporting events and other special occasions.

All musicians could find themselves having to work away from home for long periods of time.

Future prospects

Classical musicians may rise to enjoy success as solo artists, or may work in group ensembles such as orchestras in which there are chances for promotion. Diversifying into teaching is also common.

Prospects for popular musicians are varied, and depend a great deal on how successful you become. Many decide to move into a business role such as that of a manager or representative for a recording company.

Armed Forces musicians usually move across various bands throughout their career, whilst also progressing up through the standard ranks as they gain relevant management, leadership and military skills.

Advantages/disadvantages

As a musician, you could work in a variety of disciplines and with a range of different people, so the work will be stimulating and interesting.

Competition is intense in the music industry, so you will have to work extremely hard.

Qualifications and courses

ENTRY LEVEL 1

Classical musicians undertake extensive musical training and academic qualifications. Most take graded examinations in their chosen instrument/s, as well as further related courses. These include GCSE/A level music, BTEC National Diploma in music practice, music degrees at university, specialist courses at music colleges (conservatoires), and relevant postgraduate qualifications.

Popular musicians do not need to hold any qualifications for entry to the industry, but they may help as proof of your ability and dedication. Relevant courses include: GCSEs/ A levels in music or similar; BTEC National Diploma in music, music technology and music practice; HND/HNC courses; degrees in popular music or a related subject.

BTEC entry requirements are usually 4 GCSEs (A*–C) or equivalent. All degree courses require at least 2 A levels or equivalent, 1 in a related subject. Postgraduate programmes require entrants to hold a relevant first degree.

Armed Forces musicians do not need to hold any formal qualifications for entrance, but aptitude in your chosen instrument/s is expected. You will be assessed by audition at the Royal Military School of Music.

Money guide

Classical musicians employed by an orchestra usually earn between £22,000 and £40,000. Solo artists can command anything from £80 and £600 per concert.

Session musicians could earn between £120 and £350 for a three hour job, and solo musicians can earn anywhere from £500 to £2000+ a week depending on their popularity.

Armed forces musicians start on a trainee salary of about £14,000, and this can rise to £70,000+ as they are promoted in the course of their military service.

Related opportunities

- Singer p449
- Entertainer p443
- Composer/Songwriter p438

Further information

Arts Council England
14 Great Peter Street, London SW1P 3NQ
0845 300 6200; www.artscouncil.org.uk

Associated Board of the Royal Schools of Music
24 Portland Place, London W1B 1LU
020 7636 5400; www.abrsm.org

Royal Military School of Music
Kneller Hall, Kneller Hall Road, Twickenham TW2 7DU
www.army.mod.uk/music

PROPS MAKER/ASSISTANT

What the work involves

■ Props makers and their assistants are responsible for designing, changing, making and finishing the props used in theatre, video, film, television or circus work.

■ You will be working with a range of materials, including wood, fibreglass, fabric and metal, and will use a range of practical skills including carpentry, modelling and good painting ability.

■ You will spend a good amount of your time researching the historical and cultural background of the props to ensure they fit the era they represent.

The type of person suited to this work

You will need to have a mixture of practical and artistic skills in order to have the vision to design props and the ability to make them yourself.

You will be taking direction from theatre/TV producers, so must be able to listen carefully to their briefs and ideas so that you can translate them into actual props.

You will need good problem solving skills so that you can think round issues such as meeting both expectations and budget with your props.

The ability to use a variety of ICT packages, including CAD, is useful.

Working conditions

Working hours vary, but you can expect to work long hours over evenings and weekends in order to meet deadlines now and again. You will be working in small studios and prop rooms and such conditions can often be cramped.

You may also spend a good amount of time visiting suppliers for equipment, and also libraries and museums to carry out research.

You will have to wear relevant safety equipment when dealing with materials such as wood, metal, fibreglass and any chemical products.

Future prospects

The majority of props makers are freelance, so you will be employed on short-term projects most of the time. These could be for film studios, theatres, television companies, or museums.

Career progression is dependent upon building a good reputation and excellent portfolio of work. With experience, you could move into set design or take a more general role in stage management.

Advantages/disadvantages

Working in a creative industry such as theatre or film provides challenging, exciting work opportunities.

Qualifications and courses

It is possible to enter the profession without any academic qualifications, but even if you start as an assistant most employers look for at least GCSEs (A*–C) or equivalent, in English, maths and art. You will also need a good history of relevant work experience, and a lot of talent and dedication.

Most props makers have relevant qualifications, including HNDs, degrees and postgraduate diplomas, in subjects such as stage management or art. Most HND courses require that you hold at least 1 relevant A level, whereas degree courses require at least 2 A levels /H grades including art or similar. Postgraduate courses always ask for a related first degree as an entry requirement.

Most course providers also ask candidates to present a portfolio of work for entrance assessment, as well as holding the qualifications specified above.

You will be using a mixture of artistic, practical and intellectual skills which will be tiring but rewarding.

Working freelance can bring a feeling of instability and can be hard when work dries up for a month or two.

Money guide

As a props maker's assistant, you can expect to earn about £12,000. Props makers who are just starting in the industry usually earn around £15,000.

If you gain a good reputation and start to work on large productions with big budgets, you could earn £40,000+.

Related opportunities

■ Wardrobe Assistant p455
■ Make-up Artist p445
■ Stage Manager p452

Further information

The Stage Management Association
1st Floor, 89 Borough High Street, London SE1 1NL
020 7403 7999; www.stagemanagementassociation.co.uk

Creative & Cultural Skills
Lafone House, The Leathermarket, Weston Street,
London SE1 3HN
020 7015 1847; www.creative-choices.co.uk

Royal Academy of Dramatic Art
62–64 Gower Street, London WC1E 6ED
020 7636 7076; www.rada.org; enquiries@rada.org

City&Guilds

www.cityandguilds.com/myperfectjob

ENTRY 5 LEVEL

Performing Arts

CRCI: Q

ROADIE

Performing Arts

CRCI: Q

What the work involves

- Roadies are responsible for setting up a range of equipment for music concerts and events including amplifications systems, electrical cabling, stage and special effects lighting.

- You will have to move and set up heavy equipment, load and unload vans and trailers and do lots of driving around.

- You will need to maintain and fine-tune your equipment on a regular basis.

- Your work could include handling pyrotechnics, laser displays, computer/live film feeds and video links.

The type of person suited to this work

You will need to have a strong interest in music, technology and electronics. It is essential to have good communication skills and an interest in people, and to be creative and practical.

Physical fitness and stamina will be essential, and a sense of humour is a bonus in this work. Sets will have to be assembled and disassembled safely in tight deadlines so you should be able to work whilst under pressure. As most roadies are self-employed, a well-organised person with some business skills will do well with maintaining their accounts and keeping records of bookings.

Working conditions

You will have exceptionally long working hours, mainly evenings, nights and weekends, and if you are on a tour, you might be working 7 days a week. Three month contracts are typical in this line of work.

The work is very physical and there is lots of heavy lifting involved, and sometimes you could be working at heights on electrical cabling.

Future prospects

There is strong competition for jobs. The work is unpredictable and you might need another job to boost your income. Work can be seasonal, with more roadies needed for summer events.

Marketing your services will be essential for getting gigs; many roadies now use websites to advertise.

A wide range of technical skills such as stage lighting and management or sound engineering will improve your chances of employment and could enable you to secure lighting or sound jobs in film, television or theatre.

Advantages/disadvantages

Roadies work long unsociable hours and there is lots of travelling.

Very loud sounds will damage your hearing if your ears are unprotected.

You will get to attend many gigs and concerts for free.

Qualifications and courses

There are no formal entry qualifications. Most people enter this career through experience of working with a friend or other contacts. If you are under 18 you may not be able to work in some licensed premises.

If you are planning to do the more technical work you might need qualifications. Suitable courses would be in lighting, electronics, music technology, video work and sound production. Details of suitable courses are available from the National Skills Academy for Creative & Cultural Skills.

The majority of roadies will learn the trade from working with other more experienced people.

Useful skills and qualifications include a First Aid certificate, a Light Goods Vehicle or Passenger Service Vehicle driving licence and the ability to speak one or more foreign languages.

Money guide

Most roadies work freelance and your pay will depend on the gig, your experience and general availability of roadies.

As a starter, with regular work, you could earn around £12,500 per year.

A roadie with electrical, audio or video skills can earn £21,000+. With excellent technical skills, pay can rise to £30,000.

On contract to a big touring band, you could earn £35,000+.

Related opportunities

- Sound Engineer p450
- Lighting Technician p444
- Stage Manager p452
- Large Goods Vehicle Driver p607

Further information

Production Services Association
PO Box 2709, Bath BA1 3YS
01225 332668; www.psa.org.uk

The Stage Management Association
First Floor, 89 Borough High Street, London SE1 1NL
020 7403 7999; www.stagemanagementassociation.co.uk

City & Guilds

www.cityandguilds.com/myperfectjob

SINGER

What the work involves

- Singers perform in front of an audience in clubs, at gigs, on television or radio, in a recording studio, or in an opera house. They work as solo artists, or as part of a backing group, choir or chorus.

- You will spend many hours practising in order to develop and strengthen your breathing and vocal ability.

- You will need to have good diction, and be able to pronounce songs written in a variety of languages including Latin and French.

- You will work with a variety of musicians and music industry professionals, including orchestras, bands, session musicians, sound engineers, and maybe a manager.

The type of person suited to this work

You will need to have an exceptional talent for singing in order to get noticed in the music industry.

Because of the intense competition in this area, you will also need determination, self-discipline and resilience in order to cope with knock-backs and to persevere in order to achieve your goals.

You will need to be very confident in yourself and your abilities. It is difficult to hold an audience without stage presence and charisma.

Working conditions

As a singer, you can expect to work long and unsociable hours over evenings and weekends, as this is when the majority of your audience will be free.

You may have to travel long distances for gigs and rehearsals.

You could work in a variety of locations, from small clubs and theatres, to large concert halls and even outdoor venues.

Future prospects

Singing is a highly competitive industry, and opportunities for full time work are extremely limited. Because of this, most professionals supplement their income with another job, so you could look into teaching or writing songs and jingles for other artists.

Most successful singers move to London to pursue their careers, as this is where the majority of opportunities lie.

You may well work with an agent or manager at some point in your career. Their purpose is to offer you career advice and to find you singing opportunities.

Advantages/disadvantages

You will be fulfilling a passion whilst also doing your job, which is rare and satisfying.

You will be bringing pleasure to the people in your audience, no matter how big or small.

Qualifications and courses

Academic qualifications are not strictly required in order to become a singer, but they quite often demonstrate talent, commitment, and the necessary expertise to succeed in the music industry to potential employers or clients.

Relevant qualifications include GCSEs and A levels in music, BTEC courses in music, performing arts, music performance, music practice and music technology, HNC/HND courses in music-related subjects, and a degree in popular music or similar. Entry requirements for these courses vary; BTECs usually require 4 GCSEs (A*–C) or equivalent, whilst HNC/HND programmes require an additional A level, degree programmes require at least 2 A levels/H grades (often including music).

Classical singers will need to undergo far more extensive formal training, often to postgraduate level, in order to achieve the depth of specialist knowledge and technical ability required to perform in public.

Building up singing experience, through performing with choirs, in amateur productions or in talent contests, is also important in order to help you develop as a rounded performer who can hold the attention of an audience.

You will have to work long and unsociable hours.

You will have to be resilient in order to persevere despite negative feedback on occasion.

Money guide

As a solo singer, you could earn between £150 and £450 per concert. Chorus singers usually earn £70–£100. Backing singers on albums are paid £110+ for a 3 hour recording session.

If you go on to perform in the theatre, there are set rates of pay that employers must adhere to. For example, chorus members command £650 per week for performances onstage in London's West End.

Related opportunities

- Composer/Songwriter p438
- Musician p446
- Entertainer p443

Further information

The BRIT School for Performing Arts and Technology
60 The Crescent, Croydon CR0 2HN
020 8665 5242; www.brit.croydon.sch.uk;
admin@brit.croydon.sch.uk

Creative & Cultural Skills
Lafone House, The Leathermarket, Weston Street,
London SE1 3HN
020 7015 1847; www.creative-choices.co.uk;
info@creative-choices.co.uk

ENTRY
1
LEVEL

Performing Arts

CRCI: Q

SOUND ENGINEER

What the work involves

- Sound engineers set up, operate and maintain a range of technical equipment that is designed to capture, magnify and manipulate words and music.

- Theatrical sound engineers create 'sound plots', choose equipment and insert sound effects according to the instructions of the director of the production.

- Sound engineers working in the recording industry capture speech, music and other sound effects and modify them using sophisticated electronic equipment for a number of purposes including creating pop songs, adverts, computer game soundtracks, film and TV.

The type of person suited to this work

You will need a good musical ear and excellent sense of timing in order to put together pleasing and appropriate soundtracks/ background audio to a range of productions.

You should also have knowledge of both electronics and ICT systems.

Recording industry sound engineers must also have a good knowledge of both recording and post-production processes.

Working conditions

Sound engineers working in both theatre and the recording industry should expect to work varied hours that will encompass day, evening and weekend commitments.

Theatre sound engineers will spend the majority of their working day confined to a small control box which may be cramped and often is plunged into semi-darkness.

Recording sound engineers work in studios, some of which are large and air-conditioned, whilst others can be small and cramped. You will usually be working in artificial light and the atmosphere can be stressful when working against deadlines.

Future prospects

Competition for jobs is intense, and you may spend a long while proving your credentials as a runner or gofer.

You could work for a variety of employers, including theatres, opera and ballet houses, commercial recording studios or media post-production departments.

Theatre sound engineers may go on to become sound designers with greater creative input in productions, whereas many recording sound engineers move into roles as producers.

Advantages/disadvantages

You will work with a variety of people on diverse projects, so each day will bring new challenges and rewards.

Theatre and media are exciting industries to work in as there is constant cultural and technical development.

Qualifications and courses

It is possible to become a sound engineer without gaining any relevant qualifications, as many companies take on trainees as runners or assistants, and you can build your knowledge whilst you work.

Larger studios and companies do prefer candidates to hold relevant qualifications. These could include: BTEC National Certificates in live sound, stage sound, or light and sound; HNDs in sound technology or sound engineering and electronics; Foundation degrees and degrees in music production or audio technology.

Postgraduate qualifications are also offered by a limited number of providers. The University of Westminster runs an MA course in Audio Production, and the National Film and Television School offers a Diploma in Sound Recording or an MA in Sound Design for Film and Television.

For theatre sound engineers, many drama schools offer courses in theatre lighting and sound which may be useful. All good programmes are accredited by the National Council for Drama Training.

You will have to work long hours that will often fall over evenings and weekends.

Money guide

Starting salaries for sound engineers, whether they work in theatre or the recording industry, range from £13,000 to £15,000. With experience, this should rise to £30,000. Sound engineers working on large productions, with big companies or well-known artists, can earn £40,000+.

Related opportunities

- Special Effects Technician p451
- Lighting Technician p444

Further information

Professional Lighting and Sound Association
Redoubt House, 1 Edward Road, Eastbourne BN23 8AS
01323 524 120; www.plasa.org; info@plasa.org

National Film and Television School
The Registry, Beaconsfield Studios, Station Road, Beaconsfield HP9 1LG
01494 731 425; www.nftsfilm-tv.ac.uk

www.cityandguilds.com/myperfectjob

SPECIAL EFFECTS TECHNICIAN (TV, FILM AND THEATRE)

What the work involves

- As a technician you'd work to create special effects in the television and film industry.

- You might work with either physical effects, pyrotechnic, or visual. The first involves robotics, the second explosions, and the third superimposes images after filming.

- You'll work with colleagues to plan effects, create them, test them, and oversee their staging during filming.

- You may superimpose effects post filming, and will work to strict health and safety regulations, travelling to shooting locations and working long and flexible hours.

The type of person suited to this work

An interest in films and television is useful for this profession.

You need to be creative and imaginative, but at the same time practical and logical.

A visual mind is important, as you'll need to imagine how things will look on screen, and you should also be resourceful as you'll be working to a budget.

You'll be working under pressure, both with others and on your own, so need to be good at coping with all of these scenarios.

You should be adaptable and capable of coping with criticism.

Working conditions

Hours are flexible, and you should be prepared to fit around filming schedules. This may mean late nights, early mornings, and weekends.

You could work freelance, which may well mean you are very busy for a while, then unemployed for a long period of time.

When you're working, you could be travelling anywhere, sometimes for quite a while. Be prepared to stay away from home often.

Work takes place wherever filming takes place – in a studio or workshop, outdoors in the sunshine, outdoors in the rain, on location etc.

Future prospects

Once you've been working for about 10 years, you can advance to a senior technician position.

With 5 years more experience, you can move into a supervisor role.

Progression is much easier when you've built a list of contacts, and vacancies in this industry are often only advertised internally.

Advantages/disadvantages

This is a really exciting job, and seeing your hard work on the big screen can be really rewarding.

Qualifications and courses

ENTRY LEVEL 3

There is no specific entry route into this profession, but employers like to see degrees and diplomas in art subjects, especially stage crafts and animation.

Courses are available in areas such as technical arts and special effects. Most applicants take a Foundation Art and Design course prior to entry. In order to do this, you'll probably need at least 5 good GCSEs and 2 A levels or equivalent.

Relevant work experience is essential, and can be in any aspect of special effects, from theatre stage crafts to pyrotechnics and working with explosives.

When you gain employment, you will be trained whilst shadowing an experienced technician. During this time, you will also create a 'showreel' of your work to present at interviews with prospective employers.

It's a fiercely competitive profession, and you might have to face periods of unemployment.

Money guide

As a trainee, you can expect to earn between £200 and £500 a week, depending on how advanced your skills are.

Once you're a technician this can rise to about £1,250 for a week of work.

If you make it to a senior technician role, this might rise to between £3,000 and £4,000 a week.

Related opportunities

- Animator p168
- Lighting Technician p444
- Props Maker/Assistant p447
- Sound Engineer p450

Further information

The Association of British Theatre Technicians (ABTT)
55 Farringdon Road, London EC1M 3JB
020 7242 9200; www.abtt.org.uk

Broadcasting Entertainment Cinematographic and Theatre Union (BECTU), and the BECTU Special Effects Branch
373–377 Clapham Road, London SW9 9BT
020 7346 0900; www.bectu.org.uk

City& Guilds

www.cityandguilds.com/myperfectjob

STAGE MANAGER

What the work involves

- Stage managers work with designers, directors and producers, assessing and discussing what props, lighting and other stage support are needed for the production.

- You are the link between the artistic and technical aspects of all productions, as you are in charge of everything that happens on stage including calling actors, giving technical cues and moving scenery.

- You could work on numerous types of production, including theatrical performances, opera, ballet, and even music festivals.

The type of person suited to this work

You will need to have artistic flair, be practical, communicate instructions clearly and manage others confidently. Good time management skills are crucial.

The work is demanding as the successful running of the backstage support for the performance rests with you. A cool head and a sense of humour – while still being assertive – will make the work easier for you. An excellent stage manager can help create a good team atmosphere backstage between artists, props manager and stagehands.

Working conditions

You will spend long hours in theatres and studios, sometimes working into the night to meet deadlines. In addition, you will have to travel to different venues.

Finding work is not easy and can take up a huge amount of your time, so be prepared for rejection and periods without work.

Future prospects

The employment demand for stage managers has remained stable for some years. This is a competitive area of work and the opportunities for employment are not extensive. Opportunities exist in theatre companies, opera, theatre in education and touring companies.

You could be promoted to a nationally recognised position or become a company stage manager where you would do publicity and finance work as well. You could also choose to move into TV or film, becoming a director or producer.

Advantages/disadvantages

You will work long, unpredictable hours to meet production deadlines.

Permanent contracts are difficult to find.

The work is both creative and practical.

There is a great sense of achievement at the end of a successful run when everything has operated smoothly.

Qualifications and courses

Practical experience is key to obtaining work as a stage manager and is valued over academic qualifications. You could do this by volunteering or participating in student productions.

You can take a stage management course at drama school. The National Council for Drama Training accredits vocational stage management courses. You can complete a Level 3 BTEC National Award, Certificate or Diploma in Production Arts studied over 2 or 3 years full time. Entry is by interview and portfolio of practical work.

Some universities offer degrees and HNDs in technical theatre or theatre production which include study of stage management.

You could be employed as a stage assistant as part of a new creative Apprenticeship in Technical Theatre.

The Stage Management Association runs a variety of short courses for people already working as stage managers or assistant stage managers. NVQs/SVQs are available in Stage Management, and there are BTEC/SQA qualifications in relevant subjects. Some drama schools offer short, part-time courses in stage management.

Money guide

Starting out as a trainee stage manager you will earn about £14,500 per year. With experience, your annual salary can rise to £20,000+. With lengthy experience, you will be in demand, earning up to £40,000 annually.

Related opportunities

- Entertainment Manager p386
- Props Maker/Assistant p447
- Wardrobe Assistant p455
- Lighting Technician p444

Further information

EQ
Suite E229, Dean Clough, Halifax HX3 5AX
01422 381618; www.thinkeq.org.uk

Stage Management Association
55 Farringdon Road, London EC1M 3JB
020 7242 9250; www.stagemanagementassociation.co.uk;
admin@stagemanagementassociation.co.uk

www.cityandguilds.com/myperfectjob

STUNT PERFORMER

What the work involves

■ Stunt performers plan, design, practise and perform stunts in areas such as motorbike riding, car driving, diving, flying, paragliding, bungee jumping, skiing and horse riding.

■ Standing in for actors in TV, film or video productions, you will enter flaming buildings, crash vehicles, drive at speed or do dangerous stunts at sea. Sometimes, performances are in front of live audiences.

■ You could advise other performers on health and safety issues.

The type of person suited to this work

Being skilled in a range of sports, including gymnastics, trampolining, parachuting, wrestling, fencing and some of the well-known martial arts, is often useful.

Stunt performers are dedicated to their art, and committed to ensuring that their skills are highly developed. A high level of stamina and fitness is essential. You should be a risk-taker with an adventurous spirit.

You will be happy to practise every aspect of your stunts over and again until they are reproducible in all aspects, so you must be a perfectionist. You must always be aware of the dangers you face, practising long hours to make the performance appear easy!

Working conditions

Part of your working day could be spent within a studio, on location or on a film set.

You could be working indoors or out, in cramped spaces, at heights, or sometimes in bad weather conditions.

The hours will be very long, often up to 16 hours per day depending on the production, with weekend work and travelling to distant places being the norm.

Future prospects

Opportunities for live stunt work are decreasing, as digital graphics and new media can simulate stunts, so competition for work is growing increasingly fierce.

Stunt artists work anywhere in the world, with main employers being film, TV and video production companies.

You could progress into advisory work, helping film directors or advising and training other stunt artists. You could also direct action scenes.

Advantages/disadvantages

You will have the opportunity to travel the world and no two days will be the same.

Seeing the finished product on screen is rewarding.

This is difficult, dangerous work, involving many risks.

This is a very competitive area of work.

Qualifications and courses

There are no academic entry requirements for this work. However you must meet the following requirements set by the Joint Industry Stunt Committee (JISC) register in order to gain work in the UK: Be qualified in at least six categories that fall under fighting, falling, riding/driving, agility/strength or water. For example, you could be skilled in martial arts, fencing, horse riding, boxing, diving and climbing.

You must be 18 or older and have at least 1 year of experience in each category of qualification. When registering these qualifications they must not be more than 5 years old. You will also need to give the JISC evidence that you have spent a minimum of 60 days in front of the camera either as an actor or walk-on artist.

Organisations such as the British Academy of Dramatic Combat, the British Academy of Stage and Screen Combat, and YoungBlood Ltd run year-long courses, workshops and classes in stage combat for practising actors.

Equity recommends that film and TV producers only draw up contracts with stunt performers who are on the JISC register.

Money guide

There is no formal pay scale for stunt performers, and income varies greatly. Equity sets fees for stunt work with television companies and independent producers.

Recommended daily rates are £250–£370 for TV work, and £425 a day for film work.

Although the majority of stunt artists are freelance, you might enter full-time employment at around £11,000 per year. A very experienced performer may earn £25,000+ per year.

Related opportunities

■ Actor/Actress p434
■ Entertainer p443
■ Special Effects Technician p451
■ Choreographer p437

Further information

EQ
Suite E229, Dean Clough, Halifax HX3 5AX
01422 381618; www.thinkeq.org.uk

YoungBlood Ltd
20a Clovelly Rd, London W4 5DS
020 71933 207; www.youngblood.co.uk

British Academy of Stage and Screen Combat
Suite 280, 14 Tottenham Court Road, London W1T 1JY
020 8352 0605; www.bassc.org

Performing Arts

CRCI: Q

THEATRE PRODUCTION ASSISTANT/ PRODUCER

What the work involves

Production assistant

- Assisting the producer, you will have a coordinating role on the production team distributing scripts, keeping the team up-dated, and arranging rehearsing schedules.

Theatre producer

- Producers manage theatrical productions. You will select the performers, choose a suitable director, adapt scripts, coordinate and supervise the work of different departments as well as the artists. You will also be responsible for raising interest in future programmes to get financial backing.

The type of person suited to this work

Production assistant

Production assistants must be efficient, pay attention to detail and be able to work under pressure. You will need to be good at problem solving and have excellent communication skills, be methodical and have the ability to prioritise your work.

Theatre producer

You will need to be highly organised, creative and a good communicator. As part of the role is securing funds for the production, a background in finance or business could be helpful.

Working conditions

You will be working irregular hours, including evenings, weekends and bank holidays. You must be prepared to work at short notice and work overtime as productions can overrun.

Although based in an office or on set, you might need to travel to meetings with potential sponsors and other theatre staff.

Future prospects

Production assistant

This is a popular and competitive area to work in. With experience, there may be opportunities for promotion to a senior production assistant, and then producer.

Theatre producer

This is a competitive area of work at all stages of your career. Most producers are self-employed working on a contract basis. With enough experience and contacts you may be able to run your own production company.

Advantages/disadvantages

The stress of overseeing a production, while continually exploring future work, can play a big part in a producer's life.

Qualifications and courses

Production assistant

There are no specific entry requirements for this job. However, it is highly competitive and most entrants have relevant academic qualifications and/or experience.

A levels and BTEC National qualifications are available in media production. There are HNDs and degrees in broadcasting or media production. Film and Television Freelance Training (FT2) offers training for technical and production careers.

Theatre producer

A producer may have progressed from roles such as production assistant or even runner. A number will have obtained degrees or HNDs in drama, theatre production or communication.

You will work irregular hours – possibly, away from home on location for days or weeks at a time.

Working in theatre is an exciting and challenging job role; you will get to be part of a glamorous industry.

Money guide

Production assistant

£16,000–£22,000 per year is a typical salary as a trainee production assistant. You could earn up to £26,000, with some experience. £27,000–£40,000 is possible at senior levels with lots of experience.

Theatre producer

Earnings vary greatly and could start at £15,000–£25,000 in a small theatre. Established producers can earn salaries of around £50,000 depending on experience.

Related opportunities

- TV, Film and Radio Producer p430
- Artistic Director p436
- Stage Manager p452

Further information

Skillset
Focus Point, 21 Caledonian Road, London N1 9GB
020 7713 9800; www.skillset.org

WARDROBE ASSISTANT

What the work involves

- You will be responsible for assembling and sourcing the costumes needed for TV, film and theatre productions.

- You will be buying or hiring accessories and costumes, and making sure they are correctly stored and transported.

- You will be responsible for altering, repairing, cleaning and fitting costumes.

- You will need to keep a detailed record of the different costumes worn by each performer and make sure they are ready to be worn for each stage of the production.

The type of person suited to this work

You will need to be organised, accurate and be able to remain calm under pressure, especially when dealing with costume emergencies during a live performance.

It is important to have good communication and interpersonal skills as you will be working with a range of people; colleagues and professionals.

A good eye for detail, practical sewing skills and creative flair are all useful when assembling costumes.

Working conditions

You will be working unsocial and long hours the majority of the time. In theatre you will work during day rehearsals, and before and after a performance. TV/film production companies may need you to work away from home for long periods of time.

You will be sitting down, sewing and fitting costumes or running around a set helping to dress performers.

Future prospects

Most work can be found in London and other major cities, with theatres, touring companies and film/TV production companies. It is important to gain as many contacts as possible by undertaking work experience and working for free, as competition for jobs is fierce.

You can gain promotion to wardrobe supervisor and short courses are available which can enable you to have the right skills to move from theatre to film and TV work. Some wardrobe assistants move into specialist areas such as historical costumes or costume design.

Advantages/disadvantages

This is an exciting job in a glamorous industry; you may get to work with celebrities.

The pay is low for such an important role.

You can gain good insight and experience into a competitive industry enabling you to progress to senior positions.

Qualifications and courses

There are no formal entry requirements for this career; the best way to get a job is to gain practical experience. Applying to local theatre or production companies as a volunteer is a good place to start or to any student productions at school, college and university.

As competition is fierce many people study for qualifications in costume related subjects. Courses include City & Guilds certificates and diplomas in media techniques and design and craft, BTEC National Awards in Production Art, Fashion and Clothing, Foundation degrees in fashion and costume craft and degrees in Costume for the Stage and Screen.

Entry to a degree is with 5 GCSEs/S grades (A*–C/1–3) and 2 A levels/H grades. The Diploma in Creative and Media may be a useful starting point.

Drama schools and theatre schools offer full-time and part-time courses in theatre wardrobe, and other colleges offer courses in sewing and pattern cutting.

Most training is done on the job, under the supervision of a senior wardrobe assistant. It is important to develop your skills by taking short courses in costume assembling or by joining a professional association.

Money guide

You could start out doing work experience where only expenses or lunch are paid for. £30 per day is the average amount.

Your starting salary may be around £10,000, increasing to £12,000–£17,000 with experience. Senior wardrobe assistants could earn £28,000+.

Freelance rates do vary greatly depending on the job you are doing and your reputation.

Related opportunities

- Costume Designer p170
- Museum/Art Gallery Curator p356

Further information

The Society of British Theatre Designers
Theatre Design Department, Rose Bruford College, Burnt Oak Lane, Sidcup DA15 9DF
020 8308 2664; www.theatredesign.org.uk

Skillset
Focus Point, 21 Caledonian Road, London N1 9GB
020 7713 9800; www.skillset.org

City&
Guilds

www.cityandguilds.com/myperfectjob

Performing Arts

CRCI: Q

Personal and Other Services including Hair and Beauty

This is a very wide job family and covers everything from hairdressing and beauty to cleaning to wedding consulting. You can enter this career sector with a host of different skills and qualifications. What all of the jobs have in common is that they provide a particular service that a customer has asked for so you need to be good at listening to others and giving customers exactly what they want – people in this sector have a brilliant way with people. You should also demonstrate creativity and strong practical and technical skill as many of the jobs in this family require you to use specialist equipment and to have knowledge of health and safety.

In this section we look at the following jobs:

BEAUTY CONSULTANT

What the work involves

- You will work in department stores and other public locations promoting and selling beauty products on behalf of cosmetics companies.

- You will provide product demonstrations to individual customers or groups, including facials, make-up applications and manicures. You will give advice and information on cosmetic products.

- Your work may involve selling items and taking payments, managing stock levels and keeping the demonstration area attractive and presentable.

- If you are self-employed you will have to control every aspect of your business including sales, finances and marketing.

The type of person suited to this work

A sociable and professional approach is important because you will meet many customers. Working on a store counter can be fast-paced so you should be able to stay calm in busy situations. You will use your communication skills to encourage customers to find out more about your products. You should also have a strong interest in helping people make the best of themselves. For applying make-up and other products you will need an eye for design and good practical skills. Numeracy skills will help you manage stock and take payments. You should enjoy the challenge of working towards sales targets.

Working conditions

You could work between 37 and 40 hours a week, with some weekend and evening hours. If you are self-employed a lot of your hours will be in the evening.

You may have to do some lifting and carrying from the stockroom. Depending on where you work, you may wear a uniform and you will normally be expected to wear the cosmetics that you are selling.

Future prospects

Beauty consultancy offers a flexible career to people who want to combine their interest in beauty with working in sales. As well as employment within department stores, there are opportunities to work in airports and hotels. You may choose to promote and sell products from your own home. With experience, you could progress to working as a team manager and then move on to an area management role. Progression might involve changing employers and moving to a larger company.

Advantages/disadvantages

This type of work is often available on a part-time or flexible basis which may suit people with other commitments.

You might spend a lot of time on your feet which may prove tiring.

You may receive a product allowance of either discounted or free cosmetic products.

Qualifications and courses

Although formal qualifications are not generally required, GCSEs (A*–C) may prove useful, particularly in maths and English. The Diploma in Retail Business might also be helpful.

The VTCT offers Level 2 Certificates in Cosmetic Make-up and Beauty Consultancy, and NVQ/SVQs are available in Retail Skills, Customer Services, and Beauty Therapy (Make-Up). City & Guilds and BTEC both offer a Diploma in Retail Beauty Consultancy. These qualifications may be taken prior to employment or while working. Although these qualifications are not essential, they could be extremely valuable.

The Hairdressing and Beauty Industry Authority (HABIA) validates various beauty, hairdressing and barbering courses. You can also choose to do a retail apprenticeship.

If you plan on being self-employed, you must be over 18 years old. A car and driving licence would also be useful.

Training is generally in-house and may cover topics such as sales techniques, skincare and make-up techniques and stock recording and ordering.

Money guide

Starting salaries range between £11,000 and £13,000 a year. With experience you could earn £16,000 per year. At senior/management levels you could earn between £20,000 and £30,000 a year.

There are usually opportunities to earn extra income through sales of beauty products. If you are a self-employed beauty consultant you will be paid on a commission and rewards scheme only.

Related opportunities

- Beauty Therapist p459
- Hairdresser/Barber p469
- Make-up Artist p445
- Nail Technician p470

Further information

Skillsmart Retail
93 Newman Street, London W1T 3EZ
020 7462 5060; www.skillsmartretail.com

Hairdressing and Beauty Industry Authority
Oxford House, Sixth Avenue, Sky Business Park, Robin Hood Airport, Doncaster DN9 3GG
08452 306 080; info@habia.org; www.habia.org

www.cityandguilds.com/myperfectjob

BEAUTY THERAPIST

What the work involves

- You will provide a range of face and body treatments. This could include facials, massages, electrolysis and waxing treatments.

- Your work will involve cleaning and tidying the treatment room before and after each client.

- Beauty therapists provide services in beauty salons, health clubs and hotels. They also work on a self-employed basis in rented treatment rooms or from their homes.

- You may also have to complete some administrative duties and keep client records.

The type of person suited to this work

People often choose to have a beauty therapy treatment to help them relax, so you will need a calm, confident approach. An interest in helping people with a range of therapies is essential. You will need good communication skills when advising clients about the treatments they can have. A well-presented appearance and a good level of physical fitness are also important. You will work to a high standard of health and hygiene.

Working conditions

Beauty therapists work in salons, health clubs or hotels. You will generally work between 37 and 40 hours a week, including some weekends and evenings. Therapy rooms or cubicles are private, clean and warm. You could visit clients in their homes. Beauty therapists usually wear a uniform. People with allergies to beauty products may not be suitable for this role.

Future prospects

More people than ever before are seeking specialised beauty treatments so future prospects in this line of work are good. Your location can vary from being based in a beauty salon to working in a hotel or spa. With experience you could progress into a management role. You may choose to set up your own beauty therapy business or, with further experience, move into training and lecturing in beauty therapy. There are opportunities to work on cruise ships and in resorts overseas.

Advantages/disadvantages

Therapists working in health and beauty companies or clubs may be provided with free club membership and reduced cost treatments. You might find some treatments difficult to carry out if you aren't comfortable seeing people's bodies.

You can feel proud knowing you have made a customer happy after finishing their chosen treatment.

Money guide

These figures are only approximate as salaries will vary depending on location and employer.

Once qualified as a beauty therapist you could earn a starting salary of around £10,000 per year. With experience you could

Qualifications and courses

Courses include NVQ/SVQs, Vocational Training Charitable Trust (VTCT) awards, BTEC Certificate/Diploma in Retail Beauty Consultancy, International Therapy Examination Council (ITEC) awards, and City &Guilds qualifications in a range of therapies and salon management. The Diploma in Hair and Beauty Studies might also be relevant.

Universities and higher education colleges offer HNCs/Ds, Foundation degrees and degrees in beauty therapy, cosmetic science and beauty combined with hospitality or travel and tourism. Degree programmes usually require applicants to have at least 2 A levels and 5 GCSEs (A*–C). A BTEC National Diploma in Applied Science (Beauty Therapy) or an NVQ Level 3 will usually be accepted.

Trainee beauty therapists work towards NVQs/SVQs at Levels 2 and 3 in Beauty Therapy. Candidates are usually required to have some GCSEs/S grades (A*–C/1–3). Level 3 is the usual qualification for a professional beauty therapist.

Apprenticeships/Skillseekers are available for candidates aged 16–24.

Beauty therapists often extend their knowledge into holistic or alternative treatments such as massage and aromatherapy. The International Federation of Professional Aromatherapists (IFPA) accredits courses at private schools and colleges in the UK.

earn between £16,000 and £19,000 a year. At senior/management levels or if you set up your own salon you could earn over £20,000 per year.

Related opportunities

- Beauty Consultant p458
- Hairdresser/Barber p469
- Make-up Artist p445
- Nail Technician p470
- Spa Therapist p473

Further information

Hairdressing and Beauty Industry Authority
Oxford House, Sixth Avenue, Sky Business Park, Robin Hood Airport, Doncaster DN9 3GG
08452 306080; www.habia.org

British Association of Beauty Therapy and Cosmetology Ltd
Ambrose House, Meteor Court, Barnett Way, Barnwood, Gloucester GL4 3GG
0845 065 9000; www.babtac.com

City&
Guilds

www.cityandguilds.com/myperfectjob

CAR VALET

What the work involves

- Car valets clean and finish car exteriors and interiors using specialist equipment.

- You will clean every part of a vehicle or the exterior only. You could also clean the engine and help prepare cars for bodywork repairs.

- You will clear the interior of rubbish and polish the surfaces and windows. You will also clean the seats. For exteriors you will clean the bodywork and wheels.

- Car valets work for vehicle service centres, new and used car centres, garages, crash repair centres and valeting companies.

The type of person suited to this work

You should be physically fit, as jobs can take between 1 and 4 hours.

You should be able to use different types of cleaning equipment and apply your knowledge of health and safety to your work.

As you will be providing a service to customers, you will need to be a quick but thorough worker with an eye for detail.

You will be reliable and a good team player.

You should be able to cope with dirty working conditions.

Working conditions

The work is very hands on and can be tiring because it involves spending a lot of time on your feet.

You might be based outside, cleaning cars on a forecourt, sometimes in poor weather conditions.

This job requires regular contact with cleaning chemicals, so it might not suit people with allergies or skin conditions.

Future prospects

Car valeting is a key part of the sales and services end of the motor vehicle industry. You could work for a large vehicle repair company or service centre as part of a valeting team. With experience, you could progress to a supervisor role.

You could choose to set up your own valeting company. Some professional car valets offer a mobile service, going out to visit customers at their premises. With experience and further training, you could progress into a technical or sales role.

Advantages/disadvantages

Car valeting jobs may include some regular travel, either when providing services to customers on their premises, or when returning vehicles to customers.

This type of job offers the chance to work in close contact with a range of cars and other vehicles.

Qualifications and courses

No formal qualifications are required for entry to this job. Qualifications in practical or technical subjects, or previous experience in the motor trade or in cleaning work, can be an advantage.

Entrants are usually aged 17, as a full driving licence is almost always required.

Training is done on the job. Car valets may also be sent on short courses run by the manufacturers of cleaning products. The British Institute of Cleaning Science provides a Car Valeting Certificate.

NVQ Level 1 in Vehicle Maintenance and other related courses include modules on valeting. Apprenticeships in cleaning and support services, vehicle body and paint operations, and vehicle maintenance and repair are also available.

Money guide

Starting salaries begin at £12,500 per year.

With experience you could earn £18,000.

Working overtime could possibly increase your salary to around £24,000.

Related opportunities

- Cleaner p464
- Vehicle Parts Operative p499
- Motor Vehicle Technician p235

Further information

British Institute of Cleaning Science
9 Premier Court, Boarden Close, Northampton NN3 6LF
01604 678710; www.bics.org.uk

The Institute of the Motor Industry
Fanshaws, Brickendon, Hertford SG13 8PQ
01992 511 521; www.motor.org.uk

Asset Skills
2 The Courtyard, 48 New North Road, Exeter EX4 4EP
01329 423399; www.assetskills.org;
exeter@assetskills.org

City&
Guilds

www.cityandguilds.com/myperfectjob

CARETAKER

What the work involves

- Caretakers manage the security, cleaning and general maintenance of sites such as schools, colleges and office blocks.

- In some jobs, you would combine caretaking with other roles such as cleaner, gardener, porter or security attendant.

- You will be responsible for opening and locking the premises and checking building security. You will repair broken equipment and reorder supplies.

- Your work could also involve some gardening. You could also clean parts of the site or manage the work of the site cleaners.

The type of person suited to this work

Caretakers need good communication skills, because they interact closely with the people based on their premises. You may be responsible for the security of an entire site, so it's important to have a mature, honest attitude and a full understanding of emergency procedures. The ability to work independently is essential, for example when repairing broken equipment. You should also be able to work as part of a team.

Physical fitness is essential for work such as moving equipment and gardening. You will work to a high standard of health and safety at all times.

Working conditions

A 37-hour working week, which could encompass early mornings, evenings and weekends, is normal in this line of work.

Caretaking work is physically demanding. You might work outside using ladders and other tools.

Caretakers work with cleaning chemicals and wear protective clothing such as overalls. The job might not suit people with allergies or skin conditions.

Future prospects

Many locations only employ one caretaker, so you might need to move to a bigger site to progress. In larger establishments, senior caretakers have the responsibility of managing a small team of caretakers or other staff like cleaners. You could progress to a management position in a private cleaning contract company.

Advantages/disadvantages

As the premises keyholder, you could be on call for emergencies.

This job can be sociable and caretakers often build up a good working relationship with the people based on their premises.

Money guide

The starting salary for an assistant caretaker is £11,000 per year.

Qualifications and courses

No formal qualifications are required for entry to this job. Some GCSEs grades (A*–E), particularly English, maths and practical subjects, may be an advantage. However, hands-on skills and experience in basic DIY, carpentry or, painting and decorating are more important.

Experience in maintenance or security work is useful, as is a driving licence. Within some areas, for example schools, you will need to pass a police check.

Maturity is an advantage and employers often prefer older applicants with relevant experience.

Caretakers are trained on the job. It may be possible for entrants to work towards an NVQ Level 1 and 2 in Cleaning and Support Service. Caretakers can also work towards the Cleaning Supervisory Skills Certificate offered by the British Institute of Cleaning Science. A Diploma in Construction and the Built Environment could also be useful.

Studying for a NVQ Level 3 in Property and Caretaking Supervision or a NVQ Level 4 Certificate in Housing Maintenance Management can speed up career progression. Caretakers can also work towards the Chartered Institute of Housing and the Chartered Institute of Building Level 3 Certificate in Housing Maintenance.

With experience this rises to £16,000 per year.

You could earn £25,000 as a senior or mobile caretaker.

In some work areas, such as education, caretakers are offered on-site subsidised housing as part of their contract.

Related opportunities

- Cleaner p464
- Refuse and Recycling Operative p472
- Hotel Porter p142
- Labourer/Construction Operative p88

Further information

Chartered Institute of Housing
Octavia House, Westwood Way, Coventry CV4 8JP
024 7685 1700; www.cih.org

Chartered Institute of Housing – Scotland
6 Palmerston Place, Edinburgh EH12 5AA
0131 225 4544; www.cih.org/home_scotland

The Caretakers' website
www.thecaretakers.net

www.cityandguilds.com/myperfectjob

Personal and Other Services including Hair and Beauty

CRCI: RB

CARPET/UPHOLSTERY CLEANER

What the work involves

- Carpet and upholstery cleaners clean soft furnishings and carpets using special equipment, and work in a variety of private and public buildings.

- Soft furnishings include curtains, tapestries, antique fabrics, rugs and seat covers. These fabrics and carpets need special cleaning to remove dirt, smoke and grease that build up on them daily.

- You will visit the cleaning site first to assess what needs to be cleaned, and what sort of equipment and chemicals you might need. You will write an assessment of the job and what it will cost for the customer.

The type of person suited to this work

It is important to understand how fabrics and carpets are constructed as this will assist if finding ways to remove stubborn stains. You will also need good practical skills to be able to use specialist cleaning equipment and an understanding of the different types of chemicals you can use.

Excellent communication skills will be essential for talking to customers and colleagues, and you should be able to work alone and be part of a team.

Working conditions

You may need to work evenings and weekends. Most of your time will be spent on your feet and carrying around heavy equipment. You will normally be based indoors, in people's homes or public buildings.

You are likely to need to drive around to work at different locations so a driving licence will be useful. You should also be physically fit.

You might have to wear protective clothing to will protect you from dust and chemicals which may irritate your skin.

Future prospects

Carpet and upholstery cleaners are needed throughout the UK, meaning there will be lots of job opportunities wherever you live. You might work for a general or specialist cleaning company or be self-employed.

With experience you can move into managerial or training roles, or start your own cleaning business.

Advantages/disadvantages

This work brings good job satisfaction; you will be pleasing people by restoring their carpets and upholstery to perfect condition.

Qualifications and courses

There are no formal qualifications for this career. It might be helpful to have basic numeracy and literacy skills for measuring quantities of chemicals and writing quotes for customers. You will usually be trained on the job, and told about health and safety regulations.

Your employer may encourage you to take further training; there are NVQs available at Levels 1 and 2 in Cleaning and Support Services with one unit specifically for carpet and soft furnishings, a City & Guilds Level 2 Certificate in Cleaning Principles and the British Institute of Cleaning Science's Cleaning Operators Proficiency Certificate.

The National Carpet Cleaners Association has regular specialist cleaning courses such as Advanced Spot and Stain Treatment and Removal.

Apprenticeships/Skillseekers may be available for people aged 16–24 in cleaning and support services.

You could find some aspects of cleaning messy or dirty which could be unpleasant.

You have the opportunity to work for yourself and run your own business.

Money guide

The starting salary is around £11,000, with experience this can increase to £14,500. You may be able to earn up to £25,000 if you specialise in antique or tapestry cleaning.

Related opportunities

- Caretaker p461
- Car Valet p460
- Cleaner p464

Further information

The British Institute of Cleaning Science
9 Premier Court, Boarden Close, Moulton Park, Northampton NN3 6LF
01604 678710; www.bics.org.uk

National Carpet Cleaners Association
62c London Road, Oadby, Leicester LE2 5DH
0116 271 9550; www.ncca.co.uk

City & Guilds

www.cityandguilds.com/myperfectjob

CHIMNEY SWEEP

What the work involves

- Chimney sweeps help prevent chimney fires and dangerous fuel emissions by inspecting and cleaning chimney and flue systems, heating appliances and vents.

- Your work will involve using brush and vacuum equipment to clear chimneys and vents of blockages.

- You will provide information and advice to customers on the repair and maintenance of their chimneys.

The type of person suited to this work

Chimney sweeps combine their professional knowledge with practical skills to protect public safety. You will need a good knowledge of different types of chimney and flue systems. Operating brush and vacuum chimney cleaning equipment requires good manual skills.

You will visit customers in their homes, so you should have a friendly, professional attitude. In a job that involves travelling and working alone, a good level of physical fitness is essential.

Working conditions

When clearing chimneys, you will wear protective clothing, such as overalls, gloves, helmet, eye guard and respiratory protection.

Travel to different locations is a regular part of the work, so holding a driving licence is essential.

You may work unsocial hours, at weekends or evenings, to suit customers.

Future prospects

Chimney sweeping is a specialist but essential service. After gaining the relevant experience and professional qualifications, you could set up your own business, providing services within your local area. Most chimney sweeps build up a network of loyal and regular customers.

You could also offer additional roofing or ventilation services. There may be opportunities to work with another professional or to join a small specialist company.

Advantages/disadvantages

You will have the opportunity to meet a variety of people.

Most chimney sweeps work on a self-employed basis, which can lead to some job insecurity, particularly at the start of their careers.

Money guide

Most chimney sweeps are self-employed and are paid on a job-by-job basis.

Earnings will depend on a sweep's speed at the task and the hours worked. You could charge between £30 and £55 for an

Qualifications and courses

There are no formal entry requirements, but basic qualifications in English and maths are useful. Previous experience of manual work such as construction is an advantage. You would normally be trained on the job by an experienced chimney sweep.

Trainee chimney sweeps can work towards membership of the National Association of Chimney Sweeps (NACS). NACS provides an induction course accredited by CITB and City & Guilds, covering basic chimney sweeping techniques and health and safety. On completion of the training, sweeps become probationary members of NACS until they have gained sufficient experience and on-site training to work as professional sweeps.

NACS also provides an NVQ Level 2 in Chimney Engineering based on assessments in the workplace and at the NACS centre.

The other professional body for chimney sweeps is the Guild of Master Sweeps. To become a member, you must hold a City & Guilds 7641 qualification in Chimney Cleaning and successfully complete the Guild entrance exam.

NACS also provides short courses in particular areas of the work. To be qualified to carry out inspections and work on gas appliances you need to gain a certificate of competence through the Accredited Certification Scheme (ACS), leading to registration with Gas Safe.

entire sweep. If working full time you could expect to earn between £16,000 and £25,000 per year.

Related opportunities

- Heating and Ventilating Engineer p102
- Roofer p117
- Steeplejack p122
- Cleaner p464

Further information

National Association of Chimney Sweeps
Unit 15, Emerald Way, Stone Business Park, Stone ST15 0SR
01785 811732; www.chimneyworks.co.uk

Guild of Master Sweeps
London Road, Attleborough, Norfolk NR17 2DE
01953 451322; www.guild-of-master-sweeps.co.uk

City & Guilds

www.cityandguilds.com/myperfectjob

CLEANER

What the work involves

- You will be responsible for cleaning and tidying a variety of places which people either live in or visit.

- Industrial cleaners work in public buildings such as hospitals, prisons, schools and health centres and work to the highest standards to reach health and safety requirements.

- Domestic cleaners work in people's homes and may have additional tasks such as ironing and washing up.

- You will use a variety of equipment such as hoovers, mops, dusters and brooms.

The type of person suited to this work

You will need to be honest and trustworthy, as you will be entering people's homes and workplaces where valuables could be on display.

Being fit and mobile is important, as you will be on your feet for long periods, bending and stretching and carrying heavy equipment.

Good communication skills are important to interact with colleagues and clients, especially if you run your own cleaning business.

Working conditions

Working hours for cleaners do vary, as does the number of hours worked; you may be working weekends and evenings when public places are closed or standard office hours if the owner of the home you are cleaning is out all day. Hospitals would need to be kept clean 24/7.

Many cleaners are self employed and can work for different clients in one day. It would be useful to have a driving licence. It is usual for cleaners to have a uniform or wear protective clothing.

Future prospects

There is a great demand for cleaners in all sectors. You could choose to work for a cleaning company or be self employed.

Many cleaners choose to set up their own small business, or move into other jobs such as caretakers or supervise a team of cleaners.

Advantages/disadvantages

You can work different shifts that fit in well with other jobs or family commitments.

Qualifications and courses

There are no formal qualifications for this job. It may be helpful to have basic literacy and numeracy skills.

There may be Apprenticeships/Skillseekers available for 16–24 year olds in cleaning or support services.

Cleaners train whilst working, and may be able to study for qualifications such as NVQs at Levels 1 and 2 in Cleaning and Support Services or The British Institute of Cleaning Science Cleaning Operators Proficiency Certificate.

Experienced cleaners can study for an NVQ at Level 2 in Team Leading or a City & Guilds Level 3 Diploma in Cleaning Services Supervision.

You can progress to being the owner of your own cleaning business.

Some aspects of cleaning may be difficult if you are squeamish.

Money guide

The amount you earn can depend on your employer and the number of hours you work.

Most cleaners are paid hourly, around £10–13; you may earn more in London.

Related opportunities

- Caretaker p461
- Car Valet p460
- Window Cleaner p475
- Pest Control Technician p471

Further information

Asset Skills
2 The Courtyard, 48 New North Road, Exeter EX4 4EP
01392 423399; www.assetskills.org

British Institute of Cleaning Science
9 Premier Court, Boarden Close, Moulton Park, Northampton NN3 6LF
01604 678710; www.bics.org.uk

www.cityandguilds.com/myperfectjob

CREMATORIUM TECHNICIAN

What the work involves

- Crematorium technicians assist with the running of the crematorium and cemetery premises.

- Your work will involve operating cremation equipment to a high standard of health and safety. You will ensure that the cremated remains are stored and disposed of correctly.

- You will help manage the chapel and cemetery and attend cremation ceremonies.

- You will also assist with other cemetery duties, such as excavating graves and grounds maintenance. However, grave digging work is mostly undertaken by contractors working for local authorities.

The type of person suited to this work

Meeting and working with bereaved people requires a mature, sympathetic attitude. You will use your communication skills to liaise with people in the process of cremation ceremonies. A good level of physical fitness is helpful in a role that covers a wide range of activities.

It's important that cremations are undertaken to a high standard of health and safety, so you should be able to follow strict working guidelines. Office and ICT skills can be helpful in this job. The ability to work as part of a team is also useful.

Working conditions

This can be a tiring job due to the range of activities involved and the physical requirements of operating cremation machinery.

You will be on your feet for long hours.

You will need to be smartly dressed when facing the public and your outfit will usually be provided for you.

When operating machinery you will need to wear protective clothing.

You will normally work 37–40 hours a week, with some overtime including Saturdays.

Future prospects

Due to changing public attitudes, the number of cremations is increasing, as is the demand for skilled professionals.

Crematorium technicians are usually employed by local councils. With experience, you could progress to working as a senior crematorium technician and manage a team of technicians.

Advantages/disadvantages

This role provides the opportunity to provide support to people at an important and challenging time.

The nature of the job means this work can sometimes be distressing.

Qualifications and courses

There are no formal entry requirements for this type of work, and training is done on the job.

Trainees follow the Crematorium Technicians' Training Scheme (CTTS) provided by the Institute of Cemetery and Crematorium Management (ICCM). The scheme consists of a BTEC Intermediate Certificate and a BTEC Advanced Certificate. Employees may also work towards NVQ/SVQ Level 2 in Amenity Horticulture (Cemeteries and Graveyards).

Another work-based training route is provided by the Federation of Burial and Cremation Authorities' (FBCA) TEST scheme.

Experienced crematorium technicians can progress to management roles. The ICCM Diploma in Cemetery and Crematorium Management can be studied by distance learning. The ICCM also operates a Continuing Professional Development scheme for crematorium staff at all levels.

Money guide

Starting salaries are around £14,000 per year.

With experience you could earn £20,000.

At senior/management level you could earn £25,000+.

Related opportunities

- Embalmer p467
- Funeral Director p468
- Cleaner p464
- Pest Control Technician p471

Further information

Institute of Cemetery and Crematorium Management
City of London Cemetery, Aldersbrook Road,
London E12 5DQ
020 8989 4661; www.iccm-uk.com

The Cremation Society of Great Britain
2nd Floor, Brecon House, 16/16a Albion Place,
Maidstone ME14 5DZ
01622 688292; www.crematorium.org.uk

The Federation of Burial and Cremation Authorities
41 Salisbury Road, Carshalton SM5 3HA
020 8669 4521; www.fbca.org.uk

www.cityandguilds.com/myperfectjob

CRCi: RA | Personal and Other Services including Hair and Beauty

DRY CLEANER

What the work involves

- You will be cleaning clothes and fabrics which are delicate or sensitive to being washed in water; you will use chemical and steam to clean garments instead.

- You might be cleaning specialist fabrics or garments such as wool, suede, bridal wear, suits and beaded fabrics.

- You will be using potentially hazardous chemicals, although many dry cleaners now use safe and environmentally friendly products.

- You will assist customers at the counter, take payments, complete paperwork and work the cleaning machinery.

The type of person suited to this work

You will need to have good communication skills for dealing with customers and practical skills for handling the cleaning machinery. A good level of fitness would be helpful for carrying heavy items of clothing and organising cleaned garments.

You will be dealing with payments, and paperwork, so it is important to have good numeracy skills and an organised approach to your work.

Working conditions

You will be working standard hours, Monday to Friday, and usually Saturday as well. More dry cleaners are staying open in the evenings and Sundays. You are likely to work shifts which include all of these hours.

You will be working in the store, at the counter taking payments and behind the counter with the cleaning machines.

You might be exposed to some chemical fumes and there is a danger of burning yourself on pressing machines. This work wouldn't suit people with allergies.

Most stores will supply you with a uniform.

Future prospects

There are jobs available across the UK in high street dry cleaning stores or industrial cleaning plants which clean for hospitals or factories. Currently there is a shortage of dry cleaners, with more vacancies than applicants.

You can progress from an assistant position to supervisory or managerial role; it might help to gain a qualification in team leading to progress more quickly. After gaining lots of experience and knowledge of dry cleaning you could choose to open your own store.

Qualifications and courses

There are no formal qualifications needed for this work, although good numeracy and literacy skills will be helpful.

You will be trained on the job by another dry cleaner. It may be useful to have some previous experience washing clothes or other laundry work.

Many employers offer opportunities to study for qualifications part time. These include NVQ Level 2 in Dry Cleaning Operations, Level 2 Certificate in Textile Care Services and NVQ Level 2 in Dry Cleaning Service Support. The Skillsfirst QCF Awards at Levels 1–3 in Retail Skills may also be useful. The Guild of Cleaners and Launderers offers several certificates in laundry services.

All dry cleaners which use solvents must be registered and hold a permit.

Advantages/disadvantages

This is a good career if you enjoy practical work and providing a service.

You could be affected by the chemical fumes which would be unpleasant.

There are opportunities to run your own business.

Money guide

Your starting salary will be around £11,600 a year. With experience this can increase to £13,000+.

If you are in a senior position or manager of the store, you could earn between £16,000 and £30,000, depending on the reputation of the store and how well you perform.

Related opportunities

- Cleaner p464
- Car Valet p460
- Textile Operative p248

Further information

Textile Services Association
7 Churchill Court, 58 Station Road, North Harrow HA2 7SA
020 8863 7755; www.tsa-uk.org

Guild of Cleaners and Launderers
5 Portland Place, London W1B 1PW
0845 600 1838; www.gcl.org.uk

www.cityandguilds.com/myperfectjob

EMBALMER

What the work involves

- Embalmers prepare the bodies of deceased people for funerals and for viewing by their relatives. They preserve the body in the most life-like way.

- You will use specialist equipment to remove all liquids and gases from the deceased person's body and replace these with disinfecting fluid, which helps prevent infection.

- Your work will also involve preparing and cleaning the embalming equipment and treatment area.

The type of person suited to this work

You must be able to cope with working with the bodies of deceased people. A respectful approach to your work is essential. You might have to deal with distressing sights so a mature, detached and down-to-earth attitude is very important.

Embalming work involves presenting a deceased person in the most positive way for grieving relatives. A creative flair and attention to detail will help you to achieve this.

Working conditions

Embalmers work in operating rooms within funeral parlours. These are maintained to a very high standard of hygiene and kept at a low temperature.

Whilst embalming you will wear protective clothing such as latex gloves. The regular contact with chemicals means that this job may not suit people with skin conditions or allergies.

Embalming is physically demanding work and you should expect to work irregular hours and be on call.

Future prospects

Embalming is an integral part of the funeral care process, so there is constant demand for embalmers. You could gain employment with a funeral care company or you may choose to work on a self-employed basis, providing services for a number of funeral companies.

There are opportunities to work abroad. With extensive experience, you could go into teaching or training.

There are around 1,300 qualified embalmers in the UK, but the industry has a slow turnover of staff and getting in may be difficult.

Advantages/disadvantages

There are opportunities to freelance, working for a number of employers at the same time.

There are also opportunities to work overseas.

This can be distressing work, so you will need to be able to stay detached and professional.

Qualifications and courses

There are no formal entry requirements for working as an embalmer, but GCSEs/S grades including English, maths, chemistry, biology and religious studies may be useful.

Training is mainly on the job, with part-time tuition from a registered tutor at weekends or evenings, or through distance learning. Most embalmers work for qualifications awarded by the International Examinations Board of Embalmers (IEBE).

The IEBE training is modular, and trainees must pass the foundation module and test before proceeding with the rest of the training. Once you have passed the foundation module, you can register with The British Institute of Embalmers (BIE) as a student member.

The main IEBE training involves modules in anatomy, physiology, bacteriology and practical embalming, including examinations and practical work. Once you have passed these you can apply for full membership of the BIE.

Some embalmers train to work in specialist areas, such as with disaster teams, embalming the bodies of victims.

Money guide

Starting salaries begin at around £12,500 per year.

With experience you could earn £17,000.

At senior levels or, with a good reputation, it is possible to earn £30,000+.

Related opportunities

- Crematorium Technician p465
- Funeral Director p468

Further information

British Institute of Embalmers
21c Station Road, Knowle, Solihull B93 0HL
01564 778991; www.bioe.co.uk

The Federation of Burial and Cremation Authorities
41 Salisbury Road, Carshalton SM5 3HA
020 8669 4521; www.fbca.org.uk

www.cityandguilds.com/myperfectjob

ENTRY LEVEL 2

CRCI: RA

Personal and Other Services including Hair and Beauty

FUNERAL DIRECTOR

What the work involves

- Funeral directors coordinate funeral arrangements for burials and cremations.
- You will liaise with the family of the deceased, offering advice and taking note of the details they would like included in the ceremony.
- You will arrange the date and location of the funeral, transport and death notices. You will also attend the funeral.
- You might undertake embalming work.

The type of person suited to this work

You need to have a sensitive and mature attitude to your work.

Excellent communication skills and a high standard of health and safety are essential.

For liaising with local authorities and completing paperwork you will need a good knowledge of the relevant legal issues, and to be able to manage a business you will need good office and budgetary skills.

A good knowledge of different cultures and religions is also helpful.

Working conditions

Funeral directors work in funeral homes or centres based within high-street outlets or other areas.

You may work on call at weekends and in the evenings. You may also be required to work extra hours during busy times.

Funeral directors must dress smartly.

Future prospects

Most people start a career in this area by gaining experience as a funeral operative or assistant. They learn the varied aspects of the job from more experienced colleagues and work towards professional qualifications.

You could work for one of the large funeral services companies or for a smaller company. With experience, you could work as a funeral director abroad. With additional experience, you could set up your own funeral services company.

Advantages/disadvantages

Depending on the size of funeral company you work for, you may be on call on a regular basis, which can affect your personal life.

Providing a professional sympathetic service to people experiencing a very difficult time can be rewarding.

Qualifications and courses

There are no minimum academic qualifications to work as a funeral director. You will normally start as an assistant and learn whilst working. For funeral operatives/assistants with driving duties, a driving licence is essential.

BTEC and SQA offer vocational qualifications for people working as assistants and directors. The Professional Diploma in Funeral Directing is for funeral directors.

NVQs/SVQs are available in Funeral Services at Levels 2 and 3, and there is a Level 4 qualification in Funeral Services Management. The University of Bath also offer a Foundation degree in Funeral Services.

Another route is to gain the National Association of Funeral Directors' (NAFD) Foundation Certificate in Funeral Directing. This is an introductory course which candidates must have completed before they can start the NAFD Diploma in Funeral Directing (DipFD). In order to work towards this professional qualification you must have a minimum of 2 years' employment in funeral services. This includes experience of personally arranging at least 25 funerals.

Money guide

Starting salaries are around £14,500 per year.

With experience as a funeral director's assistant, you could earn £16,000–£24,000.

At senior/management level, you could earn £32,000+.

Related opportunities

- Crematorium Technician p465
- Embalmer p467

Further information

National Association of Funeral Directors
618 Warwick Road, Solihull B91 1AA
0845 230 1343; www.nafd.org.uk

The British Institute of Funeral Directors
1 Gleneagles House, Vernon Gate, South Street, Derby DE1 1UP
0800 032 2733; www.bifd.org.uk

City&
Guilds

www.cityandguilds.com/myperfectjob

HAIRDRESSER/BARBER

What the work involves

- Hairdressers shampoo, cut and style clients' hair to a range of modern or classic looks. You could also provide dry or wet shaves to male clients.

- You will discuss hair treatments with clients and may carry out colouring, tinting, perming and fixing hair extensions. You will also give advice on general haircare and hair products.

- At senior levels, you could provide training to junior hairdressers.

The type of person suited to this work

Cutting and styling hair involves close personal contact with clients so hairdressers need good communication skills and a friendly manner.

You should have an interest in fashion, a creative flair and an eye for detail. You will need manual dexterity when using specialist chemicals and equipment required to style, perm and colour customers' hair.

Sometimes you may work on reception booking appointments and taking cash, so you will have to be efficient, confident and numerate.

Some salons require staff to be able to offer a wider choice of services, such as nail and beauty treatments.

Working conditions

Most hairdressers and barbers are based in salons in high streets and other areas. Some work as mobile hairdressers, providing services to clients in their own homes.

You will do a 40-hour week, which may include Saturday. A lot of salons have late openings once or twice a week. Certain salons also open on Sunday.

Hairdressing involves bending over customers for long periods of the day, so you will need to be physically fit.

Future prospects

In a salon, you could progress to a role as senior stylist or manager. Alternatively, you could set up your own business. As a mobile hairdresser, you could provide services to people in hospitals, care homes or prisons as well as private clients.

There are opportunities to work on cruise ships. With further beauty therapy training you could work in film, television or the theatre.

Advantages/disadvantages

Regular contact with beauty products and chemicals means that this type of work may not suit people with skin conditions or allergies.

This is a very sociable job which will allow you to express your creativity.

Qualifications and courses

Some people start as unqualified assistants/trainees and progress with experience. You could study for NVQs validated by the Hairdressing and Beauty Industry Authority in Hairdressing or Barbering. Many trainees will often undertake this training through an Apprenticeship.

Some NVQs combine hairdressing with beauty therapy, and it is possible to specialise in African-Caribbean hair.

The Freelance Hair and Beauty Federation runs courses for hairdressers on establishing and managing their business, and ongoing continuing professional development courses.

Qualified hairdressers can take more specialised courses through part-time study, for example City & Guilds certificates, NVQ Level 4 in Salon Management, or a BTEC in Hairdressing and Salon Management.

Degrees and Foundation degrees in Hairdressing and Salon Management are also available.

Those with NVQ Level 2 can register as State Registered Hairdressers with the Hairdressing Council.

Money guide

As a trainee at entry level you could earn the national minimum wage of £7,342–£11,918 per year, depending on your age and the number of hours you work.

With experience and full training you could earn £13,500–£20,000. Top national hairdressers earn £30,000+.

Related opportunities

- Beauty Therapist p459
- Image Consultant p486
- Make-up Artist p445
- Nail Technician p470

Further information

Hairdressing And Beauty Industry Authority
Oxford House, Sixth Avenue, Sky Business Park, Robin Hood Airport, Doncaster DN9 3GG
08452 306080; www.habia.org

www.cityandguilds.com/myperfectjob

CRCI: RC Personal and Other Services including Hair and Beauty

NAIL TECHNICIAN

What the work involves

- Nail technicians provide a range of nail treatments to clients, including manicures, nail extensions, nail art and nail jewellery. Depending on the treatment you are providing, you will work with a range of beauty products and equipment such as brushes, stencils and airbrushes.

- You will discuss with clients their intended treatment and check their hands for skin or nail disorders.

- You will provide advice about aftercare and recommend products for nail care and maintenance.

- Your work will also include cleaning and tidying the treatment area before and after each client.

The type of person suited to this work

Nail technicians work with many people so you should have good communication skills. A professional appearance is also important. You will need excellent manual handling skills to undertake nail design work. A good knowledge of nail and beauty products is important. An eye for design and an interest in fashion are essential.

It will also be important that you are able to maintain a high standard of hygiene at all times.

If you work as a freelance technician you will need good business skills. You should also be able to cope with travelling to different work locations.

Working conditions

Nail technicians work in nail or beauty salons and other locations. Mobile nail technicians provide treatments to clients in their own homes.

Salon-based technicians usually work between 30 and 40 hours a week with some evening/weekend work.

Nail technicians come into regular contact with chemicals, so the job might not suit people with skin conditions or allergies.

Future prospects

Nail technology is a popular area of beauty and treatments are now available in nail salons, department stores and beauty and hairdressing salons.

You could work as a freelance nail technician, providing services to care homes and hotels as well as private clients. If you gain additional professional qualifications you could offer other therapies.

There are opportunities to work abroad or on cruise ships.

You could choose to teach nail treatments or become a NVQ assessor.

Advantages/disadvantages

Working as a freelancer can allow you to work flexible hours but unsocial hours are likely.

Qualifications and courses

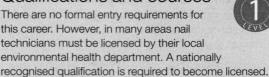

There are no formal entry requirements for this career. However, in many areas nail technicians must be licensed by their local environmental health department. A nationally recognised qualification is required to become licensed.

Relevant courses include the Vocational Training Charitable Trust (VTCT) Certificate in Nail Treatments with the option to specialise in Nail Technology or Nail Art and NVQ in Nail Services at Levels 2 and 3. A specialist unit in artificial nail systems is included in the NVQ Level 3 in Beauty Therapy. The BTEC National Award, Certificate or Diploma in Beauty Therapy Sciences includes a specialist unit in nail technology. You could also complete a CIBTAC Level 2 Diploma in Nail Treatments, an ITEC Level 3 Diploma in Nail Technology or a VTCT Level 2 Certificate in Nail Treatments, Nail Art or Nail Technology.

Apprenticeships are available to those aged 16–24.

Some salons provide bonus schemes and commission payments for product sales. Additional perks include free or reduced cost beauty treatments.

Money guide

Freelancers usually charge per job. This varies according to the nature of the treatment, from £12 to £50+.

Starting salaries are around £10,000 per year.

With experience, you could earn £11,000–£16,000.

At senior/management level you could earn £18,000–£28,000.

Related opportunities

- Beauty Therapist p459
- Hairdresser/Barber p469
- Make-up Artist p445

Further information

British Association of Beauty Therapy and Cosmetology
Ambrose House, Meteor Court, Barnett Way, Barnwood, Gloucester GL4 3GG
0845 065 9004; www.babtac.com

International Therapy Examination Council
2nd Floor, Chiswick Gate, 598–608 Chiswick High Road, London W4 5RT
020 8994 4141; www.itecworld.co.uk

www.cityandguilds.com/myperfectjob

PEST CONTROL TECHNICIAN

What the work involves

- Pest control technicians protect public health by treating and eradicating infestations of insects and vermin such as cockroaches and rats.

- Pest control technicians work in private homes, offices, shops and other sites.

- Your job may involve investigating or monitoring a site to check for pests.

- You will use a range of specialist chemicals and equipment. Your work might involve fitting traps or spraying areas with chemicals.

- In some situations you will provide advice to customers on the prevention of pest problems.

The type of person suited to this work

This job is all about protecting public health so you should be able to work to a high standard of health and safety. Working with chemical treatments and specialist equipment demands a professional approach. You will need to be calm when dealing with large numbers of insects and rodents. A strong stomach will also help you cope with working in unpleasant conditions.

Physical fitness and good manual handling skills are essential. You will need to be able to communicate and have a tactful approach when providing advice to customers. You will use your writing skills to keep records and write reports.

Working conditions

Whilst not all pest control work is unpleasant, dealing with dirty or unhygienic situations is a likely part of the job.

You will travel to different locations on a regular basis. A driving licence is essential.

Pest control technicians must wear protective clothing, such as overalls and eye goggles. They work with a range of chemicals, so the job might not suit people with skin conditions or allergies.

Future prospects

Pest control technicians provide an important service to domestic homes, factories, offices and other locations in cities and rural areas. You could run your own business or work with local councils or specialist companies.

With experience you could progress to supervising teams of staff, managing a large pest control company or working in a management role for local councils.

Advantages/disadvantages

Some employers provide extra pay for overtime.

This type of work is sometimes available on a flexible basis.

You might be faced with unpleasant situations.

Qualifications and courses

A good standard of education is required, with GCSEs/S grades (A*–E/1–5) in English, maths and science being useful. Because the job involves using specialist equipment and dangerous substances, some employers prefer candidates to be over 18 years old.

Training is undertaken on the job, supervised by an experienced technician. There might also be opportunities to attend training courses.

The entry-level qualification for the industry is the British Pest Control Association/Royal Society for the Promotion of Health Certificate in Pest Control, which equates to NVQ Level 2.

NVQs/SVQs are available in Pest Control Supervision at Level 3. The British Pest Control Association also offers a Pest Control Diploma and specialist short courses in fumigation, rodents, insects, bird management and field biology, and a Technical Inspector Certificate.

The British Wood Preserving and Damp-Proofing Association offer short courses covering insect infestation. The National Proficiency Training Council (NPTC) offers Certificates in Competence in the use of pesticides in rural areas.

Money guide

As a trainee you could start at around £12,000 per year.

With experience and qualifications, this rises to £16,500–£22,000.

At senior levels you could earn £22,000+.

Related opportunities

- Environmental Health Practitioner/Officer p35
- Refuse and Recycling Operative p472
- Cleaner p464
- Toxicologist p537

Further information

British Pest Control Association
1 Gleneagles House, Vernon gate, South Street, Derby DE1 1UP
01332 294288; www.bpca.org.uk

National Pest Technicians Association
NPTA House, Hall Lane, Kinoulton NG12 3EF
01949 81133; www.npta.org.uk

www.cityandguilds.com/myperfectjob

CRCI: RB | Personal and Other Services including Hair and Beauty

REFUSE AND RECYCLING OPERATIVE

What the work involves

■ You will collect rubbish and unwanted items and take them to an official rubbish tip or recycling depot.

■ Working as part of a team you will travel around your area, emptying bins, removing plastic sacks of waste or picking up recyclable waste.

■ Recycling operatives may have additional duties, such as sorting rubbish or collecting hazardous waste. Recycling technicians also work in recycling facilities, sorting through recycled materials in preparation for re-use.

The type of person suited to this work

A strong stomach is useful when dealing with rubbish. You should also be able to cope with getting your hands dirty.

Most companies are required to complete their rounds to deadlines, so you should be able to work under pressure.

You may also need manual handling skills to lift and move recycling collections. For work in a recycling sorting facility, you will need good eyesight and attention to detail.

Working conditions

You will wear protective clothing, such as gloves and overalls, and you will come into contact with dirt and rubbish on a regular basis. The work will involve nasty smells and some unpleasant sights.

The hours are generally around 6am–3pm, except for busy holiday periods when the amount of rubbish increases.

This type of work might not suit people with skin conditions or allergies.

Future prospects

Loaders will always be in demand as even recyclable rubbish has to be collected.

You could work for a contracting company providing services for a local authority and there are some jobs with specialist companies who collect paper or food waste.

It is likely that there will be a growth in the number of recycling jobs in local councils, contracting companies providing services to councils and recycling companies.

With experience, you could progress to supervisory or management work.

Advantages/disadvantages

For most jobs, you will have to start very early in the morning. However, this means that you will be able to finish your working day quite early.

The work is physically demanding and potentially unsafe.

Qualifications and courses

There are no formal entry requirements but you will need to be at least 18 years old and drivers must hold a Large Goods Vehicle Licence (LGV licence).

You could choose to do an Apprenticeship in Driving Goods Vehicles or in Waste Operatives.

On starting, you will have to take a short course on health and safety and then be trained on the job.

You can work towards NVQs/SVQs at Levels 1–2 in Waste Management Operations with specialist options in waste collection or recycling and Level 3 in Waste Management Supervision. You could also complete NVQs/SVQs in Recycling Operations at Levels 1–2. An NVQ/SVQ in Community Recycling is also available.

People working in supervisory roles can gain an NVQ/SVQ Level 3 in Management of Recycling Operations. It is also possible to work towards Level 3 and 4 qualifications in Environmental Conservation and Conservation Control.

Money guide

Salaries start at about £11,000 per year. With experience you could earn between £15,000 and £17,000 a year. At senior levels it is possible to earn between £18,000 and £25,000 per year.

Drivers can earn between £17,000 and £20,000 a year.

There are usually opportunities to earn extra by working overtime or during holiday periods.

Related opportunities

■ Large Goods Vehicle Driver p607
■ Loader p609
■ Removals Operative p623
■ Delivery Driver p601

Further information

Waste Management Industry Training and Advisory Board
Peterbridge House, 3 The Lakes, Northampton NN4 7HE
01604 231950; www.wamitab.org.uk

www.cityandguilds.com/myperfectjob

SPA THERAPIST/ TECHNICIAN

What the work involves

- Spa therapists provide various treatments which are designed to enhance appearance, reduce stress or improve wellbeing.

- You will offer an assortment of treatments which may include facials, manicures and pedicures, massage, body treatments like wraps and exfoliation and specialist treatments such as light therapy and lymphatic drainage.

- You will be required to talk to your clients in order to discover their specific health needs and personal expectations. You will ensure they are comfortable at all times and provide them with any necessary aftercare advice.

- You will be expected to maintain the various areas of the salon.

The type of person suited to this work

You will need a caring manner and the ability to make people feel at ease. You should be discreet and understand the role of confidentiality within the industry. It is important that you are able to work effectively as part of a team. You should have excellent dexterity, outstanding attention to detail and good time management skills. You will need to have strong personal hygiene and a smart appearance. A solid understanding of health and safety requirements would also prove beneficial.

Working conditions

Most of the work will be based in private treatment rooms which will be warm and clean, however you may be required to complete some treatments in wet rooms. A great deal of time will be spent standing and bending. Some products may irritate your skin, particularly if you are prone to such reactions.

Most spa therapists wear a uniform. Full-time hours are usually between 37 and 40 hours a week and may often include evening and weekend work.

Future prospects

You will have the possibility of working in various beauty related professions. You may choose to progress to a supervisory or management post. You could decide to combine the more practical aspects with administrative work. There is also the option of becoming a trainer or lecturer. There are numerous options available for overseas work.

Advantages/disadvantages

The unusual working hours may prove inconvenient.

Opportunities within this industry are varied and so you will have many options regarding which environment you wish to work in.

Being on your feet all day might be tiring.

You may receive bonuses, discounted/free products and the use of facilities.

Qualifications and courses

Beauty therapists/technicians need qualifications in the areas of treatment or therapy they wish to offer. It is also possible to gain experience by working in a salon and building on the treatments you are qualified to offer.

Most spa therapists hold an NVQ Level 3 in Spa Therapy, a BTEC National Diploma in Beauty Therapy Sciences or equivalent. You will need 4 GCSEs (A*–C) including English, maths and science or an NVQ Level 2 in Beauty Therapy for entry. The Diploma in Hair and Beauty Studies may also be useful.

You can also choose to do an Advanced Apprenticeship in Spa Therapy leading to an NVQ Level 3 in Spa Therapy.

If you wish to progress into management then a Foundation degree in Beauty and Spa services or a Foundation degree/degree in Spa Management will give you an advantage. Foundation degrees generally require candidates to have 1 A level, a BTEC National Diploma in beauty therapy sciences or NVQ Level 3 along with three GCSEs (A*–C), including a science subject. Degree courses generally require 2 A levels and 5 GCSEs (A*–C) or equivalent.

Money guide

Salaries range depending on location and employer.

Starting salaries for newly qualified spa therapists are usually in the area of £12,000–£14,000 a year.

After a few years that may increase to between £15,000 and £19,000.

Upon progression to management level that might swell to somewhere between £20,000 and £40,000.

These amounts may vary depending on the number of hours worked.

Related opportunities

- Beauty Therapist p459
- Beauty Consultant p458
- Nail Technician p470

Further information

The Guild of Professional Beauty Therapists
Guild House, 320 Burton Road, Derby DE23 6AF
0845 21 77 383; www.beautyguild.com

www.cityandguilds.com/myperfectjob

Personal and Other Services including Hair and Beauty

CRCI: RC

WEDDING CONSULTANT

What the work involves

- Wedding consultants organise ceremonies, receptions and other events to suit a client's plans and budget.

- You will help come up with creative ideas and themes, as well as advise the couple on etiquette.

- You will negotiate prices, book and confirm with all suppliers and keep a detailed record of costs. For example you will liaise with florists, caterers, photographers, musicians, venues and hair stylists.

- You will also help organise transport, stag and hen weekends, wedding attire and lodging for out of town guests.

The type of person suited to this work

You need to be enthusiastic and approachable. You should be a good listener and always take into account your client's ideas and wishes. You will also need the initiative and creativity to develop these dreams into a reality. A good sense of style and attention to detail is essential.

It's important to have both financial and crisis management skills. It's your job to ensure the wedding stays within budget and runs smoothly. You will need to be organised and able to multi-task.

You should be a confident and effective negotiator.

Working conditions

It's common to work 12-hour days, especially in the period leading up to the wedding. Although you can generally plan your own hours you will most likely need to meet your clients during evenings and weekends. The busiest months for weddings are February, June and December.

You could work from home or out of an office but most of your time will be spent visiting venues, suppliers and clients. A driving licence is essential.

Future prospects

Thanks to many Hollywood films profiling wedding planners the market is growing. You might work for a hotel or event-management company and start out temping as an assistant. You could also offer to plan weddings for friends, helping you to build up a portfolio.

Most wedding consultants are self-employed. Your success will depend on your reputation and how well you market yourself.

You could choose to specialise in destination weddings or work overseas.

Qualifications and courses

There are no set entry requirements for this career. A background in hospitality, event planning, design, catering or marketing is useful, especially if you want to work for a large events company.

Degrees, Foundation degrees and HNDs are available in events management.

Those with proof of more than 3 years' business trading, three client references and a satisfactory quality inspection can become members of the National Association of Professional Wedding Services who offer an Advanced Certification in Wedding Design and Management.

The UK Alliance of Wedding Planners' 2-day course which includes a work placement in wedding planning may also be helpful.

Advantages/disadvantages

This is a glamorous and creative role.

It's rewarding when you make a bride and groom's dream wedding come true.

You will be under a lot of pressure to make things perfect.

Money guide

If you work for a wedding and events planning company you can earn between £16,000 and £20,000 a year starting out. This rises to £40,000 with experience.

If you freelance, you can charge a percentage of the total cost of the wedding, an hourly rate or a flat fee. Your salary will depend on how many weddings you organise a year.

Related opportunities

- Events and Exhibition Organiser p417
- Image Consultant p486
- Entertainment Manager p386

Further information

National Association of Professional Wedding Services
Shelley Way, London SW19 1TH
020 8090 1921; www.theweddingassociation.co.uk

UK Alliance of Wedding Planners
7 Churchfield Road, Coggeshall CO6 1QE
0137 656 1544; www.ukawp.com

City&
Guilds

www.cityandguilds.com/myperfectjob

WINDOW CLEANER

What the work involves

- You will be cleaning windows and other glass surfaces in private and public buildings, using detergents.

- You will be using ladders to reach high windows or platforms and ropes for very tall office buildings. Recently the use of water pumping poles has reduced the use of ladders for health and safety reasons.

- If you are self-employed you might need to organise paperwork and collect payments.

The type of person suited to this work

Practical skills are very important for this job as you will be working at heights and with equipment. You need to be aware of health and safety issues.

It's important to respect your customers' privacy especially when cleaning windows at people's homes. Good communication skills are needed for dealing with customers, in particular if you want to run your own business.

Having a good level of fitness will help with lifting and carrying heavy equipment.

Working conditions

The hours you work will vary greatly, you may be contracted to work about 40 hours a week, in daylight hours or if self-employed, you can choose which jobs you take.

Be prepared to work in all weathers and at great heights. It is useful to have a driving licence and access to your own vehicle.

Future prospects

There are jobs available across the UK, with a great demand in towns and cities. Smaller rural areas also require window cleaners, so job prospects are good.

Health and safety regulations have been introduced to help prevent accidents at great heights. If you have access to stabilising equipment it can help you win large contracts and more work.

Advantages/disadvantages

You may have to work in poor weather conditions or at great heights which could be demanding.

You will get to meet all types of people and establish contacts.

You can set up and run your own business.

Qualifications and courses

There are no formal qualifications needed for this job, although the Diploma in Construction and the Built Environment may be useful, as will basic numeracy skills for calculating prices.

Most training is done on the job by a senior window cleaner. Health and safety issues will need to be understood.

If you are using ropes and access equipment you will need to be insured. The Industrial Rope Access Trade Association offers rope access courses.

The British Window Cleaning Academy offers courses covering window cleaning skills, water-fed pole instruction and health and safety. The NVQ at Level 2 in Cleaning and Support Services may be helpful.

With some experience you might want to study for NVQs in Team Leading or First Line Management at Levels 3 and 4.

Money guide

Starting salaries may be around £13,000, increasing to £16,000 with experience.

Self-employed window cleaners with a good reputation may earn £20,000+.

Related opportunities

- Caretaker p461
- Car Valet p460
- Care Assistant p576
- Pest Control Technician p471

Further information

Asset Skills
2 The Courtyard, 48 New North Road, Exeter EX4 4EP
01392 423399; www.assetskills.org

Federation for Window Cleaners
Summerfield House, Harrogate Road, Reddish, Stockport SK5 6HQ
0161 432 8754; www.f-w-c.co.uk

www.cityandguilds.com/myperfectjob

CRCI: RB   Personal and Other Services including Hair and Beauty

Retail, Sales and Customer Services

Jobs in this sector are suited to those of you who are very good at communicating with others and are interested in making your customers happy. Maybe you're interested in working with food and want to give your customers high quality, fresh produce. Your interest may lie in fashion retail and you could spend your time providing style advice. You should also be commercially minded and think about how your work relates to the success of the company you work for. Jobs in this sector also involve maintaining standards such as safety and quality to ensure guidelines are met, so a practical outlook can be useful.

In this section we look at the following jobs:

ANTIQUES DEALER

What the work involves

- You will be buying and selling things such as furniture, clocks, jewellery and pictures, which are either old or which people collect.

- You will go to auctions and fairs to buy things to sell in shops, markets or antique salerooms.

- You will need to develop specialist knowledge so that you can assess an object's age and value and whether it will sell at a profit.

- You will advise customers on the value of their antiques.

The type of person suited to this work

You should be fascinated by antiques and working out where they come from and what they are worth.

You will need to be interested in history and dedicated enough to travel and visit fairs and auctions all over the country and possibly abroad, searching out bargains and objects to sell. You will need to develop good specialist knowledge, know what is likely to be popular and sell quickly at a profit.

Antiques do not have fixed prices so you will need to be able to make quick decisions, and cope with the stress of buying things at auction. You will need to have good all round business skills.

Working conditions

You will work in a shop, in an antiques saleroom or on a market stall. You could be outside in all weathers and will probably have to travel to different markets.

You could be dealing with heavy objects like furniture or dusty and dirty things such as clothes and books.

Your working hours will vary a lot. Shops and stalls will be open at fixed times and on public holidays, and you could be visiting auctions or customers at any time.

Future prospects

Most antique dealers are self-employed or work in a family business, but you could start in an auction house or as a sales assistant in a larger shop.

Once you have developed contacts and knowledge of antiques and their value, you could work for yourself, perhaps starting with a market stall and expanding your business from there.

Most dealers specialise in a particular period of history or type of antique.

Advantages/disadvantages

You will be working with things that you love and have the thrill of finding bargains or rare items.

It can be a very uncertain business and prices will rise and fall as things go in and out of fashion. You can make a lot of money, but you can also lose a lot.

Qualifications and courses

No formal qualifications are needed, but enthusiasm and sales skills are useful. GCSEs/S grades (A*–C/1–3) in art, design and history are an advantage.

Entry is normally through work experience or as a trainee. Many auction houses will employ people as general workers or assistants. An NVQ/SVQ in Retail Operations can be an advantage. Auctioneers Sotheby's, Christie's and Bonhams take on graduate trainees, from a relevant degree such as history or art.

The University of Central Lancashire offers a 3-year degree in Antiques and Design Studies and a Master's by distance learning in Antiques. There are also some privately-run courses available from institutions such as Christie's and Sotheby's. Information about careers in antiques dealing and current vacancies with dealers may be available from the British Antique Dealers Association (BADA) or the Association of Art and Antique Dealers (LAPADA).

The BADA may offer advice about current vacancies with dealers. The LAPADA also offers basic guidance on careers in antique dealing.

Money guide

An assistant earns around £15,000 per year.

£20,000–£30,000 is usual for a dealer with a flair for the trade and considerable experience.

£50,000+ is possible for successful dealers or people with a high level of specialist knowledge.

Related opportunities

- Archivist p346
- Market Trader p488
- Museum/Art Gallery Curator p356
- Sales/Retail Assistant p494

Further information

British Antique Dealers Association
20 Rutland Gate, London SW7 1BD
020 7589 4128; www.bada.org

Sotheby's
34–35 New Bond Street, London W1S 2RT
020 7293 5000; www.sothebys.com

City& Guilds

www.cityandguilds.com/myperfectjob

BOOKSELLER

What the work involves

- You will be serving customers, taking money and answering queries, giving advice and ordering books.

- You will keep the shelves tidy, putting new books out and arranging displays. You will be keeping records of books and sometimes adding a classification system.

- You will be ordering books from publishers and wholesalers and keeping stock information up to date.

- You might be working with local colleges or universities to make sure you have got the books needed for their courses.

The type of person suited to this work

You will need to have a genuine interest in books and be able to keep up to date with new publications, so that you can help and advise customers.

You will need excellent communication skills for dealing with customers and sales representatives. You will work as part of a team, but should also be able to use your own initiative. It is important to remain calm and polite when the shop is busy.

Basic numeracy and ICT skills will be useful when using the tills for payments and computers for stock orders.

Working conditions

You will be working in either a small private bookshop or in one which is part of a chain of bookshops.

You will be on your feet all day, at a till, carrying heavy books and assisting customers.

You will work 39–40 hours a week, which may include weekends and evenings on a rota basis.

Future prospects

A lot of smaller book shops have closed due to competition from larger stores and the internet, so the majority of opportunities are with the big chains.

You can progress to a supervisor role or be in charge of a specific section of books. You can go on to management level or to work for head office.

You could use your knowledge and experience to open your own shop, or choose to specialise in certain types of books such as antique or second-hand.

Advantages/disadvantages

You will be using your knowledge and love of books to help other people and to keep up to date with new publications.

You could develop specialist knowledge, for example in children's books.

You will be dealing with the public, which can be rewarding but also stressful.

Qualifications and courses

There are no formal qualifications to enter this work, but most employers look for GCSEs/S grades (A*–C/1–3) in English and maths. You can enter and train for this career with qualifications at Levels 2–3 or go in with higher qualifications at Level 3 and above.

A degree in English or a degree/HND/Foundation degree in retail, business management or retail marketing can be an advantage.

Relevant courses at FE level include the Retail and Distributive Services, NVQs/SVQs in Retail Operations at Levels 2 and 3, Distributive Operations at Level 1, Customer Service at Levels 2, 3 and 4, Visual Merchandising at Level 2 and BTEC First and National qualifications in Retail/SQA National qualifications in Retail and Distribution.

Apprenticeships/Skillseekers might be available to those aged 16–24.

Money guide

Salaries vary a lot depending on the size of the shop. With large chains, you may get bonuses for high levels of sales or for meeting targets.

You can expect £12,000–£17,000 per year when you start.

With experience this can rise to £20,000.

£40,000+ a year is possible as a manager of a large bookshop with specialist departments.

Related opportunities

- Librarian p355
- Archivist p346
- Publisher/Commissioning Editor p423
- Sales/Retail Assistant p494

Further information

The Booksellers Association
Minster House, 272–274 Vauxhall Bridge Road,
London SW1V 1BA
020 7802 0802; www.booksellers.org.uk

British Shops and Stores Association Limited
Middleton House, 2 Main Road, Middleton Cheney,
Banbury OX17 2TN
01295 712277; www.british-shops.co.uk

www.cityandguilds.com/myperfectjob

CRCI: SB   **Retail, Sales and Customer Services**

BUILDERS' MERCHANT/ ASSISTANT

What the work involves

Builders' merchant

- You will be dealing with building materials and bathroom fittings. You will keep track of stock using computer or paper systems, order new stock and take deliveries.

- You will supply goods to building firms and individual builders – plumbers, electricians, plasterers – and members of the public, taking payments and using tills.

Builders' merchant's assistant

- You will work in a builders' merchants looking after the stock.

- You will handle a range of building materials, take deliveries, store deliveries properly, and keep the yard clean and deal with customers.

The type of person suited to this work

You will need to have a certain level of physical fitness for both of these positions as there will be heavy lifting and carrying involved. Asthma and allergies to dust and chemicals may be a problem.

You will need solid communication skills for dealing with customers and suppliers. You should have good numeracy and computer skills and the ability to handle money and paperwork efficiently.

Builders' merchant's assistant

You will be able to carry out instructions effectively. You should also be able to check invoices, deal with customers and possibly handle payments.

Working conditions

You will work about 40 hours a week, usually on Saturdays and sometimes Sundays. You may start at about 7.30am so that builders can buy their materials on the way to their work.

You may also need to use a forklift truck and climb ladders, which could be dangerous. You will be wearing overalls and protective boots or shoes.

You could be working outside in all weathers.

Future prospects

There are job opportunities in all areas of the country, but these vary depending on the strength of the building trade, and at present there are good opportunities.

The number of builders' merchants has increased with a lot of stores on out-of-town retail sites.

You can work part time and if you work for large merchants, or a chain, you could become a supervisor or manager. You could also work for a supplier or as a sales representative.

Qualifications and courses

Although there are no entry requirements most employers prefer applicants to have some GCSEs, including English and maths.

Previous experience within the construction industry or retailing is beneficial, as many employers view experience and personality as being more important than academic qualifications. However the Diploma in Construction and the Built Environment, the Diploma in Retail Business or the Diploma Level 1 in Construction might all be helpful qualifications.

You can choose to do an Apprenticeship in subjects such as business and administration, customer service, retail, team leading and management or warehousing and storage. The Builders' Merchants Federation (BMF) offers specialist courses in areas such as central heating, bricks, mortar and bathrooms as well as a Diploma in Merchanting.

Advantages/disadvantages

The work can be a great way of using your interest in building and knowledge of materials, tools and equipment.

There's a lot of paperwork involved in keeping track of the stock.

You could be starting early in the morning and working outside.

Money guide

Builders' merchant's assistants can start on around £12,500 a year. Once you have built on your experience and responsibilities you can expect to earn up to £20,000 per year. Delivery van drivers can earn around £16,500 a year.

You could earn more as the manager of a department or store and managers of large companies could earn £50,000+.

Related opportunities

- Sales/Retail Assistant p494
- Warehouse Manager/Worker p630

Further information

Builders' Merchants Federation
15 Soho Square, London W1D 3HL
0870 901 3380; www.bmf.org.uk

www.cityandguilds.com/myperfectjob

BUTCHER

What the work involves

- You might prepare an assortment of meat and poultry products. This could involve cutting, de-boning, trimming and slicing.

- You could offer advice to customers about varieties of meat available and preparation techniques involved with them. Some butchers offer a delivery service.

- You will take part in the everyday running of the business, visiting markets, ordering stock, taking deliveries from suppliers, organising displays and selling the products.

- Butchers can also work in the wholesale area of the industry, receiving the meat from the abattoir, then preparing and storing it for sale to the retailers or wholesale customers.

The type of person suited to this work

You will have to be meticulous and practical. You will need to have a strong understanding of and a professional approach to health and hygiene. Due to the fact you will be using sharp tools and machinery you need to be safety conscious. You should be personable, maintaining a high level of customer service. You need to have an outstanding knowledge of the various products and cuts of meat. You should have cash handling skills.

Working conditions

A retail butcher works in a shop environment with a chilled storage area. You will be expected to prepare meat in front of customers, using knives, cleavers and saws and will therefore be required to wear protective clothing, such as disposable gloves and an apron. This profession involves a great deal of standing, lifting and carrying as butchers are required to transport joints of meat. Average working hours are between 39 and 40 a week, including Saturdays and sometimes evenings and Sundays. Work starts as early as 7am.

Future prospects

With a great deal of local butchers having closed down and the ones left being small businesses, prospects are becoming somewhat limited. Supermarkets have however resurrected the idea of the meat counter over simply selling packaged meats and promotion opportunities within these chains are plentiful.

Once you have gained experience there is the option of setting up your own retail outlet. Other options include making the move into meat catering, meat wholesale or meat manufacture.

Advantages/disadvantages

You will have a great deal of customer contact and the opportunity to share your knowledge.

The amount of time spent on your feet, heavy lifting and cold temperatures may cause discomfort.

Qualifications and courses

There are no formal qualifications required to become a butcher and most people train on the job. Many employers will however want proof of a certain level of literacy and numeracy. They may require employees to have acquired English, maths and a science GCSE (A*–C) or even set aptitude tests.

Work experience in the food and drink industry is beneficial.

A good way to begin in this career is through an Apprenticeship scheme.

Many employers provide entrants with the opportunity to work towards qualifications including food safety qualifications and NVQs/SVQs in Meat and Poultry Processing at Levels 1 and 2.

The MTC (Meat Training Council) offers a range of qualifications which include the Intermediate Certificate in Meat and Poultry, the Intermediate Certificate in Meat and Poultry Management and the Intermediate Certificate in Hazard Analysis Critical Control Points (HACCP).

You could become a member of the professional body for butchers, the Worshipful Company of Butchers according to your qualifications.

Money guide

On average, a trainee butcher will earn a starting salary of around £8,000 a year.

That will increase to £12,000 once the individual has become skilled in their trade.

A butchery manager could make up to £20,000 per year.

If an individual chose to open their own shop this may increase further.

Related opportunities

- Food Processing Operative p224
- Kitchen Assistant/Supervisor p145
- Meat Process Worker p233

Further information

Meat Hygiene Service
MHS Headquarters, Kings Pool, Peasholme Green, York YO1 7PR
01904 455501; www.food.gov.uk/foodindustry/meat/mhservice/

www.cityandguilds.com/myperfectjob

Retail, Sales and Customer Services

CRCI: SB

CONTACT CENTRE OPERATOR

What the work involves

- You will be dealing with customers over the phone and using a computer to log details or find information.

- You might do telesales or telemarketing, selling, mail ordering, banking, or promoting goods and services, which could involve 'cold calling'.

- You could be doing market research, asking about people's buying habits or what services they would like from a company.

- You could be providing a service – receiving calls from customers who could be ordering goods, making a complaint, or accessing their bank accounts.

The type of person suited to this work

You should have good spoken English, with a clear voice and good hearing.

You will need excellent customer-service skills and must be able to be polite and calm when dealing with difficult callers.

For telesales or telemarketing, you will need to be motivated, persuasive and persistent.

Good ICT skills are also important.

You will probably work to targets and could be very busy so should be able to stay calm under pressure and work on your own initiative, but also as part of a team.

Working conditions

You will be office-based, usually working 38–40 hours a week. You might work shifts, which could include nights, weekends and evenings.

Call centre staff have their own workstations with a headset and computer and work as part of a team.

Meeting targets can be stressful; calls are often monitored by supervisors and staff turnover can be fairly high.

Future prospects

There has been a huge growth in call centres recently as more services are available over the phone – such as mail order and banking – and more companies are using telesales and marketing to sell their goods and services.

You could become a team leader or supervisor. You could also work abroad or establish new contact centres.

Advantages/disadvantages

There are lots of job opportunities and flexible working hours are possible.

You could utilise your customer-service and sales skills to move into related areas such as marketing or human resources.

Trying to reach sales targets can be stressful and the work can be repetitive.

Qualifications and courses

There are no formal entry qualifications, but employers generally look for at least 5 GCSEs (A*–C), including English and maths. You can enter and train in this career with qualifications at Levels 1 or 2. Previous experience of working with the public is helpful.

You could study for a BTEC Level 1 Award in An Introduction to Contact Centres, Level 2 Award in Contact Centre Skills or a Level 3 Award in Contact Supervisory Skills. City & Guilds Certificates are also available in Contact Centre Techniques and an Introduction to the Contact Centre Industry. City & Guilds also offers NVQ Levels 1 and 2 in Contact Centre Operations and at Levels 3 and 4 for Contact Centre Professionals. The Diploma in Business, Administration and Finance could also be useful.

Call centre staff can work towards NVQs in Call Handling Operations at Level 2 and 3, in Supervising Call Handling at Level 3 and Managing Call Handling at Level 4.

The Chartered Institute of Marketing offers courses on telephone selling techniques.

Money guide

You can expect £13,500–£15,500 per year when you start.

With experience, this can rise to £20,000, depending on where you work. Financial services call centres tend to pay best.

A supervisor could get £18,500–£22,500. Managerial roles pay over £25,000 per year.

Commission on sales or bonuses are possible if you meet targets.

Related opportunities

- Customer Services Assistant/Manager p483
- Marketing Assistant/Executive p414
- Sales/Retail Assistant p494
- Public Relations Officer p422

Further information

Institute of Direct Marketing
1 Park Road, Teddington TW11 0AR
020 8614 0277; www.theidm.com

Institute of Customer Service
2 Castle Court, St Peter's Street, Colchester CO1 1EW
01206 571716; www.instituteofcustomerservice.com

www.cityandguilds.com/myperfectjob

CUSTOMER SERVICES ASSISTANT/MANAGER

What the work involves

Assistant

- You will be liaising with customers, either face to face or by phone and email, in order to sell products and services such as retail goods, insurance or holiday packages.

- You could be responsible for dealing with customer enquiries, problems or complaints.

Manager

- Your role will include hiring and training customer service assistants.

- You will need to establish targets and implement different motivational techniques to ensure that staff reach them.

The type of person suited to this work

You need to have good people skills and be polite and helpful. You must be able to remain calm and patient when faced with difficult customers. You must be able to work well as part of a team, as well as on your own.

Manager

A manager needs to have excellent leadership skills and be able to motivate his or her team. Managers must also be organised, decisive and able to work under pressure.

Working conditions

You will typically work a 37-hour week, although this could be on a rota system that includes early mornings, evenings or weekends. If your company provides 24-hour assistance, you might have to work nights. There is also the opportunity to work part-time.

You could spend the majority of your time dealing with customers face to face, or at a desk with a computer or telephone headset.

Vacancies are available throughout the UK, especially in big cities and towns.

Future prospects

Opportunities are available in a wide range of different organisations including shops, call centres, banks, airports or tourist information centres.

Assistant

After gaining experience and further qualifications, you could progress into a role as team leader, supervisor and then manager.

Manager

You could progress into a job at head office or take a job with a higher salary and responsibility. You can go on to training staff or take further qualifications and work as a staff assessor.

Qualifications and courses

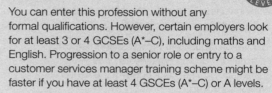

Assistant

You can enter this profession without any formal qualifications. However, certain employers look for at least 3 or 4 GCSEs (A*–C), including maths and English. Progression to a senior role or entry to a customer services manager training scheme might be faster if you have at least 4 GSCEs (A*–C) or A levels.

Manager

A degree can increase your chances of entry into a management training scheme, although any degree is accepted. Many entrants start as a customer services assistant and progress to a role as manager, obtaining qualifications while they work.

Advantages/disadvantages

Difficult customers or problems can make the work stressful.

This job can be repetitive.

There are good prospects for promotion for a customer services assistant.

You will deal with a wide range of people.

Money guide

Bonuses or commission can boost your salary.

Assistant

Starting salaries are about £10,000–£11,500 a year.

After gaining experience, this can increase to £12,000–£15,000 a year.

Manager

Starting salaries for trainee customer services managers are around £15,000–£23,000. With experience this could rise to £22,000–£27,000. Senior managers who work for large organisations can earn up to £45,000.

Related opportunities

- Sales/Retail Assistant p494
- Retail Manager p493
- Receptionist p58

Further information

Institute of Customer Service
2 Castle Court, St Peter's Street, Colchester CO1 1EW
01206 571716; www.instituteofcustomerservice.com

City&
Guilds

www.cityandguilds.com/myperfectjob

Retail, Sales and Customer Services

CRCI: SA

FISHMONGER

What the work involves

- Fishmongers prepare and sell fish, offering advice to customers on how to store and cook it. They can work in various environments including shops, supermarkets and market stalls.

- You will be required to provide customers with information such as how the fish was caught, the sustainability of its stock and whether it has been previously frozen.

- You will buy fish from the wholesaler and prepare it for retail sales. This preparation includes removing bones, skin and scales then gutting the fish and maybe cutting it into portions.

- Other tasks include preparing crab.

The type of person suited to this work

You will require good hand–eye coordination as you will be using small knives to complete detailed jobs such as filleting and taking out little bones. You will have to do messy tasks such as cleaning and gutting fish.

You should be able to stand for long periods of time. You should have a strong level of personal hygiene. You will need to be personable, as customer service is extremely important for this role. People with skin allergies may not be suitable for this job.

Working conditions

The conditions in this industry can be cold and wet. You will be expected to spend a great deal of time on your feet, moving between the counter and storage areas.

Most fishmongers will work for approximately 40 hours a week; these hours may include Saturdays with a day and a half off a week. You will frequently have to work early mornings to sign for stock deliveries. Protective clothing and footwear are required.

Future prospects

Fishmongers work in many different environments including supermarkets, small local stores and mobile fish units and so you may choose to move between them. Travelling offers a variety of new experiences and places to sell.

Other possibilities might involve supplying fishmonger stores with fresh fish or moving into other industries which require food preparation for example working with meat. You can also move into a management position or open your own shop.

Advantages/disadvantages

You will have to work early mornings.

You will have the opportunity to be creative, both in the preparation of the fish and in providing customers with advice on how best to prepare or cook it.

Spending all day on your feet and in cold temperatures can be uncomfortable.

Qualifications and courses

You do not require any formal qualifications to enter into this industry; most employers will however expect a good basic level of education including English and maths. Apprenticeships are also available; competition is fierce and so good grades at GCSE will be beneficial.

People normally begin at counter assistant level and gain on the job training either through direct entry or training schemes. Whilst working you will need to attain your basic food hygiene certification, followed by Hazard Analysis and Critical Control Point (HACCP) training.

It could also be beneficial to work towards NVQs in Retail Skills at Level 2 or Retail (Sales Professional) at Level 3, both of which contain a fish-specific unit.

There are short courses available including a 1-day introductory course, knife skills and training and the 2-day City & Guilds Seafood Retail Certificate at the Seafood Training School in Billingsgate. These courses are designed for people who have never had contact with the industry and will provide valuable practical experience.

Money guide

Pay rates vary depending on location and employer.

Fishmongers usually receive around £11,500–£13,500 a year; this figure can rise to about £19,500 per year, depending on experience. There is also the possibility of self-employment which could have a higher rate of pay.

Related opportunities

- Butcher p481
- Chef p137
- Kitchen Assistant/Supervisor p145
- Shopkeeper p496

Further information

Billingsgate Seafood Training School
Office 30, Billingsgate Market, Trafalgar Way, London E14 5ST
020 7517 3548; www.seafoodtraining.org; info@seafoodtraining.org

Sea Fish Industry Authority
18 Logie Mill, Logie Green Road, Edinburgh EH7 4HS
0131 558 3331; www.seafish.org; training@seafish.co.uk

City& Guilds

www.cityandguilds.com/myperfectjob

FLORIST

What the work involves

- Florists combine creativity with knowledge of plants and flowers to design and create floral displays. These are sold via shops and market stalls.

- You will be responsible for ordering and caring for the plants and flowers, aiding customers in choosing flowers suitable for specific occasions and creating floral displays.

- You may also be required to deliver to customers and set up displays at events.

- You will be expected to handle money, complete regular stock takes and help with the day to day running of the business.

The type of person suited to this work

You will need to be extremely creative, with an understanding of shape, colour and design. As a great deal of this job is hands-on you will need to be dexterous. A strong knowledge of plants and flowers and the care required for them is essential, along with a desire to expand that information. You will need to be patient, with good customer service skills and sensitivity to the needs of the client. You should have brilliant telephone communication skills and the ability to work within tight deadlines. Administration and sales skills are also important.

Working conditions

Florists usually work inside in a shop environment. Some travel may be required when making deliveries and so a driving licence might be needed. Those who work on a floristry stall will spend most of their time outdoors. This job involves a great deal of standing at the work bench/counter. Some shops provide uniforms or aprons. Working hours usually vary between 35 and 40 hours per week, shop opening hours are normally 9am to 5pm. This job may not be suitable for people who suffer from pollen allergies.

Future prospects

Those with a certain amount of experience and the desire to may progress to a managerial role. There is also the possibility of becoming self-employed by opening your own business once you have the required business skills. Another progression option is working as a freelance worker for a variety of businesses where you work on a contract basis, arranging flowers. Other choices include teaching floristry and becoming a professional demonstrator.

Advantages/disadvantages

You can combine creativity, skill and knowledge to create floral displays.

You will be on your feet for a great deal of time and those who work on florist market stalls will be outdoors in all weathers.

Every day will be different as you will be working with a wide range of customers towards a variety of events.

Qualifications and courses

There are no specific academic qualifications, however any formal qualifications in floristry would be advantageous.

Qualifications available include NVQs in Floristry Levels 2 and 3, Level 2 National Certificate in Floristry, Level 3 Advanced National Certificate in Floristry, BTEC National Award in Floristry, BTEC National Certificate/Diploma in Floristry and BTEC First Diploma in Floristry. The Diploma in Environmental and Land-Based Studies available at Levels 1, 2 and 3 would also be of benefit.

The requirements for entry into these courses will vary, however GCSEs (A*–E) in subjects such as English, maths and arts and crafts would be beneficial. Any other relevant experience and skills including numeracy and literacy skills might be taken into account. Work experience in a florists shop would also be valuable.

You can also choose to do an Apprenticeship in Floristry. With experience you can choose to study for a Foundation degree or degree in Floristry.

Money guide

These figures may vary depending on location and employer.

The starting salary for a florist is the national minimum wage (visit the HM Revenue and Customs website for more information).

Once experience is gained this figure may rise to around £18,000 per year and might increase again to approximately £25,000 a year once management status is reached.

Related opportunities

- Display Designer/Window Dresser p171
- Gardener/Garden Designer p270
- Landscape Architect/Designer p275
- Landscaper/Landscape Manager p276

Further information

British Florist Association
PO Box 5161, Dudley DY1 9FX
01384 213263; www.britishfloristassociation.org

Flowers and Plants Association
266–270 Flower Market, New Covent Garden Market, London SW8 5NB
020 7738 8044; www.flowers.org.uk

www.cityandguilds.com/myperfectjob

CRCI: SB   Retail, Sales and Customer Services

IMAGE CONSULTANT

What the work involves

- You will advise individuals and companies on branding, impact and appearance. This can involve style analysis, make-up advice, wardrobe management and personal shopping.

- When working with private clients you will discuss fabrics, styles, patterns and colours that will suit your client's body shape, hair and eye colour and skin tone.

- When working with corporate clients you may advise on body language, etiquette, first impressions and branding. You could also coach executives and run workshops.

- Part of your job might involve speaking on the radio as a way of promoting your business.

The type of person suited to this work

You must be aware of current fashion trends, possess a good sense of style and a great eye for colour and detail. Creativity and communication skills are essential in order to inspire clients to believe in their image. You want clients to trust you so you should be easy to talk to, uplifting and sensitive.

Self-motivation is important when running your own business. You should be able to budget well and to organise your time effectively. The ability to network and to market your brand is essential.

Working conditions

You can choose to work from home or out of a studio. Your hours will vary depending on how many clients you see and could include evenings and weekends. You will need to travel at times to a client's home or company so a driving licence would be useful.

When meeting corporate clients you will need to dress formally, and you will need to dress smartly when meeting private clients.

Future prospects

You could be an independent image consultant or work for an organisation such as First Impressions who will provide you with business support. With experience you can progress from working solely with private clients to corporate work.

You might specialise in one area, such as working with male clients or with brides. You could also move into life coaching, retail or hairdressing. Opportunities to work abroad are available.

Advantages/disadvantages

It's rewarding to help clients with low self-esteem gain confidence in their personal or professional brand.

The job can be glamorous as you may work with well-known figures in public life.

Qualifications and courses

While there are no set academic qualifications for this career, related experience in subjects such as fashion, hair, beauty or public relations is common.

The Diploma in Hair and Beauty, the City & Guilds Diploma in Beauty Consultancy or the BTEC Diploma in Retail Beauty Consultancy may be a useful starting point. Some entrants hold Foundation degrees, HNDs and degrees in subjects such as beauty therapy, cosmetic sciences, business studies or sales and marketing. You will need at least 4 GCSEs (A*–C) for HND courses and 2 A levels and 5 GCSEs (A*–C) for degree entry.

It's recommended to take a course in image consultancy approved by The Federation of Image Consultants (TFIC). Courses should cover colour analysis, style for women, style for men and cosmetic application.

You may work towards a TFIC Masters Award to improve your skills and marketability.

Starting up your own business and building up a client base can be difficult.

You might need to supplement your income when first starting out.

Money guide

Starting out you could earn between £10,000 and £15,000 per year. Once you gain experience and a regular client base you may earn up to £30,000.

If you work in the corporate sector you could earn £40,000+.

As most image consultants are self-employed your salary will depend on how well you market yourself, the area you work in and your skills. You could charge anywhere between £45 and £100 per hour.

Related opportunities

- Beauty Consultant p458
- Make-up Artist p445
- Fashion Designer p172

Further information

Hairdressing And Beauty Industry Authority
Oxford House, Sixth Avenue, Sky Business Park, Robin Hood Airport, Doncaster DN9 3GG
08452 306080; www.habia.org.uk

The Federation of Image Consultants
www.tfic.org.uk

Skillsmart Retail Ltd
93 Newman Street, London W1T 3EZ
0800 093 5001; www.skillsmartretail.com

JEWELLER

What the work involves

- Retail jewellers sell jewellery and sometimes watches, clocks and silverware in shops to customers. Other services they offer might include valuation, alteration and repair. Customer service and sales are particularly important in this industry.

- You may work for a company which specialises in selling a particular gemstone such as diamonds.

- Manufacturing jewellers create rings, necklaces, earrings, bracelets and cufflinks using metals and other materials. The items constructed might be mass-produced or individually designed and hand crafted.

- You could specialise in one area such as casting or enamelling or learn a variety of techniques.

The type of person suited to this work

A retail jeweller needs to be extremely trustworthy and security minded. You should be well turned out with good communication skills and friendly manner. You should also be capable of handling money and have any practical repair skills required.

A manufacturing jeweller needs to have an artistic flair and be highly creative. You should have good hand-to-eye co-ordination, be dexterous, patient and accurate. You should have solid problem solving skills, the ability to concentrate for long periods of time.

Working conditions

Retail jewellers work in shops, varying from small stores to larger chains. They usually work 37 to 40 hours per week; these hours may include weekends, evenings and bank holidays.

Manufacturing jewellers work in small factories, studios or workshops which are normally warm and bright. However, depending on the techniques being used working conditions could be hot, dusty, wet or noisy.

Future prospects

A retail jeweller might continue on to become a sales assistant, assistant manager or even a manager. Specialist skills can improve prospects and so learning valuation or alteration may lead to higher paid roles.

Manufacturing jewellers' prospects also improve with training and experience as they will be able to complete more challenging work. Due to the small nature of manufacturing companies progression may involve a change of employers.

Advantages/disadvantages

As a retail jeweller being on your feet all day may cause discomfort.

As a manufacturing jeweller you can be creative, putting the skills you learn to use.

Qualifications and courses

ENTRY LEVEL 2

Retail Jeweller

Although there are no set qualifications many employers will expect GCSEs (A*–C), including English, maths, art or design and technology.

Manufacturing Jeweller

Again there are no formal entry requirements; however qualifications in art, craft or design would be highly beneficial. The Diploma in Creative and Media might be helpful.

There are two ways to begin your career. The first is studying for a national certificate/diploma, HNC/HND, Foundation degree or a degree. Useful subjects include jewellery design, metalwork and 3D design. For an HNC/HND you will need 1 A level. For a degree course you will need at least 2 A levels and 5 GCSEs (A*–C). The British Jewellers' Association provides a full list of relevant courses.

The second option is to train on the job, working for a jewellery company. You can also choose to do an apprenticeship offered through The Goldsmiths' Company.

The National Association of Goldsmiths also offers professional Diplomas in Jeweller's Management, Jeweller's Gemstones and Jeweller's Valuation.

Money guide

Retail jewellers have a starting salary of around £11,200 and usually earn commission.

This may increase to about £25,000 if they reach managerial level. Senior sales consultants can earn up to £60,000.

Manufacturing jewellers usually start on a salary of around £10,500 per year; with experience this can rise to around £25,000 a year. Top salaries can be as high as £50,000 a year.

Related opportunities

- Gold/Silversmith/Engraver p175
- Sales/Retail Assistant p494

Further information

The Goldsmiths' Company
Goldsmiths' Hall, Foster Lane, London EC2V 6BN
020 7606 7010; www.thegoldsmiths.co.uk

British Jewellers' Association
Federation House, 10 Vyse Street, Birmingham B18 6LT
0121 237 1112; www.bja.org.uk

City&
Guilds

www.cityandguilds.com/myperfectjob

CRCI: SB   Retail, Sales and Customer Services

MARKET TRADER

What the work involves

- Market traders buy goods from a wholesaler or manufacturer, and then sell them from a market stall which they rent in an open-air or covered market.

- You might sell things you have made yourself at specialist craft markets.

- You will be dealing with customers, encouraging them to buy items on your stall, weighing and wrapping goods, and taking money and possibly cheques, credit and debit cards.

- As well as setting up the stall in the morning, arranging your things and keeping the stall clean and tidy, you will also pack up and clear away in the evenings.

The type of person suited to this work

You will need to be friendly and outgoing, and enjoy working with the public in an informal way, persuading them to buy your goods.

Market traders have to be fit and active to transport their goods, be on their feet all day and then pack up when the market closes. You should be prepared to work outside in all weathers, as even covered markets can be cold.

When you are buying goods you will have to know what will sell and negotiate a good price. You will deal with money and will have to do your own accounts, if you are self-employed.

You should be self-motivated and hard-working, and produce attractive, desirable products.

Working conditions

You will probably have a very early start and work from about 5am to 6pm. You will probably have to work Saturdays and often Sundays.

You might have to travel to buy the goods you sell.

You could be working on your own or with one or two other people. You could work at the same market every day or move round to several different markets during the week.

Future prospects

It can be hard to do well with a market stall: there is a lot of competition and you will need good products.

On craft markets, it can be difficult to sell things at a competitive price.

Most market traders are self-employed and you could expand by taking on staff to run extra stalls or you could open a shop.

Advantages/disadvantages

You will be your own boss, working outside in an active, practical job with lots of contact with the public.

Markets are often very lively and friendly places.

The hours can be long and strenuous.

Qualifications and courses

There are no formal entry requirements but you will need to have basic maths and English skills. Most of the training is done on the job, learning from the person you work for or from other traders.

There are some short courses you can take, usually run by the local authority, and the National Market Traders Federation (NMTF) can give advice.

You could also do short courses on running your own business, provided by small business advice services. The Diploma in Retail Business would be relevant for this line of work.

If you are selling things you have made, you will probably need to do a specialist course, for example jewellery making or a fashion course at university.

Many markets insist that traders have insurance for public liability. The National Market Traders' Federation can provide this. You will also need to apply for a market licence, from your local market office.

Money guide

When starting out you are likely to be earning minimum wage, between £7,000 and £11,900 a year.

You could earn around £15,000–£22,000 a year with some experience. A few market traders who are selling specialist goods can earn around £25,000–£30,000 a year.

Related opportunities

- Customer Services Assistant/Manager p483
- Sales/Retail Assistant p494
- Shopkeeper p496

Further information

National Market Traders' Federation
Hampton House, Hawshaw Lane, Hoyland,
Barnsley S74 0HA
01226 749021; www.nmtf.co.uk

British Shops and Stores Association Limited
Middleton House, 2 Main Road, Middleton Cheney,
Banbury OX17 2TN
01295 712277; www.british-shops.co.uk

City&
Guilds

www.cityandguilds.com/myperfectjob

MEAT HYGIENE INSPECTOR

What the work involves

- Meat hygiene inspectors visit slaughterhouses and meat stores to check that meat is being processed and produced safely and hygienically, by following relevant laws and regulations.

- You will check that live animals and poultry are healthy and disease free, and do post mortems on diseased carcases.

- You will check that animals are cared for and transported safely, that meat plants and deliveries are run safely and hygienically, and that unwanted meat or carcases are destroyed properly.

- You will write detailed reports and make sure that any action you have recommended is carried out quickly and to the right standards.

The type of person suited to this work

You will be dealing with people in lots of different organisations and at all levels, so will need to be able to establish good working relationships and deal calmly with problems.

You will need to have good written and communication skills, understand and apply laws and regulations, and have a good eye for detail.

It is a fairly active job so you will need to be fit and healthy, practical and good with your hands, and able to work to strict safety guidelines.

Working conditions

You will spend most of your time travelling to farms and processing plants. You will be wearing protective clothing, using tools and equipment and handling heavy meat carcases.

Slaughterhouses can be cold and noisy and smell strongly, and on farms you will be working outdoors in all weathers.

Meat inspectors usually work normal office hours, but might need to work evenings and weekends and work at short notice if there is a hygiene emergency.

Future prospects

Most meat inspectors work for the Meat Hygiene Service which is part of the government's Food Standards Agency. Others work for companies producing or selling food and meat products.

You will need experience in the industry before you can become an inspector. You can then progress to be a supervisor or manager for the Meat Hygiene Service or go into management in a large food company.

Qualifications and courses

All meat inspectors must hold the Royal Society for the Promotion of Health's Level 3 Diploma in Meat Hygiene and Inspection.

To get onto the course you will need to have at least 5 GCSEs/S grades (A*–C/1–3), including English and maths or a science, or Associate membership of the Meat Training Council.

NVQs/SVQs available are Meat and Poultry Processing at Level 2 and Specialist Meat and Poultry Skills at Level 3. RSPH offers a Level 2 Certificate in Wild Game Meat Hygiene to meet the food hygiene laws. RSPH also offer Level 3 and Level 4 Awards in Food Safety Supervision for Manufacturing.

Apprenticeships/Skillseekers in Food Manufacture may be available for people aged 16–24.

Advantages/disadvantages

You need to be flexible with your working hours as you may be asked to respond to an emergency at any time. You will feel satisfied that you are doing an important job; ensuring that food standards are met, meaning safe meat for the public.

Money guide

You can expect to earn £17,000 per year as a trainee inspector.

Up to £25,500 is the usual salary when you have got some experience.

You could earn £25,000–£33,000 as a senior meat inspector with qualifications and experience.

Related opportunities

- Health and Safety Adviser p40
- Trading Standards Officer p498
- Butcher p481
- Meat Process Worker p233

Further information

Food Standards Agency
Aviation House, 125 Kingsway, London WC2B 6NH
020 7276 8000; www.foodstandards.gov.uk

Meat Hygiene Service
Kings Pool, Peasholme Green, York YO1 7PR
01904 455501; www.food.gov.uk/foodindustry/meat/mservice

www.cityandguilds.com/myperfectjob

Retail, Sales and Customer Services

CRCI: SC

MERCHANDISER

What the work involves

- You will ensure that stores are stocked with products at the right quantity and price.

- You will work with retail buyers who choose different lines, and then work out the quantities of different lines needed and the amount of money to be spent.

- It will be your responsibility to decide upon the selling prices of goods and any special offers.

- You will put together budgets and sales targets, analyse sales trends, negotiate with suppliers and ensure that goods are displayed and presented in an attractive way that is consistent throughout the company.

The type of person suited to this work

You will need to be interested in your product and in predicting what will sell and how best to display it.

Merchandisers must be creative and self-motivated with initiative and confidence, because they make decisions involving large amounts of money and have to present their ideas to managers and staff.

You should be able to work well in a team and deal with people at all levels, including negotiating prices and arranging deliveries.

The job involves analysing statistics and sales figures and working under pressure to meet targets and deadlines.

Working conditions

You will mainly be based in an office in a large store, or in a head office and will probably visit other stores in your region. Most opportunities are in the South-East and big cities such as London.

You will also be visiting suppliers and manufacturers, so you might have to be away from home regularly. It is necessary to have a driving licence.

You will probably work normal office hours, but might have to work much longer at busy times.

Future prospects

You will usually start as an allocator, distributor, or merchandise administrative assistant and advance to a role as an assistant merchandiser and then to merchandiser. In a large company, you could progress to a role as senior merchandiser and then possibly manager or director. Progression depends on the talent of the individual. After gaining experience, you could also become self-employed and work as a retail consultant, or you could move into a related role such as a business analyst.

Advantages/disadvantages

This job can be stressful as you will be making decisions which will directly affect the image of your company and what the public can buy.

Keeping your finger on the pulse of fashion and future trends can be exciting.

Qualifications and courses

Most entrants to this career have a degree, or a Higher National Diploma. You might be able to get a trainee post with Level 3 qualifications but these would be very competitive and you would probably need to have retail experience as well.

Larger companies will accept degrees in any subjects, although retailing, marketing or business studies, economics or maths would be useful. It is possible to take a 2 year Foundation degree in Fashion Buying and Merchandising at The London College of Fashion.

You might be able to do an Apprenticeship if you are aged 16–24. NVQs in Supply Chain Management at Levels 2–5 and a Level 4 Diploma in Buying and Merchandising for Fashion Retail are also available.

Merchandisers are trained on the job, and can work towards professional qualifications from the Chartered Institute of Purchasing and Supply or the Chartered Institute of Marketing.

Money guide

Salaries depend on the size and location of the employer. They are typically higher in high-street chains.

Assistant merchandisers earn around £22,000–£28,000 per year. Salaries are lower for entry-level roles such as an allocator.

An experienced merchandiser could earn £37,000–£48,500.

Senior merchandisers, with responsibilities for price-setting across large companies, can earn £48,500–£65,000 and a director of merchandising can earn up to £85,000.

Related opportunities

- Retail Buyer p492
- Marketing Manager/Assistant/Executive p414
- Purchasing Manager p617
- Retail Manager p493

Further information

British Shops and Stores Association Limited
Middleton House, 2 Main Road, Middleton Cheney, Banbury OX17 2TN
01295 712277; www.british-shops.co.uk

Chartered Institute of Marketing
Moor Hall, Cookham, Maidenhead SL6 9QH
01628 427120; www.cim.co.uk

City&
Guilds

www.cityandguilds.com/myperfectjob

POST OFFICE CLERK

What the work involves

- Post office clerks provide customers with a variety of postal services along with banking services, bill payment, lottery sales, passport applications and offering advice to customers on these services.

- Tasks you will complete on a daily basis include sending important and expensive mail, selling stamps, weighing, measuring and mailing letters and parcels and dispatching mail abroad.

- Other services you may offer include banking services, passport applications, bill payments, car tax renewal, currency exchange, insurance and lottery sales.

- You might also be required to complete administrative work such as keeping accounts.

The type of person suited to this work

A post office clerk should be able to work within a team and without supervision. You should have excellent communication skills, being both polite and helpful with the ability to adjust to the needs of each client. You should have a certain level of numeracy and be able to handle money with confidence and accuracy. You will be able to cope under pressure. You should have an interest in the numerous services you will be offering along with a willingness to learn about the various forms that clients may require information on. You should have a keen eye for detail and a high concentration span.

Working conditions

If you work for a sub-post office you might be working in a newsagent, stationer or village shop. You will be working mainly at a counter but could also do some behind the scenes work in an office environment. You may be required to wear a uniform. The job will probably involve some lifting of heavy parcels. You will usually work between 35 and 36 hours per week, Monday to Friday and occasionally Saturday mornings. Part-time and flexible working hours may be arranged.

Future prospects

You could progress to the role of postmaster or training officer. Experienced post office clerks may have the opportunity to work on the post office helpline. Within this role you would answer any queries customers or sub-postmasters/mistresses had regarding the products and services that the Post Office Ltd offers.

The skills you acquire in this role stand you in good stead to move on to careers within other industries such as banking.

Advantages/disadvantages

You may, at times, find this role stressful particularly when the post office is especially busy.

You might be able to work flexible hours which suit you.

There may be some lifting involved.

Qualifications and courses

There are no set requirements for this role. Most people enter directly into employment. Training is done on the job and involves 2 weeks in a training centre followed by two supervised weeks at the counter.

Despite the lack of formal academic entry requirements it would be preferable to have achieved some GCSEs at grades A*–C, particularly in English and maths. A Higher Diploma may also be a valid qualification as this offers a mixture of academic and work related study. An aptitude for languages would also be beneficial.

Any experience of working in a customer service industry would be advantageous, as would experience of handling money. This experience might involve working in a shop as a sales assistant, working in a restaurant as a waiter/waitress or maybe as an assistant in a launderette.

Money guide

The rate of pay will vary depending on the location and the employer.

Post office clerks generally start on a salary of around £13,000. After experience this may increase to an amount somewhere in the vicinity of £18,000 a year.

A promotion to the role of postmaster or training officer would result in a pay increase.

Related opportunities

- Bank Cashier/Customer Adviser p22
- Customer Service Assistant/Manager p483
- Accounting Technician p18
- Sales Assistant p494

Further information

Royal Mail Group Ltd
100 Victoria Embankment, London EC4Y 0HQ
0845 600 180; www.royalmailgroup.com

Royal Mail Group Ltd Northern Ireland
Royal Mail House, 20 Donegall Quay, Belfast BT1 1AA

Skillsmart Retail
93 Newman Street, London W1T 3EZ
www.skillsmartretail.com

www.cityandguilds.com/myperfectjob

CRCI: SA

RETAIL BUYER

What the work involves

- You will probably work in the merchandising and marketing team of a large retail company, looking for products which fit the company image and will appeal to its customers.

- You will visit manufacturers and suppliers to negotiate prices and decide on quantities and colours. You will also check on the quality of the products.

- You will help to predict and set trends, using computers to analyse sales figures.

The type of person suited to this work

You will need to be confident and decisive because you will be dealing with large budgets.

You will need to be assertive with good communication skills to negotiate prices and make presentations to staff.

You will need to be able to analyse figures and use them to set prices and targets and check stock levels.

You should be creative, well organised and good at planning ahead, and have an eye for detail.

Working conditions

You will be office based but spend a lot of time visiting suppliers and manufacturers in this country and abroad, so will probably have to spend time away from home.

You will work standard hours but will need to work late at busy times and to meet deadlines.

Future prospects

There are job opportunities all over the country but most will be in London and the south-east of England.

In a small company there may not be much chance of promotion, but in a larger company prospects are good.

You could progress to senior retail buyer, trading manager or buying controller.

It is possible to work as a buyer in other areas, including manufacturing, the civil service and local government.

Advantages/disadvantages

This can be an exciting job and the decisions you make will affect what the public can buy and the image of the stores.

You will have a lot of responsibility and tight deadlines which can be very stressful.

Money guide

You can expect on average around £15,000–£20,000 per year when you start as a trainee retail buyer. Pay will rise to around £25,000–£45,000 as you gain experience.

£50,000+ is possible as a successful, senior retail buyer for a large company or multiple retail chain.

You could earn large bonuses if you do well.

Qualifications and courses

Entry is usually by degree, though an HND or equivalent can also be acceptable. Useful subjects include business, management, purchasing, logistics and marketing. Some specialist degrees are available in fashion buying.

The minimum entry requirements for a degree course are normally 2 A levels or equivalent. Entry into retail fashion requires a relevant qualification. It is possible to take a 2-year Foundation degree in Fashion Buying and Merchandising at The London College of Fashion. An Apprenticeship in Retail is also available.

Retail buyers are often required to study for the professional qualifications of the Chartered Institute of Purchasing and Supply (CIPS). CIPS offers a Certificate and Advanced Certificate for people employed in purchasing at a clerical level.

Entrants with an HND or degree study towards the CIPS Graduate Diploma. CIPS-accredited degrees in purchasing or business are available at some institutions, and give exemption from part or all of the Graduate Diploma.

People employed in buying can work towards NVQs at Levels 2–5 in Supply Chain Management and the Level 4 Diploma in Buying and Merchandising for Fashion Retail.

Some companies offer their own graduate training schemes, but only take on a few candidates each year.

Related opportunities

- Marketing Assistant/Executive p414
- Merchandiser p490
- Purchasing/Procurement Manager p617
- Retail Manager p493

Further information

British Shops and Stores Association Limited
Middleton House, 2 Main Road, Middleton Cheney, Banbury OX17 2TN
01295 712277; www.british-shops.co.uk

Chartered Institute of Marketing
Moor Hall, Cookham, Maidenhead SL6 9QH
01628 427120; www.cim.co.uk

Chartered Institute of Purchasing & Supply
Easton House, Easton on the Hill, Stamford PE9 3NZ
01780 756777; www.cips.org

RETAIL MANAGER

What the work involves

- Unlike a shopkeeper who owns the store and deals with manufacturers, you will be running the shop on a day-to-day basis. This could be a small or a large department store, chain, independent store or a supermarket.

- Managers recruit, train and supervise staff, encouraging them to develop their skills and meet targets.

- You will monitor sales and look at ways of improving them and oversee supplies by checking stock, placing orders and making sure you do not run out or over-order.

- The store manager has overall responsibility for everything that happens in the shop and must deal with any problems or complaints.

The type of person suited to this work

As you could be dealing with customers and complaints you will need excellent negotiation skills. You will also need to motivate, train, and sometimes discipline staff. You should be energetic and able to take responsibility and make quick decisions.

You will need an understanding of business and of relevant laws. You should be able to analyse sales figures and have creative ideas for selling and promoting goods to improve profits. You will have to be organised whilst working to targets and deadlines.

Working conditions

Many stores are open long hours, at weekends and overnight, so you will probably have to work shifts, usually over 5 days.

You will be on your feet a lot as well as doing administration and paperwork.

You may be based in one store, or be visiting several that you have responsibility for.

Future prospects

There are many opportunities but trainee posts with large chains can be very competitive.

With a large retail chain your prospects can be good and you can quickly take on more responsibilities.

You could move into other areas of the company, for example marketing or buying, and might be able to work abroad.

You could work for yourself but will need money to start up your own store.

Advantages/disadvantages

Retail is an expanding, developing business and so can offer you an exciting career with good promotion prospects.

You will have a lot of responsibility quite early in your career.

Working with the public can be demanding and stressful.

Qualifications and courses

ENTRY LEVEL 2

There are no set requirements but many stores will require 5 GCSEs/S grades (A*–C) including maths and English. Previous experience of working in retail is important.

You may pursue an Edexcel BTEC Certificate in retail or a Foundation degree or degree in retail management. Management degrees are offered by universities across the country. Advanced Apprenticeships in retail management are also available.

Many retailers offer graduate trainee management schemes and if you have a suitable degree you could pursue this fast-track option.

NVQs/SVQs are available in Retail Operations at Levels 2 and 3. Other qualifications include BTEC Retail qualifications at Levels 2 and 3 and the City & Guilds Higher Professional Diploma in Retail Management at Level 4.

Money guide

Wages vary with the company and the size of the store.

You could earn £14,300–£18,000 per year when you start as a non-graduate trainee with a large chain.

£11,000–£12,500 is likely as a trainee with a smaller company.

With experience this could rise to £21,000–£24,000.

£45,000+ is possible if you are working for a large company with a lot of responsibility. This could reach £60,000 if you are a manager in a large superstore.

You will probably also get discounts, commission and bonuses related to sales.

Related opportunities

- Retail Buyer p492
- Distribution Manager p602
- Merchandiser p490

Further information

British Shops and Stores Association Limited
Middleton House, 2 Main Road, Middleton Cheney, Banbury OX17 2TN
01295 712277; www.british-shops.co.uk

Chartered Institute of Purchasing & Supply
Easton House, Easton on the Hill, Stamford PE9 3NZ
01780 756777; www.cips.org

City&
Guilds

www.cityandguilds.com/myperfectjob

CRCI: SB   Retail, Sales and Customer Services

SALES/RETAIL ASSISTANT

What the work involves

- You will deal with customers, offering them a polite, helpful and speedy service to sell a range of goods.

- You will help keep the shop tidy and well stocked, answer questions, deal with complaints and give suggestions and advice.

- Shops range from small specialist outlets to huge department stores, so your duties will vary.

- When you are working on the till, you will take payments, give change, deal with refunds, wrap goods and arrange orders and deliveries.

The type of person suited to this work

You will need to be well presented, outgoing, friendly, polite, and be able to deal with awkward customers and stay calm when you are busy.

Sales assistants have to learn about the things they are selling, which could involve in-house training, and they must be able to help and advise customers to find what they want.

You could be working to targets and earning bonuses according to how much you sell, so will need to be persuasive but not pushy.

You should be responsible and trustworthy, and fit and active to cope with being on your feet all day.

You should be able to work within a team and on your own when required.

Working conditions

In small shops you could spend most of the time at the till/checkout. In large stores you could be working on the shop floor, helping and advising customers and fetching goods from stockrooms.

You might have to carry heavy items.

You will keep the shop clean and tidy and might wear a uniform.

You could work early or late shifts and at weekends and evenings. There are many opportunities for part-time work.

Future prospects

There are shops in all areas of the country, though large retail parks and shopping centres have meant that some smaller shops in town centres have closed.

Working in a small shop you may get to know your regulars well and be given responsibility quite quickly, but promotion prospects can be limited.

In large stores and chains you will probably get training and can quickly become a supervisor and then move into management jobs. Depending on your employer, you might have to move around from shop to shop gaining experience within different-sized shops and departments.

With significant retail experience, some sales assistants progress to occupations like merchandising or buying.

Qualifications and courses

There are no minimum entry requirements for this work. Training is provided by employers. However, larger companies may ask for 2–4 GCSEs/S grades (A*–C/1–3). You might have to pass tests in basic maths and English.

You could do a retail Apprenticeship if aged 16–24. Sales assistants can also work towards Level 1 and 2 awards, certificates and diplomas in retail skills. The Level 3 certificate/diploma also includes modules on management, visual merchandising or sales professional.

Degrees in business or retail management are also available and can speed up entry into management roles.

Advantages/disadvantages

There are lots of opportunities and you will be meeting new people.

The hours can be long.

The work can be stressful if you have to reach sales targets.

You will have very busy times and very quiet times.

Money guide

Wages vary a lot depending on the type and size of the shop and its location.

When you first start work you can expect a salary of around £11,000 per year.

With experience, this rises to £13,000–£16,000. As a supervisor you could earn up to £19,000.

You will get discounts and may get bonuses and commission on what you sell, and may get more money for working shifts.

Related opportunities

- Customer Services Assistant/Manager p483
- Receptionist p58
- Bank Cashier/Customer Adviser p22

Further information

British Shops and Stores Association
Middleton House, 2 Main Road, Middleton Cheney,
Banbury OX17 2TN
01295 712277; www.british-shops.co.uk

The British Retail Consortium
21 Dartmouth Street, London SW1H 9BP
020 7854 8900; www.brc.org.uk

City&
Guilds

www.cityandguilds.com/myperfectjob

SHOE REPAIRER

What the work involves

- Shoe repairers mend and repair shoes and other footwear. They can also repair belts, bags and briefcases, using specialist tools and materials including nail and staple guns and stitching machines.

- You will replace soles and heels by stitching or gluing on new ones and finishing them off neatly.

- A lot of shoe repairers also use specialist machinery to cut keys and do metal engraving.

- You will be serving customers, labelling the shoes they leave, issuing customers with tickets, taking payments, using a till and probably selling things like shoe dyes and polishes, belts and handbags.

The type of person suited to this work

It is important to be practical, good at working with your hands and able to do detailed work quickly and neatly. As the machinery and tools can be dangerous, you will need to be responsible and work safely, be happy wearing overalls and getting your hands dirty.

You might be dyeing shoes, so good colour vision is essential. You will need to enjoy meeting people and be able to cope with being busy and working quickly whilst customers wait for their repairs. You should be happy to work on your own or in a small team, and be able to work out costs and deal with money and payments.

You will need to have good communication skills, and have business skills if you are self-employed.

Working conditions

You will be on your feet a lot, using a range of tools and equipment. You will be using dyes and glues and it can be noisy and dirty with strong smells, so you will wear overalls.

Shoe repairers usually work around 40 hours a week, including Saturdays.

You could work on your own or with one or two others and will be dealing with the public.

Some shoe repairers work in factories repairing goods which customers have returned.

Future prospects

There are around 8,000 shoe repairers in all areas of the country but job opportunities can be limited as most are small shops only employing a few people.

Shoe repairers also work in small outlets in supermarkets or department stores.

You will learn a skill, probably including engraving, and could open your own business. You would need some money to start up, and business skills to plan your work and keep accounts.

In a large chain you could go on to management jobs.

Qualifications and courses

There are no minimum qualifications for this job but you should be able to take measurements and work with numbers.

Training is done on the job, working alongside an experienced shoe repairer. It is possible to work towards an NVQ/SVQ Footwear Repair at Levels 2 and 3. Or a Vocationally Related Qualification (VRQ) in Footwear and Leather production.

NVQs/SVQs are also available in Retail Operations at Levels 2 and 3, and a City & Guilds certificate in Retail Principles. City & Guilds also offer a Higher Professional Diploma in Retail Management.

Apprenticeship/Skillseekers might be available to those aged 16–24.

Advantages/disadvantages

You do not need qualifications and will be doing a practical, hands-on job and meeting lots of people.

You could work for yourself, running your own shoe repair outlet.

The work can be repetitive and fiddly.

Money guide

Salaries can vary a lot. Many shoe repairers are self-employed, so your salary may depend on how big the shop is, where it is and how well it is doing.

Working for someone else, you will probably earn around £10,500 per year when you start.

This could rise to £17,000 with experience and perhaps extra responsibility. Shop managers could get £21,000+.

You might get paid bonuses and will probably get discounts.

Related opportunities

- Locksmith p228
- Customer Services Assistant/Manager p483
- Sales/Retail Assistant p494
- Shopkeeper p496

Further information

MultiService Association
PO Box 9378, Newark NG24 9FE
01400 281298; www.msauk.biz

www.cityandguilds.com/myperfectjob

Retail, Sales and Customer Services

CRCI: SB

SHOPKEEPER

What the work involves

- A shopkeeper owns or manages one or more shops, such as greengrocers, bakeries, newsagents, supermarkets, fishmongers, dry cleaners, fashion retailers, jewellers and florists.

- You will be finding manufacturers and suppliers. For shops that sell foodstuffs this may mean sourcing local produce and purchasing it for the best price.

- As well as keeping the shop tidy and well stocked, you will pay staff wages and keep books and accounts.

The type of person suited to this work

You need to be determined and motivated, with a real interest in what you are doing; you should also be prepared to work long hours and to travel in order to find stock and suppliers.

You will need to be able to sell and market your goods and be confident about finding products that people want to buy.

Excellent communication skills are essential. Also important is a good business sense and being able to plan your finances and keep your accounts. You should be well organised, have some marketing, business and sales skills to succeed in this area of work.

Working conditions

Your hours and conditions will depend on what you are selling and how well you do.

Shops usually open at weekends and often in the evenings, with newsagents and convenience stores opening early and late.

Being your own boss can be stressful but also extremely satisfying and rewarding. Shops vary in size and appearance and how pleasant the working environment is will depend on its staff and clientele. You might wear a uniform and do some heavy lifting.

Future prospects

One option is to operate a franchise, for example a local convenience store, paying a larger company to use their name and sell their products.

If you are successful, you could expand by opening more or larger stores.

The trend towards large shops has meant that lots of smaller shops have closed. It's a very competitive business so you will need to find the right product.

Advantages/disadvantages

There is a lot of freedom in being your own boss: you do not have to answer to anyone else and can make all your own decisions.

You will need to develop good business skills as success will depend on your abilities.

Qualifications and courses

There are no formal entry requirements although customer service and sales experience would be useful. Business experience is also important.

NVQs/SVQs are available in Retail Operations at Levels 2 and 3, and a City & Guilds certificate in Retail Principles. City & Guilds also offer a Higher Professional Diploma in Retail Management.

Other qualifications available include the University Certificate in SME Retail Management which is offered by Manchester Metropolitan University. And some local colleges may offer evening courses in marketing and sales skills.

Local training facilities provide courses in all aspects of owning and running a business including marketing, VAT and starting a business.

If you want to buy your own store, you will need funding, either from your own pocket or through a loan from the bank. There are organisations which provide advice on opening a business, such as the National Federation of Enterprise Agencies (NFEA) and Business Link.

Money guide

Earnings can vary enormously and will depend on how successful you are, the size of the business, where it is and what you are selling.

On average, shopkeepers earn £15,000–£30,000 a year but if you do well you could earn a lot more.

If you are highly successful you could make an annual turnover of between £60,000 and £70,000+ per year.

Related opportunities

- Retail Buyer p492
- Market Trader p488
- Merchandiser p490
- Sales/Retail Assistant p494

Further information

British Franchise Association
A2 Danebrook Court, Oxford Office Village, Langford Lane, Oxford OX5 1LQ
01865 379892; www.thebfa.org

National Federation of Enterprise Agencies
12 Stephenson Court, Fraser Road, Priory Business Park, Bedford MK44 3WJ
01234 831623; www.nfea.com

www.cityandguilds.com/myperfectjob

STOCK CONTROL/ REPLENISHMENT ASSISTANT

What the work involves

- You will work in a supermarket or retail environment, refilling the shelves.

- You must be aware of where each product is, both for when you need to restock it and for when a customer inquires about the whereabouts of an item.

- Your duties will include checking to see which goods need replacing, adding labels to products, tidying the display areas and shelves and transporting goods from the stockroom.

- You may be required to order stock, take deliveries and serve customers.

The type of person suited to this work

This role involves physical activity and so you will need to have a certain level of fitness. You will be expected to, at times, work alone and unsupervised and so you must be trustworthy. You will also spend some time working as part of a team so you will need to be comfortable working with others. You must have an approachable and friendly disposition as you might need to advise customers. You might use a BHT (battery-hand terminal) or HHT (hand-held terminal) in order to keep track of stock or print labels and so you should be comfortable working with computerised equipment.

Working conditions

You will be working in a retail environment; your surroundings will vary depending on which area you choose to work in. Supermarkets can sometimes be cold. You will be on your feet for most of the day; you will be lifting and transporting sometimes heavy stock. Average working hours are about 37 to 40 a week; you will probably be on a rota and so could be working at any time of the day (or night). Part time work and flexitime are available. You might wear a uniform.

Future prospects

Working in stock control/replenishment stands you in good stead to move into other retail positions such as sales assistant or checkout operator. Your skills will be transferable to other retail environments. However, if you have not completed any qualifications progression may prove difficult.

You might be able to complete extra training whilst working which would enhance your chances of promotion. There is a possibility, with training and/or qualifications you could progress into a supervisory or managerial position.

Advantages/disadvantages

You may find the physical nature of this job tiring.

This job has a social element as it allows you to meet people from all walks of life everyday.

You might find this role repetitive.

Your job will allow you to be active.

Qualifications and courses

No formal requirements are necessary, however some employers might expect applicants to have GCSEs in maths and English grades A*–E or equivalent. Most employers will want candidates to have solid communication skills, a can-do attitude and a basic level of numeracy to know how much of each item needs to be restocked.

Retail Apprenticeships are available. This would allow you to gain valuable training whilst being paid a small salary. Many people within this industry begin on a part time basis, such as weekend or holiday work and are then offered a permanent position as and when one becomes available. Details of apprenticeships can be found on www.apprenticeships.org.uk. The salaries available for apprenticeships will vary depending on geographical location.

Previous experience dealing with the public within a relevant industry such as retail would prove beneficial when applying for a post in stock control/replenishment.

Training is done on the job and most retailers expect employees to complete an induction course and training programme. You may work towards a Diploma in Retail Skills or Customer Service.

Money guide

These figures are only approximate and will vary depending on location and employer.

On average the starting salary for this role will be around £10,000 per year. This amount could increase to approximately £15,000 with experience. If you reach the role of supervisor you can expect to earn up to £18,000 per year.

Related opportunities

- Customer Service Assistant/Manager p483
- Sales/Retail Assistant p494
- Retail Manager p493

Further information

The British Retail Consortium
2nd Floor, 21 Dartmouth Street, London SW1H 9BP
020 7854 8900; www.brc.org.uk

British Shops and Stores Association Limited (BSSA)
Middleton House, 2 Main Road, Middleton Cheney,
Banbury OX17 2TN
01295 712277; www.british-shops.co.uk

www.cityandguilds.com/myperfectjob

TRADING STANDARDS OFFICER

What the work involves

- Trading standards officers work for local government to protect consumers. You will check that any individual or company selling products or services is keeping to the law and providing a fair service.

- You will be working with a range of people and organisations. You will travel to check premises, or to follow up on a complaint from the public.

- You will be enforcing the law, leading to prosecutions but also giving help and advice to companies and to consumers.

The type of person suited to this work

You will be enforcing laws and regulations so will need to be able to take in and apply a lot of complex information.

You must have an eye for detail and make sure the reports you write are accurate because they could be used in court.

Excellent communication skills are vital because you will be dealing with lots of different people, advising them and enforcing the law. You will need to be forceful but not aggressive.

You will need to be efficient at using computers and be good at maths as you will be dealing with lots of statistics.

Working conditions

You will probably work for local government but could work for private industry advising on relevant legislation.

You will be office based but will spend time visiting places such as shops, factories, pubs and clubs which could be dirty or cold. Trading standards officers work normal office hours, Monday to Friday and possibly evenings and weekends when different business premises are open.

Future prospects

There are jobs all over the country and the work varies from cities to rural areas. You could move from local government to central government or into retail and manufacturing companies.

There is a shortage of qualified staff but trainee jobs are competitive.

It might be possible to progress to senior officer and managerial positions. As relevant laws and regulations are increasing, opportunities in private industry are growing.

Advantages/disadvantages

This can be an interesting and satisfying job where you are helping the public to get a fair deal.

You could be dealing with difficult or aggressive people.

Qualifications and courses

ENTRY LEVEL 4

To become a qualified trading standards officer, you need a Diploma in Consumer Affairs and Trading Standards (DCATS) awarded by the Trading Standards Institute, and you must be working for a local authority to achieve this.

Prior to this, you can follow a relevant degree course, such as the trading standards degree and Foundation degree. The normal entry requirements for a degree in trading standards or consumer protection are 2 A levels/3 H grades or equivalent. The degree provides exemption from certain parts of the DCATS.

Graduates from an unrelated degree subject can apply to do a Graduate Diploma in Trading Standards at Manchester Metropolitan University. Entry requirements are a 2.2 in any degree.

Non-graduates can join a Trading Standards authority as an enforcement officer or consumer adviser and follow the Accreditation of Prior Experience Learning route (APEL) before studying for the DCATS. The Trading Standards Institute also offers a Diploma in Consumer Affairs for people employed in these positions.

Money guide

As a new enforcement officer or a trainee, you could expect £16,000–£20,000 per year, although employed Apprentices earn less.

You would start on £24,000–£34,000 per year when newly qualified/graduated.

You could earn £35,000–£50,000 as a senior trading standards officer.

£70,000+ is possible for the head of a service, depending on the size of the local authority.

Related opportunities

- Environmental Health Practitioner/Officer p35
- Health and Safety Adviser p40
- Police Officer p552
- Quality Control Inspector p241

Further information

The Trading Standards Institute
1 Sylvan Court, Sylvan Way, Southfields Business Park, Basildon SS15 6TH
0845 608 9500; www.tscareers.org.uk

www.cityandguilds.com/myperfectjob

VEHICLE PARTS OPERATIVE

What the work involves

■ This job involves ordering and looking after vehicle parts and accessories and selling them to the public, garages and mechanics.

■ You need specialist knowledge of stock, and when ordering or supplying parts have to know the exact make, model and year of the vehicle.

■ You will do stock control using computerised systems or possibly keeping paper records, and reorder from warehouses or manufacturers when stocks are low. You will be checking off parts that arrive against delivery notes before placing them in a stock room.

■ As well as taking deliveries and taking orders over the phone and in person, you will use tills, take payments and sometimes invoice customers.

The type of person suited to this work

You should be interested in cars, know about a wide range of parts and accessories, and which makes of vehicles they are for. You will need to be well organised and able to research where to find more unusual parts.

You will also deal with mechanics and the public over the phone and in person, so will need to explain technical information clearly and simply.

You will need to have good communication skills, be a good team player and able to work on your own.

The job involves being on your feet a lot so you will need to be fit and active.

Working conditions

You could be working in a large shop open to the public or a warehouse used by the motor trade. You could be in a fairly small, local garage or work for a large dealership.

You might have to lift weights, move trolleys and climb ladders to reach high shelves. You will work with the public and staff from the motor trade and probably as part of a team.

Normal hours are Monday to Friday from 8.30am to 6.00pm, and you could work evenings and weekends.

Future prospects

If you work for a smaller company your promotion prospects might be limited but in larger companies you could get additional responsibility more quickly and move into managerial and supervisory roles.

You could become a trainee manager in other areas of the retail trade or move into car sales.

Advantages/disadvantages

It is a skilled job with training and you will be using your knowledge of, and interest in, cars and the motor trade.

Qualifications and courses

There are no formal entry requirements for this work, but GCSEs/S grades (A*–C/1–3) in English, maths and ICT and science are useful.

You could do an Apprenticeship/Skillseekers if you are aged 16–24. You would then take NVQs/SVQs at Levels 2 and 3. The Diplomas in Engineering and Retail, available for 14–19 year olds, could also be useful.

Trainee parts operatives can study for the Institute of the Motor Industry's Certificate (Level 2) and Diploma (Level 3) in Vehicle Parts Operations, or a City & Guilds award in Tyre Fitting. NVQs/SVQs at Levels 1–3 in Vehicle Parts Operations, Levels 1 and 2 in Vehicle Fitting, and Levels 2 and 3 in Vehicle Parts Distribution and Supply can be achieved in the workplace.

You might want to study for a Certificate in Customer Service for the Motor Industry at Levels 2 or 3 available from the Institute of the Motor Industry (IMI).

There is a lot of information to remember and the work can be repetitive.

This is a good job for those wanting to work with vehicles who do not want to be mechanics.

Money guide

You can expect £6,800–£9,000 per year when you start as a trainee.

You might earn from £10,500 to £17,000 when you have got some experience.

£20,000+ is possible as a senior vehicle parts operative.

Some employers offer performance related bonuses.

Related opportunities

■ Vehicle Sales Executive p500
■ Motor Vehicle Technician p235
■ Stock Control/Replenishment Assistant p497
■ Warehouse Manager/Worker p630

Further information

The Institute of the Motor Industry
Fanshaws, Brickendon, Hertford SG13 8PQ
01992 511 521; www.motor.org.uk

Retail Motor Industry Federation
201 Great Portland Street, London W1W 5AB
020 7580 9122; www.rmif.co.uk

www.cityandguilds.com/myperfectjob

Retail, Sales and Customer Services

CRCI: SB

VEHICLE SALES EXECUTIVE

What the work involves

- You will be selling new or used cars, motorbikes or vans; greeting customers, advising them and explaining different models, features and prices, and demonstrating cars by going out on test drives.

- Your job will include arranging finance for customers and doing paperwork for the sale and the finance.

- Garages promote their cars through advertising, special events and direct contact with customers, which may also be part of your work.

- Sales staff help keep the forecourt, salesroom and cars clean and tidy.

The type of person suited to this work

You will need to be smart, confident and outgoing with a polite, friendly manner and an ability to deal with all types of people and be persuasive without being pushy. You will need good negotiation and numeracy skills.

You should be interested in cars, know a lot about the ones you are selling and be able to explain technical features clearly and simply.

Your wages will depend on how much you sell so you will need to be motivated and determined and able to deal with stress and pressure.

Your job will also involve working out prices and deals and completing forms and paperwork accurately.

You will need to be able to work without supervision.

Working conditions

You could be working in a small, local garage selling used cars or for a large main dealership.

You will be based in a showroom but will also be outside on the forecourt and going on test drives.

You will spend most of your time dealing with customers but will also do paperwork.

Future prospects

There are currently good opportunities in all parts of the country but it is a popular industry, so jobs can be competitive, especially with the large main dealers.

Prospects are good and you can earn a lot if you do well.

In larger dealerships you can progress to senior salesperson, sales manager or dealer principal.

At management level you will probably earn bonuses linked to the sales of the whole team.

Qualifications and courses

You do not need formal qualifications to enter and train in this career, but employers will expect GCSEs (A*–C)/S in maths and English.

You can apply for a graduate training scheme run by one of the larger car manufacturers which will lead to a recognised Institute of Motor Industry (IMI) qualification.

Car salespeople receive on-the-job training, and may also work towards NVQs/SVQs at Levels 2 and 3 in Vehicle Sales, or the IMI Certificate and Diploma in Vehicle Sales. The Level 2 Certificate leads to Licentiate Membership of the IMI and the Level 3 Diploma provides Associate Membership. Sales people can also attend short courses run by vehicle manufacturers.

Advantages/disadvantages

It can be rewarding when you persuade a customer to buy a car.

You can do very well and earn a high salary.

It can be very stressful working on commission and having to meet targets and you will probably work long hours.

Money guide

Wages vary a lot. You might be on a fairly small basic salary plus commission and bonuses related to your sales.

As a starting salary you could expect £9,000–£15,000 per year. With experience this can rise to £20,000, up to £35,000 with bonuses.

In senior roles you may earn £50,000+ including commission.

Related opportunities

- Customer Services Assistant/Manager p483
- Motor Vehicle Technician p235
- Sales/Retail Assistant p494
- Retail Manager p493

Further information

Retail Motor Industry Federation
201 Great Portland Street, London W1W 5AB
020 7580 9122; www.rmif.co.uk

Institute of the Motor Industry
Fanshaws, Brickendon, Hertford SG13 8PQ
01992 511521; www.motor.org.uk

www.cityandguilds.com/myperfectjob

WINE MERCHANT

What the work involves

- You will use your knowledge of wine to buy from vineyards and suppliers and sell to the public or shops, pubs and restaurants.

- If you manage your own shop or an off-licence, you will also be responsible for supervising staff and maintaining profitability. If you sell wine over the internet or by mail order, you could be doing your own deliveries.

- You could also act as buyer for a supermarket or wine retailer. You will probably spend a lot of time abroad finding and tasting new wines, agreeing prices and checking quality.

- As an independent merchant, you will probably buy wine from companies who ship it in to the country and go to wine tastings to make selections.

The type of person suited to this work

Wine merchants are keen to develop their knowledge, finding new wines and growers and keeping up to date with new developments and tastes.

A good sense of taste and smell is needed to be able to judge the quality of a wine. You should be able to advise people what wine goes well with what food.

You must have excellent communication and customer service skills as dealing with the public and negotiating prices with growers and suppliers will be an important part of your job.

Working conditions

If self-employed you will have freedom and flexibility, but will probably work long hours.

Wine shops are often open until 10pm so you might work shifts including weekends. You will be on your feet a lot and could be lifting heavy boxes.

If you become a buyer, you may travel frequently or you could be based in a head office.

You could be working with the public, sometimes even travelling to people's homes to sell wine.

Future prospects

As supermarkets have become the biggest retailers of wine, it has become more difficult for small shops to succeed.

Large chains offer good promotion prospects. You could progress to a store manager and then to area manager.

To start your own business you will need experience, a good knowledge of wine, and money to buy stock and premises.

Advantages/disadvantages

This job will allow you to use your expertise and passion for wine. You might get to travel and work abroad.

Buyer jobs are scarce.

Qualifications and courses

There are no formal entry requirements but many new entrants have a degree or vocational qualification. Some employers prefer entrants to have 5 GCSEs/S grades (A*–C/1–3) and experience in the retail industry.

It is possible to study for the Wine and Spirit Education Trust (WSET) exams which range from a Foundation Certificate in Wines at Level 1 to the Level 5 Honours Diploma.

Other relevant qualifications include BTEC Higher National Diploma (HND) in Hospitality Management (Licensed Retail), Foundation or Advanced Certificate in Wines and Spirits qualifications offered by WSET, or a Foundation degree in Wine Business or Hospitality Management. It is also possible to take a degree in Hospitality and Licensed Retail Management.

To become an independent wine merchant you will need a premises licence and a personal licence to sell alcohol. This can only be obtained through the Level 2 National Certificate for Personal Licence Holders.

Money guide

Starting salaries are around £12,000 per year. With experience this can reach £17,000.

You might earn £18,000 as an experienced merchant or manager.

£30,000 or more is possible if you are very successful, usually running your own business, or in a top job with a big wine merchant.

Related opportunities

- Bar Manager/Licensee/Publican p134
- Retail Buyer p492
- Retail Manager p493
- Importer/Exporter p606

Further information

Wine & Spirit Education Trust
International Wine & Spirit Centre,
39–45 Bermondsey Street, London SE1 3XF
020 7089 3800; www.wset.co.uk

British Shops and Stores Association Limited
Middleton House, 2 Main Road, Middleton Cheney,
Banbury OX17 2TN
01295 712277; www.british-shops.co.uk

City&
Guilds

www.cityandguilds.com/myperfectjob

Retail, Sales and Customer Services

CRCI: SD

Science, Mathematics and Statistics

Do you have a very mathematical brain? Are you logical in how you approach tasks? Maybe you are fascinated by scientific advances and would like to be involved in future discoveries? People who work in this sector can spend long periods of time carrying out meticulous research. You may find yourself working for a variety of employers, from the health service to a cosmetics company or even a charity. You should be willing to work on your own but also be happy to present your findings in reports to others. People in this sector are very highly skilled individuals who have often been through a lot of training, and possess a questioning and inquisitive mind.

In this section we look at the following jobs:

ACOUSTICIAN

What the work involves

- As an acoustician you will manage, regulate and control sound and vibrations in various environments.

- You might work at researching material for defence, music, healthcare or telecommunications.

- Your work can include many kinds of noise, from building acoustics, architectural acoustics and aerodynamic noise to electroacoustics, environmental issues and even therapeutic uses of ultrasound, as well as diagnostic techniques.

- In your daily work you could be doing anything from advising on sound insulation to researching new ways to adapt the noise levels created by machinery.

The type of person suited to this work

If you want to be an acoustician, you should have an interest not only in how sound behaves, but in problem solving and environmental science too. You need to understand sound and acoustics, and be good at physics and maths.

You need to be creative and innovative in your approach to problem solving, and have good skills in technology for testing and planning any designs you or others create.

You should be organised, and design and plan projects methodically.

You need to be good at working with people, and have excellent communication and project management skills.

It's also important that you understand legislation and standards.

Working conditions

Working conditions vary depending exactly what job you do within acoustics. If you work in a laboratory doing research, this will probably be a 9am–5pm job.

It's rare that you'll stay in one place though: acousticians tend to move around and carry out jobs in recording and music studios, or on site. The work therefore involves standing and bending, and you may occasionally be required to lift and install heavy instruments.

You may spend time away from home and travel abroad.

Future prospects

Prospects are much better once you've registered with the IOA.

Possibilities for promotion include moving into management and supervision roles, or specialising in a particular area.

You could work freelance, or even consider setting up your own company.

Qualifications and courses

ENTRY LEVEL 5

Most jobs in acoustics require degree-level qualifications. Occasionally opportunities arise at trainee level. Relevant degrees include acoustics, sciences (particularly physics), environmental science, and subjects related to construction. For degree entry, you usually need 5 good GCSEs and at least 2 A levels including maths or a numerate science, or 3 A levels including maths and physics or equivalent. It might be helpful to take the Diploma in Science. There are also specialist postgraduate courses available in subjects such as building acoustics or transport.

Once you have a job, most employers have training programmes or graduate schemes in place.

You can also become a member of the IOA and follow courses in acoustics with them. Membership comes at different levels, and following significant contributions to the industry you may be awarded the status of Fellow. This can only happen if you are over 35 and have been working in acoustics for a considerable length of time.

Advantages/disadvantages

If you're interested in science and sound, this could be a good career option.

You won't be stuck at a desk and might get to travel to some really interesting locations. However, this does mean that you'll spend a lot of time away from home.

Money guide

When you start out, you can expect to earn between £18,000 and £22,000 a year. Once you qualify as an acoustics engineer, this could rise to about £34,000. If you become a senior acoustic consultant you might earn over £50,000 a year.

Related opportunities

- Aerospace Engineer p212
- Physicist p533

Further information

Engineering and Technology Board.
Websites: www.scenta.co.uk and www.enginuity.org.uk

Institute of Acoustics (IOA)
77a St Peter's Street, St Albans, Hertfordshire AL1 3BN
01727 848195; www.ioa.org.uk

SEMTA
14 Upton Road, Watford WD18 0JT
0845 443 9001; www.semta.org.uk

ASTRONOMER

What the work involves

■ Astronomers investigate and study the universe. Astronomy covers a wide range of areas and astronomers usually focus on a specific subject, such as planets or stars.

■ You will mainly use mathematics, physics and specialist computer software to examine the pictures and information collected by observatories.

■ You will plan and coordinate projects using specialist equipment, such as telescope systems to observe the skies and collect information.

■ Your work can include constructing new observational instruments and software to improve your knowledge about the universe.

The type of person suited to this work

As a professional astronomer you should have a keen interest in the natural world. You will also need a good understanding of the sciences. Whether you are observing the skies or analysing detailed information, you should be able to take in a range of facts and figures. You will use your decision-making skills to make informed conclusions from the information you work with.

A patient and organised approach is essential. You should be confident in working with computers to complete a range of tasks. You will also need strong communication skills and enjoy working with numbers.

Working conditions

Late or antisocial working hours can often be a feature of this type of work, whether you are based in a university, observatory or research centre. You will spend a great deal of your time working with computers.

The job may involve spending time away from home as many of the major telescopes are in remote locations.

Close observation is often part of this job, so it may be unsuitable for people with visual impairments.

Future prospects

Employment as a professional astronomer is very competitive and demands a great deal of academic study.

If you followed the academic route you could undertake original research combined with a PhD-level degree and then progress to lecturing.

You may choose to work as part of a technical team providing support for astronomy research projects.

You could progress into related jobs in engineering or electronics such as a software or electronics engineer.

Advantages/disadvantages

This job provides the opportunity to increase public understanding of the natural world.

Qualifications and courses

ENTRY LEVEL 5

A degree in physics, maths, astrophysics, geophysics or a related science is required. Specialist degrees are available in astronomy, astrophysics and space science, and in astronomy combined with maths, physics or another science.

Entry requirements for a relevant first degree are usually 3 A levels, including physics, mathematics and another science as well as 5 GCSEs (A*–C), including English and possibly chemistry.

Most entrants to this career also have a PhD or a Master's degree. Taught postgraduate courses in astronomy are available at some universities for people who have a degree in physics, maths or a related area.

To work as a research astronomer, candidates should have a 1st or 2.1 MSci or MPhys degree, followed by further study for a PhD.

University physics departments may include astronomical research groups, and some universities offer MPhil/PhD programmes specifically in astronomy.

You might have to spend a lot of time undertaking observations, which requires patience and commitment.

Undertaking research on-site can be physically tiring.

Money guide

The starting salary for a qualified astronomer with a PhD working as a postdoctoral research assistant is £25,000. With experience, you could earn £35,000 as a university lecturer. At senior levels, a salary of £65,000 is possible as a university professor.

Related opportunities

■ Geographer p520
■ Mathematician/Research Scientist (Maths) p527
■ Physicist p533
■ Geophysicist p522
■ Electrical Engineer p221

Further information

Royal Astronomical Society
Burlington House, London W1J 0BQ
020 7734 4582; www.ras.org.uk

British Astronomical Association
Burlington House, London W1J 0DU
020 7734 4145; www.britastro.org

Institute of Physics
76 Portland Place, London W1B 1NT
020 7470 4800; www.iop.org

CRCI: TD

Science, Mathematics and Statistics

BIOCHEMIST

What the work involves

- You will research a range of living organisms and processes, using specialist equipment.

- Your work may involve collating detailed information and producing reports.

- Biochemists investigate the chemistry of living organisms. They use their investigations to plan experiments and solve problems.

- Biochemists apply their knowledge and skills in many areas, including food and nutrition, agriculture, medicine, plant research and brewing.

The type of person suited to this work

You will need to be curious about biological organisms and interested in improving systems and products. You will constantly use problem-solving skills in this job. Your excellent observational skills will also be very useful. You should enjoy working as part of a team.

You will be confident in using a range of scientific equipment to gain information. You will need a patient and methodical approach for sometimes repetitive but important activities. Your strong communication skills will help you explain and record your work. Confidence in working with numbers and detailed information is also essential.

Working conditions

You would normally work in a laboratory as part of a team. You may also do some of your work in an office environment.

In some sectors, biochemists work on a shift system.

The job involves the regular use of specialist equipment which requires good manual handling skills.

As you become more senior, it is likely you will be involved with managing staff or projects.

Future prospects

Many of the products you use on a daily basis have been developed by biochemists. Biochemists have an important role in organisations ranging from research institutes to multinational companies.

If you go into research and development, you would start by working as part of a team. With experience, you would progress to planning and managing experimental work. You may choose to undertake academic research and go into lecturing or teaching.

Advantages/disadvantages

You may have to work very long hours in this job.

This type of work is often project-based which provides job variety.

Biochemistry offers a wide range of areas in which to specialise.

Qualifications and courses

A degree in biochemistry or a related subject is required for entry to this profession. Many posts also require a postgraduate qualification. A levels/ H grades including chemistry and/or biology are required for entry to a biochemistry degree. Some universities offer Foundation or bridging years as pre-degree courses for applicants who do not have the required qualifications.

Biochemists with a degree and relevant work experience are eligible to join a professional body, the Biochemical Society or the Institute of Biology.

Biochemists continue their training in service. Those with a first degree are often encouraged to study part time for an MSc or PhD.

It is possible to enter as a technician with a minimum of 4 GCSEs/S grades (A*–C/1–3), including English, maths and sciences.

If you want to work with the NHS you will need a first or 2:1 degree and will need to register with the Health Professions Council.

NVQs/SVQs are available in Laboratory and Associated Technical Activities at Levels 2, 3 and 4.

Money guide

Starting salaries for graduate trainees start at around £24,000 per year.

Post registration and with experience, as a project leader you could earn £27,500–£38,000.

At senior/management/consultancy level you can earn from £40,000 in the NHS, but pay can rise to £75,000–£100,000.

Salaries tend to be higher in industry compared with the NHS and universities, especially at junior levels.

Related opportunities

- Biotechnologist p508
- Chemist p510
- Biomedical Scientist/Medical Laboratory Assistant p507
- Clinical Scientist p512

Further information

Biochemical Society Membership Office
Portland Customer Services, Commerce Way,
Whitehall Industrial Estate, Colchester CO2 8HP
01206 796351; www.biochemistry.org

Association of Clinical Biochemists
130–132 Tooley Street, London SE1 2TU
020 7403 8001; www.acb.org.uk

Institute of Biomedical Science
12 Coldbath Square, London EC1R 5HL
020 7713 0214; www.ibms.org/

BIOMEDICAL SCIENTIST/ MEDICAL LABORATORY ASSISTANT

What the work involves

- A biomedical scientist carries out laboratory tests on bodily fluid and tissue in order to help doctors assess what is wrong with their patients. They use a range of equipment to carry out tests designed to discover abnormalities.

- Medical laboratory assistants support the work of biomedical scientists. As a medical laboratory assistant, you will carry out a variety of tasks including: sorting and labelling tissue samples, sterilising and disinfecting equipment, making up chemical solutions, separating blood serum and plasma from samples, recording and analysing information.

The type of person suited to this work

Biomedical scientist

You must be interested in science and medicine and have strong scientific skills. You must be practical, responsible, and have good IT skills. You should have the ability to supervise junior members of staff and to follow complex instructions.

Medical laboratory assistant

You need a careful, methodical approach to your work. You should be able to concentrate and pay attention to detail. You will work accurately under pressure to meet deadlines. Solid communication skills are essential.

Working conditions

Most medical laboratory assistants and biomedical scientists work in pathology laboratories within hospitals, but some work directly with patients.

Future prospects

Biomedical scientist

You will probably specialise in a specific area. In order to progress you might need a higher qualification. Within the NHS you may progress to a managerial role.

Work abroad is a possibility, especially within developing countries.

Medical laboratory assistant

Most employment is available in NHS hospitals. You may specialise or move to a related career such as a pharmacy technician. To train as a clinical or biomedical scientist you will need to study for a relevant degree.

Advantages/disadvantages

The work can be repetitive and you will probably need more qualifications to progress.

You will be performing an important part of a hospital's medical

Qualifications and courses

Biomedical scientist

You cannot become a Biomedical Scientist without registering with the Health Professions Council (HPC). To do this you must have an honours degree, accredited by the Institute of Biomedical Science (IBS) and approved by the HPC. If you complete a degree which is not accredited, you can apply to the IBS to have it assessed.

Alternatively, you can start as a trainee biomedical scientist in the NHS, whilst studying part time for 4 years to acquire an accredited biomedical science degree.

Medical laboratory assistant

There are no formal entry requirements, but 4 or more GCSEs/S (A*–C) in English, maths and a science, or an equivalent qualification such as a BTEC First Diploma in Applied Science may be valuable. Laboratory assistants can work towards qualifications such as NVQs/SVQs.

work, because you will be helping to diagnose patients' illnesses.

You may have to deal with angry doctors/patients who want results sooner than you can deliver them.

Money guide

The starting salary for an NHS biomedical scientist is between £20,225 and £26,123 a year. At an advanced level you might earn up to £38,352. A healthcare scientist at professional manager level might earn up to £64,118.

As a trainee medical laboratory assistant in the NHS you would start at around £12,177 per year. With experience this rises to around £15,107. At senior level you could earn up to £19,730 per year.

Related opportunities

- Laboratory Technician p524
- Phlebotomist p329
- Chemist p510
- Clinical Scientist p512

Further information

NHS Careers
0345 606 0655; www.nhscareers.nhs.uk

Institute of Biomedical Science
12 Coldbath Square, London EC1R 5HL
020 7713 0214; www.ibms.org; mail@ibms.org

Science, Mathematics and Statistics

CRCI: TD

BIOTECHNOLOGIST

What the work involves

- You will use biological organisms and processes to develop and adapt products. Biotechnologists work in a range of areas such as genetic engineering, electronics, food science and microbiology.

- You could work in research and development or in aspects of production such as quality control.

- Your work might involve enhancing existing products or developing new types of organisms.

- Biotechnology provides the scientific basis for agriculture, pharmaceuticals, waste management, food and medical care.

The type of person suited to this work

You will need a keen interest in science for working in any area of biotechnology. Strong observational skills and an organised approach are also essential. You should be confident working with scientific equipment and computers to manage information and undertake research.

Most biotechnologists are employed as part of a group so the ability to work as part of a team is helpful. If you work as a technician, you should be able to cope with undertaking routine but required testing activities. Biochemists in industry also need to understand the commercial applications of their work.

Working conditions

Biotechnologists usually work in a laboratory or research centre in sterile conditions to undertake experimental and testing work. You will work normal office hours, but may occasionally be on-call during evenings and weekends. Protective clothing is needed when working with micro-organisms and dangerous chemicals.

Your work is likely to involve using microscopes and electronic testing equipment, and spending time on a computer doing analysis work.

Future prospects

You could work within government research institutions or play a central role in developing and enhancing products in commercial biotechnology companies. You can progress to a supervisory role.

There is also the option to develop an academic career – this may provide additional opportunities to undertake commercial research. You can use this research to move into sales, marketing or production roles.

Advantages/disadvantages

Laboratory work, particularly at technician level, can be time-consuming and requires a lot of patience.

You will be researching and learning new things every day.

Job prospects are good as there is a range of sectors in which you can work.

Qualifications and courses

ENTRY LEVEL 7

A Master's degree in either biotechnology, bioscience or a related subject, such as microbiology, biochemistry or chemical engineering, is required for entry to this profession. For research posts, a PhD may be a requirement.

For a postgraduate course you will need a 2.1 or higher relevant first degree. These courses may run from 1 to 3 years full time.

Although rare, it is possible to become a biotechnologist with an HND or a Foundation degree in Chemical or Manufacturing Engineering by starting off as a trainee technician.

It's a good idea to do a work placement while studying as most employers also look for relevant experience.

NVQs/SVQs are available at Levels 2–4 in Laboratory and Associated Technical Activities.

Money guide

As a graduate working in a university you could start on a salary of £18,500–£24,000 per year.

With a specialist higher degree, your salary can range from £28,000 to £37,500.

Established senior lecturers can earn £38,000–£50,000.

Professors with a great deal of experience can expect to earn up to £55,000.

Biotechnologists earn higher salaries in industry.

Related opportunities

- Biochemist p506
- Biomedical Scientist/Medical Laboratory Assistant p507
- Chemist p510

Further information

BioIndustry Association
14–15 Belgrave Square, London SWIX 8PS
020 7565 7190; www.bioindustry.org

Institute of Biology
9 Red Lion Court, London EC4A 3EF
020 7936 5900; www.iob.org

Biotechnology and Biological Sciences Research Council
Polaris House, North Star Avenue,
Swindon SN2 1UH
01793 413200; www.bbsrc.ac.uk

BOTANIST

What the work involves

- Botanists study all kinds of plant life and plant biology. They are increasingly employed within industry and research in areas such as plant-cell technology and genetic engineering.

- Your work could involve managing rare plant collections, environmental conservation, horticulture, agriculture and other areas.

- You will use specialist equipment such as electron microscopes and satellite imaging technology.

- You might look into how human activity affects plants in farming, or you may try and discover useful chemicals produced by plants.

The type of person suited to this work

As a botanist you should have a real interest in science and plants. This interest should stretch to a particular field of work such as conservation. This profession will involve detailed analysis so you will need strong observational skills. You must also have a methodical approach to your work activities.

You should be comfortable working with a range of scientific equipment. However you will also need to be happy undertaking practical research work, sometimes in unpleasant weather conditions. You may also need to be a good leader as you might be in charge of junior staff, students and volunteers.

Working conditions

You could be working in one or more of the following environments; laboratories, classrooms, lecture theatres, offices and outdoors. Hours will vary, but within research and higher education you will work about 37 hours a week.

Field work takes place in all weather conditions and you may find it physically demanding. Whilst working in a laboratory you will be using specialist equipment and might be required to wear protective clothing. A driving licence may be required if you need to travel between locations.

Future prospects

Within conservation and field work, progression would entail taking on more responsibility and possibly managing others. Within the higher education sector there is a set career path leading from researcher to head of department or professor. Within industry there is the possibility of promotion. You also have the option of working as a freelance consultant and therefore being self-employed. There is the potential to work overseas in most areas of botany.

Advantages/disadvantages

There are opportunities to visit different types of outside locations on research trips.

Research jobs are often offered on a short-term basis, which can create job insecurity.

Qualifications and courses

Botanists may enter this career as laboratory technicians or technical assistants. Most entrants have a degree.

Relevant degree subjects include botany, plant biology, plant science, environmental science and ecology. A levels/H grades in biology and another science, often chemistry, are required for entry. You will also require 5 GCSEs (A*–C). The Diploma in Environmental and Land-Based Studies could be useful.

It may also be a good idea to complete some voluntary work in relevant organisations and to acquire relevant skills such as plant identification.

Good GCSE/A level choices include sciences (especially biology), maths and English. You might also want to consider geography and geology.

To work as a researcher, a postgraduate qualification is required. Candidates may enter with a PhD, or enter as a trainee researcher in a university department and work towards a PhD. In order to apply for a postgraduate qualification you will need to successfully complete a first degree.

You will have the opportunity to combine your love of plants with your passion for science.

Money guide

These figures will vary depending on location, sector and employer.

Starting salaries are around £16,000 a year. Technical assistants begin on about £18,000 per year. With experience this could increase to between £25,000 and £35,000 a year. In a senior role you could earn in excess of £45,000 per year.

Salaries within the private industry will vary considerably.

Related opportunities

- Microbiologist/Bacteriologist p530
- Ecologist p515
- Entomologist p516

Further information

Botanical Society of the British Isles
Botany Department, Natural History Museum, Cromwell Road, London SW7 5BD
www.bsbi.org.uk

British Trust for Conservation Volunteers
Sedum House, Mallard Way, Potteric Carr, Doncaster DN4 8DB
01302 388 883; www.btcv.org.uk

CRCI: TD

Science, Mathematics and Statistics

CHEMIST

What the work involves

- Chemists work in many different sectors, undertaking the analysis and use of complex scientific processes and substances on a detailed molecular level.

- As well as research and development, chemists also check that products are developed to a safe standard.

- Professional chemists are employed in a wide range of sectors, including the oil industry, pharmaceuticals, medical research and academia.

The type of person suited to this work

Chemists need strong observational skills. They must also be able to think around complex scientific problems. You will have good manual handling abilities for undertaking research with a range of scientific equipment.

Working conditions

The average chemist works about 37 hours a week. Your job could involve working in a laboratory as part of a research centre, but you may also undertake research outdoors on-site. You may have to wear protective clothing such as lab coat, protective glasses and gloves. If you are employed by a private company you may be required to work shifts organised by a rota. At senior levels, you may be involved with business development and managerial activities.

Future prospects

Professional chemists play an important role in developing and updating products and systems. Public research institutes, academic institutions and private companies employ chemists. There are also opportunities in government research, health and education. Some chemists move into areas such as law, IT, science journalism and marketing. With experience you could enter a supervisory role. There are also opportunities to teach in schools and universities. Postgraduate qualifications may improve your chances for progression.

Advantages/disadvantages

Low numbers of entrants taking chemistry degrees means that there are many opportunities.

Laboratory tasks can sometimes be repetitive and time-consuming.

Many large companies employ chemists, so promotion can be possible without moving employers.

Money guide

These figures are only approximate and will vary depending on sector, employer and location. Salary levels should increase

Qualifications and courses

ENTRY LEVEL 5

For entry to a chemistry degree, A levels in chemistry and at least 1 other science or maths is required as well as 5 GCSEs (A*–C) including maths, 2 sciences and English. It may be helpful to take the Diploma in Science. Degree courses are available in chemistry, biological chemistry, environmental chemistry, medical chemistry, and in chemistry combined with other subjects. Many institutions offer 1-year Foundation courses for candidates without the necessary scientific background.

Many chemists also have a postgraduate qualification in chemistry or in a specialist area such as materials chemistry, medicinal chemistry or pharmaceutical chemistry. You can also work towards professional membership of the Royal Society of Chemistry.

Alternatively, it is possible to enter as a technician with a minimum of 4 GCSEs (A*–C), including English, maths and 2 sciences. A levels, a National Certificate/Diploma or HNC/D in a science subject may be required.

Some posts require A levels/H grades, BTEC/SQA National qualifications, or an HNC/D. Graduates are also employed as technicians. NVQs/SVQs are available.

with the level of academic qualification. At graduate entry you can earn between £15,000 and £20,000 per year. With experience, and when established, you can expect £30,000 a year. With added responsibility, such as if you are in charge of a team or project you could expect to earn between £35,000 and £40,000 a year.

Related opportunities

- Biochemist p506
- Biotechnologist p508
- Cosmetic Scientist p514

Further information

Royal Society of Chemistry
Burlington House, Piccadilly, London W1J 0BA
020 7437 8656; Main website www.rsc.org;
Careers and jobs website: www.chemsoc.org

Association of the British Pharmaceutical Industry
12 Whitehall, London SW1A 2DY
0870 890 4333; Main website: www.abpi.org.uk;
Careers website: www.abpi-careers.org.uk

CLINICAL GENETICIST

What the work involves

- Geneticists analyse and modify human, animal or plant DNA. If working as a human geneticist, you could be involved with medical genetics or human genetic research.

- You could undertake genetic engineering in agricultural research.

- This profile focuses on clinical geneticists who are responsible for identifying and diagnosing genetic disorders. There are two main jobs in this field; cytogeneticists (studying chromosomes which contain genes) and molecular geneticists (studying DNA).

- Clinical geneticists test samples from patients, record their findings and draw a conclusion from them. They also supervise the work of others.

The type of person suited to this work

You should be an excellent communicator, both verbally and on paper. You will need to be able to work accurately and meticulously, whilst keeping to deadlines. You must have a good understanding of computers. You will need to be discreet as you will be dealing with confidential medical information. You should be able to work effectively as part of a team and be able to take on the role of a supervisor when training junior staff. You must have strong problem-solving skills.

Working conditions

You will be based in a sterile laboratory. You will have to wear protective clothing such as overalls, laboratory glasses and gloves. You will also have to ensure that you reach all health and safety standards.

As a clinical geneticist within the NHS you will be working about 37.5 hours per week, from Monday to Friday. There may also be a rota in place which covers bank holidays and weekends.

Future prospects

Genetics is a fast-developing area of science that offers the chance to work directly with patients as a medical geneticist within the NHS or directly within research in research centres and universities. You could also go on to work in research and development in industry.

In order to be promoted you will need to gather experience, responsibility and training. Once you have worked for two or three years as a registered geneticist you can begin to apply for more senior positions.

Advantages/disadvantages

You may have to repeat procedures which could become tedious.

This job contains a great deal of responsibility.

You will be working with a wide range of samples and so every day will be different.

Qualifications and courses

ENTRY LEVEL 6

An Honours degree in genetics, biomedical or biological sciences is required. In order to become a clinical geneticist with the NHS you will need a 2.1 degree in genetics or another life science. Competition to become a clinical geneticist within the NHS is fierce as there are only two training posts a year.

Two or three science A levels/H grades are normally required for entry to relevant degree courses. Chemistry and/or biology may be specified. You will also need 5 GCSEs grades A*–C.

A postgraduate qualification is desirable. In order to complete postgraduate study, you will need to successfully complete a first degree.

Training is undertaken in an accredited genetics laboratory, and follows the clinical scientist training programme lasting 2 to 3 years.

It is also possible to enter the profession at technician or trainee level with GCSEs/S grades, A levels/H grades, or equivalent qualifications in subjects such as biology, maths, science and English.

Money guide

These figures will vary depending on sector, location and employer.

The average starting salary for a graduate clinical scientist trainee is about £24,000. Once registered, you can expect to earn between £29,000 and £38,352. If you reach the level of principal clinical scientist you could earn up to £44,527. As a consultant this can increase to as much as £77,179.

You may also receive an additional allowance if you work in London.

Related opportunities

- Clinical Scientist p512
- Forensic Scientist p519
- Laboratory Technician p524
- Pharmacologist p327

Further information

Genetics Society
Roslin BioCentre, Wallace Building, Roslin, Midlothian EH25 9PP
0131 200 6392; www.genetics.org.uk

British Society of Human Genetics
Clinical Genetics Unit, Birmingham Women's Hospital, Birmingham B15 2TG
0121 627 2634; www.bshg.org.uk

NHS Careers
PO Box 2311, Bristol BS2 2ZX
0345 606 0655; www.nhscareers.nhs.uk

CRCI: TD | Science, Mathematics and Statistics

CLINICAL SCIENTIST

What the work involves

- Clinical scientists work mainly for the NHS but are also employed in the Health Protection Agency, research centres and industry.

- Your work may involve supporting doctors, suggesting suitable tests for diagnosing patients, reporting on results and recommending treatments.

- You may also research and test new methods of treatment and make recommendations on the best equipment or test materials.

- You might specialise in a particular area such as clinical embryology (the study of infertility) or clinical microbiology (identifying infections in patients caused by bacteria, fungus or parasites).

The type of person suited to this work

You should have a keen interest in medicine and science, and a desire to help others. You should have excellent observational skills. You need technical skills and the ability to use scientific equipment to get results.

You will need an organised approach for undertaking practical work and the ability to work to set deadlines. You should be able to interact well as part of a team. As a scientist you will get results by combining a logical approach with a creative flair. You should have strong computer skills.

Working conditions

You might work around 37.5 hours a week, usually from Monday to Friday, although these hours could vary depending on your specialism. You may need to work some evenings and weekends if you are on-call. You will usually work in a laboratory or within a specialist department. You may have some contact with patients. You will be working in a sterile environment, which may demand that you wear protective clothing. You might need to use ionising radiation.

Future prospects

As progression is performance based, you will need to accept more responsibility and/or take part in research and development projects to reach a more senior level. As a consultant, you would be responsible for a large department and have the chance to make important contributions to your area of expertise. There is also the option of moving between departments to gain further training. You could move into lecturing or training. There is the possibility of working abroad.

Advantages/disadvantages

You will be helping to diagnose patients and suggest treatments which will improve their quality of life.

Mistakes could lead to an incorrect diagnosis and so you will be working under a lot of pressure.

Qualifications and courses

ENTRY LEVEL 6

Entrants to this profession require a 1st or 2.1 class degree in a relevant subject, such as biochemistry, biology, chemistry, engineering, genetics, microbiology, physics or physiology. Entry to a degree typically requires a minimum of 2 A levels/3 H grades, including appropriate science subjects as well as 5 GCSEs (A*–C) including English and maths. Equivalent qualifications, such as the International Baccalaureate, Foundation degrees in Science, BTEC National and BTEC Higher Nationals and science Access to Higher Education courses may also be relevant. It might be helpful to take the Diploma in Science.

An MSc or PhD in your specialist area is an advantage. In order to apply you usually require a 1st or 2.1 in your first degree.

Clinical scientists start as Grade A trainees. The training lasts 2–3 years. On completion, candidates are eligible for state registration, and can apply for Grade B posts. In-service training continues, and many clinical scientists work towards membership of professional bodies or a PhD. After a minimum of 4 years in a training post scientists can register with the Health Professions Council allowing them to use their correct title of Clinical Scientist and work unsupervised.

Money guide

These figures vary depending on employer and location. If you work in London you will be given an additional allowance.

As a trainee clinical scientist within the NHS you could earn about £24,000 per year. Once registered, you could earn between £30,000 and £40,000 a year. This could increase to £97,478 if you become an advanced practitioner clinical scientist or consultant clinical scientist.

Related opportunities

- Biochemist p506
- Hospital Doctor p311
- Medical Physicist p316
- Radiographer p336

Further information

Association of Clinical Scientists
The Administrator, c/o The Association for Clinical Biochemistry, 130–132 Tooley Street, London SE1 2TU
020 7940 8960; www.assclinsci.org

Clinical Scientists Recruitment Centre
www.nhsclinicalscientists.info

Federation of Clinical Scientists
c/o Association for Clinical Biochemistry, 130–132 Tooley Street, London SE1 2TU
020 7403 8001; www.acb.org.uk/federation

CONSUMER SCIENTIST

What the work involves

■ Consumer scientists or home economists provide support, information and specialist services related to healthy living and eating.

■ You will be the point of communication between consumers and manufacturers. You will study what the consumer needs and provide advice on how to develop it.

■ Your work could involve developing new food products, educating people about healthy eating or assessing new cookery equipment.

■ Jobs are available within quality assurance, marketing, media and journalism, food product development, education, government, product and service development and catering.

The type of person suited to this work

You will need to have strong communication skills, which allow you to talk to people of all ages and backgrounds. You should also have an interest in food and how people live their lives within the home environment. You should have solid computer skills and a knack for describing information in a clear way, both orally and in writing. You must be creative and have proficient design skills.

Working conditions

This role may involve travelling to meetings, conferences and other environments in the UK and abroad.

Your working environment will vary according to which industry you work within. You could be in an office, kitchen, classroom, laboratory or a selection of these.

You will be working about 35 to 40 hours per week, usually from Monday to Friday. You might also have to complete reports in your free time.

Future prospects

Consumer scientists can move between industries as their services are always required. Specific industries include retail chains, marketing bodies, local authorities, magazines, television and newspapers, health authorities, producers of food, advisory and consumer organisations, hotels and restaurants, consumer pressure groups, schools, colleges and universities and many others. In most areas there is the opportunity to progress to managerial level. Promotion may involve moving to a new location within the country.

Advantages/disadvantages

You may find it frustrating when asked to complete tests in the later stages of the factory process.

This profession will give you the opportunity to move into a vast number of industries, which will aid your career progression possibilities.

You may have to complete reports in your free time.

Qualifications and courses

ENTRY LEVEL 3

HNC/Ds and degrees are available in a variety of relevant subjects, for example consumer studies/science, food studies/science, food and nutrition, food and marketing, food technology. Degrees are also available in specialist areas of consumer science, such as consumer protection or consumer psychology. To gain acceptance to a HND course you will usually require at least 1 A level and 4 GCSEs grade A*–C (or equivalent). Most degree courses expect candidates to have at least 2 A levels and 5 GCSEs (A*–C or equivalent). These requirements may vary so be sure to check with the institution. The Diploma in Hospitality could be useful.

A qualified teacher can also enter this profession. You will need GCSEs (A*–C) in English, maths and science, a relevant degree and a Postgraduate Certificate in Education.

Relevant courses at further education level include NVQs/SVQs in Food Preparation or Food and Drink Manufacturing Operations and BTEC/SQA National qualifications in Hospitality. Employers may offer in-house training leading to NVQs/SVQs.

Money guide

Salary levels vary according to employer, sector and location and so the following figures are approximate.

Starting salaries range from £18,000 to £20,000 per year. With experience, you could earn between £25,000 and £30,000 a year. At senior level you could get up to £50,000 per year. Consumer scientists working on a consultancy basis can earn £150–£500 a day.

Related opportunities

■ Chef p137
■ Dietitian p303
■ Environmental Health Practitioner/Officer p35
■ Market Research Executive p413
■ School Teacher p202

Further information

Improve Ltd
Ground Floor, Providence House, 2 Innovation Close, Heslington, York YO10 5ZF
0845 644 0448; www.improveltd.co.uk

Institute of Food Research
Norwich Research Park, Colney, Norwich NR4 7UA
01603 255 000; www.ifr.ac.uk

Institute of Food Science and Technology
5 Cambridge Court, 210 Shepherds Bush Road, London W6 7NJ
020 7603 6316; www.foodtechcareers.org

Science, Mathematics and Statistics

CRCI: TA

COSMETIC SCIENTIST

What the work involves

- The cosmetics industry requires scientists to help develop, test and produce new and existing cosmetics and beauty products, such as make-up, perfumes and haircare products.

- There are various elements to this profession, including researching new ingredients, developing cosmetic products, developing the processes used to create the product, quality control, safety testing, packaging development and regulatory affairs which involves ensuring the product meets all legal requirements.

- Most work takes place in a sterile, laboratory environment.

The type of person suited to this work

You will have an interest in the science of cosmetics, along with knowledge and skill in chemistry and biology. You will need to be meticulous, but also able to work at speed. You will need to understand statistics and have the ability to use the relevant computer software. You should have an extremely methodical approach to your work and the ability to follow instructions effectively. You must have strong communication skills, to convey information to your colleagues and clients effectively.

Working conditions

Most of your work will take place in a sterile, laboratory environment. Your job may involve handling potentially dangerous materials, so you would need to wear protective clothing. This job might involve repetitive analysis work in the laboratory, which can be physically demanding.

In addition to hands-on experimental work, your work may include using computers. Your job might involve travelling to meetings, conferences and other events in the UK and abroad.

Future prospects

Progression generally comes in the form of moving to a supervisory or managerial role, which could allow you to spend more time with the client. Alternatively, you might consider changing departments and moving into a sales or marketing position, where the scientific knowledge you have acquired would be extremely relevant.

There is also the option of self-employment, working as a consultant, providing specialist support to cosmetic companies. You might also consider lecturing on cosmetic science courses.

Advantages/disadvantages

You may find some elements of the job extremely repetitive and monotonous.

Your work will be directly influenced by the fashion industry; you will be working to predict the latest trends, which could be exciting.

This profession can be fast paced and you may find it stressful.

Qualifications and courses

ENTRY LEVEL 5

Career entry can be achieved at more than one level, including a relevant degree (cosmetic science, chemistry, chemical engineering, biology, microbiology, physics, medicine and pharmacy), Foundation degree or HNC/D. Most degree courses require applicants to have achieved a minimum of 2 A levels, which should include relevant sciences (particularly chemistry) and 5 GCSEs grade A*–C (including English and maths). Some universities may accept alternative qualifications and so you should check with the individual institution. Many colleges include a 1-year introductory (Access) course for students who have not studied the requisite science subjects at A level/H grade. Foundation degrees and HNC/HND qualifications normally expect applicants to have achieved at least 1 A level (or equivalent).

The Diploma in Cosmetic Science can be attained by distance learning, after approximately 300 hours of study. The Principles and Practice of Cosmetic Science course is a shorter course, which is particularly useful for those who have been in the industry for a while and are looking to move into supervisory or managerial roles and/or who are taking on a new field of expertise.

Money guide

Salary levels will vary according to employer, sector and location. Starting salaries are roughly between £16,000 and £23,000 per year.

With experience and training this will increase and you could earn from £25,000 to £45,000 a year.

At senior levels, such as within management, it is possible to earn over £50,000 a year.

Related opportunities

- Biochemist p506
- Laboratory Technician p524
- Pharmacologist p327

Further information

The Cosmetic Toiletry and Perfumery Association Ltd
Josaron House, 5–7 John Princes Street, London W1G 0JN
020 7491 8891; www.ctpa.org.uk

Society of Cosmetic Scientists
Suite 6, Langham House East, Mill Street, Luton,
Bedfordshire LU1 2NA
01582 726661; www.scs.org.uk and
www.cosmeticlearning.com

Royal Society of Chemistry
Burlington House, Piccadilly, London W1J 0BA
020 7437 8656; www.rsc.org

ECOLOGIST

What the work involves

- Ecologists help to protect the natural world by investigating the relationship between living organisms and their environment.

- You will undertake ecological surveys of animals and plants and monitor the state of urban and rural environments.

- You may also write reports and analyse statistical information.

- You may also advise on legal regulations, manage wildlife conservation areas and present your research at conferences or educational seminars.

The type of person suited to this work

A keen interest in the natural world is essential. It's important to be observant and methodical in your work. You will also need to be organised and work to a high standard of accuracy when collating statistics.

You will need to be comfortable working outdoors, sometimes in poor weather conditions. You must have a good knowledge of environmental policies and legislation. Good manual handling skills are important.

You will be presenting your research on a regular basis so excellent communication skills are essential.

Working conditions

Ecologists work in laboratories or research centres when undertaking analysis activities.

You would work outside in all kinds of weather conditions when undertaking fieldwork such as surveys of plants or animals. For fieldwork you would need a good level of physical fitness and good observational skills. This may make the job unsuitable for people with visual impairments.

Future prospects

Ecology offers a wide range of job opportunities; you can shape your career according to your interests. However, there is strong competition for jobs; some are available only on a contract basis and it can take time to find a permanent role.

Many types of organisations employ ecologists. You could go into scientific research, environmental management, teaching or conservation for organisations such as environmental consultancies, research bodies and private companies.

Advantages/disadvantages

This job provides the satisfaction of having a positive impact on the natural environment.

You may need to move around employers to develop your career.

You can choose to work in your specialist area, and develop your career around something you love learning about.

Qualifications and courses

Entrants require an Honours degree or above in the field of biological and earth sciences. Relevant subjects include ecology, environmental biology/management; conservation or marine biology. Additionally, many employers seek experience (as a research assistant or a conservation project volunteer), and postgraduate qualifications are increasingly an advantage.

A levels/H grades in sciences are required for entry to degrees in ecology or biological sciences. Biology A level or equivalent is a required or preferred subject for some degrees.

NVQs/SVQs are available in Environmental Conservation at Levels 2 and 3 and Environmental Management at Level 4. The Diploma in Environmental and Land-Based Studies could be helpful.

A driving licence is useful.

Ecologists with relevant qualifications and experience can become members of the Institute of Ecology and Environmental Management (IEEM). Different levels of membership are available depending on qualifications and experience. The IEEM also provides short professional development courses for its members.

Money guide

Salaries vary according to the type of organisation you work for.

Starting salaries range from around £13,000 to £19,000 per year. With experience you could earn £25,000–£45,000.

Senior/management roles in larger organisations can pay in excess of £45,000.

Related opportunities

- Environmental Scientist p517
- Environmental Conservation Manager/Officer p262

Further information

British Ecological Society
Charles Darwin House, 12 Rogers Street,
London WC1N 2JU
020 685 2500; www.britishecologicalsociety.org

Institution of Environmental Sciences
2nd Floor, 34 Grosvenor Gardens, London SW1W 0DH
020 7730 5516; www.ies-uk.org.uk

Institute of Ecology and Environmental Management (IEEM)
43 Southgate Street, Winchester SO23 9EH
01962 868626; www.ieem.net

CRCI: TD

Science, Mathematics and Statistics

ENTOMOLOGIST

What the work involves

- Entomology is the study of insects, including how they live and how they interact with their environment. Entomologists also observe the behaviour of insects to gain valuable information on the state of specific natural areas.

- As an entomologist, you could analyse and assess the effects of insect life on agriculture. Entomologists are also employed to undertake research in medicine or to support ecological and environmental conservation work.

- Work in the field might include searching for new species or studying insect ecology.

- Work in the laboratory could include developing insecticides or classifying insects.

The type of person suited to this work

You should have a methodical, logical and meticulous approach to your work and the ability to be patient and persevere when you encounter problems. You will need to be able to work effectively, both alone and within a team. As you will need to remember a great deal of information such as insect names and classifications, you should have an excellent memory. You will also require good communication, computer and leadership skills.

Working conditions

Working hours and environments will depend upon the area of entomology you work in. Research entomologists spend the majority of their time in a laboratory and will generally work regular hours from Monday to Friday. Those working in higher education will also have office hours and will spend their time in classrooms and lecture theatres, offices and laboratories.

Future prospects

Entomologists work in a wide range of areas, including agricultural research and development, ecological protection and conservation, forensics and pest control. Others go on to develop their research interests as academic professionals after gaining postgraduate qualifications.

Progression within conservation and in the field will depend on merit and responsibilities such as managing others. Within universities there is a progression path from researcher to head of department. Within industry, promotion opportunities to senior positions are available. Self-employment is a possibility.

Advantages/disadvantages

It could get frustrating when an experiment or investigation does not go according to plan.

Your work could take you all over the world.

There is a wide variety of career options available.

If you work in the field or within conservation, you might have to live and work in inhospitable environments.

Qualifications and courses

An Honours degree in a relevant field is required. There are no entomology degree courses; however biology, zoology, environmental science and biological sciences would all be appropriate. Candidates usually need at least 2 A levels/ 3 H grades including biology and 5 GCSEs/S (A*–C/1–3) for entry to relevant degree courses. You should check entry requirements with the individual university as they may vary. It might be helpful to take the Diploma in Science.

Quite often a postgraduate qualification will be required. There are numerous entomology postgraduate qualifications offered in the UK. In order to apply for a postgraduate course you must have successfully completed a first degree.

Entry at technician level requires GCSEs/S grades and A levels/H grades. Relevant subjects include biology (and other sciences), maths, English, geography and geology.

Foreign language qualifications may also prove beneficial.

Money guide

These figures are only approximate as salaries will vary depending on location, sector and employer.

Starting salaries for entomologists are usually about £16,000 per year. This could increase to around £35,000 a year once enough experience has been gathered. If you progress to the stage when you are one of the most highly regarded entomologists you could earn over £60,000 per year.

Related opportunities

- Agricultural Scientist p254
- Botanist p509
- Ecologist p515
- Environmental Scientist p517
- Zoologist p538

Further information

British Entomological and Natural History Society
The Pelham-Clinton Building, Dinton Pastures Country Park, Davis Street, Hurst, Reading RG10 0TH
www.benhs.org.uk

The Natural History Museum
Cromwell Road, London SW7 5BD
020 7942 5000; www.nhm.ac.uk

Royal Entomological Society
The Mansion House, Chiswell Green Lane, St Albans AL2 3NS
01727 899387; www.royensoc.co.uk

ENVIRONMENTAL SCIENTIST

What the work involves

- Environmental scientists apply scientific techniques to study and protect the natural environment.

- You might look for ways to ensure 'sustainable development' by discovering and experimenting with ways to reduce the damage caused to the world and our natural resources.

- You could work in pollution monitoring, conservation, energy, engineering, environmental consultancy and research or other areas.

- You will probably be advising colleagues and clients, some of whom may not have a scientific background, on the damage particular developments could cause to the environment.

The type of person suited to this work

To work in this industry you should have an interest in geography, science and environmental issues. You will need to be practical and methodical, as well as having the ability to think outside the box in order to problem solve. You will need to be meticulous in your approach to work, as the results you find could have an impact on whether developments go ahead.

Working conditions

How many hours you work and the environment you are in will depend on the specific role you take. Some environmental scientists work a 9am–5pm week but others, involved in fieldwork, will have to complete extra hours in order to meet deadlines.

When working in the field you will be outside in all weather conditions. Field roles are dependent on their geographical location and so the work field environmental scientists do varies greatly. You will also spend some time in an office and/or lab.

Future prospects

There is a growing demand for environmental scientists, mainly due to the increasing concern about climate change, global warming and other environmental issues.

You can progress to team manager or project manager, which will involve taking on more responsibilities. You could also become self-employed, working as a consultant and advising clients on a variety of environmental issues. You might also consider lecturing in environmental science.

Advantages/disadvantages

Your work will have a positive impact on the environment.

There could be opportunities to work abroad in unusual environments, such as rainforests and deserts.

You might face animosity if you refuse to approve a development.

Qualifications and courses

Most employers expect candidates to have completed an environmental science degree. However, you do not have to take environmental science as your first degree; you can continue on to postgraduate study in environmental science. Examples of relevant environmental science degrees include sustainable development or environmental management.

Most universities require applicants to have achieved 2 relevant A levels and 5 GCSEs grades A*–C (or equivalent qualifications). Relevant subjects at A level include biology, chemistry, physics, geography, English, maths and geology. Some admissions tutors will also favour foreign languages.

You do not necessarily have to have completed a degree, it is possible to start as a technician and work your way up to environmental scientist. In order to do this you will have to have achieved at least 4 GCSEs grades A*–C which should include 2 sciences, English and maths or technology. Equivalent qualifications, for example a BTEC First Diploma in science, might be considered. Many technicians also complete A levels and so you might also want to consider this.

Relevant work experience would also be beneficial.

Money guide

These figures are approximate and may vary depending on sector, employer and location.

Starting salaries range from about £18,000 to £25,000 per year. With more experience and training you could earn up to £27,000 a year. As a senior environmental scientist, with managerial duties, it would be possible to earn over £55,000 per year.

Related opportunities

- Botanist p509
- Ecologist p515
- Environmental Health Practitioner/Officer p35
- Hydrologist p523
- Oceanographer p531

Further information

Institution of Environmental Sciences
2nd Floor, 34 Grosvenor Gardens, London SW1W 0DH
020 7730 5516; www.ies-uk.org.uk

The Environment Agency, National Recruitment Service
National Customer Contact Centre, PO Box 544,
Rotherham S60 1BY
0870 850 6506; www.environment-agency.gov.uk

StudentForce for Sustainability
Oakham Railway Station, Station Approach,
Oakham LE15 6QT
01572 723419; www.studentforce.org.uk

CRCI: TD

Science, Mathematics and Statistics

FOOD SCIENTIST/ TECHNOLOGIST

What the work involves

- Food scientists undertake research, production and quality assurance work in all areas of the food industry.

- You could apply your knowledge of food, chemistry, biology and nutrition to analyse food products, set up manufacturing processes and develop food labelling.

- Your research may involve ensuring that food is safe to eat by testing it under different conditions. Alternatively, you might decrease the risk of contamination by analysing the food safety systems.

- You will be using both laboratory and computer equipment to carry out your role.

The type of person suited to this work

You will need to have a high level of ability in biology and chemistry and an interest in food and its production. You must also possess a certain level of ability in maths and physics. You will require strong communication and teamwork skills. You should be meticulous, with a keen eye for detail. You will need to be organised, with the ability to prioritise. Good problem-solving skills are key and you will need to be extremely logical. You should be able to follow strict health and safety and hygiene rules.

Working conditions

You could be working in research units, laboratories or in a factory within the quality department. The working environment will always be clean to prevent the food being contaminated and you will be required to wear protective clothing.

You will probably work somewhere between 35 and 40 hours per week and if your employer operates a shift system you might need to work weekends. This role may include travel to warehouses, factories and distribution centres.

Future prospects

You might be offered the opportunity of promotion to team leader, technical director or project co-ordinator if you work within a larger organisation. If you work for a smaller employer you might need to change companies in order to progress.

Your skills would be transferable to several related areas such as production management, marketing and buying raw materials. You could also specialise.

Working abroad may also be a possibility, especially within larger organisations.

Advantages/disadvantages

You will be able to combine your love of food with your scientific background.

You may find some aspects of the job tedious, for example if you need to repeat the same tests over a period of time.

This career has the possibility of leading to a number of areas.

Qualifications and courses

ENTRY LEVEL 5

Entrants to this profession usually have a degree, HNC/D or Foundation degree. For degree entry you will need 3 A levels, including chemistry and biology and 5 GCSEs (A*–C). HNC/HND programmes usually require 1 A level and 3 GCSEs (A*–C). The Diploma in Manufacturing and Product Design may be helpful. Some people study for a postgraduate qualification in food science before entering work.

You can enter with lower qualifications as a laboratory or quality control technician. Typical entry requirements are 4 GCSEs/S grades A*–C/1–3, including English, mathematics, chemistry and biology, or an Applied A level in science, or a BTEC National qualification in food science and manufacturing technology. Technicians can work towards NVQs/SVQs at Levels 1–4 in Food and Drink Manufacturing Operations, and at Levels 2–4 in Laboratory and Associated Technical Activities. They can also study part time for an HNC to gain promotion to food scientist. Once qualified, you can apply for registration with the Institute of Food Science and Technology (IFST).

Apprenticeships may be available.

Money guide

These figures are approximate and will vary depending on sector, location and employer.

Starting salaries range from about £20,000 to £25,000 per year. This could then increase to around £30,000–£45,000 a year, depending on experience and/or training.

At senior or management levels this could increase to over £50,000 a year.

Related opportunities

- Chef p137
- Dietician p303
- Environmental Health Practitioner/Officer p35
- Microbiologist/Bacteriologist p530

Further information

Institute of Food Science & Technology
5 Cambridge Court, 210 Shepherd's Bush Road,
London W6 7NJ
020 7603 6316; www.ifst.org or www.foodtechcareers.org

Food and Drink Federation
6 Catherine Street, London WC2B 5JJ
020 7836 2460; www.fdf.org.uk

Improve Limited
Ground Floor, Providence House, 2 Innovation Close,
Heslington, York YO10 5ZF
0845 644 0448; www.improveltd.co.uk

FORENSIC SCIENTIST

What the work involves

■ You will use your skills to provide important scientific information and help resolve legal and criminal cases.

■ By analysing samples and assessing accident and crime scenes, you will support the work of police and lawyers.

■ Your work will involve identifying anything that may be used as evidence from a crime scene, including organs, blood, bodily fluids, illegal drugs, fire arms and explosives, DNA and even paint or glass pieces. You will carry out the necessary tests to extract the information the police require.

■ You will use techniques including photography, DNA profiling, chromatography and metallurgy.

The type of person suited to this work

You need strong scientific skills and the desire to help solve crime. You will need to be confident, as you might have to make court appearances. You should be able to handle distressing situations well. You will need to pay attention to detail whilst in the field, in the laboratory and when producing reports. You will have to be able to explain scientific findings to people without a scientific background. You should be able to use statistics to interpret your findings. You must be a great communicator.

Working conditions

You will spend the majority of your time in the laboratory; however you will also need to visit crime scenes. You might have to deal with unpleasant or upsetting sights. You may also be outdoors in all weathers. You could be standing or crouching for long periods of time to examine evidence. You might have to spend time away from home. The average forensic scientist works about 35 to 37 hours per week. You may also have to spend time on-call.

Future prospects

As an assistant forensic scientist with an appropriate degree, you can progress to become a forensic scientist.

As a forensic scientist in the FSS (Forensic Science Service) you could progress to reporting officer level, delivering reports in court.

Promotion to management is generally based on appraisal reports and levels of experience. You could become self-employed by working as a forensic consultant. You might also have the opportunity to work abroad.

Advantages/disadvantages

You will be using your scientific knowledge to help the police to catch criminals, which would be extremely rewarding.

This job comes with a lot of responsibility as your evidence may be the reason someone gets convicted.

This is a varied job; no two cases will be the same.

Qualifications and courses

You will need a good Honours degree in biology, chemistry, forensic science or a related subject. Some employers may accept an equivalent professional qualification. You will usually require at least 2 A levels in relevant subjects and 5 GCSEs (A*–C) including maths and English, for degree entry. It might be helpful to take the Diploma in Science.

A lot of applicants also have an MSc in Forensic Science or a related subject. Laboratory experience is an advantage.

To enter as an assistant or technician forensic scientist in England and Wales 4 GCSEs (A*–C), including a science or maths subject along with at least 1 science A level or equivalent are required. In Scotland, a Higher National qualification in chemistry, biology or a related subject is normally required. Assistant forensic scientists often have a degree or postgraduate qualification and you will not be able to progress to a role as a forensic scientist without these.

You will be trained on the job. Once qualified, you can apply for registration with the Council for the Registration of Forensic Practitioners.

Money guide

Salary levels vary according to employer and location.

Starting salaries for trainee or assistant forensic scientists are around £14,000–£18,000 per year. After 2 or 3 years this can increase to between £25,000 and £30,000 a year. As a head of department you could earn up to £50,000 a year.

Salaries in London will normally be higher.

Related opportunities

■ Biomedical Scientist/Medical Laboratory Assistant p507
■ Chemist p510
■ Clinical Scientist p512
■ Laboratory Technician p524
■ Microbiologist/Bacteriologist p530

Further information

Forensic Science Society
18a Mount Parade, Harrogate HG1 1BX
01423 506 068; www.forensic-science-society.org.uk

The Forensic Science Service
Trident Court, 2920 Solihull Parkway,
Birmingham Business Park, Birmingham B37 7YN
www.forensic.gov.uk

Skills for Justice
Centre Court, Atlas Way, Sheffield S4 7QQ
0114 261 1499; www.skillsforjustice.com

Science, Mathematics and Statistics

CRCI: TD

GEOGRAPHER

What the work involves

- You will be undertaking research, using ICT, fieldwork and paper-based resources, to broaden public and academic knowledge of your specific field of geography.

- You can choose to specialise in either physical geography – the study of the earth, rivers, climate, land formation and oceans – or human geography – the study of humans in their environment.

- There are also several other branches of geography that come from these two; environmental, health, historical, geomatics, and pedology to name a few.

- You could use your skills and the research you have collected in a range of industrial fields, from government bodies, to private consulting firms. As a researcher for a university you will also lecture and contribute as a writer to geographical journals or articles while studying for a PhD or similar.

The type of person suited to this work

You need to have a good knowledge of your field of geography and have a genuine interest and love for what you study.

You will need excellent research and communication skills, to be able to thoroughly understand and lecture on your chosen area of study.

Being flexible, approachable and hardworking will assist your career progression and becoming an expert in your field of geography.

Fieldwork will involve travel and long hours and you must be comfortable working in unusual conditions, such as outside in extreme temperatures.

Working conditions

You could be based in a research centre, university, office or based on location during fieldwork.

You might need to work unsocial hours during fieldwork, such as weekends. Lecturing and office-based research would tend to have more standard working hours, Monday to Friday.

You will have access to a computer, and a library to assist with research. You might need to use special equipment while in the field.

Future prospects

It is important to get some work experience in a research position before applying for a fully paid job, as the competition for research positions can be fierce.

You can progress from research assistant to head researcher. If you are following an academic route you can start off as an assistant lecturer and progress to professor after completing a PhD and contributing significantly to your field of geography.

Qualifications and courses

An Honours degree or above in geography or a related field is required. Geography degrees cover varied aspects of human, economic and physical geography, but it is also possible to gain a first degree in one particular aspect, such as oceanography or global change.

Entry requirements for geography degrees vary, but often include an A level/H grade in geography. For science-based geography courses (BSc), science A levels/H grades might be required.

On completing you first degree it is the norm for researchers in academia to continue their studies to Master's and PhD level. You would usually need a good 2.1 in your first degree to progress to a Master's, and a good Master's to progress and get funding for a PhD.

The Royal Geographical Society offers opportunities for A level students to carry out sponsored fieldwork, funding for gap years and several short courses.

Advantages/disadvantages

You can work overseas, often for long periods of time, when doing field-based research.

You will need to keep up to date with any changes or developments in your geographical field of expertise. This could get stressful.

Money guide

Starting salary for a research assistant could be between £17,000 and £26,000, depending on your level of experience and if you work for an academic institution or business organisation.

After gaining experience, and acknowledgement in your chosen field of expertise your salary could increase to £30,000–£45,000. Professors contributing significantly to their area of geography can earn £50,000+.

Related opportunities

- Cartographer p82
- Planning and Development Surveyor p111
- Secondary School Teacher p205
- Town Planner/Planning Technician p128

Further information

Geographical Association
160 Solly Street, Sheffield S1 4BF
0114 296 0088; www.geography.org.uk

Royal Geographical Society (with the Institute of British Geographers)
1 Kensington Gore, London SW7 2AR
020 7591 3000; www.rgs.org

GEOLOGIST/GEOLOGICAL TECHNICIAN

What the work involves

Geologist

■ Geologists analyse and study the planet earth, including its materials, structure and history.

■ Your work may involve organising practical field and laboratory research to gain specific information. You may use your skills to support development work, for example mineral mining and the oil industry.

Geological technician

■ You will work closely with geologists, undertaking practical research work in the field and laboratory. You will collect and examine samples and produce test results.

■ You will work with other sources, for example surveys, to provide detailed information on specific geological features and aspects.

The type of person suited to this work

You should have the ability to pay close attention to detail. You will need to be meticulous, practical and logical in your approach to work. You will have to work with technical equipment and so you should have high levels of dexterity. You must be able to uphold health and safety regulations. Geologists need to be able to make important decisions and communicate well, both in person and on paper. A geological technician needs good graphical skills including computer-aided-design if they are to help produce maps.

Working conditions

The hours and working conditions of a geologist will vary considerably depending on the sector they are working in.

Geological technicians normally work 9am–5pm, Monday–Friday, with some exceptions when they have approaching deadlines.

Future prospects

Geologists could progress to a managerial role, although this may involve changing employers. There is also the possibility of becoming self employed if you work as a consultant. You could alternatively work as a university lecturer.

There are more promotion opportunities for geological technicians within larger organisations. If you choose to work for a smaller company you might need to change employers to progress. Training to become a geologist is possible.

Advantages/disadvantages

You may have difficulty gaining enough money to fund your research or projects.

Qualifications and courses

Geologist

You generally need a degree in a geosciences subject. A levels in science subjects and/or maths are usually required plus 5 GCSEs (A*–C), including English, maths and science. The British Geological Survey recruits assistant scientific officers with A levels and scientific officers with a relevant degree.

Geological technician

The usual minimum entry requirements for a junior technician are 4 GCSEs (A*–C) including science and maths. Some employers could accept a BTEC National Diploma in Science. It is possible to work towards further qualifications, such as a degree or HND. NVQs/SVQs are available at Levels 2–4.

There are job opportunities within multinational corporations which would allow you access to the latest technology.

Employers generally prefer applicants who have completed postgraduate study.

There are opportunities for international travel.

Money guide

Geologist

Starting out as a graduate you can expect to get £25,000 per year and this will increase with postgraduate qualifications. At senior levels this can increase to £40,000–£50,000.

Geological technician

Starting salaries begin at around £18,500–£24,000 per year. With experience you can expect £25,000–£35,000 a year. At senior levels this can increase to £40,000+.

Related opportunities

■ Ecologist p515
■ Geophysicist p522
■ Oceanographer p531

Further information

British Geological Survey
Kingsley Dunham Centre, Keyworth, Nottingham NG12 5GG
0115 936 3143; www.bgs.ac.uk

Cogent Sector Skills Council Limited
Unit 5, Mandarin Court, Centre Park, Warrington WA1 1GG
01925 515200; www.cogent-ssc.com

Science, Mathematics and Statistics

CRCI: TB

GEOPHYSICIST

What the work involves

- You will apply physics-based investigation techniques to explore and analyse the nature of the rocks, structures and minerals below the earth's surface. You would spend a lot of time undertaking practical work and writing up your results.

- Most geophysicists are involved with helping companies explore for oil and gas. You would help plan and organise exploration work and interpret detailed geological information.

- Geophysicists work in research in universities and research institutes and for companies involved in oil and mineral exploration.

- You will work as part of a team of geologists, engineers and/or engineering geologists.

The type of person suited to this work

You should have an interest in rock structures and a desire to travel. Your scientific and technical skills will be of a high quality. You should pay excellent attention to detail and have a methodical and meticulous approach to solving problems. You will need to have strong numeracy skills and the ability to use software packages which may be extremely complex. You should be able to communicate well, both in person and on paper.

Working conditions

You will spend some time in an office or laboratory and the rest in the field. If you are involved in data collection you will travel the world, operating from base camps.

You might also work offshore (at sea) on oil or gas platforms or ships. This work will involve being away from home for long periods of time in a confined space, living and working with the same people.

Future prospects

Construction, fuel and mineral exploration and development organisations within the public and private sectors need the skills of geophysics professionals. Developing a career in industry may mean having to move around to gain the relevant professional experience. For some jobs, this could involve spending time working overseas.

You also have the option of becoming self-employed or consultancy work.

Advantages/disadvantages

You can live and work abroad while you undertake research work.

The work can be physically demanding and may involve visiting potentially hazardous sites.

You may have the opportunity to study and observe the natural world in a variety of locations.

Qualifications and courses

ENTRY LEVEL 5

A degree in geoscience, geology, geotechnology or a related field is required. You will need 3 A levels including maths and physics and 5 GCSEs (A*–C). A levels in subjects such as biology, chemistry, maths, physics, geography or geology would be useful.

A postgraduate qualification is usually also required. Relevant postgraduate courses include the MSc in petroleum, geoscience and exploration geophysics. It is also possible to achieve a PhD in particular areas of geophysics. Pre-entry experience is desirable.

For entry at technician level, A level/H grade in physics is normally required. It may be possible to enter with an Intermediate GNVQ, SQA National at Intermediate 2, or BTEC National Diploma or Certificate in Applied Science, or to undertake an Apprenticeship in Engineering. The Diploma in Engineering could be useful

For entry to an Apprenticeship you will need 4 GCSEs (A*–C).

Some employment in this area is offered on a short-term contract basis only, which can lead to job insecurity.

Money guide

These figures are only approximate as salary levels vary widely depending on the company and sector.

Starting salaries are around £22,000 per year. With a few years of experience you could expect to be earning between £25,000 and £45,000 a year.

Once you reach a more senior level you could earn over £50,000 per year.

Related opportunities

- Environmental Scientist p517
- Geologist/Geological Technician p521
- Hydrologist p523
- Oceanographer p531
- Oil/Gas Drilling Engineer p238

Further information

British Geological Survey
Kingsley Dunham Centre, Keyworth, Nottingham G12 5GG
0115 936 3100; www.bgs.ac.uk

The Geological Society
Burlington House, Piccadilly, London W1J 0BG
020 7434 9944; www.geolsoc.org.uk

British Geophysical Association
www.ras.org.uk

HYDROLOGIST

What the work involves

- As an invaluable natural resource, water needs to be monitored and managed by hydrologists. You will help ensure that safe drinking water is available when and where it is needed.

- Your work could involve measuring river flows, rainfall, evaporation and ground water. You may assess water use in agriculture and forestry, or be involved with dealing with water-management emergencies, for example in droughts.

- Your research might involve working out potential flood risks, designing water supply systems or developing resources such as reservoirs.

- You will work with civil engineers, freshwater ecologists, chemists and other professionals.

The type of person suited to this work

You will need to have an interest in environmental protection and management and an understanding of how a water supply affects a society. You should have strong geographical, scientific, mathematical and technical capabilities.

The job calls for the ability to problem-solve and think creatively to resolve specific issues. You'll also need to be confident in using and creating maps and other ways of portraying and creating a record of a landscape.

The job demands excellent observational skills and attention to detail. You will need the ability to work with detailed factual information. You should be comfortable in communicating your work.

Working conditions

Most hydrologists work mainly within an office environment, with conventional office hours. If there is an emergency or a deadline approaching you might need to work some evenings and weekends.

You might also be required to complete time in the field. You will be outdoors, working in a variety of weather conditions and using heavy equipment, so you might need to have a certain level of physical stamina.

This job might involve travel within and outside of the UK.

Future prospects

The opportunities available for promotion will vary depending on the organisation and employer. Progression also depends a great deal on experience, skills, responsibility and merit. You may be able to increase your chances of promotion by moving to another team or geographical location in order to increase experience. To progress you should be able to manage people, projects and budgets.

Self-employment is possible if you become a consultant.

There are many opportunities to work overseas for international organisations.

Qualifications and courses

The minimum requirement for entry to the profession is usually an Honours degree in geography, environmental science, civil engineering or mathematics. For entry to a degree, students usually require a minimum of 2 A levels/3 H grades and 5 GCSEs (A*–C or equivalent). The Diploma in Environmental and Land-based Studies might be useful.

A postgraduate qualification is usually also required, normally in a subject such as engineering hydrology or water resources. You will need a relevant first degree for entry.

The Chartered Institution of Water and Environmental Management (CIWEM) accredits a number of undergraduate and postgraduate courses in the field.

Pre-entry work experience is recommended, as this is a competitive industry. You should consider completing placements during your holidays or as part of a sandwich degree.

Advantages/disadvantages

You can live and work abroad while you undertake research work.

You may have to work outdoors in the wind and rain.

Some employment in this area is offered on a short-term contract basis only, which can lead to job insecurity.

If you work within consultancy, you will have a wide variety of work available to you.

Money guide

These figures are only approximate as salary levels vary widely according to sector, location and employer.

Starting salaries range from around £17,000 to £25,000 per year. Once you have gained 5 years' experience this can rise to between £28,000 and £35,000 a year.

If you reach senior level you could earn up to £45,000 a year.

Related opportunities

- Civil Engineering Technician p85
- Geophysicist p522
- Meteorologist p529
- Oceanographer p531

Further information

British Hydrological Society
1 Great George Street, London SW1P 3AA
020 222 7722; www.hydrology.org.uk

The Chartered Institution of Water and Environmental Management
15 John Street, London WC1N 2EB
020 7831 3110; www.ciwem.org.uk

CRCI: TB

Science, Mathematics and Statistics

LABORATORY TECHNICIAN

What the work involves

- You will analyse samples of different types of substances and materials using specialist equipment.

- You could specialise in a particular area, such as microbiology or clinical chemistry.

- Your work may involve recording detailed information and developing and maintaining microbiological or other cultures.

- Laboratory technicians apply their scientific analysis and measurement skills in organisations such as the military services, the NHS, industry and scientific research institutions.

The type of person suited to this work

You will provide important factual information, so must work to a high standard of accuracy. Your patient attitude will help you undertake sometimes repetitive but important laboratory activities.

Good manual handling skills will be needed to organise laboratory equipment. You will also need good communication skills and normal colour vision. Your ICT skills will help you record and analyse a range of information. Because your work may involve potentially dangerous situations like handling bacteria and working with radiation you must work to a good standard of health and safety at all times.

Working conditions

You will most likely have standard working hours, although some employers do work on a shift or rota basis which includes early mornings, evenings and weekends. Your working day will be spent in a clean and sterile laboratory.

You will work with specialist computer software to complete your research and record activities. You could also have to carry out fieldwork at various sites outside the laboratory.

Future prospects

You will play an important role in protecting public health and help make safe, high-quality products that many of us use every day.

Scientific laboratory technicians are employed within industry, health service organisations, public research and other areas.

With further experience, you could progress to supervising a team of technicians or managing a laboratory.

Medical laboratory technicians can advance into a role as an education laboratory technician, phlebotomist, cardiographer or physiologist.

Advantages/disadvantages

Laboratory tasks can be repetitive and time-consuming and require patience.

Qualifications and courses

Entrants need at least 4 GCSEs/S grades (A*–C/1–3), including English, mathematics and a science. Equivalent qualifications such as a BTEC First Certificate or Diploma in Science may be accepted.

Qualifications at a higher level such as A levels, a BTEC National qualification, an HNC/D or a degree in a science subject might be required.

Laboratory technicians are trained on the job, and may be able to study towards NVQs at Levels 1–4 in Laboratory and Associated Technical Activities or Level 2 in Clinical Laboratory Support.

You could take the Institute of Science & Technology's Certificate in Laboratory Technical Skills at Levels 1–3 or their Higher Diploma in Analytical, Chemical or Microbiological Laboratory Techniques.

Because of the transferable nature of lab skills, you could move from one organisation to another quite easily.

In some organisations you would work on a shift basis.

Money guide

Starting salaries are around £11,000–£14,000 per year.

With experience and qualifications, you could earn up to £20,000.

As a very experienced laboratory technician, team leader or laboratory manager, it is possible to earn £30,000–£40,000.

Related opportunities

- Biochemist p506
- Biomedical Scientist p507
- Forensic Scientist p519
- Pharmacy Technician p328

Further information

Biochemical Society Membership Office
Portland Customer Services, Commerce Way, Whitehall Industrial Estate, Colchester CO2 8HP
01206 796351; www.biochemistry.org

Science Council
32–36 Loman Street, London SE1 0EH
020 7922 7888; www.sciencecouncil.org

Semta
14 Upton Road, Watford WD18 0JT
0845 643 9001; www.semta.org.uk

City&
Guilds

MARINE BIOLOGIST

What the work involves

- You will undertake practical research and analysis into animal and plant life in the world's seas and oceans. As well as academic research, you could apply your skills in fisheries, research or fish-farming development.

- You may undertake research trips above or below the sea's surface and keep detailed research records.

- By increasing understanding of the sea you will be able to make predictions about the effects man will have on the marine ecosystem and how it will cope with these changes.

- You may provide specialist advice to organisations such as governments or environmental pressure groups.

The type of person suited to this work

You should have a strong interest in science and a particular interest in marine life. You will require both a scientific understanding and practical ability. You will need to be meticulous and extremely patient. You should have good numerical and computer based skills. You must be observant and have a questioning mind. You will need to be able to analyse and interpret data effectively. You should have a certain level of physical stamina. You will need a desire to travel and not mind being at sea. You should be highly organised and able to work autonomously and as part of a team.

Working conditions

You will spend time in an office environment, laboratory and researching in the field. Whilst in the laboratory or office you will usually work normal office hours, however some projects and deadlines may require overtime.

When working on projects at sea you will probably be working longer hours. Operating at sea might mean you are away for long periods of time, in cramped and possibly uncomfortable conditions. You will be living and working with the same people.

Future prospects

There can be a lot of competition for jobs. Gaining a good level of practical experience in addition to the relevant training shows commitment and provides useful skills.

Once you have gathered enough field experience you could go freelance or alternatively, set up your own consultancy.

You could lecture students, which you could combine with completing your own research.

Working abroad is a distinct possibility.

Advantages/disadvantages

A lot of your research in the field will depend on the tides and weather conditions, which could slow down your progress.

You will use your skills and knowledge to increase public understanding of the natural environment.

Finding funding for your projects may prove problematic.

Qualifications and courses

ENTRY LEVEL 6

Candidates can either take an Honours degree in marine biology, marine science, or oceanography, or a degree in chemistry or physics, followed by a specialised postgraduate qualification. 2 or 3 A levels/H grades in relevant science subjects such as biology are required for entry to degree courses along with 5 GCSEs (A*–C). A levels in maths, technological subjects or languages would also be beneficial. It might be helpful to take the Diploma in Science.

A postgraduate qualification is an advantage and you will probably require a 1st or a 2:1 in your first degree in order to be accepted onto a Master's or PhD programme.

Entrants for research posts need a relevant degree and usually a postgraduate qualification.

If you want to apply for a technological support role you should have achieved A levels in biology, maths or geography and another science subject.

Money guide

Starting salaries tend to be at the higher end of the scale for people with a higher or postgraduate degree.

Once you are a qualified marine biologist you can expect a starting salary of somewhere between £17,000 and £20,000 per year.

With experience, salaries can increase to around £25,000 a year.

The highest earning marine biologists, who are at the top of their field can earn up to £60,000 a year.

Related opportunities

- Ecologist p515
- Environmental Scientist p517
- Oceanographer p531
- Zoologist p538

Further information

Marine Biological Association
The Laboratory, Citadel Hill, Plymouth PL1 2PB
01752 633207; www.mba.ac.uk

National Oceanography Centre
University of Southampton Waterfront Campus, European Way, Southampton SO14 3ZH
02380 596666; www.noc.soton.ac.uk

The Centre for Environment, Fisheries and Aquaculture Science
CEFAS Lowestoft Laboratory, Pakefield Road, Lowestoft NR33 OHT
01502 595106; www.cefas.co.uk

Science, Mathematics and Statistics

CRCI: TD

MATERIALS SCIENTIST

What the work involves

- Materials scientists measure, define and process materials. They help decide the types of materials to use in engineering, construction and product processing work.

- You will use your knowledge of the properties of metals and alloys, glass, ceramics and other materials in many areas of industrial research, development and production.

- You will research how and why materials react to certain conditions and how they can be used in our everyday lives.

- You will use technology and computer equipment to carry out tests on different materials, keep records of your findings and draw conclusions from the results.

The type of person suited to this work

You will need to have creative flair and you should have an inquisitive and logical mind. You will need to be meticulous. You will be able to write coherent reports and be a good public speaker, as you might need to give presentations. You will need solid computer skills. You should work well in a team environment. You should have dexterity as you will be working with a selection of test equipment. You will need good eyesight (including colour vision for some projects).

Working conditions

Material scientists in industry work normal office hours or shifts, however the more senior your role is, the longer you will have to work.

You could be working in a sterile laboratory or an industrial environment. The most common working environments for material scientists are laboratories and offices. There is a possibility you will have to complete work in the field. You may have to wear protective clothing.

Future prospects

You will have the option to change industries and purchase raw materials, work in sales, management or marketing. You could progress to become a project manager or a technical director, meaning you would be leading people in developing new products.

Alternatively, you could move into a career in teaching.

Opportunities for self-employment are limited but you could work in NDT (non-destructive testing) or failure analysis. There may be the possibility to work abroad.

Advantages/disadvantages

You will have the opportunity to apply your skills and knowledge to develop new products and provide new scientific information.

Scientists are constantly in demand in most areas of industry.

This can be a highly lucrative career.

Qualifications and courses

The usual entry qualification is a degree. Degrees are available in metallurgy and in materials science, materials technology and materials engineering. It is also possible to enter with a degree in a general science subject. A Foundation year is available at some institutions for candidates without the required scientific background.

Most degree courses expect applicants to have achieved at least 2 A levels, including maths and science, and 5 GCSEs (A*–C), including maths and English. The Diplomas in Engineering, Construction and the Built Environment as well as in Manufacturing and Product Design are also available. You could take NVQs or an Apprenticeship in Engineering and Manufacturing Technologies.

To become a chartered materials engineer, you need to have studied a 4 year MEng degree or a 3 year BEng or BSc followed by a period of professional development.

Postgraduate courses are available, and may be studied prior to entry, or through company training schemes. In order to be accepted you must have successfully completed a first degree.

Technicians need at least 4 GCSEs grade A*–C which should include two sciences (or double science), English and maths or equivalent.

Money guide

On entering this career you can expect to earn around £18,000 per year. Entry salaries tend to be higher with a postgraduate qualification. Once you have gained experience this figure can increase to £35,000 a year. Once you have reached a senior role you could earn in excess of £50,000 per year.

Related opportunities

- Biochemist p506
- Chemist p510
- Laboratory Technician p524

Further information

Institute of Materials, Minerals and Mining
1 Carlton House Terrace, London SW1Y 5DB
020 7451 7300; Main website: www.iom3.org;
Careers website: www.materials-careers.org.uk

UK Centre for Materials Education
Second Floor, Brodie Tower, University of Liverpool, Liverpool L69 3GQ
0151 794 5364; www.materials.ac.uk

SEMTA
14 Upton Road, Watford WD18 0JT
0845 643 9001; www.semta.org.uk

MATHEMATICIAN/RESEARCH SCIENTIST (MATHS)

What the work involves

- Research is conducted using mathematical theory in order to solve problems in areas such as science, engineering, finance, government and ICT. You could work at all levels of industry, research and education and help to inform the work of different organisations.

- You could study and teach pure mathematics in an academic environment or work in job roles requiring mathematical skills and knowledge, for example actuary, operational researcher or statistician.

- Your work may involve undertaking research and analysis, setting up research programmes and assessing research findings.

- In a business, you will work on a specific project such as predicting future trends in population growth or financial markets.

The type of person suited to this work

You must have a strong interest in working with numerical information to solve complex problems. You need to be logical and methodical, as well as flexible and innovative to analyse a range of problems.

Your work could help shape the activities of your company so you must have good attention to detail and be able to record your work accurately. Strong communication skills will help you explain mathematical ideas to people without a maths background. As maths-related research can take time to set up, a patient attitude can be helpful.

Working conditions

For many roles, you would work in an office and use computers to analyse information. Long hours are common in this role.

If you work in education, you will spend time teaching in classrooms and in lecture rooms. You could also spend time undertaking research.

Mathematicians who work in business, such as accountants, will spend time in meetings with their clients.

Future prospects

There is a high demand for professional mathematicians in areas such as business, finance or industry, and in companies that develop new products such as new computer software and pharmaceuticals. After gaining experience, you could progress into a managerial role. In an academic environment, progression depends on your research accomplishments.

Advantages/disadvantages

Mathematical skills apply to many different sectors, so you could move across a range of areas.

A shortage of qualified mathematicians means that there are a variety of opportunities.

A second degree could be needed to follow your chosen career.

Qualifications and courses

An Honours degree in maths is normally required to work as a professional mathematician in industry, business/finance, education or research. Degrees are available in general maths or in specific areas, for example, financial maths or business maths.

Entry onto maths degree courses usually requires at least 2 A levels/H grades including maths, and 5 GCSEs/S grades (A*–C/1–3), including English and maths. Science and or computing-related subjects are also viewed favourably. The Diploma in Engineering could also be useful.

Maths graduates are recruited directly by some companies. Most mathematicians have postgraduate qualifications, which require a first degree in mathematics, physics or another subject with a high mathematical content.

To teach maths in primary and secondary schools, maths graduates need to study for a PGCE.

It is possible to become a Chartered Mathematician with the Institute of Mathematics and its Applications after gaining an Honours degree in maths or with more than two-thirds maths content, and 3 years in employment.

Tight deadlines and the uncertainty in being able to find a solution to problems can make this line of work stressful.

Money guide

Salary levels vary widely according to employer and sector, but maths graduates earn the highest salaries of all graduates.

Starting salaries range from £20,000 to £25,000 per year.

With several years' experience you could earn £29,000–£38,000.

At senior level, possibly as a director, earnings can reach £50,000–£70,000.

Related opportunities

- Accountant p16
- Actuary p20
- Stockbroker p66
- Systems Analyst p163

Further information

Institute of Mathematics and its Applications
Catherine Richards House, 16 Nelson Street,
Southend-on-Sea SS1 1EF
01702 354020; www.ima.org.uk

Mathematical Association
259 London Road, Leicester LE2 3BE
0116 221 0013; www.m-a.org.uk

Maths Careers
www.mathscareers.org.uk

Science, Mathematics and Statistics

CRCI: TC

METALLURGIST

What the work involves

- Metallurgists apply their materials science and engineering knowledge to support product and process development in areas such as aerospace, rail, construction and oil and gas.

- You may be involved with the metal extraction process, managing projects or researching metals and materials.

- You might help develop practical solutions for production problems.

- Whatever job you do, it is likely that your role will involve aspects of quality control, project management and process/product development.

The type of person suited to this work

Metallurgists need an excellent knowledge of metals and related materials, whatever area they work in. They must also be able to understand the uses for different materials. You will need to have good communication and team-working skills. But you will also have to be confident in making decisions that could affect major industrial processes and understand the commercial impact of your work.

Your flexible approach and attention to detail will help you adapt to the changing demands of different projects. Your ICT and numeracy skills will also be important. Because you could work with potentially dangerous materials you must have a good knowledge of health and safety.

Working conditions

You might have to work in a noisy location if you are employed by a large manufacturing company. In other roles you could be based in a laboratory-style setting.

Hours vary from employer to employer, but they can be long especially if you are working to complete a specific project to a set deadline.

In many roles, you will be part of a team and could also meet with clients on a regular basis.

In some roles you may be required to write detailed reports.

Future prospects

Many industries are quite literally built on metals and related materials so there are all kinds of job opportunities.

You could undertake project management for individual companies. You could choose to work for companies that develop materials for industries such as automotive and aerospace engineering. Or you could directly manage the process of mining and extracting materials.

Advantages/disadvantages

The role can provide the satisfaction of developing new products and materials.

Qualifications and courses

The usual entry qualification for a metallurgist is a degree. Degrees are available in metallurgy and in materials science, materials technology and materials engineering. It is also possible to enter with a degree in a general science subject, such as physics or chemistry.

Entry to a relevant degree course usually requires a minimum of 2 A levels/3 H grades and 5 GCSEs/S grades (A*–C/1–3). BTEC/SQA National qualifications might be offered as alternatives.

For those seeking entry to the profession by first becoming a technician or with HNC/HNDs or Foundation degrees (in a subject such as metallurgy and materials, metals technology, manufacturing engineering or applied science) then at least 1 science A level/H grade will be required.

You can apply for a graduate training programme offered by many employers which can lead to membership of a professional institution such as the Institute of Cast Metals Engineers (ICME) and could increase job prospects.

There are opportunities to work and live abroad.

You might need to work unsocial hours for various projects.

Money guide

Starting salaries range from around £18,500 to reach £28,000 per year.

With experience and at a senior level it is possible to earn £40,000.

With chartered engineer status and considerable experience, as a senior manager you could earn £50,000+.

Related opportunities

- Materials Scientist p526
- Aerospace Engineer p212
- Laboratory Technician p524
- Structural Engineer p124

Further information

Institute of Materials, Minerals and Mining
1 Carlton House Terrace, London SW1Y 5DB
020 7451 7300; www.iom3.org; www.materials-careers.org.uk

Engineering Council UK
246 High Holborn, London WC1V 7EX
020 7206 0500; www.engc.org.uk

Institute of Cast Metals Engineers
National Metalforming Centre, 47 Birmingham Road, West Bromwich B70 6PY
0121 601 6979; www.icme.org.uk

METEOROLOGIST

What the work involves

- Information gained from observing the sky, the atmosphere and natural phenomena gives a picture of everyday weather conditions.

- As well as providing weather forecast information that is used throughout the media and to inform industries such as fishing, meteorologists undertake research into the earth's atmosphere. You could be employed by the Royal Navy, the RAF, the Meteorological Office and other employers.

- You will be using specialist computer programmes and mathematical techniques to gather information, which you will combine in order to form a weather picture.

- Within meteorology you can work as a forecaster or a researcher.

The type of person suited to this work

You should have a strong interest in the environment, science, research and climate change. You will need to excel in maths and physics. The job calls for the ability to problem-solve and think creatively to resolve specific issues. You should be happy to work in various locations, however remote.

The job demands excellent observational skills and attention to detail. You should be able to comprehend and evaluate complex information. You must be able to communicate effectively, both in person and on paper. You will be computer literate, and work well as part of a team.

Working conditions

You will generally conduct your work from an office environment, using specialised computers. When you are working in the field you could be living and working in extremely isolated areas with basic living conditions.

Researchers generally work ordinary office hours. Forecasters and observers however will usually work in shifts. When working in the field you will not usually have set hours.

Future prospects

There are three main areas that a meteorologist can work in; these are forecasting, research and teaching. You may wish to move between them in order to progress.

Once you have gained experience as a forecaster you might be able to move into broadcasting, research or consultancy work.

There are careers available at the Met office, within utility companies, shipping, insurance companies and in the armed forces. There could be the possibility of working abroad.

Advantages/disadvantages

You may have the opportunity to study and observe the natural world in a variety of locations.

You might have to work inconvenient shifts.

Qualifications and courses

ENTRY LEVEL 6

Entrants to this profession need a degree and often a postgraduate qualification. Degrees in meteorology are available, but other suitable subjects are physics, maths, computer science, oceanography and environmental science. Employers may also require A levels/H grades in maths and physics.

Relevant taught postgraduate courses are available. Subject areas include meteorology, climatology and atmospheric science. There are also opportunities to do a research PhD at some institutions.

The Met Office provides initial training for new entrants without a postgraduate qualification. The training consists of an 18-week Initial Forecasting Course, followed by 8 months' practical training at a weather station, and a 3 week Forecasting Consolidation Course. You will generally need a 1st or 2.1 and a good grade in at least A level physics to apply for a post at the Met Office.

You can also enter work at the Met Office in a support role, for which you will generally require at least a HNC/D or 2 A levels at grade C or above in maths and physics.

Relevant work experience would be extremely valuable.

There is a wide variety of work within this industry so you shouldn't get bored.

Employers increasingly require applicants to have a postgraduate qualification in a relevant subject.

Money guide

These figures are only approximate and may vary based on sector, employer and location. Starting salaries begin at around £18,000–£21,000 per year. With experience this rises to somewhere between £25,000 and £35,000 a year. If you reach a more senior level, with managerial responsibilities you could earn up to between £50,000 and £60,000 per year.

Related opportunities

- Geophysicist p522
- Hydrologist p523
- Oceanographer p531
- Physicist p533

Further information

Royal Meteorological Society
104 Oxford Road, Reading RG1 7LL
011 8 956 9500; www.rmets.org

Met Office
Fitzroy Road, Exeter, Devon EX1 3PB
01392 885680; www.metoffice.gov.uk

CRCI: TB | Science, Mathematics and Statistics

MICROBIOLOGIST/ BACTERIOLOGIST

What the work involves

Microbiologist

■ Microbiologists study microorganisms such as bacteria and viruses. They research and analyse different types of microscopic organisms to support work in medicine, agriculture, food and milk production and pollution control.

■ Your specialist skills and knowledge could be used in government defence departments, environmental conservation and medicine.

Bacteriologist

■ Bacteriologists study and analyse microscopic organisms, particularly ones that cause disease.

■ Their research provides important information on protecting against illnesses and caring for people with specific kinds of diseases.

The type of person suited to this work

You will need to be scientifically capable. You will require a high level of dexterity and you will need to be meticulous, practical and logical in your approach to work. You should also be patient as you might find you have to repeat tests.

Working conditions

Both of these professions generally work normal office hours; however these may be extended for fieldwork or to meet approaching deadlines. You will be working in a laboratory, factory or in the field.

Future prospects

Microbiologist

Microbiologists work in a range of fields. There are opportunities within the NHS and government laboratories and research centres. Microbiologists also work for private companies developing food, drink, pharmaceuticals and other products. A smaller number undertake teaching and research in universities.

Bacteriologist

Bacteriology is a specialism that most people go into after gaining experience and professional skills in related areas such as microbiology. There are a small number of opportunities within the NHS, research institutes and industry.

Advantages/disadvantages

There are opportunities to visit different types of outside locations on research trips.

Experiments can take a long time to complete and some aspects might become tedious.

Employers such as the National Health Service can offer the

Qualifications and courses

Microbiologist

Most entrants have a degree, and sometimes a postgraduate qualification, in microbiology or a related science subject. Many institutions also offer 1-year Foundation courses.

It is possible to work as a technician or medical laboratory technician. You will need 4 GCSEs (A*–C) including 2 sciences (or double science), maths and English. NVQs/SVQs are available in Laboratory and Associated Technical Activities at Levels 2–4. You could also take an apprenticeship or the Diploma in Science.

Bacteriologist

To work as a clinical bacteriologist, a 1st or 2.1 degree in a relevant subject is required and an MSc or PhD is an advantage. For entry to an academic research post, a postgraduate qualification is required. Applicants without a PhD may start as a research assistant and work towards a PhD.

You could alternatively enter as a laboratory assistant; for this you will need a minimum of 4 GCSEs including 2 sciences, maths and English.

chance to gain experience in different departments and provide well-structured career paths.

You will be handling potentially dangerous substances.

Money guide

If you begin your career as a laboratory assistant you can expect to earn between £13,000 and £19,000 a year. Newly qualified microbiologists can earn between £20,000 and £35,000 per year. Newly qualified bacteriologists can expect between £20,000 and £38,000 a year. Top salaries for microbiologists can reach £60,000 and for bacteriologists this is a bit higher at about £65,000 a year.

Related opportunities

■ Biochemist p506
■ Biomedical Scientist p507
■ Immunologist p313

Further information

NHS Careers
PO Box 2311, Bristol BS2 2ZX
0345 606 0655; www.nhscareers.nhs.uk and
www.nhsclinicalscientists.info

Society for General Microbiology
Marlborough House, Basingstoke Road, Spencers Wood,
Reading RG7 1AG
0118 988 1800; Main website: www.socgenmicrobiol.org.uk;
Careers website: www.biocareers.org.uk

OCEANOGRAPHER

What the work involves

- Oceanographers investigate how ocean organisms and structures work together.

- Your work could involve undertaking fieldwork above and below the sea's surface. You may also interpret the information you find and write research reports.

- You could specialise as a marine geologist (studying the ocean floor), marine chemist (studying the chemical composition of water and/or sediment), marine physicist (measuring the properties of currents etc) or a marine biologist (studying the plants and animals in the sea).

- The information you produce could be used by government and/or industry.

The type of person suited to this work

You will require a passion for the environment and ocean life, along with an interest in maths, science and engineering. You will need to be prepared to travel and spend time working at sea. As you may be working in the field you will need to be physically fit. You should have strong verbal and written communication skills. You will be carrying out detailed research and so will need to be meticulous, logical and practical. You will also need to be able to present your findings in front of an audience and so should have a certain level of confidence. Good team work is essential.

Working conditions

Much of your time will be spent working in a laboratory or an office, with typical office hours from Monday to Friday. Fieldwork may be carried out at sea or along the coastline. When working at sea you might be required to spend six weeks or more away from home. You will be living and working with the same people.

Future prospects

Most oceanographic work is structured around, fixed, short-term contracts and so progression can prove tricky. You might find that you have to move between employers in order to achieve a promotion. Progression is based on merit and taking on more responsibilities, such as leading a team. It is possible to become self-employed and work as a consultant. Another option might be university lecturing, where progression opportunities are easier to come by.

Advantages/disadvantages

You will be able to combine your love of the environment with your scientific ability.

Most employers expect candidates to have a postgraduate qualification.

You will have the opportunity to travel.

Money guide

These figures are only approximate as salaries will vary depending on location, sector and employer.

Qualifications and courses

ENTRY LEVEL 7

Entrants usually need a first degree. Degrees are available in oceanography and related areas, such as marine biology. Other relevant subjects include biology, chemistry, physics, mathematics and geology. A levels/H grades in sciences and maths are required.

For degree entry, candidates usually require 3 relevant A levels such as maths and science subjects and 5 GCSEs (A*–C); relevant subjects include sciences, English and maths along with foreign languages, IT and geography. It might be helpful to take the Diploma in Science.

Most employers expect candidates to hold A level/H grade in maths. It is possible to join the Merchant or Royal Navy without a degree and take additional training to become an oceanographer.

A postgraduate qualification in oceanography is a requirement for most posts. Taught courses are available in oceanography and related/specialist areas. In order to be accepted onto a Master's degree you will usually need a first degree in a science based subject. Some Master's programmes will accept graduates without a scientific background. It is also possible to do research for an MPhil or PhD.

Starting salaries begin at about £18,000–£22,000 per year; with a PhD you could start on £20,000–£22,000 a year.

Once you have gained experience as an oceanographer you could get £30,000 a year.

As a senior oceanographer, with management responsibilities you could earn £60,000 per year.

Related opportunities

- Offshore Diver p237
- Ecologist p515
- Environmental Scientist p517
- Geophysicist p522
- Marine Biologist p525

Further information

Institute of Marine Engineering, Science and Technology
80 Coleman Street, London EC2R 5BJ
020 7382 2600; www.imarest.org

National Oceanography Centre Southampton
University of Southampton Waterfront Campus,
European Way, Southampton SO14 3ZH
0044 23 8059 6666; www.noc.soton.ac.uk

The Centre for Environment, Fisheries and Aquaculture Science
CEFAS Lowestoft Laboratory, Pakefield Road,
Lowestoft NR33 0HT
01502 562244; www.cefas.co.uk

CRCI: TB

Science, Mathematics and Statistics

OPERATIONAL RESEARCHER

What the work involves

- Operational researchers use mathematical, scientific and other analytical methods to help improve the performance of organisations in business, industry and government.

- You will work closely with managers and other staff to develop practical solutions to different management and organisational issues.

- You will develop analytical models or strategies to improve a specific area or aspect of an organisation.

- You might also be involved with putting your ideas into practice within companies.

The type of person suited to this work

Operational research is all about getting practical results from in-depth analysis. So you should enjoy solving problems and applying your analytical and mathematical abilities to develop practical solutions.

You will have a strong interest in helping organisations develop and put your understanding of each company to practical use. You will need excellent communication skills for working closely with managers and other staff. Your flexible approach will help you cope with the varied demands of each project. While you will need strong ICT skills, a creative flair can also benefit you in this job.

Working conditions

You will undertake most of your work in an office setting with meetings with managers, technical specialists and staff likely to be a regular part of your job.

In the course of your work you could visit different sites in an organisation to undertake research into specific problems.

Future prospects

Operational researchers help many different organisations to develop successfully. There are increasing opportunities in manufacturing, finance and other sectors. You could move into managing an OR team or work in areas such as marketing. With more experience, you could develop a career as an OR consultant.

The Civil Service offers a well-structured career path and a range of opportunities in operational research.

Advantages/disadvantages

Strong demand in many sectors means you can develop your career in varied types of companies.

Operations research work is fast moving and you will always be learning something new.

Resolving production, resource or staffing problems for a company can be confrontational and stressful.

Qualifications and courses

The entry requirement for this profession is an Honours degree in a mathematical subject, for example maths, physics, chemistry, engineering or economics. Specialist degrees in operational research are available at some institutions and are also offered in combination with certain other degree subjects, such as maths or statistics.

For entry to a relevant degree course, applicants should have a minimum of 2 A levels/4 H grades, including mathematics. It may be possible to become an operational researcher with a degree in a non-mathematical subject if you have a good A level/H grade in maths.

A Diploma in Business Administration and Finance, Retail Business, Construction and the Built Environment, Engineering or Information Technology could also be helpful.

Some employers will require a postgraduate qualification such as a Master's in Operational Research.

The Fast Stream Development Programme offers opportunities for graduates in the Civil Service. The government's Operational Research Service scheme is open to graduates with a degree or MSc in a numerate discipline.

The Operational Research Society organises open days for undergraduates who might be interested in a career in this area. The society also offers a wide range of training courses and in-house training.

Money guide

Salary levels vary between management consultancies, the Government Operational Research Service and other employers. Starting salaries range from £20,000 to £26,000 per year. With experience and some management responsibility, you could earn £32,000–£50,000. At operational research consultant level, you could earn £100,000+.

Related opportunities

- Mathematician/Research Scientist (Maths) p527
- Statistician p536
- Actuary p20

Further information

Operational Research Society
Seymour House, 12 Edward Street, Birmingham BH1 2RX
0121 233 9300; www.theorsociety.org.uk

Government Operational Research Service
www.operational-research.gov.uk

PHYSICIST

What the work involves

- Physicists apply their understanding of matter and energy and how they work together, in industry, government research, academia and medicine.

- You could apply your specialist skills and knowledge to investigate diverse subjects, including space research, nuclear energy, electronics, defence technology and materials for industrial use.

- You might be involved with research and development work or with designing projects and experiments.

- Your role could involve developing products and systems in areas such as computing, aeronautics, transport and medicine.

The type of person suited to this work

Physicists must combine their scientific knowledge with strong problem-solving skills. You will need the confidence to work with complex numerical information and excellent attention to detail as well as a patient approach for undertaking research.

ICT skills are also important. Good written and verbal communication skills are needed to be able to explain your work clearly.

Working conditions

You will be based in a laboratory, using specialist equipment when undertaking research. This work can involve handling dangerous chemicals and wearing protective clothing.

You could spend long periods looking at and assessing information on a computer.

For some jobs evening or weekend working will be necessary. Jobs in industry may involve working shifts.

Future prospects

Physicists work at the cutting edge of science and industry. They apply their skills in areas as varied as electronics, power, communications and defence. They are employed by research institutions, government bodies and private companies to improve and develop products and systems.

You will be able to progress to supervisory or management roles, or enter into the training and teaching of physics.

Advantages/disadvantages

Physics offers the chance to develop public understanding of important scientific questions.

Working with detailed information for long periods can be very tiring.

You might have the chance to work abroad.

Qualifications and courses

ENTRY LEVEL 6

A relevant degree and sometimes a postgraduate qualification are required to work as a physicist. Entry to a degree course usually requires a minimum of at least 2 A levels/3–4 H grades, including physics and maths or equivalent, together with 5 GCSEs/S grades (A*–C/1–3) including English, maths and science.

Many institutions offer 1 year Foundation courses for candidates without the necessary scientific background which may be taught at the university or at a local partner college.

Physicists are trained on the job, and often study towards postgraduate qualifications, a PhD or the membership examinations of relevant professional bodies. For example, medical physicists must work towards the Clinical Science Diploma of the Institute of Physics and Engineering in Medicine.

For entry at technician level, an A level/H grade in physics or an equivalent qualification such as a BTEC/SQA National in science is required. Some technicians may hold a science-based degree. Technicians can work towards NVQs/SVQs in Laboratory and Associated Technical Activities at Levels 2–4.

Money guide

Salary levels vary according to employer and sector. Salaries are higher with a relevant postgraduate degree.

Starting salaries for graduates begin at £20,000, reaching £27,500 per year. With further training and qualifications salaries increase from £28,000 to £35,000.

At senior/management levels you could earn £50,000–£80,000.

Related opportunities

- Astronomer p505
- Medical Physicist p316
- Aerospace Engineer p212
- Meteorologist p529

Further information

Institute of Physics
76 Portland Place, London W1B 1NT
020 7470 4800; www.iop.org

Physics World
Dirac House, Temple Back, Bristol BS1 6BE
0117 929 7481, www.physicsworld.com

Institute of Physics and Engineering in Medicine
Fairmount House, 230 Tadcaster Road, York YO24 1ES
01904 610821; www.ipem.ac.uk

Science, Mathematics and Statistics

CRCI: TD

PHYSICS

Why study physics?

As well as an important first step towards a career in science and engineering, studying physics at college level (e.g. A level) provides a broad training in skills that are valued by all employers: an ability to grasp concepts quickly, a determination to find coherent answers, along with problem-solving, analytical, mathematical and IT skills. As Steff Gualter, TV weather forecaster says, "there are millions of students in the world, but to get a job you have to stand out from the crowd. Physics will help to give you that edge; people are always impressed by a qualification in physics."

Earning potential

Continuing with physics at university further enhances your earning potential. According to a PricewaterhouseCoopers report published in 2005, over a working lifetime the average physics graduate earns 30% more than those holding just A-levels, which compares favourably with the average for graduates in all subjects (23%) and is about double the advantage gained by studying subjects such as psychology, biological sciences, linguistics and history.

The role physicists play

Physicists play a vital role in many technology-based industries such as optoelectronics, nanotechnology, computing and renewable energy. Others work on investigating the universe; searching for extra-solar planets or looking for the remnants of the big bang. Others still, go on to apply their knowledge in healthcare (medical physics), studying the processes of the Earth (geophysics) or the climate (meteorology).

Transferable skills

The knowledge and skills that studying physics develops are important in other areas as well. Predicting future market behaviour is vital in finance, and so a physicist's ability to model complex systems is particularly valued in this sector, while a logical approach and ability to understand new technology is useful in law, for example, when patenting new inventions.

Even if you decide that you don't want to work in any physics-related industry after your degree, the skills and knowledge that you develop by studying physics will always help you in whichever area you go into. Studying physics is a good way of keeping your options open.

Simon Singh, a science writer and broadcaster says: "I think that physicists can do pretty much anything. Our training can be applied to almost any activity, and it allows us to see things in ways that might not be obvious to others."

Here are two physics graduates who have used their degrees in very different ways

Catherine Heyman is an astrophysicist

Catherine uses NASA's famous Hubble Space Telescope, as well as several large telescopes in Hawaii, to try and understand the universe. "At the moment we're trying to get funding to build telescopes up in space that are bigger and better than Hubble," says Catherine.

Catherine studied Astrophysics at university and then went on to do a PhD. "What I loved most about it was the opportunity to travel to La Palma in the Canary Islands to use the large telescopes there. My research used the data collected from these visits to find out how much dark matter there is in the universe. We now know that dark matter makes up more of the universe than normal matter (which is what we're made from), and that it surrounds our galaxy and holds it together, but we don't really know *what* it is – that remains one of the mysteries that physicists are trying to unravel."

Organisation profile **IOP** Institute of Physics

Harjinder Obhi is now a solicitor

"It was the philosophical aspect of physics that originally inspired me to study it. Particularly quantum physics and how reality may be different from what we think it is" explains Harjinder. During his physics degree, Harjinder became interested in law: "My interest was sparked by conversations with my friends. We discussed questions like 'Should man be able to patent a new form of life?' and I found those discussions fascinating, and so, after university, I studied to become a solicitor." Harjinder has worked in law ever since, and is currently employed by the internet search engine Google. "I love my job. The best things about it are the intellectual challenge and the fact that my work makes a difference across the world."

As he explains, Harjinder is not alone in moving from physics to law. "There are many people with a physics background in law. The way of thinking that physics develops is useful, as is the ability to understand technology when discussing the legal aspects of it."

Further information:

IOP Institute of Physics

For more information about careers from physics visit the Institute of Physics web-sites:
- www.physics.org/careers
- www.iop.org/careers

If you are aged between 16 and 19 and studying physics you can join the Institute of Physics for free, find out more at www.iop.org/16–19

The Institute of Physics is a scientific charity devoted to increasing the practice, understanding and application of physics.

It has a worldwide membership of over 37 000 and is a leading communicator of physics-related science to all audiences, from specialists through to government and the general public. Its publishing company, IOP Publishing, is a world leader in scientific publishing and the electronic dissemination of physics.

STATISTICIAN

What the work involves

- Statistics involves the use of mathematical techniques to collect, analyse and present large quantities of factual information.

- You will plan and undertake surveys using a range of mathematical research methods. You could apply your skills to investigate a range of subjects such as population levels, patterns of illness or national shopping habits.

- Statistical research plays a vital role in informing the activities of many areas such as government, advertising, medicine and scientific research.

The type of person suited to this work

Strong mathematical skills are essential for producing and analysing a range of statistical information. You will also need excellent problem-solving abilities to create practical solutions and collect information on specific issues.

Excellent ICT skills are needed as it is likely you will use specialist computer software. Your work could help to shape the work of different organisations, so you must have a high standard of accuracy and pay close attention to detail at all times. The ability to communicate with managers, staff and clients is essential.

Working conditions

You will be based in an office environment and spend a lot of time using computers. For some jobs you may work in a laboratory or research centre.

You will usually work 37 hours a week, with some overtime if there are deadlines to meet.

Future prospects

Statisticians investigate and research issues within the environment, medicine, business, social science and many other areas.

You could choose to develop a career in the Government Statistical Service. There are many opportunities in scientific and medical research and pharmaceutical development. Or you could choose to research and lecture on statistics in academia.

Advantages/disadvantages

Working to a high level of accuracy at all times can be very demanding.

Roles in areas such as environmental or forensic statistics are more likely with a postgraduate qualification.

As the job is often project-based, it offers a lot of variety.

Money guide

Starting salaries for graduates begin at around £20,000 per year.

With experience, you can earn £40,000, increasing to £65,000+ at senior levels.

Qualifications and courses

ENTRY LEVEL 5

The usual entry qualification is a degree in statistics, or a combined degree in statistics and another subject such as maths, economics or computer science. It is possible to enter with degrees in other subjects, providing the degree has substantial statistics content. A level/H grade maths is required for entry to a statistics degree.

Those with degrees in other mathematical subjects might enter after gaining a postgraduate qualification in statistics.

The professional examinations of the Royal Statistical Society (RSS) provide an alternative entry route for people already in relevant employment and for mature entrants.

The RSS offers courses at three levels. The Ordinary Certificate requires a GCSE/S grade in maths or the equivalent and relevant work experience. The Higher Certificate is modular and follows on from the Ordinary Certificate. The Graduate Diploma is equivalent to an Honours degree. The courses can be studied by day-release, at evening classes or by distance learning.

The Government Statistical Service has a fast-stream programme for assistant statistician recruitment. Candidates must have a 1st or 2nd class degree in a numerate subject. They offer work experience placements for students.

Statistical officer posts are also available to people with a 1st or 2nd class degree or 2 years' relevant work experience.

After 4 or 5 years' professional experience, statisticians with an approved degree or Graduate Diploma can qualify for Chartered Statistician status.

Government Statistical Service (GSS) employs over 1000 statisticians. Starting salaries range from £22,000 to £24,000.

Senior level GSS salaries are £40,000–£53,000.

Related opportunities

- Mathematician/Research Scientist (Maths) p527
- Actuary p20
- Economist p34
- Operational Researcher p532

Further information

Royal Statistical Society
12 Errol Street, London EC1Y 8LX
020 7638 8998; www.rss.org.uk/careers

Office for National Statistics
Room 1.101, Government Buildings, Cardiff Road, Newport NP10 8XG
0845 601 3034, www.statistics.gov.uk/default.asp

TOXICOLOGIST

What the work involves

- As a toxicologist, you'll study the effects of chemicals on the environment and everything within it, from humans and animals to plants.

- Work is very varied. You may find yourself working on the development of products, on testing new drugs, or lecturing and carrying out your own research.

- You may deal with poisons and drugs, or study the effects of chemicals on the environment or on human health.

- Some toxicologists work for the government.

The type of person suited to this work

You should have a strong interest in the environment, science, and public health and safety. For forensic toxicology, an interest in law is also useful.

Your level of scientific and technical knowledge should be high, and you need an excellent eye for detail as well as the ability to work carefully and accurately.

You should be able to apply scientific knowledge to practical work, and have excellent communication skills in order to explain technical and scientific information to others both verbally and in written reports.

You will also need good ICT skills.

Working conditions

The hours worked by toxicologists tend to follow the standard 9am–5pm, Monday–Friday working week pattern, and this doesn't tend to vary too much. However, if you're carrying out experimental work you might be expected to be more flexible. You might be on call on occasional weekends and evenings in case emergencies occur.

You'll spend most of your time working in a laboratory, but may sometimes have to visit scenes where incidents have taken place.

Expect to wear protective clothing most of the time, and be prepared to work occasionally with animals.

Future prospects

You can work towards being promoted to a more senior position such as project manager. This will involve spending less time with actual hands-on toxicology, and more carrying out tasks such as administration and supervision.

If you decide that this doesn't suit you, it's also possible to become self-employed and/or work on a freelance basis.

Advantages/disadvantages

Toxicology is an interesting and challenging profession, and you may be involved in exciting cases. You will constantly be learning and expanding your knowledge.

Qualifications and courses

ENTRY LEVEL 6

You'll need an Honours science degree to become a toxicologist. Relevant subjects include pharmacology or biochemistry. For entrance onto a degree course, you will need at least 2 A levels, including maths and chemistry and 5 GCSEs (A*–C).

Following your degree, it may be possible to take up a post that offers training as you work, but the usual route nowadays is to take a postgraduate qualification. Entry requirements are at least a 2.1 classification for your undergraduate degree.

After completing a Master's degree, students may choose to study for a PhD or MPhil by carrying out research into toxicology if you wish to do so. There are diplomas offered by many institutions across the UK in the subject, and you could even choose to go into ecotoxicology and may wish to study pollution or pesticide science.

There are many societies that provide qualifications in toxicology, and these include the British Toxicology Society and Federation of European Toxicologists.

It can be difficult, and you may see some distressing things. You also need to be constantly alert and can't make mistakes.

Money guide

When you start out in toxicology, you may earn about £20,000 a year.

This can increase to around £40,000 with experience.

In clinical toxicology salaries can rise to up to £65,000 a year, and in other fields this can reach £100,000.

Related opportunities

- Chemist p510
- Biochemist p506
- Biomedical Scientist p507
- Clinical Scientist p512

Further information

Association of the British Pharmaceutical Industry
12 Whitehall, London SW1A 2DY
020 7930 3477; www.abpi-careers.org.uk

British Toxicology Society (BTS)
Administrative Office, PO Box 10371, Colchester CO1 9GL
01206 226059; www.thebts.org

Council for the Registration of Forensic Practitioners (CRFP)
Tavistock House, Tavistock Square, London WC1H 9HX
020 7383 2200; www.crfp.org.uk

Science, Mathematics and Statistics

CRCI: TD

ZOOLOGIST

What the work involves

- Zoologists are involved with classifying, studying and researching all kinds of animal life. You could be involved with protecting endangered species through practical work and raising public awareness.

- Some zoologists work within industry, developing pharmaceuticals or enhancing agricultural products. Others are involved with research in their specific area of interest in academic or research institutions.

- You may choose to specialise in an area such as mammalogy (mammals), entomology (insects) or herpetology (amphibians and reptiles).

- You could work in a variety of environments including safari parks, wildlife centres and zoos.

The type of person suited to this work

You will need to have a passion for environmental issues and a love of science.

You should feel comfortable dissecting dead animals as part of your work for some roles in this area. You must be meticulous, logical, practical and patient. The ability to problem-solve is a key feature of this role. Communication skills are important as you might need to share your findings with people with little or no scientific knowledge. Leadership and computer skills are also essential.

Working conditions

If you are working in the field, you will have to base your hours upon the animals you are studying, for example if studying nocturnal animals you will have to work some nights. Your working environment will also vary depending on your area of interest. Many zoologists spend the majority of their time in laboratories or teaching in lecture theatres.

Future prospects

Whilst this is a specialist area, zoologists work for a variety of organisations such as environmental consultancies, conservation bodies, animal charities and local authorities. Others go into research and development in industry.

Many choose to work in universities which have a set progression path from researcher to head of department. Promotion within industry and government is also clearly defined. Within other areas such as conservation, progression is more limited; you made need to change employers in order to achieve promotion.

Advantages/disadvantages

There are opportunities to visit different types of outside locations on research trips.

You will use your skills and knowledge to increase public understanding of many aspects of the natural environment.

When working in the field you may find yourself in inhospitable environments.

Qualifications and courses

ENTRY LEVEL 6

A degree and, often, an MSc or PhD is required for entry to this profession. Your degree can be in zoology or a related subject, such as wildlife biology, marine biology, parasitology, animal behaviour or ecology. Most degree courses require candidates to have achieved 2 A levels and 5 GCSEs grades A*–C. An A level/H grade in biology is required for entry to these degree courses. Some courses ask for a second science, usually chemistry.

The usual entry route is a post as a trainee researcher in a university research department. Trainees work towards a PhD.

It is also possible to enter the profession at technician or trainee level with GCSEs/S grades, A levels/H grades, or equivalent qualifications including biology, maths, science and English.

Some people undertake a degree after gaining practical experience working as a zookeeper or laboratory technician. Often, admissions tutors will grant these candidates a placement, regardless of their formal qualifications.

Some institutions run one year Access courses for students without the necessary educational qualifications to catch up before they undertake their degree.

Money guide

These figures are only approximate and will vary depending on sector, location and employer. A PhD may increase your starting salary.

Your starting salary will probably be in the region of £17,000 to £20,000 per year. This may increase, with experience, to somewhere between £25,000 and £35,000 a year. As a senior zoologist you could be earning over £45,000 per year.

Related opportunities

- Ecologist p515
- Entomologist p516
- Veterinary Surgeon p283
- Zookeeper p285

Further information

British and Irish Association of Zoos and Aquariums
Regents Park, London NW1 4RY
020 7449 6351; www.biaza.org.uk

Institute of Zoology
ZSL, Regent's Park, London NW1 4RY
020 7722 3333; www.zsl.org

Institute of Biology
9 Red Lion Court, London EC4A 3EF
020 7936 5900; www.iob.org

Security and the Armed Forces

Working in the security and armed forces may give you many incredible experiences and opportunities not open to most people. You need to be an excellent team player and in some instances you may find yourself in a potentially dangerous situation, therefore it's essential that you are a great communicator. Working in this sector you can expect to spend your day absolutely anywhere! Some roles involve a lot of office work whereas others can involve spending a lot of your time on the road, or even at sea. If you're looking for a job that will be exhilarating but are able to remain calm and professional under pressure this sector could offer you a lot of opportunities.

In the section we look at the following jobs:

For similar jobs to the ones in this section turn to *Legal and Political Services* on page 361.

ARMY OFFICER

What the work involves

- The Army is responsible for defending the UK and its allies across the world, as well as taking part in peacekeeping and humanitarian operations in volatile countries.

- Army officers lead, command and train a team of soldiers on day-to-day activities, either on training exercises or on a range of combat, peacekeeping or disaster-relief missions.

- Your platoon's training, welfare and discipline will be entirely your responsibility.

- You will work within a specific professional or skill area such as medicine, dentistry, engineering, intelligence or combat.

The type of person suited to this work

You will need to have excellent self-discipline, confidence, and a natural ability to lead and motivate your team, which will consist of soldiers, non-commissioned officers and junior officers.

You must be able to keep a clear head and make sensible decisions under pressure in order to take responsibility for the safety of your team.

Initial training, with its physical and mental challenges, often comes as a shock. You will need to have determination, courage and resilience as well as a good level of physical fitness in order to get through.

Working conditions

Your hours will depend upon which specialism you have chosen to work in. Some officers work within a normal office timeframe, whilst others are required to work shifts. Hours may also be long and irregular when away on training or taking part in field-based operations.

You could be stationed anywhere in the world, and have to travel to destinations at short notice.

Officers must wear a uniform at all times.

Future prospects

Only around 1000 officer cadets are recruited each year for the training programme at Sandhurst, so entry is competitive.

Throughout your career, you will undertake further training and study for professionally recognised qualifications in order to be promoted through the ranks right up to a brigadier level after many years in service.

Advantages/disadvantages

You will be working within a close-knit team of professionals, so will build strong personal and working relationships within the job.

You may be involved in implementing large-scale peace initiatives which would be rewarding.

Qualifications and courses

ENTRY LEVEL 3

Entrants must have at least 2 A levels as well as 7 GCSEs (A*–C), including English, maths, science and a foreign language. The highest 7 GCSEs need to amount to at least 35 Advanced Level Information System points. Entrants must be aged between 17 years and 9 months and 28 years. Age restrictions are higher for those with professional qualifications.

Over 80% of the 1000 cadets accepted each year are university graduates. Some regiments and corps, such as the medical corps, might specify a particular degree as an entry requirement.

The University Officers Training Corps (UOTC) can help with degree funding by offering paid experience with the Army during your years at university. Many members of the UOTC go on to become Army officers.

You will need to pass a vigorous medical and fitness entrance test, as well as a range of interview and written tests during the selection process.

Upon entry, you will undertake intensive training in areas such as weapons handling, leadership, tactics and fitness.

You may be posted overseas for long periods of time, including over Christmas and other family events, which can be disruptive to your personal life.

Money guide

Officer cadets joining the programme straight after their A levels can expect to earn £15,286, whilst graduate entrants start on £24,000.

Once you reach the rank of lieutenant, your salary will increase to £29,000–£32,000.

If you become a brigadier, after 15–20 years with the Army, you could earn up to £98,000.

Related opportunities

- Royal Air Force (RAF) Officer p558
- Royal Navy Officer p561
- Soldier p564
- Police Officer p552

Further information

Army
www.army.mod.uk/join/join.aspx

Welbeck College
The Defence Sixth Form College, Forest Road, Woodhouse, Loughborough LE12 8WD
01509 891700; www.welbeck.mod.uk

City& Guilds

www.cityandguilds.com/myperfectjob

BODYGUARD

What the work involves

- You will be guarding your client or group, keeping them safe from harm or unwanted attention. You might also be known as a personal protection officer or a close protection officer.

- Protecting an executive on a business trip to a dangerous region of the world, an overseas royal visiting the UK, or a celebrity during an autograph-signing session could all be part of your work.

- You will be responsible for making a preliminary sweep of premises before your client arrives, setting up surveillance equipment, assessing potential threats and driving your client around.

- It is possible to be a specialist in areas such as close protection, surveillance or defensive driving.

The type of person suited to this work

This is not a first job – most have related experience and the most lucrative contracts go to those in the Special Forces or specialist close-protection police units. Also, most of the work is on a self-employed basis, so you need to have a flair for business because you will need to network and keep your accounts.

Exceptional planning skills and quick responses are essential to ensure that your client is free from harm or unwanted attention.

You will also need to be confident, physically fit to cope with the demands of the work, and have good eyesight and hearing.

Your appearance, diplomacy and communication skills also need to be top level, because you will be with your client and need to blend into the background to observe at high profile events.

Working conditions

Your work will be wherever your client goes and so this could mean lots of travelling.

You could be at risk as you would protect your client if necessary with your own body – but this is more an issue when working in dangerous areas of the world.

You will work long and irregular hours during a contract as some clients may need 24 hour protection and there will be long periods of inactivity.

Future prospects

You can progress to become a leader of a team of CPOs on assignment or establish your own business.

Very few officers are in long-term employment. The vast majority are self-employed. There is an increasing demand for good female officers.

Some progress into more mainstream security work, for example security guard or security manager. There may be opportunities to specialise in areas such as driving, and residential security.

Qualifications and courses

There are no formal entry requirements, but since 2006 there is a legal requirement for all close protection officers (CPOs) to hold a Security Industry Authority Licence (SIA) which lasts for 3 years and covers some other security sectors which also require licences.

For a Frontline Close Protection Licence, you must be 18 or over and have a Level 3 SIA-approved qualification. This could be a certificate in Protective Security by distance-learning from Buckinghamshire New University, an Edexcel certificate in Close Protection Operations or a City & Guilds Certificate in Close Protection. They all cover areas like risk assessment and surveillance. You must also have a SIA approved first aid certificate and a criminal record check.

A Diploma in Public Services is also available. Buckinghamshire New University offers a Foundation degree in Protective Security Operations.

Advantages/disadvantages

You will get to enjoy a fast-paced lifestyle and travel frequently.

Training courses are residential and expensive.

Money guide

New entrants can earn over £18,000 per year, rising to £24,000–£30,000 with experience. In high risk areas, with considerable experience, you could earn up to £100,000.

Many CPOs earn daily or hourly rates for specific contracts. These could range from £100 to £150 a day for low risk work, and £400–£500 a day in a very hostile environment or for protecting a key principal.

Related opportunities

- Army Officer p540
- Police Officer p552
- Royal Air Force (RAF) Officer p558
- Royal Marines Officer p560
- Security Officer/Manager p563

Further information

Security Industry Authority
PO Box 1293, Liverpool L69 1AX
0844 892 1025; www.sia.homeoffice.gov.uk

British Security Industry Association
Kirkham House, John Comyn Drive, Worcester WR3 7NS
0845 389 3889; www.bsia.co.uk

City & Guilds

www.cityandguilds.com/myperfectjob

CRCI: UK   Security and the Armed Forces

COASTGUARD WATCH ASSISTANT/OFFICER

What the work involves

- You will work as part of a team responding to vessels and people in distress. You will be dealing with 999 coastguard calls and radio distress calls, and will direct the efforts of the volunteer coastguard rescue officers. could may also be using the services of the Royal National Lifeboat Institution (RNLI).

- You will keep records of all activity and weather conditions, giving information to vessels and reporting anything unusual.

Watch assistants

- Watch assistants provide administrative support, keeping details of calls and rescues, and giving information to the general public.

Watch officers

- Watch officers are involved in all areas of the work and may lead coastal, sea or cliff searches and rescues.

The type of person suited to this work

You must have excellent computer skills, the ability to concentrate for long periods and a clear voice to make sure that you send rescuers to the right place.

Active search and rescue work involves carrying heavy equipment, climbing and working out at sea, all of which require a high level of physical fitness. Watch officers need good management and teaching skills to lead and train groups of auxiliary coastguards.

Working conditions

You will be located in an operations centre, using a computer and talking to others using hands-free communications equipment. Search and rescue work involves working outside in dangerous conditions. Coastguards operate 24/7 – you will be working shifts which include evenings as well as weekends and a 42-hour week.

Future prospects

This is a competitive job to enter.

You could work up to officer or sector management level. However, a limited number of senior jobs exist in this fairly small service. It is also expected that numbers will continue to drop in some areas of the service in the next few years. If you have experience and a degree, you could take a job in marine surveying within the Maritime and Coastguard Agency.

Advantages/disadvantages

With the use of satellite technology, it is possible to co-ordinate the rescue of someone hundreds of miles away from your control centre.

However, the sea is dangerous and you may arrive too late, which is an upsetting event for the whole team.

Qualifications and courses

Most people join HM Coastguard as a coastguard watch assistant (CWA).

There are no minimum entry qualifications, but GCSEs (A*–C)/S grades including English and maths, and Key Skills in Communication and Numeracy are useful. Most CWAs start as volunteers and you must be aged 16 or over to apply.

A few join at coastguard watch officer level (CWO). You will need a good standard of hearing and eyesight and a high level of fitness. You must have significant search and rescue experience and either a Coastal Skipper Licence or a Yachtmaster Certficate from the Royal Yacht Association.

Training is initially for 7 weeks at the Coastguard Training Centre. Training is then on the job with a further short course after 10–12 months. You must then pass a series of exams.

Money guide

When starting out you could earn £15,000 per year as a coastguard watch assistant. After gaining experience, this can rise to £17,800. The starting salary of a coastguard watch officer is £18,100 and can increase to £23,200. On-call allowances, plus overtime pay, can increase earnings at every level of experience.

Additional allowances are paid to those working in the Scottish Islands.

Related opportunities

- Air Traffic Controller p595
- Merchant Navy Deck Officer/Rating p610
- Police Officer p552
- Royal Navy Officer p561

Further information

Maritime & Coastguard Agency, Human Resources Team
Spring Place, 105 Commercial Road,
Southampton SO15 1EG
023 8032 9308; www.mcga.gov.uk

Port Skills and Safety Ltd
4th Floor Carthusian Court, 12 Carthusian Street,
London EC1M 6EZ
020 7260 1790; www.portskillsandsafety.co.uk

Maritime Skills Alliance
1 Hillside, Beckingham, Lincoln LN5 0RQ
www.maritimeskills.org

CRIME SCENE INVESTIGATOR/ SCENES OF CRIME OFFICER

What the work involves

- You will be collecting, storing and recording evidence such as fibres, hair and blood to help investigate crimes like burglary, accidents and suspicious deaths.

- You will use equipment and materials to lift, package and preserve evidence, such as biological samples, paint, tyre marks and fingerprints.

- Your job will involve taking photographic and video evidence of both crime scenes and victims of crime.

- You will also need to keep thorough records and attend court when required to give evidence.

The type of person suited to this work

Sifting through evidence is the main aspect of this job so you will need to be able to pay attention to detail. You will also need to be methodical and patient.

This job can be very distressing. You will need to be able to distance yourself emotionally from the crime, and be able to record the scene and collect evidence in an analytical, scientific way. Good team working skills are essential as you may be working on a project with many others.

An interest in science and technology is essential. You will need to keep up to date with developments in forensic science and technology as they will affect how well you do your job.

Working conditions

You will work both outside at crime scenes and inside at base.

You will do a 37-hour working week, including shifts, but hours might be longer at times. You could also be on-call 24-hours.

Conditions at crime scenes can be very difficult and unpleasant but you will be provided with protective clothing. You will need a driving licence.

Future prospects

Crime scene investigators are recruited by all regional police forces. Some forces only recruit civilians to do this work but a few also recruit specialist police officers. There are currently about 1800 crime scene investigators in the UK. Competition for vacancies is high.

It is possible to move into more specialised areas of work, such as the investigation of suspicious fires, or scenes where firearms have been used. There may be opportunities for promotion to senior investigator with management responsibilities. You can study for further qualifications and become a forensic scientist or specialise in fingerprint technology.

Advantages/disadvantages

Although this job has an exciting image, it can be routine and shocking at times.

Qualifications and courses

ENTRY LEVEL 5

While individual police forces will all have different entry requirements, most are now requiring applicants to have a degree. Various universities offer degrees or Foundation degrees in subjects such as forensic science and criminology. A Bachelor's degree in Crime Scene Science is available at the University of Teesside. You will need at least 2 A levels or equivalent, 1 being in science, for these degrees.

Work experience is usually required, ideally in a related area such as photography or scientific work. Previous work dealing with the public would also be an advantage.

You will need a medical exam and a background security check for this role.

Once in the job you would have a 1-month induction with your force, followed by a residential course with The National Police Improvement Agency. Specialist and refresher courses are also on offer.

You will have the satisfaction of working with a team of investigating officers and forensic scientists to gather evidence needed to trace, arrest and convict offenders.

Money guide

£16,500–£18,300 per year is usual for starting salaries.

This rises to £28,000 for experienced investigators.

£29,000–£35,000 is possible for senior investigators, depending on your local police force and responsibility level.

Related opportunities

- Forensic Scientist p519
- Police Officer p552
- Forensic Computer Analyst p548
- Private Investigator p556

Further information

National Police Improvement Agency
4th floor 10–8 Victoria Street, London SW1H 0NN
020 7147 8200; www.npia.police.uk

Police recruitment information
0845 608 3000; www.policecouldyou.co.uk

Forensic Science Service
Trident Court, 2920 Solihull Parkway,
Birmingham Business Park, Birmingham B37 7YN
www.forensic.gov.uk/html/

City&
Guilds

www.cityandguilds.com/myperfectjob

Security and the Armed Forces

CRCI: UG

CRIMINAL INTELLIGENCE OFFICER/ANALYST

What the work involves

- Your job is to protect the UK from attack and terrorism, to protect its economic wellbeing as well as to prevent organised crime such as drug trafficking.

- You will work primarily for the UK's three intelligence and security agencies: Government Communications Headquarters (GCHQ), Security Service (MI5) and the Secret Intelligence Service (MI6).

- You might be involved in military operations, counter espionage, detecting weapons of mass destruction, and identifying agents and targets.

The type of person suited to this work

This job requires you to think on your feet and be aware of the big picture. You should be a confident decision-maker, flexible and adaptable. You must be perseverant and work well under pressure.

Motivation, inquisitiveness and cultural sensitivity are essential. You need to be able to recall events accurately. Some of your work will include informing and working alongside professionals from other national and international security services so you should be a good team player.

You must keep up to date on current affairs and communications technologies.

Working conditions

Some of the posts operate shifts, which might include weekends. Starting out you will be required to work at headquarters. GCHQ is based in Cheltenham and MI5 and MI6 are based in central London. You could also be required to travel both nationally and internationally. It might be possible to work from home for some posts.

This job can become more of a way of life than a career so you should be completely dedicated and be able to keep information totally confidential.

Future prospects

You will usually work up to three years in your first role. Based on your performance and your potential you may be promoted to a more specialist role which will include more responsibility. You could be responsible for a wider geographical region or for specific analytical techniques.

You can move into policy work, projects or personnel.

Advantages/disadvantages

It's satisfying to know you are helping to protect national security.

The secrecy of the job may be difficult as you will not be allowed to talk about your work with friends and family.

Qualifications and courses

ENTRY LEVEL 4

Applicants for any post within MI5, MI6 or GCHQ must be British citizens and one or both of your parents must also be British or have substantial ties to the UK. You normally have to have been resident in the UK for 10 years prior to your application.

MI5 applicants must be aged 18 or over. MI6 applicants must be aged 21 or over and A levels/H grades or degrees may be required by some organisations. However many applicants have first degrees or postgraduate qualifications.

Graduates from a wide range of disciplines are considered. Specialist areas may require more precise subject choices, for example linguistics or computer software development. Useful degrees include criminology and criminal intelligence and analysis.

Each applicant is considered individually during the rigorous vetting procedure, known as Developed Vetting (DV) clearance. This includes medical and security clearance and may include background checks on family and friends. Recruitment can take many months.

Money guide

If you work for MI5, MI6 or GCHQ your salary will start at around £24,000. With 5–10 years of experience you could earn up to £43,000.

In addition to pay, there are excellent benefits including leisure and fitness facilities, childcare vouchers and travel assistance.

Related opportunities

- Army Officer p540
- Customs and Excise Officer p545
- Police Officer p552
- Private Investigator p556

Further information

MI5 Careers
The Enquiries Desk, PO Box 3255, London SW1P 1AE
0845 450 2152; www.mi5careers.co.uk

Secret Intelligence Service
PO Box 1300, London SE1 1BD
www.sis.gov.uk

Government Communications Headquarters
Press Office, Room A3a, GCHQ, Hubble Road, Cheltenham GL51 0EX
01242 221491; www.gchq.gov.uk

CUSTOMS AND EXCISE OFFICER

What the work involves

- You will be working as a civil servant for the Home Office, enforcing tax regulations on all goods entering and leaving the country and all goods bought and sold in the UK.

- You could specialise in customs: checking for anyone either not paying tax or smuggling in illegal items and substances.

- You could specialise in excise work: visiting traders, manufacturers and importers to check licences and accounts to make sure that the right duties are being paid on goods like petrol, alcohol and tobacco.

- You could specialise in VAT: visiting businesses to check their accounts and that the right amount of VAT is being collected.

The type of person suited to this work

If you are part of front-line detection work, investigating the entry of illegal goods into the UK, you will be involved in observing, questioning and challenging people. You will need top-notch communication and observation skills. You must be intuitive and persistent. Knowledge of or a willingness to learn a foreign language is useful.

If you work in VAT or excise, an aptitude for numbers and computers is a must, because you will be checking business accounts and watching out for sometimes quite sophisticated cover-ups.

Working conditions

Customs and immigration officers mainly work in airports, seaports and freight terminals but also may need to do outdoor surveillance work. You will wear a uniform if you are a front-line detective.

Excise and VAT officers are based in offices but also travel around their local areas carrying out checks and interviews. You will generally work office hours, Monday to Friday.

Customs officers work shifts.

Future prospects

There are about 23,000 staff based all over the country. Customs specialist staff are mainly located at air- and seaports and the Channel Tunnel. It is possible to move on to senior or management posts. There are also specialist areas within customs, for example in detection, operations and intelligence units and dog units.

Advantages/disadvantages

When dealing with front-line detection work you might have to question or detain angry or abusive people. It can be a high-pressure job at peak times.

Qualifications and courses

For an officer grade you will need 5 GCSEs/S grades (A*–C/1–3) including English and maths, and 2 A levels/H grades. Many entrants at this level have a degree. You could join at a lower level into an administration job with a minimum of 2 GCSEs/S grades (A*–C/1–3). If you do not have the minimum grades you could still enter if you sit and pass a selection test.

For those with Honours degrees at 2.2 or above, fast-stream entry is possible. This is for entry into all Civil Service departments and although a preference can be expressed, entry into customs and excise is not guaranteed.

Your training would last up to 9 months and could include some residential training courses.

All fast-stream candidates must meet the requirements of Civil Service nationality.

No two days are ever the same, especially in detection work.

It can be very rewarding to know that you have prevented dangerous items such as drugs and firearms getting into the country.

Money guide

All staff working shifts or unsocial hours are paid additional allowances.

Salaries for administration posts start around £13,000.

A Customs and Excise Officer can earn £19,500–£25,200.

Senior grades can earn up to £57,000.

Related opportunities

- Civil Service Officer p28
- Police Officer p552
- Army Officer p540

Further information

The Chartered Institute of Taxation
12 Upper Belgrave Street, London SW1X 8BB
020 7235 9381; www.tax.org.uk

General Fast Stream Programme
Pilgrims Well, 427 London Road, Camberley GU15 3HZ
01276 400333; www.faststream.gov.uk

City&
Guilds

www.cityandguilds.com/myperfectjob

Security and the Armed Forces

CRCI: UE/AB

EMERGENCY PLANNING/ MANAGEMENT OFFICER

What the work involves

- Emergency planners and managers work primarily in local government as part of a larger team to help maintain public safety, especially at times when this is threatened by an external force.

- You will be required to respond quickly to and learn from emergency situations that have arisen from natural disasters, outbreaks of serious contagious diseases, industrial accidents and terrorism.

- You will compile reports from lengthy research and planning on the most efficient ways to protect the general public should an emergency situation arise.

- You will carry out risk assessments, write safety briefs to train emergency response services and help with the recovery process after an incident has occurred.

The type of person suited to this work

You will need to enjoy working in a high pressure situation as part of a large team. You should be enthusiastic about helping to provide better public safety.

You will also need to respond quickly and calmly in an emergency and keep a level head in what may be a dangerous situation.

The job requires someone willing to work long hours, sometimes at unsociable times as well as a neat and organised person who can take comprehensive notes and present their findings accurately.

Working conditions

You may often find yourself in a highly pressured situation especially in the aftermath of a major incident so you could find yourself in danger or not knowing when you will finish the job.

You can expect travel to feature heavily as part of your job with many trips away from home a distinct possibility.

Future prospects

If you enter the career as an assistant you can expect to progress, with experience, to a management or senior role if you show signs of willingness to go where the work takes you and put in long hours.

Once you reach a more senior role you will not be working in such a hands-on environment but would provide more managerial support to your team.

Advantages/disadvantages

Your future prospects could take you all over the world to work with individuals who enjoy working as part of a close knit team.

The work has the potential to be highly distressing especially as you could be one of the first people on the scene after a major natural disaster or a terrorist attack.

Qualifications and courses

All graduates are eligible to apply to work in this profession although some degree subjects such as emergency planning and disaster management are considered more desirable in candidates applying for their first job in the field.

Many of the courses that are more directly related to the industry will be sandwich courses to give students the chance to spend a year working in the sector and gain valuable experience.

There are also more specific courses available which are geared towards a job in emergency planning but these do not guarantee a job in the sector.

Candidates who have previous experience of working in this sector or a related career will be at an advantage when applying for their first role in the industry.

Individuals who enter the profession as an assistant will take part in a lot of training on the job as well as complete several external courses as they go along many of which are run by the Emergency Planning Society. The courses available allow individuals to specialise in certain areas of emergency planning as well as gain more broad professional skills.

Money guide

A typical starting salary in the profession as an assistant is likely to be £20,000–£27,000.

You can expect this to progress to around £40,000 after 3–5 years of experience.

Senior roles come with a lot of responsibility but you could expect to earn £70,000 at this level.

Related opportunities

- Health and Safety Adviser p40
- Police Officer p552
- Firefighter p547
- Environmental Health Practitioner/Officer p35

Further information

Emergency Planning Society
The Media Centre, Culverhouse Cross, Cardiff CF5 6XJ
Tel: 0845 600 9587; Fax: 029 2059 0397; www.the-eps.org

The Emergency Planning College
The Hawkhills, Easingwold, York YO61 3EG
Tel: 01347 821 406; Fax: 01347 822 575;
epc.marketing@cabinet-office.x.gsi.gov.uk;
www.cabinetoffice.gov.uk

City& Guilds

www.cityandguilds.com/myperfectjob

FIREFIGHTER

What the work involves

- You will be dealing with a range of emergencies, not only fires but also helping at other incidents such as rescuing trapped animals and people, handling chemical spillages and assisting at road, rail or air crash scenes.

- If your team arrives on the scene before the paramedics you will have to give First Aid.

- You might give advice to organisations on fire safety and check that buildings or public events meet fire regulations.

The type of person suited to this work

You will need to stay calm in dangerous situations. People in danger tend to react in extreme ways and you will need to be good at talking to them, giving instructions, reassuring them and leading them to safety.

You need to be an excellent team player. You will be assigned to a 'watch' (a team) and need to work together to keep yourself and others safe.

You will need to be able to deal with very stressful and disturbing situations.

Working conditions

You will be based at a fire station but will go out to attend incidents. Fire stations have good facilities for eating and resting.

Working conditions can often be unpleasant and dangerous. You will wear a uniform and, when needed, protective clothing and equipment.

You will work an average of 42 hours per week, which will be divided into day and night shifts.

You can also work as a retained firefighter which means you will be on-call. Many retained firefighters have other full-time or part-time occupations.

Future prospects

The main employers are regional fire services who employ about 41,000 firefighters. Airports, the Ministry of Defence, the RAF and the Royal Navy also recruit firefighters. Some firefighters start their career as retained firefighters to gain experience. Entry is competitive.

You could move into driving fire trucks by taking an LGV licence. Promotion to supervisory and management roles is by clear grades and given on ability, but exams must also be passed.

Advantages/disadvantages

This job can be very stressful and you cannot just leave an emergency situation if your shift has ended.

Qualifications and courses

To be considered for selection as a firefighter you must be at least 18 years old. A full UK driving licence is preferred.

You will be required to pass certain rigorous physical and job-related tests (such as working within confined spaces and at heights), as well as written and psychological tests. You will also be required to undergo strict medical examinations to make sure you are fit enough to undertake demanding firefighting duties.

You must have normal colour vision and good eyesight. Glasses or contact lenses may occasionally be permitted.

Firefighters need a good general education. Some brigades may ask for specific GCSEs/S grades and some entrants have A levels/H grades or a degree. A numerical and written entrance test is required to ensure there is an understanding of problem solving and situation awareness.

You will get to know your watch very well; firefighters say they really enjoy the team spirit at work.

You need to pass demanding training successfully to qualify, and keep up a rigorous fitness and training schedule.

Money guide

As a trainee you will earn around £21,000 per year, with experience this can increase to £22,000–£28,000.

A leading firefighter can earn £28,000–£31,500 and station managers can earn up to £36,000.

Retained firefighters earn a retainer fee of around £2,600 per year. They also receive additional payments for attending fires.

Related opportunities

- Paramedic p324
- Police Officer p552
- Royal Air Force (RAF) Officer p558
- Royal Navy Officer p561

Further information

Fire Service Recruitment Information
www.fireservice.co.uk

Fire Gateway
www.fire.gov.uk/careers

Defence Fire Training and Development Centre
Manston, Ramsgate CT12 5BS
01843 823351; www.dftdc.org

FORENSIC COMPUTER ANALYST

What the work involves

■ You will be responsible for inspecting computers (and other technology such as mobile phones) for criminal activity.

■ You might be looking for evidence of identity theft, child abuse, hacking, phishing and other illegal activity.

■ Even if evidence of the crime has been deleted or corrupted you will need to retrieve it without altering it in any way.

■ You might be using specialist software and working with the police to look through files, photographs, emails and phone conversations in order to discover evidence of criminal activity. You may need to appear in court to relay your findings.

The type of person suited to this work

You will need to have a certain level of skill using computers, as well as an interest in detecting and preventing crime. You should be a patient and determined person as some investigations may take place over a long period of time. You might come across unpleasant or even horrific material and you must be able to distance yourself and deal with it objectively. You will need to be able to record your findings in a clear, coherent and logical manner. You should be able to understand the law in relation to IT crime. Articulateness and strong communication skills are essential.

Working conditions

You will spend most of your time in an office using a computer. You will generally work standard office hours (9am-5pm from Monday to Friday). Although you might need to be on call over weekends and public holidays or work overtime to meet deadlines. You might also have to attend court to give evidence.

Future prospects

Postgraduate qualifications will enhance your chances of promotion (particularly if you work within the commercial world). You could progress to the level of supervisor or line manager.

You may have to change employers in order to progress. Jobs are available with the police force, MI5, government, the Serious and Organised Crime Agency and IT firms who specialise in computer security.

Advantages/disadvantages

Your workload will be varied and opportunities are available in many different sectors.

You will spend a lot of time hunched over a computer.

If you work within a police or government sector you might help to send criminals to jail.

Qualifications and courses

ENTRY LEVEL 5

Most people who enter this career have completed a degree in IT (or equivalent computing subject). If your degree is not IT based you can take an IT conversion course. However, it is becoming more and more necessary to have a specific degree in forensic computing and information security.

In order to gain a place on a degree course you will normally require at least 2 A levels and 5 GCSEs grade A*–C. Computing, mathematics and science subjects are all relevant A level subjects.

You could alternatively complete a Foundation degree in an IT subject. These courses generally require applicants to have attained at least 1 A level and about 4 GCSEs grades A*–C (or equivalent).

There is also a Diploma in Information Technology which might be of interest.

A postgraduate degree would be extremely valuable. Entry to postgraduate programmes is reliant on the successful completion of a first degree.

Members of police staff can complete specialist training from the National Policing Improvement Agency (NPIA).

Money guide

These figures are only approximate and will vary depending on location, sector and employer. As a trainee you can expect to earn around £20,000 a year. After a year's experience, this can rise to somewhere between £25,000 and £35,000 per year. A senior forensic analyst might earn in the region of £40,000–£60,000 a year.

Related opportunities

■ Software Engineer p149
■ Crime Scene Investigator p543
■ Information Scientist p353
■ Forensic Scientist p519

Further information

The British Computer Society
1st Floor, Block D, North Star House, North Star Avenue, Swindon SN2 1FA
01793 417424; www.bcs.org

National Policing Improvement Agency
4th Floor, 10–18 Vicctoria Street, London SW1H 0NN
0800 4909 3322; www.npia.police.uk

Skills for Justice
Centre Court, Atlas Way, Sheffield S4 7QQ
0114 261 1499; www.skillsforjustice.com

IMMIGRATION OFFICER

What the work involves

- You will be working as a civil servant for the Home Office and you will be controlling the entry of people into the UK by checking the passports and visas of passengers arriving at ports, airports or via the Channel Tunnel.

- You could ask questions to find out more about them and if suspicious, conduct a more detailed interview.

- As an assistant officer you would refer to a more senior officer if you are concerned about documentation or answers to questions.

- You might work in an office processing immigration applications, dealing with appeals and conducting intelligence-based activities.

The type of person suited to this work

You will need to be confident, assertive and have the ability to work under pressure and to deadlines. You will need to be well organised, reliable and have good report-writing skills. You will need an ability to get on with people from across the world.

You should enjoy investigating and collecting information, and have the ability to write up and pass on your concerns to others in your team, or colleagues from other professions.

Working conditions

You could work in a range of places such as ports and airports where you will have access to a desk, PC, phone and interviewing area.

Some immigration officers have to undertake surveillance duties and work with other intelligence officers, but normally you will check documents and interview individuals within your office or interviewing booth.

You will work shifts that will include out of office hours and weekends.

Future prospects

Half of all immigration staff are employed in London and the South-East, at Heathrow, Gatwick and the Channel ports. The numbers of people entering the UK and asking for asylum has increased over recent years. This has impacted on the service, which has grown in numbers. Entry is competitive at officer level and the majority of entrants are graduates.

It is possible to enter at assistant grade and work up to officer grade. Placements are also possible, for example, to Immigration Visa sections at the British Deputy High Commissions overseas or to police forces around the UK.

Advantages/disadvantages

You will play an important role in helping protect national security.

This job is part of the civil service, so entry can be competitive.

The civil service offers excellent conditions of service and training.

Qualifications and courses

Assistant immigration officers have to sit a literacy and numeracy test and must attend an assessment day.

Immigration officers need no formal qualifications although most employers expect entrants to be educated to A level standard. Assistant immigration officers can apply for promotion to this level.

Applicants with a minimum of a 2.2 Honours degree can apply for fast-stream entry. This is for entry into all Civil Service departments and although a preference can be expressed, entry into Immigration is not guaranteed.

All fast-stream candidates must be UK nationals. For all other entrants, you must be a European Economic Area national, EU national or Commonwealth citizen. Swiss nationals, although Switzerland is not an EEA country, are also eligible to apply for non-reserved posts.

After a period of 10 weeks initial training, entrants are placed with more experienced officers, usually at Dover, Heathrow or Gatwick. Financial support may be available for officers wishing to learn a foreign language.

Money guide

All staff working shifts or unsocial hours are paid additional allowances.

Those working in and around London receive an additional allowance.

When starting out as an assistant officer, you earn around £18,000 per year. With experience, you can earn £20,500, rising to £26,000.

Salaries for immigration officers start at around £23,000 rising with experience to £38,000.

Related opportunities

- Civil Service Officer p28
- Coastguard Watch Assistant/Officer p542
- Equality and Diversity Officer p36
- Police Officer p552

Further information

Civil Service Careers
Unit 2–4 Lescren Way, Avonmouth, Bristol BS11 8DG
0117 982 1171; www.civil-service.gov.uk/jobs

General Fast Stream Programme
Application Helpdesk: Fast Stream Team, Pilgrims Well, 427 London Road, Camberley GU15 3HZ
01276 400333; www.faststream.gov.uk, faststream@parity.net

Home Office
Direct Communications Unit, 2 Marsham Street, London SW1P 4DF
020 7035 4848; www.homeoffice.gov.uk, www.ukba.homeoffice.gov.uk

Security and the Armed Forces

CRCI: UE/AB

PARKING ATTENDANT/ CIVIL ENFORCEMENT OFFICER

What the work involves

- You will be enforcing parking regulations for a local authority or contractors working on their behalf, patrolling and checking for illegal parking and non-payment of parking fees.

- Using a hand-held computer you will regularly check details of vehicles parked in limited-stay parking areas and issue fixed penalty tickets. You will take pictures of any illegally parked vehicles.

- You will need to arrange for vehicles to be clamped or sent to the pound. You will attend court to give evidence if any prosecution results from your work. You will have to report any suspected abandoned or stolen vehicles to the police.

The type of person suited to this work

All employers look for a polite but firm manner as well as good communication skills. You will need to be very good at dealing with people, many of whom could be feeling irate about the ticket you have just given them.

You need to be a good observer and able to follow rules and instructions. You will have to watch out at all times for illegal parking and enforce the rules.

You will meet a lot of people but you will also be working unsupervised and independently so you need to be confident, self-disciplined and reliable.

Working conditions

You will be working in the streets, in all seasons and weathers. You will need to wear a uniform and carry a hand-held computer.

You will work shifts to a total of 37–40 hours a week, including early mornings and late evenings. You might also have to work on weekends.

Future prospects

Parking attendants are now carrying out most of the duties that were formerly assigned to traffic wardens. Parking contractors are working with over 100 local authorities to enforce parking legislation. Vacancies are available with numerous main contractors.

With experience, progression is possible into a role as supervisor or trainer and then into management if suitable. However, prospects may be more limited in more rural areas.

Advantages/disadvantages

You will keep fit, walking an average of ten miles a day, five days a week carrying a 5kg pack (including your computer, printer and radio).

There is no doubt that parking attendants are not always

Qualifications and courses

You must be 19 or over. You must have a City & Guilds or Edexcel NVQ Level 2 qualification in Controlling Parking Areas or a City & Guilds Level 2 Award for Civil Enforcement Officers (Parking). However, a lot of employers will provide this training. On completion you could work towards a Level 3 course in Parking Management/Supervision or an NVQ Level 3 in Parking Clerical work.

Some employers look for at least 4 GCSEs/S grades (A*–C/1–3), including English and maths as well as experience working with the public. A full driving licence is needed for some positions.

Training is always given on entry and covers on-street enforcement activity, car park patrolling and enforcement, clamping and tow-away and CCTV operation.

popular and you might have to deal with some aggressive people.

Illegal parking can cause real problems for most law-abiding motorists and many attendants feel a sense of satisfaction from keeping the roads clear.

Money guide

Starting pay is about £13,000 per year. In certain places, supervisors' salaries can reach up to £18,000. The hourly wage is £7–£10.

Civil enforcement managers can expect £26,000–£30,000 a year.

Related opportunities

- Police Officer p552
- Police Community Support Officer p551
- Train Conductor p628
- Bailiff/Enforcement Agent p362

Further information

British Parking Association
Stuart House, 41–43 Perrymount Road,
Haywards Heath RH16 3BN
01444 447300; www.britishparking.co.uk

The Institute of Parking Professionals
Stuart House, 41–43 Perrymount Road,
Haywards Heath RH16 3BN
01444 447 300; www.theipp.co.uk

www.cityandguilds.com/myperfectjob

POLICE COMMUNITY SUPPORT OFFICER (PCSO)

What the work involves

- Police community support officers are uniformed members of the force whose role is to work within their local community, supporting the activities and initiatives of police officers.

- You will be part of the group of officers that provides visible police presence on the streets and in other public areas.

- You will be on the frontline, offering help and advice to members of the public, as well as tackling anti-social behaviour.

- Everyday duties could include crowd-control and traffic directing, dealing with minor offences, checking out abandoned vehicles, or imposing fines for acts such as littering or dog fouling.

The type of person suited to this work

You will need to be an excellent communicator, as you will encounter a range of people in your work. You must also be able to remain calm but authoritative when confronted with potentially difficult or violent members of the public.

You must be able to work effectively within a team. This means you should be able to take orders and act on your own initiative when necessary.

You should have good, accurate written skills, as you will need to produce reports on events and deal with complex paperwork at times.

Working conditions

You will work up to 40 hours on a shift basis, encompassing night and weekend work. Flexible or part time hours are available.

Although you will be based at a police station, you will work in a variety of locations including patrolling the streets, within people's homes, or in public places such as train stations.

You will be required to wear a uniform, which includes a high visibility jacket and protective hat. Additional protective equipment may need to be worn or carried on occasion.

Future prospects

Competition for entry to become a PCSO can be fierce, depending on the force you are applying to.

Experienced PCSOs are often responsible for teaching, training and guiding new recruits. There are also opportunities to move into supervisory or managerial roles within the PCSO contingent.

It is also a good role to start in if you would like to become a police officer.

Advantages/disadvantages

You will play a direct role in protecting your local community and finding solutions to problems and crime in the area.

Qualifications and courses

There are no specific entry requirements, and applicants from a diverse range of backgrounds are encouraged to apply in order to get a good representational mix across the force. You should be aged 17 years and 6 months or older.

Some employers may view your application more favourably if it demonstrates some commitment to community service schemes, or if you have undertaken a relevant course such as an NVQ Level 2, BTEC National Diploma, OCR Level 2 National qualification or HNC/D in Public Services, the Diploma in Society, Health and Development or a Foundation degree in Police Studies or Public Services.

During the application process, you will be required to sit written tests, as well as undergo medical, financial and security checks.

Upon entry, you will undertake between 3 weeks and 3 months of training. Areas covered will include relevant areas of law, self-defence, First Aid, interviewing skills, and using police communication equipment.

There are good opportunities for career development, including progression to become a police officer.

You may be confronted with difficult and dangerous situations, which can be both frightening and unnerving.

Money guide

As a new recruit to the force, you could expect to earn around £16,000. If you are working specifically for the British Transport Police, your starting salary will be slightly higher at £18,500.

Once you have gained a few years' experience, you can expect to earn £21,500.

If you reach a supervisory or managerial role, your earnings will reach about £25,000.

Related opportunities

- Police Officer p552
- Soldier p564
- Security Officer/Manager p563
- Prison Officer p555

Further information

National Police Recruitment Team
www.policecouldyou.co.uk

Security and the Armed Forces

CRCI: UG

POLICE OFFICER

What the work involves

- Police officers are responsible for safeguarding communities from crime by apprehending criminals and maintaining order.

- You will spend your time on patrol, responding to any situation that occurs whilst you are on shift.

- You will keep records, take statements, and write reports. You may need to give evidence in court on occasion, and may also give educational talks in community venues.

- Once trained, you could specialise in a department such as CID, Mounted Police, Child Protection, Drugs Squad or Traffic Police.

The type of person suited to this work

You must have excellent communication skills in order to deal with a variety of people on a daily basis whose position could range from that of a criminal who needs restraining, to a victim who needs careful treatment.

You will need to be non-judgemental, and have the ability to view situations from numerous situations.

You will need courage, initiative, and common sense in order to deal with many of the circumstances you will be presented with. You will also need to have good problem-solving skills.

Working conditions

You will be required to work 40 hours a week, covering early, late and night shifts 7 days a week. Part time or flexible working hours can usually be accommodated.

You will be based at a police station, but the majority of your time will be spent on patrol, either on foot or by car. This means you will be out in all weather conditions, and will travel to many different locations.

Future prospects

You can move upwards to the level of sergeant and inspector, and these promotions are subject to examination and interview. To progress further you must demonstrate your skills to a board of judges. You could opt to specialise in a department such as the CID, or Mounted Police.

Advantages/disadvantages

You will be meeting new challenges each day and adapting to unusual environments, which will keep you mentally and physically alert and ensures the work never gets dull.

You will be responsible for promoting safety and wellbeing in the local community, which is rewarding.

You will be required to work unsociable hours including nights and weekends.

You will have to deal with difficult, distressed, and occasionally violent members of the public.

Qualifications and courses

There are no specific academic requirements, but you must be aged 17 years and 6 months or older, and be a UK, European Union or Commonwealth citizen or a citizen from any country who has been granted indefinite leave to stay in the UK.

You could also take a relevant qualification to enhance your application. These include BTEC qualifications at Levels 2 or 3 and OCR qualifications at Level 2 in Public Services, the Diploma in Society, Health and Development, a HND/C in Public Services as well as a degree or Foundation degree in Police Studies or Criminology.

The police force operates an intensive selection process, and you will need to pass medical, fitness, eyesight, literacy, and numeracy tests. You will also be assessed using a variety of scenario exercises by which your communication, decision-making, and problem-solving skills will be judged.

You will need to pass a Criminal Records Bureau check.

Upon entry, you will undergo further officer training over 2 years through the Initial Police Learning and Development Programme (IPLDP).

Money guide

The starting salary for a student police officer is about £21,500. This will rise to £24,000 on completion of the IPLDP training programme. Once you reach the rank of sergeant, you can earn £38,000+.

Very senior officers, especially those in the larger and more active police forces, can earn in excess of £57,000.

Related opportunities

- Police Community Support Officer p551
- Police Support Worker p553
- Road Safety Officer p624
- Security Officer/Manager p563

Further information

National Police Recruitment Team
www.policecouldyou.co.uk

Civil Nuclear Constabulary
Civil Nuclear Constabulary, Building Fb,Culham Science Centre, Abingdon OX14 3DB
01235 466606; www.cnc.police.uk; jobs@cnc.police.uk

www.cityandguilds.com/myperfectjob

POLICE SUPPORT WORKER

What the work involves

- Police support workers are the first point of contact for members of the public in a police station.

- You will be responsible for answering and directing calls, passing walk-ins to appropriate members of staff, and carrying out general administrative tasks within the station.

- You will be on the front desk, so will receive firearms, knives, driving licences, and any other paraphernalia seized by police whilst on patrol. You will also be the first point of contact for missing persons and lost property enquiries.

- You will need to look after victims and witnesses when they come into the station, which may require providing first aid on occasion.

The type of person suited to this work

You must have excellent communication skills in order to deal with a wide variety of people on a daily basis, ranging from victims to aggressive detainees. Assertiveness, confidence and sensitivity are all desirable personality traits.

You should be happy working within a team, supporting your colleagues, taking directions, and working on your own initiative when required.

You will also need to adhere to confidentiality, diversity and data protection issues.

Working conditions

You will usually work a 37 hour week based on a shift pattern, which will require early morning and weekend work. There are usually part time opportunities.

You will be based within a police station, and will spend most of your time on the front desk answering queries or updating information on a computer. It is unlikely that you will need to travel in the course of your working day.

Stations can get very busy at times, so you should expect to work in pressurised and potentially stressful conditions at times.

Future prospects

The police force operates throughout the length and breadth of the UK, so there are opportunities in all regional forces.

Opportunities for promotion within a station are limited to its size. Larger establishments may have room to move you to a more senior, supervisory role whereas the smaller one will not be able to.

You could move to a more specialised area of support work, such as manning the crime helpdesk, or working in an enquiry centre.

It is possible to train as a police officer from a support role.

Advantages/disadvantages

You will be working within a close knit team, so your support work will be essential to the successful running of the station.

Qualifications and courses

There are no specific academic requirements for entry to the police force, but most employers prefer that you are educated to GCSE standard or equivalent. You must also be aged 18+, a UK or European Union national, or come from within the European Economic Area.

There are several qualifications that would be viewed favourably by employers. These include an NVQ Level 2 or BTEC First Diploma in public services, and the BTEC National Diploma in uniformed public services. Entry requirements for these courses are usually 5 GCSEs/S grades (A*–C/1–3) or equivalent, including English and maths.

If you reach interview stage, you will need to have medical, criminal record, and other background checks to assess your suitability for the role. You must declare any previous convictions prior to this stage.

Once you have been accepted onto the force, your training will be provided by a more experienced support worker and you will learn on the job. Training usually lasts between 3 weeks and 3 months.

Part time and flexible working hours are commonly available.

You will have to deal with difficult, distressed, and occasionally violent members of the public.

Money guide

The starting salary for an entry level police support worker is about £15,500.

With a couple of years' experience, this should rise to around £16,000.

If you pursue promotion and attain a high level administrative role, or become a police officer, you could earn £40,000+.

Related opportunities

- Police Community Support Officer p551
- Police Officer p552
- Secretary p63
- Civil Service/Local Government Administrator p27

Further information

National Police Recruitment Team
www.policecouldyou.co.uk

Police Oracle
www.policeoracle.com

City&
Guilds

www.cityandguilds.com/myperfectjob

PRISON GOVERNOR/ OPERATIONAL MANAGER

What the work involves

- Prison governors/operational managers are responsible for the overall running and security of the establishment.

- You will supervise security measures, make inspections, carry out disciplinary procedures, and advise both staff and inmates on behavioural standards and guidelines.

- You will also be dealing with each prisoner's casework and administration. This will include processing parole applications and complaints, and require liaison with other social and healthcare professionals.

- You will be working within strict parameters set out by the government, and must ensure that you meet their targets on service, health and safety, and prisoner welfare and development.

The type of person suited to this work

You will need excellent communication skills, including confidence, assertiveness and a motivational ability, all of which will be essential when managing and inspiring staff, and also for building effective relationships with inmates.

You must have integrity and be committed to working with vulnerable people with various social issues. This should include respect for those in your care, and for the other professionals working around you.

Working conditions

You will be expected to work on a shift basis, including night and weekend hours, in order to meet the 24 hour needs of the prison. On average, you will work a 39 hour week.

You could work in a modern prison with excellent facilities, or an older, more austere establishment that will come with maintenance problems and perhaps a less comfortable working environment.

Future prospects

Prisons are located in large cities, towns, and very rural locations, so you have a good range of options of the working conditions that would most suit you.

Prison governors are at the top of their sector, so only sideways movements are possible. You could opt to work in a specialist institution, such as one dealing with inmates with specific medical needs. Extra qualifications may be required for this.

Advantages/disadvantages

You could be responsible for turning the lives of inmates around, both by providing them with opportunities whilst serving their sentence, and also by encouraging them to pursue better lives when they leave.

You may have to control difficult and violent situations at times.

Qualifications and courses

Most prisoner governors enter the profession as a prison officer.

Generally, expectations for candidates include good health and physical fitness, Commonwealth, British or European Union nationality, no current or historical association with racist or homophobic groups, and that you have Criminal Records Bureau clearance if you are going to work with inmates under 18 years of age.

If you meet all of the criteria above, you may be asked to attend an assessment day at which employers will observe how you react to the prison environment and work-related simulations, in order to see if you would be suitable for the role.

Once you have gained experience as a prison officer you will need to work your way through supervisory and senior positions, taking relevant work-related qualifications as you go, in order to become a prison governor.

A fast-track initiative, the Intensive Development Scheme (IDS), provides an alternative route into the profession for graduates only, and is designed to encourage rapid progression through the grades into a management position.

Money guide

Prison officers start on around £17,000. Once you have worked through the grades and become a junior governor, your salary will start at around £30,000.

With experience, and on gaining the full title and responsibilities of a prison governor, you could earn between £40,000 and £75,000.

Related opportunities

- Prison Officer/Instructor p555
- Police Officer p552
- Police Community Support Officer p551
- Security Officer/Manager p563

Further information

HM Prison Service
Cleland House, Page Street, London SW1P 4LN
www.hmprisonservice.gov.uk

Scottish Prison Service
Communications Branch, Room 338 Carlton House,
5 Redheughs Rigg, Edinburgh EH12 9HW
0131 244 8745; www.sps.gov.uk; gaolinfo@sps.pnn.gov.uk

www.cityandguilds.com/myperfectjob

PRISON OFFICER/ INSTRUCTOR

What the work involves

- Prison officers are responsible for supervising inmates within a secure institution.

- You will need to build positive relationships with the prisoners in your care in order to educate and encourage them to pursue a law-abiding life.

- You could work with a variety of inmates, ranging from high risk criminals in top security institutions, to those with minor offences in low security prisons.

- Prison instructors undertake the same duties as prison officers, but are also responsible for training prisoners in order to help them develop new skills and qualifications.

The type of person suited to this work

You should have excellent communication skills and be a confident person so that you can interact positively with inmates whilst also retaining your authority when necessary.

You must be non-judgemental and have respect for the prisoners in your care. The ability to remain calm in pressurised or uncomfortable situations is also an asset.

Prison instructors should be approachable and patient. You will need to be understanding and encouraging in order to help prisoners learn and progress.

Working conditions

You will usually work 39 hours a week. Prison officers will work on a shift basis including night and weekend shifts, but prison instructors usually only work during the week.

Most work is indoors and within a prison. Prison officers will also be responsible for supervising outdoor exercise and patrolling the prison grounds. Prison instructors will work in a setting suitable for their subject, for example a workshop within the prison, or in the grounds if they are teaching horticulture.

Some travel between prisons may be expected to provide extra staffing on occasion. Prison officers may also have to escort prisoners to and from court appearances.

Future prospects

Opportunities for promotion are good, and both prison officers and prison instructors can move into a position as a senior officer or principal officer of a prison. Promotion is based solely on merit, so the more you put in the more you can get out of this career.

Advantages/disadvantages

Helping to rehabilitate and educate prisoners can be rewarding, and you will be providing an important public service.

Working in a prison environment can be claustrophobic and stifling.

Qualifications and courses

ENTRY 1 LEVEL

Entry requirements for roles as a prison officer vary throughout the UK. Generally, expectations for candidates include good health and physical fitness, Commonwealth, British or European Union nationality, no current or historical association with racist or homophobic groups, and that you have Criminal Records Bureau clearance if you are going to work with inmates under 18 years of age.

You will also need to undergo a medical and physical fitness assessment, as well as a sight test.

If you meet all of the criteria above, you may be asked to attend an assessment day at which employers will observe how you react to the prison environment and work-related simulations, in order to see if you would be suitable for the role.

Candidates hoping to become a prison instructor must hold a relevant qualification in the subject they wish to teach, such as a degree, NVQ, or City and Guilds Advanced Certificate. You will also need to hold a qualification in health and safety, and be able to demonstrate teaching or supervisory experience.

You may be faced with difficult and occasionally violent prisoners, which can be both stressful and unpleasant.

Money guide

New officers and instructors typically earn around £18,000 in England and Wales. Wages in Scotland are slightly lower at £16,000.

If you become a senior prison officer, after gaining several years of experience, your salary should rise to about £28,654.

Principal officers could earn up to £31,171.

Related opportunities

- Prison Governor/Operational Manager p554
- Police Officer p552
- Police Support Worker p553
- Social Care Worker/Social Worker p583

Further information

HM Prison Service
Cleland House, Page Street, London SW1P 4LN
www.hmprisonservice.gov.uk

City& Guilds

www.cityandguilds.com/myperfectjob

PRIVATE INVESTIGATOR

What the work involves

- You will be collecting information for a private client or a solicitor by asking questions, researching, obtaining evidence and making sense of what you find out.

- Private investigators (PIs) do a variety of different jobs such as surveillance, tracing people, serving legal documents or investigating road accidents, suspected fraud and employee backgrounds.

- You could be recording your findings using a computer, and you may be asked to present your findings in court or to a large company. You will probably take witness statements, attend court hearings and give evidence.

The type of person suited to this work

Much of the day-to-day work of this exciting sounding job is actually quite routine, so you will need to be patient and persistent and be happy with your own company.

You need to be interested in learning about the law.

You will need to have excellent communications skills, both spoken and written in order to write reports and take witness statements. You may need to calm down anxious or aggressive people when you serve legal papers or repossess their car to pay a debt.

Working conditions

Most of your working hours will be spent driving or walking around. You could be in your vehicle for hours or out in all weathers.

Hours are irregular and in some cases they could be long and include evening and weekend work.

You will be at risk of assault from aggressive individuals who you are serving with legal papers.

Future prospects

With the introduction of licensing there may be more opportunities for those with licences. A lot of the work is for legal, insurance or financial companies.

Some private investigators go on to take further qualifications and specialise in areas such as commercial piracy or insurance fraud. A few set up their own agencies and others move into supervisory or security management work. There is the opportunity to progress into a managerial or senior investigator role at bigger agencies.

Advantages/disadvantages

Private investigators are usually self-employed and so need to buy their own equipment. Licences and training will also add to the expense.

A lot of the work is routine, but PIs say that there is a lot of satisfaction when after months of patient work you manage to find the evidence your client needs.

Qualifications and courses

There are no formal entry qualifications for this work. However, many entrants have degrees or advanced level qualifications. Some employers like you to have some experience of work in the police or other security firms.

You will need a driving licence and most successful PIs work in a related job such as the police, law, customs and excise or security work first.

Applicants new to the role would benefit from having a relevant qualification, which may include an NVQ Level 3 in Intelligence Analysis, membership qualifications from the Association of British Investigators (ABI), the Level 3 Award for Professional Investigators from the ABI or a degree in an appropriate subject. You could also take the Institution of Professional Investigators (IPI) Foundation Course for Investigators or the BTEC Advanced Diploma in Private Investigation.

Your training should be accepted by the Security Industry Authority (SIA), and include the topics of the law, investigative methods, equipment and legislation.

A scheme is being introduced where a government licence issued by the SIA will be required to practise. Check with the SIA for the latest developments.

Courses are available from a number of private companies and listed by the ABI. Topics such as theft, court work, investigation and surveillance are offered. A City & Guilds Certificate in Conflict Management and Communication Skills is also available, offered through the National Investigations Group.

Money guide

Starting salaries are around £15,000 per year. Experienced investigators could earn about £30,000. Well-qualified specialists can get £100,000+.

Related opportunities

- Bailiff/Enforcement Agent p362
- Police Officer p552
- Store Detective p565
- Forensic Computer Analyst p548

Further information

Academy of Professional Investigation
The Priory, Syresham Gardens, Haywards Heath RH16 3LB
01444 441111; www.becomeadetective.com

Association of British Investigators
295/297 Church Street, Blackpool FY1 3PJ
01253 297502; www.theabi.org.uk

Institute of Professional Investigators
Claremont House, 70–72 Alma Road, Windsor SL4 3EZ
0870 330 8622; www.ipi.org.uk

ROYAL AIR FORCE (RAF) AIRMAN/WOMAN

What the work involves

- The Royal Air Force (RAF) is responsible for protecting UK airspace, performing search and rescue missions offshore and on land, transporting aid to the victims of war and natural disaster, and pursuing military action in a war situation.

- Opportunities include positions in catering, aircrew, engineering, protection and medical support.

- You will work within a team of other RAF professionals, under the guidance of an officer.

- You will also be expected to undertake general military duties, such as guarding RAF bases, and taking part in training exercises and military initiatives.

The type of person suited to this work

You should be able to work well within a team. This includes being able to follow orders, work calmly under pressure, support colleagues, and use your own initiative when necessary.

You should be self-disciplined in order to maintain high levels of fitness, mental agility, and a positive attitude to your work.

You should be good at interpreting and analysing information, both verbal and written.

Working conditions

Airmen/women usually work regular office hours, but you are required to be available for duty at all times in case of an emergency. There are also occasional social functions or other duties that need to be fulfilled over weekends.

You will be stationed at an RAF base, many of which have all the amenities of a small town.

You should be prepared to be posted overseas at short notice, and to spend long periods of time away from friends and family.

Future prospects

On joining the RAF as an airman/woman, you sign up for a minimum length of service that ranges from 12 months for non-commissioned aircrew, up to 9 years for other specialisations.

After six months or on completion of specialist training, you should be promoted to leading aircraftman/woman, and from there you can work up the ranks to the position of corporal or higher. Promotion is based on merit, so you will be rewarded for the hard work that you put in.

Advantages/disadvantages

You will work on diverse assignments within a supportive team environment, so each day will be both diverse and interesting.

There are good training schemes and potential for promotion and career progression within the RAF.

You may have to enter war situations, which can be traumatic and stressful.

Qualifications and courses

Entry requirements to become an RAF airman/woman vary according to the specialist trade you are looking to work in. Most trades require entrants to be at least 16 years old, and others set a higher age limit. The maximum age of entry is 29.

To become an RAF Regiment gunner, you do not need any formal qualifications. Most other fields require between 2–5 GCSEs/S grades (A*–C/1–3) or equivalent. If you are looking to enter as a student nurse or similar, then you will need 2 A levels or equivalent.

You will need to pass a vigorous medical and fitness entrance test, as well as a range of interview and written tests during the selection process.

It is also essential that you have been registered as a citizen of the UK, Commonwealth or Republic of Ireland since birth.

Once accepted into the RAF, you will complete an 11 week training course at RAF Halton in Buckinghamshire which will cover fitness and weapons training, followed by a 10 week aircraft training course at RAF College Cranwell in Lincolnshire.

On completion of these general elements, you will then start on more specialised training for your chosen trade, and this can take between 3 weeks and 18 months.

Money guide

On completion of your initial 6 months of training, your salary will be £16,500. After 2 or 3 years you could earn between £14,000 and £28,000 depending on your trade.

If you work as a member of non-commissioned aircrew, your salary will be around £27,200 on completion of 6 months initial training. Your salary will rise to between £32,000 and £34,000 once all your training has been completed.

Related opportunities

- Royal Air Force (RAF) Officer p558
- Soldier p564
- Air Traffic Controller p595

Further information

RAF Careers
0845 605 5555; www.raf.mod.uk

RAF Halton
Aylesbury HP22 5PG
www.raf.mod.uk/rafhalton

www.cityandguilds.com/myperfectjob

CRCI: UA

Security and the Armed Forces

ROYAL AIR FORCE OFFICER

What the work involves

- The Royal Air Force (RAF) is responsible for protecting UK airspace, performing search and rescue missions offshore and on land, transporting aid to the victims of war and natural disaster, and pursuing military action in a war situation.

- Royal Air Force officers are responsible for managing, leading and inspiring a team of airmen.

- You will occupy a specialist post within the RAF, such as that of a pilot, engineer, catering manager, or medical officer.

- You will be involved in planning and implementing various procedures from rescues to humanitarian aid drops.

The type of person suited to this work

You must have excellent communication skills as you will be responsible for briefing, leading and motivating your team. This also includes being able to listen and get on with all team members.

You will be called upon to make difficult decisions in highly pressurised situations, so must be able to think on your feet in order to reach mature, responsible conclusions.

You must be physically fit and mentally alert.

Working conditions

Officers usually work regular office hours, but you are required to be available for duty at all times in case of an emergency. There are also occasional social functions or other duties that need to be fulfilled over weekends.

You will be stationed at an RAF base, many of which have all the amenities of a small town, including shops, banks, a gym and childcare facilities.

You should be prepared to be posted overseas at short notice, and to spend long periods of time away from friends and family.

Future prospects

On joining the RAF as an officer, you sign up to a minimum length of service. This can range from 6 to 12 years according to your specialisation.

There is defined career progression through the ranks from flying officer, to flight lieutenant, squadron leader, wing commander, group captain, and further if you wish.

The training, qualifications and personal skills that come with being an RAF officer are easily transferred to a number of civilian positions.

Advantages/disadvantages

You will be responsible for training and organising a team that will carry out essential defence and humanitarian functions for the UK and the world.

You may have to enter combat situations which can be distressing and unpleasant.

Qualifications and courses

ENTRY LEVEL 3

You must be aged between 17½ and 36 to apply for an officer position with the RAF. Some specialisations impose an older age limit.

Most specialisations require applicants to hold at least 2 A levels/Highers or equivalent, and 5 GCSEs/S grades (A*–C/1–3) or equivalent, including English and maths.

Some specialisations, including engineering, legal, and the medical divisions, require a relevant degree. For entrance onto related degree courses, you will need 3 A levels/ Highers or equivalent, as well as at least 5 GCSEs/S grades (A*–C/1–3) or equivalent, including English, maths and science.

You must also be a UK, Commonwealth, or Republic of Ireland citizen since birth. For a role as an intelligence officer, you must have been a British citizen from birth.

If you meet the entrance criteria, you may be invited to attend the four day selection event held at the RAF College Cranwell, in Lincolnshire. During this process, you will have to undertake interviews, fitness and health assessments, and various aptitude tests.

The RAF also offers sponsorship to sixth form and university students.

Money guide

If you enter the RAF without a degree, as a pilot officer, you can expect to earn £23,000 as a starting salary. If you hold a degree and therefore enter as a flying officer, this will increase your starting wages to £28,000.

As a flying officer, you can earn up to £32,000.

On promotion to lieutenant, your salary should rise to between £37,000 and £44,000.

If you become a squadron leader with experience, you could earn £56,075+.

Related opportunities

- Royal Air Force Airman/woman p557
- Air Traffic Controller p595
- Army Officer p540
- Royal Navy Officer p561

Further information

RAF College Cranwell
Sleaford, Lincolnshire NG34 8HB
0845 605 5555; www.cranwell.raf.mod.uk

City& Guilds

www.cityandguilds.com/myperfectjob

ROYAL MARINES COMMANDO

What the work involves

- The Royal Marines are a specialist, highly trained, amphibious division of the Royal Navy. They carry out operations on land, in the sea or in the air. They operate in combat, peacekeeping and humanitarian situations, and also as a law enforcement agency at sea.

- You will be a commando and rifleman, working within an operational commando unit.

- You will be ready to take immediate action in any emergency or threat to national security, and this means performing to a very high standard at all times whether on land or at sea.

- You will specialise either in general duties, or in one of 26 trades which include assault engineer, mountain leader or swimmer canoeist.

The type of person suited to this work

You will need high levels of fitness, discipline, commitment and self-confidence in order to get through one of the most demanding and gruelling training programmes in the armed forces prior to qualifying as a commando.

You must be able to work well within a team and also use your own initiative when required. The ability to lead and motivate others is also an asset.

You should be level-headed and be able to react quickly and logically when under pressure. Courage and determination are also necessary in order to head into combat situations.

Working conditions

You will usually work 37 hours a week, unless you are on an operation or in training. In these instances, you could expect to work long, unpredictable hours. Even if you are not at work, though, you will always be on call in case of emergency.

You could be stationed or deployed anywhere in the world at short notice, including undertaking operations in areas of desert, jungle, and even out in the Arctic.

You will be expected to wear a uniform.

Future prospects

Within the UK, you are most likely to be stationed within the south west of England or in Scotland, as that is where the majority of naval bases are located.

You will be expected to serve with the Royal Marines for 22 years, although you can leave at any point after completing the minimum 3 years of service and giving 12 months notice.

You will be promoted on merit, so hard work should be rewarded. You could move up the ranks from lance corporal right up to warrant officer 1.

Advantages/disadvantages

You will be operating at your optimum level of mental and

Qualifications and courses

There is a rigorous selection process. You will need to attend an interview and pass a medical examination.

You will also have to undertake the Potential Royal Marines Course. This lasts 2.5 days and is designed to test your fitness, determination, stamina and mental ability. This is a gruelling assessment designed to push you to your limits, so you will have to train and prepare for it for a number of months.

You must be between 17 and 32 years of age to apply to the Royal Marines. They also require candidates to be at least 151.5cm tall and 60kg in weight.

You will also have to prove that you have been a citizen of Britain, Ireland or the Commonwealth since birth, and will have to submit to a detailed security clearance before you can be considered for entry.

physical fitness, meeting new challenges each day and adapting to unusual and inhospitable situations.

You will be working within a close knit team, providing essential services such as delivering aid or maintaining order in areas across the globe.

You are continually on call, and could be sent anywhere in the world at a moment's notice.

Money guide

New entrants to the Royal Marines at commando level receive a starting salary of £13,000.

Once you have completed your training, this should rise to about £16,000. With increasing experience you could expect to earn up to £28,300.

If you move up the ranks and reach the level of warrant officer 1 you should earn £45,836.

Related opportunities

- Royal Marines Officer p560
- Army Officer p540
- Soldier p564
- Royal Air Force (RAF) Airman/Woman p557

Further information

The Royal Marines
0845 600 1444; www.royalnavy.mod.uk/royalmarines/

www.cityandguilds.com/myperfectjob

Security and the Armed Forces

CRCI: UA

ROYAL MARINES OFFICER

What the work involves

- The Royal Marines carry out operations on land, in the sea or in the air. They operate in combat, peacekeeping and humanitarian situations, and also as a law enforcement agency at sea.

- You will be responsible for leading and managing a team both on training operations and on real missions including combat situations and peace-keeping tasks.

- You will be in charge of training your team, keeping them disciplined, and looking out for their welfare.

- You will be given the opportunity to specialise in one of 10 areas, including weapons training, signals, physical training, or as a pilot.

The type of person suited to this work

You will need high levels of fitness, discipline, commitment and self-confidence in order to get through the demanding and gruelling training programme prior to qualifying as an officer.

You must be able to lead and motivate your team, looking out for their welfare and making decisions for them in dangerous and stressful conditions.

You should be able to focus on the operations you undertake fully in order to function at your maximum level of mental and physical capacity.

Working conditions

You will usually work 37 hours a week, unless you are on an operation or in training. In these instances, you could expect to work long, unpredictable hours. Even if you are not at work, you are always on call in case of emergency.

You could be stationed or deployed anywhere in the world at short notice, including undertaking operations in areas of desert, jungle, and even out in the Arctic.

You will be expected to wear a uniform, and specialised clothing when required.

Future prospects

Competition for entry as a Royal Marines officer is fierce. You will be expected to join on a 12 year commission, and must serve at least 3–5 years of this. 12 months notice is required prior to departure.

You will normally move appointments every other year, so you will be able to experience numerous areas of work in various locations throughout your career.

Promotion is awarded on merit, and you could work through the ranks from 2nd lieutenant right up to major-general.

Advantages/disadvantages

You will be operating at your optimum level of mental and physical fitness, meeting new challenges each day and adapting to unusual and inhospitable situations.

Qualifications and courses

ENTRY LEVEL 3

Although most applicants are graduates, the minimum entry criteria are at least 2 A levels/ Highers or equivalent, and 5 GCESs/S grades (A*–C/1–3) including English language and maths.

Only men can serve as Royal Marines officers, and you must be between 17 and 26 years old to enter. You must be at least 151.5cm tall and 60kg in weight, and meet strict medical, fitness and eyesight criteria. You must also have British or dual British nationality and have lived in the UK for a minimum of 5 years.

You will attend a 3 day Potential Officers Course, which is a gruelling assessment designed to push you to your limits.

If you successfully complete the 3 day assessment, you will be invited to attend a further 2½ day interview process, during which you will sit further tests in maths, reasoning, accuracy, written communication, spatial orientation, leadership, and problem solving and undergo a series of interviews.

If you are selected to train as an officer, you will then have to complete a further 15 month programme prior to being given your own team to lead.

You will be working within a close knit team, leading them through essential operations such as delivering aid or maintaining order in areas across the globe.

Money guide

Entrants who do not have a degree can expect a starting salary of £15,000 at the start of their training, rising to £23,500 on completion. Graduates start on £24,000 and can progress to £31,200 on completion of their training.

If you become a captain, you can expect to earn between £36,100 and £43,000.

High ranking colonels can earn between £77,500 and £85,300.

Related opportunities

- Royal Marines Commando p559
- Army Officer p540
- Soldier p564
- Royal Air Force (RAF) Officer p558

Further information

The Royal Marines
0845 600 1444; www.royalnavy.mod.uk/royalmarines/

City& Guilds

www.cityandguilds.com/myperfectjob

ROYAL NAVY OFFICER

What the work involves

- You will command and train ratings, looking after their welfare, development and discipline.

- Your day-to-day work will involve you managing operations in one of four areas of duty: as a warfare officer, engineer officer, supply officer or specialist officer (for example chaplain, doctor or dentist).

- Your ship may be sent into combat or on peacekeeping duties.

- You may be tasked to do a specific job such as policing the North Sea fishing grounds or helping out in a disaster situation.

The type of person suited to this work

Officers especially need top-level leadership and communication skills as well as good judgement. You will be required to inspire ratings, be resourceful and have excellent communication skills. You should have good levels of physical fitness and stamina. You may need to work in combat zones.

You should also have a very strong sense of responsibility as your decisions may impact upon your colleagues' safety as well as your own. You should display a very high level of personal awareness and a keen sense of personal safety.

Working conditions

Most of your work will be on board a ship or submarine, or at land-based establishments in Britain or overseas. At sea, conditions can be cold, cramped and damp.

You will need to wear a uniform, and protective clothing when necessary.

Hours vary but you will usually work 8-hour turns of duty on a shift rota including weekends and holidays.

You may find yourself working in a dangerous or highly unpredictable situation.

Future prospects

There are over 7,500 officers in the Royal Navy. There are annual vacancies but some specialisms are more competitive than others. A naval college entrant usually starts out as midshipman rising to sub-lieutenant after 2 years. A graduate starts as sub-lieutenant rising to lieutenant commander by their early 30s. If you have got the right qualities you can progress on to the ranks of commander, captain and, for a few, admiral.

Advantages/disadvantages

You will be trained to a high level and will be offered a resettlement package to help you find work in civilian life when you leave.

You will be living in cramped conditions with lots of other people. However, most officers say that they enjoy the feeling of camaraderie on board and make life-long friendships.

Qualifications and courses

You will need to be at least 151.5cm tall and be of proportionate weight. A medical, with strict eyesight standards, must be passed, and you must meet the Royal Navy nationality and residence requirements. Women can still not enter the submarine or mine clearance diving branches of the Royal Navy.

There are several entry points for Officers: Non-Graduate Entry for those aged 17–26 who have at least 5 GCSEs (A*–C)/S grades including English language and maths and 2 A levels totalling 180 UCAS points/H grades.

The Defence Sixth Form College (Welbeck) focuses on gaining entry to the Armed Forces.

There is also the Defence Technical Undergraduate Scheme (DTUS) for those under 23 with 5 GCSEs/S grades including English language and maths and 240 tariff points including grade C in maths and physics. You are sponsored to complete an engineering degree before joining the Royal Navy. All candidates undergo a selection interview and medical examination before the Admiralty Interview Board (AIB). Training takes place at Britannia Royal Naval College, Dartmouth, Devon.

Money guide

Entering this career you can expect to start on £15,000 as a midshipman, but this will increase to between £20,000 and £25,000 once you have completed basic training.

As a graduate sub-lieutenant you can earn £25,000–£30,000 a year. Rising through the ranks to the level of captain could see you earning £80,000+.

Related opportunities

- Army Officer p540
- Royal Air Force (RAF) Officer p558
- Royal Marines Officer p560
- Royal Navy Rating p562

Further information

Armed Forces Careers Navy
0845 607 5555; www.royalnavy.mod.uk

Welbeck Defence 6th Form College
Forest Road, Woodhouse, Loughborough LE12 8WD
0150 1 891700; helpdesk@dsfc.ac.uk

www.cityandguilds.com/myperfectjob

Security and the Armed Forces

CRCI: UA

ROYAL NAVY RATING

Security and the Armed Forces

CRCI: UA

What the work involves

- The Royal Navy protects the UK's ports and coastline, and also undertakes international missions such as delivering humanitarian aid, entering combat, and enforcing the law on the seas.

- Royal Navy ratings work on board a ship, submarine or onshore, and are responsible for operating, maintaining and repairing technical equipment.

- You will specialise in one of the six main trades; medical, warfare, logistics, engineering, fleet air arm, or submarine.

- You will take part in naval exercises and operations both in UK and overseas waters.

The type of person suited to this work

You should be able to work within a team, reacting quickly to orders, working on your own initiative where necessary, and supporting other team members both professionally and emotionally at times.

You must be responsible and decisive and find solutions to problems under difficult or pressurised circumstances. You should also have a methodical and logical approach to your work.

You will need to have a good level of fitness, including the ability to swim and tread water for a number of minutes.

Working conditions

You will usually work 37 hours a week, which can include weekends and public holidays. You will also be on call at all times, in case of an emergency.

You could be based at sea on a ship or submarine, or in a naval station onshore. Living conditions on ships and submarines tend to be basic, and men and women always sleep in separate accommodation.

You will have to spend long periods of time away from friends and family, and may be posted overseas at a moment's notice.

Future prospects

The career progression for a Royal Navy rating is clearly mapped out. Promotion is awarded on merit so the harder you work the faster you will progress. The grades that you will move upwards through are able rating, leading rating, petty officer, chief petty officer, and warrant officer.

If you have the necessary qualifications, you could apply to become an officer. This is a popular route of career progression amongst ratings.

Advantages/disadvantages

You will be meeting new challenges each day and adapting to unusual and inhospitable situations, which will keep you

Qualifications and courses

ENTRY LEVEL 2

There are no formal qualifications for entry, but holding at least 2 GCSEs/S grades (A*–C/1–3) or equivalent is helpful. Some specialist trades have entry requirements and a higher age for admission. Typically, you must be 16 to 36 years of age to apply.

Selection takes place at local armed forces careers offices, where you will be required to take several tests including numeracy, English language, reasoning and mechanical comprehension. If you are successful, you will be invited for an interview. You must also pass a medical assessment and fitness test.

You will join the Royal Navy on a Full Career, which lasts 18 years. You can leave after completing 2.5 years training but must give 12 months notice.

Upon entry you will undertake 9 weeks basic training, followed by specialist training in your chosen trade.

mentally and physically alert and ensures the work never gets dull.

You will be working within a close knit team, supporting them both in practice and when out on real operations.

You are continually on call, and could be sent anywhere in the world at a moment's notice.

Money guide

You will enter the Royal Navy as a rating on a starting salary of £12,500.

Once you have completed your training and have qualified as an able rating, this will rise to £15,700 and, as you continue to learn and progress, could reach £26,600.

If you are promoted to the role of leading rating, your salary will increase to between £24,300 and £30,500.

Related opportunities

- Royal Marines Commando p559
- Royal Navy Officer p561
- Soldier p564
- Royal Air Force (RAF) Airman/woman p557

Further information

The Royal Navy
0845 607 5555; www.royalnavy.mod.uk

City&
Guilds

www.cityandguilds.com/myperfectjob

SECURITY OFFICER/MANAGER/ DOOR SUPERVISOR

What the work involves

- Security work is about protecting organisations, people, places, valuable goods or money.

Officer

- You might work at reception monitoring visitors and deliveries or you might patrol a site, checking for intruders or fire risks.

Manager

- You will manage a team and be responsible for their work, training and supervision. You will do security surveys, give advice on improvements and liaise with other organisations such as the emergency services.

Door supervisor

- You will stand at the entrance to a building and help control people entering and leaving, judging whether or not they should be allowed on the premises. You could also search bags and assist the police if trouble breaks out.

The type of person suited to this work

You will need to be a mature, responsible and honest person. You should be keen on technology and keep up to date with new security systems. You will also have to keep records of all incidents, so you must be happy to do paperwork.

To become a manager you will need a great deal of experience in security work as well as a talent for motivating a team of staff.

Working conditions

If you are a door supervisor you will be based in one location which could be inside, or outside in all weathers. Many security officer/manager jobs involve driving and you will spend a lot of time in a security van.

You will probably be working shifts of up to 12 hours covering days, nights and weekends. Some door supervisors or security officers work permanent nights. You may work a 48-hour week although part-time work is available.

Future prospects

This work will increasingly use sophisticated technology, computer security systems and also biometrics (fingerprint recognition systems) to control access to buildings and other secure areas. With the right training and technical ability you are likely to be in demand in this growing industry.

Advantages/disadvantages

Your promotion and earnings prospects are excellent.

You could often work alone and be put in vulnerable situations.

Qualifications and courses

Officer

All security guards must have an industry licence, approved by the Security Industry Authority (SIA). The licence is awarded to candidates who pass the two-part assessment process, usually delivered over 4 days.

For a licence you will need a City & Guilds Level 2 Certificate for security guards, a BTEC Level 2 Award or an EDI Level 2 Certificate in Security Guarding.

Manager

In addition to the SIA licence specialist managers may need specific training and experience, for example in security systems, legislation and anti-terrorist work.

Door supervisor

You will need an SIA licence which requires you to be over 18, have an SIA-approved Level 2 Certificate in door supervision and pass a Criminal Record Bureau check.

Money guide

Officer

Starting out, officers are paid up to £10 per hour. With experience this can rise to £20,000 per year.

Manager

On entry, managers earn £26,500–£28,500 per year, rising to £35,000+ with experience. Area managers can earn £50,000+ and international security managers can earn up to £70,000.

Door supervisor

Door supervisors earn up to £12 per hour; up to £17,000 per year full time. With experience this can rise to £28,000.

Related opportunities

- Bodyguard p541
- Prison Officer/Instructor p554
- Police Officer p552

Further information

Security Industry Authority
PO Box 1293, Liverpool L69 1AX
0844 892 1025; www.the-sia.org.uk

www.cityandguilds.com/myperfectjob

Security and the Armed Forces

CRCI: UK

SOLDIER

What the work involves

- The Army is responsible for defending the UK and its allies across the world, as well as taking part in peacekeeping and humanitarian operations.

- You will be involved in regular training exercises to ensure you maintain a high level of fitness and military skills so that you are ready for combat at any time.

- You will also choose to train and work within one of more than 130 different trades.

- You may be posted to dangerous areas and inhospitable environments at any time, whether for peacekeeping and aid missions, or to engage in warfare.

The type of person suited to this work

You should be able to work within a team, reacting quickly to orders, working on your own initiative where necessary, and supporting other team members both professionally and emotionally at times.

You must be extremely disciplined and responsible, with the ability to think and act logically under pressure.

You must be physically fit with excellent stamina.

You should be practical, with good manual dexterity, so that you will be able to operate various machines and equipment.

Working conditions

Your hours will depend upon which trade you choose to specialise in. Some soldiers work normal office hours, whilst others are expected to undertake shifts that encompass night and weekend work.

You could be stationed in the UK or overseas, and must be prepared for life in a number of environments including deserts, war torn cities, and mountains.

Future prospects

There is a constant demand for new recruits, so career prospects are good if you meet the selection criteria.

You will sign up for an open engagement lasting 22 years, but you can leave after serving 4 years. You must give 12 months notice prior to leaving.

All soldiers start as a private, and are awarded promotion according to their increasing levels of skill and commitment.

Advantages/disadvantages

You will be meeting new challenges each day and adapting to unusual and inhospitable situations, which will ensure the work never gets dull.

You will be working within a close knit team, supporting their work both in practice and actually out on operations.

You are continually on call, and could be sent anywhere in the world at a moment's notice.

Qualifications and courses

There are no formal qualifications for entry, but holding at least 2 GCSEs/S grades (A*–C/1–3) or equivalent is recommended. Some jobs such as vehicle mechanic have specific entry requirements.

You will need to complete the Army Entrance Test (known as BARB) and undergo an interview. Once these stages are done, you will take a physical assessment, medical, and a further interview.

Entrants aged 16 or 17 enter as a junior recruit and have to complete phase 1 and 2 training, which can take between 35 weeks and 2 years.

Entrants who are aged 18 or over will attend training programmes according to the regiment they wish to join. Adult infantry soldiers go to the Infantry Training Centre (ITC) to complete a 24 week Combat Infantryman's Course.

Those planning to join the Royal Engineers, Household Cavalry, Royal Armoured Corps or Royal Artillery attend an Army Training Regiment (ATR) where they undertake a 12 week course in weapon handling, navigation, fieldcraft, drill, health and safety, and personal administration. They then join their chosen regiment to undertake further, more specific training.

Money guide

New entrants to the Army can expect to earn £13,000. Once you have qualified as a private, this will increase to between £16,600 and £25,800. If you become a sergeant, you can expect to earn £29,400–£36,200.

In addition to a basic salary, you will receive subsidised accommodation and food, medical and dental care, discounted rail fares and subsidised nursery facilities.

Related opportunities

- Army Officer p540
- Royal Navy Rating p562
- Royal Marines Commando p559
- Royal Air Force (RAF) Airman/Woman p557

Further information

Army
www.army.mod.uk; www.armyjobs.mod.uk

Welbeck College
Forest Road, Woodhouse, Loughborough LE12 8WD
011509 891700; helpdesk@dsfc.ac.uk

City&
Guilds

www.cityandguilds.com/myperfectjob

STORE DETECTIVE

What the work involves

- You will be preventing and detecting theft or fraud in a retail outlet. You might need to chase the suspected offender and make arrests.

- Working undercover, wearing plain clothes, you will merge with shoppers, looking out for suspicious behaviour or theft.

- Using a radio you will call for assistance and listen for alerts from other staff about known offenders entering the store.

- You will make notes of any incidents and may need to use these if a decision is made to prosecute.

The type of person suited to this work

You need to have excellent communications skills as it will be your responsibility to deal with customers who have become anxious or aggressive when challenged. Your written reports will be used in court if you prosecute and you will need to be fluent and precise to get a conviction.

You must have good observation skills in order to spot suspicious behaviour and also remember the faces of known shoplifters. You should be able to plan and think ahead so that when a situation happens you can act quickly.

You will need to be mature, responsible and be able to handle difficult situations sensitively.

Working conditions

You will spend the majority of your time on your feet, in the store.

A 40-hour week is common and you may work shifts to cover long opening hours and weekends. You might wear a uniform but the majority wear their own clothes to blend in.

Future prospects

Shoplifters cost stores more than £2 billion a year so most large stores in the UK employ store detectives to minimise their losses. Some retail chains employ their own detectives, while others use agencies on a contract basis.

After gaining experience, you could become a supervisor or move into more general security management.

Advantages/disadvantages

Apprehending and successfully prosecuting shoplifters can be dangerous.

This job can be a good stepping stone into jobs such as security management.

Qualifications and courses

There are no formal entry requirements, but you will need to be able to write clearly and accurately. A GCSE/S grade in English or a Key Skill in Communication would be useful.

You will have to undergo a police check. Some employers may also do an employment history and credit check.

Previous relevant work experience is preferred, especially within the police, prison or security industry.

Training is through courses or on the job. Most companies run an induction course for new employees covering topics such as relevant criminal law and principles of investigation.

The Security Institute and the International Professional Security Association both offer courses by distance learning. This includes the NVQ at Level 2 in Providing Security Services.

The Security Industry Authority (SIA) now has a requirement for you to be licensed to operate as a store detective.

Money guide

Starting wages are usually around £12,000–£15,000 per year.

Experienced store detectives can earn up to £20,000. £28,000+ is possible for top earners.

Related opportunities

- Police Officer p552
- Private Investigator p556
- Security Officer/Manager p563

Further information

Security Industry Authority
PO Box 1293, Liverpool L69 1AX
0844 892 1025; www.the-sia.org.uk

British Security Industry Association
Kirkham House, John Comyn Drive, Worcester WR3 7NS
0845 389 3889; www.bsia.co.uk

www.cityandguilds.com/myperfectjob

Security and the Armed Forces

CRCI: UK

Social Work and Counselling Services

People who work in this sector are dedicated to caring and talking through people's problems and anxieties to improve their general wellbeing and their future prospects in life. The work requires a lot of patience, an open mind and a friendly and approachable personality. You could be helping people who are distressed and need help and guidance but equally you may be helping people who want to move on to the next stage in their careers or educational choices. Either way, you should be someone who enjoys helping people change their lives for the better. If you are interested in working in this field you need to show that you are compassionate and very good at communicating with people from all walks of life and of all ages. You should also be someone who can maintain a strong sense of professionalism as you could be in a position of trust and you must be very respectful of your clients' privacy.

In this section we look at the following jobs:

For similar jobs to the ones covered in this section turn to *Healthcare* on page 287 and *Education and Training* on page 189.

CAREERS ADVISER

What the work involves

- You will help people make realistic choices about education, training and work by listening to their ideas, discussing their interests and skills, and providing information on different jobs.

- Researching information about job opportunities in different sectors from newspapers, books, the internet or through visits to employers is all part of the role.

- Advisory work is one to one, but you could work with large groups.

- Careers advisers work with young people in schools/colleges, but also with higher education students or adults.

The type of person suited to this work

Since much of the work involves talking and listening to people, careers advisers need to have excellent communication skills.

You will need to be impartial, allowing people to come to their own decisions rather than making up their minds for them.

Careers information and guidance is largely ICT-based, so computer skills are essential, along with the ability to write reports and perform administrative tasks.

You will need to enjoy researching, as you will need to keep up to date with any changes in skills and opportunities available, and with any new qualifications and training routes.

Working conditions

Most of your work is office-based, either in a careers centre open to the public or an educational establishment.

You will travel between different educational establishments and visit employers and training organisations, which means that a driving licence may be required.

Some time will be spent in a careers centre or library, keeping up to date with job information.

Future prospects

Careers advisers work in schools, colleges, universities and adult guidance services – some will be based in one institution, others will work for several organisations.

You could move into a managerial-level post in a careers service, work for a large company as a careers manager or you could become self-employed as a consultant or researcher.

Ongoing professional development is essential.

Qualifications and courses

There are two main routes into this profession: the Qualification in Careers Guidance (QCG) or the work-based route leading to NVQ/SVQ Level 4 in Advice and Guidance. The Foundation degree in Working with Young People and Young People's Services also provides a useful background.

The QCG is a 1-year full-time or 2-year part-time course at university. People already working for a careers guidance organisation can follow a work-based route to the NVQ/SVQ Level 4.

You do not need a professional careers qualification to work as a careers adviser in higher education, although most successful candidates do have a qualification or have experience working in higher education. A specialist qualification for higher education careers advisers, the Certificate/Diploma in Careers Education, Information and Guidance in Higher Education, is available.

Advantages/disadvantages

The work is varied and can be highly satisfying.

You will work some evenings or weekends to attend school/college parents' evenings and for careers events.

The job also includes a great deal of administrative work.

Money guide

Pay is around £17,000 when training.

Salaries can reach £20,000–£27,500 when fully qualified and with some experience.

Salaries for middle management are around £35,000 and as a senior manager you can earn £55,000+.

Related opportunities

- Debt Counsellor/Money Advice Caseworker p572
- Counsellor p571
- Human Resources/Personnel Officer p41
- Teacher p202
- Youth and Community Worker p589

Further information

Institute of Careers Guidance
3rd Floor, Copthall House, 1 New Road, Stourbridge DY8 1PH
01384 376464; www.icg-uk.org

Careers Research and Advisory Council
2nd Floor, Sheraton House, Castle Park, Cambridge CB3 0AX
01223 460277; www.crac.org.uk

CRCI: V Social Work and Counselling Services

CHILDMINDER

What the work involves

- You will care for children in your own home, ensuring they are comfortable and happy.

- You will plan the children's day and keep parents informed, for example if a child has been unwell.

- You could accompany children to and from playgroup, nursery or school.

- For children aged under 5, you will have to follow the guidelines set by the Early Years Foundation Stage for play-based learning.

The type of person suited to this work

As a childminder you must be patient and caring. Creativity is needed to plan varied activities for children of different ages. You must also be adaptable and prepared to change your plans at short notice to meet the changing needs of the children in your care.

You need to share information with parents on a daily basis which means that good observation and communication skills are important.

As you will be self-employed, you will need to be organised, with good administrative and numeracy skills to work out tax and invoices. ICT skills are useful.

Working conditions

You are allowed to care for up to six children, including your own, under the age of 8 providing that only three are less than 5 years old.

You will work in your own home which may have to be altered to meet childminding standards by fitting equipment such as stairgates and socket covers.

A driving licence is useful as you may take children to playgroup or school.

You will do a lot of lifting and clearing up and will be on the go from very early morning into the evening.

Future prospects

Although the minimum age for entry is 18, most childminders are older, with experience of care work. The demand for childminders can vary regionally and at different times of the year.

Childminders can become care assistants or home care assistants, or can go on to train for similar work as a nursery nurse or registered nurse.

Advantages/disadvantages

The work will be varied and fun.

Working from home often suits people who have young children themselves.

Some jobs can be messy and unpleasant.

The hours can be very long and it can sometimes be hard work for low pay.

Qualifications and courses

Qualifications in childcare are useful. Candidates must be aged 18 or over. They, and everyone in their households over 16, must be police checked.

You could study for BTEC Certificates and Diplomas in Children's Care or Learning and Development, the Diploma in Society, Health and Development and the OCR Entry Level certificate in Child Development. A City & Guilds qualification in Early Years Foundation Stage Practice is also available. You could also take an Apprenticeship in Children's Care, Learning and Development or NVQ at Levels 2–5 in Children's Care, Learning and Development.

Childminders must register with Ofsted in England, the Care Commission in Scotland, the Care and Social Services Inspectorate in Wales and the local Health and Social Services board or trust in Northern Ireland. You need to take an introductory childminding training course and be prepared for a registration visit.

Money guide

Most childminders charge an hourly rate for each child of between £3 and £6 an hour. Your income can vary at different times of the year: for example, your hours might go up or down during school holidays.

You can expect around £6,000–£10,000 per year when starting out, rising to £15,000 when experienced. Top hourly rates are charged in London where experienced, full-time childminders can earn up to £20,000.

Related opportunities

- Children's Nurse p294
- Early Years Specialist/Nursery Worker p192
- Playworker/Hospital Play Specialist p201

Further information

National Childminding Association of England and Wales
Royal Court, 81 Tweedy Road, Bromley BR1 1TG
0845 880 0044; www.ncma.org.uk

Scottish Childminding Association
7 Melville Terrace, Stirling FK8 2ND
01786 445377; www.childminding.org

Northern Ireland Childminding Association
16–18 Mill Street, Newtownards BT23 4LU
0871 200 2063; www.nicma.org

www.cityandguilds.com/myperfectjob

CLINICAL/HEALTH PSYCHOLOGIST

What the work involves

Clinical psychologist

- You will work with people whose health problems affect their behaviour, to learn what they do and why they do it.

Health psychologist

- This is a new and rapidly growing field of applied psychology which promotes changes in people's attitudes, behaviour and thinking about health.

The type of person suited to this work

As the work is mostly about people and their behaviour, an interest in people, their personalities, abilities and interests is essential. The work involves contact with many different types of people which means you must be good at relating to others and have excellent communication skills.

Psychologists must think logically, analyse data and statistics, and work in an organised and methodical way. They need administrative and ICT skills for writing reports and analyses, and presenting information at case conferences or company meetings.

Working conditions

Clinical psychologist

Your work will take you to schools, colleges, hospitals and health centres. You may find yourself working with social services or with adolescent and child mental health services. Most clinical psychologists are employed by the NHS.

Health psychologist

You will be based in an office but you may also travel to different health centres such as hospitals.

Future prospects

Entry to psychology degrees is competitive and it takes a long time to become a chartered psychologist. The jobs available tend to be within government services, education and health, in the public and private sectors. Ongoing professional development will be important throughout your career.

Clinical psychologist

Clinical psychologists, a very large specialist area, work mainly in the Health Service but there are also opportunities in the Civil Service and private practice.

Health psychologist

Health psychology is a rapidly growing field with opportunities in many health-related areas.

Advantages/disadvantages

The work is varied, interesting and challenging. You will meet many different types of people.

Qualifications and courses

Entrants must be graduates with Graduate Basis for Chartered Membership (GBC) with the British Psychological Society (BPS). Graduate Basis for Registration (GBR) can be obtained by taking a BPS-accredited degree in psychology or a non-accredited degree plus a conversion course.

Additional postgraduate training is usually required to specialise.

Clinical psychologist

To specialise, you need to follow a BPS-accredited 3-year postgraduate training course, which is mostly hospital based. This is full time only and will lead to a Doctorate in Clinical Psychology. To start training you will need lots of experience which can be in the form of working as a psychological assistant or volunteering with the NHS.

Health psychologist

A BPS-accredited MSc and 2 years of appropriate supervised experience are essential for professional recognition. If you want to achieve chartered status and your course is not BPS accredited it is still possible to do this if you sit the BPS qualifying examination which would give you GBR.

Some people may be aggressive or even violent and you may sometimes have difficulty remaining impartial.

Money guide

Clinical psychologist

Working for the NHS you can expect your salary to start at around £26,000 whilst working as a trainee clinical psychologist. Once you reach a very senior position your salary could increase to £75,000 and more.

Health psychologist

You can expect to start on around £17,000 if you start work as an assistant. Pay rises with experience to between £27,500 and £40,000 and as a senior health psychologist with the NHS salaries can reach £60,000.

Related opportunities

- Educational Psychologist p573
- Occupational Psychologist p578

Further information

NHS Careers
0345 606 0655; www.nhscareers.nhs.uk

The British Association for Counselling and Psychology
BACP House, 15 St John's Business Park,
Lutterworth LE17 4HB
01455 883300; www.bacp.co.uk

COUNSELLOR

What the work involves

- Counsellors listen to what their clients say and ask questions in response, to help them explore, talk about and eventually resolve their problems.

- You will help your clients to see things more clearly, perhaps from a different point of view.

- You will not tell people what to do but will help them work out their next steps themselves.

- You might work with people with a range of problems or specialise in a particular area, such as bereavement, gambling, relationship difficulties or eating disorders.

The type of person suited to this work

As most of the work involves talking and listening to people, excellent communication skills are essential.

As clients come from a variety of backgrounds and have a wide range of problems, you must be able to work with people from different cultures and ethnic groups.

Counselling workers may not always agree with the views held by their clients, which means they have to be open-minded and tolerant. You must also be highly discreet as you will be given a lot of confidential information.

You need to be interested in how the mind works, and in people's welfare.

Working conditions

You will work indoors, usually sitting in a quiet, comfortable room in places such as advice centres, schools, colleges, outpatient clinics and health centres.

If you are self-employed, you might work from home, visit your clients at home, or both. Some counselling work is done exclusively over the phone.

You will work mainly with people on a one-to-one basis but also, on occasions, with couples, families or groups. Most counselling sessions last 50 minutes.

You may work in the evenings and at weekends and many counsellors work part time.

Future prospects

Most people gain voluntary experience before moving into part time paid work. They usually have experience in a career such as social work, nursing or teaching.

While the demand is increasing, there is keen competition for full time posts and many people combine counselling work with another role.

You could work in education or health, or with a specialist agency. Experienced counselling workers can become self-employed or train for a specialist area.

Qualifications and courses

ENTRY LEVEL 4

Counselling is often a second career, and maturity and experience are beneficial. It is rare for someone to enter a full time position in this field before their mid 20s. Entrants might have worked as teachers/lecturers, personal tutors, careers advisers, social workers or nurses, or in other fields.

Certificate courses in counselling skills and theory take 1 year part time. A Diploma/Advanced Diploma course lasts 2–3 years, studying part time.

To obtain the British Association for Counselling and Psychotheraphy accreditation, candidates need to have studied a course lasting 1 year full time or 2–3 years part time, and must have a certain number of hours in practice.

Advantages/disadvantages

The work can be very rewarding but also highly stressful. Starting salaries can be low, until you are fully trained and have gained some experience.

You must be able to take constructive criticism from an experienced counselling worker, therapist or psychoanalyst – both during and after completing training.

Some clients may become dependent on therapy or analysis sessions and will have to be carefully assisted to refocus.

Money guide

Expect £19,000–£25,000 per year when newly qualified.

Qualified and experienced counselling workers earn £35,000.

Earnings can reach £40,000–£50,000 with management responsibilities.

Counsellors are paid £30–£60 an hour in private practice.

Related opportunities

- Careers Adviser p568
- Debt Counsellor p572
- Mental Health Nurse p317

Further information

British Association for Counselling and Psychotherapy
BACP House, 15 St John's Business Park,
Lutterworth LE17 4HB
01455 883 300; www.bacp.co.uk

Counselling and Psychotherapy Central Award Body
PO Box 1768, Glastonbury BA6 8XP
01458 850 350; www.cpcab.co.uk

City& Guilds

www.cityandguilds.com/myperfectjob

CRCI: V **Social Work and Counselling Services**

DEBT COUNSELLOR/ MONEY ADVICE CASEWORKER

What the work involves

- It will be your responsibility to give free, impartial and confidential advice to people in serious debt.

- You will have to guide your clients through the legal procedures and represent them if they are being taken to court.

- To ensure clients are claiming available tax allowances and benefits, you will list clients' income and expenditure, then help them plan their spending by devising a budget.

- By liaising with creditors, you will try to arrange realistic repayments over a reasonable timescale.

The type of person suited to this work

People experience money problems for reasons such as unemployment and bad money management. You will need to work with very different people and be non-judgemental about their circumstances. You will need good communication skills and a confident manner so that people trust you.

Much of the work involves figures, so you do need high-level numeracy skills. It is important to be a quick-thinking negotiator to get the best deal for your clients.

Good time management is essential, as are excellent ICT skills. This job suits people who have worked in financial services.

Working conditions

You could meet your clients face to face in an office or advise them through a telephone helpline. You could also spend time in court or at meetings.

You could travel around locally, so a driving licence is useful. You will have to work some evenings, to visit your clients at home, perhaps doing shift work. Other agencies may contact you for advice on money matters.

Future prospects

Although money advisers are in demand, there are more applicants than jobs. Most openings are town- or city-based, in Citizens Advice Bureaux, advice centres or money advice units.

As funding is supported by local authorities or voluntary organisations, the majority of vacancies are for 2-year contracts.

You could progress into specialist casework. If you work for a big company, there could be opportunities for progression into a role as team leader or supervisor. You could move into other social care jobs or change to work in the financial sector.

Advantages/disadvantages

Helping clients to manage and get rid of their debt can be rewarding.

Qualifications and courses

There are no fixed minimum entry requirements but it is preferable to have a good standard of general education, including a minimum of 3 GCSEs grades (A*–C). The Diploma in Business, Finance and Administration could also be useful. In certain areas, it could be an advantage to be fluent in a minority language.

Many applicants have training and/or experience in finance or accounting, consumer advice or have worked as a volunteer for at least a year in an advice centre.

Money advisers need a detailed knowledge of the relevant laws. Short courses in specialist areas such as court procedures, housing law or bankruptcy are available.

NVQ Level 2 in Supporting Legal Advice Provision and Levels 3–4 in Legal Advice are also available. You could take a diploma, Foundation degree or degree in Advice or Legal Advice Work. The Money Advice Trust and the Citizens Advice Bureau also provide training courses for debt counsellors.

You may have to deal with rude and difficult people.

Evening and weekend work is possible in this job.

Money guide

On entry, debt counsellors can expect to earn around £19,000 per year.

Earnings can rise to £22,000–£24,000 with experience of casework.

£30,000 is an average salary for senior posts.

Earnings can be higher in London.

Related opportunities

- Accountant p16
- Financial Adviser p39
- Counsellor p571
- Welfare Benefits Adviser/Welfare Rights Caseworker p588

Further information

Citizens Advice Bureau
Myddelton House, 115–123 Pentonville Road, London N1 9LZ
020 7833 2181; www.citizensadvice.org.uk

Advice UK
6th Floor, 63 St Mary Axe, London EC3A 8AA
020 7469 5700; www.adviceuk.org.uk

Financial Services Skills Council
51 Gresham Street, London EC2V 7HQ
0845 257 3772; www.fssc.org.uk

EDUCATIONAL PSYCHOLOGIST

What the work involves

- You will work with children with social, behavioural or learning difficulties to assess their progress and their academic and emotional needs.

- You will give help and guidance, and design activities which will help them to learn.

- Your work will also involve working closely with parents and teaching professionals to broaden their understanding of the psychological needs and difficulties that children face.

- You will carry out research and keep completely up to date with new government policies and measures that have been brought in with regard to assessing a child's psychological progression.

The type of person suited to this work

You should be someone who enjoys working closely with children and accept that your work is going to involve working with those who are finding school difficult and may not be very receptive to your help.

You will need excellent communication skills as you will be working regularly with children and adults. You should make sure that you are good at explaining procedures and assessment methods in a way that is easy to understand.

You need administrative and ICT skills for writing reports and analyses, and presenting information.

Working conditions

You will spend a lot of your time in schools and colleges meeting clients, writing reports and assessing your findings.

You will run training sessions for parents and teachers as well as attend meetings in the evenings.

You will probably have to travel between different locations, so a driving licence is useful.

You are likely to be employed by the local authority but there are also opportunities to work for private organisations and to do volunteer work.

Future prospects

Most educational psychologists work for local authorities but an increasing number are self-employed as independent consultants. You will be more restricted in the way you can progress whilst working for a local authority as there are only a certain number of positions you can work up to. However you may become a senior officer in a local authority children's services department.

Being an independent consultant will give you greater opportunity to branch into different areas of psychology such as occupational psychology.

Qualifications and courses

ENTRY LEVEL 8

You will need an Honours degree in Psychology accredited by the British Psychological Society (BPS). This will qualify you for the Graduate Basis for Chartered Membership (GBC) required by all employers.

For entry to a degree course, you will need at least 2 A levels/3 H grades (A*–C) including mathematics.

Since 2006, a doctorate is also required to qualify as an educational psychologist. In order to be accepted onto this course you should demonstrate that you have a lot of work experience in the field of educational psychology. This could be in the form of working with children and young people in a variety of settings from schools to health centres. You will also have to have achieved a 2.1 or higher at degree level.

Advantages/disadvantages

The work is varied and interesting.

It can be stressful and challenging when dealing with difficult children.

Parents may not be willing to accept that their child has a psychological problem so may also be difficult to work with.

Money guide

As a graduate trainee you can expect around £26,500 per year – depending on the kind of work you do.

£50,000+ is possible in a senior post.

You will be paid an additional allowance if you work in or around London and salaries throughout the country will vary.

Related opportunities

- Youth and Community Worker p589
- Clinical/Health Psychologist p570
- Counsellor p571

Further information

Educational Psychology Postgraduate Grant Scheme
Local Government Employers, Local Government House, Smith Square, London SW1P 3HZ
020 7187 7373; info@lge.gov.uk; www.lge.gov.uk

Children's Workforce Development Council
2nd Floor, City Exchange, 11 Albion Street, Leeds LS1 5ES
0113 244 6311; www.cwdcouncil.org.uk

Association of Educational Psychologists
4 The Riverside Centre, Frankland Lane, Durham DH1 5TA
0191 384 9512; www.aep.org.uk

FORENSIC PSYCHOLOGIST

What the work involves

- You will apply psychology to the criminal and civil justice systems.

- Your job will involve direct contact with offenders to carry out assessments and you may design programmes to help in their rehabilitation.

- You may be required to present your findings on a criminal case in court.

- Your work will also include carrying out detailed research on what provokes people to carry out crimes and analyse their behavioural patterns and personality traits.

The type of person suited to this work

You should have brilliant communication skills and be able to work with people from a wide variety of backgrounds.

You must be prepared to work with criminals and be enthusiastic about helping them during their rehabilitation process.

You should not be a judgmental person and hold no prejudice against the people you are working with even if they have committed an awful crime.

You should be very good at reading people's unconscious behaviour and take detailed notes of your findings to present in reports.

Working conditions

You will spend a lot of time working in prisons, secure hospitals, police stations and mental health rehabilitation units.

You may be employed by a variety of organisations; from the NHS to Her Majesty's Prison Service to the Police Service.

Work will typically be a 37 hour week from Monday to Friday but flexible work is available. You will also find that evening and weekend work is expected of you.

If you are working in a prison you will need to become adjusted to the conditions and regulations.

Future prospects

If you achieve chartered status as a forensic psychologist there may be the opportunity to progress to a senior role. In this position you may be in charge of a complete rehabilitation scheme for a certain type of offender. You will have the possibility to work for a consultancy once you have built up enough experience. As this is a fairly new and emerging sector, there are many new opportunities to progress and branch into different areas of psychology and forensics once you have some experience behind you.

Advantages/disadvantages

You may find yourself working with people who have committed very serious crimes which can be distressing.

Qualifications and courses

ENTRY LEVEL 5

Entrants must be graduates with Graduate Basis for Chartered Membership (GBC) with the British Psychological Society (BPS).

GBR can be obtained by taking a BPS-accredited degree in psychology or a non-accredited degree plus a conversion course.

Additional postgraduate training is usually required to qualify in a specialist area.

For entry to a degree course, you will need 2 A levels/3 H grades (A*–C) including mathematics.

A BPS-accredited MSc or diploma in forensic psychology, followed by at least 2 years' supervised practice, are prerequisites for qualified status.

Helping to rehabilitate offenders back into society can be immensely rewarding.

As this is a fairly new sector you will be learning new things all the time which will make the job exciting and fulfilling.

Money guide

As a psychological assistant you can expect to start on £14,000 and there is the opportunity to receive a local pay allowance (from £1,000 to £4,000) for prisons. As a trainee in this sector, you can expect to start on £18,000–£20,000 which will increase to around £25,000–£45,000 with experience as a chartered forensic psychologist.

Senior position salaries can reach over £60,000 after 10–15 years' experience.

Related opportunities

- Clinical/Health Psychologist p570
- Counsellor p571
- Forensic Computer Analyst p548

Further information

HM Prison Service
Parliamentary, Correspondence and Briefing Unit,
HM Prison Service Headquarters, Cleland House,
Page Street, London SW1P 4LN
www.hmprisonservice.gov.uk

Division of Forensic Psychologists
The British Psychological Society, St Andrews House,
48 Princess Road East, Leicester LE1 7DR
0116 254 9568; enquiries@bps.org.uk;
www.bps.org.uk/dfp

National Probation Service
1st Floor Abell House, John Islip Street, London SW1P 4LH
www.probation.homeoffice.gov.uk

FUNDRAISER

What the work involves

- Fundraisers raise money for their charity by targeting donors and organising activities such as publicly-sponsored events, membership schemes with various benefits and corporate sponsorship.

- You will represent your charity at public events, such as dinners, giving talks to possible supporters.

- You will write strategies, reports for trustees and donors, and proposals for grants.

- You will prepare publicity material and liaise with the media, always keeping your charity in the public eye.

The type of person suited to this work

You must be good with all types of people. You should be an excellent communicator and an engaging and confident public speaker, always able to persuade people to support your charity.

You will need to be a good negotiator, with excellent writing skills to produce effective publicity material. You will have to be imaginative and creative to come up with novel fundraising ideas.

You will need to be able to organise your time and workload so you can keep running costs down to a minimum and save money for your charity.

Working conditions

You will normally be based in an office working on a computer, but you can be home-based, particularly if you work for a very small charity.

There could be pressure to hit deadlines for organising events and/or fundraising targets to meet.

You will travel fairly widely so a driving licence is useful.

You might spend time outdoors at fundraising activities.

Future prospects

It is not usual to become a charity fundraiser straight from school – most entrants have experience in sales or marketing and voluntary fundraising. Most jobs are with charities, pressure groups and non-profit-making organisations, including hospitals.

It may be necessary to move around – possibly to larger organisations – to progress your career. With experience you could move into management, become self-employed or offer consultancy advice.

Advantages/disadvantages

It's satisfying to see your charity flourish from the money you've helped to raise.

People who do not support your charity can be unpleasant at times.

You will need to work evenings and weekends.

Qualifications and courses

There are no specific entry requirements for this work although many entrants are graduates. Useful degrees include sales and marketing or business studies. You will need at least 2 A levels and 5 GCSEs (A*–C) for a degree. However experience in marketing, sales or in working for other charities can be just as important to employers. Voluntary fundraising experience is useful.

Large charities, such as Cancer Research UK, offer training schemes for entrants, while others, including Oxfam, run unpaid internships. Competition for places is fierce.

If you are trying to enter the sector from another field you may choose to do a 6 month trainee programme run by Fundraising Training Ltd.

The Institute of Fundraising runs an introductory course for charity fundraisers and a Certificate in Fundraising Management, equivalent to NVQ/SVQ Level 4, for experienced fundraisers. Short courses for people working as fundraisers/fundraising managers are also available.

Money guide

Your starting salary will be around £18,500, rising to £22,000 per year, depending on the charity.

With experience and managerial responsibilities, you could be earning £25,000–£40,000.

If you head up a fundraising department in a large charity you can earn £60,000+.

Related opportunities

- Advertising Account Executive p402
- Public Relations Officer p422
- Marketing Assistant/Executive p414
- Events and Exhibition Organiser p411

Further information

Institute of Fundraising
Park Place, 12 Lawn Lane, London SW8 1UD
020 7840 1000; www.institute-of-fundraising.org.uk

Association of Chief Executives of Voluntary Organisations
1 New Oxford Street, London WC1A 1NU
020 7280 4690; www.acevo.org.uk

Directory of Social Change
24 Stephenson Way, London NW1 2DP
020 7391 4800; www.dsc.org.uk

CRCI: V Social Work and Counselling Services

HEALTHCARE ASSISTANT

What the work involves

- Healthcare assistants help people who find it difficult to look after themselves with everyday tasks.

- Your clients could be children, elderly people or people with disabilities living in residential care or in their own homes.

- You will help them to bathe, dress, and to use the toilet or commode, and help with eating, washing, ironing, cleaning and shopping.

- Part of your time will be spent talking to your clients, helping them to write letters, budget their money or pay bills.

The type of person suited to this work

As the job involves working with people who need individual support, you will have to work out what help they need and provide it in a sympathetic and tactful way.

Healthcare assistants need to be cheerful, outgoing and friendly, as their clients may be lonely or depressed.

The job usually involves domestic work so you need to be happy and skilled at doing housework and laundry.

Helping with handling money, and writing and reading personal and business letters is work that must remain confidential, so healthcare assistants need to be very trustworthy and discreet, and able to keep clients' personal information private.

Working conditions

Most of your work is indoors but you may go out with people, for example to hospital appointments or on outings. You might have to live in for some jobs.

You need to be physically fit to help people who are unable to move around themselves; this may involve heavy lifting.

You will be expected to be very careful about health and safety issues, such as fire and hot water.

Future prospects

There are over a million healthcare assistants in the UK and demand is increasing. Many healthcare assistants work in residential homes and day-healthcare centres, but more people are being cared for in their own homes.

The main employers are health authorities, social services, private homes and voluntary agencies.

Promotion depends on qualifications and experience. With experience in healthcare work, you could train for related jobs such as social work or nursing.

Qualifications and courses

There are no fixed entry qualifications for this job. Previous experience, for example in voluntary work and/or an NVQ/SVQ in Healthcare at Level 2 is useful, and may be required by some employers.

You can study a range of relevant courses full time at school or college, prior to entry. The Diploma in Society, Health and Development and Young Apprenticeship Programme in Health and Social Care are offered to 14–19 year olds and are available for all ability levels. The National Diploma in Healthcare and A level in Health and Social Healthcare are 2-year courses, and usually require 4 GCSEs/S grades (A*–C/1–3) or a BTEC First Diploma.

Most training is work-based, and healthcare assistants can work towards NVQs/SVQs in Health and Social Care at Levels 1–3.

Advantages/disadvantages

It can be satisfying to help people in need.
You might have to work shifts, evenings, weekends and public holidays, including Christmas Day.

Some jobs can be messy and unpleasant.

Money guide

Salaries are around £13,233 per year at entry. With experience and qualifications you could earn up to £16,500.

You can earn £17,000+ in a residential post.

You will be paid more for shift work and unsocial hours, i.e. for working late hours or providing overnight healthcare.

Related opportunities

- Childminder p569
- Adult Nurse p289
- Children's Nurse p294
- Early Years Specialist/Nursery Worker p192
- Social Care Worker/Social Worker p583

Further information

General Social Care Council
Goldings House, 2 Hays Lane, London SE1 2HB
020 7397 5100; www.gscc.org.uk

NHS Careers
PO Box 2311, Bristol BS2 2ZX
0345 606 0655; www.nhscareers.nhs.uk

City & Guilds

www.cityandguilds.com/myperfectjob

LIFE COACH

What the work involves

- You will help people – independent clients or employees – to recognise and develop their special attributes and skills.

- You will coach individuals to become more successful in career matters, fitness levels, financial affairs or personal relationships. You will also help in boosting self-esteem.

- You will discuss values, attributes and beliefs and set goals with your clients for them to work towards.

- At a later stage you will review and revise the action plans you have created.

The type of person suited to this work

Once a bond of trust is established – that you are non-judgemental and hold personal information in strictest confidence – individuals will reveal their present feelings and frustrations, their future ambitions and their perceived restrictions to progress.

Besides integrity and discretion, life coaches need excellent interpersonal skills, patience and perseverance to allow clients the time to set themselves goals for change.

Working conditions

You will agree timetables with clients for coaching sessions and hold one-to-ones at their work-base or in a neutral location. Later sessions are often by phone or email. Many life coaches work with busy, highly successful chief executives, usually outside normal business hours.

Coaching sessions can be weekly, fortnightly or monthly; the frequency may change.

Future prospects

Life coaching is a relatively new field, but interest has increased as more attention is paid to developing the whole person – both within and outside the workplace.

Life coaches work as independent consultants or for business consultancy agencies. If you network and market yourself well you can build up a substantial client base. You could choose to specialise in one area such as spiritual coaching or executive coaching.

Advantages/disadvantages

There is great satisfaction in observing changes in your clients.

If clients fail to implement action plans, it can be dispiriting and frustrating.

You could have long-term coaching relationships with clients who want to work on different aspects of their lives.

Qualifications and courses

ENTRY LEVEL 5

Although there are no specific requirements to enter this area of work, you need to have gained a great deal of life experience and to have tasted many different approaches to conducting business and managing an organisation's workforce performance and delivery.

A degree in human resources work, organisations and structures, sociology or psychology would be helpful starting points. For entry to a degree course, you need a minimum of 5 GCSEs/S grades at A*–C/1–3, plus 2 or 3 A levels/H grades with an emphasis on the humanities.

There are a number of private agencies and academies offering training in life coaching, for example the Coaching Academy, where you can take a 2-day fast-track course by distance learning to focus on corporate or individual (personal performance) life coaching.

It is possible to take a longer diploma course in life coaching.

Money guide

Life coaches earn an agreed rate per session.

Working for an agency, you can earn around £60 per session plus expenses. Hourly rates for private clients could be £50–£100+ for a coaching session lasting an hour.

It is possible to earn the full-time equivalent income of between £18,000 and £24,000.

Life coaches who become well-known and sought after can charge higher fees for periods of life coaching lasting 6 months or longer.

Related opportunities

- Careers Adviser p568
- Counsellor p571
- Social Care Worker/Social Worker p583

Further information

The Coaching Academy
Hill House, 2 Heron Square, Richmond TW9 1EP
020 84399 440; www.the-coaching-academy.com

New U Coaching
Abbey Business Centre, 111 Buckingham Palace Road, London SW1W 0SR
0845 643 4371; www.newucoaching.co.uk

Social Work and Counselling Services

CRCI: V

OCCUPATIONAL PSYCHOLOGIST

What the work involves

- You will explore how organisations function and how people behave at work to improve an organisation's efficiency and employees' job satisfaction.

- You will help managers plan how they recruit and train staff, and advise on matters concerning communication between individuals in the workplace, the most effective working environment and coping with change.

- Part of your job may involve helping to recruit the right person for a particular role as well as offering support to those facing redundancy.

- You will also be working with bosses and managers to help them to understand the psychological needs of their staff so that they can maintain a stress-free environment for their staff as much as possible.

The type of person suited to this work

You should have a great interest in how organisations function and what makes people tick in the workplace. You should be comfortable working with adults and also be happy to help them progress professionally. You must be a brilliant communicator and it will also be very useful for you to have strong business skills because you will have been employed to improve the overall efficiency of a company. Your personal safety awareness should be very good as well.

Working conditions

Much of your work will take place in offices and business premises of the companies you are working for. This may involve working by yourself or as part of a team. You can expect to work around 37 hours a week from Monday to Friday but you may run or attend courses that require you to travel away and stay overnight in places. There is the opportunity to be self-employed but this is often after working for an organisation and building up your work experience.

Future prospects

Occupational psychologists work in large companies in the public and private sectors. They can work with government and public services as private consultants. Some specialise in a certain area, for example ergonomics (the interaction of people with where they work), or health and safety – studying the causes of accidents and how to prevent them.

Once you have progressed to a senior role you may set up your own consultancy.

Advantages/disadvantages

Your work will really make a difference to people's day to day lives at work which will be very rewarding.

You may be working with unmotivated or stressed individuals.

You may find that bosses are not willing to take on your advice for their staff.

Qualifications and courses

ENTRY LEVEL 5

Entrants must be graduates with Graduate Basis for Chartered Membership (GBC) with the British Psychological Society (BPS).

GBR can be obtained by taking a BPS-accredited degree in psychology or a non-accredited degree plus a conversion course.

Additional postgraduate training is usually required to qualify in a specialist area.

For entry to a degree course, you will need 2 A levels/3 H grades (A*–C) including mathematics.

Psychology graduates need to gain an accredited MSc followed by 2 years of supervised practice, or 3 years' supervised practice and the BPS Postgraduate Certificate in Occupational Psychology to become fully qualified.

If you want to achieve Chartered Occupational Psychologist status you will have to complete stage 2 of the Qualification in Occupational Psychology. One way to do this is with the BPS or alternatively you can keep a log book of your work carried out under the supervision of a qualified chartered occupational psychologist which demonstrates your progression and the knowledge that you have built up. This will then be assessed by the Division of Occupational Psychology who will decide whether to award you chartered status.

Money guide

As a trainee occupational psychologist you can earn around £18,000 as your starting salary. This can progress to around £55,000 with experience in a senior position. Salaries vary in the private sector but senior positions can carry a £70,000+ salary.

Related opportunities

- Educational Psychologist p573
- Health and Safety Inspector p40
- Recruitment/Employment Agency Consultant p59

Further information

Association of Business Psychologists
211/212 Piccadilly, London W1J 9HG
0207 917 1733; www.theabp.org.uk

The Health Professions Council
Park House, 184 Kennington Park Road, London SE11 4BU
020 7582 0866; www.hpc-uk.org

Occupational Psychology Services
Townsend Chambers, Riverhead, Sevenoaks TN13 2EL
0845 50 50 181; 01732 742 544; www.opsltd.com

PSYCHOANALYST/ PSYCHOTHERAPIST

What the work involves

Psychoanalyst

- You will help people uncover their buried, unconscious thoughts and behaviours which are disrupting and negatively affecting their daily life.

- You will see your patients 4–5 times a week over an extended period of time. You will listen during the sessions and then write down your observations after your patient has left. Your goal is to help patients achieve self-awareness.

Psychotherapist

- You will explore a person's inner conflicts and feelings in order to help alleviate their distress. Your goal is to help patients feel happy or better.

- Your treatment will be non-medical, focussing on talking through problems. Your treatment approach may include cognitive behavioural therapy, hypno-psychotherapy and psychodynamic therapies.

The type of person suited to this work

You need to be positive, empathetic and a great listener. You want to build a good bond with your patients so you should respect confidential information.

Your work can be intense at times and you will need to sympathise with your patients' problems but at the same time remain emotionally resilient. You should be observant and have a genuine interest in feelings and emotions.

Working conditions

You will work out of a consulting room that is comfortable, quiet and furnished with a couch or chair for your patients.

You will most likely work Monday to Friday but may need to work weekends and evenings to suit your clients' needs. If you work for a private practice you can decide your own hours.

This work can be emotionally demanding and you are advised to be involved in a support network, especially if you are self-employed.

Future prospects

Psychoanalyst

Most psychoanalysts are self-employed and you may choose to work part-time for a prison, school or child guidance clinic. You could become a lecturer, train graduate entrants or specialise in a particular area such as adolescent psychoanalysis.

Psychotherapist

With experience you could go on to become a manager or supervisor of other psychotherapists although this will mean you will have less clinical work. You could also become a consultant for community organisations or specialise in an area such as psychodrama.

Qualifications and courses

ENTRY LEVEL 5

Psychoanalyst

Before beginning psychoanalysis training you will need to pass three personal interviews and hold a first degree in another field such as psychiatry and counselling. For a first degree you will need at least 2 A levels and 5 GCSEs (A*–C). Training takes 4 years and must be approved by the International Psychoanalytical Association.

Psychotherapist

You will need a postgraduate qualification in order to begin training as a psychotherapist. Useful degree subjects include psychology, nursing and social work. Your course needs to be approved by the UK Council for Psychotherapists or the British Psychoanalytic Council and will be part-time over 4–6 years. Training includes personal therapy, theory and supervised clinical work.

Advantages/disadvantages

It's rewarding to see a patient overcome their problems.

You will constantly be learning more about the human mind which can benefit you as well as your patients.

Your patients might struggle with upsetting issues and this can be emotionally taxing for you.

Money guide

Psychoanalyst

Newly qualified you can earn £40,000 a year. With experience, this could rise to £60,000+. If self-employed you may earn between £45 and £70 a session.

Psychotherapist

If working for the NHS you may start out earning between £20,000 and £26,000 a year. With experience this could rise to £77,000. If self-employed or working for a private practice you may charge between £25 and £80 per hour.

Related opportunities

- Psychiatrist p335
- Counsellor p571
- Educational Psychologist p573

Further information

British Association of Psychotherapists
31 Mapesbury Road, London NW2 4HJ
020 8452 9823; www.bap-psychotherapy.org

REHABILITATION OFFICER

What the work involves

Visually impaired

- You will train people who have lost their vision or have poor vision to use their existing skills in new ways that will help them lead a normal life.

- You will assess your patients' needs before making a detailed action plan that will include teaching new ways of carrying out daily tasks, moving around with use of visual aids, providing financial and employment information and careers advice.

Hearing impaired

- You job role will be similar to a visually impaired officer but focusing instead on ways of living with hearing loss or deafness. This includes providing advice about the equipment available for hearing impaired people, such as special doorbells and amplified alarms.

- Part of your role will be liaising with other medical professionals to follow up on reports you have made about your patients' standard of living. You might also be responsible for providing training to other social and healthcare workers about sensory loss and awareness.

The type of person suited to this work

You will need to be aware of the issues that affect visually and hearing impaired people. It is important to have good communication skills and be clear when expressing yourself as your patients may rely on other senses to understand you.

You will be in contact with people of all ages and backgrounds, so it is essential you are friendly and approachable. You can act as a vital link between your patient and the outside world.

Good organisational, problem solving and assessment skills will be essential for report writing and devising action plans for patients.

Working conditions

Some of your time will be spent in an office, although a lot of time will be spent visiting patients' homes assessing their living space and daily routines. It is useful to have a driving licence and access to your own vehicle as you might be travelling around on a regular basis.

You might need to work outdoors when training a patient to use a new piece of assistive equipment or if you are escorting them somewhere.

You will be working around 40 hours a week, Monday to Friday, although you might need to visit your patients during the evenings and weekends.

Future prospects

Most positions are with local authority social care departments, voluntary services such as the Royal National Institute for the Blind and the Royal National Institute for Deaf People, and educational institutions.

Although there is no set career path in rehabilitation work, you can be promoted to supervisory and managerial roles in sensory support or you can choose to train other people to be rehabilitation officers.

There are postgraduate qualifications available in Assistive Technology and Rehabilitation Studies at Levels 7 and 8 which would speed up progression in your career.

Advantages/disadvantages

This is a very satisfying and rewarding career as you will be helping people who are in a vulnerable position.

You need to stay emotionally detached from your patients, which could be difficult as you will be spending a lot of time with them.

You might find it difficult if one of your patients is particularly stubborn or just refuses any help.

You will meet some fascinating people, learn worthwhile skills such as sign language, and make a real difference to somebody's life.

Money guide

Visually impaired

Starting salaries are around £18,000–£23,000, rising to £24,000–£30,000 with experience.

Those in more senior positions can earn £35,000+.

Hearing impaired

You could start on around £19,000–£22,300, with experience this increases to £27,000. Team leaders can earn up to £35,000.

Related opportunities

- Careers Adviser p568
- Counsellor Work p571
- Social Care Worker/Social Worker p583
- Healthcare Assistant p576

Further information

Royal National Institute of the Blind
105 Judd Street, London WC1H 9NE
020 7388 1266; www.rnib.org.uk

Skills for Care and Development
2nd Floor, City Exchange, 11 Albion Street, Leeds LS1 5ES
0113 390 7666; www.skillsforcareanddevelopment.org.uk

Social Care Association
350 West Barnes Lane, Motspur Park, New Malden KT3 6NB
020 8949 5837, www.socialcareassociation.co.uk

Royal National Institute for Deaf People
19–23 Featherstone Street, London EC1Y 8SL
0808 808 0123, www.rnid.org.uk

www.cityandguilds.com/myperfectjob

Qualifications and courses
Visually impaired

You will need a qualification in rehabilitation work. The RNIB School of Rehabilitation Studies at Birmingham City University offers a Foundation degree which is studied over 2 years. It offers work-based learning through an employer and distance learning. Entry requirements are at least 1 A level/H grade and 3 GCSEs/S grades (A*–C). The Diploma in Society, Health and Development could also be useful.

If you already have a job in a voluntary agency working with visually impaired people you can study for the BTEC Professional Diploma in Rehabilitation Studies at Levels 4 and 5. This is completed via distance learning.

Hearing impaired

There are no set entry requirements for this career. However most employers will look for GCSEs grades (A*–C) and relevant experience in social care or with people with hearing problems. It might help to have some relevant qualifications such as British Sign Language Stage 1 and the Diploma in Rehabilitation Studies available at Birmingham City University which combines a block of lectures with e-learning.

Training is on the job, with the chance to study for further qualifications; these include the Technical Officers Association's Level 3 Advanced Diploma in Technical and Rehabilitation Work with Deaf People and City & Guilds Level 2 in Supporting Users Of Assistive Technology.

There are Apprenticeships available in health and social care which could be beneficial for these careers.

As you will be working with vulnerable people you will need to undergo a Criminal Records Bureau (CRB) check.

ENTRY **5** LEVEL

RESIDENTIAL WARDEN

What the work involves

- Wardens look after the welfare of people living in supervised accommodation, including the elderly, people with disabilities, temporary hostel residents and students.

- You will make sure that meals are organised, cooked and served at set times, and that cleaning and maintenance are up to standard.

- It will be your responsibility to make sure health and safety standards are met, insurance is up to date and that security is effective.

- You will also collect rents and fees and organise social events, and sort out any disputes.

The type of person suited to this work

As you may be responsible for the accommodation of many different groups of people, it is important to be friendly and outgoing. You will also need to be understanding, patient and tolerant.

There are likely to be crises in the job so it is important to be able to cope under pressure and make decisions quickly. Problem solving skills are useful in these situations.

If you are dealing with rents and fees, being good with figures is helpful. There will be a lot of administrative work which needs a well-organised and methodical approach.

Working conditions

Most of your work will be indoors, but you may handle maintenance and repair work, using tools and climbing ladders.

You will be constantly on the go, responding to alarm calls at any hour of the day or night.

You will use ICT for administration and record-keeping.

Many accommodation wardens live on-site or in the grounds, but you might travel locally, so a driving licence is useful.

Future prospects

Although there are opportunities throughout the UK, there are few vacancies for wardens. Most jobs are in cities and major towns. The main employers are local authorities, housing associations, private companies, voluntary organisations, universities and colleges.

Promotion is likely to be from assistant warden to warden. You might have to move jobs to progress your career. It is also possible to move into management positions or other caring jobs such as social work.

Advantages/disadvantages

The work is varied and no two days will be alike.

You will get great job satisfaction from helping people.

Qualifications and courses

There are no particular qualifications necessary to become a warden. However, it would be an advantage to have previous experience of caring for people, such as nursing or working with the disabled, elderly or homeless. The minimum entry age is 20.

It is possible to study for the Chartered Institute of Housing (CIH) National Certificate in Housing as well as NVQ/SVQ Levels 2, 3 and 4 in Housing.

Qualifications in care, including NVQs/SVQs, as well as a first aid certificate, are also useful.

Wardens (managers) with the Youth Hostels Association (YHA, England and Wales) generally either start as seasonal assistants and work their way up, or are mature entrants with relevant work experience.

Some residents may be difficult to deal with.

You will work long hours, evenings and weekends, and may have to live on-site.

Money guide

Starting salaries are around £11,500–£13,000 per year.

Wages can rise to £20,000, with experience.

Earnings range from £24,000 to £32,000 for those with substantial experience – in some instances having individual responsibility for a group in supported accommodation.

Accommodation and food may also be provided.

Related opportunities

- Caretaker p461
- Hotel Manager p141
- Cleaner p464

Further information

Chartered Institute of Housing
Octavia House, Westwood Way, Coventry CV4 8JP
024 7685 1700; www.cih.org

General Social Care Council
Goldings House, 2 Hays Lane, London SE1 2HB
020 7397 5100; www.gscc.org.uk

Scottish Social Services Council
Compass House, 11 Riverside Drive, Dundee DD1 4NY
01382 207101; www.sssc.uk.com

www.cityandguilds.com/myperfectjob

SOCIAL CARE WORKER/ SOCIAL WORKER

What the work involves

Social care worker

- Your main focus will be to provide the practical, personal care for clients that has been advised by a social worker.

- You could provide live-in residential home care for the elderly, ill or disabled.

- You could also provide personal assistance/day care to someone needing help with all aspects of day-to-day living.

- Your job could also include providing outreach care such as helping drug addicts clean up and integrate into the community.

Social worker

- Working at a senior level, you will interview your clients and assess their complex problems and needs.

- You will then advise on the best package of care for your client.

- Your goal is to support people to live independently and thrive in their surroundings. This might involve helping families to stay together, protecting vulnerable people and helping the excluded to be a part of their community.

- You will keep detailed records of all your work.

The type of person suited to this work

You should be culturally aware, non-judgemental and able to engage with clients of all ethnicities, religions and backgrounds. If you're adaptable, genuine, compassionate and patient you will win your clients' trust.

Caseloads (the number of clients you will be working with at a given time) can be heavy so you need to be organised and able to multi-task. While you need to be a team-player you will also need to learn how to take the initiative and negotiate on behalf of your clients. Excellent communication skills are important.

At times your clients may become difficult and you must be confident at resolving conflict and playing the role of peace-maker. Staying calm in a crisis is essential. You also need to remain professionally detached in emotionally tense circumstances.

Working conditions

Social care worker

Depending on the role you have you may live in a residential home and work on a rota basis covering night duties or you could visit people in their own homes or work in places such as drop-in centres and youth clubs.

You might need to work in shifts to provide 24-hour care to your clients.

You could be required to carry a personal alarm or to wear protective clothing.

Social worker

You will often work within a team from other disciplines including psychologists and therapists and will be office-based. Most of your time however will be spent visiting clients at their homes. A driving licence is essential.

You will work 37 hours a week but this may include evenings, early mornings and weekends.

Future prospects

Social care worker

There are currently many government initiatives to boost community support so job prospects are good. You will most likely work for a residential care home, a nursing home or another private organisation. There are also vacancies in health services and local authority social service departments.

You could be promoted to senior care worker and with additional experience become a team manager or even a registered manager looking after an entire care home. You can do further training and qualify to become a social worker or an occupational therapist.

Social worker

There is currently a demand for qualified social workers so job prospects are high. You will most likely work for a local authority social service or for children or adult service departments within the NHS. Jobs may also be available with armed forces support groups.

After gaining experience you can vary your role by changing your specialism or by moving on within your specialism. For example you could move from child protection into foster care.

You could also become a senior practitioner or manager but this will mean you will deal more with finances and politics rather than directly with clients. Lecturing and self-employment opportunities are also possible.

Advantages/disadvantages

You have the opportunity to build meaningful relationships. You might be the only supportive person your clients know; you can make a life-changing difference to them.

No two cases will be the same, keeping your work interesting.

It's rewarding to see people reach their full potential, solve their own problems and improve their lives.

CRCI: V | Social Work and Counselling Services

Social work systems can be bureaucratic and frustrating at times.

Your work can be emotionally distressing and may put you in vulnerable situations.

Money guide

Social care worker

Starting out you may earn £11,000 and with experience this can rise to £18,000. In a senior position you can earn up to £25,000.

You could be paid on an hourly rate. If you work for a children's home you will earn between £7 and £13 an hour. If you work in a residential care home you could earn between £6.40 and £10.15 per hour.

Many care homes also provide free accommodation.

Social worker

You could start out earning between £20,000 and £29,000 a year. With experience and depending on where you live, you could earn up to £35,000.

Managers earn £42,000+.

Many employers offer additional benefits such as car allowances and child care.

Related opportunities

- Counsellor p571
- Healthcare Assistant p576
- Youth and Community Worker p589

Further information

General Social Care Council
Goldings House, 2 Hays Lane, London SE1 2HB
020 7397 5100; www.gscc.org.uk

British Association of Social Workers
16 Kent Street, Birmingham B5 6RD
0121 622 3911; www.basw.co.uk

Skills for Care
Albion Court, 5 Albion Place, Leeds LS1 6JL
0113 245 1716; www.skillsforcare.org.uk

Department of Health Social Work and Social Care Careers
0300 123 1100; www.socialworkandcare.co.uk

www.cityandguilds.com/myperfectjob

Qualifications and courses
Social care worker

Although there are no minimum entry requirements many entrants have a qualification in health and social care. You can take A levels, BTEC or City & Guilds courses in these subjects. A Diploma in Society, Health and Development is also available.

You will need to pass a Criminal Records Bureau check and register with the General Social Care Council. This means you will be bound to a national code of conduct.

Many employers will expect you to have at least 1 year of experience working in a care setting. You will also be expected to work towards NVQ Level 2 in Health and Social Care.

Social worker

You will need an Honours degree or postgraduate degree in Social Work approved by the General Social Care Council (GSCC) in order to be employed. For entry to a degree you will need at least 2 A levels and 5 GCSEs (A*–C), including English and maths. You will need a 2.2 Honours degree for entry onto a postgraduate course. Relevant subjects include social sciences, education, psychology and nursing.

A Diploma in Society, Health and Development may be useful. If you want to work with children and families, a Diploma in Children and Young People's Workforce or an Apprenticeship in Children's Care, Learning and Development may be helpful.

You will need to pass a Criminal Records Bureau check and a medical test. You must also be registered with the GSCC.

All social workers must renew their qualifications every 3 years.

ENTRY LEVEL 3

CRCI: V

Social Work and Counselling Services

SUBSTANCE MISUSE WORKER

What the work involves

- You will help people who misuse harmful substances, including drugs and alcohol, to overcome their dependencies.

- You could provide support in one-to-one or group sessions This can include counselling and care planning.

- You could offer drug treatment options to prisoners, advise on detox methods in a rehabilitation centre, prescribe drugs and medical advice in a clinic or run educational workshops in schools and youth centres.

- You could also help substance users find housing and temporary accommodation. You might accompany police patrols around clubs doing street outreach work.

The type of person suited to this work

You want your clients to trust you so you should be understanding, warm and a good listener. You need to be patient and non-judgemental as it may take substance users a long time to recover. If your clients know that you believe in them, they will develop confidence to change.

You could work with many clients at any given time and should be organised. An ability to stay calm under pressure and to maintain professional boundaries is essential.

Good communication skills are important as your role may involve educating others about the dangers of substance abuse.

Working conditions

You could be based in a drop-in centre, a clinic, prison or other community site. However a lot of your time will be spent visiting substance users in their homes or other venues. Sometimes you will be visiting shelters as many clients may be homeless. A driving licence will be useful.

You will most likely work 35–40 hours a week but these could be irregular hours including evenings and weekends. You might need to be on-call throughout the night. Part-time work is available.

Future prospects

Your job prospects are high as there are a variety of opportunities across the UK for substance misuse workers. You could work for Connexions services, drop-in centres, local authorities, housing agencies, private rehabilitation centres, the NHS, prisons, police services, charities and drug and alcohol organisations.

You could become a supervisor or manager with experience. You could also specialise in one area of treatment such as psychological intervention or drug and alcohol testing or even specialise in one user group such as young people.

Advantages/disadvantages

You have the opportunity to build meaningful relationships with clients and colleagues.

Qualifications and courses

Entry requirements vary based on the type of user you work with: with young people you will need the Common Core of Skills and Knowledge for the Children's Workforce; with adults you will need an NVQ Level 3 in Health and Social Care.

You could choose to do an Advanced Apprenticeship in Community Justice and follow the drug and alcohol pathway. The Diploma in Society, Health and Development could also be helpful. Many colleges offer an NCFE Certificate in Drug Awareness.

Voluntary experience is recommended and most employers will want to see evidence of this.

If you want to specialise in certain methods of treatment such as medicine you will need to qualify first as a nurse. For psychological intervention you will need to qualify first as a counsellor.

You will need to pass a Criminal Records Bureau check.

It's rewarding when you help a client overcome an addiction.

You might need to be on-call 24 hours a day which can be demanding.

It can be frustrating to work with uncooperative clients who don't believe they have a problem.

Money guide

In your first job, you may start out earning £19,000 per year.

With experience and team leader responsibilities you can earn between £22,000 and £30,000 a year.

As a project manager you may earn £40,000+.

Related opportunities

- Counsellor p571
- Adult Nurse p289
- Social Care Worker/Social Worker p583

Further information

Federation of Drug and Alcohol Professionals
Unit 84, 95 Wilton Road, London SW1V 1BZ
01636 612590; www.fdap.org.uk

National Treatment Agency for Substance Misuse
6th Floor, Skipton House, 80 London Road, London SE1 6LH
020 7972 1999; www.nta.nhs.uk

City& Guilds

www.cityandguilds.com/myperfectjob

Social Work and Counselling Services

CRCI: V

TRADE UNION OFFICIAL

What the work involves

- Trade union officials negotiate with employers over pay, working conditions, health and safety, dismissal and redundancy.

- Working in regional offices, you will recruit members, train shop stewards, support local officials and negotiate individual cases with employers.

- At head office, you will work on national policies and negotiate at national level.

- At all levels your role will be to bring about the best deal for the workforce by finding common ground between employers and employees.

The type of person suited to this work

It is important to have a genuine interest in people's welfare and to believe in the aims of your union. You will need to see issues from different view points.

You will spend time dealing with individuals or groups, which requires good speaking, listening and negotiating skills. Speaking in public requires confidence

Union matters involve problem-solving and negotiation which needs a patient, methodical approach and the ability to research and analyse information.

Working conditions

As a local shop steward you will have another job and attend to union business part time.

Paid officials at regional and national level are office-based.

You could travel quite extensively to meetings, tribunals and conferences so a driving licence is useful.

You will make maximum use of ICT and will probably have a lot of phone work – some after normal work hours.

Future prospects

Your prospects depend very much on the size of the union, i.e. they are greater with the large unions which are never out of the news.

Head-office posts are usually in London. After gaining experience it is possible to progress to a regional role, as organiser or secretary, or a national role.

Some people move from union work into politics by becoming councillors or MPs.

Advantages/disadvantages

The work is varied, but you may be working on one theme in preparation for a meeting.

Negotiating better pay and working conditions can be very rewarding.

Some people might be unpleasant and sometimes you have to support people you do not agree with.

You might have to work long and unsocial hours.

Qualifications and courses

Entry is typically via a branch or regional office, or by joining the staff at head office.

Head-office staff are usually qualified to degree level in the area in which they specialise, for example law, politics, industrial relations, labour studies, social policy or economics. Minimum entry requirements for a degree are 2 A levels/3 H grades and 5 GCSEs/S grades (A*–C/1–3). They might have qualified and worked in these areas beforehand or they might be direct entrants with either a relevant degree or the equivalent – such as NVQs Levels 3 and 4. Workers at union headquarters might have worked their way up from branch or regional office level.

Branch or regional office staff will have spent several years involved in union work in an unpaid or paid capacity, either as a representative, shop steward or as an administrator. There are no formal entry requirements.

A year long training scheme is run by the Trade Union Congress' Organising Academy. The majority of trainees have relevant experience, either in trade unions or campaign organisation.

Training is mainly on the job. The Trades Union Congress and General Federation of Trade Unions run regular short training programmes.

Money guide

Local shop stewards/union representatives are generally unpaid.

As a paid official you can expect around £20,000 per year on entry.

As an experienced regional or national official you could earn £30,000–£50,000.

A general secretary could get as much as £100,000.

Related opportunities

- Equality and Diversity Officer p36
- Health and Safety Adviser p40
- Human Resources/Personnel Officer p41
- Social Care Worker/Social Worker p583

Further information

Trades Union Congress
Congress House, Great Russell Street, London WC1B 3LS
020 7636 4030; www.tuc.org.uk

Scottish Trades Union Congress
333 Woodlands Road, Glasgow G3 6DF
0141 337 8100; www.stuc.org.uk

Directgov
www.direct.gov.uk/en/Employment/TradeUnions/index.htm

VOLUNTEER MANAGER

What the work involves

- You will recruit, train and organise volunteers to assist charities, hospitals, social service departments and other volunteer organisations.

- After interviewing volunteers you will match them to the kind of work that suits them.

- You will deal with administration, budgets, correspondence and report writing.

- You could also prepare publicity material and liaise with other agencies.

The type of person suited to this work

You will work with volunteers from many different backgrounds and so you must be personable as well as a good motivator. You will need tact and patience, as not all volunteers are suited to the kind of role they wish to have.

It is essential to be confident and have good communication skills to sell placements to volunteers and volunteers to placements. You will need to be flexible and adaptable.

The job will demand a good deal of administration and record-keeping, which requires excellent organisational and time-management skills.

Working conditions

You could work out of an office or from home, depending on the size of the organisation.

You will need to travel locally to arrange placements and visit volunteers, so a driving licence will be useful.

You will most likely work 40 hours a week but may need to work evenings and weekends to meet deadlines.

Future prospects

You are unlikely to start this work straight from school. Opportunities are increasing, but there is keen competition for jobs and you might have to move to another organisation or charity to gain promotion. Volunteer management provides useful experience if you would like to transfer into a career such as social work or other management posts in the voluntary sector. You will have opportunities for further training, mainly through short courses.

Advantages/disadvantages

This work is varied and challenging.

The job is fulfilling; by helping volunteers find placements you will be making a difference to people in need.

You might have to work long hours.

As with any management role, some people may be hard to work with and difficult to please.

Qualifications and courses

No formal qualifications are needed to enter this career, but relevant work experience as a volunteer is valuable.

A degree or professional qualification can be an asset. Useful subjects include community development, business studies, social care and human resource management.

Professional courses vary. The National Association of Voluntary Service Managers offers a certificate for those working in the health and social care service.

A postgraduate degree could offer you an advantage, especially in the creative or international development industries, as the job is becoming increasingly popular.

Money guide

Starting salaries are around £15,000 per year. This rises to £30,000 with experience.

Earnings can be up to £40,000 for senior staff in large organisations who have substantial supervisory experience.

Related opportunities

- Fundraiser p575
- Social Care Worker/Social Worker p583
- Education Welfare Officer p195
- Youth and Community Worker p589

Further information

Association of Chief Executives of Voluntary Organisations
1 New Oxford Street, London WC1A 1NU
020 7280 4960; www.acevo.org.uk

Directory of Social Change
24 Stephenson Way, London NW1 2DP
020 7391 4800; www.dsc.org.uk

Scottish Council for Voluntary Organisations
Mansfield Traquair Centre, 15 Mansfield Place, Edinburgh EH3 6BB
0131 556 3882; www.scvo.org.uk

www.cityandguilds.com/myperfectjob

CRCI: V | Social Work and Counselling Services

WELFARE BENEFITS ADVISER/ WELFARE RIGHTS CASEWORKER

What the work involves

- In this job you will help people cope with problems by listening, asking questions and giving impartial and confidential advice.

- You will explain people's rights on matters such as tenancy, employment, conflicts with neighbours, consumer law and finance; sometimes referring clients to other professionals.

- Helping people fill in forms to claim benefits and making phone calls on their behalf will be part of the job.

- Benefit advisers may represent their clients at tribunals, or act as advocates in a court of law.

The type of person suited to this work

As the work is mainly about dealing with people, you must have excellent people skills and the ability to remain impartial and non-judgemental. In order to explain issues very clearly to your clients, and help them to complete forms and documents, you will need excellent verbal and written communication skills.

You will be handling large amounts of information, often to find answers to queries, which means you must enjoy research and be able to grasp facts and analyse data quickly.

You need to be understanding and tactful when dealing with upset and stressed clients.

Working conditions

Benefit advisers are based in an open-access centre within a local community, town or city.

You will see clients on a one-to-one basis by appointment, but also liaise with colleagues and other professionals, such as social workers and solicitors.

You will do research using ICT to consult client records, access email and the internet. You might do shift work, including Saturdays and some evenings.

Future prospects

Advice centre work is not open to school-leavers; it suits mature people, experienced in other fields. Entry is competitive; you could gain experience in helping people through volunteering work.

Most jobs are with local authorities or charities. There are a few paid jobs with the Citizens Advice Bureau, but many posts are voluntary. Training will be given in counselling skills or benefits, for example.

Promotion prospects are limited, although every advice centre has a manager.

Advantages/disadvantages

You will get the opportunity to work with many different people.

Qualifications and courses

ENTRY LEVEL 2

There are no set minimum entry requirements, but a good standard of education is desirable.

Although a degree is not specified, many applicants have degrees in a range of subjects and/or professional qualifications.

Life experience is essential, with applicants generally having a background of working with people.

It will help if you have experience in advising/counselling work, communication, information handling, ICT skills, money management, problem solving or working with others.

Once in post, you will attend in-house training and updating courses. NVQs at Levels 3 and 4 are available in legal advice, and advice and guidance.

Depending on your advisory area, you may work certain evenings and occasional weekends.

You will have to deal with angry and upset clients; some may even have mental health problems.

Helping clients resolve their problems can be personally rewarding.

Money guide

Pay depends on where you work and who you work for.

Earnings are around £18,000–£22,000 per year on entry.

Pay can rise to £23,000–£26,000+ with experience.

Salaries can exceed £30,000 for managers or team leaders. London rates are higher.

Related opportunities

- Counsellor p571
- Debt Counsellor/Money Advice Caseworker p572
- Education Welfare Officer p195
- Equality and Diversity Officer p36
- Solicitor/Notary Public p382

Further information

Citizens Advice
Myddelton House, 115–123 Pentonville Road, London N1 9LZ
020 7833 2181; www.citizensadvice.org.uk

Citizens Advice Scotland
2 Powderhall Road, Edinburgh EH7 4GB
0131 550 1000; www.cas.org.uk

Advice UK
6th Floor, 63 St Mary Axe, London EC3A 8AA
020 7469 5700; www.adviceuk.org.uk

YOUTH AND COMMUNITY WORKER

What the work involves

- You will work with people in their local community, encouraging them to take part in local learning opportunities and community activities.

- You could be in charge of a community centre, arranging activities for people of all ages, such as youth clubs, over-60s lunch clubs and playgroups.

- Youth workers are mainly involved with young people while community workers try to make sure that people of all ages in the local community have access to opportunities.

- The work is usually with groups of people.

The type of person suited to this work

As the work involves contact with all sorts of people, it is important to be able to get on with everyone and earn their trust. You also need to be genuinely interested in the local community and in equal opportunities.

Local people have a say in what they want in their area, so you must be a good listener, able to balance local groups' ideas with local and national government policies.

Working conditions

You might be based in a community centre or in an area office.

Depending on your job, you could also be based in a school, college or Connexions centre.

You work where young people go, including drop-in centres, cafés and youth clubs; this includes attending evening and weekend sessions.

Some workers travel around their local area, so a driving licence is useful.

Future prospects

Youth and community work is a growth area. As well as roles in youth club and community centre management, there are new strands to the work with developing music, drama, art or sporting groups. Local lifelong learning adult centres also require youth and community workers.

Local authorities have a defined promotion structure but in some jobs you might have to move around to widen your experience. You could progress to work for voluntary organisations or for a specific young people's services, for example Connexions.

Advantages/disadvantages

This work provides variety and challenge.

You will play a major part in developing your local community and/or the lives of young people.

You might have to work evenings, weekends and public holidays.

Qualifications and courses

You will need to pass a disclosure check with the Criminal Records Bureau.

Youth and community work is a graduate profession from 2010.

Professional training courses will usually require GCSEs/S grades (A*–C/1–3) and A levels/H grades or equivalent for candidates under 21. Entry requirements may be waived for mature applicants with relevant experience. Graduate and postgraduate qualifications must be recognised by the Joint Negotiating Committee for Youth and Community Workers (JNC).

The types of qualification are a BA(Hons) degree, postgraduate degree and a Master's degree that have all been validated by the National Youth Agency. These qualifications vary in length, offer full-time or part-time study and include work placements. The National Youth Agency has a list of universities offering the validated youth and community work qualifications on its website.

Additional aptitudes which are needed include caring for people, and high-level skills in communication, managing and organising, and working with others.

Money guide

Once qualified you can earn between £19,000 and £25,500 per year. Salaries rise to around £30,000 with experience. For managers, pay ranges between £35,000 and £60,000.

You may be paid extra for working unsocial hours.

Related opportunities

- Education Welfare Officer p195
- Further/Higher Education Lecturer p196
- Social Care Worker/Social Worker p583

Further information

National Youth Agency
Eastgate House, 19–23 Humberstone Road,
Leicester LE5 3GJ
0116 242 7350; www.nya.org.uk

Council for Wales of Voluntary Youth Services
Baltic House, Mount Stuart Square, Cardiff CF10 5FH
029 2047 3498; www.cwvys.org.uk

www.cityandguilds.com/myperfectjob

CRCI: V   Social Work and Counselling Services

Transport and Logistics

The jobs in this sector are immensely varied because of the wide range of transport and communication links that exist today to keep our lives running. You could need a high level of technical knowledge in this sector especially for jobs such as a pilot or a train driver. But you could also be great at keeping attention to detail and maintaining schedules if logistics is more where your interest lies. Jobs in transport and logistics require very efficient and practical people to ensure that our infrastructure continues to run smoothly and safely. You may need to cope well under pressurised situations as well as be very good at communicating so that any problems can be sorted out quickly.

This section looks at the following jobs:

For similar jobs to the ones in this section see *Security and the Armed Forces* on page 539 and *Leisure, Sport and Tourism* on page 383.

Organisation Profile

Passenger transport provides a wide range of job opportunities. Below are just a few people's stories.

James – Aircraft Dispatcher at Birmingham Airport

James works as part of a team responsible for coordinating activities that make sure that flights are prepared ready for the next departure as quickly and efficiently as possible. He also has to make sure that all work is carried out safely and that the flight meets any required regulations and rules to take off.

"I have to make sure that we have correctly calculated the weights of aircraft, taking into account passengers and luggage, and help to work out how much fuel is required. It's a big pressure to make sure it's all right, but very exciting knowing that you are helping people make journeys all over the world."

Jacqueline – Train Driver in Scotland

Becoming a train driver isn't easy and requires a lot of training, which can be intense and challenging. Most people move into driving from another rail-related job, be it customer service (such as station staff or train crew) or engineering. Jacqui drives on several routes, including local services and high speed cross country routes.

"The work can be lonely, you can be in the cab of your train for very long periods on your own, but at the same time it's interesting as no one day is the same, you can face different challenges. You've got to be able to think fast, but if you do your job, and do it well, then you can really get on in the rail industry."

Dan – Bus Engineer in Bristol

Dan maintains a fleet of buses, making sure that they are road-worthy and safe. He carries out checks and fault finding and can work on areas of a bus from replacing lights and batteries to fixing brakes and exhausts and can also use high tech equipment to carry out diagnostic tests.

"I've always been interested in vehicles and grabbed at the chance to do an apprenticeship in engineering. I like the detail I have to work in, and also the feeling of making a bus engine run efficiently when it wasn't working well before. You get to learn off your mentors too, as most garages work in teams, and people can work their way up."

Alex – Transport Planner in Cardiff

Working as a transport planner provides opportunities to influence transport systems, their infrastructure and how they are used. Alex's job as a transport planner involves undertaking surveys, analysing data and drawing up designs. It is important that she understands a wide range of issues that can affect transport including the environment, health and safety and social inclusion.

"In my job you can influence how systems work – I get great satisfaction from seeing through projects to the end and making a positive impact with them. In this job you can get a variety of work; and this encourages you to develop yourself and your career."

For more information visit www.careersinpassengertransport.org

Case study

GoSkills
Moving skills forward
www.careersinpassengertransport.org

CHECK-IN SUPERVISOR

Here's Alex Broad's story

Alex works as a Check-in Supervisor for Aviance at Birmingham Airport. Aviance provides ground services to more than 15 UK airports, handling over 43,000 passengers a year and employing nearly 5,000 staff and Alex oversees passenger services for two airlines.

How Alex became a Check-in Supervisor

"My career began in the motor industry as a Sales Executive. In 1991 I joined Aviance as a Passenger Services General Agent, initially on a temporary contract. After a year I was given a permanent contract as a Lead Agent. I then moved on to the Lost and Found department where at first I was a General Agent. I rapidly progressed to head-up Lost and Found and IT for the whole of the UK. I spent a total of seven years in this department. My current position is in passenger services as a Check-in Supervisor."

A typical day for Alex

"Passenger Services includes everything from the point of making a reservation to when a passenger leaves the airport. I oversee passenger services for two airlines – Lufthansa and SAS. My role is split into two principal areas of responsibility – supervision of Check-in and what is known in the business as Airside. On the check-in side I need to make sure that staff are allocated to the right check-in desk and that the correct policies and procedures are followed for each of the two airlines. I deal with passengers with special needs or requests such as wheelchair assistance, stretchers, arranging special security clearance and even making arrangements for passengers with small pets! (Some airlines permit small animals into the cabin.) I also supervise bookings, seat upgrades, flight cancellations, general flight disruptions, and passenger complaints. We have extremely high standards of customer care and service and as a result get very few complaints.

When I am supervising Airside I am involved in dealing with everything after passengers have gone through the security check. This essentially includes supervising flight boarding and ensuring that passengers board on time and dealing with passengers on standby."

The highs and lows

"I get a lot of satisfaction from my job and there are few low points. I don't mind the shifts as I enjoy getting days off in the week, but there are times when my shifts do clash with my social life, but that is all part of it!"

What makes Alex good at his job

"As a Check-in Supervisor it is essential to have tact and diplomacy, together with the ability to diffuse situations. Good time-keeping and a flexible approach is also important. You also need to be thick skinned and learn to be proactive rather than reactive."

What the future holds for Alex

"I would like to continue climbing up the career ladder into a Senior Airline Management position."

Alex's advice for others considering a career in Passenger Services

"The skills and experience you develop in Passenger Services are highly transferable so you can do anything more or less."

AIR CABIN CREW

What the work involves

- Once you have checked the cabin, you will welcome your passengers on board and make sure they are comfortable.

- You will be responsible for making sure that customers are safely belted up and that their bags are stored away. You will demonstrate safety procedures before take-off.

- During the flight you will help to care for any young children and sick passengers, giving First Aid if needed.

- You will also serve food and drinks, sell duty-free items, ensure passengers are ready for landing and see them all safely off the plane.

The type of person suited to this work

You will need to be welcoming, friendly, well groomed, confident and caring.

You should be happy working in a team with the rest of the crew. Common sense and tact are important when dealing with a variety of situations ranging from nervous passengers to unruly passengers to medical emergencies.

It's essential to stay calm under pressure and to have a reassuring attitude.

Working conditions

You will work in a cramped, noisy, warm cabin, which in bad weather can be unstable. You may have health problems, for example ear pain from cabin pressure or jet lag from long flights.

Security incidents or accidents can cause stress and delay. Planes fly 24/7 which means unsocial working hours, but also the chance to travel all over the world.

You will have the opportunity to meet a variety of people from many different countries and cultures.

Future prospects

There is fierce competition for jobs and positions for new entrants have declined.

With experience, you could progress to working as a purser (looking after a particular cabin such as first class) and then to cabin service director or crew controller.

You could also go on to train new cabin crew.

Advantages/disadvantages

You will travel to dream destinations, but on short flights you will not always get off the plane!

No 2 working days will be the same.

While working with people can be very rewarding, you might have to deal with difficult passengers.

Qualifications and courses

Entry requirements depend on the airline. Some airlines require 3 GCSEs/S grades (A*–C/1–3), while others look for 4–5 GCSEs (A*–C)/S grades (1–3). including English and maths. You will need to be at least 18, be physically fit, and pass height and weight restrictions. You will also need a valid passport allowing unrestricted world travel. Most airlines will expect you to be able to swim 25 metres and have prior customer service experience. It is an advantage if you can speak another language or have been trained in first aid.

Relevant entry qualifications include a GCSE in Leisure and Tourism, a GCSE, AS/A level or Diploma in Travel and Tourism or BTEC Nationals in Travel and Tourism, Customer Service and Aviation Operations. Alternative routes include completion of the City & Guilds/NCFE Awards, Certificates and Diplomas in Air Cabin Crew or Customer Service and NVQs in Hospitality and Tourism, Customer Service or Aviation Operations in the Air.

Once accepted by an airline you will take part in their 4–6 week training course followed by an opportunity to take NVQ Levels 2 and 3 in Aviation Operations in the Air (Cabin Crew).

Money guide

£12,000–£15,000 per year is usual for starting salaries. With experience this rises to £16,000–£20,000.

£25,000+ is usual for senior crew.

Companies offer free flights and meals and allowances might be paid for working away from home and unsocial hours.

Air cabin crew can boost earnings with commission on in-flight sales.

Related opportunities

- Holiday Representative p388
- Tour Guide/Manager p397
- Travel Agent p399

Further information

EMTA Awards Ltd
14 Upton Road, Watford WD18 0JT
0870 240 6889; www.eal.org.uk

NCFE
Citygate, St James' Boulevard, Newcastle NE1 4JE
0191 239 8000; www.ncfe.org.uk

www.cityandguilds.com/myperfectjob

AIR TRAFFIC CONTROLLER

What the work involves

- You will be responsible for a specific section of airspace, keeping air traffic flying safely and quickly.

- Using computers, radar, radio equipment and weather reports you will check pilots' flight plans and current positions.

- You will use a radio to give pilots the instructions, advice and information they need to fly safely.

- Any difficult weather, security alerts or emergencies will mean that you would have to make quick but safe decisions.

The type of person suited to this work

You must speak clearly and confidently when sending instructions to pilots. It's essential to stay alert at all times, even when you are tired. You must be able to make quick and logical decisions and stay calm in emergencies.

When checking your pilots' flight plans you will use lots of new technology and calculate distances and angles so good ICT and maths skills are important.

The technology and software used is regularly upgraded to improve safety, so you will need to be willing to train throughout your working life.

Working conditions

You will work from 37 to 40 hours a week at a flight control centre, or in an airport traffic control tower.

As it's a 24/7 job, shift work is usual and includes early mornings, nights, weekends and holidays.

You will use computers, radar displays and radio headphones.

The lighting in the control room is kept at the right level to help you read the radar screens.

Future prospects

Most of the 2,500 UK air traffic controllers are employed by the National Air Traffic Services (NATS) and work in one of three main area control centres: Swanwick in Southampton, West Drayton near London and Prestwick in Scotland. Others work at airports.

There are regular trainee vacancies as air traffic continues to increase, although entry is very competitive.

With experience, you could manage and train other air traffic controllers.

Advantages/disadvantages

No 2 working days are the same and your job will remain interesting.

You will be well paid for the level of responsibility you take on.

Excellent training is on offer including an exciting 15 hours' flying time, but you will have to pass all your assessments.

Qualifications and courses

ENTRY LEVEL 2

The main route into this work is to apply to National Air Traffic Services (NATS). You will need a minimum of 5 GCSEs (A*–C)/S grades (1–3), including English and maths. Applicants should be 18 or over.

You will also need a good standard of health, hearing, colour vision and a clear voice.

All Key Skills are useful for this job but especially communication, information technology and numeracy skills. There is strong competition for places and entry to this profession requires the completion of many practical tests and interviews.

NATS entrants are trained at the College of Air Traffic Control, next to Bournemouth International Airport. You will start by doing an 11 month course, during which an allowance is paid. There are ongoing examinations during this period which are vital to pass in order to progress to the next stage. After graduation trainees go on to an operational airport unit for validation training. It takes 3–4 years to become fully qualified.

Money guide

Trainee air traffic controllers get a training allowance of just over £10,000 per year at college. This can rise to, £15,000–£20,000 during the validation period.

Fully qualified and with experience you can get up to £45,000.

Senior controllers in highly responsible positions earn £85,000.

Related opportunities

- Coastguard Watch Assistant/Officer p542
- Airline Pilot p596
- Helicopter Pilot p605
- Royal Air Force (RAF) Officer p558

Further information

Civil Aviation Authority
London Team, Room 703, CAA House, 45–59 Kingsway, London WC2B 6TE
020 7453 6040; www.caa.co.uk

National Air Traffic Services Ltd
Corporate and Technical Centre, 4000 Parkway, Whiteley, Fareham PO15 7FL
01489 616001; www.nats.co.uk

City&
Guilds

www.cityandguilds.com/myperfectjob

CRCI: WA

Transport and Logistics

AIRLINE PILOT

What the work involves

- You will be responsible for the safety of your passengers, crew and cargo and will need to carry out a range of safety, route and fuel checks before each flight.

- When flying you will keep in radio contact with air traffic controllers, inform and direct the crew, plan your route and use computer systems to control and monitor the aircraft.

- After each flight you will need to write a report and record any problems that took place.

The type of person suited to this work

You will need to be confident and responsible enough to take charge of your aircraft and follow the exact instructions of air traffic control. Good communication and team-work skills are essential.

You must stay composed under pressure and in emergency situations. Quick thinking and good coordination are also important.

Once you have earned your wings, you will still be regularly assessed on your health, skills and competencies, so you must be keen to keep on learning.

Working conditions

You will wear a uniform and carry company ID at all times.

You will work shifts which could include weekends, nights and public holidays. If a flight is delayed you may work much longer hours than anticipated.

You must be prepared for jetlag and spending time away from home if piloting a long-haul flight. You will spend the majority of your time sitting in a small flight deck.

Future prospects

Competition for vacancies for new pilots is intense but openings for experienced pilots are increasing.

You could be promoted to co-pilot on a long-haul flight after you have about 5 years of experience as a short-haul pilot. In order to be promoted to a captain you will need to fly 5,000 hours and this can take up to 10 years to achieve.

You could become a manager or an instructor or even work up to a senior position within a major airline.

Advantages/disadvantages

You will be at the mercy of the weather and may not always be able to minimise turbulence.

It is a thrilling job that sometimes involves travelling to exotic locations.

Qualifications and courses

ENTRY LEVEL 3

You must be aged at least 16 to begin training for a 'frozen' Airline Transport Pilot Licence (ATPL) which allows you to become a co-pilot. After enough flying hours you can unfreeze your licence and be qualified to become a captain. You need to be 21 years old to hold a full ATPL.

There are various entry routes to getting an ATPL: You can train full time over 2 years with a flying school. For this you will need at least 5 GCSEs/S grades (A*–C/1–3) in English, maths and a science.

You could also apply first for a Private Pilot's Licence (PPL) through modular training and then with an extra 150 hours flying experience apply for an ATPL.

You could train as a pilot in the armed forces, serve for a time and then take a conversion course for a civilian ATPL.

You may do a degree course in pilot training at a university which will take you to frozen ATPL status.

Training can be expensive – up to £60,000 for a full-time course. Sponsorship is possible as are scholarships from organisations such as the Air League.

Money guide

You may start out earning between £21,000 and £30,000 per year. If you are a turboprop airline captain you can earn between £32,000 and £40,000 a year.

Experienced jet pilots can reach up to £38,000 while a jet captain can earn £75,000+.

Perks include subsidised travel.

Related opportunities

- Air Traffic Controller p595
- Royal Air Force (RAF) Airman/woman p557
- Helicopter Pilot p605

Further information

British Airline Pilots' Association
BALPA House, 5 Heathrow Boulevard, 278 Bath Road, West Drayton UB7 0DQ
020 8476 4000; www.balpa.org.uk

Guild of Air Pilots and Air Navigators
Cobham House, 9 Warwick Court, Gray's Inn, London WC1R 5DJ
020 7404 4032; www.gapan.org

Transport and Logistics

CRCI: WA

AIRPORT BAGGAGE HANDLER

What the work involves

- You will be responsible for safely loading, unloading and transporting baggage, cases, and freight.

- By checking the baggage against flight lists, you will sort items to make sure you get the baggage to the right place on time.

- You will then lift the baggage onto the ramp or conveyor belt to move it onto the plane or into the baggage hall or connecting flight.

- If you spot any unusual or suspicious baggage, you will need to report it immediately.

The type of person suited to this work

You need to be alert and detail oriented when checking labels against flight lists and looking out for suspicious baggage. In order to get aircraft loaded and unloaded on a short timescale, you will need to be physically fit, fast moving and accurate.

Flexibility and a willingness to get your hands dirty are also vital, as you might need to carry out jobs such as cleaning the aircraft and keeping runways free of hazards such as snow and birds. You should enjoy working as part of a team.

Working conditions

You will work mainly outdoors in all weathers as well as in cramped spaces such as cargo holds.

You will work around 39 hours per week on a shift system. It's advisable to live near the airport and have your own transport to make it in time for early shifts.

Working near aircraft can be noisy, but you will wear ear protectors.

Your job will involve a lot of bending, lifting and carrying and you will be required to wear protective boots and a high-visibility jacket.

Future prospects

Most of the 5,000 baggage handlers in the UK work for large airlines or handling agents at the biggest airports but there are vacancies at many regional airports as well. Seasonal work is also on offer at busy holiday periods.

You may be promoted to a supervisor or manage ground transport on the runways. With further training and qualifications you could also work in cargo services or aviation management.

Advantages/disadvantages

This is a great active, fast-paced and busy role.

If you are working for an airline, one of the perks may be subsidised travel.

You may have to work outside in poor weather conditions.

Qualifications and courses

ENTRY LEVEL 2

There are no minimum entry requirements for this job. However most employers will look for GCSEs (A*–C)/S grades (1–3), including English and maths.

You will usually need to be at least 18 years old, be physically fit and pass a medical, vision and Criminal Records Bureau (CRB) check. You will also need a clean driving licence and in some cases a large goods vehicle (LGV) licence.

You may enter this job through an Advanced Apprenticeship in Aviation Operations on the Ground.

Once accepted you will be trained in all aspects of the job including barcode recognition equipment, lift equipment and operating vehicles safely and effectively.

NVQs/SVQs in Providing Aviation Operations on the Ground at Levels 2 and 3 may be available. Other qualifications available include BTEC Nationals or City & Guilds at Levels 2 and 3 in Aviation Operations or Aviation Operations on the Ground.

Money guide

Starting salaries are usually £14,000 per year.

Experienced baggage handlers can earn £17,000+.

Team leaders can earn up £22,500.

Allowances are paid for shift work and this – plus overtime pay – can increase your earnings.

Related opportunities

- Hotel Porter p142
- Removals Operative p623
- Warehouse Worker/Manager p630

Further information

Royal Aeronautical Society
4 Hamilton Place, London WCJ 7BQ
020 7670 4326; www.aerosociety.com

International Air Transport Association
IATA UK, Spencer House, 23 Sheen Road, Richmond upon Thames TW9 1BN
020 7660 0068; www.iata.org

www.cityandguilds.com/myperfectjob

CRCI: WA

Transport and Logistics

BUS/COACH DRIVER

What the work involves

- Bus/coach drivers are responsible for providing an acceptable transport service for passengers making short or long journeys.

- You will be responsible for the safety and comfort of your passengers throughout their journey, which includes ensuring that passengers are safely on or off your vehicle before pulling out, and that they are wearing seatbelts when applicable.

- You might have to work out passenger fares and issue tickets and passes if you do not have a conductor.

- You will also be responsible for checking your vehicle, coping with breakdowns and other emergencies, and driving safely at all times.

The type of person suited to this work

You will need to be an extremely competent driver.

You should have a polite and approachable manner when dealing with passengers, but have the confidence to handle disagreements or other situations which may arise on journeys.

You will need good eyesight and excellent concentration in order to remain alert for very long periods of time. Quick reactions are also useful in case you need to respond to an unforeseen event on the road.

You should be a punctual person, as you will have to adhere to a strict timetable.

Working conditions

You will work on a shift pattern, encompassing evening, overnight and weekend work. You cannot work more than 56 hours a week, or 90 hours over 2 weeks. You are also required, by law, to take a 45 minute break every 4.5 hours.

Coach drivers will be required to help passengers with luggage, and provide assistance to disabled travellers. You will have to wear a uniform.

Future prospects

There is a continuous shortage of bus/coach drivers, so job opportunities are good.

Over 80% of the workforce is employed by one of six companies; Stagecoach, First, National Express, Transdev, Arriva and Go-Ahead.

You could work anywhere in the UK, undertake long distance tour driving, or provide a transport service for specific groups such as the elderly or disabled.

You can progress to become a supervisor, service controller, or instructor within your company.

Qualifications and courses

There are no specific academic requirements, but most employers prefer that you have 4 GCSEs/S grades (A*–C/1–3) or equivalent, including English and maths.

You must hold a PCV licence, and obtain the PCV driver certificate of professional competence (Driver CPC). You cannot train for this licence until you are 18 years old, and even then you will not be permitted to drive certain routes until you reach 21.

Most companies are willing to fund employees to take the PCV licence whilst paying them a trainee wage.

PVC training lasts 4–5 weeks and includes both a theory and practical test, along with a medical. During this period, your company will also give you training in relevant areas such as customer care, disability awareness, defensive driving and health and safety.

Advantages/disadvantages

You will be providing an essential public service.
Part time and flexible hours are available so you can fit work around other commitments.

You may have to deal with difficult or distressed passengers. Driving the same route or for long periods of time can become monotonous.

Money guide

As a trainee driver, while working towards gaining your PCV licence, you could expect to earn £11,000.

Once you have gained your licence, your earnings should rise to about £16,000.

With a few years' experience, your wages could increase to £23,500.

Related opportunities

- Large Goods Vehicle Driver p607
- Taxi Driver p627
- Chauffeur p599
- Driving Instructor p603

Further information

Driving Standards Agency
The Axis Building, 112 Upper Parliament Street, Nottingham NG1 6LP
0115 936 6666; www.dsa.gov.uk or for specific Driver CPC information www.drivercpc.org

City&
Guilds

www.cityandguilds.com/myperfectjob

CHAUFFEUR

What the work involves

- Chauffeurs are responsible for driving their client to and from appointments or events, as well as the maintenance of the vehicle.

- You will have to clean the vehicle regularly, inside and out, and also undertake any minor maintenance work when necessary, or book it in to see a mechanic.

- You will be providing a personal service to your passengers, including opening and closing doors for them, assisting them in and out of the vehicle, and carrying and loading their luggage or shopping.

- You might also be required to provide a low level of security protection to your client, as well as maintaining confidentiality at all times.

The type of person suited to this work

You must be an excellent driver who observes the law and keeps cool under pressure, even when faced with endless traffic jams or unpredictable clients. You will also need to have a good awareness of safety and security, both on the road and with regard to your client.

You should have excellent interpersonal skills. You must be punctual, respectful and polite.

Good map reading skills, knowledge of basic vehicle maintenance, and a reasonable level of fitness are also helpful.

Working conditions

It is unlikely that you will work regular hours as a chauffeur, as most clients will require your services during the evenings and at weekends. Split shifts are common, where you will find yourself with 2 or 3 free hours in between appointments.

You may be required to spend nights away from home on occasion.

You will need to wear a uniform in most instances.

Future prospects

Most chauffeurs are employed by limousine companies, but there are opportunities with hotel groups, car-hire companies, park and ride schemes, tour operators, businesses and private employers.

The British Chauffeurs Guild operates a specialist employment agency for their members, through which they can find suitable opportunities.

With experience, you can command a higher salary, or you could branch into a related career such as that of a taxi driver or driving instructor.

Advantages/disadvantages

You could work for some interesting, high profile clients.

The work offers some flexibility with hours.

There is a lot of waiting around for clients, which can get boring and frustrating.

Qualifications and courses

You do not need any specific academic qualifications to become a chauffeur. The only necessity is that you hold a full driving licence. Most employers will expect this to be clean, but some do consider candidates with penalty points.

You may benefit from holding an advanced driving certificate, details of which can be found through the Institute of Advanced Motorists. This demonstrates an enhanced driving ability and additional skills that may be valued by some employers.

It is beneficial to have several years' driving experience. Not only does this demonstrate a proven ability behind the wheel, but if you are over 21 years old you will cost your employer less to insure.

There are professional courses that you could take to enhance your application and understanding of the job. These include NVQs in road passenger vehicle driving, and the ASET Level 2 Certificate in Defensive Driving. The British Chauffeurs Guild also offer a 2 day Security Chauffeur Training Course which covers the fundamental areas of chauffeuring; theory, practice, protocol, security and etiquette.

Some employers may also require you to pass a medical assessment, and a Criminal Records Bureau check, prior to taking you on.

Money guide

Salaries vary depending on your employer, but on average the starting wage for a chauffeur is usually around £18,000. With 3–5 years' experience, this could rise to £27,000.

An experienced chauffeur, especially one with advanced driving or additional security qualifications, could earn £30,000+.

Related opportunities

- Taxi Driver p627
- Driving Instructor p603
- Bus/Coach Driver p598
- Motor Vehicle Technician p235

Further information

British Chauffeurs Guild
13 Stonecot Hill, Sutton SM3 9HB
020 8641 1740; www.britishchauffeursguild.co.uk;
bcg.london@btconnect.com

Institute of Advanced Motorists
IAM House, 510 Chiswick High Road, London W4 5RG
020 8996 9600; www.iam.org.uk

www.cityandguilds.com/myperfectjob

Transport and Logistics

COURIER

What the work involves

- You will collect fragile, valuable or urgent letters and packages and deliver them within an agreed time limit.

- Once you have been allocated your job, you will travel to a collection point for pick-up. You will load up the goods and then take them to the drop-off point where you will obtain a signature for delivery.

- Motorcycle couriers may travel long distances and van couriers carry larger parcels in a town or city.

- You will need to check the lights, brakes and tyres of your motorbike, van or bicycle regularly.

The type of person suited to this work

Map-reading skills are essential. You may only be paid for the number of deliveries you do so you need to be quick and know where you are going.

You will be in constant contact with customers; collecting items, asking for instructions and getting signatures for deliveries, so you need to be good with people. You should also be reliable – you may be dealing with high value or very urgent items.

Working conditions

You will spend a lot of time travelling but with regular stops to make deliveries. Long distance or overseas deliveries might mean time away from home.

Motorcycle and bicycle couriers will be out in the weather at all times.

Courier services operate 24/7 and many couriers work on overnight deliveries.

You might have to provide your own car or van. Motorcycle and bicycle couriers usually use their own bikes.

Future prospects

The continued growth of online shopping and customer online tracking means that the demand for same and next day courier delivery is growing. However the recession has affected the industry making fewer vacancies available.

Promotion generally depends on the size of the courier company – large companies may have sales and management opportunities. It might be possible to become self-employed and start your own courier service. You could also train further and move into a related area such as large goods vehicle driving or distribution.

Advantages/disadvantages

Pay rates are good but if you are using your own transport you will have running, insurance and maintenance costs.

Making up to 20 journeys a day and possibly working 50-hour weeks make this a stressful job.

Most couriers take up the job because they are attracted to the freedom of travel. However most couriers do

Qualifications and courses

You will need to be at least 17 years old – many couriers are over 21 because of high insurance costs for young drivers. School leavers could start as bicycle couriers.

Employers ask for a full UK driving licence for driver couriers and motorcycle couriers will need the CBT qualification issued by the DVLA. Motorcycle and bicycle couriers usually use their own bikes.

Couriers driving light trucks will also need to have their C1 Category licence if they passed their driving test after 1 January 1997.

Key Skills in communication and working with others are useful.

Apprenticeships/Skillseekers are available for candidates aged 16–24.

You might be able study for an NVQ/SVQ at Level 2 in Carry and Deliver Goods and an NVQ at Levels 2 and 3 in Driving Goods Vehicles when employed.

lots of repeat deliveries in a small, often congested, urban area.

Money guide

Couriers are often self-employed and paid for individual deliveries, so earnings vary.

Employed couriers can earn £14,500 per year (£18,000 in London).

Experienced couriers can earn up to £24,000 per year (£25,000+ in London).

Couriers travelling by air may be employed by airlines on a one-off basis, receiving reduced cost flights instead of wages.

Related opportunities

- Airport Baggage Handler p597
- Taxi Driver p627
- Delivery Driver p601
- Warehouse Worker/Manager p630

Further information

Driving Standards Agency
Stanley House, 56 Talbot Street, Nottingham NG1 5GU
0115 901 2500; www.dsa.gov.uk

Institute of Couriers
Green Man Tower, 332 Goswell Road, London EC1V 7LQ
0845 601 0245; www.ioc.uk.com

www.cityandguilds.com/myperfectjob

DELIVERY DRIVER

What the work involves

- You could be responsible for the safe transportation and delivery of a variety of goods, including food and drink, parcels, and domestic appliances.

- You will be loading and unloading goods from your vehicle, and making sure that your load is secure prior to starting on your journey. You will also be responsible for ensuring that your van is well maintained and road worthy.

- You will need to organise your own delivery schedule in order to meet strict distribution times each day.

The type of person suited to this work

You will need to be an extremely competent driver and be able to focus for long periods of time.

You should have a polite manner in order to build good relationships with colleagues and customers.

Good map reading and navigational skills are helpful for finding your way round new and unfamiliar areas on a delivery. It's also important to be reliable and to stay calm in hazardous situations.

You should be physically fit, as you might need to load and unload heavy items from your van.

Working conditions

You might need to work 37–40 hours in shifts over evenings and weekends. Other companies will only deliver goods during standard working hours. Part-time work is often available.

You might work on your own or with another person who will help navigate and plan your route, and assist with loading and unloading goods.

You will spend the majority of your time in the van, and will have to drive and meet time-restricted schedules no matter what the weather. You might have to wear a uniform.

Future prospects

The rise of internet shopping has resulted in an increase in opportunities for delivery drivers; however the recession has affected the number of vacancies available.

There is demand for drivers all over the UK, so you could work anywhere, although most opportunities are found in larger towns and cities.

You could work for a variety of companies, including retail, manufacturing and supermarkets, or you could opt for self-employment.

You could also move into a related area in transport, such as an administrative or transport manager post.

Qualifications and courses

No specific academic qualifications are required for delivery drivers, but some employers prefer candidates with some GCSEs (A*–E) or equivalent, including English and maths.

You will need to hold an appropriate driving licence to work as a delivery driver. You might also find holding a licence for category C1 useful as it will allow you to drive vehicles that weigh between 3.5 and 7.5 tonnes. For this you will need to take a Large Goods Vehicle (LGV) theory and C1 practical test.

If you plan to work for a company that transports large sums of money or valuable items, you will also need an SIA licence. This can be obtained on completion of the National Open College Network (NOCN) Level 2 Award in cash and valuables transit.

Advantages/disadvantages

Part-time and flexible hours are available so you can fit work around other commitments.

You will be providing a valuable service to people, either delivering food or appliances to their homes, or transporting parcels or money safely around the UK.

Money guide

Starting salaries for full-time van drivers are usually around £11,000. With experience this could rise to between £15,000 and £18,000. Most van drivers peak at earnings of around £23,000. You can increase your wage by working overtime.

Related opportunities

- Large Goods Vehicle Driver p607
- Taxi Driver p627
- Train Driver p629
- Chauffeur p599

Further information

National Open College Network
The Quadrant, Parkway Business Park, 99 Parkway Avenue, Sheffield S9 4WG
0114 227 0500; www.nocn.org.uk; nocn@nocn.org.uk

Driving Standards Agency
Stanley House, 56 Talbot Street, Nottingham NG1 5GU
0115 901 2500; www.drivercpc.org

City&
Guilds

www.cityandguilds.com/myperfectjob

Transport and Logistics

CRCI: WE

DISTRIBUTION MANAGER

What the work involves

- You will be responsible for overseeing the control and movement of goods or raw materials held in stock.

- Using ICT, you will manage stock levels and monitor the ordering and storage of goods.

- You will also manage staff and carry out their recruitment and training.

The type of person suited to this work

Distribution is a fast-moving industry and ICT is at its centre, so you will need excellent computer skills. Like the computer programs you will use, you will need to be systematic and logical. Brilliant communication skills are also a necessity as you will have to deal with people at different levels.

It might be that the goods you have to order come from far-flung places. This means that the supply chain you will be managing might be very complex. You will also need to able to deal with the stress of making sure that you get the goods at the best price and supply them in the right condition.

Working conditions

Most of your work will be in an office, but you will also travel to meetings with suppliers or customers and visit storage depots.

Your hours will be mainly office hours, Monday–Friday, but you might have to do shift work or work weekends and evenings on a rota system.

There could be travel away from home and, for some, travel overseas.

Future prospects

There are more than 86,000 distribution managers working for a wide range of companies, including warehouse and distribution firms but also manufacturers, major retail companies, the Armed Forces and central and local government. With experience, you could progress into a senior role in business development or undertake consultancy work.

Advantages/disadvantages

As a key figure in your company, you will have the satisfaction of making sure your supply chain works and that your customers are happy.

The demands of coordinating vehicles, products, people and tight deadlines, can make this a stressful role.

Money guide

Salaries start around £19,000 per year. Experienced managers earn from £30,000. Senior managers responsible for transport schedules can earn £60,000+.

Qualifications and courses

ENTRY LEVEL 2

There are no specific entry requirements; however, many employers recruit graduates. It is also possible to work your way up from a junior post by gaining NVQ qualifications or professional qualifications.

Foundation degrees, degrees and postgraduate courses are available in areas such as logistics, transport management and supply chain management. Normally, at least 5 GCSEs/S grades (A*–C/1–3) and 2 A levels/3 H grades or equivalent are required for a degree course.

Entry for Higher National Diplomas requires a minimum of 4 GCSEs/S grades (A*–C/1–3) and 1 A level/2 H grades, a related BTEC National Certificate/Diploma or equivalent.

Other entry routes include an apprenticeship in traffic office, logistics operations management or warehousing and storage or a Diploma in Business, Administration and Finance.

People working in the industry can study for the CILT's professional qualifications. The Introductory Certificate is suitable for employees new to the profession. The Certificate is aimed at supervisors and first line managers. The Professional Diploma is intended for middle managers, including recent graduates, and fulfils the requirements for membership of the Institute.

Senior distribution managers can take the CILT Advanced Diploma or study for a Master's in Logistics.

Distribution Managers might find it helpful to take the Certificate of Professional Competence of the Department of Transport.

Related opportunities

- Freight Forwarder p604
- Importer/Exporter p606
- Road Transport Manager p625
- Warehouse Worker/Manager p630

Further information

Freight Transport Association
Hermes House, St Johns Road, Tunbridge Wells TN4 9UZ
0871 711 2222; www.fta.co.uk

Chartered Institute of Logistics and Transport (CILT)
Earlstrees Court, Earlstrees Road, Corby NN17 4AX
01536 740104; www.ciltuk.org.uk

www.cityandguilds.com/myperfectjob

DRIVING INSTRUCTOR

What the work involves

- You will teach people how to drive safely, and well enough to pass their driving test.

- You will explain basic motor and road skills as well as safe and courteous driving.

- Your role will include making your pupils aware of all aspects of the Highway Code, helping to develop observation skills and teaching manoeuvres such as reverse parking.

- It will be your responsibility to plan driving lessons to suit your pupil and give constructive criticism.

The type of person suited to this work

Not only will you need to be a good, safe driver, you will also need teaching skills. People learning to drive are often stressed and anxious, so you will need to be calm, steady and patient.

Instructors need to plan lessons to cover individual weaknesses. You will need to have quick reactions in order to prevent your pupils from causing any accidents.

As many instructors are self-employed, you will need to have a good business sense and the ability to manage your own finances.

Working conditions

Instructors can spend more than 8 hours a day sitting in the car ready to operate the dual controls to avert problems. Early morning, evening and weekend work is common as you will teach lessons at times that suit your pupils.

Instructors with lots of experience can work a 35–40 hour week. However, you might have to work longer hours to keep a steady income. This can restrict the times and lengths of holidays for self-employed or franchised instructors.

Future prospects

Driving instructors could work for driving schools, operate under a franchise, or have their own businesses. Opportunities are also available with big transport companies, the emergency services, local authorities and the armed forces.

Around 80% of instructors are self-employed. There are no restrictions on the numbers of instructors meaning there is sometimes strong competition for pupils.

You could undertake fleet driver training and instruction in driving large goods or passenger-carrying vehicles.

You could progress to a role as a trainer for new driving instructors or a driving examiner.

Advantages/disadvantages

It can be very rewarding to enable learners to become safe, qualified drivers.

Many driving instructors are self-employed.

Qualifications and courses

ENTRY LEVEL 1

You must be registered with the Driving Standards Agency as an Approved Driving Instructor (ADI). You will need to be aged over 21 and have held a full clean driving licence for 4 out of the last 6 years, with no criminal or motoring convictions. The ADI examination is in three parts: an IT-based multiple choice theory test and a video-based hazard perceptions test; a practical driving test; and a practical teaching test. Parts two and three must be completed within a year of Part one. Applicants must pass the practical driving test within three attempts.

As training can be very expensive, the majority of entrants join a training organisation or an organisation which provides franchise prospects if you complete the training.

NVQs at Level 3 in Driving Instructor and in Bus/Coach Driving Instructor are available.

If you run your own car to give lessons you will have to pay for your fuel, insurance and maintenance costs.

It may be a challenge to maintain a steady income.

Money guide

Instructors charge £10–£30 per hour for a driving lesson. Full time driving instructors could earn £15,000 as a starting salary. With several years' experience this can rise to around £23,000. Your income will be reduced by the costs of running and maintaining your vehicle or paying a franchise fee.

Full-time, experienced driving instructors can earn up to £35,000. Salaries are higher in London.

Related opportunities

- Taxi Driver p627
- Work-based Training Instructor p209
- Chauffeur p599

Further information

Driving Instructors Association
Safety House, Beddington Farm Road, Croydon CR0 4XZ
020 8665 5151; www.driving.org

Motor Schools Association of Great Britain Ltd
101 Wellington Road North, Stockport SK4 2LP
0161 429 9669; www.msagb.co.uk

The UK Driving Instructors Confederation
53 St Marys Walk, Rochester ME1 3SJ
01625 869285; www.ukdic.co.uk

City&
Guilds

www.cityandguilds.com/myperfectjob

FREIGHT FORWARDER

What the work involves

- You will organise the transport of goods across the world for importers and exporters.

- Your role will involve working out if the freight needs special handling and whether it should go by sea, road or air.

- Arranging the packing, carriage, collection and storage of the goods will be part of your job.

- You will be responsible for dealing with paperwork, applying for customs clearance and calculating insurance, transport and customs costs.

The type of person suited to this work

As you will deal with lots of different customers, some of whom may not speak fluent English, you must have excellent communication skills.

You must be determined and have excellent bargaining skills to get the best prices and terms. You will also be a good problem-solver. For example, you might have to work out how to transport a valuable racehorse from Hong Kong to the UK.

Your basic maths skills will need to be good as you will be asked to calculate exchange rates, or work out if a large piece of cargo will fit into the cargo hold of a small aircraft.

Working conditions

Most of your work will be in an office at a workstation using the telephone, computer and fax.

You will also need to travel to meet customers and contractors – this could mean being away from home.

You might need to work extra hours or shifts to cover urgent deliveries and world time zones.

Working to meet strict deadlines can make this a stressful job.

Future prospects

Freight forwarding offices are usually in cities and near airports and ports. Opportunities are growing but it is a competitive industry and it helps if you have related work experience.

As you progress, there are opportunities to specialise in specific countries and industries. You could work within the entertainment industry, shipping film and concert sets around the world, or with medical and pharmaceutical supplies. After gaining experience, you could progress to a senior freight forwarder and then to a managerial role like export office manager.

Advantages/disadvantages

This work varies. You may be specialising in, for example, moving film and TV crews and their equipment or handling perishable goods such as fruit.

You might get a chance to travel or work overseas.

Working to meet tight delivery deadlines can be stressful.

Qualifications and courses

Qualifications vary from a minimum of 4 GCSEs/S grades, including English and maths, to A levels/H grades, to the BTEC Level 3 Certificate in Logistics. Larger employers also look for a degree or language skills.

You can enter with a degree, HND or Foundation degree in a related subject, for example logistics, supply chain management, international transport or transport management. Some companies have graduate training schemes. Entry to degree courses will require a minimum of 2 A levels/3 H grades and 5 GCSEs/S grades (A*–C/1–3). For HNC/HND courses, you will normally need at least 1 A level/2 H grades and 4 GCSEs/S grades (A*–C/1–3) or equivalent like a related BTEC National Certificate/Diploma.

Other entry routes include a traffic office Apprenticeship and the Diploma in Business, Administration and Finance.

Key Skills in communications, ICT, problem solving and working with others are useful.

Training on the job includes NVQs Levels 2 and 3 in Traffic Office.

The British International Freight Association provides specialist training and a professional qualification for freight forwarders.

Certificates and Diplomas in International Trade are also available from the Institute of Export.

Money guide

Trainees usually earn around £10,000 per year.

With experience you could earn around £20,000.

£30,000+ is possible for senior freight forwarders, directors and managers.

Related opportunities

- Distribution Manager p602
- Importer/Exporter p606
- Warehouse Worker/Manager p630

Further information

Institute of Export
Export House, Minerva Business Park, Lynch Wood, Peterborough PE2 6FT
01733 404400; www.export.org.uk

Chartered Institute of Logistics and Transport
Earlstree Court, Earlstree Road, Corby NN17 4XQ
01536 740104; www.ciltuk.org.uk

City&
Guilds

www.cityandguilds.com/myperfectjob

HELICOPTER PILOT

What the work involves

- You will most likely pilot alone and will be responsible for the safety of your passengers.

- You will carry out fuel, weather and route checks before taking off and will keep in contact with air traffic controllers whilst navigating and monitoring the helicopter during the flight.

- After landing you will record your hours and details from the flight.

- You may fly for a variety of purposes including searching for missing persons, emergency work, crop spraying, photography, leisure trips or ferrying supplies.

The type of person suited to this work

You must be good with maths and physics, an excellent problem solver and a quick thinker in order to control your helicopter in all weather and in emergency situations. Good communication and team-work skills are essential.

Good coordination and attention to detail are also important. You could be flying long hours and will need stamina, forward-thinking skills and the ability to stay focused on your work.

As a pilot you are responsible for other people's safety and you must be reliable.

Working conditions

You will wear a uniform or a survival suit if flying over the sea for emergency services. Most of your time will be spent sitting alone in a small space.

Your helicopter will be single or multi-engine and it will take time to adjust to the noise and sensation.

If flying for leisure services you will most likely work during the daytime only. Emergency and business services may require you to fly through the night and on weekends.

Future prospects

There are opportunities to work in emergency services, the armed forces and for commercial companies but competition is intense for newly qualified helicopter pilots.

With 1,000 hours of flight experience and 250 hours as 'pilot in command' you can go on to get your ATPL(H) (Airline Transport Pilot Licence). You can then fly multi-engine, multi-pilot helicopters for commercial air transport. You could also set up your own air taxi service company or become self-employed.

Advantages/disadvantages

Helicopter training is expensive and you will need to raise a lot of money if you can't get sponsorship.

Qualifications and courses

You must hold a CPL(H) (Commercial Pilot's Licence) in order to fly commercially. You must be 17 years old to apply.

There are various entry routes for getting a CPL(H): You may enrol on an integrated full-time training course over 12 months. You could also apply first for a PPL(H) (Private Pilot's Licence) through modular training and then with another 500 hours study, extra flying time and exams qualify for the CPL(H).

For both of these routes you will need at least 5 GCSEs/S grades (A*–C/1–3) including English, maths and a science (preferably physics).

You need to pass a medical exam and raise money for training as sponsorships for helicopter pilots are rare. Courses can cost up to £45,000.

It is also possible to train as a pilot by joining the armed forces.

It may be difficult to get enough sleep as you could fly through various time zones.

No two days will be the same. It is exciting to not know what each flight will hold.

Money guide

Newly qualified commercial helicopter pilots can earn between £20,000 and £25,000 a year.

Experienced pilots carrying passengers can earn between £45,000 and £70,000 a year.

Related opportunities

- Air Traffic Controller p595
- Royal Air Force (RAF) Airman/woman p557
- Airline Pilot p596

Further information

British Helicopter Association
Graham Suite, Fairoaks Airport, Chobham,
Woking GU24 8HX
01276 856100; www.britishhelicopterassociation.org

British Helicopter Advisory Board
The Graham Suite, West Entrance, Fairoaks Airport,
Chobham GU24 8HX
01276 856100; www.bhab.org

Civil Aviation Authority
CAA House, 45–59 Kingsway, London WC2B 6TE
020 7379 7311; www.caa.co.uk

Transport and Logistics

CRCI: WB

IMPORTER/EXPORTER

What the work involves

- You will organise all aspects of exporting or importing goods for companies who source or sell them overseas.

- Liaising with shipping and forwarding companies, you will get the best prices, sources, quality and delivery services.

- You will deal with all the necessary financial paperwork, including invoicing and checking, and issuing letters of credit so that payment can be made.

- You will also work out accurate costings, including customs duties, insurance and forwarding charges.

The type of person suited to this work

As you will be making arrangements with a wide range of customers you need to be confident, tactful and an excellent communicator. Language skills are a real advantage.

Dealing with numbers will be one of your key strengths because you will be responsible for working out currency exchanges and import and export duties. In addition, ICT skills are vital. You must be a good negotiator as you will need to bargain with shipping and distribution companies, as well as your customers and suppliers.

Working conditions

Most of your work will be in an office using the telephone, computer and fax machine. You might need to work early mornings or late evenings if your customers or suppliers operate in a different time zone.

You may travel to meet suppliers or customers, which at higher levels could involve significant overseas travel.

Future prospects

As more products are bought and sold in a global market, the numbers of companies employing an import/export specialist have increased. Freight-forwarding, industrial, retail and specialist companies such as flower, jewellery or fruit all offer potential jobs.

Vacancies are competitive and usually require work experience in a related area. Some import/export specialists move into overseas sales management or take up consultancy work.

Advantages/disadvantages

This job is satisfying as you are helping to make the global supply chain work.

You might be under a lot of stress to meet tight deadlines and budgets.

Qualifications and courses

ENTRY LEVEL 3

You can enter export or import at different levels. While there are no set minimum qualifications, most employers will expect 4 GCSEs/S grades (A*–C/1–3) including English and maths. Others will require A levels or equivalent qualifications while many large companies will ask for an HND, Foundation degree or degree.

Useful degree subjects include logistics, supply chain management, international transport, business or languages.

Apprenticeships/Skillseekers in sales, business and administration, and logistics operations management may be available for candidates aged 16–24. Some companies offer graduate training schemes.

The Institute of Export offers professional qualifications for people working in the field of international trade. The Advanced Certificate in International Trade leads to Associate Membership of the Institute, and the Diploma in International Trade leads to Graduate Membership. These qualifications are offered at colleges of further and higher education and by distance learning. Candidates must be at least 18 years old with 4 GCSEs/S (A*–C/1–3) and 1 A level/H grade or equivalent.

You can also qualify with an NVQ/SVQ Level 2 in International Trade and Services, or an Introductory Certificate of International Trade (Institute of Export), or be 21 years old with 3 years' practical experience.

Money guide

Starting salaries at clerk level range from £11,000 to £15,000 per year. Experienced staff with more responsibility can earn up to £30,000. Import or export managers of companies with global interests can earn over £65,000.

Related opportunities

- Road Transport Manager p625
- Distribution Manager p602
- Freight Forwarder p604

Further information

Institute of Export
Export House, Minerva Business Park, Lynch Wood, Peterborough PE2 6FT
01733 404400; www.export.org.uk

City & Guilds

www.cityandguilds.com/myperfectjob

LARGE GOODS VEHICLE DRIVER

What the work involves

- You will transport thousands of tonnes of cargo in your large goods vehicle (LGV).

- You could carry loads such as livestock, fuel, chemicals, food or construction equipment.

- Your job is to deliver the cargo on time. To do this you will figure out the best route with your transport manager. You also need to calculate your mileage.

- You will sometimes help load and unload cargo, keep the goods safe, and refuel and clean your lorry after each journey.

The type of person suited to this work

You must be an excellent driver with good maths skills as you will be navigating long distances. You should be able to use your initiative and follow safety precautions. Quick reactions, good eyesight and colour vision are useful in case you need to respond to an unforeseen event on the road. It's essential to stay alert for long periods of time.

Overall, you need to be an experienced, confident and punctual driver. You should be polite when dealing with customers and also be content working on your own.

Working conditions

LGV cabs are cosy and quiet, equipped with cooking facilities, bunks, air conditioning and heating. These comforts are important as you will spend hours by yourself in your lorry, eating and sleeping in the cab.

On average you will work 48 hours a week; legally you are unable to exceed 60 hours in a week. Ten hours of night driving is the maximum you may do in a 24-hour period. Your shifts will include evenings and weekends.

Future prospects

If you work for a road haulage firm you will transport loads for multiple companies. You could also work for farms, transporting livestock, or move sporting goods for retailers. You could be employed by manufacturers, moving fleets of cars.

You could be promoted to a supervisor, become an instructor or move into driving hazardous goods. With further training you could become a manager or start up your own company, operating your own lorry.

Advantages/disadvantages

You have freedom and flexibility in your work.

The job can be adventurous as you travel to different locations.

You might need to spend long periods of time away from home which can be difficult.

It can be frustrating when you are stuck in traffic and have a deadline to meet.

Qualifications and courses

Most employers prefer candidates who have GSCEs/S grades (A*–C/1–3) in English and maths, although no formal academic qualifications are required.

You need to be over 18, have a clean driving record, pass a medical exam and hold an LGV licence category C1, C, or C+E. If you want to drive a truck with 3.5–32 tonnes you will need a C licence. A C1 licence is restricted to 7.5 tonnes. To drive up to 44 tonnes you need a C+E licence.

In order to obtain an LGV licence you need to train for the Driver Certificate of Professional Competence (Driver CPC). This requires you to do 35 hours of training every 5 years to keep your licence.

If you want to carry dangerous goods you will need to train to obtain an Advisory Dangerous Goods by Road Certificate.

The Apprenticeship in Driving Goods Vehicles may be useful.

Money guide

The pay can vary depending on where you live and who you work for. If you work freelance you may negotiate your own rate.

£14,000 a year is the typical starting salary. Once you gain a few years' experience you could start earning up to £30,000. This rises to £35,000 a year if you choose to drive a specialist fuel or chemical vehicle.

Related opportunities

- Bus/Coach Driver p598
- Taxi Driver p627
- Train Driver p629
- Driving Instructor p603

Further information

Driving Standards Agency
Stanley House, 56 Talbot Street, Nottingham NG1 5GU
0115 901 2500; www.dsa.gov.uk or for specific Driver CPC information www.drivercpc.org

Freight Transport Association
Hermes House, St John's Road, Tunbridge Wells TN4 9UZ
0871 711 2222; www.fta.co.uk

Road Haulage Association
Roadway House, 35 Monument Hill, Weybridge KT13 8RN
01932 841515; www.rha.uk.net

www.cityandguilds.com/myperfectjob

Transport and Logistics

CRCI: WE

LIFT TRUCK OPERATOR

What the work involves

- Operating a lift truck with a special fork and carrying platform, you will load, unload, move and stack heavy goods.

- You will activate the controls so that your fork or lifting gear is under the load, usually stored in pallets, cages or cases, to raise it safely. This may require manoeuvring at considerable heights.

- You will then drive the goods, being careful not to damage the load, to its destination. This could be a transport vehicle, a depot or a warehouse.

- You will also need to perform routine maintenance checks to your truck.

The type of person suited to this work

An aptitude for driving is vital. You will need to be focused and alert when manoeuvring your truck in narrow spaces, always on the lookout for potential hazards. A responsible, mature outlook is required for working to strict safety rules. You will need to be physically fit and have good coordination.

Although you will operate the truck on your own you will also need to be a team player, working alongside warehouse operatives and LGV drivers.

Working conditions

At times you will work inside a warehouse or factory and at other times outside in loading bays.

While some trucks will have cabs offering protection from the weather most of the time you need to be prepared to get cold and wet.

Operating your equipment will mean sitting in a driving seat for long periods.

Hours vary depending on your employer. You may work regular hours Monday to Friday, but many jobs include shift work covering evenings and weekends.

Future prospects

You may be employed by the manufacturing, transport, haulage, warehouse or retail industries. There are about 100,000 lift truck operators in the UK.

With experience, you can move on into supervisory or management jobs in areas such as warehousing. You could go on to train new lift truck operators. Some large employers may train you to become LGV drivers or instructors.

Advantages/disadvantages

You might work outside in poor weather conditions.

If you are keen on driving, large employers might give you the chance to move on to LGV driver training.

It can be stressful to get a load out quickly, but there's a buzz when transport leaves on time.

Qualifications and courses

There are no minimum entry qualifications for this job but basic maths is useful to work out safe loads and weights. You may have to pass a medical exam and an aptitude test. Warehouse work experience is also helpful although direct entry is possible.

You will need to be at least 18 years old to work without supervision. A driving licence is required if the truck is to be used on public roads.

Before starting work you will need to have a Construction Plant Competence Scheme (CPCS) card. To qualify you will need to pass the NVQ Level 2 in Plant Operations as well as the ConstructionSkills Health and Safety Test.

Lift truck operators can work towards the NPTC (National Proficiency Tests Council) Level 2 Certificate of Competence in Fork Lift Truck Operations or NVQ/SVQ Levels 1 and 2 in Specialised Plant and Machinery Operations.

Apprenticeships/Skillseekers may be available in such areas as Storage and Warehousing, Wholesale and Distribution, leading to NVQs/SVQs Levels 2 and 3.

Money guide

Starting wages are about £12,000–£13,000 per year.

With experience you could earn up to £16,000.

Some specialist operators can earn £20,000+.

Usually, there are shift allowances and the opportunity to do overtime.

Related opportunities

- Airport Baggage Handler p597
- Construction Plant Operator p89
- Delivery Driver p601
- Warehouse Worker/Manager p630

Further information

Association of Industrial Truck Trainers
The Springboard Centre, Mantle Lane, Coalville LE67 3DW
01530 277857; www.aitt.co.uk

National Plant Operators Registration Scheme
PO Box 204, Northwich CW9 7PL
01606 351240; www.npors.com

**City&
Guilds**

www.cityandguilds.com/myperfectjob

LOADER

What the work involves

- Loaders are operatives who load and unload goods into or out of a container or lorry.

- You will be responsible for moving goods, either by hand or using specialist lifting equipment.

- You might be operating a lift truck or a specialist lorry loader (crane) if you are loading or unloading heavy items.

- You might also have additional tasks such as cleaning the loading bay or working as a driver's mate.

The type of person suited to this work

If you like practical tasks and being outside in all weathers, this job is for you. You must be able to carefully follow all health and safety regulations as you will be working in a loading bay alongside a heavy goods operating plant. You must be fit and active.

You must be able to work well with others, for example drivers, and follow all instructions to ensure your safety and that of your team.

You should also be good at working out how items can be fitted tightly into a space, to maximise the amount of goods transported.

Working conditions

You will spend the majority of your time outside in the loading depot, or inside a large warehouse.

Hours vary. You could work regular hours, Monday to Friday, but it is often shift work and sometimes permanent night work.

There is a risk of accidents.

You will have to wear safety boots and gloves. Some employers require you to provide your own safety clothing.

Future prospects

A range of firms employ loaders, but usually expect you to do other duties. You could work for a manufacturing company moving goods from the factory floor onto wagons, or for a parcel company sorting and loading goods in delivery order, or a building materials supplier using a lorry loader to lift bricks onto a wagon.

After further training, you could progress into delivery driving or warehouse management.

Advantages/disadvantages

If you are keen on going into LGV driving, your employer may be willing to train you.

Ensuring that deliveries are loaded or unloaded quickly can be stressful.

This job provides the satisfaction of working as part of a team to get deliveries out on time.

Qualifications and courses

There are no minimum entry qualifications for this job. You will need to be physically fit and may have to pass a medical. Some employers prefer you to have a driving licence and be aged at least 18.

You might be able to take an NVQ/SVQ Level 2 in Transporting Goods by Road and NVQ/SVQ Levels 1–3 in Distribution and Warehousing Operations.

If your employer expects you to operate a lift truck, they will give you basic training approved by the Health and Safety Commission. You may also be able to work towards NVQ/SVQs Levels 1 and 2 in Plant Operations.

If your employer expects you to operate a hydraulic lorry loader you will need to take a 2-day Lorry Loader Operating Safety Course. Many employers also expect you to be a category C driver to train as a specialist lorry loader.

Money guide

Starting salaries are usually £11,500 per year.

Loaders working as specialist lift truck operators can earn up to £20,000. Hydraulic lorry loaders who also work as an LGV driver can earn up to £28,000.

Shift work or permanent nights can significantly increase your earnings.

Related opportunities

- Airport Baggage Handler p597
- Delivery Driver p601
- Lift Truck Operator p608
- Warehouse Worker/Manager p630

Further information

United Kingdom Warehousing Association
Walter House, 418–422 Strand, London WC2R 0PT
020 7836 5522; www.ukwa.org.uk

Association of Industrial Truck Trainers
Unit 20, The Spring Board Centre, Mantle Lane, Coalville LE67 3DW
01530 277857; www.aitt.co.uk

National Plant Operators Registration Scheme
PO Box 204, Northwich CW9 7PL
01606 351240, www.npors.com

City& Guilds

www.cityandguilds.com/myperfectjob

Transport and Logistics

CRCI: WE

MERCHANT NAVY DECK OFFICER/RATING

What the work involves

- The Merchant Navy consists of thousands of civilian ships, operated by individual shipping companies. They include fuel tankers and cargo ships, as well as ferries and cruise liners.

- Merchant navy deck officers are responsible for navigating ships, as well as being involved in communications and cargo handling.

- You will use satellite and radar systems in order to navigate the ship, maintain machinery and safety equipment, and train and support junior officers and ratings.

- Deck ratings are responsible for supporting the ship's officers by helping to navigate and steer the ship, as well as carrying out maintenance tasks and helping to load and unload cargo.

The type of person suited to this work

Both officers and ratings need to have good social skills in order to work successfully as part of a team. You will also need to be calm and logical in the face of emergency situations.

In addition, officers will need to have excellent numeracy skills and be able to use complex technology in order to successfully make navigational calculations. Officers will also need to have good leadership qualities, so that they inspire respect and dedication from their crew members.

Working conditions

You will expect to work shifts, known as 'watches'. These can vary in length from 4 hours on and 4 hours off, to 6 hours on and 6 hours off, or even 12 hours on and 12 hours off at times. These shifts can take place at any time.

Ratings can expect to live in close proximity to their colleagues, often in fairly cramped accommodation. Officers have their own private, en-suite cabin. Generally, good leisure facilities are provided on-board so that crew can make the most of their time off.

Future prospects

With over 20 UK shipping companies in operation, and a predicted increase in shipping activity over the next few years, prospects for Merchant Navy officers and ratings are good.

As a rating, you could gain promotion to Seaman (Grade 2), or even take a conversion course in order to progress to a position as an officer.

Officers may move into related onshore work, including shipbuilding, maritime law and ship and fleet management.

Advantages/disadvantages

You will be working within a strong team environment, so will build excellent relationships with colleagues from a variety of backgrounds.

Shift work can be exhausting.

Qualifications and courses

To become a rating, you will need to have gained GCSEs (A*–C) or equivalent, in both maths and English. You must also pass the Merchant Navy medical.

Entrants wishing to become officers can pursue one of three routes, each of which requires sponsorship by a shipping company.

You could choose to take an HND in Nautical Science, or alternatively a Foundation degree/SQA professional diploma in Nautical Science or Marine Operations. The third option is undertaking a degree in Nautical Science or Merchant Ship Operations, for which employers will require that you hold 2 A levels (including maths or physics) or equivalent, in addition to your GCSE grades.

Completion of a training course leads to the Maritime and Coastguard Agency Officer of the Watch Certificate of Competency.

You will have to spend long periods of time away from your family. This could encompass months as well as weeks.

Money guide

Trainee merchant navy ratings usually start on between £13,000 and £16,000. This can increase up to £25,000 with experience.

Newly qualified deck officers may have a starting salary of £20,000–£25,000. With experience, this should increase to around £35,000.

Ship captains can earn £30,000–£65,000+.

Related opportunities

- Merchant Navy Engineering Officer p613
- Marine Engineer p232

Further information

The Merchant Navy Association
9 Saxon Way, Caistor, Market Rasen LN7 6SG
01472 851 130; www.mna.org.uk

Merchant Navy Training Board
12 Carthusian Street, London EC1M 6EZ
0800 085 0973; www.careersatsea.org.uk;
enquiry@careersatsea.org

The Marine Society & Sea Cadets
202 Lambeth Road, London SE1 7JW
020 7654 7000; www.ms-sc.org; info@ms-sc.org

City&
Guilds

www.cityandguilds.com/myperfectjob

Organisation profile

SSTG Celebrates Thirty Years' Recruiting and Training for the Maritime Industry

At a time when the maritime industry is predicting a widening chasm over the next five to ten years between the availability of suitably qualified officers and the growing number of vessels plying the seas, the Ship Safe Training Group Ltd. (SSTG) provides an entry-route for school and college leavers wanting to directly benefit from the ever growing opportunity of a career at sea.

With over 32 years' experience, the SSTG (which operates on a not-for-profit basis for its member companies), has over 500 deck and engineering officers in training at any one time in colleges, universities and at sea. All cadets are supported by a dedicated team of training officers providing a mentoring service throughout their training, resulting in a low drop-out rate and a high level of motivation. Graduating officers have the option of taking up a posting with member companies.

The Group is currently the largest single organisation in the UK overseeing the management of young people undertaking **Honours Degree** programmes, and provides full sponsorship for cadet officers throughout their training, in effect offering school and college leavers a debt-free degree. New entrants are also provided for with courses at **Foundation Degree**, **Higher National Diploma** and **Higher National Certificate** as optional routes in to develop their careers in the maritime sector.

"There are today many exciting opportunities for school and college leavers to join the British maritime industry. This industry is continuing to expand year on year," said Ian Spreadborough SSTG Managing Director. "Ship operators are keen to attract new entrants who they can train for a career at sea and then provide with attainable opportunities for promotion. The maritime industry has the added benefit of having attractive and vibrant onshore sectors enabling qualified seafarers to take up positions in sectors as varied as maritime finance, insurance, law, education and management.

Visit the SSTG web site for entry criteria and other information www.sstg.org

Case study

CRUISING AHEAD ON THE RIGHT COURSE

Here's Jenny Grove's story

At 14, Jenny Grove was lucky to go on a cruise with her family and loved every minute of it. Her father is an Electro Technical Officer (ETO) with P&O ferries and these have been the two major influences which encouraged Jenny to become a Deck Officer in the Merchant Navy.

Jenny studies at South Tyneside College, Tyne & Wear, South Shields, the world renowned centre of vocational excellence for Marine Engineering and Nautical Science. She has been sponsored throughout her training by P&O Ferries, Dover.

Now, aged 19, Jenny's training is drawing to a close. She will be a qualified Deck Officer and able to work for any number of shipping lines around the world.

"I am getting near the end of my training now. Before I joined I worried about so many things. Would I be the only female? Would I be able to do the work? What would it be like not living at home? The list was endless." said Jenny.

"I look back at those days now and think how silly because this is such a great life and getting better all the time. **Females are capable of any job at sea whether it is Engineering Officer, Electro Technical Officer or Deck Officer**.

"I started my training with a maritime training organisation called SSTG. They interviewed me, placed me with a sponsoring company, and made all the arrangements for me to attend college. SSTG managed the whole process. They visit me at college on a regular basis and are always at the end of the phone if I need advice."

The course is phased between college "academics, underpinning knowledge and technical certificates" and sea time where you complete two NVQ portfolios. This all takes approximately three years. There's no time to get bored. After that you become a qualified Officer of the Watch and can work on any ship anywhere in the world. The promotion opportunities are excellent.

"My sponsorship agreement gives me a training allowance starting at about £4,500 which gradually rises to £7,000. My sponsorship company pays all of my tuition fees, accommodation and food, uniform allowance and travel expenses. When I am qualified my salary will be between £25,000 and £27,000, so I will leave my training debt free and be on a reasonable salary from day one.

"My sponsoring company operate ferries between Dover and Calais, one of the busiest shipping lanes in the world, so the training experience for me has been great. There's always something going on, whether it be docking, loading or navigating from one port to another. All the people on the ship are professionals but enjoy a good laugh as well and nobody gets treated differently – its all about teamwork.

"My ambition is to become the Master of a large cruise ship and travel the world. After that I will move ashore as the opportunities with my qualifications are incredible. I would recommend this industry to any young person looking to travel, get a diploma or degree qualification debt free."

There is plenty of opportunity for early responsibility and promotion and be in a position of respect. Remember 95% of our trade leaves or arrives through UK ports and although we are an island race, people here just don't appreciate or realise what a great industry this is.

If you are interested in a career in the Merchant Navy contact: Ship Safe Training Group Ltd, The Precinct Office, The Precinct, Rochester ME1 1SR; T: 01634 820 820; F: 01634 820 821; web: www.sstg.org; email: recruitment@sstg.org

MERCHANT NAVY ENGINEERING OFFICER

What the work involves

- The Merchant Navy consists of thousands of civilian ships, operated by individual shipping companies. They include fuel tankers and cargo ships, as well as ferries and cruise liners.

- Merchant navy engineering officers work with all the mechanical and electrical equipment onboard ships.

- You will work on areas of the ship such as the engines, the computer-controlled engine management systems, and the pumps and fuel systems.

- Engineering officers are based in the engine control room of a ship. They are responsible for assisting engineering officers in the repair and servicing of technical equipment.

The type of person suited to this work

You will need to be interested in working with very hi-tech machinery and enjoy learning about new, state-of-the-art technology. You will also need to be very practical and logical so that you can work quickly and efficiently to rectify problems that occur with the equipment. You should also enjoy working as part of a close-knit team and have a high level of self-discipline. Impeccable communication skills are essential for these roles.

Working conditions

You will expect to work shifts, known as 'watches'. These can vary in length from 4 hours on and 4 hours off, to 6 hours on and 6 hours off, or even 12 hours on and 12 hours off at times. These shifts can take place at any time, day or night.

You will spend the majority of your time in the engine control room or the engine room itself, where it will be hot and noisy. As an engineering officer you could be responsible for all of the ship's systems.

Generally, good leisure facilities are provided on-board so that crew can make the most of their time off.

Future prospects

There are fewer people applying to become trainee engineers now so your chances of success are good. The large shipping companies that recruit trainees are recruiting more people than they used to.

Officers may rise through the ranks to reach the level of chief engineer. Alternatively, there are also opportunities in related areas such as ship surveying or ship management.

Advantages/disadvantages

You will be working within a strong team environment, so will build excellent relationships with colleagues from a variety of backgrounds.

The relentless nature of shift work can be exhausting.

Qualifications and courses

You will need to gain five GCSEs (grade A*–C) which include science (physics or combined science awards) as well as maths and English.

To study for a Foundation degree (the most common route to this profession) will require a minimum of 120 UCAS points from your A levels which should also be taken in engineering, science-related subjects, maths and English. You can enter the profession with a science-based degree but this is not obligatory.

Merchant Navy Ratings once in the Navy can apply to do a conversion course to become an engineer. This would involve either: studying for a BTEC in marine or mechanical engineering (taking 2–3 years to complete depending on if it is a HNC or HND course) or studying for a degree in some form of engineering (usually marine) which takes up to 4 years.

To enter as a trainee, you must have sponsorship from a training organisation or from a shipping company.

You will have to spend long periods of time away from your family. This could encompass months as well as weeks.

Money guide

Trainees start on between £13,000 and £16,000. This can increase up to £22,000 with experience.

Newly qualified junior engineering officers are usually paid a starting salary of around £25,000. With experience, this should increase to between £26,000 and £50,000 depending on rank.

Chief engineers can earn in excess of £60,000.

Related opportunities

- Merchant Navy Deck Officer/Rating p610
- Royal Marines Commando p559
- Royal Marines Officer p560
- Marine Engineer p232

Further information

The Merchant Navy Association
9 Saxon Way, Caistor, Market Rasen LN7 6SG
01472 851 130; www.mna.org.uk

Merchant Navy Training Board
12 Carthusian Street, London EC1M 6EZ
0800 085 0973; www.careersatsea.org.uk;
enquiry@careersatsea.org

www.cityandguilds.com/myperfectjob

PASSENGER CHECK IN OFFICER

What the work involves

- You will be responsible for making sure that passengers and their baggage board the right aircraft.
- You will greet passengers, provide information, ask security questions and check tickets and passport details.
- Once you have weighed and put luggage on the conveyor belt you will issue boarding passes and prepare paperwork for customs.
- You could also work at the flight gate, making announcements and checking boarding cards.

The type of person suited to this work

As the public face of your airline, you will need a pleasant, confident and helpful manner with a well-groomed appearance.

You need to be confident with IT. You will use a sophisticated computer system to allocate seats, print boarding cards and baggage labels and produce post-flight figures.

You must be friendly and approachable as you will be helping passengers, including those with disabilities and unaccompanied children, from check-in, through security, and on to their flight. You will also need to be able to deal with difficult situations.

Communication skills are essential for working with your colleagues and other airport staff.

Working conditions

You will wear a uniform and work indoors at an airport.

When you are working at the check-in desk you may sit behind a counter for long periods.

If you are escorting passengers or helping with boarding at a gate, you will spend periods of time on your feet, sometimes walking quite long distances and carrying luggage.

Hours will include shifts covering evenings, weekends and holidays, to cover all the times the airport is open.

Future prospects

Employers are either airlines or the ground handling companies that work on behalf of airlines. About 70% of passenger handling work takes place at the four main airports – Heathrow, Gatwick, Stansted and Manchester – so there are more opportunities if you live within travelling distance of one of the big four. There is a lot of competition for jobs, many of which are seasonal.

You could progress to be a member of the air cabin crew, or a supervisor within passenger services.

Advantages/disadvantages

You will get to meet all types of new people from across the world.

Qualifications and courses

Entry requirements vary, but many employers prefer applicants with 3–5 GCSEs (A*–C)/S grades (1–3), including English and maths. Minimum age for entry varies from 16 to 20 years of age. You will need to be physically fit, and there may be height and weight restrictions. It's an advantage to be able to speak another language.

Key Skills in communication and information technology are useful, as is work experience with the public in a caring, catering or travel agency job.

You could study a related college or university course, for example a BTEC/SQA National Certificate/Diploma or HNC/D in travel and tourism, a GCSE/A level in Leisure and Tourism, NVQ in Aviation Operations or a degree in Travel and Tourism. Once accepted you will be trained for 4–8 weeks in all aspects of the job.

NVQs/SVQs in Handling Aircraft Passengers at Levels 2 and 3 may be available for further study.

If there is a delay to their flight, you might have to deal with difficult or demanding passengers.

If you are keen to work in an air cabin crew job then experience in this work will be a big advantage.

Money guide

Starting salaries are around £12,000–£14,000 per year. Experienced customer service agents can earn £16,000–£20,000.

At supervisory or management level you could earn up to £25,000.

Shift allowances are usually paid. There may be opportunities to earn overtime pay.

Related opportunities

- Air Cabin Crew p594
- Airport Baggage Handler p597
- Holiday Representative p388
- Tour Guide/Manager p397

Further information

GoSkills
Concorde House, Trinity Park, Solihull B37 7UQ
0121 635 5520; www.careersinpassengertransport.org

Royal Aeronautical Society
4 Hamilton Place, London WCJ 7BQ
020 7670 4326; www.aerosociety.com

City&
Guilds

www.cityandguilds.com/myperfectjob

PASSENGER TRANSPORT CLERK

What the work involves

- As a passenger transport clerk you will deal with customer enquiries regarding departure times, fares, routes, connections and disruptions on bus and rail services.

- You will use computerised systems to organise the purchase or refund of tickets and in order to issue travel cards.

- You will research the best rail or coach fares for a customer and ensure that their transport is as efficient and affordable as possible.

- You may specialise in either sales or customer enquiries but usually members of staff share these responsibilities amongst themselves.

The type of person suited to this work

You should be friendly and polite and have a genuine interest in working with the public.

Some maths and ICT skills will be necessary as you will be dealing with fares and payments.

You must be able to work quickly and efficiently so that passengers are not delayed getting to their train/bus.

As you might have to deal with customers in busy times or times when there are unexpected delays you need to have patience and the ability to deal with frustrated or angry customers.

You should have an interest in travel and customer service.

Working conditions

You will work an average of 37–40 hours each week. This may include shift work, evenings, weekends and even public holidays.

You may have the opportunity to work part-time, overtime and flexible hours.

You will be based in stations or travel centres which will function essentially as an office but you will deal with customers on the phone or as they come to the ticket office or information desk you are based at.

Future prospects

You may gain NVQs as you work in order to progress to supervisory and managerial roles.

You may be employed by any bus or coach operator or private rail companies, Train Operating Companies throughout the UK, the London Underground or Eurostar.

Qualifications and courses

ENTRY LEVEL 2

There are no formal qualifications required to enter this profession. However GSCEs in English, maths or any relevant subjects (A*–C) will be useful.

You will learn largely on-the-job, although some training might be provided.

Many companies will provide their own in-house training, or day-release training for clerical staff. If you are going into a position as a rail passenger transport clerk or a member of telephone enquiry bureau staff you will be trained in fare structures, customer care, railway geography and computerised ticket systems.

You may also be provided with training from bus and coach companies which may be provided in-house. This will involve learning how to use timetables, ticket systems, price structures and customer care information.

Advantages/disadvantages

You will have the opportunity to work in an ever-changing environment as bus and rail services are constantly updated and new customers use them each day.

At times your work may be repetitive.

Money guide

Your starting salary as a transport clerk may be around £14,500 a year.

With some experience this can increase to £17,000 a year.

With several years' experience and qualifications you can earn between £19,000 and £21,000 a year.

Related opportunities

- Customer Service Assistant/Manager p483
- Passenger Check In Officer p614
- Travel Agent p399

Further information

Customer Contact Association
20 Newton Place, Glasgow G3 7PY
0141 564 9010; www.cca.org.uk

GoSkills
Concorde House, Trinity Park, Solihull,
West Midlands B37 7UQ
0121 635 5520; info@goskills.org; www.goskills.org

www.cityandguilds.com/myperfectjob

CRCI: WA

Transport and Logistics

POSTMAN/POSTWOMAN

What the work involves

- You will sort and deliver mail to homes, shops, factories and offices in your area.
- Your day will start at the sorting office, getting your mail ready for delivery and packing your bag in the best order for your route.
- You will then deliver your mail by foot or bicycle or, in rural areas, by van. If working in a rural area you may also be responsible for delivering other goods such as milk.
- You might also be responsible for mail collections from post boxes and places of work.

The type of person suited to this work

Your round could include several hundred addresses and cover several miles a day so you will need to be fit, especially if you are doing the job on foot or by bicycle. You should also enjoy being outdoors as you will be expected to deliver the mail in all weathers.

Honesty and reliability are vital qualities in this job. You will be carrying lots of valuable and urgent mail around and you will be responsible for delivering it to the right place.

Good customer service skills and a friendly attitude are important.

Working conditions

Most of your work will be outside in all weathers. A uniform, footwear and protective clothing will be provided.

If on foot, you might have to carry your mail in bags, though there will be arrangements to transport you and your mail out to the start of your route.

Shift work with an early morning (5am) start or late evening (10pm) finish is usual. You will often work on Saturday.

You might have to walk a couple of miles in a single day or walk up steep hills and deal with minor hazards.

Future prospects

Postal delivery workers mainly work for the Royal Mail.

Recruitment tends to be steady and there are opportunities in urban and rural areas throughout the UK. Some workers start out with temporary work over the Christmas period and are retained.

It is possible to move into parcel deliveries, supervisory or managerial work.

Advantages/disadvantages

With a regular round you will really get to know your customers.

There might be some hazards on your round; you will soon learn what to avoid. All the walking or cycling will keep you fit.

Qualifications and courses

No specific qualifications are required for this job. Candidates should be aged 18 or over, and selection is by an aptitude test, a fitness assessment and interview. You might need to pass a medical examination.

The ability to ride a bicycle and/or possession of a driving licence with no more than six penalty points may be required.

Apprenticeships are available from the Royal Mail.

You will receive induction training. Further training is chiefly on the job, lasting 18 months, and can include the chance to work towards an NVQ in Mail Services at Level 2. With a minimum of 1 year's experience, you can seek advancement to supervisory or managerial levels.

Although you will have to start work by 5am if you are on the early shift, you will finish at around lunchtime.

Money guide

Starting pay for staff over 18 is £13,312 a year.

After 1 year's experience you would earn £14,820–£16,172.

£19,280 is usual for postmen/women working in outer London and £20,405 a year is common for those working in inner London.

There are additional payments for overtime and sometimes for shift work which takes place during unsocial hours.

Related opportunities

- Courier p600
- Delivery Driver p601
- Freight Forwarder p604
- Warehouse Worker/Manager p630

Further information

Royal Mail Group plc
148 Old Street, London EC1V 9HQ
www.royalmail.com

Skills for Logistics
12 Warren Yard, Warren Farm Office Village,
Milton Keynes MK12 5NW
01908 313360; www.skillsforlogistics.org

www.cityandguilds.com/myperfectjob

PURCHASING/PROCUREMENT MANAGER

What the work involves

- You will be responsible for buying the goods or services needed by a business, and providing the best value for money.

- Your first job is to find out what your employer wants to buy and how much the budget is.

- An important aspect will be to find the best suppliers and negotiate with them to get products or services at the right conditions and price.

- You will then be responsible for quality checks to make sure that the goods or services provided are of the standard agreed.

The type of person suited to this work

You must have excellent negotiation and communication skills in order to get the best quality and lowest priced goods and services for your company.

ICT and numerical skills are essential for researching, calculating costs and managing a budget. You will need to be organised and analytical and have a good business-sense.

Working conditions

You will work Monday to Friday, from 9am to 5:30pm although there can be longer hours if you work in the manufacturing industry. If your suppliers are in a different time zone to the UK, this can mean early mornings or late nights.

You will be located in a busy office, although you may travel to meet suppliers and customers which can mean time away from home.

Future prospects

Jobs are available in nearly all areas of the business sector including manufacturing, retailers, wholesale, and government organisations. Purchasing administrator jobs are competitive, but there is a shortage of qualified applicants for purchasing manager jobs.

Some buyers move into specialist areas, for example construction or chemicals. ICT purchasing is a new specialism and is predicted to grow with the expansion of e-business.

Promotion prospects are good, especially in large organisations. It may be possible to progress to a role as director. Increasing numbers of experienced managers are choosing to become self-employed and work as consultants or contract workers.

Advantages/disadvantages

If successful, you can reach high levels of responsibility, and even travel overseas, early in your career.

This job is stressful. Businesses spend over half their money on the goods and services they need to buy, so mistakes could be expensive.

Qualifications and courses

ENTRY 5 LEVEL

Employers usually ask for a degree or HND qualification. It may be possible to enter at a lower level and progress with experience and on-the-job training.

The Chartered Institute of Purchasing and Supply (CIPS) accredits some degree courses in business (with purchasing options), logistics and supply chain management, and purchasing and supply chain management.

To progress you will need the CIPS professional qualifications. You can study for a Level 2 Introductory Certificate up to a Level 7 Executive Diploma in Purchasing and Supply. These can be studied full time or part time at college, or by distance learning. The Certificate has no formal entry requirements. Once completed, you can progress to the Advanced Certificate.

After working for 3 years and completing the Level 6 Graduate Diploma, you can become a member of CIPS. You will need at least 2 A levels and 3 GCSEs (A*–C), or equivalent qualifications, or be over 21 years old with relevant work experience.

You can take NVQ at Levels 2, 3 and 4 in Supply Chain Management as an alternative route. Some universities offer postgraduate courses in purchasing, supply management and logistics.

Money guide

Starting pay for a trainee is about £18,000–£25,000 per year. For experienced purchasing administrators the salary range is £35,000–£45,000. £70,000+ is possible for senior managers and directors.

Related opportunities

- Importer/Exporter p606
- Distribution Manager p602
- Warehouse Worker/Manager p630

Further information

Chartered Institute of Purchasing & Supply
Easton House, Easton on the Hill, Stamford PE9 3NZ
01780 756777; www.cips.org

Skillsmart Retail
020 7462 5060; www.skillsmartretail.com

City & Guilds

www.cityandguilds.com/myperfectjob

THE VOICE OF THE PROFESSION

The Chartered Institute of Purchasing & Supply (CIPS) is the professional body representing the purchasing and supply management profession. With more than 60,000 members in 150 countries around the world, it is now the largest institute of its kind. As a professional body CIPS offers the internationally recognised qualifications in purchasing and supply management, part of which is the CIPS graduate diploma. Completion of the graduate diploma with proven experience of purchasing in 'the field' in turn leads to full membership of the institute, and the recognised status of MCIPS, which you can put after your name.

Best practice in action

It's not just about qualifications. CIPS exists to promote and develop high standards of professional skill, ability and integrity among all those engaged in the profession, assisting individuals and organisations. It does this through its professional qualifications programme and associated membership standard, and by providing public access training programmes and a comprehensive range of learning resources.

Helping organisations achieve and maintain the highest standards throughout their purchasing and supply management operations, contributes significantly to their effectiveness. CIPS supports organisations in a number of ways, from educating and training their staff, to improving their performance through assessment and accreditation of their purchasing and supply methods, and sharing of best practice between peer groups.

Membership of CIPS recognises your professional status and helps you to keep up to date with the latest developments through a comprehensive range of courses, conferences, publications and networking opportunities.

CIPS asks all members to sign up to a professional code of ethics – guidance and principles for best practice procurement. Find out more at www.cips.org

Read all about it

Supply Management is the magazine for CIPS members. It is published fortnightly by Redactive Media Group. All CIPS members receive *Supply Management* automatically. It is the profession's main source of news, features and comment about procurement, supply chain and related business issues.

In addition to the magazine, CIPS and Redactive jointly publish regular supplements on related subjects such as business travel, public sector procurement and career development. They also organise events and conferences. And, of course, there is a website – www.supplymanagement.com – which is updated daily with news and contains free-to-access material of the latest three issues of the magazine. It also has a huge archive of every story the magazine has published since 2000. This makes for a total of about 8,000 pieces – a hugely useful resource for all procurement professionals. You have to be a member or magazine subscriber to access the archive, but once you have signed up, you will find it invaluable.

Supply Management isn't just another old trade magazine. In the past three years it has featured interviews with Sir Alan Sugar, British Airways chief executive Willie Walsh and published special reports on China and Africa. It reflects the international nature of the profession and the institute.

This article first appeared in CIPS/Supply Management Graduate Guide 2009–10

Case study

PROCUREMENT
Fast track your career

Here's Stephen Hill's story

The transport industry was Stephen Hill's route into procurement and a role that took him to South Africa. Stephen now works as a supply chain manager and is responsible for asset management for WS Atkins, having graduated with a BA in Economics.

How Stephen came into his job

"When I graduated from Nottingham Trent University in 2004, I had no long-term vision where to specialise. My first full-time job was as an expediter for Bombardier Transportation on a national maintenance project for Virgin Trains. During my 18 months in this post, I made it my business to learn how the whole operation worked. I quickly became proficient at my role, being rewarded with a promotion and greater responsibility, working on a new fleet of East Coast Mainline trains as procurement coordinator. I was trained to use SAP business management software and, one year on, I successfully applied for a job as bids and procurement coordinator at Total Transit Systems, the turnkey rail projects arm of the organisation."

What the job typically entails

"My role at Total Transit Systems was to tender for the key elements of the $1.5 billion (£904 million) Gautrain rapid rail link in South Africa. Suppliers and the internal hierarchy can often be difficult to deal with but being confident and having an adaptable approach is important in allowing me to excel in my role. My procurement scope included station equipment, environmental and electromagnetic tests, overhead cables and design. These were all multi-million pound orders with supplier relationships being of the utmost importance. I spent a lot of time in South Africa, observing the results and managing the suppliers after contract award. I developed a good understanding of the key functions and tasks when delivering a project."

How Stephen has used his skills elsewhere

"I used these skills to work on other projects including the Nottingham Tram and the automatic people mover (an underground shuttle system) at Heathrow T5. I know it's not cool to like trains and trams but I was enjoying the industry I was in and more importantly, I had a belief and pride in the projects we were delivering."

Stephen's current role

"In 2008 I moved to WS Atkins. I am now the supply chain manager for eight Private Finance Initiative (PFI) contracts. My role is to manage suppliers for services such as mechanical, electrical, security, catering and grounds maintenance for schools, hospitals and police stations around the county. Getting the right suppliers and managing the relationships is very important.

I have developed rigorous pre-qualification processes and tender methodologies to ensure best value for Atkins, a quality service to our customers and commercial contract compliance for the client. Atkins is very supportive of my personal development, but I'm a firm believer that if you don't ask, you don't get."

Stephen's advice to others

"My advice to graduates is to make other people's business your business. That way you will find your passion and progress in your career. Every aspect of an organisation can impact on supply management and the sooner you have the knowledge, the quicker you can make more informed and strategic decisions and take on higher levels of responsibility."

This case study first appeared in CIPS/Supply Management Graduate Guide 2009–10

RAIL SIGNALLING TECHNICIAN

What the work involves

- Rail signalling technicians are responsible for installing and repairing all of the signalling and telecommunications systems that are used to support the railways.

- Equipment that you will be working on will include signal boxes, warning systems, manual lever frame boxes, and coloured light signals.

- You will also install new signalling equipment, such as GSM-R communication masts, and update existing systems.

The type of person suited to this work

You should have good manual dexterity in order to operate a range of tools and machines.

A logical approach to your work will help when tracing faults, as will the ability to understand technical drawings and engineering instructions when repairing systems. You will need good eyesight and full colour vision.

You should have a reasonable level of numeracy, and good ICT skills so that you can operate computerised machinery.

You will also need to be physically fit, as the work can include lifting and carrying heavy equipment, as well as working up ladders or in awkward places.

Working conditions

You will work around 37 hours a week, most likely in a shift pattern that could include early morning, evening and weekend work. You may also be expected to work overtime fairly regularly.

Your time will be divided between working outside, carrying out repairs trackside, and undertaking maintenance near signal boxes or within stations. You should be prepared to work in any weather conditions. You may well have to travel to various different locations each day, and overnight absence from home is common.

Future prospects

You could be employed by Network Rail, working on the UK's commercial railway tracks, or by a number of underground, metro or light rail operators such as London Underground, Metronet, Translink and the Docklands Light Railway.

With experience, you can become a member of the Institution of Railway Signal Engineers, which offers a route into becoming a registered engineering technician.

Promotion opportunities are good, and you could end up as a team manager, or even move into a consultancy role when you have built up significant experience.

Advantages/disadvantages

You will be playing an essential role in maintaining and developing the infrastructure of the UK.

Qualifications and courses

Network Rail operates a large Apprenticeship programme for those aged 16–24, as do many other employers of rail signalling technicians. Employers usually require candidates to have 3–5 GCSEs/S grades (A*–C/1–3) or equivalent, including English, maths and science. A double GCSE in engineering or a related technical subject would also be helpful.

Apprentices work towards an NVQ Level 3 in Railway Engineering (signalling), undertaking a mixture of classroom-based and on-the-job learning.

Most employers operate their own selection process on top of these academic requirements. This usually consists of a medical test, which will assess your fitness, eyesight and hearing, as well as drug and alcohol screening. Occasionally, you may also have to sit an aptitude test.

You could undertake a full time or part time course prior to looking for work as a rail signalling technician. Relevant courses include the BTEC National Certificate in Electronics and Railway Signals/Telecommunications, and the BTEC National Certificate in Signalling and Communication.

Promotion opportunities are good, and there is also the chance to undertake extra training to drive forward your career.

Working in all weather conditions and cramped surroundings can be uncomfortable and extremely unpleasant at times.

Money guide

Your starting salary as a newly qualified rail signalling technician will be about £14,000. As you gain experience, this should increase to around £22,000. If you become a senior technician, or move into a consultancy role, your salary could reach £35,000+.

Related opportunities

- Telecommunications Technician p165
- Electrician p94
- Electricity Distribution Worker p222

Further information

Railway-technology.com
Brunel House, 55–57 North Wharf Road, London W2 1LA
01207 915 9957; www.railway-technology.com

www.cityandguilds.com/myperfectjob

RAIL TRACK MAINTENANCE OPERATIVE

What the work involves

- Rail track maintenance workers are responsible for building, repairing and maintaining the rail track network across the UK.

- You will use a variety of manual and automated tools, including welding equipment, clamping machines, and cement mixers.

- You will also be responsible for inspecting the track in order to spot potential faults, which will involve walking along live tracks with trains passing nearby.

The type of person suited to this work

You will need to be fit and strong to undertake this work, as you will be lifting and moving heavy pieces of track, as well as operating powerful machinery at times. You should also have good manual skills in order to use tools effectively and safely.

You must be a good communicator so you can work effectively within a team. You should be able to listen to instructions and take direction, whilst also having the confidence to use your own initiative and help colleagues when necessary.

You should have a good awareness of onsite safety practice and a responsible attitude to your work.

Working conditions

You will work an average of 35 hours per week on a shift system. You will have to work nights and weekends regularly, as these are the times at which maintenance work causes least disruption to the train timetable.

Work usually takes place outdoors, in all weather conditions. You should be prepared to get cold and wet working in muddy conditions, and also extremely hot in the summer months.

You will have to wear protective clothing, including a hard hat, high visibility jacket and reinforced boots.

Future prospects

Network Rail employs almost all the rail track maintenance workers in the UK, and they continuously update track all around the country.

There are also opportunities with rail employment agencies, who recruit workers for specific projects managed by rail engineering contractors.

With experience, you could progress to a supervisory role, or become a specialist in a technical area such as line-laying or welding.

Advantages/disadvantages

The work is physically tiring but rewarding, as you will be working towards maintaining the infrastructure of the UK.

You will be working in a team, so the job will be sociable and you will build strong relationships with your colleagues.

Working in all weather conditions can be uncomfortable and extremely unpleasant at times.

Qualifications and courses

ENTRY 2 LEVEL

Network Rail and most other employers look for candidates with a minimum of 4 GCSEs/S grades (A*–C/1–3) or equivalent, including English and maths. A technical subject is also desirable.

Qualifications in related subjects such as a GCSE, A level or a Diploma in Engineering, or the City & Guilds NVQ Level 1 in Rail Engineering, may be helpful in demonstrating your enthusiasm for the role and securing you employment.

You will have to be fit, and most employers will ask you to take a medical assessment to measure your fitness, stamina, and also test your hearing and eyesight. You will also have to take tests for drugs and alcohol.

Some employers also require candidates to go through a Criminal Records Bureau check, as the role of a maintenance operative is critical in ensuring railway safety.

Experience in a similar construction or engineering related role may be beneficial, but is not essential.

Network Rail operates a large Apprenticeship programme for those aged 16–24.

Money guide

Your starting salary as an inexperienced rail track worker will be about £14,000.

Once you have spent a few years in the role and built up your skills, you could be earning £18,000.

Rail track workers with additional supervisory responsibilities can earn up to £25,000.

Related opportunities

- Rail Signalling Technician p620
- Stonemason p123
- Bricklayer p76

Further information

Network Rail
Kings Place, 90 York Way, London N1 9AG
020 7557 80005; www.networkrail.co.uk

Institute of Mechanical Engineers
1 Birdcage Walk, Westminster, London SW1H 9JJ
020 7222 7899; www.imeche.org; enquiries@imeche.org

City& Guilds

www.cityandguilds.com/myperfectjob

Transport and Logistics

CRCI: WD

RAILWAY STATION ASSISTANT

What the work involves

- Railway station assistants work within train stations, assisting customers, dealing with queries, and ensuring that passengers are happy.

- You may work behind a ticket desk, on an information stand, or on the station platforms so that you are accessible to passengers.

- You will need to provide assistance to wheelchair users and other people who require help boarding or disembarking from a train.

- You will check tickets, and be on the look out for any security threats or other problems within the station.

The type of person suited to this work

You will need to be a confident communicator so that you can impart information to passengers, and also field any negative comments that might be directed towards you.

You should be polite and approachable, and maintain a clean, smart appearance.

You will need good hearing and eyesight, as well as a high level of fitness in order to physically assist customers and move around the station quickly when necessary.

You should be able to work well within a team, taking instructions and helping colleagues, but also enjoy working autonomously and using your initiative.

Working conditions

You will usually work 37 hours per week, and this will include early morning, late night and weekend shifts. There are usually opportunities to undertake paid overtime work.

You will also be working within ticket offices or passenger information areas in the station. You will have to wear a uniform so that you are easily recognisable to passengers.

Future prospects

You could either work for a train operating company (TOC) or for Network Rail, within large or small train stations across the UK. There are also opportunities to work for underground or metro operators in some cities.

You could progress as a conductor or driver, move upwards to become a customer services manager, or even reach the position of station manager.

Advantages/disadvantages

You will be working in a variety of roles each day so work should not get monotonous.

You will spend a lot of time on freezing station platforms in the winter.

You may have to deal with aggressive passengers at times.

Qualifications and courses

You must be at least 18 years of age. Good communication skills and numerical ability are viewed as extremely important by employers, so most TOCs require candidates to have 4 GCSEs/S grades (A*–C/1–3) or equivalent, including English and maths.

You may also be required to pass medical assessments, which will include eyesight, colour vision and hearing tests, as well as those for drugs and alcohol use.

Employers favour candidates who have previous experience in customer relations roles, whether paid or voluntary.

Apprenticeships may be available for entrants aged 18–21.

Once employed as a railway station assistant, you will have to undergo a training period that will encompass classroom-based learning programmes including health and safety, customer care, railway operating systems and coping in emergency situations. This will be followed by practical training in the station.

Some TOCs also encourage employees to work towards an NVQ Level 2 in Rail Transport Operations as part of their training.

Money guide

Your starting salary as a railway station assistant is likely to be about £13,000. As you gain experience and knowledge, this should rise to £18,500. If you are promoted to team leader, your salary will increase to £21,000+.

Overtime is always available, so your wages can be increased if you are willing to work extra hours.

Related opportunities

- Train Conductor p628
- Train Driver p629
- Rail Track Maintenance Operative p621

Further information

Network Rail
Kings Place, 90 York Way, London N1 9AG
020 3356 9595; www.networkrail.co.uk

www.cityandguilds.com/myperfectjob

REMOVALS OPERATIVE

What the work involves

- Removals operatives move furniture, garden, household and office items into storage or to new sites. This involves carefully packing items and taking apart large items to fit into the removals van.

- You must plan how you will pack in advance to make the most of the space and to prevent damage to the goods during transit.

- You will also need to unload and unpack once you have driven the goods to their destination.

- This could involve putting furniture and other items back together again and placing them where the customer directs.

The type of person suited to this work

Your customers will most likely be stressed about moving and will rely on you to keep calm and cheerful. You should be friendly and personable.

An honest and careful approach to your work is vital as you will be dealing with valuable and fragile items on a regular basis. You should also be a team player and able to follow instructions.

It's important to be physically fit and enjoy practical work. You will be lifting and carrying large items and sometimes removing door or window frames to get items out of or into a property.

Working conditions

You will spend the majority of your time in the cab of your van. Your job may sometimes involve overnight and long-distance journeys and you should be prepared to spend time away from home.

Removals operatives usually work a 40 hour week, but some days will require working overtime until the job is finished. A lot of moves take place at weekends.

All the lifting, carrying and bending involved may put you at risk of back injury.

Future prospects

Although you will find removals companies throughout the UK, urban areas are the best place to look for vacancies as thousands of people and businesses are constantly on the move in these hubs. You may find that drops in the housing market can affect the number of jobs available.

With further training you may be promoted to a specialist packer, supervisor or manager.

You could also buy or lease a van and set up your own removal service.

Advantages/disadvantages

You might need to start early and work late, especially when legal processes can delay house removals.

Qualifications and courses

No particular educational qualifications are needed although GCSEs/S grades (A*–C/1–3) in English and maths are useful. While some firms will accept you at 16, many specify a minimum age of 18, or even 21.

If you would like to be a removals operative driver you will need a large goods vehicle (LGV) licence as well as a Driver Certificate of Professional Competence (CPC).

An Edexcel Level 1 Award or Level 2 Certificate in Commercial Moving may be useful. You can also enter this job through an Apprenticeship in Carrying and Delivering Goods.

Most people are trained on the job by experienced staff. Some firms send staff on short courses run by the British Association of Removers. Courses include removals management and specialist packing.

You may be able to take an NVQ/SVQ Level 2 in Storage and Warehousing and NVQs/SVQs Levels 2 and 3 in Driving Goods Vehicles, or other related areas.

You will be satisfied by your efforts and professionalism when you finish a move; happy customers may reward you with tips!

Money guide

Starting wages are about £10,000–£15,000 per year.

Experienced removal operatives earn around £20,000.

Supervisory staff may earn up to £30,000.

Wages can increase with overtime pay, shift allowances and tips.

Related opportunities

- Airport Baggage Handler p597
- Delivery Driver p601
- Loader p609
- Roadie p448

Further information

Skills for Logistics
14 Warren Yard, Warren Farm Office Village,
Milton Keynes MK12 5NW
01908 313360; www.skillsforlogistics.org

British Association of Removers
Tangent House, 62 Exchange Road, Watford WD18 0TG
01923 699480; www.bar.co.uk

www.cityandguilds.com/myperfectjob

Transport and Logistics

CRCI: WG

ROAD SAFETY OFFICER

What the work involves

- You will be working to reduce the number of motorists, cyclists and pedestrians injured or killed on the roads in your area.

- You will educate the public by giving presentations to groups such as children.

- Promoting national road safety campaigns by distributing leaflets and running exhibitions could also be part of your job.

- You will collect information about traffic accidents and make recommendations about how to prevent them.

The type of person suited to this work

As this job involves a lot of marketing and persuading, you will need to be an excellent communicator. You will use these skills to develop publicity materials and encourage people to behave more responsibly on the roads.

Self-confidence is vital to build good working relationships with safety engineers, police officers and local councillors.

To persuade others, you will need teaching skills and to be able to work with all age groups. You could give advice on fitting child car seats outside supermarkets, or teach small groups of young children how to cross the road safely.

Working conditions

Most of your work will be office-based, but you will also visit schools and other locations.

You will usually work 37 hours a week, Monday to Friday. Some evening work is required.

When working on-site with engineers, or when investigating accidents, you must wear high visibility clothing.

Your office work will involve using a computer to collect and analyse information.

Future prospects

Road safety officers are usually employed by local authorities. Some jobs are temporary as they are paid for by short-term government funding.

You could be promoted to manager or to a specialist post, for example in publicity, or working with schools. You might also find a job coordinating national safety and environmental initiatives, for example the National Walk to School Campaign.

Advantages/disadvantages

You will receive great satisfaction in saving lives and seeing death and injury figures reduced in your area.

There might be delays or obstacles to putting in place the safety improvement work you have recommended, which can be frustrating.

Qualifications and courses

Although there are no formal entry requirements to this job, most entrants are graduates. Useful subjects include transport management and transport safety. However, experience and personal qualities are equally as important to employers as academic qualifications. A driving licence is essential.

The Manchester College (MANCAT) is the only college in the UK that offers a BTEC Professional Development Diploma in Accident and Safety Management. For entry to the course you will need at least 1 A level and GCSEs (A*–C) in maths and English.

It is also possible to work towards an NVQ/SVQ in Transportation at Levels 3–5.

The National Staff Training Group offers a training programme for road safety officers. Phase 1 provides training for newly appointed officers. Phase 2 consists of a residential short course, and Phase 3 involves a series of seminars. Completion of Phase 2 training can lead to Associate Membership of the Institute of Road Safety Officers (IRSO).

Requirements for becoming a member of IRSO are a relevant degree, a BTEC Professional Development Diploma in Accident and Safety Management, or NVQ/SVQ Levels 3/4 in Transportation.

Money guide

Newly qualified officers earn £18,000. With experience you can earn up to £25,000 a year.

Officers with management responsibility can earn £40,000. If you are a senior manager this can rise to over £50,000.

Local authorities may offer essential car user allowances as well as bonuses

Related opportunities

- Health and Safety Adviser p40
- Police Officer p552

Further information

Employers' Organisation for Local Government
Layden House, 76–86 Turnmill Street, London EC1M 5LG
020 7296 6600; www.lgcareers.com

Institute of Road Safety Officers
www.irso.org.uk

www.cityandguilds.com/myperfectjob

ROAD TRANSPORT MANAGER

What the work involves

- You will work for a business that moves goods or passengers, planning the routes and work timetables of your drivers.

- You will oversee the day-to-day movement of your vehicles, checking that they are in the right places at the right times.

- Putting health and safety regulations into place, and monitoring compliance, will be part of your role.

- Your job will include checking costs to make sure that your company makes a profit.

The type of person suited to this work

Planning timetables, journeys and loads means that you will need to be organised. You should also be logical and enjoy using computers to manage and develop information.

You will cost up journeys, work out timetables and stick to a strict budget, so you must enjoy working with figures.

You will need to have motivational and leadership skills, as it is your responsibility to take care of your drivers.

Working conditions

Most of your work will be based in an office. You will also spend time at vehicle depots, and might need to travel to carry out spot checks on your drivers. Transport is a 24/7 business, so you might need to work shifts and weekends, or be called out in emergencies.

A passenger service vehicle or large goods vehicle licence will be useful.

Future prospects

Transport is a growing industry. You could work for a range of employers such as logistics and distribution companies, road haulage firms, manufacturers, retail chains or coach and bus operators.

It is possible to be promoted to area or general manager. Prospects are better if you are flexible about moving to a larger company or into other modes of transport.

With multinational companies there may be opportunities to work abroad.

Transport planning is currently a severe skill shortage area, and it is possible to move into it with management experience in the transport sector.

Advantages/disadvantages

No two days are the same – traffic levels, problems and weather conditions vary from day to day.

You will have the satisfaction of seeing an instant result when you make decisions. The way you manage a problem can mean happier customers.

Qualifications and courses

It is possible to enter the transport industry with qualifications ranging from a few GCSEs/S grades including English and maths, to a degree. Some companies offer Apprenticeships/Skillseekers in Logistics Operations Management.

Some companies recruit graduates to management positions. It is possible to enter with a degree in any subject. There are specialist degrees and postgraduate courses in transport management, transport planning and logistics.

Once working you can study for a variety of qualifications, including NVQ/SVQ Levels 2 and 3 in Road Passenger Transport (passenger work) and Traffic Office (freight work).

Postgraduate study is available as well. CILT offers Master's programmes in partnership with different universities.

The essential qualification to become a road transport senior manager is the Certificate of Professional Competence of the Department of Transport (Department of the Environment in Northern Ireland). This course is roughly equivalent to NVQ Level 3.

Money guide

Starting salaries are usually £15,000–£20,000 per year. Experienced managers – depending on the company's size – can earn £25,000–£45,000.

Senior managers earn up to £65,000, but the economic climate has reduced opportunities at this level. Allowances are usually paid for shift work and unsocial hours.

Related opportunities

- Distribution Manager p602
- Freight Forwarder p604
- Warehouse Worker/Manager p630

Further information

Chartered Institute of Logistics and Transport
Logistics and Transport Centre, Earlstree Court, Earlstree Road, Corby NN17 4XQ
01536 740104; www.ciltuk.org.uk

City& Guilds

www.cityandguilds.com/myperfectjob

STEWARD/CRUISE SHIP PURSER

What the work involves

Steward

- You will be responsible for keeping the public and private areas on a cruise ship clean and serviced to a very high standard. Duties may include making beds and vacuuming.

- You may serve passengers drinks in the bar area, wash glasses and keep the bar stocked and tidy.

Purser

- Pursers provide the administrative support necessary to ensure the ship operates smoothly and that passengers have a good holiday. You might work in the reception area, do secretarial duties or order various items of stock.

- As well as providing passengers services you might also support crew members by paying their salaries or updating and maintaining immigration records.

The type of person suited to this work

As you will have contact with passengers, you should be happy meeting, talking with and helping people of all nationalities. You should be polite and happy to help, and have good customer service skills.

You will need to be a dedicated employee as the work can be hard at times.

Working conditions

You will be expected to work long shifts, which for some posts can last up to 10 hours. Although cruise ships appear to be glamorous, you might work in cramped conditions or during rough weather.

You might have to share your accommodation with other members of staff.

Short-term, holiday and summer work is available.

Future prospects

In the last 7 years the cruise ship industry has become the second fastest growing sector in the UK and USA, so prospects are good.

There is a clear process of career progression. You will start as a member of crew then rise to officer as you gain skills and responsibilities.

The skills gained on board will also be useful on land in many areas of hospitality and catering (steward) or the business sector (purser).

Advantages/disadvantages

You might be away from home for months at a time.

You will be able visit lots of places around the world.

Your accommodation could be cramped and you might have to share with other crew members.

Qualifications and courses

Steward

There are no formal entry requirements for this work, but relevant experience in the leisure and hospitality industry is normally required.

Training is provided on the job, and covers subjects such as safety, health, environment, survival and rescue, fire, First Aid, etc, as well as company-specific training.

Purser

A levels/H grades or equivalent are normally required, and many employers prefer a degree in a related subject such as hospitality or travel and tourism. The normal entry requirements for a degree in a travel or hospitality subject are 2 A levels/3 H grades, or equivalent. No specific A level subjects are required.

Related experience is normally required. For senior positions, managerial experience may be required.

Knowledge of a language other than English is an advantage.

Pay is very good; accommodation and food are free while on board, and usually your salary is tax free if on a 6 month contract or longer.

Money guide

Salaries for all on-board positions are higher than for comparable jobs ashore. Salaries vary with company and liner, so contact companies directly for their earnings guide. Salaries normally start from £19,000, rising to around £25,000, with experience. A chief purser or steward can earn between £45,000 and £55,000.

Free accommodation and food, as well as tips from passengers, boost the value of earnings.

Related opportunities

- Tourist Information Centre Assistant p398
- Holiday Representative p388

Further information

International Cruise Services
36 Midlothian Drive, Glasgow G41 3QU
0141 649 8644; www.cruiseservices.co.uk,
info@cruiseservices.co.uk

www.cityandguilds.com/myperfectjob

TAXI DRIVER

What the work involves

- Taxi drivers pick up and transport passengers between destinations in a licensed vehicle for an agreed fee.

- You could either drive your own black cab (also known as a hackney carriage) or operate a private hire vehicle (more commonly called a minicab).

- If you drive a black cab, you will be able to pick up people who are waiting at a taxi rank, in the street, or those who have pre-booked. Minicabs are only allowed to carry pre-booked passengers.

- You will also need to assist passengers in and out of your vehicle, and help them with bags as necessary.

The type of person suited to this work

You will need to be personable and pleasant to passengers, but also have the confidence to handle difficult or aggressive fares should the need arise.

You should have a good local knowledge of the area in which you operate. Black cab drivers in London are required to pass a test in order to demonstrate their knowledge of the city prior to gaining a licence.

You will need a good level of numeracy, as you will be handling money regularly and need to ensure that you give passengers their correct change.

Working conditions

Your working hours will vary according to your employer. If you work for a company, you may undertake shifts that include night and weekend hours. Self-employed drivers can choose their own hours.

Most work is available in larger towns and cities, and taxi drivers are busiest on Friday and Saturday night when people are looking to go home after a night out.

You will spend the majority of your time in your vehicle, either driving passengers to their destination, or waiting for a job to come up.

Future prospects

Taxi usage is growing at a rapid rate, so job opportunities in the industry are plentiful.

Although you can work anywhere in the UK, the majority of work is focused within the larger towns and cities.

Many taxi drivers are self-employed, and with experience and knowledge you could gain an operator's licence and build up your own company.

Advantages/disadvantages

You will be dealing with a variety of people on a daily basis, so the work is sociable and interesting from that point of view.

You will be confined to your vehicle for most of your working

Qualifications and courses

It is not necessary to have any formal qualifications in order to become a taxi driver, but you do have to fulfil the conditions set out by your local licensing authority prior to them granting you a licence to work.

Criteria vary across the licensing authorities, but all require applicants to pass an enhanced Criminal Records Bureau check to prove they are not a threat to members of the local community, to have held a full driving licence for at least 12 months (3 years in London). You must also pass a medical assessment, and be over the age of 21 (18 in Northern Ireland.)

The strictest local licensing authority is that of London, which requires all registered taxi drivers to pass an extensive, knowledge-based test. It takes an average of 40 months to accumulate and learn all the necessary road information to pass.

day, and may spend long periods of time waiting around in between jobs.

You will occasionally have to deal with drunk, aggressive or distressed passengers.

Money guide

Taxi drivers who are just starting out usually earn about £12,000 for working full time hours. Figures will vary for those working part time, or undertaking significant overtime.

If you work around 40 hours a week and take a good amount of fares for the majority of the time, you could earn around £20,000.

Taxi drivers in London and other very busy cities can earn £30,000+, but they work long and often unsocial hours.

Related opportunities

- Chauffeur p599
- Tour Guide p397
- Driving Instructor p603
- Courier p600

Further information

Licensed Taxi Drivers Association
Taxi House, Woodfield Road, London W9 2BA
020 7286 1046; www.ltda.co.uk

Driving Standards Agency
The Axis Building, 112 Upper Parliament Street,
Nottingham NG1 6LP
0115 936 6666; www.dsa.gov.uk

City& Guilds

www.cityandguilds.com/myperfectjob

Transport and Logistics

CRCI: WE

TRAIN CONDUCTOR

What the work involves

- Train conductors work on passenger trains, checking and issuing tickets, and ensuring that passengers are enjoying a comfortable and pleasant journey.

- You will mainly focus on providing an excellent level of customer service to those riding the train. This will include fielding any queries or complaints, and handling rowdy passengers at times.

- You will be responsible for making announcements to notify passengers about approaching stations, times of arrival, and any delays in the journey.

- You may also need to look after passengers with special requirements, such as assisting the elderly and disabled, and keeping an eye on children travelling alone.

The type of person suited to this work

You must have excellent interpersonal skills in order to advise passengers about their journey, answer queries, deal with complaints calmly and professionally, and to maintain authority when dealing with aggressive or difficult passengers.

You should be very confident, as you will be working alone as the first point of contact for all train passengers.

You must be able to quickly and effectively deal with a number of unexpected situations.

It is also beneficial to be medically fit, and have good eyesight and hearing.

Working conditions

You will usually work 37 hours per week, according to a shift rota that will include early morning, night and weekend work. Overtime opportunities are regular.

If you work on long distance routes, you may be required to stay overnight at the destination on occasion.

Although most of your time is spent walking through the train, you will usually also have a small, private office onboard. This will have equipment for making announcements, CCTV and usually a computer terminal.

You will be expected to wear a uniform and maintain a clean, smart appearance at all times.

Future prospects

Job opportunities for conductors have decreased slightly in recent years with the introduction of driver-only trains on shorter routes. Nowadays, roles are concentrated on cross-country trains.

Most train conductors are employed by a TOC that specialises in passenger transportation. TOCs operate throughout the UK, so there are opportunities in most towns and cities.

Promotions can include titles such as senior conductor or train manager, and there may also be opportunities to move into general management within the rail sector.

Qualifications and courses

ENTRY LEVEL 2

Although there are no set qualifications for entry to become a train conductor, almost all train operating companies (TOCs) look for candidates with 5 GCSEs/S grades (A*–C/1–3) or equivalent, including English and maths.

You will need to be 18 years of age before you are legally allowed to work onboard a train. You can work within a railway station from the age of 16, which could help to build up the customer services skills that employers desire in candidates applying for conductor roles.

When you apply, you will need to pass a series of tests in order to assess your suitability. These include a full medical to gauge your level of fitness, eyesight, colour vision, and hearing.

You may also have to pass a drugs test, and may be asked to take these at random intervals in your career in compliance with the rigid safety policy that is in place regarding alcohol and drug abuse.

Apprenticeships may be available for those aged 16–24.

Advantages/disadvantages

You will be dealing with a variety of people on a daily basis, so work is rarely monotonous or boring.

You will be providing an important and valuable service to railway passengers.

You may have to deal with drunk, aggressive, or distressed passengers from time to time.

Money guide

The starting salary for a trainee conductor is about £13,000.

Once you have qualified, this will rise to £14,000.

With experience, and having gained extra supervisory responsibilities, this could increase to £21,000.

Related opportunities

- Train Driver p629
- Railway Station Assistant p622
- Rail Signalling Technician p620
- Air Cabin Crew p594

Further information

National Rail Enquiries
Freepost RSEH-TBGE-HBJJ, Customer Relations, National Rail Enquiries, Plymouth PL4 6AB
0845 748 4950; www.nationalrail.co.uk

City& Guilds

www.cityandguilds.com/myperfectjob

TRAIN DRIVER

What the work involves

■ Train drivers are responsible for safely operating trains that carry both passengers and goods around the UK.

■ You will drive the train on set routes aiming to arrive punctually at your destination, as long as there are no interferences with signalling or other unforeseen problems.

■ You must check your route carefully prior to setting off to ensure that it is still viable. You should also carry out safety-related checks on the train itself.

■ You will provide a safe and efficient service by observing railway signs, signals and speed limits, and staying alert at all times.

The type of person suited to this work

You will need to have excellent concentration and good observational skills, coupled with a responsible attitude towards safety, so that you can effectively operate a train.

You will need good eyesight and hearing, as well as quick reactions in order to respond to unexpected situations. Being able to keep calm under pressure is also an asset as difficult circumstances can arise during journeys.

You should have some mechanical or engineering knowledge so that you can carry out the necessary safety checks on the train.

You must be happy working alone for long periods of time.

Working conditions

You will usually work 35–40 hours per week on a shift system, which will include early morning, late night, and weekend work. Overtime is commonly available, and part time work can be an option.

Occasionally you might need to stay overnight at a destination if it is a long way from home, although this is more common for freight train drivers than those providing passenger services.

You will usually work alone, operating the train from the driver's cab. You may occasionally have company in the form of a driver inspector or trainee driver.

Future prospects

Most train drivers are employed by a TOC, of which there are 24 in the UK. These consist of passenger operators, light rail companies that provide underground services, freight companies, and engineering supply organisations.

With experience, you could become a trainer or an inspector of other drivers. Your company would probably fund your studies towards gaining a professional qualification in this area.

It may also be possible to move into a management role within your company or the rail sector.

Advantages/disadvantages

It can be very peaceful and pleasant driving through the British countryside on journeys.

Qualifications and courses

ENTRY LEVEL 2

Although there are no set qualifications for entry to train as a driver, almost all train operating companies (TOCs) look for candidates with 5 GCSEs/S grades (A*–C/1–3) or equivalent, including English, maths and a science subject.

You will need to be 21 years of age before you are legally allowed to train as a driver, but you can build up rail-related experience from the age of 16 working within a station, and from 18 onboard trains. This way, you can gain beneficial experience of dealing with railway passengers and understand how the industry works prior to applying as a trainee driver.

When you apply, you will need to pass a series of tests in order to assess your suitability. These include operating hand and foot controls, concentration, basic mechanical knowledge, and staying calm under pressure. You will also need to pass a medical assessment that will encompass fitness, hearing, eyesight and colour vision.

Once you have gained a position as a trainee driver, you will undergo 9–18 months of training prior to becoming a qualified driver. This will take the form of both classroom-based learning, and practical experience of driving trains.

You may have to work nights and weekends on a fairly regular basis.

It can get quite lonely being on your own in the driver's cab for long periods of time.

Money guide

Starting salaries for trainee drivers are usually about £18,000.

Once you are fully qualified, this should rise to £29,000.

With 5–7 years' experience, you could earn £35,000. If you work on mainline/high-speed passenger services, this could increase to £40,000.

Related opportunities

■ Train Conductor p628
■ Rail Signalling Technician p620
■ Large Goods Vehicle Driver p607
■ Delivery Driver p601

Further information

National Rail Enquiries
Freepost RSEH-TBGE-HBJJ, Customer Relations, National Rail Enquiries, Plymouth PL4 6AB
0845 748 4950; www.nationalrail.co.uk

City&
Guilds

www.cityandguilds.com/myperfectjob

WAREHOUSE WORKER/ MANAGER

What the work involves

Worker

- You will be responsible for checking a delivery or dispatch to make sure that the goods are in the right condition and quantity.

- Once you have approved the delivery or dispatch, you will input details into a hand-held computer terminal.

- If trained, you may drive a lift truck, or if not you may help to move or pack the goods (for example, helping to load lorries to make the best use of space).

Manager

- You will be in overall charge of the warehouse, responsible for maintaining stock levels, storing the goods safely and in the right condition, and dispatching them onwards when needed.

- Managing a team of staff, and making sure that essential health and safety training is taking place, will be part of your role.

- You will use a computer to monitor stock levels and orders, and to check the times when deliveries are due in and dispatches due out of your warehouse.

The type of person suited to this work

You must be honest and security conscious as warehouses often store valuable stock. You will need to work well in a team to get goods in and out of the warehouse quickly. The use of machinery to move and stack goods at heights can be dangerous, so you should be able to follow or implement safety regulations.

You will need excellent ICT skills as deliveries and dispatches are recorded and monitored on the warehouse's computer tracking system.

Working conditions

You will work a 37–40 hour week. Shift work is typical, with shifts at nights and weekends as well. This will include overtime at busy periods.

Worker

You will spend a lot of time on your feet and you might need to lift heavy items and climb ladders.

Manager

You will work both at a computer in an office and out in the warehouse. If you have an accredited qualification from the ECBL, you could work overseas. Knowledge of a foreign language would be helpful.

Future prospects

Warehouses are owned and managed by companies who either store large quantities of goods for their own businesses, or charge customers to store goods for them. The biggest employers of warehouse staff are retail and manufacturing companies, logistics and distribution service providers and specialist freight and haulage companies.

Some warehouses are small and only employ a few warehouse workers. Others can be the size of several football pitches and employ both management and workers.

Warehouses are becoming more computerised and some of the heavier work is being automated. This is likely to change the job in the future. Some warehouses will have fewer operatives and some are already 'lights out' warehouses with no human workers at operative level.

Worker

After gaining experience, you can progress to a role as team leader or supervisor. With additional qualifications, you can move into warehouse management.

Manager

There are good opportunities for promotion either by moving to a larger warehousing operation or into general management.

Advantages/disadvantages

You will be working to tight deadlines which can be stressful.

Working together to finish a job can foster an excellent team spirit.

Heavy workloads are common at certain periods like Christmas, although you will receive overtime pay.

Money guide

Worker

Starting pay is about £13,500, rising with experience to £17,000.

Team leaders can earn up to £24,500.

Some employers offer performance bonus schemes in addition to extra for night shifts.

Manager

Starting pay is £17,000 per year. Experienced managers can earn up to £28,000 with experience (up to £50,000+ with large companies).

Related opportunities

- Airport Baggage Handler p597
- Distribution Manager p602
- Freight Forwarder p604
- Lift Truck Operator p608

Further information

Skills for Logistics
14 Warren Yard, Warren Farm Office Village,
Milton Keynes MK12 5NW
01908 313360; www.skillsforlogistics.org

Chartered Institute of Logistics and Transport
Logistics and Transport Centre, Earlstree Court,
Earlstree Road, Corby NN17 4AX
01536 740104; www.ciltuk.org.uk

United Kingdom Warehousing Association
Walter House, 418–422 Strand, London WC2R 0PT
020 7836 5522; www.ukwa.org.uk

www.cityandguilds.com/myperfectjob

Qualifications and courses

Worker

There are no minimum entry requirements for this job. You will need to be physically fit, and a medical may be required.

Apprenticeships may be available for those aged 16–24. This leads to NVQ/SVQ Levels 2 and 3 in Distribution, Storage and Warehousing Operations. 3 GCSEs (A*–C) might be required including maths and English. ICT qualifications can also be helpful.

Most training takes place on the job. The National Proficiency Tests Council's Level 2 Certificate of Competence in Fork Lift Truck Operations may be offered by employers.

Manager

There are no specific entry qualifications. It is possible to work as a warehouse worker, gain NVQ/SVQ qualifications or the professional qualifications of the Chartered Institute of Logistics and Transport (CILT), and progress to supervisory or management roles. Good management, ICT, literacy and numeracy skills can be an advantage.

Some employers may require qualifications such as A levels/H grades. The Diploma in Retail and Business can be useful. Increasingly, companies recruit graduates. Degrees are on offer in related subjects such as logistics and supply chain management. The usual minimum entry requirements for a degree course are 2 A levels/3 H grades or equivalent.

People working in the industry can study for the CILT's professional qualifications part time at college or by distance learning. The Introductory Certificate in Logistics and Transport is aimed at new entrants and the standard Certificate is aimed at supervisors and first line managers. The Professional Diploma is intended for middle managers, including recent graduates, and fulfils the membership requirements for the Institute. New or aspiring senior warehouse managers can take the CILT Advanced Diploma or study for an MSc in International Transport and Logistics. The MSc is offered by Glamorgan University in partnership with CILT, and takes 3 years by distance learning. You can also work towards an NVQ Level 3 in Logistics Operations Management or a Foundation degree in Logistics or Transport. Qualifications in Supply Chain and Logistics at senior levels are also available from The European Certification Board for Logistics (ECBL).

ENTRY
1
LEVEL

Transport and Logistics

CRCI: WG

INDEX OF LEVELS

Level 1

Level 2

Level 3

Index

Level 6

Level 7

Level 8

INDEX

Index

INDEX OF ADVERTISERS